Year by year from 1900 to 2000

AMERICA'S CENTURY

A Dorling Kindersley Book

Dorling Kindersley

LONDON, NEW YORK, SYDNEY, DELHI,
PARIS, MUNICH, JOHANNESBURG

Editorial director: Clifton Daniel

Editor-in-chief: John W. Kirshon

Associate editor: Ralph Berens

Writers/researchers: Tom Anderson, Benton Boggs, Susan Breen, Kevin Delaney, Sean Dolan, Robert Dyer (Midwest), Edward Edelson, Philip Farber, Robert Fleming, James Forsht, John Goolrick, Esther Gottfried, Arthur Holch, Catherine Hulbert, Marjorie Hunter (Washington, D.C.), Pamela Ivinski, Marguerite Jones, Iris Kelso (New Orleans), Charles King (Canada), Jennifer Kingson (Northeast), Nicholas Lee (Northwest), Perry Leopard, Stephen Levi (Alaska), John Mariani, Susan Merrill, Roberta Oster, Edward Queen, Linda Rae, Noel Rae, Angela Read, Karen Rohan, Paige Rosenberg, Marianne Ruuth (Los Angeles), Don Schanche (Southeast), Julie Siler (Chicago), Burt Solomon, Sam Tanenhaus, William Teague (Southwest), James Tuite, Charles Turner (Hawaii), Jiri Weiss (San Francisco), Kenneth Weinstock

Historical consultant: Alan Brinkley, Professor of History,
The Graduate Center of the City University of New York

Foreword: Dr Alan F. Day, Senior Lecturer in History, University of Edinburgh

Created and produced by Jacques Legrand

© Chronik Verlag, im Bertelsmann Lexikon Verlag GmbH, Gütersloh/München 1995

This edition © Dorling Kindersley Limited, London 2000

Most of the material in this book first appeared in *Chronicle of America*, published by Dorling Kindersley in 1997

Revisions to the 2000 edition by Amber Books Limited, London

American edition 2000

2 4 6 8 10 9 7 5 3 1

Published in the United States by Dorling Kindersley Publishing, Inc.,
95 Madison Avenue, New York, New York 10016

A CIP record for this book is available from the Library of Congress

ISBN 0-7894-5339-8

Printed and bound in Germany by Mohndruck GmbH, Gütersloh

see our complete
catalog at
www.dk.com

CONTENTS

Foreword

Although as the twentieth century dawned the United States had reached almost its present geographical size, the next hundred years nevertheless saw a substantial rise in population, from 76 million to 274 million. Even if immigration in the twentieth century contributed less than in its nineteenth-century heyday, the country throughout the period continued to exercise its traditional magnetism, so that in 1990 more than twice as many newcomers settled in the US as in all other countries put together. The development of the American economy makes clear why this should be so. Having survived the devastating pre-WW2 depression America emerged from the War with its economy set on an upward path that has continued more or less ever since.

Rich or poor, immigrant or native born, all Americans have traditionally taken real pride in their system of government, and especially in its beacon, the Constitution. The dynamic nature of that venerable document is evidenced by the addition of eleven new amendments (bringing the total to 27) during the course of the twentieth century. The often terse wording of each amendment conceals the social and political struggles that led up to it: neither the ill-fated introduction of Prohibition in 1919 nor the advent of women's suffrage in 1920 was enacted without tireless campaigning and the clash of passionately held but mutually incompatible views. Nowhere is the complexity of the ratification process better shown than in the failure of the Equal Rights Amendment to gain the necessary votes in 1982.

As the twentieth century progressed, some Americans began to worry about the increasing power of the executive, the growth of what Arthur M. Schlesinger has described as the 'Imperial Presidency'. Ironically, in a country so self-consciously egalitarian as America, concerns emerged as the century drew to a close that the system was becoming too exclusive, allowing only those who possess substantial wealth to aspire to the presidency. Despite America's appearing to be the most apolitical of all industrial nations – less than half the electorate cast their ballot in 1996 – defenders respond by pointing out that democracy has survived two presidential assassinations, one attempted assassination, one resignation, and one impeachment. The system has also proved flexible enough to respond – however hesitantly and sometimes unwillingly – to the dignified struggle of Native Americans and African Americans to enter the mainstream of American political society.

During the nineteenth century the US had generally heeded George Washington's advice to avoid 'entangling alliances.' Woodrow Wilson temporarily broke this tradition of aloofness in 1917 when he committed US troops to the Allied side in the Great War, but the American public grew disillusioned with the maneuverings of the victorious European powers after the 'War to end wars.' The result was a retreat back into isolationism from which the country was only jolted by the trauma of the Japanese attack on Pearl Harbor in December 1941. Four years of bitter warfare later the US had not only finally arrived on the world stage, but bestrode it.

After WW2 the US, nuclear-armed but aware that its monopoly of such weapons could only be temporary, and determined not to repeat previous mistakes, not only continued its constructive engagement with the rest of the world but assumed the leadership of NATO, the alliance dedicated to preventing the spread of Soviet-backed Communism. Although this policy proved successful in maintaining stability in Europe, America's anti-communist crusade in Vietnam led to a war which was not only increasingly unpopular at home but was also, ultimately, humiliatingly unsuccessful in the field. The resulting scars on the American psyche have yet to heal. Toward the century's end the collapse of the Soviet Union – together with the fact that China's vast potential has not yet been fully harnessed – left the US as the only real superpower, struggling to shape a coherent response to a new world order riven by ethnic and nationalist conflict.

It is arguable, of course, that what really changed the lives of ordinary Americans profoundly and irrevocably as the century progressed, was not so much public affairs or the drama of war as the relentless flood of scientific and technological developments. Medical advances – AIDS and smoking notwithstanding – have virtually eradicated the nineteenth-century killer diseases. The burden of domestic chores has been alleviated by refrigerator, washing machine, vacuum cleaner, and freezer. Travel possibilities were extended dramatically with the advent of automobile and airplane. The space race – with its origins firmly based on super-power rivalry – may well prove to be just as significant as a source of terrestrial technological spin-off as for its achievements in lunar exploration and interplanetary investigation. Communication, entertainment, and indeed the fabric of life and society, have been transformed out of all recognition by the kaleidoscopically changing relationship of telephone, television, computer, and Internet.

By exploring such themes as they presented themselves to contemporaries, this book invites you, the thoughtful reader, to trawl back through your own memories or those of your family, to ponder on the many, subtle, and varied ways in which America transformed itself between 1900 and 2000, and to speculate on what our great-grandchildren will be writing about our present century a hundred years hence.

Agenda for a New Century 1900-1916

The United States is a nation of immigrants, a country inhabited by people whose ancestors all shared the painful experience of being uprooted from their native land to start a new life in a strange new world. From this common experience, America has earned a reputation as a land of opportunity for the world's oppressed and a "melting pot" where a variety of ethnic, religious and racial groups have mixed together to form a new culture. From 1870 to 1920, more immigrants – some 25 million – arrived in America than ever before. As they entered New York harbor, the Statue of Liberty beckoned: "Give me your tired, your poor, your huddled masses yearning to breathe free." One of the most obvious facts the newcomers faced was that the society they were joining was one undergoing a dramatic transformation.

In 1907, Henry Adams – historian, novelist, descendant of presidents – published his classic autobiography. In it, he reflected on the social and economic changes he had witnessed in his lifetime: the development of railroads and ocean liners and the telegraph; the rise of industry; the growth of cities; the explosion of technical and scientific knowledge. The world he observed around him in the last years of his life seemed so different from the one he had known as a child that he often felt himself a stranger in his own land, a relic soon to be consigned to oblivion by the forces of progress. "He could see," Adams wrote (referring to himself in the third person), "that the new American – the child of incalculable coal power, chemical power, electric power and radiating energy, as well as new forces yet undetermined – must be a sort of God compared with any former creation of nature. At the rate of progress since 1800, every American who lived into the year 2000 would know how to control unlimited power. He would think in complexities unimaginable to an earlier mind. He would deal with problems altogether beyond the range of earlier society."

The changes Adams described occurred over many decades. "With a stride that astonished statisticians," the historians Charles and Mary Beard wrote, "the conquering hosts of business enterprise swept over the continent; 25 years after the death of Lincoln, America had become, in the quantity and value of her products, the first manufacturing nation of the world. What England had accomplished in a hundred years, the United States had achieved in half the time." The Industrial Revolution had begun in America well before the Civil War; the nation's rise to economic greatness was not really as sudden as the Beards suggested. But it was true that the industrial accomplishments of the late 19th century overshadowed all earlier progress. And those accomplishments helped produce other profound changes as well. The United States was becoming not only an industrialized nation, but an urbanized one. It was changing from a fragmented and provincial society into a more centralized and consolidated one. It was moving from a position of relative unimportance in world affairs to that of a major power.

To many Americans, the dramatic changes of the age of industry were a cause for celebration and optimism. The titans of finance and industry, of course, rejoiced in their own success and in the previously unimagined fortunes they managed to accumulate. But the new affluence reached well beyond the ranks of the upper class: to the urban middle class, which grew rapidly in both size and wealth; to the agricultural world, where some farmers managed to accumulate great land holdings and establish themselves as rural "tycoons"; to the working class, where some laborers, at least, experienced slow but significant increases in their standards of living.

But the late 19th century was also a time of turbulence and crisis. For along with the undoubted benefits of economic growth came great costs. Cities were growing so rapidly that public services could not keep up with demand. Roads, sewers, transportation systems, housing, social services, government bureaucracies, public health systems: all were plunged into something approaching chaos as they strained to keep up with the changes around them. The political system, accustomed to the problems and the pace of an earlier and simpler time, reacted slowly and uncertainly to the new social problems of the new era; to many Americans, late 19th-century political life at every level was chiefly notable for its corruption. Major

demographic changes – the arrival of the millions of new immigrants from Europe and Asia, the movement of rural Americans (including, for the first time, large numbers of blacks) from the country to the city – created social and economic tensions of their own. The agricultural economy, in the meantime, suffered both an absolute and a relative decline that left some American farmers wealthy and secure, but others desperate and resentful. Some workers enjoyed significant progress in good times, but all were vulnerable when times turned bad, as they often did.

These and other problems combined in the 1890's to produce a period of crisis more severe than any since the 1860's. Industrial workers rose up in a series of major, and at times violent, protests to challenge a labor system they believed oppressed them. Farmers in the West and South, both white and black, organized a great political movement known as populism to challenge economic and political institutions they considered exploitive and dangerous. Americans of all regions and classes suffered from the effects of the most severe economic depression in the nation's history up to that point – a panic that began in 1893, that lasted for over four years and that demonstrated how interdependent the new economy had become.

The crisis of the 1890's strengthened reform impulses that had already been growing in some sectors of society for years. A few Americans saw industrialization as a menace to the world they cherished and searched for ways to stop it or escape from it. Most, however, accepted, even welcomed economic progress and sought not to impede it but to curb the instability and injustice it had brought in its wake. Growth and progress could no longer be allowed to proceed without restraints, they believed. Society needed to take steps to impose order on the growing chaos and to find just solutions to glaring wrongs. The reform impulse gathered strength in the last years of the 19th century. By the early 20th, it had acquired a name: progressivism.

Neither at the time nor since was there agreement on what "progressivism" was, so various and even contradictory were the ideas and crusades the word came to describe. Many of the "reforms" that some Americans considered progressive at the time have come to seem to later generations highly reactionary: the imposition of legalized segregation on the American South in the 1890's and the early 20th century; the continuous effort to restrict immigration; the crusade to prohibit the sale of alcoholic beverages. But at the time, many "reformers" defended even these restrictive measures as part of the effort to bring order to a disordered world. Other efforts fit more comfortably into later notions of progressive reform: civil service reform, woman suffrage, direct election of senators, public supervision of railroads and trusts, restrictions on child labor, regulation of food, drugs and other commodities affecting public health. But whatever their intent and however much they varied, most "reforms" of the progressive era had at least a few things in common: their sense that government – local, state, and ultimately national – had to play a larger role in the life of society than it had in the past; their belief that the ideal of the autonomous, self-reliant individual, an ideal that had been at the heart of America's image of itself since the founding of the republic, must now compete with the reality of an increasingly interdependent society in which individual liberties would be balanced against public needs.

At the same time, the United States was finding itself propelled into a new relationship with the world – partly as a result of the same economic forces that were remaking politics at home. As a result of the brief, and some Americans believed "splendid," Spanish-American War of 1898, the nation joined the ranks of imperial powers, acquiring overseas possessions for the first time. America also joined other nations in developing commercial ties with Japan and China. It expanded its economic and, all too frequently, its military presence in Latin America. Under Presidents Theodore Roosevelt and Woodrow Wilson (in very different ways), it attempted to become a powerful moral force in international relations. And after 1914, it found itself drawn, despite strenuous efforts to avoid it, into the greatest armed conflict in world history up to that point: World War I, which was to propel America into still another relationship with other nations and into a period of dramatic new economic growth and social change.

◄ *"The Steerage" (1907), a photographic masterpiece by Alfred Stieglitz.*

Tacoma, Washington, January. Lumberman Frederick Weyerhaeuser incorporates Weyerhaeuser Company.

Washington, D.C., Jan. 20. Negro Representative G.H. White of North Carolina introduces bill to make lynching a federal crime; it is defeated.

Washington, D.C., Jan. 25. Congressman-elect Brigham Henry Roberts of Utah unseated in House vote, on charges of polygamy.

Washington, D.C., Jan 26. Theodore Roosevelt tells friend, Henry Sprague, "Speak softly and carry a big stick and you will go far."

Chicago, Jan. 29. New baseball organization called American League formed; it fails to gain recognition from National League (→ Oct. 13, 1903).

New York City, March 5. New York University becomes site of Hall of Fame, for noted Americans.

Washington, D.C., March 20. Secretary of State John Hay announces that Germany, Russia, Britain, Italy and Japan have agreed upon Open Door policy in China (→ Aug. 14).

New Jersey, March 24. New Carnegie Steel Company incorporates, allegedly in violation of Sherman Antitrust Law (→ March 13, 1901).

New York City. Vanderbilts take control of Reading, Lehigh Valley and Erie Railroads.

New York City, Apr. 25. Cuba Company investment group allocates $8 million, to develop railroads in Cuba.

Oregon, May 22. Fire destroys 64 buildings in Lakeview.

Washington, D.C., May 22. Patent granted to Edwin S. Votey for "pneumatic piano attachment," or pianola.

New York City, June 15. Paderewski Fund of $10,000 started by virtuoso pianist Ignace Paderewski, to award American composers for best orchestral work.

Minnesota, Sept. 18. Direct primary held for coming elections; first in nation.

Boston, Oct. 15. Symphony Hall opens.

Boston. Booker T. Washington organizes National Negro Business League.

New arrivals swell U.S. population

From an Ellis Island dock, an immigrant leads his family into the future.

Proud and determined, arrivals patiently await their chance at a new life.

United States

Bolstered by a flood of immigrants streaming through Ellis Island at a rate of 100 an hour, the population of the United States has jumped to 75.9 million, up from the 62.9 million counted in the last census 10 years ago. New York is still the largest city with 3.4 million inhabitants; Chicago follows with 1.6 million. Some 3.5 million immigrants arrived in the last decade, a flow that has increased steadily except for a lull during the depression years 1894 and 1895. Ellis Island's new facilities, rebuilt after being destroyed by fire three years ago, can handle 8,000 newcomers a day. To the dismay of nativists and many labor groups, the census reported 10 million foreign-born residents and 26 million second-generation Americans. But, as a share of the total population, the foreign-born have hovered at around 14 percent for the entire century.

In fact, it is less the sheer numbers than the changing character of immigration that leads people to call for restrictions. In 1896, for the first time, the huge trans-Atlantic steamboats carried more Southeastern Europeans than Northwestern Europeans. The foreign-born population still consists mostly of Germans, Irish, Canadians, Britons and Swedes, in that order. But Slavs, Poles and Italians, settling in New York, Pennsylvania and Illinois, will soon be in the majority at the present rate. The Italians alone accounted for 100,000 new arrivals this year, up from 12,000 in 1880.

The advocates of immigration reform argue that the "new immigrants" are unskilled and uneducated, poorly equipped to contribute to the economy or the political system. Prescott Hall of the Boston Immigration Restriction League calls them "historically downtrodden, atavistic and stagnant." Even reformer Jane Addams, who works closely with Eastern Europeans, says those in Chicago are "densely ignorant of civic duties." No proof exists, however, that the new wave is any less talented than the old. The biggest hurdles are more likely the squalid conditions of urban slums and the cultural gap between tight immigrant communities and the dominant Anglo-Saxon world.

8,000 automobiles, 4 billion cigarettes

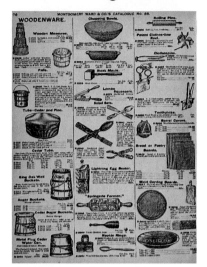

Americans can buy anything ...

New York City

The day when the average American can buy just about whatever he needs seems to have arrived – provided he has the money. Stores and mail-order houses stock an endless variety of goods. There are now at least 8,000 automobiles cruising the nation's roads. For some, the newfangled machines are too complicated; there are still an estimated 10 million bicycles and 18 million horses and mules in use. Businessmen, friends and relatives can call each other regularly on a telephone; there are at least 1,300,000 of them now in service. And for those who want to smoke but don't like to roll their own, tobacco makers produced over four billion cigarettes this year. Ah, democracy!

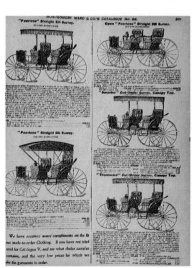

... from rolling pins to surreys from the Montgomery Ward catalogue.

U.S. finally goes on gold standard

Washington, D.C., March 14

Gold is the standard again. Using a new gold pen, President McKinley today signed the gold standard bill approved by the House, 166 to 120. Nine Democrats voted yea with the Republicans after the banking committee chairman closed debate, saying, "This is but one terrace in the height this nation is climbing to that position assured by manifest destiny." In opposition, the defeated free-silver forces charged "stealthy deceit, fraud and corruption," pledging that "the incorruptible, invincible William Jennings Bryan will drive the cohorts of corruption from power forever" in the next elections.

U.S. civil rule set for Puerto Ricans

Washington, D.C., Apr. 12

Under the terms of an act sponsored by Senator Joseph Foraker, military rule of Puerto Rico, which Spain ceded to the U.S. in the Treaty of Paris of 1898, is to be replaced by a civil government along the lines of a British crown colony. A single-chamber legislature will be popularly elected, but real power will rest in the hands of a governor and council appointed by the American president (→ Apr. 2, 1901).

U.S. and Britain sign treaty for canal

Washington, D.C., Feb. 5

A major political obstacle to the construction of a canal across Central America has been removed with the signing here of a treaty with Britain that in effect abrogates the Clayton-Bulwer Treaty of 1850. Under the terms of that agreement, both nations promised not to claim exclusive control over any canal that might eventually be built between the oceans.

The new treaty, negotiated by Secretary of State John Hay and the British Ambassador Sir Julian Pauncefote, drops British claims to a share in the canal, which will now be built by the United States alone. It is, however, stipulated that the canal be unfortified and neutral, "free and open to the vessels of commerce and of war of all nations." Criticism of this clause is heard in the Senate, where the pact must be ratified (→ Dec. 16, 1901).

Canal will be an American project.

70 dead as Hawaii is struck by plague

Honolulu, Apr. 30

Seventy people died and more than 4,000 are homeless as the result of the bubonic plague and intentionally set fires that devastated this city for four and one-half months. Health officials set the "controlled fires" after the outbreak began in December, hoping to kill the rats spreading the disease. Winds whipped the fires out of control, destroying Chinatown. Today, the plague was finally declared over.

Fifth Avenue buses begin regular run

New York City, Jan. 2

Some New Yorkers may have wondered whether the hangovers from their end-of-the-century parties were playing tricks on them when they saw a new contraption gliding down Fifth Avenue. It was the city's first autostage, or autobus. The vehicle runs quietly on electricity, carrying about a dozen passengers at a fare of five cents. Once refined, mechanics say, the bus will be a major mode of city transportation.

Trouble ahead: Casey Jones wrecks train, saves passengers

Memphis, Tennessee, Apr. 30

Train engineer Casey Jones set out on his route from Memphis to Canton, Mississippi, a little late today. Pressed to get back on schedule, he pumped the Cannon Ball express to its limit and slammed into another train at Vaughan, Mississippi. Jones died, but his brave and decisive maneuvering saved the lives of his passengers. Folks in the backwoods are calling Jones a hero. One resident said, "I've known Casey for years. He knew his locomotive and I'm sure he knew his time was up. He could've bailed out, but that would've killed a lot of passengers." Instead, Jones successfully fought to slow the speeding train and minimize the impact.

Casey Jones in the cab of Engine No. 638. Will he forget to watch his speed?

U.S. forces help crush Boxer rebels

American troops march on the Temple of Agriculture grounds in Peking. They are among the 5,000 U.S. troops led by Brigadier General Adna Chaffee, and they are allied with British, French, Russian, Italian and Japanese forces.

A few of the Boxer rebels imprisoned by the allies after the lifting of the blockade by the expeditionary forces.

Upon entering the fallen city of Tientsin, expeditionary forces discover part of the toll paid by the Chinese.

An American cavalryman and Indian troops watch over Chinese dead.

Peking, China, Aug. 14

After two months under siege by Boxer and imperial army units, the foreign legations were rescued today by a force of 19,000 British, American, Russian, Japanese and French soldiers. The diplomats, along with other foreign residents of Peking and some 3,000 Chinese Christians, had barricaded themselves in the legation quarter on June 20, when they came under attack by the rabidly anti-foreign Boxer groups. That they were able to hold out until today is due in large part to the foresight of the first secretary of the American legation, Herbert G. Squiers, who stockpiled a plentiful supply of food.

The Boxers, a secret society officially known as I Ho Ch'uan (The Righteous and Harmonious Fists), are estimated to number 140,000. They are fiercely opposed to any kind of foreign influence. Though once banned, the society has been receiving tacit support from reactionary elements that now dominate the imperial court of the Dowager Empress T'zu Hsi.

The Boxers have not tried to conceal their goals. "The will of Heaven," they declared in a placard posted in Peking last spring, "is that the telegraph wires be first cut, the railways torn up and then shall the foreign devils be decapitated."

By May, Boxer gangs had already begun a campaign of terror against any Chinese suspected of being a Christian. On May 31, attacks on foreigners began with the killing of four French and Belgian railway engineers. This was followed by the murder here of Japanese Chancellor Sugiyama. Soon after, British Admiral Sir Edward Seymour gathered an international rescue force and set out for Peking. After heavy fighting, Tientsin was occupied on July 14. The relief column then regrouped and set out for the capital 10 days ago, making its way up the Pei Ho River. At daybreak this morning, Russian Cossacks took the lead in storming the walls of this city. Although the Boxers offered little resistance in the area of the legations, there are reports that heavy fighting was going on in other parts of the city. The Dowager Empress and her court have made their way to Sian (→ Sept. 7, 1901).

Americans sweep Olympic Games

Paris, July 22

Americans made a virtual sweep of the second modern Olympics, although because of a misunderstanding some of the athletes thought they were actually taking part in the concurrent Universal Games. Winners received medals but didn't realize they were for their Olympic successes. The United States won 20 gold medals with a strong team of 55 athletes, headed by four-time winner Alvin Kraenzlein of Princeton. Most of the Americans balked at competing on a Sunday, but Kraenzlein raced and won his first gold medal on a program that was trimmed back by dropping swimming and other events.

Davis wins first tennis cup match

Longwood, Mass., Aug. 10

How appropriate it was that Dwight F. Davis should be a member of the American team that won the first International Lawn Tennis Trophy. It was Davis, a star college player, who put up the trophy. He and Holcombe Ward defeated the English pair of E.D. Black and H.R. Barrett in doubles today after each American won his singles match in the five-match series. With an insurmountable 3-0 lead, Davis was leading the fourth match when rain intervened, ending the competition.

Du Bois warns about "color line"

London, Summer

Addressing representatives to the Pan-African Conference, the noted American Negro leader W.E.B. Du Bois warned his audience that the biggest danger facing the peoples of the world in the new century is the continued existence of the "color line." Du Bois, the first Negro graduate of Harvard University, published *The Philadelphia Negro* last year. This sociological study argues that the Negro upper class, as stewards of their race, must provide the leadership necessary for liberation (→ July 13, 1905).

Hurricane in Texas takes 8,000 lives

Galveston, Texas, Sept. 8

One of the worst hurricanes and tidal waves in American history killed 8,000 people and destroyed 2,600 structures in this port city today. The hurricane's winds were estimated at 120 miles per hour and the tidal wave that swept across Galveston from one end to the other was said to have been 14 feet high. With no place to bury the victims in this sea-level strand of a city, authorities are making plans to place the corpses in boats, haul them well out to sea and simply dump them overboard. These officials say that the total damage to the city is expected to be more than $25 million.

Mosquito transmits yellow fever virus

Cuba, September

Some of the sting has been taken out of yellow fever with the discovery by Army Surgeon Walter Reed that it is transmitted by mosquito bite. Because the disease is a scourge of the tropics, Dr. Reed has been conducting his research in Cuba, where new epidemics have just broken out. He successfully produced the fever in 22 human "guinea pigs," thus proving a theory that was first proposed in 1881 by Dr. Carlos Finlay of Havana. Fortunately, none of the subjects died.

Republican McKinley retains presidency

President McKinley begins a second term with the aid of Theodore Roosevelt.

Canton, Ohio, Nov. 7

William McKinley has been re-elected President, beating William Jennings Bryan. With the Nebraska results still in doubt, McKinley has 284 electoral votes, to Bryan's 155. The President's home was connected with Republican headquarters by telegraph, and the news passed quickly to the supporters who arrived from downtown with bands playing and rockets firing. He then appeared on the porch from which he had campaigned to thank them "for the very great compliment."

President McKinley, 57, carried with him New York Governor Theodore Roosevelt as his new Vice President, and retained Republican majorities in both houses of Congress. When the results reached Roosevelt's Sagamore Hill home from the railroad telegraph three miles away, the 42-year-old hero of the Rough Riders commented: "Isn't that fine. It shows what the American people are. It shows that they want the good times to continue, and are in favor of honest money and are for the flag." The new Vice President has alarmed some Republicans by urging tighter control of the big trusts, while McKinley enjoys the support of financiers who are pleased about the new gold standard he approved in March. Bryan, the 40-year-old "Boy Orator of the Platte," based his 24-state campaign on his opposition to American imperialism.

From Dorothy in Oz to Carrie in Chicago

United States

Two very different damsels in distress star in this year's fiction. Frank Baum's children's tale, *The Wonderful Wizard of Oz*, relates the adventures of Dorothy, a little girl who falls asleep in Kansas and wakes up in Oz, a magical land that she can escape from only with the help of its mysterious Wizard. The heroine of novelist Theodore Dreiser's *Sister Carrie* also leaves a rural life for an alien world, Chicago, where she boards with her sister and brother-in-law before becoming a married man's mistress.

Olds and Firestone at first auto show

New York City, Nov. 3

Nearly 10,000 curious spectators jammed Madison Square Garden tonight for what some dubbed the "Horseless Horseshow." An exhibition staged by the Automobile Club of America, it featured the most up-to-date steam, electric and gasoline-powered vehicles. The Firestone Rubber Company and Goodyear Tire and Rubber Company also displayed the latest motorcar wheels. Particular notice was paid to Ransom E. Olds's new $1,250 Oldsmobile. A good horse and buggy costs just $400, but Detroit's Olds Motor Works hopes to sell all 400 curved-dashboard, gasoline-powered Oldsmobiles they finished this year.

$1 Brownie camera

Rochester, New York

George Eastman of the Eastman Kodak Company thinks Americans are ready for a new hobby and he's ready to help. The photography firm is manufacturing its new Brownie Box Camera and selling it for only $1. Eastman was the first to introduce transparent, flexible roll film in 1889. It now retails for 10 to 15 cents for a six-photo roll. The Brownie and inexpensive film will make it possible for thousands to become amateur photographers.

The navy's newest: John P. Holland's revolutionary submarine is 53 feet long, powered by gasoline and electric engines and is stabilized by stern-mounted horizontal rudders. It is armed with one bow torpedo tube, one bow pneumatic dynamite gun and three short Whitehead torpedoes.

Campbell's Soup, served in American homes since 1897, won awards for quality this year.

Topeka, Kansas, Jan. 1. Agnes N. Ozman receives baptism of spirit and allegedly begins speaking in tongues; first modern instance of glossalalia.

New York City, Feb. 2. Puccini's opera *Tosca* has U.S. premiere at Metropolitan Opera.

New York City, March 12. New York public library system founded with $5.2 million grant from Andrew Carnegie.

Utah, March 14. Governor vetoes bill aimed at relaxing prosecution of polygamy cases.

Philippines, Apr. 2. Emilio Aguinaldo swears allegiance to United States; former rebel leader exhorts followers to submit to U.S. rule (→ July 4).

Jacksonville, Florida, May 3. Fire destroys 2,300 buildings.

Springfield, Massachusetts, June 1. Newspapers announce public display of motorized bicycle, designed by Carl Hedstrom.

Washington, D.C., July 25. McKinley proclaims free-trade policy with Puerto Rico.

Peking, Sept. 7. Dozen nations, including United States, sign Boxer Protocol, in which Chinese agree to pay reparations for uprising; United States gets $24.5 million.

Dayton, Ohio, September. Orville Wright designs wind tunnel, with gas engine powering metal fan; it is used for flight-simulation experimentation (→ Dec. 17, 1903).

United States, Oct. 4. Columbia beats Britain's Shamrock II to keep America's Cup here.

New York City, Nov. 16. New auto speed record for mile – 52 seconds – set by French driver Henri Fournier.

Washington, D.C., Nov. 27. In wake of criticism of army's performance during war with Spain, Secretary of War Elihu Root founds Army War College.

Alabama, Nov. 28. New state constitution disenfranchises Negroes by requiring property and literacy tests, and including grandfather clause (→ Autumn, 1904).

New York City. Reformer Jacob Riis's autobiography, *The Making of an American,* published.

Morgan buys Carnegie's steel empire

Carnegie, handing the burden over.

New York City, March 13

Less than a month after J. Pierpont Morgan bought out Andrew Carnegie's steel enterprises for $250 million and created the U.S. Steel Corporation, Carnegie sailed for Scotland and his beloved golf links today. While Morgan worked out details on organization of what becomes the world's largest corporation, Carnegie declared at dockside that he has "just begun to give away money," and then turned to his thoughts of golf, calling it "one of the most bracing pastimes."

The 66-year-old self-made man, who rose from a poor youth to tycoon, has sold a complex that controls iron and steel processes from mine to mill. Carnegie is now pursuing a course he first laid out in an essay, "The Gospel of Wealth." He wrote that a rich man is but a "trustee" and that life is in two parts: first, acquiring capital, second, giving it away. In January, when Morgan agreed to meet his price, Carnegie told him, "Pierpont, I am now handing the burden over to you." The 64-year-old Morgan is credited with having stopped

Morgan, now at the top of the heap.

the run on Treasury gold in 1895 when his syndicate provided $65 million worth at a profit some called exorbitant. His new U.S. Steel trust is the largest in the trend toward gargantuan combinations.

Black gold spews from Texas Spindletop

Beaumont, Texas, Jan. 10

Oil drillers have discovered what appears to be a huge petroleum deposit a few miles from this quiet town in northeastern Texas. While the Lone Star State has no developed oil fields, geologists have long suspected that this area sits on top of a vast reservoir of oil. For years, oil has seeped up from the ground, but no one has attempted to drill a well – until now. When the well, which the oil men are calling Spindletop, hit the gas deposits, the black gold spewed at least 200 feet into the air, covering every tree, animal and person for acres around. Latest reports say that the well is still blowing oil and is still out of control. The former mayor of Toledo, Samuel Jones, who witnessed the petroleum strike, says that "It is the greatest oil well ever discovered in the U.S. It means that liquid fuel is to be the fuel of the 20th century."

A gusher comes in at the Spindletop oil well, near Beaumont, Texas.

Leftists are united in Socialist Party

Indianapolis, July 29

Quieting their family quarrels for now, the major socialist groups in America have united under one umbrella. Eugene Debs, who was not present at the new Socialist Party's founding, calls the convention a "monument above internal dissension and strife." Debs polled 98,000 votes in last year's presidential election, leading a ticket backed by his Chicago Social Democrats and a faction of the Socialist Labor Party.

Unity has been achieved, but the convention was less a monument than a melting pot. Victor Berger, the first Socialist congressman and a political intimate of Debs, led the fight for a moderate platform urging election reform and public ownership of utilities. "We are no longer a sect," he argued, "we are a political party." A Springfield, Illinois, group insisted on "only one immediate demand, the complete surrender of the capitalist class." The compromise includes demands for reform, but only as necessary steps toward revolution. Debs, publicly skeptical of unity, has vowed privately to "stick to the party through the gates of hell" (→ Nov. 8, 1910).

Whitehead claims he flew 800 feet

Bridgeport, Conn., Aug. 15

An obscure Bavarian-born inventor today claimed victory in the quest to develop a motor-driven, heavier-than-air flying machine. He is Gustave Whitehead, who settled here in 1900, and he says he flew in his steam-powered, bat-winged craft for more than 800 feet over Long Island Sound yesterday. A local newspaper reported his flight along with a fanciful sketch of the event, but skeptics question the lack of photographic proof. Meanwhile, rival aviators work away. Dayton glider designers Orville and Wilbur Wright are testing aerodynamic shapes in a long wind tunnel they built, while Samuel Langley has flown an unmanned, gasoline-powered machine.

Panic hits Wall Street

New York City, May 9

The stock market collapsed today in a panic without parallel as the result of a corner in Northern Pacific Railroad shares. As crowds descended on Wall Street, the exchange closed its gallery for the first time in history. Thousands of messengers filled the streets, earning tips that were worth many times their $4-a-week salaries.

The panic erupted after Northern Pacific opened at 170 and jumped 200 or 300 points between sales, becoming scarce at even $1,000 because it had been cornered by forces of J. Pierpont Morgan on the one hand and E.H. Harriman on the other, in their titanic struggle for control. So fierce was their fight that they actually bought more Northern Pacific than exists. Much of it was from speculators who really didn't own it, but had sold it "short," betting that it would fall before they had to deliver. When it went up instead, the speculators were trapped in the position of having to deliver stock that they didn't own, and that they could neither buy nor borrow. Quickly, they had to sell their other holdings to make good their losses. Before noon, everyone was selling everything. Speculators and average investors alike were wiped out.

When the battling giants finally agreed under court order to break their corner and let their "short" victims off the hook at $150 a share, it was too late to undo damage that could be measured by a $100 million drop in the market value of U.S. Steel alone.

Supreme Court puts new lands in limbo

Washington, D.C., May 27

The troublesome question of the constitutional status of Puerto Rico and the Philippines was at last settled today by a Supreme Court decision in what is known as the Insular Cases. The former Spanish possessions, the court has ruled, are neither foreign countries nor integral parts of the United States; their inhabitants are American nationals but not American citizens; tariffs may be imposed on goods exported to the United States; their form of government will be whatever Congress decides. In short, the newcomers are to be treated as colonies – left, as one of the dissenting judges has put it, "in an indeterminate state of ambiguous existence for an indefinite period."

Cuban regime accepts Platt Amendment

Havana, Cuba, June 12

Relying on assurances that its sovereignty will not be affected, the constitutional convention that has been meeting here since November today voted to accept the Platt Amendment as part of Cuba's new constitution. The amendment, sponsored by Senator Orville Platt and passed by Congress three months ago, authorizes U.S. intervention in Cuba if it is needed "for the preservation of Cuban independence" and "the maintenance of a government adequate for the protection of life, property and individual liberty." Cuba is also required not to compromise its independence by a treaty with a foreign power, not to borrow beyond its resources and to grant America as yet unspecified naval and coaling bases (→ July 4).

U.S. sends Taft as Governor of Philippines

Manila, Philippines, July 4

United States military rule ended here today with the appointment of Judge William Howard Taft of Ohio as civil Governor. Taft, who arrived two months ago to head the American commission charged with setting up a government, has already won over many Filipinos with his friendly ways and encouragement of Filipino participation in the territorial government. While the guerrilla war against American rule goes on in isolated areas, the rebel cause was dealt a severe blow on March 23, when Emilio Aguinaldo was seized in his hideout by Brigadier General Frederick Funston. Aguinaldo is said to have been betrayed by pro-American scouts, then to have sworn allegiance to the United States (→ May 20, 1902).

King Camp Gillette has sparked a revolution in home grooming with the invention of his safety razor. It's a big help to American men on the go.

Aguinaldo, leader of the Philippine insurrection, arrives on board an American warship following his capture. The Philippines will remain in U.S. hands.

President McKinley shot by anarchist

President McKinley is shot by an anarchist at the Pan-American Exposition.

Buffalo, New York, Sept. 6

An anarchist shot President Mc-Kinley today, but the President's doctors say he is "rallying satisfactorily and resting comfortably."

McKinley was shot twice shortly after 4 p.m. by Leon Czolgosz of Cleveland during a reception at the Pan-American Exposition. The assassin had joined a crowd of well-wishers and came to within two feet of the President. At this close range, witnesses say, he raised a hand and fired twice, using a revolver concealed in a bandage or handkerchief. One bullet struck the breast bone and was removed. The other pierced the stomach and has not yet been found.

In the pandemonium, two Secret Service men and a bystander threw Czolgosz to the ground, disarmed him and rushed him away from the screaming crowd. Nearby, the 58-year-old President protested that he was "not badly hurt," until he saw the blood spreading over his white linen. He urged that extreme care be taken in telling his infirm wife about the shooting, and asked that his assailant not be harmed.

Czolgosz is an ordinary-looking man of medium height. He was plainly dressed in black, with nothing to mark him in a crowd. The police report that Czolgosz, who has seven brothers and sisters in Cleveland, has signed a six-page confession. He says that he is an anarchist in sympathy, and influenced by Emma Goldman, but that he is not part of an organization or plot. He says he bought the weapon three days ago because the country's form of government needs changing and he wanted to get the change started. Police are guarding him from a mob estimated at 30,000. They chanted "Lynch him! Hang him!" until they were driven back by a squad of police reserves.

Vice President Roosevelt is being rushed to Buffalo from Vermont by special train. At Isle La Motte, when informed of the shooting, he exclaimed, "My God!" and declared himself so "inexpressibly grieved, shocked and horrified that I can say nothing" (→ 14).

Second treaty gives U.S. canal rights

Washington, D.C., Dec. 16

As expected, the new and revised Hay-Pauncefote Treaty, negotiated last month by the Secretary of State with the British ambassador, has been ratified by the Senate without difficulty. The new accord confirms the abrogation of the Clayton-Bulwer Treaty of 1850 with the understanding that the United States will have the sole right to build and operate a canal across the isthmus of Panama, with equal transit rights for ships of all nations; but it deletes the earlier requirement that other countries join the treaty as well as the clause that forbids fortification (→ Jan. 4, 1902).

Teddy Roosevelt sworn in as President

At 42 the youngest man ever to become President, Theodore Roosevelt brings a fiery spirit to the office.

Buffalo, New York, Sept. 14

Theodore Roosevelt took the oath of office here this afternoon, becoming the youngest President in American history. At 42, he succeeds 58-year-old William McKinley, who died at 2:15 a.m., of an infection in one of the wounds inflicted eight days ago by the anarchist Leon Czolgosz. Roosevelt, the hero of the Spanish-American War and former Governor of New York, immediately promised "to continue unbroken the policy of President McKinley." He set aside September 19 as the funeral day.

Roosevelt was the object of an intensive search in the Adirondack Mountains most of yesterday, as McKinley's condition worsened. Finally located on top of Mount Marcy, he reached a nearby village at 5 a.m by horse and fast car, transferring to special trains and finally arriving in Buffalo at 1:30 p.m. An hour later, in a borrowed high hat that did not fit, Roosevelt arrived to view the body of the President he has succeeded. He looked shaken as he left for the nearby home of his friend Ansley Wilcox. In the low-ceilinged library of Wilcox's quaint vine-covered house, which is fronted by large colonial pillars, Roosevelt was sworn in as President shortly after 3 p.m.

Czolgosz will be indicted tomorrow, with a trial and sentencing reported likely within two weeks.

Mysterious Cardiff Giant at Buffalo Expo

Buffalo, New York

Thousands of people at the exposition here who have been paying to view the 10'4" Cardiff Giant weighing 2,990 pounds have now learned that it is a hoax. Known as the "Eighth Wonder of the World," the giant was the brainchild of George Hull, a tobacco farmer from Binghamton, N.Y., who bought a five-ton block of gypsum in Fort Dodge, Iowa, and hired two sculptors to carve the giant statue. Irritated by clergymen who were always quoting Genesis ("there were giants in the earth in those days"), Hull decided to ridicule them, making a giant man-like figure out of stone and promoting it as a petrified man. He shipped the statue to William Newell's farm in Broome County, N.Y., where it was buried. After workmen digging a well discovered the huge figure, Newell charged 50 cents a look, and it became the biggest tourist attraction in the state. Newell's partner Hull spent $2,200 and earned $35,000 when the giant was sold to five businessmen. P.T. Barnum built a replica and earned even more money from the hoax.

"Bronco Buster" (1895), by Frederic Remington, on display at this year's well-attended Pan-American Exposition in Buffalo, N.Y.

Booker T. Washington, White House guest

Booker T. Washington, the educator, serves as a voice for a seen but unheard part of American society.

Washington, D.C., Oct. 16

In an attempt to improve race relations and to get better acquainted with the nation's foremost Negro educator, President Roosevelt had Booker T. Washington to dinner tonight at the White House. In office less than a month, Roosevelt is apparently already in political hot water. After the invitation was made public, Southern reaction was fierce. Some called the invitation "a crime equal to treason." A Memphis newspaper remarked that "No Southern woman with proper self-respect would now accept an invitation to the White House." Washington is the author of the best-selling autobiography, *Up From Slavery*.

President Roosevelt warns of evil trusts

Washington, D.C., Dec. 3

In his first message to Congress, President Roosevelt today pointed to "real, grave evils" in rapidly spreading trusts. He called for federal supervision of interstate trusts "in the interest of the whole people" and for a Cabinet-level secretary of commerce. But the President warned that "the mechanism of modern business is so delicate that extreme care must be taken not to interfere with it in a spirit of rashness or ignorance." Discussing organized labor, he said the eight-hour day must be honored, and women and children protected in all jobs that involve government work. He also urged aid that "helps a man to help himself" (→ March 10, 1902).

The "Colossus" pulls the strings.

Planters in Georgia still holding slaves

Anderson County, Ga., Aug. 1

Thirty-six years after the Civil War came to an end, three of the most prominent planters in this state were charged by a grand jury today with practicing slavery. The plantation owners had confined to their stockades Negroes who had never been convicted of any legal offense. The grand jury, in its report, offered evidence that some of the Negroes had also been whipped and forced to submit to other acts of cruelty. A charge of false imprisonment was filed against the violators. Many residents are shocked by the revelations, but others say they are not surprised at all.

All Oklahoma Indians granted citizenship

Oklahoma Territory, March 3

Congress voted today to grant full American citizenship to all Indians living in the Oklahoma Territory – whether they want it or not. Although the ink is hardly dry on the paper, both Indians and whites in Oklahoma and Washington are already questioning the wisdom and the full implications of the law.

Most white Americans have assumed that the Oklahoma Indians, and indeed other tribe members, have always desired American citizenship. However, both white and Indian Oklahomans have pointed out that this is not necessarily so. Congress passed a little-known act in 1890 that allowed any member of an Indian tribe living in Indi-

an Territory to apply to the United States Court at Muskogee for American citizenship. While this obviously well-intentioned move was designed to let Indians into the mainstream of American society, it was a dismal failure. Because of the Indians' pride in their traditional society and culture, the opinions of fellow Indians kept those who might desire citizenship from requesting it. In fact, only four Indians – three Cherokees and a Creek – out of the thousands who were eligible asked for citizenship. And the few who did so apparently became the object of scorn and suspicion on the part of other Indians. It would seem, therefore, that this well-intentioned act may have backfired.

Rockefeller's worth put at $200 million

New York City

Though a recent audit places the assets of John D. Rockefeller at $200 million, the world's richest man has made many times that. Following his own dictum that "A man should make all he can and give it away," the founder of the mighty Standard Oil trust has donated untold millions, including great sums to the University of Chicago and to the Rockefeller Institute for Medical Research, founded this year. But Rockefeller has also espoused the survival of the fittest, and his methods, as a result, have led more Americans to fear him than to admire him.

Adrenaline isolated

Baltimore, Maryland

Two chemists here have isolated adrenaline, the first pure hormone to be obtained from a natural source. The hormone, which is the active substance secreted by the medulla of the suprarenal glands in humans and some animals, has many therapeutic uses, including the easing of respiratory difficulties caused by asthma and allergies and the stimulation of the heart. Jokichi Takamine, a Japanese chemist, and John Jacob Abel, an American physician and physiological chemist, are credited with the discovery.

"Peskelechaco, Republican Pawnee" (c.1822) by Charles Bird King.

Red Tomahawk, an Indian who has adopted the dress of the white man.

Railroad Octopus

United States

As train lines reach out like tentacles across the continent, powerful railroad companies squeeze the life's blood out of all those who stand in their way. This is the theme of *The Octopus: A Story of California*, a gritty, realistic novel by Frank Norris. The first volume of a projected trilogy by the 31-yearold Chicagoan, *The Octopus* describes the epic battle in which a community of wheat farmers takes on wealthy railroad owners, who gain a stranglehold on the state government and newspapers.

Washington, D.C., Jan. 4.
Panama Company lowers asking price for its holdings and franchises, from $103 million to $40 million (→ 18).

Washington, D.C., Jan. 18.
Walker Commission recommends Panamanian route for proposed canal, given lowered price for Panama Company (→ June 28).

New York City, Jan. 25.
Musical *Floradora* closes after record 505 performances.

Cuba, May 20. Tomas Estrada Palma becomes first president of Republic of Cuba; United States decides to withdraw (→ Jan. 4, 1904).

Oregon, June 2. State institutes general initiative and referendum so that public can override legislative action and initiate popular vote.

Washington, D.C., June 17.
Congress passes Newlands Reclamation Act, providing for irrigation of arid lands in West through dam-building.

Washington, D.C., June 28.
Congress passes Isthmian Canal Act, authorizing President to negotiate with French for right to build canal across Colombia (→ Nov. 2, 1903).

New York City, July 12.
Twentieth Century Limited train sets new speed record, by traveling from New York to Chicago in 16 hours.

Detroit, Aug. 22 Automobile firm changes name to Cadillac, after French explorer.

Saratoga, New York, Aug. 31.
Mrs. Adolph Ladenburg introduces split skirt for horseback riding, causing sensation.

Washington, September. "Yacolt Burn" is last of forest fires that have destroyed 12 billion feet of timber in state.

Washington, D.C., Dec. 19.
United States persuades Britain, Germany and Italy to end blockade of five Venezuelan ports and enter arbitration.

United States. Song *In the Good Old Summertime* sells a million copies in first year.

United States. Saint-Gaudens completes *Victory*, winged bronze statuette of America.

DEATH

New York City, Oct. 26.
Elizabeth Cady Stanton, woman's suffrage leader (*Nov. 12, 1815).

TR resolves mine strike

Washington, D.C., Oct. 16

Anthracite mine owners have finally agreed to the appointment of an arbitration panel, ending a five-month strike in the heart of America's coal country. The pact is a triumph for President Roosevelt, who stepped into the fray after local officials began to fear fuel riots. The presidency, says Roosevelt, ought to represent the third party in labor disputes, the public. News of the owners' acquiescence was brought to Washington by J. Pierpont Morgan, who appears to be enjoying his uncharacteristic role as benign statesman in the war between labor and capital. George Baer, head of the Reading Railroad, which controls many of the struck mines, was not so statesmanlike. At an October 3 meeting with Roosevelt and the United Mine Workers, Baer fumed, "The duty of the hour is not to waste time negotiating with the fomenters of anarchy" but to "reestablish order and peace at any cost." The President says John Mitchell, leader of the U.M.W., was the only gentlemanly presence at the meeting (→ March 21, 1903).

A certificate of union membership.

Government busts one railroad trust

Washington, D.C., March 10

In a drive to revitalize the Sherman Antitrust Act, Attorney General Philander Knox has filed suit against J. Pierpont Morgan's Northern Securities firm. A holding company of sorts, the corporation controls the Northern Pacific, Great Northern and Burlington Railroads. It was set up in November as a gentlemanly resolution of a power struggle among Morgan, J.J. Hill and associates, and Edward Harriman. Morgan is said to be irate over Knox, "that country lawyer," letting the case go to court. On a February 23 visit to the White House, he reportedly told President Roosevelt, "If we have done anything wrong, send your man to my man and they can fix it up." Roosevelt, a man of clear-cut moral convictions, merely told him, "That can't be done" (→ July 4).

"Here is an enormous force let loose upon mankind," Charles Francis Adams once said of the railroads, "Not many of those who fondly believe they control it, ever stop to think of it as the most tremendous and far-reaching engine of social change that has ever blessed or cursed mankind." Photo is Stieglitz's "Hand of Man."

TR says wealth is menace and danger

Pittsburgh, Penn., July 4

Half a million people turned out today to hear President Roosevelt blast the trusts again in a "preview" of his New England tour. On his first visit to this industrial center, they cheered when the President told them that wealth "becomes a menace and danger when not used right" and urged new laws in the public interest. He recently ordered Attorney General Philander Knox, who comes from Pittsburgh, to sue to dissolve the Northern Securities Company trust that evolved from last year's corner on Northern Pacific (→ Feb. 19, 1903).

Business booming throughout America

New Jersey, Aug. 12

The economic upsurge that began two years ago shows no sign of waning.

Unemployment is at its lowest in 20 years. Industrial growth is reaching unforeseen heights. A major farm implement manufacturing company, International Harvester, was incorporated in this state today. Earlier this year, Gustavus Swift and J.O. Armour opened their huge National Packing Company plants in Chicago. And in Wyoming, J.C. Penney has announced the formation of nationwide retail clothing outlets that he calls "chain stores."

Helen Keller's "The Story of My Life"

In a reflective moment, a symbol of indomitable spirit over adversity.

Boston

Miracles happen daily in the life of Helen Keller. The 22-year-old native of Alabama, now a student at Radcliffe, lost her sight and hearing at the age of 19 months, yet, under the guidance of Miss Anne Sullivan, her teacher, she learned to read, write and, amazingly, to speak. Miss Keller relates these triumphs in *The Story of My Life*. A high point occurs when Sullivan places the hand of her 7-year-old pupil under the spout of a pump. "As the cool stream rushed over one hand," Miss Keller recalls, "my teacher spelled into the other the word water ... the mystery of language was revealed to me."

Jell-O, everybody!

New York City

Housewives bored with rich custard sweets are delighting in a new gelatin dessert called Jell-O. Children love it, and its nutritional values are being promoted as well. Originated by Pearl B. Wait, a Le Roy, New York, carpenter (his wife May coined the name), the rights to this shimmering, wobbly dessert were bought up by Orator Frank Woodward, who marketed it so well that sales this year may top $250,000.

"Automat" arrives

Philadelphia, June 9.

A new concept in self-service eating has opened on Chestnut Street – the "Automat." Patrons choose from rows of glass-fronted cases, drop in a coin or two, and out pops a freshly cooked dish. Opened by Joseph Horn and Frank Hardart, the Automat is called a great advance. Writes the *Evening Bulletin*, "The horseless carriage, the wireless telephone and the playerless piano have been surpassed ..."

The books are new, the religion old-time

United States

Charles Darwin may have cast a shadow over the Bible, but two up-to-date thinkers still espouse the old-time religion. William James, Harvard's "pragmatist" philosopher, argues in *The Varieties of Religious Experience* that belief in God is not only valuable but also practical because "the sense of union with the power beyond us is a sense of something, not merely apparently, but literally true."

Walter Rauschenbusch, a Baptist minister and professor of church history at Rochester Theological Seminary, sets forth the doctrine of Social Gospel in *Christianity and the Social Crisis*. This book holds that biblical lore can cure many of the ills created by industrialization. The liberal-minded author advocates social progress and calls upon the church to take an active role in a new holy struggle, that of bettering the lot of the working classes.

Hookworm afflicts poor whites in Dixie

Atlanta, Georgia, Feb. 10

Much of the South is poised for a drive to eradicate the hookworm, which, in the words of Dr. Charles Wardell Stiles, is the cause of "laziness" among its poor whites. While the existence of the hookworm dates back many centuries in other parts of the world, not until recently has it emerged in the American South, where it has been classified as Necator Americanus (New World hookworm). The parasitic worms, which thrive in warm and humid climates, can cause anemia, difficulty in breathing, weakness, dizziness, nausea, enlargement of the heart, abdominal pain, internal bleeding and other ailments, particularly in areas with poor sanitary conditions and among those who walk barefooted in moist soil.

Teddy averts death as carriage is hit

Pittsfield, Mass., Sept. 3

A streetcar hurtling along at 30 miles an hour came close to killing President Teddy Roosevelt and his fellow travelers today when it hit their landau. All but one of them were thrown free of the open carriage, receiving minor injuries. But Secret Service man William Craig was crushed under the car and killed instantly. The President had just delivered a speech at the park here. He was behind schedule and his driver, trying to make up time, didn't see the approaching streetcar as he spurred the four horses across the tracks. Roosevelt received a cut lip. The President, shocked by the Secret Service man's death, shook his fist at the motorman and roared, "This is the most damnable outrage I ever knew!"

Wister "Virginian" wins West again

United States

The West may already be won, but its legend survives in *The Virginian: A Horseman of the Plains*, a tale about rough-and-ready cowpunchers set in the Wyoming of the 1870s and '80s. The nameless protagonist, called simply "the Virginian," tall, brave and soft-spoken, is a model of Western valor. Readers are already repeating his retort to his nemesis, the ornery outlaw Trampus, who uses an unflattering epithet when addressing the Virginian. "When you call me that, smile!" says the hero, quickly winning his way into the heart of Molly Wood, a demure schoolteacher who has come out from Vermont to help civilize the frontier children. The author, Owen Wister, 42, is from a famous Philadelphia family.

New York City, Jan. 20.
The Wizard of Oz has premiere at Majestic Theater.

Washington, D.C., Feb. 14.
Act of Congress, signed into law by President Roosevelt, creates Department of Commerce and Labor.

Washington, D.C., Feb. 14.
Congress, at request of Secretary of War Elihu Root, establishes United States Army General Staff Corps to centralize military control.

Rochester, New York, Feb. 16.
Suffragette Susan B. Anthony donates book collection to Library of Congress.

New York City, March 29.
Regular news service opens between New York and London through use of Guglielmo Marconi's wireless system.

Nantucket, Mass., March.
Limericks, published in newspapers, become popular.

Washington, D.C., July 4.
President Roosevelt inaugurates first Pacific communications cable by sending message around world, to himself.

United States, Sept. 3.
American yacht Reliance defeats Britain's Shamrock III for America's Cup.

Detroit, Michigan, Oct. 22.
Electric Motor Vehicle Company files large suit against Ford Motor Company for patent violations.

Colon, Colombia, Nov. 2.
President Roosevelt orders cruiser Nashville to drop anchor, ostensibly to protect "free and uninterrupted transit across the isthmus" (→6).

New York City, Dec. 27. Echo song *Sweet Adeline*, by Henry Armstrong, sung for first time at Pops Sunday Nights.

Chicago, Dec. 30.
Fire in Iroquois Theater kills 588 people [public outrage leads to new theater codes across nation].

Chicago. John Dewey publishes *Studies in Logical Theory,* giving his definition of thought.

Chicago. Frank Norris publishes *The Pit,* novel about corrupt agricultural trading practices.

Atlanta, Georgia. W.E.B. Du Bois publishes *The Souls of Black Folk,* challenging views of Booker T. Washington.

Henry Ford sells first Model A, for $850

The very simplicity of Henry Ford's Model A defines a certain elegance.

Detroit, Michigan, July 23
Renowned for the success of his speedy "999" racer in the Detroit Challenge Cup auto race, Henry Ford formed a new company this year to produce the gasoline-powered "family horse," as he calls it. Today, his Ford Motor Company sold the first of these vehicles, called the Model A, for $850 to a Detroit physician.

Ford's philosophy is simply to build "more cars, better and cheaper." With financial backing mostly from local financier Alexander Mal-colmson, the company set up shop here on Mack Avenue. Ford hired 10 workers at $1.50 per day and bought parts for 650 vehicles. The Model A, which was designed last year by Ford himself and chief engineer C.H. Wills, features a two-cylinder, eight-horsepower engine that can push it to 30 m.p.h. Advertisements are boasting that "the same genius which conceived the world's record holder – the '999' – has made possible the production of a thoroughly practical car at a moderate price."

Mother Jones leads children on strike

New York City, July
Labor leader Mother Jones, still tireless at 73, has led a small army of children into New York, many of them mutilated from accidents in the textile mills. She aims to disturb President Roosevelt at his summer home in Oyster Bay, Long Island. As the parade was leaving Philadelphia on July 4, Mother Jones announced the city's "mansions were built on the broken bones, the quivering hearts and drooping heads of these children." "Fifty years ago," she cried at Coney Island, "the black babies were sold C.O.D. Today the white baby is sold on the installment plan." In fact, some 1.5 million children now work nationwide for as little as 25 cents a day. The President has announced he will not receive Mother Jones and her children.

Clearly a woman to be reckoned with.

Congress regulates railroads with law

Washington, D.C., Feb. 19
Congress moved to end the grip the nation's railroads have on commerce by enacting the Elkins Act today. The legislation will remove rebates on freight rates. Rebates worked like this: Shippers would pay regular rates to the railroads and, if they were in good favor, would receive money back. This cut into fair trade competition. Rebates have been known to breed corruption for years, but powerful rail lobbyists had worked to keep them legal. While many reformers are happy with the law, others, such as Senator La Follette of Wisconsin, feel the act does not go far enough in regulating rails (→ Jan. 30, 1905).

Helium in Kansas

Dexter, Kansas
Kansas, known for its wheat and its cattle, now has a new resource – helium. A field of the natural gas has just been discovered at Dexter. The lightest gas after hydrogen, helium has been known to exist for some time but wasn't identified on earth until 1895. It is tasteless, colorless, odorless and will not burn, making its discovery all the more remarkable. Its uses are few.

"Labor walks into House of Victory"

Washington, D.C., March 21
Ending hearings that have lasted nearly as long as last year's mine strike, the President's commission has granted most of the United Mine Workers' demands. Union recognition, however, was denied, prompting organizer Mother Jones to comment, "Labor walked into the House of Victory, through the back door." Nonetheless, the door is wide. Armed with the legal arguments of Clarence Darrow, John Mitchell's union now has a 10 percent raise for contract miners; an eight-hour day for engineers, firemen and pumpmen, and increased control over the weighing of coal. The panel may indicate a new federal willingness to stabilize the economy by arbitrating labor disputes.

Motorcar is first to cross continent

New York City, July 26

For the first time since its invention, an automobile has crossed the continent. H. Nelson Jackson, a physician from Burlington, Vermont, arrived here today after a coast-to-coast odyssey that began on May 23. He was accompanied by his chauffeur-companion, Sewall K. Crocker. Making the trip in a two-cylinder Winton, they were motivated by a $50 bet the doctor made that he could complete the grind. The car was designed and constructed by Alexander Winton, who gave up the bicycle business to produce cars. The machine has a six-horsepower, water-cooled engine that was mounted in the rear.

Herbert's "Babes in Toyland" is a hit

New York City, Oct. 13

After a troubled stint as conductor of the Pittsburgh Symphony, Victor Herbert has returned to what he loves best – writing musicals. The happy result, *Babes in Toyland*, is his first bona fide success. The book is about a couple of shipwrecked "Babes" washed up on the shores of a fabulous Toyland peopled by fairy-tale figures. From the martial *March of the Toys* to the poignant title song *Toyland*, Herbert taps a seemingly inexhaustible mine of melody.

Herbert's first bona fide success.

Boston upsets Pittsburgh, 5 games to 3, in first World Series

Huntington Avenue Ball Field in Boston is mobbed with fans as the Americans win the first World Series.

Boston, Oct. 13

The war of words between the National and American Leagues finally spilled over into the baseball field. The pennant winners of the two leagues met for a post-season showdown – though without league supervision – and Boston's Americans walked off today with an upset victory over the vaunted Pittsburgh Nationals. The upstart Bostons captured the series, five games to three, scoring a 3-0 triumph in the eighth and final game.

The Boston accomplishment convinced some critics that the American League was more than just a refuge for players who defected from the older circuit. The Nationals had outdrawn their rivals last year, but at the end of the season they made a gesture to establish peace. They and a minor league group banded into what they called Organized Baseball. National commissions will rule the leagues.

In the series, Cy Young pitched two of the Boston victories and lost once against the champions of his former league. The talents of Honus Wagner were not enough to save the Pittsburghers. The sure-handed shortstop with the remarkably strong arm got six hits in the losing cause. Patrick Henry Dougherty proved to be a standout for Boston, hitting two homers in the second contest after the Pirates had won the opening game.

Northern border set in favor of the U.S.

Washington, D.C., Oct. 20

There is good news tonight for the United States, even though it involves land more than 3,000 miles away. The American-British commission studying the boundary between Alaska and Canada has made a decision that grants the United States much of the border area territory it had claimed. The decision was not unilateral; the British commissioner sided with the Americans. The commission, which started its work in January, has disbanded, leaving border matters settled (→ Dec. 5, 1905).

Caruso debut at Met: notices fairly good

New York City, Nov. 23

The bravos still linger for soprano Marcella Sembrich's opening night *Rigoletto* at the Met. The baritone Antonio Scotti was also in excellent voice, but Sembrich as usual brought down the house. Of special interest was the debut of tenor Enrico Caruso. While he is fresh from a triumph in London and has great advance notices, critics here said he is sometimes betrayed by a rough voice and inept acting. Still, they said his singing was on the whole intelligent, passionate and generally good if never really overwhelming. He has a three-month contract and will soon sing in *Aida*.

Italian tenor Enrico Caruso.

U.S. recognizes Republic of Panama

President Roosevelt confidently shapes a new world role for the United States.

Washington, D.C., Nov. 6

Barely three days after the outbreak of a revolt against Colombian rule, the United States today recognized Panama as an independent state. The action comes as no surprise since it is an open secret that the uprising, which was largely engineered by Philippe Bunau-Varilla and other officers of the Panama Canal Company in conjunction with local dissidents, had the full backing of President Roosevelt. Indeed, it was the arrival of the cruiser Nashville in Panamanian waters, sent by the President ostensibly to protect "free and uninterrupted transit across the isthmus," that gave the signal for the outbreak of the revolt, just as it was the presence of the Nashville and other American warships that prevented the Colombians from suppressing it.

The American actions result from the rejection in August by Colombia's Senate of the Hay-Herran Treaty. Negotiations with the new Panama regime for a treaty permitting an American-controlled canal are to start soon (→ May 4, 1904).

Motion pictures get plot and narrative

New Jersey

This year, Edwin W. Porter, one of Thomas A. Edison's directors, first utilized narrative continuity, as opposed to filming skits, in *The Life of an American Fireman*, with firefighters racing to save a mother and child in a burning house. He also presented an epic nearly 12 minutes long called *The Great Train Robbery*, displaying a sense of time, space and logic. We follow each stage of the robbery, the escape and the capture of the robbers. Shot in New Jersey, the film draws long lines of avid spectators.

Chew your cheese thirty-two times

Chicago

Stuck in Chicago after being pushed out of his Buffalo, New York, cheese company by ungrateful partners, James Lewis Kraft has turned $65 into a thriving business. With a rented horse and wagon, he buys cheese from wholesalers and offers it to retail stores at a profit. Merchants are saved the trip and Kraft is saved from vagrancy. Out in San Francisco, food faddist Horace Fletcher wants to save people from a worse fate, gastronomic distress. Chew your food 32 times, he counsels.

The Olmsted legacy: parks for the people

Waverly, Massachusetts, Aug. 28

The 81-year-old park architect Frederick Olmsted died today, leaving behind acres of beautifully landscaped parks throughout the nation. After getting degrees in engineering and science, Olmsted trekked across the United States and Europe studying landscape gardening. His philosophy of using the natural landscapes in urban parks can be seen in his designs for Central Park in New York City, considered his masterpiece, and in parks that include Back Bay in Boston, and Washington and Jackson Parks in Chicago.

Toy boat lake, in New York's Central Park, Olmsted's greatest legacy of all.

Epidemic traced to "Typhoid Mary"

New York City

A typhoid fever epidemic has been traced to Mary Mallon, a cook who worked in an Oyster Bay summer house. Ten days after eating food prepared by "Typhoid Mary," several guests became sick and feverish from the highly contagious disease and were admitted to a New York hospital. After an extensive door-to-door search, Dr. George Soper of the N.Y. City Department of Health deduced that Miss Mallon was responsible. She changed jobs frequently and wherever she had worked, a case of typhoid was soon reported. Once cornered, she was told that she probably was the first known typhoid carrier in the nation. Insisting that she felt perfectly well, Miss Mallon refused to submit to a physical exam and chased Dr. Soper away with a rolling pin. A few years ago, German bacteriologists found that intestinal carriers such as "Typhoid Mary" were spreaders of the disease.

"Brown and Gold: Self-portrait" by James Abbott McNeill Whistler. The artist, an emotional and often cantankerous man, died in London on July 17 of this year.

Kate Wiggin novel, schoolgirl favorite

United States

"He who can, does," George Bernard Shaw has written. "He who cannot, teaches." One who can do both is Kate Douglas Wiggin. A Philadelphian, Miss Wiggin moved to San Francisco and in 1878 set up one of the nation's first kindergartens. She has since started writing children's books. Her latest is *Rebecca of Sunnybrook Farm*, and indications are that it will sell a million copies. The story of a precocious farmgirl and her six sisters, it has become a favorite among schoolgirls from coast to coast.

"Call of the Wild" heard by nation

San Francisco

A man's best friend is his dog, but is a dog's best friend ever a man? This question is posed in the latest adventure novel by Jack London, *The Call of the Wild*, a tale set in the rough-and-tumble world of the Klondike. The hero is Buck, a sled dog, part St. Bernard, part Scottish shepherd, who gives his all to his master, prospector John Thornton, helping him win a bet by hauling a 1,000-pound payload. But when Thornton is killed, the beastly ways of men disgust Buck, so he joins a wolfpack.

Jack London, who has been a sailor, a tramp and a gold miner, is now tasting success as a novelist.

Wright brothers' machine takes to air

Part machine and part bird, the Wright brothers' plane, Flyer, lifts off the ground and onto the pages of history.

Kitty Hawk, N.C., Dec. 17

Almost everywhere, claims of motor-driven flight have aroused skepticism, especially since the spectacular failures that sent the Samuel Langley Aerodrome machine plunging into the Potomac River on two occasions this year. But the flights by Orville and Wilbur Wright today were seen by five witnesses, mostly from a nearby life-saving station. Also, a photographer caught the Flyer just as it was leaving the ground.

Those who witnessed the tests said the Wright brothers, who have been building and flying their own gliders since 1900, hauled their 605-pound, gasoline-powered Flyer up the sandy Kill Devil Hill near Kitty Hawk this morning, and launched it four times into a freezing wind of about 20 miles per hour.

The brothers tossed a coin to determine which one would be the first to fly. The 32-year-old Orville won and climbed aboard the winged machine, dressed in his usual starched white shirt and necktie. A lightweight, 13-horsepower engine then came sputtering to life, setting the machine's two wooden propellers whirring noisily with bicycle chains.

With the 36-year-old Wilbur running alongside carrying a stopwatch, the Flyer accelerated down a 60-foot track. Finally, it took off at 10:35 on a flight that lasted 12 seconds over a distance of 120 feet. Single-minded and solitary, the Wrights rarely doubted that their machine would fly and spent little time on congratulations or, for that matter, reflecting on what could prove to be an epic achievement. Instead, they prepared for additional flights, each of which was longer than the one before it. On the fourth of the flights, Wilbur piloted the Flyer on a 59-second, 852-foot-long ascent. That "hop" came to an abrupt end when the machine nosed onto a nearby beach, crushing the frail spruce-and-muslin horizontal rudders.

Self-taught mathematicians and machinists from Dayton, Ohio, the bachelor brothers were drawn to the problems of human flight after reading about the German glider pilot Otto Lilienthal, who died in one of his unstable craft in 1896. Soon after, the Wrights began designing gliders in their bicycle shop. By 1900, they were flying them amid the favorable wind conditions at Kitty Hawk and testing new wing shapes in a wind tunnel; like nearly all their gear, including the Flyer's engine and propeller, the brothers built the tunnel themselves. They solved the stability problems that have plagued other aeronauts by coming up with a technique that is called wing warping, in which a taut cable bends the wings to help with lift and control.

Design and building expenses, including shipment to Kitty Hawk, amounted to just a little more than $1,000, compared to the $50,000 that was spent by Langley on just the launching mechanism for his Aerodrome, which was sponsored by the War Department.

The Wright brothers intend to withhold more detailed information about their machine until its innovations can be patented, and only time will tell the importance that history will accord today's claims from Kitty Hawk. But by any measure, the Flyer is a fantastic combination of craftsmanship, determination and vision.

1904

Roosevelt

Washington, D.C., Jan. 4. Supreme Court decision, in Gonzales v. Williams, rules that Puerto Ricans are not aliens and cannot be refused entry into United States (→ Dec. 6).

Michigan, Jan. 12. Henry Ford sets auto speed record of 91.37 miles per hour on frozen Lake St. Clair.

Baltimore, Maryland, Feb. 8. Two-day fire extinguished; it destroys 2,600 buildings, but there is no loss of life.

Washington, D.C., Feb. 20. United States sends circular note to belligerents in Russo-Japanese War, asking them to respect Open Door policy in Manchuria [it has no effect upon course of war] (→ Sept. 5, 1905).

New York City, Apr. 25. Will Rogers makes debut as entertainer at Madison Square Garden, appearing with Colonel Zack Mulhall's troupe.

St. Louis, Missouri, Apr. 30. Louisiana Purchase Centennial Exposition opens.→

Panama Canal Zone, May 4. Canal Zone legally becomes United States property (→ July 25, 1905).

New York City, May 20. Secretary of War Elihu Root reads letter from President Roosevelt, espousing Roosevelt Corollary to Monroe Doctrine (→ Dec. 6).

New York City, June 15. Excursion steamer General Slocum burns in East River, killing 1,030 people.

Kentucky, July 1. State legislature passes bill imposing $1,000 fine and $100-a-day penalty against institutions that admit both white and Negro students.

New York City, Nov. 19. Woodrow Wilson declares in a speech, "The Constitution was not made to fit us like a straightjacket. In its elasticity lies its chief greatness."

Albany, New York. First official road speed limits in nation set, at 10 m.p.h. in populated areas, 15 in villages and 20 on open country roads.

Washington, D.C. Deficiency Act bars Chinese laborers indefinitely; it is one of many such exlusionary laws passed.

United States. O Henry publishes *Cabbages and Kings*.

Ice cream cones, iced tea at World's Fair

Festive Hall at the St. Louis World's Fair, held this year to mark the centennial of the Louisiana Purchase, Thomas Jefferson's big land deal with France.

St. Louis, Missouri

The World's Fair has proved to Americans that not every new invention has to be the result of long, difficult trial and error. Sweltering heat appears to be very much the mother of invention here. Take, for instance, concessionaire Richard Blechtynden, whose hot tea had not been selling too well. Blechtynden thought it might help if he put ice in his tea and, sure enough, sales took off, making iced tea one of the hits at the fair. Three ice cream vendors (of the 50 stationed at the fair) now claim to have come up with the idea for edible ice cream holders made from waffle pastry.

A Syrian immigrant, Ernest A. Hamwi, says that he first rolled a Persian pastry called zalabia into a cone-shaped holder when a colleague ran out of ice cream dishes. David Avayou, a Turkish vendor, insists that he took the idea from paper cones he had seen in France. And Abe Doumar claims his "cornucopias" were being sold first, at the "Old City of Jerusalem" section of the fair. Whoever was the first to sell ice cream in cones, the idea of licking one's ice cream and then eating the container that held it seems to be a delicious new treat as well as an excellent way to cut down on waste.

Chicago, May 1. *Indiana-born Eugene Victor Debs, leader of the American socialist movement, was renominated for president today on the Socialist Party ticket. He says, "I am for socialism because I am for humanity."*

U.S., Olympic host, wins 21 first places

St. Louis, Missouri, May 14

For the first time since their revival eight years ago, the Olympic Games have come to the United States. However, the hosts showed no mercy as they captured 21 first places on the 22-event program. The only foreigner to be awarded a gold medal was a Montreal policeman. The Olympic program has been expanded to include swimming, diving and water polo. But cycling and target shooting have been dropped from the competition. The turnout of both athletes and spectators was disappointing and club athletes continued to replace those from the colleges.

Duke firms become American Tobacco

North Carolina, Oct. 19

James Buchanan Duke has reshaped his conglomerate of tobacco companies into the American Tobacco Company. It will include all the snuff, plug and cigarette makers he has bought out over the years. Duke took over his competitors by slashing prices, using automatic cigarette-rolling machines and increasing advertising. As a boy at a Quaker academy, he prophesied his future: "I'm going to be a businessman and make a pile" (→ June 1911).

Carnegie sets up fund for heroes

New York City, Apr. 15

Life-saving deeds will no longer go unnoticed if the Carnegie Hero Fund has anything to say about it. Philanthropist Andrew Carnegie, who made his fortune in iron and steel, has donated $5 million to endow the fund, which will reward those who are injured in heroic life-saving acts. Dependents of men and women who died while trying to save another's life will also be rewarded. The Hero Fund commission will investigate heroic acts, prepare reports and decide on compensation. Heroes will receive gold, silver or bronze medals, depending on the range of the heroism involved.

Steerage fare slashed; America affordable to all

New York City, May 23

The great Atlantic Ocean, once an endless sea of perils for the explorers of Renaissance Europe, has become a highway to heaven – bountiful America. A drastic cut in steerage rates goes into effect today that will allow Europeans to board a steamship with $10 in their pockets and arrive in Ellis Island less than a month later. If a decent job awaits them, they will earn the price of their passage in a week.

The new fare schedule is a result of European rivalries. Britain, Germany, Italy and France, vying for control of the seas, offer large subsidies to steamship lines. Hoping that volume will help control the routes, Inman, Cunard and the other big firms pass the savings along to passengers and use their grants to build monster ships. Inman's 11,000-ton City of Paris liner, queen of the seas since 1888, will be deposed by Cunard's 19,000-ton Caronia this year. Quarters are still cramped, but steam has mercifully cut travel time and regular schedules eliminate prolonged stopovers.

Attracting immigrants is a business for many Americans. Agents seeking laborers for American firms stand outside of Italian churches handing out leaflets and singing hymns to the Statue of Liberty's "golden door." But friends who have already made the voyage send home a more realistic picture. Half the new arrivals come with tickets paid for by contacts in the United States. They know better where to look for work and can seek out a number of government and private agencies that help channel newcomers into a niche in American society. And at the bottom line, despite a labor surplus, wages remain two to three times their levels in Europe (→ Dec. 5, 1905).

A family of Italian immigrants on the Ellis Island ferry bound for Manhattan. They, like millions of others, must still sacrifice to manage the lowered fare.

Italian mother and her three children upon arrival at Ellis Island after making the long voyage in steerage. Immigration from Italy has been growing steadily and at the present rate will lead the list with 220,000 arrivals this year.

Crossing the Atlantic Ocean in steerage is a cramped, dirty and generally unpleasant experience. But for a majority, there is simply no alternative if they want to start over and begin a new life in the land of opportunity.

Roosevelt is elected to his own full term

Washington, D.C., Nov. 9

President Theodore Roosevelt won in his own right today. Nearly complete returns show the "Rough Rider" who succeeded to the White House on the assassination of President McKinley has been elected to a full term by an electoral vote of 336 for Roosevelt to 110 for the Democratic Party's Judge Alton B. Parker. When the Roosevelt victory became certain, the President issued a statement saying that he was "deeply sensible of the honor done me by the American people in thus expressing their confidence in what I have done and have tried to do." He concluded, however, by promising: "Under no circumstances will I be a candidate for or accept another nomination."

Thus, the President has limited to only four more years his fight for such programs as his popular trust-busting campaign.

In March, the Supreme Court awarded him a resounding victory in his fight to regulate monopolistic big business that fails to operate in the public interest. By a vote of five to four, the court dissolved the Northern Securities Company railroad trust under the little-used Sherman Antitrust Act.

Promising a "square deal" for all if elected to a full term, Roosevelt ran in a campaign notable for the absence of William Jennings Bryan, the silver spokesman who lost the Democratic nomination to pro-gold Judge Parker of the party's Eastern wing (→ March 4, 1905).

The President stands for his portrait. "Theodore Roosevelt" by J.S. Sargent.

Festival is tribute to Richard Strauss

New York City, March 21

A month-long Richard Strauss Festival marking the American debut of the famed German composer-conductor has been generally triumphant. Too bad, then, that it should end on a cool note with the world premiere of his *Symphonia Domestica* at Carnegie Hall. The music isn't as dramatic as his *Don Juan* or *Till Eulenspiegel*, and many deplore its autobiographical nature. Strauss has subtitled it, *A Day in the Life of My Family*. From here, Strauss will journey to Philadelphia for two concerts at Wanamaker's Department Store – for $1,000. "True art ennobles any building," the maestro explained.

Cy Young pitches a "perfect" game

Boston, May 5

Denton True "Cy" Young became the first major league pitcher to hurl a "perfect" game when he prevented any Philadelphia player from reaching first base today. The 37-year-old hurler for the Boston Americans, who switched from the St. Louis National club in 1901, amazed fans with his control as he surpassed his performance of last September 18, when he set down the Cincinnati team without a hit. Young, who started his career with Cleveland's Nationals in his home state of Ohio, won 33 games and lost only 10 in his first year at Boston and followed that with seasons of 32-11 and 28-9.

Woman in motorcar arrested for smoking

New York City, Sept. 28

Men, says the census, now outnumber women by about 1.5 million, and they exercise many privileges denied to the female of the species. In New York today, a woman was arrested for smoking in an open automobile. "You can't do that on Fifth Avenue," a policeman lectured. There is no law against the practice, but custom dictates otherwise. But what's a lady to do when the President's daughter Alice herself smokes, even in public and probably on Fifth Avenue if given the chance. In increasing numbers, it seems, women are defying convention. Clubs, saloons and tobacco shops, at least, still offer all-male havens.

Negroes in six cities boycott "Jim Crow"

Atlanta, Georgia, Fall

This has been a turbulent year for whites and Negroes alike. Following rioting, burning and lynchings, whites are increasingly turning to "Jim Crow" (segregationist) laws to isolate themselves from the Negro community. Kentucky has officially segregated both its public and private schools. In response, Negroes have become increasingly militant in combatting this form of second-class citizenship. During this past year, Negroes have protested Jim Crow laws by boycotting segregated streetcars in Atlanta, Augusta, Columbia, New Orleans, Mobile and Houston. The racial turmoil shows no signs of waning (→ Sept. 24, 1906).

Tarbell exposes Rockefeller's Standard Oil

United States

No one is safe from the reformers, least of all a mighty financier. John D. Rockefeller is the latest to feel their wrath in *The History of the Standard Oil Company*, an exposé by Ida Tarbell of *McClure's Magazine* about the powerful company and the ruthless methods it uses to ruin rivals, plunder the earth for crude oil and buy off politicians.

The sensational findings, based on interviews with former Standard employees, first appeared last year in a *McClure's* series written by Miss Tarbell, a 47-year-old native of Pennsylvania. A graduate of Allegheny College, she taught briefly before moving to Paris, where she was hired 10 years ago by S.S. McClure, founder of the magazine bearing his name.

New York City gets shiny new subway

New York City, Oct. 27

"City Hall to Harlem in 15 minutes" has been the boast of the New York City subway since construction began in 1900. Today it lived up to the claim, as 150,000 cheering passengers jammed the gleaming, 25 m.p.h. electric cars. Chief Engineer John B. McDonald built the 15-mile line with financial backing from August Belmont. With congestion above ground growing, underground rapid transit has become a necessity. The first subway theft was also reported today. At 7:02 p.m., a passenger was relieved of a $500 diamond pin.

New steel company born in Bethlehem

Bethlehem, Penn., Dec. 10

Bethlehem Steel was incorporated today, 47 years after the nucleus of the company opened for business. Charles M. Schwab, a former U.S. Steel president, purchased an interest in the small Bethlehem Steel Company and merged it with the U.S. Shipbuilding Company last year. He will now preside over all Bethlehem Steel's activities. The firm will use the Bessemer process to manufacture steel in Pittsburgh.

Ashcan artist Robert Henri's "Young Woman in White" (1904).

Theodore Roosevelt wields Big Stick

Roosevelt, with navy in tow, turns the Caribbean into an American lake.

Washington, D.C., Dec. 6

The emergence of the United States as a world power with its own exclusive sphere of influence was highlighted today in the President's annual address to Congress in which he formulated an extension of the Monroe Doctrine that is being called the Roosevelt Corollary. Referring to recent events in Central America, the President declared that "chronic wrongdoing, or an impotence which results in a general loosening of the ties of civilized society . . . may force the United States, however reluctantly, in flagrant cases of such wrongdoing or impotence, to the exercise of an international police power."

Such police power is to be used to prevent a repetition of the 1902 incident when German, British and Italian warships blockaded Venezuela to force payment of debts on which that country had defaulted. But while deploring such armed intervention as a violation of the Monroe Doctrine, the President has shown no sympathy for countries that default. Therefore, as he put it to Secretary of War Elihu Root, "If we intend to say 'Hands off' . . . we must keep order ourselves." The newly formulated policy is likely to be applied early next year to the Dominican Republic, which recently reneged on debts that amount to some $32 million.

Despite America's acquisition of Puerto Rico and the Philippines, the President's policy is avowedly anticolonial. "I have about as much desire to annex it," he has said of the Dominican Republic, "as a gorged boa constrictor might have to swallow a porcupine wrong-end-to." Nor has Roosevelt shown any inclination to depart from the original Monroe Doctrine so far as it commits the United States not to interfere in Europe, where increasing hostility between the alliances of the great powers threatens to lead to a major war.

In automobile competition, gasoline power pulls way out ahead

Westbury, Long Island, Oct. 8

When George Heath's 90-horsepower Panhard racer whizzed past the finish line to win the first Vanderbilt Cup race today, it was new proof of the technical leaps taken by gasoline-powered cars. The race, sponsored by W.H. Vanderbilt Jr., covered a grueling 284-mile course starting in Westbury. Heath, an American, finished in 5 hours 26 minutes, as his low-slung, rakish French motorcar averaged over 50 m.p.h. At times, the speeds neared 70 m.p.h., and one vehicle, a Mercedes driven by George Arents, burst a tire and spun out of control, killing mechanic Carl Mensel.

This year, 22,130 automobiles were manufactured and sold from the Southeast to the Northwest. Steam and electric cars still abound, but as the race attests, gasoline power is unmatched for endurance and speed. In fact, New York has a new 20 m.p.h. open-road speed limit, and on September 3, an Oldsmobile driven by L.L. Whitman arrived in New York after leaving San Francisco just 33 days earlier. On August 10, St. Louis proclaimed "Automobile Day" when a 59-machine procession that left New York on July 25 crossed the Eads Bridge and entered the World's Fair grounds.

The 1904 Oldsmobile 7 is typical of the machines seen on the road. Its curved dashboard and buggy-style seat are reminiscent of the horse-drawn carriage.

Teddy mounts bully pulpit in Washington

With flags aflutter, Roosevelt takes the oath for first full term in office.

Washington, D.C., March 4

When Vice President Teddy Roosevelt moved into the Oval Office after the assassination of President McKinley in 1901, Senator Mark Hanna exclaimed, "Now that damned cowboy is President!" Last November, Teddy the Rough Rider silenced critics and was elected on his own. Today, he mounted the "bully pulpit" and delivered his presidential inaugural address.

In it, the popular, active President repeated a favorite theme: rights and duties. "We have duties to others and duties to ourselves; we can shirk neither," he exclaimed from the Capitol steps. He struck a rugged tone when he lauded America's "self-reliance and individual initiative" and, in progressive trust-busting words, he said that "accumulation of great wealth" has led to grave problems. TR ended his address with a reference to Abraham Lincoln: "We must show ... devotion to a lofty ideal ... which made great men who preserved this republic in the days of Abraham Lincoln." Roosevelt reveres Lincoln. Last night, Secretary of State John Hay gave Teddy a ring engraved with both "TR" and Lincoln's initials and a lock of his hair, snipped while he lay dying. After Roosevelt's speech, he watched the largest inaugural parade ever.

The President addresses the nation.

Supreme Court slaughters the beef trust

Washington, D.C., Jan. 30

The so-called "beef trust" was dealt a death blow today when the United States Supreme Court decided that Swift and Company was operating an illegal monopoly in violation of the Sherman Antitrust Act of 1890.

In ruling in favor of the government in Swift & Co. v. the United States, the high court held that the meat concern was acting in restraint of trade, that the effect of the company's action upon commerce among the states was not accidental.

The charge of the federal government was that "a dominant proportion" of the dealers in fresh meat throughout the country had not bid against one another in the livestock markets in order to fix prices and that they had restricted shipments of meat when that proved necessary. The government further accused the meat dealers of having sought to obtain less-than-lawful rates from the railroad companies.

The court's opinion, which was written by Justice Oliver Wendell Holmes, noted that "it is said this charge was too vague" and that it "does not set forth a case of commerce among the states." Actually, according to the Holmes opinion, when cattle are transported from one state to another and sold, interstate commerce is indeed taking place. Then, with tongue very much in cheek, Justice Holmes wrote: "It should be added that the cattle in the stockyard are not at rest" (→ March 12, 1906).

U.S. takes over Dominican finances

Dominican Republic, March 31

President Roosevelt today appointed a customs receiver for the Dominican Republic as part of his program to resolve the Caribbean country's financial problems. The republic has borrowed heavily from foreign sources and reportedly owes $32 million. Roosevelt decided strong measures were needed to prevent intervention by European powers. According to the agreement worked out with the Dominican government, the United States will control the country's customs house, its main source of income, and will allow the Dominican government 45 percent of the money collected for use domestically. The rest will be used to pay back foreign creditors. If estimates that 90 percent of customs revenues are pocketed by corrupt officials are accurate, the 45 percent allowance should not prove a hardship but a boon to the country's economy.

Roosevelt set the stage for today's action in his message to Congress last December when he stated that "in the Western Hemisphere adherence of the United States to the Monroe Doctrine may force the United States, however reluctantly, in flagrant cases of ... wrongdoing or impotence, to the exercise of an international police power."

Today's less ornate and constrictive, simpler fashions are designed to meet the changing role of woman in American society.

President helps end Russo-Japanese War

The Old World powers respectfully submit to New World diplomacy.

Portsmouth, N.H., Sept. 5

President Roosevelt's energetic efforts to get the belligerents of the Russo-Japanese War to sit down together has borne fruit. Delegates to the peace negotiations here in Portsmouth have agreed on a treaty in which the Russians are conceding to the Japanese the superior position in Korea, the principal issue over which this war has been fought.

Although the Russian government also agreed to withdraw its troops from Manchuria and to hand over to Japan part of the island of Sakhalin, its position in Asia was not harmed. The worst damage is to the prestige of Czar Nicholas II, who is the first leader of a modern European power to lose a war to an Asian one. The breakthrough in the talks came when Roosevelt persuaded Japan to drop its demand for war reparations. He had accused the Japanese of continuing the fighting for the sake of money (→ Dec. 10, 1906).

Americans get taste of pizza in Little Italy

New York City

Visitors to New York City's colorful neighborhood of Little Italy have become accustomed to sampling exotic specialties such as spaghetti and lasagna, and now a Spring Street restaurateur named Gennaro Lombardi has started to feature a new food item that the Italian immigrants here call a "pizza."

This flat, yeast bread baked with oozing, melted cheese called mozzarella and tomatoes is served in wedgelike slices that may be eaten either with fork and knife or with the fingers. Said to be a specialty of Naples, the pizza has long been a favorite there, although it is apparently not much known in the other sections of Italy.

Scot wins U.S. Open for the fourth time

Pittsfield, Mass.

Willie Anderson, a dour, uncommunicative Scot who is considered the mystery man of golf, has astounded followers of the sport by winning the United States Open championship for the fourth time. He made it three in a row with a smashing victory over Alex Smith to take it this year. Anderson had beaten Smith in the 1901 Open final, taking the playoff by a stroke. He went on to win again in 1903, this time defeating David Brown. The next year, Anderson amazed his followers by outplaying Gil Nicholls with a score of 303. Before his breakthrough, Anderson was second in 1897, third in 1898, fifth in 1899 and 11th in 1900.

Hart captures title with 12th-round KO

Reno, Nevada, July 3

Marvin Hart captured the world heavyweight boxing championship today – well, sort of. One thing is certain: He knocked out Jack Root in the 12th round here. The promoter of the fight had declared that the winner would take over the title vacated by Jim Jeffries, who quit boxing because he could not find a suitable opponent to knock out. Jeffries had held the championship since he put away a badly overmatched Bob Fitzsimmons in 1899. Jeffries, by the way, was referee in the Hart-Root fight. While it took place, Tommy Burns of Canada has been in the background, saying he is the rightful heir to the title (→ March 23, 1906).

Citing accord with U.S., Japan rules Korea

Tokyo, Dec. 21

Japan has declared Korea its protectorate, extending its control of that country into the one area that had eluded its grasp, foreign affairs. As justification for its action, Japan cited a memorandum negotiated this summer between American Secretary of War William Howard Taft and Prime Minister Taro Katsura, in which the United States recognized the Japanese control of Korea in return for Japan's pledge not to get involved in the Philippines. President Roosevelt has not protested Japan's interpretation of the Taft-Katsura memorandum, although at the time it was negotiated it was regarded as no more than a recognition of Japan's current position, not an endorsement of any future action.

Japan has been a major actor on the Korean political stage since 1895, when it overturned China's protectorate there. For a while, the Russian aspirations for Korea checked the Japanese, but Tokyo's victory in the Russo-Japanese War removed Russia as an obstacle.

Under the protectorate treaty imposed on the Korean Emperor, a Japanese regent-general will replace Korea's minister of foreign affairs and its foreign legations will be disbanded, destroying the last outpost of its already weak independence movement.

Meetings rotate; call them Rotarians

Chicago, Feb. 23

In an effort to promote high standards of practice and cooperation in business, Chicago lawyer Paul Percy Harris today founded a local organization that he calls the Rotary Club. The civilian service club will consist of at least one member from each local business or profession, without overrepresentation in any one area. Members are planning to meet at one another's offices in rotation, which explains how the organization got its name. The association said it hopes not only to foster fellowship and good will between members, but in the community as well.

States barred from setting work hours

Washington, D.C., Apr. 17

The Supreme Court ruled today that states cannot set the maximum number of hours any employee can work. By ruling so, the court overturned a New York law that sought to restrict bakery and confectionery employees to no more than 60 hours a week or an average of 10 hours a day. The state law, the court held, violated the Constitution in that it was illegal interference in the rights of both employers and employees. While conceding that such work is strenuous, the court also held there was no reasonable foundation for holding that the law in question was necessary to guard public health.

"Evening on a Canadian Lake" (1905) by Frederic Remington.

Du Bois movement urges racial equality

Fort Erie, Ontario, July 13

Responding to W.E.B. Du Bois's call for "organized determination and aggressive action," 29 Negroes from 14 states met today to formulate principles for the radical wing of the civil rights movement. Dr. Du Bois, a Harvard-educated sociologist and a reluctant entrant into politics, tells his race to "refuse to kiss the hands that smite us." The new "Niagara Movement" formalizes a split between Du Bois and educator Booker T. Washington. Washington, who runs a vocational school in Tuskegee, Alabama, says

Negroes must stake a place in the industrial economy, and only then pursue political rights. Washington's followers have taken to calling Du Bois the "professor of hysterics." His "hysteria," apparently, is the belief that without full political equality, the Negro will always be shut out of a biased economy. The Niagara Movement thus seeks manhood suffrage, freedom of speech and criticism, abolition of all caste distinctions based simply on race or color and "recognition of the principle of human brotherhood as a practical present creed."

Panama canal construction is under way

Panama, July 25

John F. Stevens arrived here today to take charge of construction of a canal across Panama. Aware that a French attempt to dig a canal ended in bankruptcy because of the toll taken by tropical disease, the noted engineer is concentrating on good housing and sanitary facilities for workers. His design calls for locks through which vessels will travel across the isthmus. The effort is being spurred by the Roosevelt administration, which created the country of Panama and negotiated a canal treaty (→ June 29, 1906).

The jungle proves a deadly opponent.

Stieglitz promotes photography at gallery

New York City, Nov. 25

The latest innovations in the expanding field of art photography can be found in the Fifth Avenue brownstone of Alfred Stieglitz this month. An editor and founder of several photographic journals as well as a photographer, Stieglitz is the leading advocate of an esthetic

rather than technical approach to photography. He brings this rather unexplored print medium closer to the status of full-fledged art by displaying in his three-room attic 100 works by members of the Photo-Secession Group, who claim to be "seceding from the acceptable idea of what constitutes a photograph."

Stieglitz's "Winter, Fifth Avenue," where the photographer's gallery is located.

Government opens insurance inquiry

Washington, D.C., Sept. 6

President Roosevelt began a comprehensive investigation today into alleged corruption among major life insurance companies. Charles Evans Hughes and William Armstrong will head the inquiry. The probe meets Roosevelt's campaign promises of last year to clean up American business. The first place the joint House and Senate committee will look is Wall Street. For years, there have been allegations that many prominent New York businessmen are tied to top-of-the-line insurance companies in defrauding the small-policy holder. The President has pledged that he won't stop here; corporations in other industries are next.

New Orleans acts to check epidemic

New Orleans, Nov. 1

City health authorities said today that aggressive measures to control mosquitoes have ended the yellow fever epidemic and held the death rate to a relatively low figure. Only 451 people died of the scourge in New Orleans compared to the more than 4,000 who died in the last epidemic in 1878. Health authorities urged citizens to oil and screen cisterns and other water containers, to place netting around beds and to apply pennyroyal or camphor to the skin. Street gutters were cleaned and oiled. Dr. Quitman Kohnke urged such measures five years ago, as soon as it was determined that mosquito bites caused yellow fever, but his pleas were ignored.

Put another nickel in the nickelodeon

United States

All across the land, in cities and small towns, storefronts are painted and embellished with colorful posters. A screen plus several rows of straight chairs and a piano are moved into a makeshift theater, an old storeroom or a new motion picture theater. The usual offerings are the 10-minute features, mainly vaudeville acts, but some film scenes as well, where larger-than-life images float across the screen, followed by an "illustrated song," sung by a soloist. And it's all for a nickel, hence the name "nickelodeons." It would seem that the "flickers" have established a firm

hold on the affections of the urban working class. The cheap amusement appeals to the vast immigrant populations of New York, Chicago and Philadelphia. Pittsburgh has also put up its first nickelodeon. Reports indicate that the very first one was built in Los Angeles, the Electric Theater, in 1902. Wherever they are, they seem to be drawing crowds, all day, every day. It is not too expensive to become the proprietor of one of these and the motion pictures may be purchased outright from companies like Biograph for 12 cents per foot or rented from the film exchanges that are mushrooming everywhere.

Festival marks visit by Lewis and Clark

Portland, Oregon, Oct. 15

Today marks the end of the Lewis and Clark Exposition. The festival commemorates the 100th anniversary of the arrival of the Lewis and Clark Expedition on the Pacific Coast and honors the progress since then. Meriwether Lewis and William Clark, representatives of President Jefferson, had come out West to explore the newly acquired Louisiana Territory. They started up the Missouri River May 14, 1804, and sighted the Pacific on November 7, 1805. An interesting sidelight to the exposition was celebration of a Western Authors' Week to demonstrate the creative force of literature that was conceived and written in the Pacific Northwest generally and in Oregon specifically. The rise of literary magazines was cited as proof that this area's writers were as prolific and professional as those anywhere in the land.

Overland Limited gets electric lights

Chicago, Nov. 8

The Union Pacific Railroad today introduced electric lighting on its luxury passenger train, the Overland Limited, which runs between Chicago and San Francisco. Passengers now will be able to light up their compartments with the snap of a switch, instead of having to rely on gas lamps. Electricity for the compartments is provided by carrying steam from the engine to a forward section of a baggage car, where it drives a generator that provides power to the entire train. The Overland is not the first train to have electric power. As early as 1887, a generator was used to light up the Pennsylvania Limited on its run between Chicago and New York. But the adoption of electric power for the Overland is certain to set off competition among other railroads to provide similar luxuries for their passengers.

"Immigrants of the right kind" welcomed

Washington, D.C., Dec. 5

President Theodore Roosevelt told Congress in his annual message today that "there is no danger in having too many immigrants of the right kind." In the face of rising nativist sentiment in some sectors fo society, the President added that he "grows extremely indignant at the attitude of coarse hostility to the immigrant." The ideal of progressive immigration policy entails "Americanization." By immigrants "of the right kind," Roosevelt meant those of whatever ethnic origin willing to learn English, embrace the values and customs of the middle class, improve themselves through education, work hard in their profession and obey the law.

In fact, studies show that most of the newcomers, and particularly their children, do yearn to become part of the mainstream, and succeed in doing so, given a chance. Thus the President concluded, "I want to implant in the minds of our

American family with roots in Bohemia; the children were born here.

fellow Americans of foreign ancestry or birth the knowledge that they have just the same rights and opportunities as anyone else in this country" (→ Feb. 26, 1907).

Vice squad closes daring Shaw play

New York City, Oct. 31

Ticket-holders who didn't make it to the premiere of *Mrs. Warren's Profession* had better get a refund. Opening night was also closing night for the daring drama by the Irish playwright George Bernard Shaw, who wrote the work in 1898 but was prevented from staging it in London, where he has lived since 1876, because of England's tough censorship laws. Much the same happened in New York as police moved in after complaints by Anthony Comstock, head of the Society for the Prevention of Vice.

The controversial Shaw, whose previous works include *Man and Superman*, *Major Barbara*, and *The Devil's Disciple*, admits that *Mrs. Warren's Profession* is not pleasant stuff. The profession in question is prostitution. Shaw, though not an advocate of that line of work, is intent on exposing its "economic basis." This theme comes as no surprise to followers of Shaw's career. Since the Fabian Society was founded in 1884, he has been a leader of the London reform group, which favors the spread of socialism.

Western mine union, I.W.W. linked to murder of ex-Governor

Caldwell, Idaho, Dec. 31

Governor Frank Steunenberg's political career ended six years ago after he brutally suppressed a Western Federation of Miners strike in the Coeur d'Alene district. He never imagined he might be endangering his life. Yesterday, however, he was torn apart by a bomb that exploded at his front gate. The motive is apparently revenge and fingers are pointing to the Industrial Workers of the World, a radical spinoff of the miners federation.

The I.W.W. is the latest of "Big Bill" Haywood's attempts to broaden the base of the Western miners. After the failure of attempts to unite with the conservative American Federation of Labor, the rugged, heavy-drinking leader presided over a January conference of left-wing unionists and Socialists in Chicago. "Fellow workers!" he bellowed, "This is the Continental Congress of the working class." A formal convention on June 27, attended by Eugene Debs and Mother Jones, proclaimed the founding of "one great union for all."

Officials suspect Harry Orchard, a member of the I.W.W., killed Steunenberg (→ July 28, 1907).

"Fabricating Steel" by Henry Bernstein. Industrialization spurs a new genre in painting, ennobling the workingman.

Washington, D.C., Feb. 24.
United States receives note from Japanese government agreeing that Tokyo will not issue passports to workers trying to immigrate to United States.

Washington, D.C., March 12.
Supreme Court, in Hale v. Henkel, holds that witnesses can be compelled to testify against their employers in antitrust suits (→ June 29).

Los Angeles, March 23.
Tommy Burns defeats Marvin Hart in 20th round to win world heavyweight boxing title.

Washington, D.C., May 8.
Law is passed giving Alaska delegate to Congress.

New York City, May 26.
Lewis Nixon announces invention of device giving submarines "eyes and ears" [sonar].

Washington, D.C., June 29.
President Roosevelt signs act of Congress, providing for a lock-type canal in Panama (→ Nov. 14).

Washington, D.C., July.
National Geographic publishes George Shiras 3rd's unique photos of animals at night.

Brownsville, Georgia, Sept. 24.
When Atlanta press urges disenfranchisement of Negroes and revival of Ku Klux Klan, violent rioting erupts.

San Francisco, Oct. 11. Board of education orders all schools to segregate Oriental and non-Oriental students (→ 15).

Chicago, Oct. 14. White Sox beat Cubs, four games to two, in all-Chicago World Series.

Tokyo, Oct. 15. Japanese government claims that segregation of schools in San Francisco violates treaty of 1894 (→ Feb. 1907).

New York City, Nov. 23.
Enrico Caruso found guilty of molesting a woman in Central Park Monkey House; he touched her left forearm with his right elbow.

Washington, D.C., Dec. 3.
Alaska's first delegate to Congress is seated.

Atlanta. Coca-Cola Company, after threats of legal action, replaces cocaine in its soda with caffeine.

DEATH

Rochester, N.Y., March 13.
Susan B. Anthony, leading suffragette (*Feb. 15, 1820).

Sinclair exposes meat-packing "Jungle"

Upton Sinclair, muckraker.

Chicago

It's no easy feat keeping your appetite after reading selected pages of *The Jungle*, a fictional glimpse of Chicago's meat-packing industry. Its 28-year-old author, Upton Sinclair, toured the city's stockyards as part of a team of investigators. What he saw has gripped – and shocked – the nation. At one point, Sinclair describes the remains of diseased cattle being processed into packaged food along with the bodies of workers who happen to fall into the mixing vats. "Sometimes they would be overlooked for days," the novelist wrote of these tragic men, "till all but the bones of them had gone out to the world as Durham's Pure Leaf Lard." This fact-based description has so outraged the public that an abashed Congress recently saved the pure food and drug bill from the edge of defeat. In addition, *The Jungle* has prompted a policy of federal meat inspection.

Sinclair, a prolific writer with half a dozen novels under his belt, welcomes the acclaim for his new book, but he feels that the purpose of his novel has been misunderstood. His true target was not the unsanitary conditions of the stockyards, he says, but the exploitation of immigrant laborers. As he commented after the passage in June by Congress of the Meat Inspection Act and Pure Food and Drug Acts: "I aimed at the public's heart and by accident hit it in the stomach."

In fact, *The Jungle* makes a direct plea for radical reform, a point made in Jack London's fiery introduction, which applauds the author's "proletarian" sympathies. Even conservative readers have been moved by the plight of Sinclair's hero, Jurgis Rudkus, a wide-eyed immigrant from Lithuania who is abused by his bosses, bilked by con men and mired in poverty. A string of setbacks causes him to quit his job and fall into criminality before he harkens to the call of socialism.

The author recently demonstrated his own commitment to the radical creed by investing his royalties in the Helicon Home Colony of Englewood, New Jersey, where 40 families, most headed by young writers, are now experimenting with communal living. Visitors to the compound have included John Dewey, William James and Emma Goldman (→ March 1907).

Steffens reveals "Shame of Cities"

New York City

What have New York, Boston and Minneapolis in common? In these cities and many others, bad government reigns, with political bosses, greedy businessmen and crooked cops in charge. Since 1902, *McClure's* has been running a serial account of the nation's great cities and their woes. Its author, Lincoln Steffens, has now gathered them in a book, *The Shame of the Cities*. "No one class is at fault . . . nor any particular interest or group or party," writes Steffens. Who is the true culprit? Ordinary people, he says, a "shameless citizenship."

Lincoln Steffens, also a muckraker.

President criticizes muckraking writers

Washington, D.C., March 17

Too much printer's ink is being wasted on the subject of corruption, President Roosevelt complained tonight in a speech to journalists at the Gridiron Club. The President, who himself does not mince words, coined a tough phrase for the new breed of fault-finding writers – Ida Tarbell, Lincoln Steffens and others – whose work often appears in publications such as *McClure's*. The chief executive called them "muckrakers," an allusion to John Bunyan's *Pilgrim's Progress*, the classic Christian allegory that features a character so absorbed in the squalid task of raking muck that he can't see a heavenly crown when it's held over his head.

The stockyards in Chicago, the focus of Sinclair's exposé of the meat-packing industry. He described diseased cattle being processed into packaged food.

San Francisco ravaged by earthquake

Amid quake ruins, Caruso in pajamas

San Francisco, Apr. 18

The Metropolitan Opera Company, with Madame Sembrich and Signor Caruso, performed a spirited *Carmen* at the San Francisco Opera House just hours before the quake hit. Minutes after the first shock, the famed Enrico Caruso sat, clad in pajamas, on his valise in the middle of the street outside the Palace Hotel this morning. Personal effects and costumes were lost, but no one in the company was hurt. The Naples-born Caruso feels the quake has "some relation to the eruption of Vesuvius." The catastrophe completely destroyed the Opera House.

Grain overcooked; now it's corn flakes

Battle Creek, Michigan

Breakfast cereal producers here were joined this year by W.K. Kellogg's Toasted Corn Flake Company, whose product was the result of an accident at the Battle Creek Sanitarium, run by Dr. John Harvey Kellogg, as cooks left some boiled grain unattended and then found it broke into crispy flakes. Now Kellogg will compete with C.W. Post, whose Postum cereal coffee and Grape Nuts have been successful.

Diamonds dug up in Arkansas field

Murfreesboro, Arkansas

John Huddleston was walking around his farm three miles from here not too long ago wondering why his land was growing such miserable crops. Kicking at the soil, he noticed two shiny objects. They were crystals. Taken to a Little Rock jeweler, they were identified as diamonds. Geologists sent to the site have discovered that Huddleston's land covers the "pipe" of an ancient volcano. Thus, they say, these diamonds may well have been spewed from the center of the planet. So far, the diamonds found have been brilliant and of an excellent luster, but most are small. The diamond mine is believed to be the only such deposit in the country.

San Francisco, Apr. 18

Day had not yet dawned when, at 5:13 a.m., deep thunder rumbled from the earth's bowels. Then San Francisco shook like a maple leaf. Its highways cracked and split; the wharves warped and creaked; steel structures swayed, and many buildings split from cornice to foundation. There were six consecutive shocks, the third, at 8:45 a.m., bringing the worst destruction. Six hours of mortal dread and nameless terror ensued as the city was tossed upon seismic waves in the most disastrous earthquake in the history of America's West Coast.

Now confusion and helpless horror reign as countless dead lie in the morgues or under fallen walls. Some 1,000 lives are feared lost. Raging fires add to the disaster. Martial law has been declared, and this afternoon four thieves were shot for looting. Military units with orders to shoot looters on sight are allied with the police to keep things under control.

Thousands of panicked citizens are trying to leave the city, which looks as if the foot of a giant had crushed an anthill. Half the population is spending the night in public squares and parks, the living hunting for the dead or missing. Both the despair and the material loss are beyond any computation (→ 19).

Fire loss worse than quake damage

San Francisco, Apr. 19

Damage from the earthquake does not begin to compare with the loss from fire. Flames have destroyed the city's business district, and sweeping winds have carried the blaze to other areas of the devastated, terrified city. Eight square miles – several hundred city blocks – are totally burned out. Nearly 250,000 people are homeless today. Many small towns along the coast and within the earthquake area have been turned into scrapheaps. Everywhere there are smoldering ruins. The loss in San Francisco itself is estimated at $250 million; losses in San Jose are put at $5 million. Oakland and surrounding regions will add heavily to the total.

The devastation of the earthquake and subsequent fire leaves the people of San Francisco dazed, confused and with little else to do but watch the city crumble.

The aftermath of the San Francisco earthquake and subsequent fire, showing the ruins of Nob Hill and the Fairmont Hotel, with Chinatown in the foreground. Nearly 250,000 residents of the city are reported to be homeless.

President gives away his daughter Alice

French celebration of the marriage and the anniversary of Washington's birth.

Washington, D.C., Feb. 17

"I can do one of two things," President Theodore Roosevelt has said. "I can be President of the United States or I can control Alice. I cannot possibly do both." Today, the greater burden was lifted. His eldest daughter, who has puffed a cigarette in public and once raced about in an automobile in the company of three men, was wed today in a splendid White House ceremony. The groom is 35-year-old Nicholas Longworth, an Ohio congressman. Alice, 21, did not wear her favorite color, the blue-gray "Alice blue," but white – her mother's wedding dress.

U.S. puts Governor in charge in Cuba

Washington, D.C., Oct. 3

President Theodore Roosevelt has appointed a Nebraska lawyer, Charles Edward Magoon, Governor of Cuba, replacing the elected President, Tomas Estrada Palma. In August, Estrada Palma asked Roosevelt for help in putting down a rebellion led by Jose Miguel Gomez and Alfredo Zayas. In response, Roosevelt sent a contingent of United States troops under Secretary of War William Howard Taft. Authority for Magoon's appointment comes under the Platt Amendment, which permits Washington to intervene if necessary to maintain order and protect Cuba's independence. The United States was also involved in Cuba after the Spanish-American War, in order to protect the strategically situated island from European powers, especially Germany. When the Americans left Cuba in 1902, the terms of the Platt Amendment were incorporated in the Cuban constitution.

Devil's Tower made national monument

Wyoming, Sept. 24

President Roosevelt today announced the designation of Devil's Tower as a national monument. This spectacular rock formation is the first place of natural beauty to be so designated. By the provisions of the recently passed Preservation of American Antiques Act, the President will be authorized to protect distinctive American geologic formations, scenic locales and other national treasures for posterity.

Hepburn Act lets I.C.C. set rail rates

Washington, D.C., June 29

Swept along on a tide of reform, railroads have nestled further into the federal embrace. The Hepburn Act, signed today by President Roosevelt, empowers the Interstate Commerce Commission to investigate and set rates. Circumscribed by Nelson Aldrich's opposition in the Senate, the bill requires that inquiries be initiated by outside complaints, and subjects all decisions to judicial review. But it does put teeth in anti-rebate laws. Teddy touts the bill as a major victory against the "malefactors of great wealth" (→ May 15, 1911)

Crime of passion: Architect is gunned down by jealous husband

New York City, June 25

The prominent architect Stanford White was brutally murdered tonight. White, a partner in McKim, Mead & White, was sitting in the Madison Square Garden Roof Theater, when a gunman came from behind and shot him in the head three times. The alleged murderer has been identified as the millionaire Harry K. Thaw. According to rumors long whispered in society, the 53-year-old White had been having an illicit love affair with Thaw's wife, Evelyn Nesbit, whom he helped put on the stage through his influence in the theater. Thaw had long suspected his wife of carrying on with White, who boasted of his passion for the lovely Miss Nesbit. A brilliant architect and a specialist in interior design, White created the furnishings for James Gordon Bennett's yacht as well as the covers of major magazines. His architectural works include Washington Arch, the Century Club and, ironically, the very building where he was slain. Thaw, charged with murder, is said to have a history of mental instability. He will be personally prosecuted by District Attorney William Travers Jerome.

Senate okays role in Moroccan crisis

Washington, D.C., Dec. 12

After bitter debate over the wisdom of American intervention in European affairs, the Senate reluctantly approved the Act of Algeciras today. The United States sent two envoys to the Algeciras Conference, which was called in January to help ease tensions that had developed between Germany and France in Morocco. According to the act, Morocco retains its territorial integrity, but France and Spain control the police force. And, the Open Door, assuring equal commercial opportunity, is to be maintained. While the Moroccan issue is a European matter, the Open Door principle also applies to the United States.

The dashing looks and manner of prominent architect Stanford White (left) may have ultimately caused his death, since his affair with Evelyn Nesbit provoked a murderous rage in her millionaire husband, Harry K. Thaw (right).

Sarah bids America a very fond adieu

The Alphonse Mucha portrayal of Sarah Bernhardt captures her grace.

New York City

Sarah Bernhardt, the dark-eyed, petite French actress who has bewitched audiences for more than 30 years, is making the final engagement of her "Farewell American Tour" at the Lyric Theater. Rivaled only by Duse as the world's greatest actress, Bernhardt is renowned for her voice, which has been likened to a "golden bell." Her Racine roles are legendary. In 1899, she appeared as Hamlet, to mixed reviews. The tour has been a grind – coast-to-coast in 62 cities – and the conditions not always the best. In some Southern cities she played in roller-skating rinks; in Texas, in tents. While in San Francisco, Madame Sarah, as she is called, gave a special recital for the prisoners of San Quentin – in French, as usual. Many Americans still hope that she can be lured back for an encore.

Pass made legal to cut football deaths

New York City, Jan. 12

Alarmed by the sharp rise in the number of deaths and injuries in college football, representatives of the Intercollegiate Athletic Association have carried out a series of rule changes, including the legalization of the forward pass. In the past, mass plays where brute strength and great weight were determining factors led to crippling injuries as well as fatalities, so much so that many college presidents have either banned the sport or threatened to do so. President Roosevelt said that the game must be made safer. As a result – in addition to the new forward pass rule – a neutral zone has been created between the offensive and defensive lines, and the offense will be required to have at least six players on the line of scrimmage before the ball can be snapped.

Welcome to Gary!

Gary, Indiana

Out of swamps and sand dunes, a steel town has been born. Gary, Indiana, named after the U.S. Steel chairman, Judge Elbert Gary, was chosen as a site for the corporation because of its good water supply and its rail transportation potential, vital ingredients for making steel.

The soaring atrium of Marshall Field's in Chicago symbolizes the range of the nation's prosperity.

TR, in Panama, is first President abroad

Astride a steam shovel at Culebra Cut, Roosevelt imbues a "can-do" spirit.

Panama, Nov. 14

President Roosevelt arrived in Panama today to inspect construction of the canal across the isthmus, establishing another precedent. Roosevelt is the first President to visit a foreign country while in office. Just four years ago, he pioneered by taking the first presidential ride in an automobile. Roosevelt sailed here from the United States on the steamer Louisiana. His Panama visit will last three days. He plans a short stay in Puerto Rico before returning to Washington.

The President finds that work on the canal is proceeding more slowly than had been hoped. Digging is disorganized, and some still oppose the decision to build a series of locks. Roosevelt views lock construction as the most effective way to deal with the difference in height between the Atlantic and Pacific sides of the isthmus. He is considering replacement of John Stevens, chief engineer, with Colonel George Goethals (→ 1910).

Nobel goes to Roosevelt for peace efforts

Oslo, Norway, Dec. 10

President Theodore Roosevelt, known more for his "big stick" than his diplomacy, was named winner of the Nobel Peace Prize today. Roosevelt, the first American to receive a Nobel, is being honored for his role as mediator in the Russo-Japanese War. Negotiations with the belligerents began in the spring of last year, and last August Roosevelt finally persuaded both Russia and Japan to have their diplomats sit down together at a peace conference in Portsmouth, New Hampshire. The Portsmouth Treaty was signed in September. Though ending a war between two countries with whom the United States has friendly relations was important, Roosevelt surely had other motives as well. Before the parley, he exacted assurances from the Japanese that they would retain the Open Door in Manchuria. While Japan won the war, it was in financial straits and there are those who speculate that without the peace conference the Japanese might have eventually been worn down by the Russians, who have made no promises about honoring the Open Door policy.

Values on Wall Street take sharp drop

New York City, March 13

A wave of liquidation shook Wall Street today, sending stock prices tumbling in their worst one-day drop since the Northern Pacific panic of 1901. Large railroads led the declines, with the Reading, Great Northern, Northern Pacific and Union Pacific lines suffering losses of 10 to 11 points. Analysts link the crash to several banks with a heavy short-term need for cash. Trading was moderate at 2.2 million shares, never approaching the level of a general panic. But today's plunge follows a long period of declining prices that business leaders attribute to President Roosevelt's trust-busting efforts. Democratic leader William Jennings Bryan has a different view. He says the public is refusing to trade in watered stock. "Must the government," he asked today, "refuse to investigate rotten management for fear the misman-aged railroad no longer will be able to fool the public into buying inflated securities?" (→ Nov. 4).

Influx of unskilled labor causing concern

Sweatshops proliferate as poorly trained immigrants swell the nation's ranks.

Washington, D.C., Feb. 26

In response to a public outcry over the flood of "new" immigrants from Southern and Eastern Europe, Congress has allotted $600,000 to form a presidential panel on immigration. Labor groups have been the most vocal advocates of immigration reform. The foreign-born make up 14 percent of the nation's population, yet they provide half the labor force. And only 15 percent of these have experience in industry. "Cheap labor, ignorant labor, takes our jobs and cuts our wages," complains American Federation of Labor President Samuel Gompers. With subsistence pay at $745 a year, immigrant wages range from an average of $722 for Swedes to $400 for Southern Italians and Hungarians.

The "new" immigrants, few of them Anglo-Saxon or Protestant, have stirred the waters of racial and religious bias. Northern Europe now accounts for less than a quarter of Ellis Island's arrivals. Many are Slavs, Slovaks, Serbs, Croats, Bosnians and Herzegovinians. And many are Jewish or Catholic. The halls of academe ring with racial theories. According to zoologist H.F. Osborn, republican institutions can only be saved by facing our primary task, "the conservation and multiplication for our country of the best spiritual, moral, intellectual and physical forces of heredity." Reformers like Jane Addams, at least, have approached immigrant ghettoes with acceptance if not respect. Addams still believes America is Thomas Paine's "asylum for mankind." The foreign-born, she says, are but "accretions of simple people who carry in their hearts a desire for mere goodness" (→ March 26, 1910).

Coast issue settled by Immigration Act

March 14

Scene in a schoolroom:
Teacher: Who was the first man?
Pupil: "Washington!"

When reminded of a man called Adam, the pupil exclaims: "Yes, if you count foreigners!"

A lighthearted depiction, perhaps, but a telling one about American attitudes toward immigrants.

President Roosevelt today issued an executive order directing that Japanese or Korean laborers, skilled or not, who have received passports to go to Mexico, Hawaii or Canada, be refused permission to enter the continental territory of the United States. This is the final chapter, except for treaty negotiations with the Japanese, in the issue growing out of the conflict with Japan sparked by the San Francisco school board's order segregating Orientals. Authority to refuse permission to certain Orientals is part of the immigration law passed February 20. The Chinese are excluded unless they can prove they are not laborers. Japanese must be admitted unless they are laborers, the burden of proof being on the government. Still, the point is that any immigrant with a passport from a nation other than the United States may be barred from entry if it is deemed detrimental to U.S. labor conditions (→ Apr. 19, 1913).

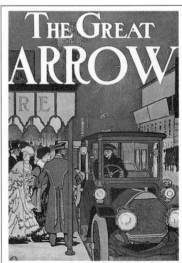

The Pierce-Arrow automobile is among the finest motorcars on the road. It is one of a class of machines designed specifically for a better class of consumer.

Good clean fight: Hurley vs. Maytag

Chicago

A washing machine operated by electricity rather than by hand has been marketed by the Hurley Machine Company here. Invented by Alva J. Fisher, the Hurley uses a small motor to spin a drum that holds clothes, water and soap. Its main competition is the Maytag Pastime, which is produced by an Iowa farm equipment manufacturer and is turned by a hand crank, like all washing machines that have been marketed since the first one appeared in the 1850's.

Hand-cranked washing machine by Maytag may get the job done, but Hurley's electric may get the buyers.

Rails can enforce racial segregation

Washington, D.C.

In a case concerning conflicting state and federal authority, the Supreme Court has supported segregation on interstate railway lines. Trains traveling across state lines, the court held, have no obligation to uphold state laws barring segregated cars. The ruling is the latest of many to validate state attacks on gains made during Reconstruction. Through "grandfather clauses" and literacy tests, Negroes have been disenfranchised in all Southern states except Tennessee, Kentucky and Maryland. Lynchings exceed 100 a year. And in all the South, high schools hold less than 8,000 Negro students (→ Nov. 1910).

Verdict split in Idaho I.W.W. murder trial

Boise, Idaho, July 28

In a murder trial that attracted nationwide attention, William "Big Bill" Haywood was found not guilty today, while his colleague, Harry Orchard, was convicted of the murder of the former Governor of Idaho, Frank Steunenberg. Haywood was acquitted mainly because of lack of evidence associating him with the crime. Orchard, on the other hand, admitted that he had placed the bomb that killed the popular Steunenberg.

The 38-year-old Haywood has been a controversial labor personality ever since he helped found the often-violent Industrial Workers of the World in 1905. He has always opposed craft unionism, favoring instead a militant industrial-union philosophy. An avowed Socialist, Haywood is hated by conventional leaders of both industry and labor. There is about him, however, a strange romanticism that seems to attract unskilled workers.

Many people who attended the sensational trial felt that the brilliant defense by the rising young lawyer Clarence Darrow was mainly responsible for Haywood's acquittal. William Borah prosecuted the state's case.

Neiman-Marcus Co. opens in Dallas

Dallas, Texas, Autumn

A major new department store has opened its doors for business here. It is the Neiman-Marcus Company and the founders say that it is specifically designed for the discriminating customers who want the "best" in both contemporary and traditional fashions. Those who have visited the store report that prices are somewhat high, although there are bargains to be found. Neiman's seems to be exactly what the French writer Emile Zola meant when he said that department stores "democratized luxury."

TR discharges 167 Negroes after riot

Washington, D.C., Jan. 15

President Roosevelt today ordered that the 167 Negro soldiers allegedly connected with a shooting spree in Brownsville, Texas, earlier this year be "discharged without honor" and "forever barred from re-enlistment." The shooting took place August 13, killing a bartender, wounding a policeman and causing pandemonium all over town. None of the soldiers, members of three army units stationed at Fort Brown there, has admitted knowing anything about the rioting. However, the President is said to be convinced that the soldiers have entered into a conspiracy of silence in order to protect the guilty.

"Three Weeks": It is banned in Boston

Boston

What is It? Every good Puritan with a young daughter knows. So does Elinor Glyn, the British novelist whose latest work, *Three Weeks*, refers to sex euphemistically as "It." A steamy tale about an adulterous Balkan queen who leads a younger man through a passionate three-week affair, the book has been banned in Boston. But Glyn, who is now touring the United States to adoring crowds, says "those who do look up beyond the material will understand the deep, pure love and the Soul in its all."

"A. Mutt" appears six days a week

America's sidekicks Mutt and Jeff.

San Francisco, Nov. 15

Under the title *Mr. A. Mutt Starts In to Play the Races*, the *San Francisco Chronicle* today began a daring experiment. From now on, Bud Fisher's comic strip adventures of bettor (and born loser) A. Mutt will appear both daily and on Saturdays. This unprecedented step is a bid to boost circulation in the wake of the success of other popular strips such as Rudolph Dirks's *The Katzenjammer Kids* in the *New York Journal*, Lyonel Feininger's *The Kin-der Kids* and *Wee Willie Winkie's World* in the *Chicago Tribune*, Winsor McCay's *Dreams of the Rarebit Fiend* in the *New York Evening Telegram*, and his *Little Nemo in Slumberland* in the *New York Herald*.

"Stag at Sharkey's" (1907) by George Wesley Bellows. The artist, a rugged individual of the Ashcan School of painting, uses his brush to capture the toughness of urban life in America through its athletic outlets.

Oklahoma becomes 46th state in union

Oklahoma City, Nov. 16

The Indian Territory and Oklahoma Territory were formally merged and admitted to the union today as the state of Oklahoma. As a territory, Oklahoma has been enjoying a healthy economy and with it a steadily increasing population since the first massive influx of migrants during the "Boomer-Sooner" days of 1889. Although Oklahoma is predominantly rural and agricultural, the bustling, modern town of Tulsa boasts a population of more than 24,000, while this state capital now is home for over 50,000 people.

U.P. news agency formed by Scripps

Cleveland, Ohio

Following the trend of collective news gathering, the Scripps-McRae League of Newspapers has created the United Press news agency. The new U.P. is likely to contribute to a standardization of news, which has proven efficient and thorough, but, critics say, mechanical. Edward Scripps started his first paper, the *Cleveland Penny Press*, in 1878. Scripps-McRae was formed in 1885 by Scripps, his half-brother George and Milton McRae by merging four Midwest dailies.

Saint-Gaudens was best U.S. sculptor

Cornish, New Hampshire, Aug. 3

America's greatest sculptor, Augustus Saint-Gaudens, died here today. Born in Dublin in 1848, Saint-Gaudens was a cameo cutter and studied at New York's Cooper Union and in Paris before setting an American standard for sculptural excellence. The sculptor's early *Silence* depicts a mysterious shrouded figure. More civic-minded is the General William Tecumseh Sherman Memorial, at the southeast entrance to New York's Central Park. Most fascinating of his works, perhaps, is the abstract memorial designed for the wife of Henry Adams in 1891.

"... and the heavens have not fallen"

Business is business: a female secretary with her Remington typewriter.

The delicate Maude Adams is best known for her role as "Peter Pan."

United States, Nov. 16

In today's issue of the *Woman's Journal,* Mrs. Ellen Richards, one of America's first woman chemists, writes: "We may discount all the scare headlines about what will happen if women do thus and so. They have done nearly everything, and the heavens have not fallen." Indeed, women increasingly contribute to the arts and sciences, and the firmament seems firmly fixed.

The Impressionist painter Mary Cassatt has led the way for other women artists. Miss Maude Adams, nee Maude Kiskadden, is queen of the stage (though it should be noted that she plays boys as often as she does grown women: currently, she fills the title role in *Peter Pan*). Edith Wharton is but one of several female novelists receiving good notices; critics praised her 1905 novel about conformity, *The House of Mirth*. There are few women in the sciences, as Mrs. Richards would concede, but females are a key part of the new technological world, working in telephone offices and sitting long days before typewriters. Participation in sports, once held improper for women, is now encouraged, Wimbledon victor May Sutton setting an example. For all these advances, women cannot vote in national elections. British suffragists plan to join American women for a rally in New York next month and pass on their lobbying strategies. It might be interesting for them to meet Professor W.I. Thomas, whose book *Sex and Society* states that the female mind is weak. The heavens may fall on him!

Arson suspected in Sinclair co-op fire

Englewood, New Jersey, March

Local police authorities now believe that the fire that completely destroyed writer Upton Sinclair's co-operative community was deliberately set. He established the socialistic, workers' co-op in this small town only a few months ago. Sinclair, author of last year's best-selling and shocking expose of the meat-packing industry, entitled *The Jungle*, is a muckraking social critic and reformer who readily admits that he is not popular in all quarters. Apparently, his unpopularity has now focused on Englewood.

A better light bulb by General Electric

New York City

A light bulb with a tungsten filament is being marketed by General Electric, which says it gives better light and is more efficient than conventional carbon filament bulbs. Tungsten's high melting point allows it to glow at a higher temperature, emitting whiter light and using less electricity than old-style bulbs. The key to using tungsten in lamps was the development of a method of drawing it into fine wires, which General Electric has achieved after years of research.

L.A. is unlikely site for motion picture

Los Angeles

As winter descended on Lake Michigan, the director and the cameraman of the Chicago-based Selig Company, having already filmed parts of a one-reel version of *The Count of Monte Cristo*, went on a desperate search for the sun. They got off the train in Los Angeles and are now shooting the remaining scenes, with local actors, behind the Sing Loo laundry downtown and on the beach at La Jolla. Another "first": Reports from Cleveland tell of a film shot in color and with simultaneous sound, depicting a bullfight, a scene from an opera and a political speech.

Phone companies offer women one of the few jobs for which they are "suited."

An American credo outlined by James

Cambridge, Massachusetts

Americans always take pride in being practical, and now a noted philosopher has stepped forward to champion their point of view. He is William James, and his new book, *Pragmatism: A New Name for Some Old Ways of Thinking*, argues that "fixed principles, closed systems and pretended absolutes" will not do for pragmatic thinkers, who turn "toward concreteness and adequacy, toward facts, toward action, and toward power." James has opportunely turned to his Harvard colleague C. S. Peirce, the logician who invented the term pragmatism.

Morgan's intervention saves Wall St.

New York City, Nov. 4

J.Pierpont Morgan is not one to fool around with the nation's economic health. At midnight, with the city's biggest banks beset by runs that had gone on for three weeks, the No. 1 banker of them all locked the trust presidents into the West Room of his 36th Street office. By 5 a.m., they pledged $25 million to salvage the banks. Morgan did his part by buying Tennessee Coal and Iron, whose dying owner was about to tear Wall Street down by declaring bankruptcy.

Morgan sent his men to Washington to clear the purchase with President Roosevelt. Before the market opened, a call came through. "All is well," said Judge Elbert Gary. Morgan, who gains mineral reserves for U.S. Steel, agrees.

Trouble began back on October 16, when Charles W. Morse and F. Augustus Heinze tried to corner United Copper and failed, sparking a run on the Knickerbocker Trust Company and the Trust Company of America. Roosevelt, who spent much of the panic period hunting bear in Louisiana, has halted his attacks on the "malefactors of great wealth." Instead, he is praising "conservative and substantial businessmen" for acting with "wisdom and public spirit" (→ May 30, 1908).

It's rumored that Morgan plans to turn the whole world into a trust.

Henry Adams pens his autobiography

Boston

Some 100 handpicked readers have been given the opportunity to revisit the life of a pre-eminent man of his time. *The Education of Henry Adams*, issued privately, is the latest work by the grandson of John Quincy Adams and himself a sometime diplomat, historian, theorist, professor and novelist. At 69, Adams views himself not as a man but as "a manikin on which the toilet of education [was] draped." The "object of study," he adds, "is the garment, not the figure."

American awarded Nobel physics prize

Oslo, Norway, Dec. 10

Albert A. Michelson today became the first American to win a Nobel Prize in science. Michelson, 54, was given the physics prize for his studies of the properties of light. Perhaps his most important experiment, done with Edward Morley, was a series of tests showing that the speed of light is the same in all directions, which confounded existing theory. An explanation was offered two years ago by a German scientist, Albert Einstein, in what he calls his theory of relativity.

Milwaukee has first inter-urban electric

Milwaukee, Wis., Oct. 28

America's first inter-urban train powered by electricity began service today between Milwaukee and Cedarburg, Wisconsin, marking another milestone in railroad electrification. The Pennsylvania and New York Central Railroads are the leaders in electrification of their commuter lines, and New York City's elevated lines, which started with steam engines, have shifted completely to electricity, citing both increased efficiency and cleanliness for the change.

Nothing sucks it up like a Hoover

Cleveland, Ohio

A light, portable vacuum cleaner is being marketed by the Hoover Suction-Sweeper Company here. Designed by James M. Spangler, the machine uses an electric motor to run a fan that sucks dirt into a disposable dust bag. Spangler has sold his patent to the Hoover Company, which is offering the device to housewives. Previous vacuum cleaners have been too bulky and expensive for use in private homes, often being so large that women could not move them from room to room.

Company dissolved by Currier and Ives

New York City

The presses of America's best lithographer have taken their last turn with the dissolution of Currier and Ives. Nathaniel Currier founded the firm in 1834 and achieved his first success with a print of the sinking of the steamboat Lexington. The talented artist James Ives, a relation by marriage, was made partner in 1857. The firm flourished until both Currier and Ives died in the 1880's, having produced over 4,000 prints documenting American historical sites, sporting scenes and social customs. The last owner is disbanding the company due to ill health and competition from photography.

"Great White Fleet" begins world tour to show U.S. might

Hampton Roads, Va., Dec. 16

America's "Great White Fleet" weighed anchor here today and left for a globe-circling tour that is expected to take about 15 months. President Roosevelt was on hand for the historic departure. From the presidential yacht Mayflower, Roosevelt personally gave the fleet its orders to "proceed to duty assigned." The President has sent the fleet of 16 battleships on its mission to convince real as well as would-be enemies, especially Japan, that the U.S. Navy is so powerful that any attack on America would be foolish if not disastrous for the aggressor. The fleet is commanded by Commodore "Fighting Bob" Evans (→ Feb. 22, 1909).

The "Great White Fleet," including the Amphitrite, Puritan and Montgomery, proves an influential arm of American foreign policy. Without firing a shot, the fleet announces to the world that the United States has arrived.

New York City, Jan. 17. A wireless message from Puerto Rico is received at Times Tower.

Collingwood, Ohio, March 4. Schoolhouse blaze kills 175 children.

Chelsea, Massachusetts, Apr. 12. One-quarter of town is destroyed by fire; 19 deaths reported.

Chicago, May 10. Socialist National Convention nominates Eugene V. Debs of Indiana for president.

Washington, D.C., May 30. In response to last year's financial panic, Congress enacts Aldrich-Vreeland Act, establishing National Monetary Commission.

Washington, D.C., June 23. Diplomatic relations between United States and Venezuela are severed because of latter's unwillingness to compensate for injuries sustained by Americans during recent upheavals.

Rome, June 29. Pope Pius X issues encyclical *Sapienti Consilio,* declaring that United States is no longer a missionary area.

Springfield, Illinois, Aug. 15. When a white woman claims a Negro raped her, community of Negroes is attacked and some are lynched..

Yellowstone National Park, Aug. 24. On road between Old Faithful and Thumb, one man holds up 17 coaches in a day, assisted by a strategic bend in road.

Detroit, Mich., Oct. 14. Chicago Cubs defeat Detroit Tigers in World Series, four games to one.

Nyack, New York, Dec. 27. Followers of doomsday prophet Lee J. Spangler sit atop a mountain awaiting end of world dressed in white gowns, "specially made for occasion."

New York City. Ex-Lax Company founded by Max Kiss, who promotes his product with filmed advertisements in movie theaters.

Utah. Dinosaur bones discovered near Jensen.

California. Construction begins on Owens Valley Aqueduct, to bring water to Los Angeles.

Boston. Van Wyck Brooks's *The Wine of the Puritans* published.

Artists open "outlaw salon" in New York

New York City, February

A rebellious group of painters known as "The Eight" has dealt a blow to the stodgy arbiter of the art world, the National Academy of Design, with the opening of an independent display of paintings at the Macbeth Gallery. Frustrated by the outdated styles and restrictive exhibition policies favored by the academy, The Eight defied convention by arranging this presentation of 63 works to compete with the National Academy's spring show, the most prestigious art exhibition in the country.

The Eight are Robert Henri, the leader, William Glackens, Everett Shinn, John Sloan, George Luks, Ernest Lawson, Maurice Prendergast and Arthur B. Davies, and they offer an array of subjects and styles, from the urban urchins of Henri, to the seaside vistas of Prendergast, whose work one critic described as "a jumble of riotous pigment ... like an explosion in a color factory." A number of the artists also treat one subject deemed controversial – the cities of America, especially New York, as they are transformed by industrialization and swelling numbers of immigrants.

Though critical opinion on The Eight has been mixed, the artistically curious have thronged the gallery in crowds of 300 visitors per hour. Despite the reservations of the art establishment, the show tallied an impressive sales figure of $4,000. Gertrude Vanderbilt Whitney proved to be an adventurous collector, buying four paintings.

Those who cannot see the show in New York will get a chance to view the "outlaw salon" as it travels across the country, spreading its message of artistic anarchy. Next stop: the Pennsylvania Academy of Design in Philadelphia.

Artist John Sloane's scenes of urban America are noted for their realism.

Singer Building sets record: 47 stories

New York City

Construction has been completed on New York's tallest skyscraper, the Singer Building. With a record 47 stories, it towers to a height of 612 feet at the corner of Broadway and John Street, with a distinctive tapering spire designed by its architect, Ernest Flagg. The building is a tribute to the heights made possible by modern construction methods. It is not expected to retain its record for long, however. Plans for a 50-story building have already been drawn up, and Frank Woolworth is said to be considering construction of a 60-story skyscraper on a site in the City Hall area.

Iron, toaster help liberate housewife

New York City

The housewife's life has been made easier by introduction of two new electric appliances, an iron and a toaster. No longer does a woman need to labor next to a hot stove to iron the family's clothes or make toast, the advertisements say. Ironing can now be done in comfort on the veranda, the Westinghouse Company tells women, while its message to husbands is, "Why not kick that stove out and get a Westinghouse electric iron?"

Film producers told to clean up their act

New York City

Ever since Edison's *The Widow Jones*, with its 20-second kiss by a homely couple, provoked howls of indignation, the makers of films are being carefully watched. Now the Society for the Prevention of Crime has convinced Mayor McClellan to revoke the license of 550 theaters until they stop showing films on Sundays and stop showing immoral films at any time. The Chicago Police Department began enforcing local censorship ordinances last year. To avert further local actions, producers have established the National Board of Censorship for self-regulation.

Labor boycott ruled in restraint of trade

Washington, D.C., Feb. 3

In a far-reaching opinion, the Supreme Court ruled today that a labor boycott of industry violates the Sherman Antitrust Act by being a conspiracy in restraint of trade. The opinion sustained a lower court decision in the case of Loewe v. Lawlor that granted treble damages to the employer as a result of a nationwide boycott organized by the hatters union to further a strike for recognition. The leader of the boycott, the hatters union, operates out of Danbury, Connecticut, which is often called the "hat city of the world." Thus, the clash has been dubbed the Danbury Hatters Case.

You just drink up and toss cup away

United States

The American paper industry always seems to be coming up with new uses for its products, uses that make life easier and more efficient. First there were paper bags, then drinking straws. Now, the International Paper Company has developed a waxed drinking cup made out of paper that is tough and nonporous. It's a sanitary way to take a beverage, and it is so cheap that you dispose of it after drinking. The product is named the Dixie Cup.

Journalism school opens in Missouri

Columbia, Missouri, April

A school of journalism has been established by the University of Missouri here and it will soon be accepting its first students. Considered to be the first professional institution of its kind in the nation, the journalism school is specifically designed to turn out the top quality working journalists and editors that the growing newspaper and magazine industries require. When William Dean Howells was asked eight years ago what the educated upper-class Americans read, he replied, "The newspapers." This school should help the reputation of the "fourth estate."

Commission is formed to save the nation's natural resources

The Teton Range of the Rockies is a stunning example of America's beauty.

Washington, D.C., June 8

President Roosevelt today announced the establishment of a National Conservation Commission. Regarding the fate of the nation's endangered natural treasures, the President said, "We intend to use these resources, but to so use them as to conserve them."

This commission is actually the outgrowth of a conference of governors that was held here last month. At that time, the President brought together the governors of the states, as well as the "representatives of the people," who included such luminaries as the Democrats' perennial presidential candidate William Jennings Bryan, the steel giant Andrew Carnegie and the railroad magnate James J. Hill. At that session, this extraordinary gathering of leaders decided it was time to do something about the country's resources – for the present as well as the future.

Roosevelt has made available every tool of the government for this landmark commission. He has ordered "every department, bureau and government establishment" to cooperate fully with the commission in its efforts to establish a national conservation policy once and for all. It was quite a meeting, one that James J. Hill called "the directors' meeting of the corporation called the United States of America." In fact, the *Wall Street Journal* has described the mission of this gathering of corporate eagles as "a radical new departure in government." The commission already seems to have achieved some concrete results. For one thing, 41 states have pledged to create their own conservation commissions and the four others are sure to follow.

Country life: American farmers thriving in new age of prosperity

Washington, D.C., Aug. 10

President Roosevelt today announced the creation of the federal Country Life Commission. Its mission is to take a comprehensive look at American rural life as it exists today. While the commission's report has not yet been published, indications are strong that its conclusions will be optimistic.

For example, the average prices of farm products have increased almost 50 percent since 1900. During the same period, the average value of farm land has increased substantially, while the value of the average farm has risen from $5,471 to $6,444. At the same time, farm foreclosures have shown a marked drop, while new machinery has been purchased and additional lands put into cultivation. The average farmer has an amazing return, or profit, on his holdings of more than $540 per year.

Relative to the city dweller, the farmer's standard of living has risen dramatically. Mail-order firms such as Montgomery Ward and Sears, Roebuck have introduced the farmer to the bountiful appliances, clothes and luxuries of the city people at reasonable prices. And the Rural Free Delivery concept has brought affordable information to the farmer's doorstep. *Editor & Publisher* magazine recently said, "The daily newspapers have never seen such a boom in circulation as they have since RFD was established." Life on the farm is good – and it's getting better.

Spring plowing in New England. American farmers are reaping lots of benefits.

General Motors formed

Detroit, Mich., Sept. 14

Henry Ford is said to be leaning toward producing just one versatile, low-priced car, but William C. Durant of the Buick Motor Company envisions turning out a wide range of motorcars. Today Durant formed General Motors, a base from which he hopes to build a vast conglomeration of automobile and parts manufacturers offering a line of machines to cover the entire spectrum of prices, styles and sizes. Thus, he reasons, under the protective wing of General Motors, no one company will be at the mercy of a changing marketplace that each year sends dozens of firms spiraling into bankruptcy.

Unlike most of Detroit's car magnates, Durant has little mechanical background. His forte is business, and his philosophy of con-glomeration is not new. By 1900, he had built a national consortium of horse-drawn buggy companies into one massive Durant-Dort Carriage Company. In 1904, at the age of 42, Durant took over the ailing Buick firm. That year, the company produced just 31 cars. Now Buick is the nation's largest automobile maker, building 8,487 this year.

Durant is said to have his eye on about 12 companies. These include Oldsmobile, the well-known manufacturer that has fallen on hard times; Oakland, the company in Pontiac, Michigan, whose Model K is this year's hill-climbing champion, and Cadillac, a big money-maker that produced 2,280 cars this year. Known for his persuasiveness, Durant will offer each of the companies huge stock holdings to join General Motors.

Ford builds the Model T

Detroit, Michigan, Oct. 1

"I will build a motorcar for the multitudes," Henry Ford has said. Today, his vision took a step toward reality, when the Ford Motor Company announced the arrival of its new Model T, a lightweight car with advanced features that will sell for $850.

The newest Ford won't win any awards for grace, but it boasts qualities not found in any automobile, much less in a low-priced model. Constructed of a tough but light vanadium steel alloy developed by Ford engineers, the Model T is built to last, with a new three-point suspension that is able to negotiate the rugged farm roads. For power, a four-cylinder, 20-horsepower engine, with a simple, easy-to-repair design, enables the car to cruise effortlessly at more than 25 miles per hour. Especially novel features are the magneto, which powers the sparkplugs while the engine runs, and the placement of the steering wheel on the left.

The first Model T was rolled out in late summer, and Ford himself took it for a triumphal test spin through the streets of Detroit. Back at the plant, he jumped from the car, slapped each of his engineers on the back and declared that he was "tickled to death" with its performance.

Ford is said to be feuding with the company's financial backers, who deplore his preoccupation with lower-priced cars. But the indomitable automaker is steadfast in his belief that the Model T is a winner. He told eager motorcar dealers recently that next year the company is planning to produce an incredible 25,000 machines.

General Motors plans to compete against Ford with sleek aerodynamic styling.

Home safe and sound, Henry Ford's first factory production Model T rests after carrying the manufacturer on an extensive hunting trip in September.

Washington, D.C., November 22. *The Postal Service bought automobiles today to facilitate rural delivery. Now the mail will always get through.*

An American family takes to the open road in their new Model T, specially designed to manage country byways. Their trip shouldn't be too bumpy.

Round-world race is won by U.S. auto

New York City, July 30

For a while, it seemed that the German team had won the great round-the-world automobile race, but in the end the honors went to the United States drivers. It seems that the Germans transported their car part of the way by rail after it was delayed by repairs en route. Their Protos was first to finish the grind in Paris, but they were penalized and the American Thomas car was ruled the winner. The Thomas received a 15-day allowance for changing its route after snow blocked its way in Alaska. The American winners were invited to visit President Roosevelt at the White House. Talking about his crossing of the United States, one German driver said: "I wish that America's roads were as nice as the people."

Ewry keeps winning gold at Olympics

Paris, July

Ray C. Ewry continues to dazzle the international track set, this time taking two gold medals in the Olympic Games. The New Yorker again won the standing high jump and the standing broad jump, as he had in the 1906 Games. Add those victories to his three each in the 1900 and 1904 Olympics for a total of 10, a figure that track experts say may never be surpassed. The number of participants, 2,082, more than doubled the 1906 turnout, but the acrimony more than doubled, too. The Finns marched flagless because they refused to carry the flag of the ruling Russians, the Irish were angry because they had to compete under the British flag, and widespread professionalism was charged. Besides, it rained a lot.

Taft and Republicans sweep national vote

Washington, D.C., Nov. 3

Republicans are singing sweet songs of success tonight as they waltz William Howard Taft of Ohio into the White House. Taft's victory over Democrat William Jennings Bryan coupled with the G.O.P.'s retention of both houses of Congress reflect the nation's satisfaction with the progressivism of Theodore Roosevelt. Teddy chose Taft as his successor. It is expected that Taft, at 300 pounds the biggest man ever to be President, will consult Roosevelt about key policy decisions. Congressman James Sherman of New York is the new Vice President. For Bryan, this is his third loss in a presidential election. He has already said it is his last. As they say in baseball, "Three strikes and you're out."

Eugene Debs, the Socialist Party candidate, was joined by other

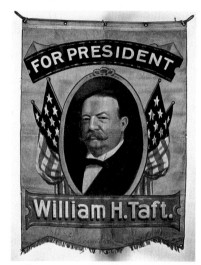

William H. Taft, 27th President.

third-party candidates, from the Prohibition National Party, the Socialist Labor Party and the Independence Party.

Johnson takes boxing title in 14 rounds

Sydney, Australia, Dec. 26

Jack Johnson finally caught up with Tommy Burns, flattened him in the 14th round and became the first Negro fighter to win the heavyweight championship of the world today. The self-styled "Li'l Arthur" (his name is John Arthur) with the bullet head and the gold-toothed grin had been challenging Burns ever since the Aussie won the title two years earlier. Burns finally agreed to take what he knew would be a terrible beating in exchange for

the lion's share of the purse. Johnson was battering Burns so badly that the police finally stepped in to halt the mayhem. Johnson is also a great defensive fighter and he has tremendous strength in his 6-foot frame. Burns, on the other hand, was, at 5 foot 7, the smallest heavyweight champion ever. The challenger taunted him throughout the fight. "Hit here, Tahmy," Johnson would say. And when Burns would take his best shot at the indicated spot, Johnson would laugh.

Mahler and Toscanini make U.S. debuts

New York City, Nov. 16

Two brilliant European conductors, Arturo Toscanini and Gustav Mahler, made their American debuts this year, both at the Metropolitan Opera. Toscanini scored a triumph as he led a cast headed by Enrico Caruso in an *Aida* that older critics said was performed just as Verdi would have wanted to hear it. The year began auspiciously on

January 1 when Mahler, reportedly ailing, all the more remarkably led a *Tristan und Isolde* that one critic described as unequaled in vitality and beauty. Mahler, who calls himself a weekend composer, has written seven symphonies. Though the Italian and the Czech take different tacks in conducting, the Met considers itself lucky this season to have two such giants on its podium.

Houdini, the master of the great escape

New York City

Harry Houdini's recent book, *The Unmasking of Robert-Houdin*, is not, as it would seem at first glance, an autobiography; it is a paean to a fellow magician, Frenchman Jean-Eugene Robert-Houdin. Still, each trick Houdini praises he does better himself and, like sleight of hand in reverse, it brings attention to his own feats. Houdini is thrilling crowds here and in Europe. After being handcuffed and locked in a box underwater, he emerges alive; he strolls through solid walls and frees himself from a straitjacket as he dangles high over the ground. Houdini was born Erich Weiss in 1874, the son of a Hungarian rabbi. Early on, he was a trapeze artist. Then, presto, he was a magician.

November 30. *TR's reputation as "The World's Constable" grew today as his Secretary of War, Elihu Root, concluded the Root-Takahira Agreement, whereby the U.S and Japan will maintain the Open Door in China.*

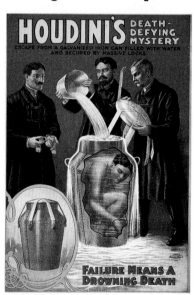

The great escape artist at his best.

Virginia, Jan. 13. After army complains about an executive order demanding increased physical fitness for soldiers, President Roosevelt rides 100 miles across Virginia to make his point.

Washington, D.C., Jan. 27. United States and England submit a long-standing dispute over Newfoundland fisheries to international court of arbitration at The Hague (→ Sept. 7, 1910).

New Orleans, Feb. 8. Napoleon's death mask, lost during Civil War, is returned to Louisiana state museum.

Washington, D.C., May 22. President Taft opens 700,000 acres of land in Idaho, Washington and Montana to settlement.

Seattle, Washington, June 1. President Taft presses gold nugget which, by telegraph, opens Alaska-Yukon-Pacific Exposition [fair attracts 80,000 people].

Washington, D.C., July 15. Taft administration requests Chinese regent to permit participation of American bankers in international railway consortium operating in China.

Fort Myer, Virginia, Aug. 2. After repeated flight demonstrations, U.S. Army buys its first airplane, from Wrights.

Peru, Sept. 2. American Annie Smith Peck, 57, is first person to climb 21,000-foot Mount Huascaran, highest peak in Peru.

Dayton, Ohio, Sept. 24. Wilbur Wright states that importation of foreign aircraft should be prohibited.

Detroit, Mich., Oct. 16. Pittsburgh Pirates beat Detroit Tigers, four games to three, in World Series.

Northampton, Massachusetts, Nov. 11. Sergei Rachmaninoff makes his U.S. debut recital at Smith College.

Cherry, Illinois, Nov., 13. Explosion in Saint Paul Mine kills 259 miners.

Washington, D.C. Congress passes Weeks Act, authorizing government to acquire White Mountain region in New Hampshire as a national forest.

New York City. Photographer Lewis Hine delivers lecture entitled "Social Photography: How the Camera May Help the Social Uplift."

"Great White Fleet" home in triumph

"Great White Fleet," after more than a year at sea, heads home to America.

Hampton Roads, Va., Feb. 22

Almost 15 months after it set sail on a historic voyage around the world, the "Great White Fleet" arrived back home today to a tumultuous welcome at the naval installation here. Officers and men of the fleet were personally greeted by Theodore Roosevelt aboard the presidential yacht Mayflower. The armada left Hampton Roads on December 16, 1907. The mission had two objectives: to show good will toward the nation's friends and allies, and to demonstrate its vast naval might to any potential enemies. The fleet of 16 battleships was originally commanded by Rear Admiral Robert "Fighting Bob" Evans. After leaving Hampton Roads, the flotilla steamed around the tip of South America and up the American West Coast. Evans became seriously ill, and was succeeded by his second-in-command, Rear Admiral Charles Sperry. After crossing the Pacific Ocean, the fleet visited Australia and New Zealand.

The crew enjoyed a three-day stay in Japan in October. Enterprising Japanese merchants sold them Mitsuokia washing powder (which supposedly rids the body of blemishes). They were also presented with large, colorful posters that urged the continuation of peaceful Japanese-American relations. Many of the sailors report that they were startled by the sincere friendliness and Oriental hospitality offered by the Japanese.

Leaving Japan, the armada traversed the Indian Ocean, passed through the Suez Canal and the Mediterranean, then headed home across the North Atlantic. The cruise covered over 46,000 miles. American diplomats at home and in the countries the fleet visited call the historic mission a great success.

Prudential Life claims it offers as much protection as the "Great White Fleet."

U.S. bans opium to curb addiction

Washington, D.C.

In a blow against the international trade in opium, Congress has voted to ban importation of the drug except for medical use. The action has been anticipated since passage of a law banning the opium trade in the Philippines two years ago. Despite American measures, trading in opium flourishes around the world. The Empress Dowager of China is trying to institute a ban in her country, but the drug is still widely available there. It is smuggled in quantities from India to most countries of Asia and Europe.

Terrier again wins Westminster title

New York City, Feb. 12

For the third year in a row, a fox terrier has won the coveted championship of the Westminster Kennel Club. There were 1,936 entrants. In fact, it was the same fox terrier, Ch. Warren Remedy, that was declared best in show for owner Winthrop Rutherford, as he was in 1907 and in 1908. The Westminster evolved from friendly competition among breeders and owners over the sleekness of their dogs. The show was first held in 1877 at Gilmore's Garden in Madison Square.

Cost of living up, family size down

Washington, D.C., Nov. 12

Government statistics show that the cost of living, which declined after the economic panic of 1907, has rebounded. Commodity prices are soaring, and there has been a 7.9 percent rise in the cost of living since the first of this year. Over the past three years, prices have risen 10.5 percent. Analysts think that the climbing cost of raw goods has pushed other prices higher, giving workers an incentive to demand higher wages. As prices go up, the number of children in families has been going down; federal census figures that were released in March showed many families have only two or three children.

Wobblies out West stage lumber strike

Kalispell, Montana, Autumn

The lumber business in Montana has almost been brought to a standstill by a series of strikes that have swept the state. Led by "Big Bill" Haywood's Industrial Workers of the World, most of the migratory workers and lumbermen have simply walked away from their jobs. The I.W.W. has also used more forceful tactics, such as strong-arming laborers who would otherwise remain at work. And there have been cases of union-sponsored arson and sabotage. The Wobblies' reliance on violence has appalled officials of the more conservative American Federation of Labor.

A boom in Bakelite

Yonkers, New York

Manufacturers are finding more and more uses for Bakelite, a new plastic material marketed last year. Bakelite was invented here by a Belgian-born chemist, Leo H. Baekeland, who named it after himself. Made from phenol and formaldehyde, it starts as a liquid and hardens into any desired shape. It is water-resistant, can be cut with a knife and is easily machined. It is also an electrical insulator. Bakelite was developed as a substitute for shellac, a natural product with limited uses, but it already is being substituted for glass and wood in many products. Its success has stimulated research efforts to create other synthetic plastic materials.

Peary gets to North Pole

Postcard showing Peary as well as Cook, who claimed he reached Pole in 1908.

North Pole, Apr. 6

After more than a month on the ice, Robert Edwin Peary reportedly reached the North Pole today. At 10 a.m., Peary ordered what was left of his expedition to halt on the "roof of the world," 90 degrees north latitude. He had achieved his lifelong goal, to stand where all points on the compass were south.

But this accomplishment has not been without sacrifice. The expedition left on March 1 with 6 Americans, 17 Eskimos, 19 sleds and 133 dogs. Today, there was only one American beside Peary, Matthew Henson, a Negro who is an old hand at Arctic travel and speaks the Eskimo language fluently. Only 4 of the 17 Eskimos remain. Most were sent back; but one, Ross Marvin, died.

The temperature was mild by Arctic standards when Peary reached the North Pole, 15 degrees below zero and dead calm. After he unfurled a small American flag, a breeze rose "from nowhere," Henson reported, and Old Glory's colors stood out against the unending white of the Arctic icecap.

Immediately after raising the flag, Peary took photos of his men at the North Pole and buried a jar with two messages for posterity. One thanked the expedition's financial backers, the Peary Arctic Club of New York. The second stated that Peary had raised an American flag at the North Pole and had formally taken possession of the entire region and adjacent areas in the name of the President of the United States.

His quest for the pole over, Peary plans to head toward the United States at about 4 p.m. tomorrow.

Congress maintains protectionist tariff

Washington, D.C., Apr. 9

Ending a bitter fight with strong class overtones, President Taft today signed a healthy tariff increase into law. Senator Nelson Aldrich, speaking for the industrial interests of the Northeast, calls the Payne-Aldrich Act a victory for economic progress. Senator Robert La Follette of Wisconsin calls it a sell-out. Leading a block of insurgent Midwestern lawmakers, he blatantly attacked the Republican mainstream for aiding the growth of trusts. According to Henry Cabot Lodge, "the amount of ruthless selfishness that is exhibited on both sides surpasses anything I have seen."

Press gets wireless

Chicago, May 3

A revolution is taking place in the news industry. For the first time, a wireless telegraphic press message has been sent; it soared on the airwaves from New York to Chicago today. Such transmissions are soon expected to be commonplace and will no doubt transform the world into a place where communication is almost instantaneous. Guglielmo Marconi pioneered radio research, when he exhibited wireless transmission in 1895. In 1901, he sent the letter "s" across the Atlantic. Last month, music was broadcast from New York's Metropolitan Opera House to the home of Lee de Forest, inventor of the three-element tube that made radio possible.

Washington, D.C., March 4. *President Taft told his wife today: "Now I'm in the White House; I'm not going to be pushed around anymore."*

"Right and Left" (1909) by Winslow Homer. The painter received most of his artistic education as an apprentice to a lithographer in the 1850's.

Four women cross country in motorcar

San Francisco, Aug. 6

The use of the automobile for pleasure driving by women got a strong boost today when four adventurous drivers arrived on the West Coast after a two-month journey across the United States. The daring women were Alice Huyler Ramsey, president of the Women's Motoring Club of New York, and her companions, Nettie R. Powell, Margaret Atwood and Hermine Jahns. They left New York on June 9 and rolled into San Francisco with great fanfare. They drove a 30-horsepower open car, built by the Maxwell-Briscoe Company, which prices its two-cylinder runabouts at $500. A recent parade of 1,000 cars in Detroit also indicated that the automobile is here to stay.

Ford: Any color so long as it's black

Detroit, Mich., Autumn

Owing to a more specialized construction line, with workers concentrating on individual parts, the Ford Motor Company turned out an unprecedented 17,700 cars this year. Henry Ford has dropped his more expensive automobiles, and now produces just the Model T, the tough, low-priced car that won a transcontinental race this summer. The company hopes to get the Model T price below the current $850, and Ford stands by his goal of making a utilitarian car for the masses, ignoring the trends of rival auto makers, who seem to be bent on appealing only to the rich. "A customer can have a car painted any color so long as it is black," Ford said this year.

U.S. forces to shield rebels in Nicaragua

Washington, D.C., Nov. 18

The Taft Administration has sent troops to Nicaragua, after receiving reports that President Jose Santos Zelaya has executed 500 rebels, including two Americans. The rebellion against the government of Zelaya, a Liberal, is led by Conservatives Emiliano Chamorro and Juan Estrada, who reportedly have received financial support from American citizens living in Nicaragua. The U.S. troops will protect the rebel stronghold in Bluefields, a city on the Miskito coast that is also a center of American business interests. Zelaya seized power from the Conservatives in 1893 and wants to form a union of the five Central American countries, with himself as leader (→ June 6, 1911).

Freud and Jung start American tour

Worcester, Mass., Sept. 10

Dr. Sigmund Freud, the noted Viennese neurologist, tonight began a series of five lectures at Clark University here. Freud is speaking on the subject of psychoanalysis at the invitation of Stanley Hall, the president of the university. The first lecture drew a large crowd, although Freud spoke in German, because of the controversial nature of the subject. One listener said that "Freud advocates free love, a removal of all restraints and a relapse into savagery." Freud is accompanied by Dr. Carl Jung, one of his most devoted disciples. The two plan to tour the East, visiting Niagara Falls and Lake Placid as well as Harvard University, before returning to Europe at the end of the month.

Harriman is dead; a railroad tycoon

Arden, New York, Sept. 9

Edward H. Harriman, one of the greatest railway builders of his time, died at his home here today at the age of 61. From his start as a Wall Street office boy, he rose to become director of the Union Pacific and Southern Pacific Railroads. His battle for control of the Northern Pacific led to the 1901 panic. Ruthless in business, Harriman took pride in having founded the Tompkins Square Boys' Club for immigrants, the first of its kind. He was also quick to aid San Francisco's earthquake victims.

"Memphis Blues"

Memphis, Tennessee

Politics and music are unlikely bedfellows. But a song recently created by trumpeter W. C. Handy for Edward "Boss" Crump's election campaign has become this season's big hit in Memphis. The title was "Mr. Crump." Because of its popularity, Handy has notated it, with an eye to publication, and renamed it "Memphis Blues." While Negro musicians have been creating blues tunes for years, this is believed to be the first that was actually written down.

Equitable, banks bought by Morgan

New York City, Dec. 2

Financier J. Pierpont Morgan may not yet own everything in the country, but he moved closer today with the acquisition of the Equitable Life Assurance Company and its banks. This marks his biggest banking consolidation to date. Morgan's disclosed resources now approach $2 billion, but his real wealth is far greater. Through interlocking directorships, his company controls or influences more than 100 of the nation's top corporations and banks with total assets of well above $20 billion.

This year's print of "The Flatiron Building - Evening" (1905) by Edward Steichen shows the former painter has turned photography into high art.

Philadelphia, August 2. *The Mint today issued a new penny to replace the Indian head penny.*

National aviation industry is taking off

Orville Wright readies his airplane for an endurance flight test in July.

New York City, December

About three dozen aeronauts, from Florida to Nova Scotia to France, are taking to the skies in powered machines. And, as spectacular records are set almost monthly, a few look to a lucrative new industry centered around airplanes.

Louis Bleriot's English Channel hop notwithstanding, Orville and Wilbur Wright are still hailed by the world's press as the "kings of the air." Orville, recovered from a crash that killed a passenger last year, dazzled the army at Fort Myer, Virginia, on July 20, when he set a duration record of one hour 20 minutes. Thousands gasped while his plane Flyer swooped in figure eights 300 feet overhead. Duly impressed, the army bought a Wright Flyer for $30,000 on August 2. On October 26, Lieutenant Frank Humphreys, trained by the Wrights,

became the army's first solo pilot.

Wilbur, meanwhile, electrified all New York on October 4, as the city was holding its gala Hudson-Fulton Celebration. Piloting a Flyer fitted with a red canoe in case of a water landing, Wilbur flew up the Hudson for 33 minutes.

The Wright brothers say they have retired from public flying, but on November 22 they announced that a new Wright Company, with $1 million in financing from August Belmont and other leading bankers, would sell airplanes to the public and the government. Rival aeronaut Glenn Curtiss, undaunted by patent suits filed by the Wrights, has started his own venture with Augustus Herring. The first Herring-Curtiss Company Golden Flier biplane has been sold to the Aeronautical Society of New York for $5,000.

Innovative Wright builds the Robie House

Chicago

Frank Lloyd Wright's new Robie House is being acclaimed as the finest achievement of the brilliant young architect. Built on the South Side near the University of Chicago for the Robie family, the structure is the latest in Wright's "prairie house" style, featuring strong horizontal lines that create a sculptural effect. Critics particularly admire the way in which Wright has made maximum use of a small lot, putting the heating and other services on the ground floor and the living quarters on the two floors above.

The 41-year-old Wright attended college for only two years and began

practicing his trade with the firm of Louis Sullivan, the acclaimed architect here. Wright split with Sullivan, who objected to his outside commissions, and designed a sensational series of buildings that won him immediate acclaim. Wright's avowed purpose is to develop a new architecture suited to the Midwest. He and others in the Prairie School use mass-produced materials and equipment. Their houses have plain walls and roomy family areas, combining comfort and convenience.

Wright also is designing innovative office buildings, most notably the Larkin Building, erected in 1904 in Buffalo, New York.

Wright's innovative Robie House, 5757 South Woodlawn Ave., Chicago, Ill.

A jaunty Frederic Remington. At the time of his death on December 26, the famous painter and sculptor stood as the undisputed illustrator of the Western frontier.

Chiricahua Apache Chief Geronimo, who died February 17, had in his later years taken up ranching, and appeared as a celebrity at the St. Louis World's Fair.

"Chinese Restaurant" by John Sloan. One of "The Eight" of the Ashcan School of art, Sloan draws inspiration from the streets of New York City.

1910

Taft

Washington, D.C., March 26. Congress amends Immigration Act of 1907 to bar entry into United States of paupers, criminals, anarchists and diseased persons.

Spokane, Washington, June 19. Father's Day is first celebrated under guidance of Mrs. John B. Dodd.

Washington, D.C., June 24. Congress passes law requiring all American passenger ships to carry radio equipment.

The Arctic, July 2. American Oscar Tamm becomes first person to cross Arctic by automobile.

Columbus, Ohio, July 11. Phil Parmelee flies a plane with a string of silk, 500 yards long, attached to it, in order to promote a department store.

Atlantic City, New Jersey, July 12. To demonstrate future of military air attacks, Glenn Curtiss drops oranges from his plane onto a ship.

Osawatomie, Kansas, August. John Brown Memorial Park, named in honor of militant abolitionist, dedicated by Theodore Roosevelt.

Hammondsport, New York, Sept. 2. Blanche Stuart becomes first American woman to fly in an airplane.

The Hague, The Netherlands, Sept. 7. International court of arbitration extends American fishing rights in Newfoundland; starts commission to arbitrate individual grievances.

Chicago, Oct. 23. Philadelphia Athletics defeat Chicago Cubs in World Series, four games to one.

Ohio. Local elections result in 58 of state's 88 counties voting to outlaw liquor.

Baltimore. Report on medical education names Johns Hopkins University as only American equal of European institutions.

New York City. Artist John Sloan joins Socialist Party and runs for assemblyman, winning only 102 votes.

DEATHS

Redding, Connecticut, Apr. 21. Mark Twain, novelist and humorist (*Nov. 30, 1835).

Chocorua, New Hampshire, Aug. 26. William James, influential psychologist and philosopher (*Jan. 11, 1842).

Taft fires Pinchot, chief U.S. forester

Washington, D.C., Jan. 7

The chief of the United States Forest Service, Gifford Pinchot, a noted conservationist, alleged last year that the Secretary of the Interior, Richard Ballinger, was unfairly selling public lands to a Morgan-Guggenheim syndicate. After Congress conducted an investigation of these charges and determined that they were unfounded, President Taft, who had long regarded Pinchot as a "radical and a crank," removed him from office. Washington insiders say that the President's removal of Pinchot is certain to raise the anger of former President Roosevelt, who had been an early supporter of the deposed chief forester.

Opera is broadcast live from Met stage

New York City, Jan. 13

Wireless operators at sea were surprised to hear the golden voice of Enrico Caruso cut through the static. They were also apparently the main recipients of this second live broadcast from the Metropolitan Opera House. The first took place last April 3. Both were managed by Lee De Forest, who invented the three-element vacuum tube, and both offered brief excerpts from *I Pagliacci* and *Cavalleria Rusticana*. In one case, with the microphones placed as closely as possible, the Neapolitan tenor sang the prologue to *Cavalleria* from behind the curtain, as is normal. The microphones were then removed before the curtain was raised.

Ballerina Pavlova makes N.Y. debut

New York City, Feb. 28

Ballet enthusiasts here were treated to the graceful and inspired dancing of the Russian ballerina Anna Pavlova tonight. The 28-year-old Pavlova made her first American appearance at the Metropolitan Opera. Pavlova entered the Imperial Ballet School in 1895, when she was 10. She subsequently became a prima ballerina of the Marinsky Theater, to which the school was attached. Her elegant and skillful dancing has taken her all over the world, including Paris, where she performed with Sergei Diaghilev's Ballet Russe and with the renowned Nijinsky. She resigned from the Ballet Russe to begin her own company in London.

Population: 92 million; less than half have high school diploma

Washington, D.C.

The U.S. population now stands at 91.9 million according to the newly released 1910 census. Of these people, almost 50 million live in rural areas while some 42 million are urban dwellers. The farm population is put at 32 million. Of the total U.S. population, 8.7 percent have immigrated to America in the last decade. In the peak year of 1907, more than 1,285,000 arrived. Over two-thirds of these immigrants made the journey on tickets prepaid by friends, relatives or businesses in the United States.

The census reveals that the immigrants do not fit a single model at all. French immigrants have the best jobs and a higher standard of living. The Irish immigrants have the highest literacy rate (97 percent). Census figures indicate that over 35 percent of New Yorkers are foreign-born and, for the most part, poor. There are 340,000 Italians in New York City as well as 540,000 Jews, mainly from Eastern Europe. Some 2,600 Armenians now live in New York, 1,900 live in Providence and over 1,100 live in Boston. Detroit reports 400 Syrians living there.

The census indicates that Americans are not particularly well-educated. Less than half of them over the age of 25 have high school diplomas, and only 4 percent have college degrees. They aren't wealthy either. The study found that the average American factory girl, for example, makes only $1.57 for a nine-hour day.

The federal census is compiled every 10 years.

"Local Industries" by John Ballator. The booming population helps fuel the growing diversity of American industry.

House revolt against "Uncle Joe" Cannon

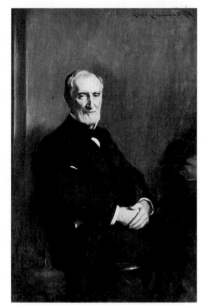

The Speaker, a muted Cannon.

Washington, D.C., March 19

Once the most powerful Speaker in the history of the House, "Uncle Joe" Cannon is now the weakest, stripped of nearly all the controls by which he had held lawmakers hostage to all his wishes. A convivial man who loves to play poker with his colleagues, Cannon, nevertheless, was a czar who held a firm grasp on every aspect of House operations – that is, until now. A revolt led by Representatives George Norris of Nebraska and Champ Clark of Missouri has left him little more than a figurehead. He lost his membership on the powerful Rules Committee, was deprived of all authority to appoint committees of the House and he no longer has the power to decide who makes a speech or a motion.

N.A.A.C.P. is organized

William Edward Burghardt Du Bois of Great Barrington, Massachusetts.

New York City, November

Crisis, the journal of the new National Association for the Advancement of Colored People, made its debut this month. According to editor W.E.B. Du Bois, it will not only "show the danger of race prejudice," but also "stand for the rights of men, irrespective of color or race." The N.A.A.C.P., founded on May 1, is an inter-racial union of Negro radicals and liberal reformers that has grown out of the National Negro Committee, founded in June of last year. Du Bois is its only Negro officer. The group's white founders include reformers Jane Addams, John Dewey and John E. Milholland. Industrialist Andrew Carnegie is among its supporters (→ Oct. 1, 1912).

Jews congregate on the Lower East Side

New York City, Autumn

New York has more people of Jewish ancestry than any other city in the United States – or in the world according to the latest census. Government figures indicate that 540,000 Jews now live in the city. The vast majority are concentrated in the shadow of the Brooklyn Bridge, on the Lower East Side.

Most of these Jews migrated to America from Central and Eastern Europe. Like most of the non-Jewish immigrants, they came for two reasons: hardship at home and the promise of a new life in America. These first-generation Jews talk freely about the "pogroms," anti-Semitic attacks, and anti-Jewish economic policies in the "old country" that literally force them to flee their "shetls," or ethnic villages. One Polish Jew says he decided to come to New York after he had seen a friend return to Poland "well dressed, with an overcoat, and a cigar in the mouth." Meanwhile, German Jews, who have been here longer, tend to look down on the new arrivals.

Teddy home after big-game trek in Africa

New York City, June 19

Colonel Teddy Roosevelt was given a hero's welcome today on his return from a year's trek in Africa hunting big game. As his 14-carriage parade proceeded from the Battery to 59th Street, crowds lining the five-mile route jubilantly waved hats and handkerchiefs. Teddy's reaction? "Bully!"

Roosevelt's safari actually ended in March. His party of six reported having bagged 13,000 specimens. Many were rare, such as the dik-dik, an antelope smaller than a jackrabbit. The more common game included lions, elephants, rhinos, leopards, cheetahs and waterbucks as well as other kinds of antelope. There was danger everywhere. On one occasion, the colonel shot and felled a bull elephant only to have its mate charge, brushing him with its trunk. But "Bwana Tumbo," as the expedition's gunbearers called him, emerged unscathed, typically stout and tanned. A journalist since he left the White House, Roosevelt has already begun working on a book about his African adventures.

A mass of humanity brings the corner of Orchard and Hester Streets to life.

The former President confidently takes the reins while on the sands of Egypt. ▷

I.C.C. to rule over all communications

Washington, D.C., June 18

Congress passed the Mann-Elkins Act today, bringing telephone, telegraph, cable and wireless firms under the umbrella of the Interstate Commerce Commission. The bill is widely hailed by communications officials who fear the rapidly growing slate of intrusive state regulations. AT&T vice president E.K. Hall hopes the action will calm public hostility that could "crystallize at any time into adverse legislation." The new law also expands the I.C.C.'s authority over the railroads. Despite efforts by President Taft to weaken it, the bill allows the commission to revise rates on its own initiative, and bars railroads from acquiring competing lines.

Ezra Pound's prose

London

Europe continues to lure leading American writers. The latest emigré is Ezra Pound, a native of Idaho who grew up and studied on the East Coast before crossing the Atlantic. His first book of verse was published in Italy in 1908; since then, he has lived in London, where his next two collections met with acclaim. Only 25, Pound has now offered his quirky prose in *The Spirit of Romance*, essays that reveal his amazing knowledge of both classic tradition and popular folk forms.

Jack Johnson knocks out Jim Jeffries

The nation's two preeminent pugilists locked in combat before a sell-out crowd.

Reno, Nevada, July 4

Jack Johnson, the Negro heavyweight champion, knocked out Jim Jeffries today in the 15th round of a bout that set off a chain reaction of race riots across the country. Eight Negroes were reported killed in the aftermath of a bout that some had thought might provide "the great white hope." But Jeffries, who was overweight and out of shape, conceded after the fight, "I couldn't come back."

Johnson was not in top form either, but he didn't have to be against a foe who had come out of a five-year retirement because he needed the cash. The sickly Jeffries, dull of eye and rubbery in the legs, was hard put to keep from keeling over under Johnson's bludgeoning. But the former champion fought on, even after a cut was opened over his eye in the sixth round. "I thought this fellow could hit," Johnson was heard to say between rounds.

On a New Orleans trolley car, a Negro who jeeringly exulted over the Johnson victory was fatally slashed by a white man.

Mann Act restricts white slave traffic

Washington, D.C., June 25

Relying on federal authority over interstate trade, President Taft signed the Mann Act today, barring the transport of women across state lines for immoral purposes. Prostitution was vaulted into the public eye in 1907 when G.K. Turner published an article in *McClure's* claiming Chicago harbored a highly organized ring of 10,000 "ladies of illfame." That year, a Pittsburgh survey counted 200 "disorderly houses"; Portland, Oregon, found 113 full-time brothels. Ex-President Teddy Roosevelt led the fight for moral legislation. The family, he insisted, must be resurrected as a bulwark against the "race suicide" of declining birth rates.

Legends at the Met

New York City, Dec. 10

The world premiere of Giacomo Puccini's *The Girl of the Golden West* at the Metropolitan Opera House was the stuff of legends. The linking of the most popular opera composer and Arturo Toscanini, the greatest conductor of Italian opera, made tickets more precious than gold. Lucky patrons heard a fiery performance of Pucciniesque lyricism, followed by 52 frenzied curtain calls. When Puccini took a bow, Met manager Giulio Gatti-Casazza placed a silver crown on his head.

Halley's comet causes thousands to panic

Few can miss the nocturnal display.

Chicago, May 18

Comet pills are selling briskly as Halley's comet reaches its nearest point to earth. Sold as an antidote for the poisonous gas mistakenly thought to constitute its tail, the pills are symptomatic of a nation in panic. Chicagoans have boarded up their windows out of the same fear, while others expect the world to end in a shattering collision. Crying "Comet!" New Yorkers bolted from a trolley when it was struck on the roof by a most earthly object, later reported to be a brick. Con men prey on the frightened and suicide levels are up. Meanwhile, the more sophisticated have been throwing nightly "comet parties."

Boy Scouts, Camp Fire Girls founded

United States

Boys and girls now have a new way to learn about cooperation, service to others and work skills. The Boy Scouts of America was founded this year by William Boyce, a Chicago publisher, to train boys, to build character through a program stressing work, outdoor play and community duty. The group is modeled after the Canadian and British counterparts. The Camp Fire Girls was started by Dr. Luther Halsey Gulick, a leader in youth recreation, and his wife, Charlotte Vetter Gulick. The Gulicks base the program on the girls summer camp they run, where they emphasize work, health and love.

Scouts raise the Stars and Stripes.

When labor strife gets out of hand

Los Angeles

"In the name of labor, labor is denied," is the cry from *The Los Angeles Times*. On October 1, an explosion ripped through the paper's plant, killing 21 people. Unionists point to a gas leak, but the paper blames the unions, saying that the cause was "dynamite by assassins." Rewards are offered, but no leads have been found. On Christmas Day, when a bomb hit the Llewellyn iron works, where a strike is in progress, investigators tied the blast to the iron workers union. In spite of Clarence Darrow's handling their defense, 38 iron workers were convicted and union president F. Ryan was sentenced to seven years in prison.

Book on Hull House

Chicago

Two decades ago, a plucky 29-year-old named Jane Addams purchased a dilapidated house in South Chicago's slums flanked by a funeral parlor and a saloon. Within a year, 50,000 poor immigrants had passed through the doors of Hull House, where a staff of volunteers gave them practical lessons in English and other subjects. Miss Addams, a pioneer in the field of social work, now writes of her famed "settlement house" in *Twenty Years at Hull House*, a best-seller that is filled with humor as well as practical advice for others who share the author's vision of a better society.

Eastman Kodak's easy-to-use portable cameras offer Americans a new way to enjoy their free time.

New football rules prohibit clipping

Chicago

Despite efforts to take the mayhem out of football, the number of injuries and fatalities has risen to the point where more changes are required. With 33 gridiron deaths recorded in 1909, the college athletic leaders have forbidden the flying tackle from behind (clipping). They have also banned the pushing or pulling of the ball carrier and interlocked interference. In addition, seven players are now required on the line of scrimmage. These changes follow others made over the past five years, first at the angry order of President Roosevelt and then by concerned college presidents who want the sport cleaned up or removed from school programs.

Socialist in House

Washington, D.C., Nov. 8

The Socialist Party of America continues to gain strength. Today, Victor Berger of Wisconsin became the first Socialist ever elected to Congress. Wisconsin is a beehive of progressive and socialist activity. In Milwaukee, Emile Seidel was elected mayor. The party was founded in 1900 and won 95,000 votes for its presidential candidate, Eugene Debs. In 1904, he pulled 400,000 votes, and in 1908, even more. Now the party is making legislative inroads (→ Nov. 5, 1912).

Time is money!

Philadelphia

The methods of Frederick W. Taylor, who calls himself the "father of scientific management," are being hailed by industry and cursed by labor. Trained as an engineer, Taylor has increased the efficiency of many factories by close observation of individual workers with the idea of eliminating all wasted time and motion. Workers, naturally, object to having all their movements studied with a stopwatch, but companies such as Bethlehem Steel that have put Taylor's ideas into action say he has saved them millions of dollars. Taylor says scientific management can make the home and society more efficient, too.

Year of air records, but it wasn't all glory

Rarely pausing to rest, ex-President Roosevelt takes to the air in St. Louis.

Cape Hatteras, N.C.

Owing to what Commander Walter Wellman called "disastrous" wind shifts, the dirigible America failed in its attempt to cross the Atlantic. On October 18, the 228-foot airship foundered in the waves off Cape Hatteras after wandering off course and losing altitude. Luckily, a British steamer rescued the crew, which was at least consoled with a 71-hour, 1,000-mile duration record.

Elsewhere this year, airplane maker Glenn Curtiss, when he wasn't training America's first aviatrix, Blanche Stuart, or new navy fliers, was giving maritime strategists the jitters with "aerial bombing" of ships with oranges. A Curtiss biplane heralded another naval breakthrough on November 14, when Eugene Ely swept aloft from an 83-foot platform fitted to the cruiser Birmingham, then flew two miles to Hampton Roads, Virginia.

At the Boston-Harvard air meet on September 12, an Englishman, Claude Grahame-White, won the $10,000 prize in a 33-mile race. On the same day, Ralph Johnson set a duration record of more than three hours in a Bleriot monoplane. Then, on October 26, Johnson set an incredible altitude record of 9,714 feet, over Long Island.

Battling disease and almost impenetrable jungles, as many as 40,000 men are employed along the route of the Panama Canal at any one time. Chief engineer George Goethals has sped up the project (→ March 23, 1911).

San Diego, Jan. 26. Glenn Curtiss demonstrates feasibility of seaplanes by flying an airplane rigged with floats, as navy officials watch in awe.

New York City, Feb. 21. Gustav Mahler conducts New York Philharmonic [last time before his death].

Arizona, March 18. Theodore Roosevelt opens dam bearing his name; it spans Salt River.

Berkeley, Calif., March 23. Former President Roosevelt states in a speech, "I took the canal zone and let Congress debate, and while the debate goes on the canal does also" (→ Aug. 24, 1912).

New York City, Apr. 11. Triangle Shirtwaist owners indicted on charges of first- and second-degree manslaughter.

Washington, D.C., May 1. In United States v. Grimaud, Supreme Court rules that federal government, not states, has control over forest reserves.

Cordova, Alaska, May 5. Irate townspeople shovel 350 tons of coal off ships in harbor, protesting government decision to close Alaska coal lands.

Indianapolis, May 30. Ray Harroun wins First 500-mile race here.

Washington, D.C., June 6. United States and Nicaragua conclude Knox-Castrillo Convention, giving United States official role in Nicaraguan internal affairs (→ Aug. 14, 1912).

Washington, D.C., June 30. It is announced that President Taft has saved nation over $42 million in last fiscal year, by requiring that all government spending estimates be submitted to him personally.

Washington, D.C., July 7. In order to protect dwindling pelagic seal population, U.S., Britain, Russia, and Japan sign treaty barring hunting above 30th parallel for 15 years.

Europe, Aug. 3. United States signs treaties with Britain and France, pledging that signers will not fight a third nation with whom a general arbitration treaty is in force (→ March 7, 1912).

Philadelphia, Oct. 26. Philadelphia Athletics defeat New York Giants in World Series, four games to two.

Triangle fire kills 146

New York City, March 25

A horrible fire this afternoon took the lives of 146 young women working at the Triangle Shirtwaist Company on Greene Street. The building was said to be fireproof, but there was no sprinkling system, and one of the two exits was bolted shut. The few employees who escaped alive said the door was kept locked to keep them from sneaking off with spools of thread. Many of the victims, mostly Italian and Jewish immigrant girls, leapt from the 10th floor to the pavement below, where some were found with their paychecks still grasped in their fists. The Women's Trade Union League places the blame squarely on the company owners. Triangle had been one of 13 firms to deny garment workers better conditions in a strike in February of last year. In fact, it is rumored that another reason the second escape door was locked was to keep out agitators (→ Apr. 11).

The Triangle Shirtwaist Company fire kills 146 and draws national attention.

Negroes to get help from Urban League

New York City

In response to a growing number of Negroes moving to cities, the National League on Urban Conditions Among Negroes has been founded. It aims to help migrants from the South find opportunities in industry and adjust to city living. Business, religious and civic groups of both Negro and white races will work to improve housing and employment conditions for Negroes.

20,000 troops sent to Mexican border

Washington, D.C., March 7

The United States today ordered 20,000 troops to the Mexican border to protect American interests. A rebellion against Porfirio Diaz, who has ruled Mexico almost continuously since 1876, has been spreading rapidly. Many of the rebel leaders are in the state of Chihuahua, across from New Mexico and Texas. The rebellion began after the election last year in which Diaz claimed victory over his opponent, Francisco Madero. Madero, leader of a reform movement whom Diaz had kept in jail through much of the campaign, fled to Texas. There he declared the elections void, named himself provisional president and urged a general uprising. Support for Madero has grown rapidly (→ Nov. 24, 1913).

Indian who founded Peyote religion dies

Cache, Oklahoma, Feb. 23

Commanche Indian Chief Quanah Parker died today in this small town. Parker, the son of an Indian chief and a white woman, Cynthia Parker, first won fame as a capable adversary of the United States Army. After finally surrendering in 1875, he founded the Peyote religion, which embraced the hallucinogenic drug, derived from cactus, in conjunction with Christian beliefs and symbols. A cultural movement as well as a religion, popular among the Indians of the Southwest, it has become institutionalized as the Native American Church.

Cadillac eliminating hand-crank starter

Cadillac's innovative electric starter will liberate drivers from the strain of hand-cranking their autos to life.

Detroit, Michigan

While countless Americans have grown to love their automobiles, few look forward to the backbreaking task of hand-cranking the engine to life, especially on a cold or rainy morning. Indeed, the hand-crank starter, which occasionally causes injuries when the crank snaps back unpredictably, is the one factor that has limited the sale of gasoline-powered vehicles to women and older men.

But the models planned for next year by the Cadillac division of Henry Leland's General Motors should change all this. Leland has recruited a young inventor named Charles Kettering, who had developed an electric motor for cash registers that provides short bursts of power. Adapted to jolt Cadillac engines into action, the battery-powered starter should send Cadillac's 1912 sales soaring past this year's impressive mark of 10,000.

Rockefeller's Standard Oil broken up

Washington, D.C., May 15

John D. Rockefeller once called the growth of huge corporations "a survival of the fittest, the working out of a law of nature and a law of God." Unfortunately for the oil tycoon, the law of the United States held sway today over both the heavens and the earth. Ending an antitrust suit launched by President Roosevelt, the Supreme Court has ordered Rockefeller's Standard Oil Company of New Jersey to divest itself of holdings in 37 firms.

In sprawling, often impenetrable sentences, Chief Justice Edward White has allegedly clarified, and many say limited, the scope of the Sherman Antitrust Act. His "rule of reason" allows that some trusts may, in fact, serve the public interest – those that combine to create economies of scale, for instance. The court's decision merely codifies the policy of selective prosecution pursued by Presidents Roosevelt and Taft for 11 years. Roosevelt repeatedly distinguished between public spirited trusts and the "malefactors of great wealth." And Taft, addressing Congress in January, warned that an all-out war on trusts would "disturb the confidence of the business community," punishing "the innocent many for the faults of the guilty few."

Standard Oil, it appears, is one of the few. Roosevelt saw Rockefeller as the personification of industrial evil, "setting the pace in the race for wealth under illegal and improper conditions." A Bureau of Corporations inquiry opened by Roosevelt revealed heavy corporate intrigue.

By 1878, Standard had "bought out or frozen out refiners all over the country," controlling 80 percent of oil output. Rebates on rail freight rates helped Rockefeller ruin middlemen. Merchants who refused to buy from Standard found their freight rates had mysteriously doubled. Commercial spies were commonplace and owners of a Standard subsidiary in Buffalo, New York, sabotaged equipment in a competing refinery. It remains to be seen whether divestment will break Standard's hold on the oil industry.

Rockefeller sits for a Lamb portrait.

American Tobacco Co. must reorganize

Washington, D.C., June

Complying with orders from the Supreme Court, the directors of the American Tobacco Company have agreed to split their firm into 14 allegedly separate units. Advocates of the plan say it will loosen founding owner James B. Duke's grip on the nation's tobacco business. Others remain skeptical. A Bureau of Corporations expert told Attorney General George Wickersham the new scheme "leaves very much to be desired if truly competitive conditions are to be reestablished."

The tobacco trust was launched in 1890 along with the Sherman Act, the instrument of its eventual destruction. Its secret was an ingenious cigarette-rolling machine, invented by Duke, and a tireless merger policy. Duke controlled 80 percent of American tobacco output and extended tentacles into Central America. But his purchase of Continental Tobacco in 1904 put him on President Teddy Roosevelt's list of "bad" trusts. Despite friendly offers of compromise, the Justice Department filed suit in 1907. The present conviction, and Standard Oil's in May, highlight President Taft's success in extending government regulation (→ Sept. 26, 1914).

Bill Larned wins seventh tennis title

Newport, Rhode Island

William "Bill" Larned, who won his first title in 1901, capped a decade of tennis excellence by capturing the national tennis championship for the seventh time. His record was compared to the reign of Dick Sears, who won seven consecutive championships starting in 1881. Larned also performed well in Davis Cup play for the United States, but he has had little support against the mighty British and Australians, who have dominated cup play. While Larned was topping the men, Hazel Hotchkiss has won three straight women's titles.

Wrigley's lasts and lasts and lasts.

"Family Group" (1910-11) by William Glackens, renowned Ashcan artist.

End of the warpath for Carry Nation

Armed with Bible and hatchet.

Leavenworth, Kansas, June 9

Mrs. Carry Nation, a temperance reformer who had a lifelong ax – or hatchet – to grind, died today at her home at the age of 64. Mrs. Nation conducted a one-woman crusade to stamp out alcohol, wielding a sharp hatchet and using it to chop up liquor crates in saloons in Kansas and across the Midwest. Born Carry Amelia Moore in Garrard County, Kentucky, she married a doctor who proved to be an alcoholic. The 21-year-old Carry left him within half a year. In 1877, she wed a lawyer named David Nation. No temperance movement supported Mrs. Nation, who supplemented her income by giving lectures and selling souvenir hatchets.

Berlin's "Alexander's Ragtime Band"

New York City

The name Irving Berlin may be new to most, but his hit song *Alexander's Ragtime Band* promises to make it a household word. First sung this year in a Chicago vaudeville act, the song became a national craze after Sophie Tucker started belting it out. Born in Russia, the 23-year old Berlin learned his craft first-hand as a singing waiter and a song plugger in Tin Pan Alley. The author of a number of vaudeville songs, Berlin warbled two of his own numbers, *Sweet Italian Love* and *Oh, That Beautiful Rag*, in last year's revue, *Up and Down Broadway*. While this year's hit song is not strictly a "rag," it nevertheless keeps the toes tapping.

"Alexander's Ragtime Band. It's the best band in the land."

Biplane limps in, first to cross U.S.

Pasadena, California, Autumn

Aviation deaths reached 100 this year, but fliers are as cavalier as ever. On November 5, with the engine of his Wright biplane dying, Calbraith Rodgers landed to a wild welcome in Pasadena, California. It was the first cross-country flight, 3,220 miles from New York in 82 hours 4 minutes. Cromwell Dixon, 19, became the first man to fly over the Rockies on September 30; two days later, he died in a crash. Glenn Curtiss raised his hydroplane from San Diego harbor, and Eugene Ely landed a Curtiss plane on the battleship Pennsylvania. On Long Island, Earl Ovington made the first mail flight, and Harriet Quimby is now "the woman aviator in trousers."

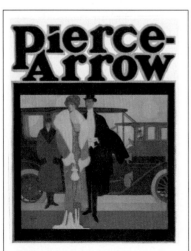

Durant, Chevrolet start auto company

Detroit, Mich., Nov. 1

William C. Durant is hoping to rebound in the auto business by joining forces with Louis Chevrolet in a new company. Durant founded General Motors three years ago, but last year his whirlwind mergers overextended the firm's capital. A banking syndicate took over, ousted Durant and put Walter Chrysler and William C. Nash in charge. Chevrolet, a Swiss-born mechanic and race-car driver who worked for Buick, will design a low-priced car to compete with the Model T. But since Ford has built an empire around the "Tin Lizzie," producing 70,000 this year for the low price of $780, the new Chevrolet Motor Car Company faces a daunting task.

Krazy Kat beware!

New York City, July 1

Poor Krazy Kat won't be around long if Ignatz Mouse has anything to say about it. The rogue of a rodent is out to "bean" the aforementioned feline with whatever object is close at hand. Bricks are his weapon of choice in the *New York Journal* comic strip *Krazy Kat and Ignatz*, the brainchild of cartoonist George Herriman. But don't worry too much about Krazy. She's in love with Ignatz and interprets his brick-throwing as a sign of affection.

Cy Young, pitching great, has retired

United States

After 22 years as baseball's premier pitcher, Cy Young has retired. The tall (6 feet 2 inches) hurler from Gilmore, Ohio, who once hurled a perfect game, has hung up his spikes after a 1911 season plagued by illness. He also pitched two no-hit games, against Cincinnati in 1897 and the New York Americans in 1908. Young, who kept the Philadelphia Americans from reaching first base in a 1904 contest, had a fling as manager during the 1907 season with the Boston Red Sox, the team with which he spent eight years and helped to win a World Series in 1903. He ended his career with 509 victories, 316 losses and an ERA of 2.63.

Studio in Hollywood

Hollywood, California

The Nestor Company has rented the Blondeau Tavern, shut by temperance enthusiasts, at the Sunset and Gower intersection, as the first film studio here. Earlier, Colonel William N. Selig built a West Coast studio in nearby Edendale, and producer Thomas Ince hired a Wild West Show for the winter, using real cowboys, Indians, wild horses and buffalo in spectacular westerns. His "Inceville" in Santa Ynez Canyon covers 20,000 acres.

Foundation set up by Andrew Carnegie

New York City, Nov. 10

After years of generously donating his money to schools, public libraries and various funds, Andrew Carnegie has set up a foundation for distribution of his vast resources. The iron and steel manufacturer's foundation, endowed with $135 million, will work to promote knowledge through educational projects and governmental and international affairs programs for American citizens as well as some British dominions and colonies. Carnegie, who will serve as the foundation's president, is particularly interested in public libraries as a means of self-education.

The philanthropist and benefactor.

New York City, Feb. 21. In declaring his intention to seek presidency again, Theodore Roosevelt is heard to exclaim, "My hat is in the ring."

Washington, D.C., March 7. Senate amends, then ratifies arbitration treaties signed with Britain and France.

Washington, D.C., March 14. Justice Department begins investigation into merger of Southern Pacific and Union Pacific Railroads.

Washington, D.C., May 1. In response to Titanic disaster, federal government orders all steamships to carry enough lifeboats for all passengers.

Washington, D.C., May 13. Senate refers to state proposal for a constitutional amendment to provide direct election of senators (→ May 31, 1913).

Seattle, Washington, July 18. Sailors raid local office of Industrial Workers of the World, burning books and furniture in street.

Washington, D.C., Aug. 2. Senate passes resolution extending Monroe Doctrine to apply to non-European countries and private foreign companies.

Washington, D.C., Aug. 24. Congress passes Panama Canal Act, permitting toll-free passage of American ships through canal, provided they are engaged in coastwide trade (→ Oct. 10, 1913).

Kentucky, Oct. 1. Lincoln Institute, dedicated to providing vocational training for Negroes, opens; Negro elite leaders such as W.E.B. Du Bois protest.

Boston, Oct. 16. Boston Red Sox defeat New York Giants to win World Series four games to three.

Chicago, Dec. 7. Dr. James B. Herrick makes first diagnosis of a heart attack in a living patient.

California. By 1912, over 5,000 Russian pacifists threatened with military service have fled to California.

DEATHS

Glen Echo, Maryland, Apr. 12. Clara Barton, founder of American Red Cross (*Dec. 25, 1821).

Dayton, Ohio, May 30. Wilbur Wright, co-inventor of airplane (*Apr. 16, 1867).

Lawrence textile strikers get pay hike

Lawrence, Mass., March 13

The *Internationale* rang out in a dozen languages today as strike leaders and workers celebrated victory and a pay raise in a heated struggle with textile mill owners. Two strikers were left dead and many injured. "Big Bill" Haywood, head of the radical Industrial Workers of the World, had warned employers they could not "weave cloth with bayonets." The last eight weeks have proved his point.

Trouble began when the first paychecks of the year showed wage cuts would accompany a two-hour reduction in the work week. The owners felt an average of $8.76 a week was too much for 54 hours. After a Polish group quit the looms on January 11, the flood gates opened. The next day, Italians at the American Woolen Company went from mill to mill on the Merrimack River and by evening, 10,000 workers had joined in; by month's end, 50,000. Fife-and-drum bands, parades and long speeches kept strikers busy. Pickets formed chains with thousands in human links circling some mills. Led by Mother Jones, women played a big role, inviting police intervention after sending their children to stay with sympathetic families in New York.

The strike, largely spontaneous, was run by the rank and file, encompassing 28 nationalities. Joseph Ettor of the I.W.W. oversaw the strike committee until he was arrested for murder after a striker was shot down during a demonstration. One labor spokesman charged that the I.W.W. seeks not a "treaty of industrial peace," but "the creation of a proletarian impulse which will eventually revolutionize society."

Businessmen, sporting flags in their buttonholes, have blamed foreign agitation for the unrest. One leading citizen is suspected of having planted dynamite in the strike district to discredit the workers. But police brutality played a bigger role in discrediting the forces of law and order. Company concessions will involve some 250,000 textile workers.

Union adds Arizona and New Mexico

Washington, D.C., Feb. 14

The Territory of Arizona today became the 48th state in the union. On January 6, New Mexico was also granted statehood. The admission of these two states has finally ended the bitter political wrangling that has been going on between the older states and the former territories over alleged special mining and land-holding groups that seemingly dominated Arizona and New Mexico for their exclusive welfare and profit. After the New Mexico bill was signed by President Taft, he said to its new citizens, "Well, it is all over; I am glad to give you life. I hope you will be healthy."

Sure! It's a cinch!

United States

Sure! You can learn to talk like young folks today. *It's a cinch!* For example, when someone treats you to something nice, like a *sundae,* say that it's just *peachy!* If somebody you know has donned stylish clothes, call the look *flossy!* Don't be *peeved* if English professors call you *lowbrow* and your new vocabulary *lousy.* Just *beat it* to a *movie* (what the old folks call a moving picture). Afterward, you can take a *joyride* in a rich friend's *speedy* automobile, and watch it being *serviced* at a garage. Easy? *Sure!*

Cherry trees, a gift from Japan to U.S.

Washington, D.C.

Japan has presented a gift of color and beauty to America. Viscountess Chinda, wife of the Japanese Ambassador, gave 2,000 tiny cherry trees to the First Lady, Mrs. Taft, as a token of friendship. The Japanese celebrate the dreamlike, flowering trees each spring. Mrs. Taft planted the first sapling during a quiet but elegant ceremony. The rest of the trees were planted along the Tidal Basin in Potomac Park. Washingtonians can expect delicate, brilliant pink blossoms each spring to accent their white marble city.

New York City, Jan. 9. *The growth of the metropolis brings with it unique perils. The Equitable Building burned today and is now encased in ice.*

Titanic goes down on maiden voyage

The mighty ship, said to be unsinkable, goes down off the Newfoundland coast.

Halifax, Nova Scotia, Apr. 15

Under a cloudless sky, the Titanic disappeared into the North Atlantic early today, leaving 1,517 people to die in freezing waters. The 700 survivors, who arrived here aboard the Cunard liner Carpathia, tell tales of a stark tragedy.

The White Star steamship, largest in the world, was four days out of Southampton, England, on its maiden voyage to New York. Its vast ballrooms and sprawling upper decks cradled the cream of high society, both London's and New York's. Some passengers paid well over $4,000 for this Atlantic crossing, while in the steerage area below it would have been difficult to find an annual income of $1,000.

The Titanic was believed to be as invincible as the Astors in their Fifth Avenue mansion. At 11:40 last night, however, even John Jacob Astor flinched when the great 46,000-ton hull brushed an iceberg for a mere 10 seconds. It was barely enough of a touch to spill a glass of champagne, but the party was over. Thomas Andrews, the engineer who had overseen the building of the Titanic, rushed starboard to find that the hull was open to the sea along a 300-foot gash.

Within minutes, six distress signals had been issued by wireless. Passengers assembled quietly on deck, calm because of their implicit trust in the best technology known to man. Officers quickly tried to fit the 2,207 people into the lifeboats – where there was really only room for 1,178, while the ballroom band struck up a ragtime medley for encouragement. As the boat listed further starboard, the English hymn *Autumn* sounded a somber note:

God of mercy and compassion
Look with pity on my pain
Hold me up in mighty waters,
Keep my eyes on things above.

It seemed only moments later, from the lifeboats, that the lucky 700 in them watched the great Titanic's bow sink, sending the stern skyward. Gravity ripped away ventilators and stanchions with the screech of grinding metal. The aft compartments filled with water and the mighty vessel vanished, leaving only the tortured wail of hundreds of human beings freezing to death in the middle of nowhere (→ May 1).

Jim Thorpe stars at Stockholm Olympics

Stockholm, Sweden, Summer

Jim Thorpe, the amazing Indian out of Carlisle, Pennsylvania, was hailed as the "world's greatest athlete" following his smashing triumphs in the pentathlon and decathlon at this year's Olympics. He was also first in the 200-meter dash and the 1,500-meter run. The King of Sweden told him, "You are the greatest athlete in the world," and Russia's Czar Nicholas sent him a silver model of a Viking ship. [Since the Olympics are for amateurs, Thorpe was later stripped of his medals and returned the gift after admitting that he had played professional baseball in 1909 and 1910. Athletes who finished second to him were moved up to first]. These Games were also notable because they included women, though only in diving and swimming.

American athletes won 13 of a possible 28 gold medals, with sterling performances by Ralph Cook Craig in the sprints and Charley Reidpath at 400 meters, as well as in a sweep of the 110-meter hurdles (→ Oct. 13, 1982).

Jim Thorpe, all-American.

New on market: Life Savers, Oreos

United States

The American hunger for new products is being amply met every day in the marketplace: this year alone has seen the introduction of many tasty treats. One favorite is cranberry sauce – a sweetened, jellied condiment produced by Ocean Spray Cranberries, a Massachusetts growers cooperative. Richard Hellmann of New York has bottled his Blue Ribbon Mayonnaise, which is said to hold its texture and freshness almost indefinitely. A Cleveland confectioner has turned out a peppermint candy with a hole in it that he calls Life Savers, because it looks like a life preserver. And this spring a new cookie – two chocolate wafers sandwiching a cream filling – called the Oreo Biscuit is a winner for the National Biscuit Co.

"Flagler's Folly" chugs into Florida

Key West, Florida, Jan. 22

The first New York-Key West train arrived here at 10:43 today with the man who built the last section of the railroad aboard. Henry Flagler and his wife, Mary Lily, debarked to the noise of firecrackers, whistles and band music. Many here had never seen a train before. Critics called the 200-mile rail extension to this southernmost point in the United States "Flagler's Folly" because of the problems of building tracks from island to island, over water and through jungles. But Flagler, Florida's pioneer developer, persisted. Today, at the age of 82, he said, "Now I can die happy. My dream is fulfilled."

Expert links crime to low intelligence

Vineland, New Jersey

The director of research at the New Jersey Training School for Feeble-Minded Boys and Girls has stirred up a great deal of controversy over his study linking inherited low intelligence with crime. Henry Herbert Goddard's paper *The Kallikak Family: A Study in the Heredity of Feeble-Mindedness* traces the ancestry of a girl named Deborah Kallikak (a pseudonym Goddard devised, from the Greek meaning "good and bad"), and discloses an unbroken path of degeneracy. Goddard has coined the word "moron," from the Greek for "sluggish," to describe an adult with the intelligence of a child.

Teddy rides Bull Moose into political fray

The former President hitches his hopes to a recognized symbol of tenacity.

Chicago, Aug. 5

The Progressive Party has nominated Theodore Roosevelt as its presidential candidate. Adopting as its symbol the bull moose (because Roosevelt always likes to compare himself to this proud, ferocious animal), the new third party offers the voters a broad range of progressive reforms, including regulation of trusts, unemployment pay, old age pensions and female suffrage. The Bull Moose convention has been a wild spectacle, much like a religious revival. Roosevelt gave his enthusiastic supporters a "confession of faith," while they responded with loud choruses of "Onward Christian Soldiers" and "The Battle Hymn of the Republic." Look out, Republicans and Democrats – the Bull Moose is loose! (→ Nov. 5).

Man jumps out of airplane with parachute

New York City, Spring

On March 1, Lieutenant Albert Berry, strapped into a parachute, climbed under the lower wing of an army biplane 1,500 feet above Kinloch Field near St. Louis and flung himself free. The 33-year-old Berry, who has made many jumps from balloons, plunged for 500 harrowing feet before the parachute billowed open. He repeated the feat soon after, then said never again.

Other aeronauts press on. Bob Fowler completed the first West-to-East continental flight on March 5; it took four months. Fowler survived an early crash, but others were not so lucky. Julie Clark became the first female air fatality in a Springfield, Illinois, crash, and Harriet Quimby, the first aviatrix to cross the English Channel on April 17, was later jolted from her plane over Boston harbor. Cross-country flyer Cal Rodgers plunged into the ocean at Long Beach on April 3.

Minimum wage law

Boston, June 4

Labor leaders are celebrating a major victory today as the Massachusetts legislature passed the nation's first law assuring a minimum wage for the state's lowest-paid workers. The hourly wage has yet to be established, but it will be set by July 1 of next year, when the law is to go into effect. It will prevent an employer from paying "slave wages." Massachusetts has been a leader in the promotion of collective bargaining plans and worker protection laws. Labor leaders will now campaign for similar legislation on the federal level.

A Dreiser tycoon

Chicago

You who dream of rising to the top, put away your morals and sharpen your claws – only the cruel survive. A survivor par excellence is Frank Cowperwood, cold-blooded hero of Theodore Dreiser's *The Financier*, who learns his life lessons by watching a lobster feast on a squid. Cowperwood becomes a human predator, devouring his foes in the business world. Dreiser admits a kinship between his hero and real-life tycoon Charles T. Yerkes; he, too, made his fortune in Philadelphia, then moved to Chicago, where the prey was more tempting.

Taft, Wilson nominated by major parties

Baltimore, Maryland, July 2

Woodrow Wilson has been nominated as the Democratic Party's presidential candidate today. After 46 ballots in which no candidate had a majority, the party turned to "dark horse" Wilson. A Virginian by birth, son of a Presbyterian minister and former president of Princeton University and Governor of New Jersey, the noted reformer recently said, "No one can worship God or love his neighbor on an empty stomach." Thomas R. Marshall, his running mate, is not so reform-minded. As he stated last month, "What this country needs is a good five-cent cigar."

Wilson will run against the Republican nominee, President Taft. Renominated by a wide margin at the G.O.P. convention in Chicago last month, he is expected to run on a pro-business platform. No political warrior, he said of the contest, "Even a rat in a corner will fight." Vice President James Sherman was also renominated (→ Aug. 5).

Debs: "Every capitalist is your enemy"

Chicago

"Every capitalist is your enemy. Every workingman is your friend." Shouted from his "Red Special" campaign train, these words are helping Socialist Eugene Debs gain a lot of attention in the presidential election campaign this year. Debs, who was nominated for the third time by the Socialist Party in Indianapolis in May, has been emphasizing that elective office is only a step on the road to revolution. "Comrades," he proclaimed in Milwaukee with great optimism, "this is our year" (→ Nov. 5).

While the Socialists illustrate their contempt for the capitalist system, for most workers the prospect of climbing that pyramid is as strong as ever.

Women get vote in three states

Washington, D.C., November

Arizona, Kansas and Oregon gave women the vote today, lifting the suffragists out of a 15-year period so dismal they refer to it as "the doldrums." From 1896 to 1910, suffrage made only six state referenda. Each lost by wide margins. For years activists have struggled for direction without a national headquarters. Elizabeth Cady Stanton's daughter Harriet stirred the waters when she returned from England in 1907 with a passion for massive parades. In California last year, the spark caught fire. Billboards, electric signs, essay contests, pageants and plays all helped a referendum win by 3,000 votes. But this month's victories give suffragists a total of only nine states. Liquor interests defeated referenda in Ohio and Wisconsin. Thinking they had Michigan won, women demanded a recount when officials claimed they lost by only 760 votes. The second total jumped magically to 100,000. To many, federal law looks like a better approach (→ March 3, 1913).

Wilson elected, pledges New Freedom

Washington, D.C., Nov. 5

In a stunning victory, Woodrow Wilson was elected President today. When he said on the campaign trail that he "wanted to restore our politics to their full spiritual vigor again, and our national life . . . to its pristine strength and freedom," the voters listened – and they responded with an overwhelming endorsement of his "New Freedom" philosophy.

In an unusual, four-cornered contest, Democrat Wilson garnered 6,286,000 votes (41 percent). The Bull Moose candidate, Teddy Roosevelt, received 4,216,000 (27 percent). President Taft, the Republican candidate, got 3,483,000 votes (23 percent), and the Socialist Party nominee, Eugene V. Debs, received about 900,000 popular votes (6 percent). In the electoral vote, it was 435 for Wilson, 88 for Roosevelt and eight for Taft.

Political analysts are already conducting their post-mortems. They note that from the outset of the campaign, Wilson's "New Freedom" theme caught hold with the

The intellectual preaches a gospel of reform and democratic internationalism.

voters much quicker – and more effectively – than did Roosevelt's "New Nationalism" program.

Roosevelt said that big business, aided and abetted by big government, would help everybody. Early on, however, Wilson began to speak of the danger of an all-powerful national state, especially with regard to the rights and freedoms of the individual. Last month, Wilson characterized this election as the "second struggle for emancipation." If Roosevelt were to win, he said, then America "can have freedom of no sort whatever."

Shot in the chest, the Bull Moose orates for 80 minutes

Milwaukee, Wis., Oct. 15

"I have a great deal to say," insisted Teddy Roosevelt after entering the presidential contest in February, "and I won't stand it for a moment" if "the discredited bosses and politicians decide against me." People wondered what creation of man *would* silence the presidential bluster. Yesterday, just after a gunman's bullet lodged in his chest, Roosevelt stood for 80 minutes to deliver the message of his Progressive "Bull Moose" Party. "Friends," he uttered upon reaching the podium, "I shall ask you to be as quiet as possible. I don't know whether you fully understand that I have been shot; but it takes more than that to kill a Bull Moose."

An intrepid hunter, Rough Rider and all-around sportsman, Roosevelt revels in public acts of bravery. From the charge up San Juan Hill to bear hunts in the Rockies to trust-busting on Wall Street, Teddy enjoys sharing danger with reporters. By his own admission, Roosevelt was "a sickly, delicate boy." But, "by acting as if I was not afraid," he says, "I . . . ceased to be afraid. Most men can have the same experience if they choose." Today, doctors say, Roosevelt is recovering, the bullet having been slowed by an overcoat, a glasses case and a folded manuscript of the speech. Would-be assassin John Chrank, an unbalanced man, is in custody.

Shot or not, Theodore Roosevelt campaigns with his characteristic dynamism.

Volcano eruption in Alaska buries town

Cordova, Alaska, June 12

One of the largest eruptions in recorded history occurred today in Katmai, on the southern tip of the Alaskan Peninsula. Geologists are estimating that the eruption hurled vast amounts of volcanic matter into the atmosphere. The small community of Kodiak, a good 100 miles from the site of the volcano, has been buried under several feet of ash.

Giant clouds of the material were driven high into the atmosphere, and experts are now predicting that the Pacific Northwest will most likely be affected by ash-laden rain for days. Interestingly, because of the manner in which the volcano erupted, geologists are predicting that it may now implode, or collapse into itself, and fill with ash. If this does happen, there is the possibility that the Katmai area will become honeycombed with vents and smoke for decades to come.

A license required for radio operators

Washington, D.C., Aug. 13

A rapid growth in the number of individuals experimenting with the new medium of radio has spurred Congress to pass the Radio Act of 1912. The bill, which became law today, requires radio operators to obtain licenses from the Department of Commerce and Labor. The first known radio program in the nation was broadcast in 1906, when Reginald Fessenden of Brant Rock, Massachusetts, read a poem and played two musical selections over the air on Christmas Eve. Many experimenters since have been developing broadcast equipment, exchanging messages over great distances. As yet, no commercial use for radio broadcasting has emerged.

Boots by L.L. Bean

Freeport, Maine, Autumn

Leon Leonwood Bean and his brother officially went into the mail order business this year, selling their popular Maine hunting boots. The company, L.L. Bean, began selling shoes when Leon Bean, a hunter and fisherman, decided to attack the problem of wet feet. Bean sent out 100 of his rubber bottom-leather top boots last year. When 90 were returned because of a defect, Bean established his policy of refunding money for returned goods – no questions asked.

Competition among auto manufacturers remains fierce for the attention of a discerning public.

Journalism school set up at Columbia

New York City, July 2

The cornerstone of Columbia University's journalism school was laid by Mrs. Joseph Pulitzer today. The ceremony came nine years after editor and publisher Joseph Pulitzer announced that his will would provide for the endowment of the school. The advisory board will include prominent journalists from Pulitzer's own *New York World* and *St. Louis Post-Dispatch* as well as from other leading newspapers in the nation. Under president Nicholas Murray Butler, Columbia University has greatly expanded during the last 10 years, advancing its original philosophy of broadening education beyond the classic 18th-century subjects.

19 in row for Rube

New York City, July 8

The amazing pitching streak of Rube Marquard is over. The New York Giants hurler, who has defeated 19 consecutive opponents since opening day, was finally stopped by the Chicago Cubs, 7-2. The streak might have been put at 20 because Rube actually won a game in relief, but the rulebook says starter Jeff Tesreau gets credit for the victory because he pitched more innings. Three runners Tesreau put on base in the ninth scored, but the Giants won after Marquard came on.

Major French film imported by Zukor

Los Angeles

Movie maker Adolf Zukor has imported the acclaimed French film *Queen Elizabeth*, starring Sarah Bernhardt and Louis Mercanton, in an attempt to give motion pictures the prestige of legitimate theater and to kill what he sees as the "slum tradition" in movies. The film is released by Zukor's Famous Players Film Company, which also makes movies, often featuring the charming Mary Pickford. Other busy new producers out here are the brothers Warner, William Fox and the amalgamation known as Universal that Carl Laemmle heads.

Marines in Nicaragua to protect regime

The marines again prove useful in enforcing U.S. primacy in the Americas.

Washington, D.C., Aug. 14

United States Marines have been sent to help the government of Nicaragua, whose stability is threatened by civil war. Nicaragua's Conservative President Adolfo Diaz requested the troops to maintain order. In 1909, after the Senate rejected a plan to help Nicaragua financially, President Taft appointed an American customs collector by executive order, thus bypassing the Senate, and New York banks made loans, taking as collateral a controlling interest in both Nicaragua's railways and its national bank. The Liberals, who feel that Diaz and the Conservatives are allowing the U.S. too much influence, have led the revolt with the slogan "Down with Yankee imperialists." With anti-American feeling prevalent, it is not clear when the marines will be pulled out (→ Feb. 18, 1916).

Taft's "Dollar Diplomacy" causes a stir

Washington, D.C., Dec. 3

Departing President William Howard Taft, whose foreign policy rarely brings anything but approbation, told Congress today that diplomacy "is an effort frankly directed to an increase of American trade." This is hardly a new policy, but Taft's rivals have made political capital by attacking it as "dollar diplomacy." Treaties with Nicaragua and Honduras that protect U.S. bankers from revolution and embezzlement have been rejected by Congress. President-elect Wilson promises to replace money with morality as the basis of U.S. foreign relations (→ Oct. 27, 1913).

Dentist Grey rides "The Purple Sage"

Zanesville, Ohio

It's no surprise to hear of a man dreaming about the Old West while trapped in the dentist's chair. But an Ohio dentist whose thoughts stray to tumbleweed and sagebrush can cause real harm. Luckily, Zane Grey put away his drill after *Betty Zane* (1904) and kept out his pen. *The Last of the Plainsmen* (1908) won the hearts of frontier lovers, but now Grey, 37, has emerged as a two-fisted storyteller with his novel *Riders of the Purple Sage*, a bigtime best-seller that may establish him as the heir of the dime novelists. It sure beats filling cavities.

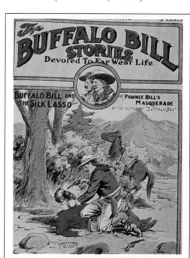

June 1. *The latest pulp novel in a series, "Buffalo Bill and the Silk Lasso," continues the adventures of the legendary frontiersman.*

Washington, D.C., March 1. Congress passes Webb-Kenyon Interstate Liquor Act, banning shipments of liquor into states where its sale is forbidden (→ Oct. 28, 1919).

Washington, D.C., March 18. President Wilson withdraws U.S. support from international industrial consortium in China, citing China's loss of "administrative independence."

Washington, D.C., Apr. 8. Woodrow Wilson becomes first President since John Adams to deliver State of Union address to Congress in person.

Washington, D.C., June 2. Department of Labor mediates first strike settlement, resolving dispute between Railway Clerks and New York, New Haven and Hartford Railroad.

Massachusetts, July 1. First state minimum wage law in effect.

Wimbledon, England, July 28. For first time since 1902, an American tennis team defeats British for Davis Cup.

Iowa, Aug. 26. Keokuk Dam, world's largest, at mouth of Des Moines River, inaugurated.

Panama, Oct. 10. Gamoa Dike explodes when President Wilson presses an electric button in White House intended to open Panama Canal to shipping (→ Aug. 15, 1914).

New York, Oct. 11. Philadelphia Athletics defeat New York Giants, four games to one, in World Series.

Philippines, Oct. 16. Governor announces more Filipinos than Americans to be on Philippines Commission, islands' ruling body (→ Aug. 29, 1916).

Mobile, Alabama, Oct. 27. President Wilson states in a speech that the United States "will never again seek one additional foot of territory by conquest."

United States. Julius Rosenwald, president of Sears, Roebuck, sets up fund providing scholarships for Negroes.

United States. Charles Beard publishes *Economic Interpretation of the Constitution*.

DEATHS

Auburn, New York, March 10. Harriet Tubman, fugitive slave and abolitionist (*1820).

Rome, Italy, March 31. John Pierpont Morgan, financier (*Apr. 17, 1837).

European art shocks the American public at the Armory Show

One critic called Duchamp's "Nude" "an explosion in a shingle factory."

Chicago, March 30

The Art Institute of Chicago this week opened an exhibition of either advanced artistic works or the insolent doodlings of lunatics, depending on one's view of modern art. The International Exhibition of Modern Art is popularly called the Armory Show after its original home at the 69th Infantry Regiment Armory in New York, where it had its premiere on February 17. Though the show was organized by the artist Walt Kuhn and the Association of American Painters and Sculptors, and a majority of its works are American, it highlights European trends, from older Post-Impressionists such as Gauguin, Cezanne and van Gogh to the new generation featuring Picasso, Matisse and Duchamp. Many Americans who prefer pleasantly realistic scenes are offended by the Cubists' geometric deformations and the strident colors of the fauvists (from fauves, or wild beasts), many of whose works are in America for the first time.

To citizens of a country that regards itself as dedicated to progress, the intentionally crude technique and unnatural colors of these "apostles of ugliness" represent the decadence and degeneration of Europe. Singled out for derision have been Duchamp's *Nude Descending a Staircase*, mocked by a contest to "find the nude," and Matisse's *Blue Nude*, burned in effigy here. The effects of the "topsy-turvyists" on American art remain to be seen.

Erector Set shown at U.S. Toy Fair

New York City

So you want to recreate the Eiffel Tower or the Brooklyn Bridge? Well, now you can with the Erector Set. A construction kit for kids, it was shown at this year's Toy Fair. Alfred C. Gilbert, the set's inventor, said: "If the idea appealed to me, I figured it would appeal to a lot of other kids." He got the idea for the set after seeing railroad power lines being constructed. Initially, he designed cardboard replicas of axles, pulleys, plates and girders. He now has what he calls, "the greatest construction toy for boys" – though some girls seem to like it, too.

Maggie and Jiggs get into the funnies

New York City

What would you do if you won the Irish Sweepstakes? For Jiggs, a former mason, the answer is simple. All he wants is to see his pals at Dinty Moore's tavern. Some corned beef and cabbage and a game of pinochle satisfy his every desire. His wife, Maggie, feels differently. She wants to forget her life as a washerwoman and enter high society … and she's taking Jiggs with her, even if she has to clobber him with a rolling pin to keep him in line. George McManus's comic strip *Bringing Up Father* was introduced this year by the Hearst newspapers.

Hopeful Pollyanna is always cheerful

United States

Hope is always on the horizon. There's nothing new about this homily – except its source, an 11-year-old orphan named Pollyanna Whittier. She's the heroine of Eleanor Porter's *Pollyanna*. When the girl turns up at the door of her rich and crotchety Aunt Polly, she is given a bed in the attic. But instead of moping, Pollyanna plays the "glad game," searching for reasons to be cheerful. Soon her optimism infects everyone in Beldingsville, Vermont, even Aunt Polly. The author is playing a glad game of her own – tallying royalties.

16th Amendment allows income tax

Washington, D.C., Feb. 25

Following ratification by Delaware earlier this month, 38 states have approved the 16th Amendment to the United States Constitution, which takes effect today. The amendment, which allows Congress "to lay and collect taxes on income from whatever source derived," was necessitated by the Supreme Court decision of 1895 that declared a tax on income to be in violation of the "direct tax" clause of Article I, Section 9, of the Constitution. No such challenge was raised to the first income tax, levied during the Civil War and lifted when peace came.

I.W.W. loses strike at New Jersey mill

Paterson, New Jersey, July

Silk workers are back at work after losing five strikers to police bullets, $4 million in wages and their bid for a halt to three-loom and four-loom shops. Spirits were lifted for a time by a pageant in Madison Square Garden. And when employers hung flags around town, strikers responded with the slogan, "We wove the flag. We dyed the flag. We won't scab under the flag." But mass arrests broke morale, sending 2,300 strikers to jail since the Industrial Workers of the World began the strike in February.

House report warns of oligarchy in U.S.

Washington, D.C., Feb. 28

A report issued today by the House Banking and Currency Committee, under the chairmanship of Louisiana Democrat Arsene Pujo, brings to a close the occasionally sensational investigation into the so-called "money trust." Among the highlights of the hearings was the dramatic questioning of J.P. Morgan by committee counsel Samuel Untermeyer, which helped prove the nation's money is controlled by a small number of financiers. The Pujo report's release is expected to help establish a federal banking system (→ Dec. 23).

Suffragettes: "Tell troubles to Woodrow"

Determined suffragettes take their cause to the main street of America.

Washington, D.C., March 3

A near-riot developed in the nation's capital today when rowdies attacked a parade of 5,000 women demanding the right to vote. Parading on the day before President-elect Woodrow Wilson's inauguration, the women carried banners reading, "Tell your troubles to Woodrow." Wilson found few well-wishers waiting to greet him.

All attention was on Pennsylvania Avenue, where angry men pushed, shoved and jeered at the suffragettes. The march was organized by Alice Paul and Lucy Burns, who had taken part in militant demonstrations led by Mrs. Emmeline Pankhurst in England.

The Misses Paul and Burns have come to the forefront of a movement that has had such leaders as Mrs. Lucretia Mott of Philadelphia, a Quaker matron; the fiery Susan B. Anthony, and Elizabeth Cady Stanton, a fine orator who was editor of *Revolution*, the militant woman's rights magazin. Mrs. Mott and Mrs. Stanton organized the landmark convention that first attracted attention to the women's rights cause in 1848. It was held at Seneca Falls, New York. Since then, victories for the movement have been few and far between. Nine states and territories have given women the right to vote. They are: Wyoming, 1838; Colorado, 1893; Idaho and Utah, 1896; Washington, 1910; California, 1911, and Arizona, Kansas and Oregon, 1912 (→ Oct. 15).

Making its debut this year: the Buffalo nickel, with an Indian head.

467 dead as floods hit in Ohio, Indiana

Dayton, Ohio, March 26

The Ohio River continued its rampage today in one of the worst floods in U.S. history. Latest reports on the five-day flood list 467 dead, 200,000 homeless and $180 million in damage. Ohio and Indiana have been devastated, with Dayton hit the hardest. Half the city is under 20 feet of water as people on roofs try to escape by sliding along telegraph lines. Houses floating away are a common sight. The National Guard has been called in and guard commanders have angrily denounced published reports that guardsmen are executing looters.

Georgia girl's death stirs anti-Semitism

Atlanta, Georgia, Aug. 26

As crowds outside the courtroom chanted "Kill the Jew," Leo Frank was sentenced to death today in the murder of Mary Phagan, a 13-year-old pencil factory worker. Frank was manager of the factory where the girl's battered body was found on April 27. She had gone to the factory on a weekend to get $1.20 due her for a day's work. Frank, who was from New York, had been president of Atlanta's B'nai B'rith, a Jewish fraternal organization. Jewish leaders say that anti-Semitism influenced the verdict.

Helen Keller urges suffrage, socialism

Philadelphia, May 5

Speaking through sign language today, Miss Helen Keller told reporters, "I am a militant suffragette because I believe suffrage will lead to socialism, and to me socialism is the real cause." An active member of the Socialist Party, Miss Keller has alienated a few Americans by her political statements, but everyone respects her accomplishments. Born healthy in 1880, she developed a fever at 19 months of age that left her deaf and blind. She has written a book, knows five languages and was graduated from Radcliffe College cum laude.

Rockefeller sets up a fund for world aid

New York City, May 14

With the idea of promoting "the well-being of mankind throughout the world," John D. Rockefeller has initiated a foundation. The industrialist, oil businessman and philanthropist has set up a fund in New York to distribute his money on a worldwide basis. Among the areas Rockefeller and his foundation are concerned with are hunger, health care, education, resolution of international conflicts and cultural development. The name of Rockefeller, who was born in 1839, is now synonymous with Standard Oil and the petroleum industry in general. Though he has been a philanthropist most of his life, this is his first international effort.

Ladies' first flights

Los Angeles, June 21

In 1906, Mrs. Mary Miller was the first woman to be a passenger in an airship. In 1910, Mrs. Blanche Stuart Scott was the first woman to make a public solo flight. In 1911, Miss Harriet Quimby became the first woman to pass the admittance test of the Aeronautics Club of America. And today Miss Georgia "Tiny" Broadwick, 18, is the first woman to make a parachute jump. How time leaps and flies!

Ford assembly line open

On the assembly line: dropping the Ford engine into the Model T chassis.

Detroit, Michigan

"Time loves to be wasted," Henry Ford has philosophized. But on the new moving assembly lines of the Ford Motor Company, the "Speed-Up King" of the American autobile industry does not intend to give it much chance.

The Ford plant has been moving toward increased worker specialization over the years, but with the assembly line, this concept takes a great leap forward. Starting last spring, Ford and production manager Charles Sorensen devised a system to pull magneto coil frames past workers by rope, as they added parts along the way. It slashed the time of building a magneto from 20 minutes to 13. By summer, the entire Model T chassis was pulled by a windlass past workers along a 250-foot stretch of the factory. The process has reduced car assembly time from 13 hours to six.

Already the innovation is reaping dividends. Model T sales more than doubled this year, to 182,809, while the price dropped to just $440. Exclaimed Ford: "Every time I reduce the charge for our car by $1, I get 1,000 new buyers."

Election of senators by direct vote set

Washington, D.C., May 31

The Millionaires' Club, as its critics have long called the Senate, may well be getting some less affluent but more responsive members, thanks to the 17th Amendment, which was ratified today. Instead of being elected by the state legislatures, where vested interests are often well entrenched, from now on senators will have to put themselves before the voting citizens for direct election. The new legislation is a victory for reformers who are also pushing for introduction of such measures as the referendum, initiative, recall, presidential preferential primaries, the Australian, or secret, ballot and, of course, votes for women.

Cather's Nebraska

United States

"O you daughters of the West!" cried Walt Whitman in "Pioneers! O Pioneers!" He would have approved of one such daughter, the flinty heroine of Willa Cather's second novel, *O Pioneers!* Alexandra Bergson is the favorite child of a hard-working immigrant sodbuster. He passes the torch to Alexandra, who skillfully runs the family farm. Her personal life yields stingier harvests, especially when tragedy overtakes her beloved brother, but this daughter of the West meets the challenge. So does Cather, a published poet whose lyric gift ennobles her song of the Plains.

Woolworth Building now world's tallest

Four years and $13.5 million later.

New York City, Apr. 24, 1913

With the flick of a switch in Washington tonight, President Wilson lit up the Woolworth Building here as it claimed the title of the tallest building in the world. Designed by the architect Cass Gilbert, the Gothic skyscraper soars 55 stories, its concrete-and-steel structure rising 792 feet above Park Place in the City Hall area. At a cost of $13.5 million, the building was financed entirely by Frank W. Woolworth, the son of a poor farmer from Watertown, New York. Beginning as a country store clerk, he put together a national chain of five-and-ten-cent stores. "The business from which this building has grown began with a five-cent piece," Woolworth said tonight.

Suffragist showing her maternal side

Rockville Centre, L.I., Oct. 15

Mrs. Wilmer Kearns, a suffragist, announced today her plans to coordinate a series of baby shows to be held in various cities of Long Island. She said she hoped to have the approval and assistance of ministers and physicians in the communities, as the shows are to be of benefit to the babies; she reasons that mothers entering their children in the contests would naturally want them to have the glow of good health, and therefore would give them good food and care. Mrs. Kearns says she ardently hopes that her effort will help "overcome the notion that suffragists are not good mothers" (→ Sept. 8, 1916).

De Mille produces film in Hollywood barn

De Mille's rival D.W. Griffith has also made a film about an Indian.

Hollywood, California

Sent to Flagstaff to film *The Squaw Man*, Cecil B. De Mille took one look at the Arizona flatlands and went on to luxuriant California. For $75 a month, he rented a barn where he recorded the simple story of an Indian maiden who saves the life of an English aristocrat, bears his child and commits suicide.

De Mille's real-life adventures were more exciting. He was shot at twice. His first negative was sabotaged. He slept in the Vine Street barn, with the owner's horses, to protect the duplicate copy. The six-reel epic, budgeted for $15,450, ultimately cost $47,000. Its first showing was a disaster; the film was wrongly perforated. After corrective surgery in New York, the first full-scale Hollywood film was a hit.

Federal Reserve created

Washington, D.C., Dec. 23

Bowing to the President's threat to keep them in session through the Christmas season, Congress has ended debate and voted to pass the Federal Reserve Bank Act. The new measure, drafted by Representative Carter Glass of Virginia, provides a major restructuring of the nation's monetary and banking system.

Under the act, the country is to be divided into 12 districts, each with its own Federal Reserve bank. These banks are privately owned corporations and are authorized to issue banknotes backed by commercial paper. They will not deal with the public but will be the central banks for each district – "bankers' banks." The system is to be overseen by a Federal Reserve Board of seven members, each appointed by the President for 14 years. All national banks are required to join the system, and state banks may also join if they qualify.

An important feature of the new system is the power given to the Federal Reserve Board to control the supply of money and credit by raising or lowering the rediscount rate. It is hoped that this will both reduce the power of the Wall Street "money trust" and prevent any repetition of the financial panic of six years ago.

A radical change in the nation's banking system has long been a high priority for reform-minded Democrats, and has been pushed hard by President Wilson as part of his attack on the privileged.

Hop ranch workers strike in California

Wheatland, California

On the Durst hop ranch near Wheatland, some 2,800 workers live in unspeakable filth and discomforts, earning 78 cents to $1 a day. An Industrial Workers of the World local formed by about 30 men is demanding improved working and sanitary conditions as well as $1.24 per 100 hops, used to flavor beer. An attempted arrest of the I.W.W. leader Blackie Ford on August 3 led to a riot in which four people were killed and many hurt. Some workers have fled, while others continue a perilous but spreading strike.

New law reduces tariffs and implements graduated income tax

Washington, D.C., Oct. 3

After six months of debate and intensive behind-the-scenes campaigning by lobbyists acting on behalf of special interests, the Senate finally voted to pass the Underwood Tariff Bill today. The measure, which provides the first major reduction of tariffs since the Civil War, cuts rates on 958 items and puts more than 100 – including steel rails and raw wool – on the free list. Rates on a few luxury items have been raised, but the overall effect is to cut tariffs from an average of 41 percent to 27 percent.

To replace lost revenue, the law calls for a graduated tax on personal income, beginning at $3,000 for single people and $4,000 for married couples (→ Jan. 24, 1916).

Wilson threatens to bar aid and sympathy for Mexican dictator

Washington, D.C., Nov. 24

President Wilson informed Mexican President Victoriano Huerta today that the United States will not give either economic aid or sympathy to his regime. In fact, Wilson said, he will take any diplomatic action that is necessary to end the generalissimo's reign. Huerta, who has been described as a sadist, alcoholic and drug addict, had Francisco Madero, the father of the Mexican Revolution, murdered in February and seized the presidency. Meanwhile, the dictator is facing a rising tide of rebellion that is spreading throughout Mexico. The rebels are led in the south by Emiliano Zapata and in the north by Francisco "Pancho" Villa (→ July 15, 1914).

Alien rights curbed

California, Apr. 19

Anti-Japanese feeling in California persists and has led the legislature, over President Wilson's protest, to adopt the Webb Act, or Alien Land Law, which forbids aliens ineligible for citizenship to own farmland in the state or to lease such land for more than three years. Ostensibly, the measure applies to all aliens, but, in practical application, it is directed at the Japanese (two percent of the state's population). The national authorities fear that this measure will jeopardize cordial relations with Japan.

Equipped with high-speed automobiles and captured federalist artillery, Mexican rebels achieve striking victories.

Copperfield, Oregon, Jan. 1. In Copperfield affair, Governor Oswald West sends his secretary to administer this railroad boom town; she declares martial law and shuts all saloons within 80 minutes.

Washington, D.C., Jan. 13. Court decides litigation over airplane-balancing patent in favor of Wright brothers against Glenn Curtiss.

Wisconsin, Jan. 20. Circuit Court declares Wisconsin's marriage law, based on eugenic principles, unconstitutional.

New York City, Feb. 13. To improve copyright laws and protect members against infringements, American Society of Composers, Authors, and Publishers (ASCAP) organized.

New York City, March. First issue of Margaret Sanger's *The Woman Rebel* is sent to 2,000 subscribers (→ Oct. 20).

Washington, D.C., May 8. Congress passes Smith-Lever Act, providing federal aid for agricultural extension programs created by land-grant colleges and Agriculture Department, formalizing cooperative farm production.

New York City, May 22. Mother Jones declares, "Never mind if you are not ladylike, you are womanlike."

New York City, July 31. As news of London Stock Exchange's closing reaches New York, most of world's exchanges follow suit, including Wall Street, because of war (→ Aug. 19).

Boston, Oct. 13. Boston Braves sweep World Series against Philadelphia Athletics, 4 to 0.

United States, December. National Security League, to upgrade national defense, founded (→ 1915).

Detroit. Cadillac develops V-8 automobile engine.

United States. Poet Robert Frost publishes his first book of poems, *North of Boston*.

United States. *The New Republic* magazine founded by Herbert Croly.

DEATHS

Barre, Massachusetts, May 26. Jacob Riis, photographer and reformer (*May 3, 1849).

Los Angeles, California, Dec. 24. John Muir, explorer and naturalist (*Apr. 21, 1838).

To sell cars to the common man, Ford offers workers $5 a day

Detroit, Jan. 5

In a move that stunned rival automakers, Henry Ford today doubled the minimum wage of his workers, to an unprecedented $5 per day. The pay raise was announced by Ford's treasurer, James Couzens, along with a plan to share $10 million from last year's profits and the addition of an extra work shift. Instead of its two nine-hour shifts, the company's Highland Park factory will operate around the clock, with three eight-hour shifts.

Referring to profits of over $37 million last year, Couzens said, "We want those who have helped us to produce this great institution to share our prosperity." Ford is also said to believe that by pioneering higher wages for workers, he will help to create a vast new market for his own product, the ubiquitous Model T car.

Tonight, the Ford factory was so besieged with job applicants that the police had to disperse crowds with firehoses. While Ford is being called everything from a socialist to a spendthrift, some see the wage hike as a shrewd move to quell unrest and labor turnover among 26,000 workers who feel increasingly dehumanized by Ford's monotonous assembly line.

In 1909, a friend warned Ford that if everybody had a car, all the horses would be frightened. But Ford replied: "I'm not creating a problem at all. I am democratizing the automobile. The horses will disappear from our highways."

Florida gets first commercial airline

St. Petersburg, Fla., Spring

Those who have not yet booked passage on the St. Petersburg-Tampa Airboat Line need no longer apply. The three-month-old airline has quietly stopped the run. Started by Tony Jannus on January 1, it was the first regularly scheduled commercial airline between cities in America. Jannus is a pilot who got the idea of ferrying passengers on the 46-mile round-trip between Tampa and St. Petersburg in a pair of flying boats. The pilot's idea quickly caught on with the tourist crowd and the Jannus business thrived. Soon he was winging his way over Tampa Bay with his plane full of wealthy thrill-seekers. But with the tourist season finished, Jannus is grounded – that is at least until next year, anyway.

A day is set aside to honor mothers

Washington, D.C., May 9

Was President Wilson thinking of his love for his mother today? He must have been, signing a joint resolution of Congress recommending that the executive departments of government recognize Mother's Day as an annual holiday. Congress proposes that the day be celebrated on the second Sunday in the month of May; this comes at the request of Miss Anna Jarvis, who wishes to honor the memory of her own mother, Mrs. Anna Reeves Jarvis, who died May 10, 1905. Miss Jarvis got the ball rolling when she petitioned Congress to create the holiday after marking her mother's passing yearly by wearing a white carnation and organizing special prayer sessions at Andrews Methodist Episcopal Church in her hometown of Grafton, West Virginia.

Tarzan of the Apes swings in America

California

Every youngster imagines his true parents are exotic strangers. And the hero of Edgar Rice Burroughs's *Tarzan of the Apes* shares this fantasy – with two big differences. First, the couple who raise him are hardly your ordinary Mom and Pop. In fact, they're apes, Kala and Tublat, who live in darkest Africa. Second, their son, Tarzan, though he thumps on his chest and swings on vines just like the other apes, isn't dreaming when he guesses he descends from different stock. His biological pater and mater – Sir John Greystoke and the Hon. Alice Rutherford – hardly envisioned a son who would wrestle gorillas. But then, who would have guessed a former light-bulb vendor and door-to-door book salesman would write a best-seller at the age of 39?

18 die in massacre at the Ludlow mine

Ludlow, Colorado, Apr. 20

National Guardsmen and security forces employed by the Colorado Fuel and Iron Company set fire to the tents occupied by striking mine workers today. When the tents went up in flames and the survivors fled, they were shot down by the guardsmen and security agents employed by the Rockfeller-owned mining company. Casualties resulting from the blaze and the subsequent shoot-out at the camp were three men, two women and 13 children.

Labor officials say the killing of the striking workers and their families by the guardsmen and hired guns was an act of cold-blooded murder. Company officials and National Guard spokesmen retort that they were simply trying to restore law and order in a situation that bordered on anarchy. They insist that if they hadn't acted, even more lives would have been lost. Residents say that this atmosphere of violence shows no signs of diminishing in the near future.

Unionism crushed in Butte mine fight

Butte, Montana, Nov. 13

Organized labor, a house divided in the copper region, has fallen after standing tall for 36 years in Butte. The state militia is gone today. But its two-and-a-half-month stay allowed mine officials to withdraw recognition from two competing unions and depose the town's Socialist mayor and sheriff.

The Western Federation of Miners local began to crumble in March of 1912 when it failed to challenge Anaconda Copper's firing of several hundred Socialist miners. In June of this year, 4,000 insurgents finally split with the miners federation, accusing it of stuffing ballot boxes and packing meeting halls with company men. The rebels blew up the old union hall and chased union president Charles Moyer out of town. But he met with Governor Stewart, and troops arrived soon after. Moyer insists he did not urge armed intervention. But the federation's leadership has shown its frontier activism is far from revolutionary.

U.S. troops depose Huerta in Mexico

Washington, D.C., July 15

Following a serio-comic invasion and much bizarre diplomacy, the United States finally suceeded in ridding Mexico – and itself – of Mexican President Victoriano Huerta. Five days ago, the Huerta forces in the federal garrison at Mexico City surrendered to the Constitutionalist General Alvaro Obregon, and Huerta capitulated. But most observers believe that the real reason for the downfall of "The Butcher" lies in the military efforts of the U.S. Navy and Marines.

After having failed to persuade Huerta to resign, President Wilson lifted the arms embargo on Mexico last February and all but gave his support to General Obregon, Huerta's rival in the Mexican Revolution. When that ploy didn't seem to topple Huerta quickly enough, Wilson decided that a military pretext would be found to hasten the Mexican's ouster. He found it in Vera Cruz. A motor whaleboat from the American warship Dolphin landed at this southern Mexican port on April 10. Its American crew was promptly arrested. Huerta's local commandant soon apologized for the inconvenience to the Americans, but Admiral Henry T. Mayo, with Wilson's enthusiastic backing, spurned the apology. A week later, Mayo told the Huerta forces they must either salute the American flag or face "the consequences." When the Mexicans did not respond, American sailors and marines swarmed ashore and took the city. American losses were listed as 19 killed and 71 wounded, while the Mexican toll was put at 126 killed and 195 wounded.

While Huerta's forces were being thrashed, he was threatening to invade Texas, to arm American Negroes and to attack Washington. Nothing came of his threats. In the meantime, the counterrevolutionary forces under Alvaro Obregon and Emiliano Zapata were scoring one success after another.

So finally, Huerta is deposed. But as one London editor said, "If war is to be made . . . by admirals and generals and if the government of the United States is to set the example for this return to medieval conditions, it will be a bad day for civilization" (→June 21, 1916).

The United States raises the flag and asserts its will in Vera Cruz, Mexico.

Mexican mountain guerrillas try but fail to defeat a superior American force.

U.S. sailors man an artillery piece in Vera Cruz, and use it with deadly effect.

President Wilson pledges neutrality as war spreads in Europe

Determined to keep us out of war.

Washington, D.C., Aug. 19

In response to the growing European war, President Wilson today reiterated his statement of August 4 that the United States is taking a neutral stance. Citing the Declaration of London of 1901, the President said that the open seas are neutral territory and that, as a maritime nation, the United States will maintain its position and will not take sides in the European dispute. In a memorandum issued today, Wilson called on the American people "to be neutral in fact as well as in name ... impartial in thought as well as in deed."

Since the assassination of the Austrian Archduke Ferdinand on July 28, pressure has been put on Wilson to support either the Central Powers – Germany and Austria – or the Allies – England, France and Russia. Pressure has also been put on the American people; since the

day last month that proved so fateful, Americans of every European ethnic background have been urged to give support to the lands of their forefathers. Many influential newspapers, including *The New York Times*, have branded the Germans the aggressor and have demanded an American declaration of war against them. Other media giants have put the blame for the war on the Allied Powers.

The truth is that Wilson and the American people have been buffeted by the propaganda efforts of

both sides. Those opposed to Germany say the war was caused by German imperialism and that Berlin's actions made the war inevita-

ble. There have been reports that the Germans have committed atrocities during their invasion of Belgium (although American war correspondents serving with the German army say the reports are not true). At the same time, those of an anti-French-British-Russian persuasion argue that American interests will not be served by Anglo-French control of the postwar world economy. Wilson will have a tough time persuading most Americans that they should be neutral "in thought as well in deed," con-

sidering the Germans' violation of Belgian neutrality and their defiance of the moral conscience of the world (→ Jan. 28, 1915).

Belgians attempt to repel the overwhelming might of the advancing Germans.

1,500 women call for peace in Europe

New York City, Aug. 29

Some were dressed in white with black arm bands; others were clad in the darkest mourning. The 1,500 women who marched down Fifth Avenue this afternoon were there to call for peace in Europe, but they appeared to hold out little hope. The large crowds watching their progress from 58th Street to Union Square were solemnly respectful. The writer and lecturer Mrs. Charlotte Perkins Gilman was among the marchers, who carried white flags embroidered with the image of a dove and the word "Peace" in gold letters.

German-Americans divided in loyalties

Washington, D.C., Autumn

Ever since the outbreak of hostilities between the Central Powers and the Allies, German-Americans have faced a peculiar and pressing identity problem. Do they support an admitted militaristic autocrat, or do they back the prime sources of American political and cultural liberalism? While many Germans are openly promoting the Kaiser's cause, others are urging intervention on the side of the Allied Powers. Some reports say the German-Americans are backing their native land in the war, but others indicate they are pro-British "all the way."

Birth control leader said to flee arrest

New York City, Oct. 20

Mrs. Margaret Sanger, advocate of birth control, is said to be on a train bound for Montreal, fleeing trial for violating the Comstock Law. The 35-year-old Mrs. Sanger has written and distributed a newspaper called *The Woman Rebel*, which makes assertions such as "a woman's body belongs to herself alone." While this paper was confiscated by the Post Office, Mrs. Sanger was not indicted until she tried to distribute *Family Limitation*, a pamphlet outlining the use of sponges, diaphragms and other birth control devices. If she had stood trial, she might have been sentenced to 45 years (→ Oct. 16, 1916).

Raggedy Ann doll

United States, Dec. 14

When 8-year-old Marcella Gruelle sadly approached her father with a faceless rag doll that she had found in the attic, he put his creativity to work. John Gruelle, a political cartoonist, wanted to please his terminally ill daughter, so he drew a face on the doll. Then his wife restuffed it and put a heart-shaped piece of candy with the words "I love you" on its chest. The result is a cheery, soft, warm rag doll with a mop of red hair. The family has named the shabby but lovable doll Raggedy Ann.

Penrod has a knack for finding trouble

Indiana

It's not easy being 12 years old and at the mercy of cruel tyrants such as parents and teachers. But Penrod Schofield, the adolescent hero of Booth Tarkington's latest novel, isn't going down without a fight. Penrod is a city cousin to another Midwesterner, Tom Sawyer. Like Tom, Penrod has an overactive imagination that lands him in some comical scrapes. And, like Tom, Penrod speaks for boys across the land, as his Indiana-born creator seems more at home in America than in England, where his "Monsieur Beaucaire" was set.

"Death" (1914) by Charles C. Buck. A face now well known.

Canal open to commerce

The task completed, the Ancon officially inaugurates the Panama Canal.

Panama, Aug. 15

One of the greatest engineering feats in history was officially completed today with the opening of the Panama Canal. To mark the occasion, a shipload of officials on board the Ancon made the 40-mile journey from the Atlantic to the Pacific – a shortcut that will lessen the voyage between the west and east coasts of North America by some 7,000 miles.

Construction, begun in 1904, has required moving an estimated 240 million cubic yards of earth by a labor force that at times reached 40,000. Total costs so far have come to $366 million. Much of the credit for the successful management of the project must go to General George W. Goethals, who was appointed chief engineer by President Roosevelt in 1907.

Yellow fever and malaria took a heavy toll until they were brought under control by Gen. William Gorgas, chief sanitary engineer. Thanks to him, the death rate was cut from 39 per 1,000 in 1906 to 7 per 1,000 now. Even so, 6,000 workers died during the 10 years it took to build the canal (→ Feb. 20, 1915).

L.A. hates and loves the movie business

Los Angeles

Local residents find the growing number of movie people something of a bother; signs outside boarding

houses proclaim: "No dogs, no actors." Young, tough movie makers, often disrespectful of private property, shoot in the streets, drawing in passers-by as needed. Still, the value of this new industry is inestimable. Since distribution of *The Squaw Man* early this year by the new Paramount company, the most notable new releases are: *Tillie's Punctured Romance* from Keystone, featuring Marie Dressler, "Fatty" Arbuckle, Charlie Chaplin and Mabel Normand; the serial *The Perils of Pauline*, starring Pearl White; Selig Company's *The Spoilers*, and D.W. Griffith's four-reel historic spectacle, *Judith of Bethulia*. Westerns are quite popular, and it seems that Bronco Billy Anderson may expect competition from William S. Hart at Ince's.

Clayton Act aids labor

Washington, D.C., Oct. 15

A major victory for labor was won today with the passage, after long and often bitter debate, of the Clayton Antitrust Act, a law that strengthens and clarifies the Sherman Antitrust Act of 1890.

Much of the act is concerned with outlawing such restrictive practices as price-cutting to force out competitors, interlocking directorates in large companies in the same line of business, intercorporate stockholdings, unfair rebates and contracts that prohibit the buyer from doing business with the seller's competitors. It also makes corporate officers personally responsible for antitrust violations.

But what has caused the unionist Samuel Gompers to hail the act as "the Magna Charta of American labor" are the provisions that exclude unions and agricultural cooperatives from laws against combinations in restraint of trade. This will prevent a repetition of the Danbury Hatters' Case of six years ago, when the High Court ruled against a union that had organized a nationwide boycott of a non-union manufacturer's products, and held the union liable for triple damages that amounted to a ruinous $250,000.

The act also limits the use of court injunctions against labor, except when there is a threat of "irreparable damage" to property, and legalizes peaceful boycotts, strikes and picketing (→ Jan. 3, 1921).

F.T.C. will enforce fair business practices

Washington, D.C., Sept. 26

Yet another reform measure that will use the power of the government to protect the interests of ordinary people was enacted today with passage of the Federal Trade Commission Act. The law replaces the Bureau of Corporations established by President Roosevelt and transfers its functions to a more powerful regulatory agency with broad powers to decide what business practices are unfair.

Abuses such as price-fixing, misleading advertising, false labeling, unfair competition and adultera-tion of products are expected to be among its targets. If the agency determines that a business is guilty of an unfair practice, it may issue a "cease and desist" order; if the order is violated, the offender may be punished by the courts. The courts may also, upon appeal, set aside an adverse finding.

The commission is to be made up of five members appointed by the president, subject to Senate confirmation, for seven-year terms. To ensure bipartisanship, no more than three members may belong to the same political party.

"Carolina Cotton Mill" (1908). For the last eight years, Lewis Hine has documented the shameful practice for the National Child Labor Committee.

Washington, D.C., Jan. 25. Supreme Court rules, in Coppage v. Kansas, that states do not have right to forbid employers from hiring because of union membership.

Washington, D.C., Jan. 28. President Wilson vetoes bill requiring immigrants to pass literacy test (→ Feb. 5, 1917).

San Francisco, Feb. 20. San Francisco Panama-Pacific International Exposition, held to mark opening of Panama Canal, ends; 13 million attended.

Washington, D.C., May 1. German Embassy warns that Americans who travel into war zone around British Isles do so at their own risk.

Berlin, Germany, June 6. German government orders U-boat commanders not to sink passenger liners without warning, even those under enemy flags (→ 9).

Chicago, June 24. Steamer Eastland explodes and capsizes in Chicago River, killing more than 800 people.

Yellowstone National Park, July 31. Dr. and Mrs. Kingman Seiler's Model T Ford is first tourist car admitted into park.

Washington, D.C., September. President Wilson agrees to reverse his policy of resisting American loans to European belligerents (→ Nov. 17).

Boston, Oct. 13. Boston Red Sox buy pitcher Babe Ruth's contract from Baltimore Orioles and put him in starting rotation; Red Sox beat Philadelphia, four games to one, in World Series.

New York City, Oct. 15. J.P. Morgan & Co. leads banking group in arranging $500 million loan to British and French governments.

Wilmington, Delaware, Nov. 30. An explosion rocks Du Pont munitions plant; sabotage is suspected.

Detroit, Mich., Dec. 10. Ford Motor Company produces one millionth automobile.

United States. *America's Coming of Age* by Van Wyck Brooks published.

DEATH

Tuskegee, Alabama, Nov. 14. Booker T. Washington, Negro leader and founder of Tuskegee Institute (*Apr. 5, 1856).

Comic masterpiece: Chaplin as "Tramp"

Charlie Chaplin's character, the Tramp, draws laughter, tears and applause.

Hollywood, California

America has fallen in love with an invincible vagabond with soulful eyes and a funny walk: "The Tramp," as created and portrayed by Charlie Chaplin. The son of music hall entertainers in London but soon fatherless and with a mother suffering a nervous breakdown, he and his brother were hungry street urchins, dancing on street corners and passing the hat for pennies until placed in an orphanage for destitute children. At 8, Charlie became a professional performer and at 17 joined a touring vaudeville company that came to the United States in 1910 and again in 1912.

Mack Sennett happened to see a performance, and in December 1913, Chaplin joined Keystone. His first film was *Making a Living*. Borrowing some clothes from "Fatty" Arbuckle, Chaplin began to develop a character in a bowler hat and baggy trousers, with a comic mustache and a cane. The Keystone Kops' roughhouse routines did not quite suit Chaplin's music hall comedy style, strongly based on pantomime. Having made 11 one- and two-reel films in three months, he began directing his own.

Now the 26-year-old Chaplin is making a new picture almost every week, and a trade paper proclaims him "the sensation of the year." Exhibitors find that they have only to put his picture on the sidewalk along with a sign, "He's here!" and they will enjoy sold-out houses.

Having just signed with Essanay for a staggering $1,250 a week (as compared to $175 a week at Keystone), Chaplin says he will make fewer films with increasing quality. He will write his own scripts about this shabby but fastidious little man, lonely and whimsical, with exquisite manners and a spirit that cannot be destroyed, just as in his new release, "The Tramp."

"Birth of Nation" condones the Klan

Hollywood, California

A "flagrant incitement to racial antagonism" or an epic? Both and more are said about D.W. Griffith's remarkable *Birth of a Nation*, the most expensive and longest film ever made, starring Lillian Gish, Mae Marsh, Robert Harron, Wallace Reid, Henry B. Walthall and Miriam Cooper. Controversy surrounded its March 3 premiere in New York and the National Association for the Advancement of Colored People has tried to bar the film, which is based on Thomas Dixon Jr.'s 1905 novel *The Clansman*, charging that it shows a distorted view of Negro history. In his passion to illustrate the Southern view of the Civil War and Reconstruction, Griffith has unwittingly sparked race riots and encouraged the revival of the Ku Klux Klan.

As a movie, *Birth of a Nation* has received critical acclaim. President Wilson calls it "writing history with lightning." The masterful Griffith, who began his film career as an actor and scenario writer in 1908 with the Biograph Company, has freed the movie screen from the restrictive methods of the stage. He moves the camera about, obtaining close-ups, distant views, fade-ins, fade-outs, angle shots and flashbacks. He rehearses scenes before shooting and takes great pains with lighting effects. Some call him "the poor man's Shakespeare," and many say the film is a landmark in cinema history as motion pictures will now be regarded as an art form.

America irate over Lusitania sinking

Coast Guard formed to protect shores

Washington, D.C., Jan. 28

The government announced today that a Coast Guard is being created and will be placed on duty "as soon as possible." The new service will be outwardly organized along traditional United States Navy lines. Its men will wear uniforms virtually identical with those of their navy counterparts and the system of ratings and ranks are also to be the same. But there the similarity ends. Not a "blue water" force, it will have the responsibility of protecting American coastal cities and waters from hostile attack. It will also be authorized to stop, search and arrest suspected smugglers and other unlawful intruders in American waters. The new service is to be placed under the peacetime command of the Treasury Department. During war, it will augment the navy (→ May 7).

U.S. "melting pot" isn't THAT melted

Washington, D.C., Apr. 19

"There is here a great melting pot," President Woodrow Wilson declared today, "in which we must compound a precious metal. That metal is the metal of nationality."

Wilson's metaphor comes from *The Melting Pot,* a 1908 play by Israel Zangwill. The newest contents of his "pot" come from Southern and Eastern Europe at a rate of one million a year. Its children, who fill a quarter of the nation's elementary schools, are soon singing of purple mountains' majesty. But many refuse to "melt." In 1913, 538 newspapers appeared in 29 foreign languages. New York Czechs meet in a five-story National Hall. And the Polish National Alliance has 800 branches. As reformer Emily Greene Balch says, "To many an immigrant the idea of nationality first becomes real after he has left his native country." So for many Americans, beset by war fever, "America first" is now a password for xenophobia. Thus the lyrics of the popular song *Don't Bite the Hand That's Feeding You:* "If you don't like your Uncle Sammy, then go back to your home over the sea."

As the Lusitania falls prey to a German U-boat, Americans question how long they can maintain their neutrality.

Washington, D.C., May 7

The Lusitania has been sunk. Incomplete reports received today indicate that the great British Cunard liner, the largest passenger ship in the world, was torpedoed off the coaast of Ireland by a German submarine. Of the 1,800 passengers aboard, 1,200 were said to have drowned. The casualty toll is reported to include at least 128 American citizens. Reaction here in the capital ranged from shock to anger to sadness. When the news reached New York earlier today, commuters at the Hanover Station on Third Avenue Elevated began singing *In the Sweet Bye-and-Bye* as the hurdy-gurdy played the traditional lament. Not at all in a sentimental mood, former President Roosevelt, who has long advocated intervention by the United States on the side of the Allies, bluntly described the vessel's sinking as an act of "piracy" and international "murder."

Now everyone is asking one question: What will President Wilson's response be to this grave incident? Ever since the submarine issue and the question of American neutral rights came up earlier this year, the President has tried to maintain a strict but traditional interpretation and observance of international and maritime law regarding non-warring nations. This is, Wilson argues, that American and other neutral ships have the right of unhindered passage on the high seas. On February 10, the President told the German government that he would hold it to "strict accountability" if any American ships were lost to its submarines. But he didn't say what his position would be if American passengers on neutral or belligerent vessels were killed.

The Germans have attacked two American vessels this year and two lives were lost. Two British ships carrying American citizens have also been sunk by the Germans, with two more Americans killed. The German government apologized for both of those incidents.

The Lusitania sinking is greatly heightening tensions between Germany and the United States. It is apparent that the Kaiser's government has upped the ante in its attempt to strangle Britain's trade by means of the submarine blockade, even if this policy means killing neutral American citizens on ships of the Allies.

Most naval experts believe that the torpedoing of the Lusitania was planned in advance. Last week, the German government published a formal warning to American citizens against traveling on belligerent passenger ships. One of the ships mentioned in that warning was the Lusitania. Because the Lusitania was carrying tons of war materiel, including a reported 4,200 cases of rifle cartridges, perhaps the German government felt justified in its extreme action.

This drastic measure, however, is certain to poison relations between Germany and the United States, perhaps fatally. In the meantime, President Wilson and Secretary of State William Jennings Bryan are reportedly drafting a firm diplomatic letter of response to the German government (→ June 6).

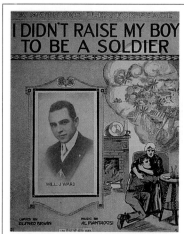

With war overseas threatening the United States, a song captures the feelings of every American mother.

Bryan quits Cabinet over U.S. war stance

"The Great Commoner" stands firm.

Washington, D.C., June 9

Secretary of State William Jennings Bryan submitted his resignation to President Wilson today. Citing irreconcilable philosophical differences with Wilson's increasingly aggressive stance toward Germany in the wake of the Lusitania sinking, Bryan said he had always advocated a pacifist, neutral position in the war and would continue to do so. The "Great Commoner" from Nebraska and former presidential candidate is expected to be succeeded as secretary by Robert Lansing, an expert in international law who shares the President's views on foreign policy (→ Sept.).

United States up in arms over naval war

Washington, D.C., Nov. 17

The Acona, an Italian merchant ship with at least 27 American passengers aboard, was sunk today and the United States is outraged. Since March, three major U-boat attacks on the high seas have convinced the United States that the Germans are a growing enemy – and one that means business. The worst affront occurred in May, when the liner Lusitania was sunk by U-boats. After that sinking, the German Ambassador, Count Johann Heinrich von Bernstorff, offered "condolences." And in response, President Wilson said that while "there is no such thing as a man being too proud to fight, there is such a thing as a nation being so right that it does not need to convince others by force that it is right."

Meanwhile, many people agree with the President's policy. Others are questioning his patience. Since the attack on the Lusitania, German U-boat commanders have been ordered to sink without warning all vessels that approach England. The Leelanaw was sunk off the coast of Scotland; the Arabic was sunk in the Atlantic. After months of what has developed into an undeclared naval war, German policy seems firm – and American resolve unsure (→ June 3, 1916).

Great White Hope wins in Havana

Havana, Cuba, Apr. 5

Jess Willard emerged today as the "Great White Hope." The 250-pound Kansas cowboy finished off the Negro heavyweight champion, Jack Johnson, in the 26th round, but there were cries of "fake" from many in the crowd of 15,000 in the Cuban capital. The fight was held in Havana because Johnson had jumped bail from his conviction for transporting a woman across state lines for immoral purposes. Did Johnson lose because he was promised amnesty if he would do so? For 20 rounds, he pounded Willard almost at will. Then he seemed to weaken. Willard caught the exiled champion with a wild right under the heart in the 25th round and finished him off in the next round with a jarring right to the jaw.

Whitney's filly wins the Kentucky Derby

Louisville, Ky., May 8.

In her first start of the 1915 season, Regret raced to victory for Harry Payne Whitney against a strong field in the Kentucky Derby. For the first time in years, powerful Eastern stables were represented in the derby. The Whitney filly, which had no trouble scoring a wire-to-wire victory, almost didn't make it to the race. It came just a day after the Lusitania was sunk off Ireland and Whitney's brother-in-law was one of the 1,198 passengers lost. But Regret was kept in the derby and became the first filly ever to win it. The Eastern stables returned to the derby because bookmakers, once barred, were allowed back to the Churchill Downs track. Star Eastern horses lured to the big race included Pebbles, the runner-up.

High court voids grandfather clause

Washington, D.C., May 15

The "grandfather clause" was declared unconstitutional today by the Supreme Court, which said that it was racially discriminatory. The court struck down Oklahoma and Maryland legislation that incorporated the clause. The case before the court concerned an amendment to the Oklahoma constitution that exempted some people from the literacy test for voters. This amendment was intended to permit whites to vote while disenfranchising Negroes. Such amendments usually exempted from literacy tests those men entitled to vote before 1867 and their lineal descendants, hence "grandfather clause." The whites could meet those conditions; Negroes could not because their slave grandfathers could not vote.

German's rampage ends with suicide

New York City, July 21

In a bizarre finish to an already incredible tale of violence, the man who bombed the Capitol in Washington and shot industrialist J. Pierpont Morgan committed suicide tonight by hurling himself headfirst from the top of a jail door.

Erich Muenter, also known as Frank Holt, died instantly in the Nassau County Jail, where he had been held for the bombing and shooting. His rampage began Saturday when a bomb wrecked a room in the Senate wing of the Capitol. During the same weekend, he invaded Morgan's Long Island home and wounded the Morgan heir in an attempt to kidnap Mrs. Morgan and their children. Muenter, a German professor, said he wanted to stop Morgan from exporting munitions.

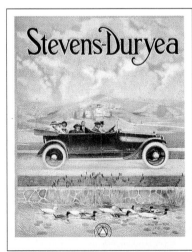

Marines in Haiti to impose order

Washington, D.C., Sept. 16

Seeking to regularize the presence of American troops in the Republic of Haiti, a treaty was signed today that in effect makes the country a protectorate of the United States. The troops will stay, to keep order and prevent any other country from interfering, and Washington will control finances, including customs. U.S. Marines landed in Port-au-Prince on July 28, a day after President Vilbrun Guillaume Sam was torn to pieces by a mob – the sixth president to meet a violent end in five years (→ Aug. 6, 1934).

German sabotage plans are exposed

Washington, D.C., Dec. 1

As the result of a startling accidental discovery, the United States government has expelled two German military attaches, Captains Franz von Papen and Karl Boy-Ed. The German representatives were sent home after an attache case belonging to the Kaiser's propaganda minister was found purely by coincidence in a New York subway car. The briefcase contained detailed documentation on plans of the Germans to launch a series of sabotage strikes against American military installations.

Cobb rips up basepaths and record book

Detroit, Michigan, October

Ty Cobb, who has been scorching the basepaths for years, has become the greatest base-stealer in the history of the sport, with 96 thefts in a season. Cobb, who helped lead the Tigers to three pennants in a row starting in 1907, hit only .240 in 1905, his first year at Detroit. But he has not been under .300 since. The outfielder stole bases almost at will, turned singles into doubles and triples and even advanced two bases on a bunt. He has led the American League in hitting since 1907. His aggressive style on the bases – some call it dirty – intimidates the rival fielders.

Ty Cobb is not a nice guy. It's rumored he sharpens his spikes.

Just what can you get for a nickel?

Washington, D.C.

During a particularly tedious recent Senate debate, Vice President Thomas R. Marshall once more observed, "What this country really needs is a good five-cent cigar!" Usually, five cents goes a long way. For a nickel, you can see a Mack Sennett Keystone Kops short or buy a copy of *The Saturday Evening Post* or get a ride in a car from an enterprising owner of an automobile. Unfortunately, some folks don't have many nickels to spare. A third to a half of all laborers work up to seven days a week, 12 hours a day to earn $30 a month.

Wireless call spans the Atlantic Ocean

New York City, Oct. 21

This year has seen major advances in wireless communication around the world. Following a research push by American Telephone and Telegraph president Theodore Vail, a radiotelephone communication was sent out from Arlington, Virginia, today and was received at the Eiffel Tower in Paris. In January, the first transcontinental link was opened, with President Wilson in Washington, Alexander Graham Bell in New York, Thomas Watson in San Francisco and Vail at Jekyll Island, Georgia, taking part in a conversation.

40,000 in Chicago protest dry Sunday

Chicago, Nov. 7

Carrying signs such as "Some folks regard it a crime to be happy," a parade of 40,000 today registered displeasure at the state law closing saloons on Sunday. Under the aegis of United Societies for Local Self-Government, scores of ethnic organizations sported the colorful garb of their native lands, such as Lithuania, Bohemia, Croatia, Poland, Italy, Denmark, Austria and Hungary. Women also participated. Typical banners read "The Sabbath was made for man, not man for the Sabbath," and "Fanatical frenzy is the parent of the blue laws."

Joe Hill of I.W.W. is executed in Utah

Salt Lake City, Utah, Nov. 19

Joe Hill died today with all the world watching. For five years the Swedish-born minstrel of radicalism wrote songs for the Industrial Workers of the World. Though no witnesses identified him and no one can figure a motive, he was convicted of having slain a grocer. Despite Hill's objections, Wobbly president "Big Bill" Haywood turned his case into a cause celebre. President Wilson, besieged by pleas, sought to save Hill from execution, but to no avail. On Hill's last day alive, he resignedly wrote Haywood, "Don't waste time mourning. Organize!"

Atlantan resurrects the Ku Klux Klan

Atlanta, Georgia, Dec. 4

An Atlanta man today resurrected the defunct Ku Klux Klan, whose white-robed members once rode the Southern countryside, terrorizing freed blacks after the Civil War. William J. Simmons, a failed preacher and salesman, has incorporated the KKK as a "purely benevolent and eleemosynary" institution. But in a ceremony late last month outside Atlanta, he and a handful of supporters set up and burned a cross, symbol of the old night riders. The Klan's early history is outlined in the popular motion picture *Birth of a Nation*.

Edgar Lee Masters visits Spoon River

United States

Sometimes simple words speak the deepest truth. At least they do in *Spoon River Anthology*, by Edgar Lee Masters, a 46-year-old lawyer who has been publishing poetry since 1898. His new book takes the form of linked graveyard epitaphs that bare the sorrows and triumphs of fiddlers, philanderers and feisty old ladies – some 250 poems. Masters's burly free verse has spared him the fate of one of his forlorn souls, "Petit, The Poet," the local bard who penned "little iambics,/ While Homer and Whitman roared in the pines!"

Three new groups to prepare for war

United States

Most Americans still agree with the popular song *I Didn't Raise My Boy to Be a Soldier*. But militarism is gaining a growing constituency. The League to Enforce Peace, the American Defense Society and the American Rights Committee were each founded this year to promote preparation for war. According to Teddy Roosevelt, their most prominent advocate, "The man who believes in peace at any price ... should instantly move to China. If he stays here then more manly men will have to defend him, and he is not worth defending."

"Edith Wilson," as painted by Adolpho Muller-Ury. Marriage to the former Edith Galt brings Wilson peace in a troubled time.

American troops killed searching for Villa

American soldiers striking a pose.

Washington, D.C., June 21

The War Department announced today that at least 18 American soldiers have been killed by Mexican forces at Carrizal, Mexico. The soldiers, members of General John J. Pershing's punitive foray against the Mexican rebel Pancho Villa, killed 29 enemy soldiers, including their commander, General Gomez. This incident comes just three days after President Wilson ordered 100,000 National Guardsmen to the Mexican border and several warships to patrol along both coasts of Mexico. Just yesterday, Secretary of State Robert Lansing warned the Mexican government that any further attacks on American forces would "lead to the gravest consequences." The killings at Carrizal earlier today have brought the United States and Mexico to the verge of war.

Animosity between the Mexicans and the Americans has been escalating steadily for six months. On January 16, Villa's men removed 16 American mining engineers from a train near Chihuahua City and shot them in cold blood. On March 9, Villa's soldiers crossed the border and sacked the tiny New Mexican town of Columbus, killing 19 Americans. The next week, President Wilson sent General Pershing with 12,000 soldiers to pursue Villa into the heart of Mexico. Because he had to bolster his sagging domestic influence, the Mexican President, Venustiano Carranza, recently informed Wilson that American forces would have to be withdrawn. Just as his note was received here on May 22, Villa's forces crossed the Texas border and killed three soldiers and a little boy in Glen Springs. As a result of this attack, members of Congress have begun calling for a full-fledged American intervention in Mexico, while the Texas Governor has asked for the military occupation of all of northern Mexico.

In the meantime, General Hugh Scott of the United States Army has reportedly requested that the War College begin drawing up contingency plans for a major invasion of Mexico. Rumors indicate that Carranza has ordered his commanders to prevent any American reinforcements from entering Mexico, and to attack Pershing's troops unless they retreat to United States territory. If a last-minute diplomatic solution cannot be found, it would appear that full-scale war is a virtual certainty.

Members of Company F, 26th Infantry, guard five captured Mexican bandits.

Treaty gives U.S. base in Nicaragua

Washington, D.C., Feb. 18

The Senate today ratified a treaty under which Nicaragua authorizes the United States to build a canal across Central America, and to build a naval base on the Gulf of Fonseca. In exchange, the United States will pay Nicaragua $3 million. Other Latin American nations such as Honduras, Costa Rica and El Salvador adamantly oppose the plan. The first two hold claims on the gulf, and all three resent what seems to be U.S. bullying.

Pasadena is site of football once again

Pasadena, Calif., Jan. 1.

In the first Tournament of Roses football game played since 1902, Washington State defeated Brown, 14-0. After that first Tournament of Roses game, football fell into disrepute and there was little interest among college presidents to continue the sport. Despite some changes, the death toll in football soared to 33 in 1909. With the legalization of the forward pass, the end of the flying wedge and other safety changes, football has been winning its way back into favor in the last few years.

Chicago is the city of the big shoulders

Chicago

Has Chicago become the nation's literary capital? Upton Sinclair, Theodore Dreiser and others have set novels there. And now the 36-year-old poet Carl Sandburg has announced himself as its bard in "Chicago," the title poem of a new collection that salutes the "city of big shoulders." Big as they are, they aren't able to support every writer. John Dewey, formerly of the University of Chicago, now philosophizes at Columbia University in New York City. His pet topic? It is still *Democracy and Education*, the title of his latest book. And Indiana's Booth Tarkington cozily depicts the life of a provincial lad in his latest work, *Seventeen*.

Wilson, urging readiness, is renominated

The climax of the Preparedness Day Parade in May was the greatest display of the American flag ever seen in New York, as depicted by Childe Hassam in "The Fourth of July" (1916). The Massachusetts-born Impressionist painter began as a wood engraver and studied at the Academie Julien in Paris.

St. Louis, Mo., June 14

The Democratic National Convention has nominated President Woodrow Wilson and Vice President Thomas R. Marshall for second terms. It is expected that Wilson will wage his re-election campaign, just as he did his nomination race, on the preparedness issue. Ever since the outbreak of the European war two years ago, most Republicans and even many Democrats have charged Wilson with being dangerously lax on the military preparedness question. The President has apparently realized the weakness of his position. In recent months, he has begun to speak out with increasing force on the twin issues of German aggression and

the need for a strong American defense establishment. On February 1, he told an audience in Des Moines, Iowa, "There is a price which is too great to pay for peace, and that price can be put in one word. One cannot pay the price of self-respect." Three weeks later, he told the Senate Foreign Relations Committee that he would not tolerate any further German infringements on American neutral rights. Last month, Wilson used his presidential influence to ensure the passage of two bills that double the size of the army and fund a naval building program that he said would give us a navy "second to none." Idealism, it seems, has been replaced by hard-nosed reality (→Nov. 7).

Bomb disrupts Preparedness Day parade

San Francisco, July

While the war years seem to have brought about a strengthening of unions in Los Angeles, in Northern California new campaigns are being waged for the open shop, this time in the guise of a preparedness measure. That, in brief, was the setting on July 22, when 10 people were killed and 40 wounded by the explosion of a bomb thrown during the San Francisco Preparedness Day Parade. Arrested for the crime were Tom Mooney, a streetcar strike leader; his wife, a music teacher; Edward Nolan of the Ma-

chinists Union; Warren K. Billings of the Shoe Workers Union, and Israel Weinberg of the Jitney Bus Drivers.

There is an uproar in the land because many feel those arrested are not guilty of the bomb-throwing. At the request of several society women, Bourke Cockran, a New York attorney and ex-congressman, will defend without charge the five people indicted for murder. In New York, 15,000 A.F.L. members from all branches of industry, will march to show sympathy for the jailed strikers (→Jan. 7, 1939).

G.O.P. picks Hughes to run for president

Chicago, June 10

Charles Evans Hughes has been selected as the Republican presidential candidate. After pre-convention booms for Elihu Root and former Governor Herrick of Ohio, the Grand Old Party chose Hughes. An Associate Supreme Court Justice and a former two-term Governor of New York, Hughes is a re-

spected liberal, a man of integrity and a bona fide intellectual. A philosophical rival of ex-President Roosevelt and his interventionist position, Hughes has criticized Wilson for weakness in foreign policy and pledges to defend U.S. rights "on land and sea." Roosevelt is not expected to give much support to the Hughes campaign (→June 14).

Wilson supports woman's suffrage, but ...

Atlantic City, N.J., Sept. 8

"I come not to fight for you, but with you!" So said President Wilson tonight at the annual convention of the National-American Woman's Party. However, his assertion that women would get the vote "in a little while" wasn't, as it seemed, his support for a woman's

suffrage amendment to the Constitution. Carrie Chapman Catt, the party leader, failed to gain his approval of such legislation. Former party president and prohibition lecturer Dr. Anna Shaw told Wilson and the 4,000 delegates, "We have waited long enough to get the vote. We want it now" (→June 4, 1919).

Wilson's support of the suffragists earns him many new campaign workers.

Wilson wins; "He kept us out of war"

"Woodrow Wilson" by E.C. Tarbell.

Washington, D.C., Nov. 7

President Woodrow Wilson was elected to a second term today. He received nine million votes to about 8.5 million for his Republican challenger, Charles Evans Hughes. Al-ready, political pundits are saying that Wilson's slogan, "He kept us out of war," (coined by Bob Wool-ey, a Democratic Party executive) was crucial in persuading thousands of erstwhile Republicans to cast their votes for him.

During the campaign, Hughes was associated with his party's ex-tremists, who favor direct Amer-ican intervention in both Mexico and Europe. The German ambassa-dor, Count Johann Heinrich von Bernstorff, prophetically informed his superiors in Berlin earlier in the year that "If Hughes is defeat-ed, he has Roosevelt to thank for it." The former President and his interventionists were recognized six months ago as an albatross around Hughes's political neck. Editor Oswald Garrison Villard said in July, "No other candidate for President within the memory of living man ever ran downhill so rapidly" (→ Jan. 22, 1917).

Birth control clinic opens in Brooklyn

Brooklyn, New York, Oct. 16

There were 150 women on line in the chill autumn air today, restless-ly awaiting the opening of Mrs. Margaret Sanger's first birth con-trol clinic in the borough. The clin-ic, at 46 Amboy Street, was well publicized through the distribution of 5,000 leaflets printed in English, Italian and Yiddish. They read in part, "Mothers! Can you afford to have a large family? Do you want any more children? If not, why do you have them?" The women seek-ing answers to the last question will get assistance from Mrs. Sanger and two aides, who have stocked the clinic with models of birth control devices and various infor-mational charts.

However, how long Mrs. Sanger will be allowed to disseminate her advice is another question. In 1914, when she was accused of distribut-ing birth control literature, she was sentenced to one month in jail. She

A defiant Margaret Sanger (left) on trial for her attempt to offer birth control to the women of America.

has spent the past year traveling in Europe to learn more about birth control methods, and came back ex-tolling the advantages of limiting families through the use of con-doms and pessaries.

Federal child labor law is finally passed

Washington, D.C., Sept. 1

After years of weak state efforts, the federal government has finally extended a hand to the nation's 1.8 million child laborers. The Keating-Owen Act, signed today, bans inter-state commerce in products made by children under 14. It also shields children under 16 from mine work, night work and work days over eight hours. In 1906, the first fed-eral child labor bill drew opposition even from the reformist National Child Labor Committee. This time, resistance was limited to the cot-ton-producing South, where mill owners argued that many children work out of necessity. Nonetheless, the bill carried 52-12 in the Senate and 337-46 in the House.

Some of America's children will no longer work in abysmal conditions.

Lumber man Boeing starts a plane factory

Seattle, Wash., July

From the moment he first beheld Puget Sound from the passenger seat of a Curtiss biplane in 1914, William E. Boeing has been hooked on flying. Soon after, the Seattle timber magnate purchased a Glenn Martin hydroplane, learned to fly, and began envisioning his own air-craft company. Not one to waste time dreaming, he built his first craft this year, a single-engine float-plane with a 52-foot wingspan, de-signed with the former navy engin-eer Conrad Westervelt. It has prov-en impressive in trials, and the new Boeing Airplane Company, with 21 employees, mostly carpenters and seamstresses, intends to build 50 Model C biplanes for the navy.

Catholics condemn doubtful morality

New York City, Aug. 21

"Alien radicalism" in the form of socialism could corrupt American youth. So says the National Com-mittee on Public Morals of the American Federation of Catholic Societies as it scored those evils it says menace the nation. Regarding divorce, the group asked for a "na-tional law so stringent" that "peo-ple of doubtful morality" could no longer take advantage of "pagan state laws" to separate "what God has joined together." The commit-tee also denounced motion pic-tures for "foisting upon our women and children immoral" films and "insidious attacks on Christianity."

Industry booms as war rages overseas

New York City

Sparked by the war in Europe, the American economy has reached new heights as the nation completes its most prosperous year in history. Foreign trade soared this year to a record $8 billion, while domestic output hit a high of $45 billion. Feeding the vast need for capital overseas, America has carved its niche as the world's creditor nation. And the funds keep flowing. John D. Rockefeller became a billionaire in September. Prices are up, but so are wages. Indeed, the biggest problem is a labor shortage created by a jobless rate that remains en-viably low.

Congress is doubling size of regular army

Washington, D.C., June 3

After months of bitter conflict between its pacifist and military preparedness wings, Congress has enacted a compromise army expansion bill. Signed into law today by President Wilson, the National Defense Act will more than double the size of the regular army over a five-year period, from 105,000 men to more than 220,000. In addition, the National Guard will be gradually brought up to a strength of over 450,000 citizen-soldiers and will be prepared for quick integration into the federal military establishment. The legislation also provides for establishing volunteer summer military camps at some colleges, where future officers are to be trained. The National Defense Act was approved partly in response to public demand for a better-prepared military establishment. A movie last year called *The Fall of a Nation* depicted an invasion of the United States by a Germanic-looking army. The movie, coupled with the sinking of the liner Lusitania by German U-boats, has resulted in a groundswell of support for a considerable American buildup of the armed forces. But it is going to require a large expenditure. As Congressman Claude Kitchin points out, when taxes have to be raised, "preparedness will not be so popular . . . as it is now" (→ 14).

Lincoln Logs invented by architect's son

Chicago

While watching construction of a Tokyo hotel, John Wright, the son of Frank Lloyd Wright, decided it was something children could do – on a smaller scale. Wright has now invented Lincoln Logs, a construction toy of wood, so kids can make their own buildings. The younger Wright had accompanied his father on the construction of an earthquake-proof hotel, the Imperial.

Third of all cars sold this year were Fords

Detroit, Michigan

When the one millionth car rolled off the assembly line at the Ford plant last year, it was just the latest milestone of a revolution in auto manufacturing. This year, Ford's mass production techniques turned out almost 2,000 cars per day, with sales of 534,000 autos representing about one-third of the industry's 1,617,000. Americans own about 3.5 million autos, and Ford is as determined as ever to expand the market by making more cars at a lower cost per car – thus at lower prices. This year, the Model T price dropped from $440 to $360, but profits soared to $59 million.

On the road. Open-air Ford Model T and owner wearing a raccoon coat.

U.S. military rules in Dominican Republic

Restoring order. American troops search huts for weapons in Santo Domingo.

Dominican Republic, Nov. 29

American military officials have declared martial law in the Dominican Republic in the wake of chaotic political and financial developments. The order, issued by Captain H.S. Knapp, included censorship of newspapers and the telegraph. Marines have been occupying Santo Domingo, the capital, since May. Unlike a similar occupation of Haiti a year ago, this one was not preceded by serious bloodshed or civil unrest. Rather, troops were sent after a series of dictators cound not avert the financial collapse of a nation heavily in debt to American and European concerns.

Wobblies battle authorities in Northwest

Everett, Washington, Nov. 5

In the heat of a six-month lumber strike, the Industrial Workers of the World are pressing their call for "One Big Union." The loudest answers so far have been bullets. Five days ago, a posse led by Everett's sheriff met a party of Wobblies and made them run a gauntlet that investigators say left "the roadway . . . stained with blood." Today, as union members arrived for a protest rally, their boat was riddled with bullets, killing five and wounding 31. Down in Seattle, authorities jailed 74 Wobblies for the murder of two deputies who were caught in the crossfire.

Talk of war sends stock prices soaring

Washington, D.C., Dec. 21

When Secretary of State Robert Lansing announced earlier today that the likelihood of American involvement in the European war was growing, stock market prices soared toward a 15-year high. Defense contractors and those in related industries apparently stand to gain by Lansing's announcement. It is obvious that investors support the warlike talk. Some of it could be tied to patriotic backing of a strong United States. But analysts suggest that one must not underestimate the attraction of wartime profit.

Americans are still entertained by the animals in the Barnum & Bailey circus, which this year is advertised by a ferocious tiger.

Progressive years restore promise of American life

Muckraking magazine, 1912, urging stronger enforcement of Pure Food and Drug Act - to halt drug abuse.

A confirmation class in La Crosse, Wisconsin, 1912. Scandinavian families predominate in the region, and the Lutheran Church plays a strong role. From 1900 to 1910, more than 190,000 Norwegians immigrated to the United States.

New York society women, members of the Woman Suffrage Party, join the parade for their right to vote.

Crusading photographer Jacob Riis, Danish immigrant, who documented "the foul core of New York's slums."

The man in the arena, Theodore Roosevelt, pictured here in 1912 after receiving news of his presidential nomination by the Progressive Party. More than any other American, the ebullient Teddy embodies the progressive era.

Senator Robert "Fighting Bob" La Follette of Wisconsin, one of the great progressive reformers in America.

American sheet music cover, c. 1908. These are years when the conservation of nature is coming into its own.

Armenians, Croats, Czechs, Hungarians, Italians, Poles, Russians, Ukrainians - they keep coming by the millions, irresistibly drawn by the promise of American life. Most are young men, who come to work and send money home.

A sharecropper family in Alabama, 1902. Despite good intentions, progress has lagged in race relations.

A faster pace sets the tone for modern times

Policeman directing traffic in Chicago. In 1906, Woodrow Wilson said, "Nothing has spread socialistic feeling in this country more than the use of the automobile. To the countryman, they are a picture of the arrogance of wealth."

John Sloan's "McSorley's Bar" (1912) depicts the drama of urban nightlife.

THE ECLECTIC FILM COMPANY'S
GREAT $25,000 PRIZE PHOTO PLAY
THE PERILS OF

Movie poster of 1914. The popular serial always ends by asking, "Next time, will Pauline be saved again?"

"Victory" (1902), a bronze statuette symbolizing America, by Irish-born sculptor Augustus Saint-Gaudens.

"And down the stretch they come!" The finish of a race at a track in Lexington, Kentucky, breeding ground for many of the finest Thoroughbreds in America.

As the song goes: "You'd look sweet upon the seat of a bicycle built for two."

"Hold your horses!" Driving a 1900-vintage "devil wagon" can be dangerous.

Saving the Dream 1917-1945

To Europeans and Americans at the time, it was the "Great War," the largest and costliest conflict in the history of the old continent and the event that propelled the United States, at least for a time, into an international system from which it had long remained aloof. To President Woodrow Wilson and to those who shared his vision, it was "the war to end all wars," a cataclysm that would force the nations to construct a new world order free of the barbarism of the old. To historians, however, it is simply World War I, a terrible conflict that resolved few of the problems that had caused it and served as prelude to an even greater war a generation later.

The United States entered the conflict on April 6, 1917, amidst a burst of patriotic fervor. But there was never any real unity in the country's view of the war, never a universal belief in the correctness of America's role. A year and a half later, the war was over. And the United States, the only nation to emerge from the conflict stronger than when it had entered it, was now clearly the pre-eminent power in the world. The country's halting effort to come to terms with that pre-eminence was one of the principal forces that shaped American history over the next 40 years. But the rise of the United States to what some have called "globalism" was not the only great historical event of the years between the World Wars. Both economically and politically, American society experienced a series of profound and at times traumatic changes that permanently transformed the nation.

Beginning in 1921, the American economy began a period of unprecedented prosperity and expansion that continued almost uninterrupted for eight years. To observers from around the globe (many of whom traveled to the United States simply to witness its achievements), the American economy came to seem one of the wonders of the world. The nation's industrial capacity grew at an unparalleled rate. The income of its citizens soared. America's position in world trade became one of unrivaled supremacy. The corporate world, after having been on the defensive for many years, basked in a widespread popularity that transformed once-despised captains of finance and industry into national heroes.

Then, in the aftermath of a frightening stock market crash in October 1929 and a gradual weakening of the economy that had been in progress for many months before it, the imposing industrial edifice collapsed and the nation plunged into the severest and most prolonged economic crisis in its history. The "Great Depression," as it quickly became known, frustrated the optimistic tactics of business leaders. By 1932, the financial crisis had brought the nation's economy (and, some believed, its social and political systems) to the brink of total collapse.

Someone asked the British economist John Maynard Keynes in the 1930s whether he was aware of any historical era comparable to the Great Depression (which was affecting England and Europe as well as the United States). "Yes," Keynes replied. "It was called the Dark Ages, and it lasted 400 years." That was no doubt an exaggeration, both of the conditions of the 1930s and of the nature of the Middle Ages. But the misery of the Great Depression was indeed profound. More than a quarter of the work force was without jobs in 1932, the worst year of the crisis; and never in the 1930s did unemployment drop much below 15 percent. On American farms, economic problems that had been developing throughout the 1920s grew suddenly far worse. Hundreds of thousands of farmers lost their land and joined the growing numbers of citizens roaming the landscape looking for work – work that generally did not exist. Men and women accustomed to poverty experienced a marked deterioration in their conditions. Millions of families accustomed to security, even affluence, experienced deprivation and economic fear for the first time. In August 1928, President Herbert Hoover had proclaimed, "We in America today are nearer to the final triumph over poverty than ever before in the history of any land." A few years later, with Hoover discredited and poverty rampant in the land, those words seemed a tinny echo of a bygone era.

Politically, the contrast between the 1920s and 1930s was almost equally striking. The election of 1920 brought to office a Republican administration determined to restore to American life what the new President, Warren G. Harding, called "normalcy." In practice, that meant rejecting many of the progressive assumptions of the previous decades of reform. Throughout the 1920s, therefore, the policies of the federal government worked largely to promote the interests of the business world, sometimes conservatively, sometimes creatively. Taxes and federal spending were sharply reduced; new, collusive relationships between business and government, and among businesses themselves, were tolerated, even encouraged. The needs of workers, farmers, and the poor were, according to the conventional wisdom, best served by attending to the health of the corporate world.

The Great Depression discredited such notions and launched a new era of reform. The Democratic Party – the minority party for most of the previous 75 years – returned to power and achieved a dominance in both local and national politics that it would not relinquish for decades. A new President, Franklin Delano Roosevelt, quickly became one of the most important, and controversial, leaders in American history. Under Roosevelt, the federal government embarked on a series of initiatives and experiments – known collectively as the "New Deal" – that dramatically expanded and altered the role of the state in national life.

By the end of the 1930s, the Roosevelt administration had drawn the broad outlines of much of the political world Americans know today. It had built the beginnings of a modern welfare system. It had extended federal regulation over numerous areas of the economy. It had presided over, and provided important legal protections for, the birth of the modern labor movement. It had created an important government presence in the agricultural economy. And it had produced the beginnings of a new "liberal" ideology that would shape reform efforts for decades to come, an ideology that remains at the center of American political debate even 50 years later.

One thing the New Deal did not do, however, was to end the Great Depression. It helped stabilize the economy in the early, desperate months of 1933, and it kept things from getting worse. But by the end of 1939, unemployment remained almost as high as it had been five years earlier and the gross national product was no larger than it had been 10 years before. Politicians, economists and others despaired at times of ever finding a solution to the economic crisis. But in 1939, another World War erupted and created a new prosperity before which all previous eras of growth quickly paled.

For a time, Americans were as reluctant to become involved in World War II as they had been to intervene in World War I. Indeed, much of America's international behavior in the 1920s and 1930s had reflected a desire to insulate the United States from any possible future wars. In the end, however, the cautious, limited American internationalism of the interwar years proved inadequate either to protect the interests of the United States or to encourage global stability. Throughout the 1920s and 1930s, the fragile world order established in the aftermath of World War I suffered a series of devastating economic, political and military blows. By the late 1930s, in the face of a new world crisis provoked by the expansionist aims of Germany and Japan, that order collapsed. Out of its ruins sprang the war that quickly engulfed the world.

The United States moved slowly even then – partly because the government itself was not certain how to act, partly because it was aware of how strongly much of the public opposed any involvement in international conflicts. But America was by then already deeply entangled in the affairs of the world despite its best efforts. Within a year, the United States was operating openly as an effective ally of Great Britain. A year later, it was actively, if unofficially, involved in hostilities. So the Japanese attack on Pearl Harbor on December 7, 1941, only confirmed what had been growing obvious for some time: that the United States was now so central to the affairs of the world that it could not remain isolated from its troubles. Four year later, with victory over Germany and Japan complete, it was clear to all that the United States of America was the greatest industrial and military power in history and had played the crucial role in saving the dream of democracy throughout the world.

◄ *"The Iwo Jima Memorial" at Arlington National Cemetery in Virginia.*

German U-boats cause rift with U.S.

A German U-boat crew cries out in victory as another ship lists and sinks.

Washington, D.C., March 20

Germany's submarine onslaught against American merchant shipping has brought the United States to the brink of war. At an imperial conference in January, the German military strategists decided to inaugurate a total U-boat war against all commerce, neutral as well as belligerent. On February 3, a German submarine sank the American liner Housatonic off the coast of Sicily, and President Wilson announced he was breaking off diplomatic relations with Germany.

Wilson addressed the Senate on January 22 and said, "Only a peace between equals can last" and that there must be "peace without victory." Despite the President's rhetoric about peace, he called upon Congress on February 26 to provide the means to achieve "an armed neutrality" to deal with the attacks on American shipping. In practical terms, this meant the arming of all American merchant vessels. But Congress still has a strong pacifist element and when the Armed Ship Bill was introduced into the Senate, filibuster resulted. Nevertheless, the measure won final approval on March 1.

The Germans now have some 120 submarines, and they can keep about two-thirds of them in operation at any one time. During the previous phase of unrestricted warfare, in 1915 and 1916, they sank about 120,000 tons of shipping a month and they accomplished that with only nine submarines operating at any given time.

But their U-boat strength is only half the story. The Germans are willing to play a card that can mean American entry into the war because they do not think the United States is much of a threat. Militarily, they rank the United States with Denmark, Holland and Chile. They are betting that the submarine campaign will bring Britain to its knees long before the Americans become involved and, should the United States finally get aroused, it is not likely to provide appreciable strength on the battlefield.

The latest U-boat effort began on February 1 and, by the end of the month, half a million tons of Allied shipping were on the bottom of the ocean. This month, the tonnage figure is approaching three-quarters of a million, and estimates for next month are more than a million. When shown the figures for lost shipping, one American admiral said, "But this means we are losing the war." His British counterpart replied, "That's right, and there's nothing we can do about it."

Actually, the British are taking measures. In an effort to restrict U-boat activity, they are attempting to seal the English Channel by creating a mine barrage across it. There are also plans to block the submarines in their bases at important ports such as Zeebrugge on the Belgian coast (→ Apr. 6).

Composer George M. Cohan's "You're a Grand Old Flag" is one of the many songs urging Americans to rally round the flag.

Germany urges Mexico to invade U.S.

Washington, D.C., March 1

Since the United States broke relations with Germany in February, all that has stood between America and war has been President Wilson's statement to Congress that he would not believe Germany hostile to the U.S. "unless and until we are obliged to believe it."

The Germans have just provided some proof, in the form of an explosive telegram, published today by the Associated Press, in which Germany urges Mexico and Japan to make war on the United States. The telegram was sent on January 16 by German Foreign Minister Arthur Zimmermann and has been in Wilson's possession since February 24. In it, Zimmermann instructs the German Ambassador to Mexico to promise the Mexican government that in return for its allegiance in the event of a war between Germany and the United States, Germany will help it "to reconquer the lost territory in Texas, Arizona and New Mexico." As the final element in the so-called Prussian Invasion Plot, Zimmermann instructed the Mexicans to seek the assistance of the Japanese.

Mexico has been the chief trouble spot of Wilson's presidency and American troops have fought there three times in the last two years.

United States enters the war "to save democracy"

Washington, D.C., Apr. 6

At exactly 1:18 this afternoon, the United States announced that it was declaring war against Germany. Peace was the thing President Wilson wanted most, and in the end he couldn't have it because of Germany's decision, in January, to inaugurate total submarine warfare against all shipping, neutral as well as belligerent. On April 2, Wilson asked Congress to recognize that a state of war existed between the United States and the German Empire. The Senate passed a war resolution two days later by a vote of 90 to 6, and the House followed suit early this morning with a vote of 373 to 50 after 13 hours of emotional debate.

In his speech asking for a declaration of war, the President said that "the world must be made safe for democracy." He added that "it is a fearful thing to lead this great peaceful people into war, the most terrible of wars. But the right is more precious than the peace, and we shall fight for the things that we have always carried nearest our hearts . . . for democracy . . . for the rights and liberties of small nations, for a universal dominion of right by such a concert of free peoples as shall bring peace and safety to all nations and make the world itself at last free."

Since the outbreak of a general European war in August of 1914, the United States, under Wilson's

President Wilson asks Congress for a declaration of war, not in search of conquest, but to ensure universal rights.

leadership, has struggled to maintain neutrality. Despite an avalanche of propaganda that came from the Central Powers as well as the Allies, the great majority of Americans has maintained a steadfast determination to avoid involvement. But this position was shaken on May 7, 1915, when the Germans sank an unarmed British liner, the Lusitania, killing more than 1,000 people, 128 of them Americans. There were difficulties with Britain as well, since it used

its vast fleet to establish a blockade of Germany. This prevented the United States from exporting food and raw materials to Germany, and the State Department sent several notes of protest to London.

Despite the many declarations of strict neutrality by the United States, it evolved as the principal source of food, raw materials and munitions that fed the Allied war machine. Wilson also permitted the British and the French to borrow more than $2 billion in the United

States to finance their war effort. The President resisted attempts by some German-Americans to institute an arms embargo against the Allies. Given these facts, it is not too difficult to understand Germany's rejection of the American claims of strict neutrality.

Naturally, Britain has praised America's entry into the war. Prime Minister Lloyd George said that "America has at one bound become a world power in a sense she never was before" (→ June 14).

Virgin Islands sold to U.S. by Denmark

Washington, D.C., March 31

The Virgin Islands in the Caribbean Sea were transferred to the United States today, putting the final touch to the most expensive purchase of land the nation has ever made. The United States paid Denmark $25 million for the islands to make sure that Germany will never have them as a military base and to protect the Panama Canal. President Wilson signed the treaty with the Danish government in January. The three important islands in the group are St. Croix, St. John and St. Thomas.

Anti-war vote cast by Montana woman

Washington, D.C., Apr. 6

Montana Republican Miss Jeannette Rankin, the only woman ever elected to Congress, stood before her fellow legislators today and declared, "I want to stand by my country, but I cannot vote for war. I vote no." A tear ran down her face. Before she was elected last November, Miss Rankin was a social worker. She has expressed the belief that women gained the vote in Montana "because the spirit of pioneer days was still alive." Clearly, she believes pacifism is a part of that same spirit.

We won't be back till it's over over there

New York City

As the song goes, "The Yanks are coming!" Was ever a more stirring call-to-arms written than George M. Cohan's *Over There*? His inspiration was immediate, the song written on April 6, the very day the country declared war. Though this may become his biggest hit, *Yankee Doodle Boy* will never be far behind. Then there's his popular theme song, *Give My Regards to Broadway*. In all, the boy born in a trunk in Providence in 1878 to vaudeville troupers Jerry and Nellie Cohan has managed, with rare success, to give America something special to sing about.

George M. Cohan's inspirational hit.

Congress orders registration for war duty

Washington, D.C., May 18

On June 5, between the hours of 7 a.m. and 7 p.m., every American male between the ages of 21 and 30 will be expected to register for a manpower draft. The Selective Service Act that has mandated the registration was approved by congressional vote today to build up the country's armed services upon "the principle of universal liability to service."

Conscription will be supervised by civilian boards around the nation. More than 10 million men are expected to be registering and about a half million will be selected in the initial draft. The concept of the draft has been the subject of a heated debate for some three years, with those who favor it arguing that it constitutes the best way to strengthen the military of the United States. Opponents of the idea, on the other hand, particularly Democrats from the South and the West, have called a draft "un-American" and "another name for slavery."

Those who support the draft insist there is nothing humanitarian or patriotic about the opposition to it, that some of the draft's critics are motivated by a fear of large numbers of Negroes becoming members of the armed forces.

As late as February, President Wilson and Secretary of War Newton D. Baker said that their preference was a voluntary system. However, that month, the two men reversed their position and authorized the bill. The Selective Service System is to be headed by the provost marshal general, Enoch H. Crowder (→ Nov. 30).

Two Liberty Loan drives fund war effort

Washington, D.C.

Some 9.5 million Americans are putting their money where their sentiments are, supporting the war effort to the tune of $4.6 billion in the second Liberty Loan drive. The Liberty Loan Act was approved by Congress on April 24. The second campaign began on October 1 and the target was $3 billion. To sell Liberty Bonds, Treasury Secretary William McAdoo enlisted famous people in many walks of life. Among them were such well-known artists as Charles Dana Gibson, James Montgomery Flagg and Howard Chandler Christy. Movie stars included Douglas Fairbanks and Mary Pickford. The Boy Scouts also lent a hand. The bonds, described as an alternative to explicit – and unpopular – taxing, pay 4 percent interest.

Anti-German feeling reaches a high pitch as officially sanctioned posters and unsubstantiated atrocity reports fan the fires of hatred in America.

Pulitzer Prizes

New York City

When newspaper tycoon Joseph Pulitzer died, he left Columbia University funds to honor the nation's best writers and the press annually. This was the first year of awards and, though the committee snubbed the novelists and playwrights, it honored biographers Laura Richards and Maude Elliott for *Julia Ward Howe* and historian J.J. Jusserand for *With Americans of Past and Present Days*. Other winners were *New York World* reporter Herbert Bayard Swope, and the *New York Tribune* for editorial writing.

Jasz, Jass, Jazz

New York City, March 17

No one spells it the same. But then, the Original Dixieland Jasz Band, now at Reisenweber's, is the first group ever to use the odd word. The advertisements for its first records, released today by Victor, call it "jass." The syncopated sounds are billed as "the First Sensational Amusement Novelty of 1917." Jazz is said to be the product of black musicians in New Orleans working from a ragout of ragtime, blues and other black musical forms. But some people fear the music may corrupt the young.

Over the past century, Uncle Sam has been used to symbolize the United States. And now artist James Montgomery Flagg, who sold his first drawing at age 12, has immortalized him – recruiting the manpower needed to win the war.

Wobbly offices raided throughout nation

Chicago, Sept. 18

After studying records seized in a nationwide raid two weeks ago, the Justice Department's raiders returned to the offices of the Industrial Workers of the World today with 166 warrants under the Espionage Act. Leading strikes this year in lumber fields and copper mines, the Wobblies have not been supportive of the war effort. The press has described them as "the waste material of creation" and advocated their elimination as the "first step in the whipping of Germany." I.W.W. is now translated as "I Won't Work," "I Want Whiskey," or "Imperial Wilhelm's Warriors."

President Wilson says they "certainly are worthy of being suppressed." The radical union has allegedly obstructed the draft. But Wobbly leader "Big Bill" Haywood has quieted the voices of discontent since the United States joined the war. Frank Little opposed Haywood, vowing to "face the firing squad rather than compromise," but somebody saved him the trouble. Little was found last month hanging from a trestle in Butte, Montana, wearing a note that read, "Others Take Notice. First and Last Warning" (→ May 16, 1918).

Russian Revolution has U.S. troubled

Washington, D.C., Nov. 11.

Russia's role in the war is in doubt. Communist radicals, intent on peace, have seized control of the Russian government from Premier Alexander Kerensky. Washington fears that the Bolshevik government will pull Russia out of the alliance, freeing Germany to concentrate its forces on its Western Front with France and Italy. Many think the new regime's leaders, Vladimir Lenin and Leon Trotsky, are paid German agents.

President Wilson is reportedly dismayed by the overthrow of a regime he has described as "a fit partner for a league of honor." The United States has refused to recognize the new Bolshevik regime. By contrast, last March the United States was the first to recognize the legitimacy of Kerensky's provisional government when it took power following the forced abdication of Czar Nicholas II. Many hoped Russia's army would be rejuvenated once freed of the Czar's mismanagement. But Kerensky was no more able to win battles or end hunger than the Czar was, paving the way for the Bolsheviks' bloodless coup d'etat.

First on the Bolshevik agenda is an immediate cessation of war. "I shall issue a few proclamations and then shut up shop," said Trotsky, the new commissar of foreign affairs. The new regime has also announced a redistribution of land to the peasants (→ Aug. 15, 1918).

American troops in France see action

Cambrai, France, Nov. 30

American troops today saw action in a major offensive for the first time since they began arriving here in June. These were Engineer Regiments who were supposed to serve only as support for British troops. But they were caught up in the combat. On November 2, the first Americans were killed near Bathelemont when German troops conducted a trench raid on the First Division.

The American Expeditionary Force, under the command of General John J. "Black Jack" Pershing, is eventually expected to total more than one million men. When American units landed in France this summer, Colonel Charles E. Stanton stood at the tomb of the French nobleman who had given so much to the American Revolution and said, "Lafayette, we are here."

At present, there are five American divisions on French soil. These include the 42nd, called the Rainbow Division because it is made up of National Guard units from almost every state; the First Division, made up of army regulars who were the first to arrive at St. Nazaire; the Second Division of marines and army regulars and the 41st Division from the American Northwest.

On October 20, the First Division entered the front lines near Luneville, a town that the army's regulars gave the nickname of Looneyville to the dismay of the local residents (→ Jan. 8, 1918).

French Marshal Joseph Joffre stands with American General John J. Pershing.

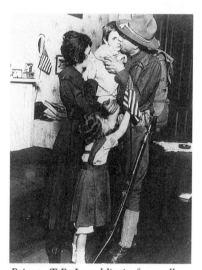

Private T.P. Loughlin in farewell.

They're off to fight the good fight.

Curbing war's foes

Washington, D.C., June 15

Stiff prison sentences and heavy fines await anyone who attempts to hinder the American war effort or help its enemies. Under the Espionage Act that won the approval of Congress today, violators can be fined as much as $10,000 and jailed for up to 20 years. Additionally, Postmaster General Albert Sidney Burleson has been given permission to bar from the mail any materials that are considered treasonous or seditious. Even before passage of the Espionage Act, the postmaster began banning publications turned out by the Socialists (→ Sept. 18).

Immigrants limited

Washington, D.C., Feb. 5

Asian workers other than Japanese will be barred from the United States and all other immigrants must pass a literacy test under the terms of the Immigration Act of 1917 that was approved today by Congress. Specifically, the new legislation excludes vagrants, illiterates, alcoholics and persons seeking to enter the United States for "immoral purposes." When the measure was first passed, it was vetoed by President Wilson. But it became law when two-thirds of both houses voted to override the President's veto (→ May 19, 1921).

Industries put under government control

Washington, D.C.

The war is rapidly coming home to America in a variety of ways, with preparations and supply affecting the day-to-day life of almost every citizen. There have been sweeping changes, and they include government controls over industry, railroading and food and fuel production; increases in the taxes on both personal income and corporations; jacked up postal rates, and even the censorship of certain kinds of mail.

After calling for "the organization and mobilization of all the material resources of the country" in April, President Wilson delegated responsibility for stepping up production and cutting down waste to the War Industries Board. He named a 41-year-old journalist, George Creel, to head the Commission on Public Information and a 43-year-old mining engineer, Herbert Hoover, to take over the Food Administration.

Other key personnel who will be in charge of regulating industry are the Treasury Secretary, William G. McAdoo, 54, who heads the Railroad Administration, and Harry A Garfield, 54, who is in charge of fuel administration.

Washington, D.C., Jan. 7.
Supreme Court rules, in Arver v. United States, that wartime draft is constitutional.

New York City, Jan. 21. New York Philharmonic Society bars all works by living German composers.

New York City, Feb. 14. George Gershwin's *Swanee* sung publicly for first time.

Washington, D.C., Apr. 8. Frank P. Walsh and former President William Howard Taft co-chair National War Labor Board, which will be a court of labor arbitration.

Washington, D.C., May 19. Federal government appropriates $1 billion for maintenance of vital railways.

Mobile, Alabama, May 21. Fire in meat market spreads throughout city, destroying 40 blocks and 200 homes.

California, July, 25. Annette Adams begins term as first woman district attorney in United States.

Europe, Aug. 10. Allies agree to formation of an independent American force under General John J. Pershing (→ 27).

Washington, D.C., Aug. 12. Post Office Department takes over control of nation's airmail service from War Department.

Upton, New Jersey, Aug. 19. *Yip, Yip Yaphank*, musical by Irving Berlin, first performed.

Washington, D.C., Aug. 27. United States rejects Pope Benedict XV's peace proposal of August 1 on grounds that German government cannot be taken at its word (→ Sept. 26).

Boston, Sept. 11. Babe Ruth's pitching helps Boston Red Sox beat Chicago Cubs in World Series, four games to two.

France, Oct. 29. Eddie Rickenbacker, leading American air ace, downs 26th enemy plane.

Washington, D.C., Nov. 5. Mid-term elections turn both houses of Congress over to Republican control.

New York City, Nov. 7. Newspapers erroneously report signing of an armistice, engendering premature public cele-·brations.

Brest, France, Dec. 13. President Wilson arrives for peace negotiations (→ Feb. 14, 1919).

United States. Willa Cather publishes *My Antonia*.

Wilson proposes 14-point peace plan

Washington, D.C., Jan. 8

In a major speech to Congress today, President Wilson presented his vision and prescription for international peace and prosperity in the postwar world. Designed to bolster sagging Allied morale and to assure the Central Powers of a fair and just treatment after the war's end, Wilson's "14 Points" program defines a new and optimistic world order. As a preface to his proposals, the President said, "We demand that the world be made fit and safe to live in ... against force and selfish aggression. The program of the world's peace is our only program." In summary, the points of the Wilson plan are as follows

1. No secret diplomacy
2. Freedom of the seas during both peace and war
3. Removal of international trade barriers and the establishment of equal international trade conditions
4. Worldwide arms reductions
5. Impartial adjustment of all colonial claims
6. No foreign interference in Russian affairs
7. Full Belgian sovereignty
8. Return of Alsace-Lorraine to France
9. Redrawing Italian boundaries with equity for all internal nationalities
10. Free, autonomous development of all nationalities within Austro-Hungary
11. Restoration of the Balkan nations and Serbian access to the sea
12. Sovereignty for the Turkish parts of the Ottoman Empire
13. An independent Poland with access to the sea
14. Creation of an international body of arbitration (a League of Nations)

The 14 Points, President Wilson concluded, are the symbol of what he called "the moral climax of this final war for liberty" (→ Apr. 14).

Activities of German-Americans are curtailed as suspicion rises

Washington, D.C., July 2

Congress voted today to repeal the charter of the National German-American Alliance. The mighty organization, boasting two million members four years ago, is silenced. Still, an uneasiness has settled across America. Are German-American neighbors loyal citizens or do they plot our government's fall? Rumors fly – spies on the Atlantic coast send messages to German U-boats. Agents incite strikes at arms plants. Even among Germans themselves, there is distrust; some recent immigrants are called "Hunnenfresser," Hun eaters, denigrators of their own people.

Yet just a few years ago, German-Americans were among the most respected of immigrants. German thinkers were widely admired, and German was taught in a fourth of the nation's high schools. When the war began, there was much empathy for the German cause. The $700,000 raised at a 1916 benefit at Madison Square Garden went to German war orphans. Opinions changed once the British cut the German telegraph cable; news went through the British service; it tells of atrocities, Huns butchering Belgian babies.

German-Americans either decry the tales or flee their identity.

Muellers become Millers, Schmidts are Smiths. Their "purer" American neighbors eradicate all vestiges of German culture: sauerkraut is "liberty cabbage," hamburger is "liberty steak." Schubert and Bach performances are banned. Berlin, Iowa, is now Lincoln.

And as for the National German-American Alliance, what crime had it committed? It had urged American neutrality in the war. And rather than face the ignominy of a forced disbandment today, the group dissolved itself and donated all of its funds to the American Red Cross (→ March 10, 1928).

WAKE UP, AMERICA!

CIVILIZATION CALLS
EVERY MAN WOMAN AND CHILD

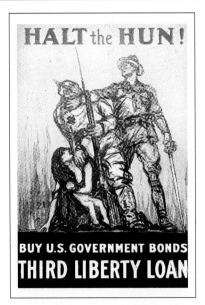

HALT the HUN!

BUY U.S. GOVERNMENT BONDS
THIRD LIBERTY LOAN

GEE !!
I WISH I WERE A MAN

I'd JOIN The NAVY

BE A MAN AND DO IT
UNITED STATES NAVY
RECRUITING STATION
34 East 23rd Street, New York

Foch given command of Pershing's troops

Pershing (right) agrees to accept the overall authority of Marshal Foch.

Western Front, Apr. 14

Ten months of bitter wrangling over who commands United States forces in France have been settled: The Americans will fight as one army under General John J. Pershing, but accept the overall strategic authority of Marshal Ferdinand Foch of France, the Allied supreme commander. When the Americans first arrived, they were larded in among the British and French forces, in piecemeal fashion when and where they seemed to be needed to plug holes or reinforce their beleaguered allies. They will campaign as a single army, although they will still lend individual units here and there (→ 30).

Americans on front lines

An American soldier is overcome by toxic mustard gas as U.S. troops advance.

Clock is set ahead to help war effort

Washington, D.C., March 31

Starting today, the sun will set at a later hour across the United States. This extension of daytime is not the result of some strange astronomical development, but a Daylight Savings Time measure that was signed by President Wilson today. Clocks are being moved forward one hour today and they will not be set back to standard time until the end of October. The change was instituted to help the war effort by cutting electricity needs. Nevertheless, it was vigorously opposed by farmers because their work day does not coincide with the new daylight hours.

Baruch takes over military industries

Washington, D.C., Apr. 5

While the War Industries Board under Bernard Baruch takes control of American industry, the War Finance Corporation, capitalized at $500 million, will be extending loans and selling bonds to assist with the war effort. The 48-year-old Baruch was given his post in May and was granted the broadest powers to make the United States function as if, from coast to coast, it were "a single factory." His responsibilities include creating and converting facilities for the war effort, setting production and delivery priorities and buying equipment for the Allied forces.

France, Apr. 30

As the German spring offensive drives toward the Marne, it has run headlong into fresh American divisions thrown into the front lines. Most of the fighting for the American Expeditionary Force is taking place at a German bridgehead near Chateau-Thierry, although the First Division had been sent to the Somme to help stop Count Ludendorff's first drive. By March, there were 325,000 Americans on French soil with more arriving every week.

The veteran German troops are busily educating the Americans in the facts of war. The shock troops called "Stosstruppen" have been raiding behind the maze of trenches that the front has become, sometimes killing army mules and stealing sacks of mail to demoralize the green American troops. The inexperience of the Yanks is shown by a joke circulating among them: "How many Heinies do you think came at us this morning, Sergeant? Oh, not too many, I'd say about three saloons full."

The German drive, now that it has reached the Marne, is beginning to slow down. At this stage of the war, a 40-mile advance is almost impossible to sustain. The French and the British have finally recovered from their initial shock and they are beginning to stage fierce counterattacks.

Back in Washington, President Woodrow Wilson has responded to the latest offensive of the German military forces by saying that "Germany has once more said that force and force alone shall decide whether peace and justice shall reign ... " (→ June 4).

Laws limit freedom of speech in wartime

Washington, D.C., May 16

"Beware that no faction of disloyal intrigue break the harmony or embarrass the spirit of our people," President Wilson warned in his 1916 inaugural adress. A year into the war, and those words seem almost prophetic. Congress today added the Sedition Act to the federal government's arsenal, which already has the Espionage and Sabotage Acts. Now, dissenters can be put in jail for criticizing the flag, government, draft or arms production. The law protects these institutions from "profane, violent, scurrilous, contemptuous, slurring or abusive language."

More than 2,000 people are in jail for hindering the draft, including anarchist Emma Goldman, former congressman Victor Berger and reformer Kate O'Hare. But as John Dewey objects, "What shall it profit us to defeat the Prussians if we prussianize our own selves?" Says Max Eastman, editor of the banned *Masses*, "They give you 90 days for quoting the Declaration of Independence, six months for quoting the Bible, and pretty soon somebody is going to get a life sentence for quoting Woodrow Wilson in the wrong context" (→ Sept. 14).

Donning French helmets, a Negro unit under a white officer holds the line.

Americans win at Marne

American 14-inch guns pound a German troop and rail center 20 miles away.

Marne River, France, June 4

The doughboys of the First Division were to reinforce the French in the Picardy sector, not to drive the Germans back. But that is what happened. The American baptism of fire was terrible. The Yanks were heavily shelled and gassed, and lost two to four times as many men as the French units in the trenches on either side of them. Nevertheless, the Americans fought back to take the strategically important town of Cantigny, though 187 were killed

and 636 wounded.

At Chateau-Thierry, a full American division was moved up to stop the German Seventh Army. The Second Division should have relieved the First at Cantigny, but it was used instead to plug the gap at Chateau-Thierry. The fighting was the worst for the Americans since the battle of Five Forks in the Civil War. The Fifth Marines had the worst of it in hand-to-hand fighting near the village of Bouresches, which they captured (→ July 1).

Airmail is started but has a way to go

Washington, D.C., May 15

Perhaps airmail is an idea whose time has come, but on today's historic start of the service it came to an abrupt end in a farm field 20 miles southeast of where it began. Lieutenant George Leroy Boyle of the Army Signal Corps crashed his JN-6H "Jenny" in the Waldorf, Maryland, area not long after his tardy Washington send-off by President Wilson and a crowd of dignitaries. Boyle's plane, which initially wouldn't even start – someone forgot to fill the fuel tank – went off course after he followed the wrong set of railroad tracks and missed Philadelphia. But for airmail, all was not lost. Lieutenant Torrey Webb had a successful take-off in New York and flew mail to Philadelphia. The new service has the President's strong backing.

Court strikes down child labor law

Washington, D.C., June 3

For a little less than two years, the ragged children of the factory had the federal government as their ally. Today, the Supreme Court broke that bond, striking down the Keating-Owen child labor law with the judgment that Congress cannot "control the states in their exercise of the police power over local trade and manufacture." Out of nearly two million working children, the law covered only the 20 percent or so who work in mines and factories. But it is there that conditions are worst. Kids in Southern mills get doused with cold water when they doze off during the night. Ten-year-old boys struggle to pick sharp slate off a speeding coal belt 14 hours a day. And these, says their radical advocate Mother Jones, are "to be the future citizens of the nation."

1.4 million women in wartime work force

Washington, D.C., March 29

Government statistics released today show that 1.4 million women have replaced men at their jobs since the United States entered the war last April. Women are doing everything from assembly-line work to delivering coal to steeple-jacking, and over 10,000 women are performing secretarial duties as yeomen in the navy. Some are

also serving without pay. Dr. Anna Shaw, erstwhile suffrage leader, chairs the Women's Committee of the Council of National Defense, which assists women in industry, aids overseas hospitals and performs a wide range of charitable acts. Even in the late hours at home, women are doing their part by knitting socks and sweaters for the boys over there.

The hilarious actor Charlie Chaplin sheds his tramp outfit for a doughboy's uniform in his latest movie, "Shoulder Arms."

New Orleans paper finds jazz a vice

New Orleans, June 20

Never mind that jazz, the musical craze sweeping the country, was born in New Orleans. The city's leading newspaper today carried a scorching editorial calling jazz, or "jass," as it is spelled in the *Times-Picayune*, "a musical vice." The newspaper urged that New Orleans "be the last to accept the atrocity in polite society . . . and make it a point of civic honor to suppress it." New Orleans has had a district of open prostitution, Storyville, but it was recently closed under pressure from the military authorities. Still, jazz thrives there in the form of ragtime piano music.

Out of the house and into the factory. American women weld bomb casings.

Meat, wheat, light curtailed by war

Washington, D.C., July 26

Housewives across the country will be combing through their cookbooks these days in search of ways to heed the call of Food Administrator Herbert Hoover today for one meatless, two wheatless and two porkless days each week. And these women and their families will have less time for evening reading, too, because Fuel Administrator Harry Garfield has proposed four lightless nights a week to conserve energy. Those with a craving for sweets will also have to sacrifice as the result of sugar rationing that has been put into effect by the United States Food Board. Under the new rationing, each person will be limited to two pounds a month.

U.S. severs ties with Bolsheviks

Washington, D.C., Aug. 15

Ambassador to Russia DeWitt C. Poole left Moscow today. His departure ends the very limited contacts the United States has with the Bolshevik regime, which it has never recognized. Poole's action was provoked by the arrest of his British and French counterparts and comes just days after the United States decided to join with Britain, France and Japan in sending troops to Russia. Although President Wilson pledged in his 14 Points address to leave Russia alone, he has decided to approve a limited military foray to stop Germany from seizing Russian supplies and to protect Czech troops marooned in Russia by the revolution (→ June 1919).

Yanks win Belleau Wood

Americans remain entrenched despite the German attempt to dislodge them.

Vaux, France, July 1

A brigade of Second Division American marines thought it would clear Belleau Wood of Germans in a few hours. Twenty days and 5,200 casualties later, the job was finally completed. One French officer described Belleau Wood as Verdun on a small scale. The Americans were slaughtered in a style that was more like the war of 1914 than 1918. The wood was a slight bulge in General Erich Ludendorff's line and the forest provided the Germans with an opportunity to hide machine-gun nests behind every boulder and fallen tree.

Militarily, the wood was useless, but the Germans had it and the Americans wanted it. The Yanks were determined to prove they were good enough to take it.

The American forces were rather pleased when a captured German officer told them that his men had fought Canadians, French and Australians, but that the American marines were the toughest. The marines also succeeded in recapturing the tiny hamlet of Vaux, just northwest of Chateau-Thierry.

In the meantime, the marines of the Third Division are holding all of the Marne crossings, with Ludendorff's drive beginning to lose steam. His attempts to capture the salient, or bulge, produced by a line running from the town of Montdidier to Noyen, appears to have failed. And this failure seems to have something special to say. The German command has lost more than 600,000 men in victories that are proving illusory (→ Aug. 10).

343 die as luxury liner sinks off Alaska

Alaska, Oct. 27

Battered by two days of storms, the luxury steamer Princess Sophia sank yesterday with 343 passengers and crew aboard. The loss of the Canadian Pacific liner as it was swept across a reef in Alaska's Lynn Canal was the worst civilian maritime disaster of its kind in American history. The 2,320-ton ship had plied the Alaska-Vancouver run since it was built in 1912.

After boarding passengers at Skagway, the Princess Sophia ran into a snowstorm. The vessel issued distress signals that were answered by government and other craft and it weathered the storm. When a second storm blew up, the steamer was lifted out of the water and tossed against a reef. With lifeboats useless and rescue ships unable to approach the reef, the Sophia went to the bottom. This morning all that could be found were four empty lifeboats washed up on a nearby island, the body of a woman and the only known survivor – a dog.

Washington, D.C., June 27. *Secretary of War Newton D. Baker ceremoniously draws the first draft number. With congressional approval of the Selective Service Act, the United States has adopted a conscription policy for the first time since the Civil War. Local draft boards, administered by a federal agency, help to determine who will serve in the Great War.*

School: It's the law

Jackson, Miss., Summer

Mississippi has finally passed a compulsory school attendance law, the last state in the union to do so. The measure was approved by the legislature this summer, but only after fierce debate. Opponents argued it would benefit Negroes who pay no taxes. Governor Theodore Bilbo, however, has advocated public education, as did his predecessor, James Vardaman, even though both men are segregationists. Vardaman once said educating a Negro "only spoils a good field hand."

OUR REGULAR DIVISIONS

Honored and Respected by All
Enlist for the Infantry –
or in one of the other 12 branches.
Nearest Recruiting Office :

Million American troops stem the tide

Doughboys establish a machine-gun nest during the Meuse-Argonne offensive.

St. Mihiel, France, Sept. 26

The St. Mihiel Salient, a bulge in the German lines near Verdun, which has been there since 1914, is no more, and the tide that threatened to put the Germans in Paris has turned and is sweeping back toward Germany instead. The operation against St. Mihiel is a portent of the future because it was basically American. The United States First Army was formally organized on August 10 with General John Pershing as its commander.

The Americans immediately went into the line holding about 50 miles of the front from Verdun to Pont-a-Mousson. Supported by the French Second Colonial Corps, the Americans were ready by September 12 for Marshal Foch's counteroffensive against the territorial gains made by General Erich Ludendorff in his spring offensive. The Americans attacked in a heavy fog that cleared in time for them to receive help from an Allied air force, commanded by Colonel Billy Mitchell,

which did a good job of breaking up German formations with machine-gun fire. Within 12 hours, the Germans were trying to get out of the pocket. But 15,000 didn't make it and were taken prisoner. In addition, some 250 guns were captured.

When General Pershing was planning his operation, he was presented with the French Eighth Army's plan, which was the size of the New York City telephone directory. Pershing came back with a plan just 14 pages long and left the rest to what he called "initiative" and "individual enterprise."

Marshal Foch, of course, had plans of his own that, when stripped of military jargon, meant that Pershing was supposed to give most of his Expeditionary Force of 999,602 to the French. In the end, Pershing was asked to launch two great attacks on battlefields 60 miles apart. The second of them would be in the Meuse-Argonne sector with Sedan as the objective. Difficult as the task seemed, with an absolutely green army and a Johnny-come-lately staff, General Pershing has succeeded in demoralizing the German forces completely and has been able to take back all the territory that the enemy had gained in 1918. The major remaining task for the Allied command now is achievement of the quick and final defeat of the Central Powers (→ Nov. 4).

Pacifist Debs gets 10 years in prison

Cleveland, Ohio, Sept. 14

Condemning those "who would strike the sword from the hand of this nation," a federal judge has sent Socialist leader Eugene Debs to prison for 10 years. Debs allegedly violated the Espionage Act in Canton in June, when he defended the I.W.W., the Bolshevik Revolution and pacifism. "The master class has always declared the wars," Debs asserted, "the subject class has always fought the battles." Refusing to contest the charges, Debs told the jury, "While there is a lower class, I am in it; while there is a criminal element, I am of it; while there is a soul in prison, I am not free" (→ March 10, 1919).

Americans, Italians rout Austrian army

Vittorio Veneto, Italy, Nov. 4

The Austrian front has broken. What began as a retreat was turned into a rout as Austrian stragglers were harassed by cavalry and Allied planes. Back in July, the 32nd Regiment of the 83rd Division of the American Expeditionary Force was sent to Italy. Actually, the unit was sent for political and morale purposes; but the Americans ended up seeing combat when the Italians crossed the Piave River and went after the Austrians, who are sick, war-weary and under strength. The greatest resistance to the Allied offensive was the high, swift water of the Piave River and many soldiers drowned in it (→ 11).

Mae West shimmy

New York City

Actress Mae West appears in "Sometime" on Broadway, introducing her "shimmy" dance. A new fad? The 26-year-old daughter of a prizefighter, West can throw a few punches of her own in the form of double entendres such as "It's better to be looked over than overlooked" and "It's not the men in my life that count; it's the life in my men." An entertainer since she was 5, the former "Baby Vamp" writes most of her own salacious lines.

A record for Babe: 29 shutout innings

Boston, Sept. 11

Boston's Red Sox clinched the sixth and final game of the World Series today with a 2-1 victory over the Chicago Cubs, but fans are still talking about the remarkable pitching of Babe Ruth that highlighted the classic. When Chicago scored in the fourth game, Ruth's record of 29 2/3 shutout innings was ended. The Red Sox salvaged that game, but lost the next. They then came back to win the sixth game. In the opener, Ruth pitched a six-hitter as he shut out the Cubs. The Babe started his career with Baltimore in 1914 and was sold that same year to Providence, a farm club of Boston. He is also quite a hitter.

The all-Negro 15th Regiment parades up Fifth Avenue in New York City, en route to an army camp. The American armed forces are segregated.

War is over in Europe: The joys and the sadness

Compiegne, France, Nov. 11

The Great War is over. The Germans signed an armistice agreement at 5 a.m. here and it went into effect at 11. Three days ago, a German armistice commission, led by Matthias Erzberger, head of the Catholic Centrists, arrived outside Allied Headquarters in the forest near Compiegne. The terms that were presented by Marshal Foch were such that it would be utterly impossible for the Germans to resume the war after the armistice has taken effect.

In the United States, there will be an opportunity to celebrate victory twice, since the United Press mistakenly reported an armistice four days ago. That report sent thousands of people pouring into the streets in celebration of an event that had not happened. President Wilson made it official this time when he informed both houses of Congress today that "the war thus comes to an end."

Under the terms of the armistice, the Germans must evacuate all the territory west of the Rhine and the Allies will establish three bridgeheads across the great river: the French around Mainz, the Americans at Coblenz and the British at Cologne. In addition to turning over hundreds of tons of war materiel to the Allies, the Germans must also surrender their holdings in East Africa, annul the treaties of Brest-Litovsk and Bucharest and continue to live under the blockade of the Allies.

The Germans obtained some mitigation of these terms by pleading the danger of Bolshevism in a nation that is on the verge of collapse. This is apparently a real danger for the Germans since the sailors' mutiny began at Kiel on October 29, and revolutionary organizations are now springing up in industrial centers throughout Germany.

The human cost of the war is unbelievable. The Allies mobilized more than 42 million men, and 5 million of them were killed, including 50,585 Americans. There were 21 million wounded combatants in all. The Central Powers mobilized 23 million men, of whom at least 3.4 million were killed. War expenditure figures differ widely, but the best guess for the Allied effort is $30 trillion; America contributed $32 billion to that total. And still, the figures do not tell the saddest story of all – the obliteration of a whole generation of young men on the Western Front. Who knows how many fine poems and scientific discoveries will never belong to humanity because the scientist and poet were destroyed in the bloom of their youth (→ Feb. 14, 1919).

"Victory Won" (1919) by Childe Hassam. At last, an end to the carnage.

Spanish flu strikes one-quarter of nation

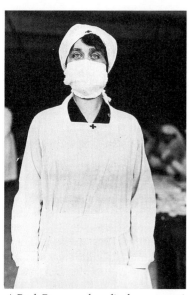

A Red Cross worker displays an anti-influenza mask she has prepared.

United States, September

One out of four people has come down with a life-threatening flu believed to have originated in Spain. Doctors have been unsuccessful in pinpointing a cure for the influenza, which is killing adults and children both here and in Europe. The Boston Stock Exchange and public buildings in several cities have been closed. In some cities, people are required to wear gauze masks in public. Philadelphia druggists are charging up to $52 for a gallon of whiskey, because it is popularly believed to be a cure for the flu. Other dubious remedies include applying onion paste to the chest and walking outdoors in the nude. In New York City alone, 400 children whose parents have died are in the care of city officials.

Wilson off to Europe for peace parley

December 4. *President Wilson boards the ship that will take him to the Versailles peace conference. Committed to the idea of making "the world safe for democracy," he sets out wholeheartedly believing that American blood has been spilled so that the world can live in peace. Under Secretary of the Navy Franklin D. Roosevelt, in top hat at center, in background (→ 13).*

Washington, D.C., Jan. 29.
18th Amendment to Constitution, mandating Prohibition, is declared ratified by states.

Washington, D.C., March 2. A Republican group, led by Henry Cabot Lodge of Massachusetts, signs statement citing opposition of 37 senators and two senators-elect to proposed League of Nations (→ 4).

Seattle, Washington, March 3. Boeing flies first international airmail run, to Vancouver, Canada.

Washington, D.C., March 10. Supreme Court rules, in Schenck v. United States, that Espionage Act does not violate First Amendment (→ Dec. 21).

Hollywood, Apr. 17. Mary Pickford joins Charlie Chaplin, Douglas Fairbanks and D.W. Griffith in forming United Artists.

New York City, June 2. Poet Carl Sandburg is awarded a Pulitzer Prize for *Cornhuskers*; Booth Tarkington wins for *The Magnificent Ambersons*.

Washington, D.C., June 4. Congress approves 19th Amendment to Constitution, which would grant vote to women; it goes to states for ratification (→ Aug. 26, 1920).

Washington, D.C., July 14. State Department permits resumption of trade with Germany.

Chicago, Aug. 14. Court rules that *Chicago Tribune* libeled Henry Ford by calling him an anarchist.

Portland, Oregon, Sept. 1. About 20,000 union members in many trades march, urging adoption of Plumb Plan for joint ownership of railroads by workers, operators and federal government, and withdrawal of U.S. troops from Russia.

Chicago, Oct. 9. Cincinnati Reds defeat Chicago White Sox, five games to three, in World Series (→ 1920).

Tucson, Arizona, Nov. 20. First municipal airport opens.

DEATHS

Oyster Bay, New York, Jan. 6. Theodore Roosevelt, 26th President of United States (*Oct. 27, 1858).

Lenox, Massachusetts, Aug. 11. Andrew Carnegie, steel magnate and philanthropist (*Nov. 25, 1835).

Triumphant Wilson offers League of Nations plan to Europeans

Italy's Orlando, Britain's Lloyd George, France's Clemenceau and Wilson.

Paris, Feb. 14

President Wilson presented his final draft for a proposed League of Nations today. In Paris for a meeting of the victorious Allies, who will work out a final peace treaty with the Central Powers, the President outlined his concept of an international organization formed and dedicated to the preservation of global peace and prosperity. The league would consist of all the nations of the world, each having an equal vote. All members would agree to turn over to the league's Council all controversies among them that might lead to war. The Council, which would consist of five small nations and France, Britain, Italy, Japan and the United States, would then arbitrate the dispute and propose a peaceful and equitable solution. A member that refused the recommendations of the Council would be liable to economic sanctions and possible joint military action by the league. In essence, Wilson's proposed league is based on an international social contract. Peace, he explained, depends "upon one great force . . . the moral force of the public opinion of the world."

When Wilson arrived in France, he was met by hundreds of thousands of well-wishers who cried out, "Vive Wilson!" (→ March 2).

Senators attack League of Nations idea

Washington, D.C., March 4

Thirty-nine Republican senators led by Henry Cabot Lodge of Massachusetts announced their opposition to the President's League of Nations covenant today and said that they intend to prevent American approval of it. The Lodge faction argues that the covenant contains no procedures for a member to withdraw, does not explicitly recognize the Monroe Doctrine and allows the league to disregard the internal affairs of member nations when it makes decisions regarding those nations. President Wilson, when he heard of the Republicans' statement tonight, condemned their "selfishness" and "comprehensive ignorance of the state of the world." So the gauntlet has been thrown down – by both sides (→ June 28).

"Acrobats" (1919) by Charles Demuth, leader in Precisionism.

Molasses swamps Boston, killing 21

Boston, Jan. 15

The commercial district of Boston was mired in deadly molasses today after a 50-foot-high iron tank owned by the Purity Distilling Company exploded, killing 21 people and wounding 40. Shortly past noon, the tank, which is situated in the North End of Boston, poured forth a two-million-gallon tidal wave of molasses. The 15-foot-high surge swamped several small homes as well as a firehouse, burying and trapping many firemen. Further injuries were caused by flying sheets of metal. The surge of molasses also caused the death of a number of horses.

An American Legion

Paris, March 15

Delegates from 1,000 units of the American Expeditionary Force met in Paris this week to form an organization of veterans called the American Legion. Its purposes are: 1) to help with rehabilitation, 2) to promote national security, 3) to promote Americanism, and 4) to help with child welfare. Over a million Americans fought in the war.

Northwest shootout against Wobblies

Centralia, Washington, Nov. 11

Armistice Day in Centralia does not apply to the war between capital and labor. A parade turned into a shootout today as the Industrial Workers of the World tried to defend their union hall from attack. The Wobblies, whose previous hall was demolished last year, say several men in the mob carried nooses. Three American Legionnaires were killed, and members of the Citizens Protective League are demanding justice. Tonight, after a blackout, the body of Wobbly Wesley Everest was found hanging, castrated and bullet-ridden. Other Wobblies survived, but are in jail (→ March 1920).

Versailles Treaty signed

Three of the "Big Four" in Paris.

Paris, June 28

The Great War was officially ended today as representatives of both the Allied and Central Powers formally accepted the Versailles Treaty. Meeting at the old royal palace near Paris, the signatory nations agreed to an accord that was originally inspired by the 14 Points program of President Wilson. But because of British-French opposition to many of these points and Wilson's subsequent acquiescence to the demands of the Allies, the final draft is hardly the idealistic and equitable document the President had once envisioned. The treaty brands the Germans as the specific aggressors who must bear full and final responsibility for the war. It also subjects them to backbreaking war reparations of $130 billion. It strips Germany of its colonial empire and essentially reduces it to the status of a small, powerless, agrarian nation. This Versailles Treaty unquestionably has flaws, but perhaps it will give the world an opportunity to get on with the business of living (→ Sept. 8).

2 West-East flights make it to Europe

Ireland, June 15

"The wonder is that we are here at all," said a dazed Captain John Alcock as he emerged from the wreckage of his Vickers-Vimy biplane today in an Irish bog. Together with American navigator Lieutenant Arthur W. Brown, the British pilot had just completed the first non-stop flight across a storm-tossed and fog-bound Atlantic, from Newfoundland to Clifton, Ireland, in 16 hours and 12 minutes. Back on May 27, all Lisbon cheered as a U.S. Navy NC-4 seaplane roared overhead, having just completed the first ocean crossing by air. Piloted by Lieutenant Commander A.C. Read, the big Curtiss biplane left New York on May 8 with two other planes. After engine failures and storms, and an Azores stopover, Read's plane had made it.

Boston Irish hail patriot De Valera

Boston, June 29

"The men who established your republic sought the aid of France; I seek the aid of America," said Irish nationalist Eamon De Valera today before an enthusiastic crowd of 40,000 at Fenway Park. The 36-year-old De Valera is one of the few surviving leaders of the failed Easter Rebellion of 1916. Like his compatriots, he was to be executed, but he was set free as public pressure mounted. De Valera was again arrested last year, but he escaped and went to America as a stowaway. Born in New York and raised in Ireland, the former mathematics professor aims to win support here for a unified, independent Ireland. Today, he said the Versailles Treaty must stress "the equality of right amongst nations, small no less than large," or it would be a "mockery."

First Triple Crown

New York City, June 29

Sir Barton swept to victory in the Belmont Stakes today and became the first horse to win the Triple Crown of racing. With Johnny Loftus in the irons, Sir Barton completed his sweep of the Kentucky Derby, the Preakness and the Belmont. It was the first time the feat has been achieved since 1875, when all three races were first run in one year. Ironically, Sir Barton almost didn't make it to the derby. A non-winner in six races, he had not competed in eight months. Also, he was 2 1/2 pounds overweight.

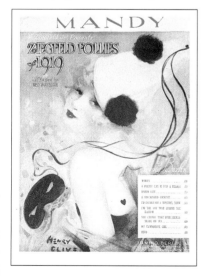

Idealist Wilson, on national tour, takes treaty to the people

Sioux Falls, S.D., Sept. 8

Faced with growing anti-League of Nations sentiment in the Senate, President Wilson has decided to take his case for ratification of the Versailles Treaty and its controversial league covenant directly to the people. Five days ago, the President launched an extensive tour of the Midwest and Far West. Advisers say that he will make about 35 major addresses during his three-week, 8,000-mile journey.

Today in Omaha, Nebraska, he said: "I can predict with absolute certainty that there will be another world war if the nations of the world do not concert the method by which to prevent it." In Sioux Falls tonight, he explained, "Some people call me an idealist. Well, that is the way I know I am an American. America is the only idealist nation in the world."

Even though his Republican adversaries in the Senate appear to be growing in strength, Wilson seems to have solid grass-roots backing among the people. Two-thirds of the state legislatures and governors have given the President their backing on the Versailles Treaty's League of Nations covenant.

A *Literary Digest* poll of newspaper editors that was taken in April suggests that the vast majority of these vital opinion-makers are in full support of the President's position. And even in the Senate, about two-thirds of the Republicans and an overwhelming number of Democrats have indicated that they favor some variation of league membership.

So even as Senator Henry Cabot Lodge and his small group of "irreconcilables" in the Senate thunder in opposition to the treaty, it would seem that President Wilson can still muster the required two-thirds majority to achieve its final approval. And the President's successful tour of the country appears to be galvanizing popular support toward that end (→ Nov. 19).

President Wilson hopes that by taking the treaty to the people, he will prevail.

Coolidge: End cop strike

National Guard restores order in Boston, endangered by strike of policemen.

Boston, Sept. 11

After stating that there is "no right to strike against the public safety by anybody, anywhere, anytime," Massachusetts Governor Calvin Coolidge today ordered the National Guard into Boston to help quell the city's police strike. The strike began two days ago when virtually all of the Boston police force refused to go to work. The mayor responded by firing the striking officers. Agreeing with the mayor, President Wilson called the strike "a crime against civilization."

With the cops off the streets, huge numbers of thugs and hooligans began roaming around. They assaulted passers-by, started fires, broke windows and looted stores. The violence did not subside until the National Guardsmen arrived late today. Spokesmen for the police say that their aims are not radical, and that their objectives are better wages and working conditions, and official recognition of their union.

Jack Dempsey takes world title with TKO

Toledo, Ohio, July 4

Jess Willard, the huge champion who regarded "little" Jack Dempsey as a joke, found the joke was on him today. In fact, Dempsey was all over him and battered the champion, 70 pounds heavier, into submission in three rounds. Willard was unable to answer the bell for the fourth round, unaware that Dempsey by then was also exhausted. Willard's idleness after taking the title from Jack Johnson, his lack of training and his age – 37 – all helped divest him of the title that he won in 1915.

A stunned Jess Willard (right) watches Jack Dempsey as the title slips away.

Scores of Negroes die in rash of race riots

Washington, D.C., December

Federal and state leaders meeting in the nation's capital are at a loss to explain this year's racial violence – or to propose workable solutions to the growing crisis. Negroes are calling the latest outbreak of lynchings and riots the "Red Summer."

The racially inspired outbreaks began in Chicago late in July after fights erupted between Negroes and white youths at a Lake Michigan beach when a young Negro, adrift on a log and unable to swim, floated into an area that was marked "For Whites Only." The white men taunted him, then watched as he drowned. When the Chicago police refused to arrest any of the whites but did arrest a Negro, a riot ensued. Gangs of white youths invaded the Negro section of town, beat its inhabitants, looted stores and burned a number of buildings. In retaliation, Negro gangs went into the white areas of Chicago and committed the same kind of outrages. By the time the National Guard restored order two weeks later, 15 whites had been killed and 178 injured, and 23 Negroes killed and at least 342 hurt. Since then, there have been at least 24 additional race riots across the nation, and 76 Negroes have been lynched. With no solutions in sight, experts say the violence may continue into the new year (→ May 31, 1921).

Vast steel strike is impressive, but it fails

Gary, Indiana, December

Demoralized by lack of funds, violence and martial law, the nation's striking steel workers are returning to their jobs in droves. Twenty people have died in the strike, 18 of them workers. In October, a clash between strikers and Negro scabs brought federal troops and martial law to Gary. Demands for union recognition, the eight-hour day and elimination of 24-hour shifts will not be met. And Judge Elbert Gary can stand by his vow that U.S. Steel "does not confer, negotiate with or combat labor unions as such." But the display of solidarity – 350,000 workers out for more than three months – rewards the effort of radical organizer William Z. Foster and proves that organized labor is returning to the steel industry.

U.S. withdraws troops from Soviet Russia

Washington, D.C., June

America's reluctant involvement in Soviet Russia's civil war is winding to a close. Having concluded that "the real thing with which to stop Bolshevism is food," President Wilson has ordered the unilateral withdrawal of 5,000 American troops now in northern Russia and has urged Britain, France and Japan to do likewise. The Allies have not succeeded in creating a democratic alternative to the Reds, which was perhaps inevitable given the disharmony that marked their intervention effort (→ Nov. 16, 1933).

Ostensibly deployed to aid the Czech Legion, U.S. troops parade in Vladivostok.

18th Amendment is enforced by new act

Washington, D.C., Oct. 28

A few months from now, America and non-medicinal alcohol part ways. Such is the gist of the Volstead Act, which will take effect January 16. After that, Americans may not legally make, sell or transport intoxicating liquors, which they like to call "hooch." The measure is designed to enforce the 18th Amendment, ratified January 29. It also prohibits the sale of liquor in restaurants, hotels and, of course, saloons. Though the bill was vetoed by President Wilson, his veto was overridden by the House and, today, by the Senate (→ Jan. 16, 1920).

Left-wing Socialists establish own party

Chicago, Sept. 1

Battered by quarrels between reformers and revolutionaries, the Socialist Party has split. Its foreign-language leaders, ousted from the Socialist convention yesterday, have formed a Communist Party on the Bolshevik model. Another faction, led by John Reed, also advocates direct action and calls itself the Communist Labor Party. Many Socialists feel, with editor Max Eastman, that their leftist brethren seek a "Russian Bolshevik Church, with more interest in expelling heretics than winning converts."

Reed to Mencken to Winesburg, Ohio

New York City

It's a long way from Harvard's Crimson to Russia's Red revolution, but reporter John Reed, 32, made the journey in time to witness the 1917 Bolshevik coup. The Harvard grad's account of it, *Ten Days That Shook the World*, has jarred thousands of Americans. Just as fascinating is H.L. Mencken's *The American Language*, a monumental study of the evolution and special uses of the language on native shores. Also special is Sherwood Anderson's *Winesburg, Ohio*, tales that give voice to the "grotesques" inhabiting a quiet American town.

Wilson breaks down; League rejected

Washington, D.C., Nov. 19

Two months after President Wilson broke down on an 8,200-mile national tour through 14 states, the Senate today voted down the treaty that would have sanctioned a League of Nations. In three separate ballots on as many versions of the Versailles Treaty, the senators effectively denied the passage of any treaty.

The first vote concerned the treaty with reservations by Henry Cabot Lodge attached; it was defeated, 55 to 39. The second ballot offered a treaty that contained fewer Lodge reservations. It was defeated by a 51 to 41 vote. And finally, the Senate considered the full treaty, without any reservations attached. It also failed, by a vote of 53 to 38.

Although the treaty would now appear to be a dead issue, the struggle apparently continues. Wilsonian Democrats still desire a League of Nations, while Republicans, and the nation, need a treaty that will legally put an end to the war.

A major factor that led to today's Senate rejection of the Versailles Treaty was the absence of President Wilson's firm advocacy of the cause he has believed in for so long. While on a speaking tour in behalf of the treaty in Denver on September 25, he collapsed with a nervous breakdown that was aggravated by a recent attack of influenza. A week later, he suffered a cerebral hemorrhage that paralyzed his left side and almost killed him. Since his near-fatal stroke, he has been incapable of performing his presidential duties. His executive responsibilities are currently being carried out by his advisers. These, according to insiders, include his wife.

Had Wilson been in good health, his dream of a postwar world based on justice, peace and prosperity might have come true. But political reality is not based on "what ifs." Tragedy is (→ March 19, 1920).

U.S., in crusading mood, deports 249 radicals to Soviet Russia

New York City, Dec. 21

"The seed of revolution is repression," counseled President Wilson earlier this month in his annual address to Congress. But no one in his Justice Department, or for that matter the nation, is listening. Today, they were too busy cheering the departure of the "Soviet Ark," which is carrying 249 aliens to the Soviet Union. Rounded up by Attorney General A. Mitchell Palmer in a series of raids last month, the 249 are considered dangerous enough to require 250 guards. But few have anything but radical beliefs to recommend their being sent out of the country.

Among the few with criminal records is Emma Goldman, who says she considers her place on the boat "an honor." Native radicals, however, are finding honor behind bars. More than 100 leaders of the Industrial Workers of the World, sentenced for sedition in August, languish in jail. Victor Berger, the first Socialist congressman, is out on appeal. Despite the resounding backing of Milwaukee voters, Congress refuses to seat him.

Economic decline and a blizzard of strikes have set the stage for the present mood. Since the end of the war, wheat prices have fallen from $2.20 to 60 cents, while a pound of cotton dropped from 40 cents to a nickel. Organized labor struck the railroad, coal, steel and construction industries. A general strike was called in Seattle that placed the city under the control of workers for several days in February. And more than 350,000 steel workers have been paralyzing the industry for the last three months.

The reaction, however, appears to far outweigh the stimulus. As journalist Walter Lippman wrote recently, "The people . . . are far more afraid of Lenin than they ever were of the Kaiser."

Funded by the American Defense Society, the National Security League and the National Civic League, a barrage of propaganda has hit the radicals. The *New York World* has charged that 10 to 15 million people have fallen under the influence of five million "Reds." Actually, membership in Bolshevik organizations is said to total less than 75,000 (→ Jan. 2, 1920).

A creeping Bolshevik slithers under the American flag. Communist revolution abroad and a wave of radical activity at home incite a "Red Scare."

New York City, Jan. 5.
Radio Corporation of America (RCA) formally founded, with capital of $20 million.

Washington, D.C., Feb. 28.
Esch-Cummins Act approved by Congress, restoring private control of railroads and setting up Railway Labor Board.

Washington, D.C., May 20.
Joint congressional resolution declares an end to state of war with Germany and Austro-Hungary [vetoed by President Wilson].

Washington, D.C., June 20.
Congress passes Merchant Marine Act, to stimulate U.S. shipping by permitting government vessels to be sold to private shipping lines.

Chicago, June.
Term "smokefilled room" coined to describe meeting place of party leaders who pick Warren G. Harding of Ohio to break Republican convention deadlock (→ Nov. 2).

New York City, July 27.
Resolute successfully defends America's Cup against British challenger Shamrock IV.

New York City, Sept. 8. First transcontinental airmail service, to San Francisco, begins.

Cleveland, Ohio, Oct. 12.
Cleveland Indians defeat Brooklyn Dodgers in World Series, five games to two.

Provincetown, Mass., Nov. 3.
Eugene O'Neill's play Emperor Jones opens, with Charlie Gilpin in title role.

Springfield, Ohio, Nov. 3.
Judge F. W. Geiger, of common pleas court, erects courtroom "ankle curtain," requested by women jurors to hide their exposed ankles.

Cicero, Illinois, Nov. 20.
Gangster Hymie Weiss fails in bid to invade Al Capone's fortified headquarters with an automobile convoy and troops [Weiss is murdered a few weeks later].

New York City, Nov. 27.
Calvin Coolidge asserts in a speech that "civilization and profits go hand in hand."

United States, Dec. 10.
President Woodrow Wilson wins Nobel Peace Prize for 1919 for work in bringing peace to Europe.

Chicago. Films Mark of Zorro, starring Douglas Fairbanks, and Dr. Jekyl and Mr. Hyde, starring John Barrymore, open.

Palmer raids net thousands of leftists

Washington, D.C., Jan. 2

In bowling alleys and pool halls, cafes, homes and offices, leaders of local radical groups across the nation were seized today. "The Department of Justice," said Attorney General A. Mitchell Palmer, "has undertaken to tear out the radical seeds that have entangled American ideas . . . the most radical socialists, the misguided anarchists . . . the moral perverts and the hysterical neurasthenic women who abound in communism."

Nearly all the 4,000 arrested are foreign-born. By the General Intelligence Office's estimate, aliens make up 90 percent of the American radical movement. And immigration rules allow deportation without trial. Wary of filing criminal suits against people whose only crime may be their political convictions, the Justice Department has left native suspects to local officials. Palmer and his deputy J.

Attorney Gen. A. Mitchell Palmer.

A young, crusading J. Edgar Hoover.

Edgar Hoover promise at least 2,700 deportations will result from this year's raid.

Government officials have been zealous to say the least. In New Jersey, it took demolition experts to identify confiscated diagrams of a phonograph. In Massachusetts, 39 bakers were released after what was reportedly a "revolutionary cau-

cus" proved to be a co-op bakery.

Prisoner treatment has not been above reproach. Captives in Boston were marched around in chains. In Detroit, 800 languish in a building with one toilet. But the Washington Post, its finger on the nation's pulse, says, "There is no time to waste on hair-splitting over infringement of liberty" (→ Dec. 25, 1921).

City slickers now outnumber farm folk

Washington, D.C.

The census this year shows a population of 105,710,620, and a general urbanization of the nation. Less than half of those people live in the country, as the urban environment continues to seduce the rural population. The number of farm residents in America has fallen below 30 percent of the overall population. The change seems to be for the

best, as the illiteracy rate has dropped to 6 percent, and since 1901 the average life expectancy of Americans has risen to 54 years from 49. The United States is producing two-thirds of the world's oil supply to help run the 15 million autos that are registered in the nation. More than 334,000 people now live in Arizona and over 960,000 people live in Florida.

Put your Baby Ruth in the Frigidaire

United States

What's cooking tonight – meat and potatoes? Naw! Americans are enjoying brand-new brand-name meals, featuring the likes of Underwood sardines, La Choy Chinese food, Maxwell House coffee (it's good to the last drop – Teddy Roosevelt once said so), Sunkist oranges, Campfire marshmallows, Kellogg's All-Bran cereal, Good Humor Ice Cream Suckers and Baby Ruth bars (named for the daughter of former President Cleveland). And to scour the pots and pans, folks are using Brillo.

Everything's easier nowadays. The ice chest is out and the Frigidaire is in. Silk stockings are out, and rayon hosiery from Du Pont Fibersilk Company is in. Still, it's tough deciding on an automobile. Do you want a Cadillac, a Chalmers-Franklin or a Chevrolet? A Maxwell, Mercedes or a Milburn Electric? A Packard, Peerless or Pierce-Arrow? A Salient, Stephens or Stutz? If you are health-minded, you might prefer a Ford Model T, because they say vibration from the "flivver" is good for the liver.

Chicago's crowded streets are typical of the nation's growing urban centers.

Eight get 25 years in I.W.W. killings

Seattle, Washington, March

Eight members of the Industrial Workers of the World were given 25 to 40 years in prison today for murders committed in defending their union hall at Centralia last fall. The jury urged leniency, but pressure for revenge won out. Since the killings, the county bar association has refused to defend Wobblies, an advertisement advocated lynching and editors of a labor paper that counseled caution have been rewarded with indictments.

Wits for lunch

New York City

Some of the bonnest of mots circulating among New York's insiders can be traced to the Rose Room of the Algonquin Hotel, on Manhattan's 44th Street. A group of writers has been meeting there to trade gossip, barbs and putdowns. Regulars include journalists Alexander Woollcott, Heywood Broun and Franklin P. Adams; poet and fiction writer Dorothy Parker, and playwrights Russel Crouse, Robert Sherwood and George S. Kaufman. Now and again, a newcomer joins the group, but at serious risk to the ego. At the Algonquin Round Table, as the club is called, the wit is razor sharp.

At Plymouth Rock, myth with cement

Plymouth, Massachusetts

The granite boulder called Plymouth Rock has a new home. Although the Pilgrims' records do not mention the rock, Elder John Faunce identified it in 1741, more than 100 years later, as the place where the Pilgrims stepped off the Mayflower. Since then, the rock has become an American symbol. However, three years after its identification, the rock was split while being dragged in pre-Revolutionary agitation. It has been cemented together and this year the Society of Colonial Dames gave the rock a granite classical monument as a home. The structure is situated on the supposed Pilgrim landing site.

Prohibition begins: America goes dry

"The Spirit of Prohibition."

Washington, D.C., Jan. 16

At 12:01 this morning, the good ship America entered the dry dock of Prohibition. To the country's many jubilant temperance workers, it signaled heaven on earth, the Anti-Saloon League proclaiming it "dry America's first birthday." To those suddenly deprived of their "giggle-water," it was something else. The many big "farewell parties" so widely predicted were generally subdued mock funerals to better, wetter days, though New York's Hotel Vanderbilt responded in style. As a band played *Goodbye Forever*, patrons were served 100 cases of the best champagne. Elsewhere, many dealers saw their stocks seized as the country's new enforcement agents, 1,500 strong, put teeth in a temperance victory.

The temperance effort grew out of colonial Puritanism. The Rev. Cotton Mather, for one, felt liquor might drown out Christianity. The Rev. Lyman Beecher, who led the American Temperance Society early in the 19th century, said "drunkards no more than murderers shall inherit the kingdom of God." Led by fervent evangelists, temperance meetings became religious revivals. By 1835, all the Protestant churches were in the temperance camp.

With the post-Civil War founding of the Prohibition Party, the Women's Christian Temperance Union and the Anti-Saloon League, the movement took a legal tack and its arguments became more practical. Industry, it said, needed sober workers. As the legal crusade gathered steam, 26 states had prohibition laws by the time America entered the Great War. In fact, temperance leaders equated winning the war with national sobriety, and by December 18, 1917, Congress had enough votes to pass a Prohibition Amendment that was ratified on January 29, 1919.

Drink up while you can. Gentlemen in straw "skimmers" raise a final toast.

Negroes organize a baseball league

Chicago

In an effort to find a place for the nation's many talented Negro players, Andrew "Rube" Foster has organized the National Negro Baseball League. Foster, manager of the Chicago American Giants, assembled eight clubs, including the Kansas City Monarchs and the Kansas City Giants, Missouri's first Negro baseball teams. Some Negro players were included on otherwise all-white teams in the late 1800s, but by 1900 they were excluded from the organized sport, including the International League. In 1906, a league of two white and four Negro teams was formed, but it lasted just that one season.

Billy Sunday "buries" John Barleycorn

Norfolk, Virginia, Jan. 16

No sooner had Prohibition killed John Barleycorn than Billy Sunday performed the burial. With 10,000 of his followers gathered here, the noted evangelist met a special train from Milwaukee carrying Barleycorn's simulated coffin. Ever a consummate showman, Sunday sent off his nemesis with the words, "Goodbye, John. You were God's worst enemy, you were hell's best friend. I hate you with a perfect hatred." Sunday comes by the burial rites honestly: he was once assistant to an undertaker. After he was ordained a Presbyterian minister, he hit the "sawdust circuit" of evangelism with spectacular results, once converting 100,000 people at a New York revival.

Evangelist Billy Sunday strikes a pose while he brings his version of salvation to millions of Americans.

Senate spurns the Versailles Treaty

An isolationist Senate feels the wrath.

Washington, D.C., March 19

The Versailles Treaty is a dead issue after its final rejection by the Senate today. In spite of general support for the accord in the Senate and from the public, disagreement over "reservations" attached by Senator Henry Cabot Lodge, the Massachusetts Republican, were ultimately responsible for the defeat. Voting to approve the treaty were 49 senators, seven short of the two-thirds majority required. Ironically, the nay votes were made up of Republicans opposed to the treaty and Democratic supporters of the treaty who, at President Wilson's request, refused to vote for it with the attached reservations.

Senator Lodge is the leader of the opposition to the treaty and its League of Nations covenant. Last March, he introduced the Republican Round Robin, signed by 39 senators, stating their opposition to the proposed league. Lodge, as chairman of the Senate Foreign Relations Committee, used a variety of stalling tactics to give the anti-league forces time to try to sway public opinion, which has favored the treaty. Lodge spent two weeks reading the full treaty aloud to the committee before starting long and often irrelevant hearings. However, in spite of his opposition, Lodge would have accepted the treaty, if some reservations were included.

Another faction of Republicans, led by Senator William Borah of Idaho, were irreconcilably opposed to the treaty. Borah and the "irreconcilables" are proponents of the traditional American policy of isolation. The Senate voted several times on the treaty last November, and it was defeated both with the reservations and without. Strong public opinion in favor of the treaty forced the Senate's vote today.

It is possible that the Democrats, with the help of some Republican "reservationists," could have put together the votes to pass the treaty if Wilson had been willing to accept Lodge's reservations. Now, however, Wilson, who convinced the Allies at the Paris peace conference of the necessity of the League of Nations and who drafted the league covenant, is blamed for the Senate rejection of the pact and the league.

Garvey preaches Negro nationalism

Garvey at the helm of his movement.

New York City, Aug. 1

Harlem's Liberty Hall today became the site of a month-long meeting of the Universal Negro Improvement Association. The national convention, initiated by Negro leader Marcus Garvey, will be attended by more than 3,000 delegates from across the United States and will feature many speakers discussing the condition of Negroes around the world. On the agenda is a bill of rights for Negroes, the announcement of a national Negro holiday to be held annually on August 31 and formation of a ship line to help interested Negroes obtain passage to Africa. The 33-year-old Garvey, a native of Jamaica, is best known for his New York-based newspaper *The Negro World*, and for his "back to Africa" campaign.

White Sox are blackened by charges they threw World Series

Chicago, Nov. 20

Can Judge Kenesaw Mountain Landis restore the tarnished image of baseball, blackened by the indictment of eight Chicago White Sox players on charges that they "threw" the 1919 World Series? Landis has been appointed baseball commissioner in an effort to win back the confidence of an American public shaken by the worst scandal in the history of the sport. In one of his first acts, he banned the eight indicted (though not convicted) athletes from organized baseball. They are Joe Jackson, Buck Weaver, Eddie Cicotte, Lefty Williams, Swede Risberg, Happy Felsch, Chick Gandil and Fred McMullin.

The eight were accused of conspiring to lose the World Series to the Cincinnati Reds in exchange for money from gambling interests. The National Commission, which was in charge of policing baseball, has been abolished and the austere Judge Landis given complete control over the game.

The most shocking indictment was that of Shoeless Joe Jackson, who had won public sympathy for his ability to rise above the background of a Southern cotton-picking family to rank with Ty Cobb and Tris Speaker as one of baseball's greatest hitters. As Jackson left the courtroom, a tearful boy reportedly pleaded, "Say it ain't so, Joe." Jackson, who received $5,000 of a promised $20,000 bribe, insisted that he had done his best in the series (he batted .375 but had some fielding lapses).

Rumors of a "fix" were widespread and bettors were putting huge amounts of money on the Reds even though the White Sox were clearly superior. Arnold Rothstein, the New York gambler, was one, knowing his group had bought off the White Sox in midseason. The signal that the "fix" was in occurred when the first Cincinnati batter was hit by a pitch. After Cicotte, a control pitcher, struck Morrie Rath in the first inning the big money poured in.

First commissioner Kenesaw Landis.

"Say it ain't so, Joe." But it is.

Olympics resumed

Antwerp, Belgium, Aug. 24

The guns of World War I were hardly silenced before plans were made to resume the Olympics, last held in 1912. Antwerp won the honor and war-torn Belgium had only a year to build a stadium, but the Games resumed on time and the United States again carried off the lion's share of medals. There were three double winners, but none of them from America. The Finns and the Yanks each won eight golds, but the big U.S. team got many seconds and thirds. Charley Paddock won the 100-meter and Allan Woodring took the 200.

From Sinclair Lewis to Scott Fitzgerald

United States

Writers are having fun with the natives. *Main Street*, by Sinclair Lewis, laces into hometown U.S.A, in this case dubbed Gopher Prairie, Minnesota. Heroine Carol Kennicott urges her neighbors to open a book now and then, but they'll have none of her high-falutin' ways. The road from Main Street to Paradise does not pass through Princeton, at least not according to F. Scott Fitzgerald, an Ivy League dropout whose first effort, *This Side of Paradise*, reads: "Here was a new generation ... grown up to find all gods dead, all wars fought, all faiths in men shaken."

Weekly broadcasts over the air waves

Pittsburgh, Penn., Nov. 2

National radio broadcasting has begun with a bang, as well as a good deal of crackle and hiss. Station KDKA has started regular weekly broadcasts by announcing the presidential election results over the air. Although less than 1,000 receivers were tuned to the broadcast, KDKA has spurred national interest in radio and, probably, in buying radio sets. Sponsored by Westinghouse, the station featured the voice of radio hobbyist Frank Conrad, and his assistant, Donald Little. Westinghouse already has plans for several more stations.

"Babe" Ruth, bought by the New York Yankees this year, earned $20,000 and hit 54 home runs.

Suffrage succeeds: Women can vote

Washington, D.C., Aug. 26

They were denied admission to the ceremony at the home of Secretary of State Bainbridge Colby today; nevertheless, the representatives of the National Woman's Party had the last word. When Colby signed the papers certifying ratification of the 19th Amendment to the United States Constitution, he was granting half the nation's population, the women of America, the right to vote. Few of the great suffrage leaders lived to see this day. Mrs. Lucretia Mott, an abolitionist and a leader of the women's rights movement, only lived long enough to see women's suffrage in the territories of Wyoming and Utah. Mrs. Elizabeth Cady Stanton and Miss Susan B. Anthony, who each fought for suffrage for nearly 50 years, had the small satisfaction of witnessing the admission of Colorado and Idaho as woman suffrage states.

The torch was passed to today's leaders, and Miss Alice Paul and Mrs. Carrie Chapman Catt tirelessly lobbied the United States Senate to pass the federal amendment last year. The exhausting state-by-state ratification process ended a few days ago when Tennessee's legislature approved the amendment.

What is women's next step? Perhaps they will try to vote out of office some of the lawmakers who denied them the power to vote.

The efforts of Mrs. Herbert Carpenter, bearing the flag in a suffrage march, and scores of thousands like her, have finally led them to the voting booth.

Advocating return to normalcy, Harding and Republicans win big

Washington, D.C., Nov. 2

Warren Gamaliel Harding celebrated his 55th birthday today by winning the presidency. Republicans Harding and running mate Calvin Coolidge, Governor of Massachusetts, easily defeated Democrats James Cox for President and Franklin Roosevelt for Vice President. The party's majority in Congress also rose as voters opted for conservatism. "America's present need is not heroics but healing; not nostrums but normalcy," Harding has said. He was chosen, one pundit said, in "a smoke-filled room," after a deadlock in the convention. Socialist Party candidate Eugene Debs won 919,799 votes as he sat in jail for sedition.

After winning election, President-elect Harding strolls through the capital.

1921

Harding

Einstein tells U.S. that it's all relative

New York City

What would it be like to ride on a beam of light? Those who attended a recent lecture at Columbia University given by the theoretical physicist Albert Einstein may have had a glimpse of this. The German mathematician and scientist gained world fame last year when a total eclipse of the sun provided an opportunity to test his "general theory of relativity." His fame has been a long time coming, since his theories first saw publication in 1905 and 1910, while he was employed at the Swiss patent office.

In 1905, he published papers on the subjects of Brownian Movement (the tendency of molecules to jiggle about when heated), the Photoelectric Effect, and Special Relativity. This last paper, and one published in 1916 on General Relativity, resulted from his meditation on the course taken by a beam of light through space. Einstein's prediction that such a beam would be bent in proximity to the sun was proven true during last year's solar eclipse.

Rx for all: whiskey

Chicago

Prohibition notwithstanding, one can still buy whiskey legally in some states of the union – whiskey prescribed by doctors for "medicinal purposes." Judging by the number of people who line up daily at the drug stores, whiskey is a popular remedy. It is now being dispensed at the rate of one million gallons a year.

Quota system curbs flood of immigration

They made it to America in time.

Washington D.C., May 19

The government acted to curb the influx of European immigrants drastically today. Congress passed the Emergency Quota Act, which restricts entrance to only 3 percent of a given nationality's American population in the year 1910, and sets a new limit of 358,000 immigrants per year. Last year alone, over 800,000 were admitted. The British, who made up 42 percent of the nation's population in 1910 will thus get 42 percent of all available visas, and Asian workers remain banned as a result of 1917 curbs. Some 40 percent of New York's 1910 population was foreign-born.

Jazz is banned in Zion (Illinois, that is)

Zion, Illinois, March 30

Along with the speakeasy and the hip flask, jazz has quickened America's postwar pulse. To some, such as temperance people, its genesis in Negro saloons and bordellos smacks of moral decadence. Therefore, the powers of Zion, Illinois, have banned its playing in public. Jazz does best in hothouses like Kansas City, where Benny Moten's Negro group plays. Moten is a protege of the ragtime composer Scott Joplin and some say his jazz is livelier than that of the all-white Original Dixieland Jazz Band. In New York, the immensely popular *Shuffle Along*, with music by pianist Eubie Blake, is building the demand for such Negro musicals.

Psychoanalyis is on everybody's mind

United States

When Sigmund Freud visited this country in 1909, he was amazed that "even in prudish America" his work was well known. Today, the descendants of Puritan repression are fixated on his theories. The young and wild welcome Freud as a scientific excuse for pursuing the pleasure principle. But even the generation that grew up with Queen Victoria is considering that sex may be more powerful than Shakespeare. To break down defense mechanisms, mass market therapy offers books like *Ten Thousand Dreams Interpreted* or *Sex Problems Solved*. Those who can afford it run off to Europe or corner psychiatrists at parties and ask for analysis as though it were a palm reading. Others pursue their own therapy, giving full reign to the libido at all-night petting parties and Theda Bara movies. Prudish America? Not anymore.

Business in schools

Chicago

Business is getting serious attention at major universities. Though the first business school opened in 1881, most of its subjects were academic, allowing little teaching in practical business experience. In recent years, Dartmouth, Chicago, Harvard and other major schools have been adding finance, banking and law to the curriculum.

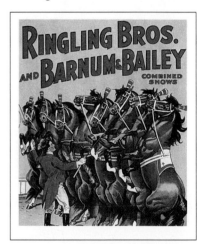

Gompers to lead A.F.L. for 40th time

Washington, D.C., June 25

Samuel Gompers was elected president of the American Federation of Labor today for the 40th time. Gompers, 71, gained prominence as head of a cigarmakers union in the 1870s, leading the fight to end sweatshop conditions in New York City. In 1886, he helped create the A.F.L., was soon elected its president and has since then been the labor movement's dominating force. Exercising what he calls "moral influence," a belief that collective persuasion befits reform better than rebellion, Gompers has led the fight for higher wages and safer conditions. The union now has 5 million members.

Gompers (right) with John L. Lewis.

Quiet Tulsa erupts; 79 die in race riots

Tulsa, Oklahoma, May 31

Residents of this small oilfield town in northeastern Oklahoma are breathing a lot easier this evening. Earlier in the day, a savage series of riots broke out, pitting Negroes against whites. The result: at least 79 people have been killed and scores wounded. Law and order were not restored until National Guardsmen sent by the Governor arrived this afternoon. Racial unrest has been plaguing this otherwise quiet town for weeks. The cause of today's violence has yet to be determined (→ May 6, 1922).

Sacco and Vanzetti held guilty of murder

The defendants on their way to a trial that is provoking heated debate.

Dedham, Mass., July 14

In a most controversial decision, a jury has declared Nicola Sacco and Bartolomeo Vanzetti guilty of first-degree murder. The case concerned the slaying of a paymaster and his guard at a South Braintree, Massachusetts, shoe factory last year. Nearly $16,000 was stolen at the time, none of which has ever been found or traced to Sacco or Vanzetti. The month-long trial has attracted national attention, with many liberals and labor groups rallying to support the Italian-born defendants. Many claim that Sacco and Vanzetti were singled out for prosecution on political grounds, since they are known anarchists in an era when anti-radical sentiment is rampant in the United States.

The case against Sacco and Vanzetti began to be formed when witnesses claimed that the murderers and thieves were Italian. The defendants were arrested when they went with two other Italians to claim a car that had been linked to the crime. Both defendants were found to be carrying guns, and both made false statements upon arrest, though the defense says they did so in fear of deportation. The money was not found in their possession, neither had a criminal record, and further evidence has been scanty.

Judge Webster Thayer, criticized by many as having been unfair to the defense, has not yet sentenced the two men (→ Aug. 23, 1927).

Taft dream comes true: He's Chief Justice

"William H. Taft" by MacCameron.

Washington, D.C., June 30

"Politics makes me sick," wrote William Howard Taft during his presidency. He always wanted to rise above politics and serve on the Supreme Court. Taft's dream came true today as President Harding named him Chief Justice. Taft brings conservatism and a respected reputation to the bench. While he advocates states' rights, many see him leaning to the liberal side on social issues. Major tasks will be to lighten the huge load of cases on the docket – the court is far behind schedule – and to unify the justices. Nearly a quarter of recent decisions have elicited strong dissents.

Troops and planes battle coal strikers

Logan County, W. Va., Sept. 5

Helped by 2,100 federal troops and cover from several planes, coal operators have warded off a retaliatory union attack. Five miners were slain earlier in labor strife here and 4,000 of their fellows were advancing on a wide front to avenge the deaths. The miners have now been halted, and 600 have surrendered to authorities. Violence has ruled coal country for two years as the United Mine Workers struggle to organize fields that are at least half non-union. Company guards patrol Logan County's borders keeping union men out. Last year in neighboring Mingo County, the labor war claimed 16 lives.

Ever new products to fit every need

United States

Drains clogged? Clean 'em fast with Drano! Rugs soiled? Vacuum 'em quick with Electrolux! No time to bake from scratch? Use Betty Crocker cake mix. No time to give your diet iodine? Add iodized salt! No time to write your grandma 3,000 miles away? Make a coast-to-coast telephone call. Too much time? Take up Ping Pong. Too much money? Buy a Lincoln! Is a meal too much? Eat a bag of Wise potato chips! Eat a Mounds bar! Eat an Eskimo Pie! Too good to be true? Buy some artificial or cultured pearls! Too much too soon? Perhaps.

Depression hurting; Hoover has job plan

Washington, D.C., Sept. 26

The country remains mired in the grimmest economic depression since the stark pre-war slump of 1914. After the brief boom that began with the Armistice, the nation has slid steadily deeper into economic distress. The gross national product, for example, has fallen by a third since 1914. There have been more than 100,000 bankruptcies. It is estimated that the number of wage-earners in the manufacturing industries has been reduced by at least 25 percent in the last two years. Government statistics indicate that almost five million workers are now unemployed, their ranks swollen by the 453,000 farmers who have lost their homesteads and land.

Commerce Secretary Herbert Hoover, presiding over a national conference about the unemployment situation, announced today a desperate two-point program to deal with the depression. He is calling on manufacturers and industrialists to reduce their prices rather than their employees' wages. Secondly, he is proposing a sweeping, federally funded jobs program for the army of the unemployed. It remains to be seen whether the corporate executives will agree to such a novel – and voluntary – plan. And his demand that the government provide jobs makes him in the minds of many either a socialist or a communist. But everyone agrees that something has to be done – and soon.

Polio strikes FDR

Campobello, New Brunswick

Tragedy has crippled the rising political star Franklin Delano Roosevelt. The former vice presidential candidate has fallen ill with poliomyelitis and doctors say he may never walk again. He won a New York State Senate seat in 1910, gained national recognition as assistant navy secretary under President Wilson and has hinted at plans to run for governor of New York. Now, many speculate that his political aspirations may be scrapped.

Drive in, eat out

Dallas, Texas, September

With millions of cars on the roads, it's become good business to cater to mobile consumers. So a Dallas candy and tobacco wholesaler, J.G. Kirby, backed by Dr. Reuben Wright Jackson, a local physician, came up with a new roadside eating idea: It's the Pig Stand, and barbecued pork sandwiches are served to drivers who never leave their cars. "People with cars are so lazy," says Kirby, "that they don't want to get out of them to eat."

Miss America pageant held in Atlantic City

Margaret Gorman in all her glory.

Atlantic City, N.J., Sept. 7

Miss Margaret Gorman, a blue-eyed, blonde 16-year-old, has won the title "Miss America" in this resort city's first major beauty pageant. Miss Gorman stands 5 foot 1 and weighs 108 pounds; her measurements are 30-25-32. She won out over six girls, but there was a separate competition for women who fit the category of "professionals," actresses and shapely athletes. Atlantic City businessmen and reporters concocted the contest to encourage tourists to remain in town beyond the Labor Day weekend. While boosters say that the event offered the most beauteous maidens in the country, actually nobody in the competition came from farther west than Philadelphia.

Socialist Debs pardoned on Christmas Eve

"I either go out a man as I came in or I serve my term to the last day."

Washington, D.C., Dec. 25

Eugene Debs stopped in at the White House today on his way to freedom. "I either go out a man as I came in," the Socialist leader had written from the Atlanta Penitentiary, "or I serve my term to the last day." Pardoned unconditionally by President Harding, Debs leaves with his pride intact. Debs's sincerity impressed Harding during their brief meeting. The two agree on nothing politically, but they do share a passion for the cowboy film star Tom Mix.

Head of the American Railway Union in the 1890s, Debs read Karl Marx while jailed for his role in the 1894 Pullman strike. Upon his release, the tall, gaunt idealist turned to socialism. He was the party's perennial candidate, running for president in 1900 through 1912 and last year, when he amassed 919,000 votes as convict No. 9653. A man who regards violence and hardball politics as abhorrent, Debs charms his following with integrity and faith. "Revolutions," he said with total confidence at his trial, "have a habit of succeeding when the time comes for them." Now, with radicalism torn by suppression and wrangling, the need for change that he expressed in prison echoes for all to hear: "If the earth and all it contains is not for the people ... then there is certainly a mighty mistake somewhere that needs the Almighty's correction."

Sports broadcasts

New York City

Americans no longer have to wait for morning newspapers to find out what's going on in sports. The Jack Dempsey-Georges Carpentier fight on July 2 in New Jersey was the first broadcast of a heavyweight title bout, and WJZ aired the play-by-play account of a World Series at the Yankee-Giant clash in New York. Dempsey was also involved in the first-ever prizefight broadcast, his easy victory over Billy Miske September 6 of last year. The first ringside description of a fight was broadcast on December 22, 1920, when Joe Lynch defeated Peter Herman in New York.

Enrico Caruso and Nellie Melba sing the praises of the Victrola.

1922

New York City, Feb. 5.
The Reader's Digest begins publication in Greenwich Village.

Washington, D.C., Feb. 9.
Congress authorizes a World War Foreign Debts Commission, to negotiate repayment agreements (→ Jan. 10, 1923).

Hampton Roads, Va., Feb. 21.
Of 45 men aboard dirigible Roma, 34 are killed as it strikes high-tension wires.

North Carolina, March 5.
At Pinehurst Gun Club, Annie Oakley hits an astounding 98 out of 100 clay pigeons.

Blackstone, Virgina, May 12.
A 500-square-foot hole created as 20-ton meteor falls to earth.

New York City, May 21.
Pulitzer Prize goes to Booth Tarkington for *Alice Adams*.

Schenectady, N.Y., Aug. 3.
First radio sound effect – two blocks of wood slapped together to simulate slamming door – produced on WGY.

Chicago, Sept. 13.
Railway shopmen end two-month national strike.

Washington, D.C., Sept. 21.
Congress passes Commodity Exchange Act, setting trade regulations on commodities.

New York City, September.
Frank I. Cobb, in *New York World*, writes, "The forgotten man was never more forgotten than he is now."

Washington, D.C., Oct. 3.
Rebecca Felton, 87, of Georgia, named nation's first woman senator, to fill vacant seat.

New York City, Oct. 8. New York Giants beat New York Yankees, four games to none, with one tie, in World Series.

Dayton, Ohio, Oct. 20. Harold Harris becomes first member of Caterpillar Club, as he parachutes safely from a crashing airplane.

New York City, Nov. 28.
Jack Savage of Britain initiates skywriting in America.

Pittsburgh. *Pittsburgh Observer* reports "a change for the worse during the past year in feminine dress, dancing, manners and general moral standards."

New York City. Walter Lippmann's *Public Opinion* issued.

Teapot Dome lease spurs Senate probe

Washington, D.C., Apr. 16

The Senate, smelling a scandal in the making, has launched an investigation into charges that Secretary of the Interior Albert B. Fall has either improperly or illegally leased out the rich Teapot Dome oilfields of Wyoming that were reserved for the navy. Persistent rumors in Washington suggest that Fall took illegal loans from oilmen Edward L. Doheny and Harry Sinclair in return for favorable leases on the Wyoming reserves as well as on reserves in California. Asked about his Interior Secretary, President Harding said: "If Fall isn't an honest man, then I'm not fit to be President" (→ March 4, 1923).

Film capital sweats under public lens

Hollywood, Calif., Feb. 6

William Desmond Taylor, one of Mary Pickford's directors, was shot to death in his Hollywood mansion the night of February 1. Mabel Normand and Mary Miles Minter had visited him that night. This latest scandal, just months after the Roscoe "Fatty" Arbuckle orgy, which left starlet Virginia Rappe dead after an alleged sexual assault by the 320-pound actor during one of his wild parties, has set tongues wagging and raised serious questions about the morals of filmland.

2 lynchings a week and legislation fails

Washington, D.C., May 6

There have been more than 50 lynchings of Negroes this year. In 30 of the cases, the Negroes were taken from the police by mobs. The most dramatic incident occurred in Kirvin, Texas, when 500 whites gathered to watch the burning of three Negroes. Meanwhile, the Dyer Anti-Lynching Bill failed in the Senate today following a long filibuster by Southerners. The bill, which called for the fining of law officers who allowed lynchings to take place, had been passed in the House (→ Sept. 15, 1923).

5 powers sign naval pact in Washington

Washington, D.C., Feb. 6

The race to build a bigger navy has been halted, at least temporarily. The world's major naval powers signed a treaty today that places a 10-year moratorium on construction of battleships and cruisers. The treaty also limits the number of all warships and calls for the destruction of some existing ships. The five nations, the United States, Britain, Japan, France and Italy, agreed to maintain battleships in a ratio to one another of 5 to 5 to 3 to 1.7 to 1.7 respectively. In order to comply with the treaty, the United States will have to scuttle 30 warships, Britain 19 and Japan 17. Much of the credit for the success of this conference belongs to Secretary of State Charles Evans Hughes, who surprised the delegates and much of the world by proposing immediate disarmament in his opening talk. Hughes's proposals were eventually accepted with few changes. Japan accepted a smaller navy after the United States and Britain agreed not to build any further fortifications on their outposts in the region, which for the United States includes the Philippines, Guam and Wake Island, and for Britain, Hong Kong. Hughes had based the battleship ratio on current naval power, but France wanted it to reflect defensive needs. Strong public pressure finally forced France to accept the ratio, but as a concession, the treaty does not place a limit on smaller ships, including subs and destroyers (→ July 21, 1930).

"Abraham Lincoln" designed by Daniel Chester French and carved by the Piccirilli brothers of New York. Dedicated May 30, the Lincoln Memorial, modeled after the Parthenon in Athens, honors both the 16th President and the virtues of tolerance, honesty, and constancy of the human spirit.

"Tales of Jazz Age," from "Babbitt" to "The Waste Land"

Under the editorship of George Jean Nathan and H.L. Mencken, "The Smart Set" parodies the fast life.

United States

The dam has burst and – to the delight of some and the horror of others – has released a flood of new literature. Some say 1922 is a banner year in the history of Western art; others mutter prayers to the gods of decency.

Consider *Ulysses*, the epic novel by the wandering Dubliner James Joyce. Ezra Pound calls it a worthy successor to the Homer *Odyssey*, which it parallels. But censors, citing the author's use of four-letter words, think otherwise. The United States Post Office in New York set fire to 500 copies of the epic smuggled from overseas. Not that readers have found solace in the new poem by T.S. Eliot, of London by way of St. Louis and Harvard. His *The Waste Land* may be filled with high-brow allusions, but it reeks of S-E-X.

Even writers who have stayed put keep bringing up subjects that in pre-war days had no place in mixed company. F. Scott Fitzgerald, spokesman for "flappers and philosophers," relates their hangovers in his novel *The Beautiful and Damned*, and in *Tales of the Jazz Age*. And satirist Sinclair Lewis has surpassed his last smash hit, *Main Street*, in *Babbitt*, which roasts businessmen, boosters and bohemians. "His motorcar was poetry, tragedy, love and heroism," Lewis writes. From Baltimore, that sworn enemy of the "booboisie," H.L. Mencken, lights into the philistines with his *Defense of Women*.

With all that searching, is it any wonder that readers are buying up Emily Post's *Etiquette: The Blue Book of Social Usage*.

The "flapper" makes her daring debut

United States, May

The trade journal *American Hairdresser* reports that bobbed hair, worn by quite a few women this spring, will stay popular for the summer. But what right-thinking woman would have her long locks shorn, would abdicate her crown of femininity? She seems the same eccentric woman who binds her breasts to make them look smaller, who wears shapeless shirt dresses that show too much ankle. Who is this woman who drinks in speakeasies, wears rouge and lipstick, rejects cotton underwear for silk, uses shocking words like "damn," "hell" and "nerts" and

The flapper drinks and smokes.

puffs on cigarettes? *Vanity Fair* calls her a "flapper."

Some adults think the girls are trying to catch the attention of today's restless, disenchanted men. These fellows don't like the responsibilities that come with wives or even girlfriends; they just want pals, so the females oblige. Some people think the opposite, that flappers neck too much to qualify as chums. In school, these girls learn all about Freud and are bent on proving his theories wrong . . . or right. Just so long as it's fun.

"The Long and the Short of It."

Mad for ads, fads

United States

Advertising proves an effective form of education. Americans now know more than ever before about halitosis, acid-stained teeth and body odor, and how these impede normal relationships. They know how to get "that school girl complexion" with Palmolive soap and how to guard the throat against excessive coughing by smoking Lucky Strikes. They have also learned it is wise to "eat more wheat," especially in the form of Gold Medal Flour. Economics is one popular course of study, as Americans begin to purchase appliances on the installment plan. "Buy now and pay later," gibberish a decade ago, now sells.

Boston puts ban on Isadora Duncan

The rebellious dancer in "Aulis."

Boston, Oct. 24

Mayor James Curley has banned Miss Isadora Duncan from further performances here after her pro-Communist remarks and exposure of her person last night. The 24-year-old dancer had offered a passionate rendition of *Marche Slav* when she suddenly told her unresponsive audience: "Life is not real here!" Then she removed a red sash from her waist (at the same time exposing herself) and held it aloft. "This is red!" she said. "So am I! It is the color of life and vigor!" She was booed off the stage.

The American-born dancer, a supporter of Bolshevism, began a dance school at a house in Moscow given her by Soviet leader Lenin. She is married to Sergei Esenin, a Russian poet.

Harding

Los Angeles, Jan. 1.
Evangelist Aimee Semple McPherson opens her $1.5 million Angelus Temple.

Memphis, Tennessee, Feb. 16.
Jazz singer Bessie Smith makes first recording, *Down-Hearted Blues.*

Washington, D.C., March 4.
Agricultural Credits Act passed, making loans available to farmers.

Montana and Nevada, March 5. Legislatures enable qualifying people over 70 to draw pensions of up to $25, setting precedent.

Washington, D.C., Apr. 9.
Supreme Court rules, in Adkins v. Children's Hospital, that District of Columbia's minimum wage for women and children is unconstitutional.

California, May 4. John Macready and Oakley Kelly are first to fly non-stop across continent, in 36 hours.

New York City, May 13.
Pulitzer Prize awarded to Edna St. Vincent Millay for *A Few Figs from Thistles* and *The Ballad of the Harp-Weaver.*

Nenana, Alaska, July 15.
President Harding hammers last spike, as Alaskan interior railroad is completed.

New York City, Oct. 15.
New York Yankees beat New York Giants in World Series, four games to two.

Washington, D.C., Oct. 24.
Department of Labor estimates nearly 500,000 Negroes have left South in past 12 months.

Washington, D.C., Nov. 6.
Colonel Jacob Schick patents first electric shaver.

Washington, D.C., Dec. 25.
First electrically lit White House Christmas tree appears.

New York City. Yankee Stadium opens; Babe Ruth celebrates with home run.

United States.
Du Pont Corporation produces cellophane.

United States. Fifteen million automobiles are registered.

New York City. Photographer Edward Steichen signs contract with J. Walter Thompson agency; birth of commercial advertising photography.

New York City. Musical *Artists and Models*, with a bare-breasted chorus, stirs widespread public outrage.

Interior chief Fall quits in oil scandal

A hapless Secretary Albert B. Fall.

Washington, D.C., March 4

Secretary of the Interior Albert B. Fall submitted his resignation to President Harding early today. The embattled Fall has been the subject of a Senate investigation since last year because of suspected illegal dealings with executives of major oil companies and the unlawful leasing of government-owned oil properties. Now the cloud over Fall's head seems to be growing daily. He apparently can't explain how he was able to spend $170,000 for improvements on his ranch in New Mexico when his annual salary is only $12,000. President Harding can't believe the Interior Secretary is guilty and has said of Fall's misadventures, "I guess there'll be hell to pay" (→ June 30, 1924).

U.S. pulling troops out of Germany

Washington, D.C., Jan. 10

President Harding today ordered American troops withdrawn from Germany to protest steps proposed by France and Belgium to enforce German reparations. The two Allies, angry at German failure to keep up reparations payments, have decided to occupy the Ruhr Valley in the industrial and coal-producing center of Germany. The British refuse to take part in any occupation, protesting that such a step is not sanctioned by the Versailles Treaty. Although the Allied Reparations Commission has determined that Germany owes $32 billion, no timetable was ever set to regulate payments (→ Apr. 16, 1924).

Bryan defeated in bid to ban evolution

Indianapolis, May 22

After a tumultuous debate, the Presbyterian General Assembly has failed to support a motion by William Jennings Bryan to cut off financial support to any Presbyterian school "that teaches, or permits to be taught, as a proven fact either Darwinism or any other evolutionary hypothesis that links man in blood relationship with any other form of life." For years, Bryan has campaigned against evolution, saying "such a conception of man's origin would weaken the cause of democracy and strengthen class pride and the power of wealth." The former presidential nominee sees this crusade as part of his long struggle on behalf of the common people.

His battle against evolution is only part of Bryan's larger fight against modernism in religion as a whole. Bryan and the other fundamentalists reject what they see as modernism's attempts to water down the fundamentals of Christianity, especially the truth of the Bible, as well as the crucifixion and resurrection of Jesus. For them, the acceptance of evolution in place of the biblical story of creation is the first step toward destroying religious truth (→ May 21, 1924).

Literary sex spawns Clean Books League

Washington, D.C.

"Foul!" is the cry reverberating through the land as steamy books roll off the presses and into the hands of eager readers. A group of outraged citizens, the Clean Books League, has fought back by mailing out leaflets that list untouchable titles such as Gertrude Atherton's *Black Oxen,* recently banned by the public library in Rochester, New York. The league, whose ranks include civic, church and law enforcement leaders, has been lobbying for the Clean Books Bill now being debated in Congress.

Dance marathons: a deadly passion

United States

"Of all the crazy competition ever invented," reports the *New York World,* "the dancing marathon wins by a considerable margin of lunacy." The madness reached its peak this year when Homer Morehouse's heart stopped beating in the 87th hour of a marathon. Homer died, but the diehards drove on, dancing to a record of 90 hours 10 minutes. Callous? Perhaps. But today's competitor will do anything for a record. Rivals have even been known to slip sleeping pills or laxatives in each other's water.

In a rare moment of rest, some of America's leaders gather. Among those seated are, from left, auto maker Henry Ford, inventor Thomas A. Edison, President Warren G. Harding and rubber magnate Harvey S. Firestone.

President Harding dies

"Warren G. Harding" (1923) by Margaret L. Williams. Death may have spared him further humiliation.

Long on common sense and short on words, the new President from Vermont displays a bountiful catch.

San Francisco, Aug. 3

America grieves the death of its 29th President, Warren G. Harding. After a tiring transcontinental trip, he stopped here to rest. Yesterday, his wife was reading him a favorable article on his presidency, *A Calm Review of a Calm Man*, when he fell into his pillow, dead of apoplexy at 57. A likable man, Harding will probably be recalled as a hapless leader. Corruption surrounded him; the presidency overwhelmed him. He once said, "My God, this is a hell of a job! I have no trouble with my enemies ... my goddamn friends, they're the ones that keep me walking the floors nights." Today, Vice President Coolidge took the presidential oath (→ Dec. 6).

U.S. Steel gives workers eight-hour day

New York City, Aug. 13

Bowing to pressure from Washington, U.S. Steel announced today that major steel firms will institute the eight-hour day. President Harding had been besieged by the clamor for reduced hours since a 1920 interchurch report detailed conditions in the steel industry. "Nothing will contribute so much to American industrial stability," said the President, "as the abolition of the 12-hour working day and the seven-day working week."

A bouquet of American beauties at the Miss America competition.

Free, flowing flapper fashions.

KKK terror spurs martial law in Oklahoma

Oklahoma City, Sept. 15

As the result of increasing racial violence, Governor J.C. Walton today activated the Oklahoma National Guard. Walton also issued an executive decree that placed the entire state under martial law. As he ordered more than 6,000 Oklahoma guardsmen to duty, he specifically blamed the rising tide of racial hatred on the Ku Klux Klan. Citing the Klan's leadership as being the primary cause of the current state of insurrection and rebellion, he proclaimed that any person found guilty of aiding the Klan's white supremacy programs would be declared an enemy of the state and subject to martial law.

The Klan is a powerful force in Oklahoma. Its members direct their philosophy of hate against not only Negroes, but also Indians, foreigners, Catholics, Jews and anyone who seems not to fit their particular concept of "American." For some years, Imperial Wizard Hiram Evans and Klan supersalesman Edward Clarke have been successful in promoting the growth of the Klan in Oklahoma, Texas and elsewhere in the Southwest. Memberships in the Klan reputedly sell for $10.

For opposing the Klan, Walton has received death threats, so his office is under 24-hour guard by state troopers. Pro-Klan state legislators have called for a special session so that impeachment proceedings can be introduced against the Governor. Walton has warned that he will jail legislators who attempt to remove him solely for his anti-Klan activities (→ March 14, 1925).

Imperial Wizard of the Ku Klux Klan rallies his followers around the flag.

For the fun of it

United States

Dr. Emile Coue, a French psychologist who recently visited the United States, urges Americans to believe that "every day, in every way, they are getting better and better." They most certainly are getting better at amusing themselves, whether it be by playing contract bridge or the Chinese game of mah jongg or roller-skating or consulting ouija boards or sitting on flagpoles or taking raisin breaks instead of tea in the afternoons or yo-yoing a yoyo (the up-and-down toy invented in the Philippines).

Luce founds Time

New York City

In this age of the airplane and the radio, news happens so quickly that it's a struggle to keep up, especially if you've got your own row to hoe. At last, the busy can find time or, rather, *Time*, the first "newsmagazine" in the country. It's the brainchild of Henry A. Luce and Briton Hadden, recent graduates of Yale, where Luce edited the campus daily. *Time* is a slim weekly, but it stretches across the whole world, condensing important and amusing events into capsule reports written in a distinctive style.

You may get a picture in your radio set

Russian-born inventor Vladimir Zworykin. Though it is still in a rudimentary phase, Zworykin's system offers endless possibilities.

New York City, Dec. 23

Imagine a picture being transmitted through your radio set. It may someday be possible. Russian-born engineer Vladimir Zworykin has demonstrated his new invention, called the iconoscope, which may make possible widespread transmission of pictures, even moving pictures. The 34-year-old engineer has produced a crude but workable system, though a commercial application may be years away. Zworykin, who learned his craft in Russia and at college in France, came to the United States after the war, and studied at the University of Pittsburgh. His work has relied on earlier experiments by the English scientist Campbell Swinton, the Russian Boris Rosing, and on Albert Einstein's photoelectric theory.

Warners to "Hunchback" to Rin Tin Tin

Hooray for Hollywood! As the movie industry grows, so too does its capital.

Hollywood, California

The film company Warner Bros. has been incorporated by Harry, Albert, Sam and Jack L. Warner, who started in the film business in 1903 with a nickelodeon in Newcastle, Pennsylvania. This year, Paramount has produced two of the biggest moneymakers ever, James Cruze's *The Covered Wagon* and Cecil B. De Mille's *The Ten Commandments*. The former chronicles the trek out West, using authentic locations and wagons, while the latter recreates Egypt in the California desert. From Universal comes *The Hunchback of Notre Dame* with Lon Chaney as Quasimodo – in an outfit that makes his suffering on screen rather genuine (it includes a 70-pound rubber lump on his back). The newest star in movies is Rin Tin Tin, a handsome German shepherd said to have been found in a trench during the World War. On the dark side, popular actor Wallace Reid has died of morphine addiction. Fame and sadness dwell in this place, which is now identified by a sign in the hills above that spells it out in letters three stories high: HOLLYWOOD.

Nation hears Silent Cal speak on airwaves

Washington, D.C., Dec. 6

The man doesn't talk much, but when he does, people listen. Thousands of Americans turned on their radios to hear taciturn President Coolidge today as he delivered the first official presidential message over the airwaves. The speech was also Coolidge's second to Congress since entering the White House after the death of President Warren G. Harding in August.

Epitomizing his free enterprise philosophy, "Silent Cal" called for tax reductions in today's speech. He also reiterated his support for the World Court and repayment of war debts by the Allies, and declared his belief that America should distance itself from the League of Nations.

Coolidge, aware that he has a sober personality, once joked: "I think the American public wants a solemn ass as a President and I think I'll go along with them."

A crowd listens carefully as Calvin Coolidge addresses Congress. Loudspeakers are set up so all can hear from a man who doesn't speak out all that much.

New Yorkers line up to hear the Thomas Sax-O-Tet at the Rivoli Theater. And no matter how hot the jazz may get, air-conditioning will keep it cool.

New York City, Jan. 1. Radios in American homes now total 2.5 million; in 1920, there were only 2,000.

Washington, D.C., March 10. J. Edgar Hoover appointed acting director of Bureau of Investigation, vowing to administer it with "no politics and no outside influence."

Washington, D.C., March 31. Supreme Court rules, in Oregon Case, that states cannot compel children of school age to attend school.

New York City, May 11. Robert Frost wins Pulitzer Prize in poetry for *New Hampshire: A Poem with Notes and Grace Notes.*

San Antonio, Texas, May 21. Presbyterian General Assembly calls evolutionary theory untenable (→ March 13, 1925).

Chicago, May 31. Nathan Leopold and Richard Loeb confess to "thrill murder" (→ Jan. 1, 1925).

Lorain, Ohio, June 28. Tornado kills 75, injures 1,037 and causes $25 million in damages.

Tijuana, Mexico, July 4. American Cesar Cardini, owner of Caesar's Place restaurant, creates Caesar Salad.

New York City, July 9. Democrats nominate John W. Davis of West Virginia for President, on 103rd ballot.

New York City, Oct. 8. National Lutheran Conference bans use of jazz in churches.

Washington, D.C., Oct. 10. Senators beat Giants in World Series, four games to three.

New York City, Nov. 30. RCA transmits photographs from London by wireless.

New York City, November. Macy's department store holds first Thanksgiving Day Parade.

New York City. Clarence Birdseye introduces process for fish freezing, suitable for immediate oven cooking.

California. Walt Disney creates his first cartoon, *Alice's Wonderland.*

New York City. Herman Melville's *Billy Budd, Foretopman,* written in 1891, found in tin box and published.

DEATH

Washington, D.C., Feb. 3. Woodrow Wilson, 28th President (*Dec. 28, 1856).

Major debut for "Rhapsody in Blue"

New York City, Feb. 12

The soaring clarinet that opens *Rhapsody in Blue* fittingly heralds the arrival of its young composer, George Gershwin. A jazz-hungry crowd fought its way into Aeolian Hall tonight for the rhapsody's debut at a concert billed as "an Experiment in Modern Music." Once inside they heard the first piece of jazz ever written for the concert hall, with bandleader Paul Whiteman at the helm and Gershwin at the piano. When it was over, America had a new piece of music unlike any other, and the 25-year-old Gershwin had passed from a promising songsmith to a famous composer. While a few critics were cool, Deems Taylor spoke for most when he praised a "genuine melodic gift and a piquant and individual harmonic sense."

Born George Gershovitz on the Lower East Side, Gershwin took to the piano when he was 12. At 15, he dropped out of school to earn

Master composer George Gershwin.

$15 a week as a song plugger in Tin Pan Alley and soon began writing songs. His first hit was *Swanee.* Recorded in 1920 by Al Jolson, it earned the composer $10,000 in royalties in that year alone. Gershwin is now teamed with brother Ira on a show to be mounted later this year – *Lady, Be Good!*

Senate override passes Army Bonus Bill

Washington, D.C., May 19

President Coolidge has lost the battle of the Soldiers' Bonus Bill. Today's Senate vote to override Coolidge's veto gives veterans the real victory, but Democrats also savor their triumph in this fight with the White House. The legislation allocates $2 billion in 20-year annuities for those Americans who served in the Great War. The Democratic Party has been in disarray of late. As comic Will Rogers puts it, "I am a member of no organized political party. I am a Democrat." But this time, party leaders united, swinging some liberal Republicans with them, to enact the bill.

"Summer, New England" (1912) by Maurice Prendergast. Despite his death on February 1, Prendergast's impact upon American art will continue to be felt. After studying in Paris (1891-94), the innovative painter returned home where he introduced Post-Impressionism to a responsive audience.

Watson's firm gets new name: I.B.M.

Endicott, New York, Feb. 14

The Computing-Tabulating-Recording Company, which produces machines that help compile such complex statistics as the United States Census, took a new name today: International Business Machines. Thomas J. Watson, president of the company, is successor to the company's founder, Herman Hollerith, who invented a method of making computations using a system of paper cards with holes punched in them. The I.B.M. machines are now used worldwide.

Crossword crazy

New York City, Nov. 24

The fans they chew their pencils,
The fans they beat their wives.
They look up words for dead birds,
They lead such puzzling lives!

So doggerel poet Gelett Burgess describes in the *New York World* today the behavior of crossword-puzzle addicts. Mania struck in mid-April when a new publishing firm called Plaza, formed by partners named Richard Simon and M. Lincoln Schuster, put out the first book of crosswords. Right off the bat, the puzzles were stumpers: the clue to three across in crossword No. 1 was "albumin from castor-oil bean." Five letters. Starts with "r." Well . . . ?

An ode to excess

United States

Have you pondered on the wonders that our world has wrought this year? Inventions with intentions good have set earth on its ear!

We have dryers that spin clothes dry, deadbolt locks crooks fail to pry, celluwipes called Kleenex for the folks who sneeze or cry.

Machines now roll the cones that scoops of ice cream call home, and ones that put the plate on plated things of chrome, and spirals on notebooks so papers do not roam.

There are marriage courses of which the co-eds tend to rave, and gizmos that give hair a permanent wave. We've got Wheaties, and writing in the sky – to advertise more things than people ought to buy.

Immigration is cut back

Newcomers to America wait patiently in the reception hall at Ellis Island.

Washington, D.C., May 26

Congress has passed the Johnson-Reed Act establishing more severe limitations and regulation of immigration than the Emergency Quota Act of 1921. Quotas based on the population of each ethnic group present in 1890 cut the maximum number of European immigrants to 164,000 per year, half of what was allowed under the Quota Act of 1921. All new entry visas must now be obtained abroad, but the most controversial piece of the new legislation completely bars Asian immigration to the United States. Despite rumors that Japan's ambassador may resign, the bill passed through the House and the Senate by an overwhelming majority. Senator George is quoted as saying, "East is East and West is West . . . Japan will recognize the full wisdom of our choice."

The quota, based on 2 percent of the 1890 census, will particularly affect East European immigrants, who have recently increased in number but were not a large contingent in 1890.

Racists across the nation have been advocating the legislation, and among its most diligent supporters was the Ku Klux Klan. "The United States once admitted everybody," claimed one advocate of the act, "but we found out that we were becoming an insane asylum."

An immigrant mother at Ellis Island keeps her children close beside her.

Teapot Dome is boiling

Washington, D.C., June 30

After two years of congressional investigations and protracted legal and judicial proceedings, it would appear that the Teapot Dome scandal has reached the boiling point. A federal grand jury today indicted Secretary of the Interior Albert B. Fall and two major oil company executives, Harry Sinclair and Edward L. Doheny. Fall's indictment charges him with the misappropriation of federal lands and oil reserves in Wyoming and California, while Sinclair and Doheny stand accused of bribery and conspiracy.

President Coolidge is singularly determined that Secretary Fall and his colleagues be brought to justice. In a blistering comment to his Secretary of Commerce, Herbert Hoover, the President said: "There are only three purgatories to which people can be assigned: to be damned by one's fellows; to be damned by the courts; to be damned in the next world. I want these men to get all three – without probation."

And that may happen. All three of the principal characters in the Teapot Dome scandal are now scheduled to face both civil and criminal charges (→ Nov. 1, 1929).

Justice blows the lid off the teapot.

Americans dominate Olympics in Paris

Paris, July 14

Paavo Nurmi, the Flying Finn, was the star of the show, but Americans won overall honors in the Olympic Games here. The United States scored 255 unofficial points to 166 for Finland, 85 for Britain, 31 for Sweden and 20 for France. After Charley Paddock was beaten at 100 meters by Harold Abrahams, a cigar-smoking, ale-drinking Briton in a major upset, America's field event stars took over and made up for some failures on the track. The coveted decathlon title went to an American, Harold Osborn, with Emerson Norton of Georgetown taking second place.

Before his death on December 13, American Federation of Labor president Samuel Gompers (right) met with Robert M. La Follette of Wisconsin, the presidential nominee of the League for Progressive Political Action. They have spent their lives fighting for the interests of the "common man."

Voters "Keep Cool With Coolidge"

"Calvin Coolidge" by J.E. Burgess.

Washington, D.C., Nov. 4

Since assuming the presidency when Harding died, Calvin Coolidge has won the hearts of many Americans with his wry wit and calm manner. Today, he won their votes for President with his laissez-faire policies and catchy campaign slogan, "Keep Cool With Coolidge." He and running mate Charles G. Dawes of Illinois scored a 382-136 electoral victory over Democratic challenger John Davis. Wisconsin Progressive Robert La Follette won six electoral votes.

Coolidge's radio address yesterday helped seal the triumph, as 30 million Americans listened. The election demonstrated the public's desire to let American business run its course with little government regulation. As Coolidge said when nominated, "America wouldn't be America if the people were shackled with government monopolies." The victory also represents the love affair the nation has with this man-of-midday-naps. Once, the President woke up from a snooze and asked, "Is the country still there?" Voters have chuckled over yarns like this: A White House guest once told Silent Cal she had a bet that she could make him say three words. "You lose," he told her.

For the first time, women won governors' races, Miriam "Ma" Ferguson in Texas and Nellie Taylor Ross in Wyoming.

Will Rogers displays wit and rope tricks

Elmira, New York, Oct. 1

Will Rogers, billed by his manager as America's Greatest Humorist, will be starting a six-month nationwide lecture tour here tonight. "If a smart man was going around the country doing this," he says, "it would be a lecture. If a politician was doing it, it would be a message." Rogers, 45, started out in the entertainment business doing rope tricks with Texas Jack's Wild West Circus. An Oklahoma native, he is proud of his Cherokee ancestry. "My folks didn't come on the Mayflower," he has said, "but they met the boat." Rogers ribs the government whenever possible, and insists that Congress has been writing his material for years.

Humble and folksy, Rogers endears himself with a unique native humor.

"Orphan Annie" gets home at Daily News

New York City, Aug. 5

Look out! That feisty, curly-haired heroine of Harold Gray's new comic strip may be a little orphan, but nothing can stop Annie! With her two true friends – her dog, Sandy, and her doll, Emily Marie – she's more than capable of handling both bratty kids and bossy grown-ups! The blank-eyed *Little Orphan Annie* began today in the *New York Daily News*.

Dawes Plan for war reparations adopted

London, Apr. 16

The committee headed by Chicago banker Charles G. Dawes has agreed on a plan to stabilize the German economy and allow the resumption of reparations to the Allied nations. As part of the Dawes Plan, Allied troops will leave the Ruhr Valley, which they occupied last year to force the Germans to keep up their payments. The German Reichsbank will be reorganized and placed under Allied supervision. The plan also sets a schedule for annual reparations payments, which will start at one billion gold marks and rise over a five-year period to 2.5 billion (→ June 7, 1929).

Moving pictures get new corporate image

Hollywood, California

As Hollywood steps up its export of manufactured fantasies five-fold and dominates the world's screens, the old "cottage industry" is evolving into a centralized and profitable product-marketing complex. Now Columbia Pictures, an outgrowth of the C.B.C./Film Sales Company, founded in 1920 by Harry and Jack Cohn with Joe Brandt, has incorporated. And Metro-Goldwyn-Mayer (M-G-M) has been established out of the Metro Corporation (formed in 1915), the Goldwyn Picture Corporation (1917) and Louis B. Mayer Pictures (1918) under the corporate control of Loew's, Inc.

President Coolidge throws out the first ball of the World Series. Once, during a nine-inning game, he uttered only four words: "What time is it?"

A TW-3 biplane, the first type to be produced by Consolidated Aircraft. Since the end of the war, innovations in aviation technology have enabled adventurous pilots to set many records, such as the one on September 28, when three army planes circled the globe in a flight time of 363 hours.

1925

Coolidge

Wyoming, Jan. 5. Mrs. Nellie Taylor Ross becomes first woman in nation to complete her late husband's term as Governor.

New York City, Jan. 8. Igor Stravinsky makes American debut, leading New York Philharmonic in program of his own works.

Chicago, Jan. 24. First total eclipse of sun in 300 years visible in Northeast and Great Lakes region.

Washington, D.C., Feb. 27. Glacier Bay National Monument, one of more accessible natural tourist attractions in Alaska, established by presidential proclamation.

Washington, D.C., March 3. House of Representatives approves resolution of adherence to World Court at The Hague.

Tennessee, March 13. Governor signs law forbidding teaching of theory of evolution in state's public school system, or any other theory denying creationism (→ July 26).

Greenwood, Mississippi, March 14. Local ministers and businessmen lead mob in lynching of two Negroes (→ Aug. 8).

Midcontinental United States, March 28. At least 800 people are killed by series of tornadoes.

New York City, Apr. 1. Dillon, Read & Co. acquires Dodge Brothers automobile company for $146 million, largest single cash transaction to date.

Osceola, Louisiana, Apr. 18. Minister, guilty of "preaching equality," is flogged and shot by mob.

New York City, Apr. 26. Pulitzer Prizes won by Edna Ferber for *So Big* and poet Edwin Arlington Robinson for *The Man Who Died Twice*.

Tallahassee, Florida, May 13. State legislature passes bill requiring daily Bible readings in all public schools.

Pittsburgh, Oct. 15. Pirates defeat Washington Senators in World Series, four games to three.

United States. Football great Red Grange quits college for pro football after signing contract with Chicago Bears.

New York City. Sinclair Lewis's *Arrowsmith* is published.

"The business of America is business"

Lucky Strike means fine tobacco.

Washington, D.C., Jan. 17

President Calvin Coolidge is a man for the times. "The business of America," he said today in a speech, "is business." And is anyone likely to disagree?

Since the 1921 recession, American industry has been humming along with the precision of a Swiss watch. Just ask Henry Ford, whose assembly lines churn out an automobile every 10 seconds. "Machinery," Ford has declared, "is the modern Messiah." But many people seem to be praying to the wizard of Detroit himself. Industrial scholars around the world are studying that special brand of scientific management that they call "Fordisimus." And the experts who run the modern factory pay attention, too, so they copy his system of high wages, low prices and an extensive division of labor. With 40 percent of American workers earning more than $2,000 a year, mass-produced commodities are provided with a ready-made mass market.

Two years ago, sociologists determined that half of the working class of "Middletown" America owned cars. Those who are still reluctant to purchase, even on credit, are subjected to an ever-growing swarm of salesmen. One-quarter of the way into the 20th century, advertisers are spending $1 billion a year trying to persuade Americans their social lives will collapse unless they use the latest deodorant, newest mouthwash, most fashionable soap or the trendiest cigarette that is being touted (→ Jan. 7, 1928).

Adman says Jesus was supersalesman

New York City

Advertising mogul Bruce Barton should have titled his book *The Man Nobody Will Recognize* instead of *The Man Nobody Knows*. The man is none other than Jesus Christ, though he's not the Son of God known to most readers. The author believes Jesus was a first-class salesman and offers a unique – or blasphemous – account of his life to prove it. According to Barton, Jesus should be seen as a go-getter who boldly "picked up 12 men from the bottom ranks of business and forged them into an organization that conquered the world." Moreover, this forerunner of today's modern hotshots charmed the pants off a world of skeptics who weren't buying his bill of goods, becoming the "most popular dinner guest in Jerusalem." How did he do it? Easy, says the adman author: by making headlines, Jesus "recognized the basic principle that all good advertising is news."

Unbeaten "Irish" win at Rose Bowl

Rockne (left) with the team captain.

Pasadena, Calif., Jan. 1.

Knute Rockne, who lifted Notre Dame from obscurity to football greatness, saw his "Fighting Irish" win the biggest prize of all by upsetting Stanford, 27-10, in the Rose Bowl today. Rockne was a star player for Notre Dame before taking over the coaching-job. His 1924 team went through the season without a defeat, helped by the forward pass, which he perfected.

"Sheik With Sheba" magazine cover. With an increase in "petting parties," a judge has condemned the auto as "a house of prostitution on wheels."

Aimee turns up; says she was abducted

Aimee Semple McPherson saves souls with a flair found in few preachers.

Douglas, Arizona, June 24

Evangelist Aimee Semple McPherson stumbled into the Calumet Hospital yesterday, overjoyed to be free of the abductors whom she said held her prisoner for the past five weeks. Mrs. McPherson, founder of the Angelus Temple in Los Angeles and noted for her dramatic revival meetings, disappeared while on a beach outing May 18. Today she told a stirring tale, which she reenacted for photographers. The abductors bagged her in blankets, she said, hid her in a secluded home and bound her hand and foot. She said eventually she broke her bonds and leaped out a window. Reporters said her clothes were quite neat despite her travails (→ 1926).

Thrill killers Leopold, Loeb serve for life

Joliet, Illinois, Jan. 1

Richard Loeb and Nathan Leopold spent the first of all their remaining New Years behind the bars of Joliet prison where they were sentenced to life terms last September for the "thrill killing" of 14-year-old Bobby Franks. In a crime that shocked the world, the two wealthy University of Chicago students said they murdered Franks for "the sport" of it. They were defended by master lawyer Clarence Darrow. By citing the theories of Sigmund Freud, a legal "first," he saved their lives, persuasively arguing that they should not be held responsible because they were emotionally deranged at the time of the crime.

Thrill killers Richard Loeb (left) and Nathan Leopold, serving life terms for what they say started as a lark.

Nine teams launch basketball league

New York City

It took a lot of compromise, but nine successful professional teams from the East and Midwest finally agreed to form the American Basketball League, the first circuit to go beyond regional limits. The two-hand dribble, which isn't used in the Midwest, was dropped. Only the Celtics, who are based in New York, failed to join the talented teams that signed up for the league. The Boston Whirlwinds dropped out early. Cleveland won the title.

Yale students toss Frisbie pie plates

New Haven, Connecticut

Has Yale University introduced a course in aeronautics? Not exactly, but undergraduates are enriching their lunches and dinners at the college cafeteria by spinning tin pie plates with stunning accuracy. The pie plates, which normally hold pies baked by the Frisbie Baking Company of Bridgeport, Connecticut, become flying objects when the young men send them sailing neatly across the dining hall tables.

Dogs save Nome after 650-mile trip

Nome, Alaska, Feb. 2

A stout-hearted team of Siberian huskies has won the "race of mercy," to deliver antitoxin to diphtheria-threatened Nome. Final relay driver Gunnar Kasson pushed through a blizzard so fierce that he often could not see the trail. "So I gave Balto, my lead dog, his head and trusted to him," Kasson said. "He never faltered. Balto led. The credit is his." The relay teams covered 650 miles, beating the nine-day record by three and a half days.

Chrysler founded; sells $1,500 car

Detroit, Mich., June 6

With its production of a six-cylinder $1,500 car, the new Chrysler Company has a job on its hands. Of more than 1,000 would-be auto makers since 1905, only 15 survive. While output is up since 1920, most folks want a cheaper ride. But Walter Chrysler is not offering a Ford-type Tin Lizzy. This former president of Buick and vice president of General Motors has a class car. It remains to be seen if the public will spend this kind of money.

February 21. First cover of "The New Yorker," by Rea Irvin, captures the intended level of sophistication of its writing and humor.

At Nashville radio, the "Barn Dance"

Nashville, Tenn., Nov. 28

To some, it is country music; to others, it's hillbilly. Whatever it is, Nashville radio station WSM is now airing it on a weekly program, *Barn Dance*. Run by announcer-manager George Hay, the first hour-long effort featured "Uncle" Jimmy Thompson, an 80-year-old fiddler who protested at the end, "Shucks, a man don't get warmed up in an hour!" He says he knows 1,000 tunes and wants to play them all. Hay has been deluged with favorable mail. Aiming at down-to-earth sounds, he plans to put on groups like The Clod Hoppers and the Possum Hunters.

A frenzy of land-buying in sunny Florida

Coral Gables, Fla., August

Florida's land boom is at the frenzy stage with the offering by promoter George Merrick of a record $75 million worth of buildings, 1,000 of them, in French, Dutch, Venetian and Chinese styles, priced at $20,000 to $100,000. The sun craze has swollen Florida's population past a million and caused a housing shortage, with tourists as well as speculators camping out along hundreds of miles of roads. Citrus groves have been devoured to provide 20 million 50-foot building lots for sale in a gold-rush-style land hysteria. Some who sold one or two years ago are now buying back, sometimes at staggering multiples of what they paid.

The lure of Florida leaves a few wealthy and too many the proud owners of wet but worthless land.

Big Bill Tilden wins sixth straight title

New York City, Sept. 2.

"Big Bill" Tilden has done it again. The master tactician of tennis, with his cannonball serve, won the national championship for the sixth consecutive time today. In addition, he led the United States to the Davis Cup championship, also for a record sixth time. There were few who thought that Tilden, who won his first national title in 1920 at the age of 27, could come close to duplicating the perfection of his 1924 triumph, when he dispatched William Johnston in 58 minutes. Yet the sheer wizardry of Tilden's strokes remained constant through a smashing 1925 season.

The nattily dressed William Tilden.

Evolution on trial: Scopes convicted

Dayton, Tennessee, July 26

Five days after concluding his role in the prosecution at the trial of John Scopes for teaching the theory of evolution, William Jennings Bryan is dead of a cerebral hemorrhage. The so-called trial of the century was indeed that. Clarence Darrow led the defense. Bryan was asked to serve for the prosecution because of his crusade against evolution. The trial opened on July 10 in a carnival atmosphere. On July 16, people finally heard the oratory they expected. Bryan's first speech enthralled the crowd, which gave him a long ovation. Dudley Field Malone responded for the defense. Bryan even told Malone, "That was the greatest speech I ever heard."

The climax came when Bryan, "the Great Commoner," took the stand. Darrow called him as an expert witness on the Bible. It was not Bryan's best moment. Questioned by Darrow, he showed an ignorance of the biblical criticism he had so long been damning. The most shocking moments came as Bryan admitted to doubts that Joshua made the sun stand still – since the earth moves – and argued that the biblical creation in six days did not mean six 24-hour days. Scopes was convicted, but the Darrow grilling left Bryan a broken man. As a reporter said, "Darrow never spared him. It was masterful, but it was pitiful."

Bryan for the prosecution.

Darrow for the defense.

Clarence Darrow rests in the heat, but he remains riveted to the proceedings.

Fitzgerald, Dreiser expose social climbers

United States

If the year 1922 was a high point in world literature, 1925 belongs to the United States. Start with F. Scott Fitzgerald. Who would have guessed the glamor boy of American literature would ripen into the sure-handed artificer of *The Great Gatsby*, an utterly splendid work. Its hero, Jay Gatsby (born Gatz), has risen mysteriously, and probably illegally, from dull poverty to gleaming wealth. At his Long Island palace – it has "a marble swimming pool, and more than 40 acres of lawn and garden" – Gatsby gives parties that are costly pretexts for winning back the girl of his dreams, a Louisville belle whose brutish husband keeps low-class mistresses

and a stable of polo ponies.

Social climbing is also the topic of Theodore Dreiser's new novel, *An American Tragedy*. Based on an actual homicide, it tells of a poor boy, Clyde Griffiths, poised on the brink of big money and love until a dark episode from his past threatens to ruin all. His dream concludes on the same note intoned this year by T.S. Eliot's poem, *The Hollow Men*:

This is the way the world ends
Not with a bang but a whimper.

There's also no room for sentimentality in the gibes of expatriate Gertrude Stein. In *The Making of Americans*, she declares: "A rose is a rose is a rose." So much for "a rose by any other name . . . "

"Both Members of This Club" (1909) by George W. Bellows is one of many powerful works on boxing by the master realist, who died January 8.

Klan marches in capital

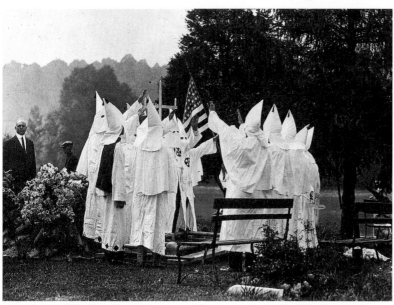

Members of the Ku Klux Klan assemble in a park in Washington, D.C.

Washington, D.C., Aug. 8

In white robes and conical caps, more than 40,000 members of the Ku Klux Klan marched through the streets of the capital today, many waving American flags. Over 200,000 spectators watched the gigantic parade, which ended at the foot of the Washington Monument. The klansmen evidently felt safety in numbers, since they did not wear the masks that they traditionally use to conceal their identities. Their costumes, however, may have provided them with some protection from the elements; it was dark and raining by the time all the marchers made it to the monument. The rain forced the white supremacist mob to cancel the massive ceremony it had planned, and to refrain from burning an 80-foot cross.

The Klan, founded in Tennessee in 1865, has carried on a reign of terror against Negroes ever since. For instance, before the 1868 election in Louisiana, it conducted "Negro hunts," murdered Republicans and left close to 500 dead. The Klan was investigated by Congress in 1871, but legislation passed against it did not last. A KKK revival that began in 1920 has swelled membership to over four million (→ Nov. 24).

Klan leader gets life term in rape death

A Grand Goblin in the night.

Noblesville, Ind., Nov. 24

D.C. Stephenson, Grand Dragon of the Indiana Realm of the Ku Klux Klan, was sentenced to life in prison today for the crimes of assault, rape and kidnapping. A sensational trial brought to light details of the capture of a young Indianapolis woman named Madge Oberholtzer, and her subsequent rape and beatings at the hands of Stephenson. Miss Oberholtzer lived just long enough to provide testimony against the Klan chief. While there has never been any evidence linking the group to the case, those who have observed the Klan don't think it is going to help the public's perception of it.

"Big Parade" brings biggest gross yet

An excited crowd packs the sidewalk in front of the Astor Theatre in New York City, awaiting show time for "The Big Parade," which has grossed $22 million.

Hollywood, California

Directed by King Vidor, *The Big Parade*, an impassioned portrait of the ordinary American caught up in war, is drawing immense audiences and has already become the biggest-grossing film ever, at $22 million. Its star, John Gilbert, has achieved worldwide popularity. M-G-M has imported a Swedish star, Greta Garbo, who came with her favorite director and mentor, Mauritz Stiller. Lon Chaney stars this year in *The Phantom of the Opera* and comedian Buster Keaton gets a lot of laughs in *Go West*. Joseph Schenck of United Artists (founded in 1919 by Charlie Chaplin, D.W. Griffith, Mary Pickford and Douglas Fairbanks) has hired a chorus girl named Lucille Le Sueur, who has been renamed Joan Crawford as a result of a fan magazine contest. An extra in *The Birth of a Nation* and a director since 1917, 30-year-old John Ford, who has transferred from Universal to Fox, shows great promise as a director. A favorite is *The Iron Horse*, which he turned out last year. William Fox has bought 450 acres on Pico Boulevard as a location ranch for Tom Mix westerns and other films, and he plans the world's largest stage with a powerhouse and generators providing enough power for a city of 60,000. Fox continues to speak out against censorship of motion pictures in the United States.

Billy Mitchell guilty

Washington, D.C., Dec. 17

Colonel William "Billy" Mitchell is guilty. In a tense courtroom, the 56-year-old champion of air power seemed relaxed as an army court-martial today suspended him for five years, finding him guilty of insubordination. The verdict follows his test sinkings of target battleships by airplanes. The colonel accused his superiors of "incompetency, criminal negligence and almost treasonable administration of national defense." But prosecuting officers branded him a "charlatan and demagogue."

Charlie Chaplin elicits laughs and tears as America's favorite little tramp in "The Gold Rush."

Washington, D.C., Feb. 26. President Coolidge signs revenue act reducing income and inheritance taxes.

Washington, D.C., Apr. 29. United States and France sign agreement reducing French war debt.

New York City, May 5. Sinclair Lewis rejects Pulitzer Prize for *Arrowsmith*, declaring that such recognition undermines writing profession.

Washington, D.C., May 20. Congress passes Air Commerce Act, giving Commerce Department control over licensing of aircraft and pilots.

United States, July 4. On America's 150th birthday, Sherwood Anderson writes, "The machine (has caused) the herding of men into towns and cities ... Minds began to be standardized as were the clothes men wore."

Washington, D.C., July 5. Government report indicates that one in every six Americans owns an automobile.

Lackawanna, New York, July 26. Sanctuary of Our Lady of Victory Church is first Roman Catholic basilica in nation.

New York City, Aug. 27. Channel swimmer Gertrude Ederle almost crushed by well-wishers.

Chicago, Sept. 15. "Jelly Roll" Morton and "Red Hot Peppers" hold recording session for RCA.

New York City, Oct. 10. St. Louis Cardinals defeat New York Yankees in World Series, four games to three.

Washington, D.C., Oct. 25. Supreme Court, in Myers v. United States, declares 1867 Tenure of Office Act unconstitutional, giving presidents right to dismiss executive officers without senatorial consent.

United States. Aimee Semple McPherson's reputation suffers when it is suspected that her so-called kidnapping was a romantic interlude.

New York City. Book-of-the-Month Club founded.

New York City. H.L. Mencken's *Notes on Democracy* published.

New York City. *The Theory of the Gene,* published by Thomas Hunt Morgan, provides basis of genetic research.

Goddard launches first liquid fuel rocket

Robert Goddard beside the rocket he has fired into the atmosphere.

Auburn, Mass., March 16

Will it ever be possible for mankind to leave the planet Earth? A new invention of the Massachusetts physicist Robert H. Goddard has caused some to speculate in that direction. The 44-year-old professor at Clark University has developed a liquid fuel rocket that soared high into the atmosphere. Interested in high-altitude flight since he was a teenager, Goddard is the author of *A Method of Reaching Extreme Altitudes*, a report that chronicles the experiments he has conducted involving solid-propellant rocket motors. Goddard's efforts and the theories that he has developed have laid the groundwork for a whole new field of study, one that some scientists think could have great potential in two areas, transportation and warfare.

Ford's work week: 40 hours, 5 days

Detroit, Michigan, Sept. 25

Some workers at the Ford factory are going on a 40-hour, five-day week, working less for the same pay than they received before. The plan, officially announced today, is based on ideas that Henry Ford outlined more than 10 years ago. The 40-hour week is going to help spread the work in these times of overproduction. The unions have praised it, but it's being condemned by some industrialists, who seem quite alarmed about Ford's pioneering pay of $6 a day.

Hall-Mills acquittal

New Jersey, Dec. 3

Mrs. Frances Hall was found not guilty today in the murder of her husband, the Rev. Edward Hall, and his paramour, Mrs. Eleanor Mills. Her two brothers were also absolved in New Jersey's longest, costliest trial. The crime took place at an abandoned farm four years ago, but Mrs. Hall was only recently accused after the *Daily Mirror* led a crusade against her. The public avidly followed the case, read the Hall-Mills love letters and was thrilled by the words of a dying pig farmer who implicated Mrs. Hall.

Mae West busted for moving navel

New York City, Apr. 26

Tantalizing, scintillating, sinful seductress. Ooo La La Lady of the Stage. Actress-playwright Mae West has been put under arrest. Her play, *Sex*, had the audiences squirming in their seats and the Society for the Suppression of Vice hot on her trail. The society's pressure got the police to close down the popular show and bust West for "corrupting the morals of youth." The play stars the author as a prostitute, swinging her hips and licking her lips. An undercover cop has said that the star "moved her navel up and down and from right to left" in a belly dance. His testimony may lead to her conviction and a jail sentence. No word as to whether she'd appeal (→ Apr. 19, 1927).

As the Roaring 20s roar on, the Charleston sets the style of the era. Developed in Charleston, South Carolina, the steps were first noted at an all-Negro review in New York in 1923. With turned-in toes, syncopated arms and flying legs, the dance even draws the older set, who do it in 4/4 time.

From Hemingway, "The Sun Also Rises"

Hemingway, expatriate in Paris.

New York City

Tales of Americans kicking up their heels in the bars and cafes of Europe have been confirmed in *The Sun Also Rises,* the first novel by Ernest Hemingway, 27. A native of Illinois who was wounded in Italy during the war, Hemingway has been in Paris since 1921 and writes for the *Toronto Star.* His *In Our Time*, a story collection, appeared last year. *The Sun*, narrated by a hard-boiled reporter wary of "all frank and simple people," stars some hell-raising young folks, mostly Yanks. Quoting Gertrude Stein in an epigraph, Hemingway writes of them, "You are all a lost generation."

"You are all a lost generation?"

United States

Vanity Fair calls them "flaming youth." And Ernest Hemingway writes of a "lost generation." But are today's young Americans truly very different from those who have gone before? Yes – and no. No previous generation saw the kind of destruction this one saw in the Great War, an experience that can crush all innocence. No previous generation has seen a machine age that renders minds as "standardized as the clothes men wore," as Sherwood Anderson writes. What generation has seen so many of its parents brazenly break the law as they flout the Prohibition Amendment? And what generation has had such privileges, from the ownership of automobiles where lovemaking proceeds unseen, to pocketing so much spending money to afford so many dreams? These youths are celebrated in the art of John Held Jr. and the words of F. Scott Fitzgerald, who wrote this year, "The parties were bigger. The pace was faster . . . morals looser." But then, doesn't every generation feel it is somehow changing the world?

John Held Jr.'s cover illustrations for "Life" magazine have made him one of the most popular artists of the day. A full-time cartoonist since the age of 16, Held has achieved tremendous fame for his simple, lively portrayals of life in the Jazz Age. When not illustrating, the versatile artist draws newspaper comic strips, including, "Merely Margie, an Awfully Sweet Girl."

Byrd and Bennett fly over North Pole

Kings Bay, Spitsbergen, May 9

Byrd and Bennett have reached the North Pole. The daring explorer Richard E. Byrd and his pilot, Floyd Bennett, returned here to an emotional reception today. Threatened by frozen fingers and engine oil leaks only 60 miles from their objective, the privately financed expedition circled the pole several times in brilliant sunlight on a flight that lasted 15 hours and 51 minutes. Their observations verify America's claim to the pole that was announced 17 years ago by Admiral Robert E. Peary and his Negro assistant, Matthew Henson.

NBC is incorporated

New York City, Oct. 9

The National Broadcasting Company, the first radio chain in the United States and a subsidiary of the Radio Corporation of America, was incorporated today. David Sarnoff, the president of NBC, first impressed RCA directors with the possibilities of radio with his blow-by-blow coverage of the Dempsey-Carpentier fight in 1921. Sarnoff, a Russian immigrant who started at RCA as an office boy, has promoted the radio business for several years. He was largely responsible for the $83 million in radio set sales RCA chalked up from 1921 to 1924.

"Mother and Child" (1905) by Mary Cassatt. The Impressionist painter's career was prematurely ended in 1914 because of failing eyesight. She died on June 14.

U.S. woman swims the English Channel

Gertrude Ederle proves that neither gender nor age need be a hindrance.

Dover, England, Aug. 6

"It had to be done, and I did it," said Gertrude Ederle, the plucky little New Yorker, after she completed her swim across the English Channel today. She thus became the first woman to accomplish the feat and easily broke the best record made by any male cross-channel swimmer. Her time was 14 hours 31 minutes. The 19-year-old Miss Ederle twice ignored the advice of her coach to come out of the water, but her father and sister cheered her on. "I am doing it for Mommy," she told them. The channel was first crossed by a swimmer in 1911 (→ 27).

"Yellow Calla" (1926) by Georgia O'Keeffe. The Wisconsin artist's work with flowers and bones is hailed as unique for the variety of emotive responses that it evokes.

Valentino is dead; long live the Sheik

"Ben Hur," "Don Juan" with musical sound, and Greta Garbo

Valentino's striking good looks made him America's leading screen lover.

Improved technology allows movie makers to leave the studio and create scenes such as the chariot race in M-G-M's "Ben Hur," featuring Ramon Novarro.

John Barrymore, starring in the big hit from Warner Bros., "Don Juan."

Hollywood, Calif., September

He died on August 23, at the age of 31, the darkly handsome Rudolph Valentino, who brought a sense of mysterious eroticism and fulfillment of dreams to the screen in movies such as *Blood and Sand*, *Monsieur Beaucaire*, *The Eagle*, and *The Son of the Sheik*. His sudden death, due to a perforated ulcer, caused mass hysteria among female fans. Thousands lined the streets at his funeral, where stars such as Pola Negri and Marion Kay broke down, sobbing loudly. A picture of Valentino meeting Caruso in heaven is being widely circulated.

Hollywood, Calif., October

More than 14,500 movie houses show 400 films a year, with the movies becoming America's favorite entertainment, ever changing and developing. Ramon Novarro plays the title role in *Ben-Hur*, the most expensive film ever made. *The Black Pirate*, with Douglas Fairbanks, uses Technicolor film with great success. *Don Juan*, with John Barrymore, just opened and is the first motion picture with a synchronized musical score, produced by a phonograph. Warner Bros., which accomplished this in association with Vitaphone, talks of a

"sound era." Fox has responded with Movietone, a sound-on-film process developed in association with General Electric. Stars are paid ever more money. M-G-M has raised Greta Garbo's salary from $550 to $5,000 a week, based on her first American film, *The Torrent*. Even football star Red Grange has been paid $300,000 for his role in *One Minute to Play*.

Interesting new releases include *Variety* from Paramount, starring Emil Jannings; *What Price Glory?* from Fox, starring Victor McLaglen and Edmund Lowe, and *The Strong Man*, with Harry Langdon

playing the "dumb clown," directed by the inventive Frank Capra. Mary Pickford, still the "essence of America," is starring in *Sparrows*.

The personality cult growing up around the movies has reached immense proportions. Valentino was a good example of this. So is Garbo. Charlie Chaplin is mobbed if he so much as ventures into the street (last year's *The Gold Rush* is still enjoying great success). And coming next year, there's *It*, with newcomer Clara Bow, the "It Girl" who offers "the same as before but more of it showing" and "a little more available."

U.S. Marshal Matheus directs the destruction of some $300,000 worth of imported liquors and wines seized from a wholesale house in Philadelphia. Similar scenes are taking place from one end of the country to the other.

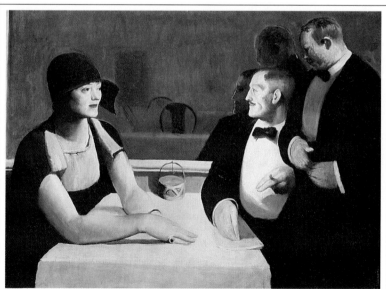

"Mr. & Mrs. Chester Dale Dining Out" (c. 1926) by Guy Pene Dubois, a Brooklyn-born painter of people of fashion who studied under Robert Henri.

Television introduced to American public

New York City, Apr. 7

The first public demonstration in America of the new invention television has shown its potential not only as an entertainment medium, but as a political tool. The first image to appear in this demonstration was that of Secretary of Commerce Herbert Hoover. A speech that Hoover was delivering in Washington was seen by a group of bankers and investors here in New York. The demonstration was set up by American Telephone and Telegraph's president, Walter Gifford, to develop interest in the remarkable invention.

Television has developed from the work of several scientists and engineers, both here and abroad. The basis of the new device is something called a cathode ray tube, which uses a beam of electricity to illuminate a phosphorous-coated screen. A crude television system was built in 1923 by the Russian-American scientist Vladimir Zworykin, who based his experiments on the work of Campbell Swinton, a British scientist, the Russian scientist Boris Rosing, and the theories of the German Albert Einstein. The system was improved upon by Scottish inventor John L. Baird, who last year produced clear images on his tube. Baird predicts that television will become a household appliance.

Hays code defines Hollywood do's, don'ts

Hollywood, California

Hollywood moguls created the Motion Pictures Producers and Distributors of America five years ago to improve the image of the industry after widely publicized scandals and pressure to create some form of film censorship. The organization, headed by Will H. Hays, is working out a code of "good taste." Regulations of the Hays Office include prohibition of "any licentious or suggestive nudity," "miscegenation," "ridicule of clergy," "inference of sexual perversion," "indecent or undue exposure" and "excessive and lustful kissing." The code urges care with themes such as "illegal drug traffic," and "justified revenge in modern times," but sex seems to be more dangerous than violence since "actual hangings or electrocutions . . . brutality and possibly gruesomenesss" may be shown "within the careful limits of good taste."

Many movie makers have found a way around the regulations: They give the public what it wants, namely sex, sin and corruption, but see to it that offenders are punished in the last 10 minutes of the movie. Cecil B. De Mille has become a master at this.

U.S. Postmaster Will Hays warns Hollywood that America will not accept any material that is considered licentious, sexually perverted or blasphemous.

Pan American wins Cuba airmail route

Key West, Florida, Oct. 19

The first airmail to Havana has gone through, just hours before the U.S. government contract deadline. A fledgling Pan American Airways, incorporated on March 8, did the job by flying seven mailbags from Key West in a floatplane rented from barnstorming pilot Cy Caldwell. Pan American president J.T. Trippe won the contract and control of Pan American because Cuban President Gerardo Machado gave him exclusive landing rights. Trippe, 28, is backed by Yale classmates, including Cornelius Vanderbilt and "Sonny" Whitney.

Paley founds CBS

New York City, Sept. 26

William S. Paley has taken over United Independent Broadcasters, a small, money-losing radio network, and renamed it the Columbia Broadcasting System. He paid $503,000 for 50.3 percent of the classical music network. The deal was closed yesterday and Paley became president today. A 28-year-old son of a Russian immigrant, Paley signed a radio advertising contract for his father's cigar business last year. Since then, he has been hankering to buy a small radio network. He reportedly spent half his savings on the company.

The "Better Buick" is but one of a new breed of automobiles that stresses a combination of design, price and function in a market that is growing more competitive.

Al Capone makes fortune in rackets

Chicago

Education, hard work and a machine gun can work wonders. Take Al Capone. After an on-the-job stint with Brooklyn's Five Points Ring, he moved to Chicago, where he arrived with the family Bible in hand, and impressively blasted his way to the top of a 700-man organization. As a result, "Scarface" now controls most of the country's bootlegging. His profits this year alone amounted to $100 million in the liquor trade, $30 million in the protection business, $25 million in gambling, and $10 million in vice and sundry rackets (→ Feb. 14, 1929).

Marines sent south

Washington, D.C.

The United States has landed 2,000 marines in Nicaragua in an effort to bolster the government of Conservative Adolfo Diaz. Washington had withdrawn its troops in 1925, but it was forced to intervene again last year in response to a Liberal revolt led by General Augusto Cesar Sandino, a fervent foe of an American presence in Nicaragua. Sandino's insurrection quickly became a full-scale civil war. The Liberals, backed by Mexico, set up their own government, under Juan Sacasa, on the east coast (→ Jan. 2, 1932).

Strike up the brand

Dear John,

Can you pick us up a few things at the store? We need some Sanka, Pet milk, Libby's tomato soup, Milky Way candy bars, Welch's grape jelly, Popsicles, Borden's homogenized milk, Hostess cakes, B&M Brick Oven baked beans, A&W root beer, Lenders bagels, Wesson oil and some Gerber's baby food. Uh, sorry, forgot to tell you. I'm expecting. And keeping that in mind, since you'll be doing more of the cooking around here, can you pick up an electric eggbeater, an automatic potato peeler, a wall-mounted can opener, a G.E. refrigerator and a Conover electric dishwasher? Thanks, dear!

Love, Mary.

Lucky Lindy hops over the Atlantic

Paris, May 21

All Paris seemed fixed upon the sky tonight, as vast throngs at Le Bourget Field strained to hear the faint hum that would signal triumph for Charles A. Lindbergh. Then, just as hope was fading, the aviator's sleek, silver-gray monoplane, which had flown 3,600 miles, from New York in 33 and a half hours, descended quietly, almost magically onto a distant runway at 10:24, setting off a hysterical rush by the cheering French. "Well, I made it," said the quiet Midwesterner as he was mobbed and carried off by the ecstatic crowd.

Lindbergh, just 25, barely got his plane off the ground early yesterday at Roosevelt Field, Long Island. The Spirit of St. Louis staggered down the runway with a huge fuel load, its engine snarling and its wings straining for lift. Once aloft, Lindy headed for Newfoundland, then out to sea, where he battled sleet, fog and exhaustion for 1,000 miles. Tonight, even Lindbergh, who navigated by dead reckoning, was astonished as he soared over the Irish coast, right on course.

The lanky flier will win a hotly contested $25,000 prize for the non-stop flight but seems surprised by the worldwide adulation his feat is generating. His main goal, he has said, is to further aviation.

Charles A. Lindbergh, son of a Minnesota congressman, developed his interest in flying during his years as a student at the University of Wisconsin. And after buying an old biplane, he began earning a living as a stunt-show pilot.

Lindbergh is hailed by adoring public

New York City

America has always loved its heroes, but nothing matches the adulation aimed at Charles Lindbergh this year. The aviator had hoped to explore Europe after reaching Paris, but President Coolidge would have none of it and sent a navy cruiser to fetch him. From a triumphant return to Washington to a parade down Broadway (featuring 1,800 tons of ticker tape) and on to a whirlwind 48-city tour in his Spirit of St. Louis, he has been feted by dignitaries and hounded by the press. "Lindbergh . . . has shown us that we are not rotten at the core," writes May B. Mullett in *American* magazine, "but morally sound and sweet and good."

Returning from Paris, the young, somewhat gawky pilot receives a hero's welcome in New York City. As tens of thousands line the streets of Manhattan for a glimpse of him, "Lindy" shows traces of the stoicism masking the dogged tenacity that helped carry him across the vast expanse of ocean.

Sacco and Vanzetti die

For the accused, the tragedy is over.

Dedham, Mass., Aug. 23

While sympathy demonstrations were being staged across the world, the switch was thrown here today, executing Nicola Sacco and Bartolomeo Vanzetti. The two Italian radicals were convicted in 1921 for the crimes of murder and theft in the 1920 robbery of a South Brain-tree, Massachusetts, shoe factory. The trial received national attention and many liberals and labor groups rallied to support the defendants. Many still believe that the evidence against Sacco and Vanzetti was slim and that the conviction and sentence were politically motivated. Both men were known as anarchists and draft evaders. Judge Webster Thayer, who presided at the trial, was recently quoted as saying of Vanzetti, "This man, although he may not actually have committed a crime . . . is . . . the enemy of our existing institutions . . . The defendant's ideals are cognate with crime."

Before his execution, Bartolomeo Vanzetti stated, "I am innocent. I am suffering because I am a radical . . . an Italian . . . "

The execution was put off while a committee named by the Governor investigated the trial. The committee upheld the court decision, saying that judicial procedure had been correct. A new trial was denied and the men were executed.

Tunney retains title after long count

Chicago, Sept. 22

Jack Dempsey was hardly the fighting machine that he was when he first fought Gene Tunney a year ago and yet – despite easy living - he almost dethroned the former marine as heavyweight champion today. But the Manassa Mauler made a fundamental mistake: He ignored the rule that he should go to a neutral corner once Tunney was down in the seventh, and the extra five or six seconds of the count enabled Gene to recover. The 104,943 people jamming Soldiers Field were shocked into silence as Tunney's knees crumpled after Dempsey's crushing left to the jaw. No one knows just how many times Dempsey hit Tunney on the way down, but it was the first time Gene has been decked in his life.

Both men had been warned that a boxer scoring a knockdown must retire to the farther neutral corner. Instead, Dempsey hovered over Tunney as he had with other floored rivals. The referee tried to tug Dempsey away, then started counting. After the "long count," Tunney recovered well enough to win the round on points. At the earlier title fight in Philadelphia, 120,757 people watched in the rain as Tunney took a 10-round decision. He battered Dempsey through every round and the beaten champ hardly looked like the young upstart who had pounded Jess Willard into a four-round defeat in 1919.

Gene Tunney is downed by Jack Dempsey. As the ref's count begins, so too does a lingering controversy.

Babe swats 60th homer

The "Sultan of Swat" watches No. 60 as he sails into the record books.

New York City, Sept. 30.

The crack of the bat was audible throughout Yankee Stadium today and 10,000 fans there knew that the moment had arrived. As the ball headed for the rightfield bleachers, they were on their feet, screaming for their hero, George Herman Ruth. The Babe had fulfilled their earnest wish, smacking his 60th homer of the season, a feat never before accomplished. Who cares that some people deride Babe Ruth as a boozer and glutton. He is also the consummate batter and the name of Thomas Jonathan Walton Zachary of the Washington Senators will go down in history as the man who served up the historic pitch – fast, low and inside. Ruth's wallop, with one on and the score tied in the eighth, also enabled the Yanks to defeat the Washington Senators, 4 to 2.

Before he crossed the plate after walloping homer No. 60, the portly Yankee slugger jogged around the bases in almost regal style. And as he did, he carefully stomped on each sack, as if he were punctuating the feat officially.

The historic homer was a tribute to Colonel Jake Ruppert, Yankee owner, who had the foresight to buy Ruth from the financially troubled Boston Red Sox for $125,000. He transformed Ruth from a stellar pitcher – he once hurled 29 2/3 scoreless innings – into a slugging outfielder. In 1920, his first year with the Yanks, Ruth lofted 54 homers and was paid $20,000. He soon became a folk hero, hitting a record 59 homers in 1921. Although ill much of 1925, he still rapped out 25 homers.

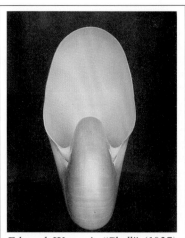

Edward Weston's "Shell" (1927), a study in detail and simplicity.

General Motors has largest dividend

Detroit, Mich., Nov. 10

General Motors announced today that it will distribute an extra $2.60 per share – the largest dividend in American history – making the total distribution to shareholders more than $65 million. The company has been offering a $1.25 regular quarterly dividend for each share of outstanding stock. Though the announcement came 20 minutes after the Stock Exchange closed, there were celebrations at several brokerage firms. The stock had traded heavily today. Analysts say that the distribution indicates that G.M. is not overly concerned about Ford's new Model A, and that G.M.'s Chevrolet is carrying its own weight in the automobile market (→ March 17, 1929).

"Showboat" sailing

New York City, Dec. 27

Broadway's new *Showboat* is likely to be a hit for all seasons, a real musical play with a serious plot and not just another musical comedy or operetta. And what musical wouldn't love to have just one of those sterling songs by Oscar Hammerstein II and Jerome Kern: *Ol' Man River, Make Believe, Why Do I Love You, Can't Help Lovin' Dat Man*, and *You Are Love*.

Bizarre auto death for Isadora Duncan

Nice, France, Sept. 14

Isadora Duncan, whose barefooted dances in sheer gowns and speeches on behalf of communism shocked the world, died a shocking death today. Miss Duncan, 47, was being chauffeured in an open car when her long red scarf, a characteristic part of her wardrobe, coiled around a spinning rear wheel. Her neck was snapped. It was the end of a tragic life, one that included several disastrous love affairs, the drowning deaths in 1913 of her two illegitimate children, Deirdre and Patrick, and the suicide by hanging of her psychotic husband, the Russian poet Sergei Esenin, in 1925.

Ain't heard nothin' yet

Al Jolson dons blackface, drops to one knee and croons to the nation.

Hollywood, California

The success of the second Vitaphone film, *The Jazz Singer*, enhanced by Al Jolson's songs and a few lines of improvised dialogue, is amazing. "Wait, you ain't heard nothin' yet," are Jolson's first quite audible words, and the response has been so great that Warner Bros. has announced there will be more "talkies." Other studios see this as a disruptive and unnecessary change and hope the fad will pass.

Meanwhile, major film makers have founded the Academy of Motion Picture Arts and Sciences to "improve the artistic quality of the film medium, provide a common forum for the various branches and crafts of the industry, foster cooperation in technical research and cultural progress, and pursue a variety of other stated objectives."

Cecil B. De Mille, a preacher's son, follows up on his formula of violence, sex and religion with another biblical epic, *King of Kings*, already a tremendous hit. It stars H.B. Warner as Jesus. The mammoth spectacle cost $2.5 million.

Spearhead points to early era of man

Folsom, New Mexico

How long has civilization existed in North America? Since Jamestown? Since Columbus? Archeologists digging in stratified earth in New Mexico have uncovered a clue suggesting that Indians inhabited the area as far back as 8,000 B.C. A stone spearhead was found stuck in the ribs of an Ice Age bison skeleton. An estimate of the date is derived from knowledge of the species of bison, which existed during the Ice Age, and from the position of the skeleton in the layers of earth and rock. The spearhead suggests that there was a civilization advanced at least to the point of a Stone Age hunting culture.

A relativist theory of history put forth

United States

Historians are beginning to question the cult of science. As usual, Charles Beard is leading the way with a relativist theory of history. In the two-volume *Rise of American Civilization,* that he and his wife, Mary, wrote, the scholar's ability to unravel the "real" past is challenged. The value of historical knowledge, says Beard, lies in how useful it is, not how it corresponds to an objective reality. In 1913, Beard's *Economic Interpretation of the Constitution* shocked scholars by attributing cynical motives to the founding fathers. Four years later, Beard left Columbia to protest the firing of anti-war faculty.

The last Model T; the first Model A

New York City, Dec. 1

Henry Ford has so stubbornly resisted changes in his beloved Model T over the years that he has been known to attack with a sledgehammer refined versions of the car presented to him by company engineers and his son Edsel. But after producing 15 million of the famous "Tin Lizzies," even Ford has had to admit that changing times have left the car behind, as rival cars like Chevrolet cut into its market. Today, though, Ford's answer to this trend, the Model A, caused a sensation when it was unveiled here. Thousands rushed to see the car, which features shock absorbers, a speedometer and more graceful lines than its utilitarian predecessor; orders already total 50,000.

Holy hell exposed

United States

Nothing is sacred to novelist Sinclair Lewis. Early on, he lambasted small-town smugness; then it was boosters. Now he has "disrobed" a man of the cloth, although the best-selling satirist seems to think a cleric needs little help peeling off his collar if a lady gives the nod. Sex is just one sinful pastime enjoyed by the title character of *Elmer Gantry*, a holy heel who uses the pulpit for his own selfish ends. Churchgoers are steaming, and no one is betting that Lewis, who spurned last year's Pulitzer Prize, will get a chance to snub the committee again.

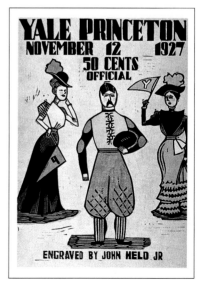

YALE PRINCETON
NOVEMBER 12 1927
50 CENTS
OFFICIAL

ENGRAVED BY JOHN HELD JR

New York City, Jan. 4. National Broadcasting Company links all 48 states to hear radio extravaganza with stars such as Will Rogers and Al Jolson.

Washington, D.C., March 10. President Coolidge signs order allocating $300 million to compensate German nationals and companies seized during Great War.

Santa Clara River Valley, California, March 13. Dam bursts 40 miles north of Los Angeles, killing 450 people as valley is flooded.

New York City, May 7. Pulitzer Prize in fiction awarded to Thornton Wilder for *The Bridge of San Luis Rey.*

New York City, May 9. *Blackbirds of 1928,* featuring an all-Negro cast, opens to popular acclaim.

Louisville, Ky., May 19. Reigh Count wins Kentucky Derby, as Shipwreck Kelly looks down from his 112-foot-high flagpole, where he has been perched for 100 hours.

Washington, D.C., May 22. Congress passes Jones-White Act, providing subsidies to American shipping industry.

Detroit, Mich., May 28. Chrysler and Dodge Motors unite in largest automotive industry merger in history.

Newfoundland, Canada, June 17. Passenger Amelia Earhardt becomes first female to cross Atlantic Ocean by plane.

Rochester, New York, July 30. George Eastman demonstrates color motion pictures.

Florida, Sept. 16. Hurricane strikes state, killing 2,000.

St. Louis, Mo., Oct. 9. New York Yankees sweep World Series, defeating Cardinals.

New York City, Nov. 6. *The New York Times* uses first moving electric bulletins to announce results of presidential election; called "zipper" because it wraps around building.

New York City. *Abie's Irish Rose* closes after record 2,400 performances on Broadway.

New York City. *The Man Who Knew Coolidge,* by Sinclair Lewis, published.

New York City. Margaret Mead, anthropologist, publishes *Coming of Age in Samoa.*

Coolidge's optimism excites Wall Street

President Coolidge remains unflappable in the face of an overheated economy.

Washington, D.C., Jan. 7

Enthusiasm kindled by President Coolidge inspired a huge volume on the booming New York Stock Exchange today. Trading was so heavy that abbreviated quotes were used, and the ticker was running 16 minutes behind transactions when the closing bell sounded. The latest surge in the soaring market follows publication of President Coolidge's assurance that he is not disturbed by unprecedented growth in loans that make it easier to buy stocks with less cash. Loans to brokers and dealers by New York Federal Reserve member banks have soared to $3.8 billion, the greatest amount in Federal Reserve history.

The President thinks that the surging loans represent a natural expansion of business in the securities market, and he sees nothing unfavorable in it. But The Nation reports that Wall Street is overflowing with "inexperienced suckers" attracted by "big, easy profits" in a "tremendous bull market" (→ Oct. 29, 1929).

Kellogg-Briand pact aims to outlaw war

Paris, Aug. 27

In a historic move designed to rid the world of war, 15 nations today signed a pact pledging to eschew the use of arms as a means of resolving international conflicts. The treaty calls on its signers to renounce war "as an instrument of national policy" and to resolve any differences peacefully. First proposed by the French Foreign Minister, Aristide Briand, as an alliance between the United States and France, the pact was broadened by the American Secretary of State, Frank B. Kellogg, to include all nations. The signers so far are France, England, Japan, Italy and the United States.

Hot Five records "West End Blues"

New York City, July 20

Judging from their recent release of *West End Blues,* Louis Armstrong's "Hot Five" get better and better. Since their first session in 1925, the group has cut some 50 records, including such gems as *Hotter Than That, Savoy Blues, Tiger Rag* and *Heebie Jeebie,* Armstrong's first recording as a "scat" singer, with vocal sounds that imitate an instrument. *West End Blues* is among the best. And for 75 cents, you can't go wrong.

Pioneering cartoon with mouse as star

New York City, Nov. 18

Steamboat Willie opened at the Colony Theater today and it did for the world of movie cartoons what *The Jazz Singer* has done for talkies. *Willie* is the first cartoon that features sound. The star of this short by Walt Disney, designed to showcase the new technology, is a mouse named Mickey, who turns the cargo of a riverboat – including the livestock aboard it – into an orchestra! Meanwhile, a replica of Otto Messmer's cartoon cat Felix is being used to monitor and to fine-tune a series of experiments with the brand new medium called television.

Mae West is "Diamond Lil" on Broadway

Mae West as "Diamond Lil." The buxom bombshell elevates the titillating to unprecedented dimensions.

New York City, Apr. 9

"When women go wrong, men go right after them." That is one of the gems that playwright-actress Mae West has given herself in *Diamond Lil*. As Lil, West unknowingly helps a Salvation Army captain knock out a white slavery ring involving a former lover. Her acting sparkles, but the writing is all rhinestone. The queen of the double entendre was last seen two years ago in *Sex*, which got her eight days in jail on a censorship charge. As she swaggered through *Lil's* opening night crowd, an admirer purred, "Your hands, your lips, your hair ... " She responded, "What-aya doin', honey, makin' love or takin' inventory?"

Hoover wins, offering chicken in every pot

Washington, D.C., Nov. 6

Herbert Hoover swept into the White House today, defeating New York Governor Al Smith in a landslide. Hoover and his running mate, Charles Curtis, were elected with promises of prosperity, saying there will be "a chicken in every pot and a car in every garage" and that America is close to "triumph over poverty." A sardonic Calvin Coolidge offered Hoover this presidential advice: "You have to stand every day hours of visitors. Nine-tenths of them want something they ought not have." Socialist Norman Thomas and Workers' Party nominee William Foster each got a handful of votes. Republicans kept control of Congress.

"Herbert C. Hoover" by Douglas Chandor. The new President offers continuity in a time of prosperity.

Make a girl happy

United States

Guys, say you've got a wonderful girl – a pippin, a peach, a sweet patootie – and you want to show you care. If you've got the dough, get her a Plymouth or a De Soto. How about a quartz clock or a Philco radio? If you're a bit short on cash, enter a talkathon or a "noun and verb rodeo" (good for 80 hours or so of entertainment) or try tandem flagpole sitting. Or take her on an old-fashioned picnic with some new-fangled foods like Velveeta cheese, Nehi soda, Peter Pan peanut butter or Rice Krispies. Of course, if your girl's actually a pill, a pickle or a priss, leave her home.

U.S. wins Olympics

Amsterdam, Netherlands, Aug. 12

There were 22 track events on the Olympic agenda, but the United States could win only one of them. Even though the Americans were able to roll up enough points to win the unofficial title, there was much evidence, first shown in Antwerp, that their dominance may be over. With European critics accusing the Americans of overconfidence, over-training and overeating, Ray Barbuti salvaged the 400 meters as the track phase was ending. Athletes in the field events saved the day for the United States, piling up 437 points, 60 more than the runner-up squad from Finland.

Poetry, fiction and all that jazz flower in Harlem Renaissance

Langston Hughes, poet.

Harlem, New York City

In the last 10 years, an important cultural movement has been spawned in the Negro ghettoes of the North. Generally referred to as the "Harlem Renaissance," the great flowering of literature, music and the arts has been stimulated by such societies as the National Association for the Advancement of Colored People and the Urban League. These groups, dedicated to the overall betterment of Negro life, along with such art-oriented societies as the Writers Guild in New York, the Black Opals in Philadelphia and the Saturday Evening Quill Club in Boston, have formed the core of a new Negro intelligentsia.

In 1925, a literary anthology titled *The New Negro*, edited by Alain Locke, included verse, fiction and nonfiction by Harlem writers. Locke's anthology, published at the peak of the Harlem Renaissance, was most influential in defining the content and direction of the movement. If Locke is Harlem's popularizer, James Weldon Johnson is its inspiration. After his pioneering novel *Autobiography of an Ex-Coloured Man* (1912), he acted as mentor to a generation of young Negro writers. Claude McKay's recent *Home to Harlem*, has proved popular with a general audience. And young Langston Hughes shows great promise in *The Weary Blues* (1926), his first volume of poetry. On stage, Negro playwrights Wallace Thurman and Garland Anderson have had productions in New York.

Jazz, of course, is popular everywhere. White people flock to the Cotton Club and Connie's Inn to hear the voices of Ethel Waters and Bill "Bojangles" Robinson, and the big-band sounds of Fletcher Henderson and especially Edward Kennedy "Duke" Ellington.

Duke Ellington and his band have played the Cotton Club for years.

The Roaring 20s: Fads, fashions and flappers

Some 78 percent of the world's autos – 24 million – are on U.S. roads.

Dancing at Tin Roof Cafe in New Orleans – no shimmying or drinking.

Police in Detroit inspect equipment found in a clandestine underground brewery. The Feds arrest 75,000 Americans a year for Prohibition violations.

Fashions of the times: The flapper dress, introduced in 1925, features a drop waist or no waist at all.

It takes two to tango. "Social dancing," says a female evangelist, "is the first and easiest step toward hell."

Tennis ace "Big Bill" Tilden, an idol of the era, learned to play at his wealthy parents' club in Philadelphia.

An American "sheba," sporting a cloche hat and knit sweater, emblems of freedom for women.

"They're desperadoes, these kids," says one writer, "the girls as well as the boys, maybe more than the boys."

1919 CHEVROLET Model 490

The 21-horsepower Model 490 Chevrolet. "In the city of Zenith," wrote Sinclair Lewis, "a family's motor indicated its social rank and where Babbitt as a boy had aspired to the presidency, his son Ted aspired to a Packard Twin Six."

Six reels of joy! Chaplin's first real feature, made in 1921, launched Jackie Coogan as a major child star.

In the morning, in the evening, ain't we got fun!

"The Bersaglieri" by George Luks. The Great War is now just a memory.

F. Scott Fitzgerald and wife, Zelda.

A flapper doin' the Charleston.

Other hits of the era: "Yes Sir! That's My Baby," "Where'd You Get Those Eyes?" and "Ain't We Got Fun."

Immigration was limited during the decade, but many newcomers have established themselves in all walks of life. They learned to speak English, served in the Great War, started their own businesses – and they have prospered.

Turn on the radio and hear "Amos 'n' Andy," "Roxy and His Gang" or "Jack Frost's Melody Moments."

The chic Fortuny gown reveals the female body by caressing its surface with shimmering pleated silk satins.

Motorized taxis wait to take passengers from Union Station in Los Angeles. You need a car in this California metropolis; its 364 square miles in 1920 reflect a 13-fold expansion since the city's founding way back in 1781.

America projects itself around the world: Main Street has no end on this cover of the popular humor magazine.

Bloody Valentine's Day

Seven of "Bugs" Moran's men are dead after a quick and brutal execution.

Chicago, Feb. 14

The floor of a Windy City beer warehouse was stained with blood today as seven members of George "Bugs" Moran's gang were gunned down in a surprise attack. Police believe Moran's rival, "Scarface" Al Capone, may be responsible for what is being called the St. Valentine's Day Massacre.

The killers, wielding machine guns, were dressed in police uniforms. This outraged Police Commissioner William Russell, who declared war on such crime. "This is war to the finish," he said. "I've never known a challenge like this."

Capone has become the king of bootlegging and gambling. His annual income has skyrocketed to about $60 million since he moved here from New York in 1920. Two years ago, he defended his "job": "What's Al Capone done, then? He's supplied a legitimate demand. Some call it bootlegging. Some call it racketeering. I call it business. They say I violate the prohibition law. Who doesn't?" Considering the tolerance, even the glamorization of Capone, it does seem that Americans want their booze, and they don't seem to care whether it's legal or not (→ Oct. 17, 1931).

Negro union gains charter from A.F.L.

Chicago, Feb. 23

The predominantly Negro Brotherhood of Sleeping Car Porters has been granted temporary admission to the American Federation of Labor. William Green, president of the federation, has been delivering a series of speeches that affirms the support of the A.F.L. for the porters brotherhood. Green hopes to help the union recruit 10,000 more members by September. He has also stressed that the A.F.L. will oppose any attempts by Pullman executives to form a company union. The brotherhood held its annual convention here this year and took up such issues as health and housing conditions of members and the mobilization of the economic power of the workers to improve their lives.

Amos 'n' Andy a hit

New Jersey

The radio program *Amos 'n' Andy*, which features Negroes as its main characters, has become so popular that it is regularly broadcast over loudspeakers at resorts such as Atlantic City. The comedy show uses white actors who speak in a Negro dialect, and portrays the main characters as hapless and humorous. The plots play on the stereotype of Negroes as being ignorant and, while millions like the show, many Negroes find it offensive.

Yale grad and crooner with a megaphone, Rudy Vallee appears in the film "Vagabond Lover."

The union blues in the age of business

United States

The union battle cry, muted by prosperity and hostility, has yielded to the hum of the well-oiled factory. Unions, recoiling from what H.L. Mencken calls "capital's vigorous and well-planned war of attrition," have lost three million members over the decade. And strikes have dropped from an average of 3,500 a year to fewer than 800.

Since the "Red Scare," labor has been saddled with the stigma of isms – communism, socialism, anarchism. The National Association of Manufacturers has named its drive for the open shop the "American Plan," and has tried to make unionism synonymous with Bolshevism. The American Federation of Labor has been accused of excluding the foreign-born and its leadership seems to be spending more time keeping leftists out than getting new workers in.

Many companies dangle the carrot as an alternative to the stick. With profit-sharing, grievance boards, recreational programs and insurance, management appears to be beating labor at its own benefits game.

Cascade Mountains get longest tunnel

Seattle, Washington, Jan. 12

Railroad president James J. Hill officially christened the new Cascade tunnel today. It is more than eight miles long and was dug through solid granite in the heart of the Cascade Mountains. Engineers with the Great Northern Railway say that it is the longest tunnel in North America. The longest railway tunnel in the world is the Simplon Tunnel in Switzerland, which is about 12.5 miles long. The construction of Hill's Cascade tunnel employed the latest civil engineering technology available. Rotary hydraulic rock drills were used to dig the tunnel, which lies several thousand feet beneath the summit of the mountain directly above it. Nitroglycerin was used for blasting out the rock.

Buck Rogers comics

United States, January

Awakening from a five-century-long sleep, a former air corps lieutenant finds himself in a devastated America overrun by Mongol invaders. *Buck Rogers*, a comic strip by Philip Nowlan and Dick Calkins, uses fantastic settings to tell stories of heroic adventure. Further heroism can be found in Hal Foster's *Tarzan* and in Elzie Segar's *Thimble Theater*, which has recently introduced a fighting sailor named Popeye.

"Soaring Steel" (1929) by Samuel Chamberlain. Photographers are finding heroism in the skyscrapers across the industrial landscape.

Academy honors movies

As movies grow so do women's roles.

Hollywood, Calif., May 17

"We want more respect," the film makers say. To focus attention on their achievements, they held a banquet last night at the Hollywood Roosevelt Hotel, where a couple of hundred movie people saw Douglas Fairbanks present artists and technicians with 15 golden statuettes, depicting a man with a crusader's sword standing on a reel of film. *Wings* won as best picture of 1927-1928, Janet Gaynor as best actress (for *Seventh Heaven*, *Street Angel* and *Sunrise*) while Emil Jannings took the prize as best actor (for *The Way of All Flesh* and *The Last Command*).

Movies are booming. Of the nation's 20,500 movie theaters, those with sound facilities have risen to 9,000, from 1,300. Musicals, such as *Broadway Melody*, *The Golddiggers of Broadway*, *Desert Song* and *The Singing Fool* are in vogue.

At the Roosevelt Hotel in New York, Guy Lombardo and His Royal Canadians are performing nightly, while Broadway has found a new favorite: handsome Britisher Archie Leach [Cary Grant], who appeared in the musical *A Wonderful Night* and then *Boom Boom*.

Young Plan eases German war debts

Paris, June 7

Thanks to a plan worked out by the Wall Street financier Owen D. Young, Germany will soon have some relief from its crippling burden of war reparations. The Young Plan reduces the total amount that the Germans must pay in reparations to $27 billion, down from the $33-billion figure that was fixed by the Allies in 1921, and allows 60 years for repayment. In spite of the loans from the United States under the U.S.-sponsored Dawes Plan, which was put into effect five years ago, Germany has been unable to meet its annual payments, due in large measure to the inflation that has devastated its economy. By ensuring that the Germans keep paying reparations, the new plan may enable the Allies to return to the United States some of the $10 billion they borrowed from it to carry on the war (→ June 20, 1931).

"Joe sent me": Speakeasies flourish under eye of Prohibition

United States

All it takes is the flash of a certain business card, a particular rhythm of knocks on a door or a whispered phrase like "Joe sent me." Nothing could be easier than slipping into a speakeasy. The estimates range from 32,000 to 100,000 illegal drinking joints in New York. A Chicago official estimated this year that there were just 10,000 in that city. To fit in the hordes who say they use them, those 10,000 would each have to be the size of a football field. Even towns in the Midwest, traditionally the driest of the dry spots, have "beer flats," "blind pigs" and "shock houses."

The clientele at the speakeasy is as varied as the drinks for sale, bricklayers and lawyers alike bellying up to the bar for potato-brewed whiskey and 60-day-old wine. Moving in among the men, and placing their orders just as loudly, are women who never would have been seen in a saloon. One of the famed speakeasy proprietors is Texas Guinan, who hails customers at her New York El Fay establishment with "Hello, sucker!" Miss Guinan has reason to be cheerful – profits are immense.

Admittedly, there are expenses, starting with installation of concealed drains where hooch can be poured in case of a raid, and the hook-up of electric switches that seal the doors when police try to drop in. There are also funds to be put aside for under-the-table distribution to federal agents and district attorneys. Some cops prefer to be paid in "liquid assets"; more than one place charges a paying customer 75 cents for a slug of gin, while an officer of the law imbibes for free. And, of course, you've got to have jack to spend on food and entertainment – people want hot jazz and cool cuisine. Meals are served at reasonable prices, because the profit margin on liquor is so high. The worst risk is indigestion. The booze is a real danger. Last year, known deaths in the nation from rotgut shot past the 1,000 mark.

Since last fall, police have increased their raids. Sometimes they are "jake foot," poorly or perfectly disguised in anything from a false mustache to a football uniform. They might make countless arrests, but the speakeasies just keep popping up. Last February, the Bar Association of New York threw in the towel, announcing opposition to Prohibition. Hearing the news, many upstanding citizens raise their shot glasses, mugs and teacups and declare, "I'll drink to that!"

At least the liquor is respectable.

Ambitious airlines invite American travelers to take to the air

AIR MAIL
is Socially Correct

Washington, D.C.

Has travel by airplane become accessible to all? A number of new American companies that provide air transport service would like the nation to think so. From the spectacle and thrill of barnstorming, air travel is apparently becoming a viable, growing industry.

Commercial service began before the war, with the huge German zeppelins flying scheduled routes in Europe. Heavier-than-air operators soon got the idea that they could make a buck with airplanes; the first scheduled passenger flights were made by the St. Petersburg-Tampa Air Boat Line, which provided twice-daily service across Florida's Tampa Bay. Its little airplane could carry only one passenger – so much for volume. The war provided a new variety of air-

craft and trained pilots and mechanics. In 1918, the United States Post Office set up a regular air route between New York and Philadelphia, to speed mail delivery. At first, it used war-surplus Curtiss Jenny biplanes; but later, the Boeing company designed the B-l Mail Boat, a plywood biplane that could land on water. In 1921, the Martin MB-l bomber, developed for the army, was converted to a mail plane and a 12-seat passenger liner. More recently, the German Fokker company has opened a factory in New Jersey to produce its giant trimotor passenger craft. American manufacturers, including Henry Ford, have improved on the tri-

motor design. The all-metal Ford trimotor, known popularly as the "Tin Goose," is earning a reputation as the most durable plane in the air.

Companies such as Colonial Airlines and North West Airlines now ply regular routes between many cities. On July 7, the Transcontinental Air Transport company opened the first coast-to-coast passenger service. The trans-Atlantic hero Charles A. Lindbergh inaugurated the Pan American Airline by flying a cargo of mail to Panama on October 2. And Universal Air Line added entertainment to the flight plan when it showed a movie aboard a flight on February 17.

Lieutenant Jimmy Doolittle is the first pilot to rely solely on instrumentation.

American novelists prove their worth

New York City

The books are just about closed on the 1920s, but the decade hardly closed down on books, despite the efforts of the Clean Books League. This year, three novels stand out, each the work of a young writer. The trio's best-known member is Ernest Hemingway, 30, the master of the blue pencil. He has stripped every ounce of fat from his prose in *A Farewell to Arms*, set during the Great War. The tale, about love and combat, is told by an American youth posted on the Italian front, where he falls for a British nurse.

The year's other blockbusters are the work of Southerners. William Faulkner, 32, comes from Oxford, Mississippi, and the odor of Confederate decay seeps from his fourth novel, *The Sound and the Fury*, about the faded fortunes of the Compsons, privileged people who have plunged into debauchery. Tautly designed, the novel twines three tour de force monologues, including one spoken by an idiot.

Thomas Wolfe, born in 1900 in Asheville, North Carolina, exhibits none of the artistic control of his rivals. In fact, his literary debut, *Look Homeward Angel*, is a rambling monster of a novel. Its source material is Wolfe's own childhood and youth and his groping search for an identity in a large, chaotic family. The driving force of Wolfe's prose has excited many readers, who eagerly await the next installment in the life of Eugene Gant.

Sociologists study typical U.S. town

Muncie, Indiana

As Americans continue to leave the farm for the town, life in the towns continues to pique the curiosity of readers. Now the subject has been approached from a new angle by a Columbia University sociologist, Robert S. Lynd, and his wife, Helen, who asked Muncie's residents what was on their minds. The answers appear in *Middletown*, a study as haunting as a tale by Sherwood Anderson. One citizen says of the rest, "These people are afraid of something: what is it?"

Detroit makes 5.3 million cars; Ford hits millionth Model A

Detroit, Michigan

Are your windows rattling more than ever? Have you noticed that, even though there are more paved roads, they are more difficult to cross? The explanation, of course, comes from the automobile manufacturers here who have now turned out 5.3 million vehicles. Ford announces that it has just built its one-millionth Model A. Introduced in January of last year, the Model A is the successor to the popular Model T. The "A" is a low-priced general-purpose car that comes in a choice of four colors and 17 body styles. All these vehicles are com-

peting for space on the nation's 695,000 miles of paved road and they are consuming about 16 billion

gallons of gasoline a year. If you're still walking, look both ways when you cross the street.

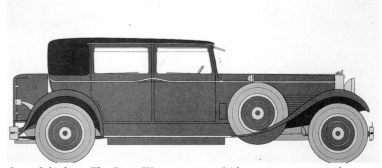

One of the best. The Stutz Weymann-type 36-horsepower sports saloon.

Black Tuesday! Wall St. in chaos as stocks crash

New York City, Oct. 29

The stock market has collapsed in a "Black Tuesday" of violent trading that was the most disastrous in Wall Street history. It was the worst by three key measurements, total losses, total turnover and the number of speculators ruined. Frantic efforts to stabilize the market were met by "must sell" orders to liquidate at any price, accelerated by insistent brokers' calls for more cash to back the record loans behind the falling stocks. The selling storm was the most catastrophic of three that began last Thursday, "Black Thursday," and erupted again Monday. The only relief today was a smart upturn at the close, believed by some to mean that the end is not far away.

In Washington, the Federal Reserve met continuously, with no lunch break and no action. U.S. Steel and American Can, however, both declared $1 extra dividends as proof of prosperity. On the New York Stock Exchange, in today's session alone, it is estimated that the loss came to $9 billion. For the month, the total is $16 billion in 240 selected issues.

Because galleries overlooking the trading floor were barred to visitors, the public drama was concentrated in brokers' offices. There, huddled around glass-domed "tickers" that typed out the stock quotations, tense faces reflected the tragic news on the tape. There were no smiles, no tears. Just a sad camaraderie of shared losses.

In Providence, Rhode Island, 57-year-old David Korn dropped dead while watching the tape, though his holdings were in no special danger. And in Kansas City, Missouri, insurance man John Schwitzgebel unsuccessfully attempted suicide with two bullets in his chest, saying, "Tell the boys I can't pay them what I owe them."

On the brighter side, New York City Mayor Jimmy Walker urged a theater owners' meeting to "show pictures that will reinstate courage and hope in the hearts of the people." Chairman Julius Rosenwald of Sears, Roebuck & Company inspired hope in 40,000 employees by guaranteeing their stock market accounts. Assistant Secretary of Commerce Julius Klein went on a nationwide radio hookup to remind the nation that last Friday President Hoover said, "The fundamental business of the country, that is production and distribution of commodities, is on a sound and prosperous basis." And Dr. Klein told the nation, "There is no reason today to change a single word of this statement of the President." But the Democratic National Committee released a contrary opinion, charging that the crisis "belongs to the party in power" and that leaders who were talking "prosperity" a short time ago are now trying to find a "scapegoat in the face of a $15 billion loss in one week of American life" (→ Dec. 31).

As the day wears on and panic grips the floor of the New York Stock Exchange, wild rumors spread through the financial district. Ambulances race to buildings where bankrupt investors are reportedly killing themselves. Whether these stories are true or not, the very spectacle of a market gone mad has drawn a crowd of thousands to the exchange building and 20 mounted officers have been rushed in to reinforce an overwhelmed police contingent. Among the desperate investors waiting to learn the fate of their life's savings, women, many of them stenographers on Wall Street, make up a sizable part of the multitude. Clearly, there is excitement in simply being near the scene. And even among those without a vested interest in the market, the chance to witness first-hand the collapse of Wall Street is just too great to resist.

Hoover tells shaky public economy is solid

Washington, D.C., Dec. 31

President Hoover exchanged New Year's wishes with reporters today, offering yet another profession of faith in America's economic future. Holiday retail receipts are running somewhat ahead of last year's totals. Earlier this month, the President told Congress that confidence in the nation's business affairs had been re-established, and the public seems to be nodding its assent. But then, according to Wall Street financier Thomas Lamont, the crash was just "a little distress selling on the Stock Exchange."

Despite the optimism of Wall Street and Washington, distress has spread quickly since October. Within two weeks of the crash, the nation had lost an estimated $30 billion. Hoover met separately with business and trade union leaders on November 21. But he has ignored voices that urge increased government spending to keep the economy from sagging along with stock prices. Instead, relying on the optimism of consumers, he has signed a tax cut of $160 million, hoping the excess funds will be pumped back into the economy rather than put away for a rainy day. "Any lack of confidence," implores the President, "in the .. basic strength of business in the United States is foolish."

Cartoonist Rollin Kirby depicts a worried investor in "Sold Out," published October 24, Black Thursday, the day the market crash began.

Chicago, Feb. 10. Federal grand jury indicts 31 corporations and 158 people on charges of operating a major bootlegging ring (→Jan. 19, 1931).

Flagstaff, Arizona, Feb. 18. Clyde William Tombaugh inadvertently discovers planet Pluto through examination of an earlier photograph.

New York City, May 4. Robert Frost wins Pulitzer Prize for poetry with *Collected Poems.*

New Hampshire, May 4. A major fire destroys most of Nashua, leaving 1,200 people homeless.

Chicago, May 11. Adler Planetarium opens in Grant Park.

Marion, Indiana, August. Two Negroes accused of killing two whites are dragged from jail and lynched by mob numbering in thousands.

Queens, New York, August. Harry Socoloff opens nation's first modern supermarket – King Kullen Grocery.

New Jersey, Sept. 3. Thomas A. Edison tests nation's first electric passenger train, from Hoboken to Montclair.

Newport, Rhode Island, Sept. 17. U.S. yacht Enterprise successfully defends America's Cup against British challenger Shamrock V.

Boston, Sept. 17. City celebrates 300th anniversary; 50,000 march through streets.

Philadelphia, Oct. 8. Athletics defeat St. Louis Cardinals, four games to two, in World Series.

Princeton, New Jersey. Institute for Advanced Study at Princeton University founded.

New York City. Elmer Davis writes in *Harper's,* "This year, when we all needed something to take our minds off our troubles, miniature golf did it . . . if we can't find bread, we are satisfied with the circus."

United States. Will Rogers says, "I never met a man I didn't like."

DEATHS

Washington, D.C., March 8. William Howard Taft, 27th President and former Chief Justice (*Sept. 15, 1857).

Silver Springs, Maryland, Mother Jones, reformer, union organizer (*May 1, 1830).

When Garbo talks, everbody watches

The sultry star in "Anna Christie."

Hollywood, California, March 15

"Gif me a viskey . . . and dawn't be stingy, baby." Those are Garbo's first spoken words on screen, in *Anna Christie,* causing the *New York Herald Tribune* today to rave about her "deep, husky, throaty contralto." One thing the elusive Garbo will not talk about is her romance with John Gilbert, her co-star in *Flesh and the Devil* and *Love.* Lewis Milestone has directed *All Quiet on the Western Front* for Universal, shooting it silent and dubbing the sound. Marie Dressler and Wallace Beery star in *Min and Bill,* which defies M-G-M's tradition of glamor. Paramount's newest star is Marlene Dietrich, who co-stars with Gary Cooper in *Morocco.*

New in Hoover era: the best and worst

United States

Signs of the times: new food – Wonder bread, Mott's applesauce; new airlines – United, TWA, American, Braniff; new inventions – windshield wipers, pinball machines; new fads – contract bridge, backgammon; new words – Hoover flags (pockets emptied and turned out), Hoover blankets (newspapers covering park bench indigents), Hoovervilles (shantytowns).

Blondie Boopadoop has beau Dagwood

Chicago, Sept. 15

In the first episode of *Blondie,* Chic Young's new comic strip, readers are introduced to the title character, a bird-brained flapper named Blondie Boopadoop. Her fondest admirer, Dagwood Bumstead, is a mild-mannered playboy and the son of a railroad tycoon. Readers suspect that they are going to become a couple, and that Dagwood's father will disinherit him.

Study sees crime getting out of hand

Washington, D.C., Jan. 10

As Prohibition reaches its 10th anniversary, President Hoover has issued a call to fight crime, much of which is related to bootlegging. His battle cry comes with the release today of the first report of a study by the Wickersham Commission that says crime is on the increase. The study, under former Attorney General George Wickersham, may result in tougher anti-crime laws, particularly in Prohibition enforcement. Forty percent of Americans favor repeal, but Hoover supports Prohibition, calling it an "experiment, noble in motive and far-reaching in purpose" (→ Feb. 10).

Hi-yo, Silver, away!

New York City

Gather round the radio. There swells the William Tell Overture, and on "a fiery horse with the speed of light, a cloud of dust and a hearty 'Hi-yo, Silver,' the Lone Ranger rides again!" Or tune in to hear the Rev. Fulton J. Sheen on the *Catholic Hour,* broadcast by NBC. And already following on the heels of radio broadcasting, the first experimental television transmissions are being beamed from station W2XBS here.

Thomas Hart Benton's "Instruments of Power," one of the murals from his "America Today" (1930) series.

A flock of firsts for female flyers

Cheyenne, Wyoming, May 15

Miss Ellen Church stepped off a United Airlines plane today, having completed the country's first flight by a female steward. She still wore the cap and hip-length shawl she had donned for the chilly flight from San Francisco. Stewardship is but one of women's advances in aviation. Two years ago, Miss Amelia Earhart flew the Atlantic, the first woman passenger to do so. One young woman, Miss Lillian Boyer, makes her living as a stunt flyer, and Miss Laura Ingalls plans to set a women's loop-the-loop record the day after tomorrow in the skies over Oklahoma.

Hughes confirmed as Chief Justice

Washington, D.C., Feb. 13

Charles Evan Hughes survived a fierce Senate debate today to gain confirmation as the nation's Chief Justice by a 52-26 vote. The former New York Governor, United States Secretary of State and associate justice will succeed William Howard Taft, who retired earlier this month for health reasons. Hughes served on the high court from 1910 to 1916, resigning to run for president against Woodrow Wilson. He is expected to add to the court's conservative slant, but is known to hold that the Constitution is an active, flexible guide to jurisprudence.

Photographer Margaret Bourke-White atop the Chrysler Building.

Population hits 122 million; L.A. is fifth

Los Angeles, California, home of Universal Studios and other dream factories.

Washington, D.C., Dec. 31

The government has released the results of the 1930 federal census, and the facts are somewhat startling. Statistics put the nation's population at 122.7 million. This represents a dramatic increase, 30 million people over the 92 million counted in the 1920 census. While New York is still the largest city, the most spectacular growth occurred in the Far West. Los Angeles has become the fifth most populous metropolis. Among the states, Arizona has experienced the most rapid growth; more than 435,000 people now live there, an increase of about 100,000 in a decade. The only state in the union to have lost population is Montana.

The census also shows that while first-generation Irish and Jewish immigrants tended to settle in the poorest inner-city slums, the next generation is moving out to the more affluent suburbs. For example, the Irish population of St. Louis has dropped by half since 1900. The same phenomenon is taking place in Harlem, once the home of more than 177,000 Jews; now fewer than 5,000 live there.

Other statistics show that the current life expectancy of the typical American is 61 years, and that there are more than 26 million cars on America's roads.

One interesting change will be taking place in the 1940 census count. When that canvass takes place, housewives will be given the official job title of "homemaker," instead of being listed as having "no occupation," as in the past.

Schmeling gets title on Sharkey's foul

New York City, June 12

For the first time in history, a world heavyweight championship has been decided on a foul. Max Schmeling, the German giant, was awarded the title today because of a low blow by Jack Sharkey that left him writhing on the canvas. It happened with five seconds left in the fourth round. Schmeling was still on the floor when the bell rang for the fifth and the German was declared winner of the title vacated by Gene Tunney. Sharkey had been ahead from the start.

Gallant Fox wins the Triple Crown

New York City, June

With Earl Sande in the saddle, Gallant Fox sped to victory in the Belmont Stakes here to became the second colt ever to win racing's Triple Crown. Last month, he won the 56th Kentucky Derby in the view of the 17th Earl of Derby ("It's darby not durby," said his lordship). Sande, in a comeback after a stint as a trainer, got Gallant Fox out of the new-fangled mechanical starting gate slowly, edged into the lead in the backstretch and romped home by two lengths.

DeMar wins 7th Boston Marathon

Boston, Apr. 20

Most dedicated runners would be happy to win it once, and just finishing it is considered a personal triumph. But today, Clarence DeMar won the Boston Marathon for the seventh time. DeMar first captured the grueling run from suburban Hopkinton to Boston in 1911; a decade passed before he won again, in 1922. After that, the Melrose athlete was almost unstoppable, repeating his victory in 1923 as well as in 1924. Then, when no one thought it was possible, DeMar confounded track buffs by taking the marathon yet again in 1927, 1928 and, incredibly, this year.

CASINO DE PARIS

JOSEPHINE BAKER

LA GRANDE REVUE

PARIS QUI REMUE

LA PLUS BELLE REVUE DU MONDE
MATINEES — JEUDIS — DIMANCHES & FETES

American-born Josephine Baker continues to delight "Tout-Paris" with her provocative dances. She may be best known for having appeared in nothing but a string of bananas in "La Revue Negre."

Disputed tariff is signed

Washington, D.C., June 17

President Hoover today placed the United States behind the highest tariff walls in the nation's history, with the help of six ceremonial pens. The President signed the tariff act and presented the pens to the six leaders who guided the measure on its stormy path through Congress. They included the bill's namesakes: Senator Reed Smoot of Utah, and Representative Willis Hawley of Oregon. The two had pressed for higher rates than the President wanted. It is believed he signed the bill mainly to calm Wall Street. On Monday, the market took a sharper drop than at any time since the November bottoming out of last year's crash.

London and Paris reacted with gloom, fearing a chill on international trade, while agricultural groups that fear higher prices for what the farmers buy moved to challenge the President, attacking the Smoot-Hawley tariff law even before the ink on it was dry.

"American Gothic," just plain farm folk

"American Gothic"(1930) by Grant Wood. In his attempt to depict the Iowa farmer, the artist has captured the spirit of rural America. The odd folks in the picture, modeled after his sister and his dentist, represent a protective father and spinster daughter. The dour couple proved popular with city as well as country folk: The Art Institute of Chicago bought the work for $300.

$116 million allocated to ease job crisis

Some 6,000 unemployed have been given surplus apples to sell for 5 cents.

Washington, D.C., Dec. 21

President Hoover today won approval of the emergency job program he wanted from Congress, and the lawmakers have adjourned for the holiday, after a session that lasted until five minutes past midnight. The measure appropriates $116 million to put the unemployed back to work on emergency construction projects. Major opponents were not so much against the idea of creating jobs in the wake of the crash as they were convinced that the President's emphasis on national voluntary community efforts is not enough. Senators Robert La Follette of Wisconsin and David I. Walsh of Massachusetts protested that 4.5 million are unemployed and that distress across the land is far worse than the President realizes. They argued against the "smallness" of the appropriation, and read into the record a number of unemployment reports they described as a "complete refutation of statements that the situation is well in hand." Senator La Follette said that he regarded the administration program as "totally inadequate." The senators left for home with La Follette's voice ringing in their ears: "I hope that when you return, you will be at least as generous as you were to corporations and income-tax payers last year" (→Jan. 7, 1931).

London naval pact ratified by Senate

Washington, D.C., July 21

The arms control effort took a step forward today as the Senate ratified the London Naval Treaty by a vote of 58 to 9. Signed in April by the United States, Britain and Japan, the pact supplements the five-power Washington Treaty of 1922, which limited the number of battleships each country could retain. The London Treaty sets ceilings for all types of warships, including cruisers, destroyers and submarines. The United States has won parity with Britain across the board, and Japan has been granted higher quotas in several categories, including submarines. Because of a dispute, however, neither France nor Italy signed the new treaty.

$45 million is voted for drought relief

Washington, D.C., Dec. 30

Relief is on the way. Congress today passed and sent to the President for his signature the first of his emergency programs. The bill appropriates $45 million to help farmers in areas that have been hard hit by either storms or drought. Calling for advances and loans to be used in farm production, including feed for livestock, it provoked a debate in which Senator James Heflin of Alabama argued: "Striking out human food and buying food for livestock puts hogs above humans and mules above men. Won't it be a glorious Christmas present to give a man money to buy food for his horse and hog and refuse it to him!" (→Jan. 4, 1931).

Sinclair Lewis wins Nobel literary prize

Oslo, Norway, Dec. 10

For the first time, the world's highest literary prize has gone to an American. Sinclair Lewis, who arrived in Stockholm aboard the liner Drottningholm, was awarded the Nobel Prize late today. The Nobel committee, which named Lewis on November 5, will gather two days from now to hear the famed satirist's acceptance speech. It should be an earful. Yesterday, Lewis sent a cable to his publisher, Alfred Harcourt, urging that he arrange for publication in full of his remarks. "Please try (to) get Sunday sections (of the) *Times* or *Herald Tribune*," the cable read in part. "Speech as it will be reported (by the) press (will) cause repercussions."

Golf Grand Slam enough for Bobby Jones

Premier golfer following through.

Georgia, Nov. 17

There are no more worlds for Bobby Jones to conquer. So with the Grand Slam of golf neatly tucked away among his laurels, Jones retired today from competition. He has run out of golfers to beat. At the age of 28, Robert Tyre Jones has won in a single year both the United States Open and Amateur and the British Open and Amateur. Jones, was especially pleased to capture the British Amateur, a new title for him. In a near gale, he won on the 19th hole. He took the United States Open in 100-degree heat with the help of his lily-pad shot, in which the ball skipped over a pond.

In all, this master of the amateurs has captured 13 championships in 14 years.

400,000 depositors find bank is closed

New York City, Dec. 11

Fearful crowds collected around the 60 branches of the Bank of United States this morning, anxious to withdraw their money, only to find the doors closed and mounted police on guard. The bank, with 400,000 depositors, blamed rumors for a run on cash, and said reopening would bring disorder. More than half its $160 million in deposits are in "thrift savings" of the lower classes. Others are concentrated in the garment industry. Many of its loans are in real estate, hard hit by the crash. To quiet fears overseas, Washington officials explained that in spite of the bank's name, there is no United States government connection with it (→ 21).

Painter Ferris dies

Philadelphia, March 18

Jean Leon Gerome Ferris, who dedicated his career in art to the depiction of American history, is dead. Ferris, son of the prolific portraitist Stephen Ferris, studied at the Pennsylvania Academy of Fine Arts and in Paris, where he was the pupil of the academic painter Jean-Leon Gerome, for whom he was named. Ferris was known for his humanizing depictions of famous Americans, whom he portrayed in both domestic and heroic scenes.

A mechanical brain

Cambridge, Massachusetts

A "differential analyzer" invented by Vannevar Bush at the Massachusetts Institute of Technology should be of great use to physicists and engineers, who can be helped by its approximations. This computer, actually an analog computing device, is a kind of mechanical brain. It does very quick, if not always very accurate, calculations. Those who need total accuracy in their figures are better off with the slower punch-card system.

Beards write "The American Leviathan"

United States

"Leviathan" means monstrous or enormous and applies in at least two ways to the new work by historian Charles A. Beard and his son William. *The American Leviathan* is, first of all, a monster of a book, with 824 fact-filled pages. And its subject is another sort of leviathan, the top-heavy ship of state that is the government of the United States. The Beards hold that the federal system has been totally transformed by modern scientific knowledge, which has created new "functions" and "has emphasized as never before the role of government as a stabilizer of civilization." The trouble, they claim, is that although technology has revamped the way the system works – in areas ranging from diplomacy to banking – it has added nothing to improve government. And it had better come up with something quick, because "historic morals and common sense" no longer suffice, as jobless millions know too well.

Harlow soars, Berkeley dazzles, Fox falls

Hollywood, California

Howard Hughes is converting his World War aviation saga, *Hell's Angels*, to sound. He began the film in 1927, but is reshooting with his 19-year-old discovery, platinum-blonde Jean Harlow, in the lead. Samuel Goldwyn has lured Busby Berkeley from Broadway to choreograph several Eddie Cantor vehicles. The trade is already talking about Busby's dizzying camera techniques for dance sequences, and Mary Pickford plans to try a musical with him. Though movie attendance is at a new high, William Fox, a top silent-era mogul, was wiped out by the Wall Street crash and had to sell his share of the Fox studio for $18 million.

Merger makes Pan Am No. 1; TWA formed

New York City, Oct. 10

Air travel is becoming more accessible as prices drop and more and larger airlines vie for business. The nation's biggest carrier is now Pan American Airlines. It became that August 21 by merging with smaller firms. A major competitor arose today with a merger of three smaller lines to form Transcontinental and Western Air (TWA). The fare from New York to the West Coast has dropped below $160. Meanwhile, new flight records are stimulating the growth of aviation. In January, Charles A. Lindbergh set a cross-country record of 14 hours 45 minutes, but in August, Frank Hawks beat that record by two hours and 20 minutes.

4 to 5 million jobless; social danger seen

"Down-and-outs" patiently wait outside New York's Doyers Street Mission.

Washington, D.C., Jan. 7

The number of unemployed in the United States now stands between four million and five million, representing a "social danger," according to the chairman of the President's Emergency Committee for Employment. Colonel Arthur Woods told the Senate Appropriations Committee today that the various construction programs across the country this year came to $2.5 billion, which he called "adequate." He testified that he agrees with Dr. Nicholas Murray Butler, president of Columbia University, that there is a danger to the social order, but not now, because "it has been foreseen." He told the committee there has been an "industrial evolution" since the days when industry met crises by firing everyone possible to cut costs. Today, he said, employers keep as many as possible on their payrolls. Asked what Congress can do to relieve the situation, Colonel Woods suggested that the senators cut the red tape that hinders conversion of appropriations into jobs.

Meanwhile, census authorities are moving apple-sellers from their lists of jobless to the category of "employed" because they say many people selling "unemployed apples" are earning a good living (→ Oct. 7).

"Cabbage Leaf" (1931) by Edward Weston. Greatly influenced by Alfred Stieglitz and Paul Strand, Weston specializes in close-range photography.

"The Star-Spangled Banner" is anthem

Washington, D.C., March 3

After nearly 150 years, Americans finally have a song that they can call their own, officially. Congress today sent President Hoover a bill designating *The Star-Spangled Banner* as the national anthem. Ironically enough in these Prohibition days, what is now a patriotic tune began as a British drinking song in colonial times, an ode to Venus and Bacchus. It was taken up by Americans after the Revolution, with new patriotic words, but it was Francis Scott Key, in 1814, who penned the words used today. The song has been an unofficial anthem for a century, and, since the 1890s, in a John Philip Sousa arrangement, was used by the military whenever an anthem was needed.

Farmers need food

England, Arkansas, Jan. 4

Over 300 impoverished farmers shouting "We want food!" stormed into town today, threatening to loot the stores unless they got food for their children. The farmers, mostly white and some armed, arrived on horses, in buggies and on foot. The march started after Red Cross aides there to help in the economic crisis said they could dole out no food because they lacked food authorization forms that had to be filled out. Local merchants met and agreed to give food to all those demanding it.

U.S. chides Japan

Washington, D.C., Jan. 2

Reacting to Japan's invasion of Manchuria last September, Secretary of State Henry L. Stimson announced today that the United States would refuse to recognize any territorial acquisitions that violate American treaty rights. Since the Japanese seizure of Manchuria violates the Kellogg-Briand Treaty of 1928, which renounces aggression, as well as the nine-power Open Door pact of 1922, Stimson has in effect condemned Japan's action. However, since President Hoover opposes any further moves, Stimson's doctrine is likely to remain just a moral condemnation.

Scottsboro Boys sentenced to die for rape

Paint Rock, Alabama, Apr. 9

Demonstrations have erupted in 28 countries today to protest the conviction of the nine Scottsboro Boys for the rape of two white girls on March 25. Eight of the Negroes were sentenced to death; one received a life sentence.

The incident allegedly occurred aboard a freight train that was traveling from Chattanooga to Memphis. Near Stevenson, Alabama, a fight broke out between groups of Negro and white youths who had hitched a ride in the freight car. Five whites were thrown from the train. They told the townspeople of Stevenson their version of the story, adding that the Negro youths were traveling with two white girls. The Stevenson station master telegraphed down the line and a posse was formed to meet the train at Paint Rock. There were indeed two white girls on the train, Victoria Price and Nancy Bates, who claimed that they had been raped.

The Negro youths fled, but nine were captured: Andy Wright, Roy White, Haywood Patterson, Clarence Norris, Charley Weems, Ozzie Powell, Eugene Williams, who is only 13, Willy Roberson, who is crippled as the result of a venereal disease, and Olen Montgomery, who is blind. The Paint Rock jurors found the girls' testimony adequate and the nine youths were convicted.

Their defense has been taken up by a Communist group, the International Labor Defense, and by the National Association for the Advancement of Colored People. The groups are presently vying for the honor of defending the Scottsboro Boys on appeal (→ Nov. 7, 1932).

Twinkies to Bahai

United States

New foods: Hotel Bar butter, Bisquick biscuit mix, Beech-Nut baby food, Hostess Twinkies, Toll House cookies. New products and inventions: Alka Seltzer, Breck shampoo, the air-conditioner, infra-red photography, Schick shavers, dry ice, coaxial cables, synthetic rubber. Also this year, the New School for Social Research opened, and the steel superstructure for the Bahai House of Worship, in Wilmette, Illinois, was completed after 21 years.

Debut of Dick Tracy

Chicago, Oct. 4

This is the town of Al Capone and Elliot Ness, of blazing machine guns and cold, hard justice. Now the innocent have another defender. Chester Gould's new comic strip, *Dick Tracy*, features an ordinary citizen who becomes a police officer after his sweetheart, Tess Trueheart, is kidnapped and her father murdered. Iron-jawed Tracy will pursue criminals relentlessly, dishing out justice daily and on Sundays in eye-for-an-eye fashion. Go get 'em, Dick!

Commission calls dry law unenforceable

Washington, D.C., Jan. 19

The Wickersham Commission report issued today left most people no wiser than before. Headed by former United States Attorney General George W. Wickersham and formally called the National Commission on Law Observance and Enforcement, the group was originally formed to study the problems of enforcing Prohibition. But it was hobbled by President Hoover's insistence that it study all national crime. The commission finds that Prohibition isn't working and can't be enforced because of general apathy, hostility and the iron grip of bootlegging. While the report suggests some mild modifications, it does not recommend repeal.

Many find the study little more than a farcical admission that problems indeed exist. As a possible remedy, the group ambiguously suggests that Congress either "adopt any system of effective control" or let the states decide Prohibition's future. This could lead to the repeal favored by the "wets," to whom the report otherwise smacks of pussyfooting and buck-passing. While the "drys" can claim it as an official victory, the report has ominous overtones for the temperance cause and portends a significant crack in their hitherto impregnable dike.

World's tallest building

New York City, May 1

A ceremony that included President Hoover and former New York Governor Alfred E. Smith today formally opened the Empire State Building, the tallest building in the world. Towering 1,245 feet over Manhattan, the Empire State has 86 floors of space, including ground floor shops and a restaurant, and above all a mooring mast for passenger dirigibles.

Officiating at the tape-cutting ceremony was the former Governor. The building's designer is the architectural firm of Shreve, Lamb and Harrison. After the ribbon was cut, President Hoover, in Washington, pushed a button that turned on the building's lights. Construction of the skyscraper is being hailed as a gesture of confidence during the Depression.

The site of the building, 34th Street and Fifth Avenue, was previously occupied by the Waldorf-Astoria Hotel and, before that, by John Jacob Astor's mansion. The skyscraper was planned during the boom years of the 1920s, but construction did not begin until 1930. The mighty structure required 400 tons of stainless steel, 10 million bricks and 6,400 windows. Constructed so it can withstand the worst storms conceivable, the top of the structure is often buffeted by winds of over 100 miles an hour.

The mooring mast surmounting the building will be available for the use of airships delivering passengers to New York City. Such facilities in the center of Manhattan, it is thought, will provide an enormous boost for the air transport industry, with the building offering a central terminal for dirigibles.

Experts say it is not likely that such an engineering feat will soon be surpassed or repeated, and the Empire State Building is likely to exist, along with the pyramids of Egypt, as a testimony to the building skills of the human race.

The 1,245-foot Empire State Building, tallest skyscraper of all, is a symbol of American confidence despite hard times. Much of the space remains vacant.

Around the world in eight and a half days

Long Island, N.Y., July 1

A world record was set today when pilot Wiley Post and navigator Harold Gatty landed their plane, the Winnie Mae, at Roosevelt Field after circumnavigating the globe in 8 days 15 hours 51 minutes. The previous record for around-the-world flight, set by the Graf Zeppelin, was 21 days. Traveling nearly 15,500 miles, the Winnie Mae made stops in England, Germany and Siberia, where it was delayed for 14 hours by bad weather, before returning via Alaska and Canada. The Winnie Mae, a Lockheed Vega high-wing monoplane belonging to Arkansas oil magnate F.C. Hall and named for his daughter, spent over 106 hours in the air.

Washington Bridge, the longest of its kind

New York City, Oct. 25

The George Washington Bridge, the longest suspension bridge in the world, was completed today, connecting Manhattan and New Jersey across the Hudson River for the first time. The bridge is 4,800 feet long and its towers rise 635 feet above the water. The four cables that support the roadway are each made up of 26,474 wires and measure 36 inches in diameter. Construction of the bridge was begun by the Port of New York Authority under the engineer Othmar Ammann in 1927. Eight spacious lanes are available, so the bridge will be a tremendous time-saver for those driving between New York and New Jersey.

"George Washington Bridge" by Berenice Abbott. After studying sculpture in Berlin, Abbott moved to Paris to perfect her photographic skills. Returning to New York in 1929, she dedicated herself to capturing the city on film.

Facing the run on banks

Citizens gather in panic outside a bank, having lost access to their money.

Washington, D.C., Oct. 7

President Hoover acted at 20 minutes past midnight to end the run on banks, 800 of which have failed. After a secret meeting with congressmen, Hoover announced a plan to mobilize banking resources against hoarding and failure. It calls for more money to strengthen the farm loan system, a privately financed $500 million revolving pool to help ailing banks and a federal agency offering loans to industry. Flying from Texas to attend the meeting, Rep. John Nance Garner found that his wife had folded a scriptural quotation within his invitation: "The spirit of the Lord watches over you and keeps you in perfect safety. His spirit is guarding, protecting, inspiring and guiding you in all your ways." Said the congressman, "I was mighty glad to read it" (→ Dec. 8).

Capone finally imprisoned, as tax dodger

Chicago, Oct. 17

America's most notorious and elusive gangster, "Scarface" Al Capone, was sentenced today to an 11-year prison term for tax evasion. Authorities have been trying for years to corral the legendary bootlegger, racketeer and killer, (he was reportedly behind the St. Valentine's Day Massacre in 1929). But Capone always dodged prosecution. This time, they've nailed him, and hard; the sentence set by the Federal Court is the stiffest ever for income tax evasion. He must also pay $50,000 in fines along with $137,328 in back taxes. Capone grew up in Brooklyn, where he dropped out of school and joined various gangs. Once, as a nightclub bouncer, he was knifed in the cheek, gaining him his fabled nickname. Moving to Chicago in 1920, he quickly rose to the peak of criminal power. With today's conviction, "Scarface" has finally lost his grip on the Chicago underworld.

"Scarface" in "his favorite pose."

Jane Addams wins Nobel Peace Prize

Oslo, Norway, Dec. 10

Miss Jane Addams, who angered many Americans during the Great War by espousing a pacifist philosophy, has become the first American woman to receive the Nobel Peace Prize. She shares the honors with Dr. Nicholas Murray Butler, founder of the Carnegie Endowment for International Peace and president of Columbia University. Twenty years ago, with the help of Mrs. Ellen Gates Starr, a college friend, Miss Addams began Chicago's Hull House. The settlement house became a model for urban betterment programs, helping the poor raise healthy families and gain self-reliance. Miss Addams, at 71 in poor health but unshakable spirit, now directs the Women's League for Peace and Freedom.

Hoover spurns dole but aids business

Washington, D.C., Dec. 8

President Hoover says business must be helped, but he opposes "any direct or indirect dole" for the needy, saying it would create more unemployment. In his State of the Union message, the President called for a $500 million emergency reconstruction program to aid business in general and railroads in particular. Speaking of the jobless, Hoover said, "The federal taxpayer is now contributing to the livelihood of 10 million of our citizens," indicating that was enough. He says that the Depression is caused by "an unjustified lack of confidence," saying that a first step toward recovery involves re-establishing confidence and thus restoring "the flow of credit which is the basis of our economic life" (→ Jan. 22, 1932).

Violent days: Cagney, Lugosi and Karloff

Hollywood, California

Movie theaters now show double features, providing the hordes of unemployed with a place to go and an affordable escape. Gangster and horror films have caught on. *Little Caesar, Public Enemy* (watch a snarling James Cagney smash a grapefruit into the face of Mae Clarke), *Dracula* with Bela Lugosi, and *Frankenstein* with Boris Karloff lead the pack. From Chaplin comes *City Lights*, a silent film except for sound effects and a musical score, composed and conducted by Chaplin himself. Silent-film extra Clark Gable, turned down by several studios because of his looks ("His ears are too big"), plays a secondary role to Leslie Howard in *A Free Soul* but delights audiences by slapping Norma Shearer around. Now he is this town's newest star, with leading ladies such as Garbo and Joan Crawford. Bing Crosby, a relaxed, engaging singer, croons his debut in Max Sennett shorts, and stage actress Bette Davis, 23, has been signed by Universal, despite having failed a screen test earlier. Carl Laemmle has reportedly said Miss Davis has "as much sex appeal as Slim Summerville," the gangling comic supporting actor.

Cagney is tough and outside the law.

Lugosi has the bite on horror films.

Lights turned out to honor Thomas Edison

The great inventor in his West Orange, New Jersey, laboratory. Although he had only three months' formal education, Edison changed the world.

West Orange, New Jersey, Oct. 18

Thomas Alva Edison, inventor, businessman and pioneer industrialist, died today at the age of 84. A colorful personality, Edison was renowned for many inventions that have changed the way Americans live, including electric lighting, the phonograph, a practical motion picture camera and a thousand other patented devices. These advances were the result of what was probably the inventor's greatest gift to American industry: organized commercial research.

Edison was born in Milan, Ohio, the son of a prosperous shingle manufacturer. A collapse of the family fortune when Thomas was 7 years old brought the family to Michigan and a frugal existence. Edison's childhood was characterized by an avid curiosity. He asked so many questions, and was so unable to adapt to the rote learning offered by public school, that his teacher decided he was "addled." He quit school and continued his education at home, taught by his mother, who was a former teacher.

At the age of 16, Edison got a job with the Western Union Telegraph Company in Boston, where he quickly earned a reputation as a rapid-fire telegrapher. At the same time, he studied Michael Faraday's writings on electricity and did experiments on his own.

He received his first patent in 1869, for an electric vote recorder. This was a commercial failure because politicians wanted to count their own votes. His first successful patent was an improved stock quotation ticker, which earned him $40,000 in 1870. This money allowed him to equip a laboratory in New Jersey, where he spent the rest of his life churning out inventions. In his memory, the lights of the nation are being turned off for one minute tonight.

Lindy's baby found dead

Princeton, N.J., May 12

The search for the kidnapped son of Charles A. Lindbergh ended today in the worst way imaginable. The decomposed body of Charles Lindbergh Jr. was found in woods less than five miles from the family home. A truck driver discovered the naked form of the 20-month-old child in a shallow grave. It was taken to the county morgue in Trenton, where the child's nursemaid, Miss Betty Gow, identified the infant as the boy once called "the fat lamb." Mrs. Lindbergh, expecting another baby soon, will not be asked to confirm the grim findings; that burden will fall on her husband, who is expected in town tomorrow, having followed up on one of many dead-end leads. Since the child vanished on March 1, there have been no firm clues as to the identity of the kidnapper other than a poorly spelled ran-

The child shortly before his death.

som note and the delivery of the baby's pajamas by a man with a German accent who was heard but was not seen (→ Apr. 3, 1936).

America's "descent from respectability"

United States

Statistics tell an ugly story these days. The jobless rate in some cities is over 50 percent; two million people wander the country as vagrants, and even Babe Ruth took a $10,000 salary cut. But numbers cannot tell the whole story. The enigma of suffering has sent people grasping for the less tangible dimension of our fate. John Dewey writes of "the breakdown of the particular romance known as business, . . . the revelation that the elated excitement of the romantic adventure has to be paid for with an equal depression." Writer Joseph Heffernan points to the "defeated, discouraged, hopeless men and women cringing and bowing as they come to ask for public aid." It is, he says, our "descent from respectability."

Once busy providers, the unemployed line up at a New York City soup kitchen.

Hoover sets up new finance agency

Washington, D.C., Jan. 22

Only recently, President Herbert Hoover suggested that "a poem can do more than legislation" to fight the Depression. Today, he traded the idea of rhymes for the reality of legislation and signed a bill creating the Reconstruction Finance Corporation. Under the leadership of Charles Dawes, the R.F.C. will dispense $500 million in loans to failing firms, mostly banks and railroads. Its appearance signals the end of the National Credit Corp., a voluntary pool through which strong banks were expected to help weak competitors. Advocates of the plan hope the loans will halt bank failures, up from 659 in 1929 to 2,294 last year, and trickle down to the millions of jobless. But liberal critics, led by New York Rep. Fiorella La Guardia, call the R.F.C. a millionaire's dole (→ July 22).

Winter Olympics

Lake Placid, N.Y., Winter

After mediocre performances in the two previous Winter Olympics, American athletes came into their own when the Games took place in their own country. The weather was unseasonably warm, and some 80,000 spectators were on hand to watch Americans score in all four speed skating events. Americans also won both bobsledding events.

Pastor leads hungry on trek to capital

Washington, D.C., Jan. 6

The Rev. James R. Cox sees hungry Americans everywhere and he wants to do something about their plight. Today, the pastor and some 18,000 unemployed men from the Pittsburgh area concluded their visit to Washington by holding a meeting with several members of Congress and President Hoover, who in 1928 had promised "a chicken in every pot." The marchers are asking for relief measures for the growing numbers of destitute. It is expected that by year's end some 13 million will be jobless. Wages have fallen by 60 percent since 1929.

Earhart flies Atlantic

Londonderry, Ireland, May 21

A Lady Lindy has flown solo across the Atlantic Ocean, the first woman to meet the challenge. Amelia Earhart landed her gold and red Lockheed Vega in a cow pasture here this afternoon, having left St. John's, Newfoundland, 15 hours and 39 minutes earlier. The 34-year-old Kansas-born aviatrix first came to public attention in June 1928 when she became the first woman passenger on a trans-Atlantic flight. She expects to rendezvous in England with her husband-business manager George Putnam before sailing back to the United States (→ July 18, 1937).

Safely down in Northern Ireland.

Norris-La Guardia Act to protect workers

Washington, D.C., March 23

Continuing its search for effective answers to the Depression, Congress today approved the Norris-La Guardia Act, placing the force of law behind labor's struggle for union recognition. Under the new legislation, owners cannot legally require non-union pledges as a condition for employment. Injunctions are curbed and jury trials granted for contempt. But most importantly, the act acknowledges labor's right to "association (and) self-organization" as a counterweight to the power of management.

Labor leaders almost universally applaud the move, hoping it will reinvigorate legions of discouraged organizers. But the battle is still uphill. Trade union rolls have been cut nearly in half, from a peak of five million in 1920, while the American Federation of Labor has shrunk from four million members to 2.5 million. An atomized labor force has been hit hard by the crash. Wage payments fell from $50 billion in 1929 to an estimated $30 billion this year, and unemployment has soared to 11 million. The economists, who think greater consumption can end the Depression are some of the bill's most vociferous backers, hoping an emboldened labor movement will push wages up.

4 from U.S. freed in Hawaiian's death

Honolulu, May 13

Four Americans convicted of killing a Hawaiian were freed today. The Hawaiian, who had been accused of raping the wife of U.S. Navy Lt. Thomas Massie, was kidnapped and killed by Lieutenant Massie, his mother-in-law and two sailors. Today, however, Hawaii Governor Judd reduced their 10-year sentences to an hour. A pardon for the four and an inquiry are being sought by U.S. senators and Clarence Darrow, the lawyer for the convicted group. Hawaiians are incensed, charging there are two sets of justice in Hawaii.

The Depression does not always discriminate in choosing victims.

Bonus Army is dispersed

A group of bonus marchers from Tennessee finally arrive in Washington, D.C.

Washington, D.C., July 28

President Hoover today ordered that federal troops under the command of General Douglas MacArthur forcibly remove the "Bonus Army" from the nation's capital. Witnesses say that the army's treatment of the unemployed veterans was little short of barbaric. MacArthur, the army chief of staff, was called in earlier today after a clash between 800 Washington police and a gathering of 5,000 veterans led to the death of two of the veterans. Leading a massed force of four troops of cavalry and four companies of infantry supported by tanks, MacArthur and his soldiers, wielding sabers and throwing tear gas, assaulted the shacks set up by the Bonus Army. The troops then burned the entire temporary settlement and dispersed the estimated 9,000 former servicemen, some say brutally. MacArthur said that he "felt revolution in the air," and was forced to use violence. But his aide, Major Dwight D. Eisenhower, described the affair as "a pitiful scene" that should not have been permitted to happen.

The Bonus Army was led by a former navy man, Roy Robertson. The veterans of the Great War, mostly unemployed, planned to go to the White House and urge that the bonuses promised them for having served in the war be paid immediately, rather than in 1945 as Congress has provided.

Shacks, put up by the Bonus Army, burn after the battle with soldiers. President Hoover believed the bonus seekers had been infiltrated by Communists.

Americans dominate Olympics in L.A.

Los Angeles, Aug. 14

The crowds were enormous, the weather was perfect and American performances were spectacular. What more was needed to make the Olympics a smashing success for the United States! No American team has ever achieved a greater haul of gold and in the unofficial points standings finished with 740.5, with runner-up Italy getting only 262.5. Despite dire predictions in a Depression year, record crowds turned out to see record performances. Eddie Tolan was the big star of the Games with two victories and his teammate, Bill Carr of Penn, took the 400 meters in 0:46.2, a time that broke both the world and Olympic marks.

"The Great I Am"

Los Angeles

The "I Am" movement founded by Guy and Edna Ballard two years ago now has over 300,000 followers. Guy Ballard claims to have received revelations from Saint Germain on Mount Shasta. Followers are called upon to visualize the "Great I Am Power" as violet light coming from heaven to surround them. They say the positive results of this will be wealth and power.

Retrial for Scottsboro 9

Seven of Scottsboro Boys with Samuel Liebowitz of New York (second from left), one of the nation's leading lawyers, who was hired to defend them.

Washington, D.C., Nov. 7

The Supreme Court has ordered a retriai for the nine Scottsboro Boys, who were accused of raping two white girls on March 25 of last year and convicted of the crime on April 9. Eight of the Negro youths were sentenced to death; the ninth was given life imprisonment. The high court granted the new trial because it said there had been improper representation by counsel.

Since the trial in Paint Rock, Alabama, the defense of the Negroes has been taken over by the International Labor Defense, an organ of the Communist Party. The Labor Defense was chosen by the parents of the youths in preference to the National Association for the Advancement of Colored People, which had also offered its services. The I.L.D. stimulated demonstrations against the convictions in 28 countries, making the case an international cause. American embassies in Europe and Latin America have been stoned and picketed. The I.L.D. has hired Samuel Liebowitz of New York, a nationally prominent lawyer, to handle the case, and has raised over $1 million to help the youths (→ Apr. 1, 1935).

Hoover clears funds for relief, housing

Washington, D.C., July 22

The federal government has decided to help millions of the hungry and homeless. Yesterday, President Hoover gave the Reconstruction Finance Corporation power to lend $1.8 billion to the states for relief and public works. Until now, the R.F.C. has served only banks and businesses. Dwindling state relief agencies offer $5 a week at best. New Orleans has barred new applicants; St. Louis cut its rolls in half, and Dallas denies aid to Negroes and Hispanics. On the housing front, with foreclosures up to 25,000 a month, the Federal Home Loan Bank Act today formed 12 federal banks to make funds available for construction (→ Nov. 8).

Rule by technocracy

New York City

Who should be the ruler of men? Plato said the philosopher; Marx said the proletariat; Rousseau said "the people." Howard Scott casts his vote for the engineer. An engineer himself, Scott leads the new Committee on Technocracy, started as a kind of temple to technology. He says technicians could govern above politics, guided by the imperatives of rationality. The technology-liberated masses would work sparingly and receive a secure living in "energy certificates."

Sultan of Swat calls shot; Series to Yanks

Babe Ruth in his most familiar pose.

Chicago, Oct. 2

Babe Ruth, stung by the taunting from the Cub bench, pointed to the spot in centerfield where he apparently planned to hit the ball – then put it there for a home run. It pointed up the consummate ease with which the Yanks were able to beat the Cubs in four straight World Series games, taking the finale by a whopping 13-6. The third game had turned out to be a home-run carnival in which Ruth and Lou Gehrig delivered two homers each, their back-to-back wallops in the fifth inning deciding a 7-5 game. In the final game, the Yanks overcame a 4-1 first-inning deficit when Tony Lazzeri hit two homers. Since 1920, the Yankees have built a dynasty, winning seven pennants and four World Series.

"Circus Elephants" (1932) by John Steuart Curry. A former magazine illustrator, Curry leads the regionalist school of American painters. He approaches all of his subjects with an absolute if not shocking realism.

New York Mayor quits in scandal

New York City, Sept. 1

He won't be leading parades anymore, or frequenting Manhattan's nightspots with the same style. The debonair and controversial Jimmy Walker resigned as Mayor today, following investigations and a hearing that disclosed evidence of improprieties. When he was questioned about a $26,000 stock gift, "Gentleman Jimmy" replied that he has "many kind friends." In fact, the Democrat was truly popular with New Yorkers, both prominent ones and average citizens, who were impressed by his creation of several excellent city services, including a comprehensive subway system and a good sanitation department.

Weston founds f-64

San Francisco

A show of photographs by the f-64 group at the M.H. de Young Museum in San Francisco marks the development of a new attitude toward photography. Unofficially led by Edward Weston, the group takes its name from the smallest lens opening on a camera, allowing for great precision and detail. The common concern of these photographers is a "straight" and unmanipulative approach to the image, as opposed to the contrived style of photography.

The Frito, the Zippo and boogie-woogie

United States

What's a hepcat like you sittin' 'round readin'? Get up and dance! Swing, do the jitterbug, the Susie-Q, the rumba, the conga, the shag, the Lindy Hop, the boogie-woogie, truckin' or the Big Apple (it's kinda like an old-fashioned square dance). Then let's catch a bite to eat – some new treat like Skippy peanut butter or Frito corn chips. Then let's light up a cigarette with a new Zippo lighter and scram, hop on America's grand new highway, Route 66, and hit the gas – 'cept there's a new tax on gasoline, isn't there?

Roosevelt elected, pledging new deal

Washington, D.C., Nov. 8

When Franklin D. Roosevelt exclaimed at the Democratic convention that he "pledged a new deal for the American people," they believed him – and took their beliefs to the polls. In an election that many experts consider the most crucial since Lincoln's victory more than 70 years ago, Roosevelt has been swept into the White House with an overwhelming plurality. The latest vote tally gives him almost 23 million to President Hoover's 15 million. Norman Thomas, the Socialist candidate, collected about 885,000 votes, while the Communist Party choice, William Foster, polled over 100,000 votes.

Just who is this 50-year old man who so soundly defeated an incumbent President who was himself overwhelmingly elected just four years ago? Roosevelt is descended from an old New York family of Dutch origin. A Harvard graduate and a lawyer, he is a fifth cousin of former Republican President Theodore Roosevelt. FDR, as his friends call him, served in the Wilson administration as assistant secretary of the navy and in 1920 he was his party's nominee for vice president. Just four years ago, he was elected

Taking hold of the reins of power.

Governor of New York. In 1921, he was stricken with polio and can walk only with heavy braces and additional support. Roosevelt married Anna Eleanor Roosevelt, who is a distant cousin, in 1905, and they have six children.

During the campaign, Roosevelt championed such traditional progressive programs as government regulation of utilities and securities, and federal sponsorship of hydro-

electric power programs. At the same time, he seems to contradict himself. At one point in the campaign, he proposed a 25 percent cut in government expenditures. Later, he said that he would consider deficit spending, if that was necessary. Contradictions notwithstanding, political experts say that his popularity stems from two primary strengths: his concern for the "forgotten man at the bottom of the economic pyramid," and his willingness to consider any economic or political program, regardless of its ideological origin. As he recently told an audience at Oglethorpe University: "The country needs . . . and . . . demands bold, persistent experimentation."

President Hoover has said that the Democrats are "exponents of a social philosophy different from the traditional American one." While this may or may not be so, the nation's voters have scuttled a Republican philosophy that wound up with the worst depression in the history of the modern world, and a President who seemed so sure of failure that, as the sculptor Gutzon Borglum remarked, "If you put a rose in Hoover's hand, it would wilt" (→ March 4, 1933).

Garbo, Barrymore star in "Grand Hotel," Muni in "Scarface"

Hollywood, California

The Academy Awards offered a surprise this year as Fredric March (*Dr. Jekyll and Mr. Hyde*) and Wallace Beery (*The Champ*) shared the best actor award. Helen Hayes won as best actress for her first film, *The Sin of Madelon Claudet*, while *Grand Hotel*, teaming Garbo and the Great Profile, John Barrymore, took best picture. Aside from the Oscars, Ernst Lubitsch crowned a decade of sophisticated comedies, often satirical looks at sex and money, with *Trouble in Paradise*. Paul Muni, triumphant in *Scarface*, as a character loosely based on Al Capone, starred in *I Am a Fugitive From a Chain Gang*, Mervyn LeRoy's look at prison abuse. Audiences also flocked to Josef Von Sternberg's *Shanghai Express* with Marlene Dietrich, Frank Capra's *American Madness*, and Rouben Mamoulian's *Love Me Tonight*.

Garbo, Barrymore in a big embrace.

Gangsters make it to the big screen.

1933

Roosevelt

Daytona Beach, Florida, March 1. Clem Sohn parachutes from a plane with "bat wings" attached to his back, sparking a new fad.

Los Angeles, March 10. An earthquake kills 120 people and causes $40 million in property damage.

Washington, D.C., March 12. To alleviate anxiety across nation, President Roosevelt addresses the people over radio hookup in first "Fireside Chat."

Raiford, Florida, March 20. Giuseppe Zangara, who tried to assassinate President-elect Roosevelt on February 15, dies in electric chair.

Washington, D.C., March 22. Congress passes Beer-Wine Revenue Act, legalizing and taxing certain beverages according to alcoholic content.

Washington, D.C., Apr. 19. President Roosevelt issues proclamation, removing U.S. currency from gold standard (→ June 15).

United States, May 1. A group of university professors issues "Humanist Manifesto," calling for a melding of religious and secular thought in response to perceived religious intolerance in United States.

New York City, May 4. Archibald MacLeish wins Pulitzer Prize for poetry with *Conquistador.*

New York City, May 7. New York Life insurance company refuses to issue new loans or policies, in an attempt to survive Depression.

New York City, June 29. Primo Carnera becomes new heavyweight champion by knocking out Jack Sharkey in sixth round.

Washington, D.C., Oct. 7. New York Giants defeat Washington Senators, four games to one, in World Series.

New York City. Mexican artist Diego Rivera dismissed from Rockefeller Center murals project for refusing to erase a picture of V.I. Lenin; the mural is destroyed.

Washington, D.C. Commission on Social Trends reports the automobile has "erased boundaries" between city and country life.

New York City. *Newsweek* and *Esquire* magazines begin publication.

"The only thing to fear is fear itself"

With the United States in desperate economic condition, President Franklin Delano Roosevelt takes charge.

Washington, D.C., March 4

As Franklin Delano Roosevelt took the presidential oath of office today, the weather matched the somber national mood: cold, rainy and gray. When Chief Justice Charles Evans Hughes began administering the oath, Roosevelt surprised the tens of thousands at the inauguration – and the millions of radio listeners at home – by carefully repeating each phrase, rather than the traditional "I do." After he was sworn in, Roosevelt turned to the crowd, not with his usual jaunty cheerfulness, but with an aura of gravity that somehow still radiated a feeling of confidence.

"First of all," began the new President, "let me assert my firm belief that the only thing we have to fear is fear itself – nameless, unreasoning, unjustified terror." With a voice beginning to show stark anger at the financiers and the bankers, Roosevelt pointed out that "the moneychangers have fled from their high seats in the temple of our civilization. We may now restore that temple to the highest truths."

Roosevelt is aware that the restoration process will be difficult, if not impossible. At present, more than one in four workers is unemployed. The steel industry is operating at about 12 percent of capacity. National income is less than half of what it was in 1930. Some 5,000 banks have collapsed, taking with them more than nine million savings accounts.

One Washington reporter describing the mood, wrote, "I come home from the Hill every night filled with gloom. I see on the streets filthy, ragged, desperate-looking men such as I have never seen before." One of the Roosevelt "brain trusters," Rexford Tugwell, said, "Never in modern times ... has there been so widespread unemployment and such moving distress from sheer hunger and cold." Even former President Coolidge has said, "I now see nothing to give ground for hope."

The President concluded his inaugural address with a hint of his proposed course of action. If traditional executive-legislative measures do not bring an end to the Depression, Roosevelt said – almost shouting – he would ask Congress "for broad executive power to wage a war against the emergency, as great as the power that would be given to me if we were, in fact, invaded by a foreign foe."

After the customary ruffles-and-flourishes performed by cavalry bugles, the President headed for the White House (→ Apr. 19).

138

The first 100 days: FDR takes bold steps

Washington, D.C., June 15

A weary Congress adjourned today after three months of the most intensive yet productive executive-legislative cooperation in American history. During President Roosevelt's first 100 days in office, the new Chief Executive sent Congress 15 messages and personally pushed 15 major pieces of legislation into law. At the same time, he gave 10 major speeches and met with both the press and Cabinet twice a week.

Roosevelt's first official act two days after taking office on March 4 was to issue an emergency executive order that temporarily closed all the nation's banks to stop the massive "runs" that threatened to destroy the entire banking system, and to buy time for their reorganization. Calling Congress into special session, he then pushed through numerous and significant - some would say revolutionary – pieces of legislation. On March 31, Congress established the Civilian Conservation Corps. FDR had the legislators abandon the gold standard on April 19. On May 12, he pressed Congress to enact the Federal Emergency Relief Act, which set up a national relief system; the Agricultural Adjustment Act, which set a national farm policy, and the Emergency Farm Mortgage Act, which enabled farmers to refinance their farms.

In another whirlwind of legislative actions, Roosevelt and Congress enacted the Truth-in-Securities Act, which called for full disclosure in the issuance of new securities, the National Industrial Recovery Act, which provided for industry codes guaranteeing fair labor practices, and the Glass-Steagall Act, which, among its other provisions, guaranteed bank deposits. And this was only the start!

Roosevelt remarked to reporters at his first press conference at the beginning of "the 100 days," "I am told that what I'm about to do will become impossible, but I am going to try it." He did, and even as traditional a conservative as William Randolph Hearst told him, "I guess at your next election we'll make it unanimous."

In the meantime, the President began broadcasting weekly "Fireside Chats" in which he described the problems he and the country were facing, and his proposed New Deal solutions. "Let us unite in banishing fear," he told his national audience on one of the broadcasts. "It is your problem no less than it is mine. Together we cannot fail."

Washington insiders are amazed at the energy of this polio-crippled President and his quick successes. Said Secretary of the Interior Harold Ickes: "It's more than a New Deal. It's a new world." Happy days may not be here yet, but they seem nearer (→ Aug. 5).

Roosevelt escapes assassin's bullet

Miami, Fla., Feb. 15

A short, wild-eyed man took aim, fired and nearly killed President-elect Roosevelt today. Chicago Mayor Anton Cermak was slain and four people were wounded. The assassin was identified as Giuseppe Zangara, a jobless bricklayer who said, "I don't hate Mr. Roosevelt personally ... I hate all officials and everybody who is rich." Just last month, Roosevelt recalled discussing assassination risks with his cousin: "I remember TR saying to me 'The only real danger from an assassin is from the one who does not care whether he loses his own life in the act or not. Most of the crazy ones can be spotted first.'"

20th Amendment moves up inaugural

Washington, D.C., Feb. 6

The lame duck period for federal officials will be shortened with today's formal adoption of the 20th Amendment to the Constitution. The reform permits the president, vice president and members of Congress to take office in January instead of March. Senator George Norris of Nebraska deserves much of the credit for the law. He argued for it for years. And the inability of lame duck President Hoover to act effectively in the economic crisis period of early this year spurred Congress to push for ratification. The new amendment will take effect after the congressional elections next year (→ Jan. 20, 1937).

"Century of Progress" expo in Chicago

The majesty of the Chicago Exposition belies the current American situation.

Chicago, May 27

In 1834, a visitor to the town of Chicago called it "one chaos of mud, rubbish and confusion." Little wonder that Chicagoans dub their World's Fair of technical advancements a "Century of Progress." The exposition, situated on two man-made parks off the shore of Lake Michigan, Burnham and Northerly Island, extends over 341 acres. The government did not provide a penny; it is entirely a realization of the dreams of Chicago's businessmen. And what dreams!

At tonight's opening ceremony, the fair was instantly lit up by a unique electrical process triggered by a beam of light captured from the star Arcturus. *Skyride*, the "highest man-made structure west of Manhattan," carries visitors between the parks in "rocket cars." One exhibit, the *Hall of the World a Million Years Ago*, boasts mechanical dinosaurs that stomp and roar. General Motors has a super-swift assembly line to visit. Promotional materials laud the futuristic steel, glass and stucco buildings, but at least one visitor, architect Talbot Faulkner Hamlin, finds them "almost without meaning," lacking in "plan, material use and proportion." However, he has nothing unkind to say of Grant Wood's *American Gothic* or Leo Katz's Mexican-influenced murals.

What has the greatest exposure at this exposition? Sally Rand, a young woman who dances with fans and seemingly nothing else.

"Century of Progress" Exposition draws national attention, and America's manufacturers, such as Oldsmobile, are quick to associate themselves with it.

N.R.A. Blue Eagle flies

Hopes for economic recovery ride on the wings of the N.R.A. Blue Eagle.

Washington, D.C., Aug. 5

Under the generalship of Hugh Johnson, the National Recovery Administration has sent its Blue Eagle into flight over cooperating businesses nationwide. The emblem, says President Roosevelt, is like the shiny night badge worn by soldiers "to be sure that comrades do not fire on comrades." New thinkers have been urging the government to bring peace to the economy since the 1880s. But it took the outbreak of a depression to turn theory into practice.

The National Industrial Recovery Act, signed June 16, forges an alliance between government and business. FDR called it "the most important and far-reaching legislation ever created" by Congress. It will, he said, assure "orderly, peaceful progress" and "wealth through cooperative action, wealth in which we can all share."

The law allows representatives of each industry to set prices, quotas, wages and hours under N.R.A. supervision. Labor spokesmen criticize the suspension of antitrust law provisions. But the act also includes a ringing endorsement of unionism and collective bargaining, and today set up a National Labor Board to hear grievances. Section 7a has been referred to as "Labor's Bill of Rights." And since June, organizers have been entering factories behind the slogan, "The President wants you to unionize."

Critics are reluctant to let the free market succumb. Senator Hugo Black said N.R.A. would give trade associations lawmaking powers not unlike those in the Italy of Benito Mussolini. Former President Hoover calls the act "fascism, pure fascism." To those who stand by laissez-faire, FDR responds: "If that philosophy hadn't proved to be bankrupt, Herbert Hoover would be sitting here right now" (→ 17).

U.S. recognizes U.S.S.R.

Washington, D.C., Nov. 16

In a move certain to stir bitter opposition from conservatives, President Roosevelt announced today that the United States was extending formal recognition to the Soviet Union. The bombshell announcement follows intensive secret negotiations conducted by Secretary of the Treasury Henry Morgenthau and Foreign Service official William Bullitt with Amtorg, the Russian trading company. In his visit here earlier this year, Maxim Litvinov, the Soviet Foreign Minister, is said to have made several pledges that laid the groundwork for the negotiations. Among other things, the Soviet Union said it would discontinue its propaganda in the United States and guarantee religious freedom at home.

Recognition, occurring 16 years after the Bolsheviks seized power, is expected to strengthen Russia as a bulwark against the increasingly expansionist Japanese. The prospect of a lucrative trade between America and the U.S.S.R. was another factor in Roosevelt's decision.

First American aircraft carrier is launched

Newport News, Va., Feb. 25

A bottle was smashed against the hull of the Ranger today, christening America's first true aircraft carrier, a ship from which planes can take off and land. There have been several previous experiments with operating planes from the decks of warships, including successful flights by Eugene Ely from a temporary wooden platform on the deck of the cruiser Pennsylvania in 1910 and 1911. In 1922, the United States Navy launched the Langley, a converted collier, as an experimental aircraft carrier. But the Ranger is the first American vessel that was designed and built from the start as a floating base for fighter planes.

Perkins announces rise in employment

Washington, D.C., Aug. 17

Good news from the capital. Secretary of Labor Frances Perkins, the first female Cabinet member in American history, says the hiring of one million workers since March has pushed the jobless rate down to its October 1931 level. Monthly industrial production nearly doubled from March to July; farm prices are up 60 percent, and stock values soared 85 percent. Still, experts fear industry is growing faster than the public's capacity to buy products. Wages, they say, must keep pace with production or the conditions that caused the Depression will continue (→ Feb. 15, 1934).

In a time of crisis, the unemployed turn to the federal government for help.

Hunger marchers in Washington, D.C. One in four Americans is out of work.

Kingfish promises to share the wealth

Senator Huey P. Long of Louisiana.

Washington, D.C., October

The Kingfish. That's what they call Senator Huey P. Long in his home state of Louisiana. Now the Senator and former Governor has a new title: author. Long has written a book in which he outlines his controversial plan for redistributing wealth in the United States. He recently denounced President Roosevelt as a "liar" for his failure to push Long's "share the wealth" plan, although Long said the President had given him a commitment. The book is titled *Every Man a King*. Roosevelt has reportedly told friends that Long is "one of the two most dangerous men in the country." The other, he said, was General Douglas MacArthur. Either, he said, could lead a revolution, Long from the left and MacArthur from the right.

Bears claw Giants

Chicago, Dec. 17

The Chicago Bears defeated the New York Giants, 23-21, today in the first championship playoff in National Football League history. The playoff became possible when the league was split into Eastern and Western Divisions. Bronco Nagurski paced the Bear attack with two touchdown passes. He was helped by a rule change that permits a forward pass to be thrown from any point behind the line of scrimmage. Thus, he could run toward the line and throw the ball as defenders left potential receivers unguarded to converge on him.

Prohibition law goes down the drain

New York City, Dec. 5

The "Noble Experiment" ended today, nearly 14 years after it began, when Utah became the 35th state to ratify the 21st Amendment repealing Prohibition. Given that both candidates in last year's presidential election – incumbent Herbert Hoover and winner Franklin Delano Roosevelt – favored repeal, its demise was a foregone conclusion for reasons long apparent.

When the Prince of Wales was asked during his 1925 visit to New York what he thought of Prohibition, he put his finger on the problem with the quip, "Great! When does it begin?" Not only didn't it work, but it also bred results contrary to its lofty aims. Saloons disappeared, but speakeasies quickly replaced them. And as crime flourished, money that might have gone into the federal Treasury ended up in the pockets of bootlegging gang-

As Americans took to the streets, Prohibition had become a national farce.

sters. As it was, the government couldn't afford an all-out fight. Genuine enforcement would have necessitated a gargantuan national police force with vastly increased powers and with expenditures of $300 million a year compared with the current average of $10 million.

Finally, Prohibition was, to a great extent, an attempt by rural America to impose its moral standards on an increasingly urbanized citizenry for whom civilized living includes the right to drink. And with the United States in the lean time of Depression, even "drys" concede that the tax on alcohol may ease the unemployment crisis.

"Invisible Man," "Duck Soup," "King Kong" and Fred Astaire

Hollywood, California

Actress Fay Wray was promised the tallest, darkest leading man in Hollywood by RKO. "I thought of Gable," she said. "When the script came, I was appalled and thought it a practical joke." Her co-star was the prehistoric gorilla, 50 times as strong as a man, known to movie audiences as King Kong of the picture of the same name. Playing the frightened girl carried to the top of the Empire State Building, Miss Wray proved that she could outscream anyone. *Invisible Man* introduces Claude Rains, who makes his non-presence felt in the H.G. Wells story. The Marx Brothers – Chico, Groucho, Harpo and even Zeppo – offer another insanely funny film with *Duck Soup*, briskly directed by Leo McCarey. Fred Astaire teams up with newcomer Ginger Rogers for his second film, *Flying Down to Rio*, offering flawlessly fluid dance numbers, while Charles Laughton and Robert Donat are both acclaimed for their roles in *The Private Life of Henry VIII*.

Meanwhile, labor organizing has come to Hollywood. Both a Screen Actors Guild and a Screen Writers Guild have been formed.

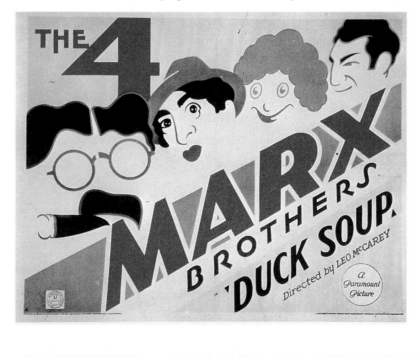

Folks may never look at the Empire State Building the same way again.

Drought grips Midwest

Abandoned farms dot the landscape as the nation's food producers give up.

Omaha, Nebraska, Autumn

After nine months without rain, Midwest farmers are in a state of panic. The Department of Agriculture had predicted a severe drought this year. Not only did the forecast come true, but the drought has proved worse than expected. One member of President Roosevelt's "brain trust," Rexford Tugwell, reported recently that the usually lush wheat crop is so sparse that the few sprigs resemble "the stubble on an old man's chin." The wheat crop is so damaged by the months of deepening drought that the Agriculture Adjustment Administration has decided not to order excess wheat plowed back into the ground – because there isn't any. Farm prices have fallen more than 50 percent in the past four years and farmers are forcibly resisting foreclosures. As Edward O'Neal of the Farm Bureau Federation remarked in January, "Unless something is done for the American farmer, we will have revolution in the countryside in less than 12 months" (→ Autumn, 1935).

Another "hobo jungle," this one in New York City, is torn down by authorities who regard such "Hoovervilles" as unsafe, unsanitary and unsightly.

More job funding; help for the dollar

Washington, D.C., Feb. 15

Congress today gave Harry Hopkins's Civil Works Administration an infusion of $950 million. Founded in November, the C.W.A. has employed more than four million people through one of the harshest winters in memory. The administration's projects – endless miles of new roads, thousands of schools and hundreds of airfields, parks and playgrounds – have won acclaim, even from conservatives. As *New Outlook* editor Al Smith says, "No sane local official ... is going to shoot Santa Claus just before a hard Christmas." The dollar got its own gift last month with passage of the Gold Reserve Act. It lets the President devalue the dollar 60 percent, using the $2 billion in proceeds for currency stabilization (→ June 6).

Abner and Flash

New York City, Aug. 20

A new comic strip made its debut today, Al Capp's *Li'l Abner*, in which a hillbilly named Abner Yokum, dumb and muscular, lolls in a Kentucky mountain pool dreaming about his Mammy's cooking. Meanwhile, in the Alex Raymond *Flash Gordon* strip, Flash is struggling to defend the planet against Ming the Merciless. C'mon, Abner – lend Flash a hand!

Townsend has plan for pension to aged

Long Beach, Calif., January

A doctor who grew keenly aware of poverty issues in his general practice has proposed a pension plan for the elderly. Dr. Francis Townsend's plan includes $200 a month for all American citizens of 80 years or more. According to Townsend, the program would not only help the elderly, but would also stabilize the economy, because the law would require that recipients spend each month's allotment within the month. The money would be raised by taxes. Since Townsend proposed the plan in a local newspaper, it has received overwhelming support from the elderly.

Bonnie and Clyde killed

G-men rub out Dillinger

Bonnie Parker with pistol and cigar.

Clyde Barrow with a sizable arsenal.

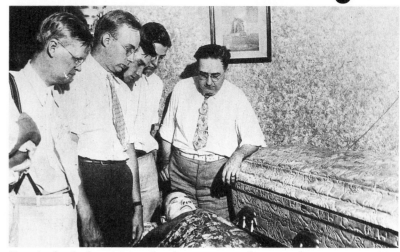

Even in death, the notorious bandit manages to fascinate the American public.

Ruston, Louisiana, May 23

The Bonnie Parker-Clyde Barrow trail of terror and death ended abruptly today as lawmen gunned them down near this northern Louisiana town. Six officers armed with submachine guns riddled the couple's bodies as they sat in a car on a lonely dirt road. Bonnie and Clyde, both in their 20s, have been accused of murdering 12 people as they roamed the Mississippi Valley, robbing banks and gas stations and fleeing the law. Six of the dead were law officers. Frank Hammer, a former Texas Ranger hired to track them down, was with the group that shot them. Bonnie, a small woman with dyed red hair, was a Dallas waitress when she met

Clyde Barrow, an ex-convict. They teamed up with Clyde's brother, Buck, and his wife, Blanche, and began their odyssey of crime. In Missouri, a town marshal told them they couldn't drink beer at a dance. Clyde killed the man. In January of last year, they narrowly escaped a police trap in Dallas and killed a sheriff's deputy. In April of last year, they shot two policemen, then crashed their car through a garage door and escaped arrest again. On one occasion, they eluded a 200-man posse that had surrounded the gang at a picnic ground near Dexter, Iowa. Another gangster, John Dillinger, once said of Bonnie and Clyde: "They're punks. They're giving bank-robbing a bad name."

Chicago, July 22

J. Edgar Hoover's G-men shot and killed John Dillinger, the nation's Public Enemy No. 1, outside a Chicago movie house today. There were 20 armed agents of the Federal Bureau of Investigation waiting for the notorious bank robber as he left the theater at about 6 p.m. Fatally wounded, the gangster fell to the ground without having drawn his pistol. Dillinger's father said, "They shot him down in cold blood." A girlfriend of Dillinger's reportedly tipped off Hoover's F.B.I. that Dillinger would be at the movie.

In a major crime career of only 14 months, Dillinger captured the public imagination with his daring

escapes from prisons and his Robin Hood approach to bank-robbing. During a Greencastle, Indiana, bank holdup last October, Dillinger spotted a farmer with $50 in his hand and asked, "Is that your money or the bank's?" When the farmer said it was his money, Dillinger said, "Keep it." Son of a prosperous grocer in a suburb of Indianapolis, Dillinger spent nine years in prison for a grocery holdup before beginning his bank-robbing career in June, 1933. Over the last 14 months, he took at least $265,000 from banks in Indiana, Ohio, Wisconsin and South Dakota.

Dillinger was the first criminal to be named Public Enemy No. 1 on Hoover's listed of wanted men.

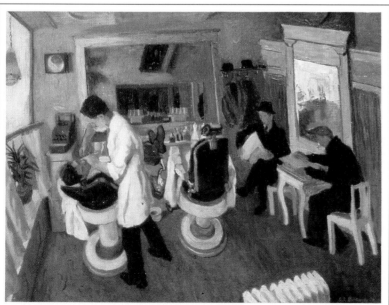

"In the Barber Shop" (1934) by Ilya Bolotawsky. Shave and a haircut.

"Festival" (1934) by Celentano. The streets of Little Italy come alive.

S.E.C. is formed to regulate market

Washington, D.C., June 6

Stock exchanges now have someone to answer to – the Securities and Exchange Commission. Following his pledge to reform abuses in securities transactions in order to prevent another stock market collapse, President Roosevelt today signed a bill to create the commission. Its duties will be to administer the Federal Securities Act of 1933 and this year's Securities Exchange Act. The commission's main objective will be to provide full disclosure to the investing public and to protect the interests of the public and investors against malpractice in the securities market. If the commission succeeds, then the days of wild speculation and excessive credit may be numbered (→ May 6, 1935).

F.C.C. will regulate broadcast activities

Washington, D.C., June 19

President Roosevelt signed a bill to create the first communications regulation agency today. With a budget of $1,146,885 and a staff of 442, the Federal Communications Commission will oversee the development and the operation of broadcast services, and help the public get quick and efficient telephone and telegraph service at reasonable rates. In addition to reducing rates, Roosevelt is especially concerned about increasing services to rural areas and overseeing technical advances. The F.C.C., which is replacing and expanding upon the Federal Radio Commission, is being created as the result of congressional approval of the Federal Communications Act on May 31.

Waterfront and textile strikes are settled

Textile workers listen to speakers at a Rhode Island mass rally; 350,000 had gone out on strike throughout the nation, fully aware of the tough days ahead.

San Francisco, Oct. 12

In less than a month, the National Labor Relations Board has settled two brutal strikes, sending out utterly conflicting signals as to its position on the industrial battlefield. Longshoremen on the West Coast today won a shortened work week with a raise in pay, recognition of their union and increased control over hiring. But not without a struggle. From May to July, 15,000 dock workers and thousands of sympathy strikers clogged every port on the coast. Dock violence here led to a general strike orchestrated by Harry Bridges, Australian immigrant and an avowed Marxist. N.R.A. chief Hugh Johnson, none too fond of Bridges, helped set off a spree of vigilante raids by urging the public to "wipe out this subversive element as you clean off a chalk mark on a blackboard with a wet sponge." The labor board, however, did not share its leader's feelings.

Textile workers were not so fortunate. On September 1, 350,000 struck the mills, charging owners with abrogating their liberal labor code. From Atlanta to Boston, National Guardsmen and strikers battled with guns and clubs. In three weeks, the United Textile Workers were broken. They agreed to a federal settlement that offered no wage hikes, no union recognition and no job protection for strikers. The settlement also sanctioned a 100 percent increase in the work load.

Baby Face and Pretty Boy bite the dust

Barrington, Illinois, Nov. 28

George "Baby Face" Nelson, the trigger-happy bank robber, was killed in a gun battle with Federal Bureau of Investigation agents near here yesterday. Nelson killed two F.B.I. agents before he was mortally wounded. His wife, Helen, dumped her husband's naked body on a road and escaped in a car. Just last month, G-men killed Nelson's equally famous partner, Charles Arthur "Pretty Boy" Floyd, near East Liverpool, Ohio. Nelson and Floyd robbed banks with John Dillinger before Dillinger was shot down in July. In April, Nelson killed another F.B.I. agent while stealing his car near the Little Bohemia Lodge at Manitowish Waters, Wisconsin. Floyd, who, like Nelson, was known for killing law officers, got his nickname from a madam known as Mother Ash who ran a Kansas City bordello. She was once said to have approached Floyd and said, "I want you all to myself, pretty boy." Floyd hated the nickname, but it stuck. He became Public Enemy No. 1 after Dillinger's death. Like Dillinger, he was known as a Robin Hood type.

"Paper Workers" (1934) by Douglas Crockwell. "The machine has destroyed a whole age of art," writes one critic, "and is busy creating a new age."

Radio priest attracts flock of five million

Father Coughlin combines radio and rhetoric to build a huge following.

Royal Oak, Michigan

Father Charles E. Coughlin has gained five million members for his National Union for Social Justice in the two months since it started. The radio priest has found a welcoming ear among many discouraged or destroyed by the Depression. He rails against big business. For Father Coughlin, the enemies are "godless capitalists, the Jews, the Communists, international bankers and plutocrats." The platform of his National Union demands the nationalization of public services, creation of a government-owned central bank and unionization of all workers. He supported Franklin Roosevelt in 1932, but Coughlin is increasingly critical of the President, and there are rumors that he will back a third party movement in the next presidential election.

"It Happened One Night" to Gable

Hollywood, California

Louis B. Mayer agreed to lend Columbia his star Clark Gable for a minor project: Frank Capra's *It Happened One Night*. Reluctantly, Gable accepted the part of the dashing reporter. Claudette Colbert did the same for her part as a madcap heiress. The film's success is overwhelming. Gable, a man's man and a woman's dream, has come to symbolize virility, and since he stripped to reveal a bare chest in one scene, the male underwear business has been losing its shirt!

Leadbelly's blues win him a pardon

Louisiana, Aug. 1

Huddie Ledbetter, that "sweet singer from the swamplands," has again sung his way to freedom. Better known as Leadbelly, the legendary blues singer was released by Louisiana Governor O.K. Allen after Leadbelly wrote a song to him pleading for a pardon. No stranger to violence, the hard-living Leadbelly has been in and out of prison since 1918. In 1925, he similarly "sweet sung" Texas Governor Pat Neff into an early release from a 30-year sentence.

Tigers choked by "Gas House Gang"

Detroit, Michigan, Oct. 9

They're a motley crew, they're the "Gas House Gang," they're the rowdy St. Louis Cardinals, and today they beat the Detroit Tigers to win the World Series in seven games. They star Pepper Martin, who rode freights to get to spring training, and 30-game winner Dizzy Dean. Great as he is, Diz was overshadowed in the All-Star Game by Carl Hubbell of the New York Giants, who fanned Babe Ruth, Lou Gehrig, Jimmy Foxx, Al Simmons and Joe Cronin in order.

Dizzy and Daffy Dean make a pitch.

American marines pull out of Haiti

Port-au-Prince, Haiti, Aug. 6

The United States withdrew its last marines from Haiti today, ending 19 years of military occupation. Although Washington will retain some control over Haiti's finances, today's action is the latest demonstration that President Roosevelt fully intends to carry out his inauguration pledge to be a "good neighbor" to Latin America, particularly by forgoing the interventionism of past decades. Last May, the United States negotiated a treaty abrogating the Platt Amendment that the Cubans hated. Forced on Cuba in 1901 as part of its constitution, this clause gave the United States the right to intervene to suppress disorder and restricted Cuba's right to make treaties and incur debts. The Americans will retain the naval base at Guantanamo Bay.

Donald Duck debut

Hollywood, California

Animator Walt Disney has given the nation a new character, Donald Duck, who makes his first appearance in the cartoon *Wise Little Hen*. This year, the 33-year-old Disney may realize a lifelong dream, a feature-length animated movie (he's talking about Snow White). Already, Oswald the Rabbit, Mickey Mouse and the Three Little Pigs have won American hearts, coming from the creative and perfectionist hand and mind of the former Red Cross ambulance driver who now heads a vast animation studio.

Sinclair loses race for coast governor

California, November

"The present depression is one of abundance, not of scarcity ... The cause of the trouble is that a small class has the wealth, while the rest have the debts ... The remedy is to give the workers access to the means of production, and let them produce for themselves, not for others ... the American way." So wrote novelist Upton Sinclair in *The Nation*. The 56-year-old Sinclair, an ardent Socialist whose novel *The Jungle* related the brutal life of workers in Chicago's stockyards, has lost his race for governor of California. He was defeated by the cautious Frank Merriam, who had almost total press support. Sinclair, running as a Democrat, based his campaign on an End Poverty in California (EPIC) plan aimed at helping the jobless and the poor.

As Hollywood continues to thrive, a star system has evolved. This year, swashbuckler Douglas Fairbanks plays in "The Private Life of Don Juan."

Blue Eagle saving Uncle Sam.

Pacific Ocean, Feb. 12. A strong gust of wind causes dirigible Macon to break up, killing two crew members.

New York City, March 7. In an effort to reduce street noise, city revokes licenses of all organ grinders.

New York City, March 19. Accusations of police brutality in case of a young Negro caught shoplifting touch off riots in which three people are killed and $200 million in damages result.

Kansas City, Mo., May 8. John Brock makes his 2,000th flight; he has flown everyday for five and a half years.

Orleans, Massachusetts, May 11. First restaurant under Howard Johnson franchise opens.

Boston, May 30. Babe Ruth's name appears in major league lineup for last time – with Boston Braves.

New York City, June 13. Jim Braddock defeats Max Baer in 15 rounds for heavyweight boxing title.

Washington, D.C., June 16. Herbert Hoover says in a speech, "Social security must be built on a cult of work, not a cult of leisure."

Detroit, Oct. 7. Tigers defeat Chicago Cubs, four games to two, in World Series.

New York City, Oct. 10. George Gershwin's musical *Porgy and Bess* opens.

Milwaukee, Nov. 9. Idzi Rutkowski, the "Mad Bomber of Milwaukee," is killed before city responds to his demands, when his dynamite cache explodes.

Detroit, Dec. 15. Lions defeat New York Giants, 26-7, in N.F.L. championship.

New York City. First Heisman Trophy awarded to Jay Berwanger, a halfback for the University of Chicago.

New York City. Clifford Odets publishes three plays: *Waiting for Lefty, Awake and Sing* and *Paradise Lost*.

DEATHS

Chicago, May 21. Jane Addams, social reformer (*Sept. 6, 1860).

Alaska, Aug. 15. Will Rogers, cowboy and humorist, in a plane crash (*Nov. 4, 1879).

N.I.R.A. is ruled illegal

Washington, D.C., May 27

The judicial branch has clamped down on the executive branch. The Supreme Court today voted unanimously that the National Industrial Recovery Act is unconstitutional. It is the first substantial act of the New Deal to be shot down. It had provided that industries be placed under codes of fair dealing that regulated wages, hours, working conditions and collective bargaining.

The court ruling came in Schecter Poultry Corporation v. United States. The court ruled that the wages and hours provisions of the codes exceeded the powers of Congress under the interstate commerce clause of the Constitution

President Roosevelt, stung by the defeat, said, "We have been relegated to the horse-and-buggy definition of interstate commerce." It is believed he will seek executive revenge for a decision that has destroyed one of his prize pieces of New Deal legislation.

Last week, the court ruled that Congress does not have the right to regulate the social welfare of workers, in declaring illegal the Railroad Retirement Act (→Summer).

W.P.A. formed, biggest work program yet

W.P.A. projects around the nation may alleviate the burden of unemployment.

Washington, D.C., May 6

At a cost of $5 billion, the most extensive public works program yet has risen from the alphabet soup of the New Deal. The Work Progress Administration, set up today under the Emergency Relief Appropriations Act, will employ one-third of the nation's 11 million jobless, according to director Harry Hopkins.

The plan will return direct relief efforts to the states. "I am not willing," President Roosevelt told Congress in January, "that the vitality of our people be further sapped by the giving of cash, of market baskets, of a few hours' weekly work cutting grass, raking leaves, or picking up papers in public parks." One-quarter of American families now depend on direct relief. As W.P.A. officials see it, their task is "to help men keep their

chins up and their hands in."

Adopted by a wide margin in the House, W.P.A. ran into fire in the Senate. Isolationists barred the use of funds for military projects. Democrats upset over FDR's non-partisan use of patronage got Senate control over appointments. Conservatives still denounce federal intrusion into the economy. To the Liberty League, W.P.A. signals the end "of the form of government under which we have lived." Liberals, on the other hand, want more of the same. Keynesians believe that $9 billion is necessary to fuel the economy. But to those the New Deal touches, it seems to instill pride. "There ain't no other nation in the world," says one North Carolina farmer, "that would have sense enough to think of W.P.A. and all the other A's" (→27).

Court strikes down Scottsboro verdict

Washington, D.C., Apr. 1

Lawyer Samuel Liebowitz and his nine Negro clients, the Scottsboro Boys, accused of raping two white girls in 1931, took their case to the Supreme Court, and today the court reversed their convictions. The court held that the trial was unfair because Negroes had been excluded from the jury. Despite the ruling, the youths have not been freed and new warrants have been sworn out by one of the girls who first brought on the trial by charging she had been raped.

Ma Barker killed in clash with F.B.I.

Lake Weir, Florida, Jan. 16

"Ma" Barker, said to be the brains of the dreaded Barker gang, was killed in a gun battle with FBI agents and local police here today. Her son Arthur ("Doc"), who was hiding out with her in a cottage, was also shot down. Ma, her husband George, and her four sons, Herman, Lloyd, Arthur, and Fred, working with other criminals, have been responsible for many bank robberies totalling $3 million. Large rewards have been offered for them, alive or dead – preferably dead. Herman was already out of the gang. He deliberately shot himself dead as police tried to arrest him in 1927.

A movie about a French princess who runs off to America and falls in love with an Indian scout.

Dust storms hit again

Dubuque, Iowa, Autumn

At least half of this state's farmers are said to have lost their land to the twin forces of depression and drought. And with the increasing severity of the dust storms that are skimming off the precious topsoil, agriculture experts say the situation is becoming even worse. The dust storms began in earnest two years ago in Texas and Oklahoma, and have gradually covered the Midwest. The biggest single windstorm swept through the so-called "Dust Bowl" this May. Tremendous clouds of dust obscured the sun as far east as the Appalachian Mountains. Here on the Plains, the dust drifts up against fences like snow in winter. And farmers report that many of their cattle eat so much dirt as they scratch for grass that they die from mudballs in their stomachs.

As one observer remarked, "The country seems to brood as though death were touching it."

Meanwhile, Congress has voted a Soil Conservation Act that should help. Sad to say, though, not even the New Deal can make the wind stop blowing.

The life of a migrant cotton worker and his family is difficult. Thousands are making their way to California via the Southwest to escape the "Dust Bowl."

C.C.C. employs 500,000

Forest Service men and C.C.C. youths lift seedlings from their beds in Oregon.

Washington, D.C., Summer

The Civilian Conservation Corps has announced that it plans to have at least half a million young men enrolled in its ranks by the end of the year. One of President Roosevelt's most popular relief programs, the C.C.C. was established in March 1933 as a way to put the growing army of unemployed youth to work and to help provide financial assistance to their families at the same time.

Under the charter of the corps, men between the ages of 18 and 25 whose families are on relief can be enrolled for a period of one year. They receive free room and board at federal camps. They are also paid a salary of $30 per month, $25 of which automatically goes to their families. The corps members are trained to work on a wide variety of projects, including reforestation, anti-soil erosion, national park construction and other public works projects.

The C.C.C. is being jointly administered by four governmental agencies. The Labor Department recruits the young men, the War Department operates the camps and the Agriculture and Interior Departments organize and supervise the work projects. While Congressmen William Green and Herbert Benjamin charge that the corps "smacks of fascism" and is little more than "a system of forced labor," most observers believe it has been a big success. The director of the corps is Robert Fechner, who was vice president of the American Machinists Union (→July 5).

Cincinnati is lit up for night games

Cincinnati, May 24

Baseball Commissioner Kenesaw Landis doesn't care much for the idea, but he did approve experimental night baseball and the first major league game was played here tonight between the Reds and Phillies. The Phillies won, 2-1, at floodlit Crosley Field. The wary commissioner has given approval for seven night games. Others in the baseball establishment have also been slow to accept the nighttime concept because they feel the national pastime was meant to be played in sunlight, as God intended. Since teams travel by train, night games could snarl schedules.

Rural homes to get electric power

Washington, D.C., May 11

President Roosevelt announced today that he has established the Rural Electrification Administration. The R.E.A., as it is to be called, will make low-cost construction loans to private companies willing to construct electrical generating and delivery systems to rural areas that are not presently being supplied. While it is estimated that nine out of 10 farms in the nation do not have electricity now, government optimists predict that by 1941, more than 40 percent of them will be equipped to receive this miracle energy of the 20th century.

Washington, D.C., May 1. *The President today used new discretionary powers to set up the Resettlement Administration, to help farm owners and tenants, such as the men in this Dorothea Lange photo, move to better land.*

Wagner Act helps labor

Washington, D.C., July 5

According to advocates of the Wagner Labor Relations Act, management and labor have agreed to a permanent truce in the industrial war, with the federal government as the peacekeeper. Signed into law today, the bill outlaws company unions and gives a reconstituted National Labor Relations Board authority to punish employers for "unfair labor practices." The three-member board will also exercise control over union elections.

The Wagner Act offers a replacement for Section 7a of the National Industrial Recovery Act, struck down by the Supreme Court in May. Section 7a protected collective bargaining, but it was rarely enforced, leading unionists to translate N.R.A. as "National Run Around." New York Senator Robert Wagner, author of the bill, told the Senate N.R.A.'s failure to uphold labor's rights while allowing price-fixing and quotas had "driven a dagger close to the heart of" the recovery drive. Unemployment, he argued, is "as great as it was a year ago." Payrolls languish at 60 percent of 1926 levels, while corporate dividends and interest have soared 150 percent. He says the "failure to maintain a sane balance between wages and industrial returns" stifles every hint of recovery. The act, he insists, is the only way to "rely upon democratic self-help by industry and labor, instead of courting the pitfalls of an arbitrary or totalitarian state" (→ Aug. 14).

Alcoholics uniting to help each other

Akron, Ohio, June 10

Bill W. and Dr. Bob S. are alcoholics. But they are facing up to their problems and hope to help others do the same through a group they have formed called Alcoholics Anonymous. The two men, one a New York stockbroker, the other a surgeon from Akron, Ohio, first began meeting last month to attack their drinking problem. Now, in a bold experiment, they hope to aid others through self-help and mutual support. For anonymity, members will be identified only by first name and last initial.

Omaha third horse to win Triple Crown

New York City, June 8

Omaha didn't do much as a 2-year-old, but Sunny Jim Fitzsimmons, his trainer, predicted that he would take the Kentucky Derby. Omaha not only won the derby but also the Preakness and Belmont, making him the third winner of the Triple Crown. The son of Gallant Fox (also a Triple Crown winner) had to wade through the Belmont mud to do it, but he beat Firethorn by a length and a half. He gave William Woodward the honor of being the only man to have bred and owned two Triple Crown winners.

Social Security is passed

As Americans grow older, they can now look forward to a brighter future thanks to Social Security. Photograph is "After Lunch" by Russell Lee.

Washington, D.C., Aug. 14

President Roosevelt signed into law today one of the most important pieces of legislation in American history, the Social Security Act. It provides a pension to Americans over the age of 65 (beginning in 1942), paid for by contributions from employee wages and matched by employers. It also gives assistance to the blind and disabled and to dependent children. At the same time, it establishes a system of unemployment compensation.

Glowing with pride because the act fulfills a campaign promise, the President called the legislation the "cornerstone" of the New Deal and a "supreme achievement." It differs from welfare in that it is not funded by taxes. However, liberal critics of the plan say the poor will pay an inordinate amount of the burden. Conservative critics say it is yet another measure pushed by the President to "Sovietize America." Some business owners are riled by the act because it cuts into their profits.

But a majority of Americans hail it as a program that is long overdue; other Western industrial nations have had a system to care for the elderly for years. The act may also allay what some see as a mood of betrayal felt by the "forgotten man" toward FDR (→ Jan. 6, 1936).

Dutch Schultz bumped off in New Jersey

Newark, New Jersey, Oct. 23

Dutch Schultz, who ran many of the underworld's bootleg whiskey operations during Prohibition, was shot down with three of his henchmen in a restaurant here today. Police said it was a gangland killing. Schultz was shot while eating at the Palace Chophouse. Some police say he was killed on orders from crime cartel boss Charles "Lucky" Luciano because he was planning to murder New York City District Attorney Thomas E. Dewey, arch enemy of the crime syndicate, an act that might have provoked a crackdown. Schultz, whose real name was Arthur Flegenheimer, also managed Harlem's numbers racket.

Dutch Schultz sits in the restaurant where he was killed by rival thugs.

Dancer and choreographer Martha Graham is rapidly becoming a major force in the development of modern dance. She has perfected a style that stresses sharp, angular movements through muscle release and contraction.

Huey Long assassinated

Baton Rouge, Louisiana, Sept. 10

Senator Huey P. Long of Louisiana died today, two days after being shot by an assassin as he walked through the halls of the state capitol. The Senator and former Governor, who has been called the first American dictator by his enemies and the champion of the little man by his friends, was walking toward the Governor's office when he was hit. His assailant was Dr. Carl A. Weiss, a Baton Rouge physician. Weiss fired at point-blank range. He was immediately shot down by Long's bodyguards. Weiss was the son-in-law of one of the Senator's political enemies, Judge Benjamin Pavy. Long was in the state capital for meetings with legislative leaders.

Elected Governor in 1928, Long attacked the "giant corporations" in populist syle. He also provided free schoolbooks for children and began a massive highway building program. He defeated an attempt to impeach him. As Senator since 1932, Long advocated a "share the wealth" program that he claimed would stave off a communist revolution.

C.I.O. is founded to reorganize labor

Atlantic City, N.J., Nov. 9

Craft unionism is "pretty small potatoes," said John L. Lewis at the American Federation of Labor convention before bloodying the nose of its main defenders. With his show of strength, the United Mine Workers boss has rallied dissatisfied A.F.L. members to the cause of industry-wide unions. Losing a vote on the issue by a 5 to 3 margin, Lewis, David Dubinsky and Sidney Hillman have formed the Committee for Industrial Organization to put pressure on the A.F.L. But the federation mainstream sees industrial unionism as a first step to communism (→ Nov. 18, 1938).

The Richard Rodgers production at New York's Hippodrome is one of several such musicals that are taking the U.S. stage by storm.

Monopoly, bingo and beer in cans

United States, December

Booming holiday sales of canned beer, bingo cards and the board game *Monopoly* reveal the mood in the land. A survey shows nearly a third of Americans drink beer at home. And nearly half of those asked said they prefer it in the newly introduced cans. *Monopoly*, a game for would-be wheeler-dealers in realty, is selling so fast its jobless inventor, Charles B. Darrow of Philadelphia, stopped looking for work. In the "O" game fad – Bingo! Keno! and Beano! – a woman undertaker was arrested in Michigan for running a 400-player Catholic Daughters of America game.

New 20th Century, old Fox in merger

Hollywood, California

The veteran Fox Company has merged with Twentieth Century, a production firm started two years ago by Joseph M. Schenck and Darryl F. Zanuck, the former production chief at Warner Bros. With Schenck as president and Zanuck as vice president in charge of production, the new 20th Century-Fox plans an ambitious production slate where technical polish and visual gloss will be emphasized. *Annie Oakley* is a current offering. At M-G-M, Rouben Mamoulian directed Hollywood's first full Technicolor feature, *Becky Sharp*.

American Airlines unveils its Douglas DC-3

Capable of carrying 21 passengers at 160 mph, the DC-3 is a major advance.

New York City, Dec. 21

American Airlines unveiled its new passenger plane, the Douglas DC-3, today. A comfortable craft, it can hold 14 sleeping berths, or 21 seated passengers, and fly at 160 miles per hour. American Airlines operates a popular coast-to-coast overnight sleeper route. Up to now, the route has been flown by Curtiss Condors, big biplanes that can accommodate sleeping berths. The new DC-3, with two big Wright Cyclone engines and a wing span of 95 feet, has a flight range of 1,500 miles, the longest of any commercial airliner. Douglas says its craft is built to last for years.

Artists and writers supported by W.P.A.

United States

Under the aegis of the Work Progress Administration, writers and artists are finding relief from the Depression. Federal Project No. 1, with a budget of $300 million, has employed 6,000 writers in collecting oral histories, researching guide books to the states and creating such useful resources as *Who's Who in the Zoo*. And artists are transforming the look of post offices and high schools by painting large murals. Critics call the program frivolous and unnecessary. But, as director Harry Hopkins points out, creative artists have "got to eat just like other people."

"Artists on W.P.A." (1935) by Moses Soyer, whose work captures a new spirit.

High court kills farm act

Washington, D.C., Jan. 6

The Supreme Court annulled the Roosevelt New Deal's farm program today by declaring the Agricultural Adjustment Act unconstitutional. The 1933 act was established to raise farm prices by lowering production. It did so because prices on agricultural products had plummeted, making rural Americans among the hardest hit by the Depression. It subsidized farmers who would take some acreage out of production, thereby creating artificial shortages. Government payments were financed by taxing the processing of food products. Critics balked at such a tax. *The New York Times* asked, "What will the great mass of consumers think of this form of sales tax, resting heavily on food?" Even President Roosevelt called it an "experiment." To a certain extent it has worked; farm prices have risen, but probably more as the result of poor harvests than from the act.

But in United States v. Butler, the high court declared by a 6-3 vote that the tax on processing unjustly benefits one group at another's expense. Dissenting opinions were strong. Justice Harlan Fiske Stone said the ruling contradicts constitutional provisions that give Congress the power "to levy taxes to provide for the general welfare."

It is believed that FDR is already working on a substitute plan to skirt today's ruling (→ Jan. 20, 1937).

67% of Americans favor birth control

New York City, Nov. 30

The aim of the Comstock Law "was not to prevent the ... carriage by mail of things which might intelligently be employed by ... physicians for the purpose of saving life or promoting the well-being of their patients." Thus Judge Augustus Hand of the Circuit Court of Appeals today upheld an earlier ruling allowing a New York doctor to put pessaries in the mail. The judge echoes public opinion: A *Fortune* poll shows 67 percent of Americans favor birth control.

Hoover Dam opens; boon for Southwest

Arizona-Nevada border, October

What is 726 feet high, 1,244 feet long and holds more than 10 trillion gallons of water? The Hoover Dam on the Colorado River. Following three years of construction, the $120 million dam will provide the main source of low-cost hydroelectric energy to much of the Southwest, in addition to flood control for the immediate region. In backing up the Colorado River, the dam also creates the 115-mile Lake Mead, the largest man-made lake in the United States.

Sarazen drives on in the world of golf

Sarazen's style sees him through.

Augusta, Georgia

Gene Sarazen is the country's premier golfer. In 1935, he won the Masters and became the only player beside Bobby Jones to score victories in three major tournaments. The others were the United States and British Opens, in 1932. Sarazen also won the P.G.A. three times, in 1922, 1923 and 1933. In the final round at the Masters, crowds were awed by his double-eagle on the 15th hole. He tied Craig Wood at 282 and won the 36-hole playoff the next day by five strokes. Sarazen began his career as a caddie and was only 20 years old when he won the P.G.A. He is the second Masters victor, Horton Smith having won the inaugural in 1934.

"Industrial" by Dacre F. Boulton. In the new machine age, artists find beauty in hard reality and even glorify concrete processes such as a construction crew erecting a building. Workers emerge as modern heroes.

"Years of Dust" poster by Ben Shahn, extolling the work of the Resettlement Administration.

FDR calls Americas ready for defense

Buenos Aires, Argentina, Dec. 1

Would-be aggressors will find the Western Hemisphere ready to take concerted action, President Roosevelt said today as he opened the Inter-American Conference for the Maintenance of Peace. FDR, who received an enthusiastic welcome from the Argentine people, spoke to delegates from 20 nations on the *Defense of Democracy*. He has been praised in Latin America for his "Good Neighbor Policy." Washington signed a treaty with Panama in March giving up America's right to intervene there. The pact also released the U.S. from the obligation to defend Panama's independence (→ Apr. 22, 1937).

Muslims in Chicago

Chicago

To escape the disputes that broke out after the death of the movement's founder, W. D. Fard, two years ago, Elijah Muhammad has moved the headquarters of the Nation of Islam [Black Muslims] from Detroit to Chicago. This movement, an amalgam of Islam, the Bible and the writings of Fard, speaks out against the "blue-eyed devils," as whites are known, and suggests that Negroes separate from whites as much as possible until Allah ends white domination. It also seems to offer a message of dignity to some Negroes in cities like Chicago.

New naval ratio set

London, March 25

Hopes for keeping peace through disarmament took a turn for the worse today as the London Naval Conference came to an end. Although the United States, France and Britain were able to agree to some limitations on the size of their warships, the conference was virtually scuttled by Japan, which quit the proceedings early. Offended by the 5-5-3 ratio, the fives being for the United States and Britain, the three for Japan, the Japanese have already served notice that they will repudiate the Washington Naval Treaty of 1922. Italy also refused to participate.

Killer electrocuted in Lindbergh case

Trenton, N.J., Apr. 3

At 8:44 tonight, Bruno Hauptmann was strapped into the state prison's electric chair. Three and a half minutes later, he was dead. The illegal immigrant from Germany had been tried and convicted for the kidnapping and murder of Charles Lindbergh's infant son. The kidnapping took place March 1, 1932, but no one was found who was a witness to the crime; he was convicted on circumstantial evidence, including the discovery of Lindbergh's ransom money at his home. His prior arrest record and escape from a German prison certainly did not help his case. His wife still maintains his innocence.

"I'm trying to say something about the despised, the defeated ... about the last ditch," says photographer Dorothea Lange of her work for the Farm Security Administration. Her "Migrant Mother, Nipomo, California," was picked up by hundreds of newspapers throughout the country in March and told the story of an itinerant woman who feeds her children on stolen frozen vegetables and trapped birds. Meanwhile, photographer Walker Evans is in Alabama, also documenting the crisis in rural America, where drought has ruined crops in 336 counties and dust has denuded at least six states.

Speed and luxury aboard Super Chief

Los Angeles, Calif., May

It will take you from Los Angeles to Chicago in record time, with air-conditioning and deluxe service. It's the Super Chief, a diesel-powered luxury passenger train. In just 39.75 hours, it crosses 2,225 miles of the Santa Fe rail route. That speed breaks the record set some three decades ago by almost six hours. There is also plenty for those who value their comfort more than speed, including Swiss stewards to serve the best in food and drink. Children will be not only well fed but entertained as well with an Indian chief in full regalia who will tell them all about the sights along the way.

Ruth, Cobb named to Hall of Fame

New York City

Babe Ruth and Ty Cobb are among the first stars named by the writers' association to baseball's Hall of Fame. The others were Honus Wagner, the Pirate shortstop, and pitchers Walter Johnson of the Senators and Christy Mathewson of the Giants. All will be enshrined in a hall planned for Cooperstown, New York. Ruth won early fame as a Red Sox pitcher, but his real fame came with the Yankees as baseball's greatest slugger, with 714 career home runs and 60 homers in one season. Cobb spent most of his years as a Detroit outfielder, batting .300 or more for 23 consecutive seasons.

Coal county conflict

Harlan County, Kentucky

Despite the best efforts of the New Deal, "bloody" Harlan County is still a fortress against unionism. Organizers from the United Mine Workers are met regularly at the county line by two-gun deputies. Late this year, several unionists had their hotel rooms teargassed and their cars dynamited. Last year, 23 organizers were jailed for three days without charges. The county prosecutor is on the coal firm payrolls as a "labor adviser." His predecessor, who tried to enforce the law impartially, was blown up in broad daylight.

How to win friends

United States

In 1889, steel magnate Andrew Carnegie preached "The Gospel of Wealth." Now another Carnegie, author Dale, preaches the gospel of "getting along with people" in his best-seller *How to Win Friends and Influence People*. An outgrowth of lectures the 38-year-old Carnegie has been giving to men and women in business in New York since 1912, this simple introduction to applied psychology outlines *Six Ways to Make People Like You,* and *Twelve Ways to Win People to Your Way of Thinking,* as well as tactics used by President Roosevelt, Clark Gable, Guglielmo Marconi and others. ▷

Rightist, leftist candidates enter the race

Socialist Thomas on campaign trail.

Detroit, Mich., September

As the campaign for the presidency heats up, three minority parties are talking more about Roosevelt than about themselves. The Rev. Charles E. Coughlin, the Detroit radio priest, who backs South Dakota Representative William "Liberty Bill" Lemke on the Union Party ticket, has labeled Roosevelt anti-God. "As I was instrumental in removing Herbert Hoover from the White House, so help me God, I will be instrumental in taking a Communist from the chair once occupied by Washington," he said.

Socialist Norman Thomas, who won 2.2 percent of the vote in 1932, is waging an uphill fight to hold his ranks against the populist magic of the New Deal. Communist Party candidates Earl Browder and James Ford are in a "united front" campaign, embarrassing the President by taking it easy on his administration, blasting the Republican candidate, Governor Alf Landon of Kansas instead (→ Nov. 4).

Americans watch rising tide of fascism

Washington, D.C., Aug. 7

Today's announcement that the United States will follow a policy of strict neutrality in the civil war that broke out in Spain on July 17 is dramatic proof of how powerful a hold isolationism has on both the nation's policymakers and its people. The war in Spain is not one between two sovereign states; rather, it is a civil war in which a democratically elected government is being challenged by a right-wing uprising led by Generalissimo Francisco Franco. His anti-government forces can be sure of getting troops, planes and supplies from the sympathetic regimes in Nazi Germany and Fascist Italy. But if the English and French follow the American policy of treating both sides equally, regardless of who is the aggressor, then the outlook for democracy in Spain is grim. Should the Loyalists lose, then Spain will be the third big European country to fall to totalitarianism.

Fascism, with its glorification of the state and its leader, its contempt for democracy and liberal institutions, its exaltation of the collective at the expense of the individual, and its love of military display and rash adventurism, first took root in Italy in 1922 when King Victor Emmanuel III appointed Benito Mussolini government leader after the "March on Rome" overthrew a weak parliamentary regime. A dozen years later, Adolf Hitler, after becoming German Chancellor, matched Mussolini's title of Il Duce by declaring himself Der Fuehrer. In both countries, freedom of the press, independent trade union and rival political parties have been abolished. National Socialism, or Nazism, seems more brutal and thorough than Italian Fascism and is also characterized by an official policy of anti-Semitism.

Parallel movements have arisen: in Norway, Vidkun Quisling's Nasjonal Samling party, in England, Sir Oswald Mosley's blackshirts. Austrian Chancellor Dollfuss was murdered largely because he resisted union – Anschluss – with Germany.

Before the Great War, most Americans opposed any role in Europe's conflicts. Results of the war brought disillusionment. Add to that preoccupation with economic ills and it becomes clear why Americans would like to believe that what happens in Europe is no concern of theirs.

Owens races to victory

Jesse Owens shatters records, showing what "non-Aryan" athletes can do.

Berlin, Germany, Aug. 16

There were 5,000 athletes from 53 countries on hand for the Olympic Games, the world was in turmoil and everyone concerned was expecting the worst. Instead, the crowds, the revenue and the performances all set records, and Jesse Owens emerged as the world's fastest athlete. He won both 100- and 200-meter dashes and the running broad jump, and was a member of the winning 400-meter relay team. The United States took eight other gold medals among the 23 track events, with notable victories being scored by Archie Williams in the 400 meters and John Woodruff in the 800 meters. Women competed in swimming, track and field and gymnastics events.

There was some embarrassment for the host country when it turned out that 10 Negroes (an alien race, Hitler had called them) were on the American team. Hitler reportedly snubbed Owens, but he apparently didn't greet any athletes other than the Germans. The Americans created their own problems. The American committee head, Avery Brundage, banned a star swimmer, Eleanor Holm, for breaking training (she sipped champagne!). And two boxers were sent home for an unnamed infraction. But their absence didn't dim the luster of the American triumph. Even several unusual rule changes imposed by the Europeans didn't keep the Americans from winning at basketball for the second Olympics in a row.

Adolf Hitler at the Berlin Games.

The Hindenburg over the Olympics.

Auto factories hit by sitdown strikes

Flint, Michigan, Dec. 30

Workers on Midwest assembly lines are threatening to grind car production to a halt. With a cry of "Shut the goddamn plant!", workers took over Fisher Body No. 2 today after finding dies being shipped to non-union plants. And in Cleveland two days ago, 7,000 sat down to protest delay of a long-awaited grievance meeting. In 45 days, the United Auto Workers have won strikes at Bendix in South Bend, Indiana, and Kelsey-Hayes Wheel and Midland Steel in Detroit. Flint and Cleveland may open the way for all-out war on General Motors.

Promises of a new deal for labor have induced a clamor for radical action. "It seems to be a custom for anybody or any group to call a strike at will," observes the C.I.O.'s Adolph Germer. In the occupied factories, strikers maintain a fierce independence. Plans are made daily at general meetings. Liaison people take off to organize "outside defense squads." Inside, the windows are covered in sheet metal; nuts and bolts are collected as ammunition. Strikers protect the machinery with military discipline, while ad hoc courts set up no-smoking and quiet zones. But at night, dancing and story-telling take over. A scene that looked like a prison seems like a palace now (→ March 12, 1937).

F.D.R. wins in landslide

Roosevelt portrait by Henry Hubbell.

New York City, Nov. 4

Overnight returns show Franklin Delano Roosevelt has won the biggest victory in election history, taking 523 electoral votes. Only Maine and Vermont went for Governor Alfred M Landon and Frank Knox. All this in the face of a *Literary Digest* poll that had predicted a Landon win. The formerly reliable *Digest* today announced it plans to change its polling method, declaring, "We may not have reached a representative cross-section of the population." The second-term victory by Roosevelt and John Nance Garner may also increase Democratic majorities in Congress.

In Topeka, Governor Landon said he was going to bed without conceding, but he congratulated President Roosevelt at 1:30 a.m. "The nation has spoken," he said. "Every American will accept the verdict and work for the common cause of the good of our country. That is the spirit of democracy. You have my sincere congratulations." A half hour later, the President wired history's worst-beaten aspirant: "I am confident that all of us Americans will now pull together for the common good. I send you every good wish."

Earlier, the Roosevelt family appeared on the porch of their Hyde Park estate, as a victory parade marched up, carrying torches and calcium flares and singing *Happy Days Are Here Again*. Laughing, the President refused radio microphones, saying, "This is just a home party." Then he happily urged photographers to hurry because, "I've got to get back and get the returns from California."

The Rev. Charles E. Coughlin's National Union for Social Justice, headed by North Dakota Representative William Lemke, polled negligible numbers. Father Coughlin himself was drubbed in his bid for a seat in the House of Representatives. The Detroit radio priest had promised he would deliver nine million votes to Lemke or retire forever from politics as well as from radio broadcasting.

New lease on Life

New York City, Nov. 23

A new magazine with a dramatic photograph on the cover and scads of pictures inside made its debut today. All readers need is a dime and they can buy *Life*, published by *Time* owner Henry Luce. He bought the moribund humor magazine of the same name because he wanted the title. Proving the adage that one picture is worth a thousand words, Luce's new magazine chronicles events in photographs. "Hundreds, perhaps thousands, of people contributed their photographic presence to the pages of this issue," the editors state. The cover was reserved for Margaret Bourke-White's image of Fort Peck Dam in Montana. She and other great photographers now have a new forum.

Shirley Temple, 8, a box-office queen

With a great smile, Shirley Temple has captured the hearts of America.

Hollywood, California

Today's biggest star is little Shirley Temple, 8 years old on April 23. The child with the curls was acting before she was 4 and was a star at 6, when her song-and-dance number *Baby Take a Bow* in the film *Stand Up and Cheer* led to a Fox contract and a special Academy Award. Her latest films are *Dimples* and *Stowaway*. Other top films are *The Story of Louis Pasteur* with Paul Muni, *Swingtime* with Fred Astaire and Ginger Rogers, Frank Capra's *Mr. Deeds Goes to Town* and *The Great Ziegfeld*. Also this year, Charlie Chaplin continues to defy convention. His *Modern Times*, with Paulette Goddard, is a silent film but still a big hit.

Chaplin and Goddard, married this year, walk off into the sunset.

At the new Automats, Americans get a meal just by inserting coins and turning knobs. A handful of change is all you need. Photo by Berenice Abbott.

Detroit, Jan. 18. Ford Motors makes 25 millionth automobile.

Cooperstown, New York, Jan. 20. Cy Young elected to Baseball Hall of Fame.

Washington, D.C., March 1. Congress passes Supreme Court Retirement Act, permitting justices to retire at age 70 with full pay (→ July 22).

Raleigh, North Carolina, March 15. First state-run contraceptive clinic opens.

Chicago, March 17. Taxi drivers launch massive strike.

New London, Texas, March 18. Schoolhouse fire kills 294 students, faculty and staff.

Virgin Islands, March 26. William H. Hastie is first Negro federal judge in nation.

Washington, D.C., March 29. Supreme Court, in West Coast Hotel v. Parrish, upholds Washington state law, requiring minimum wage for women.

New York City, May 3. Pulitzer Prize in fiction awarded to Margaret Mitchell for *Gone With the Wind*.

New York City, May 12. British King George VI's coronation is first trans-oceanic radio broadcast.

Newport, Rhode Island, Aug. 5. Yacht Ranger successfully defends America's Cup, against Britain's Endeavour II.

Washington, D.C., Sept. 1. Congress passes National Housing Act, creating United States Housing Authority to make low-income housing more affordable.

New York City, Oct. 10. Yanks defeat Giants in World Series, four games to one.

Chicago, Dec. 9. Washington Redskins defeat Chicago Bears in National Football League championship, 28-21.

New York City, December. First NBC concert with Arturo Toscanini conducting.

Jersey City, New Jersey. Mayor Frank Hague proclaims, "I am the law."

Virginia. Restoration of colonial Williamsburg completed.

New York City. *Look* magazine begins publication.

DEATH

Hollywood, California, July 11. George Gershwin, composer (*Sept. 26, 1898).

FDR: "One-third of a nation ill-housed, ill-clad, ill-nourished"

President and Mrs. Roosevelt are undeterred as they ride into a second term.

Washington, D.C., Jan. 20

Franklin D. Roosevelt began his second term as President today in a cold rain on the Capitol steps. Before a sea of ruined top hats, he spoke of the job ahead. "In this nation," he cried over the drumming of rain on umbrellas, "... I see millions denied education, recreation, and the opportunity to better their lot and the lot of their children ... I see one-third of a nation ill-housed, ill-clad, ill-nourished."

Surely many citizens share the President's vision. "Despite all the recovery we have made," said one analyst at Cleveland Trust, "we are still in the Depression." And no one suffers more under its weight than the farmer. Crop output last year, cut by drought, hit its lowest level since the Great War, except for 1934. Studies show that over half the South's farmers are tenants or sharecroppers, as are a third in the North and a quarter in the West.

Yet the last few years offer hopeful, if uneven, signs of recovery. Six million more Americans had jobs last year than in 1932. National income rose from $42.5 billion in 1933 to $57.1 billion in 1935. Railroads languish at half their pre-Depression performance figures. But Detroit's assembly lines, before sitdown strikers halted them, began to turn out cars at a healthy rate. Christmas trade last month was 12 to 15 percent above the totals for 1935. And, for what it's worth, whiskey consumption hit a post-Prohibition high in November.

The flexing of the economic indices accounts for a lot of Roosevelt's landslide. But his New Deal is far from safe. Polls show an ideological chasm between rich and poor. Of the people listed in *Who's Who*, 69 percent oppose FDR, while among those on relief, 77 percent favor him. Republicans paint New Dealers as fanatics, fascists, "theorists and impractical experimenters." By the end of the election, only 15 percent of voters wanted the next administration to be "more liberal"; 50 percent hoped to see it grow "more conservative." Still, the benefits of federal policy are legion. The P.W.A. has built homes for 21,700 families in 36 cities. The R.E.A. extends power lines far into isolated areas. The W.P.A. employs over two million jobless and the N.Y.A., the youth organization, hires hundreds of thousands of students at $5 to 30 a month.

So FDR ended his inaugural on a note of hope. "It is not in despair that I paint you that picture," he said of his earlier comments. "I paint it for you in hope ... We are determined to make every American citizen the subject of his country's interest and concern ... We will carry on" (→ Apr. 12).

Billboards cannot mask the realities of Depression life with bread lines an all too common sight. "The Louisville Flood" (1937) by Margaret Bourke-White.

Arkansas Negroes to join land co-op

Helena, Arkansas, March

A group of Arkansas Negroes may soon be owning farms on land where their grandparents worked as slaves before the Civil War. The Farm Security Administration has purchased a 5,600-acre tract of plantation land at Lakeview and plans to form a cooperative colony for Negroes. The land has been divided into 95 farms that will be allotted to colonist families. The farmers may work on the land for a trial period before committing themselves to purchasing the farms. The cooperative is going to operate a general store, a cotton gin and community schools.

G.M. gives in to strikers

Strikers sit down, wait and read the papers at the Fisher body plant in Flint, Michigan, one of the G.M. factories that workers called home for 44 days.

Flint, Michigan, March 12

Behind a vast wave of sitdown strikes, the United Auto Workers have pushed their way into General Motors. Today, a month after giving in to arbitration, G.M. directors signed a pact with the union under the watchful eye of the National Labor Relations Board. The C.I.O. hailed the victory, which designates it as the sole bargaining agent in the G.M. talks. But line workers, including the many who struck spontaneously to fight work speedups, wonder what they have won. The pact gave management "full authority" over line speed and bars strikes without sanction of the union's national officers.

For 44 days, workers made the factories their home, supplied by outside networks with everything from food and first aid to song and dance. After the New Year, the movement spread from Flint to Anderson, Indiana; Janesville, Wisconsin; Norwood and Toledo, Ohio, and Detroit and Ternstedt, Michigan. In the final 10 days of the strike, only 151 cars left assembly lines. Police and vigilante attacks in Flint, Detroit, Saginaw and Anderson failed to clear the plants. An injunction foundered on the revelation that the judge held $219,000 in G.M. stock (→ Feb. 27, 1939).

High court upholds Labor Relations Act

Washington, D.C., Apr. 12

The Supreme Court handed the administration a major victory today by upholding the National Labor Relations Act, the landmark legislation passed two years ago to benefit workers. Also known as the Wagner Act, bearing the name of its sponsor, Senator Robert F. Wagner of N.Y., the law supports the rights of workers to join unions and bargain collectively. It also prohibits employers from interfering with worker rights to join a union and authorizes investigation of unfair employment practices by a National Labor Relations Board that the law created (→ Feb. 16, 1938).

Protesters pledge opposition to war

New York City, Apr. 22

The strength of anti-war feeling was dramatically evident here today as New Yorkers massed for the fourth annual Peace Demonstration. Drawing their largest crowd to date, the demonstrators emphasized their refusal to support American involvement in any war whatsoever. American pacifism has escalated following Senator Gerald Nye's hearings on the profits made by arms producers in the Great War. Books such as Walter Millis's best-selling *The Road to War* have also persuaded many that the only way to avoid war is to eschew any foreign involvement (→ Oct. 5).

Union wins at U.S. Steel

Pittsburgh, Penn., March 2

Only last month, U.S. Steel's Benjamin Franklin Fairless reflected that his firm "has been the crouching lion in the pathway of labor." Today, lying down with the lamb, Fairless signed a pact giving bargaining rights to the C.I.O. Steel Workers Organizing Committee. The industry is in shock, its united front broken. Bethlehem, the other half of "Big Steel," has already fallen into line, with a 10 percent pay raise and a 40-hour week.

Why has Big Steel decided to deal? U.S. Steel chairman Myron Taylor, who met secretly with the C.I.O. president, John L. Lewis, has also visited the White House often of late. FDR says only that when friends get together, they naturally discuss the economy. The best answer is the steel union's 200,000 members, twice as many as enabled the United Auto Workers to bring General Motors to heel. With orders high, steel can't afford a walkout. And in a sellers' market, $100 million more in pay can be passed on in higher prices. In any case, the C.I.O. is jubilant. Said the negotiator Philip Murray, "This is unquestionably the greatest story in the history of the American Labor movement." With it, the C.I.O. steals the initiative from the A.F.L. With sitdowns threatened at Chrysler, Hudson and Firestone, Lewis had only one comment: "I have work to do" (→ July).

Dock strike ends

San Francisco, Feb. 4

The country's costliest maritime strike ended today after paralyzing all Western and some Eastern ports for 98 days. The strike, which cost the shipping industry some $7 million per day in lost revenue, has won longshoremen's unions most of their demands for control of the hiring halls, an eight-hour day with overtime pay rather than comparable time off and union recognition. Said strike coordinator Harry Bridges: "Forty thousand men are grateful. I'm only one of them."

Floods hit Midwest

Cincinnati, Ohio, Feb. 1

As lines of W.P.A. workers pass sandbags, the worst floods since 1913 are receding, leaving in their wake a devastated Midwest. The flooding began a month ago when the Ohio, Mississippi and Allegheny Rivers spearheaded a deluge that swept away a half-million homes, left a million people homeless and killed nearly 1,000. Property damage has been placed at more than $400 million, and Congress has passed an emergency relief package of $790 million.

"White Tenements" by Niles Spencer. Hard times hit the nation's cities.

Hindenburg explodes; flames kill 36

The Hindenburg's fiery end casts serious doubt on the future of dirigibles.

Lakehurst, N.J., May 6

"Oh, the humanity," cried radio broadcaster Herbert Morrison as he saw the dirigible Hindenburg erupt in flames that consumed it and killed 36 people. Morrison's anguished description of the disaster was heard across the country, on the nation's first coast-to-coast radio broadcast. Morrison, a 31-year-old announcer with WLS radio in Chicago, was assigned to cover the arrival of the Hindenburg on a trans-Atlantic trip. Listeners heard his smooth delivery suddenly turn to panic as the hydrogen in the Hindenburg caught fire.

"It burst into flames," he cried. "It's afire and it's crashing. It's crashing terrible ... It's burning, bursting into flames and it's falling on the mooring mast. This is one of the worst catastrophes in the world. Oh, the flames, 400 or 500 feet into the sky. It's a terrific crash ... the smoke and the flames now and the frame is crashing to the ground, not quite to the mooring mast. Oh, the humanity. And all the passengers."

The Hindenburg had inaugurated regular trans-Atlantic air service, making 10 round-trips between Germany and America in 1936. One-way passage cost $400. The craft began its first trip of 1937 in Hamburg on May 3, crossing the Atlantic in only 60 hours. The giant airship cruised slowly over Manhattan on its way to Lakehurst, passing over Times Square, where crowds gathered to watch for it. The Hindenburg ran into a thunderstorm over Staten Island and waited out the storm by cruising down the Jersey coast for an hour. It sailed back toward Lakehurst soon after 7 p.m. and began nosing toward the 75-foot mooring mast at the Lakehurst Naval Station.

At 7:25, when the motors had been switched off, there were two explosions just in front of the Nazi swastikas on the Hindenburg's tail. The ship was destroyed in less than a minute, as 35 of the 97 people aboard and one worker in the ground crew were killed. Heroic efforts by ground crew members saved many lives.

The disaster is a blow to the prestige of Nazi Germany, which used the Hindenburg for propaganda, as well as air service. The cause of the disaster is unknown, with speculation ranging from sabotage to static electricity that ignited hydrogen leaking from the craft.

Earhart disappears over South Pacific

Amelia christens a Ford airplane.

South Pacific, July 18

Sixteen days after the plane with Amelia Earhart and her co-pilot Frederick J. Noonan was reported lost on July 2, the navy today ended the search for the colorful aviation pioneer. The last words heard from the plane were "gas is low" and "we are flying on line of position," or on course. Earhart, 39, was the first woman to cross the Atlantic by plane, as a passenger in 1928, the first woman to make a solo flight across the Atlantic, in 1932, and the first person to fly alone from Honolulu to California, in 1935. She and Noonan were trying to circle the globe on this flight and were between New Guinea and Howland Island when the craft vanished.

John D. Rockefeller died on May 23, but he has left behind a multi-million dollar oil empire as well as a trail of shiny new dimes that he would give away to people.

Actress Jean Harlow, 26, died of uremic poisoning on June 7. Howard Hughes, her producer, set a new record this year by flying cross-country in nine hours.

Bessie Smith, the "empress of the blues," died tragically in an auto accident on September 26. She was refused admission to a segregated hospital in Memphis, Tenn.

Wallis Warfield Simpson of Baltimore became the Duchess of Windsor on June 6, when she wed the former King of England, who abdicated for "the woman I love."

Violence at River Rouge

River Rouge, Michigan, May 26

For decades, Henry Ford kept unions out of his auto empire with paternalism, high wages, profit-sharing and a host of company services. Today, he turned from the open hand to the closed fist. Richard Frankensteen, a cagey organizer for the United Auto Workers, had long sensed growing tension. Ford's 3,000-man "service department," a group of former cops and labor relations "experts" headed by Harry Bennett, has expanded espionage and agitation efforts against the union. Expecting trouble, Frankensteen invited prominent liberals to witness a leaflet drive. As the organizers and their guests lined up along an overpass here, men in felt hats approached with the greeting, "Get the hell off here; this is Ford property." Frankensteen turned to counter a blow, and was pinned by two men who pulled his coat over his head and knocked him flat, kicking him about the face and groin. Walter Reuther was bounced down the stairs, step by step. In 15 minutes, the area was cleared. Union spokesmen report 18 hurt, including four women. Bennett calls the attack a "frame-up" by the union. Frankensteen and Reuther, through bloodied teeth, disagree (→Apr. 11, 1941).

Memorial Day Massacre

Chicago, July

Eighteen strikers are dead, 10 of them shot down here on Memorial Day, thousands are streaming back to work, and still the steel union leaders refuse to admit defeat. But resolve on the picket lines has worn thin. A compromise offered July 1 at Inland Steel brought hungry strikers back to work without even a contract guarantee. And Republic, leader of the group of independents known as "Little Steel," has restarted four Cleveland plants – but without concessions.

Despite U.S. Steel's labor rapprochement in March, Little Steel violently defies compromise. "We'll go in the front door or not at all," vows Youngstown Sheet and Tube chief Frank Purcell. On May 30, a group of his guards fired on strikers from trucks, killing two and wounding dozens. On the same day, 400 miles away in South Chicago, 160 police confronted 1,500 pickets at a Republic plant. The strikers wielded car cranks, bolts and bricks; the police had guns. After the shooting, 10 strikers lay dead; of the 78 injured, five were police. The C.I.O. has criticized the White House for refusing to act against the steel firms. President Roosevelt's response: "A plague on both your houses."

Harry Bennett, chief of Ford security, among the victims of labor strife.

Golden Gate Bridge spans Frisco Bay

San Francisco, May 27

Some 200,000 people crossed the Golden Gate Bridge today to celebrate the opening of one of the 20th century's engineering marvels.

From 6 a.m. to 6 p.m., the longest suspension bridge in the world was a festival scene. At one point, as adults and schoolgirls sang such songs as *I Love You, California*, a man held up his hand and shouted "Be quiet, listen to the bridge!"

The crowd stopped and listened to an unearthly symphony of notes: a roar coming from below and high shrill sounds from the wires strung about them in four giant harps.

The festivities ended with a pageant and fireworks that bathed the bridge in a kaleidoscope of color.

The bridge, designed by engineers Joseph B. Strauss and Clifford Paine, took four years, four months and 22 days to complete. It measures 6,450 feet from anchorage to anchorage, with its main 4,200-foot span suspended on towers rising 746 feet above the surface of the bay. The bridge used up 100,000 tons of steel including 80,000 miles of wire cable. The construction, paid for by a $35 million bond issue, took 25 million man-hours and claimed the lives of 11 workers.

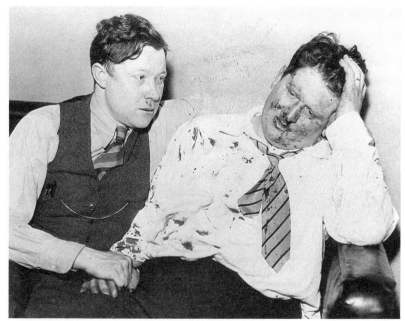

Richard Frankensteen, C.I.O. organizer, after being beaten by security men.

A spectacular accomplishment after more than four years and $35 million.

FDR loses in attempt to pack high court

Cartoonist J.H. "Ding" Darling draws the line between presidential leadership and abuse of power.

Washington, D.C., July 22

The Senate dealt President Roosevelt a severe blow today by decisively killing his plan to expand the Supreme Court. The vote was 70 to 20. Angered by the court's rulings against various New Deal programs, such as the National Recovery Act, the President had proposed that he be allowed to appoint as many as six additional justices if those 70 or older refused to retire. He argued that justices often remained on the court beyond their "physical and mental capacity." The court now has nine members, some of them older than 70.

The President's plan had been unveiled in March in a speech at a Democratic Victory Dinner. He said at that time that most of the justices were letting their personal economic ideas harm efforts by state and federal officials to deal with pressing problems. Critics, such as former President Hoover, called the plan "court packing," meant to assure court approval of questionable New Deal programs.

Hugo Black joins court despite link to KKK

Washington, D.C., Oct. 4

The nation's capital was abuzz today with the news that Associate Justice Hugo L. Black, the newest member of the Supreme Court, once belonged to the Ku Klux Klan in his native Alabama. He was appointed to the high court on August 12 by President Roosevelt and won easy confirmation a week later in the Senate, where he had served. Justice Black, now 51, joined the Klan in the early 1920s, but resigned in 1925 just before running for the Senate. He had earlier been a police court judge and then a county prosecuting attorney. It is said that the Klan, at the time he was a member, was considered to have populist leanings. Indeed, in his years in the Senate, Black was a leader of that chamber's liberals, playing a key role in New Deal legislation such as the bill to establish the Tennessee Valley Authority and a wages and hours law.

War Admiral is 4th Triple Crown victor

New York City, June 5

War Admiral won the Belmont Stakes in track record time today, the fourth horse ever to win the Triple Crown. Following up on their Preakness victory, Charlie Kurtsinger rode the son of Man o' War to a four-length triumph before a record Belmont crowd of 35,000. War Admiral missed taking the Kentucky Derby record by a second but made Governor Albert "Happy" Chandler, with $20 on his nose, a happier man. Sceneshifter, fifth to War Admiral at Louisville, was second in the Belmont. War Admiral, fractious at first, settled down to win handily.

Now shopping carts make buying easier

Oklahoma City, June

Standard Food Stores here are introducing carts that shoppers can put their purchases in. And what manner do those purchases take? They might be bottles of Aqua Velva after-shave, cans of Hormel soup, Alcoa Aluminum Foil, Niblet canned corn (with a Jolly Green Giant on the label), Pepperidge Farm bread or cans of Spam – all new this year. If the cart were wheeled outside, it might proceed to a liquor store. A recent study shows the United States is the world's largest consumer of spirits.

Joe Louis takes heavyweight crown

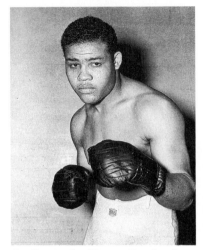

Joe Louis, the "Brown Bomber."

Chicago, June 22

Jim Braddock knocked Joe Louis to the canvas in the first round, and that may have been a mistake. In a cold fury, Louis battered the out-of-shape New Yorker for the next seven rounds before finishing him off a minute into the eighth. Louis thus became the first Negro to win the world heavyweight championship in 22 years. Braddock, eight years older than the 23-year-old challenger, was so badly beaten that the final head-jarring right left a blood stain on the canvas. Like other Negro boxers, Louis had trouble getting a title shot despite his record of 34 victories in 35 professional fights. His only defeat had been a 12th-round knockout by the German Max Schmeling.

"Bread line" by George Luks. The Ashcan artist died four years ago, but his work is immortal, here expressing the reality of the grim 30s.

Some 20,000 American Nazis gather in Yaphank, Long Island, New York, to attend the second annual German Day celebration. With the Depression continuing to take a terrible toll, people turn to the extreme right in desperation. Fully 500 half-barrels of beer were consumed at the rally.

President urges quarantine of aggressors

Chicago, Oct. 5

President Roosevelt today called upon all "peace-loving nations" to "quarantine" aggressor states that are spreading an "epidemic of world lawlessness." Alluding to the Japanese war against China as well as to events in Ethiopia and Spain, the President condemned those nations "who are threatening a breakdown of all international order and law."

Speaking here in the capital of so-called isolationist America, FDR warned that "there is no escape through mere isolation or neutrality" from the "international anarchy" caused by aggressors. "War is contagion," FDR declared, that "can engulf peoples remote from the original scene of hostilities." And he predicted that unless concerted action is taken, the Western Hemisphere will also be attacked.

Despite the President's warnings, however, isolationist sentiment is strong. Last May, Congress passed its fourth Neutrality Law in two years. An arms embargo will be imposed on aggressor and victim states, despite Secretary of State Cordell Hull's plea for discretion in applying the law in order to deter aggression. Belligerent nations will be allowed to buy only certain non-military goods such as oil and scrap iron, and will have to do so on a "cash and carry" basis, the goods to be paid for in cash and to be transported in foreign ships (→ Dec. 25).

Japan apologizes for sinking U.S. gunboat

Washington, D.C., Dec. 25

The United States today accepted Japan's formal apology for sinking the gunboat Panay on December 12. The Japanese government, which denies ordering the bombing, will pay reparations that are likely to total more than $2 million.

In the incident, Japanese aircraft bombed the boat on the Yangtze River as it was rescuing war-stranded Americans near Nanking. The attack was carried out in broad daylight despite the boat's clearly displayed American flag. Two American sailors were killed and 30 wounded. Survivors report being strafed by machine-gun fire as they sought refuge on shore.

Americans in China have come under increasing attack by Japanese forces as the Nationalists continue to lose ground. Since July 7, the Japanese have seized Peking, Tientsin, Shanghai and Nanking. In the process, they have conducted devastating bombings raids, during which American hospitals, missions and schools, though clearly marked, have often been hit.

Japan's denial that it is at war with China has given the President an excuse not to invoke the provisions of the Neutrality Acts. This has enabled Americans to provide arms to China (→March 13, 1938).

Lewis chides FDR

Washington, D.C., Sept. 3

John L. Lewis, head of the Committee for Industrial Organization, assaulted New Dealers in a Labor Day broadcast today. Angry with President Roosevelt for not backing the C.I.O. against Little Steel, Lewis spoke of betrayal. "It ill behooves one who has supped at labor's table," he scolded, "... to curse with equal fervor and fine impartiality both labor and its adversaries when they become locked in deadly embrace." He said labor sought industrial peace. But in the absence of federal help, it will use "its own economic power" to bring employers to the bargaining table.

"U.S.A." finished

New York City

The story of the United States takes a lot of telling, but for now at least John Dos Passos has uttered the last word with *The Big Money*. This installment has completed *U.S.A*, a panoramic novel begun with *The 42nd Parallel* (1930) and *1919* (1932). Other writers till smaller fields. *The Red Pony* and *Of Mice and Men*, by John Steinbeck, are both slim books. John P. Marquand tackles one man's life in *The Late George Apley*. The *Golden Boy* in the Clifford Odets play is torn between his violin and boxing. He ought to read Karen Horney's *The Neurotic Personality of Our Time*.

Photographers document the Depression

All of the misery of the times is evident in the eyes of one hapless farmer.

Photographers for the Farm Security Administration - Berenice Abbott, Walker Evans, Dorothea Lange, Russell Lee and Arthur Rothstein - use their cameras as a social force, mobilizing the public to support New Deal programs. And Margaret Bourke-White is recording the plight of Southern blacks, publishing her pictures in a book, "You Have Seen Their Faces."

Ohio, Jan. 22. A guilty verdict is handed down to 16 oil companies and 30 executives, on charges of conspiring to fix gasoline prices.

Albany, New York, Apr. 12. New York becomes first state to pass law requiring medical tests for marriage licenses.

Atlanta, Apr. 22. Air ace Eddie Richenbacker assumes control of Eastern Airlines for $3.5 million.

New York City, May 2. John P. Marquand wins Pulitzer Prize in fiction for *The Late George Apley.*

Washington, D.C., May 11. President Roosevelt upholds Treasury Secretary Harold Ickes's decision to forbid sales of helium to Germany.

Washington, D.C., June 22. Congress amends Federal Bankruptcy Act with Chandler Act; persons or firms may settle with creditors while avoiding liquidation.

New York City, June 22. Joe Louis defeats Max Schmelling in one round at Yankee Stadium to retain world heavyweight championship.

Gettysburg, Pennsylvania, July 3. President Roosevelt dedicates monument, marking battle's 75th anniversary.

St. Lawrence River, Aug. 18. Thousand Islands Bridge, connecting United States and Canada, is dedicated by President Roosevelt.

New York City, Oct. 9. New York Yankees defeat Chicago Cubs in World Series sweep.

Queens, New York, Oct. 22. Chester Carlson creates first xerographic image.

Stockholm, Sweden, Nov. 10. Pearl S. Buck receives Nobel Prize for literature.

New York City, Dec. 12. Giants defeat Green Bay Packers, 23-17, in National Football League championship.

United States. Historian Charles Beard says, "The American people surely want to stay out of the next world war. It may cost us the blood of countless American boys."

Philadelphia. Jefferson-head nickel goes into circulation.

Delaware. Du Pont Company makes first nylon products.

New York City. *Our Town,* by Thornton Wilder, published.

The "King of Swing" at Carnegie Hall

New York City, Jan. 16

With Benny Goodman leading the charge, jazz has breached the august decorum of Carnegie Hall. Goodman headed an all-star band consisting of Harry James, Ziggy Elman, Lionel Hampton, Gene Krupa and Teddy Wilson, with soloists from the Count Basie and Duke Ellington bands sitting in. The result was electrifying. Goodman's star began to rise in 1935 when his band played Hollywood's Palomar Ballroom. Bored by standard dance music, he devoted the last set to the jazz he plays best – "swing." The audience went wild and the style swept the nation. A smash hit at the Paramount Theater last year enthroned the man with the stylish clarinet as "King of Swing." Goodman has been good for jazz. Because he is white, other white Americans have more readily

Benny Goodman, "King of Swing."

accepted a music once deemed questionable. And his hiring of Negro musicians is the courageous act of a man whose convictions are as unique as his music.

New legislation lets farmers store surplus

Washington, D.C., Feb. 16

Congress passed the second Agricultural Adjustment Act today, two years after the first was shot down by the Supreme Court as unconstitutional. This act is expected to pass any judicial test, as it is funded not by a food processing tax – the downfall of its predecessor – but with general funds.

The A.A.A. of 1938 allows farmers to store excess grain and permits the federal government to lend farmers money based on their surplus. It should give stability to farm prices and incomes. In addition, it establishes the Federal Crop Insurance Corporation, which insures wheat crops against damage and loss by natural disaster.

The legislation is considered a political victory for President Roosevelt, who was frustrated by the 1936 ruling against the first act. Many observers believe that the act will help restore the American agricultural economy to where it was before the Depression (→ June 25).

"Snow White and the Seven Dwarfs" opened in February across the country to the delight of young and old. Through this first feature-length cartoon film, Walt Disney raises animation, and his reputation, to new heights.

Murrow airs Reich's seizure of Austria

Vienna, Austria, March 13

Nazi troops marched into Austria today, the CBS radio correspondent Edward R. Murrow reports. "It's 2:30 a.m., and young storm troopers are riding about the streets in trucks and vehicles of all sorts, singing and tossing oranges to the crowd," said Murrow in a live "news round-up" from Europe, the first of its kind on radio. The Austrians were to have voted in a plebiscite today to decide whether they wanted "Anschluss" – union with Germany. "We have yielded to force," said Chancellor Kurt von Schuschnigg, "since we are not prepared even at this terrible hour to shed blood." Schuschnigg resigned under pressure from Hitler and was replaced by Nazi Minister Arthur Seyss-Inquart (→ Sept. 30).

It's Superman!

New York City, June

Have you ever seen a man lift a car over his head? You can on the cover of Action Comics No. 1, where a figure in red and blue tights with a large "S" on his chest does just that! It's Superman, the brainchild of writer Jerry Siegel and artist Joe Shuster. Born on a distant planet, Superman is the possessor of powers and abilities far beyond those of mortal men. And what's more, he never has to call for a tow truck!

Mae West off radio

New York City, January

Mae West's saucy tongue has her in trouble again. In an appearance on the Edgar Bergen-Charlie McCarthy radio show, she shared some risque dialogue with actor Don Ameche during an *Adam and Eve* sketch that the Federal Communications Commission has ruled "vulgar" and "indecent." Though NBC quickly apologized, 130 stations have now banned even the mention of Mae West's name. Another upshot is that author Jane Storm is suing West, NBC and others for $10,000, charging the lines in question were pilfered from her dramatic oeuvre, *Love and Applesauce.*

Minimum wage law set

A minimum wage law could go a long way to ending scenes like this one.

Washington, D.C., June 25

America's work force got a hefty boost today when President Roosevelt signed into law the Fair Labor Standards Act, which sets a minimum wage and a mandatory ceiling on the number of work hours per week. The President, in signing the law at his home in Hyde Park, New York, predicted it would result in raising the national income to $60 billion a year, adding, "A few drops of rain have been coming from the heavens and probably will be followed by a much needed shower."

The law, which applies to most companies engaged in interstate commerce, sets the minimum wage at 25 cents an hour, eventually rising to 40 cents. It mandates a 44-hour work week, to be reduced to 40 hours over a period of time. It provides for time and a half for overtime, except in certain types of seasonal employment. It prohibits wage differentials based on age or sex. And, at last, it prohibits hiring those under 16 years of age.

Some labor leaders had opposed the bill, fearing a minimum wage would become a maximum in many jobs. But President Roosevelt hailed the law as perhaps the "most far-sighted program for the benefit of workers ever adopted in this or any other country" (→ Jan. 30, 1939).

Committee to study effects of the trusts

Washington, D.C., June 16

A panel of experts was created today to investigate the effects of monopolies on the nation's economy. The Temporary National Economic Committee, chaired by Wyoming Senator Joseph O'Mahoney, will study extensively a sector that President Roosevelt believes is stalling growth: trusts. Some feel the creation of the committee is a way to avoid adopting concrete guiding economic principles. But many feel that the concentration of wealth in America takes opportunity from the average man. One Tennessee man wrote the White House that Roosevelt's antitrust efforts bring forth hope that "burns anew."

Vander Meer, Feller blow away batters

Cincinnati, Ohio, Summer

They used to call Johnny Vander Meer the "Dutch Master." Now he will be known as "Double No-Hit Johnny." The Cincinnati pitcher held the Boston Braves hitless on June 11 and four days later totally blanked the Brooklyn Dodgers. In the American League, Bob Feller of the Cleveland Indians lived up to his nickname of "Rapid Robert" by striking out 18 Tigers in a nine-inning game, a modern record. Feller proved that he was fully recovered from the arm injury that held him to 26 games last year. Pinky Higgins of the Boston Red Sox turned in the batting exploit of the season with 12 straight hits.

FDR says South is top economic problem

Washington, D.C., July 4

President Roosevelt said today that the South is the nation's top economic problem, with conditions so severe that the entire nation is at risk. The President's remarks were made in a message to an economic conference here. It bore out many current statistics involving the South. Sickness and death rates far exceed those elsewhere in the nation. The South has 21 percent of America's population, yet earns only 9 percent of the national income. The annual wage in the South is about $865, as compared to $1,291 nationally. Common laborers earn 16 cents an hour less than those elsewhere. And while the South has the most farms of any region, the average acreage there is also the smallest, thus producing less income.

All of this, President Roosevelt told the conference, has led to "an

The South still waits for some relief.

economic unbalance in the nation as a whole, due to this very condition in the South."

"Wrong-way" Corrigan lands in Ireland

Dublin, Ireland, July 18

It was all a mistake, Douglas Corrigan said with a smile as he explained how he set out to fly from New York to California and ended up in Ireland. Corrigan, denied federal permission for a trans-Atlantic flight due to the rickety condition of his ancient Curtiss Robin J-6 monoplane, said he lost sight of the ground because of fog after taking off from New York's Floyd Bennett Field and made a wrong turn over Long Island. He says he misread his compass and didn't realize his error until he came out of the fog some 24 hours later. Corrigan, who had just set a California-to-New York speed record, said cheerfully, "I intended to fly to California but I got mixed up in the clouds and must have flown the wrong way."

Congress allots billions for works program

Washington, D.C., June 21

In the face of an unemployment figure reaching 10 million, President Roosevelt signed into law the Emergency Relief Appropriation Act today. The legislation allocates $3 billion in new funds, extending FDR's previous efforts to alleviate the recession of 1937. It will provide thousands of new work programs. Conservatives fought passage of the bill, but liberals in both houses pushed it through. In spite of the recent hard times, President Roosevelt says there is a renewed optimism in the American way of life. He said, "I sense a deep happiness that, despite the Depression, Americans are happy at surviving under a democratic form of government" (→ 25).

Artists strive to show Americans back at work. But with the Depression in its ninth year, this may be more impression than reality. "Days Without End" (1937) by Frank Cassara.

Budge is first to score a Grand Slam

Don Budge, Grand Slammer.

Forest Hills, N.Y., Sept. 24

With one last devastating cross-court backhand, Don Budge added the U.S. National title to victories in Australia, France and England, becoming the first tennis player ever to achieve a Grand Slam. In the final here, Budge attacked relentlessly to defeat his doubles partner, Gene Mako, 6-3, 6-8, 6-2, 6-1. Since winning the California boys' title in his first tournament, Budge has had a charmed career. In four years, he has compiled a 25 and 4 record in Davis Cup play and last year brought the cup to America for the first time since 1926. Budge is likely to turn pro next year.

"Clouds of war" are dispelled at Munich

Munich, Germany, Sept. 30

The crisis that has brought Europe to the brink of war appears to have eased greatly following yesterday's meeting here of the leaders of France, Italy, Germany and Britain. In a CBS radio broadcast, correspondent William L. Shirer said: "It took the Big Four just five hours and 25 minutes here at Munich to dispel the clouds of war and come to an agreement on the partition of Czechoslovakia. There is to be no European war after all." The present conference follows earlier unsuccessful meetings between Adolf Hitler and British Prime Minister Neville Chamberlain at Bad Godesberg and Berchtesgaden. Here they were joined by French Premier Edouard Daladier and Italian dictator Benito Mussolini, along with their foreign ministers. Soviet Russia was not invited, nor was the country most affected – Czechoslovakia. The accord calls for immediate German occupation of the western border area of Czechoslovakia known as the Sudetenland, which has a large German population. A plebiscite to decide the region's future was put off for a later date, but few expect it will ever be held. France and Britain have guaranteed Czechoslovakia's boundaries (→ Apr. 1, 1939).

Air records set

New York City, Sept. 3

The adventurous Jackie Cochran and the daring Howard Hughes have proved that the world is shrinking. Winning the Bendix race, Miss Cochran flew a Seversky Pursuit 2,042 miles from Burbank, California, to Cleveland, Ohio, in 8 hours 10 minutes 31 seconds. She continued to New Jersey for a west-east cross-country mark of 10:07.10. Hughes and a crew of three circled the globe in a record 3 days 19 hours 17 minutes, but landed on the wrong runway here today.

Smoking harmful?

New York City, Oct. 19

Two New Orleans surgeons said here today that lung cancer is on the rise and that smoking may be the cause. Dr. Alton Ochsner, head of surgery at Tulane University, and Dr. Michael DeBakey, his former student, addressed the American College of Surgeons. They said lung cancer cases are up sharply at Charity Hospital in New Orleans. They link this to a rise in cigarette smoking since the war. Inhaling smoke over a long period, they said, irritates the bronchial tubes.

Open Door is shut

Washington, D.C., Nov. 18

Japan has put the United States on notice that it no longer recognizes the Open Door policy. Rejecting protests that American rights had been repeatedly violated, Tokyo asserted that the United States and other countries must recognize Japan's "New Order" for East Asia. The Japanese note comes in the wake of the State Department's July decision to impose a "moral embargo" on aircraft exports to Japan, which reportedly used American planes to bomb Canton last year.

Teflon, Fiberglas

New York City

Teflon and Fiberglas, two products of great potential, were introduced to the market this year. Teflon, discovered by Roy Plunkett, a research chemist at Du Pont, is a tough fluorocarbon resin that resists corrosion even at high temperatures. It is being proposed as a coating for cookwear. Fiberglas, manufactured by the Owens-Corning Fiberglas Corporation, consists of a mass of thin, flexible glass fibers whose uses range from insulation to structural parts.

President Roosevelt counts dimes with Basil O'Connor, his ex-law partner and new chief of the National Foundation for Infantile Paralysis. The campaign, led by the President, calls upon the American people to send in their dimes, a veritable "March of Dimes," as comedian Eddie Cantor says.

Washington, D.C., May 26. *The House Committee to Investigate Un-American Activities was established today under the chairmanship of Rep. Martin Dies (right), Democrat of Texas. Here, a labor union president shows him a Communist poster with Hitler and the Pope linked arm in arm.*

Radio Martian landing terrifies Americans

Welles broadcasts to a naive public.

New York City, Oct. 30

People were crying and praying, fleeing with bundled belongings to escape death from invading Martians intent on destroying the earth. Church services were interrupted by hysterics, traffic was jammed, communication systems clogged. All due to a one-hour CBS broadcast tonight in which Orson Welles and his Mercury Theater players let loose in Howard Koch's version of H.G. Wells's novel *War of the Worlds*. Welles says he had intended to entertain his audience with an incredible story appropriate for Halloween. But of six million listeners, more than a million were

frightened by the too-realistic drama, starting with Welles's magnificent voice speaking: " ... Across an immense ethereal gulf, minds with vast intellects regarded this earth with envious eyes ... "

Dance music was interrupted by an announcer reporting gas explosions on Mars. More music, more bulletins: A flaming object, possibly a meteor, falling outside of Trenton, New Jersey. Thirty yards in diameter ... a humming sound ... something wriggling out ... "large as a bear and glistening like wet leather. Eyes ... gleaming like a serpent ... a V-shaped mouth with saliva dripping from rimless lips that seem to quiver and pulsate." Things got worse. "Poisonous black smoke ... death rays ... army wiped out ... people dropping like flies. Monstrous Martians landing all over the country ... people lying dead in the streets ... " Until the Martians themselves began to die, succumbing rapidly to disease germs ... Although there were four announcements over the hour that this was pure fiction, a tidal wave of panic swept the nation, as the rumor spread to those who did not have the radio on. At the end, Welles, now as himself, finished the make-believe ... "and if your doorbell rings and nobody's there, it was no Martian ... it's Halloween."

C.I.O. officially breaks away from A.F.L.

Pittsburgh, Penn., Nov. 18

The Committee for Industrial Organization, which has developed from an appendage of the American Federation of Labor to its chief rival in three years, has made the split official. Calling itself a Congress, the group named founder John L. Lewis as president. The C.I.O. already bans discrimination on the basis of "race, creed, color, and nationality." Radicals led by Harry Bridges tried unsuccessfully to add political beliefs to the list. Lewis, often caught defending his union against charges of communist influence, vowed privately to "lick" the leftists if they provoked a fight.

John L. Lewis, cigar in hand.

Debonair Grant and a dashing, sexy Flynn

Hollywood, California

Errol Flynn has had all kinds of real-life adventures. As a result, he has come to represent all kinds of heroes in one magnificent sexy, animal package. Currently, he and Olivia de Havilland are appearing in *The Adventures of Robin Hood*, about the socially conscious outlaw. Meanwhile, the debonair Cary Grant is showing a fine flair for screwball comedy in such vehicles as *Holiday* and *Bringing Up Baby*. The strong-minded and outspoken Katharine Hepburn spar-

kles in both these comedies, disproving beliefs that she is "box-office poison" and Dorothy Parker's quip that she "runs the gamut of emotions from A to B." A fine performance in *Boys' Town* with Spencer Tracy and his continuing role of cocky, wisecracking Andy Hardy, most recently in *Love Finds Andy Hardy*, are making Mickey Rooney a top juvenile star. Other top films are *Jezebel*, with Bette Davis and Henry Fonda, and Frank Capra's *You Can't Take It With You*, starring James Stewart.

'God Bless America'

United States, Nov. 11

Kate Smith, a home-spun singer if ever there was one, scored a coup on her radio show by offering a song that might well have been created with her in mind. Except that Irving Berlin wrote the tune, *God Bless America*, 20 years ago for his 1918 musical *Yip, Yip, Yaphank*. But it was withdrawn and never publicly sung until this *Kate Smith Hour*, marking the Great War's 20th Armistice Day. The words:
God bless America, land that I love.
Stand beside her, and guide her,
through the night with a light from above.
From the mountains, to the prairies,
to the oceans white with foam,
God bless America, my home, sweet home.
God bless America, my home, sweet home.

W.P.A. to aid music

United States, June 10

Very soon now, bands will be marching in the nation's struggle against the Depression. The Federal Music Project, one of the many arts projects of the W.P.A., will provide funds to hire more than 2,600 musicians for 38 bands and orchestras, But that's just a start – the numbers will grow. If all goes according to plan, next year should see more than 8,000 musicians performing in nearly 30 symphony orchestras, 90 small orchestras, 68 bands, 55 dance bands, 15 chamber music groups, 33 opera and choral groups and a small, special group of soloists. Governmental arts projects that are already in place include the Theater Project, which has commissioned a number of new plays, and the prolific Federal Arts Project.

Movie stars such as Cary Grant and Katharine Hepburn are part of a new breed of performers who are helping people to forget the troubles of the Depression for a few hours at a time.

Errol Flynn will always get his girl.

California, Jan. 7.
Tom Mooney pardoned for Preparedness Day bombing in 1916.

St. Louis, Jan. 16. Major General Frank M. Andrews tells National Aeronautic Association that, with only slightly more than 400 fighter planes, United States is unprepared for war.

Madison, Wisconsin, Feb. 18. University of Wisconsin refuses a donation when donor specifies that it be used only for white students.

Washington, D.C., Feb. 27. In National Labor Relations Board v. Fansteel Metallurgical Corporation, Supreme Court rules sitdown strikes unconstitutional.

New York City, Apr. 30. President Roosevelt appears on television at New York World's Fair, becoming first President to do so.

New York City, May 1. Pulitzer Prize in fiction awarded to Marjorie Kinnan Rawlings for *The Yearling.*

New York City, June 12. King and Queen of England conclude five-day tour of United States, having bolstered Anglo-American relations.

Cincinnati, Oct. 8. New York Yankees overpower Cincinnati Reds four games to none, winning World Series for fourth year in a row.

Washington, D.C., Oct. 11. President Roosevelt receives report from Albert Einstein and other leading scientists, explaining possible military application of atomic power (→21).

New York City, Oct. 15. Mayor Fiorello La Guardia formally opens La Guardia Field, as 350,000 look on.

San Francisco, November. Gangster Al Capone paroled for good behavior, despite mental instability.

Milwaukee, Dec. 10. Green Bay Packers defeat New York Giants, 27-0, for National Football League title.

New York City. Gallup Poll indicates that 58 percent of Americans believe that United States will be drawn into war.

New York City. *The Milton Berle Show* in radio premiere.

New York City. Nathanael West's *Day of the Locust* published.

U.S. recognizes Franco Spain; Hitler takes over Czechoslovakia

Washington, D.C., Apr. 1

Nearly three months after President Roosevelt, in his annual message to Congress, warned of the threat to democracy posed by the rising tide of fascism, the United States has extended diplomatic recognition to the recently victorious Spanish government of General Francisco Franco. The move, however, is not viewed as an expression of approval of the regime, but an acceptance of the reality of the situation, along the same lines as the recognition of the Soviet government. Moreover, most observers say the Franco regime has neither the means nor the intention of spreading its brand of dictatorship beyond its own frontiers.

The same cannot be said for Nazi Germany, whose armies entered Prague three weeks ago, giving the lie to Hitler's repeated pledges that cession of the Sudetenland would satisfy German demands.

Czechoslovakia's destruction has been swift. Six months after the Munich agreement, Emil Hacha, who succeeded Eduard Benes as President of the country, was summoned to Berlin and forced to sign a treaty that in effect dismembered his country. Hitler has made himself the "Protector" of Bohemia and Moravia, and has agreed to "accept" a similar position for Slovakia. On March 15, the day the treaty was signed, German forces entered Prague, and Czechoslovakia ceased to exist. By contrast, the triumph of totalitarianism in Spain has come only after a long, bitter war. Rallying to the support of the Loyalists, volunteers came from all over the world – the Garibaldi Brigade from Italy, the Thaelmann Brigade from Germany, the Abraham Lincoln Brigade from the United States. But in the end, they were no match for Franco's regular army forces, who were also aided by warplanes and troops from Italy and Germany (→ Sept. 4).

Court upholds Tennessee Valley Authority

Washington, D.C., Jan. 30

The Roosevelt New Deal, which has suffered setbacks at the hands of the Supreme Court, won a major victory today as the court upheld the constitutionality of the Tennessee Valley Authority's competition with private enterprise. The suit had been brought by the Tennessee Electric Power Company.

T.V.A. was created by Congress in 1933 during the first 100 days of the Roosevelt administration and has been under constant attack by private power sources, including a corporation headed by Wendell Willkie, a leading Wall Street attorney, who argued: "To take our market is to take our property."

In its ruling, the high court held that private utility companies have no legal right to protection from T.V.A. competition. The Tennessee authority was created by the federal government to improve the living standards in one of the nation's poorest sections, embracing seven Southern and Border states ranging from the Great Smoky Mountains to bleak hills and cotton country. By working with state and local governments, T.V.A. has promoted flood control, produced electric power and fostered the proper use of land and forests. At the outset of the project, only two of every 100 farms in the area had electric power. Many families lived on less than $100 a year. Floods often inundated farmlands, killing crops, and parts of the forests were being leveled by raging fires (→ June 30).

D.A.R. fails to stop Marian Anderson

Miss Marian Anderson, owner of a voice that comes "once in 100 years."

Washington, D.C., Apr. 9

With the giant statue of Abraham Lincoln behind her and some 75,000 people before her, Marian Anderson sang today. The world-renowned contralto was to have appeared at Constitution Hall, but the Daughters of the American Revolution refused to allow her to perform there because she is a Negro. Subsequently, Mrs. Eleanor Roosevelt resigned her D.A.R. membership and arranged today's recital. Miss Anderson, who is 37 years old, sang with the New York Philharmonic in 1925, and in 1933 she toured Europe and South America. Conductor Arturo Toscanini once said that her kind of voice comes "once in 100 years."

"Storm Brewing" (1939) by Lyonel Feininger, New York-born Cubist.

$1.5 billion is voted for W.P.A. projects

Will unemployment lines ever end?

Washington, D.C., June 30

One of President Roosevelt's major New Deal agencies, the Work Projects Administration, received a congressional boost today with an allocation of $1.5 billion. Congress also voted to reduce wages and set an 18-month limit on W.P.A. jobs. The legislation has provided jobs to millions since its conception in 1935 (then called the Work Progress Administration.) Those employed have created roads, bridges, parks, post offices and even murals in public buildings. Critics contend today's allocation will speed inflation. But Roosevelt feels it is necessary to help employ the eight million Americans now out of work.

60 nations on display as FDR opens the New York World's Fair

New York City, Apr. 30

At 3:12 p.m., President Roosevelt announced that the New York World's Fair was "open to all mankind." But not all mankind is represented at *The World of Tomorrow*: The 60 nations exhibiting do not include Germany, Spain or China, and today's crowd was relatively meager. Officals said 600,000; others put the total at 150,000. Still, the throng cheered as Albert Einstein tried in a mere five minutes to explain how cosmic rays work before he hit a switch that made those rays light up the exposition.

Perhaps most striking of all the exhibits is the Trylon and Perisphere, a 700-foot triangular tower and a sphere housing Democracity, a view of life in the year 2036. Visitors ascend escalators in the Trylon, then descend to the sphere, where revolving platforms show them futuristic films. More popular, perhaps because it is free (the Trylon and Perisphere cost 25 cents), is the General Motors Futurama. Visitors on banquette cars wind through tunnels to view the autos and highways of 1960, and they watch a new three-dimensional film using polarized glasses. With huge color photos, the Kodak exhibit introduces a color film that is called Kodachrome. At the A.T.&T. building, some people win long distance calls. NBC shows off its experimental television.

"All those who come to the World's Fair," FDR said, "will find that the eyes of the United States are fixed on the future."

Washington against the Perisphere.

National Cash Register Pavilion.

The World's Fair aglow with illuminated water spouts and fireworks. The fair does more than simply display the latest of technological wonders. It presents a moment of brilliance and of hope for "The World of Tomorrow."

Dying Lou Gehrig is "luckiest man" alive

Big Lou, defying "a bad break."

New York City, July 4

There was a terrible sadness in the crowd of 61,808 fans today as Lou Gehrig, his voice echoing through Yankee Stadium, said: "I have been given a bad break, but I have an awful lot to live for; I consider myself the luckiest man on the face of the earth." Big Lou, wasting away from the fatal amyotrophic lateral sclerosis, was retiring after a 17-year career of 2,164 games. Incredibly, he appeared in 2,130 of them consecutively, a major league record. He drove in more than 100 runs in 13 of 14 seasons and had a lifetime batting average of .340.

Sub Squalus sinks

New Hampshire, May 23

Efforts have begun to rescue the 59 men aboard the submarine Squalus, which sank today in 240 feet of water off New Hampshire during a training cruise. The navy is rushing in a 10-ton rescue chamber, which can make repeated trips to the ocean floor. The chamber will be guided by divers, who have detected signs of life in the submarine's forward torpedo room. No sounds have been heard from the aft section of the submarine. Two civilian observers were aboard the sub when it failed to surface after making a routine dive.

Airliners to Europe

Lisbon, Portugal, June 28

The Pan American Airways flying boat Dixie Clipper landed here today after a flight of 23 hours and 52 minutes that inaugurated regular airline passenger service between the United States and Europe. Pan American's base in the United States is Manhasset Bay at Port Washington, Long Island. The service is the first over the Atlantic since Germany's dirigible flights were halted after the 1937 Hindenburg disaster. The Boeing Clipper, with four 750-horsepower motors, is the first plane designed specifically for transoceanic service.

U.S. neutral as war erupts in Europe

"I have seen war and I hate war ... I hope (we) will keep out of this war."

To Adolf Hitler and his Nazis, war is the supreme test of a people's will.

Washington, D.C., Sept. 4

Following Hitler's brutal and unprovoked attack on Poland three days ago, Britain and France have honored their treaty obligation to the Poles and declared war on Germany. Broadcasting from London, Prime Minister Neville Chamberlain announced: "This morning the British ambassador in Berlin handed to the German government a final note stating that unless we heard from them by 11 o'clock that they were prepared at once to withdraw their troops from Poland, a state of war would exist between us. I have to tell you now that no such undertaking has been received and that consequently this country is at war with Germany ..." Both the British and the French agreed to come to the aid of Poland in a treaty that was negotiated on March 31. Although the Soviet Union is also a guarantor of Poland, after Moscow's stunning non-aggression agreement with Nazi Germany last month, no help can be expected from that quarter. Italy's course is uncertain, although it is expected to be pro-German. Belgium has declared itself neutral.

Neutrality is also the policy of the United States. In a Fireside Chat on Labor Day, President Roosevelt told the American people: "I have said not once but many times that I have seen war and that I hate war. I say that again and again. I hope the United States will keep out of this war ... and I give you my assurance and reassurance that every effort of your government will be directed to that end" (→ Nov. 4).

Fritz Kuhn leads American Nazis

Fritz works for his Fuehrer.

New York City, Feb. 22

They sang the *Star Spangled Banner* and pledged allegiance to the American flag, but the German-Americans at a Bund rally in Madison Square Garden proclaimed a brand of patriotism foreign to most Americans. According to leader Fritz Kuhn, "The Nazi salute is the coming salute for the whole United States." He also preaches that the world Communist movement is run by Jews. His group, founded in 1932 as Friends of the New Germany, aims at spreading the Hitler theories to sympathetic German-Americans. Under Kuhn's anti-Semitic leadership, the Bund has built its own training camps, has its own uniformed storm troopers and follows the Nazi policies. Yet it isn't especially popular, with its membership probably not being much larger than the 22,000 who attended the rally.

Congress passes "cash and carry" law

Washington, D.C., Nov. 4

Congress today passed a law allowing warring nations to buy arms from the United States, if they pay in cash and carry the materiel in their own ships. This act will enable Washington to supply Britain and France with much-needed arms.

The vote is a victory for President Roosevelt, who called Congress into special session on September 21 to seek repeal of the arms embargo mandated by the Neutrality Acts of 1935-7. Roosevelt argued that the law forced the United States to give up its right to freedom of the seas. The measure passed both houses after prolonged debate. In the Senate, James F. Byrnes of South Carolina, backed by Secretary of State Cordell Hull, led the fight against isolationist Senators William Borah, Gerald Nye, Henry Cabot Lodge Jr. and Hiram Johnson. The public seems to support FDR. A Gallup Poll shows 62 percent favor American aid to France and Britain; 29 percent favor entering the war if Hitler seems on the verge of victory (→ May 10, 1940).

Presidential panel discusses atomic bomb

Washington, D.C., Oct 21

A newly appointed Advisory Committee on Uranium met here today to consider the possibility of building weapons of almost unlimited destructive power. The committee was created by President Roosevelt after he received a letter from Albert Einstein saying that "vast amounts of power" could be released by setting up nuclear chain reactions in a large mass of uranium. There are indications that German scientists already are working on such a uranium bomb, the Einstein letter warned.

The committee is headed by Lyman Briggs, director of the Bureau of Standards. Its meeting was attended by Leo Szilard, Edward Teller and Eugene Wigner, noted physicists who fled Europe to escape Nazism. Their fear that Germany would be the first to make a uranium bomb prompted Einstein to write to Roosevelt. The committee has decided to set up an expanded group to coordinate and accelerate the work being done on nuclear chain reactions by physicists at a number of American universities.

Sad Steinbeck tale: plight of the Okies

New York City

"It don't take no nerve to do sumpin' when there ain't nothin' else you can do" is the simple wisdom of the Joad family, whose travails are the subject of *The Grapes of Wrath*, John Steinbeck's new novel. For the Joads, doing something means loading their meager possessions into a $75 jalopy and leaving the Dust Bowl for California and its promise of plenty. This tale brims with real-life details of the 250,000 "Okies" who give up their farms to head out West – where nothing awaits them but the plight of the migrant laborer.

Gulping goldfish and wearing nylons

United States

What's to like about college? Extracurricular activities, that's what. You can swallow live goldfish or chew up phonograph records liberally sprinkled with salt and pepper, followed by a milk chaser. Then there are weekend dances, where you can do the boomps-a-daisy, the chestnut tree or the chicken scratch. If you're lucky, you can hear Gene Krupa beating his skins. If you're a co-ed, you might don skatarinas (bloomers and circular skirts) and nylon stockings. Back at the dorm, you can play Chinese checkers or swap some knock-knock gags – "Who's there?" "Alma mater." "Alma mater who?" "Alma mater does is nag!"

Sports on television

Brooklyn, N.Y., Aug. 26

There are only 400 sets on which to show it, but big league baseball arrived on television today. With Red Barber in the catbird seat, a ground-level camera near home plate and one in the upper deck, the first game of a Dodgers-Reds doubleheader was televised. It was put on by W2XBS, which learned some lessons by doing a May 17 baseball game between Princeton and Columbia. Bill Stern was the announcer for this first sports broadcast by NBC-TV's experimental station.

Hollywood gems: Southern melodrama and Midwestern fantasy

Maybe he does give a damn after all.

Hattie McDaniel gives Vivien Leigh a hand, and a little useful advice as well.

Hollywood, California

A year "of genius and glitter" has taken over Hollywood as the Depression seemed to fade away. *Gone With the Wind*, a Civil War epic with Vivien Leigh and Clark Gable, attracted more curiosity and acclaim than any other film. It had its premiere in Atlanta, of course, on December 15. And then there was that grand and glorious fantasy *The Wizard of Oz*, with a wide-eyed Judy Garland singing her way into the hearts of millions; John Ford's *Stagecoach*, which made stars of Monument Valley as well as John Wayne; the dark, gothic romance of *Wuthering Heights*; *Goodbye, Mr. Chips*, starring Robert Donat; *Dark Victory* with Bette Davis and George Brent; Jean Renoir's *Rules of the Game*; Disney's *Pinocchio*; the Frank Capra *Mr. Smith Goes to Washington*, making audiences cheer Jimmy Stewart's speech on liberty; adventure stories like *Gunga Din* with Cary Grant as a Cockney subaltern, then *Beau Geste*; sophisticated comedies such as *The Women*, *Idiot's Delight* and *Ninotchka*, in which Garbo laughs; historical dramas such as *Juarez*, *Union Pacific* and *The Story of Alexander Graham Bell*; *Intermezzo* with Ingrid Bergman; *The Cat and the Canary*, featuring Bob Hope; *Destry Rides Again*, *The Roaring Twenties*, W.C. Fields's *You Can't Cheat an Honest Man* ... the list goes on and on.

In all, 388 movies were issued this year, and the average American family spent an all-time high of $25 annually to go to see them.

McHugh, Cagney and Bogart looking for trouble in "The Roaring Twenties."

Yellow brick road. "We're off to see the wizard, the Wonderful Wizard of Oz."

Depression decade: Some sing and some dance

Hollywood enjoyed a boom during the decade. Seated on the "Shall We Dance" movie set are Fred Astaire, Ginger Rogers, and George Gershwin at piano; standing behind the famed composer is his brother, lyricist Ira Gershwin.

On a rain-soaked wharf in New York City, an unattended pushcart advertises "frankfurts" with sauerkraut or onions, ice-cold soft drinks and pies for five cents. Unfortunately, for many people, such a price for lunch is too high.

"Drummer" by Ira Becker of Federal Arts Project. Swing is the thing.

Hard times, even if you have a job. San Francisco General Strike, 1934.

A full house at the Metropolitan Opera in New York City in 1937. The sad songs heard inside do not even compare with the sadder songs on the streets.

Radio comes of age, with an average of 6.6 soap operas a day, including "Our Gal Sunday" and "Search For Tomorrow." Other popular shows are "Burns and Allen," "The Jack Benny Show," "The Shadow" and "Captain Midnight".

Television, the world of tomorrow. Prilo C. Farnsworth tunes in his version of the invention, which combines radio and a cathode ray tube. Others working in the new field include Vladimir Zworykin, and John L. Baird of Scotland.

Too many say, "Brother, can you spare a dime?"

"Cold drinks inside the Red Robin Cafe" by Russell Lee, a gregarious Texan.

Defying great heights and financial depths. Photograph is by Lewis Hine.

"Ask the man who owns one." Or find the man who can afford one!

Richard Rodgers and Lorenz Hart had four hit musicals in the 30s.

The soup kitchen, an all too familiar sight. Despite the best efforts of the federal government and American industry, the economy remains stagnant.

Streamlined locomotive, The Royal Blue, races into a better future. "As a result of the revolutionary changes brought about by modern methods of production," says one hopeful writer, "America may again become a new world."

The gorgeous gams of the Rockettes, who appear at the equally fabulous Radio City Music Hall. The world's largest indoor theater, with 6,000 seats, opened in New York City in 1932. Despite the lean years, Americans get their kicks.

Washington, D.C., Jan. 26. As 1911 trade treaty with Japan expires, United States declines to renew it.

Vermont, Jan. 31. Ida Fuller becomes first recipient of a monthly Social Security payment, receiving check number 000-00-001 for $22.54.

Washington, D.C., Feb. 26. To provide a coherent air defense plan for United States, Air Defense Command is created.

Hollywood, Feb. 29. Hattie McDaniel becomes first Negro woman to win an Oscar, for best supporting actress in *Gone With the Wind.*

Camden, New Jersey, Apr. 1. RCA laboratories demonstrate first electron microscope.

Washington, D.C., May 10. Following German invasions, President Roosevelt freezes all assets in United States of Belgium, the Netherlands and Luxembourg (→June 10).

New York City, May. Pulitzer Prizes are awarded to John Steinbeck for *Grapes of Wrath* and Carl Sandburg for *Abraham Lincoln: The War Years.*

Washington, D.C., June 28. Congress passes Alien Registration Act, requiring all foreigners to be registered and fingerprinted.

Chicago, July 4. In celebration of Emancipation Proclamation, American Negro Exposition is held.

Britain, September. American volunteer fighter pilots form Eagle Squadron in R.A.F.

Cincinnati, Oct. 8. Reds win their first World Series in 21 years, defeating Detroit Tigers, four games to three.

Washington, D.C., Dec. 8. Chicago Bears defeat Washington Redskins, by record score of 73-0, to win National Football League championship.

Hollywood, Calif. *My Little Chickadee,* starring Mae West and W.C. Fields, released.

New York City. *You Can't Go Home Again,* by Thomas Wolfe, published posthumously.

New York City. *Native Son* by Richard Wright is issued.

DEATH

Hollywood, California, Dec. 21. F. Scott Fitzgerald, novelist of "jazz age" (*Sept. 24, 1896).

Population 131.6 million; Oklahoma's off

"Manhattan Skyline" (1934) by John Cunning. Asphalt jungle on the horizon.

Washington, D.C.

The nation's population climbed to a new high of 131.6 million, and average life expectancy has reached 63 years, the 1940 census shows. Signs of progress include an illiteracy rate of only 4.2 percent, the 30 million American homes that have radios and the 33 percent of farms that now have electricity. But a bitter reminder of the dust bowl is the loss of population by hard-hit Oklahoma, down 60,000 since 1930, and by South Dakota, down 50,000. California is the new home of many former Oklahomans and Dakotans.

Its population rose more than two million in the decade, to nearly 5.7 million, making it the fifth most populous state. The California climate clearly is the attraction, since Washington and Oregon experienced no such population surge.

New York is still the most populous state, with 13.5 million residents, including a large number of refugees from the war in Europe. Next in population come Pennsylvania, with 9.9 million, Illinois with 7.7 million and Texas with 6.4 million. Nevada has the lowest population, with just 110,000 residents.

Isolationists rally, urge America First

Chicago, Sept. 5
Peace or war? Which will you choose?
Should we fight for Britain?
Let's stop the rush toward war!

Those are among the slogans being voiced by the America First Committee. It is not alone. About a third of all Americans favor neutrality in the European war, and hundreds of isolationist groups are springing up this year. Most prominent are the "America Firsters," some 60,000 strong, who view President Roosevelt as a "warmonger" and his military aid to Britain as "interventionist." Their members include Charles A. Lindbergh.

Bugs Bunny debut

Hollywood, California, July 27
What's up, Doc? A new Warner Bros. Studio cartoon character, that's what! Bugs Bunny is the latest creation of cartoonist Tex Avery, whose previous characters have included Porky Pig and Daffy Duck. In the short film *A Wild Hare,* Avery comes up with another winner. According to film audiences, this rabbit's worth 24 carrots! We doubt that hunter Elmer Fudd would agree.

"Cowboy Dance" (1940), painted by Jenne Magafan for the Anson, Texas, Post Office is just one of the 1,125 murals that American artists have created in the last six years under the auspices of the Federal Arts Project.

First U.S. helicopter shown by Sikorsky

Hartford, Conn., May 15

The first American helicopter, which can take off and land straight up and down, was shown here today by Igor Sikorsky, its Russian-born inventor. The Vought-Sikorsky VS-300 is lifted by a single rotating blade above its fuselage. Sikorsky has solved the major problem of direct-lift craft, the torque created by the rotor, by putting smaller rotors turning in opposite directions at the ends of the fuselage. Germany's Focke-Wulf FW-61 has counterrotating rotors on opposite sides of the fuselage to cancel the torque. Without some such device, the craft itself would rotate.

Batman in a book

United States, Spring

Batman, the costumed crime-fighter who made his first appearance less than a year ago in Detective Comics No. 27, has already been graduated to his own title. It is Batman Comics, and it will be drawn by Bob Kane and written by Bill Finger, who together created the character (and sidekick Robin) in response to the tremendous popularity of the first comic book hero, Superman.

State Dept. still limits Jewish entry

Washington, D.C.

Despite appeals from American Jewish organizations, the State Department has been slow to relax immigration laws that limit Jewish entry into the United States. The Johnson Act of 1924 restricts entry to 2 percent of the foreign-born of any nation. From 1933 to 1937, only 33,000 Jews were allowed into America. Now, with word reaching the United States of human rights abuses in Germany, American Jewish leaders are pressing for the admission of more refugees. But the State Department asserts it is limiting entry because the nation can't support all those who seek shelter. Recently, a ship carrying more than 900 European Jews was turned away at New York harbor.

As France falls, U.S. moves from neutrality to non-belligerency

Charlottesville, Va., June 10

In a speech at the University of Virginia that marks a shift away from a policy of strict neutrality to one of non-belligerency, President Roosevelt declared today, "We are convinced that military and naval victory for the gods of force and hate would endanger the institutions of democracy in the Western world, and that equally, therefore, the whole of our sympathies lie with those nations that are giving their life blood in combat against those forces."

Lending substance to the President's words are such recent actions as his sending to Congress a military supply measure that is to provide more than $1.3 billion to build up the armed forces, and his endorsement of an agreement with the British last week to sell large amounts of American surplus or outdated military equipment.

The latter arrangement comes in response to an urgent cable sent by British Prime Minister Winston Churchill in May. Britain desperately needs military supplies to replace the vast quantitites of ammunition, artillery, tanks and other weapons abandoned on the beaches of Dunkirk. Although the bulk of the British Expeditionary Force, 200,000 men, along with 140,000 French and Belgian troops, were

A sad day for Western Civilization. Nazi troops march through Paris.

evacuated over a nine-day period from May 26, few were able to bring even their weapons with them. Meanwhile, French resistance to the invasion by the Germans continues to be fragmented, half-hearted and ineffective. Although the French have an army of 800,000 combat troops as well as trained reserves of some 5,500,000, morale is quite poor and the military is short of power both in the air and on the ground.

These are areas where the German army excels. Flushed with the recent victories in Poland, Norway and the Netherlands, the invading forces are confident and bold. They have shown themselves to be masters of Blitzkrieg, literally, lightning war, where attacking forces move not at the traditional speed of the marching foot soldier but at that of motorized infantry, backed by columns of tanks and massive support in the air. And in fact, it was the dramatic attack by German General Ewald von Kleist through the supposedly impenetrable Ardennes region of forests, crags and ravines and his drive to the English Channel that very nearly annihilated the British forces.

To add to France's disastrous situation, Italy has just declared war and an army of 400,000 is starting to invade along the Riviera. Referring to these moves by the Italians in his speech today, President Roosevelt said, "The hand that held the dagger has struck it into the back of its neighbor" (→ July 20).

Hemingway: For Whom the Bell Tolls

Havana, Cuba

From Lookout Farm, a little villa near Havana, Ernest Hemingway is enjoying the success of his new novel, *For Whom the Bell Tolls.* For the rugged author, both the moment of repose and the fact that people are buying his book in droves are unusual experiences. Hemingway is often indistinguishable from his hard-drinking, adventuresome heroes. He spent most of the Spanish Civil War reporting from the front lines and raising funds for republican Loyalists. It is not surprising then that his latest protagonist is an American volunteer in Spain engaged in a suicidal mission to blow up a bridge. Between respites in Havana, Hemingway has been covering the Japanese invasion of China.

Charlie Chaplin and Jack Oakie as the equivalents of Hitler and Mussolini in "The Great Dictator," proving comedy can be found even in tragedy.

FDR back for unprecedented 3rd term

Hyde Park, New York, Nov. 5.

President Roosevelt achieved a sweeping victory today, becoming the first man in history elected to a third term in the White House. The jubilant President, addressing a crowd outside his home here, promised to be "the same Franklin Roosevelt you have known." While he scored a decisive triumph over his Republican opponent, Wendell Willkie, carrying 38 states with 449 electoral votes, the margin was not of the landslide kind chalked up four years earlier over Alfred Landon. One reason, perhaps, was voter concern over the concept of a third term. Another may have been uneasiness over the possibility of American entry into the war now raging in Europe. FDR had less than solid support this year from organized labor, too, with John L. Lewis, president of the C.I.O., threatening to resign if Roosevelt was re-elected. But in the end, the voters signaled approval of the President's efforts to pull the nation out of the Great Depression with a monumental program of public works, relief programs, Social Security for older Americans, banking reforms, crop control and rural electrification. The Roosevelt charisma, too, was no doubt a major factor in this year's victory. While unable to walk unassisted and usually confined to a wheelchair, he has stayed close to the people by means of his Fireside Chats.

President radiates confidence as he prepares for another term.

A two-ocean navy, more planes OK'd

Washington, D.C., July 20

President Roosevelt asked for it and he got it: a powerful two-ocean navy. Congress passed a bill today to appropriate $4 billion for the building of more naval vessels for both the Atlantic and Pacific, answering the chief executive's request. Last month, funding was set aside for the construction of 50,000 fighter planes as the nation's armed services continue to stock their military arsenals. While FDR insists America has no intention of entering the European war, it is apparent he won't let the country get caught unprepared for battle (→ Aug. 18).

U.S. plans defense of the hemisphere

Ogdensburg, N.Y., Aug. 18

President Roosevelt and Canadian Prime Minister Mackenzie King have agreed to establish a Permanent Joint Board of Defense to guard North America against possible attack by Germany or Japan. The move follows last month's Declaration of Havana, a mutual defense accord that was worked out by 21 members of the Pan American Union. The declaration provides for joint action to administer French, Dutch and Danish colonies and prevent them from falling under German control (→ Sept. 3).

As Battle of Britain rages, U.S. agrees to provide old warships

Washington, D.C., Sept. 3

In an executive agreement made public today, the United States is to give Britain 50 over-age but still serviceable destroyers in return for 99-year, rent-free leases for naval and air bases in Newfoundland, Bermuda and six other sites ranging from the Bahamas to British Guiana. The deal, which has been widely discussed, is supported by 62 percent of the public, according to a Gallup Poll of August 17.

The destroyers, which date from World War I and are of the four-funnel class, are of no immediate use to the United States, but could prove vital to Britain in maintaining control of the seas in face of the German U-boat onslaught.

Also vital to England's survival is control of the skies, an issue that is still being fought out between the Royal Air Force and the Luftwaffe in what is becoming known as the Battle of Britain. The R.A.F. is said to have developed radar (radio detection and ranging) that can detect the position, speed and nature of enemy craft. And the R.A.F. has the advantage of fighting from home bases. Still, it is sorely outnumbered – 1,475 first-line craft against the Luftwaffe's 2,670.

The massive German air attacks, started less than a month ago by Field Marshal Hermann Goering, are aimed at exploiting the numerical edge and delivering a knockout blow to the R.A.F. If they succeed, the Germans will probably proceed to massive bombing raids on London and major industrial cities before invading across the English Channel. So far, however, the battle has not gone in Germany's favor. On the first day of the German attacks, R.A.F. pilots in Spitfires and Hurricanes downed 53 planes, and German losses since continue to be about double those of the British. In a tribute to the valor of the R.A.F., Prime Minister Churchill said in the House of Commons on August 20: "Never in the field of human conflict was so much owed by so many to so few" (→ Dec. 29).

Japan is angered by oil, scrap bans

Washington, D.C., Sept. 12

Joseph C. Grew, American ambassador to Japan, said today that "further conciliatory measures" toward Japan "would be futile and unwise." The advice comes as relations between the countries continue to deteriorate. Japan has strongly protested President Roosevelt's July 25 ban on exports of oil and scrap metal, materials on which Japan is heavily dependent in its war with China. Tokyo also resents a U.S. warning against its putting pressure on the Vichy government to grant Japan further bases in the northern part of French Indochina.

Draft lottery starts; No. 158, you're in!

Washington, D.C., Oct. 29

As bands played and planes flew overhead, the nation's first peacetime military draft got under way today, with Secretary of War Henry L. Stimson drawing No.158 from a bowl of capsules. Other federal officials and members of Congress then took turns at picking numbers at random, as President Roosevelt watched. To date, 16 million Americans between the ages of 21 and 36 have registered for the draft. Those in each selective service area whose numbers correspond to those drawn today will be called up for a year's service in the army.

Roosevelt says U.S. must be "arsenal of democracy"

The formidable potential of American industry is waiting to be unleashed. "Auto Industry" by Marvin Beerbohm.

Washington, D.C., Dec. 29

As the first year of the decade comes to a close, America faces a perilous threat to its existence, President Roosevelt warned tonight in his Fireside Chat. The only way to prepare, the President said, is to provide an "arsenal of democracy" for those opposing the Axis powers.

Not since "Jamestown and Plymouth Rock has our American civilization been in such danger as now," Roosevelt declared. He vowed to send the Allies as many weapons as the United States can produce, saying no dictator would stop U.S. aid from reaching those who fight Nazi Germany. He said, "No nation can appease the Nazis. No man can tame a tiger into a kitten by stroking it." But he restated his pledge to do what he could to keep America out of the war.

Just how long American non-intervention will last is uncertain. But one thing is certain: the public wants to stay out of European conflicts. A recent poll showed that 39 percent of Americans think entering the Great War was a mistake. That sentiment holds true for this war as well.

Yet, Americans are behind the recent military buildup, approving of FDR's run around possible congressional roadblocks in exchanging 50 old-model destroyers for 99-year leases on eight British naval and air bases. The President called these "outposts of security" the most strategic addition to defense since the Louisiana Purchase. The people also agreed with November's deal to give half the nation's military production to England.

If any nation can supply the Allies with enough firepower to defeat fascism, it is America. The nation's industrial productivity now surpasses any in history. America is the leading producer of autos, radios and other high technology products, steel and other items essential for war. A shift in the focus of manufacturing, using the recent allocation of $18 million for rearmament, has transformed factories into high-intensity arms production plants. With the President setting the challenge, American industrial might will further flex its muscles, to provide the punch needed to win the war (→Jan. 6, 1941).

Everybody's kicking out to the Lindy

United States

Hey, hepcat. Get down to the malt shop. Everybody's in the groove there 'cause they just got a jukebox. It takes a nickel to spin a platter and you move to the sounds of Goodman, Shaw or Dorsey or just sit back and hear the melody of some canary. Fifty cents will get you 16 tunes. If some old long hair uses his nickel to shut off the swing, you can always find an open house. If it's Saturday night, you know there's an alligator somewhere in town that's got cats kicking out and doin' the Lindy Hop.

CBS demonstrates color TV technology

New York City, Aug 29

The press got a preview of color television today as the Columbia Broadcasting System demonstrated an apparatus invented by its chief engineer, Peter C. Goldmark. The pictures are transmitted by means of a system that uses rotating color disks placed in front of the television camera and a receiver tube to enable the audience to view the pictures in color. CBS plans to begin experimental color broadcasting soon over its New York television station, W2XAB, using a high-powered transmitter situated on top of the Chrysler Building.

Willys introduces jeep to Americans

Detroit, Michigan

A tough lightweight vehicle with the carrying power of a one-and-a-quarter-ton truck and the maneuverability of an auto has been introduced by the Willys Corporation. It weighs a quarter of a ton, is powered by a four-cylinder engine and has a high clearance and a four-wheel drive that allows it to operate on rough terrain. Top speed on good roads is 65 miles per hour. The army is interested in the military uses of the vehicle, which is nicknamed "jeep," from the first letters of "general purpose" and the lovable little animal in the *Popeye* cartoon.

Disney, Stokowski offer "Fantasia"

Hollywood, California

Fantasia is Walt Disney's ambitious attempt to marry animation with classical music in collaboration with conductor Leopold Stokowski. The film's "fantasound" gives a concert-hall effect. Other new and exciting films are *The Grapes of Wrath* with Henry Fonda, about the plight of the Okies, Chaplin's *The Great Dictator*, making fun of Hitler; Hitchcock's first American film, *Rebecca*, starring Joan Fontaine and Laurence Olivier, and *The Philadelphia Story* with Katharine Hepburn, James Stewart and Cary Grant.

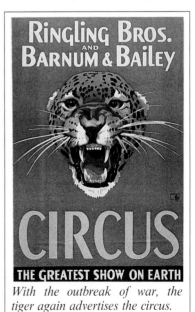

With the outbreak of war, the tiger again advertises the circus.

Washington, D.C., March 5. To provide for greater security of Panama Canal, Republic of Panama accepts U.S. air patrols beyond Canal Zone for duration of war.

Detroit, Apr. 18. General Motors now produces 50 percent of all American autos.

Washington, D.C., May 1. U.S. Defense Savings Bonds go on sale.

Washington, D.C., May 20. President Roosevelt moves Thanksgiving to last Thursday of November.

Washington, D.C., June 14. Roosevelt freezes all German and Italian assets in U.S.

Washington, D.C., June 16. American consulates in territories under German and Italian control ordered closed.

Washington, D.C., June 24. President Roosevelt pledges American aid to Soviet Union.

Washington, D.C., June 28. Office of Scientific Research and Development created by President Roosevelt.

Washington, D.C., July 26. All Japanese assets in United States frozen, in retaliation for Japanese occupation of French Indochina two days earlier.

New York City, Aug. 10. Dean Dixon, 26, leads New York Philharmonic, becoming first Negro to conduct a major American orchestra.

Washington, D.C., Sept. 11. President Roosevelt issues shoot-on-sight orders to naval commanders patrolling U.S. continental waters, warning German and Italian ships that they enter at their own risk.

New York City, Oct. 6. Yankees defeat Brooklyn Dodgers in World Series, four games to one.

Washington, D.C., Nov. 17. U.S. Ambassador to Japan Joseph Grew reports Japan may attempt surprise attack on some U.S. port (→ Dec. 6).

Chicago, Dec. 21. Bears defeat New York Giants, 37-9, in N.F.L. championship.

United States. Aerosol spray can is introduced.

New York City. *Let Us Now Praise Famous Men* by Walker Evans and James Agee issued.

New York City. Erich Fromm publishes *Escape from Freedom.*

Roosevelt calls for "Four Freedoms"

Washington, D.C., Jan. 6

President Roosevelt, citing what he called the "Four Freedoms," asked Congress today to approve a multimillion-dollar program of aid to the nations fighting the war against Nazi Germany. While still holding out hope that the United States would not be drawn into the war in Europe, the President called the proposed lend-lease program vital in promoting the defense of the nation.

"In the future days which we seek to make secure," the President told Congress, "we look forward to a world founded on four essential human freedoms: The first is freedom of speech and expression – everywhere in the world. The second is freedom of every person to worship God in his own way – everywhere in the world. The third is freedom from want – everywhere in the world. The fourth is freedom from fear – anywhere in the world."

As proposed by the President, the program would channel billions worth of weapons to Britain and its allies, the cost to be repaid within a reasonable time after the war in goods needed by the United States. The plan also would allow British warships to be repaired and refueled in American naval yards.

Preparing the nation for today's proposal, the President had said in a December Fireside Chat that he felt his re-election in November was a mandate for this country to become a great "arsenal of democracy." Although hopeful that America can stay out of war, he added: "If we are to be completely honest with ourselves, we must admit that there is risk in any course we take ... Never before since Jamestown and Plymouth Rock has our American civilization been in such danger ... If Great Britain goes down ... all of us ... would be living at the point of a gun."

The lend-lease proposal would permit the President to "sell, transfer title to, exchange, lease, lend or otherwise dispose of" ships, tanks, planes, guns, ammunition or other supplies to the Allied nations. FDR likened the plan to a man whose house is on fire and whose neighbor has lent him his garden hose. He warned of a "small group of selfish men who would clip the wings of the American eagle in order to feather their own nests" (→ March 27).

Mount Rushmore Memorial, a monument to American freedom

Mount Rushmore, S.D., Nov. 1

The faces of Washington, Jefferson, Theodore Roosevelt and Lincoln can look over the Black Hills unencumbered by scaffolding and laborers now that drilling is completed on America's latest monu-

ment, Mount Rushmore. Although workers were exhorted to "Rush More," the project was not finished before the death of its designer, John Gutzon de la Mothe Borglum, on March 6. Sculptor Borglum accepted the commission in 1925

while on the run from the state of Georgia and a memorial project he abandoned there. The Rushmore venture was not without problems. The reasons for honoring Washington, Lincoln, and Jefferson were obvious, but the choice of Roosevelt caused debate. TR's two years as a cowboy in the Dakota Territory led to his eventual acceptance.

Funding was a constant struggle. The state of South Dakota spent only $2 million, and most of that on roads. Charles E. Rushmore, the New York lawyer for whom the mountain was named, gave $5,000, the largest individual contribution. Borglum also had difficulties with contemporary Presidents. Calvin Coolidge summered a few miles from the mountain and dedicated the first drilling. But he was angered when Borglum edited a historical text he had written to accompany the monument. From 1931 to 1938, construction proceeded during the drought and windstorms that raised clouds of black dust. In terms of manpower, the project was more fortunate: None of the 360 laborers was permanently injured or killed. Yet the granite proved a difficult medium (90 percent was removed with dynamite) and the drilling moved slowly as Borglum aged. In 1938, at 71, he named his son Lincoln to finish the project.

Four faces from the past that helped shape the fortunes of the United States.

National art gallery opens in the capital

Washington, D.C., March 17

Thanks to the generosity of the late industrialist, banker and former Treasury Secretary Andrew W. Mellon, the United States can claim a federally owned collection of the highest quality art now that the National Gallery of Art has opened in Washington. Funds for the vast marble structure were provided by Mellon to house a collection to be built around the exceptional group of works he assembled over a lifetime. Highlights include paintings by Raphael, Van Eyck, Velazquez and Titian. Mellon's foresight and beneficence are especially remarkable in light of his lengthy tax battle with the federal government, which was resolved in his favor only after he died in 1937.

Watch on the Rhine

New York City, Apr. 1

Lillian Hellman has made no secret of her opinions, and her new drama may be her most forthright yet. She tackled homosexuality (*The Children's Hour*, 1934) and greed (*The Little Foxes*, 1939). Now she levels her sightsd on Nazism in *Watch on the Rhine*, which opened on Broadway tonight. The German anti-fascist hero is married to a rich American who joins him in the fight against Hitler. [The play won this year's Drama Critics' Circle Award for the best Broadway play, a first for Hellman.]

European allies to get lend-lease aid

Washington, D.C. March 27

The lend-lease bill, which President Roosevelt signed into law on March 12, has now been backed with an appropriation of $7 billion, most of which is expected to go to support a beleaguered Britain.

The program, which the President has compared to lending a hose to a neighbor whose house is on fire, with the understanding that the hose will eventually be returned, allows Roosevelt to lend or lease war material to "the government of any country whose defense the President deems vital for the defense of the United States." FDR has virtually complete discretion in administering the program.

Lend-lease will, in effect, put American industrial might at the disposition of those countries that are actually fighting the Axis powers, while it skirts the question of how such supplies are to be paid for. The financial reserves of Great Britain have disappeared almost entirely, and no one wants to see a repetition of the invidious war-debts issue that came up during

Rows of bombers await completion, and the opportunity to defend democracy.

the Great War and following it.

To its critics, however, the program will go beyond making the United States the "arsenal of democracy" and inevitably is going to drag the country into the war itself. In the words of one isolationist

Senator, Burton K. Wheeler, the bill is going to "plow under every fourth American boy." In contrast, Winston Churchill called it "an inspiring act of faith" and "a monument of generous and far-reaching statesmanship" (→ June 24).

Nation's auto makers cut production by 20% to aid war effort

Detroit, Mich., Apr. 17

America's automobile industry will shift gears beginning August 1, industry spokesmen reported yesterday. The major companies have agreed to slash production of civilian vehicles by one million units, or 20 percent, to redirect resources

toward the war effort. And today, General Motors, supplier of 50 percent of American autos, announced it would make no changes in passenger-car models this year to focus on defense needs. The auto industry has churned out vehicles at an astounding rate since America

was last at war. In 1916, there were 3.5 million autos in the nation. Last year, there were more than 31 million. Observers of American production are now able to see industry work like never before as it begins providing for the lend-lease program enacted last month.

Ford finally yields, signs pact with U.A.W.

Dearborn, Michigan, Apr. 11

Henry Ford, anti-union guardian of one of labor's last frontiers in the auto industry, opened his doors to the United Auto Workers today. Work on $158.7 million in defense contracts, he was happy to report, will continue. Ford's River Rouge plant has been shut tight since April 1, when plant managers fired three U.A.W. spokesmen just two months after a Supreme Court rebuke for discriminating against union members. Pickets blocked the 14 routes into the plant. And when a battle with Negro strikebreakers left about 200 injured, Ford gave up

all attempts to open the plant.

The world's biggest industrial unit with 85,000 workers, River Rouge is the hand that feeds the Ford empire. Without its supply of parts, 34 plants closed in two days. Back orders piled up. The government warned that defense output was languishing at 13 percent of its projected level. So when Governor Murray Van Wagoner met Ford two days ago, the 77-year-old industrial wizard was resigned. All strikers will retain their jobs; grievance procedures will be restored and a federal board will mediate wage talks pending union elections.

400,000 striking miners get $1 more

Harlan County, Ky., Apr. 28

Some 400,000 miners will descend into the shafts tomorrow with the promise of a $1 raise. For the Northern miners, this means $7 a day. Despite the efforts of Dr. John R. Steelman, the Labor Department's crack negotiator, Southern operators are sticking by their 40-cent wage differential. The month-old strike, which tied up 85 percent of soft coal production, ends as shortages threatened defense output. Five graves dug after a gunfight in "bloody Harlan" County, a scene of violence in the 1930s, are a part of the walkout's legacy.

"The Miner" (1925) by George Luks. ▷

Freighter sunk; emergency declared

Washington, D.C., May 27

The tenuous neutrality between the United States and Germany in the Atlantic has been dealt a severe blow with the sinking of the Robin Moore by the German U-boat U-69. President Roosevelt is furious because he sees it as another in a series of unpreventable events that will force the United States into war regardless of how hard his government tries to avert it. The President's reaction to the sinking was quick and vehement. In a message to Congress, he proclaimed an unlimited national emergency and he spoke of the incident as an example of "the acts of an international outlaw." He also accused Germany of a "policy of fright-fulness and intimidation," of "conquest based on lawlessness and terror on land and piracy on the sea."

The incident would never have happened if the U-boat captain, Just Metzler, had been obeying orders. Hitler does not want to provoke the Americans and he had therefore instructed his submarine chief, Admiral Karl Doenitz, to steer clear of American shipping at all costs. Nevertheless, the U-boat captain stopped the American vessel and had an officer sent on board to carry out a search. The inspecting officer came upon plane parts. Metzler then instructed the American crewmen to take to their lifeboats and ordered a torpedo fired into the freighter (→ June 14).

FDR mandates an end to discrimination

Roosevelt's opposition to discrimination is vital to its eventual eradication.

Washington, D.C., June 25

Seeking to head off a threatened march on Washington by disgruntled Negroes, President Roosevelt today mandated an end to discrimination in defense contracts and government employment. He did so by issuing an executive order establishing the Fair Employment Practices Commission, which is authorized to investigate complaints of discrimination based on race, color, creed or national origin. The President acted at the urging of his wife, Eleanor, and of Negro civil rights leaders. A. Philip Randolph, president of the Brotherhood of Pullman Car Porters, had planned to lead a march on Washington to protest widespread discrimination against the hiring of Negroes by defense industries that are under government contracts to produce arms and other supplies for Britain and other European allies in the war against Germany. The committee, an independent body within the executive office of the President, will have the authority to study complaints, hold hearings and act to end discrimination in hiring and promotion. The panel also is authorized to order training programs for those seeking jobs in defense industries. If employers fail to comply with panel rulings, they will be subject to being cut off from all government defense contracts.

Yankee Clipper hits in 56 games in row

Cleveland, Ohio, July 17

It had to happen sometime. Joe DiMaggio's record streak of hitting safely in consecutive games was halted at 56 tonight by the Cleveland Indians before a record crowd of 67,468. "Jolting Joe," who was last held hitless two months ago, bounced into a double play with the bases loaded in the eighth, his last time at bat, but the Yankees pulled out a 4-3 victory. DiMag's streak was nipped by pitchers Al Smith and Jim Bagby.

Whirlaway is fifth Triple Crown victor

New York City, June

Whirlaway was a strong-willed, fractious animal, and people said that if someone could curb his temperament, the horse could win the Kentucky Derby. So trainer Ben Jones did just that and Whirlaway, with Eddie Arcaro aboard, won not only the Derby but the Preakness and Belmont as well to become the fifth Triple Crown winner. Whirlaway tended to run on the outside rail. Jones put a one-eyed blinker on him and the problem was solved.

CBS challenges NBC on commercial TV

New York City, July 1

Commercial television broadcasting has begun here, with NBC and CBS offering competing services. NBC was first in the field, starting with broadcasts of the opening ceremonies of the New York World's Fair two years ago. It was given its license for regular operation of station W2XBS from the Federal Communications Commission today. The license calls for four hours of broadcasting a week, but NBC says it will be on the air at least 15 hours. CBS quickly matched its rival with its own telecasts. Only a few households are equipped with sets to pick up the broadcasts.

"Palmerton, P.A., 1941" by Franz Kline, master of Abstract Expressionism.

Navy pilot trainees master the quarter-mile obstacle course at pre-flight school. Although not in a state of war, the United States prepares for what may be the inevitable. The barriers of neutrality are very rapidly slipping away.

FDR and Churchill draft Atlantic Charter

Newfoundland, Aug. 12

A declaration of principles for which the war is being fought has been drawn up by President Roosevelt and Prime Minister Churchill after their secret meetings aboard the American cruiser Augusta and the British battleship Prince of Wales anchored here in Placentia Bay. The document, named the Atlantic Charter, sets forth "certain common principles" on which the two leaders "base their hopes for a better future for the world."

Among these principles are "the right of all peoples to choose the form of government under which they will live" and the outlawing of "territorial changes that do not accord with the freely expressed wishes of the peoples concerned." Also included are free international trade, full economic collaboration between all nations, freedom of the seas and "final destruction of Nazi tyranny" and a peace that will provide "freedom from fear and want."

Finally, the charter expresses the belief that "all the nations of the world, for realistic as well as spiritual reasons, must come to the abandonment of the use of force."

The charter is not an alliance or a treaty. Its significance lies in the fact that the United States of America, which is still technically neutral, has joined a belligerent nation in a statement of war aims (→ Dec. 22).

Germans sink more American vessels

Washington, D.C., Nov. 17

Relations between the United States and Germany are deteriorating by the day and the events in the Atlantic that resulted in Congress's amending the Neutrality Act seem to be propelling the country at an ever-quickening pace toward war.

October 17 saw the first American casualties in the war. Convoy SC-48 was 400 miles south of Iceland when it was attacked by a German wolf pack. Several ships were sunk. The warship Kearny took one torpedo through its bilge on that day, killing 11 men and wounding many. It remained afloat and made it to Iceland escorted by the Greer, which eluded German U-boats a month before. In response to the killings, Roosevelt told a huge audience at Washington's Mayflower Hotel, "We have wished to avoid shooting, but the shooting has started. And history has recorded who fired the first shot." Almost immediately, more Americans fell victim to the Germans. On October 31, the destroyer Reuben James, steaming 600 miles west of Ireland, took a torpedo in its port side. Of the ship's company of 160 men, only 45 were saved. All of the officers aboard were killed.

Following these events, Congress acted, on November 13, by amending the Neutrality Act, which permits the arming of all American merchantmen as well as granting them free passage to the war zones.

While Welles searches for Rosebud, Bogey hunts the Falcon

Hollywood, California

Citizen Kane marks the Hollywood debut of Orson Welles – as producer, imaginative director, cowriter and dynamic star. Its thinly disguised portrait of press tycoon William Randolph Hearst has provoked a boycott of RKO releases in the Hearst papers. But the rest of the world whispers "Rosebud," Kane's last word before his death, which prompts a reporter to try to unravel the meaning of the word. The world also hails the 26-year-old Welles as a genius. Another new director, John Huston, has guided Humphrey Bogart in a brilliant tour de force as private eye Sam Spade in *The Maltese Falcon*. Devastatingly charming Cary Grant ("I play myself to perfection") shines with Joan Fontaine in Hitchcock's *Suspicion*, while tall, handsome and laconic Gary Cooper draws audiences as the popular hero of the Great War in *Sergeant York*, which also stars Walter Brennan. *Dumbo*, about the elephant who could fly, is the year's offering from Disney and the two-faced *Dr. Jekyll and Mr. Hyde* leads his third screen life, this time with Spencer Tracy playing the title role and co-starring radiant Swedish-born Ingrid Bergman. Master director John Ford has turned his camera toward the miners of Wales in *How Green Was My Valley*, a compassionate movie about suffering and the brotherhood of man.

The treacherous Nazis are no match for the wit and cunning of Sam Spade.

The mastery of Orson Welles is drawing large crowds to his "Citizen Kane."

Roosevelt appeals to Japan for peace

Washington, D.C., Dec. 6

Negotiations over the situation in the Far East appear to have reached an impasse and war in the Pacific seems not just possible but likely. Since October, President Roosevelt has contemplated writing directly to Emperor Hirohito, and today he instructed Ambassador Joseph Grew in Tokyo to deliver the letter he wrote earlier in the week.

This unprecedented personal appeal to the Emperor is a reflection of the extreme gravity of the situation. Diplomatic tensions between Japan and the United States have steadily worsened since Washington began an embargo of oil and rice to Japan and since the July freeze of all Japanese assets in the United States. In mid-October, Fuminaro Konoye and his Cabinet fell and were replaced by General Hideki Tojo, Konoye's war minister, and a Cabinet studded with military leaders. Since then, Ambassador Grew and Secretary of State Cordell Hull have failed to reach a modus vivendi with the Japanese.

Washington has demanded that Japan cease its military adventures in the Pacific. Meanwhile, Japan has been charging encirclement by the ABCD powers (American, British, Chinese, Dutch) a charge not unlike the encirclement accusations that have been made by Adolf Hitler in Europe (→ 7).

Japanese launch surprise attack on Pearl Harbor

As the warship Shaw is shattered, so too is the nation's complacency. The United States of America has been stung, and it is unlikely to forget Pearl Harbor.

Pearl Harbor, Hawaii, Dec. 7

"AIR RAID! PEARL HARBOR! THIS IS NO DRILL!"

Those words, broadcast at 7:58 on this peaceful Sunday morning by Admiral Patrick N.L. Bellinger, shattered the complacency of the United States military. By 8 a.m., two battleships had been dealt fatal blows and hundreds of American sailors had been killed. The Japanese Empire, using aircraft carriers within 300 miles of Pearl Harbor, launched wave after wave of torpedo bombers, dive bombers and fighters against soldiers, sailors and airmen who had just started into their Sunday morning routines. The surprise element was stunning. One radar operator got some blips indicating a massive movement of planes. He looked more closely,

thought the radar was wrong or that the blips were B-17 bombers being shifted from Wake Island to Pearl Harbor and did nothing.

The first wave of Japanese aircraft, consisting of 49 high-level bombers, 51 dive bombers and 51 fighters, sighted the Oahu coastline at about 7:40 a.m. They deployed for Wheeler Field, Hickam Field and Battleship Row, which consisted of massive quays where 26 destroyers, five cruisers and eight battleships were moored. Most of the officers and men of the battleship Arizona were aboard when the first bombs and torpedoes began to rip it apart. Of its crew of 1,400, 1,103 men were killed. The Oklahoma, a 1916 dreadnought, was the next to last in line and probably the first hit. A few minutes after 8,

it rolled completely over, destroyed by three huge torpedoes in its hull. Next in line were the battlewagons Tennessee and West Virginia. The West Virginia, outboard of the pair, took six or seven torpedoes, but it was saved from the Oklahoma's fate by an exceptionally alert and well-trained crew. By the time the sailors discovered what was happening, it was almost too late, but hundreds of men were brought topside and saved.

On other ships, long lines of ammunition handlers were organized to feed the guns, which began to fire back at the swarming Japanese Zeros. On the cruiser New Orleans, Chaplain Howell Fogey, a "sky pilot," was among the ammunition passers. When a Japanese plane was hit he called out, "Praise the

Lord and pass the ammunition!"

Battleship Row tapered off at either end. The California was southernmost and the least prepared for war. It was considered completely unprepared for an admiral's inspection. Its magazine was hit and it rapidly settled into the mud.

Within two hours, the navy lost 2,000 men killed and 710 wounded, while the army and marines lost 327 killed and 433 wounded. Also killed were 70 civilians, mostly airfield workers, as were a few Honolulu residents.

By 9:45 a.m., the Japanese aircraft had returned to their carriers. But 29 did not make it back, which is a remarkable loss figure considering how completely the Americans had been surprised (→ Jan. 26, 1942).

America declares war

Washington, D.C., Dec. 11

Declaring Sunday, December 7, "a date which will live in infamy," President Roosevelt, on Monday, asked Congress to declare war on Japan. Congress hastened to comply and war was declared six and one-half minutes later. The Senate vote was unanimous. In the House of Representatives, there was one dissenting vote, that of Representative Jeannette Rankin of Montana, who also voted against American entry into the Great War.

Germany and Italy, in keeping with the terms of their Tripartite Pact, declared war on the United States today. And President Roosevelt has asked Congress to recognize that a state of war now exists.

The fact of war has come upon Americans with a bewildering sud-denness, and the mood in the country is uneasy. In Washington's Tidal Basin, one overzealous patriot chopped down four Japanese cherry trees before he was arrested. Around the White House, crowds five deep pressed against the fence railings, hour after hour. On Monday, the America First Committee hastily called a membership meeting and disbanded, calling on all Americans to back the war effort.

The great white light that burned over the White House driveway is out now. One of the President's speech writers mentioned this to a colleague; "I wonder how long it will be before that light gets turned on again?" His friend answered, "I don't know, but until it does, the lights will stay turned off all over the world."

Britain, U.S. meet to map war strategy

Washington, D.C., Dec. 22

Prime Minister Churchill and his military commanders met President Roosevelt and his generals and admirals for the first time today in order to hammer out a strategy for the long-range conduct of the war. The Arcadia Conference is an idyllic sounding name for a parley of rancorous debate and some confusion, but that is to be expected in a situation as complex as this one. After stormy discussions and major disagreements, a degree of organization was achieved. Field Marshal Archibald Wavell, now in India, has been appointed commander-in-chief of all American, British, Dutch and Australian units in the Southwest Pacific. In addition to this so-called ABDA command, an outline for a combined British-American chiefs of staff organization was set down. The Arcadia conference is regarded by most participants as the beginning of sorting out one another's motives and objectives (→ Jan. 1, 1942).

Japanese military overruns Pacific islands

Manila, Philippines, Dec. 26

The Japanese, following up on their surprise attack at Pearl Harbor, have continued to astonish the world with successful assaults all across the Western Pacific. In the early hours of December 8, Japanese naval and air forces struck almost simultaneously at Kota Bharu in British Malaya, Singora in Thailand, Guam, Hong Kong, Wake Island and the Philippines.

The blows from sea and air were immediately followed by land invasions, which were virtually unopposed. Many of the briefly trained Filipino "divisions" simply melted into the jungle when faced with the tough and disciplined veteran Japanese military units.

Elsewhere in the Pacific, British and American forces are beginning to fight back. In Kunming, China, a squadron of Colonel Claire Chennault's American volunteer group, the "Flying Tigers," shot down six Japanese raiders with no losses, and a combined force of Flying Tigers and the Royal Air Force in Rangoon, Burma, shot down several Japanese planes.

After successful Japanese landings at Luzon, Mindanao and Lingayen Gulf, American forces in the Philippines have retreated to the Bataan peninsula and to Corregidor, a tiny island at the entrance to Manila Bay (→ Feb. 28, 1942).

"A date which will live in infamy"

Clouds of black smoke replace the Japanese Zeros that have returned to their carriers in triumph. Americans are reacting with shock and anger.

The twisted hulk of the warship Arizona rests on the bottom of Pearl Harbor. It is one of 18 ships that have been destroyed by the Japanese attack.

Although the Japanese attack was a military success, it has stirred a hatred that demands revenge.

...we here highly resolve that these dead shall not have died in vain...

REMEMBER DEC. 7th!

The loss of 2,397 Americans in the assault has aroused a nation that had shown no taste for war.

Battle of Java Sea in South Pacific

Java Sea, Feb. 28

Although the United States has begun to hit back in the Pacific, the Japanese are still winning. Their latest victory was completed today in the Battle of the Java Sea. An incredibly confused tangle of ships maneuvering in the dark, the battle resulted in the loss of five Allied vessels while the Japanese suffered only one destroyer damaged.

Early in the year, the Allies put together a hastily conceived chain of command in the Pacific that was called Abdacom, which stood for American-British-Dutch-Australian Command. It was supposed to be a "Malay Barrier" to halt the Japanese octopus from spreading its tentacles into Java, Borneo and down the Malayan peninsula toward Singapore. But the "Malay Barrier" proved a myth and the Japanese hit the command area in coordinated attacks by carrier groups. Because of Japanese air superiority, the ABDA task force, under Dutch Admiral K.W.F.M. Doorman, could operate only at night. On February 4, he took four cruisers out of Surabaya in Java for a strike at Balikpapan. Japanese planes hit them and severely damaged the American warship Marblehead. Next, Doorman tried to prevent the Japanese from reaching Palembang, the great oil refinery on Sumatra. But Japanese planes did so much damage to his fleet he had to call off the attack. At this point, Doorman was replaced by Dutch Admiral Conrad Hel-

American fighter plane sweeps by as Japanese stores are hit on Wake Island.

frich, who decided on a last-ditch battle to stop the Japanese advance. He gathered up all the rag-tag ABDA forces that he could find and set out for a fight. The result was the Battle of Java Sea.

The Japanese, enjoying tactical control over the battle from its beginning, first hit the British cruiser Exeter. Four American destroyers used all their torpedoes defending it, but the British ship was badly damaged and had to leave the battle. Things only got worse for the Allies. Two Dutch cruisers, the Java and de Ruyter, were pounded by Japanese cruisers with full broadsides. De Ruyter, Helfrich's flagship, began to sink and the ad-

miral ordered the American ship Houston and the Australian Perth to run. The Allies realized that the Malay Barrier had become a trap; but it was too late. The Allied ships temporarily escaped into darkness, but on the following day, the Exeter was sunk, leaving only the Perth and Houston, which then encountered a Japanese transport force. They waded into the enemy, but soon three Japanese cruisers and 10 destroyers showed up. The Perth took several torpedo hits and went down. The Houston fought until it was dead in the water and wouldn't respond to the wheel. The American vessel just lay there until the Japanese blew it to bits (→ Apr. 9).

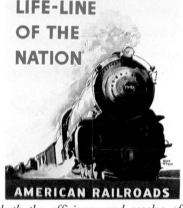

The speed with which the United States is mobilizing for war testifies to both the efficiency and resolve of the American people. Recruiting stations across the land are flooded with men, young and old, eager to sign up; the life plans of millions of families are being put on hold as sons and fathers become soldiers and leave for Europe and the Pacific. Americans have made a commitment and now they are uniting in the common cause.

Santa Barbara hit by Japanese sub

Santa Barbara, Calif., Feb. 23

A Japanese submarine shelled a Richfield Oil Company refinery at nearby Elmwood Field yesterday in the first such attack on the mainland. Most of the shells whistled harmlessly past derricks and tanks. The only damage: $500 worth of shattered wood on a pump-house roof. Southern California defense officals had rushed into action. Sirens wailed, broadcasts were halted and 30 miles of coast were blacked out. Tokyo hailed the sub's commander, Kizo Nishino, but oil officials think the raid was a personal vendetta. A few years ago, Nishino, then a tanker captain, fell on a cactus plant here, amusing the workers. The captain was heard to vow he would avenge his humiliation.

"G.I. Joe" reads Stars and Stripes

London, Apr. 17

Wherever American servicemen can be found, the newspaper *Stars and Stripes* is likely to be found as well. But most copies perform their duty in Europe, thanks to publication offices there and because the troops in the Pacific are scattered over dozens of islands. Today *Stars and Stripes* made a special contribution to the war effort by using the name "G.I. Joe." It's a term for the ordinary soldier – from Brooklyn or Boise – who bears the brunt of the fighting with no officer's clusters or bars, just a pair of dogtags and a snapshot of his girl or the family (→ June 17).

Sugar, gas rationed

Washington, D.C., May 14

The American people will start to feel the war in earnest and at home this month as many of the country's 131,669,275 inhabitants line up at schools to receive their War Ration Book No. 1, limiting each of them to one pound of sugar every two weeks. And today, some of the nation's 10 million motorists will also receive ration books. Gasoline limits of 25 to 30 gallons per motorist per month are expected.

American forces surrender on Bataan

Bataan, Philippines, Apr. 9

Quiet and modest Major General Edward P. King Jr., commander of the Luzon force under General Douglas MacArthur, has surrendered his army of 76,000 exhausted men to the Japanese. It is the greatest defeat for the American military to date. Since January, General King's mixed force of American soldiers, sailors, marines, civilians and Filipinos of all sorts had held out against an overwhelming force of Japanese under the command of Lieutenant General Homma Masahura. When King sent a flag of truce to the Japanese commander early today, he said that he felt like Lee at Appomattox. The comparison is an accurate one in that there remained only a single half ration of food in the quartermaster stores. Constant Japanese shelling, dwindling water supplies, heat and jungle humidity, and primitive or non-existent medical supplies all had taken their toll.

The battle for the Bataan peninsula began for the defending Americans and Filipinos with the fall of Manila to the Japanese on January 2. Bataan lies due west of Manila and juts into Manila Bay. South of Bataan lies the two-square-mile island of Corregidor, shaped like a tadpole, where MacArthur's remaining troops are still holding out in the island fortress that is known as "The Rock."

While MacArthur was still on Bataan, a "main battle position" was drawn across the peninsula on a line that bisects Mount Natib. Below this position another battle line, a "reserve battle position," was created. The men of MacArthur and King have fought gallantly to maintain these defensive positions, giving ground slowly to the Japanese, who have been able to push the Americans back because they are willing to make sacrifices in battle. Upon his departure to Australia in March, General MacArthur vowed, "I shall return."

The defenders had many other things to worry about in addition to the fierce firefights on the jungle floor. At the beginning of the prolonged defensive battle, there was only enough food for a period ranging from 20 to 50 days, depending on how much the planners estimat-

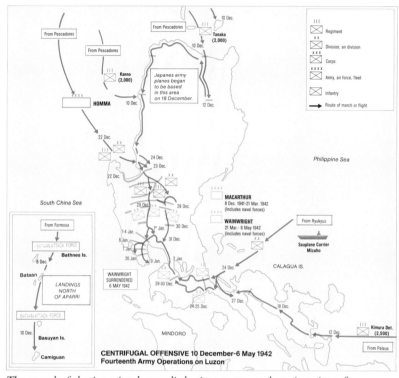

The speed of the invasion leaves little time to strengthen American forces.

ed each of the men would need to survive. In the end, the soldiers were fighting on about 2,000 calories a day – not nearly enough for troops who are waging a brutal war under terrible climatic conditions. The water was inadequate and, to make matters worse, the Japanese began to bomb and shell the peninsula from an assortment of positions that completely surround the defending Americans.

One officer put the situation this way: "Each day's combat, each day's output of physical energy, took its toll on the human body – a toll which could not be repaired ... " He added that when this fact is understood, the story of Bataan is told. Despite the communiques that have been issued by General MacArthur's headquarters and the exaggerated press reports that somehow get back to America, there have been no great battles on Bataan (→ May 6).

Americans die on Bataan "death march"

The Philippines, June

After the fall of Bataan and Corregidor, the Japanese held 76,000 American and Filipino prisoners. They had expected only 25,000 captives and were short of provisions. This was bad enough but, since a Japanese warrior is expected to die rather than surrender, they had no respect for their prisoners. A captive was undeserving of honor or respect so the road to the P.O.W. camps became lined with American corpses that had been bayonetted, shot or beheaded. Some 3,000 to 10,000 men died this way while others succumbed to exhaustion, dysentery or malnutrition.

American prisoners on Bataan.

Japanese-Americans are imprisoned

Japanese-Americans, victims of war hysteria, arrive at an internment camp.

Washington, D.C., December

Swept by a post-Pearl Harbor hysteria that portrays every ethnic Japanese as a potential saboteur, the government has taken a step without precedent in American history: it has interned behind barbed wire 110,000 of its citizens, more than two-thirds born in the United States.

At the urging of politicians and the army to remove the large Japanese-American population settled on the West Coast and in Hawaii, President Roosevelt signed Executive Order 9066 on February 19 authorizing the War Department to remove "all persons" from designated military areas. Congress has made it a federal offense to defy the army and established the War Relocation Authority to oversee the transfer.

From March through May, all Japanese Americans, including persons with as little as one-sixteenth Japanese blood and foster children brought up in Caucasian families, were told to wind up their affairs in a week to 10 days and show up at an appointed time with bed rolls and no more baggage than they could carry. Many had to sell their property at a fraction of its value to bargain hunters and junk dealers.

The army moved the ethnic Japanese to assembly centers in converted livestock stalls and stadiums throughout the West. A bare room furnished only with cots, blankets and mattresses and separated from others by a thin partition made up a family apartment.

Throughout the summer the army moved the Japanese-Americans to 10 hastily prepared relocation centers in the interior of the country: Poston and Gila Bend, Arizona; Jerome and Rohwer, Arkansas; Minidoka, Idaho; Tule Lake and Manzana, California; Topaz, Utah; Granada, Colorado, and Heart Mountain, Wyoming.

There they will live in centers encircled by barbed wire and watch towers. Guards are instructed to shoot anyone who tries to leave. All of this is taking place despite the fact that there have been no criminal charges. As a Japanese-American asked at a congressional hearing: "Has the Gestapo come to America?" (→ May 20, 1959).

Armed services get record $42.8 billion

Washington, D.C., June 30

The Senate took just 34 minutes today to approve the largest military budget in American history – $42.8 billion. The appropriation – which represents more than the entire cost of World War I – will enable the nation to support an army of 4.5 million by the end of the next fiscal year. And the cost of the war will hit Americans in their wallets, to the amount of $1.15 each per day. The bill was sent from the Senate to the House for final approval and was on its way to the White House for President Roosevelt's signature by mid-afternoon. The fiscal year ends today with the national debt at $76.6 billion and the deficit at $19.2 billion.

10,000 Nisei seek role in U.S. Army

Hawaii, June 5

Some 10,000 Americans of Japanese descent have volunteered for combat under the American flag, far exceeding the army's quota of 1,500 for the all-Nisei combat unit it is forming on the mainland. About 2,600 of these Nisei, American-born sons of Japanese immigrants, are to be sent to the mainland to train with the 442nd Combat Team. The number of volunteers seems to vindicate the policy toward the Japanese practiced by military governor Delos Emmons, who has been reluctant to carry out Washington's orders to deport Hawaii's Japanese. They make up 37 percent of the population.

Coughlin is curbed

Detroit, Mich., Apr. 14

The Shrine of the Little Flower has lost its bloom and the man in its pulpit has lost his right to publish. The man in question is the renowned radio priest, Father Charles E. Coughlin of Detroit, who has been haranguing the listening public since 1927 but who will no longer have a reading public. Under the 1917 Espionage Act, the government today banned his anti-Semitic weekly *Social Justice*.

FDR and Churchill meet on war again

Washington, D.C., June 24

Winston Churchill, accompanied by his top military chiefs, flew in from Scotland on June 17 to meet with Roosevelt and his war Cabinet. They discussed the war while traveling to and from Hyde Park, the President's residence on the Hudson River in New York. This is the second conference the two leaders have held in the United States. Chief subjects discussed have been the future Allied grand strategy as well as the deterioration of the Allied position in North Africa where German General Erwin Rommel has captured Tobruk. They also reportedly talked about the development of a new secret weapon (→ Jan. 24, 1943).

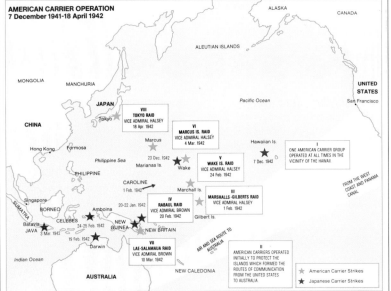

As the naval war in the Pacific expands, American military planners are relying heavily upon aircraft carriers. Originally employed to keep vital sea lanes open, they now form the backbone of the offensive strategy.

Doolittle bombs Tokyo

Colonel Doolittle's B-25 leaves the deck of the carrier Hornet bound for Tokyo.

Tokyo, Apr. 18

In a strike as surprising, though not nearly as devastating, as the Japanese attack on Pearl Harbor, Colonel James H. Doolittle and a squadron of B-25's today raided Tokyo, Nagoya, Osaka and Kobe. Completing the strike, all 16 of the American planes headed to China where they came down on darkened airfields. To prepare for the daring raid, Doolittle's men had practiced on airfields in Florida that were the size of an aircraft carrier. The pilots had to get to China

because while it was possible to launch the big bombers from a carrier it was not possible to land them on one. The men flew 688 miles to Tokyo, then an additional 1,100 miles to the field in China.

Damage to Tokyo was slight, but the raid provided a great morale boost for Americans who have had only bad news for the past 19 weeks of war. Japanese authorities have no idea where the bombers came from. President Roosevelt told the American reporters that they came from "Shangri-la."

While B-25's can take off from aircraft carriers, they cannot yet land on them.

American forces give up at Corregidor

Corregidor, Philippines, May 6

"The Rock" has fallen. After months of bombardment from sea, land and air, and fierce hand-to-hand jungle fighting, Corregidor, "the Gibraltar of the East," has fallen into Japanese hands. General Jonathan M. "Skinny" Wainwright surrendered his 2,600-man force of soldiers, sailors and marines to Lieutenant General Homma Masahura following 27 days of brutal fighting.

The prolonged defense of the two-square-mile island was made possible, in part, by an intricate system of tunnels that allowed the defenders an underground retreat from the intense Japanese shelling that tore up almost every square foot of the island. No trees were

left standing. The exact number of Americans killed may never be known, but in the final battle at least 40 lay dead in the wreckage and many times that number were wounded, filling the tunnel corridors in makeshift hospitals.

During the long siege, there were at least 1,800 casualties. Some 70 Filipinos were buried alive when a cliff collapsed, sealing their caves and dugouts. Marine officers said that Japanese casualties were at least five times as great because of their suicidal aggressiveness during the invasion of the island. At the moment of the surrender, Japanese tanks were just a few hundred yards from Malinta Tunnel, where General Wainwright's headquarters was situated (→ 8).

Battle of Coral Sea ends inconclusively

Internal explosions doomed the carrier Lexington after the Coral Sea battle.

Coral Sea, May 8

A most unusual naval battle in which the vessels of neither side could see each other ended today in the Coral Sea. The sea lies between the Equator and the Tropic of Capricorn, where the only previous conflicts have been between trading schooners and Melanesian war canoes. This battle has really been a series of events strung out over days and vast stretches of ocean, directed by leaders in huge aircraft carriers who had little or no idea where the enemy was. The result was a battle full of mistakes, some tragic and some comical. But two carriers were sunk, the Japanese Shoho and the American Lexington, which its crew had lovingly called "Lady Lex." On May 7, the light carrier Shoho was the first to go to the bottom when it accidentally en-

countered flyers from the Lexington and Yorktown. The Shoho sank in just 10 minutes and the Lexington's dive bomber commander exultantly radioed his ship to "scratch one flattop." A day later, the tables were turned when the two carrier groups finally came to grips after days of fumbling. The Japanese were shrouded in heavy overcast, but the Americans had no such protection and the Lexington took two torpedoes and two bomb hits. At the end of the battle, it seemed that the Lexington might still be saved. But suddenly, two internal explosions rocked it and Captain Frederick Sherman was forced to abandon ship. About 150 men were rescued by being lowered into motor whaleboats. The Yorktown was also hit, and lost 66 men, but it managed to survive the battle (→ June 6). ▷

American navy turns tide at Midway

A Japanese bomber scores a direct hit on the American carrier Yorktown.

The Yorktown lists to starboard during the Battle of Midway. Its loss was a severe blow; nevertheless the American fleet achieved a smashing victory.

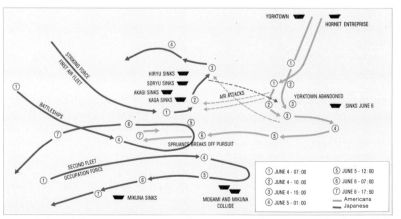

Knowledge of the Japanese command's strategy and intentions, thanks to U.S. intelligence, allows American naval forces not only to head off a major military disaster but to give chase to the retreating Japanese armada as well. Only a lack of fuel prevents the U.S. fleet from delivering one final, crushing blow.

Midway Island, June 6

Despite their overwhelming military superiority in the Pacific, the Japanese have suffered a crushing defeat in the Battle of Midway. They lost one heavy cruiser, four fleet carriers and 330 aircraft, most of which went down on their carriers. The Americans, on the other hand, lost only one carrier and about 150 aircraft.

The keys to the Japanese defeat were complacency and poor strategy. They had intended to invade both Midway Island, appropriately named because it is midway from just about anything in the Pacific, and the Aleutian chain off the coast of Alaska. Because of these fixed strategic objectives, the Americans had much greater flexibility and their admirals, Chester Nimitz and Raymond Spruance, used every bit of advantage they had. Nimitz was in overall command of the American force and Spruance commanded the carriers.

The Japanese fleet, which approached Midway Island in early June, was staggering in its size and complexity – 200 ships, including eight carriers, 11 battleships, 22 cruisers, 65 destroyers and 21 submarines. To meet this armada, the Americans had only three carriers with 233 planes, and no battleships. All the American battleships in the Pacific had been sunk or severely damaged at Pearl Harbor.

Admirals Yamamoto, who was in overall command, and Chuichi Nagumo, in command of carriers, believed that the United States fleet would not be at sea. The Americans had, therefore, the advantage of surprise. As the Japanese attacked Midway Island with dive bombers, the Americans attacked the Japanese fleet. Despite the surprise, the Americans lost the first round when 35 of the 41 torpedo bombers, relatively slow machines, were shot down. But moments later, 37 dive bombers from the Enterprise swept down on the Japanese from 19,000 feet and met almost no opposition. Three carriers were sunk in a period of just an hour.

Later in the same afternoon the carriers Yorktown and Hiryu slugged it out, and both ships were so badly damaged that they had to be abandoned (→ Nov. 15).

Eisenhower is given command in Europe

New role for Dwight D. Eisenhower.

Washington, D.C., June 25

A relatively obscure officer has been named commander of American forces in the European theater of operations. He is Major General Dwight D. Eisenhower. He served under two of the nation's foremost military leaders. He was senior aide to General Douglas A. MacArthur and, last month, General George C. Marshall assigned him to explore second-front possibilities in Britain. The 52-year-old Eisenhower, known as "Ike," was a football star at West Point, ranking 61st in a class of 164 at the Military Academy.

O.S.S. will gather secret information

Washington, D.C., June 13

America is officially in the spy business, as of today. An executive order created the Office of Strategic Services, to conduct covert operations and intelligence gathering overseas. Appointed head of the new agency is 59-year-old Colonel William J. "Wild Bill" Donovan, a World War I Congressional Medal of Honor winner who led "The Fighting 69th" Regiment. The United States has been the only major power without an intelligence service. Last July, President Roosevelt selected Colonel Donovan to be the coordinator of information, but his operation has been redesignated as the Office of Strategic Services (→ July 26, 1947).

WAAC's and WAVES join the war effort

She's doing her part in the WAVES.

Washington, D.C., July 30

An act of Congress has created the Women Accepted for Volunteer Emergency Service (WAVES) on the heels of formation of the Women's Army Auxiliary Corps (WAAC) on May 14. Mildred McAfee, the president of Wellesley College, is expected to take a leadership role among the WAVES, who like their WAAC sisters will be doing noncombat duties at home and overseas. Several hundred of the WAAC women are already in training at Fort Des Moines, and their existence has met with controversy. Some women physicians refuse to serve with the the group because they have been denied admission to the all-male Medical Reserve Corps, which they feel performs more essential work.

28 seized by F.B.I. on sedition charges

Washington, D.C., July 23

As American forces battle the Axis powers overseas, the Federal Bureau of Investigation and the Attorney General are striking at domestic enemies. Today, 28 people – including writers and publishers – were arrested on sedition charges. A special grand jury, which heard some 150 witnesses, charged that the accused plotted to "interfere with, impair and influence the loyalty, morale and discipline" of the military. They allegedly worked through publications and organizations that included the Ku Klux Klan and the German-American Bund.

On the home front

United States

What's new on store shelves? Dannon Yogurt, Kellogg's Raisin Bran, Hunt's Foods. What's on people's minds? Daylight saving time, air raids and sirens, lights dimmed on Broadway, blackout drills and saving wastepaper (Boy Scouts salvaged 150,000 tons this year). What's on bookshelves? Not much; people are donating paperbacks to victory book rallies across the country. What's on women? Trousers. Sales of women's slacks are five times what they were last year, because of factory work. What's on windows? Service flags, some with eight stars representing eight million Americans overseas.

German targets bombed

As raids on German targets increase, the Boeing B-17, known as the "Flying Fortress," shows that it can do its job in spite of anti-aircraft defenses.

Rouen, France, Aug. 17

The American Army Air Force today conducted its first major bombing raid of the war. Compared to the 1,000-plane raids the Royal Air Force has conducted, the American strike was a modest beginning that involved only 18 heavy bombers. But it is a start. Protected by an R.A.F. Spitfire cover, four bombers made diversionary raids on the French coast while 12 American B-17's struck at the railroad marshalling yards at Rouen. Weather conditions were good, enemy opposition was negligible and the raid, led by General Ira Eaker, was considered a success.

This first raid is said to be a trial operation in what is intended to be a massive joint effort by the United States and Britain. The overall strategy of the two countries is not so much to defend Britain as to gain complete air supremacy over Europe. To accomplish this task the Americans will conduct daylight raids against Germany and occupied Europe while the Britons will do the same thing at night. This division of labor was set because the United States prefers daylight bombing, which it considers more accurate, while the British prefer the night because they have fewer losses to German fighters and anti-aircraft batteries.

This raid is considered important because the first British-American effort on July 4 was hardly a success. In a raid on the Netherlands, two U.S. planes were shot down and only two managed to bomb their targets (→ Dec. 31, 1943).

BACK THEM UP!

The bombs are taking their toll.

United States, June 30. *A scrap-rubber drive begun two weeks ago has ended; everything from tires to boots was donated to keep the war rolling.*

U.S. scores big victory in Solomons

Battle for Guadalcanal begins with amphibious assault by 10,000 marines.

Guadalcanal, Nov. 15

The Battle of Guadalcanal has been a long series of naval and land clashes for control of this key island in the Solomon chain and it appears that the United States has won a major victory here. The fierce engagements got under way with an amphibious assault by the marines that was almost unopposed. By evening, 10,000 men had come ashore and the Japanese decided to retire to tunnels and emplacements. Then, in a dangerous, tedious effort, they were blasted out by hand grenades and high explosives. Japanese help came by way of "The Slot," a sea passage opposite the northern edge of the island that saw so much traffic in the next few months that it became known as the Tokyo Express. Japanese commanders underestimated the island's marine force and sent in reinforcements piecemeal, enabling the marine forces to repulse steady attacks in places that they gave names such as "Bloody Ridge" and "Hell's Corner," as well as on the Henderson Field base. Japan wasted many men in kamikaze attacks – suicide missions – against well-defended positions, losing men in a ratio of as much as 10 to 1.

By October, the marines were so firmly entrenched on the island that attempts by the enemy to take it back proved futile. At sea, the final phase was the naval battle of Guadalcanal, in which the Japanese lost two destroyers and a battleship. The Americans suffered heavier losses, including the cruiser Juneau with 700 men killed, among them all five Sullivan brothers (→ Feb. 9, 1943).

War rages on in the Pacific, but the tide seems to be turning

Solomon Islands

While Japanese and American land forces have been slugging it out for possession of Guadalcanal, both navies have engaged in a series of battles for possession of the surrounding waters. The results have been mixed, but the tide seems to have turned in favor of the United States.

Just north of Guadalcanal lies Savo, a small volcanic cone jutting up from the South Pacific. It is a piece of real estate neither side wanted but that neither side could afford to let the other have. The resulting battle was neither a decisive victory nor an unprofitable defeat. It was a bloody campaign for an unwanted island, and it cost the United States four heavy cruisers, one destroyer and 2,000 men dead.

On August 24, both navies geared up for a battle over the eastern Solomons, and this time the Americans scored a big victory. A strong carrier force – the Enterprise, Saratoga and Wasp – under Admiral Frank J. Fletcher defeated a carrier group under Admirals Nobutake Kondo and Chuichi Nagumo. In October, the Japanese again attempted to shake the marines off Guadalcanal and, when they sent reinforcements, a fierce battle was fought off Cape Esperance, north of the island. For a while, it seemed as though the Americans might lose Guadalcanal. The final engagement, called the Battle of the Santa Cruz Islands, led to the loss of the carrier Hornet, but the attrition of Japanese planes enabled the Americans to keep their grip on Guadalcanal and the surrounding waters and finally begin to turn the war against the Japanese.

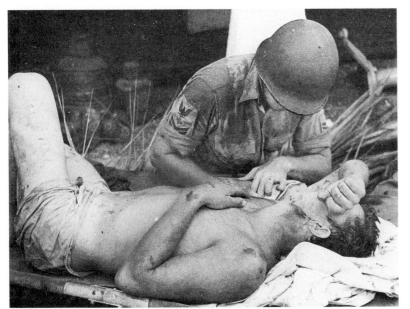

A lucky survivor of the warship Calhoun receives medical care in the Solomons.

From king of swing to king of swoon

New York City, Dec. 30

The Paramount Theater is the Mount Olympus of American pop musicians. Benny Goodman was crowned king there in 1937, and now it seems to be Frank Sinatra's turn. Never has the hall seen quite such hysterical homage and swooning. The new king is an unlikely figure, described by his former boss, bandleader Harry James, as looking like a "wet rag." But to the thousands of squealing, fainting and entranced teenagers, the 27-year-old crooner with the wraith-like voice is the Pied Piper incarnate. And in the past few years his recordings of *White Christmas*, *Night and Day* and *Fools Rush In* have helped his claim to the throne.

Speaking of records, Glenn Miller's *Chattanooga Choo-Choo* has set a new mark of one million sales, making it the first "gold record." It's also been another good year for the Andrews Sisters, always at or near the top since their 1937 hit, *Bei Mir Bist Du Schon*. This year the trio triumphed with *Don't Sit Under the Apple Tree*.

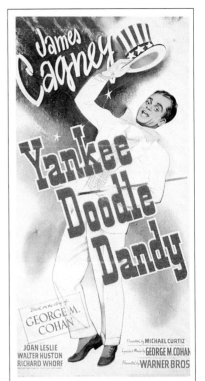

Composer George M. Cohan, who wrote "It's a Grand Old Flag" and other hits, died November 5, but his life is now on the big screen.

Atoms in chain reaction

Chicago, Dec. 2

The road to nuclear power was opened today when the world's first sustained nuclear chain reaction was achieved in a makeshift facility under the stands of Stagg Field at the University of Chicago. Though the amount of the energy released was small, it was energy from the atomic nucleus, a potentially unlimited source of power. Working in freezing conditions, a team of scientists under the direction of the brilliant Italian physicist Enrico Fermi built what they call an "atomic pile," consisting of blocks of graphite containing uranium. Fissioning of the uranium nucleus releases energy and neutrons that split other nuclei, in a potentially endless reaction. The chain reaction was kept under control by the use of rods of cadmium, which absorbs neutrons. Under Fermi's direction, the cadmium rods were slowly withdrawn from the pile. At exactly 3:45 p.m., the recorders showed that the reaction was self-sustaining, releasing enough neutrons to keep going forever.

Physicists say that the power in a few pounds of fissionable uranium could be fabulously productive, or destructive. The success today is a major step in America's growing effort to develop nuclear power.

Allies enter North Africa

Storming a beach in North Africa.

American soldiers prepare to fight.

Casablanca, Morocco, Nov. 11 .

The Allied invasion of North Africa called "Torch" is going well, but there has been more than token resistance by the French forces loyal to the government at Vichy in unoccupied France. The question of German collaboration was resolved when French batteries on Cap El Hawk, in Casablanca harbor, opened up on the British and American ships. The battleship Massachusetts, two cruisers and four destroyers were hit before the shore batteries were silenced. The unfinished French battleship Jean Bart also took part in the battle.

Before the landing operations, General George Patton gave one of his "blood and guts" speeches to the troops. "Never in history has the navy landed an army at the planned time and place," he said. "But if you land us anywhere within 50 miles of Fedala [Morocco] and within one week of D-day, I'll go ahead and win."

The landings in Algeria, at Oran, ran into even stiffer opposition than at Casablanca, but cooperation between the British and Americans got the troops ashore. The American First Division, under Major General Terry Allen, deceptively bypassed Oran in the dark, doubling back to the beaches where little opposition was met. However, at Oran harbor, big displays of American flags meant to discourage French resistance did not work. But after three days of fighting, the French gave up (→ Feb. 22, 1943).

"Casablanca" and a "Road to Morocco"

Hollywood, California

Adrift in a world at war, against a background of international intrigue, they meet, they love and they must part. The film is *Casablanca*, pairing Ingrid Bergman and Humphrey Bogart and offering witty, ironic twists. From the same country, this time with gags, the *Road to Morocco* proves a road to success for Bing Crosby, Bob Hope and Dorothy Lamour. *Now Voyager* with Bette Davis and Paul Henreid wins acclaim as does *Woman of the Year*, pairing Spencer Tracy and Katharine Hepburn for the first time. The big Academy Award winner is *Mrs. Miniver* with Greer Garson. James Cagney wins as best actor for *Yankee Doodle Dandy*. Disney's latest is *Bambi*, and Bing Crosby has recorded *White Christmas* from the movie *Holiday Inn*. Ronald Reagan, who was George Gipp in *Knute Rockne - All American* two years ago, tells his fans, "Mr. Norm is my alias. Nothing about me to make me stand out in the midway."

Clark Gable, whose wife, Carole Lombard, died in a plane crash in January while on a war bond drive, joined the armed forces, despite his age, 41. So have James Stewart, Cesar Romero, Spencer Tracy, Robert Stack and Douglas Fairbanks Jr.

Bogart and Bergman share a moment in "Casablanca" as Sam plays it again.

Muroc, California, October 1. *The XP-59, the first turbojet aircraft manufactured in the United States, was tested today by Robert Stanley, head pilot for the Bell Aircraft Corporation. Its future appears to be sound.*

U.S. defeats Japanese at Guadalcanal

American troops come ashore with Coast Guard manning the landing craft.

Two marines on Guadalcanal proudly exhibit a captured Japanese flag.

Guadalcanal, Feb. 9

Admiral William "Bull" Halsey received the following radio message from General Alexander Patch on Guadalcanal: "Total and complete defeat of Japanese forces on Guadalcanal effected today ... Tokyo Express no longer has terminus on Guadalcanal." These words mark the first major offensive victory for the United States in the Pacific and the end of seven months of bitter and savage struggle for the navy and marines. The Americans now hold some 2,500 miles of swamp and jungle-covered volcanic mountains.

The battle for the island tipped toward the United States in October 1942, and by December the Japanese were starving. Their only relief came from submarines that would sneak close to the shore at night and place drums full of supplies in the tidal waters, hoping that a favorable current would get them to the beleaguered defenders. By January, the Americans had become aware that the Japanese were planning either an evacuation or a major reinforcement, because intelligence reports showed transports and freighters being assembled at Rabaul in New Guinea. The final evacuation began slowly toward the end of January, and on the nights of February 5 and 6, Japanese transports were able to slip past the vigilant Americans and remove about 11,000 men. The marines didn't realize what had happened until they began to explore the western end of the island and found not a living soul (→ March 4).

Allies, at Casablanca, agree on 2nd front

Casablanca, Morocco, Jan. 24

President Roosevelt and Prime Minister Churchill announced today that the war will not end until they have achieved the "unconditional surrender" of Germany, Italy and Japan. Roosevelt said he was determined to destroy the "philosophies in those countries which are based on conquest and the subjugation of other people." The two leaders agreed during 10 days of meetings here to open a southern front in June or July by attacking Sicily. An invasion of Sardinia was reject-ed. The attack will be led by General Dwight D. Eisenhower. Churchill also agreed to a "maximum" buildup of forces in Britain in preparation for a cross-English Channel invasion of France.

General Charles de Gaulle participated in most of the meetings in spite of Roosevelt's objections. After the conference broke up today, Roosevelt and Churchill drove together in a car to Marrakesh, where one dinner guest said they made "affectionate little speeches to each other, and Winston sang" (→ Dec. 6).

A new penicillin

Peoria, Illinois

The potent anti-bacterial agent penicillin, accidentally discovered in a moldy culture dish in 1928, has proven too scarce to play much of a medical role. But in a chance encounter, a researcher from a government laboratory here stumbled on a new type of penicillium mold this summer on a cantaloupe at a local market. Using new deep-fermentation techniques, the laboratory hopes to grow enough of the new strain to treat every wounded soldier or infected civilian needing it.

60,000 Americans are dead in battle

Washington, D.C., February

Figures released by the government on January 5 point up the terrible price that American families are paying as their sons go into the fighting. Some 60,000 American soldiers have been killed, and many more are certain to die before the war is over. Nevertheless. with every day that passes, the American resolve to win appears to toughen. As newspaper columnist Ernie Pyle wrote of the American troops after their Tunisian victory, "Even though they didn't do too well in the beginning, there was never at any time any question about the American bravery. It is a matter of being hardened and practiced by going through the flames."

Sub commander: "Take her down"

South Pacific, Feb. 7

The powerful American submarine Growler rammed a Japanese gunboat at 17 knots today, then was spattered with machine-gun fire. Many crewmen died, as did the courageous Commander Howard Gilmore. His last words ordered the crew to "Take her down," even though he remained on the sub's bridge, bleeding from enemy shrapnel. Any delay to get him in would have lost the time needed for the vessel to get away. His action saved most of the crew and a premier sub. Gilmore will be posthumously awarded a Medal of Honor.

Allies stop Rommel in North Africa

Ike and Allied leaders review forces.

An American advance observation post in the El Guettar Valley, Tunisia.

North Africa, Feb. 22

General Erwin Rommel and his Afrika Korps have introduced the newly arrived Americans to the very tough league of mechanized desert warfare, and the lesson has been a bloody one. The Americans, under Major General George S. Patton Jr., stopped Rommel at the Kasserine Pass in Tunisia on February 19, but suffered 6,000 casualties compared to Rommel's 1,000. Of greater significance was the fact that U.S. tanks did not hold up well against German armor. The American Stuarts could not dent the heavier German tanks and the armor on the Shermans was inadequate.

On the morning of February 14, the Germans under Rommel, who had retreated westward from Libya because of British pressure, began

an assault against the Allies, hoping to buy time and to threaten their enormous supply base at Tebessa. Things might have gone better for Rommel, but he didn't have use of the 10th Panzer Division, which considerably weakened the attack. The Americans expected an assault, but they didn't anticipate its brute force. Rommel quickly cut off an infantry regiment and wiped it out. When the Americans counterattacked with an armored regiment, the Germans wiped that out as well. The Germans made steady progress for five days, breaking through the pass and advancing 70 miles into Allied territory. Rommel expected a counterattack as the advance slowed, but nothing serious developed, so he decided to pull back to the Kasserine Pass and pre-

pare an eastward counterstroke against the British Eighth Army. At one point, the Germans used a clever ruse against the retreating British, who were fighting alongside the Americans, that resulted in the capture of 700 prisoners. They placed a captured British tank at the head of their column and followed closely behind the retreating soldiers, in the hope that the Allies would assume that the tank column was not really the enemy. The plan worked and the Germans burst into the Allied ranks, causing considerable destruction and confusion.

After their initial setback, the Americans regrouped and went on the attack. Yesterday, a week after the fighting began, the battle lines had returned to what they were at the start.

U.S. bombers prevail in Bismarck Sea

New Guinea, March 4

The American Fifth Air Force today delivered the most devastating air attack against the enemy since the start of the war with the Japanese attack on Pearl Harbor. Late in February, the Japanese attempted to reinforce their garrison at Lae, New Guinea, but the Fifth Air Force, commanded by Major General George Kenney, caught the convoy of ships in the Bismarck Sea and sank eight transports and four destroyers. The damage was caused by a change in American

bomb fuses, which permitted a five-second delay. This allowed B-25's carrying 500-pound bombs to deliver them at sea level as a torpedo bomber would, and still escape.

Aided by Australia's Air Force, the Allies left Papua, New Guinea, with 207 bombers and 129 fighters. The Japanese had negligible air cover, and the Allies dropped 200 bombs on the hapless convoy. Because Japanese soldiers continued to fight back even if captured, many survivors were machine-gunned in the water (→ Dec. 26).

Coal strike halted by seizure threat

Washington, D.C., May 2

With a typical flair for drama, United Mine Workers chief John L. Lewis has ordered 500,000 miners back to work 20 minutes before President Roosevelt took to the radio to denounce his two-day strike. "Every idle miner ... is obstructing our war effort," FDR fumed after placing the mines under federal control yesterday. Labor closed ranks behind the miners, condemning a war policy that "freezes wages but permits, and indeed guarantees, a continued rise in the cost of living." Though forced to back off, Lewis has proved his skill and is likely to get his wage increase soon.

Count Fleet gallops to the Triple Crown

New York City, June 5

Count Fleet, a colt nobody wanted, even for $4,500, reached the peak of thoroughbred racing today. The Reigh Count colt won the Belmont Stakes, final leg of the Triple Crown after the Kentucky Derby and the Preakness. Count Fleet was a castoff when John Hertz bought him as a yearling and he was turned out to race when nobody would buy the horse. Because of the war, Churchill Downs has tried to discourage trips to the derby. Still, 65,000 fans showed up last month.

Churchill in capital: "V" and a pep talk

Washington, D.C., May 25

Prime Minister Churchill ended his visit to the capital today with another pep talk, and he was cheered after a press conference he held with President Roosevelt. Churchill stepped onto his chair and gave a "V" for Victory sign. Last Wednesday, the Prime Minister urged Congress to be steadfast and tenacious until the Axis powers are defeated. "We have surmounted many serious dangers," he said, but he warned that the most grave danger remaining is "the undue prolongation of the war." Churchill promised to continue in the war effort against Japan even after Germany and Italy are defeated.

Court overturns law ordering flag salute

Washington, D.C., June 14

Some call it an irony. Some call it an act of respect for the First Amendment. But on this Flag Day, the Supreme Court has ruled that schoolchildren cannot be required by state law to salute the flag. In West Virginia Board of Education v. Barnette, the high court voted 5 to 4 in favor of the Jehovah's Witnesses, holding that a statute requiring such a salute is an abridgement of the freedom of religion and expression that is guaranteed in the Constitution.

Japanese forces are defeated in Aleutians

Armed with guns and tools for construction duty, Navy Seabees drill in Alaska.

Attu, Aleutian Islands, May 29

The Seventh Infantry Division has retaken the island of Attu from the Japanese, who have occupied it since 1941, but the cost has been high. The Americans landed on the treeless, bleak and mountainous island on May 11, and encountered stiff resistance. The burden of the battle settled upon the foot soldiers because the unpredictable weather made air and naval support virtually impossible.

After two weeks of fighting, the Japanese were left with only a flat area around the Chicagof harbor base, as the American troops closed in for the kill. They were met with a banzai attack by about 1,000 Japanese, of whom 500 were quickly killed. Most of the others committed suicide, either in the traditional hara-kiri ritual of disembowelment by sword, or by a rifle shot to the head. A few Japanese continued to hold on for about a day and a half, but those followed in their comrades' footsteps rather than be captured.

In the end, the American attack force of 11,000 men lost 600 in retaking the island. The Japanese death toll was 2,351, with only 28 men taken prisoner.

"Oklahoma!" wins raves from the press

New York City, March 31

The musical *Oklahoma!* has the critics groping for adjectives, which means it's in a class by itself. Reasons are easy to find with songs like *Oh, What a Beautiful Morning, The Surrey With the Fringe on Top, People Will Say We're in Love, Out of My Dreams* and, of course, the title song. A perfect cast is headed by Alfred Drake, Joan Roberts, Howard da Silva and Celeste Holm. Equally important, it seems that Americans yearn for a sentimental, nostalgic glimpse of an era when life was more direct, less complicated than in these war-torn days. Thus, more than the rural setting of an actual state, the Richard Rodgers-Oscar Hammerstein show mythologizes a vanished state of mind.

Washington, D.C., April 13. *Roosevelt dedicated the beautiful Jefferson Memorial today in honor of the third President of the United States.*

A singing and dancing "Oklahoma!

"Use it up, wear it out, make it do, or do without"

United States

No one has lost a life wielding a hoe in a victory garden or lugging a tub of vegetable fat to the corner butcher's. Still, Americans on the homefront are doing their part, they hope, to help the boys overseas and bring the war to a swifter end. "Use it up, wear it out, make it do, or do without," is one version of a slogan going around, and so Americans are pitching in to conserve wartime materials. By year's end, however, few of the sacrifices are voluntary. Some food staples, such as butter (four ounces a week), cheese (four pounds a week), coffee and flour are rationed. Neighbors gather round a table where they once played bridge, now swapping their ration coupons. Tuesdays and Fridays are "meatless" days, and the weekly tuna casserole surprise surprises no one. What is news, however, is that, despite the 28-ounce-a-week allowance, meat consumption has actually gone up. Apparently, Americans are eating better when limits are thrust on them.

But their dress is not improved: designers have restrictions on the kind and amount of fabric they can use, and businessmen are doing without vests. Their "victory pants" lack cuffs. As for women, their dresses seem a bit on the drab side, and there is idle speculation that the hems will climb further as another sacrifice. Each American is allotted three pairs of leather shoes a year; sensible shoes are more sensible than ever.

Virtually all consumable goods have a second life, as tin and other metals, paper and nylon are recycled. Kitchen fat is processed for explosives. Rubber, found in inaccessible Asia, is one of the scarcest of commodities. Some municipalities try to ward off rubber thieves by having car owners record the serial numbers of their tires. With gas rationed and a 35 mph speed limit in effect, no one takes the car out of the garage much anyhow.

Everywhere there is delay. The trains, loaded with enlisted men or hauling war materiel, are late leaving and late arriving. Lines snake out of grocery stores, restaurants, and bars because there are too few employees waiting on customers.

Yet because manpower – and womanpower – are so much in demand, workers find themselves almost pampered. Factories have introduced coffee breaks and piped music, fringe benefits and awards for fine performance. Unfortunately, the sense of delay pervades the workplace: President Roosevelt ordered a freeze on all wages, prices and salaries, and the mandatory 48-hour week at the war plants is exhausting, coffee breaks or no. There is nothing like just going home at the end of a day, sitting in front of the old radio (factories aren't making new ones for civilians anymore) and gulping a small watered-down bottle of beer – not "sacrificing" a drop.

Norman Rockwell really hits home.   *Women help fill the nation's arsenal.*

"Victory Gardens" ease a bit of the burden on the nation's food producers.

American war production is at its peak

Washington, D.C.

The new chief of the War Production Board, Donald Nelson, said, in January 1942, "We're going to have to rely on our great mass production industries for the bulk of our increase under the war program." This has led to a staggering growth in war production. The B-24 factory at Willow Run, Michigan, employs 100,000 workers and can disgorge planes at the rate of 500 a month. Some 47,000 were produced in 1942, but this year that rose to 86,000. From December 7, 1941, to the end of this year, more than 150,000 planes were built. The figures for shipbuilding are equally impressive: 1,949 built in 1943, 1,238 of them mass-produced, assembly-line Liberty Ships (there's a new one every four days). In two years of war, 27 million deadweight tons were produced, more than offsetting heavy losses to U-boats. Output of synthetic rubber is expected to hit 800,000 tons next year. These prodigious feats have led even Joseph Stalin to toast "American productivity without which this war would have been lost."

"Penn Station at Wartime" (1943) by Joseph Delaney. On the home front, there are constant delays. People come, people go and some never return. ▷

Allies batter their way into Italy

American armor rolls through Palma, Sicily, on the way to mainland Italy.

Sicilian peasants gather sadly around a wounded soldier fighting for his life.

Naples, Italy, Oct. 3

The Allies, after three successful invasions of Italy, have conquered Sicily and worked their way up the "boot" to Naples and Foggia. The campaign began with the Sicilian invasion on July 10, when an armada of 3,000 ships unloaded 500,000 Allied soldiers along the southern beaches of the island. The Axis powers had 350,000 men to defend Italy, with six mobile German divisions at the core.

Although the landings were relatively easy, the Germans counterattacked on July 11. Armored strikes were beaten off and the British Eighth Army and the American Third began pushing north and west toward Messina. The Germans and Italians never intended to stay and fight in Sicily and they soon pulled most of their troops back to the Italian mainland. On August 17, the Allies pushed into the rubble that was Messina, and on September 21, the British began putting troops ashore on the mainland at Reggio Calabria. During this time, Italians were losing heart for the war and Mussolini's government began shaking apart, with defections to the Allies. Hitler said, disgustedly, that the Italians never managed to lose a war, no matter whose side they were on, because they were always on the winning side at the end. On September 9, Allied troops stormed ashore at Salerno, south of Naples, and continued to push north against tough German resistance (→ June 4, 1944).

600,000 flee Nazis and come to U.S.

Washington, D.C., Dec. 10

According to some of the testimony heard today by members of the House Foreign Affairs Committee, at least 600,000 people escaping persecution by the Nazis have been granted admission to the United States since 1933. Many of the refugees, such as Albert Einstein, who arrived in 1933, and composer Kurt Weill, who came two years later, are Jews. But others, such as the author Thomas Mann, who has lived in Princeton, New Jersey, since 1938, and Niels Bohr, the physicist who arrived this year, were persecuted for their secular beliefs.

U.S. agrees to join world relief body

Washington, D.C., Nov. 9

The United States has joined in a 44-nation agreement today to establish the United Nations Relief and Rehabilitation Administration. It is designed to help victims in Europe and the Far East who have suffered the most from the devastation of war. Former Governor Herbert Lehman of New York is to head the organization. The action was preceded by passage in the House of Representatives of the Fulbright Resolution, calling for an international peace organization. The Senate took up a similar proposal, the Connally Resolution.

Race rioting rocks N.Y., L.A. and Detroit

New York City, Aug. 2

As America fights a racist Hitler in Europe, racial hatred has set off riots at home. Today, a rumor of a murder in Harlem, then an argument between a Negro woman and a white policeman triggered widespread street violence, resulting in the death of five and injuries to 400.

In June, white servicemen in Los Angeles attacked blacks and Hispanics wearing "zoot" suits, the gaudy garb with long jackets and pegged pants. The assault fueled racial tension and rioting erupted. The military declared the city off-limits to servicemen before the bat-

tling was brought under control.

The worst violence erupted June 20 in Detroit, where 300,000 Southern whites and blacks have migrated to work in the war plants. In two days, 35 were killed, 600 wounded and thousands held. Thurgood Marshall of the National Association for the Advancement of Colored People said Detroit's police used "persuasion" on white rioters, but "ultimate force ... revolvers, riot guns and sub-machine guns" on Negroes. One report said of the police that they made mistakes, but "demonstrated courage, efficiency and ... good judgment."

Robeson as Othello

New York City

Last year, plans for a Broadway production of *Othello* starring Paul Robeson touched off intense debate. Will whites stand for a real-life black man as Shakespeare's Moor? Robeson opened in the title role on October 19 and the answer to the question was a record-breaking run and critical accolades – for Robeson and for co-stars Uta Hagen and Jose Ferrer. Broadway also saw a Negro cast this season in the long-awaited *Porgy and Bess*, George Gershwin's opera of 1935 about Negro life on Catfish Row in Charleston, South Carolina.

Railroads seized

Washington, D.C., Dec. 27

President Roosevelt acted firmly today in ordering the government to seize the railroads to avert a strike. Roosevelt had met for hours day after day with rail management and labor to mediate an end to the rift over a proposed wage hike. Fearing the threat to national security if workers struck, he took charge, directing the army to operate the railroads until the disputing parties reach a settlement. While a crisis has been temporarily avoided, the President will keep seeking an accord. A series of battles over salaries has raged since early spring.

Bombers ravaging German factories

Germany, Dec. 31

The German heartland is being saturated with bombs as the United States Army Air Force continues to step up the size of its daylight raids. In mid-October, the maximum number of bombers used was 400, but by this month that number has increased until three raids of 700 bombers each, per day, is not uncommon. The result is a rain of devastation on both the Rhine and the Ruhr industrial areas, and on such key cities as Regensburg, Hannover and Schweinfurt.

The principal targets are factories that are considered crucial to war production such as those manufacturing ball bearings, aircraft tires and latex rubber. But the cost to the Allies has been significant. In a raid on July 28, only 28 bombers, of a force of 120, made it to their targets. This attack was also notable for the fact that the Germans used a new weapon, an air-launched rocket that downed three B-17's (→ March 6, 1944).

Allied chiefs meet in Quebec, Teheran and Cairo to map strategy

President Roosevelt and Prime Minister Churchill hold talks in Cairo with Generalissimo Chiang Kai-shek of China and his wife. The Allies hope that postwar China will be a friend of the West and a pillar of Asian stability.

Cairo, Egypt, Dec. 6

President Roosevelt sounded upbeat today as he spoke informally with a group of American soldiers near his villa. His series of meetings with the Allies have apparently made him more confident about winning the war. "This time when we clean out the enemy," Roosevelt pledged, "we are going to clean them out thoroughly, so that they can't start another war."

The Roosevelt declaration with Premier Stalin and Prime Minister Churchill on the recently concluded Teheran Conference is equally forceful. "No power on earth can prevent our destroying the German armies by land, their U-boats by sea and their war plants from the air," it said. The leaders agreed to open a second front in Western Europe, and Stalin pledged to join the war against Japan as soon as Hitler is defeated. Roosevelt has reportedly decided to put General Dwight D. Eisenhower in charge of the cross-English Channel invasion of France. "Operation Overlord" is tentatively set for next May.

The conference, which Churchill called "the greatest concentration of worldly power that had ever been seen in the history of mankind," marked the first time that all three leaders had met. Groundwork for it was carefully laid in Moscow at a foreign ministers' meeting and in Quebec, where Roosevelt and Churchill met. In Cairo, the two leaders and China's Generalissimo Chiang Kai-shek agreed that at war's end "Japan shall be stripped of all the islands in the Pacific which she has seized or occupied since the start of the first World War." They also pledged independence for Korea (→ Feb. 11, 1945).

American forces advance on wide front in the Pacific theater

Solomon Islands, Dec. 26

Admiral William "Bull" Halsey's ability to keep the Japanese guessing and off balance has given the Americans several important victories. One reason for his success in some of the encounters was his ability to strike where he was not expected. For example, Halsey was intent on wresting the Solomons from the Japanese. Instead of hitting at Kolombangara, as would be expected, he landed on lightly defended Vella Lavella. He then returned to Kolombangara and has captured it as well.

The Solomon victories were less costly than at Tarawa, in the Gilbert Islands. There, in a direct assault, the marines took a bad hammering. They knew the tiny coral atoll would be formidable because it was defended by 3,000 troops who had built murderous beach obstacles. The marines went in against a deadly rain of fire, were caught behind sea walls, and could not advance or retreat. Some units had 50 percent casualties. Still, they took the atoll, then held it in the face of fierce counterattacks. But it cost them 3,000 men.

They did better in other island engagements in regard to casualties, but the Japanese fought tenaciously for everything they had won. At Empress Augusta Bay in western Bougainville, there were few Japanese, but the landing vehicles ran up against uncharted reefs. In spite of air support, the marines lost 78 dead and 104 wounded. At Arawe, on Goodenough Island, the enemy used machine guns to deadly effect, sinking most of the rubber landing boats the men used. Destroyer fire finally took out the machine guns (→ May 17, 1944).

A B-25 strikes Japanese ships and positions at Rabaul harbor, New Britain.

"Bound for Glory"

United States

Most autobiographers are older than 31, but most have less living under their belts than does Woody Guthrie, the Okie troubadour who has hoboed from coast to coast with a guitar in hand and tunes in his head. His story, *Bound for Glory*, has made fans of high-brow critics.

Thomas Hart Benton's "July Hay."

Washington, D.C., Feb. 29. It is estimated that black market has earned about $1.2 billion over past year.

Washington, D.C., March 4. Because of Argentina's failure to cooperate fully with Allied war effort, Acting Secretary of State Edward Stettinius says United States has adopted policy of nonrecognition toward that nation.

Washington, D.C., Apr. 30. General Douglas MacArthur releases statement that he has no intention of seeking or accepting Republican presidential nomination.

New York City, May 1. Pulitzer Prize in poetry awarded to Stephen Vincent Benet for *Western Star*.

New York City, May 8. Nation's first eye bank formed through combined efforts of 20 city hospitals.

Washington, D.C., June 13. Americans receive word that Germans have launched robot bombs against targets as distant as London.

Hartford, Connecticut, July 6. Inept fire-eaters spark a blaze during performance of Ringling Brothers and Barnum & Bailey Circus, killing 167 people, mostly children.

Atlanta, July 12. Coca-Cola Company manufactures one billionth gallon of Coca-Cola syrup.

Port Chicago, California, July 17. Ammunition ship blows up, killing 300 people.

St. Louis, Oct. 8. St. Louis Cardinals defeat St. Louis Browns in World Series, four games to two.

Washington, D.C., Nov. 18. Statistical report shows cost of living has risen almost 30 percent in past 12 months.

New York City, Dec. 17. Green Bay Packers defeat New York Giants, 14-7, in National Football League championship.

Hood River, Oregon, December. American Legion removes names of JapaneseAmericans from its military service roll of honor.

Washington, D.C. Nearly half of steel, tin and paper needed for war effort provided by people salvaging goods.

United States. Tennessee Williams publishes play *The Glass Menagerie*.

Big night at Met, but sound is jazz

New York City, Jan. 18

Following jazz at Carnegie Hall, could Jazz at the Met be far behind? Billed as the *Esquire All-Stars*, the winners of the first critics' jazz poll in *Esquire* magazine scored another "first" by introducing that hallowed hall of opera to the primal sounds of jazz. It was a formidable group: Art Tatum, Louis Armstrong, Roy Eldridge, Coleman Hawkins, Oscar Pettiford, Sid Catlett, Barney Bigard, Red Norvo and Lionel Hampton, and singer Billie Holiday. But because the concert was arranged on short notice, the group had little rehearsal and seemed weak at the seams. And though some fine solos made the evening worthwhile, they did not include any by Armstrong, whose reputation as a singer has grown as his trumpet playing has declined. Over the years his lip has taken a beating and he's no longer at ease playing very high or very fast.

Bombers blast Berlin

A B-26 Marauder, armed with 26 100-pound bombs, drops its cargo.

London, March 6

In an all-out effort to destroy the Luftwaffe, the Allies have begun bombing raids on Berlin. American and British Air Force commanders know the Germans will throw everything they have at them to defend the city, the heartland of the Reich. They also know that the Germans can ill afford a war of attrition in aircraft production. The raids are a vote of confidence for the new P-51 fighter escorts, which because of their additional fuel tanks, can fly 850 miles into enemy territory to escort the bombers.

The first raid on March 4 did not do serious damage, but today the Americans sent over 660 bombers and delivered 1,626 tons of bombs. Their losses were great: 69 bombers and 11 fighters, but the figures for downed Luftwaffe aircraft were also high. American bomber crews claimed 97 kills, while the escort fighters shot down 82 planes. One sign of weakening air strength is that the Luftwaffe sent up night fighters against the Americans in a daytime raid. Of equal significance in the ground war is the fact that the Erkner ball bearing factory was knocked out, a loss that could cripple the production of German tanks.

Prizes in the Pacific: Kwajalein, Eniwetok, Hollandia and Wake

New Guinea, May 17

The grip of the Japanese Empire in the Far Pacific is slipping as American forces continue to capture some islands and isolate others. The marines learned a deadly lesson on Tarawa in the Gilberts, where they tried to take a strongly defended island and lost 3,000 marines in the process This time the commanders have hit the Japanese where they are weakest, Kwajalein, the key to the Marshall Islands and the world's largest coral atoll. Despite the fact that it was a command center, it was lightly defended, even after the fall of the adjacent islands of Roi and Namur. The Japanese never really had a chance against the huge armada – four carrier groups, with 12 carriers – that was sent against them. Admiral Chester Nimitz next moved against Eniwetok, the far western atoll in the Marshalls. After taking nearby tiny islands, the marines and army landed against stiff but brief opposition.

The U.S. high command decided to bypass Truk and invade Hollandia, on the north shore of Dutch New Guinea. The Americans had their largest force to date for the Hollandia-Aitape operation, some 84,000 men. Carrier groups sank two enemy destroyers and downed 300 aircraft in the softening up operations. By the time they went ashore, they had total sea and air control. Japanese losses were severe at Hollandia; 1,000 of their 11,000-man force survived. The Allies next hit Wake Island to the north because they view it as a promising air base. The Japanese responded fiercely soon after the Americans landed, but the marines held on and were starting their base even before the island was secured (→ Oct. 25).

American soldiers shielded by "Lucky Legs II" advance on Japanese positions.

U.S. unveils plan for postwar peace

Washington, D.C., March 21

Secretary of State Cordell Hull called for international cooperation today as he unveiled the postwar goals of American foreign policy. Hull has been a strong supporter of the emerging United Nations and many of his goals reflect the spirit of the international body, which is yet to be formed. Hull, who has been a moderate voice in the Roosevelt administration, has been urging the President to formulate a specific policy for the governing of Germany after the war. Roosevelt is reluctant to proceed, and has told Hull, "I dislike making detailed plans for a country which we do not yet occupy." But Hull has succeeded in convincing FDR to end his support of the Morgenthau Plan, which envisages the dismemberment of Germany into agrarian states. Hull and Secretary of War Henry Stimson have called the plan "blind vengeance" (→ Oct. 7).

Meat rations end

Washington, D.C., May 3

Make that a double hamburger! The Office of Price Administration today ended national meat rationing (except for choice cuts of beef). Ironically, some Americans will now be less well nourished: The poor ate better with a weekly allowance of 28 ounces of meat than their usual income had permitted.

Allied forces enter Rome triumphant

Rome, June 4

Allied forces swept into Rome today, the first European capital liberated from the Nazis. Residents cheered the troops, who had advanced 15 miles in 24 hours, moving so swiftly that they seized 1,000 Nazi prisoners. While Rome is of little military value, the capture of the virtually undamaged city is a great morale booster. The takeover was the culmination of an offensive that broke the Gustav Line and the Hitler Line and created the Anzio breakout. Still, the German army, far from being destroyed, fights on tenaciously. After the invasions last summer, the Germans used the rugged southern half of Italy to great strategic advantage, holding on as long as they could, using rivers as defenses, then falling back to the next defendable position. The worst clash took place at the mountain stronghold of Monte Cassino, and the famous Benedictine Abbey above the town. To dislodge the Germans, the abbey was all but destroyed, a decision that caused much criticism. In the fight for Italy, the American Fifth Army worked its way up the west coast, while Britain's Eighth Army went up the Adriatic side. German resistance caused a near stalemate and, with the invasion of France near, the Allies decided on the May push with a huge cast: Americans, British, Indians, Canadians, Free French, South Africans, Poles and New Zealanders (→ Apr. 30, 1945).

U.S. troops in Rome. Coliseum is backdrop for yet another triumphal march.

Residents of Rome welcome the liberating American forces with enthusiasm.

Merrill's Marauders march through Burma

Mules assist U.S. troops in Burma.

Burma, May 18

Merrill's Marauders, officially the 5307th Composite Unit (provisional), has been giving the Japanese fits in Burma. The volunteer group, named for its commanding officer, Colonel Frank D. Merrill, was trained in guerrilla and jungle tactics in India. It has helped General Joseph Stilwell's drive to retake northern Burma. The men marched over hundreds of miles of mountainous jungles to outflank and harass the enemy. They have seized the Myitkyina airfield and if the city falls, Stilwell will have access to deliveries by means of the Burma Road between India and China.

Army seizes firm

Chicago, Apr. 26

Sewell Avery, chairman of Montgomery Ward, has hated this administration since its inception. In 1942 it took a presidential threat to make him sign a closed shop contract mandated by the War Labor Board. He has refused to renew it, and today the President turned a threat into action. Declaring the merchandising firm a war industry, FDR ordered it placed under control of the army. A righteous Avery was carried out of his office in his own desk chair. Saving his most cherished epithet for Attorney General Francis Biddle, Avery yelled, "You New Dealer!"

D-Day! Allied troops storm beaches at Normandy

American troops cross the English Channel en route to Normandy's beaches. Seasickness and foul weather complicate the task of the invading Yanks.

After their turbulent crossing, American forces take to the beaches of France. "Full victory," they were ordered by General Eisenhower, "Nothing else."

A small fraction of the Allied army wades ashore at Normandy. The size of the invading force is awesome, and so is the cost of liberating France.

Normandy, France, June 6

The Allies successfully landed about 150,000 men on the Normandy coast of France today, and Hitler's "Atlantic Wall" was breached. "Operation Overlord," the code name of the invasion of France across the English Channel, began at 6:30 a.m. and through the day – D-Day – thousands of men and tons of equipment were put ashore on five designated beaches.

The invasion began much earlier farther inland. Two divisions of Americans, the 82nd and 101st Airborne, left England at midnight and began dropping into their landing zones at about 1 a.m. High winds scattered the paratroopers and most put down far from their intended targets. Nevertheless, small groups were quickly formed and began to attack the Germans, causing more confusion and disarray than actual damage.

The resistance met at the landing beaches was less than had been anticipated because the Germans were taken almost completely by surprise. Considering the size of the invasion plan, eventually to involve almost three million soldiers, sailors and airmen, to be transported by 11,000 ships, it is amazing that the Germans did not learn the true location of the landing sites, making it the biggest secret ever kept. The nationalities of troops and the code names of the beaches, east to west, where they landed were: British troops at Sword, Canadians at Juno, British at Gold, and Americans at Omaha and Utah.

The British and Canadians went ashore against stiff opposition despite effective support from the offshore fleet. They were able to take and secure the beaches in spite of heavy losses. It was a mixed bag for American troops. There was little opposition at Utah Beach, but at Omaha the First Division faced German veterans of the 352nd Division, who held high bluffs commanding a wide view of the beach. They kept the Americans pinned down most of the day and could have pushed them back into the sea had they been better supported. The Americans finally realized that it would be wise to advance against the intense fire because staying put would get them killed. The move inland was sparked by Brigadier General Norman Cota, who calmly walked up and down Omaha Beach in withering fire, urging his troops to move farther ashore. This beach operation cost the Americans 2,000 casualties today.

The response of the Germans to the invasion was slow and confused. Hitler believed that it was only a feint. He expected the real invasion at the Pas de Calais and therefore withheld two Panzer divisions. By the time he released them late today, the Allies were safely ashore with secured beachheads. General Erwin Rommel, of Afrika Korps fame, had been designated by Hitler to stop the invasion. Rommel knew that for Germany this would be a fateful day, but Hitler had tied his hands.

By mid-day the beaches of Normandy swarmed with soldiers and tanks and the beautiful white sand was littered with bodies. Burning vehicles were everywhere and the air was heavy with pungent cordite. American Rangers stormed the Pointe du Hoc, a large protrusion used as a battery position for heavy guns. Offshore shelling had made the area around the guns look like "the craters of the moon" as one soldier described the scene, but when the emplacement was taken, the Rangers discovered that the guns were "Quakers," dummy pieces so named because they offer no resistance. As soon as the beaches were secured, the Allied command began unloading tons of equipment along with men onto "Mulberries," the huge, transportable docks or jetties (→ Aug. 25).

BUY WAR BONDS

Roosevelt approves G.I. Bill of Rights

Washington, D.C., June 22

President Roosevelt, signing the G.I. Bill of Rights today, said, "It gives emphatic notice to the men and women in the armed forces that the American people do not intend to let them down." The Servicemen's Readjustment Act (its official name) will provide housing and educational assistance for returning war veterans. The bill is set in Jeffersonian philosophy – that government should promote education. Money for a year's schooling will be offered to all veterans, and to those with special skills, funds are available for three years (→ 1947).

Americans invade France from south

Dijon, France, Sept. 11

The Allied army that invaded the south of France on August 15 has driven up the Rhone Valley via the historic Route Napoleon and linked up with units of General George Patton Jr.'s Third Army. The Sixth Army Group, under General Jacob Devers, now becomes the right flank of an enormous Allied wedge aimed at the heart of Germany.

Operation Anvil was renamed Operation Dragoon just before the landing for security reasons, and the change is significant because it symbolizes the overall squabbling that plagued the high command in planning the operation. After more of such squabbling, it was agreed that three American divisions and seven French divisions would go ashore on beaches east of Toulon. They met only light opposition, and farther inland, 25,000 members of the Free French underground eagerly rushed to join the invaders, giving them detailed information on German positions and troop movements. The German defenses were weak, consisting of reserves and second-line troops. These conditions allowed the combined Allied force to drive rapidly up the Rhone Valley. There was a brief, sporadic German defense, but nowhere was the fighting as fierce as it was in the north. By late August, Marseilles had fallen and the Allies had reached Grenoble (→ Dec. 26).

Paris rejoices as Nazi grip is broken

Paris, Aug. 25

The great race for Paris is over and the liberation of the city has become a frenzied, tumultuous celebration. Originally, the Allies had intended to bypass the French capital because the Allied commander, General Dwight D. Eisenhower, did not want the problem of feeding several million people. But General Charles de Gaulle, who led the Free French forces, began acting on his own as soon as he arrived from Algeria and told General Philippe Leclerc of the Second Armored Division to go for Paris regardless of Eisenhower's wishes. After the collapse of the Falaise pocket, which resulted in the capture of 50,000 Germans and the death of 10,000 more, all roads to the Seine were open, precipitating a mad dash for the city.

The Third Army of General George S. Patton Jr. reached Mantes-la-Jolie, 30 miles from Paris, on August 19, the day the capital rose against its occupiers. Free French forces, Communists, Socialists and students began street uprisings against the Nazis. Hitler had planned to demolish Paris rather than allow it to fall into Allied hands, but the German demolition teams waited until it was too late and, before they could act, the streets were filled with French and American troops as de Gaulle marched down the Champs Elysees and went to mass at Notre Dame.

The American novelist Ernest Hemingway, who has lived in and loved Paris, arrived with the first group of liberators. He went to visit his old friend Pablo Picasso and gave him a large box as a present. "What's in the box, Ernest?" the painter asked. "Hand grenades," Hemingway replied.

As the Allies began entering the city, the French Resistance took over the main radio station and Parisians heard the following announcement: "Parisians, rejoice, we have come to tell you that the Leclerc division has reached Paris. We are mad with happiness." The announcer then quoted Victor Hugo: "Awake, be done with shame! Become again great France, become again great Paris." After five years of darkness, the City of Lights was reborn (→ Sept. 11).

An American military column stretching for miles rumbles past smashed German armor. Now all roads lead to the long-awaited liberation of Paris.

American paratroopers display a Nazi flag found while liberating a small French village. Allied strikes behind enemy lines help distract the already surprised and confused German troops.

With the Germans in retreat, American soldiers celebrate their victory at a makeshift Paris cafe. The city as well as their spirits have been liberated.

"I have returned," says MacArthur

The Philippines, Oct. 25

As the United States Sixth Army landed on the island of Leyte, General Douglas MacArthur, with film cameras rolling, announced, "People of the Philippines, I have returned." And as ground forces began to fight it out on the large island in the center of the Philippine archipelago, the Japanese prepared a counterattack called the "Sho plan" or Victory plan. The resulting series of naval engagements left the Americans in strategic control of the entire Pacific.

The Japanese knew that losing the Philippines would mean losing the war, so they threw everything they could into this effort. It was a complicated operation, consisting of several strike forces converging on the islands the Americans had just invaded. Vice Admiral Takeo Kurita's Central Force was intercepted while still in the South China Sea and, since the Japanese had little air cover, their ships were without effective defense. American flyers hit and sank the Musashi, the largest battleship in the world. But the Japanese drew blood when they sank the small aircraft carrier Princeton.

In Surigao Strait, the Japanese sailed into a trap baited with the ghosts of Pearl Harbor; battleships raised from the mud, rebuilt and out for revenge. The Japanese had to run a gauntlet that allowed the dreadnoughts to bring their enormous guns to bear and, within an hour, several ships were sunk and Vice Admiral Ahoji Nishimura was killed. Japan's losses were huge: 26 vessels, or 300,000 tons of combat shipping, lost. The American losses were minimal (→Nov. 24).

"People of the Philippines, I have returned," announced MacArthur, at left.

The first U.S. flag is raised on Leyte during the battle for the Phillipines.

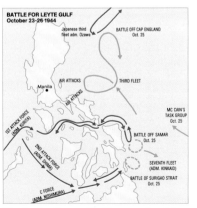

Battle for Leyte Gulf turns the tide.

FDR wins 4th term; Truman is new V.P.

Washington, D.C., Nov. 7

President Roosevelt rewrote the history books tonight as he won an unprecedented fourth term in office. Roosevelt, with his running mate Harry S. Truman, the feisty, pragmatic Missouri Senator, defeated Governor Thomas E. Dewey of New York. Democrats also kept control of Congress. Reacting to attacks, FDR had said with mock outrage: "Republican leaders are not content with attacks (on me and my family); they now include my little dog, Fala. Unlike members of my family, he resents this." Roosevelt won big in the electoral count, but his popular vote margin was smaller than before.

Lowbrow and high

New York City, Oct. 30

The Voice, sometimes called the King of Swoon, sometimes Frank Swoonatra, continues to mesmerize teenaged girls. As 10,000 bobbysoxers jostled for tickets and 700 cops tried to keep order, those who got into the Paramount Theater on October 12 squealed as Sinatra crooned tunes in a tempo described by *Life* magazine as invariably "largo alla marcia funebre."

At the other end of the cultural scale is the composer Aaron Copland, whose ballet *Appalachian Spring* was given its premiere by the Martha Graham Dance Company in Washington today. A rustic slice of Americana, it depicts a wedding in a Pennsylvania farm community. Copland uses a tune borrowed from the Shakers, *Simple Gifts*, to great effect.

World leaders agree on postwar economic, political structure

Washington, D.C., Oct. 7

Positive steps have been taken to create a framework for a new world organization to be called the United Nations. Representatives of the United States, Britain, the Soviet Union and China attended a conference at the majestic Dumbarton Oaks estate here. The Allies agreed that the new organization will be divided into a General Assembly and a Security Council whose purpose would be "to take such action by air, naval or land forces to maintain or restore international peace and security."

The conferees failed to reach agreement on two key issues raised by Andrei A. Gromyko, the Soviet Ambassador to Washington. He insisted that all 16 Soviet republics be granted seats in the Assembly. Gromyko also demanded that the Great Powers all be empowered to exercise a veto over substantive matters before the Security Council. The conference highlighted a disagreement between Britain and the U.S. Roosevelt and Secretary of State Cordell Hull believe there should "no longer be any need for spheres of influence" that countries use "to safeguard their security or promote their interests." The British like the U.N., but they also like their empire (→Aug. 8, 1945).

As Guam falls, so does Tojo's regime

Guam, Nov. 24

The Japanese have lost Guam, and with it, the battle for the Marianas, a struggle that cost them 50,000 soldiers killed in action. The July invasion of the strategically important island was fiercely contested by the enemy, and some marine rifle companies suffered 50 to 75 percent casualties. The seizure of Guam has led to an unexpected result: the fall of Hideki Tojo's government in Tokyo. Elsewhere in the Pacific, in the air battle for Formosa [Taiwan], the Japanese Typhoon Attack Force was eliminated, and Admiral William Halsey reports the destruction of 500 enemy planes (→ Feb. 23, 1945).

Glenn Miller lost

Paris, Dec. 24

Americans have apparently lost one of their most beloved music-makers – the band leader Glenn Miller, who left civilian life to play with the Air Force band. On December 16, Major Miller took a plane from England for Paris. The weather was bad, the plane never arrived and no traces have been found. Hopes that he might yet turn up were dimmed today when the 40-year-old Miller was officially listed as missing and presumed dead. The smoothly understated sound of Miller's music crystalized with the formation of his second band in 1939. His recordings of *In the Mood*, *Tuxedo Junction* and *Moonlight Serenade* have become classics. Despite Miller's absence, the band is still entertaining the Allied troops at a theater in Paris.

U.S. recoups losses in Battle of Bulge

German prisoners of war being marched out of Dutch town of Limbricht.

An American soldier views the shattered train station at Aachen, Germany.

Bastogne, Belgium, Dec. 26

It came to be called the Battle of the Bulge. In a gamble to stop the Allied advance into Germany and recapture the crucial Belgian supply port of Antwerp, Hitler secretly organized a desperate counterattack. It began on December 16, catching the Allies off guard, and punched a dangerous bulge into the American lines in Belgium. Now the Allies are hammering at the bulge and shrinking it.

The Germans had cannibalized their war machine to create two new Panzer armies under General Sepp Dietrich. They waited until bad weather had grounded Allied planes; then they hit hard.

A special English-speaking commando group, under Colonel Otto Skorzeny, the man who had rescued Mussolini, donned captured American uniforms and caused great confusion behind the American lines. When the word spread that Germans were impersonating Americans, anyone who looked suspicious was asked questions such as the names of the Brooklyn Dodgers or who married Betty Grable. The drive shattered two American divisions. The 101st Airborne was totally surrounded at Bastogne, a major junction in the Ardennes. The Germans sent word to Brigadier General Anthony McAuliffe demanding surrender, and were rebuffed with one word: "Nuts!"

The Germans' failure to take Bastogne deprived them of fuel they had hoped to capture at nearby dumps. As the Americans began retaking ground, they were horrified to find that some prisoners taken by the SS had been massacred (→ March 28, 1945).

TV networks seen

New York City, March 1

"Television promises to be the greatest medium of mass communication yet evolved," said NBC president Niles Trammell today. He predicts a vast expansion in television operations right after the war, with the creation of regional and national networks. CBS, which halted its fledgling television news broadcasts after Pearl Harbor, is also preparing for expansion.

"Kilroy was here," there and everywhere

United States

Nobody knows for certain who Kilroy is. But everyone knows his name gets around. One dictionary calls Kilroy a fictitious American created by G.I.'s who left the inscription "Kilroy was here" on surfaces all over the world. James Kilroy of Halifax, Massachusetts, says that as an inspector at a shipyard in Quincy he would chalk "Kilroy was here" on work he had inspect-

ed, and the slogan caught on.

In any case, G.I.'s and the name Kilroy have become linked, often evoking patriotic efforts back home. On assembly lines, workers are turning out cargo ships in 17 days, bombers in 13. In a year of salvage drives, the home folks collected seven million tons of wastepaper and 18 million tons of scrap metal to be made into war materiel. It's all to bring Kilroy back here.

G.I. Joe, known by his helmet.

The Big War: Sixteen million Americans in uniform

if you talk too much

THIS MAN MAY DIE

Americans are urged to keep up their guard against enemy spies. "Loose lips sink ships" is a popular phrase.

The one and only Betty Grable, the pin-up queen of the G.I.'s. This photo has made its way around the world.

On November 20, 1943, the entire crew of six that manned this gun, part of Battery F, 3rd Defense, on Bougainville, was killed by a Japanese bomb. Surrounded by enemy fire on all sides, a G.I. never knows when his time has come.

Infantry soldiers, the shock troops of the war, on the march. "Born to freedom, and believing in freedom," says FDR, Americans "are willing to fight to maintain freedom . . . We would rather die on our feet than live on our knees."

Robert W. Prescott with Curtiss P-40 of the American Volunteer Group, also known as the "Flying Tigers."

Brigadier General Benjamin Davis, America's first Negro General, pictured here in August of 1944.

The face of war. "Courage," said Mark Twain, "is resistance to fear, mastery of fear, not absence of fear."

Dancing to the sounds of Glenn Miller, in a brief but cherished moment away from the front lines of battle.

Negro soldiers in training in Louisiana in September of 1941. While the United States fights against Adolf Hitler and his racist ideology, the American armed forces remain segregated. Such a contradiction will, perhaps, end someday.

A fierce fight to the finish for the world's freedom

Irving Berlin wrote "This Is the Army," a show with an all-soldier cast, in 1942. But the composer of "White Christmas" and "God Bless America" is best loved by soldiers for his "Oh, How I Hate to Get Up in the Morning."

The United States went to war to fight for freedom and against fascism, a totalitarian philosophy that preaches hatred and religious persecution. In America, the Bill of Rights provides for freedom of religion. As President Franklin Roosevelt says, "We look forward to a world (founded on the) freedom of every person to worship God in his own way – everywhere in the world."

With their husbands, brothers and sons at war overseas, some 3.5 million American women have taken jobs on factory assembly lines, in stores and offices. For such working women, trousers have become a "badge of honor."

Waves of B-24's of the 15th Air Force fly over the Concordia Vega oil refinery in Ploesti, Rumania. After dropping their bomb loads on an oil cracking plant on May 31, 1944, they head for home base, unmindful of the bursting flak.

A kamikaze plane attack on the USS Missouri in 1945. Japanese pilots commit suicide for their country.

An aerial view of the southern tip of Manhattan. New York City is now the world's financial capital, replacing London, and its growth is symbolic of America's rise to global power and responsibilities in the wake of the war.

Bob Hope is off to entertain troops in a U.S.O. show. His theme song? "Thanks for the Memory."

Washington, D.C., Jan. 3. House of Representatives votes to establish temporary Committee on Un-American Activities as permanent body.

Washington, D.C., Jan. 15. A "dim-out" ordered for entire United States to combat shortage of fuel.

New York City, May 7. John Hersey wins Pulitzer Prize in fiction for *A Bell for Adano.*

Washington, D.C., May 10. A point system will determine priority of military discharge, taking into consideration service record, length of service and parental status.

Washington, D.C., May 25. Federal government orders reduction in military aircraft production by 30 percent.

New York City, June 23. Eisenhower quoted as saying, "Morale is the single greatest factor" in winning wars.

Washington, D.C., July 6. Executive order establishes Medal of Freedom, to honor outstanding civilian achievement.

New York City, July 28. A B-25 bomber crashes into Empire State Building, killing 13 people and injuring 26.

Hiroshima, Japan, Aug. 5. Americans drop leaflets on city, warning, "Your city will be obliterated unless your government surrenders."

Gary, Indiana, Sept. 18. Almost 1,000 white students at Froebel School boycott classes, in effort to have their Negro classmates transferred to other schools.

Detroit, Sept. 21. Henry Ford resigns as president of Ford Motor Company, and grandson Henry Ford II is elected to replace him.

Chicago, Oct. 10. Detroit Tigers defeat Chicago Cubs in World Series, four games to three.

Washington, D.C., Nov. 27. President Truman announces appointment of Gen. George C. Marshall as special envoy to China, to mediate conflict between Nationalists and Communists (→ Jan. 7, 1947).

Cleveland, Dec. 16. Cleveland Rams edge Washington Redskins, 15-14, in National Football League championship.

New York City. *Cannery Row* by John Steinbeck published.

Big Three carve up world at Yalta

Churchill, Roosevelt and Stalin convene in order to create a new world order.

Yalta, U.S.S.R., Feb. 11

Premier Stalin was more than the host today as he bade farewell to his guests in the Crimea. As Prime Minister Churchill and President Roosevelt adjourned their difficult meeting at the Livadia Palace here, it seemed apparent that Stalin was also the victor. His stunning successes on the battlefield had strengthened his hand at the bargaining table, and Stalin got almost everything that he wanted.

The Western leaders reluctantly adopted Stalin's view that Germany be divided and punished harshly when the war is over. Reparations could run as high as $20 billion, and the Soviet Union will receive half the amount. Stalin did agree to allow France to be the fourth occupying power in Germany, but the French zone will be carved out of the territory controlled by the Americans and the British.

Poland was perhaps the thorniest issue, and Stalin didn't budge. "For the Russian people," he argued, "Poland is not only a question of honor but also a question of security. Throughout history, Poland has been the corridor through which the enemy has passed into Russia." Reluctantly, Roosevelt and Churchill allowed Stalin to move his border with Poland west to the Curzon Line. The Lublin Committee, a Russian puppet, was charged with forming a new regime, and the Polish government-in-exile in London was left out of negotiations.

Stalin's influence was also recognized in the Balkans, and Roosevelt made him new promises about the Far East. In exchange for joining the war against Japan, the Russians were promised the Kurile Islands, southern Sakhalin and railroad rights in Manchuria.

Marines raise Old Glory over Iwo Jima

Iwo Jima, Feb. 23

Iwo Jima is a few square miles of volcanic ash and sand lying 700 miles south of Tokyo. Taking it from the Japanese has cost the lives of 6,800 men, and wounded 18,000 others. The U.S. high command was willing to pay the price because Iwo Jima is an ideal site for an air base from which to bomb the home island of Japan. The job of taking it went to the Fourth and Fifth Marine Divisions, under General Harry Schmidt. Battleships, cruisers and aircraft-carrier planes pounded the island relentlessly for three days before the marine landing, but the island, honeycombed with tunnels and concrete pillboxes, hid enough defenders to cause 3,000 American casualties the first day. It took four days, after the initial landing, to plant the American flag atop Mount Suribachi, where a photographer, Joe Rosenthal, caught the moment.

The battle for the rest of the island was just as tough because the enemy soldiers were dug in and had been ordered to fight to the death. The marines used satchel charges of dynamite and napalm to blast the fanatical defenders from their holes. In the end, only 200 Japanese soldiers were taken prisoner. All the others lay in the holes where they had died (→ March 4).

The flag rises on Mount Suribachi.

Enemy resistance ends in Manila

Manila, Philippines, March 4

General Douglas MacArthur had to blast the Japanese from the old walled city of Intramuros, in central Manila, with point-blank artillery fire, and most of the city is now in ruins. But that was the price that had to be paid to get it back. MacArthur's Eighth Army landed at Leyte Gulf on northern Luzon in mid-December and faced tough, often fanatical opposition to get back to the city he left in 1942. At that time, he declared Manila an open city, but the Japanese commander ignored such niceties, and the city was finally cleared in house-to-house fighting. The worst fighting occurred near the University of the Philippines, where the defenders had to be rooted out one by one. A big problem for MacArthur is the repatriation of thousands of American prisoners who suffered terribly in Japanese camps and looked like skeletons when released (→ June 22).

Patton leads U.S. troops across Rhine

General Patton leads the way.

The Rhine, March 28

A vital bridgehead across the Rhine has been secured by an armored spearhead of the U.S. 1st Army at Remagen. Once the bridgehead was secured Gen. Omar Bradley ordered all available forces to Remagen to take advantage of an incredible bit of American luck and daring. Gen. George S. Patton's troops have swept the west bank of German resistance and his troops began crossing the Rhine on pontoon bridges at Oppenheim, between Mainz and Mannheim.

On March 7, Patton's 3rd Army broke through weak German defenses at the Eifel plateau. Lt. Karl Timmerman, with an armored unit of the 1st Army, was amazed to find an intact bridge at Remagen, a small town halfway between Cologne and Coblentz. As Timmerman's men crossed the railroad bridge, explosions went off, but the bridge was not damaged (→ Apr. 25).

Collapsed bridge across the Rhine.

Beloved FDR dies; Truman steps in

Warm Springs, Georgia, Apr. 12

A shocked nation is in mourning tonight for Franklin Delano Roosevelt. The President died this afternoon at the "Little White House" in this small Georgia town. Vice President Harry S. Truman was on Capitol Hill when the President died. He was rushed to the White House, where he offered his condolences to Mrs. Roosevelt before he was sworn in as the 32nd President of the United States.

Doctors say Roosevelt passed away at 3:35 p.m., two hours after he suffered a cerebral hemorrhage. Grace Tully, his private secretary, said, "The shock was unexpected and the actuality of the event was outside belief." In recent days, Roosevelt appeared to be recuperating from the stresses of war and the Yalta Conference. His pulse was normal when Commander Howard Bruenn examined him this morning. In the afternoon, Roosevelt was sitting for a portrait by Elizabeth Shoumatoff, who had been introduced by his long-time friend, Lucy Mercer Rutherfurd. She was with Roosevelt when he slumped in his chair.

After Mrs. Roosevelt was informed of her husband's death, she said, "I am more sorry for the people of this country and of the world than I am for ourselves." When Truman asked the First Lady what he could do for her, she replied, "Is there anything we can do for you? You are the one in trouble now."

An ailing President Roosevelt with his successor, Vice President Harry Truman.

The President's casket makes its way toward Union Station and the trip home.

Ernie Pyle is killed

Iwo Jima, Apr. 18

His most recent book, published last year, was *Brave Men*. Its topic was the American soldiers, who considered Ernie Pyle one of their own. He was loved no less by readers; they studied his syndicated dispatches as intently as letters sent from a husband or son. But the beloved byline will appear no more. Today, Ernie Pyle became a casualty of the war he wrote about so eloquently. He died in the thick of the action, elbow to elbow with G.I.'s on Iwo Jima, the island taken by marines after ferocious fighting. A machine gun blast wrote the final word on Ernie Pyle. He was 45.

Marines vanquish Japanese on Okinawa

Okinawa, June 22

The beautiful island of Okinawa lies equidistant from Manila and Tokyo and it is strategically important because its fall would leave Formosa [Taiwan] isolated. The American commanders underestimated the number of defenders on the island as well as the existence of fortified defensive lines. The attackers had an easy time with landings on April 1, but then they ran up against the defensive lines. They hit the Machinato Line on April 7 and it took six days of fighting to get past it. The Japanese were, at the same time, sending massive air sorties against the surrounding fleet, using hundreds of suicide attacks. These kamikaze attacks, in which planes are deliberately crashed into their targets, caused the death of 5,000 American sailors and damaged many ships. On the island, the marines hit the Shuri Line next, causing it to collapse, then faced a last-ditch effort by the Japanese, now at the edge of the island. The two sides continued to pound each other until the Japanese defense crumbled. Rather than be taken prisoner, many Japanese soldiers leapt off cliffs to their deaths. The Americans suffered 50,000 casualties, and the Japanese 117,000, all but 7,000 of them killed (→ Aug. 2).

Americans and Russians meet at Elbe

American and Russian commanders greet each other at the Elbe River.

Allies-in-arms march through Torgau, Germany, as Third Reich collapses.

Torgau, Germany, Apr. 25

General Courtney H. Hodges of the United States First Army and Marshal Ivan Konev of the First Ukranian Army met at the Elbe River near Leipzig today and shook hands. The meeting symbolized the further collapse of the Third Reich, which has now been split in half by the conquering armies. After the Allies crossed the Rhine, the American Ninth Army and the First Army invaded the Ruhr industrial basin, encircling the Wehrmacht and trapping 300,000 men, two dozen generals and an admiral.

It is rumored that Field Marshal Walther Model committed suicide when the Ruhr pocket collapsed, though his body hasn't been found. Leaving several army corps to reduce the pocket and deal with the huge numbers of prisoners, the Americans headed for the Elbe.

About this time, General Dwight D. Eisenhower made a decision that has caused some controversy. Since the Americans and British were 200 miles from Berlin and the Russians only 35 miles, the Supreme Commander decided not to attempt to march on the city. This means that the German capital will fall into Russian hands, and Allied leaders, including Churchill, are concerned about the postwar political implications (→ May 7).

German military ousted from Italy

Milan, Italy, Apr. 30

The remainder of the Italian army surrendered to the Allies yesterday along with German forces under Colonel General Heinrich von Vietinghoff. On the day before, Mussolini's Salo Republic collapsed and Il Duce and his mistress, Claretta Petacci, were executed by partisans who hung them upside down in Milan. The army's surrender was the culmination of an Allied drive to finish off Italy that was launched on April 2. The Germans held fast for a week, but the American Fifth Army then rolled into the Po Valley and entered Bologna and Modena.

Oregon "bombing"

Lakeview, Oregon, May 5

A woman and five children in a fishing party were killed by an explosion in the mountain country near here today. The only survivor was a Pastor Mitchell of the Christian Alliance Church. "Joan, 11, came and told us that there was an object nearby," he said. "We went to investigate. It blew up and killed them all." It is reported that the "object" was a Japanese bomb, but how it got there is a mystery. The children were 11 to 13 years old.

Nazi U-boat is sunk off of Block Island

Block Island, R.I., May 6

Despite the fact that the German military machine is collapsing, the deadly war between destroyers and U-boat packs continues, as evidenced by the sinking today of a U-boat off the coast of New England. A double screen of American warships was patrolling the Atlantic north of the Azores in an effort to crush the last-gasp attempt by Admiral Karl Doenitz to destroy Allied shipping with his new snorkel-equipped submarines. Destroyer sonar picked up a blip, and two warships, the Moseby and the Atherton, were quickly dispatched. After a chase, they ran their prey to ground and sank German U-853 with all its crew.

Tragedy unveiled: Death and life at Buchenwald and Dachau

Germany, April

Some American soldiers are learning in the grimmest way what they've been fighting for all these years. As they help free the survivors at the Buchenwald and Dachau death camps, they realize one purpose of the war: to end such atrocities. Many of the G.I.'s cannot bear to look at the Nazi legacy – lifeless bodies stacked in ovens, the emaciated living hovering near death. The Americans feel foolish offering their gifts; they brought books and papers, but some survivors don't have the strength to turn a page; their eyes are sunken, they hardly see. Still, they are grateful. One Dachau prisoner tells how he felt when he saw the tanks roll in: "We were free! We broke into weeping, kissed the tank. A Negro soldier gave us a tin of meat, bread and chocolate ... We sat down on the ground and ate up all the food together. The Negro watched us, tears in his eyes."

Eyes of the death camp inmates testify to man's inhumanity to man.

Victory in Europe: Germans surrender; Hitler dead

The fight in Europe is over and Americans delight in their hard-won triumph.

Victory in Europe, jubilation in New York: Whooping it up in Times Square.

Berlin, May 7

Adolf Hitler is dead, his Thousand Year Reich is destroyed, and the war in Europe is over. The beginning of the end for Germany was the Russian drive that began on April 16. Soviet troops reached Berlin by the 22nd and surrounded the city a few days later. Hitler and his mistress, Eva Braun, the Goebbels family and a few followers remained in an underground bunker where the Fuehrer played with nonexistent armies on a large war map.

Above ground, the Russian army was blasting into rubble what Allied planes had failed to destroy. On May 1, as the last fanatical resistance was being eliminated, Hitler married Miss Braun and the two of them, followed by Joseph Goebbels and his family, committed suicide. SS troops burned their bodies with gasoline.

The next day, Russian soldiers hoisted the hammer and sickle flag atop the Brandenburg Gate. The leadership of the ruined Reich was turned over to Grand Admiral Karl Doenitz, who quickly moved to end the suffering of Germany. The Germans attempted to surrender to the Western Allies alone but the effort was spurned. Finally today, the new German leaders signed an unconditional surrender, thus making May 7 VE Day, to signify victory in Europe.

The cost of the war to the Germans proved horrendous. Unlike the Great War, which was fought on the soil of other countries, this war devastated the German homeland. Germany had mustered 20 million soldiers, half of whom were in uniform at a time. Some 3.25 million German men died from causes other than combat. A million more are listed as missing and the fate of these is not likely to be known, ever. Among the Allies, the British and the French each lost 250,000 in battle. More than six million Soviet soldiers died and the United States lost 400,000 men (→ Oct. 16, 1946).

Japan is ravaged by American bombers

Japan, August

Unlike the cities of Germany, which were well defended and built of masonry, the cities of Japan are completely undefended and built of highly flammable materials. The results have been catastrophic.

Early this year, General Curtis Lemay changed the bombing tactics. The B-29's began to bomb at night, descending to 7,000 feet for runs, and they used a far greater proportion of incendiary bombs. On March 9, Tokyo was hit by 200 Super Fortresses, a bigger version of the Flying Fortress, which delivered 1,600 tons of incendiaries. The city center, a 16-square-mile area, was destroyed. The bombers then began hitting Yokohama, Nagoya, Kobe and Osaka.

Japan's big cities have been virtually destroyed in two months of raids. And millions are homeless as the Army Air Force begins to hit the smaller cities. The United States wants to immobilize Japan's home islands before an invasion begins. Allied commanders believe such an invasion will cost over a million casualties.

B-29 bombers set Japan's cities afire.

Big Three demand surrender of Japan

Potsdam, Germany, Aug. 2

The mutuality of interests of the United States, Britain and the Soviet Union has disintegrated since the surrender of Germany, but at the Potsdam Conference here the Great Powers have come together to send a clear message to Tokyo. They have ordered the Japanese to follow Germany's example and surrender unconditionally. The alternative, they warn, is for Japan to "lay herself open to complete and utter destruction."

Of the three major leaders who participated in the conference at Yalta, only Premier Stalin has survived in power. President Roosevelt is dead and the British voters turned Prime Minister Churchill out of office. So at the conference here in Potsdam, Stalin was able to play a strong hand, and he played it forcefully. He has refused to move his troops eastward in Po-

land, he has described British accusations of repression in the Balkans as "fairy tales" and he has indicated that Soviet troops will continue to dismantle German factories and machinery (→ Aug. 10).

Atomic bombs unleashed on Hiroshima, Nagasaki

Japan, Aug. 10

The B-29 bomber Enola Gay, named after its commander's mother, dropped a single terrible weapon on the city of Hiroshima on August 6 and ushered in the Atomic Age. The bomb destroyed 80 percent of the buildings in Hiroshima and severely damaged the rest. At least 70,000 to 80,000 people were killed, many of them within a second of the explosion and its accompanying firestorm.

Sixteen hours after the bomb was dropped, President Truman called upon the Japanese government to surrender and thus avoid "a rain of ruin" from the air. Japan did not respond, and two days later Nagasaki suffered the same fate as Hiroshima. This time 35,000 people were killed, 60,000 were injured and more than 5,000 vanished. The entire city was flattened and, at ground zero, directly below the bomb's detonation, nothing at all remained standing.

During the summer of 1944, the 509th Bombardment Group began training under Colonel Paul W. Tibbets Jr., a pilot with an excellent record. Tibbets was the only member of the training group who knew the exact nature of the bomb: that it was made of fissionable material and that it would produce an explosion hundreds of times more deadly than any weapon ever known to man. The other pilots and men simply referred to their new weapon as "the gimmick." Before setting up its headquarters on Tinian Island in

As the mushroom cloud rises, mankind embarks upon a new, uncharted age.

the Marianas, the group trained secretly at Wendover Field in Utah and in Cuba, always flying the same mock mission, which was to drop a single 500- or 1,000-pound bomb precisely on target.

For the mission on which the nuclear bomb would actually be dropped, seven B-29's were assigned. Involved was a single weapon with an explosive power equal to 20,000 tons of TNT. The first atomic bomb was successfully tested in New Mexico on July 16. On

August 5, three weather planes left Tinian, followed the next day by three other Super Fortresses filled with civilian and military observers and scientific instruments. A seventh plane was in reserve. En route to Hiroshima, the crew began hearing the ominous word "atomic" for the first time and Colonel Tibbets told them to "watch your language, this is being recorded for history."

At 8:05, the escort planes pulled away and the Enola Gay began its bomb run. As the T of the bombsight on the B-29 moved over the Aioi Bridge, the bombardier let loose the 10,000-pound bomb from a height of 31,000 feet. Exactly 43 seconds later the plane filled with a bright light and the B-29 began to rock as if hit by flak. Below, there was "a fiery red core," then a huge mushroom cloud. In his mission book, the co-pilot, Robert Lewis, wrote, "My God, what have we done?"

At Hiroshima, the bomb exploded 1,850 feet above Shima Hospital, vaporizing the hospital and all its patients instantly. Of the people within 1,500 feet, 88 percent died in that first moment. Temperatures at the center reached 5,432 degrees Fahrenheit at once.

Near the hospital was the three-story Honkaua Elementary School. As Miss Horibe, a teacher, emerged from the basement, she saw another teacher, naked and covered with terrible burns. "Mother, Mother," the woman shouted to her, "this is hell on earth" (→ Sept. 2).

The Enola Gay returns safely after dropping the atomic bomb on Hiroshima.

The remains of Hiroshima shortly after the atomic bomb was exploded.

Japan surrenders: Peace settles over the world

Tokyo, Sept. 2

Aboard the new battleship Missouri today, two Japanese officials in formal morning dress and top hats surrendered to representatives of the Allied powers, led by General Douglas MacArthur, thus ending the worst war the world has ever seen. In a brief address, General MacArthur said that, with the signing, "men everywhere can walk upright in the sunlight." The end came quickly following the atomic destruction of Hiroshima and Nagasaki, and the Soviet declaration of war against Japan. The Japanese government ceased to be dominated by its military leaders and a new Cabinet went to the Emperor and persuaded him to call an imperial conference. In a deeply emotional scene, the Emperor gave his opinion that Japan must surrender. Capitulation messages were then sent to the Allies via diplomatic channels in Sweden and Switzerland.

Japan's surrender marks the end of a five-year period that has no precedent but that can only be compared with the Black Death in the 14th century, which killed a third of Europe's population and transformed the face of the continent. Not since that time have so many people been killed, wounded, displaced or had their lives so completely changed. In Asia, two huge nations, China and Japan, have been completely ruined and the colonial empires founded in the Pacific in the last century have been destroyed. China has probably suf-

fered more than any other country. It has been at war since 1937 and has had more than two million combat deaths alone; there are no realistic figures for its civilian deaths. Many of its casualties could have been avoided if it had possessed modern medical facilities. Japan suffered about the same number of combat deaths as China but its civilian losses were far fewer.

As the war comes to an end, two superpowers dominate the globe: the United States and the Soviet Union. The Russians suffered by far the more grievous wounds. More than six million soldiers were killed and 14 million were wounded. If civilian deaths are counted, the Soviet Union probably lost 20 million lives during the war – though some say 30 million. More Russian soldiers were killed in the Battle of Stalingrad than the United States lost in the entire conflict.

The Americans probably have gained more from the war than any other country. With the exception of a raid by a single Japanese seaplane, no bombs fell on the continental United States. There were 16 million Americans in uniform during World War II, and of these 400,000 were killed and a half million were wounded. But there were significant results from America's role as the arsenal of democracy. Thousands of factories and hundreds of fortunes sprang up almost overnight and, by this year, Americans had a standard of living rivaled by no one on the planet (→ 8).

Supreme Allied Commander Douglas MacArthur on the battleship Missouri.

American troops in Paris celebrate after hearing of the Japanese surrender.

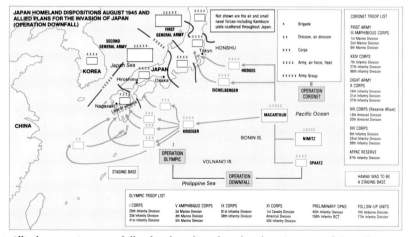
Allied strategists carefully developed a plan for the invasion of Japan. Anticipating fierce resistance and losses of one million men, Operation Downfall was intended to strike key military points, thus incapacitating enemy capabilities. With or without the atomic bomb, Japan was to be be vanquished.

Namoro Shigomitso signs the surrender documents as Allied officers look on.

Japanese-American troops most honored

Japanese-Americans fought valiantly, in part to prove how loyal they were.

Washington, D.C.

Now that the war is over, combat statistics make the internment of Japanese-Americans seem doubly shameful. Nisei soldiers not only fought with great distinction, but the 33,000 men of the Nisei 442nd Regiment and the 100th Battalion also emerged as the most decorated men in American military history. For example, the 442nd in the Italian campaign was awarded 3,600 Purple Hearts, 810 Bronze Stars, 342 Silver Stars, 47 Distinguished Service Crosses, 17 Legion of Merits and numerous other citations. More incredibly, despite heavy casualties there were no known frontline Nisei desertions as against an overall service rate of about 15 percent. In all, some 8,000 Nisei joined the army after Secretary of War Henry L. Stimson announced in January 1943, that they could do so as volunteers in segregated units. As for ingenuity, Sergeant Kenny Yasui in Burma, passing as a Japanese colonel, ordered 13 Japanese soldiers to march back to his camp as his unsuspecting prisoners.

Fair Deal promised as war economy ends

Washington, D.C., Dec. 31

As President Truman moved to replace the War Labor Board with the Wage Stabilization Board today, he was bidding the year and the war a firm farewell. The rationing of shoes, tires and most foods has come to an end, and a demand for public housing and more jobs - peacetime concerns – has begun.

In August, Truman took the first steps in the journey to normalcy, ordering a full resumption of consumer production, free markets and collective bargaining. In September, he recommended to Congress a liberal, domestic 21-point economic recovery program, because, as he explained, "every segment of our population, and every individual, has a right to expect from his government a Fair Deal." This translates in most people's minds as jobs for the returning servicemen, white and Negro. But a few women auto workers in Detroit have marched in protest against the loss of their jobs, demanding that the Fair Deal apply also to the fair sex.

"Wartime Marketing" by Bache.

The Manhattan Project now comes to light

Washington, D.C., August

The atomic bombs that wrought destruction and carnage on Japan are the product of a titanic military and scientific effort. At the peak of this top-secret "Manhattan Project," 105,000 men and women labored to unleash the terrible power of the atom; and most had no knowledge of the awesome device they were helping create.

The Manhattan Project was born on October 9, 1941, when it got a go-ahead from President Roosevelt. After Pearl Harbor, the effort grew into a frantic race, as many top officials believed that the Nazis had an atomic program. Ironically, it was Hitler's pathological anti-Semitism that gave the United States a great edge. The best minds in atomic physics, including Leo Szilard, Hans Bethe, Enrico Fermi, Niels Bohr and Edward Teller, had fled to the West to escape Nazism.

To Dr. J. Robert Oppenheimer of the University of California fell the task of organizing this awesome array of talent, while Major General Leslie R. Groves had military control of the $2 billion operation. Though it involved three huge complexes, at Oak Ridge, Tennessee, Richland, Washington, and Los Alamos, New Mexico, it was shrouded in such secrecy that even Vice Pres-

Oppenheimer and Groves examine the remains of the tower from which the first atomic bomb had dangled.

ident Truman knew nothing of it until Roosevelt's death.

On July 16, a handful of scientists huddled on a New Mexico desert to test the first bomb. Some had doubts of its working; others feared it would ignite the atmosphere. But as a blinding flash cut the pre-dawn sky and a cauldron of radioactive dust and fire rose 40,000 feet, the lanky Oppenheimer, who once described the device as "technically sweet," recalled a line from Hindu scripture: "Now I am become death, the destroyer of worlds."

U.S. and U.S.S.R. split Korea in two

South Korea, Aug. 17

In an almost casual manner, and with the stroke of a pen, Korea has been divided in two at the 38th parallel. Russian troops are occupying the northern part of the country, while American soldiers are occupying the southern segment. Following the Russian occupation, thousands of Koreans flooded back into Korea from their exile in Siberia. They had fled there during the Japanese occupation. But while they were away from their homeland, they were indoctrinated with communism. After the repatriation of the Korean population, the Russians closed off an area north of the 38th parallel, making that division a political and economic barrier, not just a military convenience (→ May 10, 1948).

Frozen orange juice, chicken and turkey

United States

It's tough to be a kid. Toys are scarce; there are no bikes, sleds, tricycles, skates or electric trains being made anymore. Kids who used to collect bubble-gum cards are settling for Defense Stamps. Girls are writing servicemen whose names are supplied by the U.S.O. Boys and girls alike are preparing CARE (Cooperative for American Remittances to Europe) packages and rolling bandages. Dinnertime is a bit better than playtime, featuring frozen foods like orange juice and Swanson and Sons' chicken and turkey. Schooltime can be frightening during air drills, but new school supplies such as ballpoint pens and wax pencils lend a sophisticated touch to the scrawl "Kilroy was here" in the margins of a textbook.

How MacArthur shapes a peacetime Japan

General Douglas MacArthur towers over Emperor Hirohito as the two awkwardly pose for photographers.

Tokyo, Sept. 8

A 29-year-old Japanese-American named Iva Togori D'Aquino is under arrest and charged with treason. Her real name means little to American servicemen. They knew her as Tokyo Rose, the broadcaster who taunted them daily with her propaganda program called "Zero Hour." She faces trial on charges that she gave wartime aid and comfort to the enemy.

General Douglas MacArthur, Supreme Commander of the Allied Powers in Japan, has pledged to bring all war criminals to trial. He has also promised to be compassionate, and President Truman has granted him a free hand. The President, mistrustful of the Russians since Potsdam, has rejected their demands to establish a "Big Four" control commission and give them a greater role in the occupation.

From his Dai Ichi Building office, MacArthur has set demobilization as his first goal. Seven million Japanese are still in uniform, at home and around the Pacific. The general's long-term goals are reconstruction and the introduction of democratic principles.

As supreme commander, he is aware that he needs the cooperation of Emperor Hirohito, and has rejected British and Russian demands that the Emperor be tried as a war criminal. "If the Emperor were indicted and perhaps hanged," he said, "military government would have to be instituted throughout all Japan, and guerrilla war would probably break out."

In a recent broadcast, MacArthur told Americans the problems in Japan must be resolved peacefully. "We have had our last chance," he said. "If we do not devise some greater and more equitable system, Armageddon will be at our door" (→ May 3, 1947).

Around the world weekly: 151 hours

Washington, D.C., Sept. 28

An Army Air Transport Command plane lifted off the National Airport runway here today to inaugurate weekly round-the-world flights. The four-engine Douglas C-54 Skymaster, nicknamed the "Globester," headed for its first stop, the Azores, with about 3,000 pounds of mail and cargo and eight passengers, including photographers and reporters. The 23,000-mile trip will take the transports across North Africa, over Southern Asia and the Pacific, then across the United States and back to Washington. Each circumnavigation will involve about 12 changes in crews and three changes in planes. The complete circuit is expected to take about 151 hours, or from each Friday to the following Thursday.

Strike shuts G.M.; anti-labor bill due

Detroit, Mich., December

Beleaguered by a wave of peaceful but debilitating labor conflicts, President Truman has asked Congress for legislation to curb strikes. Montgomery Ward, Ford and Illinois Bell have been under siege recently. But the worst blow was a strike by 325,000 General Motors workers that began November 21. Asking a 30 percent pay raise and the opening of G.M.'s books to the public, the United Auto Workers shut 80 plants in 20 states. Parts output is hurt, threatening firms that G.M. supplies. The union, with a record 1.3 million members, says the company wants "an industrial economic dictatorship." Of the Truman anti-strike plan, union spokesman R.J. Thomas merely says: "I am opposed to it."

United States joins the new United Nations

Following President Truman, Senator Arthur Vandenberg signs U.N. Charter.

Washington, D.C., Aug. 8

The United Nations, conceived in a time of war, now aims to be an instrument of peace. The organization is already a step ahead of the League of Nations, which began after the Great War. President Truman signed the U.N. Charter today, and the United States was officially a member. One reason the league failed was American refusal to join. "We had sponsored and helped establish the United Nations Organization," Truman wrote, "hoping to prevent again the too often recurring plague of humanity – war."

Sixty countries took part in the April United Nations conference at San Francisco to write the charter. It pledges to maintain world peace and security and to let the residents of colonial areas "gradually develop their free political institutions." The U.N. is divided into a General Assembly and a more powerful Security Council, where any initiative may be blocked by veto of just one of the five major powers, the United States, Britain, the Soviet Union, France and China (→ Oct. 23, 1946).

Priceless art is recovered from the Nazis

Bavaria, Germany, April

There is little room for aesthetics in war. But with fighting in Europe winding down, Generals Patton, Bradley and Eisenhower were treated this month to some of the most breathtaking sights in the history of Western art. In the Altausee salt mine and other caches in southern Bavaria, the U.S. Third Army uncovered thousands of art treasures, stolen by Nazis as spoils of war.

Some of the works were confiscated in Germany from Jewish patrons such as Rothschild, Kahn and Weil. But most of them come from France. Hitler returned many of these pieces as "loans," an act he considered a more powerful symbol of domination than outright seizure. Others were deemed too nationalistic to stay in an occupied country. These found their way to Germany, intended for a museum dedicated to Hitler's mother. The paintings, which include works by Rubens, Rembrandt, Holbein, Goya and others, are in good condition.

U.S. soldier guards a masterpiece.

The Eagle Ascendant 1946-1999

Early in 1945, as the Allied powers neared victory in Europe and the Pacific, Winston Churchill told the House of Commons, "America stands at this moment at the summit of the world." In an earlier time, such a pronouncement from a prime minister of Great Britain would have seemed extraordinary. But in 1945, it was simply a statement of the obvious. For the United States had emerged from World War II not just victorious, but supreme. As the columnist Walter Lippmann wrote that year: "What Rome was to the ancient world, what Great Britain has been to the modern world, America is to be to the world of tomorrow." In many respects, of course, the United States had been the world's most powerful nation for many years before World War II. But until the 1940s that power had not often been accompanied by a recognition of international responsibilities. The war produced a momentous change. In its wake, most Americans no longer viewed their power as a vehicle for insulating themselves from the problems of other nations; they considered it a mandate to become actively involved in trying to resolve those problems.

The nation did not, it soon became clear, have much choice in the matter. One reason was nuclear weapons, which America had brought into the world and of which it held (for a time) a virtual monopoly. Even more important was the new rivalry with the Soviet Union. That contest, eventually known as the Cold War, soon overshadowed every other consideration in international affairs and, to a great extent, in American domestic affairs.

The war also helped unleash another force, one that was at least equally important in determining the shape of postwar society: economic growth. For 10 years before the war, the United States had remained mired in a deep economic depression; some had come to believe that economic stagnation was now the norm to which the nation would have to adjust. But the war, and the massive public spending it required, not only ended the Depression, it also started the country on the road to a period of economic growth before which even the remarkable expansion of the 1920s paled. The vast new abundance this growth created affected virtually every area of American life. For members of the rapidly expanding middle class, it made possible a new level of affluence. For workers and farmers and others, it offered an escape from subsistence and poverty to a style of life previously reserved for a relative few. For those who remained economically marginal, it created new expectations and new demands.

At first, America's wealth and power seemed to insulate it from the usual frustrations of history. The Cold War was not won, certainly, but America retained a prestige and influence that the Soviet Union could not match. Social problems were not eliminated, of course, but there was widespread confidence that solutions lay within the nation's grasp. The presidency of Dwight D. Eisenhower, a genial leader who presided over a period of general calm, symbolized one side of this postwar confidence: a sense of general well-being. The presidency of John F. Kennedy, a glamorous leader who ran for office on the promise to "get America moving again," symbolized another side: the exuberance of a nation convinced that it could create a great future for itself if it only had the will and the energy to do so. When the United States first landed men on the moon in 1969, an important part of President Kennedy's vision seemed to have been fulfilled.

But the "American moment," as some have called it, did not long remain so untroubled. The assassination of President Kennedy in 1963, one of the most traumatic events in American history, came in retrospect to symbolize the beginning of a profound change in the nation's fortunes. Within two years of that tragedy, the United States was confronting powerful obstacles to both its international and domestic hopes.

The commitment to fighting communism throughout the world had led the country into a disastrous military venture in Vietnam – a conflict that continued inconclusively for more than a decade, eroding America's stature in the world and poisoning its political and social atmosphere at home.

At about the same time, a great mass movement in the American South was forcing the nation to confront the deepest national injustice of all: the oppression of America's black citizens. In the past, most white Americans had avoided confronting the problems of race, convinced that those problems were too intractable. Now, many white liberals embraced the civil rights movement, confident that the nation had the capacity to overcome even this great problem. The assault on racism produced important reforms and was responsible for improvements in the status of many black Americans. But like the war in Vietnam, it proved to be a far more difficult and costly commitment than most Americans had at first envisioned.

Finally, near the end of the 1960s, the American economy faltered. Economic growth had become the cornerstone of so many of the nation's hopes. Many Americans had come to believe the nation was now largely immune from inflation, stagnation and debilitating international competition. By the early 1970s, that confidence, too, was beginning to unravel.

Thus began the slow erosion of America's liberal euphoria – the belief that the nation had the resources and the will to do virtually everything, that it could (in President Lyndon Johnson's words) produce a "new world" and "bend it to our will." Instead, the United States entered a period of wrenching national turbulence. Urban ghettoes erupted in violence, as poor blacks struggled to draw attention to their grievances. College campuses became places of turmoil, as students raised a series of unsettling challenges to the conventions of the university and to the norms of middle class society. American women, drawing inspiration from the liberation efforts of other groups as well as from their own long history of struggle, transformed feminism from a largely intellectual stance into a powerful social movement that transformed society profoundly. Americans from almost all segments of society joined in a massive anti-war movement that shook national politics and created tremendous pressure on national leaders to end Vietnam war.

At the time, many Americans considered the turmoil of the 1960s and early 1970s the harbinger of something like a revolution. In fact, however, its principal political effect was to strengthen forces of conservatism committed to restoring order and stability to national life. The election of Richard Nixon to the presidency in 1968 (and the strong third-party presidential candidacy of George Wallace that same year) seemed to confirm the popular repudiation of liberal hopes and to express a yearning for a calmer, more familiar society. Yet America in the Nixon years did not experience stability and order. Instead, it witnessed new and even greater social and political crises: an escalation of domestic protest and social unrest, growing military frustration in Vietnam, a series of frightening economic problems, and a political scandal that forced the resignation of the President himself.

For a time in the 1970s, an uncharacteristic pessimism began to permeate America. Some spoke of the end of the "American Century," of the arrival of an "age of limits," of a future of more modest hopes and more restricted means. The humiliating end of the Vietnam War, the emergence of a prolonged energy crisis and the resurgence of Soviet military power: all contributed to a sense that America's ability to control world affairs was ebbing.

By the end of the 1970s, another vision emerged – one that combined a continued conservative retreat from the heady visions of the 1960s with a commitment to the idea of economic growth, international power and American destiny. The same belief in America's special virtues that had fueled the Cold War and the liberal crusades of the 1960s became the basis for the presidency of Ronald Reagan. For two terms, Reagan oversaw a tough foreign policy, while at home the budget deficit and unemployment grew. Reagan's unflinching pressure on the "Evil Empire" brought the Soviets to the negotiating table time and again. His successors, George Bush and then Bill Clinton, were faced with a challenge as great in its own way as any this century: the disintegration of the Soviet Union in 1991 left America as the only superpower. This produced its own uncertainties – in a world lacking an obvious single enemy, what was the purpose of overwhelming military strength? Being the "global policeman" in the Persian Gulf, in Somalia, in the Balkans, or in the Middle East, has proved a thankless and messy task, especially when the European arm of NATO is looking for a new role in a post-Cold-War world. Moreover, the accelerating economic and military emergence of China will give America ample food for thought well into the new century.

◄ "That's How It Felt to Walk on the Moon" by astronaut Alan Bean.

Millions of American workers go on strike, but without strife

"Unemployed Rally" by Brodsky.

United States

As the nation readjusts to peace abroad, the reconverting economy finds itself plagued by war at home. Aided by tax breaks, industry enjoys healthy profits; and despite postwar layoffs, unemployment hovers below 5 percent. Still, 4.5 million workers struck this year, crippling the coal, auto, electric and steel industries and interrupting rail and maritime transport. Man-days lost to strikes mounted to 113 million. But strangely absent from the battlegrounds were the guns and clubs that have "arbitrated" labor disputes in the past. As suggested in *Fortune*, management and labor have been transformed into "calm, cool, even friendly warriors."

Led by Walter Reuther, Philip Murray and John L. Lewis, labor has marched eagerly to the bargaining table. At General Motors, Reuther insisted on access to corporate books. A 30 percent wage hike, he argued, could be absorbed without an increase in prices. Loath to give labor a role in corporate planning, G.M. refused. On March 13 the union settled for an 18.5-cent wage gain after 113 days on strike.

At U.S. Steel, Philip Murray was concerned with wages, not what steel would cost. So when 750,000 steel workers returned in February after a three-week strike, they, too, had an 18.5-cent raise. But the firms used the concession as a lever to lift price controls. Their $5-a-ton price rise should amount to a net gain of $250 million on the year.

Lewis added another element to the bargaining formula when the United Mine Workers walked out in April, asking health, welfare and safety benefits. After weathering federal seizure of the mines, he got retirement and medical benefits, a federal safety code and 18.5 cents in wages. But he paid a price that may draw the lines on labor's new power. Violating a no-strike pledge to punish operators for breaking the contract, the U.M.W. walked out again in November. In three days, a court fined Lewis $10,000 and his union $3.5 million, the stiffest penalty ever imposed on a union.

"Northern Minnesota Mine" by E. Dewey Albinson. A colorful landscape.

Computer manages 5,000 steps at once

Philadelphia, February

At 30 tons, the new ENIAC computer seems a far cry from the abacus or slide rule. Designed by J.P. Eckert and J.W. Mauchly of the University of Pennsylvania, the Electronic Numerical Integrator and Calculator has 18,000 vacuum tubes and adds, multiplies, divides and computes square roots, accomplishing 5,000 steps a second. The War Department will use ENIAC for artillery computations. International Business Machines plans a much less powerful calculator, the Model 603, for commercial use.

American rockets on fringe of space

White Sands, New Mexico

From a desolate base here, scientists are firing missiles to explore the fringes of space. A Corporal rocket reached an altitude of 43 miles last year, and this year American rocketeers, aided by German scientists, are launching captured V-2 rockets. The Nazi "Vengeance" weapon, which battered London, is now being put to peaceful research purposes. The rockets that haven't tumbled off course or been obliterated at ignition are probing the mysteries of the cosmos at heights above 100 miles.

Business is terrific, under the counter

United States

"Prices soar, Buyers Sore, Steers jump over the moon" a *New York Daily News* headline exclaims, putting in a nutshell the trouble with the economy. True, people are purchasing theater tickets and cars, but doing it too often "under the counter." Goods are available on store shelves, but they disappear in an instant. In vain, people try to get new Timex watches, Ecktachrome color film, Tide detergent, French's instant potatoes, Max Factor cosmetics or electric blankets. Luckily, ice cream is not deserting its fans.

Churchill: Iron Curtain has descended in Europe

Fulton, Missouri, March

"From Stettin in the Baltic to Trieste in the Adriatic, an 'iron curtain' has descended across the Continent," Winston Churchill proclaimed here on March 5. The former Prime Minister of Britain contended that those European countries that lie behind the "Iron Curtain" are subject to growing Soviet control and that they must be considered part of the Soviet sphere of influence. "Whatever conclusions may be drawn from these facts – and facts they are – this is certainly not the liberated Europe we fought to build up," Churchill said. "Nor is it one which contains the essentials of permanent peace."

The British leader's incendiary remarks were delivered in a speech titled *The Sinews of Peace*, which he gave to an audience at Westminster College that included President Truman, and which was broadcast.

Warning his listeners that the

The British Prime Minister issues a warning in the American heartland.

Russians desire "the indefinite expansion of their power and doctrine," Churchill called on America to stand united with the British Commonwealth to discourage Russian hegemony. If the Western democracies are divided, he said, "catastrophe may overwhelm us all."

Reaction to the Fulton speech has been hostile, with many listeners considering Churchill's views unnecessarily grim, if not warlike.

An editorial in the *Chicago Sun* said that Churchill's object was "world domination, through arms, by the United States and the British Empire." *The Nation* said that Churchill was adding a "sizable measure of poison to the already deteriorating relations between the Russians and the Western powers." The *Times of London* disagreed with the wartime Prime Minister's remarks about Russia, declaring that "while Western democracy and communism are in many respects opposed, they have much to learn from each other."

The metaphor of an iron curtain is not new. In 1914, Belgium's German-born Queen Elizabeth saw between Kaiser Wilhelm's Germany and her new land, "a bloody iron curtain which has descended forever." Shortly after the Russian Revolution, Vasili Rozanov wrote, "With a rumble and a roar, an iron curtain is descending on Russian history" (→ March 12, 1947).

La Guardia: "Ticker tape ain't spaghetti"

Atlantic City, N.J., March 29

"People are hungry, and it is our responsibility to feed them," said Fiorello H. La Guardia today as he agreed to head the United Nations Relief and Rehabilitation Administration. In a passionate address here, he promised to take whatever actions are needed to feed a war-ravaged world.

The fiery former Mayor of New York implored Americans "not to overeat, not to waste," adding that "in my own city we waste enough food to feed a city of 350,000 …

I know, I picked up that garbage for 12 years." But he called Americans "kindly," saying they had "learned through a period of depression that ticker tape ain't spaghetti."

La Guardia said he intends to buy food wherever he can find it, for "wheat has no political complexion," and offered his "very personal greetings to Juan D. Peron" of grain-producing Argentina. The famed New York politician also warned that "our governments did not buy food in order to enrich a lot of black marketeers."

Fiorello La Guardia delivers fiery speech at an Italian-American labor rally.

Allies complete peace pacts with 4 ex-foes

Paris, July 1

The foreign ministers adjourned their peace conference here today after completing the treaties with Bulgaria, Hungary, Italy and Rumania. During much of the nine-week meeting, Secretary of State James Byrnes tried to improve the deteriorating relations with Moscow. He has little to show for his efforts. The Russians granted a few concessions on Trieste but showed little inclination to lift the "Iron Curtain" they have closed on Eastern Europe. By all accounts, the Russians have crushed all democratic resistance to their policies in East Germany, and Washington has halted all German reparations payments from its zone to Moscow.

"This is what makes America what it is"

Paris, July 27

Gertrude Stein is dead at 72. The American writer and patron of the arts moved in 1903 from Baltimore to Paris, where she lived with her lifetime companion Alice B. Toklas. Stein was a collector of Picasso and Matisse, then hostess of a literary salon that attracted expatriate writers, such as Hemingway and Fitzgerald, whom she called "The Lost Generation." Her 1933 autobiography was a best-seller. In 1934, she toured the United States, of which she wrote, "there is more space where nobody is than where anybody is. This is what makes America what it is."

"Gertrude Stein" by Pablo Picasso.

Philippines are free of American rule

Manila, Philippines, July 4

One of America's major ventures into colonialism came to an end today as President Truman granted the Philippines independence. The liberator of the Philippines, General Douglas MacArthur, attended the ceremonies in the nation's capital and said, "America buried imperialism here today." The United States bought the Philippines from Spain in 1898, then groomed it to be Asia's "showplace of democracy." In 1935, the Philippines became a self-governing commonwealth.

Mother Cabrini is first American saint

The Vatican, July 7

The late Mother Frances Xavier Cabrini has been canonized as a saint. She is the first American to be so honored, but countries around the world take pride in the event, for Mother Cabrini established convents and orphanages in Paris, Madrid, London, Turin and many cities in Latin America. Born July 15, 1850, in Lombardy, Italy, she became a naturalized American citizen in 1909. She died in 1917 after a long bout with malaria.

Baruch urges control of atomic weapons

Baruch in plea to U.N. commission.

New York City, July 24

"We are here to make a choice between the quick and the dead," Bernard M. Baruch, the United States representative to the United Nations Atomic Energy Commission, asserted on June 14. But hopes for the international agreement to avert the madness of a future atomic arms race that he proposed on that day now appear to be fading.

Baruch, at 75 an elder statesman of American diplomacy, challenged his listeners "to test if man can produce, through his will and faith, the miracle of peace, just as he has, through science and skill, the miracle of the atom." According to his proposal, the United States would surrender its monopoly on atomic weapons to an international authority backed by nations pledged by treaty never to develop or harness the power for military uses. Baruch insisted there could be no veto power for individual nations and called for an accord "with teeth in it," promising "swift, sure punishment for those who violate their solemn agreements."

Today, however, the Soviet delegate to the U.N., Andrei A. Gromyko, responded with a sharply worded rejection of the American proposal, which he said "could not be accepted in any way by the Soviet Union, either as a whole or in separate parts." Taking particular umbrage at the stipulation that no nation could wield veto power in a voting situation, Gromyko called it "dangerous and maybe fatal."

Little is known of the Soviet capacity to build a bomb, but most scientists and lawmakers believe the United States will retain a monopoly on its "winning weapon" for decades. Some observers feel the proposal's call for on-site inspections bothered the secretive Russians as much as the veto clause. Others questioned the wisdom of staging a dramatic demonstration of American atomic might at Bikini Atoll as the Russians were mulling over the Baruch plan (→ 26).

Fulbright program will help scholars

Washington, D.C., Aug. 1

Senator J. William Fulbright of Arkansas introduced a bill today to award academic grants to Americans for study and teaching abroad and to foreigners to study and teach here. The program will be funded by some of the proceeds from the sale of surplus federal property. Most observers believe Congress will pass this unique educational exchange plan. Fulbright is himself a Rhodes scholar and he has worked hard in Congress for the advancement of education.

"Clubfoot comet" Assault wins it all

New York City

They called Assault the "clubfoot comet" because of his strange gait, but he horse-laughed all the way to the bank after winning the Belmont to complete racing's Triple Crown. Assault was almost destroyed as a foal because of a foot injury, but he was saved for greater things, such as an eight-length victory in the Kentucky Derby, prior to his Preakness triumph. Assault's right forefoot never reached normal growth. Warren Mehrtens rides him.

Bikini Atoll is American nuclear test site

Bikini Atoll, July 26

An atomic bomb believed to be the most powerful yet developed hurled a 9,000-foot-high column of steam and churning black smoke up from the normally placid waters of Bikini Lagoon this morning. The second explosion of Operation Crossroads, it was thought to be equal to about 50,000 tons of TNT, and cut a wide swath of destruction through a flotilla of abandoned warships anchored nearby.

The weapon was the fifth of its kind to be exploded and the first to be detonated under water. It quickly sank the old battleship Arkansas and left the aircraft carrier Saratoga and the Japanese battleship Nagato listing badly. Four submarines submerged in the lagoon were also believed to have been sunk. Scientists are still puzzled by the effects of radiation, which appear to have caused many deaths among Japanese bomb victims. Nevertheless, sailors were sent in to examine the damaged ships just hours after the explosion.

This morning's blast appeared considerably more destructive than the previous Operation Crossroads test on July 1. In that demonstration, a bomb exploded 500 feet over ships in the lagoon. It destroyed the carrier Independence, but there was little damage elsewhere, prompting an unimpressed Soviet observer to remark: "Pooh."

Today's test inspired a protest in New York against the military development of atomic energy, while the Russians charged it "fundamentally undermined the seriousness of American talk about atomic disarmament" (→ Sept. 23, 1949).

July 13, 1946. *American physicists, including J. Robert Oppenheimer (second from right), inspect the new giant cyclotron at the University of California. Ions are introduced at the center of a circular magnetic field and accelerated. The wider the spiral orbit, the greater the energy produced.*

Nazi leaders hanged for crimes against humanity

Nuremberg, Germany, Oct. 16

Nine of Hitler's Nazi henchmen were hanged early this morning for committing vicious war crimes. During their trial, the defendants claimed that they were only following orders, but they showed little remorse today. Julius Streicher, the editor who once wrote, "Jewish rabble will be exterminated like weeds and vermin," shouted "Heil Hitler" as the noose was fastened around his neck. Joachim von Ribbentrop, the foreign minister, said, "My last wish is that German unity be maintained."

The defendants were all accused of committing war crimes "so calculated, so malignant, and so devastating, that civilization cannot tolerate their being ignored because it cannot survive their being repeated." The evidence included sickening films of the mass executions in concentration camps. "After the bodies were removed" from the gas chambers, one witness testified, "our special commandos took off the rings and extracted the gold from the teeth of the corpses."

Hermann Goering escaped execution by swallowing poison in his cell. Second only to Hitler, Goering directed the secret mobilization of Germany, built up the Luftwaffe and founded the Gestapo, the dreaded secret police force. During his trial, he boasted to a doctor, "In 50 or 60 years, there will be statues of Hermann Goering all over Germany. Little statues, maybe, but one in every German house."

Former top Nazis follow the trial proceedings. The chief U.S. counsel at the Nuremberg War Crimes Tribunal is Supreme Court Justice Robert Jackson.

First pilot is ejected

Patterson Air Field, Ohio, Aug. 18

Larry Lambert, a heavy-drinking sergeant with a gap-toothed grin and a penchant for fibbing, was blasted from an Army P-61 at 7,800 feet yesterday to become the first American ejected from an airplane. Lambert, whose plane was called the Jack in the Box, exudes determination. He cut off a cast on a recently broken arm to avoid worrying the project directors, and it is rumored that he is suffering from a severe hangover today. On landing yesterday, Lambert was jubilant. "I never felt it a bit," he said, presumably meaning the ejection.

Hersey's Hiroshima

New York City, Aug. 31

If you read only one article in this week's *New Yorker*, you won't miss a thing – because there's only one article in it. *Hiroshima*, by John Hersey, takes up the entire issue. A year after the first atomic bomb leveled 90 percent of the Japanese city and took 130,000 lives, Hersey recreates the nightmarish event through the eyes of six people: a poor widow with three children, a clerk, the pastor of a Methodist church, a German missionary and two doctors. Hersey's chilling account, told in no-nonsense prose, lets the atom bomb speak for itself.

United Nations meets in New York City

Queens, New York City, Oct. 23

President Truman addressed the United Nations today as the General Assembly convened in Flushing, Queens. The Assembly met in London earlier this year, but it decided to seek a permanent home in the United States. It will presumably open its headquarters somewhere in New York City, but officials are still searching for the necessary funds and an appropriate site.

In his speech, Truman attempted to ease postwar concerns, but the United Nations is fast becoming the focal point of the escalating tensions between the Soviet Union and the United States. Washington has already used the Security Council effectively to put pressure on the Russians to leave Iran under the terms of the 1942 Tripartite Treaty. The U.S.S.R. was finally shamed into leaving in May, but not before it had whipped up nationalist sentiment in Azerbaijan and Kurdistan.

Truman has been a strong supporter of the U.N. and was hoping that it would become an international forum to promote peace. It is clear, however, that the President will use the world body to oppose what he calls a "surge of Communist tyranny" (→ Oct. 24, 1949).

From Dr. Spock, advice for new parents

Common sense from Dr. Spock.

New York City

A doctor named Benjamin McLane Spock has helped lots of fathers and mothers keep their original hair. Every time they feel ready to tear it out, they read Spock's *Common Sense Book of Baby and Child Care*, which offers flexible, easygoing solutions to the problems at hand. Spock has advice for pregnant mothers, babies and children up to age 12. The doctor realizes that life is not always rosy; he has hints for raising handicapped and adopted children, and tells working mothers and separated parents how to make the best use of their time.

President Truman addresses the General Assembly of the new United Nations.

China, Jan. 7. General George Marshall's conciliation mission to China ends in failure (→ 8).

Washington, D.C., Jan. 8. President Truman appoints Marshall Secretary of State.

Washington, D.C., Feb. 10. Supreme Court upholds constitutionality of busing by public school systems of parochial school students.

New York City, Apr. 7. About 300,000 telephone employees walk off jobs in first national telephone strike.

Texas City, Texas, Apr. 16. A ship explosion kills 500 people and obliterates most of city.

New York City, May 5. Robert Penn Warren awarded Pulitzer Prize in fiction for *All the King's Men*.

Paris, July 12. Sixteen nations meet to draft proposal intended to avail themselves of economic recovery aid from United States offered under Marshall Plan.

Washington, D.C., July 18. Presidential Succession Act is passed by Congress, establishing official line of succession; it places Speaker of the House of Representatives after Vice President.

Washington, D.C., Oct. 5. Marking first time a president has addressed nation on television, Truman asks that all Americans conserve food to aid starving peoples of the world (→ Jan. 20, 1949).

New Orleans, Dec. 3. *A Streetcar Named Desire*, by Tennessee Williams, has premiere here.

Chicago, Dec. 28. Cardinals defeat Philadelphia Eagles, 28-21, for N.F.L. title.

New York City. National Basketball League, American Basketball Assocation merge.

New York City. *Meet the Press* has television premiere.

New York City. Dwight D. Eisenhower's *Crusade in Europe* published.

DEATHS

Palm Island, Florida, Jan. 25. Al Capone, infamous gangster (*Jan. 17, 1899).

Dearborn, Michigan, Apr. 7. Henry Ford, inventor and founder of Ford Motor Company (*July 30, 1863).

Truman seeks anti-Communist funds

Washington, D.C., March 12

President Truman announced a new direction in American foreign policy today as he asked Congress for $400 million to support the governments of Greece and Turkey. Truman did not mention the Soviet Union by name, but the implication was that Soviet infiltration threatens freedom in both countries. "I believe that it must be the policy of the United States to support free peoples who are resisting attempted subjugation by armed minorities or by outside pressures," he said.

Truman sought bipartisan backing for the activist policy, and polls indicate that the American people generally favor his initiative. Senator Arthur Vandenberg, the Republican chairman of the Foreign Relations Committee, had urged Truman to give a strong speech that would "scare the hell out of the country." The speech did just that. Politicians on the left fear the new policy will bring war, and the right worries that it will cost too much.

Britain will pull out of Greece at

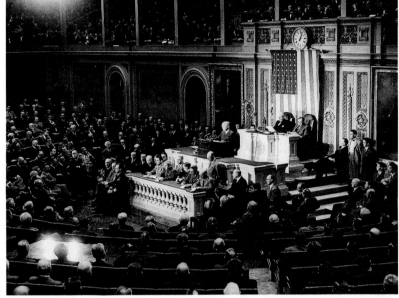

President Truman calls upon Congress to stop the spread of world communism and warns that Russian machinations are too great a threat to be ignored.

the end of the month, and Truman fears that the Russians will move into the vacuum. The U.S. ambassador has warned repeatedly that Moscow is directing and fund-

ing the Communist guerrillas in Greece. Truman has also been advised that the Soviet Union will strangle the Middle East if it controls Greece and Turkey (→ Apr. 16).

President Truman orders loyalty checks on federal employees

Washington, D.C., March 21

Only nine days after launching a new effort to contain communism overseas, President Truman has focused his attention on the home front. With $25 million at his disposal, the President has ordered all federal employees subjected to

F.B.I. loyalty checks. Agency heads will be responsible for purging their departments of employees regarded as subversives. The Civil Service Commission will screen all new applicants. On seven occasions over the past eight years, a total of 1,429 people have been dismissed after

they were charged as subversives, spies, Socialists, Communists and fellow travelers. But according to a presidential commission under A. Devitt Vanech, these types are still around. He says treason, sedition, sabotage, espionage and a variety of radicalisms must be pruned at once.

"Nude With Guitar" (1947) by Milton Avery, who is a leader of the Abstract Expressionist school.

Russians to tune in on Voice of America

Washington, D.C., Feb. 17

"One grain of truth dropped into Russia is like a spark landing in a barrel of powder," the 18th-century Frenchman, Comte de Custine, observed. The State Department, it would seem, agrees. Today, it began a Russian-language Voice of America broadcast aimed at countering what the Russians have been telling their people about the United States. Among other things, Russians are told America is a reactionary nation with slavery and cannibalism. There are a half million radios in Russia.

Truman's daughter in singing debut

Detroit, Mich., March 16

Most of the critics liked what they heard, a voice described as sweet and appealing, if inexperienced. The occasion: the singing debut of Margaret Truman on the *Hour of Music*, broadcast nationally from here with the Detroit Symphony. The soprano, performing without an audience, sang *Cielito Lindo*, *Charmant Oiseau* and, at her father's request, *The Last Rose of Summer*. The President phoned his praises from Key West, Florida. Miss Truman's public debut is in August at the Hollywood Bowl.

Baruch says nation is in a "cold war"

Columbia, S.C., Apr. 16

Bernard Baruch has added a new term to the lexicon of American-Soviet relations – "cold war." In an address before the South Carolina legislature today, Baruch said, "Let us not be deceived. We are today in the midst of a cold war. Our enemies are to be found abroad and at home." The financier used the phrase to describe the antagonism between the Communist East and the democracies of the West that has marked American-Soviet relations since the end of World War II. Baruch says the U.S. must prepare for the cold war as for any other war, by increasing expenditures on weapons and troops. To offset the inflation such an effort would cause, Baruch suggests extending the work week (→ June 5).

Marshall unveils plan to aid Europe

Secretary Marshall (front, third from left) at Harvard with fellow honorees.

Cambridge, Mass., June 5

Secretary of State George Marshall warned today that Europe's slow recovery from the war threatens international political stability, and he urged a massive American aid program to rebuild the continent. Marshall spoke this afternoon at Harvard after the university had granted him an honorary degree. "The remedy," Marshall said, "lies in breaking the vicious circle and restoring the confidence of the European people in the economic future of . . . Europe as a whole."

Marshall has been distressed by the sorry state of Europe, which Winston Churchill calls "a rubble heap, a charnel house, a breeding ground of pestilence and hate." In his recent visit to Moscow, Marshall witnessed appalling conditions. He also concluded that the Russians have no interest in the rebuilding of Western Europe, but his speech had less anti-Communist vitriol than President Truman's address to Congress. Marshall's speech was short on details, and he said the initiative for recovery must come from Europe itself (→ July).

Robinson breaks the color line in baseball

Brooklyn, N.Y., September

Some Southerners threatened to mutiny, at least two clubs threatened to strike and fans and bench jockeys rode him mercilessly, but there he was at first base, the first Negro to play in the major leagues.

Jackie Robinson was warned by Dodger president, Branch Rickey, that he had to have the courage to fight back against the bigots and he responded with his bat, hitting .295, scoring 125 runs and stealing 29 bases. Robinson was signed in 1945 to a contract with a Dodger farm club as pressure grew for the majors to hire Negroes. A football star at U.C.L.A., he went on to lead the International League in hitting and runs scored with Montreal. The Georgia-born son of a sharecropper and grandson of a slave opened the doors of integration on April 11, and in July the Cleveland Indians signed Larry Doby, the first Negro in the American League. There were some Negro players in pro ball in the late 1800s.

Jackie Robinson comes home in a triple steal against the Cincinnati Reds.

MacArthur constitution in effect in Japan

Tokyo, May 3

A historic new constitution went into effect in Japan today after it was approved by the Diet and was proclaimed the law of the land by Emperor Hirohito. The constitution greatly curtails the Emperor's power, introduces democratic principles and pledges that Japan will never again have military forces. The constitution says the Japanese people "renounce war . . . and the threat or use of force."

In a plebiscite on the constitution, Japanese women voted for the first time, and 75 percent of people eligible went to the polls. The constitution combines American and British principles. The prime minister serves four years, but is selected by the lower house of the Diet.

Much of the credit for the charter goes to the supreme commander, General Douglas MacArthur. He resisted pressure for an Allied-run military regime and pressured the Japanese to discard the ancient Meiji constitution (→ Dec. 23, 1948).

Taft-Hartley Act puts limits on big labor

Washington, D.C., June 23

Overriding a presidential veto and a barrage of invective from organized labor, Congress has passed legislation that rolls back many of the gains made by workers under the New Deal. The Taft-Hartley Act, proposed in response to a wave of postwar labor unrest, allows the President to obtain an 80-day injunction against any strike and appoint a board of inquiry to oversee collective bargaining. The act also bans the closed shop, allows states to void parts of the National Labor Relations Act and gives management greater latitude in fighting organizing drives.

Resistance to the bill was fierce. The A.F.L. described it as "conceived in a spirit of vindictiveness," the C.I.O. as "conceived in sin." A "veto caravan" of 1,450 protesters came from California to denounce the "slave labor bill." Besieged by 800,000 letters and 500,000 signatures, President Truman declared at the last minute that he would "blast hell out of the bill." It would, he charged, "reverse the basic direction of our national labor policy." His veto deepened the rift between the executive and the Republican Congress, but it may have saved the Democrats their working-class constituency.

X marks the spot to contain Russians

Washington, D.C., July

A mysterious author, X, has written an article in the current issue of *Foreign Affairs* saying the goal of United States policy toward the Soviet Union should be the "firm and vigilant containment of Russian expansionist tendencies." The author of *The Sources of Soviet Conduct* [later identified as George Kennan, a State Department Soviet expert], appears to be calling for a constant state of low-level warfare between the two superpowers.

According to the author's analysis, the Soviet Union is stubborn and intractable about its long-term objectives, yet flexible and cautious in the short-term. X compares the policy of the Communists to a fluid stream, flowing to fill all the openings available to it, yet changing direction whenever it finds a barrier in its path. He calls on the United States to stop the spread of communism by following a policy of containment and by confronting moves by "the Russians with unalterable counterforce at every point where they show signs of encroaching upon the interests of a peaceful and stable world."

Yeager breaks barrier

Captain Chuck Yeager (left) and other flight pioneers beside the rocket plane.

Muroc, Calif., Oct. 14

A sonic boom thundered across the desert here this morning, as Captain Chuck Yeager became the first man to shatter the sound barrier. Piloting a top-secret, bullet-shaped Bell X-1 rocket plane, Yeager hit a speed of 700 mph, or Mach 1.06, at an altitude of 43,000 feet.

The X-1, its fuel tanks loaded with explosive liquid oxygen, was carried aloft in the bomb bay of a B-29. As the four-engined bomber droned along at 20,000 feet, the bright orange X-1, nicknamed "Glamorous Glennis" after Yeager's wife, fell free then shot forward as the 6,000-pound thrust rockets were fired. Other planes suffer severe buffeting when approaching Mach speed, but the aerodynamically sleek X-1 sailed smoothly past the barrier.

Yeager, 24, was one of the army's hottest fighter pilots in Europe. But as the X-1 program is shrouded in secrecy, few people knew about his test-pilot activities.

U.S. armed services are now unified

Washington, D.C., July 26

President Truman today signed the National Security Act, uniting the armed services under one Department of Defense, to be headed by an official with Cabinet rank. James V. Forrestal, the current Secretary of the Navy, is slated to become the first Secretary of Defense.

The activities of the new National Military Establishment will be coordinated by a Joint Chiefs of Staff. A National Security Council will advise the president on military policy; a new information-gathering unit called the Central Intelligence Agency is established, and the Army Air Force becomes independent as the U.S. Air Force.

Both Congress and the State Department hope the new legislation will integrate domestic, foreign and military policy. Secretary of State George Marshall said last week that the weakened nations of Western Europe lie perilously near the brink of communism. The situation worsens daily, he said, and if economic aid fails, military efficiency may be at a premium. Said one State Department official: "It is later than you think."

Rosie abandons her rivets to raise babies

United States

"Hurry home, darling!" That's what women wrote their husbands overseas. And now that the men are back, the women are living happily ever after. Or are they? For some, the transition has been smooth:

While some women remain in the work force, most are finding that with the men returning the economy no longer has employment for them.

Men are now in school on the G.I. Bill, studying at the kitchen table while their wives cook dinner. Rosies have gladly abandoned riveting to raise babies. But many women are raising those babies alone.

Last year there were more divorces than ever recorded in American history, as the returning young men and waiting young women found themselves strangers. Some had not known each other well before they wed but had rushed to form a bond before death should prevent it. Other couples knew each other well before, but the war changed them. Men who were once carefree and boyish are now aloof and pessimistic; their wives hardly recognize them. As for the women, they had been holding down jobs and balancing checkbooks. All of a sudden the husband is taking charge and the woman is the inhabitant of a doll's house crammed with modern appliances.

4 million are taking advantage of G.I. Bill

Washington, D.C.

When the late President Roosevelt initiated the G.I. Bill in November 1942, he asked for quick congressional action. He got it and signed the bill into law a year and a half later. Now, more than four million veterans of the war are taking advantage of the housing, business and educational opportunities it has afforded. While a return from war is often difficult for service men and women, the bill has helped ease the adjustment to civilian life.

Men sign up for active service today to assure themselves a better tomorrow.

American nations sign defense pact

Rio de Janeiro, Brazil, Sept. 2

President Truman was on hand today to address the final session of the Rio de Janeiro Conference, where the United States and 19 Latin American nations signed the Inter-American Treaty of Reciprocal Assistance. The mutual defense pact stipulates that "an armed attack by any state shall be considered as an attack against all American states." In his speech, Truman said the treaty served as a warning to "any possible aggressor." In view of the current tensions in Europe, this appeared to be aimed at the Soviet Union (→ Apr. 30, 1948).

Record in U.S. aid to Europe's hungry

Washington, D.C., July 5

According to the Cabinet Committee on World Food Programs, over the last year the United States sent 18,443,000 tons of grain and other foodstuffs to Europe – the largest annual food shipment by any country. Commenting on the report, President Truman said that even such a record-breaking volume did not meet the "world's urgent postwar needs" and that millions of "still desperately hungry persons" need help. "We will continue to do our part to help other countries to help themselves," he said. The committee's report said that the shipments affected neither the American economy nor the nation's food supply (→ Oct. 5).

H.U.A.C. investigation into Hollywood ends with 10 blacklisted

Actors George Murphy and Ronald Reagan await their turns before H.U.A.C.

Washington, D.C., Nov. 25

An investigation into the alleged Communist infiltration of the movie industry was launched last month by the House Un-American Activities Committee. And today, in an unprecedented act of self-censorship, the film industry itself voted to bar 10 professionals who had been held in contempt of Congress.

One of the first people called before the panel was writer Ayn Rand, a friendly witness, who declared the movie *Song of Russia* propaganda.

Another friendly witness, the actor Adolph Menjou, talked of anti-American pictures that should not have been made, such as *Mission to Moscow*. Robert Taylor stated that Communist activities were found mainly in the area of screenwriting, but he mentioned "party-line stuff" among actors and he named some names. Ronald Reagan, president of the Screen Actors Guild, testified that the guild is not controlled by Communists ("99 percent of us are well aware of what's going on") and

spoke in favor of informed democracy. Gary Cooper said he had turned down a few scripts that were "tinged with Communist ideas."

Director Edward Dmytryk refused to answer some questions, citing his constitutional rights. And Emmet Lavery, president of the Screen Writers Guild, who other witnesses called a Communist, denied he was one and stated that his guild has no right to examine members on political or religious beliefs. Screenwriter John Howard Lawson said the committee was out to destroy the Bill of Rights and screenwriter Ring Lardner questioned the committee's right to question. The German playwright Bertolt Brecht spoke of the independent artist.

Charlie Chaplin sent the committee a telegram accepting an invitation to appear before them in Washington. "I understand that I am to be your guest at the expense of the taxpayers," he said, pointing out they could have seen him when they were in Hollywood "or even by means of a collect call ... While you are preparing your engraved subpoena, I will give you a hint on where I stand. I am not a Communist. I am a peace-monger" (→ Apr. 10, 1950).

"A Streetcar Named Desire" and "The Naked and the Dead"

New York City

It's hard to believe that only 20 years ago readers were scandalized by short skirts, bobbed hair and kids kissing in the front seat of a flivver. Today's writers go for stronger, often brutal stories. Take,

for instance, the Tennessee Williams smash drama, *A Streetcar Named Desire*. Set in a sweltering New Orleans slum, it reaches a climax when the genteel heroine, a faded Southern belle, is crushed in the muscular embrace of a loud-

mouthed galoot who also happens to be her brother-in-law. Some readers think the title of 24-year-old Norman Mailer's epic first novel about infantrymen in the Pacific *The Naked and the Dead*, ought to include *the Profane*.

Los Angeles, November 2. *Howard Hughes's Spruce Goose, made of wood and the world's largest plane, took to the air today, but flew only a mile.*

World Series on TV

New York City, Oct. 6

The Yanks and Dodgers served up a hair-tingling World Series that went down to seven games and provided superb fare for television viewers. An estimated 3.7 million saw the first telecast of the autum classic. Yankee relief ace Joe Page checked the Dodgers on one hit for the last five innings in the decisive game of this "subway" series today. The Bums had tied it at six-all yesterday in a game that saw a record 38 players in action. Bill Bevens missed a no-hitter by one out.

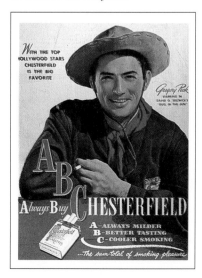

1948

Washington, D.C., Jan. 12. Supreme Court rules, in Sipeul v. Board of Regents of University of Oklahoma, that states may not use race as a criterion in judging law school applicants (→ June 8, 1953).

Bogota, Colombia, Apr. 30. United States joins 21 nations in signing Organization of American States charter.

South Korea, May 10. Under aegis of United Nations Temporary Commission, elections are held in United States-occupied South Korea, but not in Soviet-occupied North (→ Aug. 15).

Washington, D.C., May 19. Nixon-Mundt bill, requiring Communists to register with government, passed by House (→ Oct. 21, 1949).

New York City, May. Pulitzer Prize awarded to James Michener for *Tales of the South Pacific.*

Washington, D.C., June 11. Senate adopts Vandenberg Resolution, permitting U.S. to be signatory to non-Western Hemispheric defense pacts.

Washington, D.C., Aug. 15. Word received of establishment in Seoul of Republic of South Korea; Syngman Rhee is president (→ Sept. 9).

Washington, D.C., Sept. 9. U.S. learns of creation of Democratic People's Republic of Korea in Pyongyang; Kim Il Sung is president (→ June 30, 1950).

New York City, October. Dwight D. Eisenhower inaugurated as president of Columbia University.

Cleveland, Oct. 11. Indians defeat Boston Braves, four games to two, in World Series.

Maine, Nov. 2. Republican Margaret Chase Smith is first elected woman senator.

Washington, D.C., Dec. 3. Colonel Mary Agnes Hallaren sworn in as first woman officer in regular army.

Philadelphia, Dec. 19. Eagles defeat Chicago Cardinals, 7-0, in N.F.L. championship.

DEATHS

Dayton, Ohio, Jan. 30. Orville Wright, co-inventor of airplane (*Aug. 19, 1871).

Hollywood, July 23. D.W. Griffith, pioneering movie director (*Jan. 22, 1875).

United States recognizes state of Israel

Ralph Bunche (right), acting U.S. mediator, oversees Israeli independence.

Jerusalem, May 14

As midnight struck in Palestine, Jewish leaders declared the independence of the new state of Israel. The announcement, timed to coincide with the end of Britain's control over Palestine, seemed certain to commit the new nation to a war with the Arab states, who are opposed to the partition of Palestine.

Although the United States had hoped that Israel would hold off until the United Nations agreed on a timetable for peaceful partition, President Truman waited only 11 minutes before pledging America's support to the new nation and granting its government recognition. The speed with which Truman acted took many in his own State Department by surprise.

The decision to divide Palestine into a Jewish and an Arab state, with Jerusalem under international control, was made by the U.N. General Assembly last November. But the world body was unable to get the Jews and the Arabs to agree to a plan. When Britain announced on December 3 that agreement or not, it would withdraw its troops from Palestine on May 15, hope faded for a peaceful reconciliation of Jewish and Arab claims.

Washington, D.C., April 3. *The Marshall Plan goes into effect as President Truman allocates $6 billion for overseas economic and military aid, keystones in the global struggle to contain the expansion of communism.*

Toscannini conducts NBC concert on TV

New York City, March 20

A local paper describes how the customers in a Greenwich Street bar got some Teutonic mythology mixed with their malt when the television set picked up the first telecast of the weekly NBC concerts. The indefatigable Arturo Toscanini, five days shy of his 81st birthday, led an all-Wagner program. Observed one patron, "He knows his onions, dat old boid. See the signals he got?" The program was also seen in Washington, Philadelphia, Schenectady and Buffalo. The "Old Man" maintains a youthful pace, with 16 NBC concerts a year. And in two weeks he can again be seen on television, conducting Beethoven's Ninth Symphony.

Millions can now watch the Maestro.

High court forbids prayer in schools

Washington, D.C., March 8

The Supreme Court added another brick to the "impregnable" wall separating church and state today. In McCollum v. Board of Education, the court ruled that a time set aside by public school districts at the start of each school day for prayer violates the Constitution. Lawyers for the state of Illinois argued that the First Amendment only forbids government preference of one religion over another. But, Justice Hugo Black held that "both religion and state can best work to achieve their lofty aims if each is left free from the other within its respective spheres."

Soviets blockade Berlin

Berlin, West Germany, June 26

Operation Vittles is under way. The West has launched a massive airlift of food to Berlin in response to the Soviet blockade of the Allied sections of the city. The blockade began two days ago when the Russians stopped all rail, road and barge traffic from the Western zone of Germany into Berlin, citing "technical difficulties" as the cause. A more likely reason is Soviet anger at the introduction by the Allies of a new currency into the Western zone to prevent the Russians from flooding it with counterfeit money, as they had been doing. According to an Allied estimate, 2,500 tons of food a day will have to be flown into Berlin to prevent the population from starving (→ May 12, 1949).

U.S. soldiers and German civilians unload coal during the Berlin airlift.

Armed forces integrated

Washington, D.C., July 30

President Truman issued an executive order today forbidding segregation in the nation's armed services. The President said that racial discrimination should end "as rapidly as possible." He also established the President's Committee on Equality of Treatment and Opportunity in the Armed Service to study the matter. The integration order is expected to create turmoil among Southerners. While nearly a million Negroes served in the military in World War II, most were confined to segregated and cheaper quarters. The President's campaign for racial equality took a major step four days ago when he ordered an end to discrimination in federal hiring.

The President rules Negroes may no longer be segregated in the military.

Rail strike blocked

Washington, D.C., May 10

Like his predecessor, President Truman has acted forcefully to end a strike threat by the nation's rail workers: He ordered the government to seize the railroads. Today's action averted a strike that union leaders had set. The army will operate the trains just as it did in 1943 when President Roosevelt seized them. Truman also intervened in a rail strike two years ago. It is hoped that mediation will end this dispute quickly, as it did in 1943 and 1946.

Citation triumphant

New York City, June

Citation has proved to be one of the few young colts that have lived up to their early promise. After a 27-for-29 record as a 2-year-old, he romped to victories in the Kentucky Derby and Preakness and wrapped it all up with a Triple Crown sweep by taking the Belmont Stakes. "He's the greatest I've ever seen," said jockey Eddie Arcaro, who in taking his fourth Derby surpassed a record shared by Earl Sande and Isaac Murphy.

Big lens dedicated

Mount Palomar, Calif., June 3

Amid a prevailing sense of gloom over science's role in the atomic age, astronomers dedicated a giant telescope here today to the peaceful pursuit of knowledge. With a 200-inch lens, the instrument will peer eight times deeper into space than any other telescope. Said one speaker: "Man spends his energies in fighting with his fellow man over issues which a single look through this telescope would show to be utterly inconsequential."

Draft is reinstated

Washington, D.C., June 24

President Truman signed the Selective Service Act today, reinstating a peacetime draft. It will require all men between the ages of 18 and 25 to register with the government for military duty, with all 19-year-olds eligible to be called up for 21 months of service. Between 200,000 and 250,000 men are expected to fill the ranks in the first year of conscription. Tension in both Europe and Southeast Asia is believed to have precipitated the legislation.

Eastern Europe falls into Soviet orbit

Washington, D.C.

Despite hope for a united Europe, an impenetrable barrier – an Iron Curtain – has riven East and West. Under the powerful arm of Soviet Premier Stalin, coalition governments have given way to Communist rule in Poland, Rumania, Hungary, Bulgaria and Czechoslovakia.

Poland, with a history of animosity toward the Russians, was the first to go. As Stalin insisted, "any freely elected government would be anti-Soviet and that we cannot permit." The Rumanians had helped the Nazis invade Russia, and the popular King Michael was ousted last

December. Bulgaria, historically friendly to Russia, leaned easily to the left. King Simeon gave up his throne in 1946, and the Communists were soon ruling the Fatherland Front. In Hungary, control over farm policy gave the Communists popular appeal by means of land reform. The Czechs, victimized by a coup in February, had tried for middle ground, but to no avail. And in Yugoslavia, Marshal Tito firmly resisted, and was brusquely expelled from the Soviet alliance this year. Hearing of Tito's "disloyalty," Stalin snarled, "I will shake my little finger and there will be no more Tito."

New York City, June 25. *Joe Louis (right) rocks "Jersey Joe" Walcott with a powerful right. Punching and jabbing, heavyweight champ Louis successfully defended his title by scoring an 11th round knockout.*

Alger Hiss indicted for perjury as Whittaker Chambers talks

Whittaker Chambers, an editor at "Time" magazine and former Soviet agent, is the principal witness in the government case against Alger Hiss.

New York City, Dec. 15

Whittaker Chambers led a group of investigators and reporters to a pumpkin patch on his Maryland farm earlier this month, where he produced evidence that has resulted in the grand jury indictment today of Alger Hiss for perjury. This sordid tale of espionage and backstabbing has Republicans excited and Democrats embarrassed.

The story starts in 1937, when Chambers, a Soviet agent at the time, is alleged to have received secret State Department documents from Hiss, then a department official. Chambers, now an editor at *Time* magazine, told the House Un-American Activities Committee that Hiss provided the documents and other strategic data that Chambers passed along to the Russians as part of a widespread pre-war Communist spy ring. Hiss, now president of the Carnegie Endowment for International Peace, denied the allegations before a federal grand jury and sued Chambers for libel. That denial is the basis for today's perjury charge.

California Rep. Richard M. Nixon has pursued the case, bringing it to national attention with the charge that the Truman administration is more interested in covering up the facts than in seeking out the truth. Truman, in showing support for Hiss, called the charges against him a "red herring." But, in a dramatic presentation, Chambers opened up a hollow pumpkin which he said served as a "drop," and pulled out three rolls of microfilm that contained secret State Department papers. The trial is expected to begin next year (→ 1949).

Polaroid magic

United States

Push a button. Pull a tab. Wait a minute. And there you have an instant snapshot, developed and printed in the camera. That's the appeal of the $95, five-pound Polaroid Land Camera, designed by the inventor Edwin Land. It produces a black-and-white photo that can be removed from the back of the camera. Just coat it with a varnish to protect its surface.

Congress seeks end to rising inflation

Washington, D.C., Aug. 31

Back in November 1946, President Truman ended wage and price controls. It seemed like a good idea at the time. But today, an Anti-Inflation Act became law in response to skyrocketing inflation. Statistics show that a house costing $4,440 in 1939 costs $9,060 now. Clothing is up 129 percent, food 129 percent, home furnishings 93.6 percent. Only gas and electricity have had a cost decrease. In addition to the new anti-inflationary measures, the Federal Reserve has imposed limits on installment buying, hoping consumers will continue to pay for homes and other large items sooner than later.

Dixiecrats, Progressives offer alternatives

Washington, D.C.

This year's presidential election offers alternatives to the Democratic and Republican candidates. In July, two parties tossed candidates into the fray. The States' Rights Democratic ticket nominated South Carolina Governor Strom Thurmond at its convention. Known as "Dixiecrats," the party denigrates the civil rights campaign promoted by President Truman.

Alabama's Governor Dixon delivered the keynote speech, saying Truman's policy "wants to reduce us to the status of a mongrel, inferior race, mixed in blood, our Anglo-Saxon heritage a mockery."

A few days later, the Progressive Party chose Henry Wallace, a Vice President under Roosevelt and recently fired as Truman's Secretary of Commerce. The parties are likely to splinter Truman's support.

New York City, August 16. *The Babe standing before a huge crowd celebrating the 25th anniversary of Yankee Stadium, "The House That Ruth Built," five days ago. Today, baseball's greatest slugger died of cancer.*

38 gold medals go to U.S. Olympians

London, Aug. 14

The postwar Olympics seemed to be the best-kept secret in this blitzed-out city, but once under way, they turned out to be a smashing success – especially for the United States. American athletes among the 6,000 competitors on hand rolled up 662 points, with 38 gold medals. Sweden was second best, scoring 353 points. One of the biggest American stars was 17-year-old Bob Mathias of California, who rolled up 7,139 points to win the grueling decathlon – on a rain-soaked track. The only political flap came up when some of the Czech and Hungarian athletes refused to return to their homeland behind the Iron Curtain and asked for asylum in the West.

McDonald's is open

San Bernardino, Calif., December

Taking their cue from self-service retail stores, Richard and Maurice McDonald have opened a hamburger drive-in with no carhops and no options on the burgers. Prewrapped with standard condiments ("Buy 'em by the bag," says McDonald's sign), they cost 15 cents; french fries are a dime, milk shakes 25. The idea has yet to attract a public that is used to car-side service.

Quik, Dial, Honda: "brand" new world

United States

As new products arrive on the market, Americans wonder how they ever did without Honda motorcycles, Land Rovers, Michelin radial tires, Porsche sports cars, heat-conducting windshields, non-glare headlights, Nikon 35-mm. cameras, Salton Hottrays, color newsreels, Scrabble and Dial soap. How did they do without a Baskin-Robbins chain? Would they have wasted two quarters on what they now buy with a Franklin 50-cent piece? Would they have drunk tea instead of Nestle's Quik? And what would they have called bikinis if the island had not been bombed (maybe "next-to-nothing-atoll")?

Truman defeats Dewey

An exuberant Harry Truman mocks the skeptics who said it couldn't be done.

Washington, D.C., Nov. 3

The *Chicago Tribune's* headline screamed: "Dewey Defeats Truman." This early report was dead wrong as Harry S. Truman won a full term in the White House yesterday in one of the biggest political upsets in American history.

Give 'em Hell Harry and his running mate, Alben Barkley, defeated the heavily favored Thomas E. Dewey, Governor of New York, and his vice presidential nominee, Earl Warren, at dawn when the vote in Illinois pushed the Democrats over the top. Democrats also regained control of Congress, sweeping in on

the President's coattails. Truman pulled out the election with his whistle-stop tour of the nation. On it, he was at his best. He described the Republicans as "bloodsuckers with offices on Wall Street, princes of privilege, plunderers." He tickled the electorate by saying that the polls predicting Dewey would win were like "pills designed to lull the voter into sleeping on Election Day. They ought to call them sleeping polls." The victory is even more remarkable in that the Progressive and Dixiecrat Parties each took over a million votes from the Democrats (→ Jan. 20, 1949).

Japanese leaders hanged for war crimes

Tokyo, Dec. 23

Seven Japanese officials, including two former prime ministers, were hanged today following their convictions as war criminals. No photographs were allowed. Witnesses say none of the men expressed remorse. Each shouted "Banzai!" as he walked to the scaffold.

Former Prime Minister Hideki Tojo was in power for most of the war. He attempted suicide unsuccessfully to avoid trial. Koki Hirota was Prime Minister in 1936-37 and oversaw the signing of the Anti-Comintern Pact with Germany and Italy. An 11-judge civilian tribunal convicted the two of "crimes against peace." The supreme com-

mander, General Douglas MacArthur, endorsed the verdicts, with little negative reaction.

MacArthur was severely criticized for refusing to block the executions of two Japanese generals in Manila in 1946. Military tribunals convicted Masaharu Homma, the leader for the Philippines invasion, and Tomoyuki Yamashita, the "Tiger of Manila," of war crimes. Evidence did not link either directly to the Bataan death march, where many Americans died on the way to war camps. Editor H.L. Mencken charged that MacArthur simply executed two men who beat him "in a fair fight" on the battlefield (→ Sept. 8, 1951).

U.N. hails Mrs. Roosevelt's rights efforts

New York City, Dec. 10

People from around the world stood and applauded Mrs. Eleanor Roosevelt today for her efforts in winning passage of the United Nations Declaration of Human Rights. The President of the U.N. General Assembly, Dr. Herbert Evatt, said she "has raised a great name to an even greater honor." Mrs. Roosevelt thanked everyone in her usual self-effacing way. A U.N. delegate since 1945, the wife of the late President has long been active in humanitarian causes, with no issue too large or too small for her attention. In 1942, when wartime gas rationing began, Mrs. Roosevelt looked beyond the economic factors. She said that people on farms would have to stay home and "never see another soul for weeks and weeks." She cares.

The former First Lady never rests in the fight for humanitarian causes.

New on television

New York City

Television is rapidly becoming a permanent part of American lives. Shows that began this year include *Candid Camera*, *The Milton Berle Show*, *The Toast of the Town*, *Arthur Godfrey's Talent Scouts*, *Philco Television Playhouse* and *Studio One*. A Philco television set installed in a Capital airliner flying between Washington and Chicago works so well that video will be put on other flights. The Screen Actors Guild says that when a film is televised more than once in a locality, there must be "some additional payment for actors."

Tiny transistor may recast electronics

Murray Hill, N.J., July

It is only a minuscule metal disk with an even smaller germanium crystal soldered onto one face. But the Bell Labs physicists who displayed their creation this month say it will revolutionize electronics. The transistor, according to its inventor, Dr. William Shockley, amplifies electric current without a heated filament or other costly components. It may replace bulky vacuum tubes, making radios both smaller and more portable.

Kinsey sex report

Bloomington, Indiana

Dr. Alfred C. Kinsey specializes in insects. But his study of humans has made the University of Indiana professor a household name. It all began in 1938, when Kinsey started compiling dossiers about the sexual practices of American males. He eventually interviewed some 5,000 men, who related details about their preferences, habits and partners. At last, Kinsey's findings – long kept under lock and key – have been released in *Sexual Behavior in the Human Male*, a scholarly work with just enough spicy details to make it a runaway best-seller.

Celebrity endorsements are proving a lucrative marketing tool.

Truman sworn in, offers poor nations aid

Washington, D.C., Jan. 20

Inaugurated as President today, Harry S. Truman offered "a bold new program" for underdeveloped areas and denounced communism as "a false philosophy." For the first time, television carried the inaugural as far west as Sedalia, in Truman's home state of Missouri. In all, 10 million people looked on, many times more than watched all previous inaugurations combined. The President outlined a four-point program, supporting the United Nations and world trade and denouncing communism. As Point Four, he said, we should "help the free peoples of the world lighten their burdens." The project will provide technological skills, knowledge and equipment to poor nations.

"President Harry S Truman," man from Missouri, by Greta Kempton.

Lady wrestlers, roller derby and pizza

United States

Some nice things for women this year: prepared cake mixes, Pillsbury "Bake-offs," Revlon's "Fire and Ice," ripping needles for sewing machines, boned bras, decolletage bras, scented bras (by Love-E), mother-daughter matching playsuits and Gorgeous George, the wrestler. For men: roller derbies, pyramid clubs, Sara Lee cheesecake and lady wrestlers. Nice things for couples: LP record catalogues, canasta and the pizza pie. An article in the *Atlantic Monthly* says, "You eat it, usually sitting in a booth in a bare, plain restaurant, with a mural of Vesuvio on the wall, a jukebox, and a crowded bar. The customers are Italian families, Bohemians, lovers, and – if a college is nearby – students and faculty members." Some things kids like: Silly Putty and more pizza.

"Rose and Driftwood" (1932) by San Francisco-born Ansel Adams, who this year published "My Camera in Yosemite Valley." Originally trained as a pianist, Adams did not dedicate himself to photography until 1930. Since that time, as an ardent conservationist, he has focused on nature.

Champ for 11 years, Louis calls it quits

United States, March 3

Joe Louis, boxing's popular and durable heavyweight champion, is hanging up his gloves. The "Brown Bomber," who limited his boxing to exhibition tours for the past eight months, said he is retiring after 11 years as champ. Since beating Billy Conn in a rematch that drew one of the richest gates in history, Louis knocked out Tami Mauriello in 1946 and defeated Joe Walcott twice, but he is obviously losing the blinding jab and lethal hook that won him world fame. The 35-year-old Louis, who is in dire need of money to pay back taxes, said he would box exhibition matches in an effort to pay his debts.

World-circling flight sets 94-hour record

Forth Worth, Tex. March 2

Another air record was set here at 10:31 a.m. today when Captain James Gallagher landed his Boeing B-50, Lucky Lady II, on the same runway at Carswell Air Force Base from which he had taken off 94 hours and 1 minute earlier. In the meantime, Captain Gallagher had completed the first non-stop round-the-world flight ever attempted.

Traveling eastward, Lucky Lady II was refueled in flight four times during the 23,452-mile journey: over the Azores, Saudi Arabia, the Philippines and Hawaii.

The feat is yet another triumph for American aviation, which has been breaking one record after another. On October 14, 1947, Captain Charles Yeager, flying a Bell X-I, became the first pilot to break the sound barrier. On January 5 of this year, Captain Yeager set a climbing speed record of 13,000 feet per minute. Then, on February 8 an Air Force XB-47 flew from Moses Lake, Washington, to Andrews Air Force Base in Maryland in 3 hours 46 minutes, setting a speed record of 607.2 miles per hour. And in a less dramatic technical development in this emerging nuclear era, the Air Force recently test-dropped a 42,000-pound bomb, the world's heaviest, from the bay of a B-36.

In "South Pacific," box office magic

New York City, Apr. 7

With their new musical, *South Pacific,* Richard Rodgers and Oscar Hammerstein are working at the same, high level as *Oklahoma!,* but in a palm-tree scene a world away. Based on stories by James Michener, the plot features the wartime romance of an American nurse and a French plantation owner. As Nellie Forbush and Emile de Becque, Mary Martin and Ezio Pinza are magical in songs like *A Cockeyed Optimist* and *Some Enchanted Evening.* With the largest advance sale in history, *South Pacific* should be around a long time. And with the advent of long-playing records, the financial reward may be staggering.

Snowy California

California, January

In Palm Springs and Santa Barbara, commonly known for semitropical weather, it's snowing. San Diego, on the Mexican border, got its first snow in its 99-year weather history. The virtually unprecedented snowfall, covering Los Angeles and coastal areas in depths up to one foot, is crippling traffic and menacing Southern California's fruit and vegetable farms.

Senate ratifies North Atlantic Treaty

American might assures NATO its necessary strength and credibility.

Washington, D.C., July 21

By a vote of 82 to 13, the Senate today ratified the North Atlantic Treaty which commits the United States to a mutual defense alliance with 11 other countries. This is the first time in its history that the United States has entered into such a treaty in peacetime, and is yet another milestone in the nation's assumption of the role of leader of the free world in the cold war.

The treaty, signed in Washington on April 4, includes Canada, Britain, France, Belgium, Italy, the Netherlands, Luxembourg, Norway, Sweden, Ireland and Iceland. Its principal purpose, as set forth in its preamble, is to "safeguard the freedom, common heritage, and civilization of their peoples, founded on the principles of democracy, individual liberty and the rule of law." To that end, "an armed attack against one or more of them in Europe or North America shall be considered an attack against them all." The pact is drawn up under Article 51 of the U.N. Charter, which provides for regional security arrangements.

Ratification, though opposed by a handful of diehard isolationists, was virtually a foregone conclusion after the passage last year by a 64-4 vote of Senator Arthur H. Vandenberg's resolution urging President Truman to encourage collective security arrangements. Public opinion also strongly backs the North Atlantic Treaty Organization (NATO) accord, with 67 percent approving. Not surprisingly, Communist opposition has been shrill. The *Daily Worker* called it "International Murder, Inc."

Western observers say that the need for strong measures to counter the aggressive policies of Russian-dominated communism has been made evident by recent events in Europe: the Communist coup in Czechoslovakia, the moves to subvert Greece and Turkey, and most glaringly, the blockade of Berlin.

By joining NATO, the United States has served notice that it does not intend to sit on the sidelines while aggression has its way and intervene only later, as happened in World War I and II. Instead, aggressors now know they will have to reckon with the full might of the United States from the outset. And this, it is hoped, will prevent World War III (→ Sept. 1, 1951).

Year-long Allied air lift breaks Soviet Union's blockade of Berlin

Berlin, Germany, May 12

The Berlin Airlift, which for 321 days has brought food, clothes, fuel and other essential supplies to the beleaguered citizens of the Allied sectors of this city, is coming to an end. Thanks to an agreement worked out under United Nations auspices in New York, Soviet authorities have reopened the city to road, rail and canal communication with the West.

During the blockade, some 2.5 million tons of supplies were flown in by American and British planes at a cost estimated to exceed $200 million. Only three "air corridors" were available to the supply planes, which at times were landing at the rate of one a minute.

Much of the credit for the successful management of the operation is being given to General Lucius D. Clay, the autocratic 4-star general who is military governor of the United States occupation zone in Germany. From the start, he had a clear view of the strategic issues involved. "A retreat from Berlin," he said, "would have serious if not disastrous political consequences in Europe. I do not believe that the Soviets mean war. However, if they do, it seems to me that we might as well find out now as later."

Young Berliners cheer as an American airplane brings them more food.

Charles wins title that Louis vacated

Chicago, June 22

Ezzard Charles is the new heavyweight champion of the world. The quiet Georgian, who as a boy didn't even like prizefighting, outpointed Jersey Joe Walcott in a 15-round contest to gain the title vacated by Joe Louis. Charles found his talent for boxing at age 16 and went on to win 42 amateur fights in a row before turning pro at 18. He patterned his style after that of Joe Louis but said, "It didn't work out for me." Charles is an admittedly cautious fighter, which reduces him in the eyes of some critics, but he can box furiously when he is cornered. And though his knockout record is not notable, he walloped a lot harder than most of the experts expected.

Auto industry fueling postwar economy

"Graceful as a yacht," the ad says, "the smart car for young moderns."

Detroit, Michigan

The airlines may have stolen the spotlight for technological innovation, but it is the auto industry that provides the spark for postwar recovery. During the war, auto plants turned out one-fifth of the nation's military goods. Now Ford, Chrysler and General Motors have returned to the consumer market with a vengeance. A record six million cars rolled off American assembly lines this year, outstripping the rest of the world's output. G.M. reported profits of $500 million for the first three quarters, and offered dividends totaling an unprecedented $190 million. And with Detroit using steel, rubber and glass, prosperity spreads widely. Consumers glad to be rid of wartime rationing seem eager to buy.

Soviets detonate Bomb

Washington, D.C., Sept. 23

A major shift in the balance of power between the Soviet Union and the West was disclosed today with the announcement by President Truman that the Russians have succeeded in detonating a nuclear bomb. Though it was suspected that the Russians were working on an atomic weapon, it was generally believed that they were at least three years from their goal. The news means that the United States can no longer rely on its exclusive ownership of nuclear weapons to counterbalance the Soviet advantage in conventional weapons and land forces. The problem is not immediate, because the United States has a substantial stockpile of atomic weapons under the control of the Atomic Energy Commission, but its monopoly is now at an end.

While that monopoly lasted, the United States was widely praised for its offer to share its nuclear technology with the rest of the world, although under conditions that would prevent any country from using this knowledge for other than peaceful purposes. Since this would entail on-site inspection, the offer was turned down by the Russians on the grounds that such inspections would be used as an excuse for espionage. Now, however, it would seem that the reason for the Russians' refusal was a desire to conceal the fact that they were working on a bomb of their own.

Today's news will almost certainly lead to an acceleration of the arms race, with the emphasis on developing a hydrogen bomb. While technically more complicated than a fission bomb, a thermonuclear device would be 100 times more powerful (→ May 12, 1951).

U.N. cornerstone laid in New York City

New York City, Oct. 24

In an open-air plenary meeting of the General Assembly, the cornerstone of the United Nations building was laid today at a ceremony whose speakers included President Truman and Secretary-General Trygve Lie. The 18-acre site between 42nd and 48th Streets, bounded by First Avenue and the East River, was acquired in 1946 with an $8.5 million gift from John D. Rockefeller Jr. The American architect Wallace K. Harrison is heading an international team of architects working on plans for a 39-story Secretariat Building, domed General Assembly Hall and a long, low Conference Building.

The Secretariat Building is expected to be ready for at least partial occupancy late next year. In the meantime, the organization, after moving from temporary premises in London, then Hunter College in New York, is now in the Sperry Gyroscope building at Lake Success, Long Island (→ Oct. 14, 1952).

500,000 steel workers strike; get pension

Pittsburgh, Penn., Nov. 11

Even in the age of collective bargaining, the strike is labor's indispensable weapon. That was once again proved by United Steel Workers president Philip Murray, who has sent the last of 500,000 men back to work with pensions funded fully by the steel firms. For 77 days, Murray held off while federal mediator Cyrus Ching and a presidential fact-finding board did their work. He gave up on a wage raise, but insisted the firms pay for welfare and pensions. Company-funded welfare, retorted U.S. Steel, would "strike a blow at the principle of self-help and dignity." So in the age-old tradition of union self-help, 500,000 steel workers struck on October 1. Their action paid off.

Pound gets prize in mental institution

Washington, D.C., Feb. 19

From a hospital for the criminally insane, Ezra Pound today accepted the $1,000 Bollingen Prize for Poetry. The honored work, *The Pisan Cantos,* was finished in a U.S. Army prison in Italy, where the poet stood accused of making pro-Mussolini radio broadcasts during the war. Upon return, he was pronounced "insane and mentally unfit for trial." Pound has disavowed Fascism, but the judges still saw fit to defend their choice. "To permit other considerations," they stated, "than that of poetic achievement to sway the decision would destroy the significance of the award."

Communists take Peking as Americans ask who lost China

Peking, China, Oct. 1

With the proclamation here today of the People's Republic of China by the victorious 56-year old Mao Tse-tung, nearly one quarter of the world's population – some 500 million people – have come under the rule of a Communist government. To cold warriors, who view communism as a monolithic structure bent upon world conquest, it is a staggering blow, and the search for scapegoats is sure to start soon. American right-wing Republicans are already pointing the finger at the Democratic administration, which refused to intervene on behalf of the collapsing Nationalists. Secretary of State Dean Acheson is a key target, and there is already talk of Communist sympathizers entrenched in the upper reaches of the State Department.

However, the man who may be responsible is Chiang Kai-shek, the Nationalist generalissimo who has taken refuge along with the remnants of his army on the offshore island of Formosa [Taiwan], where he is protected by the American navy. Corrupt and inefficient, the Nationalists quite simply lost the support of the Chinese people, particularly the vast rural majority who were attracted by the Communists' promises of radical land reform. The Communists are also perceived to have taken a more active role in the wartime fighting against the Japanese (→ Dec. 8, 1950).

Peking falls to Communist forces.

11 Communists sentenced under Smith Act

New York City, Oct. 21

All but one of 11 leading Communists were sentenced today to five years in prison and a $10,000 fine for conspiracy to overthrow the United States government by force and violence. The 11th received only three years because of honorable military service during World War II. Judge Harold R. Medina set the sentence one week after the jury convicted all 11 men under the Smith Act of 1940. The charges stem from the activities of the Communist Political Association during an attempted reorganization in 1945. The men who received five years were Eugene Dennis, 44 years old and general secretary of the Communist Party of the United States; Gus Hall, 39, the Ohio chairman; John B. Williamson, 46, the party's national labor secretary; John Stachel, 49; Henry Winston, 35; John Gates, 36; Irving Potash, 47; Gilbert Green, 43; Carl Winters, 43, and Benjamin J. Davis Jr., 46, who is a New York City Councilman and chairman of the party's legislative committee. Robert Thompson, 34, New York State chairman, was sentenced to three years. Hundreds of demonstrators gathered in front of the courthouse on Foley Square protesting the convictions and sentences. In 1941, the Trotskyite Workers Party came under the scrutiny of the Smith Act; 12 members were convicted (→ Sept 23, 1950).

Hiss testifies he was never a Communist

New York City

Alger Hiss, the former State Department official who has been accused of handing over government secrets to Soviet agent Whittaker Chambers in the 1930s, testified in June that he was never a Communist and that he never transmitted any department documents to anyone. The case has captured national attention with a series of dramatic circumstances: a secret drop for microfilm in a pumpkin patch; claims by Representative Richard Nixon that the Truman administration was hiding the truth about Hiss, as well as stories circulating widely that the State Department is a "Communist breeding ground" (→ Jan. 25, 1950).

The defendant Alger Hiss (seated).

"Death of a Salesman" wins a Pulitzer

New York City

"A salesman has got to dream, boy. It comes with the territory." These words, from Arthur Miller's *Death of a Salesman,* could serve as the epitaph for every generation of Americans that lives from hope to hope, sure that someday its ship will come in. The dream is the American dream, and it goes sour in Miller's two act-drama. The loser is Willy Loman (that is, "low man"), an aging salesman "way out there in the blue, riding on a smile and a shoeshine." All his life, Willy has waited for better times, and now, as the wheel spins down, he's got no chips left, only a long-suffering wife and a pair of troubled sons who haven't grown up. Miller, 34, whose modern-day tragedy excited audiences and critics alike, has himself ridden off with something more substantial than "a smile and shoeshine" – the Pulitzer Prize.

A different prize is awarded in "The Lottery," the spooky title story of a collection by Shirley Jackson. It describes a ritual in a make-believe American town: Citizens draw lots with a bizarre prize for the "winner" – death by stoning.

No Flying Saucers, the Air Force insists

Dayton, Ohio, Dec. 28

Get the barbecues back out, because our skies were declared free of flying saucers by an Air Force report today. Project Sign, better known as project saucer, began on December 22, and investigated 244 sightings. These were explained as hallucinations, misinterpretations, hoaxes and natural phenomena, but for 23 percent of the cases the only answer was psychological malfunction. Major General L.C. Craigie headed the project.

Pogo and his pals back on comic page

New York City, May

Pogo is back! Walt Kelly's comic strip, last seen earlier this year in the *New York Sun,* now defunct, has been picked up for nationwide distribution by the Hall Syndicate and it is going to appear locally in the *New York Post.* Set in the Okefenokee Swamp, the strip describes the adventures of a mild-mannered little opossum named Pogo and his best friend, an outspoken, cigar-chomping alligator by the name of Albert.

C.I.O. throwing out Communist unions

Cleveland, Nov. 5

The Congress of Industrial Organizations is getting rid of its Communist albatross. Former president John L. Lewis's willingness to bring radicals into the C.I.O. has subjected the group to repeated attacks. This week at its annual convention, president Philip Murray seized the offensive. The United Electrical Workers and the Farm Equipment Workers, Murray insisted, were "diabolical apostles of hate" who "lied out of the pits of their dirty bellies." Both Communist-led unions were ousted. Panels were named today to investigate 10 other unions.

Burial mounds gain federal protection

McGregor, Iowa, Autumn

The Department of the Interior has announced that it will soon establish an Effigy Mounds National Monument about 15 miles from this small farming community in northeastern Iowa. Residents have long known and talked about the mysterious fortifications and burial mounds nearby. Anthropologists are of the belief that these earthen works were built in prehistoric times by American Indians. As a national monument, the rich archeological sites will be protected by the federal government from harm by careless visitors as well as looters.

TV firsts: Lone Ranger, Kukla, Quiz Kids

Hollywood, California

Now he is going to ride into our living rooms, that mysterious, masked stranger, as *The Lone Ranger* makes its debut on television along with *Quiz Kids, Original Amateur Hour, Captain Video and his Video Rangers, The Goldbergs,* and *Kukla, Fran and Ollie.* Milton Berle is the top-rated television entertainer and music lovers are hailing NBC for offering the Toscanini concerts. The Academy of Television Arts & Sciences handed out its first Emmy Awards at the Hollywood Athletic Club on January 25. Winners include a ventriloquist and her puppet, an adaptation of de Maupassant's *The Necklace* and *Pantomime Quiz Time.*

With Indian scout Tonto by his side, the Lone Ranger rides into the sunset and millions of American homes.

New York City, Jan. 25. Alger Hiss sentenced to five years in jail on two counts of perjury.

Washington, D.C., Feb. 7. U.S. grants formal recognition to South Vietnamese regime of Bao Dai (→ May 8).

Washington, D.C., Feb. 20. Supreme Court rules, in U.S. v. Rabinowitz, that police may search, without a warrant, a limited area under control of an arrested suspect.

Washington, D.C., Apr. 10. By refusing to review contempt convictions of two film writers, Supreme Court upholds right of congressional committees to force witnesses to reveal their political affiliations.

Washington, D.C., April. In a speech to Newspaper Publishers Association, former President Herbert Hoover says, "I suggest the United Nations should be reorganized without the Communist nations in it."

New York City, May 1. Gwendolyn Brooks becomes first Negro woman poet to receive Pulitzer Prize, for her collection *Annie Allen*.

New York City, May 1. Richard Rodgers, Oscar Hammerstein and Joshua Logan win Pulitzer Prize for *South Pacific*.

Washington, D.C., July 7. Government implements use of draft, to increase size of military.

Washington, D.C., July 17. President Truman comments, "If you tell Congress everything about the world situation, they get hysterical. If you tell them nothing, they go fishing."

New York City, Oct. 7. Yankees sweep Philadelphia Phillies in World Series.

Washington, D.C., Dec. 8. President Truman imposes ban on trade with People's Republic of China (→ Feb. 2, 1953).

Brussels, Belgium, Dec. 19. North Atlantic Council names General Dwight Eisenhower Supreme Commander for Allied Powers, Europe.

Cleveland, Dec. 24. Browns defeat Los Angeles Rams, 30-28, for N.F.L. title.

New York City. Cartoonist Herblock coins terms "McCarthyism."

New York City. *The Betty Crocker Cookbook* published.

McCarthy flaunts "subversives" list

Washington, D.C., Feb. 22

"I have here in my hand," announced the junior Senator from Wisconsin, "a list of 205 . . . names that were known to the Secretary of State as being members of the Communist Party and who nevertheless are still working and shaping policy in the State Department." The ladies of the Wheeling, West Virginia, Republican Women's Club were shocked. Joe McCarthy barreled ahead. "The bright young men who are born with silver spoons in their mouths," he observed, "are . . . the worst," and they are led by Secretary of State Dean Acheson, a "pompous diplomat in striped pants with a phony British accent."

This was the scene on February 9. McCarthy had been chosen by Republicans to speak on Lincoln's Birthday. No one had expected a scandal. Until then, McCarthy's activities in Congress had gained scant attention. He was a tireless worker for a bottled drink firm, earning the nickname "Pepsi-Cola Kid." He had called a Wisconsin foe a "pinko," but never went beyond the usual cold war rhetoric.

"I have here in my hand a list of 205 names . . .," Senator McCarthy claims.

But McCarthy always excelled at self-promotion. As a campaigner, he called himself "Tail-gunner Joe" though he spent most of his time pushing paper in the marines. Senate Majority Leader Scott Lucas says McCarthy's anti-Communist ploy has made him the "the greatest headline hunter in the world." A week after McCarthy's speech, neither the news media nor Congress could ignore him. Two days ago, the Senate heard McCarthy discuss 81 anonymous cases. Today, the Foreign Relations Committee was assigned to investigate. State Department security chief John Peurifoy says anyone implicated will be fired "by sundown" (→ July 20).

Coplon convicted of spying for Soviets

New York City, March 7

A weak smile crossed the face of former Justice Department employee Judith Coplon and she paled as she heard a jury report a guilty verdict today on charges that she spied for the Russians. Her friend, Valentin Gubitchev, still listed as a member of the Soviet Foreign Ministry, was also found guilty. According to the jury, the two conspired to pass secret documents to the Russians at the height of the cold war. Both face stiff jail terms, to be determined on Thursday.

The convictions seem to mirror a mood among some government officials, a feeling that subversion is threatening America's national security. Prosecuting attorney Irving Saypol said after the trial, "We in the government are not oblivious to the sinister attempts to undermine us and we shall continue aggressively and forthrightly to vindicate our laws and protect our country."

Lewis wins nationwide truce in coal fields

Washington, D.C., March 6

After 10 months of fruitless talks and brutal work stoppages, there is coal peace and John L. Lewis has won his United Mine Workers their first industry-wide contract. The miners have been out for a month. An injunction had worried Lewis, who bears the scars of heavy fines. But his miners insisted, "No contract, no work." A judge cleared away the injunction and President Truman gave in, ordering the mines seized and a panel set up to rule on "just compensation," which means a raise and better welfare benefits.

John L. Lewis makes case for his miners before a committee of the Senate.

TWA changes its name and expands

New York City, Apr. 27

The dynamic world of American aviation is continuing its postwar expansion. Transcontinental and Western Air, Inc. (TWA) changed its name today; the company will henceforth be called Trans World Airlines. And the firm has placed a major order for a fleet of long-range, four-engine pressurized Constellation planes with Lockheed. In another recent aviation development, an Avro turbojet transport plane made the New York-Toronto flight in one hour last week; but experts predict that civilian jet transportation will not be commercially viable before the end of the decade.

U.S. to help French battle Indochinese

Paris, May 8

After conferring with French officials, Secretary of State Dean Acheson announced today that the United States is prepared to help the French defeat a rising Communist insurgency in Indochina. The French military has occupied the old colonial possession since the end of World War II, but Communist forces under Ho Chi Minh have announced their determination to liberate Cambodia, Laos and Vietnam from the French Union. Acheson is expected to offer France up to $10 million in economic and military aid (→ Apr. 7, 1954).

"Woman I" (1950) by Willem de Kooning, Abstract Expressionist.

U.S. backs South Korea against North

Washington, D.C., June 30

The United States will give all necessary military and economic aid to the Republic of Korea in the face of the Communist attack from North Korea, the State Department announced today. President Truman is steadily escalating the American response to the Communist moves. When the North Koreans crossed the 38th parallel five days ago, Truman simply said the United States supported its South Korean allies. But three days ago, the President authorized Douglas MacArthur, commanding general of American Far East forces in Tokyo, to provide the Republic of Korea troops with American naval and air power. And today, MacArthur reported that the Communist forces are so powerful that only the introduction of American ground forces can stop them. Accordingly, Truman has given MacArthur the authority to commit American infantry units as soon as possible. American intelligence sources report the North Korean army numbers about 89,000 men, supported by Russian-made T-34 tanks. The South Koreans' army consists of less than 38,000 soldiers, most of them poorly trained and without anti-tank weapons of any sort.

Three days ago, Truman explained America's position: "To return to the rule of force in international affairs would have far-reaching effects. The United States will continue to uphold the law" (→ July 7).

MacArthur to direct Korean campaign

Washington, D.C., July 7

President Truman has appointed General Douglas MacArthur to head the United Nations Command in Korea. Acting on a U.N. Security Council request today that he appoint a senior American general to direct all U.N. forces, the President immediately turned to MacArthur, conquerer of the Japanese in World War II and now head of the American Far East Command. MacArthur is expected to name a field commander in Korea but will lead the overall war effort from his Tokyo headquarters (→ Sept. 15).

MacArthur says only American soldiers can stop powerful Communist forces.

U.S. troops, arriving in July, prepare a 75 mm recoiless gun on the front lines.

Panel calls McCarthy charges a "Big Lie"

Washington, D.C., July 20

A majority on Senator Millard Tydings' panel has concluded that Senator Joseph McCarthy's "charges of Communist infiltration of and influence upon the State Department are false."

"A fraud had been perpetrated upon the Senate," the report asserts. McCarthy's "nefarious" plot, say committee Democrats, utilized the "technique of the Big Lie" for personal and political gain. Indeed, most of McCarthy's evidence was covered earlier by four House committees, none of which found cause for alarm. The F.B.I. and the Civil Service Commission have already purged from federal payrolls 2,000 people suspected of being radicals.

But the tempest is far from over. Senator Henry Cabot Lodge's dissenting report calls the inquiry "superficial and inconclusive." McCarthy sees it as "a green light for Reds" and charges that F.B.I. evidence had been "raped and rifled." The senator is now pursuing the case of Far East scholar Owen Lattimore, whom he calls "the top Russian espionage agent" in the United States. But his wrath embraces the "whole group of twisted-thinking New Dealers (who) have led America near to ruin at home and abroad" (→ March 26, 1952).

U.S. troops swarm ashore at Inchon

U.S. infantrymen lay down fire and lob grenades as they overrun enemy lines.

American and South Korean troops search prisoners after the Inchon landing.

Guns of the North Carolina open fire on enemy installations at Inchon. Naval bombardment helps to make the difficult landing a little less so.

Korea, Sept. 15

The United Nations Command has announced that U.N. forces launched a major amphibious assault at Inchon this morning and operations are still being conducted. According to preliminary reports, the invasion was led by the United States First Marine Division and the Army's Seventh Infantry Division. The operation is being supported by an Allied naval armada of more than 200 ships and dozens of planes.

General Douglas MacArthur, chief architect of the daring plan, has command of the operation and is directing the invasion from the Seventh Fleet flagship, the Mount McKinley. The huge water-borne invasion has been expected for some time; the location comes as a surprise to many veteran military analysts. Because of its low tides and many mud flats, the harbor of Inchon is considered by amphibious warfare experts to be a nightmare. Others say that is precisely why MacArthur chose Inchon. His invasion forces achieved complete surprise and have suffered only minor casualties. While the objectives of the invasion of this port city on South Korea's west coast have not been announced, observers see the assault as designed to relieve the pressure on American units besieged to the south inside the "Pusan perimeter." MacArthur's men are likely to push eastward to the capital city of Seoul (→ 26).

Truman seizes rails as wartime action

Washington, D.C., Aug. 25

President Truman ordered the government to seize the railroads today to avert a strike. With the nation involved in the Korean conflict, it is feared that a work stoppage could threaten the stability of the country and the President is not willing to risk that. The rail union was offered an 18-cent per hour raise for yardmen, but management would not extend that increase to trainmen. In a show of solidarity, the union moved to strike, realizing that Truman might seize the lines as he did briefly in 1946 and again in 1948. The army will operate the rails until a settlement is reached.

62,000 reservists called up by army

Washington, D.C., Aug. 4

With the war in Korea heating up, President Truman today ordered the army to ready 62,000 reserves for military duty. The troop alert comes as part of the United Nations agreement to stop the Soviet-backed attack by North Korea against the South. Some see the conflict as a way to bolster the world organization's power. Political columnist Thomas Stokes has written, "Korea can be the beginning of a new era under a strengthened U.N., in which our leadership can be notable."

American invasion force liberates Seoul

Korea, Sept. 26

General Douglas MacArthur announced today that United Nations forces had recaptured Seoul. Spearheaded by elements of the United States First Marine Division and the Army's Seventh Infantry Division, the U.N. troops launched the attack on the capital four days ago.

The army troops, reinforced by the South Korean 17th Division, struck Seoul from the south, while the marines hit the North Koreans from the west. According to reliable estimates, the South Korean capital was occupied by 8,000 North Korean soldiers. American military sources say the Communist defense was formidable, with many reports of massed suicidal attacks against the advancing American forces. American losses have apparently been high. One marine company of 206 men suffered 176 casualties. On the plus side, Lieutenant Harry L. McCaffrey of the army's 32nd Infantry Regiment and his men killed 500 enemy soldiers, destroyed five tanks and captured 40 trucks. McCaffrey has been awarded the Silver Star. The struggle for Seoul has been ferocious. A British war correspondent, Reginald Thompson, said, "Few people can have suffered so terrible a liberation" (→ Oct. 20).

First jet dogfight, and the U.S. wins it

Korea, Nov. 8

In history's first all-jet dogfight, Lieutenant Russell J. Brown of the United States Air Force shot down a Russian-built North Korean MIG-15 fighter today. Brown, piloting an F-80 Shooting Star, was flying escort for 70 B-29 bombers whose mission was to destroy bridges at Sinuiju, just south of the Yalu River on the North Korean-Chinese border. After evading heavy anti-aircraft fire, Lieutenant Brown and the other escorts were attacked by many MIG's at 18,000 feet. Air Force spokesmen report that all the American aircraft made it back to their bases (→ Dec. 5).

Security legislation to curb Communists

Washington, D.C., Sept. 23

Congress voted today to override President Truman's veto of the Internal Security Act. The law requires all Communist groups to report the identity of their officers and how they spend funds. It also bars any Communists from defense jobs. A Subversive Activities Board will enforce the law. Truman feels the act is unconstitutional and that it would drive Communists underground, thus hindering steps to contain them. Both houses of Congress collected the two-thirds majorities to override (→ Jan. 21, 1953).

Chinese flood across Yalu into Korea

Korea, Dec. 5

The massive Chinese military intervention in North Korea 10 days ago has broken the back of the advance by United Nations forces toward the Yalu River. Both the American and South Korean armies have suffered extremely heavy casualties and are engaged in a rapid but organized retreat. The American Eighth Army, the major fighting force in North Korea, has completely withdrawn to sites south of the 38th parallel. The other main American force, the 10th Corps, is engaged in a fighting retreat from northeastern Korea, near the Chosin Reservoir, toward the port city of Hungnam. Forward units of this battered group, mainly marines, and some army infantrymen, are being evacuated aboard a flotilla of navy ships standing by in the Hungnam harbor.

The Chinese Communists have been threatening to intervene in the war ever since September, when General Douglas MacArthur announced that he planned to carry the war to the Yalu River. The Chinese made good their warning on November 26, when an estimated 550,000 Chinese soldiers carried out a series of frontal attacks on American positions.

Last month, General MacArthur seemed on the verge of a brilliant military victory. With a degree of ironic understatement, he has acknowledged that "we face an entirely new war" (→ March 15, 1951).

U.S. troops pass through the carnage wrought by the Chinese as they retreat.

American soldiers surrender to members of the Chinese Communist Army.

North Korean capital seized by U.N. force

Korea, Oct. 20

With American troops in the lead, United Nations forces captured Pyongyang today. The United States Eighth Army under General Walton Walker crossed the 38th parallel into North Korea 11 days ago under direct orders from President Truman and the Joint Chiefs of Staff. Military observers here say that with South Korea cleared of Communist troops, the war is entering a new phase. Whereas the Americans entered the war in June only to defend their South Korean ally, the strategy is now to conquer North Korea and unify the two Koreas under a pro-Western government. General Douglas MacArthur reportedly informed the President of this plan on September 29. And when the General and the President met at Wake Island last week to discuss American war goals, Truman told reporters, "There is complete unity in the aims and conduct of our foreign policy." According to General MacArthur, the U.N. forces can conquer North Korea by Thanksgiving, and most American troops can be withdrawn to Japan by Christmas. When he was asked by Truman about the chances of Chinese or Soviet intervention in the war, MacArthur simply replied, "Very little" (→ Nov. 8)

From its encircled beachhead at Hungnam, the United States 10th Corps is successfully evacuated. The orderliness of the operation saved many lives.

Faulkner accepts Nobel, warns of timidity

From William Faulkner, a warning.

Oslo, Norway, Dec. 10

For years he toiled in obscurity, his books out of print, his bills paid by Hollywood hackwork. But hard times are over for William Faulkner, this year's winner of the Nobel Prize for Literature. The dapper 53-year-old Mississippian delivered his acceptance speech here today and the world is likely to sit up and take notice. Referring to the atomic bomb and its impact on the modern mind, Faulkner accused younger writers of giving into fear and evading the eternal "problems of the spirit." He lamented that to some there is only the question: "When will I be blown up?"

Will TV create a "nation of morons?"

Boston

"If the television craze continues with the present level of programs," says Daniel Marsh, president of Boston University, "we are destined to have a nation of morons." A national survey shows children watch TV 27 hours a week, only 45 minutes less than their hours in school. New shows – no relation to the Marsh comments – include *Your Show of Shows, The Garry Moore Show, The Kate Smith Hour, The Steve Allen Show, What's My Line?, The George Burns and Gracie Allen Show* and *Truth or Consequences*. In March, RCA exhibited a tube to usher in the color era.

Garry Moore in a moronic moment.

Kids dig Sugar Pops and Smokey Bear

United States

How do you entertain kids today? Buy them toy guns, spurs, boots and other Hopalong Cassidy items. Serve them Sugar Pops for breakfast and take them to a lecture by Smokey Bear. Explain how nifty new inventions work: the Otis elevator with self-opening doors, phototransistors and Sony tape recorders. Teach the youngsters how to square dance or even do the mambo. Let them watch a Cinerama movie. Or take them out in search of Unidentified Flying Objects.

Forget about cash, join Diners Club

New York City, February

Frank MacNamara, head of a small commercial finance firm, was embarassed the other night. So he decided to launch a business venture. He had run up a formidable bill entertaining guests at a restaurant here before realizing his wallet was back home. This is never going to happen again, he vowed. MacNamara and a friend, Ralph Schneider, now offer a Diners Club card, allowing its 200 bearers to charge food and revelry. Made of cardboard, it lists the 28 participating establishments on the back.

Minneapolis Lakers win basketball title

Minneapolis, Minnesota

The nation's leading basketball teams finally got together in 1947 in one league – except for the Globetrotters – and this year, when the skirmishing ended, the Minneapolis Lakers were at the top of the heap. They won the championship of the National Basketball Association, an amalgam of the American Basketball Association and the National Basketball League. In the end, five teams fell by the wayside and 17 survived. George Mikan was outstanding for the Lakers as they defeated Syracuse for the title.

Ralph Bunche wins Nobel Peace Prize

Oslo, Norway, Dec. 10

The Nobel Peace Prize went to United Nations diplomat Ralph J. Bunche today for his work in mediating the conflict between Jews and Arabs in the Holy Land. Dr. Bunche is the first Negro American to win the Nobel Peace Prize. The grandson of a slave, the 46-year old Bunche graduated from the University of California and received his M.A. and Ph.D from Harvard. In 1946, after two years at the State Department, he joined the U.N. and became chief negotiator of its Palestine Commission in 1948.

The Fords – Benson, Henry II and William – with one of their models. The company thrives as Americans take to the road in record numbers.

Celeste Holm, Bette Davis and Hugh Marlowe take a ride in the film "All About Eve," which has won the Oscar for best picture of the year.

Truman declares state of emergency

Washington, D.C., Dec. 16

Because of deepening strain on both military and economic resources brought about by the Korean War, President Truman has declared a state of national emergency. In a broadcast to the American people last night, Truman said that he needed extraordinary executive powers to overcome the great crises now facing the country. He promised that the United States would continue to fight to preserve the ideals of the United Nations – "the principles of freedom and justice," and to build up our armed forces and those of our allies. The President also said that "we will expand our economy and keep it on an even keel." He closed his dramatic speech with a somber request that every citizen "put aside his personal interests for the good of the country."

Analysts say Truman's emergency proclamation is a masterpiece of political strategy. It allows him the temporary authority to build up the nation's defense capabilities gradually rather than alarming both its allies and enemies by ordering a full-scale mobilization effort. The declaration also enables him to impose politically unpopular tax increases, wage and price controls and resource allocation measures.

Two Puerto Ricans try to kill Truman

Washington, D.C., Nov. 1

An attempt by two Puerto Rican nationalists to kill President Truman today ended in a gun battle in which one of the gunmen and a police officer were killed. The gunfight took place outside Blair House, where the President is staying during White House renovations. The second gunman was arrested. This week saw riots in Puerto Rico over whether the territory should be free. Truman supports a move for independence. But the territory is subordinate to the U.S. in offshore matters (→ July 24, 1952).

"Lonely Crowd"

United States

Do Americans today differ from their predecessors? Yes, say social scientists David Riesman, Nathan Glazer, and Reuel Denney, whose acerbic study, *The Lonely Crowd*, claims a new species of American is afoot. An urbanite, he tends to be "other-directed," that is, he apes the behavior of others, from friends and acquaintances to "those with whom he is indirectly acquainted," chiefly through the mass media. The result? Conformity. For although "all people want and need to be liked by some of the people some of the time, it is only the modern other-directed types who make this their chief source of direction and chief area of sensitivity."

It's Charlie Brown, small-fry everyman

United States, Oct. 2

A new daily comic strip made its debut today. Charles Schulz's *Peanuts* is the work of a young cartoonist who wouldn't take no for an answer. Under the title *Li'l Folks*, the strip was rejected by a half-dozen major newspaper syndicates. But Schulz persisted, much like his central character, Charlie Brown, a hapless young everyman who waxes philosophical at each new defeat and who happens to share with his creator a first name, a barber father and a basic mistrust of adults.

Census: 150 million

Washington, D.C.

The first census since World War II shows the American population at 150.6 million people. Urbanites make up 64 percent of that figure while there are only 5.4 million family farmers. The nation's newest war effort, in Korea, has decreased the number of unemployed to fewer than two million, and on another economic note, the average weekly wage in industry has hit a new high of $60.53. Illiteracy has dropped to 3.2 percent, a new low, but a study at the University of Michigan shows that half the population does not read books anyway. Germans and Italians are the largest immigrant groups, and Arizona has the largest Indian population.

Faces from the front lines in the Far East

Another generation shares the conclusion of General William Tecumseh Sherman after the Civil War: "I am tired and sick of war. War is hell."

Washington, D.C., Jan. 15. President Truman proposes $71.5 billion budget, over half of it to go to the military (→Jan. 21, 1952).

Washington, D.C., Jan. 26. Economic Stabilization Administration freezes most wages and mandates price ceilings for goods and services.

Washington, D.C., Apr. 16. In recalling General MacArthur, President Truman states, "In the simplest terms, what we are doing in Korea is this: We are trying to prevent a third world war" (→19).

Chapel Hill, North Carolina, Apr. 24. Univ. of North Carolina admits first Negro student.

Washington, D.C., Apr. 25. Servicemen's Indemnity Act signed into law by President Truman, providing sum of $10,000 to be paid to survivors of servicemen killed since beginning of Korean conflict, or any who die in future.

Rochester, New York, April. Rochester defeats New York Knicks, four games to two, in N.B.A. championship.

New York City, May. Pulitzer Prize awarded to Carl Sandburg for *Complete Poems.*

New Jersey, June 14. A human birth is shown on television for first time.

Illinois, July 12. Race riot, which erupted when a Negro family attempted to move into Chicago suburb of Cicero, prompts Governor Stevenson to call out National Guard.

Washington, D.C., Aug. 1. Tariff concessions to Eastern-bloc nations canceled by President Truman.

Korea, Sept. 3. Major Louis L. Sebille wins first Medal of Honor for air combat against ground artillery.

New York City, Oct. 10. Yanks defeat Giants in World Series, four games to two.

Englewood, New Jersey, Oct. 10. Transcontinental dial telephone service inaugurated.

Los Angeles, Dec. 23. Rams defeat Cleveland Browns 24-17 in N.F.L. championship game.

Hollywood, Calif. Films this year include *A Streetcar Named Desire, The African Queen* and *A Place in the Sun.*

New York City. *From Here to Eternity,* by James Jones, published.

Back on offensive, U.S. retakes Seoul

For the first time in military history, helicopters are used to ferry troops.

A tank of the U.S. First Division rumbles through devastated Chunchon.

Korea, March 15

American military authorities announced today that Seoul has been recaptured from Chinese and North Korean troops. The battle for Seoul began last week when General Matthew B. Ridgway, Eighth Army commander, launched Operation Ripper. His forces included nine divisions: six American and three South Korean. The offensive opened with a massive American artillery barrage and an infantry assault by the 25th Division against enemy positions on the Han River, 20 miles east of Seoul. After three days of bitter fighting, the Chinese began to withdraw. American military commanders report that their advance to Seoul was severely hampered by torrential spring rains and mudslides from hills surrounding the capital city. On most days, the Americans could advance only a mile or so. When they finally arrived in Seoul today, virtually all the Chinese and North Korean soldiers had been pulled out.

Army officials believe that the Communist evacuation is perhaps a ploy designed to draw the United Nations forces farther north, toward the 38th parallel, where the Chinese and North Korean troops can then launch a counterattack. But most military experts insist that Operation Ripper has been an unqualified success and that U.N. forces, with their superior aerial reconnaissance capabilities, will not be drawn into such a trap.

The capture of Seoul marks the fourth time in nine months the city has changed hands (→Apr. 11).

Rosenbergs are sentenced to death for selling atomic secrets

New York City, Apr. 5

Julius and Ethel Rosenberg, convicted of espionage last week, were sentenced today to die in the electric chair for revealing secrets of atomic weapons to the Soviet government. The law under which they were sentenced allows for the death penalty only if the act is committed during wartime, and though the Soviet Union was America's ally at the time, the Rosenberg crime occurred around June of 1944. Explaining his sentence today, Judge Irving R. Kaufman said, "The nature of Russian terrorism is now self-evident. Idealism as a rationale dissolves." Julius, who is 32, and Ethel, 35, are the parents of two young sons, and have stoically maintained their innocence during the proceedings, which began on March 6. Emanuel Bloch, who represented the Rosenbergs, described them today as "victims of political hysteria" and attributed their sentence to "extraneous political considerations having no legitimate or legal connection with the crime charged against them."

Bloch announced that he will file for an appeal with the Second Circuit Court and then with the United States Supreme Court should that fail. This will serve to stay the executions scheduled for May 21 at Sing Sing prison. Judge Kaufman, who during the trial often directly questioned Julius as to his Communist involvement, described the Rosenbergs as agents of a hostile totalitarian nation (→June 19, 1953).

Sugar Ray captures middleweight title

New York City, Feb. 14

Has there ever been a boxer so smooth and clever as Sugar Ray Robinson? Most experts say no. Their opinion was reinforced tonight as Robinson, for five years the world welterweight champion, added the middleweight title to his list by finishing off Jake LaMotta in the 13th round. Sugar Ray, who was born Walker Smith, has reigned as welterweight champion since he outfought Tom Bell in 15 rounds in 1946. With no more welterweights to conquer, he opted to turn his boxing skills to the heavier division and pecked away at Jake LaMotta's brutal style.

22nd Amendment limits presidency

Washington, D.C., Feb. 26

The 22nd Amendment was ratified today, placing a limit of two elected terms on the presidency, with succession from the vice presidency with two years of service to count as a full term. Nevada was the 36th state to ratify, fulfilling the requirement of three-quarters of all states for passage. There has been no limit on how many terms a president could serve. Nobody before Franklin Roosevelt served more than two full terms. Foes of the reform say it cuts presidential accountability. But most say it appropriately limits presidential power.

Nevada atomic test

Las Vegas, Nevada, Feb. 6

The fifth and final detonation in a series of atomic bomb tests was carried out here today under the auspices of the Atomic Energy Commission. Shock waves from the explosion were felt in this resort town 45 miles from the test site, and the flash is reported to have been visible in San Francisco. Radioactive particles, resulting from earlier tests, have been found in snowfalls as far east as Rochester, New York, but the Atomic Energy Commission says the levels of radiation are far too low to have harmful effects (→ Oct. 10, 1963).

Truman fires a recalcitrant MacArthur

The buck stops here, not in Korea.

Washington, D.C., Apr. 11

In a momentous decision that came as a shock yet was not really that unexpected, the chief executive today formally relieved General of the Army Douglas MacArthur, the senior general in the United States Army, of all commands, including that of United Nations commander in Korea.

From the outset of the Korean War, personal and philosophical differences have plagued the Truman-MacArthur relationship. In July of last year, MacArthur conferred with President Chiang Kaishek of Nationalist China without Truman's permission. A month later, the general sent the influential Veterans of Foreign Wars a scathing indictment of Truman's Formosa policy. In his message, the

general blasted the President for supporting the argument of "those who advocate appeasement and defeatism in the Pacific." When the Chinese intervened in Korea, MacArthur lambasted the administration for not letting him bomb bases inside Chinese territory. And when Truman recently announced that a cease-fire was being considered, MacArthur said that if favorable terms for the United States couldn't be achieved, he would back the bombing of Chinese bases. Six days ago, Congressman Joseph Martin read before the House of Representatives a letter the general wrote him attacking Truman's policy of a limited Korean war. Suggesting

a full-scale war against China and possibly the Soviet Union, he added that "... we must win. There is no substitute for victory."

When Truman received word of the letter, he conferred with the Joint Chiefs of Staff, who unanimously backed the President's decision to relieve MacArthur. In his announcement, Truman explained that "If I allowed him to defy the civil authority, I myself would be violating my oath to uphold and defend the Constitution."

President Truman has appointed Lieutenant General Matthew B. Ridgway to succeed MacArthur as commanding general of the United Nations forces in Korea (→ 16).

General Douglas MacArthur inspects the French battalion of the United Nations forces near the town of Wonju before beginning his journey home.

MacArthur: "Old soldiers never die; they just fade away"

Washington, D.C., Apr. 19

In an emotional address before both houses of Congress that was broadcast nationally on radio and television, General of the Army Douglas MacArthur gave his official farewell today to the American people. Fired last week by President Truman, the old warrior recounted his 52 years of military service in war and peace. Speaking eloquently and with intense sentiment, he closed his historic speech with a quote from a traditional British barrack-room ballad. "Old soldiers never die," he said, "they just fade away" (→Nov. 27).

MacArthur, hero of the Asia campaigns, is cheered in New York on April 20.

U.S. detonates H-bomb

Marshall Islands, May 12

The explosive equivalent of several million tons of TNT was released here today on the tiny atoll of Eniwetok as scientists of the Atomic Energy Commission detonated the world's first thermonuclear device – the H-bomb.

While most of the details concerning the bomb's design and construction are secret, scientists have long known of the tremendous energy that could be released if the nuclei of heavy hydrogen, deuterium, could be made to combine. This, after all, is the method by which many stars, including the sun, create their heat. But to make the nuclei react, temperatures of several million degrees would be required. The only way of achieving such heat on earth is by nuclear fission, using an atomic bomb of the kind dropped on Hiroshima as a trigger for the fusion bomb.

Much debate has surrounded the project; those opposing it included most of the members of the General Advisory Committee of the A.E.C. But news that the Russians had begun to test their own atomic weapons late in 1949 tipped the scale, and on January 31, 1950, President Truman approved the project.

Lady Senator, a quiet voice of conscience

Washington, D.C., August

Margaret Chase Smith has been tactful in opposing McCarthyism since her "Declaration of Conscience" last year. "I don't want to see the Republican Party," she had announced, "ride to victory on the four horsemen of calumny – fear, ignorance, bigotry and smear." Her honesty got her dropped from two G.O.P. posts and isolated in her own party. Smith, one of Washington's hardest workers, now speaks out through her votes. Liberals like her, but as the first woman elected to the Senate, she still contends with the patriarchs who have dubbed her "the girl scout with a mission."

Margaret Chase Smith of Maine.

UNIVAC, electronic computer, unveiled

Philadelphia, June 14

A powerful new electronic digital computer was unveiled here today by Remington Rand. It is UNIVAC (Universal Automatic Computer), the first such machine to be put on the market. The first customer will be the Census Bureau. The computer was designed by the physicist John W. Mauchly and the electronics engineer J. Presper Eckert, who developed the first large electronic digital computer, ENIAC, in 1945. UNIVAC includes revolutionary new features such as mercury delay lines for memory and magnetic tape for input instead of the punched paper used in the past.

The United States is largest U.S. ship

Newport News, Va., June 23

Barely 15 months after its keel was laid, the United States was "floated out" today after a simple ceremony that was in marked contrast with the elaborate rituals that usually accompany launchings. Designed by William Francis Gibbs, the nation's leading marine architect, the ship was built at a cost of $77 million, three-quarters of which was paid by the government. At 990 feet, it is America's largest ship, and only 40 feet shorter than the Queen Elizabeth. After its fitting-out and sea trials, the United States is scheduled to sail on its maiden voyage next year, when it is hoped that it will capture the famed Blue Riband for the fastest trans-Atlantic crossing.

From bed vibrator to power steering

Detroit, Michigan

This is the year to start taking it easy. Buy yourself a Chrysler with power steering and cruise the new New Jersey Turnpike. Check into a hotel and nap on a vibrating mattress with foam pillows. When you get home, open the garage door with a push-button control in your car. Next, take a television course from Marquette University, collect trading stamps, try a Dacron suit (you won't like it). Quit worrying over cavities: chew sugarless gum. Don't let Dennis the Menace's antics upset you. And if your ulcer is acting up, remember this: research findings at Duke University show that burned toast, strong tea and milk of magnesia are antidotes for poisons of an unknown nature.

Senator Kefauver airs U.S. crime problem

New York City, March 13

A reputed underworld "boss" upstaged the Senate Crime Investigating Committee's chairman, Estes Kefauver, today when Frank Costello took the stand and became television's first "headless star." After the bashful Costello protested that shots of his face jeopardized his privacy, the cameras trained on his hands, arms and chest instead. The effect mesmerized crowds gathered around the 2.5 million sets tuned in to the spectacle as the close-ups of his nervous hands conveyed intense emotion. Senator Kefauver is probing alleged links between the country's racketeers, its businessmen and public officials.

The heat is on, as the Kefauver crime committee hearings are televised.

The end may be in sight in Korea. As U.S. Marines fire rockets at Communist forces, the enemy's resistance is not nearly so stiff as had been expected.

Millions love Lucy, Roy and color TV

That zany redhead and sidekicks.

New York City

I Love Lucy, half an hour of fun with the Queen of Comedy, alias Lucille Ball, and her real-life hus- band, Desi Arnaz, is an instant suc- cess. Other television premieres in- clude *The Roy Rogers Show*, *The Jack LaLanne Show* for fitness fans and the soap opera *Search for To- morrow*. At this year's Emmy Awards, Imogene Coca and Sid Caesar took best acting awards and their program, *Your Show of Shows*, won the best variety show award. On May 2, the first live coast-to- coast hook-up was achieved, and the Radio Corporation of America is now broadcasting color programs from the Empire State Building. RCA has announced that it plans to give CBS the tri-color television tube for research to iron out current color problems. Last year, there were 3.8 million TV households (9 percent of all the homes in the country) and the number is con- stantly increasing.

U.S. joins alliance for Pacific defense

San Francisco, Sept. 1

With the signing here today of the Tripartite Security Treaty, gen- erally known as the ANZUS pact, the United States has joined Aus- tralia and New Zealand in a mutu- al security agreement designed, at least in part, to counter the threat of Communist expansion in South- east Asia. The treaty also sets up a Pacific Council composed of the three foreign ministers to coordi- nate mutual defense plans.

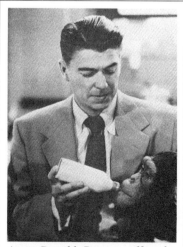

Actor Ronald Reagan offers his scene-stealing friend a snack in spoof called "Bedtime for Bozo."

Pact gives Japan sovereignty again

San Francisco, Sept. 8

The restoration of full sovereign rights has been accorded Japan un- der terms of a treaty signed here today by the United States and 47 other nations. At the same time, a mutual security agreement has been signed by the United States and Ja- pan; in return for military bases, U.S. forces will assume responsibil- ity for the defense of Japan, whose constitution forbids it to maintain armed forces (→ Feb. 27, 1952).

"Catcher in Rye"

New York City

Young Americans have found a spokesman in 16-year-old Holden Caulfield, narrator of *The Catcher in the Rye*, the first novel by J.D. Salinger, 32, and a best-seller. Hol- den – tall, skinny, hapless and screamingly funny – deplores the "phonys" who rule the roost at Pencey, the high-tone prep school where he gets the boot. On impulse, he flees to New York City and checks into a flophouse. Holden has become a symbol of plain-talk- ing to teens, but some bluenoses are crying "foul language." How would Holden respond? Probably with his pet expression: "That kills me."

Truce is forged in Korea

Troops of the U.S. 25th Infantry Division cross a narrow footbridge in Korea, as negotiators finally hammer out a truce in what was called "a police action."

Panmunjom, Korea, Nov. 27

After five months of haggling, United Nations and North Korean negotiators have finally taken the first concrete step that will, they hope, lead to the end of the war. After today's meeting, both sides announced that they will observe a truce along the entire battle line that stretches across the width of the Korean peninsula. If the nego- tiators fail to settle the other two major remaining items on their ar- mistice agenda – specific provi- sions for enforcing the armistice, and the exchange of prisoners of war – it will expire in one month, on December 27.

Because of the inflexible posi- tions taken on these two critical points by both the Americans and the North Koreans, the establish- ment of a final peace may prove exceedingly difficult. One of the negotiators, General Matthew B. Ridgway, the American comman- der of U.N. forces, has stated: "We have much to gain by standing firm. We have everything to lose through concession. With all my conscience, I urge we stand firm." With Amer- ican casualties exceeding 22,000 since talks opened in July, Ridg- way's tough stand may become im- possible to maintain, either militar- ily or politically (→ Dec. 5, 1952).

FROM OUT OF SPACE.... A WARNING AND AN ULTIMATUM!

THE DAY THE EARTH STOOD STILL

As science and technology make giant strides, so does science fiction.

New York City, Jan. 29. Herman Wouk wins Pulitzer Prize for *The Caine Mutiny*.

Washington, D.C., Feb. 27. Treaty concluded with Japan, allowing United States military bases on Japanese territory.

Washington, D.C., Apr. 2. Veteran diplomat George F. Kennan appointed U.S. ambassador to Soviet Union.

Minneapolis, Apr. 15. Lakers defeat New York Knicks in N.B.A. championship, four games to three.

Azores, Apr. 26. Destroyer Hobson and aircraft carrier Wasp collide in Atlantic, killing 176; Hobson sinks.

New York City, June 25. Journalist Edward R. Murrow inaugurates television news show *See It Now*.

London, July 7. Superliner United States wins Blue Riband.

Washington, D.C., July 24. Death sentence for Oscar Collazo, who tried to assassinate President Truman, commuted by President to life imprisonment.

New York City, July 31. General Douglas MacArthur is appointed chairman of board of Remington Rand Company.

Brooklyn, N.Y., Oct. 7. Yankees defeat Dodgers in World Series, four games to three.

Washington, D.C., Nov. 25. George Meany elected president of A.F.L., following death of William Green on Nov. 21.

Cleveland, Dec. 28. Detroit Lions defeat Browns, 17-7, for N.F.L. title.

Hollywood, Calif.. *The Jackie Gleason Show*, starring Gleason and Art Carney, has its premiere on television.

Washington, D.C. Republican vice presidential candidate Richard Nixon says, "Adlai [Stevenson] is the appeaser ... who got his Ph.D. from Dean Acheson's College of Cowardly Communist Containment."

Springfield, Ill. Democratic presidential candidate Adlai Stevenson says, "Eggheads of the world unite. You have nothing to lose but your yolks!"

New York City. John Steinbeck's *East of Eden* issued.

New York City. Ralph Ellison publishes *The Invisible Man*.

Truman's budget allots 75% for arms

Washington, D.C., Jan. 21

Calling it a weapon in the fight for security and peace, President Truman has submitted to Congress the biggest peacetime budget in the nation's history. More than 75 percent of it is earmarked for major national security programs, with some $6 million for the expansion of atomic energy programs. The President's new budget would produce a deficit of more than $14 billion, but he says that this ought to be trimmed by means of higher taxes. Republicans oppose raising taxes and charge that Truman thinks spending solves all problems. The President calls Congress's tactic of percentage cuts unconstitutional.

Mad about comics

New York City, November

An entire generation of American children has gone Mad! *Mad Comics* No. 1 went on sale early this month and is a runaway hit. Published by E.C. Comics and edited by Harvey Kurtzman, *Mad* is the first humor comic book to parody every aspect of American culture, including comics, movies, television magazines and advertising. It follows on the heels of other successful E.C. titles, such as *Tales From the Crypt*, *The Vault of Horror*, *The Crypt of Terror*, *Weird Science*, *Weird Fantasy*, *Two-Fisted Tales*, *Incredible Science Fiction* and *Frontline Combat*.

Dinner by the TV

United States

It's the year to get off your duff! Dive into the Vinylite swimming pool, go bowling at an alley with automatic pinsetters, cut the grass with a motorized lawnmower. Do some flying saucer watching, race a hot rod, lead a panty raid, spin the propeller on top of your beanie and make like a whirlybird. Take up parachuting and break this year's record of 124 jumps in a day. Donate to a telethon, study psycholinguistics, down some No-Cal ginger ale and try to chew a Swanson TV dinner energetically – while watching television, of course.

McCarthy files libel suit

Senate colleagues have reacted bitterly to McCarthy's tactics and attacks.

Washington, D.C., March 26

Joseph McCarthy, for two years the storm center of the Senate, will take his tempest into court. Today, he filed a $2 million libel suit against Connecticut Democrat Senator William Benton. Since September, Benton has sought McCarthy's expulsion from the Senate. The Red-baiting Wisconsin lawmaker, he charges, accepted an illegal gratuity from the Lustron Corporation and perjured himself by telling Congress he implicated 57, not 205, officials in the February 1950 speech that set off a wave of national hysteria. Last week, Benton urged the Senate to vote on the issue, calling McCarthy's tactics Hitleresque.

The accused seems to revel in the martyr's role. His suit maintains that he "has been libeled, defamed, held up to ridicule, disgrace, scorn and obloquy and has suffered injury to his good name and reputation."

McCarthy has achieved his reputation with such feats as persuading the Washington police to set up a unit "to investigate links between homosexuality and communism." Last week, he called fellow Republican Newbold Morris "either the biggest dupe or the biggest dope in all history." Morris denounced the inquiries of McCarthy and the Senate Permanent Investigations subcommittee as "mental brutality" and "ghastly distortion." "In the last three years," he roared, "you have created an atmosphere so vile the people have lost confidence in their government" (→ Aug. 31, 1954)

April 15. *The Boeing YB-52 bomber on its maiden flight. Dubbed the Stratofortress, the Air Force's newest plane has eight engines and a 185-foot wing span that give it the capability of striking deep into enemy territory.*

High court rules steel seizure illegal

Washington, D.C., June 2

The Supreme Court dealt the nation's steelworkers a blow today, ruling that President Truman overstepped his powers when he nationalized the mills April 8. As Justice Hugo Black read the decision, pickets gathered at mills across the country. Truman intended to give the United Steelworkers a 26.5-cent wage and benefit increase and a union shop, as proposed by the Wage Stabilization Board. This, the court ruled, infringed on the right of Congress to make law. Three dissenting justices pointed to the President's war powers, arguing that he moved "only to save the situation until Congress could act."

U.S. first: A year without a lynching

Tuskegee, Alabama, Dec. 30

According to a report from the Tuskegee Institute, this has been the first year, since officials began keeping records 71 years ago, that no lynchings have been reported. Interestingly, the racially motivated violence seems to have declined without the benefit of Congress passing any of the anti-lynching legislation brought before it during this period. The absence of lynchings seems to parallel a recent decline in the membership and popularity experienced by the white supremacist Ku Klux Klan, an organization that has been responsible for many of the lynchings since the end of the Civil War.

Immigration quotas are set by Congress

Washington, D.C., June 27

The United States Senate today passed the Immigration and Naturalization Act over President Truman's veto, restricting and restructuring immigration into the country. The legislation establishes quotas based on national origin percentages as of 1920. Total immigration has been limited to 154,657 a year, and visas will be allotted with priority given to foreigners with "high education, technical training, specialized experience, or exceptional ability." In vetoing the bill, Truman said it would "intensify the repressive and inhumane aspects of our immigration procedures." The bill passed two days later.

U.S. stockholders number 6.5 million

Washington, D.C., June 30

More than 6.5 million Americans own a share in the nation's business, 76 percent of them earning less than $10,000 a year after taxes. These figures "clearly show that vast numbers of people have a direct stake in the ownership of business enterprise," according to the Brookings Institution, which conducted the study for the New York Stock Exchange. The 135-page survey released today shows that 28 percent bought stocks in the hope that they would go up, 22 percent for dividends, 10 percent because their brokers called them sound, and 8 percent because a family member worked for the company.

Republicans like Ike for presidency ...

He's commanding yet amiable, so what's not to like about Ike?

Chicago, July 11

It's Eisenhower and Nixon. The general won the Republican nomination for President on the first ballot today, and the senator got the vice presidential nomination by acclamation. Thus end the hopes of Ohio Senator Robert A. Taft, unsuccessful for the third time. As the second roll-call of the first ballot began, General Eisenhower was still nine votes short, with favorite sons such as California's Governor Earl Warren holding out in hopes that the general would fade in later rounds. But Minnesota's Harold Stassen delegation switched, providing the winning margin (→ 26).

Korea War G.I. Bill

Washington, D.C., July 16

President Truman signed into law today the Veterans' Readjustment Assistance Act, known as the G.I. Bill of Rights. The legislation will help veterans of the Korean War in much the same way as the G.I. bill served World War II vets. It provides those returning from military service in Korea with education benefits, housing, loan and business guarantees and other kinds of financial aid. The World War II program sent millions of veterans to college and was seen as a great success. Truman and an overwhelming majority in Congress expect this act will prove equally fruitful.

Bob Mathias stars

Helsinki, Finland, Aug 3

Led by star decathlete Bob Mathias, the United States has claimed victory in the 1952 Olympics, coming from behind to edge out the Soviet Union. Mathias, the one-man track team, pulled a muscle and still broke his own world record in the decathlon. Victories in the shot put, 400-meters, 100-meter hurdles, javelin and discus gave him a point total of 7,887. At 21, he says he may retire from the sport. Lifting the Americans past the Soviets on the last day were middleweight boxer Floyd Patterson and the U.S. basketball team, which defeated the Russians 36-25 for the gold.

...while Democrats go madly for Adlai

Stevenson, an admired intellectual.

Chicago, July 26

In a boisterous session that lasted past 2:30 a.m., the Democratic Party has nominated Illinois Governor Adlai E. Stevenson to run for President. After resting, they selected Alabama Senator John J. Sparkman as his running mate. Saluting Stevenson's victory, President Truman told the cheering throng, "I am going to take my coat off and help him win." Governor Stevenson told the delegates, "I have asked the merciful Father to let this cup pass from me. But, from such dread responsibility one does not shrink in fear" (→ Nov. 5).

It is the envy of every American child. This top-of-the-line Schwinn comes equipped with whitewalls, light and, for that extra flair, tassled handlebars.

Ike wins: A general in the White House

The President-elect and Vice President-elect confer at Eisenhower's residence.

New York City, Nov. 5

General Dwight D. Eisenhower was elected 34th President of the United States today in a Republican landslide that carried both houses of Congress. Almost complete vote returns show nearly 34 million for Eisenhower, who campaigned against "Korea, Communism and Corruption," to 27.3 million for Adlai Stevenson, who said he tried to "talk sense to the American people." Taking the stump more actively than any other retiring chief executive, President Truman turned out to be a big issue himself. Republicans say the vic-tory is a repudiation of the Truman Fair Deal. On communism, the role of the new Vice President, Richard M. Nixon, in the investigation of Alger Hiss was a major factor, and Eisenhower's pledge to go to Korea is believed to have been decisive. In the grand ballroom of the Commodore Hotel here, it was 2:05 a.m., when the President-elect, his wife, Mamie, at his side, said he will not give "short weight" to his job. Stevenson, in Springfield, said he "felt like a little boy who stubbed his toe in the dark. He was too old to cry, but it hurt too much to laugh" (→ Jan. 20, 1953).

President-elect visits U.S. troops in Korea

G.I.'s hold their ground while next President holds to his promise to visit.

Seoul, Korea, Dec. 5

President-elect Eisenhower today secretly fulfilled his campaign promise: "I will go to Korea." Under a news blackout until one hour after he took off for home, the general's three-day visit ranged from the snow-covered front lines to a meeting with President Syngman Rhee. Eisenhower leaves convinced that achieving victory might require "enlarging the war." He believes Korea must have outside help "for a long time" to keep fighting Communists, and he promised the Western Allies will see it through together, in spite of differences. Eisenhower wore double-breasted civvies when he started in Washington, but he changed to army woolens with no insignia except that of his old European command. At the front, he was saluted by the unrehearsed thunder of rocket fire just as the First Marine Division band finished *Ruffles and Flourishes*. Surprised, the general asked, "What are they dropping in here?" One of the officers nearby explained to him that a pilot had attacked enemy positions somewhat farther away than it seemed, with sound carrying far and fast in the 8-degree temperature (→ July 27, 1953).

Checkers speech helps Nixon cause

Wheeling, W. Va., Sept. 24

On a campaign stop here, General Dwight D. Eisenhower says his running mate "is completely vindicated as a man of honor," following Senator Richard Nixon's dramatic explanation on TV of his $18,235 "supplementary expense" fund. In Hollywood last night, the senator said he had never personally used any of his millionaire supporters' fund. Then he disclosed one gift. It was a little dog that their daughter Trisha had named Checkers. "We're gonna keep it!" Nixon said, adding he's "not quitting." Tonight, Ike read aloud a telegram from Nixon's mother and said her son is all right with him.

Lillian Hellman takes her stand

Washington, D.C., May 20

Lillian Hellman, the playwright and activist accused of Communist sympathies, today wrote John S. Wood, chairman of the House Un-American Activities Committee, concerning a subpoena calling for her appearance before the committee tomorrow. Miss Hellman wrote, "I am most willing to answer all questions about myself ... But to hurt innocent people whom I knew many years ago in order to save myself is, to me, inhuman and indecent and dishonorable. I cannot and will not cut my conscience to fit this year's fashions." She may reluctantly take the Fifth Amendment.

New York City, October 14. *The United Nations today opened its first session in its new home, in America to ensure the organization's success.*

Eisenhower

Eisenhower takes the oath on television

As Vice President Richard Nixon looks on, Dwight D. Eisenhower takes the oath of office. He led Americans in war and now will lead them in peace.

Washington, D.C., Jan. 20

All America watched the biggest television hookup in history today as Dwight D. Eisenhower was sworn in as the 34th President of the United States. The New York Stock Exchange slowed to half its normal volume as millions left their usual pursuits to gather around TV sets and view the first inaugural ever telecast from coast to coast. Compared with the 10 million who watched four years ago on networks linked only as far west as Missouri, 21 million sets could receive 118 stations from New York to California today.

As many as 75 million people viewed the events in Washington, from schools and bars, offices, factories, homes and restaurants. At luncheon clubs, scheduled speakers were canceled in order that members would be able to watch history in the making, sometimes on several sets at once. The Astor Hotel used five screens in one room to give 300 luncheon guests close-up views denied to the 550,000 who crowded Washington curbs and elbowed for the best vantage points they could find. Radio was there, too, potentially reaching 98 percent of all the homes in America.

13 Reds convicted in conspiracy plot

New York City, Jan. 21

After a nine-month trial and a seven-day jury deliberation, a verdict was delivered today, convicting 13 Communists of conspiring to teach and advocate the overthrow of the United States government by force. Those facing sentencing next week include two founders of the Communist Party here, Alexander Bittelman and Alexander Trachtenberg. Judge Edward Dimock praised the jury's handling of the case. The foreman said, "We deliberated long and arduously and gave every possible consideration to each defendant. But after all was said and done, it was the only verdict we could reach" (→ Aug. 24, 1954).

U.S. girl, 17, wins world skating title

Davos, Switzerland, Feb. 15

Tenley Albright, a 17-year-old from Boston, has become the first American to win the world figure-skating championship but she had to overcome dreaded poliomyeletis to do it. Miss Albright won all seven votes of a panel of judges today and completed a sweep of the skating events by Americans. Hayes Alan Jenkins of Ohio captured the men's championship. For Miss Albright, the victory capped a six-year comeback against the crippling disease, helped by skating exercises that she began at the age of 9. Miss Albright was runner-up in the 1952 Winter Olympics to Jeannette Altwegg of England.

McDonald's arches

Phoenix, Arizona, May

In search of an eye-catching look for their hamburger shops, Richard and Mac McDonald have discarded professional architects' ideas and decided on an oddly shaped building with a tilted roof, big windows, red-and-white tiles, a neon figure of a chef named "Speedee" and two sheet-metal parabolic "golden arches" with neon stripes that make the place look like a cross between an airport conning tower and a spaceship. It's quite a sight.

Wright, master builder, gets retrospective

New York City, November

The Solomon R. Guggenheim Museum is honoring the design and structural innovations of America's pre-eminent 20th-Century architect, Frank Lloyd Wright, with a retrospective exhibition of his work. Called *Sixty Years of Living Architecture*, it traces Wright's career, from the influential "prairie houses," which echo the horizontal lines of the Midwestern plains, through his latest skyscraper project. Wright, one of the first architects to work in concrete, made stunning use of the new technology in the Falling Water project: a house dramatically cantilevered over a waterfall. Wright is now working on a building for the Guggenheim that will feature spiral ramps.

Innovative architect Frank Lloyd Wright unveils his model of the Oklahoma skyscraper Price Tower.

Rosenbergs executed in electric chair

Ossining, New York, June 19

Julius and Ethel Rosenberg died in the electric chair tonight, convicted of selling atomic secrets to the Soviet government. They are the first civilians to be put to death under the General Espionage Act of 1917. The day was characterized by futile appeals to Judge Irving R. Kaufman, who sentenced them on April 5, 1951, judges of the Federal Circuit Court, the United States Supreme Court, and President Eisenhower, who refused executive clemency for a second time.

The trial opened on March 6, 1951, with an indictment charging the Rosenbergs with espionage dating back to June of 1944. Although the Espionage Act does allow for the death penalty during wartime, it has been noted that the Soviet Union was an ally of the United States, not an enemy, at the time of the crime. In every appeal, it was the serious nature of America's current relationship with Russia that served as justification for the sentence. Said President Eisenhower today, "I can only say that, by immeasurably increasing the chance of an atomic war, the Rosenbergs may have condemned to death tens of millions of innocent people all over the world."

In New York City, more than 5,000 people gathered on Union

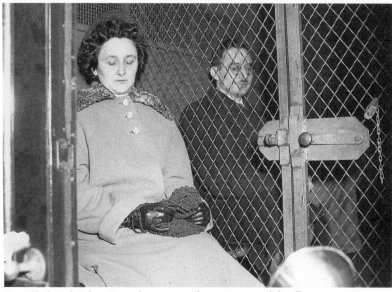

For Ethel and Julius Rosenberg, appeals, protests and finally execution.

Square today to protest the execution. Representatives from the New York Clemency Committee of the National Committee to Secure Justice in the Rosenberg Case denounced Eisenhower, calling him "bloodthirsty." In another speech, the Rosenbergs were described as "freedom-loving people who were to die for world peace and American democracy." The implication that the Rosenbergs' conviction was part of a conspiracy involving Senator Joseph McCarthy was a key theme of the New York protest,

but the appeals and speeches accomplished nothing.

At 8:04 p.m., Joseph Francel pulled the switch that sent Julius Rosenberg to his death, and seven minutes later Ethel joined her husband. On Union Square, the police ordered the sound system shut off and the crowd began to sing the spiritual *Go Down Moses*. In a letter Ethel wrote to the President on June 6, she asked "whether that sentence does not serve the ends of 'force and violence' rather than an enlightened justice."

Cochran surpasses the speed of sound

Edwards AFB, Calif., May 18

Attaining a speed of over 760 miles an hour as she flew her F-86 Saber jet over Rogers Dry Lake, Jacqueline Cochran today became the first woman to pilot a plane faster than the speed of sound. While she was about it, she also set a new international record of 652 mph for a 100-kilometer closed course. Miss Cochran was raised in a foster home and left school after third grade to work in a cotton mill. Receiving a pilot's license in 1932 after only three weeks of training, she became the second woman ever to win the Bendix transcontinental race and the first to ferry a bomber to England during World War II.

It's a country awash in fads, and these youngsters are enjoying one of the latest. With the aid of specially designed "glasses," you, too, can see the likes of Mighty Mouse jumping off a page of Three Dimension Comics.

American aircraft fired on by MiGs

Alaska, March 14

The cold war has turned hot for American pilots. For the second time in four days, an American aircraft has come under attack by MiG fighters. A weather observation plane of the Strategic Air Command was fired upon today by one or two MiGs over international waters off Siberia. The Americans returned the fire, but no one was hit. On March 10, Czech Air Force MiGs shot down an American F-84 Thunderjet on routine patrol over the American zone in Germany. The pilot in that attack, which was the first on a United States plane since the start of the cold war, parachuted safely. He had not been wounded.

Miller's "Crucible"

New York City

Critics of Senator Joe McCarthy and of the House Committee on Un-American Activities often liken their proceedings to a witch-hunt. Now Arthur Miller, himself a victim of the "Red Scare," explores the analogy in *The Crucible*, which recreates the 1692 Salem trials. The play focuses on the persecution of John Proctor, who was hounded to death for his beliefs.

"Little Mo" wins tennis Grand Slam

New York City, Sept. 7

"Little Mo" has done it! Maureen Connolly, who at the age of 16 won the United States singles title, proved her claim as the best woman tennis player in the world by scoring a Grand Slam. With her victory at Forest Hills today, she completed a sweep of all four major championships in a year, the first woman ever to do so. In addition to the United States title, she won Wimbledon and the French and Australian Opens. Miss Connolly began playing tennis when she was 10 years old after having won many prizes in the horse-show ring. She grew interested in tennis when her family moved near the city courts in Balboa, California.

Monroe and Hefner and a moon of blue

Some things speak for themselves.

Hollywood, California

Sexy is in! Marilyn Monroe is in three movies – *Niagara*, *Gentlemen Prefer Blondes* (with Jane Russell, too) and *How to Marry a Millionaire* – as well as on the cover and as a nude centerfold in the first issue of *Playboy*, a new magazine published by Chicago-born Hugh Hefner. Otto Preminger has released *The Moon is Blue* without the blessing of the Production Code. Other hit films include *Shane*, *From Here to Eternity*, *Roman Holiday* and *Julius Caesar*.

War in Korea finally draws to a close

Panmunjom, Korea, July 27

Three years, one month and two days after it began, the Korean War has finally ended. Meeting this morning at 10 o'clock, senior Communist and United Nations delegates assembled, with few friendly gestures or kind words, for the ceremony. As dozens of journalists, photographers and military officials looked on, the senior representative of each side – General William K. Harrison for the United States and General Nam Il for North Korea – signed nine copies of the armistice agreement.

Actually, there was little to do when the representatives came together today, except to approve the armistice agreement formally. The three long-disputed obstacles to a peace agreement have already been resolved. The exchange of war prisoners has been started; the specific armistice details have been worked out, and the maverick President of South Korea, Syngman Rhee, who once violently opposed the agreement, has finally come around to supporting it.

The Korean War has been a costly conflict for limited objectives. Estimates put U.S. casualties at more than 55,000 dead and 102,000 wounded. But the count has not yet been completed (→ Nov. 17, 1954).

"... and our flag was still there."

Books: Science, fiction and science fiction

United States

The democratic experience has yielded a melting pot of books this year as three up-and-coming writers add spice to the native broth. One of these men is the son of a Harlem preacher; another is Jewish and ghetto-bred, and the third descends from venerable New England stock. James Baldwin, 29, is exploring the lives of inner-city churchgoers in *Go Tell It on the Mountain*, his first novel. The narrator of *The Adventures of Augie March*, the third novel by Saul Bellow, 38, exults in being "an American, Chicago born." John Cheever, 41, a prep-school dropout, flashes his verbal pedigree in a second set of stories, *The Enormous Radio*.

Other writers are peering past national borders. James Michener, 46, has gone Korean in *The Bridges of Toko Ri*. Science fiction writer Isaac Asimov, 33, resumes his galactic travels in *Second Foundation*, capping a trilogy. And some wags think B.F. Skinner has located a world all his own in *Science and Human Behavior*.

Scrabble, TV Guide

United States

Men: Is all you ever think about making it to first base? Or better yet, hitting a home run? Then maybe you're one of the 15 million people who attended major league ball games this year. Or maybe it means you like the new girlie magazine *Playboy*. Women: Do you prefer men who are the egghead type? Who like to play Scrabble? Who'd rather read *TV Guide*? Then join the 30 million people a year who attend performances of classical music and you'll probably find your man.

The new Massachusetts Senator John Kennedy, and his 24-year-old bride, Jacqueline, enjoy his family's home at Hyannisport.

McCarthy acquiring foes in own party

Washington, D.C.

Senator Joseph McCarthy, that water-cannon of political assault, seems a bit nostalgic for old Democrats in high places. On November 24, he was still bashing former President Truman, insisting that his administration was "crawling" with Communists. Those are the old enemies. McCarthy, however, is not short on new foes, even in his own party. Most politicians are still cowed into silence, but President Eisenhower has assailed the senator's tactics, insisting that those attacked have a right to meet their accusers "face to face." Ike is angry over the rift in the Republican Party McCarthy has caused but does not want an ugly battle with him.

"42nd Street Nocturne" (1953), by Xavier J. Barile, shows a marquee with this year's controversial movie "The Moon Is Blue," a saucy comedy "spiced by more than a dash of sex" and in which the word "virgin" is used for the first time - to the shock of many an American moviegoer.

San Francisco, Jan. 14. Actress Marilyn Monroe marries New York Yankee baseball great Joe DiMaggio.

Washington, D.C., March 1. Senate confirms Earl Warren, as Chief Justice of Supreme Court.

Washington, D.C., Apr. 1. President Eisenhower signs bill establishing United States Air Force Academy in Colorado.

Minneapolis, Apr. 12. Lakers defeat Syracuse Nationals, four games to one, to win N.B.A. championship.

New York City, May 3. Charles A. Lindbergh wins Pulitzer Prize for *The Spirit of St. Louis*.

Atlantic City, New Jersey, Sept. 11. Miss America pageant, with Bert Parks as host, becomes first nationally televised beauty contest.

North America, Sept. 27. United States and Canada set up Distant Early Warning (D.E.W.) Line of radar north of common border.

Cleveland, Oct. 2. New York Giants win National League's first World Series victory since 1946, sweeping Cleveland Indians.

Hollywood, Oct. 3. *Father Knows Best* has TV premiere.

Washington, D.C., Oct. 25. Eisenhower holds first televised Cabinet meeting.

Washington, D.C., Nov. 2. Democrats regain both houses of Congress, in mid-term elections.

Washington, D.C., Nov. 17. Senate ratifies mutual defense pact with Republic of Korea.

New York City, Nov. 19. CBS public affairs program *Face the Nation* has TV premiere.

Cleveland, Dec. 26. Browns defeat Detroit Lions, 56-10, for N.F.L. championship.

Washington, D.C. Poll shows that 78 percent of Americans believe it important to report to F.B.I. relatives or acquaintances suspected of being Communists.

New York City. New York Stock Exchange has its best year since 1933, with 573,374,622 shares traded.

Hollywood, Calif. *On the Waterfront* released, starring Marlon Brando, Karl Malden and Eva Marie Saint.

Eisenhower explains: "You have a row of dominoes set up..."

President Eisenhower speaks out.

Washington, D.C., Apr. 7

Comparing the situation among Asian nations to a row of dominoes, President Eisenhower today expressed his concern that the conquest of Indochina by Communist forces could result in a disaster for the free world.

Noting that 450 million people are already living under Communist dictatorships in Asia, the President explained, "You have ... what you would call the 'falling domino' principle. You have a row of dominoes set up, you knock over the first one, and what will happen to the last one is the certainty that it will go over very quickly."

He pointed out that the entire island defense chain – meaning Japan, Formosa [Taiwan] and the Philippines – might be flanked, which would threaten both Australia and New Zealand.

In its effort to combat the threat of communism in Indochina, the United States is also now mobilizing a multinational coalition.

The President says that stopping Communist expansion must be given high priority. Earlier in the year, he called for a "New Look" in defense policy, one that would rely on atomic weapons and on strike forces to meet the threat wherever it might erupt. Speaking of this evolving new defense policy, Secretary of Defense Charles E. Wilson described it as getting "a bigger bang for the buck" (→ Oct. 23).

U.S. launches Nautilus, first atomic sub

Groton, Connecticut, Jan. 21

As an enthusiastic crowd of over 12,000 ship workers and spectators looked on, First Lady Mamie Eisenhower christened the nation's first nuclear-powered submarine, the Nautilus, today.

Named in honor of the submarine built by the inventor Robert Fulton in 1800, the vessel has a top speed of 30 knots and cost $55 million. Because its high-speed turbine engines are powered by an atomic reactor that needs no air, the submarine is expected to be able to circumnavigate the globe without having to surface.

Today's ceremony was a personal triumph for 54-year-old Rear Admiral Hyman Rickover, the outspoken Russian-born advocate of using nuclear energy to power submarines and other naval craft. As head of the naval reactors branch of the Atomic Energy Commission, and head of the nuclear power division of the navy, Admiral Rickover was the man responsible for directing the planning and construction of the Nautilus. A controversial figure because of his contempt for red tape and his unorthodox ways, Rickover was promoted to his present rank only after intense pressure was applied by Congress to a reluctant navy.

First Lady Eisenhower christens the submarine Nautilus as thousands watch.

Salk polio vaccine given to children

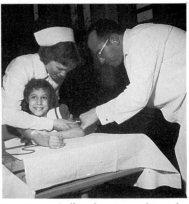

Dr. Jonas Salk administers his polio vaccine to a still-smiling recipient.

Pittsburgh, Penn., Apr. 12

The disease most feared by parents may soon be eradicated, following today's licensing of polio vaccines. The results of testing by virologist Dr. Jonas Salk of the University of Pittsburgh showed the vaccines to be safe and 70 percent effective. He tested 400,000 children with three vaccines: He and his colleagues had previously discovered that polio was caused by three viruses. The vaccines for each of the viruses were injected separately in every child. The government licensed the vaccines today, two hours after the results of the testing were made public. Scientists are hopeful that the vaccines will end the disease, which infected 21,000 individuals in 1952 alone.

Communist threat tops O.A.S. agenda

Caracas, Venezuela, March 1

Communist infiltration in Latin America is at the top of the agenda as the Organization of American States convenes here today – the first time it has met since 1948. Against the background of a Communist-dominated government in Guatemala, the United States will recommend outlawing the Communist Party in the Western Hemisphere. While the United States believes it is going to get broad support, some members will be focusing on the "bread and butter" issues, including the formation of a trade council that will deal with economic matters.

Four Puerto Ricans open fire in House

Washington, D.C., March 1

Screaming "Viva Puerto Rico!" four Puerto Rican nationalists began firing from the spectators' gallery in the House of Representatives, wounding five congressmen. Some 25 shots were fired before police officers entered. The governor of Puerto Rico says these nationalists are part of a small faction. Earlier this year, Puerto Rico rejected a resolution that would have meant independence for the territory.

Crewcuts are cool

United States

What college girls are looking for in college boys: cool crew cuts, neat flattops and ducktails. Preferably, they have lots of bread and a dragster or a Mercedes 300 SL with fuel injection. Nice if they're cadets at the new Air Force Academy who might someday fly the new supersonic F-100 Supersaber. These guys should also be smart enough to remember Armistice Day is now Veterans' Day. A plus if they look like Audie Murphy. What the boys are looking for in girls: blondes (by Miss Clairol) wearing felt skirts with poodle appliques. All right if they have the "raccoon look" of heavy mascara, and hopefully, they can dance the cha-cha-cha. Grace Kelly lookalikes do fine.

Drama of Army-McCarthy hearings captivates American public

Washington, D.C., Aug. 31

In a distinct anticlimax to the marathon television spectacle of the Army-McCarthy hearings, the Senate Permanent Investigations subcommittee has mildly condemned both sides. According to the panel's Republican majority, Senator Joseph McCarthy allowed counsel Roy Cohn to attempt to put pressure on military officials to promote an aide named G. David Schine. Secretary of War Robert T. Stevens, the report said, vacillated in dealing with Cohn. Last year, Cohn and Schine virtually ran the investigations subcommittee, which McCarthy normally chairs. McCarthy had charged that Stevens held Schine "hostage" to halt a Senate inquiry into subversion in the army.

From late April through early June, however, the plot was secondary to the drama itself. Most Americans – sometimes 20 million at a time – were glued to the television set for at least a few of the 187 hours. Two million words of testimony poured forth, much of it screamed, shouted, squalled or sputtered through clenched teeth.

The proceedings opened with a speech by Karl Mundt, the rotund Republican who filled McCarthy's chair for the eight weeks. The hearings, he proclaimed, would be run with "dignity, fairness and thoroughness." It was there that the facade of parliamentary procedure

Chief counsel Roy Cohn feeds the fuel that keeps Senator McCarthy in action.

ended. From the very first question, McCarthy imposed his own staccato pace. "Point of order, Mr. Chairman!" he interrupted, until schoolboys were imitating him in parks and playgrounds everywhere. Mundt was so obviously torn between his allegiance to McCarthy and his role as impartial moderator that one commentator labeled him the "tormented mushroom."

With everyone else abdicating, it was left to Army counsel Joseph Welch to supply the voice of reason. More than anyone, Welch was responsible for turning McCarthy's panel, his weapon of destruction for so long, into the vehicle of his

own decline. With patience and humor, the long-faced Bostonian took Cohn apart, leaving him short-tempered and brutal before the cameras. But even Cohn flinched as McCarthy cast aspersions at a young aide on the Welch staff. Welch shed his lawyerly self-control completely. "Until this moment Senator," he cried, "I think I never really gauged your cruelty." And through watery eyes: "Have you no sense of decency, sir, at long last? Have you left no sense of decency?" In the solemn Senate Caucus Room, a burst of applause hinted that a cowering nation was having its long-awaited catharsis (→ Dec. 2).

G.E. hires Reagan

Schenectady, New York

General Electric has hired actor Ronald Reagan as host for its television anthology series, *The General Electric Theater*, and to tour its plants to speak on the virtues of free enterprise and the American way. Reagan has played rather square romantic leads in some 50 films, but his performances in *King's Row* (1942) and *The Hasty Heart* (1950) have won praise. Earlier, he was host of TV's *Death Valley Days* western series for three years.

The G.E. series, which began without a host in February of last year, will offer a wide range of material – from adventure to biblical drama, light comedy and melodrama. Reagan will also act in some of the presentations.

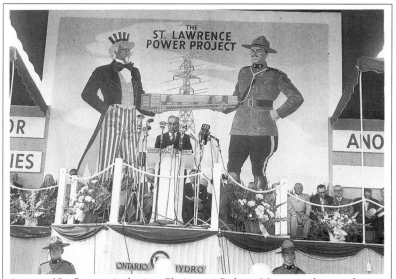

August 10. *Power Authority Chairman Robert Moses is the speaker at ceremonies inaugurating the St. Lawrence Power Project. Such joint ventures by the U.S. and Canada underscore the unique relationship between the two nations, which share an unguarded border almost 4,000 miles long.*

Supreme Court strikes down "separate but equal"

Washington, D.C., May 17

The case of Brown v. the Board of Education has culminated in a unanimous Supreme Court decision that overturns previous decisions permitting the segregation of public schools by race. The long-standing "separate but equal" policy was declared unconstitutional because "separate educational facilities are inherently unequal," as the opinion written by Chief Justice Earl Warren stated.

The case began in 1950 when the National Association for the Advancement of Colored People decided to initiate a large-scale effort aimed at abolishing educational segregation. The N.A.A.C.P. put more than $100,000 into research and a campaign. A team of lawyers headed by Thurgood Marshall was assembled. Other members of the team included Robert L. Carter, Jack Greenberg, Louis Redding, James Nabrit, George E. C. Hayes, and Spotswood Robinson 3d. Many

Mrs. Nettie Hunt explains to her daughter, Nikie, what the court ruling means.

of the arguments presented by the N.A.A.C.P. were based on social and psychological research material gathered by Kenneth Clark. As a result of this campaign, in 1953 the Supreme Court ordered five school desegregation cases to be brought before it. The current decision, which began in a Topeka, Kansas, school district, sets a precedent that guides decisions in the other cases presently before the court, and in future cases.

The "separate but equal" doctrine had its roots in a precedent that was set by the Massachusetts Supreme Court in 1849. A Negro, Benjamin F. Roberts, sued the city of Boston for damages when his 5-year-old daughter was refused admission to a white public school. The case was argued with no success and the supreme court of Massachusetts rejected the appeal. The "separate but equal" doctrine was further established by an 1896 case that involved a New Orleans Negro who was arrested and convicted for having attempted to ride in a white railroad car. The defendant, Homer Plessy, then appealed to the Supreme Court, but was rebuffed with the ruling that the maintenance of "separate but equal" facilities was a "reasonable" use of state police funding and power. The court further ruled it had not been the intent of the 14th Amendment to abolish segregation (→ May 31, 1955).

Ike promises more help to South Vietnam

Washington, D.C., Oct. 23

President Eisenhower wrote a letter to the President of South Vietnam early this month, promising more American support for that country, it was disclosed today. In his note to Ngo Dinh Diem, Eisenhower did not specifiy what type of assistance, military or economic, the United States is going to provide the Southeast Asian country in its struggle against a growing Communist insurgency. The President's position, however, is clear. He said in April that South Vietnam is like a domino among other dominoes, or nations, in that part of the world: if one of them falls to the Communists, then the rest of the democratic nations of Southeast Asia will inevitably be brought down too (→ Feb. 23, 1955).

Can charwoman Ella Watson one day become a congresswoman? Why not? Photo by Gordon Parks.

Giant new carrier

Newport News, Va., Dec. 11

American naval power received a major boost here today with the launching of the aircraft carrier Forrestal, the first of a new class of carriers. With a length of more than 1,000 feet and a top speed of more than 30 knots, the new carrier is larger and faster than those of the Essex class, and at 59,650 tons it is the world's largest warship. Over the next 12 years, the navy expects to add at least seven more flattops of the Forrestal class. Plans are also in the works for an even larger carrier that will be driven by nuclear power.

Anti-Communists take over in Guatemala

Washington, D.C., Oct. 30

Guatemala's newly installed anti-Communist government, which came to power with the support of the United States Central Intelligence Agency, is going to receive $6,425,000 in United States aid. The road to the change in government began in June when rebels under Colonel Carlos Castillo Armas invaded Guatemala. In 11 days, they ousted the ruler, Jacobo Arbenz, replacing his Communist-controlled regime with a military junta. Last month, Colonel Armas was installed as president.

Major new U.S. highway system planned

Washington, D.C., July 12

A major new road-building program that would cost $5 billion a year for the next 10 years was proposed today on behalf of the administration by Vice President Nixon. While the main emphasis would be on constructing a network of interstate and intercity highways, provisions would also be made to help local "farm-to-market" travel. The program comes at a time when the number of American families who own a car has risen to 70 percent. A blue ribbon panel, probably to be headed General Lucius Clay, will study methods of financing the program, which, if approved, will be the largest public works venture in American history.

As the number of Americans taking to the roads continues to increase dramatically, the highway system is being expanded to handle the load.

Congress puts curbs on U.S. Communists

Washington, D.C., Aug. 24

The Communist Party, caught in a game of political hardball, has been deprived of its rights under the law. Hurt by charges of softness on communism, Democrats led by Senator Hubert Humphrey proposed making party membership punishable by a $10,000 fine and five years in jail. Rushing in to take a public stand, the senators passed the proposal unanimously. Then the provision died in conference. But the bill that made it to the floor stripped the party of its rights and deprived Communist unions of National Labor Relations Board protection. Of 346 legislators present, just two voted nay.

A nation under God

Washington, D.C., June 14

President Eisenhower signed a congressional resolution today that alters the words of the Pledge of Allegiance. The resolution adds the words "under God," changing the phrase "one nation indivisible" to "one nation, under God, indivisible." At the signing, the President said that it served to rededicate the nation to its divine source and provided meaning to a world that recently experienced cruelty and violence and where a materialistic philosophy of life deadens millions.

Comics crackdown

New York City, October

Comic book publishers banded together this month to establish the Comics Code Authority, a self-regulating body created to assure parents of the wholesome content of their children's reading material. Code-approved comics will carry a seal similar to the Good Housekeeping Seal of Approval. The adverse impact of comic books on the emotional development of children was an issue first raised by psychiatrist Frederic Wertham in his book *Seduction of the Innocent* and later explored by Senator Estes Kefauver's subcommittee hearings on juvenile delinquency, which resulted in a public outcry against comic books.

McCarthy condemned for misconduct

Washington, D.C., Dec. 2

Casting off a yoke of fear, the Senate voted 67 to 22 today to condemn Senator Joseph McCarthy for abusing his colleagues. "We can probably get the sentence commuted to life in prison," quipped the senator from Wisconsin. But no amount of humor would dispel the consequences. The report avoided the term censure, but only three other senators in history have been so rebuked. Said Democrat Mike Monroney, McCarthy will be "buried back with the classified ads."

Sensing his demise, "Tail-Gunner Joe" lashed out at his attackers. Ralph Flanders had introduced the censure resolution, noting McCarthy's "habitual contempt for people." McCarthy called him "senile." He said the committee that recommended his censure, led by

McCarthy supporters assemble at New York's Pennsylvania Station on their way to Washington to encourage him in his crusade against communism.

Mormon Senator Arthur Watkins, was a "lynch party." McCarthy's attacks on the Watkins panel and on an elections subcommittee were the immediate grounds for censure. But the rebuke stands as a condemnation of his four-year barrage of anti-Communist innuendo.

This Babe's a lady

United States

From a double Olympic track champ in 1932, Mildred "Babe" Didrikson has gone on to become winner of the U.S. Women's Open golf championship for the third time. The slim Texan became a pro after winning the women's national championship in 1946 and becoming the first American to take the British title in 1947. She also won the Open from 1948 through 1950.

G.M.'s 50 millionth

Flint, Michigan, Nov. 23

The 50 millionth General Motors car rolled off the assembly line here today, marking the start of a nationwide celebration. To commemorate the event, the custom-made Chevrolet sport coupe was gold-painted and manufactured with 60 gold-plated parts. General Motors was established in 1908, but it took 10 years to produce its first car. The company is now the largest auto maker in the nation, having turned out 2.8 million cars last year for a record-breaking sales figure of $10 billion. President Eisenhower said today that the anniversary epitomized "the industrial, scientific and creative genius of our people."

Eight nations set up East Asian defense

Manila, Philippines, Sept. 8

A new weapon has been added to the arsenal being prepared in the effort to contain communism in Southeast Asia. It is an eight-nation defense alliance established here today. Known as the South East Asia Treaty Organization, it affirms the rights of Asian and Pacific people to self-determination and equality. Members of the new alliance, in addition to the United States, are Britain, France, Australia, New Zealand, the Philippines, Pakistan and Thailand. Unlike the North Atlantic Treaty Organization, the South East organization, to be known as SEATO, does not provide for a unified military command. Moreover, it does not obligate the United States or other members of the alliance to act militarily except in the event of a specific Communist danger.

"Papa" Hemingway reels in Nobel Prize

Oslo, Norway, Dec. 10

His beard has grown grizzly and the lean body has gotten a mite soft in the middle, but Ernest Hemingway, 55, still reigns as the he-man of American letters. And today the outdoor athlete with the sinewy prose landed the biggest literary fish of them all, the Nobel Prize for literature. He had lately flopped with the critics, but his 1952 novella, *The Old Man and the Sea* (1952), the poignant story of an aging fisherman who won't accept defeat – even when sharks circle his battered skiff – has put "Papa" back on top. Now Hem can ease into old age without being reduced to telling fish stories – about, say, the prize that got away.

Ernest Hemingway with a swordfish he caught while on location for filming of "The Old Man and the Sea."

Washington, D.C., Jan. 4. United States awards $2 million in damages to 23 Japanese fishermen who sustained injuries as a result of hydrogen bomb testing on Bikini Atoll.

Washington, D.C., Jan. 19. President Eisenhower becomes first President to conduct a televised news conference.

Washington, D.C., Feb. 9. Senate ratifies U.S.-Nationalist China Mutual Security Pact.

Syracuse, N.Y., April. Syracuse Nationals win National Basketball Association title by beating Fort Wayne Pistons, four games to three.

Washington, D.C., May 19. According to Federal Trade Commission, business mergers have increased three-fold over a five-year period.

Detroit, June 6. Ford Motor Company signs agreement with United Auto Workers that, aside from providing a wage increase, also grants funds for laid-off workers.

Purchase, N.Y., July 13. First executive jet, Beech Paris, goes on display.

Anaheim, Calif., July 18. Illustrator Walt Disney opens Disneyland theme park.

Oceanside, N.Y., Aug. 2. Mrs. Sheldon Rubbins becomes first female cantor in history of Judaism.

Washington, D.C., Aug. 21. Department of Commerce estimates U.S. investments abroad total $26.6 billion.

New York City, Oct. 4. Brooklyn Dodgers defeat New York Yankees in World Series, four games to three.

Washington, D.C., Dec. 12. Upon opening national headquarters, evangelist Billy Graham comments, "I just want to lobby for God."

New York City, Dec. 12. Ford Foundation makes $500 million educational grant, largest in history.

Los Angeles, Dec. 26. Cleveland Browns defeat Rams, 38-14, for N.F.L. title.

New York City. *Family of Man* photo exhibit opens at Museum of Modern Art.

New York City. *Why Johnny Can't Read,* by Rudolph Flesch, published; examines American education.

President authorized to defend Formosa

Washington, D.C., Jan. 28

As the Formosa Straits crisis continues to heat up, President Eisenhower has received full authority from Congress to take whatever military action he deems necessary to repel a Chinese Communist assault on Generalissimo Chiang Kai-shek and his Nationalist army. The Nationalists have taken refuge on Formosa [Taiwan] and nearby islands. The resolution, which passed the House 410 to 3 and the Senate 83 to 3, is without precedent in the country's history. It was requested by President Eisenhower to avoid the criticism leveled at President Truman for entering the Korean conflict without congressional backing.

Just what steps should be taken in the present crisis is left to the President's discretion. On January 22, he ordered three aircraft carriers from Pearl Harbor to join the Seventh Fleet, which is patrolling the Formosa Straits. But it is not clear whether he intends to offer full protection to Quemoy and Matsu, two small islands close to the mainland that are heavily garrisoned by the Nationalists. Secretary of State John Foster Dulles favors a hard-line course, but the President seems to be following a policy of deliberate vagueness. "We do not believe in giving blueprints to the Communists of just what we will or will not do," he has said.

This is especially so in the case of nuclear weapons. At least five times last year he resisted advice to launch a nuclear attack against mainland China. "With modern weapons," he has said, "there can be no victory for anyone" (→ Feb. 9).

U.S. sends military advisers to Vietnam

Washington, D.C., Feb. 23

Because of the increased success of the pro-Communist forces operating in South Vietnam, the United States will send a small force of military advisers to the Southeast Asian nation. The State Department said today an American Military Advisory Group is being formed and will be based in Saigon. The group will only give advice to officers and senior enlisted men in the South Vietnamese armed forces. According to State Department officials, the Americans will not be sent into active combat either as a unit or with the Vietnamese troops. President Eisenhower sent a group of 200 technicians to South Vietnam last year to assist the French before the Battle of Dienbienphu, but they were withdrawn soon after, and France was defeated (→ Apr. 28, 1956).

"Downtown Kansas City in Winter" by Fred Bergere. Everything is up to date in the Midwest metropolis, including skyscrapers and shopping centers.

Einstein, citizen of the U.S., is dead

One of the world's greatest minds.

Princeton, N.J., Apr. 18

Albert Einstein, one of the great scientists of the world, died at his home here today. He was 76. Intrigued by the nature of light, the German-born physicist lent new meaning to the concept of space and time with his theories of relativity, for which he was awarded the Nobel Prize in 1921. Moving to the United States, he became a citizen in 1941 and a popular figure, admired for his warmth and common touch. When not working, he loved to play the violin and to sail.

Sanders, Landers and coonskin caps

United States

Disneyland has just opened in Anaheim, California, but the country seems to be one big amusement park. Where else are commercial goods such a source of fun? Where else are there new food items such as the Kentucky Fried Chicken of Colonel Sanders and the Special K of Kellogg? Where else roll-on deodorants, a Texas-style department store such as Neiman-Marcus, an *Ann Landers Says* column, the conservative William F. Buckley's *National Review* and the liberal *Village Voice?* And what land lavishes on its kids Uncle Wiggley and Snakes and Ladders board games or Davy Crockett coonskin caps?

School integration: Deliberate speed

Washington, D.C., May 31

Following up on last year's decision in Brown v. the Board of Education, the Supreme Court today announced its directives for school segregation on a national basis. The guidelines call for local boards to draw up their own plans for ending the separation of white and Negro schoolchildren "with all deliberate speed." This is a major disappointment for the National Association for the Advancement of Colored People, which had hoped the court would announce a specific time limit. Under this plan desegregation is already proceeding in many states, and, though not an easy process, it is expected that hundreds of school districts will be integrated by year's end (→ Dec. 5).

$1 wage minimum

Washington, D.C., Aug. 12

Minimum-wage workers will receive an extra 25 cents an hour beginning next March 1. President Eisenhower signed an amendment increasing the minimum wage from 75 cents to $1 today. Under the Fair Labor Standards Act of 1938, usually called the Wages and Hours Law, the minimum wage was set at 40 cents an hour. Since then the law has been periodically amended.

Ike, at summit, proposes "open skies"

The plan would allow reconnaissance planes to take pictures for study.

Geneva, July 21

As Soviet Premier Nikolai Bulganin listened silently, President Eisenhower today unveiled a dramatic proposal to ease cold war tensions. Speaking at the summit conference here, Eisenhower said his plan would reduce the possibility of "surprise attack, thus lessening danger and relaxing tensions."

He suggested that the United States and Soviet Union exchange a "complete blueprint of our military establishments, from one end of our countries to the other." And he called for the two nations to open their skies and allow reconnais-

sance planes to "make all the pictures you choose and take them to your own country for study." He said the two nations "admittedly possess new and terrible weapons," and therefore urged that "we take a practical step, that we begin an arrangement very quickly, as between ourselves – immediately."

Britain and France like the plan. United Nations officials were said to be wary. The summit participants include Prime Minister Anthony Eden of Britain, Premier Edgar Faure of France and Soviet Communist Party First Secretary Nikita Khrushchev.

Number 1: "Rock Around the Clock"

United States, May

Bill Haley didn't know what to call his music when he first slipped a blazing rhythm and blues beat into his unique brand of country swing. But "rock 'n' roll" now suits him just fine. His new hit, *Rock Around the Clock,* fizzled on the charts last year, but it has jumped to No. 1 after it was included in the hit movie *Blackboard Jungle.* The film's marriage of rock 'n' roll and the juvenile delinquency theme proved irresistible to teenagers and it even sparked a riot or two. But as other rock 'n' rollers like Little Richard, Bo Diddley and Chuck Berry begin to crowd more sedate chart staples such as Perry Como, some critics have labeled the music "dirty, and as bad for kids as dope."

Enter I.B.M. 700's

New York City, Aug. 1

A major challenge to Remington Rand, whose UNIVAC computer has been considered the leader in the industry, has come with the introduction today of I.B.M.'s 700 line of computers. Masterminding the I.B.M. entry into the field is Thomas Watson Jr., who recently took over management of the international company from his legendary father.

Everybody is getting into the act. Senator Estes Kefauver, Tennessee Democrat, sports the coonskin cap that's been made famous by television's "Davy Crockett." No American boy and no presidential hopeful should be without one.

Television offers fantasy, facts and fun

United States

We have come a long way. In December 1945, 81 percent of respondents in a Gallup Poll had never seen a television set in operation. In 1946, there were 10,000 sets and six stations each programming 10 hours a week. By June 8, 1948, when NBC began *Texaco Star Theater* with Milton Berle's pie-in-the-face brand of comedy, movie theaters and restaurants took a beating, proving the power of the new medium.

Television personalizes the political process, as when Senator Richard Nixon, Republican candidate for Vice President, told a national audience about his personal and political finances in his "Checkers"

speech on September 23, 1952. On January 19, 1953, all America went "aaah" as Lucille Ball's character on *I Love Lucy* gave birth to Little Ricky. Then the McCarthy hearings and the televised bus boycott in Montgomery, Alabama, took us right to the spot.

For children, there is *Captain Kangaroo* weekday mornings. New shows include *Davy Crockett,* with the Alamo hero and king of the wild frontier played by 6-foot 5-inch Texan Fess Parker, the thrilling anthology *Alfred Hitchcock Presents* and the soap opera *As the World Turns.* And film studios have even started producing films for TV and allowing theatrical releases to be shown.

"Gunsmoke" is roaring across the television screens like a runaway stagecoach. Every week millions of Americans tune in to see plain folks go through the trials and tribulations of the Wild West – and even live to tell about it.

Dean lived too fast and died too young

Hollywood, Calif., Sept. 30

Driving his Porsche to Salinas to compete in a race, actor James Dean, 24, was killed in a highway crash today. Dean had a brief but spectacular screen career. In just a little over a year, his popularity soared and many regarded him as a personification of the alienated American youth of today. This year, he played a tender but rebellious boy in *East of Eden* and gives an equally outstanding performance as a restless teenager in *Rebel Without a Cause*, due for release next month. He had just finished the movie *Giant* with Elizabeth Taylor and Rock Hudson.

The rebel who ignited a generation.

Back of the bus no more

When Rosa Parks sat in the front of the bus, things really started moving.

Montgomery, Alabama, Dec. 5

When the Cleveland Avenue bus pulled up to a stop on December 1, 43-year-old Rosa Parks entered and took a seat at the front. That would not seem to be a particularly remarkable event, except that Rosa Parks is a Negro and, as such, has always been relegated to the rear seats. When Miss Parks refused to give up her seat to a white man, the bus stopped and she was arrested.

That evening, other Negro women from Montgomery gathered to call for a boycott of the city buses. Negro leaders met the next day to call for a widespread bus boycott today. The pastor of the Dexter Avenue Baptist Church, the Rev. Martin Luther King Jr., was chosen to head the publicity campaign and inform Montgomery's 50,000 Negroes of the boycott. He was then elected president of the Montgomery Improvement Association's boycott committee.

Normally, 75 percent of the bus passengers are Negro and today's boycott was effective. The demands of the Improvement Association do not include immediate desegregation, so it is not supported by the National Association for the Advancement of Colored People. But the boycott will go on until Negroes are treated as equals (→ March 1956).

A Monroe doctrine that's all about sex

Hollywood, California

She is Fox's biggest box-office draw and Hollywood's newest sex goddess: Marilyn Monroe, 29. She wiggles, she pouts, she speaks in a husky, whispery voice and exudes a both inviting and wholesome sensuality with equal parts of reality and humor. She has proven to be a big enough star to survive the disclosure of nude photos ("I was hungry") and that her mother is in an asylum. While at work on her new movie, *The Seven-Year Itch*, she divorced baseball hero Joe DiMaggio after a nine-month marriage. The next movie she makes will be *Bus Stop*.

Marilyn in "The Seven-Year Itch."

Eisenhower suffers mild heart attack

Denver, Colorado, Sept. 26

President Eisenhower suffered a mild heart attack three days ago. While he is resting comfortably now, the pulse on Wall Street has slowed to an alarming pace. The New York Stock Exchange lost some $44 million, making today the market's worst in history. Financial experts say Ike's illness is the reason for the dramatic fall; investors shy away from activity in times of national crisis. And a serious illness to a popular president constitutes a crisis. Ike asked aides to be candid with the public about his condition. He feels the secrecy surrounding President Wilson's illness early this century was a mistake.

"Aspects of Suburban Life: Golf" by Paul Cadmus. In the 10 years since the end of World War II, the American middle class has developed its own way of life. Young couples marry, head for the suburbs, buy houses and start families. The nation's new role as world leader and its unprecedented prosperity have given its people the means to regain a life lost during 20 years of depression and war. For millions, the American dream is a reality.

A.F.L. and C.I.O. form single union

New York City, Dec. 5

In the cavernous 71st Regiment Armory, 16 million workers were united today into one House of Labor. Ending their 20-year estrangement, the American Federation of Labor and the Congress of Industrial Organizations merged under the leadership of the A.F.L. president George Meany. Since the time of C.I.O. founder John L. Lewis, the craft-oriented A.F.L. has come around to accepting the C.I.O.'s industry-wide organizing methods. The two labor giants have agreed that recognition will be given to both craft and industrial unions, and that both groups will stop raiding sister unions for members.

Eisenhower

Montgomery, Ala., Jan. 30. Home of the Rev. Martin Luther King Jr. is bombed.

Washington, D.C., March 12. In Florida ex. rel. Hawkins v. Board of Control, Supreme Court draws distinction between primary and secondary schools and professional programs, saying latter must integrate without delay (→ Dec. 21).

Philadelphia, Apr. 7. Warriors defeat Fort Wayne Pistons, four games to one, in N.B.A. championship.

South Vietnam, Apr. 28. U.S. Military Advisory Group assumes responsibility for training of South Vietnamese army (→ July 9, 1959).

New York City, May 7. Pulitzer Prize in fiction awarded to MacKinlay Kantor for *Andersonville.*

Washington, D.C., May 23. To reduce certain crop yields, Congress passes a measure providing $750 million per year, subsidizing farmers who reduce their production.

United States, July 16. Ringling Brothers and Barnum & Bailey Circus gives last performance under a tent.

Washington, D.C., July 19. Secretary of State John Foster Dulles withdraws American offer to help Egypt with construction of Aswan High Dam because Egypt has been dealing with Soviet Union (→ Nov. 5).

Washington. D.C., Sept. 14. 63-year-old female patient at George Washington University Hospital is first person to undergo a lobotomy.

California, Nov. 6. D.S. Saund is elected to House of Representatives, becoming first Congressman of Asian ancestry.

New York City, Dec. 30. Giants defeat Chicago Bears, 47-7, for N.F.L. championship.

Hollywood, Calif. Top films this year include *Bus Stop, Giant, The Ten Commandments* and *Invasion of the Body Snatchers.*

New York City. Grace Metalious's *Peyton Place* is a best-seller.

New York City. William Whyte publishes *The Organization Man,* describing corporate pressure to conform.

Dulles: "If you are scared to go to the brink, you are lost."

Washington, D.C., Jan. 16

In a forceful defense of the Eisenhower administration's foreign policies, Secretary of State John Foster Dulles disclosed today that the United States has been on the "brink" of war on three occasions during the last three years.

In an article in *Life* magazine titled *How Dulles Averted War,* the 68-year-old secretary pointed to the conflicts in Korea and Indochina and the question of Formosa [Taiwan] as the three occasions when the United States was on "the verge of war."

In explaining his diplomatic policies, Dulles said: "You have to take chances for peace, just as you must take chances in war. Some say that we were brought to the verge of war. Of course we were brought to the verge of war. The ability to get to the verge without getting into the war is the necessary art. If you cannot master it, you inevitably get into war. If you try to run away from it, if you are scared to go to the brink, you are lost."

He added, "We walked to the brink and we looked it in the face. We took strong action."

Secretary Dulles, who had been a vigorous critic of former President Truman's policy of "containment" of communism, has long been an advocate of the use of the threat of massive nuclear retaliation as a deterrent to aggression by the Soviet Union.

Secretary John Foster Dulles believes U.S. must use its power to the fullest.

"My Fair Lady"

New York City, March 15

Eliza Doolittle has been reborn on Broadway in *My Fair Lady,* one of the wittiest musicals ever seen on the American stage. Except for the ending, this tuneful version is scrupulously faithful to George Bernard Shaw's *Pygmalion* as Julie Andrews's cockney Eliza is browbeaten by Rex Harrison's imperious Professor Higgins into learning the King's English. With this sparkling work, Alan Jay Lerner and Frederick Loewe fulfill the promise of their enchanting *Brigadoon.*

Will they bury us?

Moscow, November

The cold war is thriving in the freezing Moscow winter. Premier Nikita S. Khrushchev has gleefully offered Western diplomats here these chilling words. "Whether you like it or not, history is on our side. We will bury you." With less glee, one of the nuclear bomb inventors, J. Robert Oppenheimer, said America and Russia "are like two scorpions in a bottle, each capable of killing the other but only at the risk of his own life ... The atomic clock ticks faster and faster."

Drive-ins booming

United States

There are now 7,000 drive-ins across the country, more than triple the number in 1950. And because 11 percent of all cars sold are station wagons, the movies must often be kiddie fare. Regular movie theaters charge that drive-ins drive out their customers, and indeed, a drive-in can be just as comfy. In the winter some drive-ins supply heaters. But many people are staying home to watch TV, turned off by high theater admission prices ($2 in N.Y., $1.50 in Los Angeles).

U. of Alabama sued for banning Negro

Montgomery, Ala., March 1

A recent court order has allowed a Negro woman, Autherine Lucy, to enroll as a student at the University of Alabama. On February 7, only a day after her enrollment, the white student body rioted, leading the university to suspend Miss Lucy. Now, the National Association for the Advancement of Colored People has stepped in to help by filing a discrimination suit against the university. Although the Supreme Court ruled last year that public schools must desegregate, the ruling has not been applied in practice to colleges. In addition, the N.A.A.C.P. has not been effective in this Southern state (→ 12).

A B-57 light bomber equipped to test Boeing "Bomarc" supersonic interceptor missile components. Since the advent of the atomic bomb, planners of modern warfare have been relying more and more on technological advances. American planes are flying higher and faster, rockets are firing farther and more accurately and the possibilities brought on by the computer appear limitless. Man is slowly relinquishing the art of war to his machines.

Delinquency linked to absent parents

St. Louis, Missouri, June 6

Ellsworth Bunker, president of the American Red Cross, told its annual national convention today that "absentee parents" are the major cause of juvenile delinquency. While some might argue with that diagnosis, no one would dispute the prevalence of this social ill.

It is estimated that half the thieves arrested in New York are under 21, while in Los Angeles 20 percent of all crimes are committed by teenagers. The majority of auto thefts in larger cities are attributed to youths. A book this year by professors at Brooklyn College and the University of Chicago, *Delinquency: The Juvenile Offender in America Today,* looks hard for delinquency's causes. Everything from endocrine glands to comic books are said to be partly at fault; "broken homes" are frequently in the background of these offenders, but are not necessarily the primary factor. It says that the media and movies take their toll: James Dean in *Rebel Without a Cause* is as much a reflection of teenage angst as an instigator of crime. But psychologists say that rarely are these youths in leather jackets and slicked-back hair asked why they do what they do or what's on their minds. Which, the analysts feel, might be a reason in itself.

Elvis rocks America

Elvis has all of the right moves.

New York City

Elvis Presley is a phenomenon. Music critics call him "unspeakably untalented and vulgar," a clergyman branded him "a whirling dervish of sex" and business boomed for a Cincinnati car dealer who promised to smash 50 Presley records for each customer. But while adults recoil in horror from the 21-year-old's high-energy pelvic gyrations and defiant sneer, delirious teenage fans bought seven million copies of his records this year.

Two years ago, Presley was a Memphis truck driver making $35 a week and aching to sing. Sam Phillips of Sun Records, who felt that a white artist who could per-form with the abandon of the best Negro stars would take the segregated pop charts by storm, was awed by Presley's raw talent and charisma. Local hits followed, and so did performances that sent female fans into such a frenzy that Presley was at times nearly mauled.

This year, Presley exploded onto the national charts with *Heartbreak Hotel, Don't Be Cruel* and *Blue Suede Shoes.* A brazen, high-voltage performance on a September 9 Ed Sullivan show grabbed a record TV audience of 54 million, but television censors have seen enough. His next appearance, in January, will show just his face.

American girls know what they like.

Pollock, Abstract Expressionist, dies

East Hampton, L.I., Aug. 11

A single-car crash today took the life of Jackson Pollock, a leading Abstract Expressionist painter. Pollock, who was born in Cody, Wyoming in 1912, studied at the Art Students' League in New York. Stimuli for his work of the 30s included the Social Realism of Thomas Hart Benton, his teacher, and the Mexican mural movement.

Pollock's discovery of an original signature style, the "drip" paintings dating from 1947, is recognized in avant-garde circles as a benchmark in modern art, though the public found it cryptic. "Jack the Dripper," as he was dubbed, would lay a huge canvas on the floor, then pour and drip house paints directly from the can onto its surface. The resultant work is not an image of an object, but rather an abstract "all-over" organization of skeins of pigment that emphasizes the gestural component of painting. Extremes of ecstasy and anxiety are suggested, and Pollock's personal troubles have often been read into these paintings. Although he was painting figures once more in the early 50s, the drip works won Pollock privileged status among such Abstract Expressionists as Barnet Newman, Franz Kline, Clyfford Still, Mark Rothko and Willem de Kooning.

April 19. *The girl from Philadelphia has become a real princess with her marriage to Monaco's Prince Rainier. Grace Kelly's charm and beauty make her the perfect choice for the regal role.*

Andrea Doria sinks following collision

Nantucket, Mass., July 26

In a dense fog, two luxury liners collided just before midnight yesterday, killing 50 people. The Italian vessel Andrea Doria sank 11 hours after being struck by the Stockholm, a Swedish ship. The accident, which occurred 60 miles south of Nantucket, was reportedly caused by radar blindness. The Stockholm, a 40-foot hole in its bow, slowly made it to port. Some 1,650 people were rescued by four ships. Not all were so fortunate: one man said his wife vanished through a gaping hole in the Andrea Doria. Some passengers said the crew failed to sound an alarm or announce information about the rescue effort.

Girls: Wear his ring around your neck

United States

For the girl who has a steady: a gold necklace to put his ring on. Think Elvis Presley's the most? Buy an Elvis Presley key chain. And while you're in a buying mood, stock up on some of the new items on the market this year, such as Comet cleanser, Raid to do in bugs and Imperial margarine. Or just stay home and enjoy the TV commercials of Bert and Harry Piel, of Betty Furness and Westinghouse, of Julia Mead and Lincoln-Mercury. Should a young woman tire of men and materialism, consider the path of M.E. Tower, who has become the first woman ordained as a Presbyterian minister.

April 25. *As Rocky Marciano retires, he leaves behind an amazing record. He is the only heavyweight champ never to have lost a professional bout and won 43 of 49 fights by the knockout route.*

Ike wins 2nd term with landslide vote

Voters endorse Eisenhower's course.

Washington, D.C., Nov. 6

Dwight D. Eisenhower was re-elected President today, scoring a landslide victory over Adlai E. Stevenson. The most impressive triumph since Franklin D. Roosevelt buried Alfred Landon, it makes Ike the first Republican in this century to win successive presidential elections. At 66, the World War II hero again carries the 43-year-old Vice President Richard Nixon into office with him. Voters backed the Republican contention that the nation needs Ike's experience, and rejected the Democrats' view that he is too old, a "part-time President" who delegated too much authority during his recent illnesses.

Bus segregation is unconstitutional

Montgomery, Alabama, Dec. 21

In a mass meeting, Montgomery's Negro citizens have agreed to end a year-long boycott of the city's bus system, a decision based on the city's announcement of compliance with a November 13 Supreme Court ruling that has declared segregation on buses unconstitutional. In offering an explanation of how this victory for Alabama Negroes was achieved, the Rev. Martin Luther King Jr., leader of the boycott, said, "Nonviolence is the most potent technique for oppressed people." King and 100 other Negroes had been arrested back in March for conducting an illegal boycott. Dr. King's case was settled with payment of a $500 fine. But it seemed a small price to pay because the case has led to desegregation in several Southern states (→ Feb. 1957).

American Negroes no longer have to turn right into the "colored waiting room."

Larsen is perfect

Brooklyn, N.Y., Oct. 10

Don Larsen pitched a perfect game today, the first in the major leagues in 34 years. In setting down 27 batters in a row, he also turned in the first no-hitter in a World Series as the New York Yankees defeated the Brooklyn Dodgers, four games to three. Larsen uses a unique no-windup delivery.

Russians trounce Americans at Olympics

Melbourne, Australia, Dec. 8

The United States took a drubbing from the Russians in the total Olympic standing but once again proved superior in track. The Soviet Union headed the standing, 722 to 593, using its own measure, or 622 to 497, using the European method. It also collected more medals than the Americans, 99 to 74, and more gold, 37 to 32. Bobby Morrow, 21-year-old sprinter from Abilene, Texas, proved to be the American star, winning both dashes with no trouble. Lee Calhoun and Glenn Davis accounted for hurdles victories, Charlie Jenkins took the 400 meters and Tom Courtney the 800. Bob Richards vaulted to an Olympic mark.

Hungarians revolt; U.S. won't act

Washington, D.C., November

While Hungarian rebels battled the tanks and troops of the Soviet army, the United States offered little more than moral support, backing for a resolution at the United Nations and asylum for refugees. The Hungarian rebels, encouraged by Radio Free Europe broadcasts, had hoped for American intervention. But the response of the United States was tempered by fear of a possible land war in Europe or a nuclear showdown. Inspired by Polish riots earlier this year, the Hungarian uprising began on November 5. The rebels enjoyed five days of freedom before the Soviet army crushed them.

U.S., Soviets agree in the Suez Crisis

Washington, D.C., Nov. 5

In one of their rare moments of accord, the United States and the Soviet Union today voted to support a United Nations call for an immediate cease-fire in Egypt as well as the withdrawal of French and British military units. Britain and France, America's usual allies, vetoed the resolution but the two are expected to comply. An invasion by English, French and Israeli forces was triggered by the Egyptian seizure of the Suez Canal in August. After the Russians threatened to intervene, the United States warned Britain, France and Israel that it did not intend to support them.

Arthur Miller and his new bride, Marilyn Monroe, meet Sir Laurence Olivier and Vivien Leigh. Both Miller and Monroe fans were surprised by the marriage of the playwright and the Hollywood goddess on June 29.

Washington, D.C., Jan. 28. Secretary of Defense Charles Wilson informs House Armed Services Committee that draft dodgers were harbored by Coast Guard during Korean conflict.

Washington, D.C., Feb. 25. Supreme Court, in Butler v. Michigan, holds that states do not have constitutional right to bar from sale materials that might be corrupting to minors.

Boston, Apr. 13. Boston Celtics defeat St. Louis Hawks, four games to three, in N.B.A. championship.

Greenville, South Carolina, Apr. 22. Stating that struggle is now against Communists and integration, Ku Klux Klan announces it is opening membership to Roman Catholics.

Bonn, West Germany, May 2. Secretary of State John Foster Dulles tells North American Council that United States will maintain its forces in Europe at current levels.

New York City, May 6. Diplomat and historian George F. Kennan wins both National Book Award and Pulitzer Prize for *Russia Leaves the War.*

New York City, May 6. Massachusetts Senator John F. Kennedy awarded Pulitzer Prize for *Profiles in Courage.*

Detroit, September. American Motors introduces nation's first compact car, the Rambler.

Nevada, Sept. 19. First United States underground nuclear tests begin.

New York City, Oct. 10. Milwaukee Braves beat New York Yankees, four games to three, to win World Series.

Cape Canaveral, Dec. 17. First Atlas I.C.B.M. tested by army.

Detroit, Dec. 29. Lions defeat Cleveland Browns, 59-14, for National Football League title.

Philadelphia. *American Bandstand* makes TV debut on ABC.

New York City. Dr. Seuss publishes *The Cat in the Hat* and *The Grinch Who Stole Christmas.*

New York City. *Atlas Shrugged* by Ayn Rand issued.

DEATH

Bethesda, Maryland, May 2. Joseph McCarthy, controversial U.S. Senator (*Nov. 14, 1908).

U.S. would respond to Mideast attack

Washington, D.C., Jan. 5

Any Communist aggression in the Middle East could result in American military intervention, according to President Eisenhower. Speaking before Congress today, the President asked the legislators for the power to use force to oppose any such aggression. He said that he would use American troops if requested by a nation that had come under attack, but only while he conducted "hour-by-hour" consultations with Congress and in accordance with the United Nations charter. The President also said he would seek $400 million for Mideast aid over two fiscal years.

Jasper Johns waves the American flag

New York City

Jasper Johns has said that he paints the American flag because he had a dream about doing so. *Flag on an Orange Field* joins the series of works on this theme begun in 1954 by the young painter from South Carolina. Little is known of Johns's work before that because he destroyed his youthful output. Done in encaustic, a technique combining paint and wax that is little used by contemporary artists, the flags, like the targets he paints, embody an alternative to Abstract Expressionism being developed by Johns and Robert Rauschenberg.

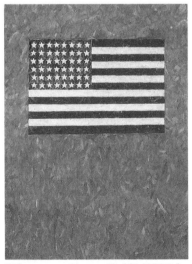

"Flag on an Orange Field" (1957) by Jasper Johns, who tests the limits.

King heads Southern Christian Leadership

The Rev. Martin Luther King Jr. has become a symbol of change in America.

Atlanta, Georgia, February

With a popular base developed during last year's Montgomery, Alabama, bus boycott, Negro leaders from 10 states have organized the Southern Christian Leadership Conference. The Rev. Dr. Martin Luther King Jr., along with Bayard Rustin and Stanley Levinson have established the interracial society to coordinate the activities of nonviolent protest groups throughout the country. The goals of the Leadership Conference include full citizenship and "total integration" into American life for Negroes. Dr. King will head the new organization. Another key member of the group is Ella Baker, who was a field secretary for the National Association for the Advancement of Colored People and an organizer for the Urban League. Baker will organize mass meetings to win support for the S.C.L.C. And Dr. King plans a national tour on which he will speak in over 200 localities. He is becoming known as an excellent spokesman and dynamic organizer. He was ordained a minister in 1947 and led Montgomery's Dexter Ave. Baptist Church. His role in the bus boycotts led to his jailing and the bombing of his house (→Aug. 29).

Communist Party in America in decline

New York City, December

The Communist Party, chained to Moscow and isolated from the American worker, is fading into obscurity. At a national committee meeting this month, the hard-line followers of William Z. Foster ousted reformer John Gates and deserted the "revisionist" *Daily Worker,* the party's official organ. At the party congress in February, Gates had the votes to force a break with Moscow, but backed off to save party unity. Since then, his faction has quit en masse. As one exiting New York leader complained, out of 160 members "a couple of dozen come to meetings; we sit around and argue about Hungary and Leninism. What the hell else is there to do?"

707 airliner crosses U.S. in record 3:48

Baltimore, Md., March 12

A National Airlines Boeing 707 broke a speed record for cross-country passenger flight when it arrived here today non-stop from Seattle in just 3 hours and 48 minutes. The four-engine jet transport carried 42 passengers and a crew of 10 on the 2,330-mile trip. The Boeing Airplane Company, which was founded by William Edward Boeing in 1916, introduced the 707 model on July 15, 1954. Replacing the outmoded piston engine, the 707 was the first American jet transport and on its maiden flight reached a cruising speed of 600 miles per hour. Built for intercontinental travel, it is capable of carrying 219 passengers.

Gibson first Negro to win Wimbledon

Wembley, England, July 6

Althea Gibson, born in a run-down cabin on a South Carolina cotton farm, has won the most coveted prize in tennis. She is the first Negro to win the All-England title at Wimbledon, in fact the first ever to take any major tennis tournament. Miss Gibson, who grew up on the streets of Harlem in New York, started by playing paddle tennis there and graduated to the bigger game. She won the New York State Negro girls' championship in 1945 and 1946 and the national title in 1948. In 1950, she broke the color line when she played at Forest Hills.

Sun-heated building

Albuquerque, N.M., Aug. 1

The nation's first totally sun-heated commercial building was dedicated today. The structure, appropriately named the Solar Building, uses the energy of the sun to generate heat during the day. Special battery-like collectors save the excess energy produced during the day, and it is then put to use heating the building at night. The innovative heating system was designed by Frank H. Bridgers and Donald Paxton.

Donning his trademark white bucks, now a nationwide fad, pop singer Pat Boone croons his way into the hearts of millions of Americans with such hits as "Love Letters in the Sand." Boone prides himself on his clean-cut image.

Basie band makes history, at Waldorf

New York City, June 15

The quick, breathless rhythms of the Count Basie Band are now making history at the Starlight Roof Room of the Waldorf-Astoria Hotel. It's the first Negro band ever to perform there. Ella Fitzgerald is also on hand. The Count's popular group seems to have played everywhere else, and pieces like *One O'clock Jump*, *Taxi War Dance* and *Jumpin' at the Woodside* are international favorites. After the Waldorf, the band heads for the Newport Jazz Festival. Later this year, the Count meets the Queen – or vice versa – in a Command Performance at London's Palladium.

Balloon 20 miles up

Forbes, North Dakota, Aug. 20

Paving the way for future space travelers, an Air Force balloonist has spent a record 32 hours suspended near the limits of Earth's atmosphere. Major David G. Simons landed near Forbes in his pressurized gondola after the flight took him to an altitude of 101,486 feet, nearly 20 miles up. An officer overseeing the test said it proved man can live in space. He said he would call for rapid development of manned rocket-powered vehicles.

Freed's radio show rocks 'n' rolls 'em

New York City, May 4

Alan Freed's old music teachers may be wondering just where they went wrong. The 35-year-old disk jockey has forsaken his classical roots to set an entire generation of teenagers rocking and rolling with his nightly radio show, which is now serving up the likes of Elvis Presley and Buddy Holly to a spellbound national network audience. Freed's live rock 'n' roll shows are also wowing young crowds, though a psychologist attending a recent extravaganza here warns the music could induce "medieval types of spontaneous lunacy," even "prehistoric rhythmic trances." But a 13-year-old fan begs to differ. She calls Freed "the mostest."

Rights act overcomes Thurmond filibuster

Civil rights movement continues as Negro students accompany whites to school.

Washington, D.C., Aug. 29

After much wrangling in the Senate, the Civil Rights Act finally won approval today. The major opposition came from Southern legislators, most notably from Senator Strom Thurmond of South Carolina, who broke all records by speaking for 24 hours and 18 minutes, making his performance the longest personal filibuster in history.

The Civil Rights Act was first proposed last year by President Eisenhower. The section of the bill that allows the Justice Department to bring suit on behalf of Negroes who are denied the right to vote was not included in the original draft, but was added later at the suggestion of Attorney General Herbert Brownell Jr. The bill was passed in the House and made its way to the Senate in June.

Title III of the bill, which would have allowed the Justice Department to sue to protect a civil right, was deleted from the act, partly because of Senator Richard Russell's argument that he doubted that the President actually understood the provision. The rest of the bill passed easily.

The Civil Rights Act establishes a commission to obtain facts, suggest further legislation, and amend the United States Code to affirm the right to vote or to sit on a jury regardless of race, color or previous condition of servitude. Opponents of the bill attached an amendment providing that, in cases of contempt arising under the act, a judge might impose a fine or sentence without jury trial (→ Sept. 25).

Britons and Yanks mark colonial events

Jamestown, Virginia, Oct. 16

This year has produced both British and American interest in commemorating two important colonial events. In a re-creation of the Mayflower's voyage of 1620, the 180-foot Mayflower II arrived in Plymouth, Massachusetts, on June 13, 54 days after having left Plymouth, England. A crowd of 25,000 people waited at the landing, while thousands watched the event on television. Today, Queen Elizabeth II paid a visit to Jamestown, Virginia, to commemorate the 350th anniversary of the first permanent English settlement in the New World.

A meeting on common ground.

Troops help integrate in Little Rock

Negro student Johnny Gray strikes back during the integration of Little Rock.

Federal troops escort Negro students up the steps and through the front door.

"The Problem We All Live With," by Norman Rockwell, seems to capture the quiet determination of one small child in the struggle for equality.

Little Rock, Ark., Sept. 25

Disputed and widely publicized for nearly a month, the integration of the Little Rock Central High School has finally taken place, with the help of 1,000 paratroopers and 10,000 Arkansas National Guardsmen ordered into federal service by President Eisenhower.

The election of Orval Faubus as Governor of Arkansas recently was hailed as a victory for liberals in Arkansas. The issue of race was never spoken of during the campaign. So it came as somewhat of a surprise when Faubus posted National Guardsmen outside Central High as a court-approved integration plan was to be implemented. As a first step toward total desegregation, nine Negro children were to attend the school. On September 5, the children were turned away when they attempted to attend their first classes at the school.

Commenting on the opposition of Governor Faubus to integration, the President said, "The federal Constitution will be upheld by me by every legal means at my command." On September 9, F.B.I. agents in Little Rock presented a 400-page report to a federal district judge who requested that the United States government enter the case. On September 20, after a hearing, the judge issued an injunction against Governor Faubus's attempts to impede integration.

On Monday, September 23, the guardsmen were gone and the children were able to enter the school. A mob of about 1,000 whites gathered outside it and there was talk of dragging the Negro children out of the school and lynching them. By noon, the order came from city authorities to take the children out. The N.A.A.C.P. said they would not attend school again without assurance that the President intends to protect them from the mob. The mob stayed at the school for two days. Today, the federal troops intervened and the Negro pupils entered Central High as the mob was dispersed. The paratroopers and guardsmen remain posted and may stay for the school year.

Eisenhower commented on the events by saying, "Mob rule cannot be allowed to override the decisions of our courts" (→ Sept. 1959).

Sputnik prompts a frenzied failure

Cape Canaveral, Fla., Dec. 6

Its national prestigue shaken by the Soviet launchings of Sputnik I and II, the United States is racing to gain an equal footing on the high ground of space. Today, however, the American answer to Sputnik, the Navy Vanguard rocket bearing a 3 1/4-pound grapefruit-sized satellite lifted two feet off its Cape Canaveral, Florida, launching pad only to collapse in a raging inferno. The spectacular failure was blamed by some experts on the tremendous political pressure to rush the program along. But space scientists don't promise to slacken their pace as the Russians dazzle the world. More powerful Jupiter and Atlas rockets are being hurried for future satellite attempts (→ July 29, 1958).

First atomic plant produces electricity

Shippingport, Penn., Dec. 18

The nation's first atomic power plant began generating electric energy today. The plant was opened by the Duquesne Light Company in conjunction with the Atomic Energy Commission, as authorized by the Atomic Energy Act of 1954. This allows industry, with A.E.C. licensing, to use nuclear fuels to run atomic power plants. An A.E.C. report on nuclear accidents says that a worst-case scenario at a 200-megawatt reactor may kill 3,400 people within a 45-mile radius.

"West Side Story"

New York City, Sept. 26

West Side Story has exploded on the American stage like a bomb thrown at decades of conventional, musical romance. True, it retells the Romeo and Juliet tale, but the warring gangs – the white Jets and the Puerto Rican Sharks – are right from the switchbladed streets of contemporary New York. The language thumbs its nose at the traditional gentility of the genre, and the hammering beat of Leonard Bernstein's music breaks like a new, overpowering wave. All in all, it's a revolutionary work.

1958

Eisenhower

Washington, D.C., March 3. President Eisenhower and Vice President Nixon reach an arrangement whereby, should chief executive become disabled, the Vice President would temporarily assume presidential duties.

New York City, March 11. Robert Penn Warren wins National Book Award and Pulitzer Prize for *Poems, 1954-1956.*

St. Louis, Apr. 12. St. Louis Hawks defeat Boston Celtics, four games to two, for N.B.A. title.

Moscow, Apr. 13. Texan Van Cliburn wins first prize in prestigious Tchaikovsky Piano Competition.

New York City, April. Ford Thunderbird unveiled, at International Automobile Show.

Arlington National Cemetery, Va., May 30. Burial ceremonies held for unknown soldiers of World War II and Korean conflict.

New York City, May. International News Service and United Press merge, to form United Press International.

Washington, D.C., June 16. Supreme Court rules in Kent v. Dulles that State Department has no right to refuse passports based upon political affiliations or views.

Washington, D.C., Aug. 6. President Eisenhower signs Defense Reorganization Act, giving defense secretary greater control over military.

United States, Sept. 26. Yacht Columbia successfully defends America's Cup against British challenger Sceptre.

Milwaukee, Oct. 9. Yankees win World Series, four games to three, over Braves.

New York City, Oct. 26. Pan American World Airways inaugurates first American jet service to Europe.

New York City, Dec. 28. Baltimore Colts defeat New York Giants, 23-17, for N.F.L. title.

New York City. American Express Company introduces credit card service; 500,000 use card by end of year.

United States. *Three Flags* painted by Jasper Johns.

Hollywood, Calif. *Vertigo,* starring James Stewart, released.

Vice President Nixon greeted by hostile crowds in Latin America

Washington, D.C., May 15

Vice President Richard Nixon returned to cheers today after a tumultuous 18-day Latin American tour that saw him besieged by violent mobs in Peru and Venezuela. The Vice President was welcomed home by an estimated 15,000 people at the airport and about 85,000 along his route to the White House.

His trip, which began with a visit to Argentina, grew violent May 8 when he reached Lima, Peru. Nixon had been scheduled to meet a student group at the University of San Marco. In a dramatic gesture, against the advice of his security staff, he ventured into a mob of demonstrators outside the university. He was spat upon, hit by a stone, shoved and booed. An hour later, he and his staff fought their way past 2,000 demonstrators outside his hotel. Similar violence beset him in Caracas, Venezuela.

President Eisenhower said in his welcoming address, "The occurrence of these incidents has in no way impaired the friendship be-

Vice President Nixon meets with the President. Despite his violent reception in Latin America, Nixon is rapidly developing an expertise in foreign affairs.

tween the United States and any other single one of our sister republics to the south."

Nixon said the Latin American masses support the United States, and that a "minority element" of Communists was to blame for the disturbances. He said Communist leaders stirred up crowds by exploiting local economic problems.

Millionth at I.B.M.

New York City

Less than a century since writing machines were invented, International Business Machines has produced its millionth electric typewriter. The first marketed typewriter, by E. Remington & Sons in 1874, only produced capital letters. Since I.B.M. introduced electrics in the 1920s, the company has made typing more popular and versatile.

Bums, Giants move

New York City

In Brooklyn, the Gowanus Canal was running high with the tears of the Faithful. In Manhattan, they were saying, "Say it ain't so, say it ain't so." The Dodgers, those beloved Bums, were moving to Los Angeles, and along with them the Giants were leaving the hallowed Polo Grounds and heading for San Francisco. It was all part of baseball's growing pains and the lure of gold out West. In 1954, the St. Louis Browns became the Baltimore Orioles and in 1955 the Philadelphia Athletics moved to Kansas City.

Michigan's Mackinac Bridge is dedicated

Mackinaw City, Mich., June 28

It is considered an engineering marvel, stretching about five miles to link upper and lower Michigan. Today, the Mackinac Bridge was formally dedicated. It is the world's longest suspension bridge, the suspension part of it measuring 8,614 feet, which is some 2,000 feet longer than the Golden Gate Bridge across San Francisco Bay. Alto-

gether, the "Mack" spans 26,444 feet. It cost $100 million and took nearly four years to build, but it is soon to pay off because it will stimulate economic growth in northern Michigan. Governor G. Mennen Williams said it will be a "key link in America's system of modern arterial highways, as a gateway to the great outdoor vacationland of northern Michigan."

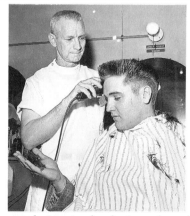

King Elvis loses his crown. Presley may rock America but he is ready and willing to serve it as well. When he was called up for duty in the army March 24, millions of his fans came out to catch a glimpse of their cropped idol.

N.A.S.A. is to vie with Soviet in space

Washington, D.C., July 29

Congress feels that the United States must not be outdone by the Soviet Union in the space race. To compete with the Russians, the legislature passed a bill today allotting millions of dollars for the creation of the National Aeronautics and Space Agency to coordinate space technology research. Even many economic conservatives voted for the program, spurred into action by the successful launching last year of Sputnik, the first man-made satellite. America put up its first satellite, Explorer, January 31. But the Soviets are still ahead. N.A.S.A. is to start work on a manned space craft immediately (→ Apr. 9, 1959).

Dr. King is stabbed

New York City, September

The Rev. Dr. Martin Luther King Jr., leader of the Southern Christian Leadership Conference, and a principal spokesman for the cause of civil rights, was stabbed by a Negro woman while in Harlem to promote his new book, *Stride to Freedom*. The woman is thought to be deranged. Dr. King is a Baptist minister and an eloquent advocate of non-violent protest as a means of gaining equality for Negroes. He is expected to recover from the injury.

Marines go to Lebanon

Once again the United States Marines see action, this time in the Middle East.

Washington, D.C., July 15

President Eisenhower sent 5,000 marines to violence-torn Lebanon today to help preserve that country's government in the wake of internal revolts and a coup in neighboring Iraq. The troops, along with sea and air support, landed in Beirut and occupied its airport. The President said that the number of marines would be increased if necessary, but that they would be "withdrawn as rapidly as circumstances permit."

Their mission is to show support for President Camille Chamoun's government. Eisenhower said Chamoun sent an "urgent request" for help yesterday, after developments in Iraq. Chamoun said, "Without an immediate showing of United States support, the government of Lebanon would be unable to survive," Eisenhower reported.

Lebanon has been racked by an insurrection for two months, since violence broke out along the Syrian border. The crisis worsened yesterday after the Iraqi regime was ousted violently. Eisenhower says Syria and Egypt – which make up the United Arab Republic – are responsible for the trouble.

U.S. acts to temper Chinese island spat

Washington, D.C., Oct. 1

Although President Eisenhower has committed the United States to protecting the Chinese Nationalist islands of Quemoy and Matsu – a move criticized by Senate leaders – the administration has also called for Taiwan to reduce its garrison there. A White House official said today if the Chinese Communists would stop bombing the islands from the mainland, talks could progress and the Nationalist force from Taiwan could be cut. The Communists have been shelling Quemoy since August. In September, the mainland Chinese extended their territorial limits to 12 miles, including the small islands.

"Affluent Society"

Cambridge, Massachusetts

Americans may not be as well off as they think, writes Harvard economist John Kenneth Galbraith in his new book, *The Affluent Society*. In such chapters as *The Theory of Social Balance*, *Security and Survival*, and *Labor, Leisure and the New Class*, Galbraith ties such ills as inflation and recession to a materialistic public and to the stale policies of timid leaders.

Americans go crazy for Hoola Hoops

United States

Last year's Frisbie fad has sailed off and this year the hoop-la is for the Hoola Hoop. The new hullabaloo began at about mid-year in Southern California when Arthur Melin and Richard Knerr decided to promote and sell a version of bamboo hoops that they had heard Australian schoolchildren used. With some chemists at a plastics factory, they designed a tubing of material called Grex (a form of polyethylene), which when stapled end to end formed a hoop. It was dubbed a Hoola Hoop, and now there are over 20 other manufacturers, calling it "Whoop De Do," "Hoop Zing" and other forgettable names. By this fall, 25 million have been sold at about $3 each. Millions of kids are delighted, and millions of adults have sore hips.

"Baltimore" by Palmer Hayden. In big cities and suburbs, American prosperity is unprecedented, symbolized by such features as fins on cars.

A new fad makes the rounds.

Nautilus under the ice

Reykjavik, Iceland, Aug. 8

In an achievement fraught with strategic implications, the world's first atomic-powered submarine, the Nautilus, has pioneered a new route beneath the frozen wastes of the Arctic. The feat, disclosed by the White House today, took the ship 1,830 miles under the polar ice cap from Point Barrow, Alaska, to the Atlantic near Spitsbergen, Norway, in just four days.

The Nautilus was designed and built under the direction of Rear Admiral Hyman G. Rickover and was commissioned on September 30, 1954. With just a few pounds of enriched uranium, the ship can "steam" for over 60,000 miles without refueling and can submerge for weeks while cruising at over 20 knots. "Operation Northwest Passage" began on July 23, when the 300-foot-long craft left Pearl Harbor with a crew of 116 led by Commander W.R. Anderson. The Nautilus passed directly beneath the North Pole on August 3 and reached Iceland yesterday.

On an ominous note, the Nautilus has proven that the fleet of Polaris submarines scheduled to be deployed starting in 1960 could hide under the polar ice cap while armed with thermonuclear missiles. Experts say the Russians have no atomic submarines, but they concede that, like most strategic advantages in the nuclear age, this one is not likely to last forever.

Ike adviser Adams ousted after scandal

President Eisenhower and White House aide Sherman Adams in happier times.

Washington, D.C., Sept. 22

President Eisenhower's chief of staff, Sherman Adams, reluctantly resigned his post today amid a storm of scandal. A congressional panel concluded that Adams received expensive gifts, an oriental rug and a vicuna coat, for using his influence at the Securities and Exchange Commission and the Federal Trade Commission to help Boston industrialist Bernard Goldfine.

The impropriety tarnishes the reputation of the President, who was once described by the diplomat George Kennan as "the nation's number one Boy Scout."

Adams quit to minimize the embarrassment to his boss and the Republican Party. He declared his innocence in a televised resignation speech, saying, "I have done no wrong." He blamed a Democratic "campaign of vilification" for his downfall. Eisenhower has supported Adams, saying, "How dreadful it is that cheap politicians can so pillory an honorable man."

The scandal seems to have contributed to a dramatic slump in Ike's popularity. In the first half of his second term, opinion polls show a drop in approval from 79 percent to 49 percent. Democrats say the decline will help them pick up seats in this year's congressional elections.

"Hang down your head, Tom Dooley"

United States

If parents were lucky this year, they might have heard the dulcet harmonies of the Kingston Trio wafting in from their kids' rooms. But the pounding beat and raucous shouts of Little Richard's high-powered rock 'n' roll stomp *Good Golly, Miss Molly* were the norm, as the new music continued to climb the charts.

The Kingston Trio emerged from the smoky folk clubs of San Francisco to move a huge, mostly college-aged audience with pensive folk ballads such as *Tom Dooley*. The Everly Brothers hit it big with the lilting country-tinged harmonies of *All I Have to Do Is Dream*, as did 17-year-old Ricky Nelson from TV's *Ozzie and Harriet* with *Poor Little Fool*.

Joining Little Richard among the rockers were Chuck Berry, whose ringing guitar and lyrics about cars and girls were pure poetry with kids on hits like *Johnny B. Goode*, Texas's Buddy Holly and the Crickets, with *Think it Over*, and J.P. *Big Bopper* Richardson.

American rocketry gets a big boost

Cape Canaveral, Fla., Nov. 28

The National Aeronautics and Space Administration reported the first successful launching of an Intercontinental Ballistic Missile today. The Atlas rocket hit its target in the South Atlantic, some 5,500 miles from its launching pad. The achievement helps restore confidence in space and defense technology after last month's semi-failure of the Pioneer. That satellite was launched to reach the moon's orbit, but it burned up and fell to Earth a third of the way to its destination. However, it did travel higher, 68,000 miles above the Earth, than any other space vehicle.

Effort is made to close education gap

Washington, D.C., Aug. 23

Is Johnny dimmer than Vladimir? Many observers of American education see students here falling behind their Soviet counterparts. A *Life* magazine editorial has commented, "The schools are in terrible shape ... the spartan Soviet system is producing many students better equipped with the technicalities of the Space Age." It blames poor curriculums, crowded classes and poorly paid teachers for the lag. Today, Congress acted to close the gap with the National Defense Education Act. It provides $1 billion, mostly in the form of student loans on the college and graduate level.

The national struggle goes on. In a rare moment of peaceful change, white and Negro students walk side by side on the first day of school integration in Louisville, Kentucky. This year alone, about one million student days were lost across the nation because of school closings to thwart integration.

1959

Eisenhower

New Cuban ruler pays a visit to the U.S.

Fidel Castro, Cuban revolutionary.

Washington, D.C., Apr. 15

Premier Fidel Castro of Cuba arrived in the United States today for what he termed a "truth operation," to counter "propaganda" against the Cuban Revolutionary Government. The 32-year-old former guerrilla leader, wearing his trademark green military fatigues, was greeted by 1,500 supporters, as well as State Department officials.

His visit grew from an invitation to address the American Society of Newspaper Editors, which has since been criticized for barring radio and television coverage of the event, scheduled for next Friday.

The United States recognized the new regime in January, a week after Castro's troops ousted dictator Fulgencio Batista. Many of Batista's forces have fled Cuba or been imprisoned or executed. The new government, nominally headed by President Manuel Urrutia Lleo, but in fact by Castro, has promised to hold free elections (→ July 6, 1960).

Fly coast to coast with American Airlines

Los Angeles, Jan. 25

It was not very long ago that it took days to travel from coast to coast. Not any more. American Airlines announced today that it is opening same-day passenger service east-to-west as well as west-to-east between New York and Los Angeles on its Boeing 707 jets. The service is the first of its kind. Industry experts expect other airlines to be offering similar flights soon. Last month, Pan American World Airways inaugurated regular trans-Atlantic service on Boeing 707's from New York International Airport to Paris. It was the first American airline to offer the jet flight. It takes a third less time than on a propeller plane.

Sandburg addresses Congress on Lincoln

Washington, D.C., Feb. 12

Carl Sandburg accomplished two nearly impossible feats today: He pulled the nation's two parties together and, more remarkably, he

Sandburg sings Lincoln's praises.

reduced the members of Congress to silence. The occasion was the sesquicentennial of Abraham Lincoln's birth, and Sandburg, whose massive biography of "Honest Abe" won the Pulitzer Prize in 1939, sang Lincoln's praises on the floor of Congress. The usual yawns, snores, whispers and tapping pencils echoed through the hall as the white-haired bard strode to the podium. But Sandburg, unfazed, let his lyric cadences do their work, as he read his opening sentence. "Not often in the story of mankind does a man arrive on earth who is both steel and velvet, who is as hard as rock and as soft as drifting fog, who holds in his heart and mind the paradox of terrible storm and peace unspeakable ... " A hush fell over the congressmen, who seemed bewitched by Sandburg's address.

Three rock stars die in plane crash

Buddy Holly, talented Texan.

Mason City, Iowa, Feb. 3

Rock 'n' roll fans were shocked today by the deaths in a small-plane crash here of three top stars, Buddy Holly, Richie Valens and J.P. "Big Bopper" Richardson. The plane, which plunged to earth after taking off in snowy conditions, was to fly the singers to a show in Fargo, North Dakota. Holly, 22, was beloved for hits such as *Peggy Sue*, Valens, 17, for *La Bamba* and Richardson, 24, for *Chantilly Lace*. Teenage fans have "lost" other heroes as well lately, Elvis Presley to the United States Army, top disk jockey Alan Freed, done in by a payola scandal, and Little Richard, whose searing hits included *Long Tall Sally* and *Lucille*, who has left rock 'n' roll in order "to make peace with Jesus."

Cranberry scare

Washington, D.C., Nov. 9

A weed-killer (ATZ) that has caused cancer in rats has contaminated some cranberry bogs in Oregon and Washington, the Department of Health, Education and Welfare said today. No contamination was found in the cranberry-growing states of New Jersey, Wisconsin and Massachusetts, but the scare caused stores and restaurants to avoid the fruit. The industry claims the contaminant is in so small an amount that it is harmless.

Able, Baker, Pioneer IV and Explorer IV

Cape Canaveral, Florida

The United States, lagging far behind the Soviet Union in the space race, succeeded in launching the first orbiting weather station on February 17. And since then, the new National Aeronautics and Space Administration has staged impressive otherworldly feats.

On May 29, two monkeys were rocketed 300 miles into space in the nose of a Jupiter rocket, then plucked safely from the Caribbean, 1,700 miles from the launching site here. The space travelers, a rhesus monkey named Able and a smaller squirrel monkey, Baker, were to show what effects weightlessness and high speed may have on mammals. NASA has now selected seven human astronauts and plans to send the first on a space trip within two years.

On March 13, a camera aboard a research rocket took ultraviolet pictures of the sun at an altitude of 123 miles, and on March 4, a gold-plated 13.4-pound Pioneer IV probe sped past the moon on its way to a perpetual orbit around the sun. Images of Earth transmitted from these satellites as well as from the 147-pound Explorer IV, launched on August 7, are forever altering the perspective of mankind.

St. Lawrence Seaway is officially opened

St. Lambert, Quebec, June 26

Queen Elizabeth and President Eisenhower today formally opened the St. Lawrence Seaway linking the Atlantic Ocean with the Great Lakes. The Canadian government, which bore 80 percent of the $750 million cost, was represented at the ceremonies by Prime Minister John Diefenbaker.

The seaway completion brought an end to years of controversy in both the United States and Canada regarding the desirability of the project. Washington was at first reluctant to participate, but changed its mind when Ottawa threatened to go ahead alone, building the entire seaway within its own territory.

More than 500 homes and 6,500 inhabitants along the Canadian shore had to be relocated to higher ground because of the flooding of Lake St. Lawrence. The 2,350-mile waterway allows bulk carriers of up to 730 feet long to pass through the system of canals, locks, rivers and lakes as far inland as Duluth, Minnesota. The seaway will have a major economic impact on both countries. It makes possible the exploitation of the iron ore deposits of Quebec and Labrador and it changes Canada from a net importer to an exporter of iron ore, mostly to the United States.

Sub with I.C.B.M. is launched by navy

Groton, Conn., June 9

Members of the United States Navy saluted the crew of the atomic submarine George Washington today as the vessel left its dock at the famous shipyard here. It is the first sub launched that carries and can fire intercontinental ballistic missiles, the powerful longrange Polaris rockets. The Joint Chiefs of Staff herald the George Washington as another advance to close the gap between Soviet and American weaponry. It is expected that the submarine will fire a test missile later this summer.

Ailing "Lady Day" finds peace at last

New York City, July 17

The melancholy song that was Billie Holiday's life ended in a hospital here today. She was 44. Before her death, she was arrested in her bed on a drug charge. The police confiscated her magazines, radio and Whitman's chocolates. "Lady Day" lived an unbelievably tough life, fed by the kind of bittersweet pride that can be heard in her recording of *Fine and Mellow*. As for the mysterious, haunting quality of her singing, someone said, "It ain't the blues. I don't know what it is, but you got to hear her."

"Lady Chatterley" still too hot for U.S.

Washington, D.C., July 21

Thirty-one years after it first appeared – in a private edition in Italy – D.H. Lawrence's *Lady Chatterley's Lover* is still too hot for American postal workers to handle. Today, Postmaster General Arthur Summerfield called the novel, about a torrid liaison between a married woman and her virile gamekeeper, "obscene and filthy" and banned it from the mails. This angered American fans of the English writer, who died in 1930. But they shouldn't feel cheated. The book is illegal in England, too.

Integrated schools open in Little Rock

Little Rock, Ark., September

Two high schools here have reopened this year with token integration – three Negro students at Hall High School and three at Central High. The presence of police is assuring the safety of the children. The mob violence and tension that characterized similar attempts in the past two years seem to be dissipating. This year's action is based on a decision by the newly elected Little Rock board of education and represents what some consider to be merely a first step in achieving equality for all (→ Apr. 1960).

Upon his death on April 9, the architect Frank Lloyd Wright left behind an enduring legacy. Wright's innovative designs, from the "Falling Water" house to the Guggenheim Museum, have influenced an entire generation of architects and have set American design on a unique course.

Moscow kitchen debate

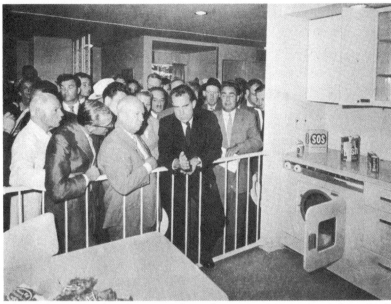

Khrushchev: "You don't know anything about communism except fear of it."

Moscow, July 24

Heated exchanges between Soviet Premier Nikita Khrushchev and Vice President Richard Nixon did not take place at the Kremlin. They began unexpectedly today in a model kitchen.

Khrushchev challenged the Vice President as Nixon was formally opening the United States National Exhibition before scores of reporters and television cameras. The show features a model American home equipped with all the latest domestic technology, including a washing machine and kitchen gadgets. It prompted the Soviet leader to say that "Americans should

not think the Russian people will be astonished to see these things." Russian homes, he asserted, have modern conveniences.

The exchange between the two men reached a boiling point when it moved from a comparison of the standard of living in each country to war between the two nations over West Berlin.

Referring to the recent threats by Premier Khrushchev to "free" West Berlin from American control, Vice President Nixon said that neither country should be given the ultimatum to "accept dictation or fight," cautioning that "if war comes, we both lose" (→ Sept. 27).

Alaska, Hawaii join USA

President Eisenhower unveils the new United States flag, resplendent with its 50 stars. The latest stars represent recently welcomed Alaska and Hawaii.

Honolulu, Hawaii, Aug. 21

Hawaii lost the race with Alaska to become the 49th state, but today, with a proclamation signed by President Eisenhower, it became the 50th star on the American flag.

Alaska became the 49th state on January 3, after Hawaii's non-voting delegate to Congress, John A. Burns, acceded to the Democratic leadership in Washington and agreed to a one-year delay. The nation's northernmost land had struggled for 42 years for the privilege of statehood. Its acceptance into the union was the first since 1912, when President Taft made Arizona the 48th state. Covering one-fifth the

area of the rest of the United States, Alaska is the nation's largest but least populous state.

Hawaii has been ready for statehood for nearly a decade, having adopted a state constitution in 1950. The delay was marked by a long series of congressional hearings on the threat of communism in the islands. No proof of such a threat was established, but seven residents were convicted of conspiring to topple the government. The Supreme Court overturned their convictions. Still, the stigma prevailed to the moment Congress approved statehood, with most of the opposition coming from the South.

Van Doren sweating for the cameras.

TV quiz contestants admit role in rigging

Washington, D.C., Nov. 2

Charles Van Doren, a 33-year-old assistant professor of English at Columbia University, confessed today that he has lived a lie for three years. During 14 appearances on *Twenty-One*, he got the questions in advance, enabling him to win $129,000. Others have come forward telling tales of rigging: Hank Bloomgarden, who won $98,500 on the same program, and two $4,000 winners on *The $64,000 Challenge*, a clergyman and a salesman. As a result of the scandal, the Federal Trade Commission will try to rid television of deceptive practices (→ Jan. 17, 1962).

Detroit, November 19. *The Ford Edsel has a 120-inch wheel base, contour seats, self-adjusting brakes and a driver-operated lubrication system. But fewer than 100,000 were sold in two years, and today it was discontinued.*

Khrushchev tours U.S.

Premier Khrushchev speaks following his arrival at Andrews Air Force Base.

New York City, Sept. 27

Soviet Premier Nikita Khrushchev was a happy man today as he sped to the airport after a 12-day tour of the United States, his first. "Let us have more and more use for the short American word, O.K.," Khrushchev said after he signed several accords with President Eisenhower at Camp David. The Premier had a fine time in Hollywood and on his visit to an Iowa farm, but, he was disappointed when he could not visit Disneyland for "security reasons." He spoke of world disarmament at the United Nations General Assembly, toured an I.B.M. plant in San Francisco and ate his first hot dog on his tour of the farm belt (→ May 17, 1960).

Americans are said to be status seekers

United States

It's open season on Americans. Readers have already been lambasted for being "other-directed" (David Riesman) and materialistic (John Kenneth Galbraith). Now, it seems, they are also hung up on what the neighbors think. So says Vance Packard, author of *The Status Seekers*, a withering look at the nation's class system; white- and blue-collar groups are being driven apart and the wedge is a college education. On the matter of status, ironically, Packard's critics dismiss him as *only* a journalist who has been encroaching on the exclusive turf of the sociologist.

Record steel strike, 116 days, is ended

Washington, D.C., Nov. 7

Under the Taft-Hartley Act, the Supreme Court has ordered an 80-day halt to the longest steel strike ever. And as union counsel Arthur Goldberg says, "From the Supreme Court, the only appeal is to God." So 500,000 workers returned to work after 116 days. President Eisenhower told both sides of their "obligation" to resolve all differences, the worst of which is the issue of labor's right to stop automation from eating up jobs. Most workers are happy to be back at work, but some resent the injunction. "How would Ike like it," said one striker, "if we told him he couldn't play golf for 80 days."

It's a gas! Get with it in a go-cart!

United States

If you think a go-cart is a gas, this is another year of great fads for you. Make the scene by parachute jumping. Get with it by trying some phone booth packing (the record to beat is 25 in a booth). Take up bowling or sailing. Become a member of the Chicago Buddhist Temple or Maharishi Mahesh Yogi's Spiritual Regeneration Foundation. But please, keep in mind the findings of a *Look* magazine poll on moral attitudes, which states that America's moral relativity is based on group acceptance. In other words, you should do whatever you want to do – as long as the neighbors are doing it too.

Films: "Ben Hur," "Some Like It Hot"

Hollywood, California

William Wyler's big-budget production of *Ben Hur*, with Charlton Heston, has been the year's top-grossing picture. Meanwhile, foreign films such as *La Dolce Vita*, *Breathless* and *The 400 Blows* were also successful. To combat the popularity of television, Hollywood went for the big laugh, and got it with Billy Wilder's brilliant farce *Some Like It Hot*, with Marilyn Monroe, Tony Curtis and Jack Lemmon. Monroe is proving to be a gifted comedienne with a hilarious innocence about her.

Doris Day and Rock Hudson entertain in *Pillow Talk*, Sandra Dee is a cute *Gidget*, while former child star Elizabeth Taylor confirms her versatility in the chilling *Suddenly, Last Summer*, with Katharine Hepburn and Montgomery Clift. Otto Preminger strains Production Code limits in *Anatomy of a Murder*, dealing with rape. And Alfred Hitchcock offered *North by Northwest*, a playful thriller with Cary Grant and Eva Marie Saint.

Independent film makers, unhampered by studio traditions, are experimenting, and some stars, such as Burt Lancaster, Marlon Brando, Richard Widmark, Kirk Douglas and William Holden, forgo star salaries for profit participation. Now location shooting and production of films at far-off studios are threatening the old Hollywood system.

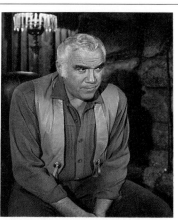

One hundred years after the first cattle drive, westerns predominate on television: Lorne Greene in "Bonanza" and Clint Eastwood in "Rawhide."

Charlton Heston plays "Ben Hur"

Curtis and Lemmon "Like It Hot."

The 1950s: A time of tranquility and prosperity

A nuclear test is conducted in the ongoing arms race with the Soviets. Lots of people worry about the Bomb.

The decade is filled with funny fads, from stuffing phone booths to coonskin caps to twirling hoola hoops.

President Eisenhower, affectionately known as Ike, presides over an era of seemingly endless tranquility, when the Yankees always seem to come in first and the United States of America always seems to be on top of the world.

The 50s are a time of mostly peaceful progress in civil rights - of integration - when Negroes in all walks of life register their grievances and stand up for the rights guaranteed, but too often denied them, by the Constitution.

A time when the nuclear family prospers, when everybody heads for the suburbs, when a convertible with whitewall tires is it, and when situation comedies on television, such as "Leave It to Beaver," actually seem to mirror real life.

The Barbie doll, a sensation when introduced in 1959. Is she a symbol of the ideal woman of the future?

William Levitt converted a Long Island potato field into a prefabricated suburban community in 1949. In the next 10 years, his four-room $7,990 homes with outdoor barbecue, washing machine and built-in TV set sold fast.

In the wake of the suburban housing boom comes the baby boom, when America is a special land for kids.

When the United States of America leads the world

The only cloud on the horizon is Soviet Russia, the Communist enemy headed by Premier Nikita Khrushchev, the funny-looking little man who in 1956 said, "Whether you like it or not, history is on our side. We will bury you."

What the Barbie doll is to little girls, toy trucks are to little boys. In gravel driveways and on dirt mounds across the nation, future engineers spend hours digging and building an even better landscape than the one around them.

Elvis Presley, the man responsible for the emergence of rock 'n' roll. His "Hound Dog," "Don't Be Cruel" and "Love Me Tender" were instant hits.

The one and only Marilyn Monroe, the woman responsible for putting sex back in American life. "It's nice to be included in people's fantasies," she says.

The "New Look," introduced by Christian Dior of Paris in 1947, has revolutionized women's fashion.

Baseball's dynasty lives happily ever after: New York Yankee slugger Mickey Mantle, catcher Yogi Berra and manager Casey Stengel, stars of a ball club that won eight pennants and six World Series victories in the 10 years from 1950-59. Mantle won the Triple Crown in 1956, and Berra was M.V.P. in 1951, 1954 and 1955.

Sit-ins, cutting edge in a war on bias

Greensboro, N.C., April

Throughout the South, Negroes have adopted a non-violent protest technique that has been dubbed the "sit-in," to combat discrimination at lunch counters, cafeterias, libraries, churches and beaches. The trend toward this type of protest got started on February 1, when four Negro college students refused to move from a Woolworth lunch counter in Greensboro, when they were denied service. The action quickly spread to lunch counters in more than 50 Southern towns. This led to wade-ins at all-white beaches, read-ins at libraries, and kneel-ins at racially segregated churches. Many Negro students have been arrested for the protests, and the National Association for the Advancement of Colored People has stepped in to defend quite a number of them. Among the highly respected people lending their assistance to provide lessons in non-violent protest for the students in Greensboro are the Rev. Dr. Martin Luther King Jr., head of the Southern

Students of North Carolina A&T College stage a sit-in at Woolworth's lunch counter in Greensboro, N.C. A white woman refuses to sit with Negroes.

Christian Leadership Conference, George Simpkins, the N.A.A.C.P. aide, and Len Holt of the Congress of Racial Equality.

Sit-ins at Nashville, Tennessee, led to 76 arrests, but they have forced politicians and businessmen to deal with the Negro community and a favorable resolution is believed to be near. There were 43 arrests at a Raleigh, North Carolina, sit-in. Race riots broke out after sit-ins and wade-ins at Chattanooga, Tennessee, and in Biloxi, Mississippi, where 10 Negroes were wounded by whites (→ May 7).

Sub Triton circles globe under water

Delaware, May 10

The American nuclear-powered submarine Triton poked its conning tower above the waves off Delaware just before dawn today, completing a record underwater circumnavigation of the globe. It took 84 days and covered 41,500 miles, retracing much of the route of the 16th-century explorer Ferdinand Magellan.

The 7,750-ton Triton is the largest and most powerful sub in the world. Captain Edward L. Beach, who is also the author of the best seller *Run Silent, Run Deep*, wrote in his log that "one can almost become lyrical thinking of the tremendous drive of the dual power plant of this great ship." The sub, with 183 aboard, left its Groton, Connecticut, base February 16. One aim was to test the endurance of humans deprived of sunlight and fresh air; a psychologist reported high morale, except when smoking was banned. The feat also raises the nuclear stakes: missile-carrying Polaris subs will soon roam the seas.

Basketball's Lakers move to Los Angeles

Los Angeles

Basketball has finally joined major league baseball and football in moving to California. Hit hard by the retirement of George Mikan, the Minneapolis Lakers have moved their National Basketball franchise to Los Angeles. The club had declined on the court and at the box office since Mikan's departure, but the outlook is changing. The Lakers now have Elgin Baylor, who scored 71 points in one game, and his partner, Jerry West, a rookie out of West Virginia. After a slow start, West quickly improved.

Golf is becoming the sport of choice among many Americans, thanks to the fact that it is favored by people like President Eisenhower, who spends a lot of time at it, and Arnold Palmer, who won the Masters again this year.

Soviets down U-2; summit wrecked

Population nearing 180 million mark

New York City

The national census report shows the population is now 179,323,175. This indicates that the annual average growth has been 18.5 percent since 1930. New York State, whose population increased by only 13.2 percent in the three decades, to 16,782,304, will lose two of its 43 seats in the House of Representatives because of a proportionate drop in relation to some states. California will gain eight seats, for a total of 38. The census shows large population gains in Nevada, Florida, Alaska and Arizona. Other statistics show the number of women over 14 who work is up, from 25 percent in 1940 to 34 percent now.

Will new computers slash work force?

Washington, D.C.

American industry is being seduced by the capabilities of computers. Last year, the first automated computerized control system was installed at a Texaco refinery, and for the first time banking is using MICR (Magnetic Ink Character Recognition). Languages such as FORTRAN are economically attractive because they allow computers to do the work of humans. Though 2,000 computers are in use, analysts point out that workers are always needed to run them.

Montreal captures its 5th straight cup

Montreal, Apr. 17

The Montreal Canadians have taken the Stanley Cup again, the first team ever to win it five straight times. They also won their third National Hockey League title in a row, beating Toronto by 13 points in the standings. In the playoffs, the Canadians went on to sweep Chicago, then Toronto, to win the cup in a minimum of eight games. The Montreal star was Jacques Plante, who excels despite 200 stitches in his face, a nose that has been broken four times, a fractured skull and two broken cheekbones.

Paris, May 17

The Big Four summit meeting here never got off the ground after the Russians downed an American U-2 spy plane over Soviet territory and captured its pilot, Francis Gary Powers, on May 1.

The talks stalled when President Eisenhower refused to meet a demand to "apologize for past acts of aggression" against the Soviet Union and to punish "those responsible" for the U-2 incident. He did agree to stop the spy flights over the Soviet Union. These were the conditions that Premier Nikita S. Khrushchev said must be met before he would participate in the Paris summit discussions with Eisenhower, Britain's Prime Minister Harold Macmillan and French President Charles de Gaulle that had been scheduled to get under way on May 15.

But today, the summit meeting

"The Fantasticks"

New York City, May 3

This evening, 150 New Yorkers left the Sullivan Street Playhouse, a tiny theater in Greenwich Village, humming wistful bars from *Try to Remember*. The song is a highlight of *The Fantasticks*, a musical that opened tonight on a stage as bare as the one in *Waiting for Godot*. The show was written by two University of Texas graduates, Harvey Schmidt and Tom Jones.

Eisenhower returns from Latin America

Puerto Rico, March 3

President Eisenhower returned to American soil today after a 10-day Latin American tour, which his aides said showed that backing of the United States there is at the highest level since World War II. Eisenhower's worst moments came on the flight home, when an engine of his plane lost power and it had to land in Suriname. The calm of his trip to Brazil, Argentina, Chile and Uruguay contrasted sharply with the violent demonstrations that erupted on Vice President Nixon's 1958 tour.

Soviet citizens examine the wreckage of Gary Powers's downed U-2 spy plane.

that never really began ended officially. When the spy plane was first shot down, the State Department said it was a weather plane that had strayed from its course. But Moscow had the pilot as well as parts of the aircraft. Eisenhower admitted the truth (→ Aug. 17).

Birth control pill is approved for market

Washington, D.C., May 9

The Food and Drug Administration today approved the use of a contraceptive pill. The hormonal tablets, which are said to be nearly 100 percent effective in preventing pregnancy, were tested over several years by women in Puerto Rico under Planned Parenthood supervision. One in five women reported nausea and/or a gain in weight. There have been no reports of tumors or unusual cysts; indeed, preliminary studies have shown a reduction in the expected numbers of uterine and breast cancer cases. The pills are to be placed on the market early next year under the brand names of Norlutin and Enovid, and one month's supply is expected to cost $10 to $15. Mrs. Margaret Sanger, the life-long advocate of birth control, is reportedly quite pleased with the news.

"People in the Sun" (1960) by Edward Hopper. A leader of the American realist school, Hopper uses a psychological approach. Whether painting people taking the sun or a lonely office worker, he always remains detached.

Kennedy's image outshines Nixon's in series of TV debates

In the nation's first series of televised presidential debates, Senator John Kennedy and Vice President Richard Nixon square off on the major issues.

New York City, Oct. 22

The great presidential television debates have ended, and according to the Gallup Poll, Senator John F. Kennedy is the winner. Going into the series of four all-network programs, Gallup had Vice President Richard M. Nixon leading, 47 to 46, with 7 percent undecided. Coming out, it's Kennedy on top, 51 to 45, with 4 percent on the fence.

Political pundits and television critics alike believe that most of the shift came as early as the first of the four debates. They say both men handled themselves well, but they think Kennedy just looked better on the tube. On the radio, it sounded like a standoff, but on television, the senator from Massachusetts seemed healthy and vigorous, while the Vice President appeared haggard under a coat of pancake makeup intended to hide his heavy stubble. Only recently out of the hospital, where he lost weight recovering from a knee injury, Nixon also wore a shirt collar that was half a size too big. He regained his weight with milk shakes, but never won the sympathy that he did in 1952 with his emotional television chat about the Nixon family's finances and Trisha's dog Checkers.

Other factors aside, it is believed the series of four nationwide debates served to erase the Nixon advantage of being better known. Observers say the senator was able to come out "on top because he started far behind" (→ Nov. 9).

Patterson regains title, first to do so

New York City, June 20

For 359 days after his first loss to Ingemar Johansson, Floyd Patterson smoldered. His pride hurt, he was determined to defeat the young Swede in their rematch, and he did with a vengeance. Patterson caught Johansson with a knockout left hook in the fifth round and thereby became the first boxer ever to regain the world heavyweight title. The Swedish champion had been floored earlier by a hook, but he arose at the count of 9. For Johansson, it was his first defeat in 23 bouts; for Patterson it was the 36th victory in 38 fights. Such fighters as Joe Louis, Jack Dempsey and Jim Corbett were among those unable to recapture the title.

Biggest ship ever

Newport News, Va., Sept. 24

The Enterprise, the world's biggest ship and first nuclear-powered aircraft carrier, was launched today in the James River. Measuring 1,101 feet and displacing 83,350 tons, the ship is the largest vessel ever built. Its eight nuclear reactors drive four massive propellers, each as high as a two-story house. Capable of speeds above 30 knots, the vessel, built at an estimated cost of $365 million, could travel 20 times around the world non-stop.

Wilma Rudolph, Cassius Clay and Russians star in the Olympics

Rome, September

The Soviet Union outpointed the United States again in the Olympics, but there were some shining performances in the losing cause. Wilma Rudolph captured the headlines with her three gold-medal performance in track, Americans scored a brilliant sweep of the hurdles and a brash young boxer from Louisville, Kentucky, Cassius Clay, took home the top prize for light heavyweights. The leggy Wilma ran the 100-meter final in 11 seconds for a record and ran a brilliant anchor in the 400 relay. An American, Rafer Johnson, set a decathlon record. Clay outboxed an experienced Polish Olympian in his final. Lee Calhoun paced the sweep of the 110-meter hurdles.

"The Library" (1960) by Jacob Lawrence, who uses art to study Negro life.

U-2 pilot Powers gets 10-year term

Moscow, Aug. 17

Francis Gary Powers, pilot of the American U-2 spy plane shot down near Sverdlovsk on May 1, showed no emotion in the crowded courtroom today as he was sentenced to 10 years in a Soviet prison and work farm for espionage against the Soviet Union. He is not permitted an appeal, but his family says that it will ask Premier Nikita Khrushchev for a reprieve. The pilot was not given the death penalty because, the court said, he expressed "sincere repentance and confession of his guilt." Powers said he was following orders from the C.I.A. (→ Feb. 10, 1962).

Elvis Presley waves his farewell to the army that drafted him in 1958 and his hello to the legions of his waiting fans. On returning from Germany, Elvis intends to pick up his career where he left it, with 14 million-selling records in a row.

Beehive: Whole lot of teasin' goin' on

United States

Things are looking up – literally. Rocket models are taking off, balloon satellites and cosmonauts are circling the globe, and people are craning their necks to view the tops of beehive hairdos. Figuratively, things are looking up too. Barbie doll has a new boyfriend, Ken. Sports nuts have the American Football League, and players have Astroturf. People want to laugh; sales of comedy records are soaring. People want racial equality: 70,000 Negroes and whites are staging sit-ins in more than 100 cities this year. And in California, where a law was just passed to reduce auto fumes, it may soon be possible to look up and see the sky.

Harvest of Shame

New York City, Nov. 25

In an uncompromising exposure of filth, despair and grinding poverty, Edward R. Murrow took us into the lives of millions of migratory farm workers tonight. We saw pickers stacked vertically in trucks while the picked products traveled in cool elegance. We met a mother of 14 children who worked 10 grueling hours for $1. *Harvest of Shame* on CBS was this year's *The Grapes of Wrath*, brilliantly and compassionately reported by Murrow.

"International Surface No. 1" (1960) by Stuart Davis. After studying under Robert Henri at the age of 16, Davis learned to apply his unique form of Cubism to the sights and the sounds of everyday life in modern America.

JFK wins presidency by close shave

His looks and charm make the new President a natural in the television age.

Washington, D.C., Nov. 9

In one of the closest elections in American history, Senator John F. Kennedy has won the presidency by a plurality of less than half of 1 percent, or less than two votes per precinct. The outcome remained uncertain for long hours, and 52 electoral votes remain in doubt, but the Democratic candidate's total now amounts to 300 votes, or 31 more than required.

The popular vote was so close that the incumbent Vice President Richard M. Nixon stopped short of conceding at 3:20 this morning, though he told supporters at the Ambassador Hotel in Los Angeles that it looked as though Senator Kennedy had won, and he was going to bed. Instead, he stayed up, to see the Kennedy margin shrink to almost zero. Not until almost 1 in the afternoon, New York time, did he telegraph his formal concession, telling the President-elect, "I know that you will have the united support of all Americans as you lead the nation in the cause of peace and freedom." In reply, the President-elect congratulated the Vice President on "a fine race," and told him he knows the nation "can count on your unswerving loyalty."

"To all Americans," President-elect Kennedy said, "the election may have been a close one, but I think that there is general agreement that a supreme national effort will be needed in the years ahead to move this country safely through the 1960s. I ask your help, and I can assure you that every degree of mind and spirit that I possess will be devoted to the long-range interests of the United States and to the cause of freedom around the world. So now," he concluded, "my wife and I prepare for a new administration and for a new baby. Thank you."

At 43, the 6-foot 1-inch Kennedy enters the White House as the second youngest chief executive in American history (Theodore Roosevelt was 42), and as the first Catholic to hold the office. He defused the religious issue when he told the Houston Ministerial Association he believes in complete separation of church and state. If he could not resolve a conflict between conscience and his office, he said, he would resign. (→ Jan. 20, 1961).

The King of Hollywood is dead but the realm continues to thrive

Hollywood, California

"The King" is dead. On November 16, Clark Gable, 59, died after a heart attack. Not only women loved him; his hulking frame and outspoken manner made him a working man's hero. His last role was in *The Misfits* with Marilyn Monroe and Mongomery Clift, written by Monroe's husband, playwright Arthur Miller, and directed by John Huston. At the Academy Awards, *The Apartment*, with Jack Lemmon and Shirley MacLaine, won top honors, while Elizabeth Taylor (*Butterfield 8*) and Burt Lancaster (*Elmer Gantry*) won the best acting awards. Kirk Douglas is star of the epic *Spartacus*, and *Psycho*, with Anthony Perkins and Janet Leigh, is scaring millions. Hitchcock says this is the last film he will shoot in black and white.

Arthur Miller (at top), Eli Wallach, John Huston, Montgomery Clift, Marilyn Monroe and Clark Gable (far right) on location while filming "The Misfits." For decades, Gable ruled the screen with his manly appearance and demeanor.

President Kennedy: "Ask what you can do for your country"

President Kennedy exhorts the American people to join his New Frontier.

President Kennedy and the First Lady on their way to the inauguration.

Military-industrial threat seen by Ike

Washington, D.C., Jan. 17

In a farewell address that has startled people in the capital, President Eisenhower tonight warned against "the acquisition of unwarranted influence by the military-industrial complex." National leaders had expected a soft and sentimental goodbye from the old soldier winding up 50 years of public service. Instead, his address bristled with warnings to America to guard its liberties from a "conjunction of an immense military establishment and a large arms industry." He concluded with a prayer that "all peoples will come together in peace guaranteed by mutual respect and love."

President's brother is Attorney General

Washington, D.C., Jan. 21

Just hours after his brother took the oath as the new Attorney General, President Kennedy was joking about it tonight. Speaking at the Alfalfa Club, a bigwigs' dining club, the President said that he doesn't see anything wrong with giving his brother a little legal experience "before Robert goes out to practice law." Robert Kennedy was sworn in with the rest of the new Cabinet on this first day of his brother's administration following mostly indulgent Senate hearings. The President is known to believe that the closeness with his brother outweighs considerably any lack of seasoning on Robert's part.

Washington, D.C., Jan. 20

President Kennedy stirred the nation and the world today with an inaugural address that is being acclaimed by Democrats and Republicans alike as one of the best in memory. In a temperature of 22 degrees, the young President addressed a crowd that had braved an eight-inch overnight snowfall, telling them: "Ask not what your country can do for you. Ask what you can do for your country. Let the word go forth from this time and place, to friend and foe alike, that the torch has been passed to a new generation of Americans – born in this century, tempered by war, disciplined by a hard and bitter peace, proud of our ancient heritage – and unwilling to witness or permit the slow undoing of those human rights to which this nation has always been committed, and to which we are committed today at home and around the world."

The President declared that the United States was prepared to "pay any price, bear any burden, meet any hardship, support any friend, oppose any foe to assure the survival and the success of liberty."

President Kennedy spoke about new negotiations with the Soviet Union, and he issued this exhortation to the American people: "Let us begin anew. Let us never negotiate out of fear. But let us never fear to negotiate."

"Woman VIII" (1961) by Willem de Kooning. Born in Rotterdam, Holland, in 1904, de Kooning came to the United States in 1926. His technique in Abstract Expressionism has made him one of the nation's foremost painters.

Peace Corps to aid those in poor lands

Washington, D.C., March 1

Beginning to develop his New Frontier, President Kennedy today signed an executive order to launch the Peace Corps, an organization to aid undeveloped countries. The program, directed by Kennedy's brother-in-law, R. Sargent Shriver, will train American volunteers to help "liberate independent nations from the bonds of hunger, ignorance and poverty," Kennedy said. The program will train people of all ages to teach skills such as agriculture and public health. Peace Corps workers will not be paid but will be given training, transport and living expenses.

The missile race

Washington, D.C.

Though fears of a "missile gap" have faded, America continues to build a huge arsenal of intercontinental ballistic missiles. The Russians are now said to have 50 missiles, while the United States can fire over 100 Atlas and Titan nuclear-tipped rockets. America plans to build 700 Minuteman missiles, which have been test-fired from impregnable underground silos. Powered by solid fuel, a Minutemen can be fired in seconds. Armageddon is as near as the pressing of a button.

23rd Amendment gives D.C. the vote

Washington, D.C., March 29

The 23rd Amendment was ratified today, granting residents of the District of Columbia the right to vote in presidential elections. It gives to the district "a number of electors of president and vice president equal to the number of senators and representatives in Congress to which the district would be entitled if it were a state, but in no event no more than the least populous state." Kansas became the 36th state to ratify the amendment. To some it seems incredible that the district had to push for such reform, charging racism to those who opposed it; the population is predominantly Negro.

Bay of Pigs invasion ends in disaster

Washington, D.C., Apr. 24

President Kennedy has accepted full responsibility for the failed Bay of Pigs invasion, even though the plan was hatched under the Eisenhower administration. As Kennedy noted, "There's an old saying that victory has a hundred fathers and defeat is an orphan."

The small force of anti-Castro Cubans, with the support of the United States Central Intelligence Agency, landed a week ago. Within days, Castro's troops had wiped out the rebel beachhead. At last count, 743 men had been captured.

The action has been condemned worldwide. In Congress, Senator Wayne Morse, Democat of Oregon, called the invasion "a colossal mistake." But for the most part, domestic criticism has been scant, pending a full investigation.

Tensions with Cuba had been mounting since the Castro government moved toward the Communist sphere. In January, Eisenhower broke diplomatic relations with the island nation.

Without proper back-up support, Cuban anti-Communist forces were doomed.

Officials say Eisenhower had been planning the invasion for months. Kennedy was faced with a decision: drop the effort, and possibly damage morale in the anti-Castro camp, or proceed with the risky venture. Proponents said the invasion had to take place swiftly, before Castro got enough Soviet arms to repulse any attack. Opponents said the time was not yet ripe (→ Oct. 28, 1962).

400 Green Berets ordered to Vietnam

Washington, D.C., May 11

President Kennedy has ordered a contingent of 400 Special Forces soldiers and 100 military advisers to South Vietnam. Today's White House statement comes at a time when most unofficial estimates of the number of advisers there total about 2,000. The Special Forces troops are better known as "Green Berets" because of their distinctive headgear. Specially trained in jungle warfare and counter-insurgency tactics at Fort Bragg, North Carolina, these soldiers have the mission of training and advising an estimated 320,000 South Vietnamese troops in their war with the Communists. Aides close to Kennedy say the President believes that these additional forces will enable South Vietnam to win the war without the direct involvement of American fighting units. But Kennedy's chief military adviser, General Maxwell Taylor, argues that the U.S. will have to provide 8,000 additional soldiers (→ Oct. 26).

Is television just "a vast wasteland"?

United States, May

One youngster calls television "chewing gum for the eyes" and the general mediocrity of the medium has prompted hard-hitting Newton N. Minow, 35, the New Frontier's chairman of the Federal Communications Commission, to put broadcasters on notice that station licenses won't be automatically renewed from now on. He says "performance" will be judged against "promises." What does he think of present performances? "A vast wasteland" of "game shows, violence, formula comedies about totally unbelievable families, blood and thunder, mayhem, violence, sadism, murder ... And most of all, boredom." The top networks, NBC and CBS, have been trying to produce more "blue ribbon programs," and Minow himself did praise *CBS Reports* and NBC's *Project 20*.

Familial bliss at its televised best.

Dr. Kildare always saves his patient.

"Freedom Riders" attacked in South

Segregationists block the path of buses that are about to leave the station.

Montgomery, Alabama, May

Organized by James Farmer of the Congress of Racial Equality (C.O.R.E) along with members of the Student Non-Violent Coordinating Committee, a Freedom Ride campaign has set out from Washington, D.C., on a bus tour of the South. This racially integrated collection of riders is testing Southern compliance with regulations for desegregation recently enacted by the Interstate Commerce Commission, and orders along similar lines from federal courts. Riders have been attacked, harassed and arrested along the route. Whites in Anniston, Alabama, attempted to burn their bus, and a Birmingham mob attacked and beat the demonstrators. A par-

ticularly violent attack in Montgomery prompted Attorney General Robert Kennedy to send out 600 federal marshals to restore order, while Alabama declared martial law and sent in the National Guard. At Jackson, Mississippi, 27 of the riders were arrested.

Farmer, of C.O.R.E., has long been involved with national anti-discrimination protests. He graduated from Wiley College with a divinity degree in 1941, but he has refused ordination on the grounds that congregations were segregated. Greatly influenced by the non-violence tactics of Gandhi in India, Farmer has stressed such non-violent protest, including the use of the sit-in and the Freedom Ride. Popu-

lar as a writer, radio commentator and speaker, Farmer donates his earnings to C.O.R.E.

The first of the Freedom Rides took place in April 1947, with a similarly integrated group touring the South, but the action did not receive nearly the attention of the ride this year. Non-violent sit-in protests have been widespread, resulting in the arrest of more than 3,600 Negro students, and the desegregation of churches, beaches, lunch counters and other public facilities in some 100 Southern cities. These activities have been aided by the Southern Christian Leadership Conference and the National Association for the Advancement of Colored People (→ Oct. 1, 1962).

A beaten Freedom Rider awaits aid.

A young President encourages fitness

Washington, D.C., July 19

President Kennedy has called on the schools of the nation to seek out their underdeveloped pupils and work with them to improve their physical capacity. The President, in an unusual postscript to this morning's news conference, suggested that each school prepare a program of basic physical development, exercise and achievement. He urged the schools to adopt the recommendations that have been made by the National Council on Physical Fitness, which said such a program ought to encompass both boys and girls and ought to "use valid fitness tests" to evaluate the progress of the pupils.

X-15 at 4,070 mph

Edwards AFB, Calif., Nov. 9

Major Robert White streaked to a new speed record for winged craft today in a needle-nosed X-15 rocket plane. The plane dropped from a B-52 "mothership," then zoomed off to a speed of 4,070 mph, reaching a height of over 100,000 feet before gliding back to a desert landing here in California. The jet black X-15 suffered a cracked outer windshield from the tremendous heat and pressure, but Major White said that he was "never in danger." On October 12, White piloted the X-15 to a new record altitude of 215,000 feet.

The Alliance for Progress in Latin America

Punta del Este, Uruguay, Aug. 17

The United States and 19 Latin American nations today signed a charter creating the Alliance for Progress, a 10-year economic effort backed by $20 billion in long-term financing from the United States. Cuba cast the lone dissenting vote.

The alliance is aimed at providing not only economic betterment to the region, but accompanying gains in education, health, housing and agriculture. The United States representative, Treasury Secretary Douglas Dillon, then said that support under the program would be disbursed in relation to each nation's cooperation in furthering

democracy and freedom.

Many of the delegates to the Inter-American Economic and Social Conference called the alliance "a turning point in the history of the Americas." But the Cuban envoy, Major Ernesto "Che" Guevara, bitterly denounced the plan as "an instrument of economic imperialism." Dillon replied that the United States has no intention of giving the Cuban regime funds so long as it remains "under the control" of the Soviet Union. Dillon will visit Venezuela before going home.

The long-range program of Latin American aid has the strong backing of President Kennedy.

"Come on, baby, let's do the twist"

PNew York City

From the moment Elvis Presley first gyrated across American television screens, teenagers have been caught in a feverish quest for new dance steps. But nothing compares with the full-blown craze being generated this year by Chubby Checker's *The Twist*. Checker, born Ernest Evans, recorded the Hank Ballard tune last year, but it didn't catch on until the 19-year-old did it on TV's *American Bandstand*. Overnight, the twist had replaced such crazes as the mashed potato at teen sock hops, and, unlike other dance sensations, it has been irresistible for many adults.

If proof is needed that we're out of the 1950s, here it is in the twist. The dance is sweeping the nation, a sure sign that society is loosening up.

Americans are in space

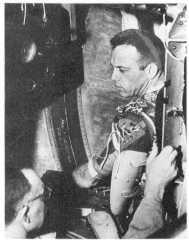

Astronaut Alan B. Shepard Jr., 37, America's first man in space. "What a beautiful view!" he exclaimed.

Cape Canaveral, Fla., July 21

"We are behind," said President Kennedy after Soviet cosmonaut Yuri Gagarin orbited the Earth in April, "and it will be some time before we catch up." But two Americans have since hurtled into space, and the President has expanded his New Frontier by pledging to put a man on the moon within 10 years.

On May 5, Navy Commander Alan B. Shepard Jr., 37, rocketed 115 miles into space via an Army Redstone missile trailing a yellow-orange tail of flames. Shepard, cramped into a tiny Mercury capsule, was weightless for just five minutes, barely long enough to peer down at the Caribbean and exclaim, "What a beautiful view!" As the capsule parachuted into the Atlantic just 15 minutes after liftoff from Cape Canaveral, the nation was both exultant and relieved.

Captain Virgil "Gus" Grissom, 35, duplicated the sub-orbital feat today, though the capsule sank after splashdown and the astronaut was barely saved from drowning.

American astronauts have yet to orbit the Earth, but on May 25, Kennedy said: "I believe this nation should commit itself to achieving the goal, before this decade is out, of landing a man on the moon and returning him safely to earth" (→ Feb. 20, 1962).

Maris hits 61 home runs in 162 games

New York City, Oct. 1

Roger Maris has smashed the home-run record that some baseball experts said would stand forever. The Yankee slugger belted his 61st home run, one more than Babe Ruth, in the final game of the season. Of course, he needed a 162-game season to do it, eight more games than Ruth had in setting a mark that has stood for 34 years. Maris socked No. 61 off Tracy Stallard, a Boston rookie, and got the only run in the 1-0 Yankee victory. Maris also led the league in runs batted in with 142.

Wood, Newman and Tracy at the movies

Wood as the no-nonsense Maria.

Hollywood, California

Stimulating new films include *West Side Story*, combining Leonard Bernstein's music and Stephen Sondheim's lyrics, and starring Natalie Wood, George Chakiris and Rita Moreno in a New York gang war saga. Other standouts: *The Guns of Navarone*, with Gregory Peck and David Niven, *The Hustler*, with Paul Newman and George Scott, the Italian *Two Women*, with Sophia Loren, *Judgment at Nuremberg*, with Maximilian Schell and Spencer Tracy, *Breakfast at Tiffany's*, with Audrey Hepburn and George Peppard, and *A Raisin in the Sun*, with Sidney Poitier.

Kennedy at the summit

President Kennedy and Premier Khrushchev size each other up in Vienna.

Vienna, June 4

President Kennedy introduced himself at the start of his five-day summit tour of Europe as "the man who accompanied Jacqueline Kennedy to Paris." During the last two days in Vienna, the President introduced himself to Soviet Premier Nikita Khrushchev as a man able to cut through diplomatic red tape.

The fact that Kennedy managed to arrange a summit meeting with the Soviet leader was a victory in itself. The men held "frank and courteous" negotiations just a year after Khrushchev refused to meet with "cowardly, piratical" Americans in the doomed Big Four summit in Paris. The Russian already has kind words about Kennedy. "I don't agree with this man," he told an aide, "but I can talk with him." Actually, analysts say Khrushchev likes dealing with Kennedy because he is a diplomatic novice.

The two agreed that Laos should be neutral and independent and that there must be a cease-fire there. Their positions on Germany were restated: Kennedy warned Khrushchev the United States would go to war to defend Berlin. Khrushchev wants the city's status renegotiated and says he will sign a peace treaty with East Germany. On a nuclear test ban treaty, Khrushchev still wants three-man inspection teams with each man having a veto. In talks with France, the President pledged closer contacts on NATO.

President and Mrs. Kennedy visit with French President de Gaulle. "I am the man," quips Kennedy, "who accompanied Jacqueline Kennedy to Paris."

New York City, Jan. 17. Television quiz show contestant Charles Van Doren and others convicted of game show fixing.

Cooperstown, New York, Jan. 23. Jackie Robinson elected to Baseball Hall of Fame.

Washington, D.C., Feb. 10. United States trades Soviet spy Rudolph Abel for captured U-2 pilot Gary Powers.

Boston, Apr. 18. Celtics defeat Los Angeles Lakers, four games to three, in N.B.A. championship.

Christmas Island, Australia, May 6. Nuclear submarine Ethan Allen tests first sub-launched atomic missile.

New York City, May 7. Theodore White wins Pulitzer Prize for *The Making of the President, 1960.*

Paris, June 3. Airline disaster takes lives of 111 prominent Atlanta citizens.

New Haven, Connecticut, June 12. Receiving honorary degree from Yale, President Kennedy comments, "It might be said now that I have the best of both worlds. A Harvard education and a Yale degree."

Newport, Rhode Island, Sept. 24. U.S. yacht Weatherly defeats Australian challenger Gretel for America's Cup.

Washington, D.C., Oct. 10. After revelation that thalidomide has caused birth defects in Europe, President Kennedy signs legislation banning use in United States.

United States, Oct. 14. Harry Truman comments, "If former President Eisenhower had understood the Monroe Doctrine, we would not have any trouble in Cuba today."

San Francisco, Oct. 16. New York Yankees defeat San Francisco Giants in World Series, four games to three.

California, November. Richard Nixon, defeated gubernatorial candidate, announces retirement from politics, stating, "You won't have Nixon to kick around any more."

New York City, Dec. 30. Green Bay Packers defeat New York Giants, 16-7, for N.F.L. title.

DEATH

New York City, Nov. 7. Eleanor Roosevelt, former First Lady (*Oct. 11, 1884).

Friendship 7 puts John Glenn in orbit

Astronaut John H. Glenn Jr. enters the spacecraft Friendship 7 as he prepares to lead his country into space.

Cape Canaveral, Fla., Feb. 20

John H. Glenn Jr. today became the first American to make an orbital flight, whirling around the Earth three times before splashing to a safe landing in the Atlantic at 2:43 p.m. The 40-year-old astronaut completed the flight despite a series of difficulties that at one time raised concern that his Mercury spacecraft might disintegrate as it attempted to return to Earth.

Glenn, a Marine Corps lieutenant colonel, waited a long time for the flight. It had been postponed 10 times since December because of bad weather or technical problems. Today, he was awakened at 2:20 a.m. and again entered the spacecraft, which has been named Friendship, about an hour later. The countdown proceeded smoothly, and Glenn was rocketed into orbit at 9:47 a.m., as some 100,000 spectators on the nearby beaches of Florida cheered and millions watched on television.

All went well at first, as Glenn reported frequently to ground sta-

tions around the globe that his condition was "fine." But a problem developed when the jets designed to maintain the spacecraft's orientation began to malfunction. They were guided by an automatic system that fired squirts of hydrogen peroxide from the jets to keep the craft at its designed attitude. Instead of firing the small control jets, the system began to fire larger jets for more radical corrections, raising the danger that all the fuel might be consumed. Glenn met the problem by shifting to a manual control system, called fly-by-wire.

A greater danger arose when instruments read at ground stations indicated that the spacecraft's heat shield had become detached from the main capsule body. Without the heat shield, Glenn and the spacecraft would have been consumed by the high temperatures generated as the capsule plunged back into the atmosphere. Worried that their instruments were giving a false reading, ground technicians changed the sequence of re-entry events to keep

the heat shield in place even it it was detached. The changes retained the braking rockets that bring the capsule out of orbit, rather than jettisoning it early. Fears about the heat shield proved unwarranted.

While he was in orbit, Glenn received congratulations from President Kennedy by radio telephone and saw the lights of Perth, Australia, turned on in tribute as he flew over. "Oh, that view is tremendous," he exclaimed at one point. Glenn fired the braking rockets successfully and splashed into the Atlantic near Grand Turk Island in the Bahamas, 700 miles southwest of Cape Canaveral, where he was picked up by the destroyer Noa. His flight was two orbits more than flown last April by the Soviet cosmonaut Yuri Gagarin, the first man in space, but far short of the 17-orbit flight of Gherman Titov in August. But it is still a major step toward making the nation competitive in space and the most impressive achievement of the American space program to date (→ July 11).

Moving of peasants started in Vietnam

Saigon, South Vietnam, March 22

A special team of United States Army advisers and troops of the Army of South Vietnam (ARVN) have begun Operation Sunrise. The objective of Sunrise, a so-called "pacification" operation, is to transfer loyal South Vietnamese peasants from five hamlets in Binh Duong Province, a known refuge for Communist insurgents, to Bien Cat District, an area where the ARVN maintains control and the villagers can live in safety. The South Vietnamese will regard those remaining in the hamlets as Vietcong soldiers or sympathizers, and treat them accordingly – which means the "enemy" hamlet will probably be destroyed (→ May 17).

Steel yields to Kennedy

President Kennedy's resolve forces the steel industry to drop price increases.

Force sent to Laos: "act of diplomacy"

Washington, D.C., May 17

The White House announced today that President Kennedy is ordering a small contingent of American naval and ground personnel to Laos. The message asserted that the United States recognizes the sovereignty of that nation and will work for the preservation of its neutrality under Prince Souvanna Phouma. Kennedy is convinced that both the Communist Pathet Lao and the North Vietnamese are out to undermine and ultimately overthrow the Laotian government. Since Kennedy does not want to appear to be sending troops into Laos for combat, he carefully called their introduction an "act of diplomacy" (→ Nov. 2, 1963).

A tour of the White House with Jackie

Washington, D.C., Feb. 14

Mrs. John F. Kennedy took millions of television viewers on a personal tour of the newly restored White House on a CBS News broadcast this evening. Accompanied by correspondent Charles Collingwood, Mrs. Kennedy related the history of the presidential mansion including the East Room, the Red Room and Lincoln's bedroom. The First Lady narrated the $100,000 production and the President discussed the renovations and the importance of history.

Washington, D.C., Apr. 13

U.S. Steel officials have tested President Kennedy's mettle, only to find it as tough as their own. Today they rescinded price increases announced April 10 after the President, in excoriating terms, accused them of public irresponsibility in their "pursuit of private power and profit." Treating the planned increase as virtually traitorous at a time when he was asking unions to rein in their wage demands, Kennedy said it was unacceptable that "a tiny handful of steel executives could show such utter contempt" for the American people.

Seven firms in all had followed U.S. Steel's lead. When two of them, Inland Steel and Bethlehem Steel, changed their minds, U.S. Steel gave in. The possibility of collusion led Attorney General Robert Kennedy to order a grand jury investigation under the antitrust laws. And Albert Gore of Tennessee introduced three related bills in the Senate, one of which would amend the Sherman Antitrust Act so that courts could more easily break up monopoly practices.

Reaction in Congress was predictably split. The Republican leader, Everett Dirksen of Illinois, said Kennedy was "looking in the wrong place for the basic cause of inflation." Privately, the President said, "My father always told me that all businessmen were sons of bitches, but I never believed it till now."

Chamberlain soars to 100-point game

Hershey, Penn., March 2

It was a night when Wilt Chamberlain could do nothing wrong. The new coach of the Philadelphia Warriors, Frank McGuire, wanted Wilt the Stilt to go to the basket as much as possible and the Big Dipper obliged with 100 points. He was virtually a one-man show in leading the Warriors to a 169-147 victory over the New York Knicks. Wilt got 36 baskets and 28 of 32 free throws. The performance evoked new complaints that his height, 7 feet 3 inches, was ruining the sport.

An elegant White House tour guide.

No prayer in school

Washington, D.C., June 25

The Supreme Court today handed down its decision in the case of Engel v. Vitale, also known as the Regents' Prayer Case. By a vote of 6-1, the court held that the recitation of a prayer written by a state agency for use in the public schools violated the establishment clause of the First Amendment. In his opinion, Justice Hugo Black stated that no government has the "power to prescribe by law any particular form of prayer ... to be used as an official prayer ... " This decision is expected to result in a storm of protest.

S.D.S. issues credo

Port Huron, Michigan, July

The young activist group Students for a Democratic Society has issued a manifesto, *The Port Huron Statement*, seeking an "agenda for a generation" of radical politics. Tom Hayden drafted the credo at the group's convention here. In it, he calls for "participatory democracy" to overcome a sense of powerlessness in society. S.D.S. was started two summers ago in New York City by Al Haber and Hayden to support civil rights and to oppose militarism. "We may be the last generation in the experiment with living," said Hayden.

Basketball's Wilt the Stilt in action.

Marilyn Monroe is dead

Her sultry looks enticed millions but masked her warmth and intelligence.

Hollywood, Calif., August 5

The last of the love goddesses is gone. Marilyn Monroe (nee Norma Jean Baker) rose from a childhood of deprivation, foster homes and mistreatment, including rape, to become the whole world's symbol of the eternal female. She married at 16 to escape her surroundings. Working as a paint sprayer in a defense plant in 1944, she was discovered by an army photographer and became a pin-up girl and a model. In August of 1946, Fox signed her to a contract for $125 a week. From small parts as a dumb blonde, she moved on to starring roles in *Bus Stop*, *Some Like It Hot* and *Let's Make Love*. Director Joshua Logan called her "pure cinema ... the most authentic film actress since Garbo." But her health and confidence were stretched to the breaking point. In her last movie, *The Misfits*, Clark Gable looks at her and remarks, tenderly: "You're the saddest girl I ever saw." She divorced her third husband, playwright Arthur Miller (her second was baseball hero Joe DiMaggio) last year. In June, she began the movie *Something's Got to Give*, but was fired. This morning, the 36-year-old star was found lifeless in bed. The death was called a suicide, but questions have been raised.

Telstar communications satellite in orbit

Communications in the space age.

Andover, Maine, July 11

Americans today watched the first transmission of television signals from Earth to a space satellite and back again. The revolutionary Telstar communications satellite, sent into orbit early this morning, received signals from an American Telephone & Telegraph ground station here for 17 minutes and flashed them back to be rebroadcast across the United States. Stations in England and France also received the signals, marking the start of an era of trans-Atlantic TV transmission. The first broadcasts from Europe to America via Telstar, a $50 million A.T.&T. project, will take place tomorrow (→ Jan. 25, 1964).

Negro enrolls at Ol' Miss

Oxford, Mississippi, Oct. 1

Accompanied by federal marshals, James Meredith crossed a riot-torn campus today to become the first Negro student at the University of Mississippi. Burned-out cars, tear gas canisters and broken glass littered the campus where an angry mob of thousands gathered Sunday night to try to block Meredith's registration. Federal troops held the mob off with tear gas, but two people were killed and 28 marshals were wounded by gunfire in the melee. Those slain were a French reporter, Paul Guihard, and Ray Gunter, an Oxford resident. Over 200 people were arrested. Unknown to the crowd, Meredith had been installed in a dormitory room on campus at 6:30 p.m. Sunday.

While the riot raged on through the night, President Kennedy and his brother, Attorney General Robert Kennedy, directed federal operations from the White House. Mississippi Governor Ross Barnett, who had vowed he would go to jail to block integration, did not appear on campus. Both Kennedys talked with him by telephone during the day trying to reach a peaceful solution, but the negotiations broke down. The President then went on national television at 10 p.m. and appealed for order. "Americans are free ... to disagree with the law," he said, "but not to disobey it."

Meredith, 29, is a native Mississippian and a former sergeant in the air force (→ May 13, 1963).

U.S. troops arrive on campus to ensure that the university will be integrated.

Nobel for Steinbeck

Oslo, Norway, Dec. 10

It was no *Winter of Discontent* for John Steinbeck, who accepted the Nobel Prize today, but next season may become a *Silent Spring*, says Rachel Carson, who claims insecticides sneak 500 alien chemicals into our bodies. Other best-sellers this year: *Sex and the Single Girl* by Helen Gurley Brown; *Pale Fire* by Vladimir Nabokov; *The Guns of August* by Barbara Tuchman; *One Flew Over the Cuckoo's Nest* by Ken Kesey; *Fail Safe* by Eugene Burdick and Harvey Wheeler, and *Six Crises* by Richard M. Nixon.

Fine films featured

Hollywood, California

Movie-goers flock to see *Lawrence of Arabia* with Peter O'Toole, Anthony Quinn and Omar Sharif; Sean Connery as James Bond in *Dr. No;* Gregory Peck's brilliant acting in *To Kill a Mockingbird*; *The Miracle Worker* with Anne Bancroft and Patty Duke; *Days of Wine and Roses* with Jack Lemmon and Lee Remick; Bette Davis and Joan Crawford in *Whatever Happened to Baby Jane?*; *Long Day's Journey Into Night* with Katharine Hepburn, *How the West Was Won* and *The Manchurian Candidate*.

Missiles of October place the world at the brink

Washington, D.C., Oct. 28

A week of unprecedented worldwide tension that drove the United States and the Soviet Union to the brink of a thermonuclear confrontation ended today. Faced by an unwavering American President, Soviet Premier Nikita Khrushchev retreated, agreeing to remove from Cuba missiles that American military experts said could have wiped out the nation's defenses in 17 minutes. Khrushchev acted after getting a pledge from Kennedy not to invade Cuba. "I understand very well your anxiety and the anxiety of the people of the United States," Khrushchev said in a conciliatory letter to the President today.

Until yesterday, it was not clear that the crisis could be resolved peacefully. The Pentagon reported that a U-2 spy plane had been shot down over Cuba. Thousands of air force reservists were being called up. Florida looked like a D-Day invasion zone. Khrushchev was offering to withdraw his weapons, but only if Kennedy dismantled American missiles in Turkey.

"This is the first real, direct confrontation between the superpowers," said a United Nations aide, "and we all feel pretty powerless."

At the White House tonight, reaction to the diplomatic and military victory is restrained. The President will undoubtedly reap domestic political benefits, but administration insiders say that the global fallout is more important. "The need for a confrontation with the Soviets had been obvious for some time," one Kennedy adviser told *Newsweek*. "They were putting the pressure on us all around the world."

The President had been aware for weeks that the Soviet Union might be supplying Cuba with sophisticated new middle-range nuclear weapons. He received the evidence he needed to prove his case early on the morning of October 16. Aerial reconnaissance pictures showing a missile in Cuba were brought to Kennedy while he was still in bed.

During the next 48 hours, the White House inner circle considered an invasion of Cuba, but it was feared that Khrushchev would retaliate by seizing Berlin. On the afternoon of October 18, Kennedy asked Soviet Foreign Minister Andrei Gromyko about the missiles. Gromyko pulled a note from his pocket with the prepared answer. "Training by Soviet specialists of Cuban nationals in handling defensive armaments is by no means offensive," it asserted. Discussion was resumed at the White House after Gromyko's departure. It ended when Kennedy told his advisers, "The greatest danger of all is to do nothing." He used the same phrase four days later, when he addressed the nation on Monday the 22nd.

When he spoke to 50 million Americans on television, Kennedy was direct and determined. He accused Khrushchev of lying when he said the weapons were merely defensive, and he charged they could be launched against "most of the major cities in the Western Hemisphere." The President stated that an air and naval blockade would examine all ships approaching Cuba to determine whether they were carrying weapons. He demanded a withdrawal of all offensive weapons on the island and warned that the United States would retaliate if the weapons were fired at any country in the hemisphere. "Aggressive conduct, if allowed to go unchecked and unchallenged," Kennedy said, "ultimately leads to war."

In Cuba, the speech was interpreted as a declaration of war. Castro ordered a complete mobilization. In Europe, Kennedy's speech was applauded wholeheartedly.

By the middle of the week, Kennedy was receiving mixed signals from Khrushchev. He proposed a summit meeting at the same time that Soviet ships were voluntarily turning back from Cuba. But the Premier was also promising to retaliate for the blockade. On Thursday, he agreed to a U.N. proposal to stop sending missiles to Cuba if the United States ended the blockade. But on Friday, intelligence indicated that work was speeding up on Soviet bases in Cuba.

With the crisis finally ended, President Kennedy has seemingly won and Khrushchev has lost. But there could be a second dispute soon, possibly over Berlin. "The path we have chosen is full of hazards," Kennedy said. "The cost of freedom is always high, but Americans have always paid it."

Picture released by the Department of Defense showing Soviet ballistic missile installations at Sagua La Grande, Cuba. This and other intelligence photographs prove beyond any doubt that the Soviet Union has turned Cuba into a nuclear missile site a mere 90 miles off the coast of the United States.

President Kennedy (right) confers with his closest adviser, brother Robert.

Integration in Alabama

Governor George Wallace confronts Deputy Attorney General Nicholas Katzenbach at "the schoolhouse door" of the University of Alabama.

Birmingham, Ala., June 11

Alabama Governor George Wallace vowed he would "stand in the schoolhouse door" to block integration. He did so today, but was brushed aside as National Guardsmen under federal orders escorted two Negro students, Vivian Malone and James Hood, into the University of Alabama's Foster Auditorium to register for classes.

The victory is the first for the Kennedy administration in its continuing struggle with Wallace. Attorney General Robert Kennedy met with the Governor in April, attempting to reach a peaceful resolution. He left in frustration, Wallace still vowing to defy federal integration orders. "It's like a foreign country," Kennedy complained. "There's no communication."

The struggle in Alabama is still far from its conclusion. Wallace insists he will continue to challenge the constitutionality of federal "interference" in the affairs of his state (→ 12).

King out of jail; protesters score gains

Birmingham, Ala., May 13

A relative calm has settled here after weeks of racial protest and violence. Federal troops are quartered at Fort McClellan, just 30 miles away. President Kennedy sent troops in after bombs exploded at the motel of the Rev. Martin Luther King Jr. and at the home of his brother. Rioting broke out after the bombing. Birmingham business leaders announced last week that they will desegregate lunch counters and hire Negroes for clerical and sales jobs. Dr. King told a crowd at a rally, "These things would not have been granted without your presenting your bodies and your very lives before the dogs and the tanks and the water hoses of this city!" Millions across the nation watched on television May 3 as officers directed by Birmingham public safety director Eugene "Bull" Connor turned fire hoses and snarling police dogs on children who were demonstrating.

Dr. King was jailed April 12 and, while held, wrote a 20-page message to clergymen. Called *Letter From the Birmingham Jail*, it explained his thoughts on civil disobedience: "I submit that an individual who breaks a law that conscience tells him is unjust, and who willingly accepts the penalty of imprisonment in order to arouse the conscience of the community over its injustice, is in reality expressing the highest respect for law" (→ June 11).

President requests $14 billion tax cut

Washington, D.C., Jan. 24

President Kennedy presented a tax bill to Congress today that would cut personal and business taxes by nearly $14 billion over the next three years. The bill is designed to stimulate the economy by giving the biggest breaks to low-income groups and small businesses. By 1965, the measure would reduce personal income taxes by 6 to 26 percent; corporate taxes and taxes withheld from paychecks would each drop 5 percent. On the other hand, the bill will not allow certain "loopholes" such as untaxed profits on stock option trades and deductions for minor casualties.

129 entombed as submarine sinks

Boston, Apr. 10

The nuclear submarine Thresher with 129 men aboard was lost today in stormy waters 220 miles east of Boston. The Thresher submerged at 9 a.m. in a test dive designed to reach its maximum depth of more than 1,400 feet. It never resurfaced. Searchers found an oil slick in the area of the dive, where the Atlantic is 8,400 feet deep. Admiral George Anderson, chief of naval operations, said the navy had no good theory to explain the disaster.

Birmingham, September 10. *Negro students Floyd and Dwight Armstrong enter an elementary school as integration proceeds.*

Evers of N.A.A.C.P. slain in Mississippi

Jackson, Mississippi, June 12

Medgar Evers was working late, but he called his wife, Myrlie, three times, each time saying, "I want you to know I love you." Just after midnight, a car door slammed and a shot rang out. Evers had been shot. He died soon after. A field aide in the National Association for the Advancement of Colored People, Evers was called "Mississippi's Martin Luther King." At a rally June 7, he said he would gladly die to make a better life for his family. [Byron de la Beckworth, a Greenwood, Mississippi, white, was tried twice for Evers's murder. Each trial ended in a hung jury] (→ 19).

California passes N.Y. in population

California, Autumn

There are more people in the state of Big Sur than in the state of the Big Apple. The official count is not complete, but population experts say California has surpassed New York as the nation's most populous state. At mid-year, New York had 17,708,000 and California had 17,590,000. But the traditional late summer migration to the West has put California ahead, and with the state's tendency to breed odd life styles, many feel, way out.

JFK: No "colored" signs on foxholes

Washington, D.C., June 19

While speaking to help the passage of his new equal rights bill, President Kennedy noted, "No one has been barred on account of his race from fighting or dying for America; there are no 'white' or 'colored' signs on the foxholes or graveyards of battle." Kennedy's bill, sent to Congress on the day of the funeral of Medgar Evers, a Negro leader who was shot to death, would guarantee equal rights in public facilities and give the attorney general power to sue for enforcement of the 14th and 15th Amendments. Kennedy holds that segregation is immoral (→ Aug. 18).

Kennedy at Berlin Wall

JFK at the Berlin Wall, near the Brandenburg Gate, where East meets West.

West Berlin, Germany, June 26

"All free men, wherever they may live, are citizens of Berlin. And therefore, as a free man, I take pride in the words, 'Ich bin ein Berliner'" ("I am a Berliner").

With this rousing declaration, President Kennedy today won thunderous applause from a crowd of about 150,000 West Berliners packed into the plaza facing the Rathaus, or city hall. Among those standing with the President on the balcony, which was draped with an enormous American flag, was West Berlin's popular mayor, Willy Brandt.

The President, who is on a 10-day visit to Europe, also took a look at the Berlin Wall as he visited Checkpoint Charlie. Although the wall has certainly succeeded in stemming the exodus of East Germans, who until two years ago were voting with their feet for freedom and prosperity, it has also served as a symbol to the rest of the world of Communist repression.

Birmingham, Alabama, September 15. *Police examine the wreckage left by a bomb that exploded at the 16th Street Baptist Church. Segregationists have gone beyond individual lynchings to widespread threats and murder in an effort to stop integration. In this case, four Negro children were killed and 17 were injured while they were attending Sunday school.*

Big powers agree to curb nuclear testing

Washington, D.C., Oct. 10

The Limited Nuclear Test Ban Treaty, which has been ratified by the Senate, signed by President Kennedy and agreed to by the Soviet Union and Britain, goes into effect today. Although only a modest step toward disarmament or even arms control, it constitutes an important victory for environmentalists: by allowing only underground testing, it will go far to curb the radioactive fallout that results from above-ground detonations. Many countries are expected to sign the treaty, with the notable exceptions of France and China (→ June 1, 1972).

Meredith graduates with class of whites

Oxford, Mississippi, Aug. 18

James Meredith, the first Negro to attend the University of Mississippi, became its first Negro graduate today. Mississippi Governor Ross Barnett tried to block Meredith's degree, but the state college board overruled him. The campus, where a riot erupted the day Meredith arrived to register in 1962, was quiet. Among those who looked on as Meredith was presented with his diploma was his father, "Cap" Meredith, the son of a slave (→ 28).

Newport sensation: a kid named Dylan

Newport, R.I., July 28

Some 47,000 fans of the booming East Coast folk music scene flocked here this weekend for a festival of tunes from Pete Seeger, Joan Baez, and Peter, Paul and Mary. Most hadn't bargained for a performance with the power to change lives. But Bob Dylan, a 22-year-old songwriter with the tattered appearance and social conscience of Woody Guthrie, the lyricism of Rimbaud and the defiance of James Dean, simply mesmerized the crowd with works like *Hard Rain*, *Talkin' John Birch Society Blues* and *Blowin' in the Wind*, an anti-war song that is stirring a generation.

King to 200,000: "I have a dream"

U.S. gets hot line to Soviet Union

The Rev. Dr. Martin Luther King Jr. waves to thousands of his followers.

Washington, D.C., Aug. 28

In the largest civil rights demonstration ever, more than 200,000 non-violent protesters gathered at the foot of the Lincoln Memorial today to hear Dr. Martin Luther King Jr., president of the Southern Christian Leadership Conference, describe his vision of the future of race relations in the United States. "I still have a dream," Dr. King told the rapt audience. "It is a dream chiefly rooted in the American Dream. I have a dream that one day this nation will rise up and live out the true meaning of its creed: 'We hold these truths to be self-evident, that all men are created equal'." As the crowd cheered each repetition of his refrain, "I have a dream," King described a land where whites and Negroes would be brothers, and where his people would be "free at last, free at last, thank God Almighty, free at last."

Also at the rally to help speed the passage of civil rights legislation, were the folksingers Bob Dylan, Joan Baez and Peter, Paul and Mary, the legendary singer-dancer Josephine Baker and the baseball great, Jackie Robinson. The day also gave the Negro leaders a chance to meet President Kennedy.

King's speech turned the tone of the event from a party into a crusade. But though his words moved the hearts of a nation, it remains to be seen whether Congress will be moved to action (→ May 26, 1964).

Washington, D.C., Aug. 30

With a simple exchange of routine test signals, the so-called "hot line" between the White House and the Kremlin has been put into service. The need for a direct link that can be used in the event of emergencies such as an accidental nuclear firing emerged during the Cuban missile crisis last year, when there were dangerous snags in communication between the Soviet and American governments. The system will use both a wire telegraph service and a radio telegraph service. For security reasons all messages will be encoded. The sender will use his own language for the messages, which will be sent and received by bilingual teleprinters at either end.

Art going pop

New York City

The Solomon R. Guggenheim Museum succumbed to pop art's appeal this year by staging a pop show of its own. Claes Oldenburg's soft sculptures, Andy Warhol's silk-screened portraits and the comic-strip canvases of Roy Lichtenstein have all angles covered: they satirize, laud and echo American values. Lichtenstein finds most modern fine art "despicable" and says that many artists could get away with "hanging a wet paint rag."

Friedan: Housewife isn't happy at all

United States

Mrs. Betty Friedan, a 42-year-old psychologist and housewife, has published *The Feminine Mystique,* a book that takes the boredom of housewives very seriously. After research and in-depth interviews, Friedan has concluded that women are unfulfilled and must develop their identities. She blames such forces as Freud, Margaret Mead and Madison Avenue for fooling women into thinking that cooking and cleaning should be satisfying enough. Her solution? A *New Life Plan for Women* that emphasizes work outside the home.

South Vietnamese Premier is assassinated as conflict worsens

Saigon, South Vietnam, Nov. 2

The South Vietnamese Premier, Ngo Dinh Diem, and his brother Nhu were murdered today by a group of military leaders headed by General Duong Van Minh. Trying to escape from the royal palace after Minh's coup d'etat, they were arrested and placed in an armored personnel carrier, where they were killed. Diem has been described by his detractors as an insufferable autocrat and a tyrant – but he was a fierce anti-Communist. A skilled leader, he had nevertheless alienated the Buddhists, the intellectuals and South Vietnam's urban middle class with his blatant corruption and oppression. Because Ambassa-

dor Henry Cabot Lodge and senior aides felt the war could not be won under a Diem regime, they were said to have encouraged Minh to plot his overthrow, probably with the administration's knowledge.

Meantime, more American soldiers are dying in the growing Indochinese conflict. In January, five American helicopters were downed and three crewmen killed. Dozens of G.I.'s have been killed this year.

Diem's murder has complicated the American position in South Vietnam. President Kennedy said the United States could play only a supporting role to Diem in what he felt would be a farce if it were not such a tragedy (→ Aug. 7, 1964).

A Buddhist monk who opposes the regime protests by self-immolation.

President Kennedy is slain by assassin in Dallas

Dallas, Texas, Nov. 22

President John F. Kennedy was killed today when a sniper fired three rifle shots at the presidential motorcade as it drove along Elm Street in downtown Dallas. Texas Governor John B. Connally, who rode in the President's car with his wife and Mrs. Kennedy, was seriously wounded in the attack. The Governor is at Parkland Memorial Hospital, where he is listed in serious condition. Mrs. Kennedy and Mrs. Connally were not wounded.

While the nation was still in shock at the loss of its elegant, dynamic and popular young President, the momentum of the government continued. Just 98 minutes after the death of President Kennedy, Lyndon Baines Johnson, the 55-year-old Vice President who had been in the motorcade several cars behind the President, took the 34-word oath of office aboard Air Force One and became the 36th President of the United States. Jacqueline Kennedy stood beside Johnson while he took the oath, her stockings and shocking pink skirt still spattered with her late husband's blood. She had just arrived in the hearse that carried Kennedy's casket to the plane to be taken to Washington for burial.

A few hours after the shooting, the Dallas police arrested Lee Harvey Oswald and later charged him with the murder. Oswald, 24, is a former marine who became a Soviet citizen in 1959 before returning to the United States in 1962. He was active in the Fair Play for Cuba Committee. He is believed to have fired at least three rifle shots at the President from the sixth floor of the Texas School Book Depository, where he had been employed as a clerk.

The shooting occurred at 12:35 p.m. just as the 12-car motorcade was nearing the end of its 10-mile tour and passing the textbook warehouse. As the shots rang out, the crowds scattered, people fell to the ground or ran for cover and some screamed and wept after the President took a lethal bullet in the back of his head. The first bullet to strike the 46-year-old President had hit him in the back below his collar bone.

"Oh no! Oh no!" Jacqueline Kennedy cried over and over, cradling his head in her lap as the limousine raced to the Parkland Memorial Hospital three miles away. At 1 p.m., John F. Kennedy, America's youngest elected President, was pronounced dead, a victim of what he had called a "dangerous and untidy world." At 2:41 p.m., Air Force One took off from Love Field carrying a new President and Kennedy's body home (→ 24).

President and Mrs. Kennedy join Texas Governor John B. Connally in a limousine for the ride to the Merchandise Mart. The day was so beautiful that the President had asked that the car's protective bubble be removed.

Oswald shot down as TV cameras roll

Dallas, Texas, November 24

Lee Harvey Oswald, the man accused of killing President Kennedy two days ago, was shot dead today in the basement of a jail as he was being moved to a tighter security prison. Jack Ruby, a Dallas nightclub owner, fired a revolver at point-blank range into Oswald's stomach. He died instantly, in view of 50 reporters, Oswald's police escort and millions of TV viewers. Oswald died without confessing to Kennedy's murder. There has been speculation that Ruby killed Oswald to keep him from testifying, but the vengeance motive is held more likely. Ruby could get the death penalty (→ 25).

Kennedy is buried and nation grieves

Washington, D.C., Nov. 25

President John F. Kennedy was buried today with full military honors in Arlington National Cemetery. A million mourners lined the streets of Washington and millions all over the world attended the ceremony through radio and television. Following the flag-draped casket drawn by six gray horses were 92 foreign leaders and the Kennedy family. The procession moved from the Capitol rotunda to the White House and then on to St. Matthew's Roman Catholic Cathedral for a short requiem mass before the burial at Arlington. His widow, Jacqueline Kennedy, lit the eternal flame at his grave (→ Sept. 27, 1964).

John F. Kennedy Jr. snaps a salute as his father's casket passes. The boy's calm demeanor, the beauty of his innocence, touches his family and the entire nation as they mourn the President's loss. It was John-John's third birthday.

Washington, D.C., Jan. 17. Panama breaks diplomatic ties with United States (→ Apr. 4).

California, Jan. 25. Echo 2, first American-Soviet communications satellite, launched, to relay radio signals worldwide (→ July 31).

Washington, D.C., Feb. 29. President Johnson announces that Lockheed Corporation has produced a jet capable of speeds greater than 2,000 mph.

Washington, D.C., Apr. 4. United States concludes agreement with Panama, resuming diplomatic relations and negotiating settlement of grievances.

Boston, Apr. 26. Celtics beat San Francisco Warriors four games to one, for N.B.A. title.

Baltimore, Maryland, May 21. Baltimore Lighthouse becomes world's first nuclear-powered lighthouse.

Prince Edward Island, Virginia, May 26. Supreme Court rules county public schools, shut to avoid integration, must reopen and integrate (→ July 3).

Alaska, May 27. "Good Friday Quake" strikes; 114 killed.

New Orleans, Louisiana, May 30. After 133 years, last streetcar runs on Canal Street.

Cape Canaveral, Florida, July 31. About 4,000 photographs of lunar surface received from Ranger 7 before it crashes on moon (→ March 23, 1965).

Washington, D.C., Sept. 14. Theologian Reinhold Niebuhr receives Medal of Freedom.

Newport, Rhode Island, Sept. 21. Yacht Constellation successful in defense of America's Cup against British challenger Sovereign.

St., Louis, Oct. 15. Cardinals top Yankees, four games to three, in World Series.

New York City, Nov. 21. Verrazano-Narrows Bridge, world's longest suspension bridge, officially opens.

Cleveland, Dec. 27. Browns defeat Baltimore Colts, 27-0, for N.F.L. title.

Philadelphia. Kennedy half-dollar issued.

DEATH

Washington, D.C., Apr. 5. Douglas MacArthur, General of the Army (*Jan. 26, 1880).

Beatles invade America

John Lennon takes the lead as Britain's "Fab Four" rock 'n' roll America.

New York City, Feb. 10

"It's B-Day! It's 6:30 a.m.! The Beatles left London 30 minutes ago! Heading for New York!" It was all the kids awakening to transistor radios on February 7 needed, as thousands besieged Kennedy Airport to offer the Liverpool quartet a shrieking, frenzied welcome to America.

The Beatles – John Lennon, 23, Paul McCartney, 21, George Harrison, 21, and Ringo Starr, 23 – shaped their music and shaggy haircuts playing in rowdy Hamburg clubs. Returning to England, the prolific Lennon-McCartney writing team started churning out hits last year. They've sold six million records, and *I Want to Hold Your Hand* is now No. 1 here.

Pandemonium has followed the group everywhere this weekend, as obsessed fans even mobbed a befuddled cop, shouting "He touched a Beatle!" But if anyone doubted Beatlemania's impact, last night the group captured a record TV audience of 73 million on the Ed Sullivan Show, singing over the hysterical squeals of their fans. Said Ringo: "So this is America. They all seem out of their minds."

Surgeon General: Cigarettes cause cancer

Maybe it isn't so glamorous after all.

Washington, D.C., Jan. 11

An expert committee appointed by the Surgeon General today declared cigarette smoking a "health hazard of sufficient importance to the United States to require remedial action." In a 150,000-word report, the 10-member panel said cigarettes are the leading cause of lung cancer and bronchitis and are involved in other forms of cancer, heart disease, ulcers and other diseases. Surgeon General Luther L. Terry called the report "the most comprehensive ... analysis ever undertaken" of the smoking-health controversy and said he would advise all smokers to stop.

LBJ fights poverty; seeks $962 million

Washington, D.C., March 16

President Johnson sent a request to Congress today for $962 million to fight poverty. LBJ has given the destitute a high place on his presidential agenda. In his January State of the Union address, he lamented, "Unfortunately, many Americans live on the outskirts of hope – some because of their poverty, and some because of their color, and all too many because of both." He also said the administration is "declaring unconditional war against poverty." Congress is expected to approve the request. Johnson, a former majority leader of the Senate, is a great persuader among his old colleagues. He is also passionate about helping the poor, drawing from Michael Harrington's 1962 book on social injustice, *The Other America* (→ Jan. 4, 1965).

"Times a changin'"

New York City, February

"Be-bop-a-lu-la, she's my baby" may have been poetry enough for an earlier generation of music fans, but as Bob Dylan sings on his new album, *The Times They Are a Changin'*. The enigmatic songwriter hitchhiked from Hibbing, Minnesota, to Greenwich Village two years ago and took the folk world by storm, giving a new depth to popular music with lyrics on social injustice and the horrors of war.

Clay defeats Liston

Miami Beach, Fla., Feb. 25

Cassius Marcellus Clay is the new heavyweight champion of the world. Against all odds, he demolished the gargantuan Sonny Liston tonight with a seventh-round technical knockout. Some experts even wanted the fight called off because Liston might hurt "little" Cassius permanently. Instead, Clay buzzed Liston for three rounds and Sonny was so befuddled that he missed and missed again. This made him tired and angry. Some coagulant put on Liston's eye rubbed off on Clay in the fourth and blinded him, but Liston didn't follow up. He couldn't come out for the eighth.

Civil Rights Act passed

President Lyndon Johnson hands out pens used during the signing of the landmark Civil Rights Act. Attorney General Robert Kennedy (center) and the President appear to have put aside their personal differences for the day.

Washington, D.C., July 3

Providing many new measures and agencies to combat inequities based on race, sex, color, religion or national origin, the Civil Rights Act passed by Congress was signed into law today by President Johnson. He, as well as President Kennedy before him, lobbied intensively for the bill, which prohibits racial discrimination in public accommodations, employment, unions and federally funded programs. Passage of the bill required the Senate to impose cloture for the first time on a civil rights bill, to end a fili-

buster by Southern senators. The bill is the most sweeping civil rights legislation in American history and, as President Johnson said in a television address, it may help to "eliminate the last vestiges of injustice in America." The act will be of great benefit, it is hoped, to the country's 22 million Negroes.

President Johnson said he signed the legislation to "close the springs of racial poison." The measure codifies President Kennedy's policy of treating discrimination as a moral evil (→ July).

Race riots hit New York

Negro rioters flee from advancing policemen during the chaos that has gripped Harlem. The death of a Negro youth at the hands of an officer has released a sense of anger and frustration that is prevalent in most inner-city ghettos.

New York City, July

Riots in the state of New York have led to over 1,000 arrests, six deaths and the wounding of hundreds. Earlier this month, the first of the riots began when an off-duty police officer killed a 15-year-old Negro boy in Harlem. Negroes attacked police and white-owned stores with fire bombs. One person was killed, at least 140 injured and 500 arrests were made. The rioting spread from Harlem to predominantly Negro areas of Brooklyn, and raged for several days.

A similar riot exploded in Roch-

ester on July 24 when police arrested a Negro man for allegedly molesting a Negro woman at a dance. It was rumored that the man was abused by police during the arrest. Five people died in the violence and 750 were arrested for looting, possession of illegal weapons and rioting. About 75 percent of those arrested were Negro. To restore order, the National Guard was called out by Governor Nelson Rockefeller. These riots constitute the first serious racially motivated mob violence in a Northern state since the 1940s (→ Aug. 4).

24th Amendment outlaws poll taxes

Washington, D.C., Jan. 23

The use of poll taxes in federal elections, a controversial symbol of racial discrimination in the South, became unconstitutional with the ratification of the 24th Amendment today. President Johnson called the act a "triumph of liberty over restriction." Five Southern states still require voting fees. Texas and Virginia have already set up a two-tiered registration that will preserve the poll tax in state and local elections. Ironically, the tax began as a democratic advance, replacing restrictive property qualifications.

Court rules malice is key in libel case

Washington, D.C., March 9

The Supreme Court today overturned a $500,000 judgment against *The New York Times* by an Alabama court in the case of The New York Times Co. v. Sullivan. Protecting freedom of speech, the high court ruled that in order for a government official to collect damages for libel against a publisher, the official must prove that the publisher showed "actual malice." *The Times* was sued by Montgomery city commissioner L.B. Sullivan for having printed an advertisement about racism in Alabama.

Hoffa found guilty of fraud, conspiracy

Chicago, July 24

For the second time in a year, James Hoffa, chief of the Teamsters union, has been convicted of serious crimes. Today, a federal jury found Hoffa guilty of mail fraud and conspiracy to abuse the union's pension fund. In March, a Tennessee jury convicted him of attempting to bribe a previous jury in a case that ended in mistrial. Tennessee Judge Frank Wilson told Hoffa, "You stand here convicted of seeking to corrupt the administration of justice . . . of having tampered with the very soul of this nation."

Congress irate at Tonkin Gulf attack

Washington, D.C., Aug. 7

After reports of two North Vietnamese attacks on American destroyers earlier this week in the Gulf of Tonkin, Congress has overwhelmingly backed President Johnson's request for broad emergency powers. By a unanimous vote in the House of Representatives and an 88 to 2 vote in the Senate, the Southeast Asia Resolution (which some legislators call the Gulf of Tonkin Resolution) has become law. The resolution, vaguely worded, says Johnson has full congressional authority "to take all necessary measures to repel any armed attack against the forces of the United States and to prevent further aggression." Thus Congress gave him virtually every power he needs to deal with this growing conflict – except a formal declaration of war.

The Gulf of Tonkin crisis erupted on August 2 when the navy destroyer Maddox reported having been attacked by North Vietnamese torpedo boats. The Maddox said it returned fire and called in fighter planes from the carrier Ticonderoga. The Americans sank two of the three boats and damaged the other. Two days later, the navy said, Communist boats attacked the Maddox and the destroyer Turner Joy, both in international waters. In response to the second attack, which Washington said was unprovoked, the

American ships and aircraft carriers at sea. The reported attack by North Vietnamese vessels in the Gulf of Tonkin has led to firm U.S. retaliation.

President ordered a retaliatory attack by navy fighter-bombers on the North Vietnamese oil tanks and torpedo boat bases at Vinh. The next day, the President justified the attack, saying, "Aggression unchallenged is aggression unleashed."

After Johnson announced the strike at Vinh, he met with 18 congressional leaders from both parties seeking a statement of support for his overall policy in Southeast Asia. And he got it. Senator Frank Church said it was time to "rally 'round" the flag. And Senator Barry Goldwater warned, "We cannot allow the American flag to be shot at anywhere on earth if we are to retain our respect and prestige."

Senator Wayne Morse opposed the resolution, questioning both its purpose and the wisdom of open-ended commitments. Others doubted there had ever been an attack on the destroyers, and accused the President of over-reacting or seeking a pretext to expand his own powers (→ Nov. 1).

Reagan makes plea for Barry Goldwater

Sacramento, Calif., October

Governor Ronald Reagan of California is doing all he can to elect fellow conservative Barry M. Goldwater to the White House. Reagan made a televised speech this month, exalting the G.O.P. nominee's political savvy, intelligence, toughness and experience. Reagan has become a popular leader in the West, where Goldwater must win if he is to have a chance in the election. The plea should help bridge the gap in recent polls that show President Johnson leading Goldwater, who was nominated in July after a speech in which he said, "Extremism in the defense of liberty is no vice ..." (→ Nov. 3).

F.B.I. finds bodies of 3 rights workers

Philadelphia, Mississippi, Aug. 4

The bodies of three civil rights workers, James Chaney, Andrew Goodman and Michael Schwerner, were discovered buried in an earthen dam near Philadelphia today. F.B.I. agents reportedly got a tip on the location. The three had been missing since June 21, when they were accused of speeding and taken to the Neshoba County jail. They had driven to Philadelphia to investigate the burning of a Negro church. Chaney, a Negro, was from nearby Meridian. Schwerner and Goodman were New Yorkers who had come to Mississippi for the summer to help register Negro voters. Fingers have been pointed at the county sheriff's office, but no arrests have been made yet (→ Dec. 10).

Mass in English

St. Louis, Mo., Aug. 24

This evening the Rev. Frederick R. McManus of Catholic University performed the Roman Catholic Mass in English for the first time ever. The event, part of the 25th anniversary meeting of the Liturgical Conference, is a result of the modernizing of the Roman Catholic Church at the Second Vatican Council. This English version was adopted by the American bishops last April, and next month the bishops will decide when to put it into general use in this country.

At the first New York World's Fair since 1940, which opened April 22, visitors view exhibits emphasizing "peace through understanding."

"William James, The Varieties of Religious Experience" by Boty.

Johnson retains presidency with landslide

Lyndon Johnson in the Oval Office.

Washington, D.C., Nov. 3

Lyndon Baines Johnson defeated Republican challenger Barry M. Goldwater by a lopsided margin in today's presidential election. Johnson called the victory for himself and his running mate Hubert Humphrey "a mandate for unity."

Political experts disagreed about whether the election is a "mandate." But it is clear that voters rejected Goldwater's conservatism, particularly on racial integration. In the campaign he said, "There's a freedom to associate and there's a freedom not to associate." Johnson used remarks like this to paint Goldwater in the colors of the radical right, saying, "Extremism in the pursuit of the presidency is an unpardonable vice." He also depicted the G.O.P. as nuclear hawks and the Democrats as peacekeepers: "There is no such thing as a conventional nuclear war." Democrats held on to both houses of Congress. And Robert Kennedy was elected a senator from New York.

Warren report says Oswald acted alone

Washington, D.C., Sept. 27

The Warren Commission investigating the assassination of President John F. Kennedy has found that Lee Harvey Oswald, the accused assassin, acted alone. The report states it did not find evidence of a conspiracy in the November 22 shooting. The commission, headed by Chief Justice Earl Warren, further states that Oswald fired three shots from the easternmost window on the sixth floor of the Texas School Book Depository building on Elm Street. The report also recommends that killing of a president or vice president be made a federal crime. The report reprimanded the F.B.I. for having failed to alert the Secret Service that Oswald was in the region during President Kennedy's visit.

Rebels hit air base of U.S. at Bien Hoa

Saigon, South Vietnam, Nov. 1

Vietcong guerrillas attacked the United States Air Force base at Bien Hoa today, killing four American servicemen and wounding 12. Five planes were destroyed and many were heavily damaged. According to officials at the base, the Communists launched a heavy mortar barrage. Then, as the shellfire lifted, enemy demolition units cut through the perimeter wire, exchanged fire with the American defenders and tossed explosive charges at the planes parked there. The base, which is about 10 miles northeast of Saigon, supports various types of combat aircraft, including the versatile B-57 Canberra light bombers that are used for ground support as well as aerial reconnaissance missions (→ Feb. 7, 1965).

Olympics in Japan

Tokyo, Oct. 24

Don Schollander captured four swimming gold medals and American track stars swept 10 of 24 events in the Olympic Games that wound up today. Schollander set world records in the 100-meter and 400-meter free-style races and added gold medals in two relays. For the first time, an American won the 10,000 meters, Billy Mills breaking the Olympic record by cutting 50 seconds off his own best time. Bob Hayes tied the world mark of 10 seconds in the 100-meter sprint.

Protest at Berkeley

Berkeley, Calif., Nov. 12

The campus has been in turmoil since the University of California banned political activities here. The ban caused a 32-hour sit-in October 1 and 2 and unrest continues. President Clark Kerr says he will not allow "intimidation to replace reason" as the standard for school policy and denies the university is trying to prevent student participation in the civil rights movement. Led by Mario Savio, students have formed a Free Speech Movement to guard their constitutional rights.

King receives Nobel

Oslo, Norway, Dec. 10

The Rev. Martin Luther King Jr., who brought the concepts of non-violence to the American civil rights movement, won the Nobel Peace Prize today. He is, at 35, the youngest recipient of the award. The Baptist preacher first came to national attention when he led bus boycotts in Montgomery, Alabama. He later headed the Southern Christian Leadership Conference, a group that teaches the techniques of non-violent protest to civil rights activists (→ Jan. 11, 1965).

"Dr. Strangelove"

Hollywood, California

The best movie around is *Dr. Strangelove or: How I Learned to Stop Worrying and Love the Bomb*, a black comedy on atomic annihilation with Peter Sellers and George Scott, followed by Julie Andrews's film debut in *Mary Poppins*; James Garner and Julie Andrews in *The Americanization of Emily*; a scary *Hush... Hush Sweet Charlotte* with Bette Davis and Olivia De Havilland; the Beatles romp, *A Hard Day's Night* and *The Pink Panther* with Peter Sellers and David Niven.

LBJ shows off his cattle-herding abilities during a luncheon with the press. The Texan has always retained close ties to the land of his birth.

October 25. *Another band out of Britain. The Rolling Stones, led by Mick Jagger (left), are introduced to Americans on "The Ed Sullivan Show."*

Arizona, Jan. 8. Lorna Elizabeth Lockwood is first woman named chief justice of a state supreme court.

New Orleans, Jan. 11. Negro players boycott American Football League's all-star game to protest racial bias in New Orleans (→ March 25).

Pleiku, Vietnam, Feb. 7. U.S. military advisers' compound struck; eight Americans die (→ March 17).

Cape Kennedy, Florida, March 23. Gemini III launched, orbiting Earth three times and splashing down in Atlantic (→ Apr. 6).

Cape Kennedy, Apr. 6. National Aeronautics and Space Administration launches first commercial satellite, Early Bird, designed to relay telephone and television signals (→ June 3).

Midwest, Apr. 11. Tornadoes strike seven states, killing 271 people and injuring 5,000.

Boston, April. Celtics defeat Los Angeles Lakers, four games to one, in N.B.A. championship.

Washington, D.C., June 7. Supreme Court rules that televised coverage of criminal trials violates due process.

Washington, D.C., Aug. 8. Congress passes Omnibus Housing Act, providing new funds for low-income housing.

Minnesota, Oct. 14. Los Angeles Dodgers defeat Minnesota Twins, four games to three, in World Series.

St. Louis, Oct. 28. World's tallest monument, 630-foot Gateway Arch designed by Eero Saarinen, completed.

East Coast, Nov. 10. Power restored following greatest electrical failure in history, which blacked out seven states and Ontario for two days.

Atlanta, Dec. 8. Delta Airlines puts first DC-9 jet into service.

Space, Dec. 16. Walter Schirra and Thomas Stafford, aboard Gemini 6, achieve first rendezvous of manned orbiting spacecraft when they maneuver within one foot of Gemini 7.

Berkeley, California. Term "Flower Power" coined by Allen Ginsberg, at anti-war rally.

Hollywood, Calif. Top films this year include *Dr. Zhivago, The Sound of Music, Help* and *The Pawnbroker*.

U.S. goes on the offensive in Vietnam

American marines patrol in a village suspected of harboring Vietcong soldiers.

Captured Vietcong guerrillas, tethered to one another, are marched away.

Vietnam, December

When the history of the Vietnam War is written, 1965 will be remembered as the year the United States went from an advisory to a combat role and from a defensive strategy to a full-blown offensive one.

After American bases at Pleiku and Quinhon were attacked in February with significant casualties, President Johnson dramatically escalated the role of the air force. On February 13, he ordered the air force and navy to commence Operation Rolling Thunder, a vast bombing campaign directed against military targets in North Vietnam. He began a dramatic buildup of combat personnel in March when the first two battalions of marines landed at Danang. American troop strength at the end of 1964 was 23,000; it is now over 154,000.

By last August, the United States had begun regularly engaging the enemy in battalion-sized offensives. On August 21, marines destroyed a huge Vietcong force in Quangngai Province during Operation Star Light. By late November, the First Cavalry had sought out and soundly defeated thousands of enemy soldiers who gathered at Iadrang in the Central Highlands to cut South Vietnam in half. Although the troops of the cavalry achieved a decisive victory, both sides suffered tremendous casualties. The total of American combat deaths this year has passed the 1,500 mark (→ March 1966).

President Johnson pledges Great Society

Washington, D.C., Jan. 4

President Johnson outlined his domestic aims tonight in his State of the Union address, calling for the creation of a "Great Society." Although he conceived his program last May, tonight he expanded on it. Like the New Deal and Fair Deal before it, the Great Society is designed to help the politically and economically impoverished. It is founded on the premise that poverty and racial strife beleaguer the whole nation. As he has said, "The Great Society rests on abundance of liberty for all. It demands an end to poverty and racial injustice – to which we are totally committed."

He asked federal support for urban renewal, health care, education and the basic needs of the poor. The President hopes to capitalize on his huge electoral victory and a solid Democratic-controlled Congress to enact voting rights legislation. He appealed to the House and Senate tonight for such enactment. It is expected that by month's end he will also ask Congress to support a health care plan for the elderly and aid to education.

Many political experts believe Johnson has the potential to pass as many of his Great Society proposals as Franklin D. Roosevelt did his New Deal initiatives (→ July 30).

Woman immolates self over Vietnam

Detroit, Mich., March 17

In a ghastly scene more appropriate to a horror movie than day-to-day life, an elderly woman publicly burned herself alive today to protest the growing American involvement in Vietnam. Witnesses described how Mrs. Alice Hertz, aged 72, sat down in the street, doused herself with gasoline, and set fire to her clothes. By the time onlookers put out the flames, Mrs. Hertz was critically burned. She was rushed to a local hospital, where she died. No surviving family members have been found (→ Dec.).

Malcolm X silenced by assassin's bullets

New York City, Feb. 21

Black leader Malcolm X is dead today at the age of 39, shot by assassins as he was beginning to address an audience of 400. His death was apparently not caused by the white members of society he so often spoke against, but as the result of quarreling within the Black Muslim movement. Born Malcolm Little, he served 10 years in prison, beginning in 1946. While there, he became a convert to the Black Muslim organization that was led by Elijah Muhammad. Disagreements with Muhammad led Malcolm X to found his own group, the Organization for Afro-American Unity. The two sects continued to feud, ultimately resulting in the assassination.

Malcolm X, the fiery Afro-American leader, addressing Muslim followers shortly before he was assassinated.

March to Montgomery

The Rev. Dr. Martin Luther King Jr. and other civil rights leaders at the head of the procession that marched from Selma to Montgomery, Alabama.

Montgomery, Alabama, March 25

Overcoming weeks of violence and intransigence, more than 25,000 people poured into Alabama's capitol today, affirming the right of Negroes to vote. With the protection of federal troops, Negroes accompanied by sympathetic whites marched 54 miles from Selma to the capitol building. The Rev. Dr. Martin Luther King Jr. addressed the crowd from the capitol steps with the flag of the Confederacy waving overhead.

The euphoria of the march soon ended. Viola Liuzzo, wife of a Detroit union official, was killed by whites who attacked her as she took groups of marchers back to Selma. The Selma march has been marked by violence from the beginning. On March 6, state troopers, some on horses, waded into a group of marchers at the Edmund Pettus Bridge near Selma. The sight on the television news of marchers being beaten and trampled has stunned the nation. After another march, a white Unitarian minister, the Rev. James Reeb, was clubbed, and died two days later. In February, Jimmy Lee Jackson, a 26-year-old black demonstrator, was beaten, and died seven days later (→Aug. 6).

Electric Bob booed

Newport, R.I., July 25

Bob Dylan seems determined to follow his own instincts as his music becomes more energized and his lyrics grow personal and imagistic. Tonight, however, he ran headlong into a backlash from folk purists as he took the stage here dressed in flamboyant clothes and armed with an electric guitar and high-wattage back-up band. As hundreds booed, an unperturbed Dylan offered searing versions of *Maggie's Farm* and *Like a Rolling Stone*.

Single life in L.A.

Los Angeles

The mating instinct often drives young people to the big cities in search of the Right One. There they find the usual singles meeting places, bars, clubs, dance halls. But most singles find this scene artificial and unpleasant. A Los Angeles realtor now has a possible solution. He has put up a "Singles Only" apartment project, a natural setting for people to get to know each other, with community rooms, pool, game rooms and planned parties.

Do your own thing, Krishna or Watusi

United States

Good vibes from overseas. The Beatles and James Bond toys were imports, as were the I Ching from the Orient, Krishna Consciousness from India and macrobiotic food. As for home-grown pleasures, there are computer dating, G.I. Joe, Allan and Midge dolls and body painting. Girls in go-go boots and mini paper dresses do the watusi, the frug and the swim. They're groupies or some guy's old lady. Everyone smokes, and if it's tobacco, don't blame Madison Avenue, because the F.T.C. has proposed warning messages on cigarette packs. In fact, don't listen to the bad vibes, just do your own thing!

Liston is flattened in two minutes by a taunting Cassius Clay

Lewiston, Maine, May 25

Cassius Clay knocked out Sonny Liston tonight for the second time as fans cried, "Fake! Fake! Fake!" They would have been even more upset if they had heard a taunting Clay say before the battle that he would win it in one minute 49 seconds of the first. One observer with a stopwatch reported Liston hit the canvas at 1:48 and, except for a timing mix-up, would have been counted out at 1:58. The official time was incorrectly set at a minute. The brash champion threw a short right hand that caught Sonny on the chin. Liston teetered like a huge redwood about to topple in the forest, then fell. He tried to get up, but his glazed eyes signaled his bewilderment. It was all over.

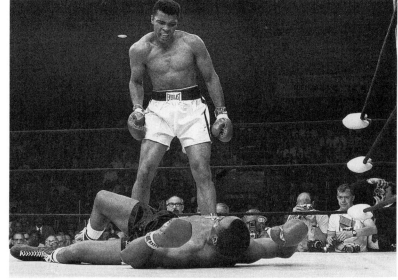

Champ Cassius Clay tells a floored Sonny Liston: "I told you I had a surprise." ▷

American astronaut takes a stroll in space

Edward White performing in space.

Houston, Texas, June 3

Astronaut Edward White 2nd took the first American walk in space today, spending 20 minutes floating outside his Gemini 4 spacecraft during the third orbit of its scheduled four-day flight. White and James McDivitt were lifted into space at 11:16 a.m. When the spacecraft was 150 miles above Australia, White opened its hatch, stood up and floated into space at the end of a 25-foot gold-plated nylon tether. He remained outside the spacecraft longer than planned, using all the fuel of a jet gas gun provided to propel himself. "This is the saddest moment of my life," White said ruefully as he had to return to the spacecraft (→ Dec. 1966).

Dominican turmoil eases

Santo Domingo, Aug. 31

The political turmoil that has plagued the Dominican Republic since the 31-year dictatorship of Rafael Trujillo ended with his assassination in May 1961 seems to be easing. A provisional government headed by 44-year-old Hector Garcia-Godoy has been formed with the backing of the United States and the Organization of American States. Since Garcia-Godoy is acceptable to the supporters of the deposed president, Juan Bosch, under whom he served as foreign minister, and to the right-wing of the army, hopes are high that the compromise will hold and the 22,000 American troops, here since April, will be able to return home.

Although the United States intervention was first justified as needed to protect American lives, it was obviously based on the fear that Santo Domingo under Juan Bosch might become another Cuba. However, the charge that he was a stalking horse for Communists has been vigorously denied by Bosch, the exiled professor who became president three years ago in the first free election since 1924. Washington's intervention is widely resented here as typical gringo imperialism. The O.A.S. has authorized an Inter-American Peace Force, but it consists almost entirely of the American forces already here.

Truman host to LBJ for Medicare signing

Independence, Missouri, July 30

It was a touching moment at the Harry S Truman Library here today when the Medicare Social Security Bill was signed into law by President Johnson.

The 81-year-old former President Truman was the first chief executive to recommend that a federal program be established to provide health insurance for the elderly under the auspices of the Social Security operations. And Truman was touched by the tribute that was bestowed upon him by President Johnson. Said LBJ, who was a congressman from Texas when the former Missouri senator was President, "The people of the United States loved and voted for Harry Truman, not because he gave them hell – but because he gave them hope."

The new Medicare legislation expands an existing insurance program by providing hospital care, nursing home care and out-patient diagnostic services for the senior citizens of the country. As it goes into effect, more than 19 million Americans will be eligible to receive the new assistance (→ Sept. 9).

New agency to run housing program

Washington, D.C., Sept. 9

Continuing his pledge to provide shelter for the poor, President Johnson today signed the Omnibus Housing Act, creating the Department of Housing and Urban Development. The new Cabinet-level office will administer the program for housing and urban renewal, which includes a plan to grant financial aid for low-income homes. Named by Johnson to head the department is Robert Weaver, the first Negro Cabinet member (→ Oct. 11, 1966).

Americans active in Vatican Council

Rome, Oct. 4

American bishops are playing a major role in the proceedings of the Vatican Council. Last month, the council adopted an American-written *Declaration on Religious Liberty*. The Americans have also been instrumental in drafting a document stating that the Jews are not to blame for Jesus's crucifixion. Today, Pope Paul VI is in New York City, where he celebrated an open-air mass in Yankee Stadium and later spoke at the United Nations.

The war in Vietnam is beginning to polarize the nation. A growing number of Americans are questioning the role of the United States as casualties continue to mount. By the end of this year, the number of American servicemen in the small Southeast Asian nation passed the 150,000 mark. And as some young men of college age burn their draft cards in protest (left), even older citizens (right) join demonstrations to "stop the war machine."

Voting Rights Act guards Negro ballot

Washington, D.C., Aug. 6

The Voting Rights Act, which prohibits states from using poll taxes, literacy tests or other techniques to curtail voter registration among minorities, has been signed into law by President Johnson. Rigorously debated in Congress, the new legislation also makes it possible for federal examiners to insure compliance with the law in those states that have a history of voter discrimination. The Justice Department is expected, very soon, to announce a list of places where these examiners may be sent.

Signing the bill, President Johnson proclaimed that "three and a half centuries ago, the first Negroes arrived ... They came in darkness and ... in chains ... The story of our nation and of the American Negro are like two great rivers. Welling up from that tiny Jamestown spring they flow through the centuries along divided channels. ... When the Liberty Bell rang out in Philadelphia, it did not toll for the Negro. When Andrew Jackson threw open the doors of democracy, they did not open for the Negro. It was only at Appomattox, a century ago, that an American victory was also a Negro victory. And the two rivers, one shining with promise, the other dark-stained with oppression, began to move toward one another" (→ 16).

"Burn, baby, burn": Watts in chaos

Stores go up in smoke during rioting in the depressed area of Los Angeles.

Los Angeles, Aug. 16

The arrest of Marquette Frye, a 21-year-old Negro, was the spark that ignited five days of rioting in Watts, a Negro section of Los Angeles. His arrest for drunken driving, and subsequent allegations of police brutality, produced an explosion of racial tension that had been building throughout the nation for years.

The riot, which decimated the streets of Watts, was responsible for 34 deaths, over 1,000 injuries and 4,000 arrests. Some 200 businesses were destroyed, and 700 severely damaged. Property damage has been estimated at $40 million. Most of it was caused by Negroes who, outraged by the reports of police brutality, and by their impoverished and humiliating lives, attacked whites and police, fired guns and smashed and burned buildings. A witness to the violence said, "There were a lot of young hoods and agitators. But there were a lot of others who were just discontented and took advantage of the situation for emotional release."

It has been suggested that radical groups such as the Black Muslims helped to incite the riot by preaching violence against whites. A heat wave may also have served to raise tempers.

On August 13, it became clear that the police and riot control squads had little chance of quelling the violence. Therefore, 20,000 National Guardsmen were called out by California Governor Edmund Brown and a curfew from 8 p.m. to sunrise was established over a 35-mile area around the rioting. Still, it required more than two days for the soldiers to bring the area under control.

President Johnson said of the rioting: "It is not enough to simply decry disorder. We must also strike at the unjust conditions from which disorder largely flows." The President is now promoting legislation for restoration of the sacked ghetto, which has become a symbol for racial strife and urban deterioration across the nation. A commission of eight men, led by the former Director of Central Intelligence John A. McCone, will investigate the causes of the riot.

While Watts was in flames, similar rioting broke out in Chicago between August 12 and 14, after a Negro woman was killed by a fire engine driven by whites. It took 500 Chicago policemen to subdue more than 1,000 rioters. Some 80 people were injured and 140 arrested (→ March 25, 1966).

Quotas lifted from immigration policy

Liberty Island, Oct. 3

The path to the American Dream became more accessible today as President Johnson signed the Immigration Bill at a ceremony in New York harbor. It ends most national origin curbs. It also raises the annual ceiling to 120,000 Western Hemisphere immigrants a year and 170,000 from the rest of the world, with a limit of 20,000 from any one nation. In encouraging refuge for those from oppressive regimes, LBJ said: "The future holds little hope for any government where the present holds no hope for the people." A ship of Cuban emigres is due here later this week.

Spirit of America races 600.601 mph

Bonneville Flats, November 15. *Craig Breedlove broke the world's record for ground speed today, traveling at 600.601 mph in his Spirit of America.*

Nader on bad cars; Leary on good trips

United States

Sixty years ago, Upton Sinclair's *The Jungle*, a novel about meat packing in Chicago, pushed the nation to the brink of vegetarianism. Now consumer advocate Ralph Nader, 31, has motorists pining for the days of the horse and buggy with his expose *Unsafe at Any Speed*, a high-octane indictment of auto safety standards. The good news is you can travel far without a car. So says Harvard's Dr. Timothy Leary, whose *Psychedelic Reader* plots another sort of trip that is available to those who taste the hallucinogenic nectar of LSD, or in Leary's words, who "tune in, turn on, drop out."

American G.I.'s search and destroy in Mekong Delta

American troopers leap out of their helicopters and into the fray.

A wounded medic aids his fallen comrades as a rescue helicopter arrives.

South Vietnam, March

American forces have scored resounding victories in two recently completed search-and-destroy operations in the Mekong Delta region of South Vietnam. In Operation Marauder, which began the first week in January, troops of the 173rd Airborne Brigade engaged and destroyed an entire Vietcong battalion and the headquarters of a second battalion. Some 20,000 troops of the First Cavalry Division, aided by South Korean marines and South Vietnamese infantrymen, began another search-and-destroy campaign code-named Operation Masher/White Wing January 24. Military chiefs offered a "body count" of the enemy as a way of indicating the success of the effort. For the six weeks of the campaign against nine Communist battalions, they reported killing 1,342 enemy soldiers, capturing 633 and seizing 1,087 suspected Vietcong.

While the search-and-destroy operations have been militarily successful, they have been terrible for the civilians caught in the fighting. President Johnson and Prime Minister Nguyen Cao Ky agreed at their Honolulu talks February 8 that these operations must be accompanied by non-military efforts to "win the hearts and minds" of civilians. Otherwise, the war could easily be lost. The leaders pledged to improve medical care and education and to build a real political democracy in Vietnam (→ June 29).

Georgia House bars Bond for war stand

Atlanta, Georgia, Jan. 10

Julian Bond, the 25-year-old civil rights activist, was denied a seat in the Georgia legislature today because of his opposition to the Vietnam War. Legislators insisted Bond was disloyal to the United States because he said he admired draft-card burners. The vote barring him from a House seat was 184-12. Bond and seven other Negroes were the first of their race to be elected to Georgia's legislature since Reconstruction. Bond is a leader in the militant civil rights group, the Student National Coordinating Committee (S.N.C.C.) (→ May 15).

Seagren pole vaults to record 17 feet

Albuquerque, N.M., March 6

How high can man soar on his own power? For decades, the 17-foot pole vault, like the 4-minute mile, was considered unattainable. Today, Bob Seagren vaulted 17 feet 3/4 inch and set a world indoor record. The improvement in Seagren's performance has been remarkable considering the fact that last year he could do no better than 16 feet 4 inches outdoors. He seems certain to clinch an Olympic berth for 1968 and is expected to break records along the way. Another American, Fred Hansen, vaulted 17 feet 4 inches outdoors in 1964.

Celtics win eighth N.B.A. title in a row

Boston, April

The Boston Celtics have won their eighth straight National Basketball Association Championship – their ninth in 10 years – by defeating the Los Angeles Lakers in a seven-game series. However, the coach who presided over this dynasty, Red Auerbach, has announced that he is retiring. Bill Russell, the great shot-blocker, was named to replace him. The Celtics proved that as good as Bob Cousy was, they could win after his departure. Cousy, who left the Celtics in 1963, had made the All-N.B.A. first team for 10 years in a row.

Wave of anti-war protests sweeps country

Washington, D.C., May 15

Thousands of people marched and chanted in the nation's capital today to protest the deepening American involvement in Vietnam. They surrounded the White House and vowed to throw congressional supporters of the war out of office. Today's demonstration was the latest in a series of anti-Vietnam protests. At the University of Chicago, hundreds of students seized the administration building for three days. In New York, students shouted at the president of City College and sat on the floor outside his office.

The war seemed close to home yesterday as 400,000 students took the selective service qualification test. Those who score under 70 risk losing the 2-S deferment. Critics say the exam increases the war's burden on the poor and uneducated. Harlem lawmaker Adam Clayton Powell Jr. said the tests remind him of Nazism because they "weed out the intellectually deprived or socially undesirable by conscripting them for cannon fodder."

President Johnson called war critics "nervous Nellies," and stopped just short of branding them unpatriotic. He accused them of "turning on their leaders, their country and their fighting men." At Princeton, Johnson's admonition to critics to "cool it" was greeted with frigid silence. "This war is unconstitutional," the protesters' signs read. "Who are we to police the world?" (→Oct. 22, 1967).

B-52's hammer Hanoi

Wave upon wave of B-52 bombers strike at Hanoi with devastating effect.

H.E.W. offers birth control services

Washington, D.C., Apr. 1

The government has taken bold steps to provide contraceptives for those in need. The Department of Health, Education and Welfare is spending $3.1 million this year on family planning services. President Johnson says all families should have access to services which "allow freedom to choose the number and spacing of their children." Despite opposition from the Catholic Church federal funds for birth control will almost double yearly.

N.O.W. issues bold women's manifesto

Washington, D.C.

Calling for "true equality for all women in America," the National Organization for Women has promised to oppose vigorously any party or candidate who "ignores the principle of full equality between the sexes." N.O.W. leader Betty Friedan says women are "in relatively little position to influence or control major decisions." But N.O.W. plans to mobilize the women's vote and work on legislation to fight sex discrimination (→Aug. 26, 1970).

Saigon, South Vietnam, June 29

For the first time in the war, North Vietnam's key cities of Hanoi and Haiphong have been blasted by waves of B-52 heavy bombers. The North Vietnamese capital and primary port cities had been considered off limits because Pentagon officials repeatedly have said that bombing strikes on these centers might provoke either Russian or Chinese intervention – or both.

The decision to bomb Hanoi and Haiphong is the latest step in the U.S. effort to destroy the North Vietnamese military machine in an undisguised campaign of attrition. On April 12, B-52's based on Guam bombed targets near the Laotian border. And last month, the big bombers hit enemy forces on the Cambodian side of the Caibac River in western South Vietnam.

The B-52's, originally designed to deliver nuclear weapons, carry a conventional bomb load of 58,000 pounds. Flying at a height of 50,000 feet, these giant bombers cannot be seen or heard – until each rains down its three dozen 2,000-pound block-busting bombs.

While the bombing of Hanoi and Haiphong is admittedly a strategic gamble, Pentagon officials believe this dramatic new phase in the air war will ultimately prove decisive in bringing about the defeat of North Vietnam (→Oct. 25).

Masters & Johnson on human sexuality

United States

Human Sexual Response, the first book to utilize extensive experiments on human subjects to study sexual behavior, is based on an 11-year research program run by authors Dr. William Masters, a gynecologist, and Virginia Johnson, a psychologist. They studied and filmed the sexual activities of over 600 male and female volunteers ranging in age from 18 to 89. The book dispels old myths, providing detailed measurements of the sexual cycle, orgasms, and physiological patterns vital for treating sexual problems.

G.M. offers apology to crusader Nader

Washington, D.C., March 22

General Motors executives apologized publicly to safety crusader Ralph Nader today for having private detectives pry into his sex life and political beliefs. Company president James M. Roche and other officials admitted before a congressional committee that they ordered the investigation of Nader because of his book, *Unsafe at Any Speed*, which pointed out the safety flaws of the automobiles. Roche agreed with Senator Abraham Ribicoff that the snooping techniques used by detectives G.M. hired were "unworthy of American business."

American draftees are sworn into the army. The war in Vietnam keeps expanding, and the administration, determined to see it through to a successful conclusion, calls up ever-increasing numbers of young men.

Race riots inflame Atlanta, Chicago

Impelled by poverty, hunger and hopelessness in the midst of an affluent society, some ghetto dwellers loot local stores in full view of policemen.

Atlanta, Georgia, Sept. 11

Racial violence erupted again in Atlanta, where militant young Negroes shouting "Black Power" attacked cars and police vehicles with chunks of concrete last night. Atlanta police, who battled rioters with tear gas three days last week, worked to prevent another major outbreak. The Atlanta riots, which started after police shot a Negro suspect they said was fleeing, have dramatized the deep split between young militants and more moderate civil rights leaders. Atlanta Mayor Ivan Allen Jr. has blamed Stokely Carmichael, national chairman of the Student Non-Violent Coordinating Committee, for the rioting and Carmichael, who popularized the "Black Power" slogan, has been arrested and charged with inciting the violence. The Rev. Martin Luther King Jr. has criticized the rioting. Negro ministers and businessmen have gone door to door in Negro neighborhoods trying to bring order.

Dr. King left Atlanta for Chicago, where he has been leading marches to demand better housing for poor people. In early September, under the watchful eye of some 2,000 bayonet-wielding National Guardsmen, King led a march on Cicero, Illinois. Roving gangs of whites attacked the marchers with flying bottles and rocks, shouting "Kill 'em!" or "Tar and feather 'em!" The riots initially broke out in Chicago in mid-July only days after King launched his crusade. The National Guard was called in following three days of looting and burning (→ 12).

2 brutal killing sprees horrify nation

United States, Aug. 1

Two killing sprees have again stamped the country as a land of senseless violence. On July 19, Richard Speck, 26, was arrested in Chicago for the gruesome slaying of eight student nurses. He forced his way into their dormitory with a knife and gun, bound their hands with bedsheets, then strangled five and stabbed three. A ninth escaped by hiding under a bed. Today, in Austin, Texas, Charles Whitman mounted the 27-story University of Texas tower and opened fire on the people below, killing 16 and wounding 30. The 90-minute slaughter ended when he was killed by an off-duty policeman. Whitman had killed his wife and mother the night before. The 25-year-old honor student was a former marine.

As the war progresses, the introduction of new technologies such as the variable-sweep wing of the F-111B fighter increases American firepower.

Miranda case backs rights of suspects

Washington, D.C., June 13

"You have the right to remain silent. Anything you say may be used against you in a court of law." If an arresting police officer does not inform a suspect of these and other rights, the accused has been denied liberties, according to a Supreme Court decision today.

The court ruled in the controversial Miranda v. Arizona case. Weighing Fifth Amendment guarantees against self-incrimination, a 5-4 majority held that a confession obtained by police is invalid if the suspect is not told of his rights, including the right to have a lawyer present. The case came to the high court after convicted rapist Ernesto Miranda appealed, charging he had been denied his Fifth Amendment rights in confessing to his crime. Critics say that the decision will allow more criminals to go free on procedural technicalities. But proponents applaud the ruling as a victory for civil liberties and protection against police entrapment.

Black Power splits civil rights groups

Stokely Carmichael of S.N.C.C. coined the term "Black Power."

United States, July 9

"Black Power." The Congress of Racial Equality has endorsed it. The National Association for the Advancement of Colored People rejects it. Roy Wilkins, leader of the N.A.A.C.P., says his group "will have none of this ... It is the ranging of race against race on the irrelevant basis of skin color. It is the father of hatred and mother of violence." But C.O.R.E. says, "Black Power is not hatred. It is a means to bring Black Americans into the covenant of brotherhood, ... a unified Black voice reflecting racial pride in the tradition of our heterogeneous nation." Student Nonviolent Coordinating Committee chairman Stokely Carmichael gave birth to the phrase. He spoke of "Black Power" during a June Mississippi voter registration march (→ Aug. 26).

Mini-skirts a la mod

United States

Its a mod, mod, mod, mod world. Minis are bearing thighs for all the world to see, pushing Mom's morality further into the dark ages. Flower children are packing up and taking off to blow their minds on LSD. In the hippie havens of California, the Bible gives way to Tarot cards; the disco steps aside for the psychedelic Day-Glo dance hall, complete with strobe lights and electric Kool-Aid; and Elvis surrenders to the Stones and the Grateful Dead.

Child Nutrition Act gives food to kids

Washington, D.C., Oct. 11

"I know what it is like to teach children who are listless because they are hungry – and realize the difference a decent meal can make in lives and attitudes of school children." With those words, President Johnson signed the Child Nutrition Act today. It grants federal funds to feed impoverished students and is another Johnson initiative to help the nation's schools. Last year, he signed the Elementary and Secondary Education Bill. Many of the school supports come from recommendations by the LBJ-appointed task force on education, headed by John Gardner, president of the Carnegie Corporation (→ Nov. 11).

Johnson, warned of failure, meets with Ky

Prime Minister Nguyen Cao Ky (left) is also an air force vice marshal.

Manila, Philippines, Oct. 25

Faced with a deteriorating political and military situation in South Vietnam, President Johnson began talks yesterday with South Vietnamese Prime Minister Nguyen Cao Ky and leaders of the other nations involved in the war. Warned 10 days ago by Secretary of Defense Robert McNamara that neither the heavy bombing campaigns nor the pacification programs have been effective enough to bring North Vietnam to the peace table, Johnson and the allies have issued a series of three statements designed to reassure the North Vietnamese of their limited war aims and thus hopefully speed up the peace process. The leaders announced today that while they remain dedicated to peace in Vietnam, they also promised to remove the allied troops from South Vietnam within six months after the war ends. In another statement, the Declaration of Peace, they said: "We do not threaten the sovereignty or territorial integrity of our neighbors, whatever their ideological alignment. We only ask that this be reciprocated."

In addition to President Johnson and Prime Minister Ky, those participating in the Manila talks include President Park Chung Hee of South Korea and President Ferdinand Marcos of the Philippines. Australia, New Zealand, and Thailand have also been participating in the conference (→ Feb. 24, 1967).

$1 billion to rebuild 60 to 70 U.S. cities

Washington, D.C., Nov. 3

One might think of it as a War on Decay, urban decay. And with the signing today of the Demonstration Cities and Metropolitan Redevelopment Act, the first battle has been won. President Johnson, after signing the legislation, said, "I believe this law will be regarded as one of the major breakthroughs of the 1960s." The Model Cities Act, as it is called, provides nearly $1 billion in federal funds over two years for 60 to 70 "demonstration" cities for the reconstruction of their cores. It works with local arms of government and will be an experiment in inter-governmental administration.

"In Cold Blood"

United States

What do you get when you fuse story-telling skills with dogged research? A "non-fiction novel." This is what Truman Capote calls his *In Cold Blood: A True Account of a Multiple Murder and Its Consequences*. A first printing of 100,000 sold out nearly overnight. The book is a blow-by-blow account of the brutal 1959 killing of a wealthy Kansas farm family, the Clutters. Capote reviews the lives of the victims, probes the minds of the cold-blooded murderers, Dick Hickok and Perry Smith, and follows them to Death Row and their execution.

Pop is growing up

United States

On the jacket of their innovative new album, *Revolver*, the Beatles gaze introspectively from behind dark glasses. The made-for-TV Monkees were a hit this year, but they were out of step with the new-found maturity of many pop musicians: Bob Dylan offered the far-ranging *Blonde on Blonde*, the Beach Boys, *Pet Sounds*. The Byrds soared with *Eight Miles High*, piloted by Jim McGuinn's shimmering guitar, but it was often banned for suspected drug allusions. More danceable but no less creative were Motown's Supremes and Miracles.

Gemini: docking and walking in space

Houston, Texas, December

Project Gemini has paved the way for the landing of an American on the moon within this decade. With 10 two-man missions, the $1.35 billion program has pioneered long-duration flights, maneuvering, rendezvous and docking techniques and "walks" in space. These will be essential in the coming Apollo lunar missions.

In the first mission on March 23 last year, Gemini 3, the new capsule and a Titan 2 rocket were tested. In June astronaut Edward White was the first American to "walk" in space, spending 20 minutes swooping about with a gas-powered jet gun. Gemini 5 stayed up for the eight days required for a moon flight. And in December, Gemini 6 and 8 met in space after a 100,000-mile chase. Gemini 7 astronauts Frank Borman and James Lovell Jr. stayed in space a record 14 days.

This year, Gemini 8 completed the first space docking, with an Agena rocket on March 16. Pilot Neil Armstrong likened it to "parking a car," though a faulty rocket soon forced a premature end to the mission. On the final flight, Gemini 12, Edwin E. Aldrin Jr. spacewalked for 5 1/2 hours on November 15, after an Agena link-up (→ Jan. 27, 1967).

Walt Disney dies; ruled empire of fantasy

Hollywood, Calif., Dec. 15

Walt Disney, who gave us Mickey Mouse, Donald Duck and many other fabulous characters, died of lung cancer today at the age of 65. But the empire he built with the help of his life-long collaborator, Ub Iwerk, a team of artists, ever-growing inventiveness and a great sense of fantasy, will live on. The Chicago-born animation pioneer became king of family entertainment through his fantasy park Disneyland in Anaheim, animated features such as *Snow White*, *Fantasia* and *Bambi*, nature films such as *The Living Desert* and regular films such as *Mary Poppins*.

The great showman at his zenith.

Washington, D.C., Jan. 10. Supreme Court, in United States v. Lamb, rules criminal charges may not be brought against Americans for visiting nations forbidden by State Department.

Cambridge, Mass., Jan. 18. Albert De Salvo, confessed "Boston Strangler," sentenced to life for armed robbery, assault and sex offenses.

South Vietnam, Feb. 24. U.S. forces shell targets inside North Vietnam for first time (→ May 14).

Washington, D.C., March 16. Senate approves first bilateral treaty signed with Soviet Union since 1917, providing framework for greater diplomatic ties.

New York City, Apr. 21. Stalin's daughter, Svetlana Alliluyeva, arrives in U.S. after defecting in New Delhi, India.

New York City, May 1. Anne Sexton wins Pulitzer Prize in poetry, for *Live or Die.*

Washington, D.C., May 11. With installation of one millionth telephone, half of all world's telephones are in United States.

San Francisco, May 24. Philadelphia 76ers defeat San Francisco Warriors four games to two, for N.B.A. title.

Chicago, Aug. 15. Pablo Picasso's gift to city unveiled, steel sculpture weighing 163 tons and standing 50 feet high.

Washington, D.C., Aug. 30. Senate approves appointment of Thurgood Marshall to Supreme Court, first black to be seated on high court.

Newport, Rhode Island, Sept. 18. U.S. yacht Intrepid defeats Australian challenger Dame Pattie for America's Cup.

Boston, Oct. 12. St. Louis Cardinals defeat Red Sox in World Series, four games to three.

Mississippi, Oct. 20. Jury convicts 11 of 18 in 1964 slaying of three civil rights workers; deputy sheriff of Neshoba County among the guilty.

Stanford, California, Dec. 14. It is announced that Stanford University biochemists have successfully synthesized D.N.A.

Hollywood, Calif. Top films this year include *The Graduate, In the Heat of the Night* and *Bonnie and Clyde.*

Vince Lombardi's Packers defeat Kansas City in first Super Bowl

Lombardi at the halftime break in the Super Bowl, the new N.F.L. title game.

Los Angeles, Jan. 15

Winning was the only thing for Coach Vince Lombardi and the Green Bay Packers today when they went into the first Super Bowl, and the Kansas City Chiefs were the victims of a 35-10 drubbing. The winning ingredient was pinpoint passing by Bart Starr; he completed 16 of 23 tosses. Jim Taylor's line-busting enabled the Packers to mix their attack sufficiently to keep the Chiefs off balance. Over the last seven years, a varied assault backed by a strong defense has built a Packer football dynasty, with a succession of Green Bay teams leading the league five times. Unfortunately, the stadium was only two-thirds full today.

3 astronauts burn to death on launching pad in Apollo tragedy

Cape Canaveral, Fla., Jan. 27

Astronauts Virgil Grissom, Edward White and Roger B. Chaffee died tonight when a flash fire swept through their Apollo capsule during a simulated countdown. The three astronauts, rehearsing for the first Apollo space flight, were consumed in a blaze made more intense by the 100 percent oxygen atmosphere of their spacecraft. They are the first astronauts to die in a spacecraft, after 16 successful Mercury and Gemini orbital space flights.

The countdown was only 10 minutes from the simulated liftoff that would have completed the test when the fire broke out. The launching crew was watching on closed-circuit television when there was a sudden flash on the monitor, then a torrent of smoke and fire. Smoke drove rescue crews back as they tried to enter the capsule. The cause of the fire is unknown, as is its effect on plans to reach the moon in this decade (→ July 24, 1969).

Two major combat operations are launched north of Saigon

Washington, D.C., May 14

The Pentagon today announced the conclusion of the biggest combined American-South Vietnamese effort of the war. Operation Junction City, which was launched February 22, involved 22 American and four South Vietnamese battalions. In fierce fighting against veteran North Vietnamese forces in Tayninh Province north of Saigon on the Cambodian border, at least 282 Americans were killed and over 1,500 were wounded. The Communists did not list casualty figures.

This offensive follows the huge assault of January 8 to 26, Operation Cedar Falls, which was spearheaded by the American First and 25th Infantry Divisions and supported by South Vietnamese. In that attack, enemy headquarters and bases in the "Iron Triangle" area 25 miles north of Saigon were destroyed and a supply of rice seized that would feed 13,000 enemy soldiers for a year. Also seized were a half million pages of Communist military documents.

The latest escalation of the war began February 24 when marines shelled enemy positions in North Vietnam and United States aircraft mined rivers north of the demilitarized zone, both for the first time. In April, B-52 bombers were deployed to the U-Tapao airfield in Thailand for long-range strikes against North Vietnam (→ Sept. 30).

Infantrymen leap from their "Huey." Though the helicopter was introduced into combat during the Korean War, its full impact is only now being realized.

Ali stripped of title for resisting draft

Ali, formerly Clay, formerly champ.

Houston, Texas, Apr. 30

Muhammad Ali, who boxed his way to the top of the fistic heap as Cassius Clay, has been stripped of his world heavyweight championship for resisting the military draft. When Ali balked at taking the step that would have put him in the service, the boxing association voted to take away his title. There is also a possibility of criminal prosecution. Ali, who claimed exemption as a Black Muslim minister, said, "I cannot be true to my belief in my religion" by joining the military. Ali has fought twice this year, beating Ernie Terrell February 6 and scoring a six-round knockout of Zora Folley March 22. He looked stale despite a busy 1966 in which he defeated five so-called Bums of the Month (→ June 28, 1971).

25th Amendment sets succession line

Washington, D.C., Feb. 10

The 25th Amendment to the Constitution was ratified today, assuring clear lines of succession to the presidency. "It's a happy day," said Senator Birch Bayh of Indiana, "A constitutional gap that has existed for centuries has finally been filled." The law provides for transfer of power to the Vice President if the President is incapacitated and allows the chief executive to name a Vice President if the spot is vacated. Previously, the position stayed vacant until the next election.

Detroit race riot worst in U.S. history

Detroit, Mich., July 30

The worst race riot in the nation's history has ended here, leaving 38 people dead and sections of the city in charred ruins after four days of terror. Damage from the looting and fire-bombing has been estimated at $500 million. "It looks like Berlin in 1945," said Detroit's Mayor Jerome Cavanaugh.

The rioting in Detroit may have been the worst in deaths and destruction, but cities across the nation are being torn by racial violence. Forty have been hit in the past week alone. Since the July rioting in Newark, New Jersey, racial strife has erupted in some 70 cities, including Atlanta, Boston, Philadelphia, Birmingham, New York and Cincinnati.

After the Detroit riots, President Johnson commented: "We have endured a week such as no nation should live through: a time of violence and tragedy." A newspaper in Stockholm observed: "It threatens to become a revolution of the entire underclass of America."

The rhetoric was strong among many black groups. At a conference on black power in Newark last week, H. Rap Brown, new president of the Student Non-Violent Coordinating Committee, called on Negroes to "wage guerrilla war on the honkie white man," adding, "I love violence." Brown was arrested in July when fires broke out in Cambridge, Maryland, after he urged a crowd of 400 young blacks to "burn this town down."

The rioting in Detroit started after police officers raided an after-hours nightclub where black-power advocates often gather and arrested 75 blacks. Flames soon erupted over Detroit's West Side as arsonists tossed fire bombs into stores that had just been looted. In some neighborhoods where there was looting, a shocked Mayor Cavanaugh reported "a light-hearted abandon, a carnival spirit."

Offering reasons for the riots, sociologists have pointed to unemployment, poor housing and hopelessness in the ghettoes. Michigan's Republican Governor George Romney said Great Society programs had raised false hopes among Negroes. "They are bitter and frustrated," he said (→ Feb. 29, 1968).

A group of Michigan National Guardsmen with bayonets fixed on their rifles advance toward rioters.

A guardsman stands ready while a section of Detroit burns around him.

Police arrest black looters during race rioting in Newark, New Jersey.

Troops stand guard as residents return to view the wreckage after Detroit riots.

Flower children flock to San Francisco for "Summer of Love"

A colorfully bedecked and beaded hippie walks by a psychedelic glass shop on a street in San Francisco.

San Francisco, Summer

"We want the world, and we want it now," thundered Doors lead singer Jim Morrison this year. But many kids figured as long as society was ravaged by war, injustice and materialism, they would do just as well to heed drug guru Timothy Leary's advice and simply drop out. And what better place to do that than in San Francisco, where, as Scott McKenzie warbled in one hit song, everyone was sure to be wearing flowers.

The San Francisco "Summer of Love" began, more or less, in June at the Monterey Pop Festival. With the Beatles' masterpiece, *Sgt. Pepper's Lonely Hearts Club Band* as a beacon, the feeling that rock music had come into its own merged with a high-flying counterculture movement. About 50,000 kids, many with hair even longer than the Beatles' and dressed in a riot of colors, got high on everything from LSD to the communal vibes and grooved to a fantastic array of artists. There was the driving Memphis soul of Otis Redding, the cerebral ragas of Indian sitarist Ravi Shankar and a cavalcade of bands from California, including the Mamas and the Papas, Byrds, Jefferson Airplane, Grateful Dead and Buffalo Springfield. Newcomers like The Who and Janis Joplin were overpowering, while a young guitarist named Jimi Hendrix blew minds – and eardrums – with a brilliant display of stratospheric sounds and incandescent showmanship.

After the festival, the word had spread, and as the media declared San Francisco's Haight-Ashbury section a "Hippie Haven," thousands flocked here. Although the festival mood lingered all summer, as communes formed and acid rock bands played free concerts, the city soon felt the strain. Living space grew scarce, crime soared – and hard drugs wreaked havoc. One hippie called the Haight area "as bad as the squares say it is."

But the local music scene still thrives, with groups like the Airplane and Dead embarking on free-form psychedelic jams laced with lyrics of peace, love and flowers.

Making music and watching the world go by. A drummer takes in the sights and sounds of "the" summer.

Elsewhere, though, the groups couldn't help but reflect an outlook shaped by nightly violence on the TV news. "There's something happening here ... There's a man with a gun over there," sang the Buffalo Springfield in *For What It's Worth*, a song about street fighting on the Sunset Strip in Los Angeles, while the Doors descended into a nightmare world of Oedipal psychosis and carnivalesque organ sounds on *The End*. The "Summer of Love" has some ominous overtones.

Glassboro summit is a cordial success

Glassboro, N.J., June 25

After conferring for 10 hours over a three-day period, President Johnson and Soviet Premier Aleksei N. Kosygin have gone their separate ways. Their talks, which covered such topics as Vietnam, the Middle East and disarmament, although officially described as cordial, have clearly been inconclusive. The meetings were held at Glassboro State College in southwest New Jersey. The site was selected mainly for reasons of protocol: it is precisely half way between the White House and the United Nations, where Kosygin has just addressed a special session of the General Assembly, called to discuss the recent Arab-Israeli war.

Public broadcasting

Washington, D.C., Nov. 7

President Johnson has signed the Public Broadcasting Act of 1967. It establishes a 15-director corporation that will use public and private funds to subsidize non-commercial television and radio. News, public events and cultural and educational programs are to be offered. Initial federal funding of this "network of knowledge" is $9 million. The Carnegie Corporation and CBS have pledged $1 million each, the United Auto Workers $25,000.

Millions of Americans shedding hang-ups

Model Twiggy in minidress.

United States

To parents surveying the times through horn-rimmed glasses, the world of youth may look confusing. Colleges, which have doubled enrollment since 1960, are breeding a new hedonism. Co-ed dorms bring the sexes together. Mini-skirts, introduced last year, are now ubiquitous. Skin is bared and hang-ups shed at "Be-In's," psychedelic, dionysian attacks on the American success ethic. Far Eastern gurus offer spiritual guidance to a host of peaceniks. And San Francisco is host to 100,000 hippies. So confusion may be part of growing up, but to a new generation of iconoclasts looking at the times through shades, everything is beautiful.

Esalen Institute offers group gropes

San Francisco, September

Hugging, slapping and cuddling its way to success, the Esalen Institute, founded on the Big Sur, has now opened a branch at San Francisco's First Unitarian Society Church. Founded in 1962, the Esalen is dedicated to helping people redefine themselves and their relationships through the abandonment of words and the adoption of physical sensation. Everyone from the State Department officer to the housewife is enrolled in a weekend course. Resident fellows attend for two semesters, paying just $3,000 for the insights that fondling and tickling can bring.

A Ryun mile record two years running

Bakersfield, Calif., June 22

For the second year in a row, Jim Ryun has lowered the world record for the mile run. He deftly paced himself in the Amateur Athletic Union meet today, clipping two-tenths of a second off the mark of 3 minutes 51.3 seconds that he set last July at Berkeley. He posted a zippy 3:53.2 in the NCAA championships at Compton. Ryun, who at 16 was the youngest American to make the Olympic team, was ill for the Tokyo Games, but he quickly rebounded in 1965. Ryun recaptured the spotlight from foreign runners who have been shaving the mile mark for three decades.

U.S. forces in war rising to 525,000

Washington, D.C., Sept. 30

President Johnson has signed a $70 billion defense appropriations bill – the largest money bill that Congress has passed in its 177-year history. A huge part of the new funds – and the new 10 percent surcharge on the income tax proposed by LBJ in July – will be used to finance the military effort in Vietnam. The President reported six weeks ago that after conferring with General William Westmoreland he had decided that 47,000 more combat and support soldiers must be sent to Vietnam. When these troops have arrived there next June, the total of American military personnel in Vietnam will come to about 525,000 (→ Jan. 21, 1968).

Brainwashed?

Detroit, Mich., Sept. 4

The *Detroit News* has withdrawn its endorsement of Michigan Governor George Romney for the Republican presidential nomination. Romney, who earlier endorsed the Vietnam War, was asked today why he now calls the war a "tragic mistake." Romney said that on a 1965 Vietnam visit he had been brainwashed by generals and diplomats. The *News* says it now backs New York Governor Nelson Rockefeller, "who knows what he believes."

McNamara resigns as head of defense

Washington, D.C., Nov. 29

Defense Secretary Robert McNamara sent shock waves through Washington today when he announced he was resigning to become president of the World Bank. Liberal historian Arthur M. Schlesinger Jr. called the resignation "ominous and scary." Critics of the Vietnam War charged McNamara had been forced out by Pentagon hardliners. The secretary has not been a dove on the war, but he has criticized the continued bombing of North Vietnam. Earlier this year, he said the bombing would not "seriously reduce the actual flow of men and materiel to the south."

March on the Pentagon

With the march under way, a protester taunts military police at the Pentagon.

Arlington, Virginia, Oct. 22

Bonfires burned into the early hours today as demonstrators continued to jeer the helmeted military police protecting the Pentagon. The protest against the Vietnam War began yesterday afternoon as tens of thousands spilled across the Memorial Bridge from the Lincoln Memorial to the Pentagon. The demonstration started peacefully, and "Dump Johnson" banners outnumbered Vietcong flags. Many protesters were students who had been bused to Washington.

Tempers began to flare as radicals led by David Dellinger and Jerry Rubin confronted thousands of guards wielding rifles and tear gas grenades. The radicals' organization, the National Mobilization Committee to End the War in Vietnam, had vowed to shut down the Pentagon, and a small group did manage to break briefly into the fortress. They were quickly expelled, with more than a dozen protesters injured. Hundreds were arrested, including Dellinger and novelist Norman Mailer.

The march here capped a week of anti-war protests in San Francisco, Los Angeles, New York and Madison, Wisconsin (→ Nov. 11).

"Eve" (1967) by B.M. Jackson. As this realistic painting of a rural home adorned with the Stars and Stripes shows, many Americans still display an old-fashioned kind of patriotism. But others believe that the nation is in an illegal war that cannot be sanctified by wrapping it in a flag.

500 labor leaders meet to oppose war

Chicago, Nov. 11

Cracks appeared today in organized labor's support for President Johnson's conduct of the war in Vietnam. Some 500 officials from the A.F.L.-C.I.O. and independent unions met to urge an "immediate and unconditional end to the bombing of North Vietnam" and a negotiated settlement of the war. The declaration had little effect on the President, who is standing firm on Vietnam despite his decline in the polls. He still has many labor leaders in his corner, including George Meany. At a dinner for the A.F.L.-C.I.O. president, Johnson blasted critics of the war as "calamity howlers" and "forces of division" (→ Dec. 8).

Dr. Spock arrested

New York City, Dec. 8

Anti-war demonstrators were no match for the New York police this week as they tried to shut down the army induction center. More than 500 protesters were arrested. Baby doctor Benjamin Spock and poet Allen Ginsberg were among those taken into custody. So was Cathleen Fitt, daughter of the assistant secretary of defense for manpower. Her father is the man who decides how many men get drafted every month (→ March 6, 1968).

McCarthy will run anti-war campaign

Washington, D.C., Nov. 30

Senator Eugene McCarthy of Minnesota announced today that he will challenge President Johnson for the Democratic nomination in at least four primaries next spring. McCarthy, an outspoken critic of the Vietnam War, says the conflict has created a "moral crisis in America," while the administration has "set no limit to the price which it is willing to pay for a military victory." McCarthy's entry gives a new legitimacy to the anti-war movement, but few think he will stay in the race all the way. Many feel he is a "stalking horse" for Robert Kennedy (→ March 12, 1968).

Miami, Jan. 14. Green Bay Packers beat Oakland Raiders, 33-14, in Super Bowl II.

South Vietnam, Jan. 21. About 5,000 American marines are isolated and under attack by 20,000 North Vietnamese in Khesanh (→ 31).

Washington, D.C., Jan. 30. Clark Clifford confirmed by Senate as Defense Secretary.

Washington, D.C., March 16. Senator Robert Kennedy of New York announces intention of seeking Democratic presidential nomination (→ 31).

Saigon, South Vietnam, Apr. 8. About 100,000 American and South Vietnamese troops begin offensive against Communist forces in 11 provinces.

New York City, May 8. William Styron wins Pulitzer Prize for *The Confessions of Nat Turner.*

Lewisburg, Louisiana, May, 11. Seven Sisters Oak, with a diameter of 36 feet 10 inches, made president of Louisiana Live Oak Society.

Los Angeles, May. Boston Celtics defeat Los Angeles Lakers, four games to two, for N.B.A. title.

Saigon, South Vietnam, July 3. General Creighton Abrams replaces General William Westmoreland as U.S. commander in Vietnam.

Moscow, July 15. Aeroflot and Pan American World Airways open direct service between U.S. and Soviet Union.

St. Louis, Oct. 10. Detroit Tigers defeat St. Louis Cardinals in World Series, four games to three.

New York City, Nov. 5 Shirley Chisholm is first black woman to be elected to United States Congress.

United States. William Burroughs observes, "The youth rebellion is a worldwide phenomenon that has not been seen before in history."

United States. Books published this year include Tom Wolfe's *The Electric Kool-Aid Acid Test,* Eldridge Cleaver's *Soul on Ice,* Arthur Hailey's *Airport* and John Updike's *Couples.*

DEATH

Westport, Connecticut, June 1. Helen Keller, leader of the handicapped (*June 27, 1880).

Reds launch a massive Tet offensive

American troops fight back in the city of Hue. Much of the ancient capital was seized by North Vietnamese forces as they launched their Tet onslaught.

U.S. soldiers watch from behind a wall as an artillery shell explodes.

A wounded Vietnamese mother and her child, caught in the offensive.

Americans watch results of bombing against the North Vietnamese. The enemy has launched repeated assaults from the zone between the North and South.

Washington, D.C., Jan. 31

North Vietnamese and Vietcong forces have launched a massive offensive throughout South Vietnam, Washington confirmed today. The campaign began yesterday with a series of coordinated attacks aimed at American and South Vietnamese troops in the northern and central provinces. In the past 24 hours, an estimated 84,000 Communist combat troops – and an equal number of support forces – have struck at virtually all the provincial capitals and major cities in South Vietnam, incuding Saigon and Hue.

In Saigon, a North Vietnamese suicide squad blew a hole in the wall of the United States Embassy last night, killing two army military policemen. The North Vietnamese occupied the embassy yard for five hours, until they were all killed by other military policemen and marine guards at the embassy this morning. Fighting is continuing on the outskirts of Saigon.

Communist forces have also attacked and captured the port city of Hue. Early word indicates that civilian casualties are extremely high, and there have been many reports of North Vietnamese atrocities.

The Tet offensive has been expected for some time by American military leaders. Their intelligence officials received word last week of the coming "decisive campaign," a contest that the Vietcong soldiers were being told would produce the "final victory." Last week, President Johnson was informed by General William Westmoreland, the American commander in Vietnam, that he believed the Communist attack would come just before Tet, the Vietnamese lunar New Year – even though a truce between the two sides was in effect for the holiday period.

With the news that some 5,000 marines are besieged by at least 20,000 North Vietnamese soldiers at Khesanh and with the yearly cost of the war now approaching $25 billion, opposition to America's continuing commitment to the Saigon government is certain to increase. The Tet Offensive, if it is successful, may convince many American "doves" that the "light at the end of the tunnel" is dimmer than ever (→ Feb. 24).

Americans counter Vietcong offensive

Washington, D.C., Feb. 24

In the aftermath of the Communist Tet offensive, the United States is gearing up for a renewed military effort against the North Vietnamese and Vietcong. Pentagon officials say fighter-bomber planes from the nuclear-powered aircraft carrier Enterprise have begun major air strikes against the Communist capital of Hanoi. And General William Westmoreland, commander of United States forces in Vietnam, has again asked that more troops, 206,000 of them, be sent to reinforce his men in South Vietnam. Last month, 14,000 air force and navy reservists were called up to bolster the American position in Korea so that additional regular forces could be sent to Vietnam (→ May 10).

Johnson will step down

A weary, deeply concerned President Johnson at work on his historic speech.

Washington, D.C., March 31

President Johnson stunned the nation tonight when he announced unexpectedly on television that he does not intend to run for re-election. "I shall not seek and I will not accept the nomination of my party as your President," Johnson declared as he stared purposefully at a camera in the Oval Office.

The President's appearance tonight had been billed as an address to the country on the war in Vietnam. In his speech, he admitted that the conflict had created "division in the American house," and he went on to say that he would not "permit the presidency to become involved in the partisan divisions that are developing."

Johnson's conduct of the war has created deep divisions in the country and eroded his standing in the polls. The latest Gallup poll says only 26 percent of the people favor Johnson's handling of the war. An NBC poll released after the New Hampshire primary indicated half the Democrats were not even aware of Senator Eugene McCarthy's position on the war. Analysts concluded that much of McCarthy's support was as much anti-Johnson as it was anti-war (→ June 6).

McCarthy's surprise in New Hampshire

Concord, N.H., March 12

Senator Eugene McCarthy surprised the White House tonight by capturing 42 percent of the vote in the New Hampshire Democratic primary. McCarthy, who trailed President Johnson by just 7,000 votes, predicted that he will win the next race in Wisconsin. "I think I can get the nomination," McCarthy said. "I'm ahead now." After predicting that Johnson would "murder" McCarthy in the primary, the President's operatives were reduced to fighting from the gutter and talking of the senator as a "peace-at-any-price fuzzy thinker." McCarthy, who was helped by thousands of student volunteers here, says he owes it to them not to drop out of the race when Senator Robert Kennedy tosses his hat in the ring (→ 16).

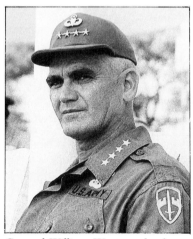

General William Westmoreland.

"Come clean for Gene" McCarthy.

Cronkite joins cry against war effort

United States, March 6

Walter Cronkite, breaking a code of neutrality among major newscasters, has opposed the Vietnam War on national TV. Last night in a special report, Cronkite said a trip to Vietnam left him deeply disillusioned. He believes the war to be futile and immoral. "We have too often been disappointed by the optimism of the American leaders," he said, "to have faith any longer in the silver linings." Cronkite joins a growing group of prominent Americans who have publicly denounced the war effort (→ June 6, 1969).

The New Jersey uses its 16-inch guns off North Vietnam. The firepower of the navy and air force is awesome, but the enemy keeps coming on.

Panel warns nation on racial division

Washington, D.C., Feb. 29

The United States is "moving toward two societies, one black, one white, separate and unequal," says a report from the President's National Advisory Commission on Civil Disorders. The report ties recent widespread rioting to "white racism" and urges programs of job creation, bans on discriminatory practices and a reorganization of welfare systems. Headed by Illinois Governor Otto Kerner, the commission also recommended new riot-control and arrest-processing methods (→ Apr.).

Martin Luther King murdered; riots besiege nation

A photograph of the Rev. Dr. Martin Luther King Jr. that was taken shortly before the civil rights leader was felled by a sniper's bullet in Memphis.

Coretta Scott King mourns the loss of her husband with characteristic dignity.

Memphis, Tennessee, April

An assassin's bullet has put an end to the life of the Rev. Dr. Martin Luther King Jr., but apparently not to his influence. On April 4, the 39-year-old Baptist preacher and civil rights activist was leaning over a second-floor motel balcony, talking to fellow activist Jesse Jackson, when he was felled by a shot from a high-powered rifle. The assassin, who escaped, is thought to be a white man who was staying at a cheap boarding house less than 100 yards from the motel. Police think the man escaped in a white Mustang. The rifle was found about a block from the scene of the crime.

That night, Senator Robert Kennedy tried to console a crowd in Indianapolis. "What we need in the United States," he said, "is love and wisdom and compassion toward one another, and a feeling of justice toward those who still suffer within our own country, whether they be white or they be black."

Dr. King, who was in Memphis to help organize a strike by garbage collectors, was known as an advocate of non-violent protest to achieve racial justice. In spite of his stance, Bobby Kennedy's words and the efforts of black leaders to calm King's followers, rioting has broken out in Memphis and in 124 cities across the nation. More than 68,000 soldiers were called out to end the violence. At least 40 blacks and five whites are dead. Over $45

million in property was destroyed and more than 20,000 people were arrested. In the nation's capital alone, seven people were killed, more than 1,000 injured and over 7,000 arrested. It took more than 15,000 troops to stem the rampage. There were also major outbreaks in Baltimore, Chicago and Pittsburgh.

In the midst of the rioting, on April 9, Dr. King was buried in Atlanta, Georgia, after a nationally televised funeral march through the city. On April 11, President Johnson signed the Civil Rights Act of 1968, curbing discrimination in housing. He also signed a law making it a crime to cross state lines for the purpose of inciting a riot.

By April 15, much of the rioting had come to an end. In Chicago, however, continued violence led Mayor Richard Daley to tell police to "shoot to kill" anyone suspected of looting, rioting or arson.

King had been strangely unconcerned about threats on his life. The day before the assassination, he told a Memphis church congregation, "We've got some difficult days ahead. But it really doesn't matter with me now. Because I've been to the mountain top. Like anybody, I would like to live a long life, (but) I've seen the Promised Land. I may not get there with you, (but) we as a people will get (there) ... So I'm happy tonight. I'm not fearing any man. Mine eyes have seen the glory of the coming of the Lord."

Federal troops try to restore order in the nation's capital. The murder of Dr. King shattered black America at a time when it was making great strides.

A young black runs down a street in New York's Harlem as firemen attempt to put out a blaze. A night of chaos followed the assassination of Dr. King.

Robert Kennedy is killed in California

U.S., Vietnam open peace talks in Paris

Paris, France, May 10

After a successful series of military operations, the United States has started peace talks with the North Vietnamese. Last month, the army's First Cavalry Division finally rescued the 5,000 besieged marines at Khesanh. Other concurrent offensives have secured the areas around both Saigon and Hue. Now, apparently with a "carrot-and-stick" strategy in mind, American peace negotiators Cyrus Vance and Averell Harriman met today with North Vietnamese representative Ha Van Lau, to work out preliminary agendas and formats for subsequent discussions. After their initial meeting this afternoon, Vance said the first session was "cordial and businesslike." The talks resume tomorrow (→Oct. 31).

Broadway's "Hair"

New York City, Apr. 29

The most visible sign of the times – long tresses sported by men – is celebrated in the new "rock musical" *Hair*. The tale of a hippie's rebellion against "The Establishment" is untidy, but its fresh, contemporary sounds are a welcome infusion to mainstream fare. The song *Aquarius* limns the idealistic ethos with what a critic called its "harmony and understanding, sympathy and trust abounding."

King's heir leads poor to the capital

Washington, D.C., June 23

It was hot and humid in the nation's capital, but over 50,000 people marched a mile with the Rev. Ralph Abernathy in an effort to show legislators how many people live in abject poverty, burdened by discrimination. Abernathy is successor to the slain Rev. Martin Luther King Jr. as head of the Southern Christian Leadership Conference, and the march was originally conceived by King. Despite the non-violent techniques proclaimed by King and Abernathy, there have been instances of vandalism and violence among the marchers.

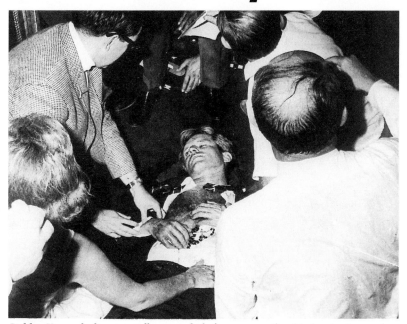

Bobby Kennedy lies mortally wounded, four years after his brother's murder.

Los Angeles, June 6

Life slipped away from Senator Robert Kennedy early this morning, 25 hours after he was shot by a gunman in a kitchen corridor of the Ambassador Hotel. The death of the vibrant senator is hard to explain to a land overrun by violence and a family numbed by tragedy. "All I can say is, good Lord, what is this all about?" lamented Richard Cardinal Cushing, a friend of the Kennedys. "We could continue our prayers that it would never happen again, but we did that before."

The accused assassin, Jerusalem-born Sirhan Sirhan, waited for Kennedy while the senator gave his California primary victory speech. Sirhan allegedly fired twice with a .22-caliber revolver that can be purchased easily for $32. Eight other people were wounded. The gunman was wrestled to the ground by eight Kennedy friends, including pro football star Roosevelt Grier, Olympic champion Rafer Johnson and author George Plimpton.

The murder, just two months after the assassination of the Rev. Martin Luther King Jr., fueled new conspiracy theories, but authorities said Sirhan acted alone. His diary shows him to be virulently anti-Jewish, and Kennedy was a strong supporter of Israel.

Kennedy had refused police protection in Los Angeles and his own bodyguard was unarmed. Congress is now moving to provide Secret Service protection to all major presidential candidates (→Aug. 29).

Radical students rule Columbia University campus for a week

New York City, Apr. 30

One of the decade's most publicized protests ended tonight when 1,000 police officers cracked down on the week-long student takeover of Columbia University. Some 700 people were arrested and 148 hurt in the confrontation as the police cleared five student-occupied buildings, including the ransacked office of university president Grayson Kirk. A school official admitted there were "breakdowns in the police action." Students countered the nightsticks by kicking, biting and hurling anything at hand.

About 5,000 students took part in the demonstrations, which were led by Mark Rudd, president of the Students for a Democratic Society, and joined by the Students' Afro-American Society and residents of Harlem. They protested the proposed erection of a university gym, and Columbia's ties with the Institute for Defense Analysis. The gym, to be built in an adjacent black area, was seen as a "racist" symbol of Columbia's disregard for black neighborhoods. The Defense Department project was scored as aiding the Vietnam War. The students also sought a restructuring of the university to give them greater participation. An emergency faculty committee agreed to drop the gym project but not the Defense Institute affiliation. During the week, acting dean Henry Coleman and two other officials were held captive for more than 24 hours.

Students camp out in front of Low Memorial Library on the Columbia University campus, expressing frustrations felt by many Americans, as student activism reaches a level unprecedented in American academic history.

Chicago: The whole world's watching

Chicago policemen break up a demonstration at the Democratic convention.

Chicago, Aug. 29

A splintered Democratic Party nominated Hubert Humphrey as its presidential candidate on the first ballot tonight. Humphrey defeated Senator Eugene McCarthy by more than 1,100 votes, but the party he will lead against Richard M. Nixon is far from united. The convention was haunted by the ghost of the slain Robert Kennedy; a move to draft his young brother, Ted, nearly split the party, and the platform committee refused to embrace opponents of the Vietnam War.

All week Chicago was badly divided, and nowhere were the divisions more visible than in the blood-spattered streets near the conven-

tion Amphitheater. Ten thousand young people came to Chicago to protest the war, but flower power was no match for police power. "Kill 'em, kill 'em," the police shouted as they charged. "Pigs, pigs, oink, oink," the demonstrators screamed back. One witness heard an officer yell, "We'll kill all you bastards," as he clubbed a protester. And as news cameras rolled and clubs flew, the protesters chanted, "The whole world's watching! The whole world's watching!"

Some 700 demonstrators were hurt and 650 arrested. Police reported 80 of their men injured. Critics said the cops acted like Nazis, but Mayor Richard Daley backed

the 20,000 police, National Guardsmen and soldiers. "How would you like to stand around all night," he said, "and be called names not even used in a brothel house?"

The worst violence unfolded tonight, as demonstrators tried to march south from Grant Park to the Amphitheater. Inside the convention hall, nervous security guards caught up in the violent scene scuffled with and clubbed some delegates and newsmen. Walter Cronkite, the normally reserved CBS anchorman, called the guards "thugs." At the podium, Connecticut's Senator Abraham Ribicoff stared at Daley and said, "With George McGovern as president, we wouldn't have Gestapo tactics in the streets of Chicago." The mayor's reply was not printable. McGovern of South Dakota had been in the running for the nomination.

Faced with anarchy in the party, Humphrey turned to Edmund Muskie of Maine, a quiet friend in the Senate, as his running mate. In his acceptance address, Humphrey urged his party to look to the future. "If there is any one lesson that we should have learned, it is that the policies of tomorrow need not be limited by the policies of yesterday," he said. But the platform committee defeated a bid to insert a plank urging a halt to bombing in Vietnam. For that reason, perhaps, many notables, including McCarthy and Ted Kennedy, did not join Humphrey at the podium (→ Dec. 1).

Warhol wounded

New York City, June 3

Andy Warhol clings to life tonight, wounded in the chest under circumstances as weird as any of his avant-garde film plots. Valeria Solanis, 28, lesbian head of S.C.U.M. (Society for Cutting Up Men), was hired by Warhol to star in his film *I, a Man*. Today, when he refused to film a script she wrote, she shot him three times. Warhol won fame with silk-screen portraits of himself and Marilyn Monroe. He first attracted notice with realistic paintings of huge Campbell's soup cans. The fortyish Warhol had a successful career as an illustrator before making celebrity his profession.

James Ray seized in King's murder

London, June 8

James Earl Ray, the man accused of having assassinated the Rev. Dr. Martin Luther King Jr. on April 4, was arrested at the London airport today as he was disembarking from an airliner. Using a Canadian passport, Ray was traveling under the name Ramon George Sneyd. Ray has been accused of shooting the civil rights leader while King was in Memphis to help organize a strike among predominantly black sanitation workers. The murder was the last of several assassination attempts against King and inspired mass protests and rioting across the nation. Ray will be tried for the murder in a Memphis court (→ Oct. 27).

10% war surcharge

Washington, D.C., June 28

To help offset the expense of the Vietnam War, Congress passed a 10 percent surcharge on income taxes today. Critics say the tax exemplifies the high cost of the war and the great gains of arms contractors; corporate profits have soared since escalation of the American involvement in Vietnam. The Johnson administration recently turned down a proposal for an excess profits tax. When the surcharge was initiated, leaders of 13 major corporations sent wires to congressmen encouraging its passage.

Oct. 1. *Yippie leader Abbie Hoffman plays with a yo-yo after appearing before the House Un-American Activities Committee.*

Peace demonstrations are attracting thousands of people from all walks of life. The conflict, which seems to roll on and on, has affected almost every American, whether through the loss of a loved one in Vietnam, or an increase in taxes. One thing that everyone now wants is a speedy end to the war.

U.S. ends bombing of North Vietnam

Washington, D.C., Oct. 31

President Johnson announced tonight that American aerial and naval bombing of North Vietnam will stop tomorrow in order to further the possibilities of a negotiated peace. He made it clear, however, that the end of the bombing does not mean that an end to the long war is at hand. As the President said, "There may well be very hard fighting ahead." Johnson's decision to halt the bombing was apparently approved in advance by the leaders of Congress. It is reported that the South Vietnamese government was opposed to a bombing halt that did not include equivalent concessions on the part of the North Vietnamese (→ Feb. 23, 1969).

Chicago cops chided

Washington, D.C., Dec. 1

The Chicago police force was severely criticized today for the attacks on demonstrators at the Democratic convention. A presidential panel, headed by Milton Eisenhower, concluded that the reaction of the officers could "only be called a riot." The report did accuse the protesters of having provoked the police with "obscene epithets ... rocks, sticks, bathroom tiles and even human feces." But the committee accused the police of having used "unrestrained and indiscriminate" violence (→ Feb. 18, 1970).

A wounded marine in Vietnam wears a "flower power" arm sling.

Nixon ekes out victory

The people hear his call for a restoration of "law and order" in the nation.

Washington, D.C., Nov. 5

Richard M. Nixon squeaked past Hubert H. Humphrey today to win the presidency in one of the closest votes in history. With 95 percent counted, Nixon appears to be a minority victor. As counting continues, he has 29,726,409 votes to Humphrey's 29,677,152, while the American Independent Party's law-and-order candidate George Wallace of Alabama nears the 10 million mark, apparently making good on his promise to deny the White House to the Democrats. Following a long, tense night, Nixon held off

delivering his victory remarks until 11:35 a.m., when he thanked his tired but happy supporters. The President-elect described Vice President Humphrey's losing fight as "gallant and courageous," then went on to speak about a campaign incident in the little town of Deshler, Ohio. "I suppose five times the population was there in the dusk, almost impossible to see, but a teenager held up a sign, 'Bring us together.' And that will be the great objective of this administration at the outset, to bring the American people together".

Genesis in space

Space, Dec. 24

With their TV camera transmitting the first close-up images of the barren lunar surface, the Apollo 8 astronauts read a Christmas message to millions back on "the Good Earth" tonight. The space voyagers, Colonel Frank Borman, Captain James A. Lovell Jr. and Major William A. Anders, became the first men to orbit the moon at 4:59 a.m. Tonight, Borman described the moon as "a vast, lonely and forbidding sight," and Lovell called Earth "a grand oasis in the big vastness of space." The astronauts then took turns reading about Creation from the Book of Genesis. Borman concluded, saying "Merry Christmas. God bless all of you, all of you on the Good Earth."

Pueblo crew, held for a year, released

Panmunjom, Korea, Dec. 22

The 82-man crew of the Pueblo, led by its captain, Commander Lloyd M. Bucher, crossed the Bridge of No Return today, bringing along the body of a shipmate who was killed when the vessel was seized by North Korean patrol boats on January 23. Though full of sophisticated intelligence-gathering equipment, the ship carried only two machine guns and was not escorted at the time of its capture. Nevertheless, the prospect of a court-martial awaits Commander Bucher for having surrendered his ship without a fight and for having signed a confession that he was within North Korean territorial waters when seized (→ May 6, 1969).

Kubrick's "2001"

Hollywood, Calif.

Arthur C. Clarke wrote the short story *The Sentinel* 18 years ago. Now director Stanley Kubrick has transformed it into *2001: A Space Odyssey*, a $10 million science fiction film of dazzling imagery and visual splendor. With stunning special effects, it contrasts human frailty – in the conflict of earthlings and HAL, a computer that goes mad – with a mystical vision. Keir Dullea plays the astronaut.

Black militancy is displayed at Olympics

Mexico City, Oct. 27

Black athletes who were seeking a way to protest the treatment of blacks in the United States found their opportunity after Tommy Smith and John Carlos finished first and third in the Olympic 200-meter dash today. As medals were given out and the *Star-Spangled Banner* played, Smith and Carlos each held a dark-gloved fist aloft. Heads bowed, they defiantly refused to look at the flag. They were suspended from the Games and expelled from the Olympic Village. The demonstration was made in lieu of a Black Power boycott of the Games that never developed. With the help of Smith and Carlos, the U.S. team won 45 gold medals; the Soviets 30 (→ Dec. 6, 1969).

Smith and Carlos (right) raise fists.

Nixon begins "Vietnamization" plan

Wounded and weary U.S. troops.

Vietnam, literally a quagmire.

Due to recent policy changes, American troops are beginning to be withdrawn.

Washington, D.C., July 8

In accord with President Nixon's plans for a gradual disengagement from the Vietnam War and for turning over the burden of the fighting to the South Vietnamese military forces, the first American combat unit left Saigon today. A battalion of soldiers from the Ninth Infantry Division was flown out of Tan Son Nhut Airport for its permanent headquarters at Fort Lewis, Washington. The gradual withdrawal of American combat forces has been planned since June 8, when the President announced that 25,000 American troops would be sent home by the end of next month. Administration spokesmen say that even more American soldiers are going to be withdrawn if the South Vietnamese army shows it is capable of containing enemy military efforts.

The "Vietnamization" process began April 26 when the American 77th Field Artillery turned over its equipment to a South Vietnamese army artillery unit in the southern Mekong River region. In the same month, American military officials announced that all South Vietnamese units have been equipped with M-16 rifles along with most of the helicopters that will be needed for independent combat operations. It is expected that the South Vietnamese forces will be taking over the ground combat role completely by 1972 (→ Nov. 16).

Oil leak smears Santa Barbara area

Santa Barbara, Calif., Feb. 9

"It's plugged." This brief comment from Union Oil signals victory in the 12-day fight to choke an undersea oilflow that has been going on since January 28. Some 231,000 gallons spilled into the Pacific, smearing 30 miles of beaches and killing waterbirds and marine life. But the trouble, caused by Union's Platform A, 5.5 miles off Santa Barbara, is not over. An oil slick covers 800 square miles. Governor Ronald Reagan has declared Southern California shores a disaster area, the clean-up goes on and so do protests against oil drilling.

Smothers Brothers get the ax at CBS

New York City, Apr. 4

"They're a little more topical than we anticipated," a CBS aide said a while ago about the Smothers Brothers, Tommy and Dick. "We're trying to make people aware of what's going on today," says Tommy. But CBS Program Practices, which the brothers call "Big Daddy Memo," has the final say on what goes out over CBS airways, and it seems to be in constant conflict with the comedy team over lines and skits about Vietnam, the administration and other "controversial" topics. Today, the conflict led to cancellation of *The Smothers Brothers Comedy Hour.*

Berrigans convicted in anti-draft action

Baltimore, Maryland, June 6

Fathers Daniel and Philip Berrigan, along with the other members of the Catonsville Nine, were convicted in state court today of charges stemming from the destruction of selective service records in May of last year. The Nine, who were found guilty on similar charges in federal court last November, burned the files of the Catonsville, Maryland, Draft Board to protest the Vietnam War. The Berrigans have orchestrated similar protests before and the two Roman Catholic priests have become heroes to anti-war activists (→ Nov. 15).

Neil Armstrong on moon: "The eagle has landed"

"That's one small step for man, one giant leap for mankind," said astronaut Neil Armstrong from the "magnificent desolation" of the moon.

Houston, Texas, July 24

"Houston, Tranquility base here. The Eagle has landed." As these words crackled 238,000 miles through the blackness of space four days ago, humanity was awed by the news that two American astronauts, Neil A. Armstrong and Colonel Edwin E. Aldrin Jr., had landed on the moon. Soon after, Armstrong, 38, emerged from the spidery lunar lander. And as a television camera transmitted the otherworldly images to an audience of perhaps 600 million, the astronaut slipped softly onto the bleak, powdery lunar surface at 10:56 p.m., delivering the already immortal line, "That's one small step for man, one giant leap for mankind."

The mission, the culmination of a decade-long effort and an age-old dream, began on July 16, when Apollo XI blasted off from Pad 39-A at Cape Kennedy, Florida. With Lieutenant Colonel Michael Collins, 38, the astronauts thundered into Earth orbit atop a 363-foot-high Saturn V rocket, then

fired for a trajectory to the moon. Four days later, Armstrong and Aldrin, 39, crawled from a narrow hatchway into the frail four-legged Lunar Module (LEM) and separated from Collins, who continued circling the moon in the Apollo capsule. "Eagle has wings," exclaimed Armstrong as he piloted the LEM into a descent of 200 feet per second. But 300 feet from the landing spot in the airless, waterless Sea of Tranquility, the astronauts were startled by a treacherous, boulder-strewn moonscape. Calmly, Armstrong detached the computer control and, as fuel ran low, guided the craft to a smooth plain, touching down at 4:17 p.m. "We're breathing again, thanks a lot," intoned a mission controller in Houston.

Within six hours, Armstrong had stepped into history; and 19 minutes later Aldrin joined him amid what he called the "magnificent desolation." The explorers wore 185-pound suits but they "kangaroo-hopped" over the low-gravity moonscape, which Armstrong said

had "a stark beauty all its own." For over two hours, they collected samples and set up instruments and an American flag. From Washington, President Nixon told them that "for one priceless moment in the whole history of man the people of this Earth are truly one."

Indeed, Earth did seem united, as hundreds of millions from all political backgrounds thrilled to the feat. Tibet's Buddhist leader, the Dalai Lama, predicted, "Man's limited knowledge will acquire a new dimension of infinite scope," while Charles Lindbergh, the first man to solo across the Atlantic non-stop, spoke of "a flowering of civilization to the stars." But a black leader, the Rev. Jesse Jackson, wondered, "How can this nation swell and swagger with technological pride when it has a spiritual will so crippled?" Picasso dismissed the whole fuss, saying "I have no opinion about it, and I don't care."

On July 21, at 1:55 p.m., the Lunar Module lifted toward a rendezvous with Collins in his solitary

orbit 69 miles above. Today, after a flawless return voyage, Apollo XI parachuted safely into the Pacific. It was the end of a week that Nixon, aboard the nearby carrier Hornet, called "the greatest in the history of the world since Creation" (→Apr. 17, 1970).

Apollo XI lifts off in a fiery blaze.

Woodstock: A coming together for rock, drugs, sex and peace

At Woodstock, Jimi Hendrix played a raucous "Star-Spangled Banner."

A young girl shows her sentiments up front as a friend paints her body.

Bethel, New York, Aug. 17

It is disbanded now, the Woodstock Nation of 400,000, a peaceful kingdom that for this one brief weekend was united by good vibrations. When farmer Max Yasgur turned over his 600-acre farm outside Woodstock to the agents of the Who, Jefferson Airplane and other groups, he had no idea of the eventual impact of the Aquarian Exposition. There were traffic jams, long exposures of nudity, acid trips (one person died of a bad one), casual sex and peace signs. One reporter estimated that 90 percent of the crowd was smoking marijuana. Despite all the anti-establishment trappings, it was one very peaceful event. Those within hearing distance of Jimi Hendrix, the Band, Janis Joplin et al cheered and waved, while those farther off just rocked to the bass beat that moved the ground beneath them.

On two nights, that ground was thick mud, churned up by downpours. People shared plastic bags for impromptu cover and they lent one another room in huts built of collapsible chairs. It was a time of coming together, and as cars roll out of Bethel tonight, there is a sense that they are all rolling in the same direction, revving to a common beat.

Ted Kennedy guilty in Kopechne case

Martha's Vineyard, Mass., July 25

Following the death of Mary Jo Kopechne that made Chappaquiddick a synonym for shame, Senator Edward M. Kennedy pleaded guilty today to a charge of leaving the scene of an accident. That accident happened a week ago, July 18, as Kennedy drove his companion away from a party of married men and younger women at Martha's Vineyard. At Chappaquiddick, the car plunged off a narrow bridge into a pond and Miss Kopechne drowned. Kennedy didn't report the accident until 10 hours later. He said he had "repeatedly dove" in rescue attempts, had been in "a state of shock," and did not realize what had happened until he awoke in his motel the following morning. Miss Kopechne, a 28-year-old Washington secretary, had once worked for Robert Kennedy.

Wiretapping of King and others revealed

Chicago, June 13

In testimony heard today in a federal court, it was alleged that the Justice Department has illegally eavesdropped on those suspected of subversion. Last week in Houston, Texas, witnesses testified that the F.B.I. set wiretapping devices on telephones of the Rev. Martin Luther King Jr. They were allegedly set after President Johnson had established limits on surveillance. It is no secret that F.B.I. chief J. Edgar Hoover disliked King, once calling the civil rights leader "the most notorious liar in the country." Formal charges are expected to be filed against those to blame for the taps.

Actress slain in Manson cult murder

Los Angeles, Aug. 10

The pre-dawn horror of August 9 left five people dead, with the words "HELTER SKELTER" and "PIGS" written in blood on the walls. The cultists, including young women from middle-class backgrounds and directed by Charles Manson, invaded the home of Sharon Tate and her husband, film director Roman Polanski (he was in London at the time). The band ritualistically slaughtered the beautiful actress, who was eight and a half months pregnant, three guests and a passer-by. Tonight, Manson's gang murdered a couple elsewhere in the city (→ March 29, 1971).

2 Illinois Panthers slain in police raid

Chicago, Dec. 6

In a wild shoot-out on the west side of the city tonight, the police killed Fred Hampton, leader of the Illinois chapter of the Black Panthers, and Mark Clark, a party leader from Peoria. The killing, which took place during a police raid on the Panthers' Illinois headquarters, is only the latest in a series of confrontations between police and Chicago's black population. Several young blacks have been shot by the police under questionable circumstances, and some blacks have shot at policemen. In two years, confrontations with police have resulted in the deaths of 28 Panthers (→ Apr. 20, 1971).

Stabbing incident mars rock concert

Tracy, Calif., Dec. 6

Believers in the Woodstock Nation were jolted awake tonight by a fatal stabbing at a rock festival headlined by the Rolling Stones. A crowd of 300,000 swamped the Altamont Speedway here for a show that also included the Jefferson Airplane and Grateful Dead, and there was violence right off the bat as Hell's Angels motorcycle gangs policed the stage. Jefferson Airplane singer Marty Balin was hurt trying to stop a fracas, and as the Stones began Sympathy for the Devil violence erupted with the stabbing of Meredith Hunter. Some link the violence to the hiring of Hell's Angels in exchange for free beer.

"Buffalo Dancers" by Awa Tsireh. Native Americans, long relegated to second-class citizenship, are uniting to awaken the country to their needs.

Massive anti-war rallies

Peace symbols come to Washington.

Washington, D.C., Nov. 15

The largest anti-war demonstration in the capital's history unfolded peacefully today as 250,000 people marched from the Capitol to the Washington Monument. Across the continent, nearly 200,000 people rallied in San Francisco's Golden Gate Park. "All we are asking is give peace a chance," they chanted.

The Washington protest was led by familiar faces in the movement, Senators Eugene McCarthy and George McGovern, Coretta King, wife of the slain civil rights leader, Benjamin Spock, author of the infant-care book, and folksinger Arlo Guthrie. "It takes little wisdom,"

Mrs. King said, "to realize that if it was unwise and inept to have gotten into this war in the first place; to stubbornly persist in staying in it becomes stupid and evil."

There were tense moments when counter-demonstrators clustered near 12 coffins containing names of American servicemen who have died in Vietnam. The situation was defused when they were allowed to add the names of civilians slaughtered by the Vietcong in the Tet offensive. Only one arrest was reported during the protest.

President Nixon, who vowed to ignore the demonstrations, spent much of the week solidifying support for his Vietnam policy. House members passed a resolution endorsing his "efforts to negotiate a just peace in Vietnam," and he made a dramatic appearance to thank them. "When the security of America is involved, when peace for America and the world is involved, and the lives of our young men are involved," Nixon said, "we are not Democrats, we are not Republicans, we are Americans." The President avoided the harsh language he used earlier to criticize campus revolt, discord and the violation of "old standards" and "old principles." Middle America, Nixon seems to believe, stands behind his efforts to end the war with honor (→ Feb. 25, 1970).

Massacre at My Lai

Washington, D.C., Nov. 16

Hundreds of Vietnamese civilians were massacred by American troops 18 months ago, Defense Department officials have disclosed, and senior officers of the Americal Division have allegedly been covering up the atrocity. On March 16 of last year, Task Force Barker, a battalion-sized unit of the Americal, launched a search-and-destroy operation against suspected Vietcong sympathizers in the hamlet of My Lai, part of the Song My village in Quangtri Province. The commander of Charlie Company apparently believed every Vietnamese in My Lai was either Vietcong or a sympathizer, and he ordered his men to burn and destroy the hamlet completely. No enemy forces were encountered in the attack. But the American soldiers swept through My Lai and killed every person in the hamlet – mainly old men, women and children. There were several sexual assaults on the women, including one gang-rape. The number of victims in the immediate vicinity of My Lai is estimated at 175 to 200. Army sources report that some 450 civilians were probably killed by troops of Task Force Barker in the overall Song My village complex. Murder charges are expected to be filed against some of the participants in the My Lai massacre (→ Apr. 30, 1970).

"The Making of a Counterculture"

United States

Two new tracts are spreading the gospel of the New Left. Theodore Roszak takes an academic slant in *The Making of a Counterculture.* Scorning science and reason ("the myth of objective consciousness"), he laments "the final consolidation of a technocratic totalitarianism in which we shall find ourselves ingeniously adapted to an existence wholly estranged from anything that has ever made the life of man an interesting adventure." The only antidote is a "standard of truth" pegged to "illuminated personality."

Roszak's plan pales beside the visionary ramblings of Jerry Rubin, Chicago Seven defendant and co-founder, with Abbie Hoffman, of the Yippies. In *Do It,* Rubin predicts a "Youth International Revolution," staged by "tribes of long hairs, armed women, workers, peasants and students." The White House is slated to "become one big commune." Las Vegas has yet to lay odds on Rubin's assertion that the Pentagon "will be replaced with an LSD experimental farm."

Agnew: "Effete corps of impudent snobs"

Washington, D.C., Autumn

President Nixon has sent Vice President Spiro Agnew on a speaking tour of the nation – to brand the opposition and "divide on authentic lines." It has produced a barrage of heavy-handed, yet colorful, rhetoric hurled at the anti-war movement and the news media.

Agnew described war protesters as "anarchists and ideological eunuchs." Of the liberal news people, he said, "A spirit of national masochism prevails, encouraged by an effete corps of impudent snobs who characterize themselves as intellectuals." He also called journalists "nattering nabobs of negativism." Americans, he says, want "a cry of alarm to penetrate the cacophony of seditious drivel." Nonetheless, with dozens of lives lost weekly in Vietnam, "seditious drivel" sounds more and more like heartfelt compassion to a lot of Americans.

"Patriotic Boy" by Diane Arbus. As this photograph shows, there is continuity amid all of the change.

Riot policemen plunge into a crowd of angry demonstrators in front of the instrumentation laboratory at the Massachusetts Institute of Technology in Cambridge on November 5. Many of the nation's research and development centers are targeted by protesters because of ties to the defense industry.

The Sixties: "There's something happening here"

President Kennedy claps along as daughter, Caroline, and son, John Jr., romp in the Oval Office. The First Family captured the hearts and imaginations of the American people and symbolized the vigor of a new generation.

A decade of demonstrations. Students in Des Moines, Iowa, the heartland of America, like young people throughout the country, express their outrage at perceived injustice and war, appropriating the V for Victory sign for peace.

Smoking "grass" or "pot," one of the more prevalent practices of kids today. At least one-third of college students have tried marijuana, and some have used LSD, mescaline and other hard drugs in an effort to escape from reality.

1963 Corvette Sting Ray Coupe, one of the hottest cars on the road. Automobiles have taken on a longer, lower, leaner look, with the Ford Mustang and the GTO among the most popular in a mobile society that worships wheels.

A Mercury rocket poised on the launch pad. JFK's dream of putting a man on the moon has been realized.

Bob Dylan and Joan Baez. "You don't know what is happening," Dylan sings, "do you, Mr. Jones?"

Dustin Hoffman pensively considers what Mrs. Robinson has to offer. The film "The Graduate" illustrates what many college graduates are now asking themselves: Is money and a comfortable suburban life style all there is?

"... There's a man with a gun over there ..."

A peace symbol – in the jungles of Vietnam. Perhaps no one wants an end to war more than the soldier.

While racial turmoil rages back home, the hardships of war continue to draw many Americans together.

On February 1, 1968, a South Vietnamese police chief executes a captured Vietcong officer with a single pistol shot to the head. This photo, by Eddie Adams of the Associated Press, has come to symbolize the horror of the war.

A fixed bayonet points out over the rubble-strewn, riot-torn West Side of Detroit in the long, hot summer of 1967. Tanks had to be used to restore order. Said Mayor James Cavanaugh of his city: "It looks like Berlin in 1945."

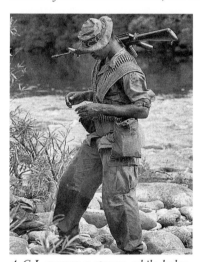

A G.I. crosses a stream while balancing his M-16 on his neck. Is there light at the end of the tunnel?

A major hugs his wife, clad in height of fashion, as he returns from Vietnam. There's no place like home.

National Guardsmen on patrol in Newark, New Jersey, one of 70 American cities torn by race riots in 1967. "We have endured a week such as no nation should live through," said President Johnson. "A time of violence and tragedy."

Purple smoke directs an evacuation chopper during the fierce battle for Ashua Valley. Although the United States has made a sizable military commitment to the defense of South Vietnam, final victory seems as elusive as ever.

309

New York City, Jan. 8. National Football League and American Football League form N.F.L. Players Association.

New Orleans, Jan. 11. Kansas City Chiefs defeat Minnesota Vikings, 23-7, in Super Bowl IV.

Vietnam, Jan. 26. Lieutenant Everett Alvarez sets record for longest time spent as prisoner of war by any American – 2,000 days.

Space, Apr. 17. Explosion of oxygen tank aboard service module prevents Apollo 13 from landing on moon (→ July 31, 1971).

Louisville, May 2. Diane Crump becomes first woman jockey in Kentucky Derby, finishing 12th on Fathom.

New York City, May 4. Jean Stafford wins Pulitzer Prize, for *Collected Stories.*

New York City, May 8. Knicks win N.B.A. title, four games to three, over Los Angeles Lakers.

Washington, D.C., June 15. Supreme Court, in Welsh v. United States, rules that moral conviction is equivalent to religious credo in qualifying for conscientious-objector status.

Chicago, June 26. American Medical Association votes to allow doctors to perform abortions for social and economic reasons (→ July 1).

Washington, D.C., Aug. 12. President Nixon signs Postal Reorganization Act, making postal service independent government corporation.

Newport, Rhode Island, Sept. 28. U.S. yacht Intrepid successfully defends America's Cup against Australian challenger Gretel II.

Baltimore, Oct. 15. Orioles defeat Cincinnati Reds in World Series, 4 games to 1.

Washington, D.C., Dec. 3. House subcommittee rejects an impeachment charge against Supreme Court Justice William O. Douglas by Michigan Representative Gerald R. Ford.

Washington, D.C., Dec. 29. President Nixon signs into law Occupational Safety and Health Act, establishing occupational standards.

Hollywood, Calif. Top films this year include *Patton, M*A*S*H* and *Woodstock.*

Chicago Seven hear fate

Jerry Rubin, Abbie Hoffman and Rennie Davis during a break in the trial.

Chicago, Feb. 18

In a trial that reached comic heights unparalleled in American jurisprudence, the "Chicago Seven" were found not guilty of conspiring to incite a riot. But five of the defendants – Rennie Davis, David Dellinger, Tom Hayden, Abbie Hoffman and Jerry Rubin – were convicted of crossing state lines with intent to cause a riot. Presiding Judge Julius Hoffman handed them five-year sentences, the maximum term. The other two defendants, John Froines and Lee Weiner, were acquitted on both counts.

During the course of the trial, the five were also given contempt-of-court sentences, as were their lawyers, William Kunstler and Wil-

liam Weinglass. The trial was the result of the riots during the 1968 Democratic National Convention in Chicago. There were originally eight defendants. But Bobby Seale, leader of the Black Panthers, was granted a separate trial after having conducted a one-man war against the judge, who tagged him with 16 contempt-of-court charges. Their confrontation, which characterized the trial as a whole, bordered on Theater of the Absurd as Seale was ordered bound and gagged after having called Judge Hoffman a "racist," a "fascist" and a "pig." After the sentencing, the wife of defendant Abbie Hoffman was expelled for shouting at the judge, "We'll dance on your grave, Julie!"

Earth Day spotlights the environment

United States

Looking to the future and finding a picture clouded with exhaust fumes and sewage, Americans are mobilizing to protect their environment. On April 22, designated "Earth Day" by environmentalists, millions left their homes to participate in clean-ups, marches and teach-ins.

And perhaps none too soon. Demographics experts say the Earth's population may reach a saturation point of 3.6 billion by the year 2000. Americans alone pile up waste at the rate of

3.5 billion tons a year. Each of the 87 million cars driven in the United States emits 1.5 pounds of pollutants daily. And at least five percent of drinking water nationwide is contaminated.

The message is beginning to reach Washington. In November's elections, voters rejected six of the 12 lawmakers with the worst environmental records. In October, an Environmental Protection Agency was created with William Ruckelshaus as its director. And the Clean Air Act, passed in December, mandates pollution-free cars by 1975.

Anti-war protesters burn bank on coast

Santa Barbara, Calif., Feb. 25

Anti-war demonstrators set fire to a Bank of America branch in the troubled Isla Vista area near the University of California at Santa Barbara as rock- and bottle-throwing rampages continued for a second night. The crowd numbered over 1,000, but some were onlookers and objected to the violence as having little to do with issues. The climate around the campus has been tense since an "anti-establishment" instructor was dismissed, and the arrest of a student activist set off the "burn, baby, burn" and "death to corporations" rage. Police cars have been hit with rocks and one was set afire (→ May 4).

Joe Frazier wins heavyweight title

New York City, Feb. 16

Joe Frazier has solved the question of who will succeed Muhammad Ali now that the world heavyweight title has been vacated. The 26-year-old ex-Olympic champion thrashed every contender, topping off his streak today by putting away Jimmy Ellis in five rounds. Frazier provided some fun and money to the 200 Philadelphia "investors" who owned his contract. Frazier, though taller than Rocky Marciano, was compared to him in style and, like Rocky, he is undefeated.

Nation's population passes 203 million

Washington, D.C., Nov. 30

The 1970 census places the nation's population at 203,184,772, a 13.3 percent increase over 1960 and the smallest rise since the Depression 1930s. The biggest increase was in the South, eight million. California (20 million) passed New York (18.2 million) as the most populous state. The largest Asian group is the Japanese, with 597,000, followed by 435,106 Chinese. Of 1.5 million Puerto Ricans, 817,000 live in New York. There are five distinctly Byelorussian churches in the U.S.

U.S., Vietnam units sent into Cambodia

Washington, D.C., Apr. 30

President Nixon announced today that American and South Vietnamese forces have entered Cambodia. As he spoke, 40,000 cavalry and paratroopers were still crossing into the "Fish Hook" region just over the South Vietnamese-Cambodian border. On a map in his Oval Office, the President pointed out alleged Vietcong bases, shaded in red. The soldiers' objective, he claimed, is not to kill enemy forces, but merely to destroy supplies and drive the Communists from their sanctuaries. As such, he said, the operation is "not an invasion," but a necessary extension of the Vietnam War. "If, when the chips are down," Nixon said, "the world's most powerful nation, the United States of America, acts like a pitiful, helpless giant, the forces of totalitarianism and anarchy will threaten free nations and free institutions throughout the world."

Support for the President's war policy is down to 48 percent from a high of 65 percent in January, and the incursion will send it lower. But Nixon argues it is "indispensable" to the success of Vietnamization, the process by which the war is being turned over to the South Vietnamese. "I would rather be a one-term President and do what I believe is right," he said, "than to be a two-term President at the cost of seeing America become a second-rate power" (→ Feb. 8, 1971).

Kent State: Four are dead in Ohio

Kent, Ohio, May 4

Student dissent over the American invasion of Cambodia exploded in death at a university today. It did not happen at Berkeley. It happened at usually apathetic Kent State. Four unarmed students were killed by National Guardsmen.

Ohio Governor James Rhodes ordered the guard to the campus after bottles were thrown at police on Friday, May 1, and firebombs were thrown into the building of the Reserve Officer Training Corps (R.O.T.C.) on Saturday. Rhodes, who tied the violence to the "Communist element," vowed, "We are going to eradicate the problem."

The tired and nervous guardsmen moved in on a group of students who were holding an anti-war rally that Rhodes had banned. When the students refused to disperse, the guard fired tear gas. The students responded with rocks and cement. At 12:25 p.m., the unit commander says, his men heard a shot. They then unleashed a volley of gunfire at some students 25 yards away. Four were killed and 10 wounded.

Student leaders say the dead were all innocent bystanders, including 19-year-old William Schroeder, an R.O.T.C. member. Allison Krause, also 19, was with her boyfriend and had "just stopped to look around and see what was happening." Krause's shocked father wondered, "Is this dissent a crime? Is this a reason to kill her?" The Justice Department will investigate (→ May).

Ohio National Guardsmen fire tear gas as students congregate on campus.

A young coed grasps her head in horror as one of her fellow students lies dead in a pool of blood after National Guardsmen opened fire on protesters. Many of the guardsmen were no older than the students at whom they were firing.

Sympathy strike for peace at 451 colleges

Washington, D.C., May

The student protest against the war in Vietnam is gathering momentum all over the country. The large rallies this month here and in New York are attracting the biggest headlines, but the anti-war fervor is also felt in many small towns. The student strike center at Brandeis University says that protests have either shut down or curtailed activities at 451 colleges and universities.

This month, many students decided that megaphones alone will not end the war. They descended on the nation's capital to lobby congressmen against the war. A delegation from the University of Washington even managed to hand President Nixon an anti-war petition signed by 8,500 people. One student said, "The system can be worked within. We'll go back and tell the rock throwers." Attorney General John Mitchell is less sanguine. He is said to believe that "the students are abysmally ignorant of the facts they are complaining about."

The anti-war protest continues to spark violence. Police killed two students at Jackson State College in Mississippi. In New York, 70 people were hurt as construction workers backing the war fought with protesting students and secretaries on Wall Street (→ Oct.).

The United States recently purchased from Britain for use in Vietnam 12 V/STOL Harrier planes, which are able to take off and land vertically.

Women march in force for equality

Thousands of women take to the streets to back the Equal Rights Amendment.

New York City, Aug. 26

American women across the nation celebrated 50 years of suffrage today by demanding equal rights under the law, guaranteed by a constitutional amendment. In some cities, women stayed off their jobs, which usually pay just 58.2 percent of a man's salary for equal work.

In New York, police estimated that 10,000 women marched up Fifth Avenue (the demonstrators put the number at 50,000). In Washington, D.C., the law forbids government workers to strike, but they marched with placards on their lunch hour. Some protesters ascended the Capitol steps and warned they would watch their senators closely when the Equal Rights Amendment is debated this fall. In Detroit, New Orleans, Indianapolis, San Francisco and Los Angeles, women took to the streets, some encountering hostile pushing and shoving from onlookers. In Boston, construction workers held counter-demonstrations, with signs reading "Hardhats for Soft Broads." But nothing stopped the women from demanding why they are forbidden to drink at some bars, why airline attendants lose their jobs when they have children, why there are so few women in Congress. Betty Friedan, author of *The Feminine Mystique* and organizer of the day's strike, said the turnout "exceeded" her "wildest dreams" (→ March 22, 1972).

Strange case of the invisible billionaire

Paradise Island, December

It was Thanksgiving, well before dawn when the helicopter deposited Howard Hughes atop the Britannia Beach Hotel here in the Bahamas. Or did it? The 9th floor is sealed as tight as the resort workers' lips. Hughes, in seclusion since 1950, is fleeing a power struggle in his Las Vegas empire ($100 million in land and seven casinos). The 64-year-old billionaire was orphaned at 17 and took over his father's Hughes Tool Co. Since then he has produced films, piloted planes, bought and lost TWA and now disappeared. He is worth $2 billion.

What's in, and out

United States

What's in: ergonomics, psycho-technology, encounter groups, sensitivity training, radical chic, Mickey Mouse watches, quadraphonic sound, safety tops on medicine vials, a woman jockey in the Kentucky Derby, women generals in the army and a woman in the air force who is also a nun. What's out: hassles, putdowns, preppies, hype, the blahs, blame in divorce (California has no-fault divorce) and blame in auto accidents (Massachusetts has no-fault auto insurance). And New York is out millions of dollars if someone wins its lottery.

New York adopts liberal abortion law

Albany, New York, July 1

Like Hawaii and Alaska, New York has adopted a liberal abortion law. It goes into effect today. More than 1,200 women here have applied for abortions, operations that will cost up to $500. The law is virtually "abortion on demand," with no questions asked regarding the circumstances of the pregnancy. In 16 other states, laws are also liberal, making concessions to a woman's mental and physical health. In the rest of the nation, however, many women are still going to back-alley practitioners at the risk of losing their lives (→ Jan. 22, 1973).

Two rock stars fall

Los Angeles, Calif., Oct. 4

The excesses of stardom have taken two of rock's most talented and flamboyant performers, Jimi Hendrix and Janis Joplin. Hendrix, 27, was found dead of a sleeping pill overdose in London on September 18. A radically imaginative guitarist with the Experience, Hendrix changed the face of music with a fiery technique merging blues with electronics and a striking, sensuous stage show. Joplin, also 27, won fame singing in a raspy, passionate style with Big Brother and the Holding Co. Today in Los Angeles, she died of a heroin overdose.

Panel condemns student protest violence

One of the angriest men in America.

Washington, D.C., October

A presidential commission has harsh words for students who use violence to protest the Vietnam war. "Students who bomb and burn are criminals," the panel concluded. President Nixon appointed the panel after the killings at Kent State and the deadly explosion at an army research center at the University of Wisconsin. The panel advised the President that he must solve a political crisis that "has no parallel in the history of the nation." Without singling out administration spokesmen like Vice President Spiro Agnew, the commission said divisive rhetoric must end. Otherwise, "the survival of the nation will be threatened" (→ Nov. 3).

"Benign neglect"

Washington, D.C.

The last several years have seen the rise of a nationally active civil rights movement, the passage of Civil Rights Acts, the non-violent campaigns of the Rev. Martin Luther King Jr., the assassination of King and race riots across the nation. In the wake of controversy and headlines, Nixon aide Daniel Patrick Moynihan has been quoted as saying, "The issue of race has been too much talked about ... We may need a period in which Negro progress continues and racial rhetoric fades ... a policy of benign neglect." This is not the kind of policy that will sit well with radical groups such as the Black Panthers or Black Muslims.

"Silent Majority"

Washington, D.C., Nov. 3

President Nixon addressed "the great Silent Majority of my fellow Americans" tonight in a nationally televised speech, asking for support against anti-war "demonstrations in the streets." His message coined a new demographic category. Who are those in the Silent Majority? The President says they are the vast number of quiet, conformist citizens, living by traditional American values, not those responsible for "old standards violated, old values discarded," as he has said. The speech was intended to isolate dissenters. The Vietcong "cannot defeat or humiliate the United States." Nixon said. "Only Americans can do that" (→ March 1, 1971).

Nixon

Miami, Jan. 17. Baltimore Colts defeat Dallas Cowboys, 16-13, in Super Bowl V.

Hollywood, Calif., January. *All in the Family* has TV debut.

Laos, Feb. 8. Supported by American air power, Vietnamese army moves into Laos in effort to cut Communist supply lines (→ March 24).

New York City, March 4. James McGregor Burns wins National Book Award and Pulitzer Prize for *Roosevelt: the Soldier of Freedom.*

Washington, D.C., March 23. Citizens of District of Columbia elect first non-voting congressman since 1875, Walter E. Fauntroy.

Laos, March 24. In face of large losses, Vietnamese army ends efforts to cut Communist supply lines in Laos (→ 29).

Washington, D.C., Apr. 14. President Nixon announces end of trade embargo against People's Republic of China.

Washington, D.C., May 1. Amtrak, the National Railroad Passenger Corporation, begins operations.

Washington, D.C., May 25. Nixon signs bill halting U.S. production of Supersonic Transport jets (SST).

Milwaukee, May. Bucks win N.B.A. title, sweeping Baltimore Bullets.

Washington, D.C., June 28. Supreme Court finds state underwriting of nonreligious instruction in parochial schools unconstitutional.

Washington, D.C., June 28. Ex-champion Muhammad Ali cleared by Supreme Court of draft-dodging charges.

Washington, D.C., Sept. 21. Congress extends military draft for two years, with increased pay and benefits.

Orlando, Florida, Oct. 1. Disney World opens, at cost of $500 to $600 million.

Lake Havasu City, Arizona, Oct. 10. Relocated London Bridge reopens here.

Baltimore, Oct. 17. Pittsburgh Pirates defeat Baltimore Orioles, four games to three, in World Series.

Washington, D.C., Nov. 12. Senate adopts proposal making money paid for child care a deductible business expense.

A "new revolution" is urged by Nixon

Washington, D.C., Jan. 22

President Nixon today called upon Congress to help with "a new American revolution in which power is turned back to the people." In his State of the Union message, he called for revenue-sharing to "renew" state and local government. A Congress controlled by Democrats is cool to Nixon's "revolution," which *Time* magazine describes as "part flimflam." One correspondent says Nixon's revolution has been floated out there on "oratory, with no roots in the realities of Congress, labor unions, industry or Middle America."

President Nixon in the Oval Office.

My Lai: Calley is guilty

Lieutenant William Calley leaves the courtroom shortly before the verdict.

Fort Benning, Georgia, March 29

In the most celebrated military court-martial of the Vietnam conflict, First Lieutenant William Calley was found guilty today. He was charged with the murder of 22 Vietnamese civilians in the My Lai massacre of March 1968. The prosecution argued that Calley had personally directed and participated in the brutal killing of unarmed innocent men, women and children in the hamlet of My Lai. Calley pleaded not guilty on the grounds that he was only following orders given by his company commander, Captain Ernest Medina. He will be sentenced later this week (→ Aug. 11).

Charles Manson is sentenced to death

Los Angeles, March 29

Charles Manson and the three women in his hippie "family" today were sentenced to death in the gas chamber following their January conviction for the gruesome murder of actress Sharon Tate and six others. Before their sentencing, the four were ejected for shouting at the judge. One of them, Susan Atkins, warned the court, "It's going to come down hard. Lock your doors. Protect your kids." The three women said that they had been high on LSD at the time of the murders, and insisted that Manson himself was innocent.

The eyes reflect the cultist's mind.

7,000 protesting war arrested in capital

Washington, D.C., May 3

Local police, the army, marines and guardsmen have stopped anti-war demonstrators from closing down the capital. But critics say the lawmen themselves broke the law by arresting everyone in sight, with total disregard for constitutional standards. More than 7,000 demonstrators were herded into the District of Columbia jail, a football field and the Coliseum. The crackdown had the full support of the President. "Short of killing people, Nixon had given Attorney General John Mitchell a blank check," one official said. He called it "overkill." Some anti-war leaders fretted that this protest by "crazies" threatened the real peace cause (→ June 30).

A variation on the Stars and Stripes.

Capitol is bombed

Washington, D.C., March 1

The Weather Underground today claimed responsibility for the bomb blast that destroyed a Senate bathroom at 1:32 a.m. The blast cracked walls, shattered windows and caused some $300,000 in damages. A telephone caller warned the Capitol switchboard earlier that a bomb would go off to protest "the Nixon involvement in Laos." The President called the bombing a "shocking act of violence." Senator George McGovern called it "barbaric," but noted it was prompted by the massive American bombing in Indochina (→ May 3).

N.Y. Times prints Pentagon Papers

Washington, D.C., June 30

The Supreme Court says *The New York Times* can resume publication of the top-secret *Pentagon Papers* about America's involvement in the Vietnam War. The court ruled today that the government has failed to show that its order to block news articles prior to publication is constitutional under the First Amendment. By a vote of 6 to 3, the justices thus upheld the right of *The Times* and other papers and ended the restraint imposed by the courts at the request of Attorney General John Mitchell, who claimed publication of the Pentagon study would cause "irreparable injury" to national defense. Today's decision apparently ends the spec-

tacular battle between the Nixon White House and the press over the government's right to secrecy versus the public's right to know.

The source of the 40-volume leak is believed to be the former Defense Department analyst Daniel Ellsberg, who is said to have offered the files to *Times* reporter Neil Sheehan. Working in secrecy, 30 *Times* reporters and editors helped Sheehan process the huge study, which was commissioned by Defense Secretary Robert McNamara, who was increasingly upset by the course of the war.

The first installment on the front page of the Sunday, June 13, issue of *The Times* was drily headlined: "Vietnam Archive: Pentagon Stu-

dy Traces 3 Decades of Growing U.S. Involvement." The six pages of documents and the two installments that followed drew little attention until the White House action forcing suspension of the series. *Times* publisher Arthur Sulzberger justifies the report as "a part of history that should have been made available a long time ago." *Times* managing editor A.M. Rosenthal believes, "the essence of journalism is to make information available. How could we say to our readers, 'We know, but you can't know'?" The articles, which have now been resumed, are based on 2.5 million words that are classified "secret, top secret or top secret-sensitive" (→July 12, 1974).

26th Amendment: 18-year-olds vote

Washington, D.C., July 25

President Nixon formally certified the states' ratification of the 26th Amendment to the Constitution today. The reform extends last year's law that gave 18-year-olds the right to vote in national elections, by granting them the vote in all elections. The Supreme Court struck down a provision of the 1970 act that gave 18-year-olds the vote in state and local balloting. The court held that Congress lacked authority to set age requirements in state elections, that it would have to be done through constitutional reform. A campaign for the 26th Amendment was started, and it won ratification easily.

High court O.K.'s busing for integration

Washington, D.C., Apr. 20

In its most important ruling on race relations since the Brown decision of 1954, the Supreme Court today unanimously upheld busing and redistricting as tools for integrating American schools. To the chagrin of many Southerners, the ruling curbs only "state-imposed segregation," thus largely exempting Northern states where barriers to integration are de facto, rooted in housing patterns rather than law.

Ironically, segregation is worse in the North than in the old slave states. Some 58 percent of Northern blacks attend schools that are

80 to 100 percent black, compared with 39 percent in the South. The N.A.A.C.P. will challenge courts to apply the ruling in the North. But last week Southern conservatives and Northern liberals killed a $20 billion desegregation plan offered by Connecticut Senator Abraham Ribicoff, who decried Northern "hypocrisy." "I do not see," he said, "how you can ever point your fingers at a Southern senator or a Southern school district and tell them that they are discriminating against black children when you are unwilling to desegregate schools in your own cities" (→Dec. 30, 1974).

U.S. turns over ground war to Vietnamese

Washington, D.C., Aug. 11

Secretary of Defense Melvin Laird says that as of today, ground operations in Vietnam will be conducted solely by the South Vietnamese Army (ARVN). These forces were reported to be doing quite well in their independent operations against the battle-hardened North Vietnamese regulars.

They conducted a highly successful attack on the Parrot's Beak region of Cambodia in February. Earlier this spring, they began a two-month campaign in eastern Laos to disrupt the Communist supply line along the Ho Chi Minh

Trail, although the success of that effort was questionable. Ever since the Tet Offensive of 1968, South Vietnamese forces have improved dramatically. In the past two years, they have carried out three times as many operations as they did in 1966 and 1967, and suffered fewer casualties proportionately. One senior American officer says South Vietnam's forces "have demonstrated their ability to work without United States advisory assistance and have done remarkably well." He said that Vietnam's military ability is high and its success seems assured (→Apr. 16, 1972).

Robin Brosset (left) and Paula Moye seem to have overlooked the controversy.

A peace flag adorns American tank on the South Vietnam-Laos border.

Police attack ends Attica prison revolt

Attica, New York, Sept. 13

The Attica prison rebellion was crushed today when 1,500 state troopers stormed the facility, indiscriminately firing on both prisoners and hostages. A total of 31 prisoners and 9 hostages were killed in the attack, while 28 hostages were rescued unharmed. The uprising began when about 1,000 convicts seized control of the prison and took hostages. The assault, backed by Governor Nelson A. Rockefeller, came after four days of talks failed to produce a settlement. It also took place despite an injunction issued by a federal judge that met a prisoner demand that there would be no reprisals against them.

Jesus is superstar

New York City, Oct. 17

With the new *Jesus Christ, Superstar*, showbiz has conferred its ultimate if anticlimactic accolade. With melodies by Andrew Lloyd Webber, the rock musical is a sure-fire crowd-pleaser – tuneful, colorful and, with amplified sound, very loud. It also reverses the usual course of a musical by having first been a smash-hit rock album before ever having been staged. The show had inevitably sparked a reaction from certain Judeo-Christian critics. Some are grumbling about blasphemy, while others regard it as anti-Semitic.

U.S. astronauts take a spin on the moon

The Lunar Rover allows the astronauts to examine a greater area of the moon.

The Moon, July 31

Shouting "Man, oh, man!" like a pair of teenagers with a hot rod, two astronauts set off for a drive across the desolate lunar surface today. They covered about five miles in the four-wheeled, electrically powered Lunar Rover for what astronaut David R. Scott called "exploration at its greatest."

Colonel Scott, 39, landed on the moon yesterday with his Apollo 15 colleague Lieutenant Colonel James B. Irwin, 41. They set their Lunar Module Falcon, down in the arid Sea of Rains, near the Hadley Rille and Apennine Mountains. As astronaut Major Alfred M. Worden, 39, piloted the Apollo 15 command ship Endeavor in a lunar or-

bit above, Scott and Irwin today became the sixth and seventh men to walk on the lunar surface. Scott stepped off the Falcon ladder at 9:26 a.m., followed by Irwin, who likened the surface to "soft-powdered snow," eight minutes later.

After unfolding the 10-foot-long Lunar Rover from Falcon's descent stage, the astronauts wheeled off at 5 mph for a "rock and roll" ride over the bumpy moonscape. They will spend two days on the moon before rejoining Worden. Because of budget constraints, just two more moon landings are planned, but scientists of the National Aeronautics and Space Administration still hope astronauts will be roving Mars in the late 1980s (→Jan. 5, 1972).

Wage-price limits are being relaxed

Washington, D.C., Nov. 14

Frozen prices and wages began to thaw today, as President Nixon's campaign against inflation entered Phase II. With the end of Nixon's three-month total wage-and-price freeze, the nation now enters one year of broad mandatory controls that will let both wages and prices rise again, but not by very much. Labor, which was denied retroactivity for wage increases delayed by the freeze, now appears ready to go along with an overall wage-ceiling guideline set at 6.6 percent per year. Prices will be permitted to go up enough to cover higher costs, but not enough to produce an increase in profits.

Record G.M. recall

Detroit, Mich., Dec. 4

General Motors said today it will recall nearly 6.7 million cars – the largest recall in auto history – because of engine mount problems. The company acted after the government issued a safety bulletin warning owners of Chevrolets built between 1965 and 1969 that their cars could go out of control if the engine mounts broke. In a letter to the National Highway Traffic Safety Administration, G.M. denied any safety problems but said that it would recall the cars to install restraints to prevent engine runaways if the mounts break.

Helicopters move troops rapidly.

Some new ways, and yearning for the old

United States

The radical way of life of the late 1960s seems to be turning into the mainstream attitude of the early 70s. Many traditional barbers have gone out of business or become hair stylists in response to unisex hairdos. A Yankelovich poll indicates that 34 percent of the population believes marriage is obsolete, up 10 percent from 1969. Films seem geared only to youth, as polls reveal that three-fourths of all moviegoers are under 30 years old. A survey of women at a major Eastern college showed that 18 percent would stop working if they became mothers, compared with 59 percent in 1943.

Smile buttons would have been frowned on a few years ago, and hot pants would have had their hems rolled down. Still, not everyone is into the up-front scene: 75 percent of the public polled opposed publication of the *Pentagon Papers,* and Senator George McGovern drew some harsh criticism when he said that every senator who backed the war in Vietnam is "partly responsible for sending 50,000 young Americans to an early grave." A lot of people are like Archie Bunker of TV's *All in the Family,* nostalgic for the days when we didn't have a welfare state and a meathead for a son-in-law. Right on!

The Nixon family at Christmas.

Washington, D.C., Jan. 2. Cigarette advertisements banned from airwaves.

Washington, D.C., Jan. 5. President Nixon approves $5.5 billion for NASA, to develop and build a reuseable space shuttle (→ July 17, 1975).

New Orleans, Jan. 16. Dallas Cowboys 24-3 winners over Miami Dolphins in Super Bowl VI.

New York City, Jan. 20. Dr. Juanita Kreps elected first female governor of New York Stock Exchange.

Washington, D.C., March 22. Senate ratifies Equal Rights Amendment to Constitution (→ July 15).

New York City, Apr. 13. Joseph Lash wins Pulitzer Prize, National Book Award for *Eleanor and Franklin.*

North Vietnam, Apr. 16. American planes bomb Hanoi and Haiphong for first time in four years (→ May 8).

Hollywood, Calif., April. Charlie Chaplin given special Academy Award, for his "incalculable effect" on film.

Los Angeles, May 7. Lakers defeat New York Knicks for N.B.A. title, four games to one.

St. Louis, June 26. Air Force unveils F-15 jet fighter.

Reykjavik, Iceland, Sept. 1. Bobby Fischer becomes first American world chess champion by beating Boris Spassky of U.S.S.R. in 24-game match.

Washington, D.C., Sept. 14. Senate approves pact with Soviet Union, imposing freeze on offensive nuclear weapons.

Cincinnati, Oct. 23. Oakland A's defeat Cincinnati Reds, four games to three, in World Series.

Atlanta, Nov. 9. Andrew Young elected South's first black congressman since Reconstruction.

Hollywood, Calif. Movies out this year include, *The Godfather, Cabaret, Last Tango in Paris* and *Play it Again, Sam.*

DEATHS

Washington, D.C., May 1. J. Edgar Hoover, first F.B.I. director (*Jan. 1, 1895).

Kansas City, Missouri, Dec. 26. Harry S Truman, 33rd President of United States (*May 4, 1884).

Nixon pays historic visit to Red China

President Nixon, escorted by Chou En-lai, reviews a military honor guard.

The President and Mrs. Nixon atop the Great Wall. When asked his thoughts, Nixon said, "I think you would have to conclude that this is a great wall."

Shanghai, China, Feb. 28

The first visit ever made by a president of the United States to China ended today as Richard Nixon, accompanied by Mrs. Nixon, Secretary of State William Rogers, Henry Kissinger, the national security adviser, and a large entourage left this bustling city for home.

Before departing, the President and Premier Chou En-lai issued a joint statement, the Shanghai Communique, which summarizes the issues on which they have either come to an agreement or acknowledged their differing positions.

Foremost among these issues is Taiwan. The United States has abjured the "two-China" policy, recognized Taiwan as an integral part of China and agreed to "the ultimate objective of the withdrawal of all United States forces and military installations." The communique makes no mention of the 1955 defense treaty that binds the United States to the Nationalist regime, but it was reaffirmed yesterday by Kissinger during a news conference here. The Chinese leaders, for their part, have indicated that they are in no hurry to settle the Taiwan issue, and they understand that it would be politically impossible for President Nixon to abandon the Nationalists.

The Chinese are also understood to have promised that they will not intervene militarily in Vietnam, and have indicated that they regard American defense ties with Japan as a guarantee against a possible resurgence of Japanese militarism rather than as a threat. Both sides agreed to increased cultural and scientific contacts, but as yet there is to be no restoration of regular diplomatic ties. Implicit throughout has been the recognition that the countries share important common ground in their desire to restrain Soviet expansionism. This mutual interest has been the pragmatic basis of the whole venture.

The trip has been a diplomatic and public relations triumph for the President. Few who saw it will forget the sight of Nixon, the Republican President of the world's foremost capitalist country, shaking hands with the legendary Mao Tse-tung, the 79-year-old founder of the People's Republic of China.

U.S. to mine ports of North Vietnam

Washington, D.C., May 8

President Nixon has ordered the aerial mining of Haiphong and six other North Vietnamese harbors. In addition, he has sent air force and navy planes deep into North Vietnam to interdict all major sea and land routes used to transport enemy war supplies. Nixon's actions come as a direct response to the Communist Easter offensive, the largest such operation since the Tet offensive of 1968. The North Vietnamese army began the huge offensive on March 30, when it threw 14 divisions, supported by over 200 Russian-built tanks and 130-mm. guns, against outnumbered South Vietnamese forces in the country's northern provinces. In order to support the beleaguered South Vietnamese troops, on April 16, Nixon ordered the resumption of full-scale air and naval bombing of strategic North Vietnamese cities and military bases. Nevertheless, the Communist troops succeeded in capturing the key towns of Anloc, Dakto and Quangtri.

American military observers say Nixon's order to mine the North Vietnamese harbors will probably have little immediate effect on the fighting in the South. But the ever-confident American military predicts that the return of American air and naval power to North Vietnam will encourage the South Vietnamese forces to hold their ground and ultimately repel the Communist invaders (→ Dec. 30).

Nixon-Brezhnev summit

Nixon and Soviet General Secretary Leonid Brezhnev sign the arms treaty.

Washington, D.C., June 1

Declaring that "the foundation has been laid for a new relationship between the two most powerful nations in the world," President Nixon reported to a joint session of Congress today on his recent visit to Moscow, the first such visit by an American president. After landing at Andrews Air Force Base, Nixon flew by helicopter to Capitol Hill to address the joint session.

While at the summit meeting, where he conferred mostly with General Secretary Leonid Brezhnev, the President concluded talks for the SALT, or Strategic Arms Limitation Treaty. These are in fact two treaties, the ABM, or Anti-Ballistic Missile, Treaty and the Interim Offensive Weapons Agreement. The first allows each country to deploy only two anti-ballistic missile defense systems. Thus, each side is giving up attempts to achieve

immunity, and the "balance of terror," with its promise of "mutual assured destruction," will remain as the principal guarantor of peace.

The offensive weapons pact freezes the number of intercontinental missiles for the United States at 1,764 and for the Soviet Union at 2,568. The Russians are allowed more because the American missiles are technologically superior.

Agreements on trade, technical and scientific cooperation, and a joint space effort were also signed. It is hoped that, along with SALT, these will help initiate an era of cooperation and detente.

But the President tempers optimism with caution. "Maintaining the strength, integrity and steadfastness of our free world alliances," Nixon says, "is the foundation on which all of our other initiatives for peace and security in the world must rest" (→ Nov. 24, 1974).

Gunman tries to kill candidate Wallace

Laurel, Maryland, May 15

The campaign of George Wallace has not ended, in spite of an assassination attempt that may relegate the Alabama Governor to a wheelchair for the rest of his life. While speaking at a campaign rally, Wallace was hit by bullets in the stomach, shoulders, arms and spine. The gunman, seized moments after he fired the shots, was identified as Arthur Bremer, who apparently had been following the Wallace campaign for some time, planning the assassination.

High court shelves the death penalty

Washington, D.C., June 29

In setting aside the death sentences of two men for murder, and one for rape, the Supreme Court ruled by a 5-4 vote today that the death penalty as usually enforced represents cruel and unusual punishment and is thus unconstitutional. But the separate majority opinions differed in their reasoning, hinting that the ruling might have been different if state death penalties had met certain, non-discriminatory standards. The defendants were represented by the National Association for the Advancement of Colored People, which has led a national campaign against the death penalty. The last execution was in June 1967 (→ July 2, 1976).

Burned children from Trang Ban, South Vietnam, flee after napalm struck their school during a raid.

Jury in California clears Angela Davis

San Jose, Calif., June 4

Angela Davis, the black activist, was found not guilty of murder, kidnapping and conspiracy charges today. It took the white jury 13 hours to reach the verdict. The charges were filed when guns used in a San Rafael court-escape murder case were traced to her. The 28-year-old Miss Davis first won national attention when she was dismissed from a teaching position for being a Communist. When the jury announced the not-guilty verdict today, Davis broke into sobs.

Liberated women start Ms. magazine

New York City, July 15

The second issue of *Ms.*, the feminist magazine created by journalists Gloria Steinem and Letty Cottin Pogrebin, is in the mail. For $1, the August issue offers articles on Marilyn Monroe, vaginal self-examination, essays by Kate Millett and Angela Davis, a short story by Alice Walker and articles on how television, film and theater misrepresent women. Of course, there are advertisements, too, such as the one showing an A.T.&T. phone operator with sideburns (→ Nov. 21, 1977).

Demonstrators opposed to the war in Vietnam burn the flag as an act of protest in Berkeley, California.

Nixon is re-elected in landslide victory

Washington, D.C., Nov. 7

Richard M. Nixon was re-elected President today with the highest percentage ever amassed by a Republican: 60.7 percent of the vote. Nixon's triumph resembles the landslide victories of Presidents Franklin D. Roosevelt and Lyndon B. Johnson.

His success comes 10 years to the day after Edmund Brown beat him in the race for governor of California. After that loss, he told reporters, "You won't have Nixon to kick around any more, because, gentlemen, this is my last press conference." Often dogged by questions about his campaign financing, Nixon entered the White House after the narrowest of victories over Vice President Hubert Humphrey four years ago, and now caps his career with an enormous personal achievement, winning in every state but Massachusetts. George McGovern conceded shortly before midnight in a telegram pledging support for the President's goals of "peace abroad and justice at home." In two televised statements from the White House, President Nixon, who will turn 60 just before his second term begins, called on the nation "to get on with the great tasks that lie before us." He promised that there would be "a peace with honor in Vietnam" and "a new era of peace throughout the world."

States will share in federal revenue

Philadelphia, Oct. 20

President Nixon flew to Independence Hall by helicopter today to sign the $30.2 billion revenue-sharing bill during his only Pennsylvania campaign appearance, described as "official" business. The idea of signing at the historic location was that of Philadelphia Mayor Frank Rizzo, the former police chief, who has campaigned energetically for Nixon, though a Democrat himself. The President proposed revenue-sharing in his 1971 "new American revolution" State of the Union message. State and local governments are to benefit for five years.

Watergate break-in: Where will it lead?

Was President Nixon involved?

Washington, D.C., June 20

The break-in at Democratic National Committee offices in the Watergate complex last week has become the basis of a million-dollar lawsuit against the Republican Committee to Re-elect the President. Democratic Chairman Lawrence F. O'Brien announced the suit today, calling the break-in "a blatant act of political espionage." Meanwhile, the F.B.I. has subpoenaed records of the hotel where the alleged burglars were registered. They are anti-Castro Cuban exiles who conferred recently with E. Howard Hunt, a C.I.A. retiree who worked as a White House consultant. Hunt refuses to cooperate with the F.B.I. White House press secretary Ronald Ziegler says Hunt was recommended by Charles W. Colson, special counsel to the President, who has "assured me that he has in no way been involved in this matter." Also today, former Attorney General John Mitchell, who now heads the Committee to Re-elect the President, said, "This committee did not authorize and does not condone the alleged actions of the five men apprehended" (→ March 23, 1973).

Porno films, acupuncture, Jesus freaks

United States

Problems? This year has solutions. Under the weather? Try health food or acupuncture. Having a crisis of faith? Talk to a Jesus freak or a believer in Transcendental Meditation. Trouble with your libido? Join the millions watching pornographic films. Trouble with a spouse? Take her (him) out to dine, perhaps at one of the thousands of new fast-food chains. Home robbed too often? Buy a plasticcard-operated lock-and-key system. Tired of taking out the garbage? Give it to Union Electric, St. Louis, which uses trash as boiler fuel. Burn, baby, burn!

Opposition to the war in Vietnam has come from virtually every sector of American society, but now that veterans of the conflict have joined in the protests, the peace movement is taking on a new dimension. If those who were in the war are criticizing U.S. involvement, something must be amiss.

Bombing off again; is peace at hand?

Washington, D.C., Dec. 30

After four confusing, contradictory and painful months of bombing-then-talking and talking-then-bombing, the United States is again calling a halt to the bombing of North Vietnam.

The last American combat force was withdrawn from South Vietnam on August 12. After discussions with North Vietnamese representatives in Paris, national security adviser Henry Kissinger announced October 26 that "peace is at hand." The next day, President Nixon halted the bombardment of Hanoi and Haiphong.

But since then, American B-52 bombers have conducted the largest aerial attack of the entire war. Dozens of the giant planes carried out a massive, around-the-clock "carpet bombing" campaign. On television, Senator George McGovern has described it as "the most murderous aerial bombardment in the history of the world." And it has been costly. The American air force has lost about 20 B-52's to anti-aircraft fire as well as surface-to-air missiles.

But once again, the Communist negotiators in Paris have shown a willingness to hold peace talks. And the President has again called a halt to the bombing. So, does all this mean that peace is now really close at hand? (→ Jan 27, 1973).

Spitz Olympic king with 7 gold medals

Munich, West Germany, Sept. 4

Mark Spitz finally lived up to his promise in the Olympics here. A big disappointment in 1968, when as a brash youngstser he was expected to make a gigantic splash in Olympic diving, he came of age at Munich by taking seven gold medals. Spitz even splashed to a world mark in the 200-meter butterfly, an event in which he finished last at Mexico City. Tragedy overshadowed these Games when Arab terrorists scaled the fence of the Olympic Village and stormed the compound of the Israeli athletes. In the shootout, 11 Israelis were murdered.

1973

Nixon

New Orleans, Jan. 8. Sniper atop Howard Johnson motel kills one police official and seven other people.

Washington, D.C., Feb. 15. United States and Cuba conclude five-year extradition treaty (→ June 3, 1977).

Washington, D.C., Apr. 2. I.T.T. admits having offered C.I.A. funds in 1970 to oppose Chile's Marxist President Salvador Allende (→ Dec. 4, 1975).

Chicago, Apr. 26. Chicago Board of Options Exchange, first of its kind, opens.

New York City, May 7. Pulitzer Prize awarded to Frances Fitzgerald for *Fire in the Lake.*

Los Angeles, May 10. New York Knicks defeat Lakers, four games to three, for N.B.A. title.

Los Angeles, May 29. Run-off election makes Thomas Bradley city's first black mayor.

Washington, D.C., June 27. Clarence Kelley appointed director of F.B.I.

Washington, D.C., July 1. President Nixon signs law ending all U.S. military activity in Indochina (→ Apr. 30, 1975).

Washington, D.C., Sept. 21. Senate confirms Henry Kissinger as Secretary of State.

Boston, Oct. 3. Six blacks burn a white woman to death.

Oakland, California, Oct. 21. A's defeat N.Y. Mets, four games to three, in World Series.

Washington, D.C., Oct. 25. President Nixon puts military on worldwide alert in anticipation of Soviet Union's intervening in Mideast.

New York City, Nov. 6. First coast-to-coast hot air balloon flight completed by Malcolm S. Forbes.

Oslo, Norway, Dec. 10. Henry Kissinger shares Nobel Peace prize with North Vietnam's Le Duc Tho.

Washington, D.C. Pentagon reports 45,997 Americans were killed in combat and 10,928 died from other causes since 1961 in Vietnam.

DEATH

San Antonio, Texas, Jan. 22. Lyndon B. Johnson, 36th President of United States (*Aug 27, 1908).

U.S. role in Vietnam War is ended

Paris, France, Jan. 27

The official cease-fire agreement that effectively ends the American combat role in the Vietnam War was signed here today. According to the statement agreed to by Henry Kissinger and North Vietnamese negotiator Le Duc Tho, the cease-fire order will take effect at 8 a.m. tomorrow (Saigon time). The agreement also stipulates that the North Vietnamese will release all American prisoners of war and that all American troops will be removed from South Vietnam. In addition, it calls for the end to foreign military intervention in Laos and Cambodia, and for the establishment of an international force to supervise the truce itself.

After the controversial, devastating American bombing of Hanoi and Haiphong last month, President Nixon ordered air and naval operations against North Vietnam to cease as of January 15. Four days ago, Kissinger and Le Duc Tho formally announced that the cease-fire accord had been reached and that it would be officially implemented today.

The American response to the cease-fire has been more of a feeling of relief than celebration. When he announced the agreement earlier today, President Nixon never used the word "victory" to describe the termination of America's role in the war. Rather, he continuously referred to the cease-fire as having achieved "peace with honor" for the United States (→ July 1).

As war role ends, so does U.S. draft

Washington, D.C., Jan. 27

On the same day that President Nixon announced that the Paris peace accords have finally ended the Vietnam War, Secretary of Defense Melvin Laird has also called an end to the military draft. He told the press this afternoon that because the conclusion of the war would result in a reduction of military manpower requirements, the draft will no longer be needed. Secretary Laird says that the postwar military forces will consist entirely of volunteers.

Secretary of State William Rogers signs the accords ending U.S. combat role.

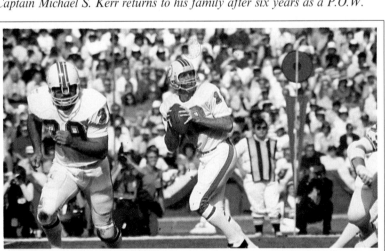

Captain Michael S. Kerr returns to his family after six years as a P.O.W.

January 14. *Quarterback Bob Griese of the Miami Dolphins in the Super Bowl against the Washington Redskins. Miami won the championship by a score of 14-7, finishing the season with an unprecedented 17-0 record.*

Watergate men sentenced; one may talk

Washington, D.C., March 23

James McCord, the Watergate conspirator, seems ready to talk. Judge John Sirica today delayed McCord's sentencing and agreed to hear him next week. Also today, the judge sentenced G. Gordon Liddy to prison for up to 20 years in a case that is increasingly embarrassing the Nixon administration. Five other men who pleaded guilty to a charge of second-degree burglary at the Democratic national headquarters were sentenced "provisionally" to 35 to 40 years. McCord, Nixon's political chief of security, told Judge Sirica he is under "political pressure to plead guilty and remain silent." He was arrested at the Watergate complex on June 17, with Bernard Parker, Frank Sturgis, Eugenio Martinez and Virgilio Gonzalez, all involved earlier in clandestine work against Cuba's Premier Fidel Castro. Liddy, of President Nixon's re-election staff, was arrested outside.

Today's sentencing is the latest Watergate development casting a shadow on the White House. Judge Sirica has complained that much about the intrigue remains shrouded in secrecy. Though McCord appears ready to talk, he says that members of his family have expressed "fear for my life if I disclose knowledge of the facts," either publicly or privately.

Larry O'Brien, Democratic Party national chairman, has gone to court charging that the burglaries are "political espionage" (→ July 30).

Sioux Indians ousted from Wounded Knee

Wounded Knee, S.D., May 8

In what has been called the "Second Battle of Wounded Knee," the 120 remaining occupiers of that Indian hamlet have surrendered to federal agents under an agreement reached by the two sides. Only about half the occupiers were Indians. The battle of 1890 was the last major conflict between Indians and white Americans. Unlike that one, which saw nearly 200 Indians killed, this one was relatively bloodless. Nevertheless, two Indians were killed and several injured during the 70-day skirmish with some 250 officers. Wounded Knee is on the Oglala Sioux reservation.

The confrontation began when some 200 supporters of the militant American Indian Movement, led by Dennis Banks and Russell Means, took over the hamlet and presented the government with a list of grievances that included broken treaties and violations of civil rights. The government has agreed to look into the charges. During the siege, federal agents arrested about 300 people trying to enter or leave the village, including four members of a television crew who were charged with "aiding a civil disorder." Wounded Knee itself was virtually burned down, with damages put at $240,000.

Sioux Indians camp out at Wounded Knee during their occupation of the area.

2 top Nixon aides testify

Dean testifies before the committee.

Senator Sam Ervin leads the panel.

Washington, D.C., July 30

Former top Nixon aides John D. Ehrlichman and H.R. Haldeman again ringingly denied guilt in testimony before the Senate Watergate Committee today. Winding up five days of testimony, Ehrlichman repeatedly challenged former Nixon counsel John Dean, who has implicated his ex-associates. Ehrlichman, who left his job as chief White House domestic adviser to prepare for his appearance, said, "I do not apologize for my loyalty to the President." Then, taking Ehrlichman's place at the witness table, former White House chief of staff H.R. Haldeman joined in the attack on Dean. Haldeman invoked still-secret White House tape recordings as proof that Dean "did not keep us fully and accurately informed on Watergate." The committee has no way to check on the matter because the President refuses to release the tapes, the existence of which was casually revealed July 16 by surprise witness John Butterfield, another former White House aide. The committee asked for the tapes on July 17, but the White House said they were presidential papers. Commenting on today's testimony, House Republican leader Gerald Ford said, "I personally respect John Ehrlichman. I think it premature to form conclusions." But Ohio Democrat Wayne Hays said, "Ehrlichman acts like a Nazi. Part of the Nazi program was to tell a big lie, over and over until it was believed" (→ Nov. 17).

High court allows abortion in Roe v. Wade

Washington, D.C., Jan. 22

The "right of privacy ... is broad enough to encompass a woman's decision whether or not to terminate her pregnancy." Having stated its position, the Supreme Court today overturned all state laws that restrict or deny a woman's right to obtain an abortion during the first trimester of pregnancy. A Texas case, Roe v. Wade, brought the explosive issue to the court. A state law had permitted abortions only to preserve a woman's life, but the court has ruled that "the unborn have never been recognized in the law as persons in the whole sense."

Anti-abortion forces led by the Catholic Church are appalled by the decision; they argue that a fetus is a human being from the moment of conception and must be protected from murder. Feminists hail the ruling, rejoicing that no more will women die of abortions botched by back-alley practitioners.

A few questions still linger: Will abortions be affordable to the poor? How are states going to interpret their right to "protect a woman's health" and regulate second-trimester abortions? And will pregnant teens need parental permission for the procedure? (→ Dec. 7, 1977).

Nixon: I'm not a crook

Disney World, Florida, Nov. 17

President Nixon took the Watergate offensive today, assuring the 400 editors at the Associated Press Managing Editors convention that he is no crook. "I welcome this kind of examination," he said, "because people have got to know whether or not their President is a crook. Well, I'm not a crook. I've earned everything I've got."

Near the monorail to the Magic Kingdom, the beleaguered President denied all charges and told editors from 43 states that he will not resign. Shifting his counter-offensive into high gear, the President answered a dozen questions about the latest Watergate events. The editors' questions ranged from recent revelations that White House tape recordings containing key conversations are missing, to the famous "Saturday Night Massacre." On that night, October 20, Attorney General Eliot Richardson resigned rather than follow the White House orders to fire the Watergate special prosecutor, and his deputy was also fired for refusing. The prosecutor was discharged anyway.

At Disney World today, President Nixon said the reason "there are difficulties in hearing" some of the White House tapes is that "this is no Apollo system." It cost only $2,500, he told the editors, and "I found it was a Sony, a little Sony" with "these little lapel mikes in my desks" (→ March 1, 1974).

Members of the new Committee to Impeach the President take advantage of a federal court's decision to permit marches in the White House area.

President sees oil embargo causing crisis

The embargo of Arab oil-exporting nations is causing chaos at gas stations across America, where motorists wait hours for their turn at the pumps.

Washington, D.C., Nov. 7

Against a background of rapidly rising fuel prices and long lines at gas stations, President Nixon went on television this evening to warn Americans of "the stark fact" that they are facing the worst energy crisis since World War II.

The basic cause of the shortage is last month's oil embargo by the Organization of Petroleum Exporting Countries to punish those who backed Israel in the Middle East war. But Nixon also sees the crisis as part of a long-term problem: With only 6 percent of the world's population, America consumes one-third of its energy output. So while Nixon favors increasing energy supplies by constructing more nuclear plants, deregulating natural gas prices and building the Alaskan pipeline, he feels equal importance must be given to conservation.

To meet the crisis, he favors emergency measures such as year-round daylight saving and a national speed limit of 50 mph. For the long term, there is Project Independence, to make the nation self-sufficient in energy terms by 1980 (→ Apr. 18, 1974).

Secretariat is a Triple Crown winner

New York City, June 9

Even longtime racing fans could hardly believe their eyes. Here was Secretariat, with Ron Turcotte in the saddle, winning the Belmont Stakes, the test of champions, by an amazing 31 lengths. Some were calling him the fastest thoroughbred that ever lived. He clinched the first Triple Crown in 25 years after setting a track record in the Kentucky Derby and winning, but not in record time, the Preakness. The Belmont gave Secretariat a 12-for-15 record, but in one race he was disqualified from first. The large Virginia-bred chestnut thoroughbred, with earnings totaling well over $1 million, will be put to stud at the end of the year.

President restricted by War Powers Act

Washington, D.C., Nov. 7

Congress handed President Nixon his worst legislative defeat today by overriding his veto of the War Powers Act limiting his authority to send armed forces into overseas combat. In a crushing blow to presidential power. the House overrode the veto by a margin of four votes, the Senate by a margin of 13. A total of 111 Republicans sided with the Nixon opponents. In his veto, the President, whose stature is being eroded by Watergate developments, said the measure is "clearly unconstitutional." He said that it would "seriously undermine this nation's ability to act decisively and convincingly in times of international crisis."

Gerald Ford is V.P. as Agnew resigns

Washington, D.C., Dec. 6

Gerald R. Ford has taken the oath as 40th Vice President of the United States, replacing Spiro T. Agnew, who resigned in disgrace before pleading no contest to a charge of income tax evasion. Ford was sworn in with his wife, Betty, their children and President Nixon at his side. He was the first chosen under a new constitutional procedure for replacing a vice president. Sixty years old and a veteran of 25 years in Congress, Vice President Ford has been House minority leader since 1965. Today, he inspired friendly laughter when he said, "a funny thing happened to me on the way to becoming Speaker of the House of Representatives."

Chicago. *The Sears Tower, the world's tallest building at 110 stories or 1,450 feet, 104 feet higher than N.Y.'s World Trade Center.*

Washington, D.C., Jan. 3. President Nixon signs amendments to Social Security Act providing automatic cost-of-living allowance.

Houston, Jan. 13. Miami Dolphins beat Minnesota Vikings, 24-7, in Super Bowl VIII.

Washington, D.C., Jan. 31. Congress passes Child Abuse Prevention and Treatment Act.

United States, January. *Happy Days* premieres on ABC-TV.

New York City, May 7. Poet Robert Lowell awarded Pulitzer Prize for *The Dolphin*.

Milwaukee, May 12. Boston Celtics beat Bucks, four games to three, for N.B.A. title.

Cincinnati, June 14. Dr. Henry Heimlich announces new technique for saving life of a person choking on food.

North Philadelphia, Penn. July 29. Four bishops ordain 11 women to Episcopal priesthood in defiance of church law (→ Sept. 16, 1976).

Washington, D.C., Sept. 4. United States establishes formal diplomatic ties with (East) German Democratic Republic.

United States, Sept. 17. Yacht Courageous defeats Australian challenger Southern Cross, for America's Cup.

Washington, D.C., Oct. 8. President Ford offers economic reform program, dubbed Whip Inflation Now (W.I.N.).

Oakland, California, Oct. 17. A's beat Dodgers, four games to one, in World Series.

Hartford, Connecticut, Nov. 5. Ella Grasso becomes nation's first female state Governor elected in her own right.

Fullerton, California, Nov. 13. Graduates of Monterey Institute of Frisbee Dog Studies compete in first all-dog Frisbee competition.

Hollywood, Calif. Top films this year include *Godfather, Part II* and *Chinatown*.

DEATHS

New York City, May 24. Edward Kennedy "Duke" Ellington, jazz composer and musician (*Apr. 29, 1899).

Washington, D.C., July 9. Earl Warren, ex-Chief Justice of United States (*March 19, 1891).

Hawaii, Aug. 26. Charles A. Lindbergh, aviation pioneer (*Feb. 4, 1902).

Patty Hearst, kidnapped heiress, helps radical captors rob bank

Patty Hearst, now calling herself "Tania," as she appeared before bank cameras during the robbery.

San Francisco, Apr. 15

Patty Hearst, missing since her abduction by Symbionese Liberation Army members two months ago, showed up for three minutes during an armed bank robbery this morning, then disappeared again as the bandits got away.

Surveillance cameras photographed Patricia Campbell Hearst, the 20-year-old daughter of millionaire newspaper publisher Randolph Hearst, as she entered the Sunset District branch of San Francisco's Hibernia Bank with four of her captors. She pointed a .30-caliber carbine as the army's leader, "Cinque" Donald De-Freeze, shouted, "This is a holdup. This is the S.L.A. This is Tania Hearst." During the holdup, Patty

"Tania" Hearst screamed at the small startled group of employees and patrons, "Keep down or we'll shoot your f— heads off," according to a 66-year-old bank guard, Edward E. Shea. During the getaway with $10,960, DeFreeze shattered the bank's glass doors with a spray of bullets and left two people lying wounded on the street.

Patricia Hearst's part in the robbery and her relationshp with her captors are not clear. Her April 3 taped message said she had "converted" to their cause, but photos taken by the bank camera show she may be an unwilling accomplice. Miss Hearst is seen under the gun of at least one other bandit throughout the robbery (→ Sept. 18, 1975).

Court says schools must teach English

Washington, D.C., Jan. 21

The Supreme Court ruled today that public schools must teach English to foreign-speaking students. The case involves a San Francisco school system that did not provide English instruction to some 1,800 Chinese-speaking pupils. To neglect them, the court maintains, is racial discrimination. Justice William Brennan, author of the majority opinion, wrote that "students who do not understand English are effectively foreclosed from any meaningful education."

Evel Knievel fails in daring cycle leap

Twin Falls, Idaho, Sept. 8

With a guarantee of $6 million hanging in the balance, Evel Knievel failed in his effort to rocket 1,600 feet across Snake River Canyon in a motorcycle-like vehicle today. Instead, the daredevil made a nose-first crash-landing on the rocks of the river bank. His only injuries were some superficial cuts and bruises. The failure was caused by a tail parachute that opened prematurely on takeoff. The big crowd on the rim of the canyon worried that the wind might blow Evel's rocket in its direction.

OPEC lifts embargo on oil sales to U.S.

Vienna, Austria, Apr. 18

Except for Libya and Syria, the Arab members of the Organization of Petroleum Exporting Countries today voted to resume exports to the United States and most other countries embargoed last year for supporting Israel in its war against the Arabs. There will, however, be no rollback in prices, which have risen from an average of $4 a barrel before the crisis to $12 now. The news cheered Americans who have been coping with long lines and limited sales at gas stations (→ May 2).

Jury orders 5 tried in Watergate case

Washington, D.C., March 1

A grand jury dealt President Nixon two staggering blows today; first, by issuing criminal indictments against his top aides, John Ehrlichman and four others; second by giving Judge John J. Sirica sealed evidence for delivery to the House panel considering impeachment of the President himself. Today's proceedings took just 13 minutes in a courtroom that is too small to handle the huge number of people who want to attend the proceedings (→ Aug. 8).

Winnebago Indians dancing during a tribal powwow. Native Americans have struggled to preserve their heritage in the face of a changing world.

Amid energy crisis, oil profits surge

Washington, D.C., May 2

While the energy crisis continues to strangle consumers of gas and oil, the only clear winners seem to be the oil firms. As demand outruns supply, prices have skyrocketed, and taken profits along. In the last quarter of 1973, Exxon profits rose 59 percent, and in the first quarter of this year, Occidental Petroleum's soared 748 percent. In response to oil profiteering and the ongoing shortages, Congress, prodded by President Nixon, has approved creation of a Federal Energy Administration to develop conservation measures, advise on foreign trade, administer gas rationing and curb windfall profits (→ Apr. 18, 1977).

Kissinger shuttle scores in Mideast

Geneva, Switzerland, May 31

After 32 days of commuting between Jerusalem and Damascus, Secretary of State Henry Kissinger took another step toward peace with his "shuttle diplomacy" today, this time persuading the anti-Zionist President of Syria, Hafez al-Assad, to agree to a troop disengagement in the Golan Heights. Back in January, after a week of shuttling between Egyptian President Anwar el-Sadat and Israeli Premier Golda Meir, Kissinger arranged a similar Egyptian-Israeli disengagement.

A note of concern over nuclear energy

Morris, Illinois

They open to the sky like ominous vats and many think they are the panacea for America's energy woes. Nuclear cooling cones are popping up in great numbers; 42 plants are now operating. The Atomic Energy Commission says by 1980 the U.S. will have 100, generating 102,000 megawatts of power. But some people are wary. In Morris, site of Dresden, one of the nation's first plants, a citizen said: "Dresden is also the name of a city leveled by fire-bombing in World War II. I hope that's not an omen."

Aaron blasts his 715th

Aaron swings into history. He started with the all-black Indianapolis Clowns.

Atlanta, Georgia, Apr. 8

With a towering drive over the fence in left-center field 385 feet away, Hank Aaron hit his 715th homer today to became the leading home-run hitter in baseball history. He erased Babe Ruth's 39-year-old record, one that he tied four days earlier. Aaron, a 40-year-old Atlanta Braves outfielder, hit his fourth-inning home run off Al Downing, enabling the Braves to beat the Dodgers, 7-4. Hank's reaction? "All I could think about was that I wanted to touch all the bases."

A big baseball fan, Georgia Governor Jimmy Carter presented Aaron with a license plate marking the epic homer. It read "HLA715" for Henry Louis Aaron. Hank, who was born in Mobile, Alabama, began his career with the Indianapolis Clowns of the Negro American League.

The Hammer, as Aaron is called, came up to the majors with Milwaukee, which became the Atlanta Braves. When newly acquired Bobby Thomson broke an ankle in 1954, Aaron stepped into the lineup and hit .280 as a rookie. He has been named to every National League All-Star team since, and was named the most valuable player in the loop in 1957, when he led the Braves to victory in the World Series. Some experts have called him the greatest natural right-handed hitter of all time.

"Old Faithful" keeps visitors entertained faithfully. The most famous of the 200 geysers in Yellowstone National Park erupts about every 65 minutes.

Ehrlichman is guilty in Ellsberg break-in

Washington, D.C., July 12

President Nixon's former chief domestic adviser, John D. Ehrlichman, became the highest aide to be convicted in the web of Watergate cases today. A jury of six men and six women found Ehrlichman and three members of the White House "plumbers" unit, which staged the Watergate break-in, guilty in a bizarre aspect of the *Pentagon Papers* case that involved the secret papers that were made public by Daniel Ellsberg. The jury decided that Ehrlichman conspired with the others in the break-in at the office of Ellsberg's former psychiatrist, in an effort to find papers that would discredit Dr. Ellsberg.

Nixon in Mideast and Soviet Union

Moscow, July 3

Concluding his third summit meeting with General Secretary Leonid Brezhnev, President Nixon left Moscow for home today. Although there was no major arms-control breakthrough, the summit furthered the general process of detente and the two leaders agreed to meet again before the end of the year. The Nixon trip follows last month's six-day tour of the Mideast, designed to firm up the recent peace settlement, which was largely the result of American diplomacy.

Baring bottoms and feminist power

Nukes no! Nudes yes! Thousands of college students, some in Nixon masks, tennis shoes and nothing else, are baring their buttocks in this year's streaking fad. Women also are making waves, such as Massachusetts state representative Elaine Nobel, who admitted she was a lesbian before being elected, and Janet Hayes, who came to power in San Jose, California, as the first woman mayor of a major city. Girls play Little League baseball and 11 women are now Episcopal priests. Is it a coincidence that businesses catering to singles net $40 billion a year?

▷

Nixon, cornered, resigns as President

Washington, D.C., Aug. 8

Snarled in Watergate and prodded by the threat of impeachment, President Richard M. Nixon has resigned the presidency as of noon tomorrow. In effect, he named his own replacement when he nominated Gerald R. Ford 10 months ago as successor to Vice President Spiro T. Agnew, who quit in disgrace. Speaking from the Oval Office tonight, the 61-year-old Nixon was delivering his second farewell in 12 years. After losing a gubernatorial race in California in 1962, he told reporters, "You won't have Nixon to kick around any more." Tonight, seemingly calm in an anguish-laden White House, he said he would have preferred to "stay on and fight as my family unanimously urged. I have never been a quitter." His remarks recalled to many the famous television appearance in 1952 in which he fought off charges of irregular finances with help from the family dog, Checkers.

"To leave office before my term is completed is opposed to every instinct in my body," Nixon said tonight. "But as President I must put the interests of America first.

Farewell to a disillusioned nation.

By taking this action, I hope that I will have hastened the start of that process of healing so desperately needed in America." The departing President then expressed his deep regrets for "any injury that may have been done. I would say only that if some of my judgments were wrong – and some were wrong – they were made in what I believed at the time to be the best interests of the nation."

As the first President in history to resign, Nixon removes himself from the threat of impeachment, but not from the onrushing wave of Watergate, because he appears to lack immunity, and the incoming President Ford says that he has made "no deals" (→ 9).

Nixon, in a TV address on April 30, released edited transcripts of the tapes.

Ford is President, declaring "long national nightmare is over"

Washington, D.C., Aug. 9

Emotions were high today as the resigning President Richard Nixon said tearful farewells and Gerald R. Ford took the oath to succeed him, declaring, "Our long national nightmare is over." Ford, who was elected Vice President on Nixon's nomination, offered some emotional parting remarks to the President, whose letter of resignation was received by Secretary of State Henry Kissinger at 11:35 a.m. It read: "Dear Mr. Secretary: I hereby resign the office of President of the United States. Sincerely, Richard Nixon."

Tears streaked Nixon's face as he told his staff, "Others may hate you. But those who hate you don't win unless you hate them – and then you destroy yourself." As the Nixon family left for California, President Ford urged the nation to pray for them. "May our former President, who brought peace to millions, find it for himself," said the new President. Ford, 61, is an ex-college football hero and a 25-year veteran of the House (→ Sept. 8).

Chief Justice Warren Burger administers the oath of office to President Ford.

Parents seek ban on "vulgar" books

West Virginia, Sept. 3

Holden Caulfield doesn't have many friends in West Virginia. The J.D. Salinger novel *Catcher in the Rye*, where Holden "lives," is one of many books being deemed "vulgar" by parents of schoolchildren in this state. Hundreds of angry parents, led by fundamentalist ministers, picketed the opening of the school year today with a call to ban texts that they feel are obscene and blasphemous. The protesters are to meet with the school board to negotiate an end to the dispute.

Rockefeller sworn in as Vice President

Washington, D.C., Dec. 19

After four months of investigation by 300 F.B.I. agents, Nelson Aldrich Rockefeller was sworn in today as 41st Vice President of the United States. "There is nothing wrong with America that Americans cannot right," the new Vice President said. Rockefeller, whose family is worth about $1.3 billion, becomes the second Vice President in little more than a year to attain the office under the recent 25th Amendment, which authorizes a president to fill a vice presidential vacancy without an election, although the consent of Congress is required.

Rocky, scion of a wealthy family. "There is nothing wrong with America that Americans cannot right."

Congress lifts ban on record access

Washington, D.C., Nov. 21

Congress voted today to override President Ford's veto of the Freedom of Information Act of 1974. As a response to former President Nixon's abuse of "executive privilege," the amendments to the 1966 act prohibit the government from "arbitrarily or capriciously" denying access to offical documents. It puts the burden on the government to justify the classification of documents. And it forces federal agencies to act quickly on requests for information. The reform is regarded by some as a defeat for presidential power. Others believe it is only the beginning of congressional curbs on the executive branch in the wake of Watergate.

Nixon pardoned by Ford

Washington, D.C., Sept. 8

President Ford has pardoned former President Nixon – the man whose actions made Ford chief executive. The pardon is unconditional for all crimes Nixon may have committed in the White House. The pardon's timing surprised many because it came without warning on a Sunday morning and because it is a sharp reversal from the position his aides ascribed to him when Ford became President. Press secretary J.F. terHorst resigned today in protest, but Leon Jaworski's office said the Watergate special prosecutor believes the pardon is lawful and "accepts the decision."

In his announcement, President Ford said he issued the pardon because "the tranquility to which this nation has been restored by the events of recent weeks could be irreparably lost" by the year or more it would take to conduct a trial.

The pardon was flown out to Nixon in California by a White House lawyer who said that "a pardon has to be accepted after it is offered." Ten minutes later, the former President released a statement that said, "No words can describe the depths of my regret and pain at the anguish my mistakes over Watergate have caused the nation and the presidency." Nixon added that those events are "still in my mind a confusing maze of events, decisions, pressures, and personalities ... which grew from a political scandal into a national tragedy" (→ Feb. 21, 1975).

Summit yields arms pact with U.S.S.R.

Vladivostok, U.S.S.R., Nov. 24

The momentum that led to three Nixon-Brezhnev summits in two years continues as President Ford ends two days of talks here with Soviet leader Leonid Brezhnev. Planned only as a get-acquainted meeting, the talks have produced an arms pact that extends the 1972 SALT treaties limiting strategic arms. Details haven't been issued, but it is known that both sides agreed to limit the number of MIRVs (multiple independently targetable re-entry vehicles) and to resume SALT talks in January. Secretary of State Henry Kissinger, who laid the basis for the pact, said a cap has been put on the arms race for 10 years (→ June 18, 1979).

Violence erupts as busing starts in Boston

Boston, Dec. 30

Three months of often-violent protests over court-ordered busing resulted in punitive action today against three Boston school officials for their failure to enforce integration measures.

Trouble began on September 12, when students opposed to desegregation in Boston schools rioted. Many white pupils boycotted classes and attacked black students. Police escorted buses to South Boston High School, and tried to defuse tension. On October 15, fighting reached a peak. Seven students were hurt and police were called out after a white girl was assaulted by 20 blacks, igniting gang wars.

Governor Francis Sargeant requested help from the National Guard. But President Ford said federal troops "should be used only as a last resort." His stance prompted criticism from civil rights leaders.

Rioting has subsided. But opposition to busing continues, despite court insistence that it is necessary to attain equality in education (→ March 11, 1975).

Ali KO's Foreman in Zaire to regain title

Kinshasa, Zaire, Oct. 29

Muhammad Ali became the second heavyweight in boxing history to regain the world championship today when he knocked out George Foreman midway through their title fight in this exotic African setting. Only Floyd Patterson, in 1960, had won back a lost heavyweight title. The 32-year-old Ali knocked out 25-year-old Foreman in the eighth round of a 15-rounder to the chant of "Ali kill him" from most of the fans at the pre-dawn (for TV transmission) fight.

The Louisville slugger, after taking the best Foreman had to offer, sent his rival to the canvas with a one-two combination that convinced those cynics who thought Ali could not get back into fighting shape. Foreman, who had flattened three earlier challengers in less than five minutes each, was a 3-1 favorite. In a reversal of his usual strategy, Ali dropped his tricky dancing tactic and let Foreman flail away at his body. When Foreman tired, Ali let loose with bursts of left and rights.

Bewilderment marks the face of a child in the middle of busing controversy.

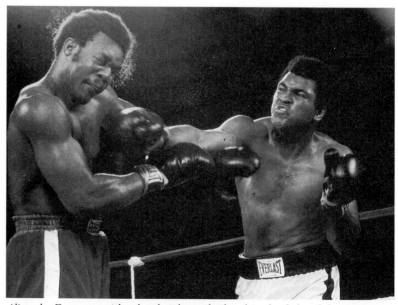
Ali rocks Foreman with a hard right to the head in the fight of the year.

New Orleans, Jan. 12. Pittsburgh Steelers defeat Minnesota Vikings, 16-6, in Super Bowl IX.

Detroit, Jan. 20. To stimulate sales, major auto makers offer rebates to customers purchasing new cars.

Minnesota, Jan. 26. U.S. Geological Survey announces discovery of oldest known scientifically dated rock, some 3,800 million years old.

Washington, D.C., Feb. 14. In nation's first acquisition of territory in almost 60 years, Northern Mariana Islands become U.S. commonwealth.

Saigon, South Vietnam, Apr. 4. Air Force C-5 transport plane, carrying 300 Vietnamese children and their caretakers to United States, crashes, killing over 200 people.

New York City, Apr. 16. Dumas Malone wins Pulitzer Prize for biography *Thomas Jefferson and His Times.*

Phnom Penh, Cambodia, Apr. 17. Cambodian government toppled by Communist Khmer Rouge rebels (→ Apr. 30).

Alaska, May 27. State Supreme Court legalizes marijuana use in the home.

Oregon, June 16. State is first to ban sale and use of aerosols containing chlorofluorocarbons.

Washington, D.C., June 30. Supreme Court holds that criminal defendants have right to conduct own defense rather than accept court-appointed counsel.

Orange, New Jersey, Aug. 21. Renee Richards, former navy officer who underwent surgical sex-change, wins first tennis match as woman athlete.

Boston, Oct. 22. Cincinnati Reds beat Red Sox, four games to three, in World Series.

Washington, D.C., Oct. 25. Soviet-American grain pact concluded, binding Russians to buy six million to eight million tons of American grain a year, beginning in 1976.

Washington, D.C., Nov. 29. President Ford signs legislation requiring states to provide free education for handicapped between ages of 3 and 21, effective within five years.

Hollywood, Calif. Top films include *Jaws, One Flew Over the Cuckoo's Nest, Nashville.*

Watergate principals get prison sentences

Co-conspirators Haldeman and Ehrlichman could serve up to eight years.

Washington, D.C., Feb. 21

The three most powerful men in the Nixon administration have been sentenced to prison terms that range from two and a half to eight years for their Watergate cover-up crimes: former Attorney General John Mitchell, former White House chief of staff H.R. Haldeman and former chief domestic adviser John Ehrlichman, along with former Assistant Attorney General Robert Mardian, who drew a lesser sentence. Federal Judge John Sirica denied Ehrlichman's request to do his time on an Indian reservation instead of in prison. Haldeman's attorney brought up the recent presidential pardon, protesting, "whatever Bob Haldeman did, so did Richard Nixon." Judge Sirica offered no comment. Neither did Nixon, now golfing behind the walls of Walter Annenberg's estate in Palm Desert, California.

Mitchell saved his remarks for reporters: "It could have been a hell of a lot worse. They could have sentenced me to spend the rest of my life with Martha." A judge in New York today denied Mrs. Mitchell's request for a quick divorce trial, stating that her husband's sentence was no excuse for bypassing the normal six-month waiting period (→ July 8, 1976).

"Trail Riders" by Thomas Hart Benton of Missouri. With his death on January 15, the American art world lost one of its best regional painters.

F.B.I. abused data on political figures

Washington, D.C., Feb. 27

J. Edgar Hoover, the late director of the Federal Bureau of Investigation, made improper use of files that he collected on political activists, a House of Representatives subcommittee was told today. Attorney General Edward Levi said that Hoover, who died in 1972, kept documents with derogatory information on presidents, on congressmen and on a variety of prominent people. The Attorney General's testimony indicated that at least three Presidents – John Kennedy, Lyndon Johnson and Richard Nixon – had data collected regarding congressmen and senators who opposed them (→ May 19, 1976).

Clemency is over

Washington, D.C., March 31

President Ford's clemency program for Vietnam-era military deserters and draft evaders ended today. A total of 22,500 men of a possible 124,400 applied for an opportunity to "earn a return" to American society under the program. Charles E. Goodell, chairman of the Presidential Clemency Board, described most of the applicants as "unfortunate orphans" of a system that favored those who were "educated, clever, articulate and sophisticated" (→ Jan. 21, 1977).

Segregation debate is shifting to North

Washington, D.C., March 11

The Commission on Civil Rights issued a report today, indicating that Southern schools are more integrated than their Northern counterparts. The study underlines a changing trend: resistance to racial mixing is stiffer in the North, as evidenced by the recent violence in Boston, Detroit and Denver over school busing. Opponents of busing won a major victory last year when the Supreme Court ruled in Milliken v. Bradley that Detroit's program was unconstitutional. But civil rights leaders are still striving for school integration, including support for busing (→ June 28, 1978).

Americans evacuate as Saigon falls to Communists

22,000 more fled by boat and were picked up by United States Navy ships in the South China Sea.

The number of Americans killed in 10 years of fighting exceeded 46,000, with 10,000 more dying of related causes; more than 300,000 were wounded. South Vietnamese losses topped 184,000. North Vietnam released no figures. The American troop strength in Vietnam peaked at 543,400 in 1969 before President Nixon began withdrawal.

American losses in Vietnam far exceeded those suffered in Korea. They were substantially lower, however, than the 291,557 American battle deaths recorded in World War II or the 50,585 of World War I. Nor did they approach the level

of total losses on both sides in the Civil War – 360,000 on the Union side, 258,000 for the Confederacy.

Nevertheless, the long conflict in Asia was one of the bleakest episodes in the nation's history. The war caused grievous wounds in society that may take a generation or more to heal. To avoid conscription, thousands of American young men fled to Canada and other countries, vowing that they would never return to the land of their birth. Riots and demonstrations were common on college campuses, and the unpopularity of the war was a major influence on the course of American politics and relations with the other powers of the world.

Although serious involvement in

Emergency evacuation by helicopter.

Saigon, South Vietnam, Apr. 30

The Vietnam War ended today with the unconditional surrender of South Vietnamese forces to the Communist Vietcong. Though the event took place thousands of miles from Washington, many Americans feel the Vietcong have handed the United States its first military defeat in 200 years as a nation. The 1,000 Americans remaining in Vietnam were evacuated by military helicopters, as were thousands of Vietnamese who feared for their lives under Communist rule. Secretary of State Henry Kissinger estimated the number of Vietnamese refugees evacuated at 56,000. Some

As the withdrawal continues, South Vietnamese desperately seek any way out.

Victims of the Communist advance.

Vietnam began under two Democratic Presidents, John Kennedy and Lyndon Johnson, it reached its greatest intensity during the Republican administration of President Nixon. In spite of Nixon's repeated attempts to achieve a peaceful solution, it became a contributing factor in the President's eventual resignation at a time when he was under threat of impeachment.

President Ford, who succeeded Nixon, said that with the end of the fighting in Vietnam it was time to "look ahead to the many goals we share and to work together on the great tasks that remain to be accomplished" (→ May 7).

Ford declares turbulent Vietnam era over

Washington, D.C., May 7

President Ford has declared the end "of the Vietnam Era" in a speech announcing the termination of veterans' benefits. The fall of Saigon, he said, "closes a chapter in the American experience. I ask all Americans to close ranks, to avoid recrimination about the past."

But old wounds were opened as the North Vietnamese drove into Saigon. Two years after the embarrassment of withdrawal, it seemed the United States had lost again. Conservatives decried a half-hearted effort. "We failed," said General William Westmoreland. "We let an ally down," said Ronald Reagan, blaming "the most irresponsible Congress in history." Liberals gave

cautious advice. "What we've learned is that there aren't American answers for every problem in the world," said Senator Hubert Humphrey. Radicals cheered as Tom Hayden, founder of Students for a Democratic Society, called the fall of Saigon "the rise of Indochina."

Amid the torrent of words, a few stark facts elude argument. Hundreds of thousands of Americans were killed or maimed; 7 million tons of bombs fell and $141 billion was spent. Figures endure as does the pain they represent. At least one veteran abhors Ford's plea for what he called national amnesia. Said Thomas Hyland, "My brother-in-law wakes up every day without his legs. How can he forget?"

Alexander Calder, after 40 years, is still at work creating mobiles.

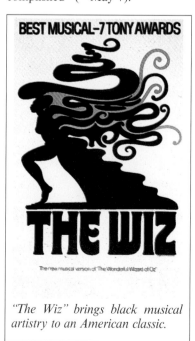
BEST MUSICAL – 7 TONY AWARDS

THE WIZ

The new musical version of "The Wonderful Wizard of Oz"

"The Wiz" brings black musical artistry to an American classic.

C.I.A. is accused of domestic spying

Washington, D.C., June 10

The Central Intelligence Agency, whose charter bans "internal security functions," systematically spied on alleged radicals during the administrations of Presidents Johnson and Nixon. According to the report of an eight-man panel headed by Vice President Nelson Rockefeller, the agency amassed 13,000 files on domestic dissidents by illegally scrutinizing mail from the Soviet Union. It used wiretaps and break-ins to police its own employees and held a defector in solitary confinement for three years. But the panel blames the Presidents, not the C.I.A. Johnson, for one, insisted that foreign money was behind the student anti-war effort. Rockefeller says the violations were "not major." But Senator Frank Church, who is investigating the C.I.A. on foreign assassinations, disagrees. "Ours is not a wicked country," he said, "and we cannot abide a wicked government" (→ May 19, 1976).

Apollo and Soyuz reach detente in space

The link-up in space proves Americans and Russians can work together.

Houston, Texas, July 17

Astronaut Thomas Stafford and cosmonaut Aleksei Leonov shook hands today as the Apollo 18 and Soyuz 19 docked in the first joint American-Soviet space mission. The rendezvous occurred four days after Apollo was orbited from Cape Canaveral, Florida, and Soyuz was launched from the Tyurtam space center. Apollo and Soyuz will remain docked for two days, while the six American and Soviet crew members exchange visits and perform experiments together before returning to Earth (→ Apr. 14, 1981).

35 nations sign accord in Helsinki

Helsinki, Finland, Aug. 1

After 22 months of negotiations, leaders of the 35 member nations of the Conference on Security and Cooperation in Europe gathered here today to sign the Final Act, a statement of principles "guiding their mutual relations." Among these are recognition of all national boundaries as they were at the end of World War II, settlement of disputes by peaceful means, non-intervention, and a commitment to "take positive action" to promote personal liberties. President Ford praised the pact for its "moral commitments aimed at lessening tensions," but critics charge that it has sold out the Baltic states and East Germany to the Soviet Union. They also question the commitment of the Soviet Union to personal liberties and they point to its invasion of Hungary in 1956 and Czechoslovakia in 1968 as examples of how the Russians interpret the principle of non-intervention.

Cambodians seize U.S. merchant ship

Phnom Penh, Cambodia, May 14

American air, sea and ground forces attacked Tang Island in the Gulf of Siam today in retaliation for the Cambodian seizure two days ago of the United States merchant ship Mayaguez and its 39-man crew. The ship and crew were released before the American attack took place. Three Cambodian gunboats were destroyed by American jet fighters in the course of the attack, and the Communist defense shot down three United States helicopters. American losses included one marine killed in the fighting on the island and the 14 crewmen in the downed helicopters.

Sony VCR's invade the United States

United States

The nation's dance crazes, which include the bump, the hustle and the robot, have a mechanical air about them. And why not? America has gone techno-illogical, loving gizmos never sold at five-and-ten-cent stores (which have been replaced by 69-cent discount stores). Digital records and Sony videocassette recorders (VCR's) move into our homes; word processors electrify our offices and computers zip us through the supermarket checkout. Only skateboards and mood rings don't need motors. Pet rocks, while not requiring remote control, may need to be kept on a leash.

Aircraft from carrier Coral Sea rescue marines under Cambodian attack.

President Ford teams up with pro golfer Jack Nicklaus, who has won the Masters five times, the PGA four times, and the U.S. Open three times.

Ford survives pair of attempts on his life

San Francisco, Sept. 22

An attempt to assassinate President Ford was foiled September 5 as Lynette "Squeaky" Fromme, a follower of mass murderer Charles Manson, stepped from a crowd on a Sacramento sidewalk and aimed a loaded .45-caliber automatic pistol at the President from point-blank range. Miss Fromme, 27, wearing a long red dress and red turban, was wrestled to the ground by a Secret Service agent, Larry Buendorf, as she screamed repeatedly, "It didn't go off!" Experts determined that the pistol's loading mechanism had not been operated properly. None of the four live rounds in the clip had been loaded into the firing chamber.

Today, the second attempt on the chief executive's life occurred here in San Francisco when Sara Jane Moore, a 45-year-old part-time police informer and sometimes radical, pulled a .38-caliber revolver from her purse while standing in a crowd across the street from the Hotel St. Francis and fired a single shot at the President from a distance of about 40 feet. A bystander, Oliver "Bill" Sipple, slapped Mrs. Moore's arm, causing the bullet to go astray. The slug, a flat-nosed projectile designed to cause a massive wound, smashed into a planter box near where the President stood, ricocheted off the pavement and, finally spent, struck a nearby cab driver.

U.S. saves New York City from bankruptcy

Washington, D.C., Dec. 9

Two days before New York City would have defaulted on its loans, President Ford today signed legislation authorizing the Treasury to lend the financially strapped city $2.3 billion annually until June 30, 1978. The loans will have to be repaid at the end of each city fiscal year (June 30) at an interest rate one percentage point higher than the current Treasury borrowing rate. Opponents of the bill said it would drain the American taxpayer, create more federal control over local government and encourage fiscal irresponsibility in local governments. Proponents felt the loan would not be enough to keep the city from bankruptcy.

The twin towers on shaky ground.

Patty Hearst seized in raid by the F.B.I.

San Francisco, Sept. 18

After a 19-month search, F.B.I. agents caught up with Patty Hearst today. They arrested the 21-year-old publishing heiress who was kidnapped February 1 of last year by Symbionese Liberation Army members and later joined their cause. Patricia Campbell Hearst gave up meekly to the F.B.I. at her apartment in the Mission District. She faces bank robbery and other charges. The F.B.I. believes that with today's arrest of Miss Hearst and three friends they have rounded up the last of the S.L.A. members.

C.I.A. linked to assassinations, Chile coup

Washington, D.C., Dec. 4

The Central Intelligence Agency, according to two congressional panels, encouraged coups in several countries and sought the assassination of at least two world leaders. Today's report concluded that the United States spent $13.5 million to keep Chilean Marxist Salvador Allende out of office. After his election, the C.I.A. financed an anti-Allende newspaper and encouraged the 1973 coup in which the leftist leader was killed.

Last month, Frank Church's Senate panel revealed that the C.I.A. plotted to kill Premier Patrice Lumumba of the Congo (now Zaire) and Premier Fidel Castro of Cuba. American officials "encouraged or were privy to" coups that killed Vietnamese President Ngo Dinh Diem, Chilean General Rene Schneider and dictator Rafael Trujillo of the Dominican Republic. In 1963, on the day President Kennedy was killed, the C.I.A. was reported to be equipping a Cuban dissident with a poison-tipped pen designed to kill Castro. According to the panel, the agency also hired Mafiosi to kill the Cuban leader. The Church report is the first official indication that the United States employed assassination as an instrument of foreign policy (→ May 19, 1976).

Seton is canonized; first U.S.-born saint

Vatican City, Sept. 14

Elizabeth Bayley Seton today became the first person born in the United States to be cannonized as a Roman Catholic saint. Mother Seton, who was the founder of the Sisters of Charity of Emmitsburg, Maryland, converted to Catholicism shortly after the death of her husband and was active in aiding the small American Catholic community of the early 1800s in attaining some organizational structure. In addition to founding the order, she was responsible for building schools, orphanages and hospitals.

Deng Hsiao-ping shows the President how it's done. The renewal of ties between the United States and China has altered international politics.

Doctorow goes from Ragtime to riches

New York City

The ragtime music craze crested in the early 1900s, but the form has found new life, thanks to *Ragtime*, the best-seller by E.L. Doctorow. The novel examines the country before World War I and finds it to be a familiar place – fraught with racism and hatred, laced with scandal, money and sex. Doctorow's prose rhythms give his story a bright syncopated beat, and he adds a medley of real-life celebrities, including Henry Ford, Houdini, anarchist Emma Goldman, and Scott Joplin, the king of ragtime.

A midshipwoman at U.S. Naval Academy. Admission of women to the military academies is turning traditions upside-down.

Miami, Jan. 18. Pittsburgh Steelers beat Dallas Cowboys, 21-17, in Super Bowl X.

Washington, D.C., Jan. 31. Supreme Court, in Buckley v. Valeo, rejects limits on political campaign spending.

Washington, D.C., Apr. 13. Secretary of State Kissinger warns that Communist success in any West European country will adversely affect U.S. policy toward that country.

New York City, May 3. Saul Bellow wins Pulitzer Prize, for *Humboldt's Gift*.

Washington, D.C., May 24. First commercial supersonic transport, Anglo-French Concorde, lands at Dulles International Airport.

Snake River Valley, Idaho, June 5. Teton River Dam bursts, releasing 80 billion gallons of water, which causes about $1 billion in damage.

Phoenix, Arizona, June 8. Boston Celtics beat Suns, 4 games to 3, for N.B.A. title.

New York, July 8. For his obstruction of justice during Watergate, ex-President Nixon is disbarred in New York.

Minneapolis, Sept. 16. Episcopal Church approves ordination of women to priesthood (→ Sept. 16, 1977).

West Point, New York, September. Some 700 cadets at Military Academy suspended for violating honor code.

Washington, D.C., Oct. 4. Sec. of Agriculture Earl Butz resigns over racist comment.

New York City, Oct. 21. Cincinnati Reds defeat New York Yankees in four-game sweep of World Series.

Alabama, Oct. 25. Governor George Wallace pardons Clarence Norris, last surviving Scottsboro Boy.

Plains, Georgia, Nov. 14. President-elect Carter's church is integrated.

Chicago. In *Playboy* interview, Jimmy Carter says, "I've committed adultery in my heart many times."

Hollywood, Calif. Hit films this year include *Rocky* and *Network*.

DEATH

Houston, Texas, Apr. 5. Howard Hughes, eccentric billionaire (*Dec. 24, 1905).

Americans migrate south to the Sun Belt

"Storm over Taos" by John Marin. Warmth and beauty attract Northerners.

Washington, D.C., Feb. 7

"Go West, young man," was the old adage. Well, the direction has changed. Northern city dwellers are moving south at an unparalleled rate, according to a new Census Bureau report. Spurred by a number of developments, not the least of which is air-conditioning, the Sun Belt grew twice as fast as the North over the last 25 years. Florida has doubled its population since 1960; and Arizona shows a growth rate of 25 percent over the last five years, the highest in the nation.

The migrants, it seems, bring prosperity with them. Businesses, attracted by low wage scales and tax bills, are relocating in warmer climes. Lear Jet moved to Tucson, Greyhound to Phoenix and Shell to Houston. From 1967 to 1972, manufacturing employment increased 7 percent in the Sun Belt, while dropping 12 percent in the North. Professionals are escaping the rat race of New York and Chicago in packs. And the growth of Sun Belt universities has been causing a "brain drain" on the North.

Southerners also benefit from a $13 billion net gain in federal funds after taxes; Northerners lose $20 billion. And with the lion's share of defense contracting centered in the Sun Belt, Northerners will certainly think twice before reprising the Civil War.

High court, in shift, OK's death penalty

Washington, D.C., July 2

In a series of companion cases, the Supreme Court ruled today that laws in Florida, Georgia and Texas permitting imposition of the death penalty are constitutional. In Jurek v. Texas, the court voted 7-2 to reverse its 1972 decision outlawing capital punishment. Texas officials hailed the decision, hoping the high cost of violent crime will be a deterrent. Justices Thurgood Marshall and William Brennan dissented, adhering to the 1972 view that the death penalty violates the Eighth Amendment protection against "cruel and unusual punishment."

U.S. Olympic stars: Jenner, swimmers

Montreal, Canada, July 8

The image of Bruce Jenner waving a small American flag on his victory lap in the decathlon provided a poignant memory of the 1976 Olympics. The flag had been handed to him by a small boy after his race. The swimmers from America made the greatest impact in the unofficial point standings, by winning 12 of 13 events. John Naber was the individual star with records in both backstroke events. The United States had threatened to withdraw from the Games over a Canadian ban on the flag of Communist China, but relented.

Agency to oversee intelligence units

Washington, D.C., May 19

Closing a three-year battle between Congress and the intelligence community, the Senate has set up a 15-member agency with broad powers to oversee the nation's intelligence activities. Observers had been worried that a recent spate of congressional leaks would jeopardize attempts to police the C.I.A. and the F.B.I. In February, the Pike Committee report showed up in the pages of the *Village Voice*. It placed C.I.A. spending at $10 billion (three times the announced figure) and blasted Secretary of State Henry Kissinger's "passion for secrecy." Kissinger calls the panel "a new version of McCarthyism."

An Apple with byte

Mountain View, Calif., Apr. 1

A company called Apple that intends to make and sell small computers for personal use has been started by two young engineers, Steven Jobs and Stephen Wozniak, who have a total of $1,300 in capital and plan to assemble their computer in a garage. Both men work for established electronic companies but see great possibilities in personal computers. They originally planned to sell 100 computers for $50 each to make a quick profit, but local stores already have placed orders for four times that number.

State law barring gay sex is upheld

Washington, D.C., March 29

The Supreme Court ruled today that states have the right to enforce laws banning homosexual acts. The decision upholds a ruling of a Virginia court that prohibited such activities, even between consenting adults in the privacy of their own homes. The high court's ruling is a reversal of its record of the last 10 years, which had expanded guarantees of privacy. Civil liberties groups and gay activists are outraged over the decision and are planning to protest it. But social conservatives believe it appropriately curbs "abnormal behavior."

National revelry marks 200 years of independence

United States, July 4

A bicentennial is worth two centennials, and then some. The frolics of 1876 were no match for the festivities of 1976; the first centennial was mostly celebrated by feeding from a simple picnic basket or watching an amateur marching band perform without the benefit of Sousa. The year 1976, however, offered a splendid show of 225 tall-masted ships, the opening of a great aviation museum, a 10-mile-long international parade and, briefly, the largest American flag ever, a banner boasting stars as big as bath-tubs. As for meaningfulness, there may be segments of the population unhappy with the current state of social and political affairs, but 1976 delivers more of the promises of 1776 than 1876, 100 times over.

Today, New York played host to Operation Sail, as the ships of 30 nations were elegantly navigated through New York harbor. Visitors crowded the wharves and New Yorkers found perches in skyscrapers to get a glorious view. One thing they did not get to see was the immense flag along the side of the Verrazano-Narrows Bridge that had been sewn by volunteers hailing from Marblehead, Massachusetts. Because planners failed to provide vents to let the high winds though, the flag was quickly torn to shreds. In Washington, D.C., thousands of visitors were welcomed to the Smithsonian Institution's new

National Air and Space Museum and 33.5 tons of fireworks were sent up near the normally sedate Lincoln Memorial. The Boston Pops Orchestra played the *1812 Overture,* punctuated by harmonious howitzers. President Ford rang the Liberty Bell in Philadelphia, Chicago swore in 1,776 citizens, and in Los Angeles an *All Nations, All Peoples* conga line swayed to the Pacific. New Orleans retired to a jazz marathon last night; San Antonio rose to a balloon race this morning. Small-town U.S.A. did its duties, too, with pie-eating, baton twirling and greasedpole shinnying contests.

People who thought hard about what *independence* means enjoyed the holiday less. The July 4th Coalition held a mostly peaceful protest in Philadelphia, drawing attention to the fact that its members (blacks, Indians, gays and feminists) were all created equal but lost ground the instant they stepped into society. Others who reviewed America's democratic traditions felt its people weren't so badly off: true, a President just resigned in disgrace, but that isn't bad for nearly 200 years of chief executives. One writer noted how content people seem with the new President, and wondered if they would have liked him any less if they had voted him into office. But most Americans focused on the revelry at hand. Will the tricentennial outdo it?

Americans remember those patriots who fought and died to win liberty.

Independence Hall in Philadelphia is carefully preserved as a symbol.

The British are coming! Across the country, Americans are staging re-enactments to commemorate the pitched battles of the War for Independence.

"Old Ironsides" sails again. The warship Constitution is back in the water, this time as a symbol of America's strength and dedication to freedom.

The colonial Minuteman is best remembered for his heroic convictions.

The Stars and Stripes Forever. Old Glory, illuminated in all its majesty.

Slowdown gives economic issue to Carter

Washington, D.C., October

The stagnating economic recovery that experts keep trying to predict away is stubbornly hanging on to poison Republican fortunes in next month's election. The rate of expansion slowed from 9.2 percent in the first quarter to 4.5 percent in the second. Leading economic indicators dropped in August for the first time in a year and a half. Unemployment did fall from 7.9 to 7.8 percent in September, but only after rising three months in a row. And according to the Census Bureau, 25.9 million Americans are poor, the highest number since 1970.

With the figures bared to the public eye, the first presidential debate, on September 23, quickly became a nationally televised forum on economic policy. President Ford, defending his record, spoke of a glass half full. He took credit for creating four million jobs and bringing the total number of employed Americans to 88 million, "the most in the history of the country." Jimmy Carter insisted that Ford's tenure has seen a 50-percent increase in unemployment. Both are correct. A 14-percent rise in the cost of living has sent women and teens flocking into the labor force faster than the economy can produce new jobs.

The two candidates also clashed on taxes. Ford offered a $28 billion cut, while Carter argued that most of the benefits would go to corporations and "special interests."

Ford trips on Soviet issue in Carter debate

Ford's uncertainty about Soviet sway over the East bloc is troubling voters.

15 percent of adults functionally illiterate

Washington, D.C.

Tfgrx pj kuuyl mxstqv, lpqw. To you, the above collection of letters holds no meaning. To millions of Americans, this "sentence" means as much as any other; it is a cluster of symbols that cause embarrassment, frustration, harm. According to a Census Bureau report, 15 percent of all American adults are functionally illiterate, living blindly in a world of written words. The impact of illiteracy on the individual is clear: a parent can't read to his child, can't decipher antidote instructions on a bottle of roach poison in an emergency. When a whole society is involved, the problem multiplies. In the face of these figures, literacy foundations have been pushing harder for the government to provide some assistance.

San Francisco, Oct. 6

President Ford declared tonight, "There is no Soviet domination in Eastern Europe." The President made the statement in the second of two televised campaign debates with the Democratic presidential nominee, Jimmy Carter, broadcast from the San Francisco Palace of Fine Arts.

Carter said he would like to see Ford convince Americans of Polish, Czech and Hungarian descent that their ancestral homelands are not under the "domination and supervision of the Soviet Union behind the Iron Curtain."

Ford accused Carter of "looking with sympathy" toward the idea of having a Communist government in the North Atlantic Treaty Organization, which he said would destroy the alliance. Carter denied that he had ever advocated such a course for Italy, saying it would be a "ridiculous thing for anyone to do who wanted to be President of this country" (→ Nov. 2).

Mysterious "Legionnaires" flu kills 28

Philadelphia, Aug. 26

The death toll from the mysterious influenza-like disease that struck the Pennsylvania American Legion convention here last month now stands at 28, and epidemiologists say they have no clues to its cause. The outbreak was first spotted by Dr. William Campbell, a family doctor who noted similar symptoms in three of his patients who attended the convention. Studies found 180 cases across the state. Patients have an unusual pneumonia with high fever and a persistent cough. The largest force of federal investigators ever assembled combed the Bellevue-Stratford Hotel, the convention site, in vain. Speculation on the cause ranges from an unidentified toxic substance to a new kind of bacteria.

California asserts patient's right to die

Sacramento, Calif., Sept. 30

Governor Jerry Brown signed into law today California's Natural Death Act, dubbed the "right-to-die" law, the first of its kind in the nation. Its application, however, is limited. A patient's natural-death directive must be witnessed by two persons, neither of whom is related to the patient nor involved in his medical treatment. At least two physicians must certify to the patient's imminent terminal condition as well as to his or her mental competence to make the decision. The patient can cancel the directive at any time. The controversial statute contains a strong statement that this in no way condones mercy killing or euthanasia.

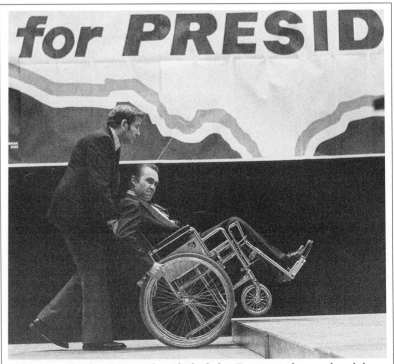

Taking to the hustings with a little help. Permanently paralyzed by a would-be assassin in 1972, George Wallace runs again for the White House.

Americans win all Nobels but Peace

Stockholm, Sweden, Dec. 10

Americans have scored a near sweep of the 1976 Nobel Prizes. The literature winner was Saul Bellow, the Canadian-born novelist who lives in Chicago. Conservative economist Milton Friedman won the economics prize and William Lipscomb Jr. was the chemistry winner for his work on compounds called boranes. Baruch Blumberg and Daniel Carleton Gajdusek shared medicine honors for virus research, and Burton Richter and Samuel Ting won for discovering a subatomic particle. Mairead Corrigan and Betty Williams of Northern Ireland won the Peace Prize.

U.S. to name firms in boycott of Israel

Washington, D.C., Oct. 8

The Commerce Department announced today that it will publish the names of all American firms that are asked to join the Arab boycott against Israel, and whether or not they do. The announcement was in compliance with a pledge made on television by President Ford during his debate with Jimmy Carter, who denounced American acquiescence in the embargo as "a national disgrace." A Commerce Department report of September 30 found that 94 percent of American firms went along with the boycott.

Bermuda Triangle claims another ship

Bermuda, Oct. 15

A 590-foot cargo ship with a crew of 37 is missing in the Bermuda Triangle, the ocean area between Bermuda, Puerto Rico and Norfolk, Virginia, where over the years hundreds of men, ships and planes have reportedly vanished without explanation. The Panamanian-registered Sylvia L. Ossa, was bound from Brazil to Philadelphia with a cargo of iron ore. It had radioed that its arrival would be delayed because of gale winds and high seas. Then it fell silent. Coast Guard planes are searching the area.

Carter retakes White House for Democrats

Jimmy Carter goes to Washington.

Washington, D.C., Nov. 2

In one of the closest elections of the century, Democratic Party nominee Jimmy Carter was elected President of the United States today, defeating the Republican incumbent, Gerald Ford.

The outcome split the nation on East-West lines. Carter won the South and a number of key states including New York, Pennsylvania, Texas, Ohio, two states in the upper Midwest and Hawaii. Ford won most of the Midwestern stastes and all of the West except Hawaii. Although Ford won 27 states to Carter's 23 and the District of Columbia, Carter obtained 279 electoral votes to Ford's 241.

It was the eighth time in the nation's history that a sitting president had been defeated. The last previous occasion was the Franklin D. Roosevelt triumph over Herbert Hoover in 1932. Carter was the first candidate from the "Deep" South to be elected since the Civil War, although another Southerner, Texan Lyndon Johnson won in 1964.

Tom Wolfe proclaims the "Me Decade"

New York City

Writing in *New York* magazine, satirist Tom Wolfe has called this the "Me Decade." Chronologically, 1976 is smack in the middle of "meness," and there are some statistics to bear Wolfe out. One report reveals three out of five marriages end in divorce, and one out of five children lives in a one-parent home. Is it a coincidence that the teenage SAT scores are so low? What were parents doing while their children's average scores dropped to 472 in math and 453 in English (from 501 and 480 in 1968)? Perhaps they were joining the Me generation, filling up on bran to live longer (bran cereal sales climbed 20 percent this year), or worrying more about the numbers on their paychecks than those on their kids' tests. No longer, it seems, are people willing to risk life and limb to march for peace, harmony and civil rights. Unless, of course, the price is right.

Cadillac Eldorado is last convertible

Detroit, Mich., Apr. 22

The last assembly-line convertible built in the United States, a white Cadillac Eldorado, rolled out of the factory today. Doomed by auto air-conditioners and freeway speeds, convertibles have steadily lost market share since 1965, the peak year, when more than 500,000 were sold. Chrysler, Ford and other General Motors divisions stopped convertible production earlier, but Cadillac kept making them until its last supplier of convertible soft tops went out of business. This model is likely to become a collectors' item.

A Watergate movie on whistle blowers

Carl and Bob bask in the glory.

Washington, D.C.

What's happening in the news can be tomorrow's successful film, as demonstrated by *All the President's Men*, in which Robert Redford and Dustin Hoffman portray Bob Woodward and Carl Bernstein, the *Washington Post* reporters who broke the news of the Watergate scandal in 1972. The picture was actually considered before the book was written and published in 1974. Redford, irate over the abuse of public trust, got in touch with Woodward and Bernstein and grew fascinated by the story. The two reporters have written a second best-seller, *The Final Days*. Also a best-seller is *Blind Ambition: The White House Years*, by John Dean, former White House counsel.

For John Beasley, 20, repainting the house plain old green didn't seem to fit the bicentennial spirit. So, with brush in hand, he created a patriotic masterpiece. He says dad thinks it's "kind of cool," but mom is not amused.

Carter calls energy crisis battle "the moral equivalent of war"

Washington, D.C., Apr. 18

The nation must wage "the moral equivalent of war" to overcome an energy crisis that could lead to "national catastrophe," President Carter told the nation in a televised address from the Oval Office tonight. Unless the United States reduces energy consumption, Carter said, its spending on imported oil could rise from the current $36 billion a year to $550 billion by 1985, an increase he said, that "will threaten our free institutions." The energy goals he set for 1985 include a cut in the annual energy growth rate to 2 percent from today's 4 percent and a reduction of 10 percent in gasoline consumption.

Public opinion polls show half the public believes there is no energy crisis or that it is artificially created. To counter that skepticism, the President released a Central Intelligence Agency report predicting sharp oil price increases unless a major conservation program is begun.

Carter did not give details of his plan, but he said it would depend on financial sacrifices and changes in living habits. "With the exception of preventing war, this is the greatest challenge that our country will face in our lifetimes," he said somberly. "The energy crisis has not yet overwhelmed us, but it will if we do not act quickly" (→ Sept. 13).

President Jimmy Carter and First Lady Rosalynn broke convention by walking a part of the way to the White House on Inauguration Day, January 20.

"Roots," TV event

New York City, Feb. 1

Alex Haley's *Roots* began with a birth in an African village in 1750 and ended seven generations later at a black professor's funeral in Arkansas. Haley is that professor's son. The ABC series ran an unprecedented eight consecutive nights with more than 51 percent of all television sets tuned in each night. The nightly audience of 80 million was the biggest ever for a TV show.

Gilmore executed; first in a decade

Utah, Jan. 17

Gary Gilmore's death wish came true tonight when the killer of two men was executed by a firing squad at the Utah State Prison. It was the first time the death penalty has been carried out in the nation since 1967. Gilmore, who twice tried to commit suicide in prison, became highly publicized because of his demand that he be executed. After a last-minute challenge to the death penalty by the American Civil Liberties Union, the Supreme Court refused to grant a stay of execution.

Carter pardons all Vietnam draft evaders

Washington, D.C., Jan. 21

Acting promptly to fulfill a campaign pledge, President Carter today granted a full pardon to all Vietnam-era draft evaders, providing they had not engaged in violent acts. The amnesty was not extended to those who entered the forces and then deserted, but an immediate study was promised to consider upgrading discharges that were less than honorable.

The presidential pardon was criticized by some who thought it went too far, and by others who felt it did not go far enough. Senator Barry Goldwater, the 1964 Republican presidential nominee, called it "the most disgraceful thing that a President has ever done." But Democratic Senator Edward Kennedy called his action "a major, impressive and compassionate step toward healing the wounds of Vietnam".

February 18. *The space shuttle Enterprise, scheduled to make orbital space flights in 1979, got its first test run today on the back of a Boeing 747.*

U.S. to reduce aid for rights violators

Washington, D.C., Feb. 24

Following through on President Carter's campaign pledge to make human rights a top priority, Secretary of State Cyrus Vance today announced cutbacks in foreign aid to three offenders, Argentina, Ethiopia and Uruguay. Strategically important countries such as South Korea, where civil rights are also abused, do not face aid cutoffs now, but there will be more American pressure for better conditions. The step comes a week after Carter wrote Andrei Sakharov, the dissident scientist, pledging to urge broader human rights in the Soviet Union (→ March 22, 1981).

Vast pipeline will bring oil from Alaska

A project of epic proportions, the Alaska pipeline carries oil over 800 miles.

2,000 at Seabrook besiege atom plant

Seabrook, N.H., May 2

Sponsored by a group called the Clamshell Alliance, a demonstration to halt the planned nuclear reactor at Seabrook drew a crowd of 2,000 today. The protesters occupied the site, saying they would remain until plans for the atomic plant were abandoned. About 1,400 of the demonstrators were arrested, loaded into buses and brought to court. A similar, but smaller demonstration occurred last August, when more than 100 were arrested. "If they keep building, we'll come back with 18,000," said an alliance leader. Use of nuclear energy has raised environmental concerns.

Spanking held legal

Washington, D.C., Apr. 19

"Spare the rod, spoil the child" is the old adage, and the Supreme Court seems to agree. Today, in a 5-4 decision, the court ruled that spanking schoolchildren does not violate Eighth Amendment protection against "cruel and unusual punishment." But the court did say that school officials who use "excessive" force in disciplining students are subject to criminal penalties. It also said sufficient protection against such abuse exists. In dissent, Justice Byron White called spanking a "barbaric" punishment.

Valdez, Alaska, July 28

After more than a month of delays, spills and false alarms, the first barrel of North Slope oil has arrived in Valdez. This year-round, ice-free port on Prince William Sound will be the southern terminus of the TransAlaska Pipeline System, known as TAPS.

Completed on May 30 at a cost of $8 billion, TAPS will channel two million barrels of petroleum a day from the Prudhoe Bay oilfield on the shore of the Arctic Ocean. The 800-mile trail of 48-inch pipe is considered by many to be the technological wonder of the age. With 78,000-above ground supports, TAPS crossed more than 800

rivers, the longest being the Yukon, where a 2,290-foot bridge had to be built for both pipeline and road traffic. Although laying the pipeline was expensive, it will more than pay for its cost when the estimated seven billion recoverable barrels of oil are extracted.

Though Prudhoe is the largest oilfield on the North American continent, it is modest when compared to the oilfields of the Middle East. Nevertheless, economists estimate that, on the basis of current needs, Alaskan oil from this one field will enable the United States to reduce its imports from the Middle East and elsewhere by more than 15 percent.

It's Seattle Slew

New York City, June 11

He was not the kind to win any beauty contest for horses and, in fact, was sold at auction for a very modest $17,000. But races aren't won by looks or money and today Seattle Slew accomplished the toughest task in horse racing as he swept to the Triple Crown. He did this by taking the Belmont Stakes, where he was the 2-5 favorite as a result of his victories in the Kentucky Derby and the Preakness. The undefeated colt outraced Run Dusty Run, who also chased him in the first two legs.

Ray is recaptured

Tennessee, June 13

James Earl Ray and six other convicts were found today, three days after their escape from Brushy Mountain State Prison. They got away with the help of a bogus fight staged by fellow inmates. Ray is serving a 99-year sentence for the murder of the Rev. Dr. Martin Luther King Jr., and the escape fueled national skepticism. Despite the finding that Ray acted alone, many believe he was involved in a conspiracy and regarded the escape as an engineered effort to silence the one man who might air the truth. Governor Ray Blanton, citing the cost and security problems, has asked the federal government to take charge of Ray.

"Moonies" held to be brainwashed, given back to parents

California, March 24

California Superior Court Judge S. Lee Vauris ordered a group of five adult members of the Unification Church placed in the temporary custody of their parents today. In issuing his order, Judge Vauris said it would appear that the Rev. Sun Myung Moon's Unification Church (Moonies) exerted a brainwashing influence on the young adults, making it impossible for them to consciously choose to remain with or leave the church. The Unification Church has acquired great notoriety in this country and many feel that this case is directed against the church itself and would not have been heard had it involved one of the regular denominations.

Critics question how the Rev. Sun Myung Moon controls his young followers.

New diesel cars need 40% less fuel

Detroit, Mich., Sept. 13

Reacting to the energy crisis, General Motors today introduced a new line of diesel cars whose major selling point is a claimed 40 percent mileage advantage over gasoline-powered autos. This diesel, available first in full-size Oldsmobiles, is a modification of G.M.'s 350-cubic inch gasoline engine and will be built in a new $500 million plant near Lansing. General Motors acknowledges that its diesel has the traditional faults of such engines, including greasy exhaust fumes, noise and slow starting on cold days, as well as a price $1,000 higher than conventional models, but it is counting on the low cost of diesel fuel and the new energy consciousness of American drivers.

Foreign cars pour in

Detroit, Michigan

Auto imports hit a new high this year, with foreign car makers expected to sell 2.1 million vehicles, capturing nearly 20 percent of the American market. Imports, mostly Japanese, account for 40 percent of all sales in some Western states. American auto companies are fighting back by reducing prices of their small cars, which have suffered the greatest sales decline, and introducing new models designed to compete directly with the most popular Japanese subcompacts.

Farrakhan leads separatist Muslims

Chicago, December

Louis Farrakhan, formerly Malcolm X's successor at Temple No. 7 in Harlem, has led a group of followers out of the World Community of al-Islam in the West. The separatists dislike the drift toward orthodox Islam and away from racial separatism that has marked the Black Muslim movement since Elijah Muhammad died. Farrakhan has reorganized the old Nation of Islam (Black Muslims) along the strict separatist and racial lines that distinguished the movement at its start.

Elvis, king of rock, gone

By the time of his death, Elvis had gained weight and given in to drug abuse.

Memphis, Tennessee, Aug. 16

Elvis Presley died at his Graceland mansion today. He was 42. Rock 'n' roll might still be an innocuous hillbilly genre had Elvis Aaron Presley not shown up. Born in Tupelo, Mississippi, to working-class parents, Presley had a voice brushed with a shade of Southern blues. When parents heard his first hit, *Heartbreak Hotel*, in January 1956, they knew they didn't want their teenagers to hear it, and when they saw him gyrating on the Ed Sullivan Show in September of the same year, they didn't want him seen, either. But his songs *Hound Dog*, *Don't Be Cruel*, *Love Me Tender* and *Blue Suede Shoes*, and his films, including *Viva Las Vegas* and *Jailhouse Rock*, had an irresistible appeal to a generation longing to seem a little more dangerous than it really was.

Elvis lived on the edge: He took up karate and earned a black belt, stayed up at night and slept by day and had several lovers after his five-year marriage to Priscilla Beaulieu. Though a near teetotaler, he took amphetamines and barbiturates, and though physicians have blamed his death on a "cardiac arrhythmia," rumors are that he succumbed to a drug overdose, a king who sadly dethroned himself.

Serving an energy-hungry America. The Indian Point nuclear plant in New York State is one of several such facilities providing the new source of power.

Episcopalians split over women priests

St. Louis, Mo., Sept. 16

In a reaction to the ordination of women to the Episcopal priesthood, several conservative Episcopalians have left the Protestant Episcopal Church of America to organize a new denomination, the Anglican Church in North America. At a three-day meeting, the 1,700 dissidents adopted a charter for the new denomination and declared themselves to be true heirs to the Anglican tradition. The dissidents view the ordination of women as contrary to the historical doctrines of Anglicanism and say it puts the Americans at odds with Anglican churches in other nations. While women's ordination was the catalyst for the separation, the split had been long in the making.

$2.65 wage floor

Washington, D.C, Nov. 1

President Carter signed legislation today to raise the minimum wage for workers to $2.65 an hour. The bill also mandates a rise in the hourly minimum to $3.35 in 1981. Unions wanted this year's increase to be $3. Some union leaders feel the President did little to help their cause. *Congressional Quarterly* reported, "Only after months of negotiations did labor succeed in gaining administration support (for the bill.)" Low wage-earners see it as a step in the right direction.

Divorced Catholics allowed to remarry

Washington, D.C., Nov. 10

At their annual meeting, Roman Catholic bishops announced today that Pope Paul VI has ended the automatic excommunication imposed on divorced American Catholics who remarry. It was last year that the bishops asked the Pope to lift the excommunication first imposed by the Plenary Council of Baltimore in 1884. The bishops said the aim of this step was to extend reconciliation to divorced and remarried Catholics and to encourage them to regularize the status of their marriages.

Irate farmers: "No dough, no grow!"

Washington, D.C., Dec. 10

Thousands of tractors rumbled into Washington, Atlanta, Denver and some 30 other state capitals today to demand increased crop support from the government. The farmers are planning their first national strike since 1932, and one sign reads "No Dough, No Sow, No Grow." Critics doubt that the farmers, traditionally hard to organize, can be mobilized. But, said Bill Schroeder of Colorado, "If I work, I lose money. If I sit on my rear, I lose money. What would you do?" Since 1973, farmers have suffered a drop in net annual income from $9,950 to $5,300, while costs continue to climb. Protesters say a bushel of wheat worth $2.70 on the market costs $5.06 to produce.

Abortion funds cut

Washington, D.C., Dec. 9

Congress has placed strict curbs on the use of federal Medicaid financing of abortions. Previously, Medicaid covered all abortions considered "medically necessary." But now they are limited to those for physically ill women and the victims of incest and rape. Abortion rights activists fear that poor women will again become victims of dangerous "back-alley" abortions.

U.S. signs away canal

The end of a U.S. monopoly. President Carter could not have chosen a more polarizing issue to tackle. Built with United States money, know-how and muscle, the Panama Canal represents to many America at its industrious best.

Washington, D.C., Sept. 7

The leaders of the United States and Panama agreed today that the Panama Canal shall be Panama's canal by the year 2000 – if the American Senate ratifies the treaty. President Carter and Brigadier General Omar Torrijos signed accords that would revoke the treaty of 1903 under which the United States built and controls the canal.

The Senate must approve the new accord by a two-thirds majority before it can take effect. Under its terms, American control of the canal will expire on the last day of 1999, but the United States will still be authorized to "counter any threat to the canal's neutrality." A bitter fight is likely in the Senate, because of American pride in the canal and strong feelings about its importance to national security.

Torrijos urged Senate "statesmen" to approve the new treaty. He pointed out that the original one was not signed by a Panamanian, but by a Frenchman acting on the behalf of a small nation that had recently seceded from Colombia.

Of discos, muscles and "Star Wars"

Hollywood, California

Disco seems to be contagious after *Saturday Night Fever*, a new film in which John Travolta puts his best foot forward as the intense and moody Brooklyn youth who yearns for glory and finds it as king of the discos. The latest media trend king, Travolta has inspired vast numbers of inner-city dancers. Clad in silk shirts and skin-tight pants, they are flocking to discos across the country and writhing under multi-colored strobe lights to the sounds of the Bee Gees and Donna Summer.

Elsewhere in the world of film, Woody Allen presents another personal picture, witty *Annie Hall*, with himself and Diane Keaton. Arnold Schwarzenegger muscles his way to stardom via *Pumping Iron*. Good and evil fight in George Lucas's forceful *Star Wars*, a fantasy inspired by the work of mythology scholar Joseph Campbell. It's loaded with spectacular effects, and people return to see it again and again. Steven Spielberg alienates no fans with his huge hit, *Close Encounters of the Third Kind*. In *Julia*, Jane Fonda is playing Lillian Hellman, Vanessa Redgrave is her brave friend and Jason Robards is Dashiell Hammett. Liza Minnelli and Robert De Niro make music in Martin Scorsese's big band-era musical *New York, New York*. And the movies refight World War II in Richard Attenborough's $25-million *A Bridge Too Far*.

National Women's Conference meets to plan feminist future

Two ladies of liberty. Ardent feminists from around the country express their hopes and dreams for an America without sex distcrimination.

Houston, Texas, Nov. 21

On November 18, at the start of the four-day First National Women's Conference, a flaming torch led a phalanx of marchers through Houston. The torch had traveled 2,500 miles from Seneca Falls, New York, site of the first women's convention in 1849, and one woman runner after another had carried the flame on the trek across the country. Now marching behind it were 2,000 delegates, led by tennis star Billie Jean King, politician Bella Abzug and the N.O.W. founder Betty Friedan, all holding hands and linked by womanhood. Later, First Lady Rosalynn Carter stood shoulder to shoulder with former First Ladies Betty Ford and Lady Bird Johnson.

Clearly, the conference at Houston has had form. Has it had function? Its resolutions are many: It calls upon Congress to establish full employment, thus making more jobs available to would-be working women. It seeks sex education at all school levels, including the elementary grades. It urges voluntary, flexible-hour child care. It demands enforcement of the Federal Equal Credit Opportunity Act of 1974. And minorities in the women's movement have not been forgotten: special attention is demanded for disabled women, Hispanics, blacks, Indians and the elderly of all races. So much for demands. As delegates disperse, they know the hard part is ahead: working to get the demands met (→ June 30, 1982).

John Travolta is stayin' alive in "Saturday Night Fever," a film that celebrates the latest fad – disco dancing – sweeping the nation.

160,000 miners end longest strike

Washington, D.C., March 24

Keeping the United Mine Workers and the coal operators at the bargaining table, says Labor Secretary Ray Marshall, is like "trying to corral quicksilver." But today the efforts paid off. After a record 16 weeks on strike, 160,000 miners approved a pact to raise wages from $7.80 to $10.20 an hour over three years. The union, however, is broke and torn by dissension. Nearly half the rank-and-file opposed the contract, which requires annual contributions to a health plan. According to one West Virginia union official, strikers voted yea "just because they (were) hungry."

Sneaker sales soar

Chicago

Some call them tennies or tractor treads. Some call them felony flyers, gumshoes, plimsolls, pussyfooters, perpetrator boots or simply gym shoes or sneaks. Basically, they are sneakers and basically they account for 50 percent of all shoe sales. In a country where 30 million people play tennis, other millions play racquetball and one person in nine runs almost daily, their feet have gone to their head.

U.S. acts to curb nuke proliferation

Washington, D.C., March 10

President Carter today signed the Nuclear Non-Proliferation Act, placing strict curbs on the export of fissionable materials. The law requires the renegotiation of all agreements with recipient nations. The United States seeks to gain veto power over re-export and over the reprocessing of spent fuels into material capable of producing weapons. Western Europeans, who rely on the United States for over half their nuclear fuel, have already expressed grave reservations. Sources say West German Chancellor Helmut Schmidt, who is scheduled to meet with Soviet leader Leonid Brezhnev next month, may seek to buy more uranium from the Russians.

U.S. and Japan discuss economic malaise

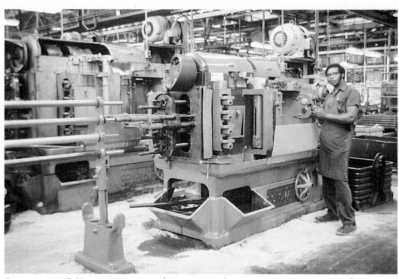

International Harvester uses color as an inducement to increase productivity.

Washington, D.C., May 3

Accompanied by Foreign Minister Sunno Sonoda, and Minister for External Economic Affairs Nobuhiko Ushiba, Premier Takeo Fukuda met today with congressional leaders to discuss Japan's troubled economic relationship with the United States. The meeting was arranged by former Senate majority leader Mike Mansfield, now ambassador to Tokyo, in hopes of heading off protectionist laws aimed at halting the loss of American jobs to Japan. There is a vast surplus of Japanese exports over imports. Last year, there was an $8.9 billion trade imbalance with the United States.

Fukuda has come ready to make concessions. Exports of Japanese cars to America, which totaled 1.9 million last year, are to be cut back to 1977 levels; steel exports will be pared 10 to 20 percent, and color TV sets to 30 percent below 1976 levels. Fukuda has also promised to stimulate domestic consumption by $7 billion to $10 billion a year, thus creating opportunities for American exports, but he has resisted suggestions that Japan spend more on defense (→ Dec. 17, 1987).

New law raises age of retirement to 70

Washington, D.C., Apr. 6

As President Carter signed a law to raise the mandatory retirement age for most Americans from 65 to 70, Representative Claude Pepper beamed with pride. The senior congressman from Florida, who lobbied hard for the bill, called this "a happy day for millions of American elderly." Opponents of the change say it will disturb employment practices, taking jobs from women, the young and minorities. But Labor Department studies indicate it will have no long-term effects on the economy and, in fact, may even result in a saving from undistributed Social Security payments. Senior citizen groups applauded the legislation as a morale booster for older people.

Carter will hold off on a neutron bomb

Washington, D.C., Apr. 7

President Carter today indefinitely "deferred production" of the neutron bomb. This "enhanced radiation weapon" has caused much public debate because of its effectiveness against human beings, and the fact that it does relatively little damage to buildings. This makes it more likely to be used, its opponents argue. Ultimately, the President said, the decision on developing the weapon would be influenced "by the degree to which the Soviet Union shows restraint in its conventional and nuclear arms programs." The Defense Department, in the meantime, will modernize the missiles and artillery delivery systems to be used if Carter should change his mind.

Californians vote vast cut in property tax

Sacramento, Calif., June 6

After a hard and often rancorous campaign, in which there was as much mud-slinging as debate, Proposition 13 has been approved by an overwhelming majority of the California voters.

The proposition, which restricts property taxes to no more than 1 percent of assessed valuation, got under way as part of a campaign to put a limit on the powers of the state's legislature. But California politics aside, the vote appears to have turned into the starting gun for a nationwide effort to roll back what many property owners all over the country feel are exorbitant property taxes.

The California property owners have long felt that their representatives in Sacramento were overtaxing them to support social programs from which they did not benefit. Noting the overwhelming vote of support, Howard Jarvis, father of the tax reform movement, said today that it was a clear indication of the end of the days of "spend, spend, spend."

Property tax reform organizations throughout the nation have been keeping a close eye on the kind of reception Proposition 13 would receive. A victory by a wide margin in California, many of their leaders believe, may carry the message that there is also sentiment for federal tax reform in California as well as other states.

Bakke wins reverse discrimination ruling

Washington, D.C., June 28

In what many call the most widely anticipated ruling of the decade, the Supreme Court decided today that fixed racial quotas are unconstitutional. In a case brought by Allan P. Bakke against the University of California Medical School at Davis, the justices ruled that Bakke was a victim of reverse discrimination. While public educational institutions had to recognize the need for minority students, the court ruled that no school could set fixed quotas. Many jurists are not sure what the ruling means. All that has been outlawed are fixed racial quotas. The ruling does not do anything about any other form of discrimination (→Feb. 13, 1979).

Challenging the "social engineers."

The star who made women's tennis shine

Forest Hills, New York

Equal pay for equal play, Billie Jean King insisted, and she made it work. She became the leading force in putting women's tennis on a par with men's and along the way reigned as the nation's foremost female player. Billie Jean, short of legs but stout of heart, became in 1971 the first woman to win more than $100,000, and by 1975, Chris Evert was earning $300,000 a year. King nurtured the Virginia Slims circuit, a separate tour which brought women greater attention. She helped equalize United States Open prize money for men and women. And it was her passion and intensity that got World Team Tennis off the ground. Meanwhile, she won four U.S. Open singles titles and rushed to more Wimbledon crowns than any other player.

Her most public triumph came in September of 1973 when she beat "male chauvinist pig" Bobby Riggs. She called this the "culmination of 19 years of tennis." Before a Houston crowd of 30,492 and with millions watching on TV, she won, 6-4, 6-3, 6-3. Breaking gender boundaries in sports, a traditionally male enclave, King has become a source of inspiration for the women's movement in a way that transcends her contribution to tennis.

Harvard introduces new core curriculum

Cambridge, Mass., May 2

"Changing undergraduate education," says Harvard president Derek Bok, "is like trying to move a graveyard." But his faculty did just that today by approving a core curriculum. A backlash against the 60s, the plan requires students to take 10 courses in five basic areas. Dean Henry Rosovsky says it will ensure "literacy in the major forms of intellectual discourse." But many criticize the program's European bias. One student called it "a step back ... to the old English idea of spoon-feeding students."

Mormon priesthood is opened to blacks

Salt Lake City, Utah, June 9

Spencer W. Kimball, president of the Church of Jesus Christ of Latter Day Saints (Mormons), announced today that the church had received a revelation allowing black males to be admitted to the Mormon priesthood. The letter announcing the revelation states that "all worthy male members of the church may be ordained to the priesthood without regard for race or color." The church has never offered an explanation for the exclusion of blacks except that there "were reasons known only to God."

Billie Jean shows her stuff. Aside from her amazing record of 21 American titles, King has been pivotal in achieving recognition for women's tennis.

The Ford Fairmont is one of the American automotive industry's latest attempts to combine ample passenger room with increased fuel economy.

American balloon is 1st to cross Atlantic

Paris, Aug. 17

They missed the Eiffel Tower by about 60 miles, but three natives of Albuquerque, New Mexico, have become the first human beings ever to cross the Atlantic Ocean by balloon. Ben Abruzzo, Max Anderson and Larry Newman piloted the Double Eagle for 138 hours and six minutes, a record for balloon flight. They will return to the United States next week by some faster, more secure means of transport. A reception at the White House will be one of the first stops. Then, not yet satisfied with a mere hop across the ocean, the three travelers are planning a 30-day balloon trip around the world.

Ethics law signed

Washington, D.C., Oct. 26

Some may question President Carter's economic policy or his ability to lead. But none question his ethical integrity. So it is fitting that he signed the comprehensive Government Ethics Law today. It requires United States legislators, judges and members of the executive branch to make financial disclosures, and it changes the guidelines for federal employees returning to the private sector. It also sets procedures for picking special prosecutors to examine charges of impropriety in the executive branch.

Ali wins title third time

A little older, but again the greatest.

Spinks, no match for Ali tonight.

New Orleans, La., Sept. 17

It was vintage Ali. He floated like a butterfly and stung like a bee. And in the end, Leon Spinks was no longer the world heavyweight champion. Ali was champ, for the third time, a feat never achieved in boxing. He outfought Spinks, who said after tonight's bout, "My head wasn't in it." His head was in it long enough to be jarred by stinging left jabs from the 36-year-old Ali. Spinks had taken the title away from Ali in February on a decision, when Ali's rope-a-dope and peek-a-boo strategy – bobbing up and down, weaving in and out – wasn't working. Ali said after that bout, "I want to be the first man to win the championship back for a third time."

After the fight, its promoter, Bob Arum, offered some clues to the reverse in fortunes that led to Ali's victory. "Leon was out every night, disco dancing," said Arum. "He was running around. He didn't deserve to win." Even his manager walked away from Spinks's corner after the fifth round, leaving the Superdome before the bout ended. "Ali wasn't tougher than last time," Spinks said, "but my mind wasn't ready." As for Ali and the earlier fight, Arum said "he didn't move in Las Vegas because he didn't train. Now he moved." Questioned later about retirement, Ali was evasive.

Carter announces anti-inflation plan

Washington, D.C., Oct. 24

In a nationwide address on television this evening, President Carter unveiled a voluntary program that he said would put a rein on the country's inflation by means of wage and price standards, inflation "insurance" for workers and continued deregulation of government-controlled industries. "Of all our weapons ... competition is the most powerful," the President said, referring to his plans for deregulating the surface transportation industry, as the airlines industry has been. Carter said that the recommendations would result in a reduction of inflation by between 1 and 2 percentage points.

Rockwell is dead

Stockbridge, Mass., Nov. 8

America's best-loved illustrator, Norman Rockwell, died today at the age of 84. Rockwell, who first studied at the Art Students' League in New York, gained fame for his magazine covers. From 1916 to 1963, Rockwell did 322 covers for the *Saturday Evening Post*. In designs like *Girl With Black Eye* and the *Look* cover that featured John F. Kennedy and the Peace Corps, Rockwell succeeded in portraying Americans as they wished to be seen, with patriotism, kindness and a gentle humor.

President Carter is joined by retired Admiral Hyman Rickover (left) and Captain Peter Hekman on a visit to the nuclear-powered missile cruiser Mississippi, during its commissioning at the base in Norfolk, Virginia.

Las Vegas, Nevada. *This city has changed enormously since the Mormons first settled here in 1855 and left two years later. Since 1931, when gambling was legalized, "The Strip" has always proved a good bet for high rollers.*

Cleveland defaults; first city since 30s

Cleveland, Ohio, Dec. 16

Cleveland today won the dubious distinction of becoming the first American city since the Depression to go into default. The city owes $14 million to six local banks, which have yet to take court action to collect. A major part of the problem is a political battle between Mayor Dennis Kucinich and the City Council. According to a report in the *Wall Street Journal*, Cleveland "has the financial capacity to get out of the predicament, if only its leaders can work in harmony." In fact, Cleveland bonds are now in brisk demand. One of the city's resources is a fairly low tax base.

Affirmed wins it all

New York City, June 10

It took a photo-finish camera to rule that Affirmed had won the Belmont Stakes in one of the most dramatic finishes ever in this third leg of the Triple Crown. The photo showed Affirmed had a margin of a head over Alydar, who also ran second to Affirmed in the first two legs of the series, the Kentucky Derby and Preakness. Affirmed and Alydar ran head and head for the last half-mile of the mile-and-a-half grind but the Harbor View colt bobbed his head just at the finish. Steve Cauthen rode Affirmed.

Reggie Jackson, "Mr. October," leads the Yankees to World Series win over Dodgers, 4 games to 2.

Tragedy at Jonestown

A scene of indescribable horror. The mass suicide in Guyana brings into focus the power a cult leader, Jim Jones in this case, can have over his followers.

Jonestown, Guyana, Nov. 18

Representative Leo J. Ryan was killed today and hundreds more are reported dead in a bizarre murder and mass suicide at an American religious cult community in this South American country. Ryan, 53, was reportedly killed by followers of the Rev. Jim Jones, a controversial California religious figure. Some 900 of Jones's followers then committed mass suicide.

The congressman had gone to Guyana to investigate reports that members of the Jones community were being held prisoner. Ryan and several aides and reporters with him were fired upon by some of Jones's associates after leaving the community and trying to board a plane bound for the United States.

Reports from the area indicate that hundreds of the cultists then swallowed a concoction of Kool-Aid and cyanide – at Jones's direction – and that Jones himself also committed suicide. Hundreds of bodies, adults and children, have been found in the Guyana jungle around Jonestown. There were no marks of violence. Not one living person was found in the camp.

Jones moved his San Francisco-based People's Temple to a 27,000-acre land grant in Guyana four years ago. His followers included blacks and whites who believed in his vision of racial harmony.

Gay Frisco official and Mayor killed

San Francisco, Nov. 27

Former Supervisor Dan White, 32, walked into City Hall today in a rage. He shot and killed Mayor George Moscone, 49, a father of four, then Supervisor Harvey Milk, 48. Why? The Mayor had not reinstated White, who had quit his job November 10 but changed his mind a week later. Milk was a different case. White, a self-proclaimed defender of family and morals, hated homosexuals, and Milk, a leader in gay politics, was the first openly gay city official. Dianne Feinstein, board president, was sworn in as temporary mayor.

More Indochinese refugees accepted

Washington, D.C., Nov. 28

The United States plans to admit 21,875 more Indochinese refugees in addition to the current quota of 25,000 a year. They would include both Cambodians and Vietnamese. Attorney General Griffin Bell, who formulated the plan, said today that he would proceed unless Congress balked. He also said that Congress should consider a broader admissions policy. The majority of the new refugees would be "boat people" such as the 2,500 aboard the Hai Hong, who were accepted on November 17 after Malaysia had denied them permission to land.

Kennedy and King conspiracy victims?

Washington, D.C., Dec. 30

President John F. Kennedy and the civil rights leader, the Rev. Dr. Martin Luther King Jr., were not killed by gunmen working alone, contrary to previous evidence, the House Select Committee on Assassinations asserted today. Based on reports from acoustical experts, the committee believes President Kennedy was shot at from a grassy knoll in Dealey Plaza as well as from the Texas School Book Depository in 1963. The committee said there was a "likelihood" that Dr. King's convicted killer, James Earl Ray, worked with his two brothers or for a businessman who offered $50,000 for King's death.

Dallas all the rage

Dallas, Texas

CBS has brought soap opera to prime time in the form of *Dallas*, a series about the complicated lives of a wealthy Texas oil family, the Ewings. Head of the family is J.R., a crooked-wheeling and dirty-dealing villainous hero, who gets what he wants any way he can. The part is played by Larry Hagman, himself born in Texas. While the series *Dallas* is growing in popularity, so is the real city. Attracted by seemingly unlimited job and housing possibilities, more than 1,000 families move to Dallas each month.

Mikhail Baryshnikov, who defected from the U.S.S.R. in 1974, dances in the "Nutcracker Suite."

New York City, Jan. 15. *The Stories of John Cheever* earns Cheever both National Book Critics Circle Award and Pulitzer Prize.

Miami, Jan. 21. Pittsburgh Steelers defeat Dallas Cowboys, 35-31, in Super Bowl XIII.

Texas, January. William P. Clements is first Republican elected Governor of Texas since Reconstruction.

New York City, Feb. 9. Nelson Rockefeller's will leaves $13.5 million worth of art to Museum of Modern Art and Metropolitan Museum of Art.

Washington, D.C., Apr. 6. Because of Pakistan's attempts to build a uranium-enrichment facility, all United States aid is terminated.

Seattle, Washington, June. Seattle Supersonics defeat Washington Bullets, four games to one, for N.B.A. title.

Washington, D.C., July 25. President Carter appoints Paul Volcker chairman of Federal Reserve Board.

Detroit, July 31. Chrysler Corporation reports second quarter losses of more than $207 million (→ Dec. 20).

Washington, D.C., Aug. 31. Government reveals that Soviet Union maintains combat-ready contingent of 2,000 to 3,000 troops on Cuba.

Washington, D.C., Oct. 17. Special prosecutor clears President Carter and brother Billy of wrongdoing related to business loans obtained through banker Bert Lance.

Baltimore, Oct. 17. Pittsburgh Pirates defeat Baltimore Orioles, four games to three, in World Series.

Cincinnati, Dec. 3. Eleven fans die of asphyxiation trying to get into rock concert by The Who.

Washington, D.C., Dec. 13. A suit brought by conservative congressmen to block termination of Taiwan treaty dismissed by Supreme Court.

United States. Ronald Reagan says, "For the average American, the message is clear. Liberalism is no longer the answer. It is the problem."

United States. Books published include, Tom Wolfe's *The Right Stuff* and Norman Mailer's *The Executioner's Song*.

Carter: Peace has come

A diplomatic miracle: Jimmy Carter links Egypt's Sadat and Israel's Begin.

Washington, D.C., March 26

Building on the success of last year's Camp David accords, which set the framework for a settlement in the Middle East, President Anwar el-Sadat of Egypt and Prime Minister Menachem Begin of Israel signed a peace treaty this evening in a ceremony held in a huge tent on the south lawn of the White House. Clasping hands with the two leaders, who shared the Nobel Peace Prize last December, a jubilant President Carter proclaimed, "Peace has come."

But, as the President was careful to point out, the treaty is only "a first step on a long and difficult road." No other Arab country, not even Jordan or Saudi Arabia, the two that are friendliest to the United States, has taken part in the settlement. The status of Jerusalem is vague and it will be many months before Israeli troops withdraw from the Sinai Peninsula. The future of the Israeli-occupied West Bank of the Jordan River is also unclear, and a likely source of future contention. And both leaders can expect to pay a heavy political price – Begin at the hands of right-wing Israelis who are reluctant to give up Sinai settlements, and Sadat at the hands of other Arab states, which are already treating him as a pariah and will almost certainly end their oil-financed subsidies.

President Carter comforts Joan Kennedy, Senator Edward Kennedy's wife, during dedication ceremony of the Kennedy Library in Cambridge, Mass.

46% in U.S. attend segregated schools

Washington, D.C., Feb. 13

A report from the Civil Rights Commission disclosed today that 46 percent of the nation's minority students still attend segregated schools. This is in spite of a national desegregation effort that began with the Supreme Court's 1954 ruling in Brown v. the Board of Education that "separate educational facilities are inherently unequal." The court followed this decision with a directive for school boards to integrate "with all deliberate speed." It has also been suggested that many schools in traditionally segregated areas have enacted only token desegregation to comply with the directives (→ Nov. 2, 1983).

Marking past victories and failures.

Divorce rate soars 69% over a decade

United States

Sociologists say clothes with designer labels, bumper stickers and T-shirts with slogans like "Kiss me, I don't smoke" express a wish for connection with other people. If there were ever a disconnected time, this is it. The divorce rate is up 69 percent since 1968. The average marriage lasts 6.6 years, and 40 percent of children born this decade will spend some of their youth in a one-parent home. Backgammon may be popular now, but it takes two to play; electronic games like Chess Challenger may have lasting appeal for our solitary society.

OPEC oil price up; U.S. to curb imports

Washington, D.C., July 15

Since the Organization of Petroleum Exporting Countries (OPEC) has set the average price of a barrel of oil at $23.50 – a rise of over $7 in the past three months alone – President Carter today announced an energy program that in 10 years would bring oil imports down to 1977 levels. Conservation and development of new energy sources, including nuclear power, are major features in the program, which would cost $140 billion. At last month's Tokyo "energy summit" meeting of the seven major industrialized democracies, the United States agreed to hold oil imports to 8.5 million barrels a day.

Silkwood avenged

Oklahoma City, May 18

A jury has awarded $10.5 million to the Karen Silkwood estate in a suit against the Kerr-McGee plutonium plant for negligence in radiation poisoning. Silkwood, an exemployee, was poisoned in 1974 by plutonium in her apartment. No one knows how it got there, and the damage it did fortified the judge's contention that the material was so inherently dangerous that Kerr-McGee could be liable. Silkwood was killed in a car crash before her case was decided and there have been rumors of foul play.

MX missile system to cost $30 billion

Washington, D.C., June 7

President Carter today announced plans to build the MX mobile intercontinental ballistic missile for $30 billion. The MX, which stands for "missile experimental," will entail the production of 200 vehicles, each weighing 120,000 pounds and carrying as many as 10 warheads. Each of the warheads has the explosive power of 335 kilotons, 22 times the power of the bomb dropped on Hiroshima. The MX will replace the Minuteman-3 missile currently deployed in underground silos in the Western part of the country.

Nuclear disaster at Three Mile Island

Harrisburg, Penn., March 31

A faulty cooling system at the Three Mile Island nuclear power plant has caused the worst nuclear accident in the history of the United States. Two days ago, a combination of human error and stuck valves allowed the fissioning core of the reactor, normally submerged in water, to become exposed to air. The highly radioactive fuel rods that make up the core began to melt, releasing radioactive gases. Although officials say that it is unlikely, the danger remains that a bubble of radioactive hydrogen within the containment vessel might explode, which would cause a greater release of radiation. It is also still possible that a complete meltdown might occur, allowing the entire molten contents of the core to be released into the environment. Only a small amount of radiation has actually escaped so far, federal officials say, but the inside of the reactor is highly contaminated and it is still considered too hot to approach.

Governor Richard Thornburgh of Pennsylvania has advised the

The cooling towers of the Three Mile Island nuclear power plant jut into the Pennsylvania sky. While the damage from this accident may well prove to be slight, it raises serious doubts about the feasibility of nuclear energy.

evacuation of children and pregnant women from within a five-mile radius of the damaged plant. A general evacuation, he has said, will not be necessary. President Carter, who holds an advanced degree in nuclear physics, has announced that he plans to make an inspection of the accident site.

Anti-nuclear protesters are planning to stage a demonstration tomorrow at the state capitol. The failure of the Three Mile Island reactor may serve to confirm what anti-nuclear protesters have been predicting for several years now. There have been protests to halt the construction of new atomic plants at several sites, including Seabrook, New Hampshire.

U.S. and Soviet agree on SALT II treaty to set missile limits

Washington, D.C., June 18

Right after signing SALT II, a new agreement with Soviet leader Leonid I. Brezhnev in Vienna to limit strategic arms, President Carter returned home to address a joint session of Congress today and to deliver a strong plea for treaty approval. The pact, the result of tough bargaining between Secretary of State Cyrus Vance and Soviet Foreign Minister Andrei Gromyko, limits each country to 2,250 missile launchers. No more than 1,320 of them may be equipped with multiple warheads (MIRV's), with further restrictions on bombers that can use long-range cruise missiles.

Prospects for Senate ratification are uncertain. Carter points out that with this treaty the Russians will have a third fewer missile launchers and bombers by 1985 than they would have had if they kept on building at the present rate. And he stresses that the treaty allows the United States to keep developing its MX missile.

Senator Henry Jackson and other hard-liners call the terms too favorable to Moscow and say the deal smacks of "appeasement." But liberals like Senators William Proxmire and George McGovern say the pact does not do enough to limit nuclear arsenals (→ Dec. 8, 1987).

President Carter and Leonid Brezhnev agree to a problematic arms treaty.

Carter says a crisis of confidence threatens America's future

The President senses a "crisis of confidence" and appeals to self-reliance.

Washington, D.C., July 15

President Carter said today that the United States faces a "crisis of confidence" at least as serious as the energy crisis, and called for measures to stem both problems. In a nationally televised speech, Carter outlined a six-point program of energy initiatives that he said would save 4.5 million barrels of oil a day by 1990.

During his 33-minute address, Carter said the nation has spiraled downward into self-doubt since the assassination of President Jonn F. Kennedy, the Vietnam War years, the Watergate scandal and the current inflation and energy crises. He called for Americans to recapture their old spirit of self-reliance.

Carter's energy plan would limit oil imports, require utilities to cut their oil use, allow the President to ration gasoline and establish or strengthen government boards that regulate energy consumption.

House Speaker Thomas "Tip" O'Neill Jr. described the speech as "one of the strongest and best the President has made." But some Republican leaders expressed the view that it showed an indecisive President. John B. Connally, a Republican presidential hopeful, said, "The crisis of confidence is one of the President's own making." And George Bush, the former Director of Central Intelligence, said that the speech raised questions about "how much follow-through, courage and leadership the President will have in his own country."

Inflation soaring; interest rates fluctuate

Washington, D.C., Oct. 10

With the consumer price index up by 13.3 percent, the largest rise in 33 years, the balloon of inflation continues to expand. Countermeasures by Federal Reserve Chairman Paul Volcker created fears among the nation's money managers when he announced that the Fed would curb the money supply. This is a significant departure from past practice, though the result is the same. When money is made scarce, interest rates are driven up. But with no benchmark to go by, rates fluctuated wildly. Said one trader, "They're going up and down like a roller coaster." In one day alone the federal funds rate rose to 15 percent, then dropped to 7 percent. Bonds plummeted by record amounts as investors sought better long-term returns.

Wall Street reacted like a yo-yo. After setting a year high of 897.61 the day before Volcker's move, the Dow Jones fell 40 points in the next two days. Heavy trading included today's volume of 81.6 million, the largest in history. Many investors, caught in a "margin squeeze," sold at a loss. But the dollar seemed to gain strength – one of Volcker's aims (→ Apr. 16, 1980).

Young sees P.L.O., is out of U.N. job

New York City, Aug. 15

Andrew Young, the first black American delegate to the United Nations, has resigned over his controversial talk with the Palestine Liberation Organization's U.N. observer. He said the meeting was unplanned, but he was chided by Secretary of State Cyrus Vance for breaching American policy, which bars such contacts. Young favors recognition of the P.L.O., a stance the Israelis oppose. He said the Israeli government decided to make the meeting a public issue.

Congress bails out struggling Chrysler

Washington, D.C., Dec. 20

Is the bastion of capitalism adopting socialism for corporations? In the biggest bailout ever by the United States government, Congress has approved a $1.5 billion loan to the ailing Chrysler Corporation. The firm gets the matching-type loan if it can raise $5 billion privately. Part of the loan deal would be a three-year wage freeze for the unionized workers. All this has led Senator William Proxmire of Wisconsin to ask, "Are we going to guarantee businessmen against their own incompetence?" But as some people in industry say, as Detroit goes, so goes the nation. Or does it? (→ May 13, 1980).

Four are shot dead opposing the Klan

Greensboro, N.C., Nov. 3

Four demonstrators opposing the Ku Klux Klan were killed today when Klan sympathizers opened fire on them with automatic weapons and shotguns. The four, and a fifth person who was wounded, were members of the Communist Workers Party, conducting a "Death to the Klan" march. The assailants tried to flee in two vehicles but were seized near the scene by the police. All 12 were charged with murder and conspiracy to commit murder (→ Nov. 17, 1980).

Righteous indignation: Women protest over pornography. During the past decade the proliferation of sexually explicit material has shocked many.

Beirut, October 4. *Civil rights leader Jesse Jackson turns to world affairs as he meets with the P.L.O.'s Yasir Arafat to talk about the Mideast.*

Ailing U.S. Steel shuts 10 factories

Pittsburgh, Penn., Nov. 27

Citing unfairly priced imports and excessive environmental spending, U.S. Steel is closing 10 plants, shutting parts of six others and laying off 13,000 workers. It will also trim its product line and raise its prices. The nation's biggest steel producer blames the government for its predicament, particularly the $1.8 billion it must put out by 1983 to comply with clean-air standards. Analysts reply that the company deliberately delayed meeting the requirements. They also claim that the steel industry, but especially U.S. Steel, has been slow to modernize and thus to respond to foreign competition (→ July 1986).

99% now own TV, but 41% like it less

Washington, D.C., March 1

More Americans have TV sets than ever before, but is television any better? In a *Washington Post* poll today, 99 percent said they owned a set. But only 17 percent said the shows were better now than five years ago, and 41 percent said they were worse. The *Post* found TV watching has declined, with 54 percent watching less than they did five years ago. More than a third said they would pay a small fee to get rid of commercials, which they found too long, loud and untrue.

Haves to have-nots

Washington, D.C., Dec. 31

It isn't what it used to be, $1 million, so more people are making it. U.S. Trust reports that 520,000 Americans are millionaires, or one in every 424 of us. On the other side of that coin, the Commerce Department says that about 25 million people, 11.6 percent of the population, earned less in 1979 than the official poverty level of $7,412 (for a non-farm family of four). The 1979 median family income, $19,684, was up 11.6% from a year ago but inflation took all but three-tenths of 1 percent of it. The 1979 median incomes: white families, $20,520; Hispanic, $14,320; black, $11,651.

Iranian militants seize U.S. Embassy

Angry Iranian students burn the American flag and shout "Death to America!"

Some of the hostages seized by Iranian militants who raided the U.S. Embassy.

Teheran, Iran, Nov. 20

A mob of 500 Iranian students seized the United States Embassy here on November 4, taking 90 hostages. The takeover has turned into a diplomatic nightmare and the situation continues to deteriorate as President Carter begins to hit back. Carter's latest actions have been to freeze all of the considerable Iranian assets in the United States and to send a naval task force to the Indian Ocean, where carrier-based jets and helicopters would be within easy striking range of Iran.

Meanwhile, American television audiences have been shocked to see blindfolded members of the United States Marines embassy guard, with their hands tied behind their backs, as they were paraded before TV cameras while students chanted "Death to America, Death to Carter, Death to the Shah." Effigies of Uncle Sam and Carter were burned and scores of American flags were spat upon, trampled and burned in the street.

The United States immediately sent mediators to Iran to seek the release of the hostages, but they have met with little success. The students, who have the support of Ayatollah Khomeini's government, continue to take a hard line even though a trickle of hostages, mainly women and blacks, have gained their freedom. There are still 52 Americans in captivity.

The deposed Shah is hospitalized in the United States. His arrival set off the embassy attack and the students are demanding his return to Iran (→ Apr. 25, 1980).

End of a decade in Hollywood: Down memory lane at the movies

Hollywood, California

Kramer vs. Kramer was the big winner at this year's Academy Awards. Dustin Hoffman took the prize as best actor while Sally Field won for *Norma Rae*. Among other films audiences have applauded lately are *All That Jazz*; Woody Allen's *Manhattan*; *Star Trek - the Motion Picture*; *Being There* with Peter Sellers; *Apocalypse Now,* and *The China Syndrome*. The 70s offered a wide variety of films, starting in 1970 with George C. Scott as *Patton* and James Earl Jones as the

first black heavyweight champion in *The Great White Hope. Love Story* sold a lot of handkerchiefs. In 1971, *Carnal Knowledge* and *Klute* won respect for Ann-Margret and Jane Fonda, respectively. William Friedkin's *The French Connection* and Stanley Kubrick's *Clockwork Orange* were stand-outs. In 1972, Diana Ross played Billie Holiday in *Lady Sings the Blues* and Liza Minnelli dazzled us in *Cabaret*. Marlon Brando was a double sensation in Bertolucci's *Last Tango in Paris* and *The Godfather*. In 1973 Jack

Lemmon in *Save the Tiger* and Tatum O'Neal in *Paper Moon* were noteworthy, as were *The Sting* and *The Exorcist*. With 1974 came *Chinatown* and in 1975 everyone was talking about *One Flew Over the Cuckoo's Nest* and Steven Spielberg-directed *Jaws*. The bicentennial year sent conflicting signals with *All the President's Men, Bound for Glory, Network, Rocky* and *Taxi Driver*. In 1977, there were *The Turning Point* and *Julia*. And last year Bette Midler acted her heart out in *The Rose*.

Carter bans grain sales to Soviet Union after Afghan invasion

Washington, D.C., Jan. 4

President Carter intends to back up his tough talk concerning the recent Soviet invasion of Afghanistan. He has halted delivery of 17 million metric tons of grain that had been earmarked by the Russians for their livestock herds. The eight million tons that were ordered in 1976, however, will be delivered.

In a television address to the nation, Carter described the Soviet invasion as "an extremely serious threat to peace" and added that an Afghanistan ruled by Moscow is a threat to both Iran and Pakistan. In addition to the grain embargo, Carter intends to suspend sales of high technology, such as advanced computers and oil drilling equipment, until further notice. Soviet fishing in American waters will be curtailed, leading to the loss of 350,000 tons of fish this year. And all new cultural and economic exchanges have been canceled. The President is also considering pulling the United States out of the

Afghani students demonstrate against the December 1979 Soviet invasion of their nation. They attacked the Soviet Embassy and lowered the Soviet flag.

Olympics Games that are to be held in Moscow this summer.

To prevent losses to farmers, the government plans to buy the grain intended for the Soviet Union at current market prices and store it.

The Russians have responded by calling Carter "wicked and malicious." They claim their action in Afghanistan is not an invasion but a move to support a legitimate government in Kabul (→ Apr. 24, 1981).

Windfall oil tax

Washington, D.C., Apr. 2

Thanks to the decontrol of oil prices, American oil tycoons stand to earn an extra $1 trillion by 1990. But because of the Windfall Profit Tax Act signed today by President Carter, $227 billion of it will go to the Internal Revenue Service. Real profits should be about $221 billion, which the tax does not cover. It's after the new, higher profits.

Silver market crash corners the Hunts

New York City, March 27

A $5-per-ounce plunge in the price of silver today to $10.80 may wipe out the Texas billionaire brothers Nelson and Bunker Hunt. Their activity last year drove the price up from $6 to its January peak of over $50. But when they began to issue silver bonds, their evident need for cash steadily drove the market down for a record 15 consecutive days, wreaking havoc on Wall Street. As a result, the Hunts have been left holding the silver-lined bag.

U.S. captures hockey title at Olympics

Lake Placid, N.Y., Feb. 2

An American team made up of itinerant players and a few collegians accomplished the seemingly impossible feat of winning the hockey gold medal at the Olympic Games today. The United States six scored a 4-2 victory over Finland, and earlier had upset the mighty Soviet team. The dramatic finish set off a joyous demonstration here

that reverberated across the United States. The result of the game was announced at a matinee in New York's Radio City Music Hall, and the audience cheered, then sang the *Star-Spangled Banner*. The result of the Olympic series was a vindication of what is known as American hockey, in which players utilize more of the ice for passing and use harder body checks.

Going for gold! The U.S. hockey team won the Olympics as America cheered.

Carter admits U.S. is hit by recession

Washington, D.C., Apr. 16

With unemployment up and personal bankruptcies the highest in five years, President Carter today conceded what everyone else is saying. The economy, he observed, "has slowed down and probably entered a recession." He said it will be "mild and short" but that the arch-enemy, inflation, would rise for several more months. Most economic indicators are bad. February-March production was down and housing starts fell 21.8 percent to their lowest rate since 1975. The Federal Reserve has increased farm loans and Carter said he favored a congressional expansion of federally backed mortgages (→ Dec. 19).

Disaster in Iran's desert

The rescue attempt was a complete fiasco, as this helicopter wreckage shows.

Labor leader to sit on Chrysler board

Rockford, Illinois, May 13

Trying to insure labor support for its recovery program, the beleaguered Chrysler management has placed United Auto Workers president Douglas Fraser on its board of directors. Fraser, who used to work on a Chrysler assembly line, is the first union leader ever elected to the board of an American company. Nearly 500,000 shares were voted against him. Several stockholders took the floor to argue that a labor spokesman would not pursue the interests of the firm. But Chrysler president Lee A. Iacocca, unwilling to jeopardize a $1.5 billion government loan approved last week, gave Fraser his support (→ Feb. 27, 1981).

Computer's alarm almost starts war

Washington, D.C., June 6

A false alarm reporting a Soviet missile attack put American nuclear strike forces on alert today, defense officials say. They attribute the mistake to a malfunction of a computer at North American Defense Command headquarters in Cheyenne Mountain, Colorado. It took only three minutes to discover the mistake, but the alert, which resulted in 100 bomber crews armed with nuclear weapons starting their engines, lasted 20 minutes. It is the second such alarm in three days. The cause is being investigated.

Washington, D.C., Apr. 25

A United States military expedition to free the hostages held by Iran met with disaster today after a helicopter collided with a transport plane at a staging area in the Iranian desert. Eight Americans were killed and several more were injured in the fiasco. After an early morning report at the White House on the failed mission, a stony-faced and haggard President Carter appeared on national television to tell the nation what happened. He gave few details, but said he had "ordered the cancellation of an operation in Iran that was under way to prepare for a rescue of our hostages. The mission was terminated because of equipment failure. During the subsequent withdrawal,

there was a collision between aircraft on the ground at a remote desert location."

None of the casualties resulted from military action. The President said that the mission was not motivated by hostility toward Iran or the Iranian people and that there were no Iranian casualties. The operation involved helicopters, C-130 Hercules transport planes and 100 men and it took place 200 miles southeast of Teheran.

The Iranians celebrated the failure of the rescue mission at a rally that was staged in front of the occupied American Embassy, and a broadcast from Teheran announced that the Iranians "had inflicted defeat and flight upon Americans and their mercenaries" (→ Jan. 21, 1981).

Patents permitted on living organisms

Washington, D.C., June 16

Living organisms can be patented, the Supreme Court ruled today in a case that takes on added significance in the era of genetic engineering. In the case of Diamond v. Chakrabarty, the court ruled in favor of General Electric, which filed for a patent on an oil-eating bacteria created by research scientist Ananda Chakrabarty. Scores of patent applications for organisms produced by genetic engineering already have been filed, and the court's decision will give a major boost to the fledgling biotechnology industry.

Mt. St. Helens blast shocks Northwest

Mount St. Helens, Wash., May 18

In one of the most spectacular displays Mother Nature has offered the Northwest this century, Mount St. Helens erupted at 8:32 a.m. today. With a rumble that registered 4.1 on the Richter scale, the volcano hurled almost a cubic mile of earth and ash into the atmosphere. Destruction is widespread, with hundreds of square miles of trees flattened by the blast and Spirit Lake clogged with ash. Naturalists say it will take a decade for the Washington area to recover.

Jimmy Carter, a peanut farmer, with brother, Billy, and Ronald Reagan, chopper of wood. Reagan's ideological outlook has turned the presidential race into more than just a referendum on the Carter administration.

18 people are dead in Miami race riots

Miami, Florida, May 19

National Guardsmen armed with shotguns are patrolling Miami's streets today after rioting that has cost 18 lives and more than $100 million in damage. Officials say it is the worst race riot since the Newark and Detroit outbreaks of 1967. Crowds of enraged blacks surged into the streets Saturday night after a white jury in Tampa acquitted four white policemen in the death of a black businessman. The policemen were accused of having beaten the man to death.

U.S. 226 million: Latins, Asians, Bosnians, Acadians and Manx

Washington, D.C.

There are 226,504,825 people in the United States, according to the latest census. A majority of Americans come from somewhere else, and more keep coming. While Los Angeles is acknowledged as a melting pot – it has become the first city in the nation where the bulk of the population is made up of Latin Americans and Asians – the rest of the country is also an exotic mixture with some 70,000 Albanians, 820,000 Acadians (bringing Mardi Gras to New Orleans), 80,000-plus Amish, up to 100,000 Basques, 600,000 Carpatho-Rusyns, about 750,000 Croatians, four million Dutch or people of Dutch descent, 2,500 Afghans, 1,100 Georgians, 435,000 Greeks, 21,000 Icelanders, 10,000 Indonesians, more than a million Lithuanians, up to 30,000 Macedonians, 50,000 Manx (from the Isle of Man), over five million Poles and their descendants, up to 30,000 Serbs, 30,000 South Africans, 20,000 Thais, over 487,000 Ukrainians, 3,500 Bangladeshi, 300,000 Dominicans and so on. About 500 Burmese arrive annually, as do 2,000 Armenians. In Detroit live 70,000 Arabs. Boston was and remains the center for Albanian Americans. Most Cossack (Ukrainian) groups are based in New Jersey. Chicago is the center for Bosnian Muslims. Miami has the largest concentration of Cubans and is officially a bilingual city.

Hispanic residents in Miami take the oath of citizenship at a naturalization ceremony. Despite its problems, America remains a beacon of hope and light.

Bulgarian periodicals have a circulation of 7,000. More than a million people have migrated from Central and South America since 1820. And since then, over 500,000 West Indians, descendants of slaves, have arrived. There are presently six Hindu temples serving Indians in New York City. Over 1.5 million Scots, 740,000 French and five million Italians have immigrated to the United States. In Hawaii, Chinese make up 7 percent of the population (the biggest concentration of Chinese in America) and have an average income 40 percnt higher than Chinese on the American mainland.

After Gamal Abdel Nasser took power in Egypt and turned his land toward Islam, many Coptic Christians migrated; up to 85,000 have come to America since 1966. Since the founding of Israel, over 300,000 Jews have arrived; about half settled in New York. The three cities with the largest Greek populations are New York, Chicago and Washington, D.C. In North Dakota and Montana live about 6,000 Hutterites, teaching their children German and practicing Christian communal living. The number of illegal aliens in America is estimated at 3.5 million to 6 million (about half from Mexico) (→June 22, 1981).

Games in U.S.S.R.; U.S. leads boycott

Moscow, August

The United States and 50 other nations were missing from the competition, but the Soviet Union held the Summer Olympics as scheduled and they turned out to be quite successful. A total of 36 world records were set despite the absence of talented athletes from countries that joined in the boycott to protest the Soviet invasion of Afghanistan. However, the security was so strict that the athletes had to forgo the traditional victory laps. The Soviets accounted for 80 gold medals, but such athletes as eight-medal winner Aleksandr Dityatin might not have done nearly so well against the world's best.

Cuban boatlift ends

Miami, Florida, Sept. 26

Fidel Castro abruptly ended a sealift that poured 125,000 Cuban refugees into the United States. On Friday, Cuban soldiers forced more than 100 boats from the United States out of Mariel harbor without passengers. Castro offered no explanation for closing the open door he gave some Cubans five months ago. Miami Mayor Maurice Ferre said Castro opened prison doors to some of Cuba's worst criminals. "He flushed his toilets," said Ferre (→Apr. 19, 1982).

Larry Holmes foils comeback bid by Ali

Lost the fight, but still the greatest.

Las Vegas, Nevada, Oct. 2

It's all over for Muhammad Ali. The former heavyweight champion, in his effort to win the title for a fourth time, ended his career at the age of 38 tonight, sitting weary and beaten on a stool, unable to come out for the 11th round of what was to have been a 15-round fight. He was no match for his former sparring partner, Larry Holmes, the 30-year-old undefeated champion. It was Ali's manager, Herbert Muhammad, who put an end to the one-sided contest in which the former Cassius Clay could land no more than 10 blows in 10 rounds. Many in the crowd wept at the defeat of one of boxing's greatest champions.

Falwell: "Get in step" with conservatism

Trenton, N.J., Nov. 10

The Rev. Jerry Falwell held a revival meeting on the steps of the New Jersey State House today. Or was it a political rally? Falwell, who reaches an audience of 18 million with his television ministry, founded the Moral Majority two years ago to spread the church's conservative agenda. This year, the group spent $3 million opposing liberal Senate candidates. Today, he told liberals to "get in step with conservative values or be prepared to be unemployed." Falwell's group supports family values and a strong defense and opposes abortion, pornography and homosexuality. "God created Adam and Eve," says Falwell, "not Adam and Steve."

Crossing the line between church and state? Jerry Falwell wants to restore morality through political channels.

NATO warns Russia on role in Poland

Brussels, Belgium, Dec. 12

Nine days after President Carter warned that Soviet military intervention in Poland would have "most negative consequences," the ministers of the NATO countries, prodded by Secretary of State Edmund Muskie, have issued a statement that intervention would mean the end of detente and would "fundamentally alter the entire international situation." Strikes and political unrest are in their sixth month in Poland. Despite reassurances by First Secretary Stanislaw Kania that his country's commitment to the Warsaw Pact remains firm, the Kremlin leaders are concentrating troops on the Polish border.

Reagan in a landslide

He's proud to be an American. Ronald Reagan pledges to revive national spirit.

Washington, D.C., Nov. 4

Ronald Wilson Reagan, a former movie star and television personality, was elected President today, toppling Jimmy Carter, the Democratic incumbent. At age 69, the one-time California Governor is the oldest man ever elected to the nation's highest office.

Returns showed a surprisingly strong Reagan victory, sweeping the East, Middle West and even what had been President Carter's stronghold in the South just four years earlier. Reagan received 489 electoral votes, almost twice the 270 needed to win, while Carter took just 49. George H.W. Bush was elected Vice President.

The outgoing President is the first elected incumbent to lose since Franklin D. Roosevelt ousted Herbert Hoover in 1932 early in the Depression. Gerald R. Ford, an incumbent, was defeated four years ago by Carter. But Ford was never elected to the office. He was serving the unexpired term of Richard M. Nixon, who resigned under threat of impeachment.

Prime rate zooms to 21.5 percent

New York City, Dec. 19

As of yet, no bright rays have dispelled the fog of recession. On the contrary, the nation's prime lending rate - the minimum charge on corporate loans – has just hit 21.5 percent after rising over 4 percentage points in the past month. This is the highest since April, when it began to fall. The Federal Reserve has also raised the discount rate. Banks link the rate rise to an increased demand from corporations. They say that they have also been hit by a rise in the federal funds rate to nearly 19 percent. This is the amount those in the financial circle charge one another for an overnight "quick-fix."

Who shot J.R.?

Hollywood, Calif., Nov. 21

Last season's final episode of the television series *Dallas* left J.R. Ewing shot by an unidentified assailant. Tonight, in the first episode of the fall season and after five months of ballyhoo and speculation, it was revealed that Kristin Shephard, played by Mary Crosby, did it. The show had the highest ratings ever for a regular television series: 88.6 million viewers.

Record loss for Ford

Detroit, Mich., Dec. 31

Chrysler isn't the only auto company running on empty. Ford has suffered a third-quarter loss of $595 million, a record for American corporations. Ford's 1981 deficit could thus hit $1.5 billion. Factors cited are the recession, high interest rates and Japanese competition. Rumors are spreading of G.M. rebates next year similar to those now offered by Chrysler.

All-white jury clears Klansmen of murder

Fanning the flames of hatred. It is not so prominent today, but the Ku Klux Klan is still an insidious force.

Greensboro, N.C., Nov. 17

Six supporters of the Ku Klux Klan were acquitted today of murder charges by an all-white jury in the 1979 killings of five anti-Klan demonstrators in Greensboro. After a week of deliberations, some jurors said they believed the defendants acted in self-defense. The charges stemmed from a November 3, 1979, "Death to the Klan" march by the Communist Workers Party in this textile city. Four marchers were killed when two carloads of white men opened fire on them and a fifth died later of wounds from the shooting. Five other men are also facing murder charges, but have yet to be tried. Signe Waller, the widow of one of the slain marchers, said, "I was so outraged I could hardly talk," after hearing the verdict.

Imagine . . . music without John Lennon

New York City, Dec. 8

John Lennon, musical icon and passionate spokesman for pacifism, died a victim of violence today. The former Beatle was returning home after a night of recording with wife, Yoko Ono, when a man stepped out of the shadows and fired four bullets into his back. When police arrived, they found an unemployed amateur guitarist named David Chapman thumbing through J.D. Salinger's *Catcher in the Rye* as he awaited arrest. Until today, Lennon was enjoying an emotional comeback after several years of seclusion. He was, as the title of his new single proclaims, *Starting Over*. By midnight, hundreds of mourners had gathered by candlelight outside the Dakota apartments where he lived, singing, "All you need is love. Love is all you need."

"Some say I'm a dreamer," John Lennon sang plaintively. Now, for the ex-Beatle, "the dream is over."

Hostages freed as Reagan takes over

Washington, D.C., Jan. 21

A few minutes after Ronald Reagan was sworn in yesterday as 40th President of the United States, the 52 American hostages in Iran were boarding a plane in Teheran, bound for West Germany and freedom after 444 days of captivity. Former President Carter had hoped the Iranian affair would end on his watch, but it was not to be.

Reagan made no mention of the hostages in his brief inauguration speech. He urged the nation to "begin an era of national renewal" and said that our new priority is to curb government. "Government is not the solution to our problem, government is the problem," the new President said. His first official act will be to freeze federal hiring. After his speech, the President, wearing a charcoal-gray suit, accompanied First Lady Nancy Reagan, wearing a bright red coat, down Pennsylvania Avenue in an open limousine while they waved to enthusiastic crowds lining the way.

The hostages could have been freed earlier, but there was a last minute snag. The Iranians challenged the appendix to the formal financial agreement that allowed the return of $8 billion in Iranian assets that had been frozen by the U.S. government after the takeover of the American Embassy by militant Iranian students on November 4, 1977. Executive State Minister Behzad Nabavi, Iran's chief negotiator, said the appendix was a surprise and that, upon examination,

Ronald Reagan talks of a nation reborn, one rededicated to preserving liberty.

he discovered that the change of one word meant a potential loss of $900 million to Iran. The dispute was settled, however, by Deputy Secretary of State Warren Christopher and Algerian intermediaries. As soon as the hostages were released, President Reagan disclosed that "some 30 minutes ago the Algerian planes bearing our prisoners left Iranian air space and they are now free of Iran."

Former President Jimmy Carter flew to Wiesbaden, West Germany, to greet the hostages on behalf of President Reagan.

Following an hour-long meeting with the hostages at the United States Air Force Hospital, Carter charged that many of the hostages had been mistreated by their Iran-

ian captors. "Our Americans were mistreated much worse than was previously believed," he said. "The acts of barbarism which were perpetrated on our people by Iran can never be condoned." According to former White House aides of Carter, the hostages had been subjected to "mock firing squads," to games of Russian roulette and to other forms of mental as well as physical torture. One marine sergeant, John McKeel Jr., told his mother that his captors had informed him that she was dead and that they would let him come home to attend her funeral if he told them what they wanted to know. Iran had denied that it was responsible for any abuse of the American captives (→ 27).

President welcomes the hostages home

Washington, D.C., Jan. 27

Two days after setting foot on American soil, the American hostages released by Iran were honored at a reception in the White House. President Reagan greeted the 52 Americans on the South Lawn of the White House after a motorcade through Washington where a crowd of 200,000 people cheered them. The reception was attended by hostages and their families, as well as the families of the eight soldiers who died in the aborted rescue attempt last April.

Welcome home. The Ayatollah drove a final stake into the Carter presidency.

President seeks cut in budget and taxes

Washington, D.C., Feb. 18

Warning that the United States is fast approaching "a day of reckoning," President Reagan today proposed a sweeping economic plan that would cut the budget as well as reduce certain taxes. His proposal, in a televised speech to Congress, calls for spending $695.5 billion in the coming fiscal year, $41.4 billion below the amount sought by former President Carter. The new plan would trim individual and business taxes by $53.9 billion. While raising military spending by $7.2 billion, it would slash such domestic programs as student loans, public service jobs, food stamps, welfare payments and free school lunches.

U.S. lends Chrysler $400 million more

Detroit, Mich., Feb. 27

In a deeper hole than previously estimated, Chrysler may yet roll again. The corporation will be given $400 million more by the Congressional Loan Board after having met several conditions. One is that its United Auto Workers employees approve a $644 million wage-benefit cut. Another concerns Canada, which will lend the company about $170 million. Chrysler is to repay it by investing some $850 million in Canada this year. Last year Chrysler broke an American corporation record by losing $1.71 billion.

North Dakota tops Kansas wheat total

Bismarck, North Dakota

Leadership in the nation's wheat production has unexpectedly shifted. Harvesting 338 million bushels this year, North Dakota passed Kansas as the leading producer. Frost kept Kansas from sharing in a national increase of 10 percent over last year's record-setting volume. But, in one of the economy's many ironies, healthy harvests can mean hard times. With the market glutted, grain prices are plummeting, and Washington has ordered a 15 percent cut in planting.

Reagan survives attack

President Reagan waves to the crowd moments before his assailant strikes.

Washington, D.C., March 30

President Reagan was shot and gravely wounded today as he was leaving the Washington Hilton Hotel after addressing a labor convention. Also wounded were his press secretary, James Brady, and two security officers.

The President was reported to be in "stable" condition tonight after two hours of surgery at George Washington University Hospital, just blocks from the White House. "The prognosis is excellent," Dr. Dennis S. O'Leary reported. "He is alert and should be able to make decisions by tomorrow."

Just minutes after the shooting, officers arrested John W. Hinckley Jr., 25, a resident of Colorado, and charged him with having attempted to assassinate the President. He is being held without bond.

When he arrived at the hospital, the 70-year-old President attempted to reassure his wife and friends that he was fine. "Honey," he told his wife, Nancy, "I forgot to duck." The President then winked at his chief of staff, James A. Baker 3rd. After that, he next turned to Edwin Meese 3rd, his chief White House counselor, and quipped: "Who's minding the store?" Later, in the operating room, the President remarked to his surgeons with a chuckle: "Please tell me you're Republicans."

Most seriously wounded in the shooting spree was Jim Brady, the press secretary, who suffered severe head wounds (→ June 21, 1982).

Security agents draw their guns as three others are wounded in the attack.

U.S. will act to cut influence of Soviets

Washington, D.C., March 22

In a reversal of the human rights policies of the Carter administration, Secretary of State Alexander M. Haig Jr. told Congress today that the major concern of the Reagan White House will be to contain and turn back Soviet influence in the developing world. "It does no good to pretend in our policies or our proclamations that (Soviet activity) is not the most serious threat to world peace we're facing today," Secretary Haig said this week in his public testimony on Capitol Hill. He said such Carter era concerns as human rights and South African apartheid would be subordinate to dealing with the Soviet Union.

El Salvador to get more U.S. support

Washington, D.C., March 2

The State Department today announced plans to expand military assistance to El Salvador, and White House sources are saying that the Reagan administration is considering even greater support for the Salvadoran economy. The military package will total $25 million and the economic aid will come to as much as $225 million. El Salvador's military has been severely criticized by human rights groups for alleged terrorism, including the murders of three Catholic nuns and a lay worker in December 1980.

Honolulu at the top of living-cost list

Honolulu, Hawaii

Fueled by a heavy influx of Japanese money and wealthy tourists, prices in Honolulu have risen to give the city the highest cost of living rate in the country. All over Hawaii, residents are organizing to oppose rampant development. Here, however, the tourist trade is too lucrative to resist, and hawkers abound, offering "freebies" as lead-ins to land and condominium sales pitches. "A $32.50 show for $10," says one. "Jim Nabors. He does a half-hour of Gomer Pyle."

First Columbia shuttle flight orbits Earth

Want a lift? The success of the shuttle marks a new era in space exploration.

Edwards AFB, Calif., Apr. 14

The Columbia, the world's first reusable spacecraft, has touched down gracefully in the California desert, completing the first flight of America's proposed fleet of space shuttles. Riding atop a spectacular plume of smoke and fire, the shuttle was piloted into orbit two days ago by astronauts John W. Young and Robert L. Crippen. The winged orbiter circled the Earth 36 times during a flight of 54 hours 22 minutes. The flight provided the opportunity to deploy a variety of scientific equipment, as well as to run general tests of all systems aboard the new spacecraft. The only potential trou-

ble spot came when the orbiter lost a few of the ceramic tiles from its heat shield, apparently during the launching. The damage was relatively minor and did not interfere with the flight schedule. Designing and constructing the ceramic tile shield was one of the greatest difficulties to be overcome in the production of the shuttle. National Aeronautics and Space Administration officials say that the Columbia could be ready for its next flight within six months. Three additional orbiters are being built to meet the space agency's rigorous schedule of one flight every two weeks (→ June 13, 1983).

Celebrating the triumph of liberty. Americans mark the 200th anniversary of the Battle of Yorktown with a re-enactment of the Revolutionary War's decisive military encounter. In October 1781, a French-American force of 17,000 cornered a smaller British force under General Cornwallis at Yorktown, Va., forcing their surrender and securing American independence.

Reagan fires striking air traffic workers

Washington, D.C., Aug. 12

The 15,000-member Professional Air Traffic Controllers Organization has challenged Ronald Reagan head on, and lost. Rejecting an annual raise of 11.4 percent, the union struck on August 2. In three days, the President had fired 2,000 of them for refusing to return to work. "Dammit," he exclaimed, "the law is the law, and the law says they cannot strike." Within a week, the union was fighting for its life, with fewer than 5,000 members left. Its president, Robert Poli, who had backed Reagan in the election campaign, blasted the administration's "scorched earth" policy; but a Gallup poll showed he had only 29 percent of the public behind him.

Of the other 71 percent, many were angry that safety worries had forced them to desert the airports. The Federal Aviation Administration got traffic back to 75 percent of normal using non-strikers and 500 military controllers. But, feeding the flames, Poli has announced that "chaos" prevails inside the control towers. Airlines put losses since the strike crisis at $35 million.

When the smoke clears, Reagan may be the big winner. With widespread public approval, he has projected a tough image both at home and overseas. In the words of one aide, "He wanted to jut his jaw out." Asked if he felt bad about firing so many workers, he replied, "You bet. But the law is the law."

Air traffic control union strikers challenged the new President, and lost.

President resumes Soviet grain sales

Washington, D.C., Apr. 24

President Reagan fulfilled his campaign pledge to resume grain sales to the Soviet Union today by lifting the embargo Jimmy Carter imposed after the Russian invasion of Afghanistan in 1979. This was the President's first major political decision since he was wounded on March 30. The embargo had denied 13 billion metric tons of grain as well as phosphate fertilizers, which were later included in the ban. Sales of soybeans, meat and other non-grain products will also resume, but restrictions on high-technology products and permission to fish in American waters are still in effect.

Williams conviction ends Abscam trials

Washington, D.C., May 1

Senator Harrison A. Williams has been convicted on nine charges related to the "Abscam" operation. He is the last of eight legislators to be sentenced. All were found guilty. "Abscam," short for "Arab Scam," began when F.B.I. agents posing as Arab sheiks offered several politicians bribes in exchange for political favors. Williams, a New Jersey Democrat, and seven men in the House of Representatives were named as having accepted bribes. Williams is the third American senator ever convicted on criminal charges while in office, and the first since 1905. He faces up to 18 years in prison and Senate expulsion.

Atlanta has suspect after 28 blacks die

Atlanta, Georgia, June 21

A 21-year old black photographer was charged today with the murder of one of 28 black children and young adults slain in Atlanta over the last two years. Wayne B. Williams was charged after tests linked fibers found on the victim with evidence taken from his home. He was implicated in the death of Nathaniel Cater, 27, whose body was found May 24 in the Chatahoochee River. Williams, who proclaims his innocence, is the first person officially accused in any of the killings of 23 children and five adults since they began in the city (→ Feb. 27, 1982).

Supreme Court gets first woman justice

Washington, D.C., Sept. 25

Chief Justice Warren Burger today swore in the 102nd Supreme Court justice, who is also the first woman on the court: Mrs. Sandra Day O'Connor. On July 7, President Reagan nominated her to fill the vacated seat of Associate Justice Potter Stewart, and confirmation was swift. Mrs. O'Connor, 51, has a firm Republican record, favoring the death penalty and urging balanced budgets. However, she has backed the right of women to choose abortions and supports most civil rights legislation. She, her lawyer husband and three adult sons live in Paradise Valley, Arizona.

President wants $180 billion for arms

Washington, D.C., Nov. 18

President Reagan has proposed a weapons package that will cost $180 billion over six years as a "strategic program which America can afford." The program calls for cancellation of the mobile basing system proposed by President Carter in favor of "super-hardened" silos for MX missiles. It also calls for 100 B-1 long-range bombers to replace the aging B-52's, a program that was cut by Carter, and the radar-evading "Stealth" bomber. At a time when many domestic programs have been cut, Reagan's plan actually costs less than many had expected. The response to his plan in Congress has generally been favorable.

Launching the buildup. Two unarmed Minuteman III's are tested.

9,700 become citizens in mass ceremony

Los Angeles, Calif., June 22

Memorial Stadium was a shrine of nationality today as 9,700 immigrants became citizens in the biggest naturalization ceremony the country has ever held. The mass swearing-in dramatizes a surge in immigration that brought 808,000 new arrivals in the last year. Most are from Asia and the Pacific. They represent the fastest growing ethnic group in the country, one that has swelled from 1.5 million to 3.5 million during the 1970's. Optimism dominated the ceremony. Said one Vietnamese, "It is great to be an American. There is so much opportunity here" (→ June 23, 1982).

Reagan responds to Libyan terror threat

Washington, D.C., Dec. 10

The White House acknowledged today having receiving detailed intelligence reports that a Libyan-trained terrorist squad has entered the United States with the intention of killing President Reagan and other officials. Reagan commented to reporters: "I think in view of the record you can't dismiss them out of hand. On the other hand, they're not going to change my life much." He declined to comment further on security moves. F.B.I. sources say that the reported assassination plan, which appeared in a *Newsweek* article this month, was exaggerated (→ Apr. 16, 1986).

I.B.M. personal computer promises to revolutionize the office

New York City, August

International Business Machines has introduced its long-awaited version of the personal computer, a move experts say will give new impetus to the revolution in office automation. A first evaluation is that I.B.M.'s P.C. is no great advance over presently available personal computers, but that its arrival is significant in several major ways.

For millions of people, the fact that I.B.M. has put its name on a personal computer means that the machine is more than a fad. Purchasing agents who have been reluctant to buy personal computers now can say they're going with a P.C. made by the company that dominates the industry. For I.B.M., introduction of the P.C. is a revolutionary move. The strength of the company has been in large mainframe computers, which offer centralized data processing. Personal computers, which make for office decentralization, could cut main-frame sales. But the P.C. success of firms such as Apple Computer could not be ignored.

One advantage of the I.B.M. computer is that it offers more memory than most personal computers. Other key factors include its choice of an operating system, the set of basic instructions that runs a computer. I.B.M.'s choice promises to become the standard in an unstandardized field. Small companies reportedly already are busily copying the P.C. of I.B.M.

Will it byte? Americans now face the task of learning to use the computer.

Immune deficiency disease identified

Washington, D.C.

A disease that has caused a number of deaths within the nation's homosexual community and among Haitian immigrants to the United States has been identified by doctors in America and in France. Called human lymphotropic virus-III (HLTV-III) at the National Cancer Institute, the ailment has been given the name AIDS, for Acquired Immune Deficiency Syndrome. It is spread by the exchange of bodily fluids through sexual contact, use of contaminated hypodermic needles or blood transfusions. The virus destroys T lymphocytes, white blood cells that help defend the body against disease. AIDS deaths usually occur from massive systemic infections or cancer. Known cases of the disease have been limited to homosexual men, but the potential for epidemics exists (→ Oct. 22, 1986).

New Reagan budget shows a huge deficit

Promises kept. President Reagan's call for cuts in social programs and a rise in funds for arms shows he meant what he said in the election campaign.

Washington, D.C., Feb. 6

President Reagan asked Congress today for an unprecedented shrinkage of domestic spending. However, even if such cuts were approved, the deficit would still stand at a startling $91.5 billion in the coming fiscal year.

"We are putting the false prosperity of overspending, easy credit, depreciating money and financial excess behind us," Reagan said in his budget message. "Our task is to persevere, to stay the course, to shun retreat, to weather the temporary dislocations and pressures that must inevitably accompany the restoration of national economic, fiscal and military health."

While proposing deep slashes in domestic spending, the President called for an expansion of the nation's military strength, despite the huge overall budget deficit. His proposal was greeted with deep skepticism in both political parties. The Democrats called it "unfair" and "unworkable," while several members of the President's own party expressed shock at the size of the deficit. The President attributed the size of the deficit to the heavy spending policies of earlier administrations (→ Dec. 10, 1985).

U.A.W. trades a cut in pay for security

Detroit, Mich., Feb. 28

For the first time in the history of the recession-torn auto industry, workers have taken wage and benefit cuts in exchange for job security. Ford chairman Philip Caldwell hailed the "cooperation and trust" displayed in negotiations, but fear played as large a role. Some 55,000 United Auto Workers were laid off at Ford, and in a month, General Motors closed seven plants. The new contract pledges Ford to share profits, support laid off workers with 15 years' seniority, and avoid closing their plants by shifting work to outside suppliers. In return, the union gives up regular pay raises and defers cost-of-living increases.

Allies in training. Washington is committed to keeping El Salvador out of the hands of Communists and believes that a competent military force is the way to do it.

Antitrust suit ends the Bell monopoly

Washington, D.C., Jan. 8

American Telephone & Telegraph has agreed to sell two-thirds of its assets, ending a seven-year antitrust suit that cost the communications monolith $360 million. A grim Charles Brown, the A.T.&T. chairman, said, "It's exactly what the government wanted." And Justice Department officials seemed to be pleased. But Ma Bell loses only its 22 local phone operations, the sluggish sector of its business. Left with long-distance service, Bell Laboratories research and Western Electric manufacturing, a lean A.T.&T. is now free to explore the new frontiers of the communications revolution.

TV ads deregulated

Washington, D.C., Nov. 23

Broadcasters and the Justice Department agreed today to end restraints on the length and frequency of television commercials, now at a maximum of eight and a half minute an hour. The Federal Communications Commission chief wants TV ads totally deregulated, making owners as free to operate as newspapers, with no limit on contents or amounts. Networks have their own ad guidelines and claim some are stiffer than the old code.

Getty is the envy of other museums

Malibu, Calif., November

While other museums struggle to mantain operations, the J. Paul Getty Museum is required by law to spend at least $51 million every year in order to maintain its status as a private foundation. Getty left virtually his entire estate, valued at $1.1 billion, to the art museum that he founded in 1953. Museum officials were surprised to learn that the money, amassed from the vast Getty oil operations, was bequeathed with no strings attached. The museum, which is now housed in a building copied after the Villa dei Papiri in ancient Herculaneum, has drawn up plans to expand into three facilities.

Anti-nuclear rally in N.Y. biggest ever

New York City, June 12

An army of 550,000 protesters, the biggest America has seen, flooded New York today to appeal to the United Nations Special Session on Disarmament. "One, two, three, four," they sang, "we don't want a nuclear war. Five, six, seven, eight, we don't want to radiate." Spurred to action by President Reagan's hard line, the peace drive is at its apex. But with wars raging in the Falklands and Lebanon, U.N. Secretary General Javier Perez de Cuellar said peace hopes "are further from our reach now than they were four years ago." Of protests, Reagan said American foreign policy will "not be set in the streets."

Hope for E.R.A. expires

Proponents of E.R.A. fell three states short in their campaign for change.

Smugglers of illegal aliens are indicted

Albuquerque, N.M., June 23

A federal judge today handed down indictments charging 38 people with smuggling some 24,000 illegal aliens a year into the United States. For 11 months, undercover immigration agents posing as drivers watched the ring from the inside. Their reports detail a huge business, grossing over $24 million annually. Clients were shipped out of six hotels in Mexico, mainly to Chicago, but also to sites in California, Michigan and New York. In a related Supreme Court ruling arrived at earlier this month, children of illegal aliens were given the right to tuition-free education in public schools (→Sept. 26, 1983).

Handguns banned by San Francisco

San Francisco, June 28

Legislation banning private possession of handguns was signed into law here today by Mayor Dianne Feinstein. She said it is the "first time a large city has spoken out and said we have had enough of the death, dismemberment and desecration of our society from the handgun." The statistics convinced her: In 1979, handguns killed eight people in Britain, 48 in Japan, 34 in Switzerland, 52 in Canada, 58 in Israel, 21 in Sweden, 42 in West Germany and 10,728 in the United States. The board of supervisors approved the ordinance 6 to 4.

Washington, D.C., June 30

Millions of women feel that "We the people" is an empty phrase because the Equal Rights Amendment failed to become a reality today. The amendment, which would have been the Constitution's 27th, fell three states short of ratification. Humorist Erma Bombeck once said of the proposed law that its words have never been so misunderstood since the four words "one size fits all." For Representative Martha Griffiths, who sponsored it, and the National Organization of Women that fought for it, the amendment would have prevented the denying or abridging of rights on account of sex; equal work would have received equal pay, and equal opportunity would have been guaranteed,

regardless of the whims of individual state legislatures.

For one homemaker, Phyllis Schlafly, who will be enjoying a victory ball tonight celebrating the triumph over the amendment, it would have meant that her daughters could be drafted in case of a war. Countless times she stressed that women already have special societal privileges and that equal rights would threaten them. Foes of Mrs. Schlafly see irony in the idea of a woman campaigning for an issue – in effect acting as politician, promoter and activist – with the goal of insisting that the only place she belongs is in the home.

Presbyterians unite

Hartford, Conn., June 29

The General Assembly of the United Presbyterian Church today voted to merge with the Presbyterian Church, U.S.A. The latter group approved the accord June 15. The merger, which heals a division caused by the Civil War, has been years in the making. If approved by the presbyteries, it will make the denomination the fourth largest in the country and leave the Southern Baptist and American Baptist Conventions as the only remaining denominational division from the Civil War period.

Knoxville plays host to World's Fair

Knoxville, Tenn., May 1

The 1982 World's Fair opened its gates today, beginning a scheduled 184-day run in which millions of visitors will see a complex of exhibitions geared to the energy crisis of the 1970s. Opening ceremonies were attended by President and Mrs. Reagan, scores of dignitaries and thousands of tourists. Nearly two million advance one-and two-day tickets have already been sold to the Southeast's first World's Fair ever. Although a few exhibitions were not entirely ready by today's deadline, all but one of them were open. Some critics say the fair's theme, "Energy Turns the World," is already outdated.

Survival of the fittest. Braniff, the nation's eighth largest airline, filed for bankruptcy May 13 as the industry restructures under deregulation.

World's Fair finally comes to Dixie ▷

U.S. poverty level highest since 1967

Washington, D.C., July 19

After 12 months of recession and 18 of the Reagan presidency, more Americans are poor than at any time in the last 15 years. A new Census Bureau report places the current poverty rate at 14 percent, up from 11.1 percent in 1973. Last year saw the annual incomes of 2.2 million people fall below the official poverty line, set at $9,287 for a family of four. Blacks, many of whom say they have suffered disproportionately under Reagan's budget cuts, sustained the largest income drop. Their poverty rate is 34.2 percent, compared to 26.2 percent for Hispanics and 11.1 percent for whites. Median family income fell 3.5 percent to $22,390 (→ Dec.).

USA Today in color

Virginia, Sept. 15

A new national newspaper published by the Gannett Company, USA Today, made its debut today. The full-color paper carries lots of national news, comprehensive sports, entertainment and business sections and eye-popping graphics. Gannett president Allen Neuharth hopes to appeal to a wide audience. "I think it will sell," he said. So do the firm's shareholders: A reported $30 million was invested just to get it off the ground.

Marines join multi-national force in Beirut

U.S. Marines try to bring peace to Lebanon, a troubled land in the Mideast.

Beirut, Lebanon, Sept. 19

Marines of the 32nd Amphibious Unit landed in Beirut on August 25, taking up positions in the port area recently abandoned by the French. President Reagan announced on August 20 that he was ordering 800 marines to Beirut as part of a multi-national group supervising the withdrawal of Palestinian and Syrian fighters from the beleaguered city. The deployment of marines is part of a plan negotiated by American envoy Philip Habib and accepted by the Lebanese, the Palestinians and the Israelis. Reagan said that the marines would stay in Lebanon no longer than 30 days and would perform "a carefully limited non-combat role." He said they would be withdrawn if any party in the dispute attempted to draw them into the fighting.

Removal of the Palestine Liberation Organization fighters was proceeding as the marines were landing. Almost 400 Palestinian guerrillas left by ship on August 21 for Cyprus and then were flown to Iraq and Jordan. The next day, King Hussein of Jordan greeted the soldiers and told them that they had "held the flag high and fought well for (their) rights" (→ Apr. 18, 1983).

Reagan gets $98 billion tax hike

Washington, D.C., Aug. 19

Responding to heavy lobbying by President Reagan, Congress has approved a bill to increase taxes and reduce spending in the coming fiscal year. Overall, the measure would increase taxes by $98.3 billion and cut federal outlays by $17.5 billion in order to trim the deficit during the current recession. Much of the tax increase would affect businesses by speeding the collection of corporate payments as well as by limiting tax breaks for some firms. A lesser amount of the increase would come from individual taxpayers, mainly by improving collections. The bill had strong support from House Speaker Thomas P. "Tip" O'Neill.

It's the Cats' meow

New York City, Oct. 7

Critics took like catnip tonight to the new British musical, *Cats*. The spectacle, based on T.S. Eliot's *Old Possum's Book of Practical Cats*, presents a fantasy world of larger-than-life felines in an equally large junkyard as they vie to get into Cat Heaven. Andrew Lloyd Webber's music is mostly clawless, but it purrs along nicely and the audience seems to find their never-never world a pleasant change – indeed the cat's pajamas.

Red and stunning. Bill Blass introduces his latest line of evening wear, reflecting America's return to style, elegance and formality.

Washington, D.C., October 13. *Preparing for America's future today. President Reagan is joined by job trainees as he signs the Job Training Partnership Act. Despite his professed distaste for government intervention, Reagan feels business and government can cooperate to promote growth.*

Singer Kate Smith receives the Medal of Freedom. Generations of Americans recall her thrilling version of "God Bless America."

Tylenol laced with cyanide kills seven

Chicago, Oct. 5

Seven people are dead in Chicago after using a Tylenol pain reliever in capsules laced with cyanide, and a man in California has been stricken after swallowing Tylenol capsules that had been contaminated with strychnine. Today, Johnson & Johnson, the manufacturer of the aspirin substitute, recalled all Extra Strength Tylenol. The contamination was apparently the result of deliberate tampering with the product, although the perpetrator has not been identified and the motive remains unclear. It is also not clear whether there is any connection between the incidents in Chicago and California. Federal authorities announced they are going to meet with the drug companies to work out new regulations that could protect the public against further tampering with over-the-counter products.

Recession takes over; industry grinds to lowest level in 34 years

Washington, D.C., December

As the economy sputters into its 18th month of recession, experts are still looking for signs of recovery. A third of the industrial capacity lies idle. Interest rates stay stubbornly high. The jobless rate hit 10.8 percent last month, putting more people on unemployment benefit lines than at any time since the Great Depression. In the view of Harvard economist Otto Eckstein, "The economy is probably in the worst shape that it has been in nearly half a century."

As in the 1930s, the condition extends worldwide. Western Europe suffers from 10.3-percent unemployment. And the nations of the third world languish under a $626 billion debt burden.

At home, record deficits seem to suffocate the recovery. Housing starts and car sales are up. Renegade members of the Organization of Petroleum Exporting Countries are cracking the production quotas

An idled oil rig symbolizes the recession that is gripping the nation. Jobless figures have soared, but the President says good economic times lie ahead.

to lower oil prices. And conservatives hope Reagan's 10 percent income tax cut and 7 percent rise in defense spending will generate both demand and supply. But with a deficit of $110.7 billion, neither tax cuts nor increased spending are likely to win long-term support.

EPCOT, world of tomorrow, opens today

Florida, Oct. 1

If you are about as old as former Mouseketeer Annette Funicello (40), the Experimental Prototype Community of Tomorrow may be just right for you. Walt Disney World's EPCOT, opening today, promises educational fun for adults. Covering 260 acres and entered through an 18-story geodesic dome called Spaceship Earth, it offers among its many exhibits Journey into Imagination, a Kodak-sponsored video and music festival, and the Universe of Energy, an Exxon-supported show that somehow makes sense of solar-heating displays and odiferous lava flows.

Barney Clark is first to get artificial heart

Salt Lake City, Utah, Dec. 22

His own defective heart replaced by a plastic and metal artificial one on December 2, retired dentist Barney Clark has recovered enough to take his first steps since the operation was performed. The 61-year-old patient was close to death from heart failure before the operation. The mechanical heart, named the Jarvik-7 after its inventor, Robert Jarvik, was placed in Clark's chest by a surgical team headed by Dr. William C. DeVries at the University of Utah Medical Center. The device has been implanted successfully in animals, but this is the first human application.

The Experimental Prototype Community of Tomorrow Center at Lake Buena Vista, Florida, is a companion park to nearby Disney World, in Orlando, opened in 1971. Disneyland amusement park in Anaheim, California, opened its gates in 1955. All three provide fun and education to all visitors.

Tribute to the fallen. Designed by Yale University architecture student Maya Yang Lin, the Vietnam Veterans Memorial in Washington was dedicated on November 13. The names of more than 58,000 dead inscribed in the black granite testify to the terrible cost of the war in Vietnam.

1983

Washington, D.C., Jan. 7. Reagan administration lifts arms embargo against Guatemala, citing significant human rights improvements.

Pasadena, Calif., Jan. 30. Washington Redskins beat Miami Dolphins, 27-17, in Super Bowl XVII.

Medina, N.D., Feb. 13. Gordon Kahl, extremist foe of federal income tax, and his son kill two U.S. marshals, who stopped them at roadblock.

New York City, Apr. 18. Alice Walker wins Pulitzer Prize and American Book Award for *The Color Purple.*

Montgomery, Ala., May 24. Jesse Jackson is first black man to address legislature here.

Philadelphia, May 31. The 76ers defeat L.A. Lakers, 115-108, for N.B.A. title.

Space, June 13. Pioneer 10 becomes first spacecraft to leave solar system; it has been aloft for 11 years (→ 18).

Washington, D.C., June 21. First giant panda offspring born in United States dies three hours after being delivered by Ling-Ling.

Cape Canaveral, Fla., Sept. 30. Shuttle Challenger, first spacecraft launched at night, carries into orbit first black astronaut, Guion Bluford (→ Feb. 7, 1984).

Hollywood, Fla., Oct. 5. Delegates to A.F.L.-C.I.O. convention endorse Walter Mondale as Democratic presidential nominee; first such labor endorsement of a candidate for presidential nomination (→ Nov. 3).

Philadelphia, Oct. 16. Baltimore Orioles defeat Philadelphia Phillies, four games to one, in World Series.

Beirut, Lebanon, Dec. 4. Eight American marines killed at airport by Syrian troops, as U.S. planes attack Syrian bases in Lebanon (→ Feb. 24, 1954).

United States. Estimated 4.1 million VCR's are sold in America this year.

United States. Automobile production up by 10.2%; personal income rises by 6.3%, and new home construction is up 60%.

Hollywood, Calif. Top films of year include *Terms of Endearment, Tender Mercies.*

First black elected Mayor of Chicago

Washington, breaking the barriers.

Chicago, Apr. 13

The first black man to be elected Mayor of Chicago, Harold Washington, won by a narrow margin in one of the fiercest races the city has known. Some 82 percent of Chicago's 1.6 million registered voters went to the polls, a record turnout for the city. Washington received 51 percent of the vote, and his white opponent, Bernard Epton, got 48 percent. Though most blacks voted for Washington, and most whites voted for Epton, as expected, there were more whites voting for Washington than there were blacks voting for Epton. Washington said, "We have kept faith."

Demonstrators against abortion march in Washington, D.C. No single issue since the Vietnam War has so divided Americans.

Reagan aims high with space shield idea

Washington, D.C., March 23

President Reagan has proposed construction of an anti-ballistic missile (ABM) system that would render nuclear missiles "impotent and obsolete" and that would hold out "the promise of changing the course of human history." Using charts and graphs to illustrate the growing Soviet effort to build a worldwide offensive military force, Reagan today urged American scientists to "turn their great talents" to developing a system that would destroy Soviet missiles before they reached their targets. He sees the project as a first step in an "intensive effort to define a long-term research and development program to begin to achieve our ultimate goal of eliminating the threat posed by stategic nuclear missiles."

If this program is approved, it would signal a fundamental shift in the nuclear strategy of the United States, which for 35 years has been based on massive retaliation to deter an attack. The new Reagan system would employ a wide range of sophisticated technology, including lasers, microwave devices, particle beams and projectile beams, and would be based both on land and in space.

Some critics have argued that the President's proposals would be in violation of the 1972 ABM treaty with the Soviet Union. But administration aides have denied this. Their position is that deployment of such a system was barred but not research and development of one.

Reagan declares Soviet "evil empire"

Orlando, Florida, March 8

Describing the Soviet Union as an "evil empire," President Reagan called upon a group of Protestant evangelicals to oppose a nuclear arms freeze and to return to a political philosophy based on "respect for the rule of law under God." The President described himself as being out of step with modern secular ideas that have discarded "the time-tested values upon which our very civilization is based." In addition, he told his audience it must not rest until abortion on demand has been outlawed.

Reagan also renewed his plea for a constitutional amendment that would permit prayer in public schools. He defended the administration's policy of notifying the parents when a clinic provides a birth control drug or devices to a minor. This so-called "squeal rule" has come under attack as violating a student's right to privacy. The President maintains that the parents' rights supersede those of "Washington-based bureaucrats and social engineers."

Jailing of Japanese held grave injustice

Washington, D.C., Feb. 24.

Citing "racial prejudice, war hysteria and failure of political leadership," a congressional committee today formally condemned the internment of Japanese-Americans during World War II. The report of the Commission on Wartime Relocation and Internment of Civilians described the relocation as "unique" and blamed President Roosevelt in particular. According to the report, Roosevelt agreed to release inmates only after the 1944 elections, thus avoiding any political backlash. The commission may recommend financial compensation for surviving victims.

American doctors call for boxing ban

Chicago, Jan. 13

The *American Medical Association Journal* has reported new evidence suggesting that chronic brain damage is prevalent among prizefighters. An editorial in the journal called for the banning of the sport. If the sport is to continue, the editorial went on, steps should be taken to improve monitoring a boxer's condition before, during and after a fight. In the study of 38 boxers that led the AMA to call for the ban, more than half showed some brain tissue loss or atrophy. A fighter in this condition is commonly referred to as being "punch drunk."

Beirut embassy bombed

Terrorists strike again. Americans and Lebanese search rubble for survivors.

Beirut, Lebanon, Apr. 18

The United States Embassy in Lebanon was demolished today by a car bomb containing 300 pounds of TNT and driven by a man who perished in the suicide attack. Dozens of people are feared dead and over 100 wounded. The exact number of casualties will not be known until rescue workers, digging round the clock, complete their grim task of pulling bodies out of the twisted ruins. The central part of the horseshoe-shaped building collapsed, leaving only shattered masonry, all that remained of offices and balconies. The dead and wounded are primarily American embassy staff,

marine guards and Lebanese clerical workers. Civilians who were at the embassy applying for visas were also among the casualties.

A group calling itself Islamic Jihad (Holy War) claimed responsibility for the blast, telephoning a news office immediately after the explosion. In a departure from usual practice, the Central Intelligence Agency acknowledged that its top Middle East analyst, Robert Clayton Ames, had been killed. Most of the C.I.A.'s Beirut staff was reportedly wiped out. Witnesses said they saw a large van force an entrance through the driveway of the embassy (→ Oct. 23).

Report on education: "A Nation at Risk"

Washington, D.C., Apr. 26

The country's educational standards, according to a bipartisan commission, "are ... being eroded by a rising tide of mediocrity that threatens our very future as a nation and as a people." The panel, formed two years ago by Education Secretary T.H. Bell, surveyed research, commissioned studies and held hearings across the country. Its report, *A Nation at Risk*, says that "if an unfriendly power had attempted to impose on America the mediocre educational performance that exists today, we might well have viewed it as an act of war."

The panel recommended a tightening of high school requirements and college admissions standards; extended school days and years; "far more homework"; higher pay for teachers, and "master teachers" to train new instructors.

The panel avoided controversy, but its report has become a political football. Carl Perkins, head of the House Education and Labor Committee, praised the call for more educational funding, but noted it followed "three years of administration efforts to cut back." President Reagan, however, lauded the "call for an end to federal intrusion" and vowed to continue working for "tuition tax credits ... voluntary school prayer and abolishing the Department of Education." One thing is sure: The findings will get a response from Washington. As the panel so ominously warned, "History is not kind to idlers."

Williamsburg is host to economic summit

Williamsburg, Va., May 30

The annual summit meeting of the seven industrialized nations came to a close today, leaving several divisive issues unresolved. The leaders of the United States, Canada, England, France, West Germany, Italy and Japan met in this uniquely American setting ostensibly to discuss the recent global recession and such specifics as the ballooning American budget deficit and how open the Japanese markets are or are not. Despite President Reagan's declaration that "recovery is what this summit is all about," America's allies came here principally hoping to gauge Reagan's anti-Soviet stance. The President's support for such controversial measures as East Bloc trade restrictions and the deployment of American missiles in Western Europe continues to strain the Western alliance. In a pre-summit concession, the administration agreed to resume talks on long-term grain sales to the Russians, but the move did little to turn the meeting into more than a telegenic success.

Sally rides shuttle, a woman in space

Cape Canaveral, Florida, June 18

Expressing regret that it has taken the United States so long, Dr. Sally Ride shot up into space on the shuttle Challenger today. She is the first American woman to do so. As the shuttle rose, watchers chanted, "Ride, Sally, ride." Dr. Ride, 32, is a woman for all seasons: a fine tennis and rugby player, a physicist and a Shakespeare scholar. In graduate studies at Stanford University, she studied the behavior of free electron lasers. Noted for her calm under pressure, she faces the task of using a robotic arm to maneuver an errant satellite into the shuttle's cargo bay (→ Sept. 30).

Ex-newscaster wins in sex bias case

Kansas City, Mo., Aug. 8

"Too old, unattractive and not deferential enough to men," 38-year-old Christine Craft was nevertheless smart enough to sue her employer, Metromedia, for unlawful demotion. A jury awarded her $500,000 in damages this afternoon. When hired as a co-anchor at KMBC-TV in 1981, she said she had no intention of being "made over" as a stereotypically fashionable anchorwoman. Eight months later she was demoted to reporter status. Television executives say the court ruling sets a bad precedent. It also happens to curb their authority (→ Jan. 13, 1984).

Marching in the heartland of America. Representatives from around the nation kick off National Gay and Lesbian Pride Week with a parade through Des Moines, Iowa. Always on the periphery of American society, many homosexuals say that only through activism can they win equal rights.

Bomb rips Marine compound in Beirut

As American marines search for bodies of their comrades in Beirut, at home officials are asking what went wrong with security and who was to blame.

Beirut, Lebanon, Oct. 23

Shortly after dawn today a TNT-laden truck was driven into the United States Marines' headquarters building and detonated. The resulting explosion killed more than 200 sleeping marines and completely destroyed the building. Two minutes later, a second truck blew up a French paratrooper barracks about two miles away, killing 47 French soldiers and wounding 15. The marine death toll exceeds the number of casualties in any single day of the Vietnam War.

Pentagon officials say that a big Mercedes truck filled with 2,500 pounds of TNT breached a barbed wire fence surrounding the marine compound, swerved between two sentry posts, crashed through a chain-link gate and drove into the lobby of the four-story cinder block building where it was detonated by the driver. A sentry reported that the driver was smiling as he entered the lobby. The force of the blast created a crater 30 feet deep and 40 feet wide and hurled bodies 50 feet into the air. Surviving marines and Lebanese firemen struggled to unearth the dead and injured from the enormous pile of rubble that had been the headquarters. They managed to extinguish a fire before it could reach a load of ammunition that had been stored in the basement.

President Reagan expressed outrage over the "vicious, cowardly and ruthless" attack and asserted that the United States was determined to remain in Lebanon. This blast, occurring six months after a car bomb attack on the American embassy in Beirut, has raised serious questions about marine security precautions (→ Dec. 4).

U.S. irate after Soviets down Korean airliner, killing 269

New York City, Sept. 1

The Soviet Union's destruction of a South Korean airliner flying from New York to Seoul has produced a cry of outrage from the international community. The Boeing 747 evidently strayed off course and was shot down by missiles from a Soviet fighter.

According to Korean Airlines, among the 269 passengers and crew who died were 81 South Koreans, 61 Americans, 28 Japanese, 16 Filipinos, 10 Canadians, six Thais and four Australians. One of the American passengers was Representative Larry P. McDonald, head of the ultraconservative John Birch Society.

There is much speculation as to why Flight 007 strayed off course and flew directly over the Kamchatka Peninsula and Sakhalin Island where strategic Soviet bases are situated. Navigational equipment had been installed after a 1978 incident in which a Soviet plane fired on a South Korean jetliner, killing two passengers and forcing it to land on a frozen lake near Murmansk. The Soviet news agency Tass said that an intruder plane, which did not respond to signals or warnings, had been shot down.

President Reagan condemned the downing of flight 007 as a "horrifying act of violence." Secretary of State George Shultz said, "The world is waiting for the Soviet Union to tell the truth." The plane was fitted with three separate navigational computers and it is considered extremely unlikely that all three would have failed at the same time.

Outpouring of anger against the Russians spreads quickly around the world.

Sailing cup leaves America first time

Newport, R.I., Sept. 26

For the first time in its 132-year history, the America's Cup will be leaving the United States. The symbol of yachting supremacy the world over was won today by an Australian boat that came from behind in all four races of the series. "It was pretty frustrating," said H.C. Herreshoff, who was navigator of the losing Liberty. "Everyone worked very hard and yet we were losing," he said of the critical fifth leg, when the Australia II again overtook the Liberty. "We were all doing everything we could to hold them off." Herreshoff added, "It hurts pretty bad. It will hurt for a long time."

Liberty (foreground) sails to defeat.

Million are caught crossing border

Washington, D.C., Sept. 26

Spokesmen for the Immigration and Naturalization Service say that so far this year it has caught more than one million illegal aliens trying to slip into the United States. The vast majority of them are Hispanic, fleeing either the poverty of Mexico or the political instability and poverty of Central America. According to the immigration service, most of them cross the long and difficult-to-guard border along the Rio Grande River in southern and far-western Texas.

Dr. King's birthday is national holiday

Washington, D.C., Nov. 2

President Reagan today signed legislation that will make the birthday of the Rev. Dr. Martin Luther King Jr. a national holiday. According to the holiday provisions, the celebration, including the closing of schools and public facilities, will take place on the third Monday in January. The bill will take effect in January of 1986. Dr. King, who was born in 1929 and assassinated in 1968, is being honored because of his work in bringing the techniques of non-violent protest to the civil rights movement. The Baptist leader preached a doctrine of harmony and equality among all people (→ Dec. 2).

Jesse Jackson plans to seek presidency

Washington, D.C., Nov. 3

Black civil rights activist Jesse Jackson announced today that he will toss his hat into the ring as a Democratic candidate for President. The 42-year-old Baptist minister worked closely with the late Rev. Martin Luther King Jr. and has been active in such civil rights organizations as the Congress of Racial Equality and the Southern Christian Leadership Conference. Before he announced his bid for the nomination, Jackson had begun a major voter-registration drive among blacks (→ July 20, 1984).

Anti-war TV fare drawing millions

Hollywood, Calif., Nov. 20

After 251 episodes and 14 Emmy Awards, the television screen went dark March 2 on the TV series *M*A*S*H*. Over 125 million people watched the antics of Hawkeye and the rest for the last time – the biggest TV audience ever for a non-sports program. Tonight, a film on the horrors of nuclear war, *The Day After*, drew over 100 million viewers. As the town of Lawrence, Kansas, was devastated, the point was made that nuclear war is neither "winnable" nor "survivable."

Americans take Grenada

General George Vessey (center) confers with marines during the invasion.

Grenada, Oct. 25

A force of American marines and rangers today invaded the tiny island of Grenada, where the United States says a "brutal group of leftist thugs violently seized power." President Reagan said he ordered the attack because he is concerned about the welfare of some 1,100 American citizens on the island. The world press and many Democratic members of Congress reacted negatively to the invasion, which is the first military intervention in this hemisphere by the United States since the 1965 invasion of the Dominican Republic.

In defending his actions, Reagan said he responded to a formal request from the Organization of Eastern Caribbean States to restore order in the region. Washington agreed to become part of a multinational effort with contingents provided by Antigua, Barbados, Dominica, Jamaica, St. Lucia and St. Vincent.

In the fighting, against inferior Cuban troops, 16 Americans died and 77 were injured. The death toll of the Cubans is not known, but 630 were taken prisoner. An English journalist reported 47 mental patients killed when the United States bombed a hospital by mistake.

Before the invasion, Prime Minister Maurice Bishop of Grenada had been placed under arrest by military commander General Hudson Austin and Deputy Prime Minister Bernard Coard, both Marxists with strong Soviet and Cuban ties.

Objective achieved. American troops guard captured Cubans and Grenadans.

G.M., Toyota agree to joint car venture

Washington, D.C., Dec. 20

The Federal Trade Commission has given approval to a joint venture between the Japanese Toyota company and General Motors, America's biggest auto maker. The two will build and operate a factory in Fremont, California, where they will be able to produce up to 250,000 East-West hybrid cars. Although American auto production was up this year, Japanese and other foreign cars have recently taken a big bite out of the American market. New car buyers have been buying smaller, more efficient imports in preference to larger American models. This move may regain some of the market for G.M.

Washington to end racial hiring quotas

Washington, D.C., Dec. 2

The Reagan administration has announced its intent to end hiring quotas for blacks set by the Equal Employment Opportunity Commission. The commission was created by the Civil Rights Act of 1964 to end discrimination in employment that might be based on race, color, religion, sex or national origin. Minority hiring quotas have been one of its tools to achieve integrated hiring practices. The agency also promotes voluntary programs by employers and unions to end discrimination (→ Jan. 17, 1984).

America is wired for cable television

New York City

The networks are aware of a steady loss of viewers as more and more people turn to cable television. The number of subscribers to the 20 basic services and 10 extra-pay services now totals 25 million. Basic cable averages a 16.4 percent share of the audience from 9 a.m. to 11 p.m. However, the Entertainment Channel, devoted to cultural events, is ending service because of heavy losses. But HBO, Showtime, Playboy, Disney and the Movie Channel are doing well.

Missouri, Jan. 13. A federal jury awards newswoman Christine Craft $325,000 in damages against KMBC-TV of Kansas City, which was accused of firing her because of her age and appearance.

Washington, D.C., Jan. 17. Commission on Civil Rights votes to discontinue use of numerical quotas, in employment promotion of blacks.

Tampa, Florida, Jan. 22. Los Angeles Raiders beat Washington Redskins, 38-9, in Super Bowl XVIII.

Lebanon, Feb. 24. Last of U.S. Marines are withdrawn.

New York City, Feb. 25. *Ironweed* by William Kennedy wins Pulitzer Prize in fiction.

Boston, June 12. Celtics defeat Los Angeles Lakers, four games to three, for N.B.A. title.

Hollywood, Calif., June 19. Motion Picture Association of America creates PG-13 film rating, meaning "some material may be inappropriate for children under 13."

Orlando, Florida, June. Donald Duck's 50th anniversary celebration held, at Walt Disney World.

Washington, D.C., July 3. Supreme Court, in Gomez Bethe v. U.S. Jaycees, rules that Jaycees cannot exclude women from full membership.

Albany, New York, July 11. New York becomes first state to institute compulsory seat belt law.

Mississippi, July 13. A 48-page collection of unpublished poems by William Faulkner given to University of Mississippi.

New York City, Oct. 1. Olympic ceremonies organizer Peter V. Ueberroth named commissioner of baseball.

Detroit, Oct. 14. Tigers defeat San Diego Padres, four games to one, in World Series.

New Jersey, Dec. 20. Bell Labs invents megabyte chip, capable of storing four times as much data as any other.

Hollywood, Calif. Top films include *Amadeus, Beverly Hills Cop* and *Ghostbusters.*

DEATH

Martha's Vineyard, Mass., June 30. Lillian Hellman, playwright and screenwriter (*June 20, 1907).

Kissinger study suggests $8 billion in aid for Central America

Washington, D.C., Jan. 12

A committee headed by former Secretary of State Henry Kissinger named to investigate alternatives for improving the situation in Central America today finally issued its recommendations. They include an $8 billion economic aid program and a substantial increase in military aid to the government of El Salvador. The National Bipartisan Commission on Central America was created by President Reagan in 1983 to develop recommendations on American policy in the region. The report is largely in agreement with the administration's current Latin America policy. The only major change involves linking aid to El Salvador to gains in human rights.

Kissinger, still shaping policy.

Salvadoran guerrillas on the march.

The five-year economic aid package doubles current levels of assistance provided by the United States.

The report proposes that American aid form the basis for long-term programs of reconstruction and development that would include the elimination of violence and the development of stable democratic institutions. Efforts to improve social conditions and a more equitable distribution of wealth were also recommended. The panel urged that all barriers to Central American imports be removed and that other nations extend duty-free trade to the region. Both long-term and short-term stabilization programs called for "realistic objectives" to improve living conditions

in Central America. Included are a reduction in malnutrition, a lowered infant mortality rate, a slowing of the population growth, elimination of illiteracy, access to primary health care and increased educational opportunities.

The commission says the main security threats to the area and to American interests there are Soviet and Cuban activity in Nicaragua.

Reprentative Michael D. Barens, Democrat of Maryland, one of the eight congressional advisers to the commission, was sharply critical of the report. "Our real objective in the region is peace," he said, "and the whole thrust of the report is that the way to achieve peace is by sending more guns."

Marxist Nicaragua: A Soviet proxy?

Reagan tells U.S. it now stands tall

Washington, D.C., Jan. 25

President Reagan said today that "America is back – standing tall, looking to the 80s with courage, confidence and hope." The President's State of the Union address was upbeat and optimistic, but he mentioned problems such as the huge increase in the federal deficit. He proposed a bipartisan approach to the deficit with the goal of a $100 billion reduction over three years. The administration is going to study a plan that calls for simplification of the entire tax code as well as a plan to construct a permanent space station.

The fashion designs of Oscar de La Renta utilize bold colors and simple lines to accent the woman.

2 astronauts trip the light fantastic

Space, Feb. 7

In a balletic display 170 miles above the Earth, two astronauts flew through space today totally free of their Challenger shuttle. "That may have been one small step for Neil, but it was a heck of a giant leap for me," joked Captain Bruce McCandless 2nd, paraphrasing Armstrong's famous line when he set foot on the moon. The astronaut, along with Lieutenant Colonel Robert L. Stewart, maneuvered with a jet backpack worthy of Buck Rogers. The walks were a happy note on a troublesome mission that included two wayward satellites.

Texas O.K.'s study of evolution as fact

El Paso, Texas, Apr. 14

The Texas board of education today repealed a decade-old rule requiring textbooks used by Texas schools to teach evolution "as only one of several explanations of human origins" and to present it as a theory and not as fact. The rule had come under indirect attack by the governor's select committee on education, which blamed the board for the state's weakness in science teaching. The repeal also was hastened by a decision of the state attorney general that it was unconstitutional and that he would not defend the board against lawsuits filed as a result of it.

Socal acquires Gulf in record merger

New York City, June 15

Stockholders of the Gulf Corporation have approved what will be the largest corporate merger in history. Pending approval by the Federal Trade Commission, Standard Oil of California will acquire Gulf for $13.2 billion, or $80 a share. With the stroke of a pen, Socal would enlarge its oil and gas reserves by 1.97 billion barrels, more than any firm could hope to gain through exploration in a decade. The new conglomerate would be the third largest oil firm in the country, behind Exxon and Mobil, but lawyers claim antitrust legislation poses no barrier.

Democrats pick woman for Vice President

Geraldine Ferraro breaks a barrier.

Mondale-Ferraro, that's the ticket.

San Francisco, July 20

Representative Geraldine Ferraro of New York became the first woman in American history to be chosen as a nominee for Vice President on a major party ticket. The 48-year-old legislator was hand picked as his running mate by Walter F. Mondale, the Democratic nominee for President, and was approved for the slot today by delegates to the party's convention in San Francisco. "She's a woman, she's ethnic, she's Catholic," said one Mondale aide in explaining why she was chosen for the ticket. "We have broken the barrier."

Mrs. Ferraro is slim and attractive and a shrewd politician. A lawyer, she was an assistant district attorney in Queens County before her 1978 election to Congress. The daughter of an Italian immigrant, she is married to a Manhattan real estate developer, John Zaccaro, and they have three children. She, like many women, has kept her maiden name for professional purposes.

Some strategists view her selection as an effort by the presidential nominee to fire up the party's seemingly hopeless effort to topple President Reagan, the Republican incumbent, by attracting women voters. Others feel it is a gamble. However, Mrs. Ferraro has the support of many top party leaders, including Governor Mario Cuomo of New York and House Speaker Thomas P. "Tip" O'Neill (→ Nov. 6).

Reagan, in China, promotes wider trade

Peking, China, Apr. 30

The United States, which is now China's third largest trading partner, will play an even larger role in its economic growth as a result of agreements signed here today by President Reagan. American investments, which already exceed $700 million, will increase as tax law changes and bureaucratic streamlining clear the way for joint ventures in offshore oil exploration and the development of electric power systems. Reagan has also agreed to sell nuclear reactors and technology for peaceful uses, despite the fact that China has not signed the 1968 Nuclear Non-Proliferation Treaty.

Trade with China has boomed in the 12 years since President Nixon made his historic visit to China, rising from $4.9 million in 1971 to $5.5 billion in 1981. A major boost came in 1979 when China won most-favored-nation status, qualifying it for U.S. Export-Import Bank financing. Last year, China canceled a 4.4-million-ton grain purchase in retaliation for American textile quotas. But a January visit to Washington by Premier Zhao Ziyang smoothed matters and cleared the way for today's accords.

Preparedness and peace. President Reagan reviews American troops in Honolulu before he flies to Peking.

The Reagans atop the Great Wall. Since 1972, relations between China and U.S. have been on firm ground.

Agent Orange fight wins fund for vets

New York City, May 7

A huge class-action suit filed by Vietnam veterans against seven chemical companies was settled out of court today just hours before jury selection was to begin in the trial. The companies agreed to pay $180 million as compensation if the veterans drop all claims against the companies. Veterans assert that exposure to Agent Orange, a herbicide used in Vietnam, led to high rates of cancer, nerve, skin and liver damage. While the companies deny any link between Agent Orange and the medical problems, they are ready to pay.

Court tightens law on political asylum

Washington, D.C., June 5

The Supreme Court ruled today that the alien who seeks refuge in America must prove he faces "a clear probability" of persecution in his native country to avoid deportation. The decision is less lenient than a lower court's, which allowed refuge if an alien showed a "well-founded fear" of persecution. The ruling was unanimous but, to the surprise of many, its lack of breadth fails to define a distinct standard for political asylum. John Paul Stevens, who wrote the majority opinion, said, "That issue is not presented in this case" (→ May 2, 1986). ▷

L.A. Olympics open with celebration and close with U.S. gold

Greeting an adoring crowd. Team members Edwin Moses and Sharon Weber lead the other members of the American squad in a march around the track at the Los Angeles Coliseum, where the Olympics are being held this year.

Los Angeles, July

In an appropriate Hollywood setting, not far from the heart of Tinseltown, the 1984 Olympic Games got off to a glitzy start, staged a star-spangled finish, and crammed lots of excitement in between. When the Olympic flame flickered and died, the United States was in possession of 83 gold medals, 81 silver and 30 bronze. It would not have been that easy had the Soviet team not stayed home in retaliation for the boycott of its 1980 Games by 50 nations. This year, West Germany was second in medal production with 59. Even without the Communist bloc nations, 7,000 athletes from 140 countries took part, making it the largest national representation in Olympic history.

The opening ceremony included thousands of pigeons, a 1,000-voice choir, a 100-piece orchestra, gospel singers, break dancers, square dancers, a 750-member marching band and 84 pianists playing *Rhapsody in Blue*. The closing program had fireworks, a laser show, a simulated flying saucer suspended from a helicopter and singing and dancing on a 23,000-square-foot stage.

Among America's leading individual stars was Greg Louganis of Mission Viejo, California, who won both platform and springboard diving events.

Sullivan first U.S. woman to walk in space

Space, Oct. 11

Dr. Kathryn Sullivan had a fine view of Cape Cod and the rest of planet Earth during the first space walk by an American woman this morning. Following in the "steps" of 38 American men and one Soviet woman before her, Dr. Sullivan, 32, started her jaunt at 11:46 a.m. Working with Commander David Leestma, she completed a difficult refueling operation, monitored a set of 10 tools and snapped several photographs of Leestma and Earth. As the three-hour round neared completion, a safety cap for a valve on the airlock's hatch fell off and wandered out of sight. After a brief search the astronauts recovered it and reboarded (→ Jan. 28, 1986).

Indian rights leader gives himself up

Rapid City, S.D., Sept. 13

Indian leader Dennis Banks has surrendered to legal authorities. A fugitive for nine years, he was sentenced last month to three years in prison for his part in the Custer County Courthouse riot of 1973. An Oglala Sioux, he is a founder of the American Indian Movement (AIM), established in Minneapolis in 1968. Banks and fellow AIM leader Russell Means have been demanding that the federal government return to native Americans tribal lands ceded to them at a time in the 19th century when Indians were being ousted from prime land.

American balloonist first across Atlantic

Savona, Italy, Sept. 18

An American making the first solo balloon flight across the Atlantic crash-landed in Italy today and walked away with a record. Actually, he was flown by helicopter from the landing area to a hospital in Nice, suffering from a broken ankle. Joe W. Kittinger reached Savona with rain and strong winds lashing his 10-story-tall balloon. The flight from Maine covered 3,535 miles and lasted 84 hours. Kittinger, 56, said he had been hoping to set down in Moscow. The previous record distance for a solo balloon flight was 2,475 miles.

Feds bail out bank with $4.5 billion

Chicago, July 26

Offering a shot in the arm to the ailing banking industry, the Federal Deposit Insurance Corporation announced today it would give Continental Illinois an infusion of $4.5 billion to cover bad loans. The aid package is one of the biggest ever offered to a private business. It gives the government an 80 percent stake in the bank and leaves federal regulators in charge of policy. Experts say Continental's new managers will steer the bank away from large corporate clients, but keep its role as an international lender.

Bankers fear the action will slow deregulation. But, plagued by the 1982 recession and a host of bad investment decisions, many of them may have no choice. "This isn't the go-it-alone path we aspired to," said departing Continental chief David Taylor, "but it was the best course open to us."

Most American bank failures since 1938

Washington, D.C.

Despite the continuing economic recovery, 79 banks failed this year, more than in any other year since 1938. The figure pales in comparison to the 4,000 that went under in 1933 without federal insurance to back deposits. But the Federal Deposit Insurance Corporation lists a record 817 banks as problem cases. Many are burdened by loans to the troubled agriculture, energy or real estate sectors of the economy. Others, like Jake Butcher's United American Bank of Knoxville, Tennessee, seem to be victims of widespread fraud. Whatever the cause, the failures have put pressure on banks to raise reserves, which some warn could slow economic growth.

Quincy Jones bestows yet another honor on the reclusive and eccentric Michael Jackson at the Grammy Awards. Jackson's distinct sound and fancy footwork have made his "Thriller" the best-selling album in history.

Reagan romps to victory

A winning team. President Reagan has won the heart of America's voters.

Washington, D.C., Nov. 6

President Ronald Reagan was re-elected today, soundly defeating Democrat Walter F. Mondale by carrying 49 of the 50 states. The President, the oldest man ever to occupy the White House, had campaigned on the slogan, "It's morning again in America," and, indeed, his landslide victory seems to indicate that America's voters approved of his performance over the past four years. Vice President George Bush also was re-elected.

Mondale, Vice President under Jimmy Carter, had taken a risk by conceding during recent months that he would propose a tax increase to reduce the country's enor-

mous deficit. The President, on the other hand, declared that only "over my dead body" would there be any increase in taxes.

As a band played *Hail to the Chief*, the President entered a ballroom in Los Angeles to greet his supporters as they chanted: "Four more years." The smiling President said: "I think that's just been arranged." Promising to extend the economic and military policies of his first term, Reagan added: "You ain't seen nothing yet."

The Democratic campaign had been hampered by disclosures involving the tangled financial problems of the vice presidential candidate, Geraldine Ferraro.

Cuba takes back criminal refugees

Washington, D.C., Dec. 15

The United States and Cuba have agreed that Cuba will accept the return of 2,746 criminals and mental patients who entered the United States during the Mariel boatlift in 1980. President Fidel Castro announced the decision Friday night, but he denied that those who will return were criminal or mentally ill when they left Cuba. The Cubans being returned were among some 129,000 refugees who arrived in the United States in boats from the port of Mariel. Thousands of them are still confined to refugee camps and prisons.

Pro-abortion nuns facing expulsion

Vatican City, Dec. 18

A Vatican spokesman today confirmed that 24 American nuns who signed a statement supporting a woman's right to choose an abortion have been threatened with expulsion. The statement, which appeared in a full page advertisement in *The New York Times* October 7, was signed by several prominent Roman Catholics. It affirmed their belief in a woman's right to choose an abortion. The Vatican said that the Sacred Congregation for Religious and Secular Institutes had written letters demanding that the nuns retract their statement.

U.S. bishops issue critique of capitalism

United States, Nov. 11

America has failed to provide its people with a just economic system. That is the thrust of a draft *Pastoral Letter on Catholic Social Teaching and the Economy* presented at the the annual meeting of the National Conference of Catholic Bishops today. The 120-page document is to be discussed during the coming year before the final draft is issued next year. The letter recognizes the positive impact capitalism has had in providing a high level of production but states that the tremendous inequality that continues to pervade the country is immoral. Homelessness and hunger in a country as wealthy as the United States are only two examples the letter uses to illustrate the failure

of society and individuals to create an equitable economic system. The bishops said: "We believe that the level of inequality in income and wealth in our society and even more the inequality on the world scale today must be judged morally unacceptable." They argue that the federal government should be playing a greater role in overcoming this inequality.

The issuance of the letter seems to be a victory for the those bishops who argued for a spectrum of approaches to contemporary moral and social problems over those who preferred a concerted effort against abortion. The three issues upon which the bishops have chosen to center are economics, abortion and nuclear weapons.

Fair at New Orleans closes with lawsuits

New Orleans, Nov. 11

The New Orleans World's Fair closed today as a financial fiasco and a national flop, but with thousands of local residents mourning its closing. While contractors and others who lost money on the fair were planning lawsuits, visitors to the New Orleans area crowded onto the fairgrounds for one final, fabulous fling. One couple said they had used their season tickets to attend the fair 145 times since

its opening on May 12.

The failure of the fair was attributed to inadequate financing, poor marketing, the city's location and a negative reception from the nation's press. Some experts said such an exposition is "a tired idea" and the New Orleans fair may be the last such show. Fair officials expected 11 to 12 million visitors, but only 7 million came. The fair emphasized New Orleans jazz and Louisiana's Cajun culture.

Bruce Springsteen is "Born in the U.S.A."

United States

Singing about hard-luck cases yearning for hope against a fading American dream, Bruce Springsteen stirred millions this year with *Born in the U.S.A.* From the opening strains of the album's title song, about forsaken Vietnam vets, to the melancholy *My Hometown*, the album presented a grim view of American society, yet one tinged with a tough-minded compassion and wary optimism. Even President Reagan jumped on the bandwagon this summer, invoking the name of the New Jersey singer while campaigning. But "The Boss" would have none of it. Countering Reagan's *Morning in America* theme, Bruce said that he had seen places where "It's midnight, and like, there's a bad moon risin'."

One of the hardest driving rock stars in America, "The Boss" has breathed new life into old-time rock 'n' roll.

New Orleans, Jan. 3. Rotating blackouts instituted across southeast Louisiana leave 70,000 people without electrical power.

Palo Alto, California, Jan. 20. San Francisco 49ers defeat Miami Dolphins, 38-16, in Super Bowl XIX.

New Orleans, Apr. 4. Tulane University cancels school's basketball season, after allegations of point shaving and illegal payments.

New York City, Apr. 24. Pulitzer Prizes awarded to Alison Lurie, for *Foreign Affairs*, and Studs Terkel, for *The Good War: An Oral History of World War II*.

Pittsburgh, May 2. Heads of U.S. Steel, LTV Steel, Bethlehem Steel, Inland Steel, Armco dissolve their 30-year-old coordinated bargaining committee.

Boston, June 9. Los Angeles Lakers defeat Boston Celtics, four games to two, for N.B.A. title.

Washington, D.C., July 1. Supreme Court rules that public school teachers may not enter parochial school classrooms, to provide remedial or enrichment instruction.

Mississippi, Aug. 15. Tourists flock to Tupelo, Elvis Presley's birthplace, to mark eighth anniversary of his death.

Maine, Aug. 25. Bar Harbor Airlines plane crashes, killing 13-year-old Samantha Smith, who had visited Soviet Union upon invitation from Soviet government.

Kansas City, Oct. 27. Royals defeat St. Louis Cardinals, four games to three, in World Series.

New York City, Nov. 26. Random House will pay $3 million for rights to official biography of President Reagan by Edmund Morris.

Texas, Dec. 11. State court upholds $11 billion damage award Texaco must pay Pennzoil for undermining its bid to acquire Getty.

St. Louis, Missouri. Anheuser-Busch sells 68 million barrels of beer this year, greatest volume ever.

Hollywood, Calif. Hit movies this year include *Out of Africa*, *Prizzi's Honor* and *Kiss of the Spider Woman*.

Westmoreland ends suit against CBS

New York City, Feb. 17

In a surprise move, General William C. Westmoreland dropped his libel suit against CBS today, as the case was within days of going to jury. The retired general agreed to an out-of-court settlement in which no money changed hands. Westmoreland filed his $120 million suit after a CBS documentary, *The Uncounted Enemy: A Vietnam Deception*, implied that Westmoreland deceived the government and the public about the troop strength of the Vietnamese enemy. A joint statement makes it appear that CBS is standing by its broadcast and that Westmoreland construes the CBS statement as an apology.

Capital Cities buys ABC for $3.5 billion

New York City, March 17

Capital Cities Communications and the American Broadcasting Company shook hands today on a deal by which Capital Cities bought ABC for over $3.5 billion, provided stockholders, the Department of Justice and the Federal Communications Commission approve. The surprise deal is the largest ever in the entertainment industry. To keep off "unfriendly suitors" until the merger is final, Capital Cities put down a $53 million option to buy 5.3 million shares of ABC common stock at $118 a share. ABC has 214 affiliated stations; Capital Cities owns newspapers, magazines and cable TV systems.

Union Carbide sued over India disaster

New York City, Apr. 8

The Indian government filed suit against Union Carbide Corporation in Manhattan District Court today for unspecified damages arising from the December 1984 gas leak at the company's plant in Bhopal. The suit stated that 1,700 people died and 200,000 were injured in the lethal leak. India seeks compensatory damages for the victims as well as punitive damages "in an amount sufficient to deter Union Carbide ... from the willful, malicious and wanton disregard of the rights and safety of the citizens of those countries in which they do business." It is reported that India might settle out of court.

Chavez trying to revive Farm Workers

Tehachapi Mountains, Calif.

High in the Sierra headquarters of the United Farm Workers, isolated from the rank and file, Cesar Chavez is trying to rekindle the energy he rode to national prominence in the 1960s and '70s. Some 42 percent of Californians have joined his new grape boycott, a tactic that once forced dozens of growers to bargain with the U.F.W.

Chavez began the union in 1962 when migrant workers, ignored by the New Deal, had no bargaining power. A long strike in 1965 had pickets chanting "Viva la Huelga" ("Long Live the Strike") on national television. Liberals and clergy flocked to support Chavez, and by 1975, he had 50 contracts in the grape industry alone. Now he has three. Chavez drifted into meditation, holistic health and encounter groups. Union officials deserted in droves, calling him a dictator. But Chavez remains committed. "The workers," he says, "will ask me to leave when they are ready."

Supreme Court bars moment of silence

Washington, D.C., June 4

In a 6-3 ruling today, the Supreme Court struck down an Alabama law that required a moment of silent meditation at the beginning of each school day. In another chapter of the school prayer debate that has agitated the country off and on since the court's 1962 decision in Engel v. Vitale, the court stated that a moment of silence was not in itself unconstitutional if used for some purpose such as bringing order to a classroom at the beginning of the day. In the Alabama case, the court found that the intent of the law was explicitly to promote religion and thereby violated the First Amendment of the Constitution as applied to the states by the 14th Amendment.

The school prayer issue, however, does not seem destined to go away soon. President Reagan has called for a constitutional amendment allowing required prayer in schools, and bills are regularly introduced into Congress with that intent. The Rev. Jerry Falwell of the Moral Majority has made it a major element in the agenda of that political organization, in spite of the fact that board meetings of Moral Majority itself do not begin with a prayer because of the possibility that any particular prayer would offend some members.

San Francisco. *Invented by Andrew Hallidie, a British-born businessman, in 1867, charming, efficient cable cars have been running here since 1873.*

Reagan stirs uproar by visiting Bitburg

Bitburg, West Germany, May 5

President Reagan's short visit to a military cemetery in Bitburg today in the midst of the annual Western economic summit meeting drew protests from American and European Jews. The protests, aides to the President said, marred the summit aspects of the trip.

Reagan delivered an eloquent speech after visiting the cemetery where 2,500 German soldiers, 49 of them SS men, are buried. He condemned Nazi atrocities and hailed the 40 years of German-American friendship. Despite the President's sentiments and an earlier visit to the Bergen-Belsen camp, holocaust survivor and scholar Elie Wiesel said of the Bitburg visit, "We have been wounded ..." Jews in Europe and the United States had urged Reagan not to go to Bitburg. Hundreds turned up to protest.

T.W.A. hijack drama comes to an end

Damascus, Syria, June 30

The 39 American hostages on the T.W.A. flight hijacked by Arab terrorists 17 days ago are free. A spectacular convoy sped them to Damascus from the Beirut slum where they were held captive after removal from the aircraft. Also today, two of the hijackers still guarding the plane strode into an airport lounge and bragged to reporters about "the ability of the oppressed to control America." Hooded in pillow cases, the pair concluded with the slogan: "America is the great Satan." The freed hostages said they will never forget the screams of fellow passenger Robert Stethem, a navy diver, before he was murdered. The passengers hailed purser Uli Derickson for her brave calm. So far, the Shiite terrorists have failed in their demand that the Israelis free Palestinians, as the price for today's release.

Hijackers talked with journalists and labeled America "the great Satan."

On television, President Reagan told terrorists that America "will fight back against your cowardly attacks." Reporters also heard the President declare in a microphone test, "Boy, I'm glad I saw *Rambo*, last night. Now I know what to do next time."

Treasure hunter unearths Spanish galleon

Key West, Fla., July 21

"It's the mother lode! We're sitting on silver bars!" cried diver Andy Matroci as he splashed to the surface. So ends Mel Fisher's obsessive 16-year search for the Nuestra Senora de Atocha, a treasure-laden Spanish galleon that last saw sky in 1622. To the archeologists with Fisher's Treasure Salvors Inc., the ship is a "virgin time capsule." To the trip's 700 investors, it is 60 pounds of gold and 47 tons of silver worth close to $400 million. For Fisher, it may be a small consolation for the loss of his son and daughter-in-law, who drowned in the search for the Atocha.

Growing homeless ranks face bitter winter

Washington, D.C., December

As the winter winds begin to howl through the streets of the urban North, a legion of homeless people once again faces the perennial challenge of survival. Unemployment may be the lowest in five years, but homelessness is worse than at any time since the Depression. No one really knows how bad; estimates range from 350,000 to 3 million. But the facilities are inadequate for handling even the best-case scenario. Only 91,000 shelter beds exist in the whole country. A public outcry has forced higher expenditures in some states. But corporate contributions to health and human services are down. And the Reagan administration has slashed spending on low-income housing. As one Department of Health and Human Services official explained, "We think it is a local problem."

Live-Aid concert for African famine relief

At the Live-Aid benefit, Madonna shows her navel for a good cause.

Philadelphia, July 13

"To me this is not a pop concert, to me this is not a TV show," said Irish singer Bob Geldof of today's Live-Aid extravaganza, "to me this is simply a means of keeping people alive." The all-star intercontinental rock fete was organized by Geldof to raise money for African famine relief. Centered at Wembley Stadium in England and Philadelphia's JFK Stadium, the shows included Sting, Paul McCartney, U2, Dire Straits, The Who, Madonna, Crosby, Stills, Nash & Young, Bob Dylan and Led Zeppelin. Geldof hopes the shows, TV broadcasts to 152 nations and phone pledges will raise $50 million. As Woodstock alumnus Neil Young said, "This time you know it's going to help."

As the nation becomes more aware of the plight of the homeless, many are blaming the government for not doing enough to alleviate the awful situation. ▷

Pete Rose breaks Ty Cobb's record

Cincinnati, Ohio, Sept. 11

One of baseball's most enduring records, held by Ty Cobb since 1928, has gone the way of most "unbreakable" marks. Pete Rose of the Cincinnati Reds got a line single for the 4,192nd hit of his 23-year career, surpassing the Cobb record, and followed that six innings later with a triple for No. 4,193. The feat of the 44-year-old Cincinnati hero touched off a seven-minute standing ovation and a fireworks display. There were tears in Pete's eyes. "The only other time I remember crying was when my father died," he noted after belting out his record hit off Eric Show of the San Diego Padres.

Smashing performance. Pete Rose gets a single and jogs into history.

Rebuffed by CBS, Turner eyes MGM

Atlanta, Georgia, Aug. 7

Broadcaster Ted Turner is determined to become a media mogul. Rebuffed in his "hostile" takeover bid for CBS, he is going for the MGM/UA Entertainment Company for about $1.5 billion ($29 a share). He would kick back UA to major stockholder Kirk Kerkorian for $470 million ($9 a share). If Turner can raise the money, he will run a major Hollywood theatrical, TV and home video supplier and own a library of 2,200 films, 600 of them silents, many classics.

U.S. now debtor nation

Washington, D.C., Sept. 16

In a few years, the United States has fallen from its lofty position as the world's largest lender, to a shaky place in the debt cellar. According to figures issued today by the Commerce Department, the nation will accumulate a current accounts deficit of $130 billion this year, the largest in the world. It will be the first time since 1914 that the United States has owed foreigners more than they have owed to this country. At 3 percent of the gross national product, the figure doubles the previous high of 1.5 percent, reached during the 1870s, when the developing West absorbed huge quantities of foreign capital.

Not surprisingly, economists disagree on the effects of the historic shift. Borrowing appears to have few intrinsic pitfalls as long as the capital is used for productive investment. Certainly America developed on foreign money throughout the 19th century. But industrial production has been stagnant for a year under a flood of imports. And the future promises an even greater drain on investment capital. The debt may hit $1 trillion by 1990, with interest and dividend alone equaling the 1985 total deficit. Dependence on foreign money also opens America further to international fluctuations. As an official at the Institute for International Economics put it, "If there was a run on the dollar tomorrow, we'd be hurt."

Reagan's new revolution: tax revision

Washington, D.C., May 28

Labeling it a "second American Revolution for hope and opportunity," President Reagan has proposed a far-reaching plan to reshape the federal income tax system. The losers, he said in a message to Congress, would be "those individuals and corporations who are not paying their fair share or, for that matter, any share."

The plan would replace individual tax rates, now ranging from 11 to 50 percent, with three new rates of 15, 25 and 35 percent. Families of four with incomes of about $12,000 or less would pay no taxes. And the top corporate tax rate would drop from 46 to 33 percent.

The plan would retain deductions for charitable contributions as well as interest payments on all primary residences, but it would eliminate many other tax breaks, including deductions to help offset state and local tax payments. It also would limit deductions for interest payments on second homes.

Reaction to the plan was mixed on Capitol Hill. Dan Rostenkowski, chairman of the House Ways and Means Committee, said "the battle for reform will be long and tough." He predicted some changes would be made, that the Congress would not rubber-stamp the plan.

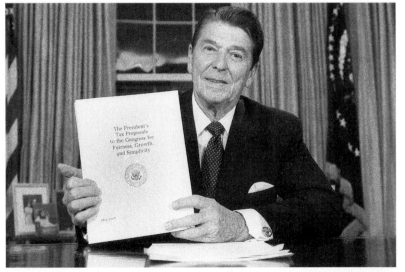
Going to the people. President Reagan unveils his tax program on television.

U.S. curbing trade with South Africans

Washington, D.C., Sept. 9

President Reagan announced today that the administration will impose economic sanctions against South Africa. In a policy reversal, Reagan said he would prohibit most loans, computer sales and nuclear technology deals with the Pretoria government in an effort to end its policy of apartheid against South African blacks. Critics of the President refuse to give him much credit for the action, saying it comes only after a public outcry, both here and abroad, against South Africa's program of oppression. It is expected that other Western nations will follow Reagan's lead with economic sanctions of their own.

Coretta King and children join a protest at the South Africa Embassy.

Montgomery Ward dropping catalogue

Chicago, Aug. 2

After 113 years of mailing catalogues and merchandise to customers, Montgomery Ward is going out of the mail-order business. The company will send its final issue in December. Montgomery Ward was founded in 1872 in a livery stable loft with $2,400 in capital and a single-sheet brochure listing a few dry goods items. It began catalogue sales before its nearest competitor, Sears, Roebuck & Co. Now officials say the catalogue business is losing money.

Law intends to end U.S. deficit by 1991

Washington, D.C., Dec. 10

President Reagan today signed into law a radical revision of the budgeting procedures, requiring an end to the federal deficit by 1991. The President praised it as "an important step toward putting our fiscal house in order." The new law was sponsored by Representative Phil Gramm of Texas and Senators Warren B. Rudman of New Hampshire and Ernest F. Hollings of South Carolina, and bears their names. To achieve gradual elimination of the monumental national debt, the new law would require cuts in many programs if Congress fails to agree to reductions in the deficit (→ June 6, 1986).

Frank Zappa zaps plan to censor rock

Washington, D.C., Sept. 19

From Presley to Prince, rock music has always exploited shock value. But Tipper Gore, wife of Senator Albert Gore and founder of the Parents' Music Resources Center, has seen enough. At a congressional hearing today she urged warning labels on "offensive" albums. Folksinger John Denver and heavy metal icon Dee Snider disagree. And rock's daring experimenter Frank Zappa likened the center's demands to "some sinister kind of toilet training program to housebreak all composers and performers."

The President and the First Lady, reviving frontier spirit of the West.

Superpower summit

The Communist and the Cold Warrior set course for an era of cooperation.

Geneva, Switzerland, Nov. 21

In the latest of the 10 summit meetings held since World War II between the leaders of the United States and the Soviet Union, President Reagan today opened discussions on a wide range of topics with General Secretary Mikhail Gorbachev. Meeting at the Chateau Fleur d'Eau outside Geneva, the President greeted Gorbachev with a firm ceremonial handshake. The two men strolled in the wintry Swiss wind, then adjourned to a warm fireplace with their advisers to begin tough negotiations on arms control and human rights. According to reliable sources, Gorbachev quickly told Reagan he must abandon his touted "Star Wars" space defense program. And the President, just as quickly, refused to do so. While this event might have ruined other summit meetings right from the start, insiders say that in spite of their differences, Reagan and Gorbachev did seem to hit it off personally and that agreements on their broad agenda still may be reached.

While the President is debating "Star Wars" with the Soviet leader, Nancy Reagan is engaged in "style wars" with Raisa Gorbachev. But the First Lady is keeping a sense of perspective about their alleged fashion rivalry. Says she, "I think that's a little silly. I mean there are very important things being discussed here, and what somebody wears or doesn't wear really isn't terribly important."

Youth from Russia to be U.S. citizen

Los Angeles, Oct. 3

Walter Polovchak, the Ukrainian youth who ran away from his parents five years ago rather than return to the Soviet Union, won the right to seek United States citizenship today. He became an adult. The Chicago youth celebrated his 18th birthday on a television program here. Polovchak came to the United States with his parents six years ago, but refused to go back to the Soviet Union with them a year later. "I'm celebrating my freedom today." said Polovchak.

Largest atom lab opens in Illinois

Batavia, Illinois, Oct. 13

The Fermi National Accelerator Laboratory is the home of the world's largest atom smasher, a huge accelerator that measures four miles in diameter. Switched on for the first time today, the enormous device has produced energy levels three times higher than any previously achieved. The accelerator is expected to help the United States regain the lead in high-energy physics that was lost to a European consortium in the 1970s. As a research tool, the device is unequaled.

President signs costliest farm bill

Washington, D.C., Dec. 23

With quick strokes of his pen, President Reagan today signed into law the most expensive federal farm bill in American history. The $169 billion expenditure includes a huge fund reserved for crop insurance and long-term, low-interest loans to the economically distressed farming sector. This law comes after a year of farm protests. In January, 10,000 people held a rally in St. Paul, Minnesota, to protest low farm prices and high interest rates. The next month, a crowd of more than 14,000 gathered at Iowa State University in Ames to demand immediate federally funded farm credits.

Chris Evert at 30 just keeps winning

New York City

Chris Evert, once the darling of women's tennis, is now perhaps the most consistently dominating figure in the sport's history. In 1971, at 16, her backcourt patience and trademark two-handed backhand took her to the U.S. Open semifinals. For five straight years in the '70s, she held the No. 1 spot, streaking to 125 straight clay court wins. For 11 years she made the semifinals of every Grand Slam event she entered. And this year, at 30, Evert won in Paris, still unwilling to give ground to the young and eager.

Evert, a powerhouse of the game.

New Orleans, Jan. 7. Chicago Bears defeat New England Patriots, 46-10, in Super Bowl XX.

Hanover, New Hampshire, January. Group of Dartmouth students opposed to college's divestment of funds in South Africa stage midnight sledge-hammer attack on campus protesters' shanties.

New York City, Feb. 26. Robert Penn Warren named first official poet laureate of United States by Librarian of Congress Daniel Boorstin.

Florida, March 6. Divers recover Challenger crew compartment, containing remains of astronauts (→June 9).

New York City, Apr. 17. Pulitzer Prizes awarded to J. Anthony Lukas, for *Common Ground* and Larry McMurtry, for *Lonesome Dove.*

Washington, D.C., Apr. 23. House of Representatives approves Garrison Diversion Project in North Dakota, though project is scaled back from 250,000 to 131,000 acres.

New York City, Apr. 27. A video pirate transmits protest over cost of pay television to millions watching Home Box Office television.

Detroit, Apr. 28. General Motors becomes biggest U.S. company, replacing Exxon.

Tuscon, Arizona, May 1. Eight Christian activists convicted, of smuggling and harboring illegal aliens (→Nov. 7).

Washington, D.C., June 9. President's commission on Challenger disaster pinpoints fault on a defective "o-ring" seal on one of solid fuel booster rockets (→Sept. 29, 1988).

Philadelphia, June 18. Academy of Fine Arts acquires 1,000 works by Thomas Eakins.

Washington, D.C., June 23. President Reagan states: "The one thing that I do seek are judges that will interpret the law and not write the law."

Atlanta, Oct. 1. Ex-President Carter officially opens Carter Presidential Center.

New York City, Oct. 27. Mets beat Boston Red Sox, 4 games to 3, in World Series.

Las Vegas, Nov. 22. Mike Tyson knocks out Trevor Berbick in second round, for World Boxing Council title.

Shuttle Challenger explodes; 7 killed

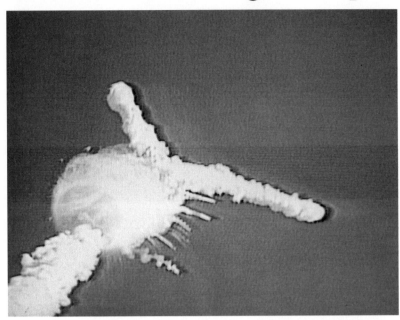

Tragedy in the sky. Booster rockets careen away from the space shuttle.

A quiet moment for Challenger crew members. Christa McAuliffe is at left.

Cape Canaveral, Fla., Jan. 28

The space shuttle Challenger exploded into a massive orange fireball today 73 seconds after liftoff, killing all seven astronauts aboard. The shocking scene was witnessed by thousands of spectators here, while millions who were watching their televison screens stared in disbelief. The worst catastrophe in the history of American space exploration, the tragedy has closed down the country's space shuttle program indefinitely.

The winged spacecraft lifted off flawlessly at 11:38 a.m., after delays related to unusually cold temperatures. Many in the crowd of spectators were students, cheering for Christa McAuliffe of Concord, New Hampshire, who was to have been the first schoolteacher in space. As Challenger soared to a height of nine miles and a speed of 2,900 feet per second, Commander Francis "Dick" Scobee said, "Roger, go with throttle up, up," signaling a power increase. But the craft was suddenly engulfed by a massive eruption of its liquid hydrogen tank at 11:39; its two solid fuel boosters continued to fire, leaving two smoke trails across the cloudless sky. Thousands of pieces of debris fell into the Atlantic.

The other members of the Challenger crew were Commander Michael J. Smith, Dr. Judith A. Resnik, Dr. Ronald E. McNair, Lieutenant Colonel Ellison S. Onizuka and Gregory B. Jarvis. Space officials have not determined the cause of the tragedy (→March 6).

Scientology guru writes kinky novel

New York City, Jan 24

Once upon a time, L(afayette). Ron Hubbard wrote science fiction. Then he gave it up to found the Church of Scientology, a religion whose main goal, say skeptics, is lining Hubbard's pockets. In any case, Hubbard's back in sci-fi and is at work on a 10-volume work ("dekalogy" in Hubbardese) titled *Invader's Planet.* The maiden novel, *Mission Earth,* came out today. It is weak in the science and fiction areas, but it has lots of kinky sex.

AIDS silence ends; condom use urged

Washington, D.C., Oct. 22

"The silence must end." That was the message of Surgeon General C. Everett Koop's report on acquired immune deficiency syndrome today. The study urged education for schoolchildren on the causes of the disease and condom use by adults not in "mutually faithful monogamous relationships." Teenagers should abstain from sex, according to the report, which also tries to allay fears that AIDS is spread through casual contact.

Wall Street plagued by insider trading

New York City, Nov. 18

In the midst of its greatest boom in history, Wall Street has been shaken to its foundations by scandal. Ivan Boesky, one of the nation's richest arbitrageurs, has pleaded guilty to buying and selling stocks based on illegal information. He will pay $100 million as penalty for his involvement in the insider trading game. Half of that total represents illegal profits, half is a civil penalty. He will also be barred from the securities industry for life.

Ad agencies merge into world's largest

New York City, Apr. 27

Three major advertising agencies today agreed to merge and create the largest agency in the world. The agencies – BBDO International, the Doyle Dane Bernbach Group and Needham Harper Worldwide – bring in some $6 billion a year in billings. "We want to be nothing less than advertising's global creative superpower," according to Allen G. Rosenshine, chairman and chief executive officer of BBDO. He added that the merger will offer extra resources for major clients and diversity for restless, creative-talent employees. Advertising has grown increasingly important as products become more alike and rely on extra "hype" to distinguish themselves.

Oil prices plummet; Southwest hurting

Houston, Texas

When oil hit a low of $10.77 a barrel this year, most Americans applauded. A Merrill Lynch analyst viewed it as "a huge tax break." Experts said drivers would save $23 billion, heating consumers $12.5 billion, truckers $7.7 billion and farmers $1.1 billion. But the Southwest is not smiling. Oil output is off 800,000 barrels a day; profits are off 50 percent; foreclosures, bankruptcy and unemployment are endemic, and bank failures in Texas are up 119 percent.

Boston Celtics win 16th N.B.A. title

Boston, June 8

The Boston Celtics won their 16th National Basketball Association title today, but the score could have read Bird 114, Houston 97. It was Larry Bird at his best, doing all and playing all but two minutes in the decisive sixth game in the best-of-seven series. He got 29 points even though he was double- and triple-teamed. He broke up Rocket plays and forced 11 first-quarter turnovers. He even untangled the net for the officials.

U.S. bombs Libya for terrorist attacks

Terrorism gets punished. Libya is hit hard by the American reprisal raid.

Washington, D.C., Apr. 16

Last night's surprise American raid on Tripoli has taken the lives of Colonel Muammar el-Khadafy's 15-month-old adopted daughter and two American pilots. President Reagan told a meeting of businessmen here today, "We would prefer not to have to repeat the events of last night. What is required is for Libya to end its pursuit of terror for political goals." The President ordered the attack in retaliation for Libya's "direct" role in the April 5 bombing of a West Berlin discotheque popular with American servicemen. Sounds of bombs and guns in Tripoli were heard clearly by Americans listening to radio broadcasts live from the scene. The 18 bombers striking from a base in England were hampered by Paris's refusal to let them cross French air space. An additional 15 planes took off from American aircraft carriers in the Mediterranean just before the White House began a briefing for some key congressmen.

Republican Senator Richard Lugar said today that the briefing began early enough so that the raid "could have been called off" if the legislators had insisted. But the Democratic Senate leader Robert Byrd, who was present at the briefing, strongly dissented. "We were not consulted," he said. "We were notified of a decision that had already been made."

U.S. to recognize new Philippine regime

Washington, D.C., Feb. 27

The Reagan administration announced today that it will give full diplomatic recognition to the new Philippine government headed by Corazon C. Aquino. The decision by Washington to recognize Mrs. Aquino as the legal head of the new Philippine government is a severe blow to former President Ferdinand Marcos, who still claims to have won the presidential election three weeks ago.

For years, Marcos headed a regime that was known for its corruption and its indifference to a 20 percent unemployment rate, with two-thirds of the Filipino people living in poverty. The Marcos government also had been implicated in the political assassination of many enemies, including Mrs. Aquino's husband, opposition leader Benigno Aquino.

Incoming: New Philippine President, Corazon Aquino, greets the people.

Outgoing: Ferdinand Marcos, ousted Philippine leader, reaches Hawaii.

What Asian influx may mean for U.S.

Los Angeles, June 29

As the number of European newcomers to the United States steadily declines, Asians are flocking to America's shores. And these Asians now account for half of all legally admitted foreigners. And as Thais, Indians and others pursue the American dream, experts are beginning a serious examination of the long-term effects on American society.

The sights and sounds of the East are enveloping entire communities. Surgeons, entrepreneurs and laborers are creating urban microcosms of their homelands; their children are excelling in school, and Asians often economically surpass other Americans and minorities. In short, most are succeeding.

But many experts warn that self-supporting socio-economic enclaves are rapidly supplanting the need for assimilation. Economic success can now be achieved with only a marginal understanding of American life. But there are some who believe that should the current trend continue, future national unity might be endangered.

▷

National debt passes the $2 trillion mark

Washington, D.C., June 6

The omnipresent federal budget deficit, long the talk of economic pessimists, has now reached such absurd proportions – $2 trillion – that it can no longer be ignored. According to Keynesian economic theory, a moderate federal debt is no cause for concern so long as sustained growth keeps pace with it. It is a fact, however, that the deficit has doubled over the past five years, and this has experts on both the left and the right deeply worried.

Much of the American debt has been incurred by what many call a spending-happy Congress, but consumer debt, business debt and foreign debt have significantly added to the problem. Spending far more than it takes in, the United States has created what some consider to be an artificial prosperity. True or not, no nation can continue amassing huge debts without a day of reckoning. Should foreign financial institutions call in their United States loans, the effects could be extreme. In the final analysis, Americans must find a long-term, programmatic solution, lest that day of reckoning be worse than need be.

Star Wars system wrecks Iceland summit

Reykjavik, Iceland, Oct. 13

The once-promising arms meeting between President Reagan and Soviet leader Mikhail Gorbachev broke up late yesterday. According to administration spokesmen, the talks ended because of the continuing U.S.-U.S.S.R. impasse over Reagan's refusal to drop the "Star Wars" space defense program. The Russians offered to make major cuts in their medium- and long-range nuclear weapons system, but only if the Americans would agree to stop both the testing and deployment of space-based weapons envisioned in the President's so-called "Strategic Defensive Initiative." Reagan apparently said he would not do so, and the talks came to an abrupt and confused end.

Observers say that when the talks suddenly stalled, Reagan and Gorbachev were on the verge of a comprehensive agreement that would have severely cut back the deployment of both intermediate and long-range nuclear weapons systems. It is expected that discussions on arms control will resume next year when experts of both countries meet at Geneva (→ Dec. 8, 1987).

Steel in crisis as imports flood America

Washington, D.C., July

The steel crisis hit a new level this month as LTV, the nation's second largest steel firm, filed for bankruptcy. Since 1982, the rusted industry has lost $7 billion under the pressure of heavy imports, which have seized a 25 percent share of the market, up from 14 percent 10 years ago. And the market itself is shrinking; cars are smaller, plastics are on the rise and computers are replacing heavy equipment.

Some analysts blame the high cost of labor. LTV supports two pensioners for every worker on the payroll. But unionists have grown compliant in the face of mass layoffs that have thinned the ranks of steelworkers from 450,000 to 200,000 since 1979.

Labor has led the call for federal help. Says union president Lynn Williams: "The steel industry – and industrial America in general – will continue to disintegrate if vigorous action is not taken." But the administration will not impose import quotas and hurt consumers. Says the Commerce Department, "It's a fact of life that changes in technology and demand affect an industry's ability to compete. Some people win, some people lose." Most analysts say the losers will be the big, integrated firms. Decentralization, it appears, is steel's key to survival.

Industry gives way to service sector

Washington, D.C.

"This nation is becoming a nation of hamburger stands," said the A.F.L.-C.I.O. in 1974, "a country stripped of industrial capacity and meaningful work, ... a service economy ... busily buying and selling cheeseburgers and root beer floats."

The intervening years have in fact witnessed what is called the "hollowing of American industry." Beset by competition from abroad, American firms shift output to low-wage nations, or they import products, becoming marketers and distributors for foreign firms. Since 1953, manufacturing fell from 30 to 21 percent of gross national product.

Service industries have taken over, creating 10 million jobs in seven years, while 1.5 million were lost in manufacturing. A few economists see the shift as a healthy adaptation to international competition that will allow America to specialize in high-tech services. But most of the new jobs offer low pay and low productivity growth. "The McDonald's counter jobs will offset the McKinsey consultant jobs," says one expert. And industries like trucking, banking and computers rely directly on manufacturing for demand. As a Japanese Toyota director said bluntly, "You can't survive with just a service industry."

New York City, July 4. *Fireworks light up the Statue of Liberty as America marks the lady's 100th birthday. Thanks to careful restoration, this gift of the French people will stand for another century as a symbol of freedom.*

The United States Bullion Depository at Fort Knox, Kentucky, has held the nation's gold reserves since 1936. It is the gold here that the currency is based on and it is against these reserves that Congress is able to borrow.

High court upholds affirmative action

Washington, D.C., July 2

The Supreme Court today approved the practice of affirmative action to remedy past discrimination against minorities. The 6-3 decision is a blow to the Reagan administration, which has fought to remove employment preference on account of race, color or gender. Assistant Attorney General William Reynolds, speaking for President Reagan, called the ruling "disappointing." But Benjamin Hooks, head of the National Association for the Advancement of Colored People, called it a "significant rebuke to the Reagan administration's pernicious efforts to destroy affirmative action."

Workers hash out beef with Hormel

Austin, Minn., Sept. 12

The P-9 local of the United Food and Commercial Workers Union wearily voted to end a bitter yearlong strike at the Hormel meatpacking plant here today. The new contract restores hourly wages to the levels of the early 1980s, before they were cut from $10.60 to $8.25. The strikers, who have weathered the National Guard and condemnation of their national union leaders, received no guarantees that they will be rehired.

Law offers amnesty to illegal migrants

Washington, D.C., Nov. 7

President Reagan today signed a landmark immigration bill that bans the hiring of illegal aliens. It also offers legal status to immigrants who can prove that they have lived here continuously since January 1, 1982. There are an estimated three million illegal aliens in the United States. The bill imposes fines ranging from $250 to $10,000 on employers who violate its provisions. The President insists it will remove "the incentive for illegal immigration by eliminating the job opportunities." He added, "Future generations of Americans will be thankful for our efforts to humanely regain control of our borders."

"How the Reagan Revolution Failed"

Washington, D.C.

In 1980, David Stockman was, at 34, the wunderkind of the Reagan team, point man on the-slash-and-trim attack. Four and a half years later, the savant of supply-side economics quit his job as budget director and got a job on Wall Street. Now he's back in the news with *The Triumph of Politics: How the Reagan Revolution Failed*, a memoir that depicts the President as a muddle-headed leader who'd rather tell anecdotes than face tough issues.

Iran arms deal revealed

Washington, D.C., Nov. 13

The Reagan administration has confirmed a flood of worldwide reports that it indeed has been sending Iran weapons – against both United States law and official policy – for some time. The bizarre story began to break last week when a pro-Syrian Beirut newspaper, *Al Shirra*, ran a story that said the United States had sent Iran spare parts and ammunition for jet fighters. The newspaper also reported that the United States had airlifted weapons from the Philippines to Iran in four C-130 cargo planes.

Al Shirra also said that White House assistant Robert McFarlane had met in September with Iranian officials in Teheran, who asked for military equipment. About the same time, a spokesman for a Danish maritime union reported that Danish ships had carried at least five loads of arms and ammunition for the United States from Israel to Iran.

By shipping arms to Iran, the Reagan administration has violated the spirit if not the letter of a long string of federal laws that are designed to stop any arms transfers, direct or indirect, to Iran. In addition, the arms sales run totally counter to the administration's worldwide campaign to embargo the sale of all military weaponry to Iran.

Despite a flurry of official "no comments" along with "off-the-record" responses, most observers say

President faces the nation's press.

that the objective of the arms sales was to win the release of the American hostages now held in the Mideast, and to establish some degree of relations with the government of the Ayatollah Khomeini.

The arms deal was reportedly organized and carried out by a "crisis management" group within the 46-member National Security Council staff. In addition to McFarlane, a prominent member of the team is marine Lieutenant Colonel Oliver North, a decorated Vietnam veteran and deputy director for political-military affairs at the Security Council. He helped plan the 1983 invasion of Grenada and the April bombing of Libya (→ July 1987).

Americans do it again. The experimental airplane Voyager becomes the first to circumnavigate the globe non-stop without refueling on December 23. The 25,012-mile trip took nine days three minutes 44 seconds. Piloted by Richard Rutan and Jeana Yeager, Voyager holds 1,500 gallons of fuel.

The Presidential Palace, better known as the White House for obvious reasons, has become the symbol of the American presidency. Home to the nation's chief executives since 1800, the three-story, 100-room mansion has endured the British torch, three expansions and total reconstruction.

New York City, Jan. 13. *Today* show celebrates 35th anniversary on television.

Pasadena, California, Jan. 25. New York Giants defeat Denver Broncos, 39-20, in Super Bowl XXI.

South Pacific, Feb. 4. Yacht Liberty regains America's Cup by defeating Australian challenger Australia II.

Washington, D.C., March 18. Congress votes to raise rural highway speed limit from 55 miles per hour to 65.

Los Angeles, June 14. Lakers defeat Boston Celtics for N.B.A. title.

Los Angeles, July. Motorists on freeways use guns to vent traffic frustrations.

New York City, Sept. 11. Anchorman Dan Rather walks off set during *CBS Evening News* over disagreement with management; screen goes blank for five minutes.

Los Angeles, Oct. 1. Host Johnny Carson celebrates 25th anniversary of television's *Tonight Show*.

Washington, D.C., Oct. 23. Senate rejects President Reagan's nomination of Robert Bork for Supreme Court associate justice.

Minnesota, Oct. 25. Twins defeat St. Louis Cardinals in World Series, four games to three.

New York City, Nov. 11. Vincent Van Gogh's painting *Irises* sells for $53.9 million, highest price ever for an auctioned painting.

Washington, D.C., Nov. 15. Mr. Potato Head vows to Surgeon General C. Everett Koop that he is giving up his 35-year-old pipe smoking habit, as part of American Cancer Society's anti-smoking campaign.

New York City, Nov. 17. Columbia University loses 40th straight football game, setting an all-time record.

Chicago, Nov. 23. Mayor Harold Washington's sudden death precipitates a heated power struggle among city's black and white aldermen.

Hollywood, Calif. Top films this year include *Platoon, Wall Street, Broadcast News, The Untouchables, The Last Emperor* and *Empire of the Sun.*

Evangelist Bakker toppled in sex scandal

Smiling down from on high, though there doesn't seem much to smile about.

Springfield, Missouri, May 6

The governing board of the Assemblies of God voted today to strip Jim Bakker of his ordination. Bakker has been in the midst of a sex and money scandal since early this year. The founder of the tremendously successful PTL Club television ministry has admitted to a "sexual encounter" in December of 1980 and claims to have been blackmailed as a result. Since news of Bakker's indiscretion became public, donations to PTL (Praise the Lord, People That Love), which previously received over $100 million a year from viewers, have fallen sharply (as have donations to other television ministries).

When Bakker resigned as head of PTL March 20, the new governing board of the ministry was headed by Jerry Falwell, the founder of the Moral Majority and host of the *Old Time Gospel Hour.* This was an unusual development since Falwell has been outspoken in his opposition to the Pentecostal movement. Still, it points to important contact between various elements within the so-called religious right.

The scandal over Jim Bakker's sexual liaison with Jessica Hahn has been titillating the country for months. Stories about Bakker and his wife and partner Tammy Faye have been widely reported. Their luxurious style of life, Tammy's heavy use of makeup and their seeming unawareness of public opinion have also been material for satire and humor.

Marvel or albatross? Scrapped by President Carter but salvaged by President Reagan, the B-1 bomber is intended to replace the aging B-52. Many Americans, however, question whether it's worth $283 million per plane.

Andy Warhol, guru of Pop Art, is dead

New York City, Feb. 21

After surviving the excessive life style of his acolytes and an assassination attempt by the lone member of S.C.U.M. (Society for Cutting Up Men), Andy Warhol died today of complications resulting from surgery. After working in commercial illustration, Warhol initiated the Pop Art movement with his deadpan representations of banal objects, from Campbell's Soup cans to dollar bills and celebrities such as Elvis Presley and Marilyn Monroe. Warhol manufactured his own stars, from the people who were associated with his studio, The Factory, and his films.

Andy Warhol took art to its extremes, creating a new genre in the process.

Robot at sea finds Civil War's Monitor

Hatteras, N.C., July 23

A deep-sea robot descended 220 feet to survey the Monitor, a warship that sank 125 years ago. The small armored ship, built for the Union navy in the Civil War, fought only one battle against the Confederate enemy before it went down with a crew of 20 in a storm off Cape Hatteras. The navy and other organizations are leading a 10-day survey using electronic devices to learn whether the ship is salvageable. The Monitor was equipped with many "firsts," including armor plating and a flush toilet.

G.E. divests itself of electronics unit

Fairfield, Conn., July 22

General Electric announced today that it is selling its $3 billion-a-year consumer electronics operations to Thomson S.A., the electronics company run by the French government. The G.E. move stunned the electronics industry, with Zenith now the only major American manufacturer of videocassettes and TV sets. John Welch, chairman of General Electric, said consumer electronics has been a company "stepchild." In light of Japanese competition, the Americans have increasingly been bowing out of the price-cutting wars.

General Electric's TV, VCR, radio, telephone and tape recorder units will all go to Thomson, one of the world's largest electronics companies, in exchange for $800 million and Thomson's medical equipment business, a sector where G.E. is expanding. Some 31,000 employees will transfer to Thomson.

Colonel Oliver North takes the stand

Washington, D.C., July

After seven months of invoking the Fifth Amendment's protection against self-incrimination, Lieutenant Colonel Oliver North has finally told his version of the Iran-contra affair and his role in it. Testifying before Senate and House investigating committees under a grant of limited immunity, North spent six full days artfully defending his actions in the illegal arms-for-hostages deal, saying that "I assumed that the President was aware of what I was doing and had, through my superiors, approved." He claimed that he had sent five memoranda to the President through Admiral John Poindexter, Reagan's national security adviser, requesting permission to divert money from the Iranian arms sales to the contras. North's hard-hitting testimony left the impression that the late director of the Central Intelligence Agency, William J. Casey, had masterminded

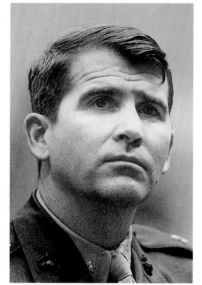

North: American hero or villain?

the financing of the contras with profits from the Iranian arms sales. North said that Casey referred to this operation as "the ultimate irony, the ultimate covert operation."

Referring to Casey as his "personal friend and adviser," North said that he had "never disagreed with any of the things I was doing."

North's testimony has evoked mixed reactions. Democratic Senator Daniel Inouye, presiding over the hearings, said that the Iran-contra arms-for-hostages operation was a naked attempt to create a "secret government within our government." In a *Time* magazine poll conducted two weeks ago, 60 percent of the respondents said they sympathized with the 43-year-old marine officer, but only 51 percent saw him as totally truthful. Still, 69 percent felt he should not go to jail for his Iran-contra activities.

North was described by Neil Livingstone, a former counter-terrorist colleague, as a man who came "into the N.S.C. as an easel carrier and ended up as the world's most powerful lieutenant colonel." He has also emerged as a loose cannon, or an American hero (→ Nov. 19).

America faces up to Japanese challenge

Washington, D.C.

Launching a new attempt to fight off Japan's economic challenge, Congress barred Japanese construction firms from public works projects on December 17. On the high-tech battleground, President Reagan imposed high duties on Japanese electronics in March. And in January, a Pentagon-C.I.A. study convinced semiconductor firms to cooperate in order to keep America ahead in the silicon chip race.

Why such an uproar? Soaring exports in automobiles, textiles, televisions and computer chips have given Japan bigger trading profits than any other nation. As the world's biggest creditor, the small Pacific nation spreads its capital far and wide. In 1985, the Japanese bought $6 billion worth of American real estate. Mazda, Mitsubishi, Honda and Fuji-Isuzu are opening plants in the Midwest. And American industry appears to be abdicating in the face of the onslaught. Says economist Nestor Terleckyj, "If Ford ... can make money by making loans, it will become a bank and let the Japanese make more and more of its cars." But with the American corporations providing services instead of making things, and the balance of payments going in their competitors' favor, the American role in the world economy may soon be far different from what it was in an earlier time.

Japan-bashing: U.S. legislators smash a Toshiba radio with zeal.

Black American middle class is growing

New York City, August

The total of middle-class blacks in America has more than doubled between 1969 and 1984, according to an article in *Ebony* magazine. The report defines "middle class" as taxpayers with an income between $20,000 and $50,000. While nearly half of all white families are middle class, the article says, only about 30 percent of black families fall into the category. Two-fifths of middle-class blacks, *Ebony* reports, have some college education, while one-fourth have completed four years of advanced schooling. Although these statistics show some gains for blacks, a report from the National Urban League says that Reagan policies have hurt them.

In the wake of the Iran-contra affair, President Reagan assembles the National Security Council staff to outline its new system of operation.

Stock market tumbles by 508 points

Panic! The New York Stock Exchange goes wild as millions of dollars are lost.

New York City, Oct. 19

The stock market plunged 508 points today. The debacle was described by the New York Stock Exchange chairman as "the nearest thing to a meltdown that I ever want to see." The rout was the worst day in history, wiping out more than $500 billion in stock equity. It came on an awesome volume of 604 million shares, almost double the previous record set last Friday, when stocks plunged 108.35 points. After topping out at a record 2,722.42 on August 25, the Dow Jones industrial average has plummeted 1,000 points, or 36 percent – nearly three times the calamitous decline that ushered in the Great Depression.

With the tape running two hours late, desperate stockholders flooded phone lines in vain. It seemed everyone who owned mutual fund shares wanted to switch to any other kind, all at once, so that almost no one could get through with an order. One official at Kemper Financial Services said, "We've just seen a genuine panic." Fidelity, which increased its 24-hour telephone staff by 20 percent over the weekend, expects 200,000 calls tomorrow, up from 115,000 today. In a business that loves a laugh, the head of Drexel Burnham's equity desk said, "This is not a laughing matter." At Shearson Lehman Brothers, traders tacked up a sign: "To the lifeboats!"

The White House tried to buoy spirits with news that President Reagan was watching the collapse "with concern," and that he remains certain "that the underlying economy is sound." But the stockholders wanted more, studying tickers and television in search of answers that they failed to find. One New York actor said that he was being battered, but couldn't get through to his broker so he could sell out. Others were holding firm. "The only way for people to stop something like this," one of them advised "is to stop the panic and hold their stock" (→ Feb. 2, 1988).

Fairness Doctrine abolished by F.C.C.

Washington, D.C., Aug. 4

The Federal Communications Commission, in a historic action expected to fuel a war with Congress, today scrapped a 38-year-old policy requiring broadcasters to air all sides of controversial issues. In a unanimous vote, the F.C.C. said the Fairness Doctrine is unnecessary because of the number of radio and television stations serving the nation and may be unconstitutional since it gives the government editorial control over broadcasters. A storm of protest comes from citizen groups and Congress. The F.C.C. said the ruling did not affect "equal time," "reasonable access" or "issue-responsive programming."

Pope says Catholics must not dissent

Detroit, Mich., Sept. 19

Pope John Paul II, in a statement issued today, ignored the request of American bishops that he affirm his belief in freedom of speech. Instead, the Pope declared that dissent from the Magisterium was incompatible with being a Catholic. This statement is destined to fuel the continuing controversy over dissent in the Roman Catholic Church in America. All during his trip to the United States the pontiff praised its Constitution but reminded Catholics that the church is not a democracy.

Pope, in the U.S., is firm on dissent.

United States retaliates against Iran for attacks in Persian Gulf

The long arm of America. U.S. makes Iran pay for attack in Kuwaiti waters.

Washington, D.C., Oct. 19

The navy reported today that two of its warships have shelled an Iranian oil platform in the Persian Gulf. According to Pentagon sources, the two destroyers approached the platform, announced their intention to attack, and called for the workmen to abandon it. After the Iranians had climbed down from the platform, the American warships threw salvo after salvo of 5-inch cannon fire at the rig, leaving it ablaze.

The strike retaliates for an Iranian missile attack, on October 16, on a U.S.-flagged tanker off Kuwait. In May, an Iraqi missile hit the U.S. frigate Stark, killing 37 sailors. (→ July 1988).

Superpowers sign first missile reduction treaty

Washington, D.C., Dec. 8

The United States and the Soviet Union formally agreed to the first comprehensive arms control treaty in the nuclear age today. Coming after the serious breakdown in their arms limitations talks in Reykjavik, Iceland, President Reagan and General Secretary Gorbachev announced the terms of the far-reaching Intermediate Nuclear Forces (I.N.F.) treaty, which will go into effect as soon as the legislatures of both nations complete the ratification process.

The treaty calls for the elimination of ballistic and Cruise missiles that have striking ranges of up to 3,500 miles. Under the terms of the treaty, the United States is to dismantle and destroy its 102 Pershing-2 missiles now based in West Germany and its 256 ground-launched Cruise missiles currently in place in Britain, West Germany,

Thousands of warheads still exist, but the world can rest a little easier.

Italy and Belgium. In turn, the Russians have agreed to destroy 132 SS-4 and SS-12's as well as 441 SS-20 missiles, each of which car-

ries three warheads. The treaty means the Russians have agreed to destroy more than four times as many nuclear warheads (1,500)

as the Americans (350). Elimination of the intermediate-range missiles will result in the reduction of the combined American-Soviet inventory of nuclear warheads by about 4 percent.

To insure that both sides comply with the I.N.F. treaty, a comprehensive set of verification procedures will be implemented. Observers from the United States will be stationed in the Soviet Union. In turn, Soviet inspectors will be posted in America. Each team of observers will carry out 20 scheduled inspections during the first three years of the treaty. Other "surprise" inspections will be conducted if either team regards it as necessary. The first team of Soviet inspectors is to be stationed at Magna, Utah, while its American counterpart will be stationed in Votkinsk, about 600 miles from Moscow (→ May 31, 1988).

Iran-contra report blames the President

Washington, D.C., Nov. 19

The House and Senate committees investigating the Reagan administration's handling of the Iran-contra affair have concluded that "the common ingredients of the Iran and contra policies were secrecy, deception, and disdain for the law." The 690-page congressional report states, "The ultimate responsibility for the events in the Iran-contra affair must rest with the President ... If the President did not know what his national security advisers were doing, he should have." The minority reports of the committees took issue with the majority position, which it termed a bunch of "hysterical conclusions."

Riots by Cubans rock 2 Southern prisons

Officials use helicopter at riot scene.

Atlanta, Georgia, Dec. 4

Cuban inmates at the federal prison here released 89 hostages today, ending the 11-day riot over plans to return the prisoners to Cuba. Riots here and at a detention center at Oakdale, Louisiana, left one man dead and more than 20 injured. The Oakdale center is a charred ruin and the Atlanta prison severely damaged. The Oakdale riot ended November 29. The riots began after President Reagan announced a plan to deport the inmates, who arrived in the 1980 boatlift from the Cuban port of Mariel. Most committed crimes in the United States and were awaiting deportation. Cuba has agreed to accept the inmates.

Amerasian children find home in America

Bangkok, Thailand, Dec. 31

They were greeted with gifts of American flags and picture books titled *This Is America* when they arrived in Bangkok today. A group of 65 of the many Vietnamese fathered by Americans during the Vietnam War are headed to the land of their fathers – the United States. They left Vietnam, some with family members, under the renewal of a resettlement program stalled for two years. The program, which be-

gan in 1979, has resettled 4,000 Vietnamese-Americans in the states. At least 10,000 are still in Vietnam. The process was halted by Hanoi in 1986, because of the complexity of screening procedures; the United States has since simplified the process. Most of these Amerasians, whose average age is 18, expressed a desire to see their fathers. Many noted the pain of growing up with a Western face in Vietnam, and hoped for a new acceptance.

15 billion photos

Rochester, N.Y., January

The photographic exposure took up to eight hours when first invented, but now, 150 years after the debut of photography, the snapshot rules. Americans click their shutters 15 billion times a year, taking an average of 155 photos per household. Some 400 million rolls of film are purchased by the 95 percent of American families who own cameras. What would Louis Daguerre, who published the first photography manual 150 years ago this month, have to say about the new Fujicolor Quick Snap, the first throwaway camera?

Workers stitch a quilt bearing the names of AIDS victims to be displayed in the capital in November.

New Orleans, Jan. 31. Washington Redskins defeat Denver Broncos, 42-10, in Super Bowl XXII.

Los Angeles, Jan. 21. Lakers defeat Detroit Pistons, four games to three, for N.B.A. title.

Washington, D.C., Feb. 5. United States indicts Panama's General Manuel Noriega, on drug smuggling charges.

Washington, D.C., Feb. 18. Anthony Kennedy is sworn in as Associate Justice of Supreme Court.

Washington, D.C., March 13. I. King Jordan becomes president of Gallaudet University, institute of higher learning for deaf, following series of protests by students opposing earlier appointment of president who can hear.

New York City, March 31. Pulitzer Prize awarded to Toni Morrison for *Beloved*.

Phoenix, Arizona, Apr. 4. Governor Evan Mecham removed from office by state legislature, because of campaign fund diversions.

Atlanta, May 5. Eugene Antonio Marino installed as archbishop of Atlanta, becoming nation's first black Roman Catholic archbishop.

Washington, D.C., June 14. White House chief of staff Howard Baker resigns post after having restored order to White House in wake of Iran-contra affair.

Atlanta, July 21. Michael Dukakis of Massachusetts nominated for President (→ Aug. 17).

Hollywood, Calif., Aug. 12. Film *Last Temptation of Christ* released, sparking protests across nation.

New Orleans, Aug. 17. George Bush nominated for President (→ Nov. 8).

San Diego, California, Sept. 9. Catamaran Stars & Stripes defeats challenger New Zealand, for America's Cup.

Gulf of Mexico, Sept. 17. Hurricane Gilbert batters Texas coast with 218 mph winds, worst in state history.

Los Angeles, Oct. 20. Dodgers defeat Oakland A's, four games to one, in World Series.

Hollywood, Calif. Movies this year include *Bull Durham*, *Big* and *Working Girl*.

Evangelist Swaggart falls from grace

Jimmy Swaggart of the Bible belt.

Baton Rouge, Louisiana, Feb. 21

In yet another installment of religion and sex, the television evangelist Jimmy Swaggart has admitted to visiting a prostitute. "I have sinned against you, and I beg your forgiveness," said Swaggart in a tear-flooded confession to his congregation. Swaggart, a flamboyant preacher, was among the most virulent in denouncing Jim Bakker last year when a sex scandal rocked the latter's ministry. Swaggart, who called Bakker a "cancer on the body of Christ," was forced to humble himself after church officials were shown photographs of Swaggart's visit to a prostitute.

The Bakker and Swaggart scandals have brought television ministers under greater public scrutiny. This will increase in the future as Pat Robertson's campaign for the presidency develops. Robertson, founder of the 700 Club television ministry, is an outspoken representative of fundamentalist Christianity and political conservatism. It remains to be seen whether these scandals will affect the Robertson campaign.

Troops in Honduras to warn Sandinistas

Washington, D.C., March 19

The State Department said today that 3,000 soldiers of the 82nd Airborne Division are being airlifted to bases in Honduras. They will serve as reinforcememts for the 3,000 troops that have moved to the area over the past several months. Secretary of State George Shultz says that the American forces will not actively participate in any Honduran military action against Sandinista troops. The Nicaraguan soldiers have reportedly been crossing the border into Honduras in "hot pursuit" of contra forces taking refuge in that country. Honduran jet fighters have bombed Sandinista troops twice this week after they chased contra soldiers into Honduras.

State Department officials said the administration believes that the reinforcememt of American forces will serve to inhibit the Sandinistas while giving a psychological boost to the contra troops (→ 24).

The 82nd hits the ground during Golden Pheasant operation in Honduras.

Sandinistas reach truce with contras

Washington, D.C., March 24

News received from Nicaragua today confirms that the pro-Communist Sandinista government has signed a temporary cease-fire agreement with the contra rebels. At a news conference in Managua, President Daniel Ortega reportedly said to his old foes, "We are here together determined to bury the ax of war and raise the olive branch of peace." In response, contra leader Alfonse Calero noted, "Today we have taken a first and firm step to end this fratricidal war."

The terms of the cease-fire require that the Sandinista government release its 3,000 contra prisoners; in return, the contras have promised to recognize the Ortega regime as being the legitimate government of Nicaragua and to refuse further military assistance from foreign governments.

Farmers better off

Washington, D.C., Feb 15

America's farmers seem to be more prosperous now than at any time in this decade. While at least 10 percent of farmers are in debt, their cash income has reached $58 billion, up from, $37 billion in 1983. Farm debt has dropped more than 28 percent since 1983. The continuing drought in the South and Midwest, however, is expected to take a heavy toll on agriculture later in the year.

Computer use cut by Stock Exchange

New York City, Feb. 2

Big-time traders who make a killing buying and selling giant blocks in split seconds won't have the help of the New York Stock Exchange's Super Dot electronic order system any more. Moving against the kind of trading some blame for the October crash, Big Board directors have decided that during big swings the system will be barred to giant traders who program their computers to take advantage of small differences between the prices of stocks and stock index futures.

Income disparities growing in nation

Washington, D.C., Apr. 30

According to the Census Bureau, the economic separation between the upper-income and lower-income Americans keeps growing. A sampling of some 60,000 American homes showed incomes averaging $36,300. And while the annual income for the top 5 percent rose by over $6,000 during the 1980s, average income for the poor decreased by more than $7,000.

The study illustrates the uneven success of the economic boom of the mid-1980s. The growth of a service economy and the premium placed on technological know-how have left many less educated workers, particularly those formerly employed in heavy industries, with few opportunities. The need for temporary employees has risen, but such jobs rarely provide adequate family-supporting income.

America in decline?

United States

As the American Century nears an end, some fear the nation's glory days will end "not with a bang but a whimper." One gloomy seer is Paul Kennedy, author of *The Rise and Fall of the Great Powers: Economic Change and Military Conflict From 1500 to 2000*. The Yale professor says the United States, now a victim of "imperial overstretch," will sink under global commitments while other nations grow stronger.

Pentagon unveils Stealth bomber

Washington, D.C., Apr. 20

The U.S. Air Force today released pictures of the B-2 or Stealth bomber, a project it has kept secret for 10 years. The artist's rendering shows a tailless, multiple-engine boomerang-shaped craft that resembles the YB-49 Flying Wing developed by Northrop in the late 1940s. The plane is built from materials that make it virtually invisible to radar. The air force would not provide information regarding the bomber's dimensions, size of crew and payload.

Reagan visits changing Soviet Union

Ronald Reagan in the heart of what he once called "the evil empire."

Moscow, May 31

President Reagan's trip to the Soviet Union has had mixed results so far. According to Howard Baker, White House chief of staff, Reagan and Soviet leader Mikhail Gorbachev collided almost immediately after they met formally. Sparks flew as Reagan assailed the Soviet Union's human rights record. One Russian spokesman said flatly, "We don't like it when someone from the outside is teaching us how to live, and that is only natural." So far, the two leaders have produced no significant agreements. But they recognized the need of continuing the thaw in the cold war and of maintaining a dialogue on the crucial issues of disarmament and the resolution of regional conflicts.

While Reagan has had his problems with Gorbachev, he apparently is well-liked by the Soviet people. Today, he met with 600 students and intellectuals at Moscow State University and was welcomed with enthusiasm. Explaining why the President is so popular with the Russian people, a Soviet editor said, "Reagan is a simple man. He likes astrology, and he was an actor."

In spite of his initial conflict with Gorbachev, it seems that Reagan has begun to realize that the "evil empire" he spoke about in earlier years is perhaps no longer all that evil, and that the era of "perestroika," or economic restructuring, and "glasnost," or openness, represents a new and positive phase in the U.S.-Soviet relationship (→ Dec. 7).

After four decades, the cold war just may be finally ending

New York City

The year 1988 will pass into history as the year the cold war ended, say those who think Mikhail Gorbachev means what he said at the United Nations December 7. Though the Russian Revolution "radically changed the course of world development," the Soviet leader said, "today we face a different world, for which we must seek a different road to the future." He said "closed" societies are impossible, because "the world economy is becoming a single organism." He also spoke out for individual rights, calling freedom of choice "mandatory." The Gorbachev remarks came four decades after the term "cold war" first came into use, a time when Stalin called on the Soviet Union to defend itself because there would be wars as long as there were capitalist nations. Moscow swallowed neighbors, dropped an Iron Curtain around them and entered an arms race. Gorbachev told the U.N. to "let historians argue who is to blame for it," and proceeded to proclaim the cold war over, saying he will reduce Soviet arms, use capitalist economic techniques and allow political freedom. So powerful is his message that he is winning such unlikely allies as British Prime Minister Margaret Thatcher. She feels the cold war is indeed over and "it is in the Western interest" for Gorbachev to succeed But many in Washington still hold back, causing some to think they mean "nyet" when they say "not yet." Gorbachev is waiting for a sign from Vice President Bush.

Yellowstone National Park is burning

Forest fires ravage Yellowstone.

Yellowstone Park, Wyo. July 27

The oldest national park in the nation is ablaze and firefighters said today that they haven't been able to control the 12 separate wildfires. One experienced park official called it "the worst inferno I've seen in 17 years." The fires have consumed more than 88,000 acres of lush timber land and are threatening to isolate the famed geyser Old Faithful. Fortunately, the park is so large - 2.2 million acres – that the animals can stay out of the path of the fires and still have plenty of room to roam. Authorities at the park say that the fires are not likely to be completely extinguished until the extended drought is broken by some good rains.

While the fire has blackened the mountains this year, experts say that no permanent harm has been done. The fire releases nutrients in the form of burned trees and other vegetation, which is an excellent form of natural fertilizer. Also, as the heat from the fire warms the pine cones, they open and drop the seeds that one day will grow into a new generation of trees. As one of the park officials put it, "Life and geysers go on."

Crack and other drugs plague inner cities

United States

"Our children are hooked on drugs that have come straight from the pit of hell," a Brooklyn minister said recently. Indeed, the inner cities of America are being ravaged by crack, an inexpensive, mind-numbingly addictive form of cocaine. In the ghettos, where the family barely exists as a social unit, almost a whole generation is being swept into a netherworld of drug addiction and violent street gangs, armed with semi-automatic weapons, who kill to keep control of drug-selling zones. Older addicts, more likely to use narcotics such as heroin, face the added danger of AIDS, which is spread by shared hypodermic needles. The older addicts are often the parents of crack users, completing a cycle of despair.

Drugs are no stranger to the streets, but crack, a cocaine derivative, is particularly heinous, leaving violence in its wake. Mural by Keith Haring.

Americans return to space with Discovery

Cape Canaveral, Fla., Sept. 29

The shuttle Discovery blasted flawlessly into orbit today, heralding a long-awaited comeback for the beleaguered American space program. An unspoken tension surrounded the launching, at 11:37 a.m., reaching a peak as the Discovery, riding the familiar billowing white smoke trail, passed the 73-second mark, the point at which the Challenger exploded, plunging NASA into a somber 32 months of redesign of the shuttle fleet and reassessment of the nation's space goals. Six hours later the craft's five-man crew launched a $100 million communications satellite. Said one official: "We're back in business, and it hasn't been easy."

Age of Discovery begins anew.

Gulf war ends; U.S. downs Iran airliner

Washington, D.C., July

The "on again, off again" war between Iran and Iraq drew to a close this month in spite of a deadly error by an American destroyer that many had feared would prolong the conflict. Only 16 days after an American ship shot down an Iranian airliner with 290 passengers aboard, Iran's Ayatollah Khomeini on July 20 agreed to the United Nations cease-fire plan. On Teheran radio, Khomeini recalled he "had promised to fight to the last drop of my blood and my last breath." Changing this decision, he said, "was more deadly than taking poison." But he said he decided to end the war "based only on the interest of the Islamic republic."

One frightening aspect of the airliner tragedy was that the destroyer Vincennes mistakenly identified the big airliner as a hostile fighter plane and downed it only days after the speaker of the Iranian Parliament, Hojatolislam Hashemi Rafsanjani, had stated that Teheran was willing to accept an immediate cease-fire. After the plane was downed, Washington apologized for the loss of life and tried during its inquiry to calm the troubled waters.

The war caused a million casualties and involved the United States as defender of oil routes in the gulf.

Atlantic City, N.J., June 27. *Mike Tyson walks away from a floored Michael Spinks; he earns $200,000 a second and retains his heavyweight title.*

Gorbachev, at the U.N., offers troop cuts

New York City, Dec. 7

Mikhail Gorbachev announced today that he is willing to make major troop and weapon reductions in Eastern Europe. Speaking before the United Nations General Assembly, the Soviet leader said that he would reduce the Red Army in Europe by at least 500,000 soldiers and 10,000 tanks. These proposed cuts would shrink Soviet military personnel by 10 percent and armor strength by 25 percent. Although the Gorbachev offer has startled some Western observers, his plans to shift the Soviet military strategy from an offensive to a defensive posture has been under discussion for some time. Over the past three years, the Russians have stated that a large-scale conventional war in Europe would be almost as catastrophic in its results as would a nuclear war. Their military leadership has now been instructed to make the prevention of war, rather than victory in one, their principal objective.

Although the proposed Soviet reductions are significant, the Warsaw Pact forces will still have a decided superiority over NATO in manpower, tanks and artillery. Nevertheless, President Reagan expressed satisfaction with the Gorbachev offer, saying, "I heartily approve" of the plan. President-elect George Bush, echoing "the Gipper," stated simply, "I support what the President says."

U.S. talks to P.L.O.

Carthage, Tunisia, Dec. 16

The United States and the Palestine Liberation Organization began formal talks here today, ending Washington's 13-year ban on contacts with the P.L.O. Resumption follows by just two days P.L.O. chairman Yasir Arafat's acceptance of three American conditions. In an about-face, Arafat now says he recognizes Israel, renounces terrorism and accepts United Nations Security Council Resolutions 242 and 338 as the basis for Middle East peace. Today's historic 90-minute meeting is seen by many observers as a potential breakthrough in the conflict.

U.S.-Canada pact

Ottawa, Canada, Dec. 24

Overcoming fears that Canada might lose its economic independence, the House of Commons today "chose an instrument that promises more jobs and more wealth for future generations of Canadians." In a 141-111 vote, Canada's legislative body approved a major free-trade agreement between Canada and the United States. Designed to increase the gross national product of the two nations and counter the economic integration of Western Europe that is set for 1992, the pact provides for the elimination of all tariffs and trade barriers between the world's largest trading partners.

Selling out America

United States

The latest economic crisis to hit the nation is the apparent "selling out" of major industries and assets to foreigners, particularly the British, Japanese, Canadians and Dutch. Foreign investment in the United States, now running at $200 billion a year, has increased six times since 1974. Some states are even competing to attract the business. The phenomenon has three main causes: the cheap dollar, strong consumer markets here and a huge capital surplus overseas. At the current rate, however, all reducible assets (that is, those except land) in the country will be sold in 50 years.

Is America happy?

New York City, Dec. 24

The Fordham Institute for Innovation in Social Policy reported today that problems in America, from the growing income gap to the teenage suicide rate, are getting steadily worse. How, then, explain a Gallup poll showing 56 percent of the public content with "the way things are going." Maybe facts are no match for feeling, reality a puny rival of dreams. Despite homelessness, joblessness, drugs, AIDS and a rising cost of living, many look back on the nation's history with a sense of gradual gains for all, saying that life, liberty and happiness have come in their own sweet time.

George Bush sweeps to 40-state victory

Washington, D.C., Nov. 8

George Herbert Walker Bush, a decorated hero of World War II, was elected President of the United States today, winning 40 of the 50 states to defeat Governor Michael Dukakis of Massachusetts, his Democratic challenger. The final tally showed Bush with 426 electoral votes to 112 for Dukakis. He will take office January 20, succeeding Ronald Reagan, whom he served as Vice President for eight years.

Bush, a New Englander who made his fortune in the oil fields of Texas, is the first sitting Vice President elected to the nation's highest office since Martin Van Buren in 1836. The Bush running mate, Senator Dan Quayle of Indiana, was elected Vice President.

Bush: Assuming Reagan's mantle.

This year's campaign was viewed by many voters as one of the most negative in the nation's history. Bush repeatedly attacked Governor Dukakis on such issues as a dirty Boston harbor, prison furloughs for felons and the death penalty, accusing him of being too liberal. During their nationally televised debates, as well as in stump speeches, Bush often avoided taking firm stands on critical issues. But he did slam the door on any rise in taxes, despite the soaring national debt. The next President's stand on this crucial issue is almost certain to lead to an intense political struggle with Congress, which stays in control of the Democrats in spite of the Dukakis defeat.

Snoopy, Charlie Brown and Lucy catch the Spirit as they bang the drum for Old Glory. The Peanuts gang typifies the way we like to think American kids grow up in an average community, happy, secure and above all, free.

Huge oil spill in Alaska

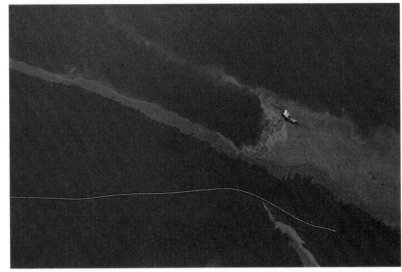

A massive operation to clean up crude oil spilt by the Exxon Valdez.

Alaska, March 30

President Bush today called the spill of 11 million gallons of crude oil a "major tragedy." A week after the 987-foot supertanker Exxon Valdez ran aground on a reef soon after sailing from Valdez, shocked experts estimate that oil has spread over 500 square miles of Alaskan waters and coated hundreds of miles of coastline. The millions of gallons of crude have poured into Prince William Sound, an area rich in marine wildlife and economically crucial to local fishing communities. Angry environmentalists say the clean-up will take years and cost millions. Federal authorities are questioning the ship's captain, Joseph Hazelwood, who is reported to have been in his cabin at the time of the accident.

George Bush sworn in as 41st president

Washington, D.C., Jan. 20

George Bush today took the oath of office to become the nation's 41st president. He thanked President Ronald Reagan for "the wonderful things you have done for America," but implied that his administration would not be a carbon copy of his predecessor's. In what is perhaps a comparison with the Reagan presidency, Bush vowed "to celebrate the quieter, deeper successes that are made not of gold and silk, but of better hearts and finer souls."

Bush is flanked by his wife, Barbara, and predecessor Ronald Reagan.

Two Libyan fighters shot down by U.S.

The U.S. presents its case at U.N.

Washington, D.C., Jan. 5

The Reagan administration has firmly rejected Libyan claims that yesterday's downing of two Libyan fighters by U.S. Navy aircraft was unprovoked.

Defense Secretary Frank C. Carlucci said two F-14 Tomcats, on combat air patrol from the carrier USS John F. Kennedy, fired their missiles defensively. The Libyan planes, two MiG-23 Floggers, approached in a hostile manner and the F-14s opened fire when the MiGs were just 14 miles away, Carlucci added. Both Libyan pilots parachuted into the sea.

This was the second time U.S. and Libyan warplanes have clashed during the Reagan administration. In 1981, Navy fighters downed two Libyan jets over the Gulf of Sidra.

February 11. *The Rev. Barbara Clement becomes the Episcopal Church's first woman bishop.*

Colonel North convicted

Washington, D.C., May 4

The long-running Iran-contra affair at last reached a conclusion of sorts today.

Marine Lieutenant Colonel Oliver North was convicted in federal court on three of 12 counts against him. The jury found that North, a National Security Council aide during the Reagan administration, destroyed and falsified documents, used public funds to pay for a personal security system and aided the obstruction of Congress. But he was acquitted of the most serious charges, one of which was lying to Congress. U.S. District Court Justice Gerhard Gesell fined North $150,000, gave him a three-year suspended sentence and ordered him to perform 1,200 hours of community service. Gesell said North should be viewed as a "low-ranking subordinate working to carry out the initiatives of a few cynical superiors." The trial disclosed much about secret arms sales to Iran and the diversion of funds to Nicaraguan contras. The administration's refusal to release classified documents permitted only circumstantial light to be shed on the roles played by Reagan and then Vice President Bush (→ June 11, 1990).

Blast kills 47 seamen aboard USS Iowa

The battleship's huge 16-inch guns explode during training mission.

Atlantic Ocean, April 19

A 16-inch gun turret – the world's largest naval guns – blew up today on the U.S. battleship Iowa. These awesome guns can fire a shell weighing one ton up to 23 miles. The explosion killed 27 sailors who were inside the 17-inch-thick hardened-steel walls of the turret, and a fire tore through the interior to the deck, killing 20 more. The blast occurred as the ship fired a broadside during exercises in the Atlantic, 300 miles northeast of Puerto Rico.

The 58,000-ton warship, built in 1943, is one of the biggest as well as the oldest battleships afloat. She is one of four World War II Iowa-class battleships taken out of mothballs by President Reagan in his drive to give the United States a 600-ship navy. The Iowa was outfitted to carry Tomahawk sea-launched cruise missiles with nuclear warheads.

Today's mystery blast was the first in a U.S. warship's gun turret since 1972, when 20 were killed and 36 injured on a heavy cruiser off Vietnam. The last main-gun explosion on a U.S. battleship took 43 lives aboard the Mississippi during World War II.

Lucille Ball dies; all America loved Lucy

The zany comic was a TV delight.

Los Angeles, April 26

Lucille Ball, perhaps America's best known comic, died today of an aortal rupture at the age of 77. She is best known for her portrayal of the accident-prone hatcher of ridiculous schemes on the television show "I Love Lucy," which ran from 1951 to 1957, with more than 1,000 episodes. The show, which also starred her husband, Desi Arnaz, was the first to be filmed rather than broadcast live, and was also the first to be filmed before a live audience. "I Love Lucy" won five Emmys and continues to delight TV viewers in syndication.

U.S. sanctions after Beijing massacre

Washington, D.C., June 5

Barely 24 hours after Communist Chinese troops killed more than 2,500 pro-democracy students in Beijing, President Bush today suspended all U.S. arms sales to China for an indefinite time.

The White House, however, rejected calls to impose economic sanctions or break diplomatic relations with China. Outraged politicians on Capitol Hill are calling for a firmer U.S. response to the brutal crushing of anti-Communist demonstrations on Tiananmen Square. Live television coverage of the events brought the full horror of the massacre into millions of American homes.

Flag burning is free speech, says Court

Washington, D.C., June 21

In a controversial decision, the Supreme Court has ruled that burning the American flag is "expressive conduct," and therefore a constitutionally protected form of free speech. The case, Texas v. Johnson, dates from 1984, when protesters at the Republican Convention in Dallas burned the flag, chanting "America, the red, white and blue, we spit on you." Gregory Johnson, one of the protesters, was found guilty of violating a Texas law proscribing flag desecration and was sentenced to a year in prison. The issue cropped up in the 1988 presidential race; President Bush came out in favor of anti-desecration laws.

June. *Tim Burton's magnificent "Batman," with Jack Nicholson playing the deliciously evil Joker and Michael Keaton in the role of the Caped Crusader, is a mega-hit nationwide immediately after its release.*

Muslim extremists execute U.S. hostage

Body of Lt. Col. William R. Higgins, videotaped by his Shiite captors.

Beirut, July 31

A pro-Iranian terrorist group claims to have hanged a senior U.S. military officer, Lieutenant Colonel William R. Higgins. The killing was apparently carried out by a group called the Organization of the Oppressed of the Earth. According to President Bush, Americans "were shocked right to the core" to see a shadowy half-minute videotape showing Higgins hanging by a noose. The American officer had been attached to a U.N. observer force in Lebanon until his abduction on February 17, 1988. Higgins's Shiite captors said the execution was in retaliation for the Israeli kidnapping of Sheik Abdul Karim Obeid, a leader of the pro-Iranian Party of God. Israeli commandos seized the sheik in southern Lebanon three days ago.

Pete Rose banned from game for life

New York City, Aug. 24

Pete Rose has been banned from baseball for life, but continues to deny allegations that he placed bets on ball games. In March it was revealed that Peter Ueberroth, then commissioner of baseball, was investigating "serious allegations" against Rose involving gambling. Commissioner A. Bartlett Giamatti's decision today to ban Rose from the game was the result of a deal in which Rose signed a statement stating that the commissioner had a "factual basis" for banning him, while Giamatti agreed not to make "formal findings or declarations" on the charges.

Hurricane Hugo lashes shores of Carolinas

East Coast, Sept. 21

Hurricane Hugo, the most destructive storm to hit the U.S. in two decades, struck Georgia and the Carolinas after midnight last night. Coastal areas of the Carolinas were wracked by 135-mph winds, and 17-foot walls of water crashed over homes. Damage is expected to climb into the millions.

Puerto Rico and the Virgin Islands were the first to feel Hugo's destructive force. The storm left at least 25 dead, hundreds injured and 100,000 homeless in a matter of hours after the storm reached the islands on the 17th. Widespread looting was reported from the Virgin Islands, and 1,000 military police were flown in to restore order.

Wrecked pleasure boats litter the coast of the Carolinas in Hugo's wake.

Bush commits billions to drugs crusade

Washington, D.C., Sept. 5

In a televised address to the nation, President George Bush tonight launched a major offensive against drugs. Showing viewers a bag of crack, Bush urged Americans to work together and said: "Drugs are sapping our strength as a nation. Let there be no mistake, this stuff is poison." The $7.86-billion plan is aimed at reducing both supply and consumption of drugs in the U.S. by 10 percent by 1992 and by 50 percent by the end of the century. Money will also be spent on more prisons and for more police to control what has become a $110-billion industry.

Hotel queen Leona guilty in tax case

New York City, Aug. 30

"Only the little people pay taxes," said Leona Helmsley, but that remark has come back to haunt her. Mrs. Helmsley, president of Helmsley Hotels, Inc., the company founded by her husband, was tried on charges of defrauding the government by claiming personal expenditures as business deductions. Today she was convicted on 33 counts of tax evasion. The bill for back taxes from the years 1983-85 comes to a total of $1.2 million (→ Apr. 15, 1992).

July 22. *American racer Greg LeMond wins the Tour de France by just eight seconds as France celebrates the bicentennial of its Revolution.*

September 22. *America's songwriter, Irving Berlin, dies.*

San Francisco devastated by earthquake

A house lists like a sinking ship while ruins smolder in San Francisco.

San Francisco, Oct. 19

At exactly 5:04 p.m. two days ago, an earthquake measuring 6.9 on the Richter scale struck the Bay area. More than 200 people are feared dead. From its epicenter northeast of Santa Cruz on the San Andreas fault, tremors reached north to Sacramento and south to Los Angeles. There was severe damage on the Bay Bridge, where a span collapsed, on Interstate 880, where a half-mile upper section of the highway fell onto the lower one, killing 42, and in the Marina district, where older, less "earthquake-safe" buildings were demolished and a ruptured gas main sparked an inferno. Baseball fans at Candlestick Park held their breath as the stadium swayed, halting the third game of the World Series.

A collapsed part of Bay Bridge.

Evangelist Bakker gets 45-year term

Charlotte, N.C., Oct. 24

Jim Bakker, wearing stone-washed jeans and handcuffs, was led out of a Charlotte courthouse today after being sentenced to 45 years in prison and a $100,000 fine. He had been convicted on October 5 of fleecing followers of his now-bankrupt PTL (Praise the Lord, People That Love) ministries to the tune of $158 million. The 24 counts of fraud and conspiracy are related to the Heritage USA Christian theme park and PTL, both of which he founded.

Judge Robert "Maximum Bob" Potter, who heard the case, stated: "Those of us who do have religion are sick of being saps for money-grubbing preachers and priests." Lawyers for Bakker said that he will appeal the verdict.

October 6. *The inimitable Bette Davis, star of such classics as "All About Eve" and "Jezebel," died in a Paris hospital today of breast cancer at the age of 81.*

U.S. forces launch invasion of Panama

Panama City, Dec. 20

An estimated 24,000 U.S. troops swept into Panama early today as the Bush administration moved to topple the country's corrupt dictator, General Manuel Antonio Noriega.

Noriega has gone into hiding and is being hunted by U.S. forces. Panama's strongman has already been replaced by Guillermo Endara, who had been elected president by the Panamanian people in a contest voided by Noriega. The U.S. operation, code-named "Just Cause," began with three simultaneous attacks against pro-Noriega strongholds in the capital. U.S. forces quickly took control of much of the area, although they are being harassed by snipers belonging to Noriega's fiercely loyal Dignity Battalions. About 200 civilians, and 19 U.S. and 59 Panamanian soldiers are reported dead. President Bush wants Noriega to stand trial in the U.S. on drug-trafficking charges, and has offered a $1-million reward for information leading to his capture (→ Jan. 4, 1990).

West rejoices over fall of Berlin Wall

United States, Nov. 10

America and its NATO allies are elated today following the dismantling of the world's most visible symbol of Communist oppression. The Berlin Wall, a 28-mile-long concrete and barbed-wire barrier that had divided Berlin ever since August 1961, has fallen at last. East Germans can now freely travel to the West.

Yesterday's historic event came 26 years after President John F. Kennedy stood by the Wall and declared: *"Ich bin ein Berliner."*

Big Apple elects its first black mayor

New York City, Nov. 7

David Dinkins, former Manhattan borough president, has been elected mayor of New York City. The 62-year-old Democrat beat Edward Koch, the outgoing mayor, in the primaries, and then his Republican opponent, former federal prosecutor Rudolph Giuliani. Dinkins won with a majority of the black vote and about 30 percent of the white vote. He inherits a city burdened with a massive budget deficit, AIDS and drugs problems, and more than 50,000 homeless.

U.S. troops stop and search suspected partisans of General Noriega.

1990

Bush

New York City, Jan. 10.
Time Inc. acquires Warner Communications Inc. for $14.1 billion.

Cove Neck, N.Y., Jan. 25.
A Colombian Boeing 707 crashes on approach to Kennedy Airport, killing 73.

Moscow, Jan. 31.
McDonald's opens its first restaurant in the U.S.S.R.

Tokyo, Feb. 11.
James "Buster" Douglas flattens fellow American Mike Tyson to win world heavyweight title.

Hollywood, Calif., March 26.
Bruce Beresford's *Driving Miss Daisy* wins four Oscars.

Augusta, Georgia, April 9.
Briton Nick Faldo edges out U.S. golfer Ray Floyd to win U.S. Masters.

Ohio, June 14.
Flash floods caused by violent thunderstorms leave 33 dead.

Philippines, June 27.
All 260 Peace Corps volunteers told to leave country due to fears for their safety.

Channelview, Texas, July 5.
A blast at a chemical plant kills 17 workers.

Plainfield, Illinois, Aug. 28.
A tornado leaves 29 people dead and 297 injured.

Helsinki, Finland, Sept. 9.
Presidents Bush and Gorbachev agree that Iraqi troops must withdraw from Kuwait.

Washington, D.C., Oct. 9.
Judge David H. Souter joins the U.S. Supreme Court following the retirement in July of Justice William J. Brennan.

Oakland, Calif., Oct. 20.
Cincinnati Reds defeat Oakland A's to sweep World Series.

Washington, D.C., Oct. 26.
Mayor Barry is sentenced to six months in jail for possession of cocaine.

Washington, D.C., Dec. 31.
Census Bureau puts population of the U.S. at 248,709,873, or 10.2 percent more than in 1980.

Hollywood, Calif.
Top fims include *Pretty Woman, Dances With Wolves, Home Alone* and *Total Recall*.

DEATH

New York City, Apr. 15.
Greta Garbo, American actress (*Sept. 18, 1905).

Gen. Noriega faces drug charges in Miami

En route from Panama to Miami.

Miami, Jan. 4
Panama's fallen strongman, General Manuel Noriega, stood in a U.S. courtroom today charged with drug trafficking. "Pineapple face," as his opponents call him, was arrested when he left the Vatican embassy in Panama City, where he took sanctuary 10 days ago following the U.S. invasion of Panama. If found guilty, Noriega faces a jail term of up to 145 years and over $1.5 million in fines on today's charges. More criminal charges are likely. Noriega's alleged links to the C.I.A. are sure to figure in his defense and may prove an embarrassment to President Bush, a former C.I.A. director (→July 10, 1992).

F.B.I. sting nabs Washington's mayor

Washington, D.C., January 19
Marion Barry, one of America's best-known black politicians, was secretly videotaped smoking a pipeful of crack, a highly addictive form of cocaine, the F.B.I. said today. The filming took place shortly after the mayor of the nation's capital had been lured to a hotel room in the city by an ex-girlfriend. F.B.I. agents arrested Mayor Barry as he lit the pipe.

The popular 53-year-old mayor, who strongly denies any wrongdoing, now faces a possible prison sentence (→Oct. 26).

Eighty-seven die in New York disco fire

New York City, March 25
The Happy Land Social Club, a Bronx discotheque, became a nightmarish inferno tonight. Firefighters from a neighboring station managed to put out the blaze quickly, but that was not enough to avert tragedy. When they entered the small, windowless club, they found the dance floor littered with bodies. All but one of the 88 people in the club when the fire broke out died from smoke inhalation. "It was so tightly packed that all the oxygen was consumed by the fire within seconds," said a policeman. Police have arrested a suspect on charges of arson.

Rescue teams work through the night to retrieve the dead and injured.

January 25. Hollywood's sultry beauty, Ava Gardner, dies at 68.

U.S. Perrier scare

United States, Feb. 14
Yuppies will be deprived, temporarily at least, of one of their favorite thirst quenchers.

Traces of benzene, a carcinogen, have been discovered in sparkling mineral water bottled by Perrier. The French company has recalled its entire stock of 160 million bottles from the world market. The chemical was originally found in bottles examined in the U.S., but has since been found in supplies exported to Denmark, Japan and Britain as well. Perrier says the problem was apparently caused by dirty filters at its plant in Vergeze, in southern France.

Jan. 28. San Francisco 49ers quarterback Joe Montana stars in Super Bowl XXIV, in New Orleans. The 49ers defeated the Denver Broncos 55-10.

386

Two American hostages freed in Beirut

Lebanon, Apr. 30

Frank Reed, the American college administrator held hostage by the pro-Iranian Islamic Jihad group since September 1986, was released into Syrian custody in Beirut today. His freeing, following that of another U.S. hostage, Robert Polhill, eight days ago, gives hope that all Western hostages may soon be out. The Iranians are making it clear that much depends on President Bush's response to their latest "gesture of goodwill." The White House has thanked Syria's President Assad for facilitating the release of the two hostages.

When Reed appeared on television this evening, the effects of his long ordeal were only too apparent. He said he had been blindfolded for much of his captivity.

Bob Polhill was held for 1,183 days.

Major flaw found in NASA space telescope

Houston, June 27

The Hubble Space Telescope, which was launched in April from the shuttle Discovery, is myopic. One, if not both, of the $1.5-billion telescope's mirrors, which focus images so that pictures can be taken, has an incorrect curvature. This results in a condition that NASA scientists compare to near-sightedness. The space agency had high hopes for the Hubble telescope; pictures taken from space would provide more profound detail and be intensely clearer than those made from earth. The defects could have been detected during pre-launch tests, but the tests were not performed because of constraints of time and money.

Former N.S.C. head sentenced to jail

Washington, D.C., June 11

Retired Admiral John Poindexter today became the seventh former Reagan administration official to be found guilty of wrongdoing in the Iran-contra affair.

Poindexter, who served as the President's national security adviser for a year, was convicted on April 7 on five felony counts of conspiracy, obstructing Congress and making false statements to legistators about his role in the plot. Today, a federal judge sentenced Poindexter to six months in jail for his involvement in secret arms sales to Iran and the diversion of profits to Nicaragua's contra rebels despite a congressional ban. None of the other defendants already tried and found guilty have been sent to jail (→ Sept. 16, 1991).

April 5. *Amid considerable fanfare, Donald Trump's giant new casino venture, the extravagant Trump Taj Mahal, opens in Atlantic City, New Jersey.*

Bush makes U-turn on campaign tax vow

Washington, D.C., June 26

Today's presidential about-face could not have come at a worse time for George Bush. As Republican leaders are gearing up for November's mid-term elections, Bush has admitted he can no longer stick to the most memorable pledge of his 1988 presidential campaign: "Read my lips: no new taxes."

The president's embarrassing reversal was motivated by the urgency of the budget crisis. In a memo, Bush coyly refers to "tax revenue increases" as a means of attempting to deal with the spiraling deficit. Republicans and Democrats alike are anxious to cut the deficit, and so far there has been little sniping at Bush's U-turn. Rises are most likely in indirect taxes rather than income tax.

How the New York Post saw it.

Brando's son Chris arrested for murder

Los Angeles, May 16

Marlon Brando's 32-year-old son, Christian, was arrested today and charged with the murder of his half-sister's French companion, Dag Drollet.

Police believe that Christian shot Drollet at the Brando residence here during a violent argument, apparently because he was opposed to the young Frenchman's relationship with Cheyenne, Christian's half-sister (→ Feb. 28, 1991).

Superpower discord on united Germany

Washington, D.C., June 3

There was a time when U.S.-Soviet summits were headline-grabbers. Now that superpower relations are warmer, they seem mostly routine.

At the core of the second Bush-Gorbachev meeting was the Soviet leader's attempt to convince the U.S. President that when East and West Germany reunify on October 3, the new nation should not be a NATO member. Gorbachev even suggested that a united Germany could be a member of both NATO and the Warsaw Pact. Bush rejected both Soviet proposals.

Show biz mourns Sammy Davis Jr.

Los Angeles, May 16

Sammy Davis Jr. could do it all: He was a singer, dancer, actor, musician and mime. He began his career at the age of 3 in a vaudeville act with his father and uncle. A star of the Las Vegas nightclub scene, he ran with the Rat Pack, which included his pals Dean Martin and Frank Sinatra. In 1956 he debuted on Broadway in *Mr. Wonderful* and on the screen in *The Benny Goodman Story*. Hard living led to ill health – kidney, heart and liver problems – in the latter part of his life. He died today after a long battle with throat cancer.

Sammy Davis Jr. was just 64.

Bush draws 'line in sand' for Saddam

Thousands of American troops are being airlifted to Saudi Arabian bases.

Washington, D.C., Aug. 8

Just six days after Iraqi forces swept into Kuwait, the first contingent of U.S. troops landed at Dhahran today. The forces being deployed in Saudi Arabia include units of the 82nd Airborne Division, of the Marine Corps as well as U.S. Navy and Air Force assets.

As Iraqi armor was massing on Saudi Arabia's northern borders, President Bush went on nationwide television this evening to denounce Iraq's "naked aggression" and explain his objectives in the first major crisis of the post-Cold War world. Bush told Americans that the troops being airlifted into the region had drawn "a line in the sand." If President Saddam Hussein crossed it, there would be war. He added that chief among U.S. aims was the unconditional with-drawal of Iraqi forces from Kuwait. Bush also expressed concern for the safety of the hundreds of Americans and other Westerners taken to Baghdad after being seized in Kuwait. Saddam, who formally annexed the oil-rich emirate today, has warned that their lives will be in danger if their countries take military action against Iraq. Bush is calling on NATO allies and Arab states to join a multinational coalition to oppose Iraq (→ Nov. 29).

Neil Bush involved in S & L scandal

Denver, Colorado, July 10

The savings and loan scandal that has rocked the administration and banking circles became a personal crisis today for President George Bush.

Neil Bush, one of the President's five children, has been implicated in the collapse of Denver's Silverado Banking, Savings and Loan Association. The collapse of the institution, of which Neil Bush was a director, has resulted in a $1-billion loss to the federal government.

Although it seems highly unlikely that he will be prosecuted, the President's son has been accused by federal regulators of conflicts of interest as a result of his financial dealings with the bank and several of its chief borrowers. The bailout of the hundreds of insolvent S & Ls will probably cost the federal government $500 billion over the next 40 years.

Ready for "Mother of all Battles".

Atlanta wins battle for 1996 Olympics

Tokyo, Sept. 18

Six cities had battled for the honor of hosting the 1996 Olympic Games. Manchester, Melbourne, Belgrade and Toronto were early casualties of the voting today.

That left Athens, the sentimental favorite and birthplace of the modern Olympics in 1896, and Atlanta. By a comfortable 51 votes to 35 the International Olympic Committee meeting in Tokyo awarded the Games to Atlanta. The Atlanta delegations's carefully costed proposals and the prospect of lucrative television contracts won the day.

Census controversy as results come in

Washington, D.C., July 1

The U.S. Census Bureau estimated the population at 251,394,000 today. This estimate is higher than the actual count: Early results put the number at just under 246 million, but the final total, to be reported in December, is likely to be higher. Six years of planning and $2.5 billion went into the census.

This year's census had many firsts. Computers were used more than ever before, and a computerized map that showed the nation block by block was developed to help in enumeration. New questions were designed to take into account the evolution of family groups, including gay households. Only 26 percent of households with children under 18 included a married couple. For the first time an attempt was made to count the nation's homeless population.

One in four Americans is a member of a minority group. Asians and Pacific Islanders, the fastest growing group, accounted for 2.9 percent of the population. Hispanics made up 9 percent of the population, and blacks 12.1 percent.

Despite a bid to increase accuracy, there are charges of undercounting. Results are used to determine the number of seats in the House of Representatives for each state, as well as for the apportionment of federal and state funds. Even broadcast advertising rates for different regions are determined by census figures (→ Dec 31).

Sept. 9 *Pete Sampras, 19, the youngest to win U.S. Open, beats Andre Agassi 6-4, 6-3, 6-2.*

American Tom Curren wins World Surf Championship in France.

JDL founder Kahane shot in Manhattan

New York City, Nov. 5

Rabbi Meir Kahane, the U.S.-born Israeli politician who founded the Jewish Defense League in 1968, was shot to death in a Manhattan hotel tonight. Kahane was hit by two bullets reportedly fired by an American of Egyptian descent as the rabbi was leaving a meeting with his supporters. The suspect was arrested. Kahane had spent a year in a U.S. jail for plotting to make bombs before moving to Israel in 1971. There he founded the extremist and anti-Arab Kach political party. In 1988, he lost his seat in the Knesset, or parliament, after Israel banned Kach for its "Nazi-like," anti-democratic policies.

Rabbi Kahane, a militant Zionist

$600-million fine for junk-bond king

New York City, Nov. 21

Former Drexel Burnham Lambert whiz kid Michael Milken, who made a colossal fortune on Wall Street during the 1980s trading in so-called "junk" bonds, was today sentenced to a 10-year jail term, three years on probation and $600 million in fines.

The 44-year-old bond trader, who earned $550 million in 1987 alone – the highest paycheck in history – had pleaded guilty to securities violations and helping to file false income tax returns. He had persuaded investors to buy high-risk, high-yield "junk" bonds used in corporate takeovers.

U.N. backing for war to free Kuwait

New York City, Nov. 29

President Bush, who says he has "had it" with Saddam Hussein's intransigence, has won a crucial battle at the United Nations.

The Security Council voted today to approve use of military force against Iraq if Iraqi troops do not withdraw from Kuwait by January 15. Cuba and Yemen were the only nations to vote against the resolution, while China abstained. The U.N. ultimatum, which also calls on Iraq to free all hostages, gives the U.S. and its Desert Shield allies in the Gulf about six weeks to bolster their military presence in the region (→ Jan. 1991).

Italian mogul buys slice of Hollywood

Hollywood, Calif., Nov. 1

Promising to restore the studios to their former greatness, Italian entrepreneur Giancarlo Parretti has won a hard-fought battle to buy MGM-United Artists for $1.3 billion.

Dubbed the "mystery mogul" by the press, Parretti's ever-growing media empire now spans the Atlantic. Parretti, a farmer's son, launched his Hollywood takeover bid after purchasing the French Pathé Cinéma group. However, French authorities are already asking whether Parretti has the full support of his financial backers (→ Dec. 30, 1991).

Aid to Soviet Union announced by Bush

Washington, D.C., Dec. 12

In a bid to alleviate the looming threat of famine and civil strife, President Bush today agreed to send an aid package to the Soviet Union.

The wide-ranging package includes emergency medical supplies, credits to buy $1 billion worth of U.S. grain and long-term assistance to improve the country's infrastructure. Overturning previous administration policy, which made aid conditional on the Soviets relaxing emigration laws, Bush explained that he wanted to help the Soviet people "stay the course of democratization" (→ July 17, 1991).

Republican setback in mid-term voting

United States, Nov. 6

As is often the case in mid-term elections, voters tend to favor the party that failed to win the White House two years earlier. Today's voting results run true to form, with the Democrats picking up eight seats in the House of Representatives and gaining one in the Senate. Democrats now control 56 seats to the G.O.P.'s 44, while they have 268 House seats to the Republicans' 167.

Politicians and media commentators are attributing today's Republican losses to President Bush's June 26 backdown on his 1988 campaign promise not to increase taxes to cut the budget deficit.

October 14. *Leonard Bernstein, composer of "West Side Story," dies at the age of 72.*

Nov. 22 *President Bush and his wife, Barbara, are in Saudi Arabia to spend Thanksgiving Day with the soldiers of Operation Desert Shield.*

Political Correctness: How's that again?

United States

Mao once asked, "Where do correct ideas come from?" While that puzzler may go unanswered, most would agree that ideas, correct or not, are transmitted by language. The modifier "politically correct," or PC, was originally used by those on the left, somewhat ironically, to describe a range of progressive thought. To spread PC ideas, PC lingo was needed. The proponents of PC speech say that they are battling racism and sexism. Critics say that they are massacring English with Orwellian newspeak.

Here are some examples of the Brave New English:
Differently abled: disabled
Temporarily abled: not disabled
Enslaved person: PC for slave, preferable because it emphasizes the personhood of the oppressed
Eurocentrism: the belief that Western culture is superior
Herstory, hystery: feminist replacements for history
Human animal: non-speciesist replacement for human
Longer-living: old
Mutant albino genetic-recessive global minority: white people

Tampa, Fla., Jan. 27.
The New York Giants win Super Bowl XXV by defeating the Buffalo Bills, 20-19.

Los Angeles, Feb. 28.
Marlon Brando's son, Christian, is jailed for 10 years for the killing of his half-sister's lover.

California, June 16.
Former President Reagan denies having delayed the release of U.S. hostages in Iran to win the 1980 election.

Washington, D.C., July 10.
President Bush lifts economic sanctions imposed on South Africa in 1986.

Washington, D.C., July 24.
The government announces that no further space shuttles will be built.

Washington, D.C., Sept. 16.
A federal judge orders all Iran-contra charges against Oliver North dropped (→ Dec. 24, 1992).

Indianapolis, Sept. 16.
U.S. gymnast Kim Zmeskal, aged 15, wins a gold medal at the world championship.

Minneapolis, Oct 27.
The Minnesota Twins beat Atlanta Braves to take World Series, four games to three.

Las Vegas, Nevada, Dec. 15.
Rodeo star Ty Murray of Texas wins the title of world champion all-round cowboy.

Moscow, Dec. 25.
The U.S.S.R. disintegrates as President Gorbachev resigns.

Los Angeles, Dec. 30.
Control of MGM-Pathé is awarded to Crédit Lyonnais, a French bank, after the arrest for tax fraud of studio owner Giancarlo Parretti.

Hollywood, Calif.
Top films of the year include *Thelma and Louise, Robin Hood: Prince of Thieves* and *Terminator 2.*

DEATHS

La Jolla, Calif., Sept 24.
Theodor S. Geisel (Dr. Seuss), author (*March 2, 1904).

Santa Monica, Calif., Sept 28.
Miles Davis, jazz trumpeter (*May 25, 1926).

Santa Monica, Calif., Nov. 5.
Fred MacMurray, actor (*Aug. 30, 1908).

Canary Islands, Nov. 5.
Robert Maxwell, British publisher, owner of *New York Daily News* (*June 10, 1923).

Operation Desert Storm frees Kuwait

The U.S. carrier Theodore Roosevelt launches its aircraft against Baghdad.

Gen. Norman Schwarzkopf, commander of the allied forces, briefs the press.

U.S. armor slices through battered Iraqi defenses on Kuwait's border.

Persian Gulf, January

The U.S. went to war at dawn on the 17th. Operation Desert Storm, placed under the overall command of General Norman Schwarzkopf, began with waves of high-tech bombing raids on Baghdad. The Iraqi capital was hit by dozens of laser-guided "smart bombs" dropped by USAF F-117 Stealth aircraft. Over the next days, U.S. and allied planes launched thousands of raids over Iraq and Iraqi-occupied Kuwait. While President Saddam Hussein's forces hunkered down in bunkers, Iraq retaliated by launching Scud missiles at Israeli cities, killing at least four Israeli civilians. U.S. bases in Saudi Arabia were also targeted by Scuds.

Ground troops went into action on January 29 after a column of Iraqi armor and infantry crossed the Kuwaiti border and seized the Saudi town of Khafji. Three days of fighting forced an Iraqi retreat, but left 12 Marines dead.

Feb. 28

The Gulf war is over. President Bush went on nationwide television yesterday at 9 p.m. to announce: "Kuwait is liberated. At midnight tonight, exactly 100 hours since ground operations began, all coalition and United States forces will suspend offensive combat operations." This morning, the people of Kuwait City, who have endured six months and 25 days of Iraqi occupation, are celebrating their new-found freedom. Their country is in ruins. Before withdrawing, the defeated Iraqi troops set fire to hundreds of Kuwaiti oil wells, and a thick pall of smoke hangs over the emirate. In Saudi Arabia, allied commanders are counting the cost of the short, brutal war. A total of 148 U.S. servicemen were killed in action, and 472 were wounded. The allies estimate that 150,000 Iraqis were killed. Tens of thousands were captured or surrendered. The turning point in what Saddam Hussein called the "mother of all battles" came two days ago when the U.S. 82nd and 101st Airborne Divisions and the 7th Corps reached the Euphrates River in southern Iraq. Supported by British and French units, the U.S. forces trapped six divisions of Iraq's elite Republican Guard (→ Apr. 19).

U.S. mounts aid operation to save Kurds

USAF aircraft drop supplies to refugees who wait in makeshift camps.

Iraq, Apr. 19

Several thousand U.S. troops are moving into northern Iraq to set up camps for the 500,000 Kurdish refugees struggling to survive near the Turkish border. U.S., British and French aircraft are dropping food and medicine to the starving refugees, who fled to the area to escape from Iraqi troops.

Following the failure of a Kurdish revolt against Saddam Hussein, President Bush decided to create a safe haven for the Kurds. Lieutenant General John Shalikashvili, the U.S. commander in the area, has told Baghdad that the U.S. will not tolerate overflight of the safe haven by Iraqi military aircraft.

Book's salacious details ruffle Reagans

California, Apr. 9

An angry Ronald Reagan struck back at Kitty Kelley, the author of an unauthorized biography of his wife, Nancy, dismissing the book's salacious claims as "flagrant and absurd falsehoods" that went beyond "the bounds of decency." The book includes allegations of adultery, marijuana use and child abuse, and characterizes the former first lady as mean, greedy, deceitful and manipulative.

Kelley countered: "Everything is documented ... I spent four years doing this book and talked with 1,000 people." The book is a tremendous success, and Simon & Schuster, the publishers, have ordered 150,000 extra copies to add to the 600,000 already in print.

Kitty Kelley: controversial author.

Court upholds curb on family planners

Washington, D.C., May 23

In a 5-4 ruling, the Supreme Court today upheld regulations issued under the Reagan administration which forbid family planning clinics to "encourage, promote or advocate abortion," or to hand out written material on the subject. Judge David Souter, the only justice appointed by President Bush, voted with the majority, despite his earlier observation that the regulations "may preclude professional speech" (→ June 29, 1992).

Ivana Trump gets large settlement

New York City, March 20

The 13-month public feud between Donald Trump and his ex-wife Ivana has been resolved with an agreement to settle the affair out of court.

The divorce agreement, which was announced by the millionaire real estate developer today, gives the former model $10 million, their mansion in Connecticut and their apartment on the East Side of Manhattan. "I'm very happy that it worked out so well," he said.

Ex-Senator Tower dies in plane crash

Brunswick, Georgia, Apr. 5

This afternoon a twin-engine turboprop dove into the woods and crashed, just two miles from its destination here. Among the 23 people killed in the crash was John Tower, the former Texas senator. Tower, whose nomination by President Bush for defense secretary was rejected by the Senate in 1989, had recently published a book of memoirs, *Consequences*, in which he struck back at his critics, especially Georgia Senator Sam Nunn.

Video of beating in L.A. causes outcry

Los Angeles, March 15

Four Los Angeles police officers were indicted today following the March 3 beating of a black motorist, 25-year-old Rodney King.

The incident was taped by a bystander trying out a new video camera. The tape shows four officers repeatedly clubbing King as he lay on the ground. The videotape has been shown on television news programs across the country, and has led to a nationwide outcry against police brutality. There have also been calls for the resignation of Los Angeles Police Chief Daryl Gates (→ May 2, 1992).

Minimum wage is $4.25 per hour

Washington, D.C., Apr. 1

The national minimum wage has been raised to $4.25 per hour. This increase, from the previous minimum of $3.80 set in April 1990, comes as a result of legislation passed by Congress and signed into law by President Bush in November 1989. Critics of the increase claim that it will cause hardships for small businesses and increase unemployment.

A lower training wage of $3.61 was set for workers 16 to 19 years old in the first six months of their first job. This training wage will expire on March 31, 1993.

March 20. *Sony Corp. signs a $1-billion multi-year contract with pop star Michael Jackson.*

March 25. *Kevin Costner's film, "Dances With Wolves," receives no less than six Oscars.*

Bush taken to hospital for heart problem

Bush reassures reporters.

Bethesda, Maryland, May 6

A smiling President Bush left the National Naval Medical Center today, apparently eager to get back to work after spending two days in the hospital.

He had been rushed to Bethesda after suffering from irregular heart rhythms while jogging at the Camp David, Maryland, presidential retreat. It seems the President's busy schedule was at least partly responsible for the trouble. Bush, aged 66, was given two heart-regulating drugs after his doctors decided against an electric shock procedure to stabilize his heart rhythm. This avoided the need for sedation, a move that would have required a temporary transfer of power to Vice President Dan Quayle.

Historic address by Queen Elizabeth II

Washington, D.C., May 16

Queen Elizabeth today became the first British monarch to address a joint session of the Senate and the House of Representatives. She reminded Congress of Britain's contribution to the Gulf War and the two countries' alliances in previous wars, but also joked about her height. "I do hope you can see me today," she said. When she had spoken earlier at the White House she was almost invisible behind the microphones. The high points of the Queen's trip were the speech to Congress and a visit to a poor neighborhood, where she was embraced by an admirer. The Queen is not accustomed to such American familiarity: Touching the monarch is against royal protocol.

Congress applauds the Queen.

Texas picks fast French train system

Austin, Texas, May 28

By 1998 Texans should be able to travel by rail between Houston, Dallas and San Antonio at speeds of up to 185 miles per hour. Passengers will be whisked from downtown Houston to central Dallas in just 90 minutes.

The Texas High Speed Rail Authority today awarded the franchise for the triangular 600-mile route to a group using existing French *Train à Grande Vitesse*, or TGV, technology. This was chosen over Germany's ICE system. The cost of the privately financed project has been set at $5.7 billion.

June 10. *Cheering New Yorkers give a rousing ticker-tape welcome to veterans of Operation Desert Storm at a victory parade on Broadway.*

Thurgood Marshall retires from Court

Washington, D.C., June 27

Thurgood Marshall, the first black ever to serve on the U.S. Supreme Court, retired today after 24 years of distinguished but often stormy service. The 84-year-old justice cited failing health but said he will remain on the bench until his successor has been confirmed by the Senate. Justice Marshall, who came to the Supreme Court on October 2, 1967, has been a staunch liberal and ardent defender of civil rights. His greatest legal victory came in 1954, when the court banned segregation in "separate but equal" public schools (→ Oct. 15).

New financial woes hit New York City

New York City, May 10

Mayor David Dinkins today presented the New York City Council with his "doomsday budget," a plan developed in response to the city's worst fiscal crisis in a generation.

The proposed budget calls for cuts of $1.5 billion in municipal services. The Central Park Zoo would be closed, more than 29,000 employees, including 2,800 teachers, laid off and a quarter of the city's 295,000 street lights turned off. The cutback plan would affect every agency except the police and jails. It calls for the elimination of many educational, sanitation and preventive health programs. In addition, Dinkins has asked for $1 billion in tax increases to help eliminate a deficit that could reach $3.4 billion for the fiscal year beginning July 1. By law, the city must begin the fiscal year with a balanced budget. "No adjectives can explain the consequences of cuts so large," said the mayor. "For unless our friends in labor, in the legislature, in the governor's office, in the Municipal Assistance Corporation and in the City Council step forward and help out, the unthinkable will become the unavoidable."

June 9. *U.S. tennis star Jim Courier wins the French Open.*

U.S. to sign vital Antarctic protection pact

Washington, D.C., July 4

President Bush announced today that, despite lingering doubts about some aspects of the pact, the United States will sign a tough international agreement to ban mining and oil exploration in the Antarctic for at least 50 years.

The new accord is aimed at protecting Antarctica's fragile environment and wildlife and promoting scientific research there. The pact, which will not come into force until it is ratified by its signatories, is to be added to the 1961 Antarctic Treaty. That 30-year-old accord strictly prohibits weapons testing and the dumping of nuclear waste in the Antarctic.

A 50-year respite for Antarctica.

Sprinter Lewis sets sensational record

U.S. runner delights the crowds.

Tokyo, Aug. 25

"This is the best race of all time, the best sprinters in the best race," exulted Carl Lewis, who set the world record for the 100-meter sprint today at the World Track and Field Championships, an event rivalled in importance only by the Olympics. Lewis finished at 9.86 seconds, followed by two fellow Philadelphia natives. Kenny Burrell, who had set the previous record in June at 9.90, led the race until the final 10 meters and finished at 9.88, and Dennis Mitchell came in third at 9.91 seconds.

Lewis was world champion in 1983 and 1987 and won gold medals in the 1984 and 1988 Olympics, but this is his first individual world record.

July 1. *Actor Michael Landon, aged 54, dies of cancer.*

West hails failure of Soviet coup bid

Washington, D.C., Aug. 23

White House officials breathed a sigh of relief today. Four days ago a group of Soviet hardliners, including senior K.G.B. and military officers, announced that they had taken control of the Soviet government. When the dramatic coup attempt unraveled, President Bush was one of the first Western leaders to telephone Gorbachev and express his support. Gorbachev survived the coup, but his authority has been badly shaken (→ Dec. 25).

Bush refuses blank check for Gorbachev

London, July 17

President Mikhail Gorbachev will be returning to the Kremlin practically empty-handed.

It was the first time that a Soviet leader had been invited to attend a Western economic summit. Gorbachev had come here in the hope of persuading President Bush and the leaders of the world's six other wealthiest nations, known as the Group of Seven, to agree to a massive Western aid package. However, Bush and John Major, the British Prime Minister, argued that Gorbachev's latest economic reform proposals were not radical enough to create a viable free-market economy. Despite this rebuff, the G7 leaders agreed to share their nations' technical know-how so that the Soviets can press ahead with their efforts to modernize their economy (→ March 11, 1992).

As George Bush meets leaders, Barbara visits HIV patients with Lady Diana.

Brooklyn race riots sparked by accident

Brooklyn, New York, Aug. 22

A measure of calm has returned to Crown Heights after four days of rioting. Tension between the Jewish and black communities here flared into violence after a tragic car accident three days ago. A car in a motorcade of the Lubavitcher sect's grand rabbi hit two black children, killing one of them. An ambulance regularly used by the Lubavitcher community did not pick up the injured child. Angry crowds of blacks quickly formed, chanting anti-Semitic slogans. Just hours later, a Jewish scholar from Australia was stabbed to death by a group of young blacks. Rioting ensued, and 84 police and at least 25 civilians were injured in the next three days.

Dozens of youths are arrested during three days of bitter racial clashes.

Navratilova palimony case ends in deal

Judy Nelson settled out of court.

Texas, Sept. 11

Tennis star Martina Navratilova and her former lover, Judy Nelson, have made a tentative financial deal to settle the palimony claim brought by Nelson in June. Nevertheless, their relationship is still far from love-all.

Nelson will receive an undisclosed sum, but still claims that she and Navratilova had an agreement entitling her to half of Navratilova's earnings, estimated at $5 million to $9 million over the seven years during which they had a relationship. Navratilova says she was defrauded and disputes the validity of the cohabitation agreement. Nelson says she is not just after the money: "It's about Martina honoring a contract."

Tough U.S. refuses Israel a vital loan

Washington, D.C., Sept. 13

Israel is enraged at President Bush because he has refused a loan guarantee of $10 billion to build housing for Soviet immigrants in Israel. Bush has said that in order to "give peace a break" in the Middle East he would ask Congress to defer consideration of the Israeli request. He also said the loans cannot be used to build housing in the Occupied Territories. The glitch in U.S.-Israeli relations comes as Washington is trying to organize Mid-East peace talks (→ Oct. 30).

Computer giants to share technology

New York City, Oct. 2

I.B.M. and Apple, fierce rivals ever since Apple was founded in the 1970s, have agreed to form an alliance which they hope will boost lagging sales.

The two computer giants announced plans to make their products compatible and develop a family of powerful new microprocessors. I.B.M. and Apple have also decided to create "open" systems which will allow consumers to mix and match as they buy hardware and software.

Senators focus on sexual harassment

Clarence Thomas is confirmed despite allegations by Anita Hill.

Washington, D.C., Oct. 15

Senate hearings that have thrust sexual harassment to the forefront of American debate ended today. Clarence Thomas, a federal appeals court judge, was confirmed as a Supreme Court justice by a vote of 52-48. Thomas was accused of sexual harassment by Anita Hill, a law professor who had worked for him. Hill said that the judge made lewd suggestions to her, boasted of the size of his penis, and described pornographic movies he had seen, mentioning in particular one starring "Long Dong Silver."

Judge Thomas denies all the charges. Accuser and accused are both black, both graduates of Yale law school, and one of them is lying. Thomas is passionate, eloquent, outraged that anyone should question him. Hill is calm, deliberate and restrained. The hearings were televised live, and more people watched them than tuned into the daytime soap operas.

Thomas is a conservative, and President Bush nominated him in order to cement the conservative majority on the court. Liberals tried to stop him, and Hill's allegations were leaked to the media, changing the focus of the hearings from judicial philosophy to questions of sexism and abuse of power.

Loner kills 22 in a Texas gun rampage

Killeen, Texas, Oct. 16

A man crashed his pick-up truck through the window of a restaurant and pulled out a semi-automatic pistol and slaughtered 22 people before killing himself.

Gregory Kennard, 35, jumped out of his truck and cried, "This is what Bell County has done to me!" Then he opened fire on people waiting in line in the cafeteria. Customers hid under tables as the gunman walked through the restaurant shooting and reloading his gun with 17-round magazines. After the killer was hit by police gunfire, he shot and killed himself. At least 20 people were wounded, and they were taken to three different hospitals in the area. Many of them are in critical condition.

U.S. backs Mid-East peace conference

Madrid, Oct. 30

President George Bush, flanked by Soviet leader Mikhail Gorbachev and U.S. Secretary of State James Baker, today attended the opening of crucial Mid-East peace talks.

As Bush and Gorbachev made their opening remarks, Yitzhak Shamir, Israel's premier, sat impassively at the huge table, facing the Palestinian delegation. The conference, sponsored by the U.S. and the Soviet Union, marks the beginning of the first direct negotiations between Israelis and Palestinians. All sides at the talks stress that today's meeting is just a start, adding that the road to peace in the Middle East will be long and tortuous (→ Aug. 11, 1992).

Oct. 23. *Fires rage for three days through Oakland and Berkeley, Calif., leaving at least 24 dead, and damage is estimated at over $1.5 billion.*

Magic Johnson is HIV-positive, will retire

Los Angeles, Nov. 8

America is shocked by the revelation that one of its top sports stars, the L.A. Laker forward Earvin "Magic" Johnson, has tested positive for the virus that causes AIDS. The star – described today by President Bush as a "hero" – made the announcement himself yesterday. The item dominated TV news bulletins for two reasons: first, because Johnson is hugely popular, and second, because he says he contracted the disease through heterosexual sex. Johnson, who is 32, intends to retire from basketball and devote his time to campaigning for greater awareness of AIDS among heterosexuals. Until now, most Americans had linked the disease with homosexuals and drug users.

Basketball legend to fight AIDS.

End of an era as Pan Am ceases flying

Miami, Dec. 4

The end of the road came today for one of America's greatest commercial aviation pioneers.

Pan American World Airways, the 64-year-old airline founded by Juan Trippe, ceased operations, a victim of deregulation and a deep recession in the industry.

Pan Am, burdened by huge losses and operating under court protection from its creditors since January, is the third major U.S. airline to fold this year. The carrier's demise comes after a decision by Delta Air Lines to withdraw from a deal that would have helped Pan Am emerge from bankruptcy. Delta announced yesterday that it would not put up any more money to keep Pan Am flying.

Last Pan Am flight lands in Miami.

Last U.S. hostages freed from Lebanon

Free at last: Joseph Cicippio, Terry Anderson and Alann Steen.

Damascus, Syria, Dec. 5

Associated Press correspondent Terry Anderson, the last of the 17 U.S. citizens who have been taken hostage in Lebanon since 1984, is free. Anderson, who was held for a total of 2,455 days – more than any other American hostage – will now be flying to Germany to join two other U.S. hostages, Alann Steen and Joseph Cicippio. They were released earlier this week. Shortly after Anderson was freed, he was reunited in Damascus with his fiancee, Madeleine, and their 6-year-old daughter Sulome – whom he had never seen. The release of the three Americans leaves two Germans as the only Western hostages held in Beirut.

William Kennedy Smith acquitted of rape

Senator Ted Kennedy's nephew is cheered as he leaves the courtroom.

Tragic Kimberly dies of AIDS

Florida, Dec. 8

Kimberly Bergalis, 23, who was infected with the AIDS virus after being treated by a dentist with HIV, died today. Doctors reacted with skepticism when Bergalis insisted in September, 1990, after the dentist died of AIDS, that she had not contracted the disease through sexual intercourse, intravenous drug injections or a blood transfusion. But the Centers for Disease Control established that the strain of HIV with which she was infected was identical to that of her dentist.

Rate cut boosts ailing economy

United States, Dec. 30

The economic year is ending on an upbeat note. Experts claim the end of the recession is in sight. Traders on Wall Street have been on a buying spree since the Federal Reserve cut the discount rate 10 days ago, from 4.5 to 3.5 percent, its lowest level since 1964. The Dow Jones industrial average rose 8.6 percent in 10 days, ending the year at a record high of 3,168.83. The annual inflation rate stands at just 2.9 percent, compared with 6.1 percent last year.

West Palm Beach, Fla., Dec. 11

The jury took just 80 minutes to acquit William Kennedy Smith of raping a 30-year-old woman at the Kennedy family's Florida estate last March. The trial had been televised throughout the country and sharpened the debate about "date rape" and the difficulty of proving sexual assault. Smith admitted that he had had sex with the woman, but claimed that she had consented. In the end, it was his word against hers, and the jury found that there was insufficient evidence to prove the charges. Senator Edward Kennedy, Smith's uncle, was among those who gave evidence, saying that he had heard no screams on the night of the alleged assault.

Bush is taken ill at state dinner in Tokyo

Aides and agents rush to assist the President as he keels over and vomits.

Tokyo, Jan. 8

President Bush's misfortune tonight will surely be remembered as the most public case of an intestinal flu attack ever. As video cameras taped the formal state dinner, the President turned white as steamed rice, flopped backward in his chair, vomited on the Japanese Prime Minister and hit the floor as Secret Service agents scrambled to assist him. Bush's visit was focused on "jobs, jobs, jobs." He was accompanied by the heads of the Big Three U.S. automakers, but met stiff resistance from Japanese officials reluctant to open their markets to U.S. trade.

Silicone breast implants cause scare

Hemlock, Michigan, January 14

Dow Corning Co. plants here and in Arlington, Tennessee, which make silicone breast implants, have been shut down, at least temporarily. On January 6, the Food and Drug Administration called for a 45-day moratorium on the use of the implants and asked producers to halt distribution. New information on the safety of implants, including the possibilty that silicone in the body may lead to inflammatory autoimmune disease, will be examined by an advisory panel. Officials of Dow Corning say they are sure the implants are safe, and have scientific tests which prove it, but stopped production in compliance with the FDA's request.

Jan. 26. *Another disappointing year for the Buffalo Bills, defeated in Super Bowl XXVI by the Washington Redskins, 37-24, in Minneapolis.*

Danger signs for American economy

United States, Feb. 24

To say the least, the economic signs are worrisome. The unemployment level reported on January 10 was the highest since 1987, at 7.1 percent. A week later, I.B.M. announced its first ever annual loss, $564 million for 1991. On January 30, TWA, with a debt of nearly $2 billion, was added to the long list of airlines seeking Chapter 11 protection against creditors. Today General Motors announced its largest loss ever, $4.5 billion for 1991, preceded earlier this month by Ford's posting of a record annual loss, at $2.3 billion.

Serial killer gets life for 15 murders

Milwaukee, Feb. 17

One of the most gruesome criminal cases in U.S. history ended today with the sentencing of Jeffrey Dahmer to 15 consecutive terms of life in prison. There is no possibility of parole.

Last month Dahmer, 31, pleaded guilty to the murder, mutilation and dismemberment of 15 men and youths, most of them black gays. He also confessed to acts of cannibalism and necrophilia during a killing spree that lasted several years. Dahmer then pleaded not guilty by reason of insanity. The jury of seven men, one of them black, and five women rejected the insanity plea two days ago, ruling that the accused was not suffering from a mental disease at the time of the killings.

Jeffrey Dahmer listens to verdict.

Tyson given six-year term for rape

Indianapolis, March 26

The boxing career of the world's youngest heavyweight champion came to a jarring halt today. Five years after he won the world title, 25-year-old Mike Tyson was sentenced to 10 years in prison, four of them suspended, after being found guilty of one count of rape and two counts of criminal deviant conduct. Tyson was convicted for the rape of a Miss Black America contestant, Desiree Washington, in his Indianapolis hotel room last year. The ex-champ was led off to prison after the verdict was announced and will have to serve at least three years of his term (→ March 25, 1995).

Former heavyweight boxing champion is driven to court to hear the verdict.

Nixon slams Bush policy on Russia

Washington, D.C., March 11

Former President Richard M. Nixon is back in the limelight. His charges that the Bush administration has provided "pathetically" inadequate aid to Russia have stung the White House.

Today, Nixon stressed there was no rift between him and Bush, but reiterated his call for stronger U.S. support for democratic reform in Russia. Nixon has warned that if Russian President Boris Yeltsin were to be overthrown by hardliners, Bush and his administration would have to face the question of "who lost Russia."

Disney exports Magic Kingdom to Europe

The $4-billion Euro Disney theme park opens just outside Paris.

April 10. *Former tennis champ Arthur Ashe announces that he is HIV-positive (→ Feb. 6, 1993).*

Marne-la-Vallée, France, Apr. 12

Euro Disneyland opened its gates to the public today in the suburbs east of Paris. The opening of the $4-billion complex was celebrated last night with a show featuring stars of film, stage and song that was seen on television by 100 million people around the world.

Euro Disney can handle an estimated 50,000 to 60,000 guests a day, and six hotels decorated in different American themes with 5,200 rooms have been built on the grounds to accommodate them. To staff the enormous complex, the largest hiring campaign ever seen in France was launched. Euro Disney has hired 14,000 "cast members," efficient, smiling and clean-cut, *à l'américaine.*

Wal-Mart founder dies of cancer at 74

Little Rock, Arkansas, Apr. 5

Sam Walton, one of the richest men in the country, died of cancer today at the age of 74. Walton was the founder and chairman of Wal-Mart, a chain of discount stores which sells everything from jeans to popcorn to car stereos. There are 1,735 Wal-Mart stores, with an average floor space of more than 86,000 square feet, situated in rural areas and small towns in 42 states. Since Walton opened the first Wal-Mart Discount City in 1962, the company has become the largest and most successful retailer in the United States.

NASA bird peers into cosmic past

Washington, D.C., Apr. 23

Scientists believe that they have finally found the Holy Grail of cosmology. A NASA satellite, the Cosmic Background Explorer, or COBE, has found evidence of huge, wispy clouds of matter near what could be "the edge" of the universe. These clouds explain how galaxies were produced after the Big Bang, the cosmic explosion scientists say created the universe. The clouds date back 15 billion years, just 300,000 years after the Big Bang. COBE's findings were announced here today at a meeting of the American Physical Society.

April. *Vintage B-25s are launched from a carrier off San Diego to mark 50th anniversary of General Doolittle's historic bombing raid on Tokyo.*

Rioters ravage Los Angeles after King verdict

Resentment flares into violence, looting and arson in South Central area, as police struggle to restore order.

Los Angeles, May 2

An uneasy calm has returned to this battered city, where the death toll of three days of rioting stands at 37. National Guard troops and federal law-enforcement officers are patrolling South Central, the area where the worst of the rioting took place. The White House has placed 5,000 soldiers and Marines on standby outside the city.

The rioting erupted soon after the acquittal of four white Los Angeles police officers who had been charged with beating a black motorist, Rodney King. The jury at the trial in Simi Valley did not include a black. As police watched helplessly, violence and looting quickly spread from the predominantly black South Central area to adjoining communities. More than 1,500 people have been injured, dozens of them critically, and property damage is estimated at $600 million.(→Apr.17,1993).

U.S. Navy rocked by Tailhook sex scandal

Washington, D.C., June 26

At last year's convention of the Tailhook Association, a private group of active-duty and retired naval pilots, drunken male Navy and Marine Corps aviators made women run a gauntlet along a hallway in a Las Vegas hotel, touching and grabbing them in a sexually aggressive manner, according to the 26 women, half of them naval officers, who claim to be the victims. Today the Defense Department suspended the investigation into the sexual harassment scandal, saying that the naval officers who were conducting it might be suspects themselves.

May 16. *Billionaire Bill Koch, skipper of America³, sails to victory in the America's Cup, ahead of the Italian entry, Il Moro di Venezia.*

Supreme Court upholds abortion rights

Washington, D.C., June 29

In a politically explosive decision destined to figure prominently in the presidential election campaign, the conservative-dominated Supreme Court today upheld a ruling giving states the power to restrict the right to have an abortion. The court stopped short of overturning its own historic 1973 ruling in the case of Roe v. Wade, which enshrined abortion as a constitutional right. The vote was 5-4. The decision satisfies neither side in the bitter abortion fight, which has divided America for nearly 20 years.

The battle involves both President Bush and his likely opponent, Bill Clinton. The President said he is pleased with the court's decision to uphold "reasonable restrictions on abortion." The Arkansas Governor warned that a woman's right to an abortion was now "hanging by a thread," and only a Democratic victory would preserve that right.

Johnny Carson ends 30-year run on NBC

Burbank, Calif., May 22

A chapter of television history closed with Johnny Carson's last "Tonight Show." With tears in his eyes, the legendary 66-year-old entertainer told millions of viewers and the invited audience of friends, family and staff members: "It has been an honor and a privilege to come into your home all these years and entertain you." Carson, who took over the show from Jack Paar in 1962, was the highest-paid personality in the history of television, earning an estimated $2,380 per minute of airtime.

"Tonight Show" host retires.

Florida reels in wake of Hurricane Andrew

Bill Clinton beats Bush

Life must go on despite massive destruction of property in the Miami area.

At 46, Governor Clinton is the first baby-boomer to reach the White House.

Florida, Aug. 25

After devastating much of Dade County south of Miami, Hurricane Andrew is crossing the Gulf of Mexico, on its way to the Louisiana coast. At least 15 people have been killed, and damage estimates range from $15 to $20 billion, more than for any other natural disaster in the history of the U.S. Andrew wrenched trees from the ground, mowed down houses and picked up boats, car and planes, flinging them into the air. Miami and Coconut Grove were virtually under martial law, as riot-equipped police and 15,000 National Guard troops went on patrol to prevent looting.

U.S. sends troops to aid starving Somalia

Mogadishu, Dec. 9

U.S. Marines and Navy frogmen stormed ashore at dawn today ready to do battle with the Somali gunmen who have been holding their famine-stricken country to ransom. The troops were confronted not by bandits, but by the press, tipped off by U.S. officials. The plan is to secure the airport and harbor areas before moving out to get food and medicine to Somalis in the hinterland, where thousands have died of starvation. Followers of rival warlords Mohammed Farah Aidid and Mohammed Ali Mahdi have pulled out of the capital under a U.S.-brokered agreement (→ Oct. 3, 1993).

United States, Nov. 4

The results of yesterday's voting are in. Americans have chosen their 42nd president, Arkansas Governor Bill Clinton. The 46-year-old Democrat will be the first U.S. president of a post-World War II generation.

The first candidate from his party to be elected president since Jimmy Carter in 1976, Clinton campaigned as a "New Democrat," combining traditionally Democratic liberal social themes with calls for greater fiscal responsibilty and closer cooperation with business.

Clinton received 43 percent of the popular vote, well ahead of President George Bush, who received 38 percent, and pulled in 370 electoral votes, much more than the 270 needed to win. A third party candidate, the Texas billionaire Ross Perot, won an unprecedented 19 percent of the popular vote. Perot, who ran on a deficit-reduction platform, may have lost some of his support when he abandoned the race after the Democratic Convention in July, only to jump back in in October.

The President-elect has begun to outline the priorities of his presidency. Creating new jobs, reducing the deficit and reforming the health-care system will be the primary domestic goals. Clinton also revealed his foreign policy objectives: he wants to move forward in global trade talks and peace talks between Israel and its Arab neighbors, complete arms agreements with Russia, aid the famine victims in Somalia and work toward an end to the civil war in the former republics of Yugoslavia (→ Jan. 20, 1993).

U.S. marines hit Somalia's beaches at dawn in a huge relief operation.

Aug. 9. *Michael Jordan, Magic Johnson and fellow Dream Team members celebrate their Olympic victory in Barcelona. U.S. athletes won 108 medals, including 37 gold and 34 silver, to the former U.S.S.R.'s total of 112.*

Pasadena, Jan. 31.
The Dallas Cowboys defeat the Buffalo Bills 52-17 in Super Bowl XXVII.

Waco, Texas, Feb. 28.
Four federal agents are killed in a shoot-out with the Branch Davidians, an apocalyptic cult (→ Apr. 19).

Pensacola, Florida, March 11.
A doctor who performed abortions is murdered outside a clinic by an anti-abortion activist (→ May 12, 1994).

Washington, D.C., April 22.
The Holocaust Museum opens.

Washington, D.C., April 28.
The armed forces ban on women combat pilots ends.

Washington, D.C., June 7.
Congress hears testimony of mysterious ailments afflicting thousands of Gulf War vets.

Phoenix, June 20.
The Chicago Bulls defeat the Phoenix Suns to win their third straight N.B.A. championship.

New York, June 24.
The F.B.I. arrests eight men on charges of plotting to blow up the U.N. building.

Iraq, June 26.
The U.S. launches a missile attack on Iraqi intelligence headquarters in retaliation for a plot to assassinate former President Bush.

Washington, D.C., July 20.
White House aide Vincent Foster commits suicide (→ June 30, 1994).

Washington, D.C., Aug. 23.
The National Archives opens nearly all files relating to the assassination of President John F. Kennedy.

Somalia, Oct. 3.
Twelve U.S. soldiers are killed in a failed raid to capture leaders of Mohammed Farah Aidid's militia.

Atlanta, Oct. 23.
The Toronto Blue Jays beat the Philadelphia Phillies to win the World Series.

Manassas, Virginia, Nov. 10.
John Wayne Bobbitt is acquitted of marital sexual assault; his wife claimed she cut off his penis because he had raped her (→ Jan. 21, 1994).

Houston, Dec. 10.
NASA astronauts repair the faulty Hubble Space Telescope.

Hollywood, Calif.
Top films of the year include *The Fugitive*, *The Firm*, *Sleepless in Seattle* and *Aladdin*.

Clinton is inaugurated

Bill Clinton, the nation's third-youngest President, takes the oath of office.

Washington, D.C., Jan. 20
William Jefferson Clinton took the oath of presidential office from Chief Justice William H. Rehnquist today, swearing to "preserve, protect and defend the Constitution" on his grandmother's King James Bible. Tens of thousands of spectators turned up on the Mall on this bright, chilly day to witness the inauguration on the steps of the Capitol. The ceremony included a prayer led by the Reverend Billy Graham and a poem read by Maya Angelou. The new President's inaugural speech took "renewal" as its theme, and he challenged Americans to "answer the call" to service and sacrifice in order to "reinvent America."

Tennis champion Arthur Ashe dies of AIDS

New York, Feb. 6
Arthur Ashe, one of America's most loved and respected athletes, has died at the age of 49 of pneumonia brought on by AIDS. Ashe was not only a tennis champion, but also a human-rights and AIDS activist, *Washington Post* columnist, TV sports commentator and author of a history of America's black athletes. He was the first black athlete to win a Grand Slam event, in the first U.S. Open in 1968, and the first to win the Wimbledon men's title, in 1975.

Jan. 6. *Dizzy Gillespie, the innovative trumpeter who helped create the bebop style and introduced Cuban rhythms into jazz, dies of cancer at 75.*

Bomb attack under World Trade Center

New York City, Feb. 26
A bomb exploded in an underground parking garage between the 110-floor twin towers of the World Trade Center at lunchtime today. Five people were killed, and hundreds were treated for smoke-related injuries. A fire raged for two hours, sending smoke billowing into the streets and up to the 96th floor of the towers. Fire fighters worked into the night to get people out of the buildings. Some people were rescued by helicopter from the roof, but workers and visitors managed their own evacuation for the most part. The towers accommodate 55,000 workers and 80,000 visitors each day (→ June 24).

A huge hole was opened between the garage and commuter train station.

March 15. *One of the worst winter storms this century lashes the eastern U.S. from Atlanta to Boston, leaving at least 93 people dead.*

Rodney King verdict eases tensions in LA

Los Angeles, April 17

Los Angeles has been a tense city for the last week. The jury in the civil-rights trial of four policemen accused in the beating of Rodney King went into deliberations last weekend. Gun sales were up and the National Guard standing by in anticipation of a repeat of last year's riots. The tension was lifted today when the jury came in with its verdict. Sgt. Stacy Koon, the ranking officer present at the beating, was found guilty of allowing excessive force to restrain King. Officer Laurence Powell, who was seen to strike most of the blows against King in the video of the beating made by a bystander, was convicted of using excessive force. The other officers, Theodore Briseno and Timothy Wind, were acquitted.

Waco standoff ends in fiery tragedy

Waco, Texas, April 19

Ranch Apocalypse, as the headquarters of the Branch Davidian cult has been nicknamed, burned today after an armored-vehicle assault by federal agents.

The F.B.I. has been in a standoff with the cult since February 28, when four federal agents were killed in a failed surprise raid on the compound. The heavily armed cult was led by the charismatic David Koresh, who told his followers that the end of the world was nigh. The F.B.I. alternated tactics of negotiation and harrassment, at one point playing Tibetan chants to drive out the Davidians.

Early this morning a negotiator warned the cult that tear gas would be injected into the compound to force them to give themselves up. Warnings broadcast on loudspeak-

The assault ends a 51-day siege of the cult headquarters by U.S. federal agents.

ers were ignored, and the F.B.I. began their assault. F.B.I. snipers say they saw two people setting fires about noon. The blaze spread rapidly, engulfing the buildings as police

and reporters watched helplessly. About 90 adults are believed to have been inside; nine escaped from the self-inflicted inferno. Among the dead are at least 17 children.

Last call for laughs on tap at Cheers bar

Boston, May 20

The cast of the hit show *Cheers* gathered here at the Bull & Finch, the bar that served as a model for Sam's watering hole, to watch the final episode. Advertisers are betting that huge numbers of Americans will join them: They're paying $650,000 for each 30-second spot aired during the special 98-minute show. *Cheers*, which debuted on September 30, 1982, was a critical as well as a popular success. The show won 26 Emmy awards and was nominated for 111, and it was seen in 38 countries around the world.

A grand total of 275 episodes.

Mystery illness hits Navajo reservation

Navajo Reservation, May 31

A mysterious illness researchers are calling "unexplained adult respiratory distress syndrome" has killed 12 people here on the Navajo reservation that is located at the meeting point of the states of Arizona, New Mexico, Colorado and Utah. The victims, not exclusively Navajo, first notice mild flu-like symptoms, then hours or days later suddenly die from respiratory failure. Navajo nation President Peterson Zah is encouraging residents of the reservation to collaborate with the medical authorities.

Navajo President Peterson Zah urged cooperation with U.S. authorities.

Spielberg's Jurassic dinos invade theaters

United States, June 10

Steven Spielberg's heavily hyped new movie, *Jurassic Park*, roared into theaters across the country today. The stars are, of course, the dinos, and their development began more than two years ago. New computer graphics software – more than 200 programs – and robotic technologies, including a life-size T-rex using flight simulator machinery, were designed to bring them to life. The movie's marketing campaign is bronto-sized, including T-shirts, toys and a new *Jurassic* ride to be built at Universal Studios' theme park.

June 12. *More than 60,000 easy riders gather in Milwaukee, Wisconsin, to celebrate the 90th anniversary of the creation of Harley-Davidson "hogs."*

Pentagon can't ask, gays mustn't tell

Washington, D.C., July 19

President Clinton and the Joint Chiefs of Staff have reached a compromise on gays in the armed forces. "Don't ask, don't tell, don't pursue" is the new rule. "Don't ask" means that although the ban on homosexual conduct is not removed, the military may not ask recruits if they are gay. "Don't tell" means that gays cannot declare their homo-

The new policy is controversial.

sexuality, because showing "propensity or intent" to engage in homosexual acts is forbidden. "Don't pursue" means that only "credible" evidence of homosexual acts is cause for dismissal. Going to gay bars or reading gay magazines would not suffice to launch an investigation, for example.

Midwest is drowned in record floods

The Mississippi has been above flood stage since June 27, and 20 million acres of farmland have been inundated.

Midwest, Aug. 1

The United States has seen the worst flooding in recorded history. The Father of Waters, as Native American tribes called the Mississippi River, and its tributaries overflowed their banks and the walls and levees built to protect Midwest farms and towns.

The first of many crests was recorded near Saint Paul on June 26. The upper Mississippi became unnavigable, with trees, dead animals and other detritus being rapidly swept along by the current, and a 500-mile stretch of the river was closed to shipping. Since June 27,

the Mississippi has been above flood stage. Mid-July brought hope in the form of blue skies, but those hopes were dashed as new rains, and with them new record crests, came. The Midwest now resembled a great lake. Its raging rivers were a muddy brown, and the standing water stank and was dangerous, polluted with fertilizer, sewage, diesel fuel and other contaminants.

The end of July saw the climax of the flooding. The Missouri and Kansas rivers, at their convergence near Kansas City, both set records on July 27. The Kansas reached 55 feet, and the Missouri reached 49

feet. The Mississippi's largest crest came today, when it reached 49.5 feet at Saint Louis.

The flood's toll is monumental. The homes of 38,000 families have been damaged, and 20 million acres of farmland are underwater. At least 50 people died due to the catastrophe, and 70,000 were driven from their homes. The damage is estimated at $12 billion.

The Great Flood of 1993 seems to have come to an end, but much work remains to be done. It will take weeks for the river to recede to its normal levels, and the massive cleanup will last several months.

Aug. 12. *The pope was diplomatic, avoiding direct references to abortion when he met with Clinton on his arrival in Denver for World Youth Day.*

Aug. 28. *Thousands gather in Washington, D.C., to mark the 30th anniversary of Martin Luther King's historic "I have a dream" speech.*

Deficit-reduction plan barely passes

Washington, D.C., Aug. 6

Bill Clinton's deficit-reduction plan has scraped through Congress after much heated debate and presidential arm-twisting. No Republicans voted for the plan, and the President had to work the phones all week to get enough Democrats to back his budget. The House passed the bill yesterday with a vote of 218 to 216, and tonight Vice President Al Gore cast the tie-breaking vote in the Senate. The plan combines higher taxes, never a vote-getter in Congress, with a freeze of discretionary spending at 1993 levels. Increases hit incomes above $115,000, and a higher percentage of Social Security benefits for individuals who make more than $34,000 are taxable.

Rabin and Arafat sign historic accord

Recognition and Palestinian autonomy are the first steps to a lasting peace.

Washington, D.C., Sept. 13

History was made today on the White House South Lawn when two bitter enemies shook hands. It was Yasir Arafat, chairman of the P.L.O., who extended his hand to Israeli Prime Minister Yitzhak Rabin, who briefly hesitated, then took it, to seal an agreement on Palestinian self-rule. President Clinton praised the two leaders and thanked Norway's government, which brokered the secret talks that led to the accord. The agreement gives Palestinians a measure of self-rule immediately in Gaza, Jericho and parts of the West Bank. Much more work will be necessary to reach the ultimate objective of today's accord – a country shared by Jews and Arabs in peace.

Hillary presents her health plan on Hill

Washington, D.C., Sept. 29

First Lady Hillary Clinton has dazzled Congress with her performance as the White House's chief representative for its health-care reform plan. She said that the White House was open to compromise on methods for reform but insisted that the end result be a guarantee for every Amerian of "a comprehensive package of benefits that can never be taken away." It remains to be seen if the momentum of this early success will hold up through the legislative process to become law.

'Air' Jordan says goodbye to Bulls

Deerfield, Illinois, Oct. 6

The world's greatest basketball player and perhaps its most famous sportsman announced his retirement from the game here today. "I have no more challenges," explained Michael Jordan. "I had achieved everything in basketball I could." Jordan has led the Chicago Bulls to three straight championships, being named MVP in all three series. He has the game's highest scoring average in the regular season, 32.3 points a game, and in the playoffs, 34.6 points (→March 19, 1995).

Brady bill regulates handgun purchases

Washington, D.C., Nov. 24

Concern about violent crime has reached a point where the influence of the powerful National Rifle Association could no longer prevent passage of gun-control legislation. The Senate today enacted a bill imposing a five-day waiting period during which background checks will be made on handgun purchasers.

"How sweet it is," said James Brady, the Reagan aide who was wounded in a 1981 assassination attempt on the President and for whom the bill was named.

'I'm innocent' says Jackson live on TV

Santa Ynez, Calif., Dec. 22

Michael Jackson, fighting back tears in a four-minute speech broadcast live on TV, denied that he had sexually molested a 13-year-old boy. He called an examination of his genitals by criminal investigators a "horrifying nightmare." The results could be used to verify the boy's description of discoloring spots on the singer's skin. Jackson decried the treatment of the story "terrible mass media" and said, "I ask all of you to wait to hear the truth before you label or condemn me."

Aug. 16. *Cancer claims the life of movie star Stewart Granger, 80.*

Sept. 12. *Raymond Burr, TV's Perry Mason, dies of cancer at 76.*

Oct. 7. *Princeton's Toni Morrison wins the Nobel Prize for literature.*

Dec. 4. *Rocker Frank Zappa dies just before his 53rd birthday.*

Detroit, Jan. 6.
Figure skater Nancy Kerrigan's knee is badly bruised by crowbar-wielding assailant (→ Feb. 27).

Manassas, Virginia, Jan. 21.
Lorena Bobbitt, who cut off part of her husband's penis, is found not guilty by reason of insanity of malicious wounding.

Atlanta, Jan. 30.
The Buffalo Bills lose an unprecedented fourth straight Super Bowl to the Dallas Cowboys, 30-13.

Seattle, April 8.
Rock star Kurt Cobain, 27, of the group Nirvana, kills himself with a shotgun.

Alexandria, Virginia, April 28.
C.I.A. agent Aldrich Ames is sentenced to life in prison for spying for the Soviet Union.

Singapore, May 5.
An American teenager, Michael Fay, receives four strokes of a cane for vandalism.

Washington, D.C., May 12.
Congress passes a bill banning violence, blockades and threats against abortion clinics.

Houston, June 22.
The Houston Rockets defeat the New York Knicks to win the N.B.A. championship.

Washington, D.C., Aug. 25.
Congress passes Clinton's crime bill, which budgets for more police on the streets, crime-prevention programs and the building of prisons and bans assault weapons.

Los Angeles, Oct. 12.
Steven Spielberg, David Geffen and Jeffrey Katzenberg announce the creation of a new movie studio.

Las Vegas, Nov. 5.
George Foreman, 45, beats Michael Moorer, 27, to retake the world heavyweight title.

Hollywood, Calif.
Top films included *Pulp Fiction, Schindler's List, Four Weddings and a Funeral, The Lion King* and *Forrest Gump.*

DEATHS

Big Sur, California, Aug. 19.
Linus Pauling (*Feb. 28, 1901), who won Nobel prizes for Peace and Chemistry.

Connecticut, Sept. 11.
Stage and screen actress Jessica Tandy (*June 6, 1909).

Delaware, Nov. 18.
Big Band leader Cab Calloway (*Dec. 25, 1907).

Major earthquake jolts Los Angeles

The earthquake hit just before dawn, spreading mayhem and killing dozens.

Los Angeles, Jan. 18
Aftershocks measuring 4.7 on the Richter scale added further damage to the devastation caused by a 6.6-Richter-scale earthquake which struck here yesterday at 4:31 a.m. local time.

The tremor was the strongest to have hit the city this century. Freeways crumbled, water mains burst and fires spread from the area where the quake was centered, in the suburban San Fernando Valley at the city's northern edge. Property damage has been estimated in excess of $7 billion, and 34 people have died. It could take this urban region with a population of 9 million – tens of thousands of whom are now homeless – more than a year to repair the damage.

Winter Olympics a hit despite media frenzy over Tonya and Nancy

Not a good day for Tonya Harding.

Lillehammer, Norway, Feb. 27
The two million visitors to this year's Winter Olympics nearly unanimously proclaimed them the best ever. They certainly were for the U.S.; the team won more medals here, 13, than in any other Winter Games. Skiers Tommy Moe and Diann Roffe-Steinrotter and speed skater Dan Jansen won golds.

Unfortunately the intensive press coverage of the tension between figure skaters Tonya Harding and Nancy Kerrigan somewhat overshadowed Kerrigan's winning a silver medal. Harding denies charges of being involved in a bizarre attack on Kerrigan on January 6.

Silver, not gold, for Nancy Kerrigan.

We don't spike our smokes, say CEOS

Washington, D.C., April 14
Six chairmen from the biggest American cigarette companies appeared before Congress today to deny claims by the Food and Drug Administration that they spike smokes with extra nicotine to keep their customers hooked. Phillip Morris took ABC to court last month over a TV documentary making the same accusation. If the F.D.A. decides that the companies do add nicotine, cigarettes could be prohibited like cocaine and heroin.

Jan. 22. *Telly "Kojak" Savalas, who turned 70 yesterday, dies of cancer.*

Death claims two American icons: Nixon and Jackie

Nixon worked hard in his later years to reclaim his place as a great U.S. leader.

Jacqueline Kennedy Onassis was a role model for many American women.

New York, April 22

Richard M. Nixon, who died today at 81, was probably America's most controversial politician. His presidency came at a time when the country was divided, and it remains split in its view of the man. Nixon's successful 1946 and 1950 California campaigns for the Senate won him the nickname "Tricky Dicky" because of his tactics of accusing his opponents of being communist sympathizers. As Vice President to Dwight Eisenhower, he developed the foreign policy expertise which would serve him well later. He won much acclaim for his "kitchen debate" with Soviet leader Nikita Krushchev over the relative merits of capitalism and communism. Elected President in 1968 by a narrow margin in the popular vote, his 1972 re-election was a landslide. The Watergate scandal led to his resignation and deepened his reputation as a devious, vengeful and even paranoid politician. But his foreign policy triumphs, especially the opening up of relations with China and initiating detente with the Soviet Union, have been widely praised. In recent years his legacy has undergone revision, and he has taken a role of grey eminence to U.S. presidents.

New York, May 19

Jacqueline Kennedy Onassis was loved and admired by Americans and around the world. Her struggle against lymphatic cancer was revealed earlier this year; she died today at the age of 64.

Jacqueline Bouvier was born on July 28, 1929, to a rich Republican family whose French ancestors fought with the Americans in the Revolutionary War. She was dubbed "Queen Deb of the Year" when she came out in New York society in 1946. Working as a photojournalist she interviewed the young Massachusetts Senator John F. Kennedy, whom she had previously met at a Washington party. Her beauty and sophistication helped create the Camelot myth of her husband's presidency. When he died, her courage was lauded, and she gave strength to a nation in mourning. Her later marriage to an older Greek shipping tycoon, Aristotle Onassis, at first caused some controversy in the U.S. For many, she would always be Jackie Kennedy, but for others, she became a symbol of international high society – Jackie O. For the last few years, she epitomized the successful businesswoman, working as an editor for Viking and Doubleday.

June 6. *President Clinton and leaders of the World War II allies gather on the beaches of Normandy, where 50 years ago the D-Day invasion launched the battle on the continent to free Europe from the clutches of Nazism.*

Whitewater findings favor White House

Washington, D.C., June 30

No White House officials will be charged with breaking laws in connection with their receiving briefings on an investigation into Whitewater said Robert Fiske, the special counsel appointed to look into the matter, in his first findings.

The Whitewater affair takes its name from an Arkansas real estate development in which President Clinton invested while governor of the state. James McDougal, who was a partner in Whitewater with Clinton, ran Madison Guaranty Savings and Loan, which later went bankrupt. The investigation centers on the question of whether money was diverted from the S&L to pay Clinton's 1984 gubernatorial campaign debt or to the coffers of the Whitewater Development Corp.

Today's findings concern the Washington phase, or the question of whether the White House was illegally briefed about an earlier investigation by the Resolution Trust Corp. into whether funds had been diverted. Fiske is now turning to the Arkansas phase: his investigation of the Whitewater real-estate company dealings themselves.

Fiske had also looked into the death last year of a close friend and aide of Clinton's, Vincent Foster. He found that Foster did indeed commit suicide and that there was no evidence that concern over the Whitewater affair contributed to his severe state of depression.

Millions watch fall of American hero O.J. Simpson

Los Angeles, June 17

A white Ford Bronco led a group of California Highway Patrol cars and a fleet of television news helicopters across the freeways of Los Angeles County as thousands of people stared and millions more watched on TV. In the Bronco was movie star, corporate spokesman and former football hero O.J. Simpson. Simpson led the pack to his home and then gave himself up. Earlier today, he had failed to appear for an agreed-upon arraignment on charges of murdering his former wife and another man.

Nicole Simpson, 35, and Ron Goldman, 25, a waiter at a restaurant that she frequented, were found dead from multiple stab wounds on Monday the 13th. Police found blood stains on Simpson's vehicle and in his driveway. Simpson, who had flown to Chicago the night of the murder, was asked to return for questioning.

After the police announced that Simpson had disappeared, his lawyer, Robert Shapiro, described him as suicidal and released a note he had written. "Please think of the real O.J., not this lost person," he wrote. Police located the Bronco in Orange County by tracing cellular phone calls. The 40-m.p.h. chase began at 6:25 p.m., ending when Simpson led the convoy to his home at 8:50 p.m. (→ Jan. 27, 1995)

Fans waved "Go Juice" signs as the former football star was chased by police.

First World Cup U.S.A. is won by Brazil in a penalty shootout

Brazil's fourth soccer world championship came after 120 scoreless minutes.

Pasadena, July 17

After two hours of unadventurous and goalless play on both sides which emphasized defense over fancy footwork, Brazil won the penalty shootout which gave them the victory over Italy in the final game of the World Cup.

The first soccer championship to be held in the U.S. saw the host team ousted by Brazil 1-0 in the second round. A smashing success, World Cup U.S.A. drew more spectators than any before. Total attendance in the sweltering heat was 3,567,415 – more than 68,000 per match – compared to the 2.5 million who turned out for Italia 90.

Castro threatens a flood of emigrants

Guantanamo Bay, Aug. 24

Cubans are taking to the Strait of Florida by the thousands in rickety boats, rafts and even inner tubes to head for the U.S. Fidel Castro, angered by a huge demonstration in Havana earlier this month and by the U.S. policy of automatically granting asylum to Cubans who flee the country, has threatened to stop blocking their exit. President Bill Clinton ended this policy last week, and today ordered the expansion of the U.S. Navy base here, where the asylum claims of the "balseros," or boat people, will be reviewed.

Aug. 1. *Graceland meets Neverland: Lisa-Marie Presley, Elvis's daughter, says that the rumors that she had married Michael Jackson in May are true.*

Aug. 16. *The Age of Aquarius meets Generation X in Saugerties, N.Y., for Woodstock II, 25 years after the original "days of peace, love and music."*

Race, IQ and class debate rages in U.S.

United States, Oct. 19

The United States is currently embroiled in a controversy over the relationship of intelligence to race and class. The debate, which has often raged in the U.S., has been rekindled by three new books: *Race, Evolution and Behavior: A Life History Perspective* by J. Phillipe Rushton, *The Decline of Intelligence in America: A Strategy for National Renewal* by Seymour W. Itzkoff and especially *The Bell Curve: Intelligence and Class Structure in American Life*, which has attracted most of the media's attention, by Charles Murray and Richard Herrnstein, who died last month.

All three books assert that IQ is a real and accurate indicator of intelligence and that it is correlated to job success and rates of crime and other social pathologies. The authors say that a low-IQ underclass is reproducing more quickly than what Murray and Herrnstein have called the "cognitive elite," lowering the intelligence of the country. They also point out that blacks make up a large proportion of this underclass and that blacks as a group score lower on IQ tests than whites.

While some people say the books spell out a hard truth that the country must face, others discount them as unscientific and racist. Many scientists reject the value of IQ tests, and there is little if any agreement on how much of a person's intelligence is inherited.

U.S. invades Haiti

Haiti, Sept. 19

American soldiers seized Haiti today and did not fire a shot. As the announcements from loudspeakers in army helicopters flying over Port-au-Prince put it: "We're not at war. We're here to restore democracy and supply humanitarian aid." The United Nations Security Council had approved a U.S.-led invasion to drive out the military government and restore the president they had forced into exile, Jean-Bertrand Aristide. An 11th-hour agreement brokered by Jimmy Carter, which calls for junta leader Raoul Cédras to step down, circumvented a bloody battle with his forces.

Strike cancels Series

New York City, Sept. 14

"Nineteen ninety-four – the season that struck itself out," is how former baseball commissioner Peter Ueberroth defined the cancellation of the season and the World Series by major league owners. The players strike that led to the decision began August 12, when the players rejected a proposal by the owners calling for a 50-50 split of industry revenues and a salary cap. Bud Selig, the acting commissioner, announced the cancellation by a fax in which he said: "This is a sad day. Nobody wanted this to happen, but the continuing player strike leaves us no choice but to take this action." The owners voted last night; all but two, Peter Angelos of Baltimore and Marge Schott of Cincinatti, signed the resolution to kill the Series. Angelos agreed with the decision but wanted to change the wording; Schott, however, wanted to continue the season with replacements. "Let's see the real players instead of the million-dollar babies," she said.

President Clinton has said that perhaps baseball's anti-trust exemption should be reviewed. A bill modifying the status failed in the Senate last night, but Congress is still considering a repeal (→ April 2, 1995).

Republicans take the Hill in elections

Washington, D.C., Nov. 9

Republicans won control of both houses of Congress, for the first time in 40 years, in yesterday's elections. In the Senate, 53 of the 100 seats are now Republican, and in the House there are now 230 Republicans and 204 Democrats. Voters turned out Democratic governors as well, including New York's Mario Cuomo, defeated by George Pataki; a majority of the statehouses are now Republican. Republicans say the results are a rebuke by voters to Bill Clinton, who said today, "They sent us a clear message – I got it."

Cooperation between the White House and the new majority will be difficult. Although Bob Dole, the Senate's Republican leader, seems willing to make deals with the president, Jesse Helms, likely to head the powerful Senate Foreign Relations Committee, and Newt Gingrich, expected to be the next House Speaker, are more combatitive. Both these right-wing Southerners have built reputations as "bomb throwers" and have blasted Bill Clinton at every opportunity. The Grand Old Party is now preparing to capitalize on their electoral momentum and vote on the points – such as a balanced-budget amendment and tax cuts – of the "Contract With America," their campaign platform, in the first 100 days of their new majority (→ Jan. 24, 1995).

Gingrich is expected to be Speaker.

"Forrest Gump" is the surprise hit of the summer, having taken in $222 million. Disney's "The Lion King," at $257 million, is at the top of the heap.

Oct. 20. *Hollywood's humane tough guy, Burt Lancaster, shown here with Deborah Kerr in "From Here to Eternity," dies of a heart attack at 80.*

Washington, D.C., Jan. 2.
Marion Barry, who spent six months in prison for a 1990 drug conviction, returns as the capital's mayor.

Miami, Jan. 29.
The San Francisco 49ers beat the San Diego Chargers 49-26, to win Super Bowl XXIX.

Washington, D.C., Jan. 31.
President Clinton says he will create a $20 billion line of credit to Mexico to help save the peso.

Cape Canaveral, June 1.
Woodpeckers are the latest headache for the space shuttle program. Birds damage insulating foam on the launcher's fuel tank. NASA is using decoy owls to scare the birds away.

Seattle, Washington, Aug. 24.
Microsoft launches its much-hyped Windows 95 software globally at midnight, amid a worldwide media blitz.

Los Angeles, Sept. 28.
The jury in the O.J. Simpson trial is finally facing the prospect of freedom, having become the longest-sequestered jury in legal history. (→ Oct. 1)

New York City, Oct. 20.
Cuban leader Fidel Castro is in New York for the fiftieth anniversary celebrations at the United Nations.

Jerusalem, Israel, Nov. 4.
Israeli prime minister Yitzak Rabin is assassinated by right-wing fundamentalists after leaving a peace rally.

Dayton, Ohio, Nov. 21.
US negotiator Richard Holbrooke brokers a peace deal accepted by all the factions in the war-torn former Yugoslavia.

Los Angeles, Dec. 30.
The top-grossing movie this year is *Batman Forever*, which took $187 million.

DEATHS

Washington, D.C., Feb. 9.
J. William Fulbright, former Democratic Senator, who inspired Fulbright Scholarships (* April 9, 1905).

California, June 29.
Lana Turner, "Sweater Girl' and star of *The Postman Always Rings Twice* (1946). (* 1920).

Clinton's agenda fails to sway Republicans

Washington, D.C., Jan. 24

House Speaker Newt Gingrich jumped up to applaud Bill Clinton's call, in his State of the Union speech for "leaner, not meaner" government, but for most of his 82-minute address, the new Republican majority remained stonily silent. Bob Dole, the Senate majority leader, said that the President was "going to run into reality pretty quick." The reality is that the Republicans are preparing an offensive on the way Washington now works. They plan to dismantle many welfare programs, pass a balanced-budget amendment, repeal last year's assault-weapons ban and decrease U.S. contributions to the U.N., all projects opposed, at least in part, by the President.

President's State of the Union speech.

Big Blue gives green light for blue jeans

Armonk, N.Y., Feb. 3

I.B.M., the home of the dark conservative suit and no-nonsense tie, has lightened up its unwritten, but nonetheless strict, dress code. Employees will now be able to wear whatever they think is appropriate to the office.

Big Blue has joined a large number of American companies that are relaxing dress codes. Many have instituted "Dress-down Fridays," a day when employees can drop their stuffy three-pieces and dresses for jeans and loafers. Law firms and banks, even "The Company," the C.I.A., have gone casual for the entry to the weekend.

O.J. Simpson's defense slams 'rush to judgement' by prosecutors

Los Angeles, Jan. 27

Americans, shocked at the brutal slaying of Nicole Simpson and Ronald Goodman, have been waiting for this moment for seven months. How would football hero O.J. Simpson respond to the charges that he killed his former wife and her friend? Today, Simpson takes his case into bookstores with *I Want to Tell You*. "How can anybody say I killed this woman," he writes in his new book. "Don't they understand I'd jump in front of a bullet for Nicole?"

Prosecutors presented a different Simpson in their opening arguments this week. They portrayed an abu-

sive man bent on controlling his ex-wife. State attorneys said O.J.'s motive was simple, "If he couldn't have her, nobody else could." They presented a trail of blood and hair linking the victims to Simpson by way of a bloody glove found at his home.

The defense, which wound up its first arguments yesterday, said the prosecution condemned Simpson in a "rush to judgement at any cost," which ignored other suspects and leads. Sloppy police work was magnified by racism, they said, focusing on Detective Mark Fuhrman, who found the notorious bloody glove. He planted it, they insist.

Jan. 22. *Rose Fitzgerald Kennedy (*July 22, 1890), the mother of the 35th President of the United States, dies of pneumonia at 104.*

Feb. 6. *Lieutenant Colonel Eileen Collins, 38, NASA's first female shuttle pilot, prepares for Discovery's rendezvous with Russia's Mir space station.*

Hoops king Air Jordan reclaims his throne

Indianapolis, March 19

"I'm back" was all Michael Jordan's press release said, and that was enough. For two weeks, since the three-time National Champion and MVP announced he was quitting baseball and started working out with his old club, the Bulls, basketball fans have been waiting for those two words.

Tonight, His Airness graced the court once again, only to lose his comeback game against the Indiana Pacers in overtime, 103-96. Jordan took 16 minutes to sink the first of only 7 of 28 shots from the field, but that didn't matter. The important thing is – as Pacers coach Larry Brown put it – "The Beatles and Elvis are back."

He's back after a 21-month absence.

Tyson released after 1,095 days in prison

Southington, Ohio, March 25

Mike Tyson, one of the most promising heavyweight boxers the world has ever seen, returned to his palatial mansion here today. The former champ, wearing an Islamic prayer cap and saying nothing to reporters and fans, had earlier left the prison near Indianapolis where he has spent the last three years. Tyson was convicted in 1992 of the rape of a Miss Black America contestant, Desiree Washington. The big question now is what the future holds in store for the man who became the world's youngest heavyweight champ. Experts say he could make $50 million from his first fight, and millions more if he tries to recapture the world crown.

The former heavyweight champion.

Major league strike ends after 234 days

Chicago, April 2

The 234-day strike by major league baseball players has come to an end. After a four-hour meeting here today, team owners accepted the players' offer to return to the diamond. Two days ago, a federal judge ordered owners to restore free-agent bidding, salary arbitration and the anti-collusion provisions of baseball's expired collective bargaining agreement, fulfilling the players' conditions for ending the strike. The owners only alternative would have been to institute a lockout.

Greenback plunges to new record lows

New York City, April 10

The U.S. dollar's steady downward spiral over the past weeks got worse today, when the greenback hit a new postwar low of 80.15 yen.

Germany and Japan have been buying dollars to prop up the U.S. currency but complain that the U.S. Federal Reserve is not doing enough to stop the fall. They blame the Fed's policy of "benign neglect" for the drop and say the U.S. has an obligation to support its currency because of the dollar's status as the world's reserve currency.

Terrorism hits Oklahoma

Oklahoma City, April 19

A car bomb tore a nine-story hole in the Alfred Murrah federal building here at 9:00 this morning. The massive blast could be heard as far as 30 miles away, and the bomb is estimated to have been 1,000 to 1,200 pounds.

As many as 100 people have died in the attack, but rescue workers are still searching the rubble for victims. Nearly half of the 550 people who work in the office building are still unaccounted for, and it is feared that many of them have perished. The building housed offices of the Drug Enforcement Administration and the Bureau of Alcohol, Tobacco and Firearms and other federal workers as well as a childcare center.

Theories on the responsibility for the bombing range from Middle Eastern terrorists to Colombian drug cartels to parties seeking revenge for the federal raid two years ago on the Waco headquarters of the Branch Davidians religious cult, in which some 80 people died. President Clinton, speaking just hours after the attack, vowed to swiftly bring to justice the "evil cowards" who perpetrated the attack.

March 13. *Flooding due to heavy rain has turned 39 of California's 58 counties into disaster zones, killing 12 people and devastating farmland.*

The bombing of the Murrah building in Oklahoma City comes on the second anniversary of the federal raid on the Branch Davidian compound in Waco.

Heatwave wilts Windy City

Chicago, Illinois, July 16

The final death toll from Chicago's recent high temperatures of 106°F will be about 400, predicts the Cook County medical examiner, Dr. Edmund Donoghue. Cook County morgue is filled to capacity with heat-induced fatalities, with a further 300 bodies being held at funeral homes. The authorities have had to resort to using refrigerator trucks to store bodies.

In New York, eleven people died when temperatures soared to 100°F, although thermometers are now registering a welcome return to normal.

Oklahoma bomb suspects in court

McVeigh at the time of the bombing.

Oklahoma City, Aug. 15

Timothy J. McVeigh and Terry L. Nichols have pleaded not guilty to charges of causing the explosion that destroyed federal offices in Oklahoma City, killing 167 people. The two accused, who were described as army deserters, have links with white supremacist militias. They were indicted by a grand jury on August 10. A third ex-soldier, Michael Fortier, pleaded guilty to a separate charge of knowledge of the intention to carry out the attack.

The prosecution argued that the two alleged conspirators robbed a gun dealer in Arkansas to finance the crime and then raided a Kansas quarry for dynamite and fuses. These were used to set off a homemade bomb of diesel fuel and fertilizer. McVeigh is further charged with parking the truck containing explosives in front of the Federal building and detonating the bomb.

Investigators believe that the bomb was a revenge attack on the FBI for its role in the Branch Davidian cult deaths. The device was detonated on April 19, the second anniversary of the bloody end to the Waco siege. President Clinton has pledged to crack down on terrorism and quasi-military groups.

Unabomber manifesto published

Washington, D.C., Sept. 19

The *Washington Post* has published a 35,000-word manifesto by a serial bomber known as the Unabomber.

The document, entitled *Industrial Society and its Future*, attacks politicians on both sides of the spectrum. It rails against modern technology and calls the Industrial Revolution "a disaster for the human race". It also urges the overthrow of the industrial apparatus. The self-styled "anarchist" had vowed to end his 17-year campaign of terror if the *Post* or the *New York Times* published his manifesto in full, although he did not rule out further attacks on property.

The *Post* has been criticized for giving publicity to a terrorist but the FBI welcomed the move, hoping that it will lead to information. The newspaper's editors defended their decision to publish, insisting that it was in the public interest. Copies of the manifesto have been given to university academics, to see if any recognize the writing of a colleague or ex-pupil. The Unabomber, so-called because his initial targets were universities and airlines, has been linked to several connected bombings. The most recent was in April 1995, when the chief lobbyist for the California Forestry Association was killed by a mail bomb in Sacramento.

O.J. acquitted

Los Angeles, Oct. 1

After just four hours' deliberation, the jury of ten men and two women have found O.J. Simpson not guilty of murdering his ex-wife Nicole Brown Simpson and her friend, Ronald L. Goldman. Judge Ito announced the verdict today. The case exposed national racial divides. Many whites were convinced by Simpson's record as a wife-beater and prosecution allegations of jealousy. Many blacks have welcomed Simpson's release, accepting the defense argument that he was set up by the LAPD. In a major turning point, the chief police witness, Mark Fuhrman, was shown to be a bigot and a racist.

Historic peace accord for West Bank

Washington, D.C., Sept. 28

President Clinton scored another foreign policy triumph when Israeli Premier Yitzak Rabin and the Palestine Liberation Organisation's leader Yasser Arafat signed an historic peace agreement. The accord extends Palestinian self-rule on the West Bank of the Jordan. Israeli troops will withdraw from the so-called occupied West Bank in ten days. Palestinians will take over control of administration and law and order, to prepare for elections to a Palestinian legislative council. Hardliners on both sides have denounced the peace process. Arafat faces stringent opposition from the Islamic militant group Hamas while Israeli ultranationalists, who regard the West Bank as part of Greater Israel, likened Rabin to a traitor and a Nazi. Until two years ago, both the US and Israel regarded Arafat as a terrorist. Now, however, international observers hope that the agreement will offer a lasting solution to the Israeli-Palestinian conflict.

May 29. *Actor Christopher Reeve, who played* Superman, *was riding in Virginia and seriously injured his neck when his horse refused a jump. Doctors fear he may be paralyzed.*

Clinton smiles as Israeli Yitzak Rabin and Palestinian Yasser Arafat shake hands.

Million Man March marks day of atonement

Washington, D.C., Oct. 16

Even though the final number of marchers fell short of the million promised, today's twelve-hour rally in Washington, D.C. was still the biggest gathering of people of color in the history of the United States. The Mall was thronged with 600,000 orderly and attentive participants: 150,000 more than the memorable 1963 Civil Rights march led by the Reverend Martin Luther King.

Louis Farrakhan, the organizer of the "Million Man March", is leader of the controversial black Muslim separatist group, Nation of Islam. He has been criticized in the past for racism against Jews and whites. Today, however, he called on black men to look inward to examine their own shortcomings and scrutinize their own behavior. He demanded an end to violence except in self-defense, respect for black women and a rejection of rape and drugs. He also used the occasion to make a verbal attack on the white founding fathers of the United States, and Abraham Lincoln and President Clinton. A boycott of shops and businesses had been called to coincide with the march, and black women were asked to stay home in solidarity. Political leaders were divided in their support for the march, with the National Black Caucus in favor but with women's groups and the National Association for the Advancement of Colored People opposed. Prominent African-Americans who spoke to the crowds included author Maya Angelou and the Reverend Jesse Jackson. General Colin Powell turned down an invitation to speak, explaining that he did not wish to increase Farrakhan's standing in the black community.

Speaking out against racism in Austin, Texas, President Clinton praised the march and its message but criticized Louis Farrakhan.

The Capitol building is the backdrop for the Million Man March organized by Louis Farrakhan to raise awareness of black America.

Powell will not run for President

Alexandria, Virginia, Nov. 8

Colin Powell, 58, ended months of speculation when he announced that he will not seek the Republican nomination for President in 1996. Last month, Powell admitted that he was contemplating a presidential campaign. Opinion polls indicated that he was favorite to unseat Clinton. In a news conference today, Powell, who was the highest-ranking black officer ever in the US Army, said that his commitment to politics did not match his dedication to the military. His decision will disappoint many, who had hoped that Powell would become the first black President. Powell's liberal views on affirmative action, the right to choose, and social welfare differ starkly from those held by the Republican Party's right wing, who were fiercely opposed to his nomination.

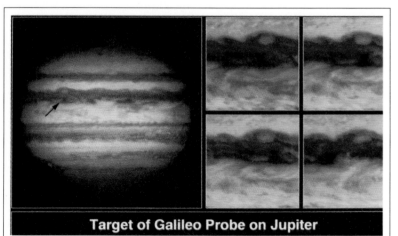

Target of Galileo Probe on Jupiter

Dec. 7. *The space probe Galileo launched a capsule into Jupiter's atmosphere. The mission yielded our first close-up pictures of the planet's surface.*

Showdown leads to shutdown

Washington, D.C., Dec. 16

The government has ground to a halt again. "Non-essential" government workers in the Commerce, Housing and Education departments have been sent home for the second time since mid-November. The compromise bill passed to resolve the November shutdown has failed to prevent a repeat occurrence.

Ongoing hostilities between the Republican Congress and Senate and the White House mean that only six out of thirteen financial bills have been passed this year. This has led to a gap in government funding. President Bill Clinton has vetoed three bills, including the radical budget reconciliation bill.

Congress, led by fiscal conservative Newt Gingrich, has clashed repeatedly with the White House over spending and social policy. The Republicans are determined to eliminate the budget deficit by the year 2002. They want Clinton to agree to a balanced federal budget, and with this objective in mind they successfully blocked his efforts to extend the federal debt limit in November. An opinion poll taken during the last federal shutdown indicated that 48 percent of Americans blamed the Republican Congress for the present crisis, with only 27 percent holding the President responsible.

Clinton's fortunes could improve further, just in time for next year's all-important election race.

Newt Gingrich and Senate leader Bob Dole prepare for more talks.

Blizzard of '96

Huge snow falls mean that commuters have to ski across Times Square.

New York City, Jan. 10

The East Coast has been hit by a blizzard described by the National Weather Service as of "historic proportions." States from Virginia to Massachusetts have been covered in 1.5 – 3 feet of snow by the "Blizzard of '96". It is estimated that the storm could leave at least 100 people dead and cause an estimated $1 billion worth of damage. Airports in Washington, D.C., Philadelphia, Baltimore and New York were closed and New York City received its worst snowfall in 48 years. Commuters endured extra-long delays in frozen conditions, the Mercantile and Commodities market was shut and the Stock Exchange opened late. Schools were closed on January 8 and 9, an almost-unheard-of event, and there was no postal service.

The weather delayed the return to work of government officials after the latest federal shutdown. Cross-country skiing proved the best way of crossing Central Park.

Multi-millionaire accused of murder

Pennsylvania, Jan. 28

John Eleuthier du Pont has been arrested for the murder of Olympic gold-medal wrestler Dave Schultz. Du Pont is a scion of one of America's wealthiest families. He coached the US Olympic pentathlon team in 1976 and had set up a training center for wrestlers at his estate at Newton Square. Schultz was one of a squad of athletes living and training there.

Schultz was shot dead three days ago at Newton Square. Du Pont was arrested after a 48-hour siege. A renowned marksman and notorious eccentric, he barricaded himself into his mansion to evade arrest. Police managed to seize him when he was tricked into emerging to inspect his boiler, which they had switched off.

Liggett liability

New Orleans, Louisiana, March 13

America's fifth-largest cigarette company, the Liggett Group Inc., has admitted liability in the largest class-action suit of the anti-smoking lobby. The so-called Castano case was brought by a consortium of over 60 law firms in the name of "all nicotine-dependent persons". The company will help to finance nicotine-withdrawal programs.

Liggett's decision to settle is the first time that a tobacco company has agreed to pay damages to a plaintiff. It shattered the decades-old front the industry had presented in past legal battles and quashed the recent efforts of the Food and Drug Administration to regulate tobacco.

The four other firms involved fear that the landmark decision opens the way for litigation. They attacked the settlement and said that the damages agreed were minimal.

Liggett reached separate agreements with Florida, Louisiana, Massachusetts, Mississippi and West Virginia, which were suing for reimbursement of money spent on Medicaid for various smoking-related illnesses. These states agreed to drop their lawsuits in return for $5 million dollars toward healthcare budgets. Liggett also agreed to relinquish 2.5 percent of its pre-tax profits over the next 25 years.

March 25. *The Department of the Interior partially re-opens the Glen Canyon Dam to create an artificial flood. The aim is to unleash 117 million gallons of water to clean up the Colorado River. Scientists hope that the action, which mimics that of a natural flood, will stir up sediment, benefit wildlife and improve fertility on the river's beaches.*

"Unabomber" held

Theodore J. Kaczynski – as suspected Unabomber he attracts media attention.

Lincoln, Montana, April 3

A 16-year manhunt ended yesterday when FBI agents arrested a man they believe to be the Unabomber. Theodore J. Kaczynski was apprehended in a tiny shack outside the small town of Lincoln. Kaczynski, now a recluse, is a Harvard graduate and former mathematics professor at Berkeley. He has been charged with possessing sundry bomb-making materials. Unabomber attacks on universities, airlines and computer stores have killed three people and injured 23.

His brother David tipped off the FBI when he noticed similarities between papers he found at his mother's former home in Illinois and the Unabomber manifesto that was published last year by the *Washington Post.*

Lazier wins

Buddy Lazier celebrates his win.

Indianapolis, Indiana, May 26

Indy car-racing fans today were spoilt for choice, but most watched the Indy 500 rather than the US 500. A split between the Indy Racing League and the Championship Auto Racing Team (CART) was responsible for the duplicate fixtures. CART hoped that its star line-up would be a draw but the Indy 500 was a more dramatic contest. Buddy Lazier, a relative unknown, who two months ago sustained back injuries, won by a narrow margin – after arriving on crutches. Jimmy Vassar had a more predictable win in Michigan in the US 500.

Ban on landmines

Norman Schwartzkopf.

New York City, May 16

President Clinton has ordered the destruction of four million anti-personnel mines following last week's UN agreement to impose a limited ban on their deployment. Last month, General H. Norman Schwartzkopf, known as "Stormin' Norman" after his staunch role as US commander in the Gulf War, called for an end to the use of landmines in war. He was one of 15 retired generals and admirals to sign an open letter to the President in the *New York Times.* The general added that such a ban was "not only humane, but militarily responsible".

Atlanta bomb rocks the centenary Olympics

The morning after the night before – the destroyed sound tower graphically shows the bomb's devastating effect.

Atlanta, Georgia, July 27

An uncredited terrorist explosion shattered the harmonious and festive atmosphere at a concert in the Centennial Olympic Park at 1:25 this morning and left two people dead. The crude pipe bomb, which was placed near a sound tower, injured a further 111 people. A police official commented it was a miracle that more people were not fatally injured.

A 911 emergency call just 18 minutes earlier was the sole warning that there was a bomb planted somewhere in the park. The caller's voice was described as that of a white US male. In consequence, the FBI believes that domestic terrorists are responsible for the attack.

Security at the Games has now been stepped up, as federal and state agents search through the bomb debris and scour the park and the surrounding area for clues to identify the perpetrators responsible for the incident.

It's show time as the Olympics celebrates its

Atlanta, July 19. *The fabulous opening ceremony for the one hundredth Summer Olympics in Atlanta. The performers are seen forming the five Olympic rings and the number 100.*

Dominique Moceanu, left, Kerri Strug, center, and Shannon Miller salute the flag after being awarded the gold in the women's team gymnastic competition. Strug injured her left leg following her vault, but bravely carried on.

Proud Carl Lewis – his phenomenal success in the long jump continued as he won his fourth gold medal.

President Clinton with swimmer Michelle Smith of Ireland, who was a triple gold medallist.

Stefka Kostadinova of Bulgaria gained the gold in the high jump.

In the exciting and eagerly awaited men's 100-meter race, American Dennis Mitchell (right) was pipped at the post by Donovan Bailey of Canada (left) who gained the gold, while Frankie Fredericks of Namibia (center) took silver.

centenary in Atlanta in record-breaking style

Britain's Matthew Pinsent (left) and Steve Redgrave take off on their gold medal run in the men's coxless pairs. Steve Redgrave went on to win his fourth consecutive gold medal in the event.

Golden-shod Michael Johnson celebrates after winning the 200-meter race in the world record time of 19.32 seconds.

Russia's Andrej Chemerkin jumps for joy to celebrate his world record lift of 260-kg in the Clean and Jerk at the weight-lifting competition.

Muhammad Ali with the basketball Dream Team – Ali's medal replaced the one he won in 1960 but threw away in protest over racism.

The jubilant athletes of the 4 x 100-meter relay team proudly wave the Stars and Stripes in the traditional lap of honor as they win gold.

Hideous disaster hits TWA Flight 800

The cockpit of the ill-fated TWA Flight 800 is hauled from the Atlantic.

Smithstown, New York, July 26

Searchers today found two engines from the tragic Trans World Airlines (TWA) Flight 800 on the ocean floor.

All 228 people on board were killed when the 747 jetliner plunged into the Atlantic Ocean off the coast of Long Island on July 17. Disaster struck just half an hour after takeoff from New York's Kennedy International Airport. The flight was bound for Paris. Many eyewitnesses saw the burning fragments of the aircraft fall into the sea.

While investigators scoured the ocean floor for forensic evidence, grieving families waited in agony for the bodies of their loved ones to be recovered. The US Coast Guard searched in vain for survivors, assisted by civilians and fishermen from Long Island.

Divers recovered the voice recorder a week later. The so-called black box indicated a brief noise immediately before the tape ended and the plane crashed. The black box of Pan Am Flight 103 recorded a similar sound shortly before a bomb on board exploded above Lockerbie in Scotland in 1988. Experts have not ruled out a terrorist attack, although they are still exploring the option of mechanical failure.

Flight 800 is the latest in a series of aviation tragedies. In May a Valujet DC-9 crashed into the Everglades. Canisters of oxygen in the hold which were wrongly labeled as empty were implicated. The Federal Aviation Authority appointed hundreds of new safety inspectors and the Transport Department was urged to ensure that airlines operated within strict safety guidelines.

Dole accepts republican nomination

San Diego, California, August 15

Senator Robert Dole has beaten off his rivals to take the Republican nomination for President. His victory ended a dramatic political contest. With the Democrat nomination a lackluster affair, the Republicans dominated headlines. Dole staked his political career on taking the nomination and last May gave up the Senate seat he held for 27 years.

In his acceptance speech to party members in San Diego, he promised to honor the Republican pledge to balance the budget. He also spoke of the need for "inclusion" and "compassion". Today's unity contrasts with the partisan campaign that preceded it. When he lost the New Hampshire primary to right-wing commentator Pat Buchanan, Dole declared that the battle for the Republican nomination was "a race between the mainstream and the extreme" and branded his rival as intolerant. To underscore his commitment to the center, he has named moderate Jack Kemp – once a contender for the nomination – as his running mate.

Tupac Shakur gunned down

Las Vegas, Nevada, Sept. 12

Rap star Tupac Shakur, 25, has died of gunshot wounds He was shot four times on his way to a nightclub six days ago. His death has once again raised the issue of violent lyrics and macho posturing. These have been blamed for a number of incidents, with record companies only too happy to foster a tough image for their artists. Fans are mourning the rap star as a victim of the violence devastating the black community, even though his own lyrics glamorized violence.

Tupac Shakur, victim of violence.

Clinton condemns church burnings

Greeleyville, S. Carolina, June 12

President Clinton urged all Americans to unite to rebuild black churches destroyed by arson attacks. In the last 18 months, more than 30 churches have been burned down across the southern states. Southern churchmen last week lobbied Washington, D.C., over the burnings. So far, evidence of a conspiracy has not been found, although racism is widely held to be a factor in some, though not all, of the attacks. Few of the cases have been solved.

Surge of ceremonies as naturalizations hit an all-time high

Salma Carunia Carter, formerly of India, proudly waves her Stars and Stripes.

Irving, Texas, Sept. 17

Ten thousand new US citizens were sworn in at a mass naturalization rally today. People from 113 different countries pledged allegiance to the Stars and Stripes at Texas Stadium in Irving. There will be an even bigger ceremony in San Jose, California, tomorrow.

Experts attribute the sharpest rise in naturalization seen to date to anti-immigration laws and hostile public sentiment, although there are accusations that the Clinton administration is trying to turn out large numbers of Democratic voters before the election.

Israeli-Palestinian peace plan stumbles

Washington, D.C., Oct. 2

A two-day emergency summit presided over by President Clinton ended in deadlock today. Despite valiant diplomatic efforts by the US, Israeli prime minister Benjamin Netanyahu and PLO leader Yasser Arafat failed to reach agreement on crucial issues. The talks were called to rescue the Middle East peace process after the recent outbreak of violence in the West Bank and Jerusalem. Clashes over Muslim holy places in Jerusalem left at least 70 people dead last month. Last year's bright hopes for a lasting peace now seem to be dashed by recent events.

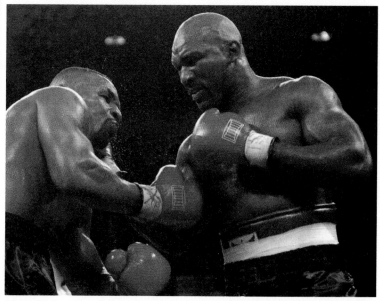

Nov. 9. *In one of the biggest surprise upsets in boxing history, the 11-1 underdog Evander Holyfield defeats Mike Tyson in a technical knockout in the eleventh round to win the World Boxing Association heavyweight title.*

NCOs suspended over sex claims

Aberdeen, Maryland, Nov. 10

Fifteen NCOs were suspended at a US Army training base in Maryland after allegations of sexual harassment, serious sexual misconduct and intimidation.

Investigations first began in September after a female student at Aberdeen Proving Ground filed a complaint against an instructor on the base. Since then, more than 20 other female students have come forward with similar allegations. All the complainants were students just out of basic training, who were being instructed in additional skills such as weapons repair. Aberdeen deals with more than 11,000 trainees annually, and more than a fifth of them are women.

This latest case again raises awkward questions from critics about alleged widespread and systematic sexual abuse in the armed forces. In an effort to eradicate these alleged problems, the army has just introduced a toll-free hotline and has launched a full investigation into this issue.

The Navy and Marine Corps introduced a sexual harassment hotline in 1992 and the Air Force did likewise in 1994.

California okays marijuana

Sacramento, California, Nov. 5

Fifty-six percent of Californian voters approved a measure to allow seriously ill patients to use prescribed marijuana under a doctor's supervision. Arizona voters have approved a similar measure. The illegal drug is reported to relieve pain and nausea. Aids carers also allege that marijuana counters certain unpleasant side-effects of legal drugs used to treat the virus.

Growers can now legally sell marijuana for the first time in 30 years.

Denis Peron, founder of the Cannabis Buyers' Club, smoking a joint to celebrate the new law.

Blockbusters break all records at the box office

Aliens in a massive spacecraft blow up the White House just for kicks in ID4.

Los Angeles, Dec. 30

The top-grossing films this year were Twentieth-Century Fox's *Independence Day* ($306 million), Warner Brothers' *Twister* ($241 million) and Paramount's *Mission: Impossible* ($180 million).

All three were holiday releases, in a summer that distributors hailed as the best ever.

Independence Day (*ID4*) broke the $100 million mark just one week after its release over the July 4 weekend. It ousted *Mission: Impossible* as this year's record-breaker – the Tom Cruise vehicle opened over Memorial Day weekend and took $74.9 million in six days. With *Twister* also doing strong business, US distributors are celebrating what looks like being the biggest summer ever.

The three top box-office smash hit movies were unashamed all-action roller-coasters, with little romance but masses of adrenaline and, in the case of *ID4*, pleasing incidental humor, notably from Jeff Goldblum and Will Smith.

Moviegoers enjoyed expensive and impressive set-pieces in each film. Invading aliens blow up the White House in *Independence Day*, frenetic meteorologists chase tornadoes right across the midwest in *Twister*, while in *Mission: Impossible* Tom Cruise gets embroiled in complicated espionage set-ups in Central Europe.

After all this present day and future-set action, audiences now seem ready for a change of pace. The avowedly romantic desert-and-adultery period epic *The English Patient*, with a strong, predominately European cast, has done good business in theaters since it opened in October.

New Orleans, Jan. 26.
The Green Bay Packers beat the New England Patriots 35–21 to win Super Bowl XXXI.

Washington, D.C., Feb. 4.
President Clinton's State of the Union address praises the U.S. as the world's most diverse democracy, but calls on all Americans to repair the breach in the country's racial divide.

Media, Pennsylvania, Feb. 25.
John E. du Pont is found guilty of third-degree murder for the January 1996 killing of Olympic gold-medal wrestler David Schultz, having been declared mentally incompetent in September 1996.

Los Angeles, March 7.
The Return of the Jedi hits the big screen again, completing a "special edition" cinema re-release – with improved special effects and added sequences – of George Lucas' 1970s *Star Wars* trilogy. The first part, *Star Wars*, grossed $35.9 million on the first weekend of its return early this month.

Washington, D.C., April 24.
915,900 people were granted permanent resident status last year, reversing a four-year decline in legal immigration.

Miami, Oct. 26.
The Florida Marlins win the baseball World Series, beating the Cleveland Indians in the 11th inning to take the seven-game series 4–3.

New York City, Nov. 4.
Rudolph Giuliani becomes the first Republican mayor of New York to win re-election since Fiorello La Guardia in 1937.

Washington, D.C., Nov. 13.
The F.B.I. announces the end of its 16-month investigation into the July 1996 crash of TWA Flight 800 after finding no evidence of criminal involvement.

Washington, D.C., Dec. 2.
Attorney General Janet Reno announces that she will not not be appointing a special prosecutor to investigate alleged fundraising irregularities by President Clinton and Vice President Al Gore in 1996.

DEATHS

Massachusetts, April 12.
Nobel Prize-winning biologist George Wald (*1907).

Fort Worth, Texas, July 25.
Golfing great Ben Hogan, four-times winner of U.S. Open, aged 84 (*Aug. 13, 1912).

Diana dresses auctioned

New York City, June 25

British royal finery was up for sale tonight as 79 of Princess Diana's most glamorous evening gowns were auctioned for charity at Christie's New York. Telephone bidders competed with a 1,100-strong gathering of Manhattan socialites in the Park Avenue auction rooms, raising more than $3.2 million for various charities. The most expensive sale was a velvet silk Edwardian-style gown in inky blue, which Diana wore to the White House in 1985 for a dinner at which she danced with John Travolta. The dress, designed by Victor Edelstein, raised $200,000, a record for an item of clothing sold at auction. Since Diana and Prince Charles divorced in 1996, she has had little use for formal gowns; the idea of auctioning them reportedly came from Prince William.

This 1994 silk dress fetched $65,000.

Tiger Woods blazes trail in Masters

Tiger burns bright as he shakes hands with previous winner Nick Faldo (left).

Augusta, Georgia, April 15

At just 21, Tiger Woods is the youngest-ever winner of golf's prestigious U.S. Masters tournament. Although he was already favorite to win before play even commenced, Woods went on to break the all-time scoring record and established the largest-ever margin of victory, winning by a 12-stroke lead and 22 under par. His final score was 70-66-65-69 – 270. His fans are asking: "Can he now win the Grand Slam?" Woods is the first man of color to win a major golf championship. The site of this victory, Augusta's National Club, was a symbol of national segregation until 1975, when Lee Elder first broke the color line.

Tobacco companies strike deal

Wigand and attorney Motley hear news.

Washington, D.C., June 20

Leading tobacco companies have agreed a deal worth $368.5 billion over 25 years that will settle most legal claims against them. This is welcome news to supporters of the claim, like whistleblower Jeffrey Wigand. The breakthrough follows months of talks with the Attorneys General of 40 states who were suing the tobacco industry to recover public money used in the healthcare of people made ill by smoking. Of the total amount, $360 billion will meet the states' Medicare bills over the coming quarter-century. The deal guarantees the tobacco industry immunity from future state and class-action lawsuits. Also, punitive damages will not usually be awarded against the industry – except in cases of future misconduct. The companies agreed to limit advertising and meet targets for reducing smoking by the young. The deal now requires legislation by Congress.

Jan. 6. *Dr. David Ho is* Time *Magazine's 1996 Man of the Year. The AIDS researcher has discovered a treatment that all but eliminates the HIV virus.*

Clinton's second inauguration

Washington, D.C., Jan. 20

William Jefferson Clinton was today inaugurated for his second term as President, with Al Gore again his second-in-command. The President, chastened by his often stormy first term, made a low-key speech. He spoke of the need for a "government humble enough not to try to solve all our problems" and committed himself to balancing the budget. Although the Democrats won the Presidential race, the Republicans have retained control of Congress.

O.J. found liable

O.J. now faces financial troubles.

Santa Monica, CA, Feb. 10

On February 5 a civil jury found former football star O.J. Simpson liable for the deaths of his ex-wife Nicole Brown Simpson and her friend Ronald L. Goodman, in a case brought by the families of the deceased. The jury found that there was a "preponderance of evidence" that Simpson had "wilfully and wrongfully" caused Goldman's death by stabbing. It awarded $8.5 million compensation to the Goldmans. Today a further $12.5 million was awarded to each family in punitive damages.

Ronald Goldman's father, Fred, began the civil proceedings when he filed a wrongful death lawsuit against Simpson. He says he brought the case in the interests of justice. A jury in an earlier criminal prosecution found Simpson not guilty on two counts of murder.

As this was a civil case, Simpson will not have to serve a custodial sentence, but the judgment means he is facing financial disaster.

Cult suicide

San Diego, CA, March 28

In a mass suicide pact, 39 men and women have taken their lives by taking a drug overdose washed down with vodka. They were apparently convinced that an Unidentified Flying Object hidden behind the Hale-Bopp comet would take them to the stars. All 39 were members of a cult led by a figure known as "Father John." They were dressed identically in black pants and sports shoes, with faces and chests covered with a purple shroud. The well-planned suicides took place over a period of seven days. All appear to have been voluntary.

The bodies of the cult members were discovered on Wednesday, March 26, at the luxury Rancho Santa Fe mansion, by a former cult member and his employer, a Beverly Hills computer expert. The group had sent their former colleague a package which contained details of their planned suicide, along with videotaped goodbye messages. They told him that by the time he received their letter they would have "shed their containers." They seemed to be "quite jovial and excited about moving on to this next stage."

Tyson bites Holyfield

The ear was sewn back together.

Las Vegas, June 28

Tonight's much-hyped world heavyweight title boxing bout between Mike Tyson and Evander Holyfield ended in uproar after Tyson savagely bit off part of his opponent's ear in round three and was immediately disqualified. Tyson claimed that he used his teeth in retaliation for a head butt from Holyfield, but the fight referee declared the butt accidental. Defending champion Holyfield, who caused an upset when he took Tyson's World Boxing Association title in 1996, was rushed to the Valley Hospital Medical Center, where his ear was repaired.

Mike Tyson's career now lies in tatters. He faces the possibility of being banned from all forms of boxing when the Nevada Athletic Commission rules on the case later in the year.

U.S. shares British grief over loss of Princess Diana, "Queen of Hearts"

Diana's coffin arrives at the Abbey, watched by members of the Royal family.

London, Sept. 6

First Lady Hillary Clinton and former U.S. Secretary of State Henry Kissinger today attended the funeral of Britain's Princess Diana in Westminster Abbey. The Princess died in Paris on August 31 after the limousine in which she was traveling crashed at 85mph in a road tunnel. The car's driver, Henri Paul, and Diana's companion, Dodi Fayed, son of Egyptian millionaire Mohammed al-Fayed, were also killed in the accident.

The news of the Princess' death at the age of 36 plunged Britain and Diana's many friends world-wide into mourning. In London vast crowds flocked to Diana's Kensington Palace home, leaving a mountain of floral tributes. In the United States President Clinton declared: "Hillary and I are profoundly saddened by this tragic event." Diana's griefstricken sons – Princes William, 15, and Harry, 12 – were among the members of the Royal Family who somberly escorted the coffin into the Abbey. Hollywood celebrities including Steven Spielberg, Tom Cruise and Nicole Kidman were present at the service and billions around the world watched on TV.

Gingrich gets reprimand

Washington, D.C., Jan. 21

Newt Gingrich was given an official reprimand by the Congress Ethics Sub-committee, just 14 days after he was re-elected as House Speaker by a narrow margin. The committee also imposed a fine of $300,000 on him. Republican Gingrich has admitted that he funded a politically partisan college course using tax-exempt charitable contributions and that he misled Congress over the affair.

The scandal has severely dented Gingrich's reputation for being tough on both fiscal and moral questions. The Republican Party may now find it much more difficult to pursue President Clinton and Vice President Al Gore over allegations of improper methods of fund-raising during last year's election campaign.

M Veigh sentenced to death for bomb attack

Denver, Colorado, Aug. 14

Timothy McVeigh, convicted in June of first-degree murder for the 1995 Oklahoma City bombing in which 168 people were killed, was today sentenced by U.S. District Judge Richard Matsch to death by lethal injection. In court 29-year-old McVeigh made his first public statement since he was arrested, quoting from a 1928 Supreme Court dissenting opinion by Justice Louis Brandeis: "Our government is the potent, the omnipresent teacher. For good or ill, it teaches the whole people by its example." He offered no apology and showed no signs of remorse.

Many interpret his implied statement that he was taught violence by the government as confirmation that the bombing was intended to avenge the 80 people who died in 1993 when the F.B.I. brought to an end the siege of the Branch Davidian religious sect buildings in Waco, Texas. The attack on the Alfred Murrah building in Oklahoma City on April 19, 1995, took place on the second anniversary of the siege's end at Waco.

McVeigh, who was trained in the use of explosives by the U.S. Army, was sentenced to death on each of 11 charges – including murder and using a weapon of mass destruction – of which he was convicted in Denver on June 2. The murder charges, brought forward by the prosecution led by Joseph Hartzler, covered the deaths of eight federal law officers in the bomb explosion.

Joseph Hartzler, lead prosecutor.

Mayhem in U.S. financial markets

Trading was suspended on October 27 to avert market meltdowns.

Manhattan, Oct. 28

The crisis in Asian financial markets has brought turmoil to Wall Street over the last two days. Yesterday in Hong Kong fears of rapidly rising interest rates led to a fall of 5.8 percent in the Hang Seng index and on Wall Street the Dow Jones suffered its largest ever single-day fall, dropping 554.26 points to close at 7161.15. Today the Dow looked to be going into free fall – losing a further 186 points in early trading, but then it dramatically rallied to rise more than 400 points and close up by 337.17 – the largest ever one-day rise – at 7498.32. Some 905 million shares were traded on Wall Street today, another record.

Hubble captures brightest star

Los Angeles, Oct. 7

NASA's Hubble space telescope has taken pictures of the brightest star yet discovered – 10 million times brighter and 100 times more massive than the sun. Named the Pistol star for the pistol-shaped nebula that surrounds it, the star lies an estimated 25,000 light-years from Earth. It is invisible to the naked eye and to regular telescopes because of dust clouds in the Milky Way. An infrared camera aboard the Hubble in Earth orbit took the pictures released by University of California scientists today. Hubble is proving an invaluable aid to astronomers. On February 14 this year two astronauts aboard the space shuttle *Discovery* gave the telescope its billion-mile service during a space-walk.

Army sexual harassment report

Washington, D.C., Sept. 11

A U.S. Army report released today concludes that sexual harassment is found throughout the service, "crossing gender, rank, and racial lines," and is so common that many soldiers view it as a "normal part of army life." The 10-month investigation included interviews with 35,000 commanders and soldiers, following complaints at an army training center in Aberdeen, Maryland, where one drill sergeant was jailed for rape. The Army has stated it will improve basic training and equal opportunities programs and increase supervision of the drill sergeants.

July 4. *The Mars Pathfinder rover vehicle today finally touched down on the Red Planet, after a seven-month journey from Earth.*

Versace murdered

The Miami mansion where Gianni Versace was brutally murdered.

Miami, July 15

Italian fashion designer Gianni Versace was murdered at the gate of his South Beach mansion this morning. An unidentified gunman fired two shots into the back of Versace's head and the designer died in an ambulance on the way to the hospital. The murder plunged the fashion world into mourning and a gala ceremony in Rome was cancelled. Tonight the sidewalk on Ocean Drive is strewn with flowers left by well-wishers. Law officers have not established a motive for the attack on the 50-year-old entrepreneur. Versace was openly gay and the F.B.I. suggest that suspected gay serial killer Andrew Cunanan, 27, may have been involved.

Michael Kennedy dies in ski tragedy

Death revives talk of Kennedy curse.

Aspen, Colorado, Dec. 31

Tragedy has struck the Kennedy clan once again. Michael Kennedy, the 39-year-old son of the late Senator Robert F. Kennedy, was killed today in a bizarre skiing accident on the Copper Bowl slope of the 11,200 ft Aspen Mountain in Colorado. He was playing a game of catch with members of his family, and attempting to use a video camera to record the game, when he collided with a tree. He was pronounced dead on arrival at the hospital. Weather conditions were fine and Kennedy was an experienced and skillful skier.

Kennedy headed the Citizens Energy Corporation, a non-profit body providing household fuel to the poverty-stricken. He was once widely considered a likely candidate for Congress but his political ambitions faded after revelations of an affair with the family's teenage babysitter led to his separation from his wife Victoria. The scandal also impacted adversely on the campaign of Michael's brother Joseph, a Democrat congressman, to become governor of Massachusetts. Another brother, David, died in 1984 after overdosing on drugs.

Now the members of this great political family, already chastened by so many untimely deaths, must put aside their New Year celebrations and gather for another memorial service. The funeral is planned for January 3.

World Trade Center bombers convicted

New York, Nov. 12

A federal jury has convicted two men of murder and conspiracy for their part in the February 1993 bombing of the World Trade Center, in which six died and more than 1,000 were hurt. Prosecutors said that Ramzi Yousef, a 30-year-old of uncertain nationality, masterminded the outrage to force an end to U.S. aid to Israel; his Palestinian accomplice Eyad Ismoil, 26, drove the truck containing the bomb into the Center's carpark. Both men fled the U.S. after the attack but were apprehended abroad in 1995. Yousef is already serving a life sentence following his 1996 conviction for plotting to blow up 12 U.S. airliners.

Clinton accused of sexual harassment

Little Rock, Arkansas, Aug. 22

President Clinton is to suffer the indignity of a sexual harassment suit while in office. U.S. Federal District Judge Susan Webber Wright today refused to dismiss the suit, which was brought against the President by Paula Jones, a former Arkansas state employee. Jones' allegations include that in May 1991 Clinton, then Arkansas governor, exposed himself and made sexual propositions to her in a hotel room. The judge set a trial date of May 26 next year. Jones' lawyers will be able to subpoena witnesses when the case enters its discovery phase next January.

July 1–2. Hollywood loses two of its greatest leading men: Robert Mitchum (left), aged 79 on July 1 and James Stewart (89) on July 2.

Jury convicts Nichols of conspiracy and manslaughter in Oklahoma bombing

Denver, Colorado, Dec. 23

A second man may face the death penalty for his role in the Oklahoma City bombing of 1995. Following the sentencing to death of Timothy McVeigh in August, his alleged accomplice, Terry Nichols, was today convicted by a federal jury of conspiracy and involuntary manslaughter.

Unlike McVeigh, Nichols was not found guilty on murder charges covering the deaths of eight federal law officers in the blast. When the bomb blasted the Alfred Murrah federal building in Oklahoma City on April 19, 1995, Nichols was more than 200 miles away on his farm in Kansas. But the federal jury that convicted him was satisfied that he had helped to plan and pay for the attack and to construct the explosive device. Nichols, now 42, met McVeigh in the U.S. Army in the 1980s and they were driven by a contempt for the federal government. The conspiracy charge carries a possible death penalty.

Unabomber changes plea to guilty

Kaczynski's mother and brother.

Sacramento, CA, Jan. 22

The trial of the man accused of being the Unabomber, the woodland recluse who killed three and wounded 23 in an 18-year bombing campaign, has ended before it began. Offered a guarantee that he would be spared the death penalty, Theodore Kaczynski this afternoon changed his plea to guilty on 10 charges. He will be jailed for life without parole.

Kaczynski, a 55-year-old former Berkeley math professor, was arrested in April 1996 at the Montana log cabin that he had built in 1969 after quitting academia – and from which he had conducted his violent anti-technology protest. In the last few weeks Kaczynski tried to sack his defense lawyers, angry that they wanted to portray him as deranged, and asked to be permitted to mount his own defense constructed around his long-term belief that humanity was a victim of technology. A federal psychiatrist found him to be a paranoid schizophrenic – and thus subject to delusions and prone to violence – but also declared him mentally competent to defend himself.

Kaczynski's brother David, whose tipoff to the F.B.I. led to the arrest, today said that he and their mother, Wanda, felt the plea bargain to be an "appropriate, just, and civilized resolution to this tragedy in the light of Ted's diagnosed mental illness." Prosecutor Robert Cleary said that the families of the victims had been consulted about the plea bargain. "The Unabomber's career is over," he said.

Chicago Bulls win NBA Championship

Salt Lake City, June 14

Ecstatic Chicago Bulls fans are celebrating their heroes' third straight NBA World Championship. At the Delta Center here tonight the Bulls beat the Utah Jazz 87–86 to take a 4–2 finals victory – after "His Airness" Michael Jordan shot the decisive basket with just 5.2 seconds remaining on the clock. Bulls' Coach Phil Jackson declared: "I don't know if anyone could have written a scenario as dramatic as this." It is the Bulls' sixth World Championship in eight years, but the future may not be so bright. Jackson looks unlikely to return next year – and the 35-year-old Jordan, who quit basketball in 1993 only to return in 1995, is himself threatening to retire once more.

Titanic victory

Cameron delights in his triumph.

Los Angeles, March 23

"I'm the king of the world!" exploded *Titanic* director James Cameron, clutching the Oscar for Best Director and echoing the words of the character Jack Dawson in the movie. Tonight Cameron's 194-minute drama about the ill-fated 1912 ocean liner avoided all icebergs as it sailed to triumph, scooping 11 Oscars and so equaling the best-ever sweep of the Academy Awards made by *Ben Hur* in 1959.

Aside from Best Director, the $200 million *Titanic* – the most expensive movie ever made, but also the first to gross $1 billion – won Best Picture as well as nine other Oscars. *Titanic*'s young leads Leonardo DiCaprio and Kate Winslet missed out, though – Best Actor and Best Actress went to Jack Nicholson and Helen Hunt respectively for their parts in *As Good As It Gets*.

March 26. *Bill Clinton, welcomed to Cape Town by President Nelson Mandela, becomes the first U.S. President to visit South Africa. He called for "mutual respect and mutual reward" between the two countries.*

Woodward makes plans to go home

Free at last, Louise (left) with mother Sue, sister Vicky and father Gary.

Boston, June 16

Louise Woodward, the British au pair at the center of a controversial child murder trial, is tonight planning to return to her home in northern England. Last October 31 Ms Woodward was convicted of the murder of Matthew Eappen, an eight-month-old baby in her care, only for the trial judge 11 days later to reduce the conviction to manslaughter and sentence her to 279 days' imprisonment. She was freed because she had already served this time on remand, but had to remain in the U.S. pending an appeal. Today the Massachusetts Supreme Court upheld the conviction and the sentence. The child's parents, Sunil and Deborah Eappen, have now filed a civil lawsuit against Woodward.

Feb. 20. *Aged 15 years 255 days, U.S. skating prodigy Tara Lipinski becomes the youngest ever winner of an individual gold medal in the Winter Olympics in Nagano, Japan.*

Clinton denies having sexual relations with former aide Monica Lewinsky

Washington, D.C., Jan. 27

President Clinton yesterday issued an emphatic denial of recent allegations that he had an adulterous affair with former White House aide Monica Lewinsky, and that on December 28 last year he asked her to deny the affair when she made her deposition to lawyers in the Paula Jones sexual harassment case against the President. He said: "I did not have sexual relations with that woman, Miss Lewinsky. I never told anybody to lie, not a single time. Never."

The allegations, which appeared in the press six days ago, sparked a storm of speculation in the media that Clinton might be forced to resign. Today First Lady Hillary Clinton gave an interview on NBC. She spoke of the need to fight a "vast right-wing conspiracy" against his presidency.

The Lewinsky story emerged in the discovery phase of the Paula Jones case as her lawyers attempted to establish a pattern of adulterous behavior on Clinton's part. On January 17 Clinton had become the first sitting President to testify as defendant in a court case when he spoke under oath to Jones' lawyers in Washington. The most potentially damaging allegations are that the President attempted to entice Lewinsky to commit perjury on his behalf and that on January 17 he committed perjury himself by denying the affair with her while under oath.

Kenneth Starr was authorized to extend his investigation into Clinton's involvement in the Whitewater property deal in Arkansas to include the allegations concerning Lewinsky. He is said to be armed with tape recordings containing details of Lewinsky's relations with the President.

Lewinsky hits the headlines.

Tornadoes hit southern states

Devastated industrial buildings make grim viewing for Al Gore (center).

Nashville, Tennessee, April 17

Latest reports suggest that as many as 60 people have been killed and more than 160 injured by the violent storms and tornadoes that have been battering the southern states this month. Vice President Al Gore today visited storm-ravaged Nashville, where a tornado yesterday wrecked up to 400 downtown buildings and 500 homes in the east of the city, and said "I'm truly inspired by the way the community has pulled together." Nashville had no fatalities, but yesterday's storms, with winds of up to 260 m.p.h., killed six people in Tennessee, two in Arkansas, and three in Kentucky.

Earlier this month, a tornado swept through Alabama, Georgia, and Mississippi, killing 30 and injuring 160. According to the Storm Prediction Center, 102 people have been killed by storms and tornadoes since January.

McGwire hits major league record

McGwire blasts his 70th home run. It soared 370 ft into the left field seats.

St. Louis, Sep. 27

Mark McGwire, St. Louis Cardinals' brawny big-hitter, beat off the challenge of Chicago Cubs' Sammy Sosa in the dramatic home-run contest that has gripped major league baseball this year. The Cardinals' "Big Mac" ended the season today with a new major league record of 70 home runs, four ahead of Sosa.

The two men have been going neck and neck after the records in a personal contest memorable for the hitters' easy-going mutual respect and for their heroics on the diamond. Both smashed Roger Maris' 37-year-old record of 61 homers – McGwire on September 9 against the Cubs and Sosa on September 13 against the Milwaukee Brewers. Only last Friday Sosa edged ahead, hitting his 66th home run off Jose Lima of the Houston Astros, but the same night McGwire matched him with his 66th, off Shayne Bennett of

the Montreal Expos.

Sosa stalled on 66, but the 6 ft 5 in and 250 lb Big Mac powered on. Yesterday he hit two more homers – 67 and 68 – in the Cardinals' 7–6 defeat by the Expos. He despatched the final two today in the Cardinals' 6–3 victory over the Expos – number 69 came off Mike Thurman in the third inning and number 70 off Carl Pavano in the seventh.

The chase really hotted up in June when Sosa hit 20 homers in one month. On June 30, with almost three months to go, Sosa had 33 and Big Mac 37. Both have been good-natured and modest throughout. When he beat the record on September 9 McGwire celebrated with Maris' children – Maris himself died in 1985, aged 51. McGwire spoke warmly of his forerunners – Maris and the legendary "Sultan of Swat," Babe Ruth, whose 1927 record of 60 home runs Maris beat in 1961.

U.S. embassy bombings

Washington, D.C., Aug. 10

The government is taking a hard line in the wake of bomb attacks that hit U.S. embassies in eastern Africa on August 7. A blast in the Kenyan capital, Nairobi, killed at least 253, including 12 U.S. citizens, and injured 5,000, while in the Tanzanian city, Dar-es-Salaam, a bomb killed 10, though none of them were U.S. citizens, and injured 75. Secretary of State Madeleine Albright today offered $2 million of government money for information leading to the conviction of the terrorists. Islamic militants are believed to be behind the attacks. Osama bin Laden, the 45-year-old Saudi-born financer of Islamic terrorism now resident in Afghanistan, declared in a June interview with ABC that he was planning attacks on U.S. targets.

A soldier raises a flag in the debris.

Bob Livingston resigns over scandal

Washington, D.C., Dec. 19

Speaker-elect Bob Livingston dramatically quit during today's presidential impeachment debate in the House of Representatives, after calling on President Clinton to resign.

Two days ago Republican representative Livingston, 55, admitted the truth of media reports that he had committed adultery in his 33-year marriage – despite his high moral stance on the President's sexual misdemeanors. Today he

declared "I must set the example that I hope President Clinton will follow."

Following the Republicans' disappointing showing in the November 3 mid-term elections, Livingston announced on November 6 that he would challenge the House Speaker, fellow Republican Newt Gingrich, and on the same day Gingrich resigned. Livingston was elected by the Republican majority in the House of Representatives on November 18.

July 3. *Brush and forest fires in Florida force more than 70,000 people to evacuate their homes.*

May 14. *Singer and Oscar-winner Frank Sinatra, dubbed "the Voice," dies in LA age 82.*

Swiss banks compensate victims of Holocaust

Brooklyn, Aug. 12

Credit Suisse, the Swiss Bank Corporation, and the Union Bank of Switzerland have announced a $1.25 billion settlement with Jewish groups in compensation for the loss in World War II of deposits made by thousands of Jews. Survivors of the Nazi Holocaust and their heirs brought a class action against the banks on October 3, 1986, and in June this year rejected an offer of $600 million. The banks admit mistakes in handling the contents of deposit boxes and bank accounts belonging to Jews.

Estelle Sapir claimed on the account of her father, Joseph, a Holocaust victim.

Operation Desert Fox terminated

Washington, D.C., Dec. 20

Operation Desert Fox – a four-night U.S.-British air bombardment of Iraq – ended last night and was today hailed a success by Defense Secretary William Cohen. Desert Fox was unleashed December 16 to punish the Iraqi regime of Saddam Hussein for its recent repeated refusals to cooperate with agreed United Nations inspections of possible weapon-production sites. The inspections were provided for in the 1991 ceasefire that ended the Gulf War.

In 650 air sorties and 400 cruise missile attacks, Desert Fox hit 100 Iraqi targets, including the Baghdad military intelligence H.Q. and 11 weapons facilities. There were no U.S. or British casualties. Cohen said the mission was planned to keep civilian deaths to a minimum and that its goal – "to weaken Iraq's military power" – had been achieved.

The attack was condemned by Russia and China as a violation of the U.N. charter. General Hugh Shelton, however, called Desert Fox a "job extremely well done," and added that the U.S. would maintain a "significant" military presence in the Persian Gulf area to deter future aggression by President Saddam.

Clinton's grand jury testimony broadcast to the nation

Washington, D.C., Sept. 21

Americans today got to judge for themselves President Clinton's August 17 testimony to the grand jury investigating allegations that he committed perjury and attempted to obstruct justice in trying to cover up his relations with former White House intern Monica Lewinsky. A four-hour video tape of the testimony was broadcast on TV. The President admitted to "inappropriate intimate physical contact" with Ms Lewinsky but said that this "did not consist of sexual intercourse" and "did not constitute sexual relations." After the screening the Pres-

ident's job-approval rating promptly rose by six points to 66 percent – a full 10 percent higher than it had been in January before the Lewinsky saga began.

The President's popularity has held firm throughout the investigation, which the U.S. public has had the chance to follow in exhaustive detail. Independent Counsel Kenneth Starr's 445-page report into it was presented to Congress on September 9 and then made public on September 11 after the House of Representatives voted to release it.

On the day of his grand jury testimony, President Clinton made a

TV address watched by 150 million in which he admitted to a relationship with Ms Lewinsky that had been "not appropriate" and "wrong" but said that his January 26 denial of sexual relations with her had been "legally accurate" – although he had given a "false impression" by not providing more information. In early September he made a number of public apologies, but still denied that he had committed perjury, obstructed justice, or tried to suborn Ms Lewinsky. On September 9 he declared himself "determined to redeem the trust of all the American people."

U.S. launches cruise missiles

Arabian and Red Seas, Aug. 20

At 1:30 p.m. Eastern Standard time today, U.S. ships launched simultaneous Tomahawk cruise missile attacks against targets officials describe as a terrorist camp in Afghanistan and a manufactory of nerve gas ingredients in the Sudan. President Clinton said that intelligence information had convincingly suggested that groups affiliated to the Afghan-resident financer of terrorism, Osama bin Laden, had been behind this month's attacks on the U.S. embassies in Tanzania and Kenya. Today's missiles on centers associated with these groups had been to pre-empt a further "imminent threat" to U.S. national security.

Silicone implant compensation

Bay City, Michigan, July 8

A total of around 170,000 American women who say that rupturing and leaking of their silicone-gel breast implants caused them to suffer immune system and other health problems will share $3.2 billion compensation under an agreement that was announced here today. The deal allows Dow Corning Corporation, manufacturer of silicone implants, to emerge from Chapter 11 bankruptcy protection, in which it has languished since 1995. The Food and Drug Administration effectively banned silicone-gel implants because of associated health risks in 1992 and more recent implants use a saline gel.

Oct. 29. *Senator John Glenn at 77 becomes the oldest man in space. He takes off aboard the space shuttle Discovery for a nine-day mission to take part in experiments investigating the effects of weightlessness on aging.*

Washington, D.C., Jan. 1.
Official figures reveal a 2.5 million rise in the population of the U.S. in 1998 to a new total of 271,645,214.

Washington, D.C., Jan. 6.
Dennis Hastert is elected Speaker of the House of Representatives.

New York, Jan. 12.
The baseball which Mark Mc-Gwire hit for his record 70th home run in 1998 is auctioned for $3,005,000, the most money ever paid for a sport object.

Washington, D.C., Jan. 19.
President Clinton does not mention his impeachment trial during his State of the Union address. He declares that the U.S. is enjoying "the longest peacetime economic expansion" in its history, adding "America is working again. The promise of our future is limitless."

Miami, Jan. 31.
The Denver Broncos beat the Atlanta Falcons 34–19 in Superbowl XXXIII. Falcons star Eugene Robinson plays after earlier being arrested for allegedly propositioning a policewoman posing as a prostitute.

Jasper, Texas, Feb. 25.
White supremacist John King, 24, is sentenced to death by lethal injection for the murder of African American James Byrd Jr. in June 1998.

New York, Mar. 3.
An estimated 70 million audience – the highest in U.S. TV history for a news program – watches ABC's two-hour interview with Monica Lewinsky.

Los Angeles, Mar. 21.
The movie *Shakespeare in Love* wins seven Oscars.

New York, Mar. 29.
The Dow Jones breaks the 10,000-point limit and stays above it for the first time in history: it closes at 10,006.78.

Montgomery, April 15.
The Alabama House of Representatives repeals the state's constitutional ban on interracial marriages.

Oklahoma and Kansas, May 3.
Tornadoes kill at least 47 and injure hundreds.

New York, Dec. 4.
Regular passenger flights from New York to Havana, Cuba, start again after almost 40 years.

DEATH

Hertfordshire, England, Mar. 7.
Bronx-born movie director Stanley Kubrick (*July 26, 1928).

Denver school massacre

In the wake of the shooting, one survivor seeks comfort in her mother's arms.

Denver, Colorado, April 20

Two high-school juniors today brought devastation to the quiet Denver suburb of Littleton, slaughtering 12 fellow students and a teacher at Columbine High School before killing themselves. Twenty-three people were hurt. Survivors reported that Eric Harris (18) and Dylan Klebold (17) targeted their attack on ethnic minority students and athletes. They ran through the school yelling and laughing as they fired four handguns and planted over 50 homemade pipebombs.

When members of SWAT teams summoned to Columbine entered the school they found the corpses of the killers in the library. Bomb squad experts are still making the site safe, and have found two propane bombs in the school kitchens. Harris and Klebold were members of a clique calling themselves the "Trenchcoat Mafia," said by students to be fascinated by satanism and the Nazis. Harris left a note at home blaming the attack on teachers and parents and claiming that he had been driven to it by students who had ridiculed him.

The attack has again focused public attention on gun laws and the ease of gaining access to firearms. There are calls for the National Rifle Association to postpone its annual convention scheduled to be held in Denver in early May, but the NRA appears committed to pressing ahead with the event.

Jan. 3. *An Iowa resident digs out his driveway. The Big Freeze killed around 90 people on January 2–6 as temperatures hit record lows.*

Michael Jordan decides to retire

Chicago, Illinois, Jan. 13

He was the greatest, but now he's gone. Michael Jordan announced his retirement from basketball today, ending a glittering career in which he has won six NBA World Championships and five Most Valuable Player awards and notched the highest career scoring average in the history of the game.

When Chicago Bulls coach Phil Jackson stood down at the end of last year's triumphant season, Jordan was restless and reportedly did not take to new coach Tim Floyd. The decimation of this season due to an owner-player labor dispute that was only resolved last week made matters worse.

'Air' Jordan powers to the hoop.

U.S. nuclear secrets leaked to China

Washington, D.C., May 25

Secrets of U.S. nuclear technology were leaked to the People's Republic of China for more than 40 years from the 1950s, according to the report of a congressional committee chaired by Christopher Cox. The 700-page report, released today, calls the leak the worst ever lapse in U.S. security and says that secrets about submarine technology were passed to the Chinese as late as 1997. The committee criticized security in the weapons research establishments of Los Alamos and Sandia, New Mexico, and the Lawrence Livermore in California and warned that security problems continue even in 1999.

Gore runs for President

Carthage, Tennessee, June 16

The 2000 presidential election race is on. Vice President Al Gore, 51, today announced himself as a candidate for the Democratic nomination. He distanced himself from the sexual scandals that have engulfed Clinton's second term by emphasizing his happy family life, and tried to focus attention on the strength of the economy. But he lacks the campaigning charisma of his predecessor, and in recent polls has trailed his likely Republican opponent, George W. Bush, the 52-year-old Governor of Texas. Bush, the son of former President George Bush, declared for the presidency on June 12 at Cedar Rapids, Iowa, and with his new brand of "compassionate conservatism" seems to be building up unstoppable momentum in the race for the Republican nomination.

Al Gore joins the election race.

NATO war in Yugoslavia is halted

Washington, D.C., June 10

NATO has suspended its 78-day bombing campaign against Yugoslavia, launched without U.N. backing on March 24. Yugoslav President Slobodan Milosevic had refused to end campaigns against separatist fighters in Kosovo, a largely ethnic-Albanian province of the main Yugoslav republic, Serbia. During the war, NATO was prevented by lack of ground troops from pursuing its declared humanitarian aims and bloody and widespread "ethnic cleansing" of Kosovan Albanians by Serbian forces occurred. Today President Clinton pledged humanitarian aid for Kosovans but warned the Serbs to expect no help while Milosevic remains in power. Last night in Macedonia Yugoslav and NATO generals signed an agreement providing for the withdrawal of the 40,000-strong Yugoslav army and special police units from Kosovo by June 21. A peacekeeping force of Russian and NATO troops, including US Marines, is poised to move in.

March 8. *"Joltin' Joe" DiMaggio, the graceful New York Yankees baseball star who married Marilyn Monroe in 1954, dies in Florida aged 84.*

Clinton acquitted on Lewinsky charges

The San Francisco Examiner runs a special afternoon edition.

Washington, D.C., Feb. 12

President Clinton today declared himself "humbled and very grateful" after the U.S. Senate acquitted him on charges of perjury and obstruction of justice that related to his alleged attempts to cover up an intimate relationship with former White House intern Monica Lewinsky.

The Senate did not come close to the two-thirds majority required to remove an impeached President from office. It voted 55–45 to reject the first article of impeachment – that the President had perjured himself when denying in his grand jury testimony on August 17 last year that he had sexual relations with Ms Lewinsky. The vote on the second article – that the President attempted to obstruct the course of justice in the investigation into the Paula Jones sexual harassment case against him – split 50 votes to 50.

Polls showed that most Americans did not believe that the crimes of which the President was accused merited his removal from office. While 80 percent believed that he was guilty of the charges on which he was impeached, 75 percent thought he was doing a good job in the presidency.

Doctor Death sent to jail

Pontiac, Michigan, April 13

Dr. Jack Kevorkian, the controversial advocate of euthanasia for the terminally ill who is called "Doctor Death" by his opponents, was today sentenced to 10–25 years in jail. The prison term follows his March 26 conviction for second-degree murder in the case of Thomas Youk, a 52-year-old sufferer from Lou Gehrig's disease who died on September 17 last year after Kevorkian administered a lethal injection.

Kevorkian, 70, admits to having been present since 1990 at 130 euthanasia deaths, but Youk's case was the first in which the doctor administered the final injection rather than assisting the patient in the act. Dr. Kevorkian videotaped the event and passed the tape to CBS, who aired it on the *60 Minutes* current affairs TV show. He had previously been cleared three times on assisted suicide charges, while a fourth proceedings had been declared a mistrial. He was also today sentenced to 3–7 years' imprisonment for administering controlled substances. Mr Youk's widow, Melody, spoke in support of Kevorkian at the sentencing hearing, emphasizing that her husband had wanted to end his life. At the trial earlier this year Kevorkian was unable to call on testimony concerning Youk's suffering after the judge ruled it irrelevant in a case of murder.

John F. Kennedy Jr. dies in air crash

Washington, D.C., July 25

The nation once again joined the Kennedy family in mourning today as a magnificent Mass was held in the National Shrine of the Immaculate Conception in memory of John F. Kennedy Jr., the 38-year-old son of President Kennedy. With his wife Carolyn Bessette Kennedy and her sister Lauren Bessette, JFK Jr. died when the private jet he was piloting crashed into the Atlantic Ocean west of Martha's Vineyard, Massachusetts, at around 9:40 p.m. on Friday July 16.

He had been flying to the Vineyard for his cousin Rory's wedding scheduled for the following day. The party was reported missing at 2 a.m. on July 17 and early that day Americans hoped against hope that they would be found alive. But that hope dwindled away. Their personal belongings began to be washed ashore and their bodies were eventually found and brought ashore on July 21.

JFK Jr., dubbed "the world's

Mourners left flowers at John Kennedy Jr.'s New York apartment building.

most famous son," lived his entire life in the glare of press attention. Born on Thanksgiving Day 1960, in the very month in which his father was elected President, every infant development of "John-John" was eagerly watched and reported. He was just under three years old when his father was killed in Dallas, and the image of the boy saluting his father's coffin was one of the most devastating of that tragic time. He founded the New York-based political magazine *George* in 1995 but said that he had no plans for a political career himself.

Hollywood movies gross billion-dollar ticket sales

Fans wait hours in line to see George Lucas' "Star Wars" prequel.

Los Angeles, Nov. 29

The adventures of Woody the cowboy and space ranger Buzz Lightyear are the talk of the town again after the computer-animated *Toy Story 2* grossed a whopping $57.4 million over the Thanksgiving Day weekend. Disney's much anticipated sequel to 1995's *Toy Story* also has a role for Barbie, the girls' doll who on March 9 celebrated the 40th anniversary of her first appearance in stores.

It has been a bumper year for Hollywood with the highest grossing summer in movie history, drawing $2.9 billion in ticket sales across the U.S. and Canada. The top hit of the Labor Day weekend was the supernatural thriller *The Sixth Sense*, which grossed around $28 million over the weekend. However, the biggest grosser this year was George Lucas' *Star Wars: Episode 1 – The Phantom Menace*, which has taken more than $420 million in 1999. Over $130 million has also been earned by the surprise horror success *The Blair Witch Project*, which was made for around $60,000 only.

Yankees hailed

New York, Oct. 29

World Series heroes the New York Yankees were today acclaimed in a ticker-tape parade along the Canyon of Heroes, lower Broadway, then given the keys to the city of New York by Mayor Rudy Giuliani. On Wednesday night the superb pitching of veteran Roger Clemens and runs by Chuck Knoblauch, Derek Jeter, Bernie Williams, and Jim Leyritz carried the Yankees to a 4–1 victory over the Atlanta Braves that clinched a 4–0 series sweep. It is the Yankees' third World Series triumph in four years and their 25th in all – fans are hailing them as baseball's "team of the millennium."

Mars probe silent

Pasadena, Dec. 4

A $165-million NASA probe landed on Mars yesterday at the climax of an 11-month mission – and then went quiet. Scientists have been waiting for the first transmissions of data about the red planet's climate and surface composition from the Mars Polar Lander, but in vain. Trouble has dogged the mission – 10 weeks ago mathematical errors caused the Lander's sister ship, the $190-million Mars Climate Orbiter, to crash into the planet. The latest breakdown may be due to minor misalignment of antennae or to another crash.

Oct. 9. *Annie Lennox of Eurythmics performs for NetAid to combat global poverty. Online donations raised $1 million and corporate sponsors gave $11 million.*

Trade meeting sparks Seattle riots

Shooting sprees

Gunman Furrow in custody.

Flower power demonstrators were among those who delayed the opening of the WTO conference on November 30.

Seattle, Washington, Dec. 4

Riot police used rubber bullets and tear gas against crowds of protesters who have gathered here to disrupt the four-day meeting of the World Trade Organization, whose talks collapsed today without agreement. The demonstrators accuse the WTO of promoting the interests of corporations while failing to protect workers' rights and the environment. To keep order on the streets National Guardsmen and state police were called in and night-time curfews were imposed in downtown Seattle. Some protesters indulged in various acts of violence, smashing storefront plateglass and daubing graffiti. Four hundred protesters were arrested Wednesday.

The WTO was forced to cancel a reception for the 135 member delegations scheduled for Wednesday evening. Visiting the conference, President Clinton condemned the violence but supported the rights of peaceful demonstrators and urged the WTO to keep its eye on "the big picture."

Mirroring the disorder on the streets, the WTO talks fell apart. African, Caribbean, and Latin American countries refused to accept proposals for greater central control over labor standards.

Las Vegas, Aug. 11

Fugitive gunman Buford Furrow Jr. surrendered to the F.B.I. here today in the wake of a major manhunt in the states of Washington and California. Yesterday Furrow, a 39-year-old former psychiatric patient with documented links to the Aryan Nations white supremacist group, injured five people when he opened fire on a Jewish Community Center in Los Angeles then later shot dead Filipino mailman Joseph Santos Ileto. Furrow reportedly later claimed that the attack on the community center was a "wake up call to America to kill Jews."

The incident is only the latest in a series of horrific shooting incidents. On July 2–4, 21-year-old Benjamin Nathaniel Smith killed two people and injured four others in a three-day drive-by spree in Chicago in which he fired at strangers from his moving car. He eventually killed himself on July 4 in Salem, Illinois.

On July 29, 44-year-old Mark Barton shot dead nine people and injured more than 12 others in Buckhead, Atlanta, seemingly because of the fact that he had lost some $300,000 as a day trader over the Internet. On the evening of the same day, Barton shot himself. Police later found that he had earlier killed his second wife as well as his two children.

Nov. 13. Britain's Lennox Lewis (right) defeats American Evander Holyfield on a unanimous points decision in Las Vegas to become the undisputed heavyweight boxing champion of the world.

July 4. Tennis great Pete Sampras celebrates Independence Day by beating fellow-American Andre Agassi to win the Wimbledon men's singles for the sixth time.

From east to west, city by city, hour by hour, the

Due to security concerns the firework celebrations in Seattle are brought forward to 9 p.m. Refusing to let this dim their party spirit, an enthusiastic crowd watches the 605 ft- (185 m-) tall Space Needle being bathed in light.

Pink confetti, made to resemble cherry blossom, rains down on a crowd of two million celebrating the new millennium in Times Square, New York, under the strict supervision of 8000 police officers – more than twice the regular number.

Fireworks and city lights are reflected in the waters of the Atlantic Ocean at the two-mile Copacabana Beach, Rio de Janeiro, Brazil, where an enormous beach party is underway. Offerings of white flowers and candles are made to Iemanjá, sea goddess of the candomblé cult – a traditional part of Brazilian new year festivities. More than three million people attend and watch the magnificent firework display.

Earth welcomes the new millennium

Just minutes after midnight the Pittsburgh skyline is illuminated in colorful celebration of the new year.

Hundreds of thousands watch as a large "2000" lights up on the 555 ft- (170 m-) tall Washington Memorial.

A storm of fireworks breaks over Washington, D.C. In the background the Washington Memorial and in the left foreground the Iwo Jima Memorial provide reminders of American history as the country enters the new millennium. As part of the festivities President Clinton sealed a 20th-century time capsule which will be reopened in 100 years.

Australia is one of the first countries to welcome the new millennium – television pictures of the fireworks on the Sydney Harbour Bridge are beamed across the world. Around one million people have gathered at the harbor to watch the extravaganza of light and sound. It is the first time that fireworks have been let off above the Opera House (bottom left).

The morning after – Partygoers in Times Square, New York, left behind around 30 tons of waste.

As midnight sweeps around the world, the night

Celebrations at Badeling Pass on the Great Wall of China, north of Beijing, attract vast crowds. China indulged in a second round of parties on February 5, at the start of the Chinese lunar calendar's Year of the Dragon.

Celebrations at the Century Altar in Beijing, where a new eternal flame, "the Sacred Flame of China," is lit.

Pope John Paul II celebrates Mass at Santa Maria Maggiore in Rome.

On the Champs Elysees in Paris a line of eleven giant Ferris wheels, pointing toward the distant Arc de Triomphe, are illuminated just after midnight.

Crowds celebrate in Red Square, Moscow, a few minutes after midnight.

A barrage of fireworks and more than 5000 spotlights illuminate the sky above the Parthenon, the ancient temple on the Acropolis in Athens. A 200-strong choir, orchestra and Byzantine dancers provide entertainment.

sky is lit up by non-stop celebration

Since the huge, enigmatic pyramids in the desert at Giza, near Cairo, were built around 2500 BC they have witnessed the beginning of five successive millennia. Thousands of people gather on the Giza plateau to watch a spectacular laser show illuminating these ancient structures.

In London Prime Minister Tony Blair fires a laser across the Thames River toward the newly built giant wheel to mark the start of an extravaganza of fireworks, entertaining millions who have gathered in the capital.

In the first moments of the new year fireworks burst from the 984 ft- (300 m-) tall Eiffel Tower and rain down over Paris.

Germany celebrates the new year with fireworks over the Brandenburg Gate in Berlin, which recently became once again the capital of a reunited country.

The century's presidents

During the course of the 20th century eighteen presidents have guided their country through its frequently turbulent years. From the Republican William McKinley, in office as the 19th century gave way to the 20th, through the Democrat Bill Clinton, who saw the arrival of the 21st, each president has made it his aim to strengthen a nation still comparatively young and to steer it toward the fulfillment of its full potential.

Each has used his own particular combination of geographical origin – California to Virginia, Texas to Vermont – religion – Methodism to Society of Friends, Roman Catholicism to Disciples of Christ – and profession – lawyer to soldier, actor to farmer – to bring a unique perspective to bear on his awe-inspiring task. Some presidents have made their mark in troubled or even violent times; others have made their mission social reform or the consolidation of tranquillity. Whatever their background, whatever their strengths or their weaknesses, whatever their fate, these eighteen men have between them presided over a remarkable period which saw their country, and its place in the world, transformed out of all recognition.

William McKinley

Lived: Jan. 29, 1843–Sept. 14, 1901
Birthplace: Niles, OH
Married: Ida Saxton
Profession: Lawyer
Religion: Methodist
Affiliation: Republican
Term: 1897–1901, 25th President
Nickname: Idol of Ohio

Warren Gamaliel Harding

Lived: Nov. 2, 1865–Aug. 2, 1923
Birthplace: Corsica, OH
Married: Florence De Wolfe
Profession: Publisher
Religion: Baptist
Affiliation: Republican
Term: 1921–1923, 29th President
Nickname: None

Theodore Roosevelt

Lived: Oct. 27, 1858–Jan. 6, 1919
Birthplace: New York City, NY
Married: A. Lee, E. Carow
Profession: Lawyer
Religion: Dutch Reformed
Affiliation: Republican
Term: 1901–1909, 26th President
Nickname: TR, Trust Buster

Calvin Coolidge

Lived: July 4, 1872–Jan. 5, 1933
Birthplace: Plymouth, VT
Married: Grace Goodhue
Profession: Lawyer
Religion: Congregationalist
Affiliation: Republican
Term: 1923–1929, 30th President
Nickname: Silent Cal

William Howard Taft

Lived: Sept. 15, 1857–March 8, 1930
Birthplace: Cincinnati, OH
Married: Helen Herron
Profession: Lawyer
Religion: Unitarian
Affiliation: Republican
Term: 1909–1913, 27th President
Nickname: None

Herbert Clark Hoover

Lived: Aug. 10, 1874–Oct. 20, 1964
Birthplace: West Branch, IA
Married: Lou Henry
Profession: Engineer
Religion: Society of Friends
Affiliation: Republican
Term: 1929–1933, 31st President
Nickname: None

Woodrow Wilson

Lived: Dec. 28, 1856–Feb. 3, 1924
Birthplace: Staunton, VA
Married: E. Axson, E. Galt
Profession: Professor
Religion: Presbyterian
Affiliation: Democrat
Term: 1913–1921, 28th President
Nickname: Schoolmaster in politics

Franklin Delano Roosevelt

Lived: Jan. 30, 1882–April 12, 1945
Birthplace: Hyde Park, NY
Married: Eleanor Roosevelt
Profession: Lawyer
Religion: Episcopalian
Affiliation: Democrat
Term: 1933–1945, 32nd President
Nickname: FDR

Harry Truman

Lived: May 8, 1884–Dec. 26, 1972
Birthplace: Lamar, MO
Married: Bess Wallace
Profession: Public Official
Religion: Baptist
Affiliation: Democrat
Term: 1945–1953, 33rd President
Nickname: Give 'Em Hell Harry

Gerald Rudolph Ford

Lived: July 14, 1913–
Birthplace: Omaha, NE
Married: Elizabeth "Betty" Bloomer
Profession: Lawyer
Religion: Episcopalian
Affiliation: Republican
Term: 1974–1977, 38th President
Nickname: Jerry

Dwight David Eisenhower

Lived: Oct. 14, 1890–March 28, 1969
Birthplace: Denison, TX
Married: Mamie Doud
Profession: Soldier
Religion: Presbyterian
Affiliation: Republican
Term: 1953–1961, 34th President
Nickname: Ike

James Earl Carter

Lived: Oct. 1, 1924–
Birthplace: Plains, GA
Married: Rosalynn Smith
Profession: Farmer, Public Official
Religion: Baptist
Affiliation: Democrat
Term: 1977–1981, 39th President
Nickname: Jimmy

John Fitzgerald Kennedy

Lived: May 29, 1917–Nov. 22, 1963
Birthplace: Brookline, MA
Married: Jacqueline Bouvier
Profession: Public Official
Religion: Roman Catholic
Affiliation: Democrat
Term: 1961–1963, 35th President
Nickname: JFK, Jack

Ronald Wilson Reagan

Lived: Feb. 6, 1911–
Birthplace: Tampico, IL
Married: Jane Wyman, Nancy Davis
Profession: Actor, Public Official
Religion: Presbyterian
Affiliation: Republican
Term: 1981–1989, 40th President
Nickname: Dutch

Lyndon Baines Johnson

Lived: Aug. 27, 1908–Jan. 22, 1973
Birthplace: near Stonewall, TX
Married: Claudia "Lady Bird" Alta
Profession: Public Official
Religion: Disciples of Christ
Affiliation: Democrat
Term: 1963–1969, 36th President
Nickname: LBJ

George Herbert Walker Bush

Lived: June 12, 1924–
Birthplace: Milton, MA
Married: Barbara Pierce
Profession: Public Official
Religion: Episcopalian
Affiliation: Republican
Term: 1989–1993, 41st President
Nickname: Poppy

Richard Milhous Nixon

Lived: Jan. 9, 1913–April 22, 1994
Birthplace: Yorba Linda, CA
Married: Thelma Ryan
Profession: Lawyer, Public Official
Religion: Society of Friends
Affiliation: Republican
Term: 1969–1974, 37th President
Nickname: Dick

William Jefferson Clinton

Lived: Aug. 19, 1946–
Birthplace: Hope, AR
Married: Hillary Rodham
Profession: Public Official
Religion: Baptist
Affiliation: Democrat
Term: 1993– , 42nd President
Nickname: The Comeback Kid

Development of the Union

How a tiny enclave grew to embrace half a continent

After the ratification of the Constitution by the original thirteen colonies, the first new state was Vermont, which entered the Union in 1791. By the time of the last nineteenth-century admission – Utah in 1896 – there were 45 states in the Union.

During the nineteenth century Americans imposed their mastery on a vast and unknown continent. Land was acquired through negotiation, annexation, and war. Thomas Jefferson purchased the Louisiana territory from the French government in 1803 for fifteen million dollars, at a stroke

doubling the area of the United States. Then, during the administration of James Polk between 1845 and 1849, the area increased again by fifty percent. During these years the US annexed Texas from Mexico, continued negotiations with Britain over the Oregon territory, and fought a war with Mexico that led to the acquisition of what would become California and New Mexico. The west was not tamed by a simple westerly movement of people. Settlers first occupied the Midwest and California and then spread to the nation's vast

inner spaces. Interior migration accelerated after 1870 when the burgeoning railroad network made the journey to the Great Plains and the Far West easier and quicker.

The process of admitting states was scarred and complicated by slavery, which reached even into the western territories. Compromises achieved over the issue in the constitutional debates of 1787 provided no permanent solution as pro- and anti-slavery groups struggled fiercely to defend their rival, incompatible views. In the Missouri

Compromise of 1820 the admission of a new slave-owning state, Missouri, was counterbalanced by the admission of non-slave-owning Maine (which had been part of Massachusetts). Under yet another compromise, when California was admitted as a free state in 1850 the principle was adopted of allowing territories to decide on the issue of slavery themselves. The tensions finally resulted in the temporary fission of the Union when the southern states seceded in 1861, and a bloody 4-year Civil War was needed to restore the Union.

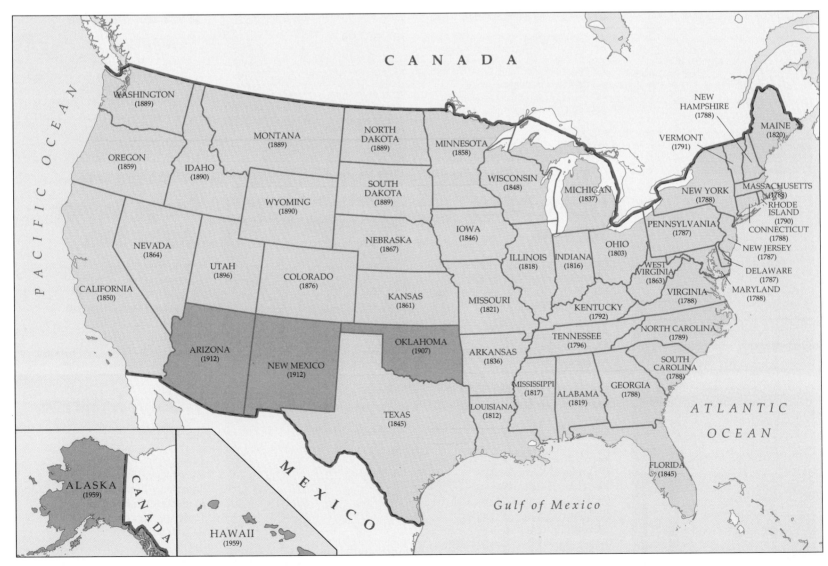

Profiles of the five states that joined the Union during the 20th century

Alaska

Capital: Juneau
Entered Union: Jan. 3, 1959
49th state
Nickname: The Last Frontier
Population: 609,000
Rank by population: 48th
Total area: 591,000 sq. mi.
Rank by area: 1st
Largest cities: Anchorage, Fairbanks, Juneau
State bird: Willow ptarmigan
State flower: Forget-me-not

Alaska and the Aleutian Islands were discovered in 1741 by Vitus Bering, a Dane working for the Russians. Most of this vast territory was unexplored in 1867 when Secretary of State William Seward arranged for its purchase from the Russians for $7.2 million, a cost of some two cents per acre. This deal was ridiculed as "Seward's Folly."

In the late 19th century, the Gold Rush led to a massive influx of people. The 1890 census showed a total of only 32,052 Alaskans; the 1900 census counted 63,592.

A huge reservoir of oil and gas was discovered near Prudhoe Bay, on the Arctic Coast, in 1968. Crude oil is conducted by the Trans-Alaska pipeline, completed in 1977, to the port of Valdez. Tourism, furs, wood, and fisheries are other industries important to Alaska's economy.

Arizona

Capital: Phoenix
Entered Union: Feb. 14, 1912
48th state
Nickname: Grand Canyon State

Population: 4,462,300
Rank by population: 23rd
Total area: 114,000 sq. mi.
Rank by area: 6th
Largest cities: Phoenix, Tucson, Mesa, Tempe, Glendale, Scottsdale
State bird: Cactus wren
State flower: Flower of the Saguaro cactus

Arizona's name derives from the Indian word "arizonac" or "little spring." Marcos de Niza, a Spanish friar, was the first European to explore the territory, arriving in the late 1530s in search of the fabled Seven Cities of Gold. Fort Tucson was founded by the Spanish in 1776. Most of the territory became part of the U.S. after the Mexican War, and the southern part of the territory was added by the Gadsden Purchase of 1853. It was in Arizona that Indian chiefs such as Geronimo and Cochise fought against frontiersmen, and the state has one of the nation's largest Indian populations.

Arizona's chief industries include aeronautical, electrical, and communications equipment. The state produces much of the nation's copper. Tourists also flock to visit the Grand Canyon.

Hawaii

Capital: Honolulu
Entered Union: Aug. 21, 1959
50th state
Nickname: Aloha State
Population: 1,186,602
Rank by population: 40th
Total area: 6,471 sq. mi.
Rank by area: 47th
Largest cities: Honolulu, Pearl City, Kailua, Hilo
State bird: Hawaiian goose
State flower: Yellow hibiscus

Hawaii was first settled in the 6th century by Polynesians. In 1778, Captain James Cook of England landed there and named the group the Sandwich Islands. During most of the 19th century the islands remained a native kingdom. Queen Liliuokalani was deposed in 1893 and the Republic of Hawaii was established. Following its annexation, Hawaii became a U.S. territory in 1898.

The attack by Japanese forces on the naval base at Pearl Harbor, on December 7, 1941, led to the U.S. entry into World War II.

Hawaii is a chain of volcanic and coral islands nearly 1,600 miles long. Most of these are tiny, while the eight main ones are Hawaii, Maui, Oahu, Lanai, Kauai, Niihau, Kahoolawe, and Molokai.

New Mexico

Capital: Santa Fe
Entered Union: Jan. 6, 1912
47th state
Nickname: Land of Enchantment
Population: 1,736,931
Rank by population: 36th
Total area: 121,593 sq. mi.
Rank by area: 5th
Largest cities: Albuquerque, Santa Fe, Las Cruces, Roswell
State bird: Roadrunner
State flower: Yucca

Indians first lived in New Mexico about 10,000 years ago. The first European to visit the region is believed to have been Alvar Nunez Cabeza de Vaca. In 1598, the first Spanish settlement was established on the Rio Grande. Much later, in the early 1820s, New Mexico became a province of Mexico. Most of the territory was acquired by the U.S. as a result of the Mexican War. During the Civil War, Confederate forces captured much of the area.

New Mexico became effectively linked to the rest of the U.S. in 1881, on completion of the southern trans-continental railroad.

Since 1945, when the first atomic bomb was tested at Trinity Site, New Mexico has been a leader in energy research.

Oklahoma

Capital: Oklahoma City
Entered Union: Nov. 16, 1907
46th state
Nickname: Sooner State
Population: 3,317,000
Rank by population: 28th
Total area: 69,919 sq. mi.
Rank by area: 18th
Largest cities: Oklahoma City, Tulsa, Lawton, Norman
State bird: Scissor-tail flycatcher
State flower: Mistletoe

Oklahoma, a name derived from two Choctaw Indian words meaning "red people," has been nicknamed the Sooner State for the homesteaders who tried to enter the area and claim land sooner than it was legal to do so. The Spanish were the first Europeans to explore Oklahoma in 1541. Since Oklahoma achieved statehood, it has changed from a rural to an urban state, from an agricultural economy to one based on industry. Its population increased until the times of the Dust Bowl and the Depression. Massive emigration ensued, and the population did not begin to grow again until the 1950s.

Oil has made Oklahoma a rich state. It is a major center for military activities and its plains produce bumper wheat crops.

The century's statistics

Every ten years the U.S. Bureau of the Census collects detailed figures about the economy and people of the United States, providing a striking social and economic overview. The last census was taken in 1990 and another is due in 2000. All figures for 2000 are based on official estimates.

Population

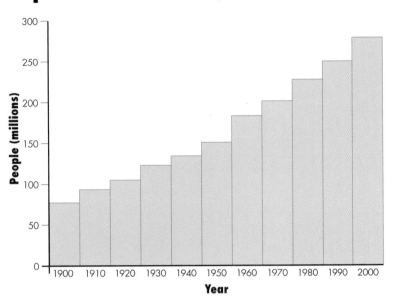

A steady increase

Between 1800 and 1900 the U.S. population grew 15 times larger, from around five million to around 75 million. That astonishing rate of growth slowed in the 20th century, but the number is still increasing: in 2000 the U.S. is about 3.5 times more populous than it was at the turn of the last century.

Urban/rural population

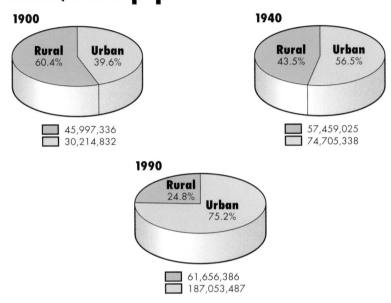

Ever-growing, more crowded cities

America's movement of population from country to city is replicated across the globe in the 20th century. In the 1990 census the most heavily populated state was New Jersey with 1042 people per square mile while Alaska, at the other extreme, had an average of one person per square mile.

Immigration

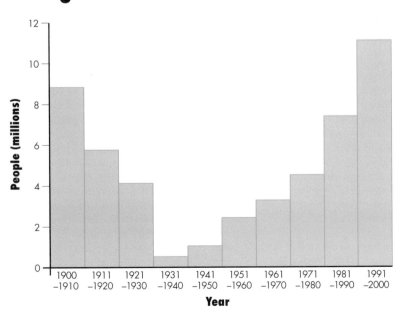

"The land of the free"

The 20th century began with a great influx of European immigrants seeking work and, often, freedom from persecution. Immigration was cut back by the draconian Johnson-Reed Act of 1924. Asia and Mexico – rather than Europe – are the main sources of the new boom in immigration at the century's end.

Labor force

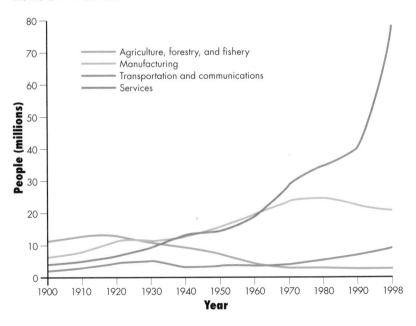

The "service economy"

The numbers working in agriculture, forestry, and fishery rose in the first two decades of the century, then began a decline which became rapid after 1950. The number of people employed in the service sector of the economy exploded in the 1990s and shows no sign of flattening out.

438

Social trends

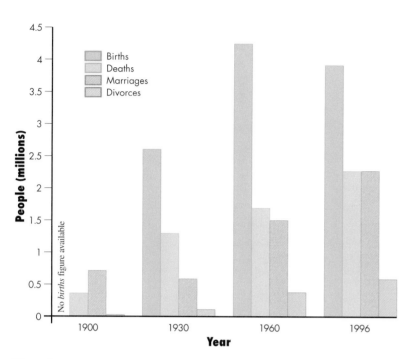

Changing ways

The number of births increased steadily until the 1960s, since when the rate has been declining. The divorce rate rose rapidly in the second half of the century. Although in the 1990s the number of marriages showed a slight decline, in 1996 the rate was still comparatively high at 8.9 per 1,000 people.

Most populous cities

1900		
1	New York City, NY	3,437,202
2	Chicago, IL	1,698,575
3	Philadelphia, PA	1,293,697
4	St Louis, MO	575,238
5	Boston, MA	560,892
6	Baltimore, MD	508,957
7	Cleveland, OH	381,768
8	Buffalo, NY	352,387
9	San Francisco, CA	342,782
10	Cincinnati, OH	325,902

1996 (Estimated)		
1	New York City, NY	7,380,906
2	Los Angeles, CA	3,553,638
3	Chicago, IL	2,721,547
4	Houston, TX	1,744,058
5	Philadelphia, PA	1,478,002
6	San Diego, CA	1,171,121
7	Phoenix, AZ	1,159,014
8	San Antonio, TX	1,067,816
9	Dallas, TX	1,053,292
10	Detroit, MI	1,000,272

New York defies change

New York City has remained top of the heap throughout the 20th century. Los Angeles arrived in the 1920s: tenth most populous city in 1920, rising to fifth by 1930. At the century's end Philadelphia's population is in decline but figures show Phoenix to be the fastest-growing city of the 1990s.

Transportation

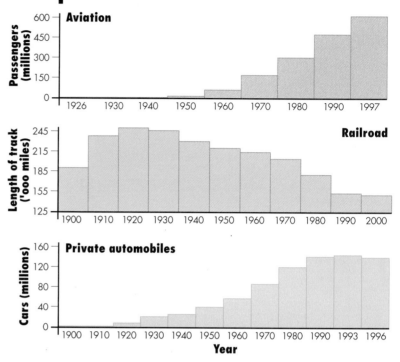

Rise and fall of the railroad

In 1900 the Wright Brothers had not yet invented the airplane, and motor cars were the preserve of the rich. The railroad was enjoying a golden period which lasted beyond the end of World War I, but later in the century it endured a steady decline while the automobile and aviation industries boomed.

Gross National Product (GNP)

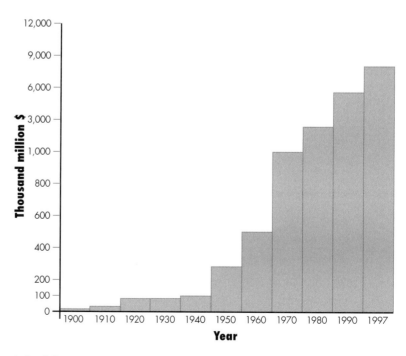

A healthy economy

The country's GNP (the total value of goods and services produced) increased steadily throughout the first half of the century. After World War II the rate of increase accelerated further, and the economy became the biggest in the world.

441

454

455

Picture Credits

Some agency names have been abbreviated in this index. The list below provides full names of picture agencies:

Am. Railroads: Association of American Railroads
AMNH, Smithsonian: American Museum of Natural History, Smithsonian Institution
Appomattox: "Surrender at Appomattox" by Tom Lovell, © 1988 The Greenwich Workshop, Inc., Trumbull, CT, 800/243-4246
Ass. Press: Associated Press
Becker: Becker Collection
Bettmann: The Bettmann Archive, New York
Bourke-White, Time-Life: Courtesy of Margaret Bourke-White, Time-Life Magazine
Brown: Courtesy of the John Carter Brown Library
Can. Railways: Canadian National Railways
Chrysler: Chrysler Museum
CHS: Courtesy, Colorado Historical Society
Cinematheque: Cinematheque de Paris
Cleveland Museum of Art: The Cleveland Museum of Art, Hinman B. Hurlbut Collection
Coca-Cola: Courtesy of The Coca-Cola Company
DeSomma: DeSomma, Vincent
Eastman: International Museum of Photography at George Eastman House
Equitable Life: Courtesy of the Equitable Life Assurance Society of the U.S.
Ferris: J.L.G. Ferris, Estate of
Gables: Photo Courtesy of the House of Seven Gables Settlement Association
Granger: Granger Collection, New York
Kendall Whaling Museum: The Kendall Whaling Museum, Sharon, Massachusetts, USA
Kirshon: Kirshon, John
Mary Evans: Mary Evans Picture Library
National Portrait Gallery, Smithsonian: National Museum of American Art, Smithsonian Institution
Metropolitan: Metropolitan Museum of Art
Modern Art: Museum of Modern Art, New York
NJHS: From the Collection of the New Jersey Historical Society
NMAA, Smithsonian: National Museum of American Art, Smithsonian Institution
NMAH, Smithsonian: National Museum of American History, Smithsonian Institution
NYHS: Courtesy of the New York Historical Society, New York
NYPL: New York Public Library
NYPL, Map Division: New York Public Library, Map Division
Paramount: Paramount Pictures
Reuters/Bettmann: Reuters/Bettmann Newsphotos
Sears: Sears Archive
Sipa: Sipa Press, New York
Smithsonian: Smithsonian Institution
Seaver: Seaver Center for Western History Research, Natural History Museum of Los Angeles County
Teich: Lake County (IL) Museum, Curt Teich Collection
UPI/Bettmann: UPI/Bettmann Newsphotos
Vicksburg: "The Union Fleet Passing Vicksburg" by Tom Lovell, © 1989 The Greenwich Workshop. Inc., Trumbull, CT, 800/243-4246
Walt Disney: © The Walt Disney Company

While every effort has been made to trace copyright holders, the publishers apologize for any unintentional error or omission and would be pleased to rectify them in future editions.

The position of the pictures is indicated by two letters: B: bottom, T: top, M: middle, L: left, R: right, X: middle left, Y: middle right, SP: spread

Credits are given for pages 434 to 435 from left top to bottom and right top to bottom

8 TM: Bettmann – **BM:** Granger
9 TGL, BL, TR: Granger – **BR:** Bettmann
10 All pictures from Bettmann
11 TM: Granger
– **BL:** General Dynamics Corporation
– **BR:** JL International
12 TX, TR: Bettmann – **BM:** Granger
13 BR: Bettmann – **BL:** Gillette
14 TL: Granger – **MY:** Bettmann
– **BR:** Houston Museum of Art
15 TL: Bettmann – **TR, BX:** Granger
– **BY:** National Archives
16 TY: Granger
– **BR:** Georgia O'Keefe, Estate of
17 TY: Bettmann – **BR:** Granger
18 All pictures from Bettmann
19 TR: UPI/Bettmann – **BL:** Granger
– **BR:** Bettmann
20 TL: Granger – **BL:** Bettmann
– **BR:** National Gallery of Art
21 TR: Granger – **BL:** Bettmann
22 TM: Bettmann – **BM:** Granger
23 TR, BR: Granger – **BL:** Bettmann
24 BL: Bettmann
25 TM, BR: Granger – **BL:** National Gallery of Art
26 All pictures from Bettmann
27 TL: Bettmann – **BR:** Granger
28 TR: Granger
– **BL:** Georgia O'Keefe, Estate of
29 BR: NMAA, Smithsonian – **TR:** Kirshon
30 BM: Bettmann – **TX, MR:** UPI/Bettmann
31 All pictures from Granger
32 All pictures from Bettmann
33 TR, TL: Granger – **BX:** Marshall Fields
34 MM: Granger – **BR:** JL International
35 ML: Maytag Corporation – **TR:** Granger
– **BR:** Cleveland Museum of Art
36 TX, BM: Granger – **TY:** Bettmann
37 TR: Granger – **BR:** Bettmann
38 BM: National Archives
39 TM: U.S. Department of the Interior
– **BM:** Granger
40 MR, BR: Bettmann
– **ML:** Granger
– **BL:** U.S. Postal Service
41 TR: Becker – **BR, BL:** Granger
42 TM: Bettmann – **BM:** Granger
43 TM, BR: Granger – **BL:** Bettmann
44 TL: JL International – **BL:** Eastman
– **BR:** The Creators
45 TL, BL: Bettmann
– **MR:** Office of Alumni Relations, University of Chicago
– **BX, BR:** National Archives
46 BR: NMAA, Smithsonian
47 BL, TR: Granger – **BR:** Bettmann
– **TL:** Architect of the Capital
48 TM, BR: Bettmann – **BL:** Granger
49 TR, BL: Bettmann – **BR:** Granger
50 BM: Bettmann
51 TR, TL: Bettmann – **BR:** National Gallery of Art – **BL:** Wrigley's Company
52 TL: Bettmann – **TR, BR:** Granger
– **BL:** JL International
53 BR: NYHS
54 TL: Mary Evans – **BL:** Bettmann
– **BR:** Granger
55 TL: Bettmann – **BR:** Granger
56 TR: Bettmann – **BL:** Granger
57 TR, BR: Bettmann – **BL:** JL International
58 TM: JWT Archives
59 TM: Bettmann – **BM:** Granger
60 TM, BL: Bettmann – **BR:** Granger
61 TL : Granger – **BR:** Bettmann
62 TR: Granger
63 All pictures from Bettmann
64 TL, MM: Bettmann
– **BL: NMAA,** Smithsonian
65 TL: Bettmann – **BR:** Eastman
– **BL:** Granger
66 TM: NYPL – **BR:** Granger
67 TR: Ferris **BR:** Ferris
68 TL: Bettmann – **BL, BX, BY, BR:** Granger
69 All pictures from Granger
70 TX: Bettmann – **MM:** UPI/Bettmann
71 TL: National Gallery of Art
– **BR:** Bettmann
72 TL, BL: Granger – **TR:** Bettmann
73 TR, BL: Bettmann – **BR:** Granger
74 TM: Olson, Dr. Richard F.
– **TR, ML, MR:** Bettmann
– **MM, BL, BR, TL:** Granger
– **BM:** UPI/Bettmann
75 TR: Bettmann – **MM:** JL International
– **MR, ML:** Granger
– **BL, BR, TL:** National Archives
76 FP: Granger
78 TM: Bettmann – **BX:** Granger
79 All pictures from Bettmann
80 All pictures from Granger
81 TR: UPI/Bettmann – **MY, MR:** Bettmann
82 All pictures from Granger
83 All pictures from Bettmann
84 TL: Bettmann – **BR:** Granger
– **BL:** NYPL
85 TR, BR: Granger – **BL:** Bettmann
86 All pictures from Bettmann
87 TR: National Gallery of Art
– **BL, BR:** Bettmann
88 TM: Granger – **BX:** Modern Art
89 TL, BL: Bettmann – **BR:** Bettmann
90 TL, BR: Bettmann – **BL:** Granger
91 BR: Granger
92 TY, TR: Bettmann – **BM:** Granger
93 TX: Granger – **MR, BR:** Bettmann
94 TL, BX: Granger – **BL, TR:** Bettmann
95 All pictures from Bettmann
96 TY: Migdail-Smith Shari
– **BX:** JL International – **BR:** Granger
97 TM, ML: UPI/Bettmann
– **BX, BR:** Granger
98 TR: Bettmann – **BL, BR:** Granger
99 BR: Granger
100 TL: Granger – **TR, BR, MX:** Bettmann
– **BL:** JL International
101 All pictures from Bettmann
102 TL, MR: Granger – **TX, BL:** Bettmann
– **BX:** Houston Museum of Fine Art
103 TR, BL: UPI/Bettmann
– **TL:** Bettmann
– **BR:** Rivoli Theater, New York
104 TY: UPI/Bettmann – **BM:** NMAA, Smithsonian
105 TL, BL: Granger – **TR:** Bettmann
– **BR:** UPI/Bettmann
106 TL, TR: Granger – **BL:** Bettmann
– **BR:** General Dynamics Corporation
107 TX: JL International – **TR, BR:** Granger
108 TL, BR: Granger – **TR:** Bettmann
– **BL:** New Yorker Magazine Inc.
109 TY, TR, MR: Bettmann
– **ML:** UPI/Bettmann
– **BR:** National Gallery of Art
110 TL, TR, BR: Granger – **BL:** Bettmann
111 All pictures from Granger
112 TL, BL, BX: Granger – **TR:** Bettmann
– **BY:** National Gallery of Art
– **BR:** NMAA, Smithsonian
113 TL, TR, BR: Granger – **TM:** Bettmann
– **BL:** UPI/Bettmann
114 BM: Bettmann – **BR:** JL International
115 All pictures from Granger
116 TL, BL: Granger – **TR:** UPI/Bettmann
– **BR:** National Archives
117 All pictures from Granger
118 TM: Bettmann – **BM:** JL International
119 TR, TL, BR: Granger – **MX:** Bettmann
120 TL, TX, BM, BL, BR: Granger
– **TR:** National Archives
– **ML, MX, MR, MY:** Bettmann
121 TL: National Gallery of Art
– **TY:** Bettmann
– **TR, ML, MR, BR:** Granger
– **MM:** DeSomme
– **BL:** Cincinnati Art Museum
– **BM:** National Archives
122 TM: Bettmann – **BY:** Granger
123 TX: Granger – **BR:** Bettmann
– **BL:** NMAA, Smithsonian
124 MM: Bettmann – **TL:** JL International
– **BR:** Granger
125 TR: UPI/Bettmann – **BY, BR:** Granger
126 TX: Granger – **BR:** Equitable Life
127 TM: JL International – **BR:** Granger
– **BL:** Bourke-White, Time-Life
128 All pictures from Bettmann
129 TX: Bettmann – **BL, BR:** Granger
130 TM: UPI/Bettmann – **BM:** Metropolitan
131 BR: Bettmann
132 TR, BR: Bettmann
– **BL:** NMAA, Smithsonian
133 All pictures from Granger
134 TY: Bettmann – **BM:** Granger
135 TR: Bettmann
– **BR:** National Archives – **TL, BL:** Granger
136 TM, BL: Bettmann
– **BR:** National Gallery of Art
137 All pictures from Granger
138 TM: UPI/Bettmann
139 TR: Bettmann – **BR:** Teich
140 All pictures from Bettmann
141 TR, BM: Bettmann – **TL:** UPI/Bettmann
– **BR:** Granger
142 All pictures from Bettmann
143 TL, TX, TR: Bettmann
– **BL, BR:** NMAA, Smithsonian
145 TR, TL, BR: Granger – **BL:** Bettmann
146 All pictures from Bettmann
147 ML: Bettmann – **TR:** UPI/Bettmann
– **BR:** Library of Congress
148 TR: Library of Congress
– **BR:** UPI/Bettmann – **BL:** Granger
149 TR, BL: Granger
– **BR:** NMAA, Smithsonian
150 TR: Bettmann
– **BM:** NMAA, Smithsonian – **BR:** Granger
151 BM: Bettmann
152 TR, BR: Bettmann
– **BY, TL:** UPI/Bettmann
153 TX: Bettmann – **TR, BR:** Granger
– **BL:** JL International
154 TM: Bettmann
– **BM:** Bourke-White, Time-Life
155 TL: UPI/Bettmann – **BR:** Bettmann
156 TL: Granger
– **TR, BX, BY, BR:** Bettmann
– **BL:** UPI/Bettmann
157 ML, BL: UPI/Bettmann – **BR:** Bettmann
158 TL, BL, BR: Bettmann – **TR:** Granger
159 All pictures from Granger
160 TY: Bettmann – **BM:** Cinemateque
161 TL, TR: Bettmann
– **BR:** NMAA, Smithsonian
162 TL: UPI/Bettmann
– **BL:** March of Dimes Birth Defects Foundation – **BR:** Bettmann
163 TR, TL: Bettmann – **BY, BR:** Granger
164 MR: UPI/Bettmann
– **BM:** National Gallery of Art
165 All pictures from Bettmann
166 TL: Granger – **ML:** UPI/Bettmann
– **TR:** Bettmann
167 TX, TR, MR: Granger – **BR:** Bettmann
168 TL: Granger – **ML: NMAA,** Smithsonian
– **MX, MR, TR:** National Archives
– **BL:** National Portrait Gallery, Smithsonian
– **BR:** UPI/Bettmann
169 TL: Library of Congress
– **TR:** National Archives – **MX, BR:** Granger
– **MR, ML:** Bettmann – **BL:** Am. Railroads
170 All pictures from NMAA, Smithsonian
171 TR: UPI/Bettmann – **BR:** Granger
172 TM: Bettmann
173 TR: NMAA, Smithsonian – **BR:** Granger
174 BM: Granger
175 TR: Bettmann
– **BR:** National Gallery of Art
176 TR: UPI/Bettmann – **BL:** NMAA, Smithsonian – **BR:** Bettmann
177 All pictures from Granger
178 T: UPI/Bettmann
179 TR, BY, BR: Granger – **MR:** Bettmann
180 TR, BX. BR: Bettmann
– **BY:** UPI/Bettmann
181 TR: JL International – **BR:** UPI/Bettmann
182 TL: Bettmann – **BL:** JL International
183 TL: UPI/Bettmann – **BL, MR:** Bettmann
– **BL:** JL International
184 TL, ML, TR: Bettmann
– **BL:** JL International
185 TR: Granger
– **BY, BR, TL, BL:** Bettmann
186 TL: Bettmann – **BL, BR:** Granger
187 TY, TR: Bettmann – **BL, BR:** Granger
188 All pictures from Bettmann
189 TX, TR: UPI/Bettmann
– **BY, BR:** Bettmann
190 TR, BL: Bettmann
– **BR:** Granger
191 TY: JL International
– **TR, MR:** Bettmann
– **BR: NMAA,** Smithsonian
192 TL: Bettmann – **ML:** UPI/Bettmann
193 TM: UPI/Bettmann – **BL, BR:** Bettmann
194 TY: UPI/Bettmann – **BM:** Granger
195 TR, BL, BR: Bettmann
– **MR:** UPI/Bettmann
196 TL, ML, BL: Granger
– **BR:** JL International

197 TR, MR: Bettmann – **BR:** Granger
198 TM, MM: Bettmann
– **BL:** JL International
199 TM, BR: Bettmann – **MM:** UPI/Bettmann
200 BX, BR, TL, TX, TR, ML, MY, BL:
Bettmann – **MR:** UPI/Bettmann
201 TL, BL: Granger – **TR, MR:** Bettmann
– **BM:** National Archives
– **BR, ML:** UPI/Bettmann
202 TM: UPI/Bettmann – **BX:** Bettmann
203 TR, MR, BL: UPI/Bettmann
– **TL:** Bettmann
204 TL, BX: Bettmann
– **ML, BL:** UPI/Bettmann
205 TL: Bettmann – **TR, BR:** Granger
– **BL:** UPI/Bettmann
206 TM: Bettmann – **BL, BR:** Granger
207 TR, MR, BR: Bettmann
– **BL:** JL International
208 TL: Bettmann – **TR:** UPI/Bettmann
– **BL:** NMAA, Smithsonian
209 TL: Bettmann – **BR:** UPI/Bettmann
210 FP: America's Team - We're No. 1
by Alan Bean
212 All pictures from NMAA, Smithsonian
213 TM: UPI/Bettmann – **BL:** Bettmann
– **BR:** Granger
214 TX: Bettmann – **BL:** UPI/Bettmann
215 TR: Granger – **BR:** UPI/Bettmann
– **BL:** Bettmann
216 TR: UPI/Bettmann
– **BX:** NMAA, Smithsonian
217 All pictures from UPI/Bettman
218 TM: UPI/Bettmann – **BL:** Granger
219 TM: JL International – **BR:** Granger
– **BL:** UPI/Bettmann
220 TM, MR: Bettmann – **BM:** UPI/Bettmann
221 TX: UPI/Bettmann – **TR, BR:** Bettmann
222 TL: Bettmann – **BM:** UPI/Bettmann
223 TR: UPI/Bettmann – **TR:** Bettmann
– **BR:** Granger
224 TY: Bettmann – **BM:** High Museum
of Art, Atlanta
225 Bettmann – **BM:** UPI/Bettmann
226 BR: Granger – **TL:** Bettmann
227 TR: UPI/Bettmann – **BR:** Bettmann
228 All pictures from UPI/Bettmann
229 TR: Bettmann – **MR:** UPI/Bettmann
– **BL: NMAA,** Smithsonian
230 TL: UPI/Bettmann – **ML, BL:** Bettmann
231 All pictures from UPI/Bettmann
232 TL, TR, BR: Bettmann
– **BL:** UPI/Bettmann
233 TY, BR, BR: Bettmann
– **TR:** Granger – **MY:** UPI/Bettmann
234 TM: UPI/Bettmann – **MM:** Granger
235 TX: UPI/ Bettmann – **MR, BR:** Bettmann
236 All pictures from UPI/Bettmann
237 TR: UPI/Bettmann – **TL, BR:** Bettmann
– **BL:** JL International
238 TR: Bettmann – **BR:** Granger
239 ML, BL: Bettmann
– **BR:** Smithsonian
240 TL: Bettmann – **TR:** UPI/Bettmann
– **BR:** Granger
241 All pictures from UPI/Bettmann
242 TM: Bettmann – **BM:** UPI/Bettmann
243 TR, BL: UPI/Bettmann – **TL:** Granger
– **BR:** NMAA, Smithsonian
244 TX, MR: UPI/Bettmann – **BM:** Bettmann
245 TR: UPI/Bettmann – **BR:** Bettmann
246 TM: UPI/Bettmann – **BR:** National
Archives – **BL:** Library of Congress
247 All pictures from Bettmann
248 TR: UPI/Bettmann – **BM:** NMAA,
Smithsonian
249 TM: Granger – **BL:** UPI/Bettmann
– **BR:** Bettmann
250 TM: UPI/Bettmann – **ML, MR:** Granger
– **BM:** NMAA, Smithsonian
251 TR: Bettmann – **BR:** Granger
252 All pictures from UPI/Bettmann
253 TR, TL: UPI/Bettmann – **BR:** Bettmann
254 TR: UPI/Bettmann – **BX:** JL International
255 TR, BR: UPI/Bettmann – **BL:** Granger
256 TL, ML: UPI/Bettmann
– **BL:** National Archives
257 TR, BR: UPI/Bettmann – **BY:** Granger
258 TM, BR: UPI/Bettmann
– **BL:** National Archives
259 TR: UPI/Bettmann – **BR:** Bettmann
260 TX, TR: UPI/Bettmann – **BX:** Bettmann
261 All pictures from Bettmann
262 TL: Bettmann – **TR, BR, BL:** UPI/Bettmann
263 TL: UPI/Bettmann
– **BY, BR, BL, BX:** Bettmann
264 TL, TR, TX, ML BM: UPI/Bettmann
– **MR:** Bettmann
– **BL:** Mattel Toys – **BR:** Jeanette Hall
265 TL: Bettmann – **TR:** Tonka Corporation
– **ML, MR:** Granger
– **BL:** Cincinnati Art Museum

– **BX, BR, BY:** UPI/Bettmann
266 TR, BR: UPI/Bettmann – **BX:** Bettmann
267 TR: UPI/Bettmann
– **BR:** NMAA, Smithsonian
268 TL, BR: UPI/Bettmann
– **BL:** NMAA, Smithsonian
269 TM: UPI/Bettmann – **BR:** Granger
– **BL:** NMAA, Smithsonian
270 TM, MM: UPI/Bettmann
– **BR:** NMAA, Smithsonian
271 TR, BR: UPI/Bettmann – **BY:** Bettmann
272 All pictures from UPI/Bettmann
273 TR, BR: UPI/Bettmann – **TL:** Bettmann
– **BL:** Granger
274, 275 All pictures from UPI/Bettmann
276 TL: Granger– **MR, BL:** UPI/Bettmann
277 All pictures from UPI/Bettmann
278 TM: National Archives
– **BR:** UPI/Bettmann
279, 280, 281 All pictures from UPI/Bettmann
282 TM: UPI/Bettmann – **BX:** Granger
283 TL, TR: UPI/Bettmann
– **BR:** Granger
284 TM, BL: UPI/Bettmann
– **BR:** NMAA, Smithsonian
285, 286, 287 All pictures from UPI/Bettmann
288 TL: Granger – **BL, BR:** UPI/Bettmann
– **BM:** Bettmann
289, 290, 291, 292 All pictures from
UPI/Bettmann
293 TM: Bettmann – **BR:** Granger
294, 295, 296 All pictures from UPI/Bettmann
297 TM: UPI/Bettmann
– **BM:** National Gallery of Art
298 to 305 All pictures from UPI/Bettmann
306 TL, TX: UPI/Bettmann
– **BL:** NMAA, Smithsonian
307 TM: Keystone – **BL:** UPI/Bettmann
– **BR:** NMAA, Smithsonian
308 BR, TL, MR: Bettmann
– **TR, ML, BL, BX:** UPI/Bettmann
309 TL: Granger – **TX:** Bettmann
– **TR:** Wide World Photos
– **ML, Y, MR, BR, BL:** UPI/Bettmann
310 TM: UPI/Bettmann
311 to 322 All pictures from UPI/Bettmann
323 TM: UPI/Bettmann
– **BM:** National Park Service
324, 325 All pictures from UPI/Bettmann
326 TM: UPI/Bettmann – **BM:** National
Gallery of Art
327 TL, TR, MM, BL: UPI/Bettmann
– **BR:** Granger
328 All pictures from UPI/Bettmann
329 TR: Kirshon – **BL:** UPI/Bettmann
– **BR:** Bettmann
330 TM: National Gallery of Art
331 All pictures from National Park Service
332 to 335 All pictures from UPI/Bettmann
336 TM: Sipa – **BM:** UPI/Bettmann
337 TM, BL: UPI/Bettmann
– **BR:** JL International
338, 339 All pictures from UPI/Bettmann
340 TX, TY, BL: UPI/Bettmann
– **BR:** Bettmann
341 to 344 All pictures from UPI/Bettmann
345 TM: TM: Sipa – **MM:** UPI/Bettmann
346 All pictures from UPI/Bettmann
347 TM: Sipa – **BX, BY:** UPI/Bettmann
348 to 351 All pictures from UPI/Bettmann
352 MR, TL: UPI/Bettmann
– **BL:** National Park Service
353 TR: UPI/Bettmann – **BM:** International
Business Machines
354, 355, 356 All pictures from
UPI/Bettmann
357 TR, BR: UPI/Bettmann
– **BL:** Walt Disney
358 All pictures from UPI/Bettmann
359 TL: Sipa – **BR:** UPI/Bettmann
360 to 365 All pictures from UPI/Bettmann
366 BM: Bettmann
367 to 370 All pictures from UPI/Bettmann
371 TM, BY: Sipa – **BX:** Reuters/Bettmann
372 All pictures from UPI/Bettmann
373 TR, BL: UPI/Bettmann – **BR:** Granger
374 TM, MR: Sipa – **BM:** UPI/Granger
375 All pictures from UPI/Bettmann
376 TL: UPI/Bettmann – **BR:** Sipa
– **BL:** Reuters/Bettmann
377 TM, BR: Reuters/Bettmann – **BL:** Sipa
378 TX: Sipa – **BM:** Bettmann
379 TM: Reuters/Bettmann
380 TL, BR: Sipa – **TR:** UPI/Bettmann
– **BL:** Kirshon
381 TR: Sipa – **BR:** JL International
382 TL: Orth/Sipa
– **TR:** Savino/Sipa
– **BR:** Sobol/Sipa
– **BL:** Trippett/Sipa
383 BR: Suu/Joffet/Sipa
– **ML:** Trippett/Sipa

– **TR:** US Navy/Sipa
384 BL: BL: Allsport
– **TL:** Bermann/Sipa
– **MR:** Bob McNelly/Sipa
– **BR:** Sipa
385 BR: DOD
– **M:** Joffet/Sipa
– **TR:** Lehr/Sipa
– **TL:** Rex Features
386 BL: Rex Features
– **TL:** Sipa
– **TR:** Sunshine/Sipa
– **BR:** Win McNamee/Sipa Sport
387 TR: New York Post – **BR:** Popperfoto
– **TL:** Robert Pohill/Sipa
– **BL:** Savino/Sipa
388 TM: Gromik/Sipa Sport
– **BL:** Savino/Sipa
– **TL:** Topham Associated Press
– **BR:** Topham Picture Library
389 MR: Emerson/Maras/Sipa
– **TL:** Sipa
– **BL:** Witt/Sipa
390 TM: Halley/Sipa
– **BM:** Sipa – **M:** Witt/Sipa
391 BR: Joffrey/Asian/Barthelemy/Sipa
– **BL:** Morris/Sipa
– **TR:** Press Association/Topham
– **TL:** Rex Features
392 BL: Chesnot/Sipa
– **BR:** Colin/Sipa Sport
– **M:** Rex Features – **TL:** Rex Features
– **TR:** Rex Features
393 TR: Rex Features
– **BR:** Savino/Sipa – **BL:** Sipa
– **ML:** Sipa – **TL:** Sipa
394 BL: B. Ward/San Francisco Chronicle/
Sipa – **TL:** Popperfoto
– **TM:** Popperfoto
– **TR:** Rex Features
395 ML: Associated Press
– **TR:** Joe Rimkus/Miami Herald
– **MR:** Rex Features
– **TL:** Sipa Sport
396 TL: Akihiro Mishimura/Sipa
– **BR:** Orton/MIL. Jour/ Sipa
– **BL:** Star Tribune/Sipa
397 ML: Boulat/Sipa
– **BR:** Courtesy of Mark Pyle
– **BL:** Nina Bermann/Sipa
– **TM:** Nina Bermann/Sipa
398 BL: Klein/Sipa Sport
– **TL:** Lee Celano/Sipa
– **BR:** Rex Features/Sipa
399 TL: Christoper Brown/Sipa
– **BR:** Jean-Michel Psaila/Sport/Sipa Sport
– **TR:** Sobol/Sipa
400 T: Bob Strong/Sipa
– **M, BR:** John Mantel/Sipa
– **BL:** Luc Delahaye/Sipa
401 T: Ft Worth Star Telegraph/Sipa
– **ML, BL:** Sipa – **BR:** Schlabowske/Sipa
– **MR:** Groshong/Sipa
402 TR: Mac Bride/Sipa
– **TL:** Chavez/Sipa
– **BR:** Abramson/Sipa
– **BL:** Stanley/Denver Post/Sipa
403 TM: Villard/Sipa
– **BL:** Sunshine/Sipa
– **BX:** Boutefeux/Sipa
– **BY:** Mantel/Sipa
– **BR:** Ruding/Sipa
404 TM: Taylor/Mooney/Sipa
– **ML, MR:** Razliki/Sipa
– **BM:** Sipa
405 TL: Tripett/Sipa
– **TR:** Hulton Deutsch/Sipa
– **BL:** Boulat/Sipa
406 TR: Hartog/The Outlook/Sipa
– **ML:** Walsh/Action Images/Sipa
– **BL:** Niviere/Sichov/Sipa
– **BR:** Strong/Sipa
407 MR: Tripett/Sipa
– **BR:** Rex/Sipa – **BL:** Sipa
408 TM: Tripett/Sipa
– **BL:** RPN/Sipa
– **BR:** NASA/Sipa – **M:** Sipa
409 TR: Lash/Don King Productions/Sipa
– **TL:** Smith/Sipa
– **BR:** Edmund Evening News/Sipa
– **BL:** Stevens/Sipa
410 T: Longstreath/Ass. Press
– **BL:** Hulshizer/Ass. Press
– **BR:** Mills/Ass. Press
411 T: Helber/Ass. Press
– **BL:** Beebe/NASA/Ass. Press
– **BR:** Lee/Ass. Press
412 T: Drew/Ass. Press
– **BR:** Robbins/Ass. Press
413 TL: Lammers/Oakland Tribune/Ass. Press
– **TM:** Strattman/Ass. Press
– **TR:** Ass. Press

– **B:** Gaps III/Ass. Press
414 TL: Lipchitz/Ass.Press
– **TR:** Ragan/Ass. Press
– **X:** Sladky/Ass. Press
– **Y:** Paquin/Ass. Press
– **BL:** Borea/Ass. Press
– **BR:** Mills/Ass. Press
415 TL: Maury/Ass. Press
– **TR:** Mills/Ass. Press
– **Y:** Draper/Ass. Press
– **BL:** Gaps III/Ass. Press
– **BR:** Longstreath/Ass. Press
416 T: Krupa/Ass. Press – **Y:** Wiese/Ass.
Press – **B:** Sharp/Ass. Press
417 X: Terrill/Ass. Press – **Y:** Morris/Ass.
Press – **B:** C20th Fox/Kobal Collection
418 T, TR, M: Associated Press (AP) – **BR:**
Katz Pictures Ltd (Time Inc.)
419 All pictures Associated Press (AP)
420 All pictures Associated Press (AP)
421 T, X: Associated Press (AP) – **Y, BL:**
Corbis Sygma
422 All pictures Associated Press (AP)
423 All pictures Associated Press (AP)
424 All pictures Associated Press (AP)
425 All pictures Associated Press (AP)
426 All pictures Associated Press (AP)
427 All pictures Associated Press (AP)
428 All pictures Associated Press (AP)
429 All pictures Associated Press (AP)
430 TL: Popperfoto – **TR:** Sipa-Press, Paris
– **B:** Associated Press GmbH Frankfurt
431 TL, TR: Associated Press (AP) – **X,
BR:** Sipa-Press, Paris – **BL:** Associated
Press GmbH Frankfurt
432 TL, BR: Sipa-Press, Paris – **TR, X, BL:**
Associated Press, GmbH Frankfurt – **M:**
Popperfoto
433 T, BR: Associated Press GmbH
Frankfurt – **Y:** Associated Press (AP) **L:**
Sipa-Press, Paris
434 Granger, Bettmann, Library of
Congress/Sipa Bettmann, UPI Bettmann
435 Bettmann, Sipa (Paris), Topham
Picture Library, Bettmann Archive NY – **B:**
Corbis Sygma

Jacket Credits:

Front:
L: Corbis-Bettmann
M: Rex Features
TR: Stu Segal
MR: Nasa
BR: The Granger Collection

Spine:
T: UPI/Corbis-Bettmann

Back:
TL: UPI/Corbis-Bettmann
TR: Rex Features
MR: Frank Spooner Pictures
BR: Rex Features